AF891579

HEIKE ALPS, DENIZ GÜNAL und SANDRA SCHUH (Hrsg.)

Annäherungen an das japanische Recht

Schriften zum Internationalen Recht

Band 245

Annäherungen an das japanische Recht

Festschrift für Heinrich Menkhaus zum 70. Geburtstag

Herausgegeben von

Heike Alps, Deniz Günal und Sandra Schuh

Duncker & Humblot · Berlin

Bibliografische Information der Deutschen Nationalbibliothek

Die Deutsche Nationalbibliothek verzeichnet diese Publikation in der Deutschen Nationalbibliografie; detaillierte bibliografische Daten sind im Internet über http://dnb.d-nb.de abrufbar.

Satz: 3w+p GmbH, Rimpar
Druck: Beltz Grafische Betriebe, Bad Langensalza

ISSN 0720-7646
ISBN 978-3-428-19611-1 (Print)
ISBN 978-3-428-59611-9 (E-Book)

Gedruckt auf alterungsbeständigem (säurefreiem) Papier
entsprechend ISO 9706 ♾

Verlagsanschrift: Duncker & Humblot GmbH, Carl-Heinrich-Becker-Weg 9,
12165 Berlin, Germany | E-Mail: info@duncker-humblot.de
Internet: https://www.duncker-humblot.de

Vorwort der Herausgeberinnen und Herausgeber

Diese Festschrift ehrt Heinrich Menkhaus zu seinem 70. Geburtstag, den er am 27. Dezember 2025 beging. In Japan wird das 70. Lebensjahr *koki* (古希) genannt. Die Kombination der Schriftzeichen „古“ (*ko* = alt) und „希“ (*ki* = selten) entstammt einem Gedicht des Dichters Dù Fǔ (杜 甫) aus der Tang-Dynastie, in dem es heißt: „人生七十古来稀“, was übersetzt werden kann als „Das Erleben des 70. Geburtstags ist seit jeher eine große Seltenheit“. Auch wenn das Erreichen dieses Alters heute keine Seltenheit mehr ist, so ist es doch ein Grund zu feiern und das Lebenswerk des Jubilars besonders zu würdigen, etwa durch diese Festschrift.

Mit Vollendung des 70. Lebensjahres erfolgt auch die Emeritierung der Professoren an der Meiji Universität, an der Heinrich Menkhaus lehrt. Entsprechend emeritiert der Geehrte zum Ablauf des akademischen Jahres am 31. März 2026.

Das Wirken von Heinrich Menkhaus hat nicht nur in Deutschland, sondern auch in Japan tiefe Spuren hinterlassen. Dies wird nicht zuletzt daran deutlich, dass dem Jubilar zwei weitere Festschriften in Japan gewidmet wurden:

1. als spezieller Band Nr. 4/5, Doppelnummer 2026 der Zeitschrift 法律論叢 (*hōritsu ronsō*, wörtlich: Juristische Aufsätze) der Juristischen Fakultät der Meiji Universität,
2. unter dem Titel „ドイツ法と日本法の架け橋・法学教育におけるドイツ法研究の意義“ (*doitsu-hō to nihon-hō no kakehashi, hōgaku kyōiku ni okeru doitsu hōkenkyū no igi*, übersetzt: Eine Brücke zwischen dem deutschen und dem japanischen Recht – Die Bedeutung des deutschen Rechts im Studium des Rechts), herausgegeben von Nakamura Anna, Doi Kazushige und Funabashi Akiko, erschienen im Verlag Keiso Shobo, Tokyo.

Die Wirkgeschichte des Jubilars als Brückenbauer zwischen dem deutschen und japanischen Rechtskreis geht weit zurück. Von 1987 bis 1989 war er Stipendiat am Japanischen Institut für Rechtsvergleichung (日本比較法研究所, *nihon hikakuhō kenkyūjo*) an der Chuo Universität in Tokyo und beschäftigte sich insbesondere mit dem japanischen Wirtschaftsrecht. Bis 1993 war er Wissenschaftlicher Mitarbeiter am Deutschen Institut für Japanstudien in Tokyo. Aus dieser Tätigkeit gingen diverse Publikationen zum japanischen Finanz- und Kapitalmarktrecht hervor. Bis 1995 war Heinrich Menkhaus Geschäftsführer des Ständigen Büros der Europäischen Gesellschaft für Japanforschung (*European Association for Japanese Studies, EAJS*) im niederländischen Leiden. Daraufhin stellte er als Leiter der Abteilung Recht und Steuern der Deutschen Industrie- und Handelskammer in Tokyo seine Fähigkeiten in der juristischen Praxis unter Beweis.

Duncker & Humblot · Berlin | https://doi.org/10.3790/978-3-428-59611-9.2025.423786

Im Jahr 2001 verschrieb sich Heinrich Menkhaus ganz der Wissenschaft und übernahm die Professur für Japanisches Recht an der Philipps-Universität Marburg. In dieser Funktion veröffentlichte er mit einer großen Bandbreite zu rechtsvergleichenden Themen, etwa dem japanischen Arbeitsrecht, Handels- und Gesellschaftsrecht und der deutsch-japanischen Rechtsgeschichte.

Neben seiner wissenschaftlichen Tätigkeit setzte und setzt sich Heinrich Menkhaus in tragenden Funktionen für den akademischen Austausch zwischen deutschen und japanischen Wissenschaftlern ein. So ist er seit 2003 – mithin seit über 20 Jahren – Vorsitzender des Vorstandes der Deutschen Gesellschaft der JSPS-Stipendiaten e. V. in Bonn. Weiterhin war er von 2002 bis 2016 Vorsitzender des Vorstandes der Deutsch-Japanischen Gesellschaft für Arbeitsrecht e. V. und von 2005 bis 2012 Vorsitzender des Vorstands der Gesellschaft für Japanforschung e. V.

Nach Gastprofessuren an der Chuo Universität, der Hitotsubashi Universität und der Bond University in Australien zog es Heinrich Menkhaus schließlich im Jahr 2008 erneut nach Japan, um den Lehrstuhl für Deutsches Recht an der Meiji Universität zu übernehmen. Gewissermaßen spiegelbildlich zu seiner früheren Tätigkeit an der Universität Marburg, bildet er seither japanische Juristen aus und macht diese mit den Methoden der Rechtsvergleichung im Allgemeinen sowie dem deutschen Recht im Besonderen vertraut.

Im Laufe der Jahre hat Heinrich Menkhaus vielen jungen deutschen und japanischen Juristinnen und Juristen die Möglichkeit eröffnet, im akademischen Austausch den Weg nach Japan bzw. Deutschland zu finden. Auch wir, die Herausgeberinnen und Herausgeber dieser Festschrift, konnten dank des Jubilars an der Chuo Universität intensiv zum japanischen Recht forschen und wertvolle fachliche wie persönliche Erfahrungen sammeln. Hierfür bleiben wir Heinrich Menkhaus in ewiger Dankbarkeit verbunden.

Mit unserem Dank stehen wir nicht allein. Für seine herausragende Rolle im akademischen Austausch zwischen Deutschland und Japan wurde Heinrich Menkhaus im Jahr 2001 mit dem Bundesverdienstkreuz am Bande, im Jahr 2023 mit dem Deutsch-Japanischen Freundschaftspreis des Verbandes Deutsch-Japanischer Gesellschaften e. V. und im Jahr 2024 mit dem Orden der Aufgehenden Sonne, goldene Strahlen mit Rosette des japanischen Kaiserhauses (旭日小綬章, *kyokujitsu shōju shō*) geehrt.

Auch wenn er auf ein erfolggekröntes Leben zurückblicken kann, ist der Jubilar unverändert aktiv und plant weitere wissenschaftliche Veröffentlichungen. Damit können wir uns auch in Zukunft auf spannende Ergebnisse seiner Arbeit freuen.

Wir bedanken uns zudem bei der Deutsch-Japanischen Gesellschaft für Arbeitsrecht e. V. für die großzügige Förderung dieser Festschrift. Schließlich bedanken wir uns auch herzlich bei den Autorinnen und Autoren für ihre wertvollen Beiträge, wie bei dem Verlag für die Unterstützung und Betreuung.

Gemeinsam wünschen wir dem Geehrten alles Gute für viele weitere Jahre!

Heike Alps, *Deniz Günal* und *Sandra Schuh*

Grußworte der Kinder

Lieber Papa,

in einer der Festschriften, die Dir in Japan gewidmet worden sind, haben wir erzählt, wie beeindruckt wir von Deinem Mut, Deinem Weg und Deiner Haltung sind. Jetzt möchten wir darüber sprechen, wer Du für uns bist – nicht nur als Professor, sondern als Vater.

Wir haben viel mit Dir erlebt – und vieles erst später verstanden. Wir erinnern uns, wie wir mit Dir Bücherregale aufbauten – nicht nur ein paar, sondern ganze Wände voll. Deine Bibliothek war riesig, sie war und ist ein Teil deiner Identität. Es machte Dich glücklich, wenn du dort in den Büchern blättern konntest. Man sah es an Deinem Gesicht – oder später an den Brillenabdrücken auf Deiner Stirn, ein stiller Beweis für Dein konzentriertes Lesen.

Du hast oft mittags auf dem Teppich geschlafen – mit einem Buch auf der Brust. Du hast wirklich jedes einzelne davon gelesen, auch wenn wir es als Kinder kaum glauben konnten. Wenn wir nicht schlafen wollten, hast du gesagt: „Soll ich euch eines meiner Bücher geben?" – und es funktionierte.

Was wir damals nicht verstanden, begreifen wir heute: Du hast Dein Leben dem Wissen verschrieben.

Und auch Dein Ruf war überall spürbar. Als Kinder konnten wir die Dimension noch nicht erfassen – wir wussten nur, dass sich viele Menschen mit großem Respekt, teils fast ehrfürchtig, vor „Herrn Professor Dr. Menkhaus" oder in Japan „Menkhaus-sensei" verneigten. Wir wurden oft zu besonderen Empfängen mitgenommen, zu Vorträgen, zu Veranstaltungen in Botschaften oder Institutionen. Du hast Menschen beeindruckt – durch Deine Haltung, Deinen Geist, Deine Art zu sprechen.

Was uns vielleicht am tiefsten geprägt hat, war Deine moralische Klarheit. Du hast uns gezeigt, was es heißt, für das Richtige einzustehen – auch wenn es unbequem ist. Du wolltest nie Anwalt werden, weil Du niemanden vertreten wolltest, der nicht im Recht war. Als wir einmal ein Apple-Tablet gefunden haben, war für Dich sofort klar: Wir versuchen alles, um den rechtmäßigen Besitzer zu finden. Du hast uns beigebracht, dass Integrität kein Ideal ist – sondern eine Haltung.

Du bist der Vater, der morgens am Frühstückstisch Zeitung las – oder sie sich in Streifen schnitt, um Informationen festzuhalten. Der Vater, der im Anzug im Garten arbeitete. Der Vater, der Gefühle nicht in Worte fassen konnte, aber dessen Gesicht oft mehr sagte als hundert Sätze. Du schreibst uns E-Mails – manchmal mit Rechtschreibkorrekturen zu unseren Texten –, und bist immer da, wenn wir Dich brauchen. Deine Ratschläge? Meist rechtlich abgesichert – und trotzdem voller Herz.

Duncker & Humblot · Berlin | https://doi.org/10.3790/978-3-428-59611-9.2025.423787

Und Dein Humor – Papa, was sollen wir sagen. Deine Kalauer waren und sind legendär. Niemand fand sie lustig. Außer Dir. Und genau deshalb mussten wir jedes Mal mitlachen – spätestens, wenn Du mit hochrotem Kopf prustend über Deinen eigenen Witz gelacht hast. Einmal hast Du ernsthaft gefragt, warum ein Tisch nicht laufen könne – schließlich habe er doch vier Beine.

Und hier einer von uns zurück: Papa-Witze sind wie guter Rotwein – sie brauchen Zeit … und nicht jeder verträgt sie.

Früher haben wir oft nicht richtig zugehört, wenn Du uns von Geschichte, Politik oder Geografie erzählt hast. Deine Erzählströme waren lang, Deine Fakten unerschöpflich. Aber Du hast nicht aufgehört – und heute danken wir Dir genau dafür. Denn mit Dir zu sprechen heißt zu lernen, zu staunen, zu lachen. Du bist unser wandelndes Lexikon – nicht, weil Du alles besser weißt, sondern weil Du alles mit uns teilen willst.

Du beginnst Sätze mit: „Damals, 19-hundert-irgendwas …“ oder: „Nach meinem Wissen müsste das so um 17-hundert passiert sein …“ Und schon sind wir in der nächsten Geschichte, mitten in einem historischen Exkurs. Früher war uns das manchmal zu viel. Heute ist es eines unserer liebsten Rituale mit Dir.

Du hast nie Dinge getan, um gesehen zu werden. Du hast überzeugt – durch Substanz, nicht durch Schein. Das prägt uns bis heute. Auch in unserem beruflichen Tun: Wir setzen auf Qualität, auf Haltung, auf das, was bleibt. Still, stark, echt – wie Du.

Du bist für uns kein perfekter Vater – aber Du bist der beste, den wir uns hätten wünschen können. Weil Du immer Du geblieben bist. Weil Du uns liebst – auf Deine Weise. Weil wir es fühlen – jeden Tag.

Deine Zeit ist noch lange nicht vorüber – im Gegenteil.

Wir wünschen uns, dass Du uns noch viele Jahre erhalten bleibst – als Vater, Großvater, Geschichtenerzähler, wandelndes Lexikon und Produzent großartiger Kalauer.

Wir wünschen uns, dass auch Deine Enkel Dich so erleben dürfen, wie wir es durften. Und wenn sie eines Abends nicht schlafen wollen, wirst Du vielleicht fragen: „Soll ich Euch eines meiner Bücher geben?“ Vermutlich werden sie Dich mit großen Augen anschauen – und plötzlich ganz brav ins Bett gehen. Und vielleicht wird es ihnen genauso gehen wie uns damals: Sie schlafen ein – und wachen Jahre später mit großem Respekt auf.

Lieber Papa, wir lieben es, Deine Kinder zu sein. Und wir lieben Dich.

Mit tiefer Zuneigung und großer Dankbarkeit,

Deine Kinder

Alisa und *Keiho*

Grußworte der Schwestern

Lieber Heiner,

wir feiern Deinen 70. Geburtstag – ein besonderer Meilenstein, der uns alle sehr freut. Auch wenn Dich Dein beruflicher Erfolg nach Tokyo gebracht hat, ist da immer Deine Verbundenheit zur Heimat. Trotz der Entfernung hast Du nie den Kontakt und die Nähe zu Deiner Familie verloren. Das zeigt, wie tief die Wurzeln in Deinem Herzen verankert sind und wie wichtig Dir die Familie ist.

Wir sind dankbar für all die schönen Erinnerungen, die wir teilen, und für den Zusammenhalt, der uns verbindet – egal, wo auf der Welt wir sind. Möge Dein neues Lebensjahrzehnt Dir Gesundheit, Glück und Zufriedenheit bringen.

In Liebe,

Deine Schwestern *Gabi* und *Steffi*

Duncker & Humblot · Berlin | https://doi.org/10.3790/978-3-428-59611-9.2025.423788

Inhaltsverzeichnis

Duncker & Humblot · Berlin | https://doi.org/10.3790/978-3-428-59611-9.2025.423789

Verständigung – Studium des japanischen Rechts

Von *Heike Alps*

Dr. Heike Alps, LL.M. (Chuo Universität, Japan) ist Rechtsanwältin, Fachanwältin für Arbeitsrecht, Mediatorin und als Referentin für Grundsatzfragen und Recht für den Betriebsrat der Salzgitter Flachstahl GmbH und den Konzernbetriebsrat der Salzgitter AG tätig. Sie ist Lehrbeauftragte für die Vorlesung „Einführung in das Japanische Recht" an der Martin-Luther-Universität Halle-Wittenberg und begleitet in dieser Funktion regelmäßig Studienreisen der Vorlesungsteilnehmenden nach Japan. Heike Alps verbrachte über 3 Jahre zu Forschungszwecken in Japan. Prof. Dr. Heinrich Menkhaus ist ihr Doktorvater.

Ich habe Prof. Dr. Heinrich Menkhaus vor über 20 Jahren in Marburg kennengelernt. Auf meine Frage, ob er die Rolle als mein Doktorvater übernehmen würde, sagte er unter einer Bedingung zu: ich sollte meine Forschung nicht auf Informationen in deutscher und englischer Sprache beschränken, sondern mich mit japanischsprachigen Quellen auseinandersetzen. Das war von Anfang an sein Credo. Das Eintauchen in ein Thema und das wirkliche gegenseitige Verstehen gelingen nur über die Sprache. Ich stimmte zu, ohne wirklich darüber nachzudenken, was für eine Herausforderung vor mir lag. Dieser Tag in Marburg stellte für mich eine Lebensweiche und es begann eine Reise, die bis heute andauert.

Eine der schönsten Erinnerungen aus den Vorlesungen von Heinrich Menkhaus, die ich in Marburg besuchen durfte, stammt aus einer Veranstaltung zu feindlichen Übernahmen (*tekitai-teki baishū*, das habe ich bis heute nicht vergessen). Heinrich Menkhaus berichtete von einem wunderbaren Kinofilm, der von feindlichen Übernahmen handelte, kam aber nicht auf den Namen. Die Studierenden und ich rätselten, in welchem Film sich Hollywood vorwiegend der feindlichen Übernahme gewidmet habe. Wir wussten es nicht und zum Glück fiel es Heinrich Menkhaus dann selbst wieder ein: Pretty Woman. Ich muss heute noch schmunzeln, wenn ich daran denke und ich finde es einfach wunderbar, dass es jemanden auf diesem Planeten gibt, der den Blockbuster Pretty Woman als Film zum Gesellschaftsrecht wahrgenommen hat. Toll.

Von Anfang an habe ich Heinrich Menkhaus als integren Menschen mit einem klaren Moralkompass erlebt, als unbestechlichen Menschen der Wissenschaft, auf den ich mich in jeder Lebenslage immer verlassen konnte. Das ist nicht selbstverständlich und ich weiß es sehr zu schätzen. Dank seiner Unterstützung durfte ich drei Jahre in Japan verbringen und dort an der Chuo Universität in Tokyo für meine Master- und Doktorarbeit forschen. Diese Zeit war prägend und wird mir immer in besonderer Erinnerung bleiben. Im Wohnheim, in dem ich untergekommen war, lernte ich die unterschiedlichsten Menschen kennen, die aus verschiedenen Kultur- und Sprachkrei-

Duncker & Humblot · Berlin | https://doi.org/10.3790/978-3-428-59611-9.2026.431118

sen stammten. Uns einte das Interesse an Japan und an der japanischen Sprache. Gelebte Völkerverständigung.

An der Chuo Universität erlebte ich dann im Bereich der juristischen Forschung, wie sehr auch das gemeinsame Interesse am Recht der jeweils anderen Brücken baute. Besonders von den japanischen Professorinnen und Professoren, die sich vergleichenden Studien des japanischen und deutschen Rechts widmeten, wurde ich mit offenen Armen empfangen. Sie unterstützten meine Forschung wo sie nur konnten. Wir hatten regelmäßige Austauschrunden, in denen ich Fragen zum japanischen Recht stellte und selbst Fragen zum deutschen Recht beantwortete. Es war eine wunderbare Symbiose, in der wir alle voneinander profitierten und dazulernten. Die gegenseitige Akzeptanz, Diskussionen auf Augenhöhe und die Bereitschaft, sich auf rechtliche Ideen und Entwicklungen eines anderen Kultur- und Rechtskreises einzulassen, die eigenen rechtlichen Strukturen auf diesem Wege zu überprüfen und zu überdenken, waren der Kern dieses wissenschaftlichen Austausches.

Seit dieser für mich sehr wertvollen Erfahrung ist es mir ein Anliegen, den Austausch zwischen japanischen und deutschen Juristinnen und Juristen auch selbst zu fördern und jungen Studierenden eine Möglichkeit zu bieten, ihren persönlichen und juristischen Horizont zu erweitern. Gemeinsam mit Gregor Stevens, Vorsitzender Richter am Landgericht Potsdam, gestalte ich seit 2017 einen Lehrauftrag für die Veranstaltung „Einführung in das Japansiche Recht" an der Martin-Luther-Universität Halle-Wittenberg. Ins Leben gerufen hat dieses Angebot Prof. Dr. Henning Rosenau, Professor für Strafrecht, Strafprozessrecht und Medizinrecht. Die Vorlesung besteht aus vier Semestern, die sich in die Bereiche Allgemeines Zivilrecht, Besonderes Zivilrecht, Strafrecht und Öffentliches Recht aufteilen. Ein Ziel neben der Vermittlung der japanischen Rechts ist, dass die Studierenden das deutsche Rechtssystem durch den Vergleich mit den jeweiligen japanischen Regelungen besser verstehen und zugleich erkennen, dass es verschiedene Möglichkeiten gibt, auf rechtliche Fragestellungen zu antworten.

In Deutschland gibt es erfreulicherweise zahlreiche Formate an Universitäten und Instituten, die Studierenden einen Einblick in das japanische Recht gewähren. Einige stelle ich im Folgenden vor:

- Beginnen möchte ich mit dem Kompetenzzentrum Japan des Max-Planck-Instituts für ausländisches und internationales Privatrecht in Hamburg, das im Jahr 2025 unglaubliche 40 Jahre Forschung zum japanischen Recht feiern konnte. Das Zentrum wurde unter der Leitung von Prof. Dr. Harald Baum bekannt für (rechtsvergleichende) Forschung zum japanischen Zivil-, Handels- und Wirtschaftsrecht und entsprechende Publikationen zum japanischen Recht. Mit der Zeitschrift für Japanisches Recht (ZJapanR) gibt das Institut die weltweit einzige Zeitschrift heraus, die regelmäßig die aktuellen Entwicklungen des japanischen Rechts in westlichen Sprachen dokumentiert und analysiert. Seit 2020 leitet Dr. Ruth Effinowicz das Zentrum.
- Die Abteilung für Japanisches Recht (mittlerweile als Bereich der Abteilung für Ostasiatisches Recht) der Fernuniversität Hagen kann auf eine über 30-jährige Geschichte zurückblicken und bietet u. a. den berufsbegleitenden Weiterbildungsstudiengang „Grundlagen des Japanischen Rechts" über zwei Semester in Teilzeit an.

Nachdem Prof. Dr. Hans-Peter Marutschke dem Institut fast 20 Jahre vorstand, leitet seit 2020 Jun.-Prof. Dr. Julius Weitzdörfer die Abteilung.

- Die Goethe Universität Frankfurt am Main hat im Jahr 2008 das Interdisziplinäre Zentrum für Ostasienwissenschaften (IZO) eingerichtet. Prof. Dr. Moritz Bälz mit seiner Professur für Japanisches Recht und seine Grundlagen ist einer der Direktoren des IZO und für den japanbezogenen Bereich der Forschung zuständig. Zum Angebot der Goethe Universität gehören auch Vorlesungen zum japanischen Recht.
- An der Universität Augsburg besteht seit 2021 eine Forschungsstelle für Japanisches Recht, die sich der Erforschung des japanisches Rechts und der Vernetzung mit der japanischen Rechtswissenschaft widmet und sowohl Vorlesungen zum japanischen Recht anbietet als auch in regelmäßigen Abständen eine Summer/Winter School über mehrere Tage organisiert. Prof. Dr. Johannes Kaspar und Dr. Oliver Schön, Vorsitzender Richter am Landgericht München, bieten als Direktoren der Forschungsstelle ebenfalls Vorlesungen zum japanischen Recht an.

An der Universität Halle-Wittenberg wollen Gregor Stevens und ich einen Beitrag dafür leisten, dass die künftigen Generationen von Juristinnen und Juristen ihre Sicht durch den sprichwörtlichen „Blick über den Tellerrand" erweitern. Wir laden japanische Gastwissenschaftler und Gastwissenschaftlerinnen zu den Vorlesungen ein, um die Diskussion zu den unterschiedlichen oder auch ähnlichen Regelungen des deutschen und japanischen Rechts nicht einseitig von deutscher Seite aus zu führen, sondern unter japanischer Beteiligung. Dieser Austausch erweist sich als sehr fruchtbar für alle Beteiligten.

Die Vorlesung im Hörsaal in Halle ist das eine, besser ist immer das wirkliche Erleben. Dankenswerterweise bietet Prof. Rosenau den Studierenden in regelmäßigen Abständen an, an einer Studienreise nach Japan teilzunehmen, die ich gemeinsam mit Gregor Stevens begleite. Die letzte Reise fand im Jahr 2024 statt und führte uns von Tokyo über Hiroshima nach Kyoto und zurück.

Auf den Studienreisen besuchen wir mit den Studierenden das Parlament, den Obersten Gerichtshof, nehmen an einer Gerichtsverhandlung am Distriktgericht Tokyo teil und zeigen ihnen ein japanisches Gefängnis von innen. Der Besuch der deutschen Botschaft sowie einer Anwaltskanzlei und der dortige Austausch mit deutschen Juristinnen und Juristen, die in Japan arbeiten und den Studierenden eine mögliche berufliche Perspektive aufzeigen, gehören ebenso dazu wie der Besuch einer japanischen Universität mit juristischer Fakultät. Letzterer fordert von den Studierenden ein gesteigertes eigenes Engagement, da wir gemeinsam mit den japanischen Studierenden und deren Professoren und Professorinnen ein Seminar abhalten. Die Themen werden vor der Reise festgelegt. 2024 haben wir uns mit der Todesstrafe beschäftigt. Alle, die an der Studienreise teilnehmen und auch die japanischen Studierenden bereiten Kurzvorträge zu ausgewählten Fragen in englischer Sprache vor. Nach den Vorträgen diskutieren wir über die jeweiligen Standpunkte und im Anschluss an das Seminar geht der Austausch in gemütlicher Atmosphäre bei einem gemeinsamen Essen weiter. Auch in die Geschichte und Kultur Japans tauchen wir mit den Studierenden ein, besuchen Tempel und Schreine und – meiner Ansicht nach ein

Muss in diesen Zeiten von Unsicherheit und kriegerischen Auseinandersetzungen in der Welt – Hiroshima mit seinem Friedensmuseum zum Gedenken und zur Dokumentation des Atombombenabwurfs auf Hiroshima. An diesem beklemmenden Ort wird jedem klar, dass das Streben nach Frieden unverzichtbar ist.

Von den Studierenden, die an den Vorlesungen zum japanischen Recht und einer der Studienreisen teilgenommen haben, haben sich bereits mehrere für längere Aufenthalte in Japan entschieden und sind für ein oder zwei Semester zum Studium und zum Erlernen der japanischen Sprache in Tokyo gewesen. Es freut mich sehr, dass unsere Vorlesung an der Universität Halle-Wittenberg einen Beitrag dazu leistet, ein Interesse für Japan, das Land, die Kultur und das Recht zu entfachen und dass die Studierenden ihre eigenen Erfahrungen in Japan machen können. Deshalb wünsche ich mir, dass sich die Angebote zum japanischen Recht an den deutschen Universitäten noch lange halten werden.

Lieber Heinrich, Du hast auf mein Leben einen großen Einfluss genommen und dafür möchte ich Dir herzlich danken. Du hast Dich für mich verbürgt zu einem Zeitpunkt als wir uns noch nicht lange kannten und mir den Weg zu einem dreijährigen Aufenthalt in Japan geebnet. Mein Aufenthalt in Tokyo und an der Chuo Universität ist eine unvergessene Zeit, die mich sehr geprägt hat, mir Lebensfreundschaften geschenkt und die mir viele Türen geöffnet hat. Zwei dieser engen Freundschaften verbinden mit Deinen Kindern Alisa und Keiho. Der Austausch mit Alisa, meine Besuche in ihrem Atelier und das Tragen ihrer besonderen Mode sind zu meinem Glück ebenso elementare Bestandteile meines Lebens geworden wie meine Verbundenheit zu Japan: Susumu Ai eben – Fortwährende Liebe.

Sustainability, Big Tech and Artificial Intelligence

How Japan Tackles the Hot Topics of EU Competition and Regulatory Law[1]

By *Carmen Appenzeller*

Dr. Carmen Appenzeller, LL.M. (Columbia) is a Senior Associate in the Tokyo office of Herbert Smith Freehills Kramer GJBJ. She has been based in Japan since 2019 after having qualified in Germany and worked in Brussels. Her current practice focusses on advising Japanese clients on German, EU and international competition law and regulatory matters.

Japan has a strong tradition of creating and developing its legal system through comparative legal studies. Unlike Western jurisdictions, where legal frameworks have gradually evolved over centuries through precedents and statutes, Japan's legal system underwent rapid Westernization during the Meiji era. With no comparable domestic legal tradition to fall back on, Japan adopted rules from foreign legal systems, notably using an early draft of the German Civil Code as the blueprint for its own Civil Code.[2] This established a tradition of close links between legal practitioners, the judiciary, officials, and academics in both Germany and Japan.

Professor Menkhaus has played a significant role in facilitating this exchange, organizing conferences and connecting legal professionals from both countries. This is not only because of the extraordinary breadth of topics that his academic interests cover, but also due to the large network of contacts in the German-Japanese legal community that Professor Menkhaus has built up. It was at one of these events that we first met after I had heard his name since I first became interested in the connection between German and Japanese lawyers and legal traditions.

While the legal exchange between Japan and Germany continues to flourish, the Japanese legislator looks increasingly to developments at the level of the European Union (EU) for inspiration. The EU sees itself as a global trendsetter of regulation, especially since enacting the General Data Protection Regulation (GDPR) which has indeed impacted businesses and inspired lawmakers well beyond the EU's Internal Market.

---

[1] Heartfelt thanks go to Yusuke Takamiya (Partner at Mori Hamada, Tokyo) for inspirational discussions that have informed this article. This article was prepared with the assistance of Microsoft 365 Copilot, which provided research and drafting support. All arguments and views expressed in this article are the author's own.

[2] Cf. *Menkhaus*, History of German-Japanese Scientific Relations in the Area of Legal Science, pp. 107 et seqq., in: Deutsche Gesellschaft des JSPS-Stipendiaten e. V. (ed.): 10th Anniversary of the Deutsche Gesellschaft der JSPS-Stipendiaten e. V. (2005), available at https://www.jsps-club.de/fileadmin/veroeffentlichungen/Festschriften/Festschrift_10_Jahre_JSPS-Club.pdf.

Duncker & Humblot · Berlin | https://doi.org/10.3790/978-3-428-59611-9.2025.418778

The EU's unique legal nature, with its competence subsidiary to Member States, means its laws must focus on regulating cross-border goods and services, and competition law has been at the centre of the EU's legal system from the first.[3] There is now likely no sector that is more emblematic of cross-border impacts than digital business models. This may be one reason the EU's legislative and executive branches have focused on digitalization and sustainability, addressing the impacts and challenges of disruptive technologies such as artificial intelligence (AI) and renewable energy. Furthermore, legislation that concerns novel phenomena not yet addressed under national law may be politically easier to agree at EU level than the harmonisation of other areas of law that are steeped in national legal traditions.

This contribution examines how Japan has mirrored EU competition and regulatory law at the examples of competition law relating to sustainability cooperations, the ex-ante regulation of Big Tech, and AI legislation. It explores how the European Commission (EC) and the Japan Fair Trade Commission (JFTC) address the complexities of integrating sustainability goals with competition law, the tailored approach of Japan's Smartphone Software Competition Promotion Act (Smartphone Act or SSCPA) compared to the EU's Digital Markets Act (DMA), and Japan's "light touch" regulatory approach to AI in contrast to the EU's comprehensive AI Act.

I. Competition Law Enforcement Relating to Sustainability Cooperation

1. Setting the Scene

Sustainable development refers to the ability of society to consume and use the resources available today without compromising the ability of future generations to meet their own needs. It encompasses activities that support economic, environmental and social (including labour and human rights) development.[4]

Sustainability cooperation involves businesses working together to achieve environmental and social goals, such as reducing carbon emissions, promoting renewable energy, and ensuring fair labour practices. Such collaborations can be crucial for addressing challenges of global scale, such as climate change or resource depletion. An early example of a sustainability cooperation is the Fairtrade initiative which aims at improving working conditions for farmers and workers in developing countries.

That said, the interaction between competition law and sustainability cooperation can be complex. Traditional competition law focuses on preventing collusion by keeping competitors ignorant of other market players' commercial strategies, and, in principle, mistrusts initiatives where competitors align their behaviour to achieve a common goal. Concerted practices between competitors with the object or effect of

---

3 Articles 85 et seqq. of the Treaty of Rome, 25 March 1957.

4 Communication from the Commission – Guidelines on the applicability of Article 101 of the Treaty on the Functioning of the European Union to horizontal co-operation agreements (Horizontal Guidelines), OJ C 259, 21 July 2023, p. 1, para. 517, available at https://eur-lex.europa.eu/legal-content/EN/TXT/?uri=uriserv%3AOJ.C_.2023.259.01.0001.01.ENG&toc=OJ%3AC%3A2023%3A259%3ATOC#ntc364-C_2023259EN.01000101-E0364 with reference to UN Resolution 66/288 adopted by the General Assembly on 27 July 2012.

restricting competition are prohibited, unless such cooperation entails tangible efficiencies that benefit consumers (cf. Article 101(3) of the Treaty on the Functioning of the EU, TFEU). Are sustainability goals considered beneficial for consumers in the sense of competition law? This question has been controversial, especially so where sustainability efforts could lead to an increase in prices for consumers.[5] For instance, in an early decision, the Dutch Authority for Consumers & Markets (ACM) held in the "*Chicken of Tomorrow*" case that an animal welfare initiative did not entail net benefits for consumers and was therefore an unjustified restriction of competition.[6] In its assessment of consumer benefits, the ACM found that the monetary value consumers attribute to the increased animal welfare standards under the proposed initiative was less than the expected increase in chicken meat prices, thereby netting a loss for consumers.[7]

The International Chamber of Commerce (ICC) has warned of the "chilling effects" of competition law on sustainability cooperation and called for practical guidelines from competition enforcers.[8] The ICC pointed to the difficulty of potential collaborators in self-assessing whether the efficiencies of their planned initiative would be considered sufficient to justify any restriction of competition. Such self-assessment is always complex, but even more so for sustainability initiatives because these often aim at regional or even global effects. The ICC points to three main challenges: First, the onus is on the companies to prove that specific efficiencies accrue to consumers; second, the legal test for justifying restrictions of competition is typically strict, and varies between competition authorities; third, each authority has different procedures for granting pre-approval, consultation or letters of comfort for sustainability cooperations.[9]

Given the promotion of sustainability and carbon neutrality is an important political goal both in the EU (see below 1.) and Japan (see below 2.), both jurisdictions' competition authorities have made efforts to encourage companies in this regard.

---

5 Cf. *Nowag*, Sustainability and Competition Law: An International Report, in: Kellezi/Kobel/Kilpatrick (eds.): Sustainability Objectives in Competition and Intellectual Property Law (2024), pp. 3–26, available at https://link.springer.com/chapter/10.1007/978-3-031-44869-0_1.

6 *ACM*, ACM's analysis of the sustainability arrangements concerning the 'Chicken of Tomorrow' (January 2015), available at https://www.acm.nl/sites/default/files/old_publication/publicaties/13789_analysis-chicken-of-tomorrow-acm-2015-01-26.pdf.pdf.

7 The ACM has since revised its earlier guidelines, now also providing a "safe harbour" for agreements that are necessary for achieving environmental benefits if consumers in the relevant market receive an appreciable and objective part of the advantages, see *ACM*, ACM's oversight of sustainability agreements (4 October 2023), para. 23, available at https://www.acm.nl/en/publications/policy-rule-acms-oversight-sustainability-agreements.

8 *ICC*, When Chilling Contributes to Warming. How Competition Policy Acts As a Barrier to Climate Action (2022); available at https://iccwbo.org/wp-content/uploads/sites/3/2022/11/when-chilling-contributes-to-warming-2.pdf.

9 Id. p. 13.

2. Legal Assessment in the EU

a) Sustainability Chapter in the Horizontal Guidelines

After much deliberation, a dedicated chapter on "sustainability agreements" was added in the EC's Horizontal Guidelines of 2023.

First, it is clarified that sustainability agreements are not regarded as capable of raising competition law concerns where they do not negatively affect parameters of competition, such as price, quality, choice or innovation.[10] Examples are agreements that aim solely at ensuring compliance with sufficiently precise requirements or prohibitions in legally binding international treaties, agreements or conventions,[11] agreements that do not concern the economic activity of undertakings, but their internal corporate conduct,[12] agreements to set up a database containing general information on sustainability criteria of suppliers' operations but which do not constrain the parties in their purchase decision,[13] and agreements relating to the organisation of industry-wide awareness campaigns, provided that they do not amount to joint advertising of specific products.[14]

Next, the assessment of sustainability agreements under Article 101(1) is laid out in principle and in relation to sustainability standardisation agreements in particular. Generally, restrictive behaviour that may ordinarily be considered a restriction by object needs to be assessed as to its effects on competition where the main object of an agreement is the pursuit of a sustainability objective.[15] This diverges from normal principles, where a restriction by object is presumed to present a sufficient degree of harm to fall under Article 101(1) irrespective of its effects on competition.

Sustainability standardisation agreements are used to specify requirements that producers, processors, distributors, retailers or service providers in a supply chain have to meet in relation to a wide range of sustainability metrics, such as the environmental impacts of production.[16] The main competition concerns in this respect are price coordination, foreclosure of alternative standards, and the exclusion of (or discrimination against) certain competitors.[17]

---

10 Horizontal Guidelines, para. 527.

11 Id., para. 528.

12 Id., para. 529.

13 Id., para. 530.

14 Id., para. 531.

15 Id., para. 534. The following factors should in particular be taken into account when assessing the effects of a sustainability agreement: the market power of the parties participating in the agreement; the degree to which the agreement limits the decision-making independence of the parties in relation to the main parameters of competition; the market coverage of the agreement; the extent to which commercially sensitive information is exchanged in the context of the agreement; and whether the agreement results in an appreciable increase in price or an appreciable reduction in output, variety, quality or innovation (id., para. 535).

16 Id., para. 539, with reference to United Nations Forum on Sustainability Standards, available at https://unfss.org/home/objective-of-unfss/.

17 Horizontal Guidelines, para. 546.

The Horizontal Guidelines contain a "soft safe harbour" for sustainability standardisation agreements, which means that appreciable negative effects on competition are regarded as unlikely as long as all of the following six conditions are met:

(1) The procedure for developing the sustainability standard must be transparent, allowing all interested competitors to participate in the process leading to the selection of the standard.

(2) The sustainability standard must not impose any compliance obligations on undertakings that do not wish to participate.

(3) Binding requirements can be imposed on the participating undertakings to ensure compliance, but applying higher sustainability standards must remain possible.

(4) Commercially sensitive information may be exchanged, provided that it is objectively necessary and proportionate for the development, implementation, adoption or modification of the standard.

(5) Effective and non-discriminatory access to the outcome of the standard-setting process must be ensured.

(6) The combined market share of the participants must not exceed 20% on any relevant market affected by the standard, *or* the standard must not lead to a significant increase in the price or a significant reduction in the quality of the products concerned.

Where a sustainability agreement is considered to restrict competition, the Horizontal Guidelines lay out how the conditions of Article 101(3) TFEU apply.[18] Of particular interest is the test for taking collective benefits into account when assessing whether consumers receive a fair share of the benefit resulting from improved production, distribution, technical or economic conditions. In essence, undertakings must be able to demonstrate that the consumers in the relevant market substantially overlap with the beneficiaries of the sustainability agreement, and that the share of the collective benefits that accrues to the consumers in the relevant market outweighs the harm suffered by those consumers as a result of the restriction.[19] How severely this requirement limits the possibility for justification under Article 101(3) TFEU is illustrated by the example in paragraph 585 of the Horizontal Guidelines:

> "[C]onsumers may buy clothing made of sustainable cotton that reduces the use of fertilisers and water on the land where the cotton is cultivated. Such environmental benefits could in principle be taken into account as collective benefits. However, in this case there is unlikely to be any substantial overlap between the consumers of the clothing and the beneficiaries of the environmental benefits, as these occur only in the area where the cotton is grown. Therefore, it is unlikely that these collective benefits would accrue to the consumers in the relevant market. They could therefore only be taken into account if and to the extent that consumers of the clothing are willing to pay more for clothing that is made of sustainably grown cotton".

18 Id., paras. 556 et seqq.

19 Id., para. 570.

In conclusion, the impact on price of a sustainability agreement is still a central consideration, both in terms of assessing whether the "soft safe harbour" applies as well as in considering whether an exemption under Article 101(3) TFEU is available.

b) Challenges From a Practical Perspective

In addition to the general guidance in the Horizontal Guidelines, the EC "is committed to provide information guidance regarding novel or unresolved questions on individual sustainability agreements".[20] According to the EC's Informal Guidance Notice[21], the EC may provide guidance on novel or unresolved legal questions to increase legal certainty. While the EC will not consider hypothetical questions, it is possible to consult the EC in relation to agreements that are envisaged, provided planning has reached a sufficiently advanced stage for a request to be considered.[22] This, however, can present pitfalls: the informal guidance process provides no protection against self-incrimination. The EC can therefore initiate an antitrust investigation if it takes the view that the facts presented in the request for guidance indicate a possible violation of competition law. This is in line with the fundamental expectation that undertakings shall self-assess their behaviour, based on the nuanced precedent of EU case law and the EC's decisional practice and public guidelines.

The "chilling effect" of the EU approach is two-fold: publicity and exposure. Pursuant to para. 22 of the Informal Guidance Notice, guidance letters will be published on the EC's website, which could be undesirable if an initiative is not yet sufficiently mature to be publicly announced. More importantly, the protection granted for seeking guidance are weak: Neither is the EC prevented from opening an infringement investigation against the applicant instead of providing the desired comfort letter, nor would a comfort letter afford legal protection against national proceedings, litigation or subsequent investigation by the EC itself (cf. paras. 19, 25 and 27 of the Informal Guidance Notice). Sustainability initiatives typically present novel questions, primarily because the efficiencies of any infringement depend on a highly fact-specific assessment of the collective benefits. If the EC will only provide guidance on cooperations that are sufficiently advanced, this means that in practice, a considerable exchange of information, likely commercially sensitive, has already taken place. Should the EC deem the cooperation not to be exempt from Article 101(1) or not sufficiently justified under Article 101(3), there is a considerable risk that the parties have *nolens volens* notified the EC of their own violation of competition law. If such a worst-case outcome materialises, applicants might have been better served to self-report a suspected violation by applying for leniency.

---

20 Id., para. 515.

21 Commission Notice on informal guidance relating to novel or unresolved questions concerning Articles 101 and 102 of the Treaty on the Functioning of the European Union that arise in individual cases (guidance letters) (Informal Guidance Notice), OJ C 381, 4 October 2022, pp. 9–13, para. 7, available at https://eur-lex.europa.eu/legal-content/EN/TXT/?uri=OJ%3AJOC_2022_381_R_0007.

22 Id., para. 9.

From the EC's homepage, it appears that the EC has, in fact, not issued a single guidance letter since the Informal Guidance Notice was published.[23] It remains possible to consult informally with the EC, although from anecdotal evidence, companies are also hesitant to avail themselves of the informal consultation option.

c) Cartel Enforcement Against Sustainability Initiatives

When looking at the EC's approach towards sustainability initiatives, two recent cartel cases stand out. In both cases, the EC imposed multi-million fines against car manufacturers for concerted practices related to sustainability. In the AdBlue case, Mercedes (the leniency applicant), Volkswagen, Porsche and BMW were found to have infringed competition law by communicating about the tank size of AdBlue and other aspects of emissions-reducing technology.[24] This coordination was, according to the automakers, aimed at helping to establish a customer-friendly infrastructure for refilling AdBlue, which is essential for operating the emissions-reducing technology in diesel engines. However, the EC found an infringement by object in the form of a limitation of technical development.

The second, recently settled case relates to an industry-wide agreement between automakers regarding their end-of-life vehicle (ELV) recycling measures. The EC found that 16 major car manufacturers, facilitated by the industry association ACEA, agreed not to pay car dismantlers for processing ELV and to limit their efforts of promoting recyclability of vehicles.[25]

The fines imposed, in both cases through settlements, were considerable: around EUR 875 million in total in the AdBlue matter and around EUR 458 million in total in the ELV recycling case. In both cases, the main harm lies in the omission to invest or promote sustainability goals more. The AdBlue case attracted particular criticism because the initiative was aimed at technological improvement, and while the competitors discussed alignment on tank sizes, these were not actually implemented.[26] In view of the novelty of the case, the EC provided guidance to the companies under investigation on those aspects of their cooperation which did not violate competition law, while fining the conduct that, in the EC's view, constituted a violation. However, as both the AdBlue and the ELV cases settled, no detailed reasoning was provided and the EC's "novel approach" is not being tested in court. The chilling effect is clear:

---

23 The only guidance (although not concerning a concrete initiative) in recent years was published on allowing limited cooperation among businesses, especially for critical hospital medicines during the coronavirus outbreak (EC, press release of 8 April 2020, available at https://ec.europa.eu/commission/presscorner/detail/en/ip_20_618), arguably an unprecedented situation of emergency.

24 Commission Decision, Case AT.40178 – Car Emissions, OJ C 458/16 of 12 November 2021, summary available at https://eur-lex.europa.eu/legal-content/EN/TXT/PDF/?uri=CELEX:52021AT40178(02).

25 Commission Decision, Case AT.40669 – End-of-life vehicle recycling of 1 April 2025, press release available at https://ec.europa.eu/commission/presscorner/detail/en/ip_25_881.

26 BMW Press release of 8 July 2021, available at https://www.press.bmwgroup.com/deutschland/article/detail/T0337552DE/kartelluntersuchung-gegen-automobilhersteller:-eu-kommission-laesst-anschuldigungen-gegen-bmw-group-weitgehend-fallen.

novel theories of harm coupled with high fines for sustainability agreements make engaging in such initiatives appear particularly high-risk.

3. Legal Assessment in Japan

In line with the global trend, the JFTC also considered the interaction between competition and sustainability issues and whether any action towards clarification was needed.[27] In March 2023, the JFTC published its Guidelines Concerning the Activities of Enterprises Toward the Realization of a Green Society Under the Antimonopoly Act (Green Guidelines).[28]

a) Development of the "Green Guidelines"

The Green Guidelines materially differ in their scope from the Sustainability Chapter in the EC's Horizontal Guidelines as they focus exclusively on environmental considerations, notably the reduction of carbon emissions.[29] The JFTC's express purpose for publishing the Green Guidelines is the further promotion of companies' efforts in terms of competition policy, given that the efforts of companies toward the realization of a green society are expected to be even more active and take shape in the coming years. In that, the Green Guidelines set a markedly different tone than the Sustainability Chapter in the Horizontal Guidelines. Where the EC aims at encouraging sustainability cooperation by providing greater clarity how they would be assessed under competition law, the JFTC seems to understand competition law as a tool to actively promote sustainability initiatives.

Given their stand-alone nature, the Green Guidelines can address sustainability considerations more comprehensively than the Sustainability Chapter in the Horizontal Guidelines, touching on joint activities (Part I), possible restraints on trading partners' business activities (Part II), the abuse of a superior bargaining position (Part III), the review of business combinations (Part IV), and dedicating a whole chapter to the consultation process offered by the JFTC (Part V). With 74 pages containing 84 case studies (as opposed to 14 pages and 5 examples of EC guidance), the JFTC's guidance is very specific and comprehensive by international standards. This notwithstanding, the initial version of 2023 was criticised for not being sufficiently detailed. To address this critique, after only one year, the JFTC published revisions to the Green Guidelines to address such criticism and reflect insights from consultations.

---

27 Cf. e.g. the CPRC's 20th International Symposium "Green Growth and Competition Policy" on 25 March 2022 (information available at https://www.jftc.go.jp/cprc/events/symposium/2021/220325sympo.html); *JFTC*, Interim Report "Competition Policy Issues Related to Measures Using Economic Methods in Global Warming Countermeasures/Issues in the Domestic Emissions Trading System", published 31 March 2022, available at https://www.jftc.go.jp/houdou/pressrelease/cyosa/cyosa-sonota/h22/10033102.html.

28 JFTC, Guidelines Concerning the Activities of Enterprises, etc., Toward the Realization of a Green Society Under the Antimonopoly Act, revised as of 24 April 2024, available at https://www.jftc.go.jp/en/pressreleases/yearly-2024/April/240424EN2.pdf.

29 *Takamiya/Shiozaki*, Japan Fair Trade Commission publishes "Green Guidelines" (June 2023), available at https://awards.concurrences.com/IMG/pdf/jap.pdf?119382/96345e2b5e7b4104559e12f8d441e40d9640a1bab587e8bab64b74a4e34e0d85.

The influential business association Keidanren in its comments on the first draft of the Green Guidelines had called for various amendments, including two important points: First, to recognize carbon emissions reduction as a pro-competitive effect[30] and second, to clarify rules on information exchanges in preparation of a sustainability initiative.[31] The first point was reflected by an addition in the 2024 update to the Green Guidelines at footnote 4, which now states that "excellent products" may also include products that contribute to reducing greenhouse gases during production or use.[32] The latter was addressed by adding example cases 5[33] and 8[34] to the Green Guidelines in 2024.

b) Active Consultation Process

The JFTC actively encourages companies to engage in consultations under the two alternative consultation procedures that are generally available. Parties can seek the JFTC's guidance either through the more formalised Prior Consultation System (事前相談制度, *jizen sōdan seido*) under the Prior Consultation Guidelines[35] or by obtaining oral advice informally.[36] The number of "green-related inquiries" increased from around 10 cases in the fiscal year 2023 to over 20 cases in the first 3 quarters of fiscal year 2024, and the JFTC is considering another update of the Green Guidelines amid the rising demand for further guidance.[37]

The JFTC published several consultation cases (with the consent of the consulting companies), both before and after the Green Guidelines were released. A case that garnered wide attention was the Shunan Complex consultation, published in February 2024.[38] Idemitsu Kosan and four other petrochemical companies consulted the JFTC about their intention to cooperate to change electricity generation at the Shunan Complex (where each of the collaborators had production sites) from fossil fuels to ammonia. The JFTC recognized that the cooperation pursued the legitimate aim of

30 *Keidanren*, Opinion on the "Draft Approach to the Antimonopoly Act on the activities of business operators and other entities toward the Realization of a Green Society" (13 February 2023), point 1, available in Japanese at https://www.keidanren.or.jp/policy/2023/010.html.

31 Id. point 2.

32 Green Guidelines, p. 2 fn. 4.

33 Case 5 of the Green Guidelines illustrates that information permissible that is aimed at gaining the understanding of business partners and customers that prices are rising due to implementing measures to reduce greenhouse gas emissions.

34 Case 8 of the Green Guidelines sets out a clean team arrangement to exchange commercially sensitive information that is required for an initiative to switch raw materials with the intention of reducing greenhouse gas emissions.

35 Guidelines on Prior Consultation System for Activities of Businesses (Prior Consultation Guidelines), 1 October 2001, available at https://www.jftc.go.jp/en/legislation_gls/imonopoly_guidelines_files/priorconsultationsystem.pdf.

36 Cf. Green Guidelines, p. 69.

37 Statement of the Secretary General Tetsuya Fujimoto on the JFTC's initiatives for the realization of a Green Society, Press Conference on 26 February 2025, available at https://www.jftc.go.jp/en/about_jftc/index_3_250226.html.

38 JFTC, Joint Actions by Petrochemical Complex Operators to Achieve Carbon Neutrality (in Japanese) available at https://www.jftc.go.jp/dk/soudanjirei/r6/r5nendomokuji/r5nendo02.html.

significantly reducing carbon dioxide and that although the costs of the products manufactured in the Shunan Complex would be affected, there was no substantial restrictions on competition.[39]

Why is the Japanese consultation process more popular than the EC's? The Prior Consultation System shares certain features with the EU's Informal Guidance in that it is a written procedure at the end of which the applicant's name as well as the details of the consultation and response shall be published (point 3(3) of the Prior Consultation Guidelines). However, the JFTC in practice publishes prior consultation cases with the consent of the applicants only. More importantly, the JFTC has strongly and successfully promoted the consultation process for sustainability initiatives,[40] and even though the Prior Consultation Guidelines do not formally grant immunity to applicants, corporates are taking up the offer. Consultation, both formal and informal, is also deeply ingrained in Japanese administrative processes generally and the JFTC's in particular. Overall, it appears the JFTC has managed to assuage, at least to some extent, the fears of companies to expose themselves to liability for well-meant cooperation.

c) Sustainability Considerations in Merger Control

The JFTC recently applied the reasoning of the Green Guidelines in a merger control case. Kubota Corporation and Nippon Chutetsukan Corporation consulted the JFTC about the proposed establishment of a manufacturing joint venture to produce ductile iron pipes, which are widely used in Japan as water pipes.[41]

The JFTC applied the test set out in the Green Guidelines[42] for business combinations, which consists of three legs that must be met cumulatively:

(1) The business combination has an inherent effect of increasing efficiency;

(2) The increase in efficiency is feasible, and

(3) The increase in efficiency will increase the welfare for consumers.

The JFTC found that the parties planned to manufacture ductile iron pipes using electric furnaces, which emit less CO_2, than the current cupola furnaces, and that neither party on its own would have achieved the introduction of electric furnaces at an

---

39 Prior to that, the JFTC had already published positive replies on a consultation relating to joint research by four transportation machinery manufacturer for new technology using carbon-free fuels, cf. JFTC: Consultation Case Study "Joint research by a transport machine manufacturer for a new technology that uses carbon-free fuels", 2023, available at https://www.jftc.go.jp/dk/soudanjirei/r6/r5nendomokuji/r5nendo01.html. Before the Green Guidelines were adopted, the JFTC published guidance to an association of retailers' guidelines to charge 3 yen per plastic bag, cf. JFTC, Consultation Case Study "Efforts to unify unit prices by trade associations in response to charging for plastic shopping bags", 2019, available at https://www.jftc.go.jp/dk/soudanjirei/r2/r1nendomokuji/r1nendo12.html.

40 Cf. JFTC website "Efforts of the Japan Fair Trade Commission to Realize a Green Society" (in Japanese) available at https://www.jftc.go.jp/dk/greentorikumi/.html.

41 See Kubota, Press Release (7 August 2023), available at https://www.kubota.co.jp/news/2023/management-20230807.html.

42 Green Guidelines, p. 61.

early stage, which constituted an efficiency (criterion 1). Further the switch to electric furnaces was expected to reduce carbon dioxide emissions by a considerable amount compared to the conventional method, making the improvement in efficiency feasible (criterion 2). Finally, the substantial reduction in carbon dioxide emissions is seen as an improvement in quality, leading to increased consumer welfare (criterion 3). Therefore, the JFTC held that all three criteria for "efficiency" under the Green Guidelines were met and did not oppose the transaction, despite the 3-to-2 type of combination and a combined market share of around 70%.[43]

II. Ex-Ante Regulation of Big Tech Companies

1. Setting the Scene

Building up an economic ecosystem to gain a competitive advantage is regarded a hallmark of commercial success, be it for established corporations or start-ups.

At the same time, landmark cases of competition law deal with conglomerates which have become so large that they are deemed detrimental to the proper functioning of the market. The break-up of the Standard Oil Corporation into 34 distinct corporations ordered by the U.S. Supreme Court in 1914[44] is an early example of a corporation being deemed too large (and: financially successful) for the good of the economy as a whole. An example from Japan is the dissolution of the *zaibatsu* (財閥, lit. "asset clique") ordered during the Allied occupation after Japan's surrender in the Second World War.

In the 21st century, competition enforcement has focused on "GAFA" – short for Google, Apple, Facebook and Amazon. Both in the EU and in Japan, competition authorities have investigated alleged abuses of Big Tech's dominant market position. Notable decisions by the EC include the Shopping,[45] Android[46] and AdSense[47] cases against Google; the investigation of Apple's mobile payments[48] and App Store prac-

---

43 Cf. JFTC, Kubota/Nippon Chutetsukan/JV, 27 March 2025, para. 6.2(1)(e), available in Japanese at https://www.jftc.go.jp/houdou/pressrelease/2025/mar/250327_kiketsu_kn_gairyaku.pdf.

44 Standard Oil Co. of New Jersey v. United States, 221 U.S. 1 (1911).

45 Case AT.39740 Google Search (Shopping) of 27 June 2017, available at https://competition-cases.ec.europa.eu/cases/AT.39740, which the Court of Justice of the European Union (CJEU) ultimately upheld, see CJEU, Case C-48/22 P of 10 September 2024, available at https://curia.europa.eu/juris/document/document.jsf?text=&docid=289925&pageIndex=0&doclang=en&mode=lst&dir=&occ=first&part=1&cid=10331300.

46 Case AT.40099 Google Android of 18 July 2018, available at https://competition-cases.ec.europa.eu/cases/AT.40099, appeal before the CJEU pending, see CJEU, Case C-738/22 P.

47 Case AT.40411 Google Search (AdSense) of 14 July 2016, available at https://competition-cases.ec.europa.eu/cases/AT.40411, overruled by the General Court, appeal pending before the CJEU, Case C-826/24 P.

48 Case AT.40452 Apply Mobile payments, closed with commitments on 11 July 2024, available at https://competition-cases.ec.europa.eu/cases/AT.40452.

tices;[49] an investigation of Facebook's marketplace;[50] and Amazon's e-books terms,[51] buy box[52] and marketplace.[53]

However, the EC's GAFA cases highlight a general shortcoming of ex post regulation.[54] After lengthy proceedings, which can extend up to ten years and involve significant resource expenditure on both sides, the EC's GAFA decisions faced court battles in Luxembourg. However, even where upheld, these decisions do not provide clear guidance on acceptable behaviour, leaving companies to self-evaluate and adjust their practices, only to potentially face a new investigation by the EC. This protracted process is not economically viable for many competitors, especially those whose business models rely on fair platform access, or for business partners suffering from abusive terms. Market realities change too quickly for such protracted loops of trial and error.

Another notable issue was that national enforcement began to diverge, with the German government even amending the German Competition Act to include provisions regulating "undertakings of paramount significance for competition across markets" (cf. Section 19a Competition Act).[55] Consequently, the EC began considering the implementation of novel instruments of competition law,[56] finally adopting the Digital Markets Act (DMA) in 2022.[57]

The structure of digital markets in Japan exhibits significant differences from that of the EU. Unlike the EU, Japan is characterized by the presence of substantial homegrown players. Notably, Rakuten and LY Corporation have each developed their own extensive digital ecosystems. While these ecosystems contain services that do overlap in certain areas with those of GAFA (such as market places, search and messag-

49 Case AT.40437 Apple – App Store Practices (music streaming) of 4 March 2024, available at https://competition-cases.ec.europa.eu/cases/AT.40437.

50 Case AT.40684 Facebook Marketplace of 14 November 2024, to be published at https://competition-cases.ec.europa.eu/cases/AT.40684.

51 Case AT.40153 E-book MFNs and related matters (Amazon), closed with commitments on 4 May 2017, available at https://competition-cases.ec.europa.eu/cases/AT.40153.

52 Case AT.40703 Amazon – Buy Box, closed with commitments on 20 December 2022, available at https://competition-cases.ec.europa.eu/cases/AT.40703.

53 Case AT.40462 Amazon Marketplace, closed with commitments on 20 December 2022, available at https://competition-cases.ec.europa.eu/cases/AT.40462.

54 Cf. OECD, Competition policy in digital markets. The combined effect of ex ante and ex post instruments in G7 jurisdictions, 2024, available at https://www.oecd.org/en/publications/competition-policy-in-digital-markets_80552a33-en.html.

55 Cf. for an overview of further national cases *Podszun*, Introduction, para. 11, in: Podszun (ed.): Digital Markets Act, 1st ed. (2024).

56 Cf. for an examination of the factors leading to this shift in approach: *Podszun* (fn. 55), para. 10; *Cini/Czulno*, The Origins of the Digital Markets Act. Explaining Policy Change, Vista Policy Paper (2/2022), available at https://fasos-research.nl/vista-jmn/files/2022/10/VISTA-Policy-Paper-02-Cini-and-Czulno-10-2022.pdf.

57 Regulation (EU) 2022/1925 of the European Parliament and of the Council of 14 September 2022 on contestable and fair markets in the digital sector and amending Directives (EU) 2019/1937 and (EU) 2020/1828 (Digital Markets Act), OJ L 265, 12 October 2022, pp. 1–66, available at https://eur-lex.europa.eu/legal-content/EN/TXT/?uri=uriserv%3AOJ.L_.2022.265.01.0001.01.ENG&toc=OJ%3AL%3A2022%3A265%3ATOC.

ing), the dynamics are different because each of the Japanese ecosystems has a unique mix of services, going beyond GAFA for instance by offering telecommunication and/or financial services. Furthermore, Japanese incumbents are adept at catering to local consumer preferences, which may give them a competitive edge over foreign entrants. This is somewhat different from the EU, where consumer preferences across the Internal Market are not as homogeneous, and local players may struggle to develop sufficient scale to compete with GAFA. It can be said that the entry of GAFA into the Japanese market has intensified competition, spurring Japanese competitors to further enhance their services. Perhaps unsurprisingly, while the Japanese government studied the developments in Europe very closely, it has taken a narrower approach to regulation. The focus of the JFTC's market study of 2023[58] and the Cabinet's Report on mobile ecosystems of the same year[59] was on mobile operating systems and apps, and the SSCPA of 2024[60] mirrors this narrower scope.

2. Digital Markets Act (EU)

a) Scope of Application

The scope of the DMA is novel as it applies exclusively to "gatekeepers" rather than any market participant. A gatekeeper is a company that has a significant impact on the internal market, provides a core platform service which is an important gateway for business users to reach end users and currently or in the foreseeable future enjoys an entrenched and durable position in its operations.[61] The DMA contains quantifiable thresholds for each criterion: A "significant impact" shall be presumed to exist where an undertaking achieves at least EUR 7.5 billion in annual turnover in the EU in each of the past three financial years or its average market capitalisation was at least EUR 75 billion in the last financial year (Article 3(2)(a) of the DMA). An important gateway with an entrenched and durable position presumably exists where a core platform service is provided to at least 45 million monthly active end users in the EU and at least 10,000 yearly active business users in the EU, during each of the last three financial years (Article 3(2)(b) and (c) of the DMA).

An undertaking that meets these presumptions shall notify the EC to this effect, and the EC may then designate that undertaking as a gatekeeper within the meaning of Article 3 of the DMA, thus obliging the designated undertaking to conform with the obligations of the DMA.

---

58 *JFTC*, Market Study Report on Mobile OS and Mobile App Distribution (February 2023), available at https://www.jftc.go.jp/file/230209EN_hontai2.pdf.

59 *Secretariat of the Headquarters for Digital Market Competition*, Competition Assessment of the Mobile Ecosystem (June 2023), available in Japanese at https://www.kantei.go.jp/jp/singi/digitalmarket/kyosokaigi/dai7/siryou2s.pdf; summary available in English at https://www.kantei.go.jp/jp/singi/digitalmarket/pdf_e/documents_230616.pdf.

60 スマートフォンにおいて利用される特定ソフトウェアに係る競争の促進に関する法律 (Act on Promotion of Competition for Specified Smartphone Software), law no. 58 of 2024, available at https://laws.e-gov.go.jp/law/506AC0000000058/20251218_000000000000000.

61 Article 3(1) of the DMA.

A total of seven gatekeepers have been designated to date:[62] Alphabet, Amazon, Apple, Booking, ByteDance, Meta and Microsoft. The designated core platform services are intermediation services (Google Maps, Google Play, Google Shopping, Amazon Marketplace, App Store, Booking.com, Meta Marketplace), operating systems (Google Android, iOS, iPadOS, Windows PC OS), social networks (Tiktok, Facebook, Instagram, LinkedIn), messenger services (WhatsApp, Facebook Messenger), video sharing (YouTube), search (Google Search), browser (Google Chrome, Apple Safari), and ADS (Google, Amazon, Meta).

b) Obligations of Gatekeepers

Once designated, gatekeepers are automatically required to adopt or omit certain behaviours (cf. Article 5 of the DMA). These obligations build on decisions by the EC based on Article 102 of the TFEU.[63] In short, gatekeepers are obliged to:

- Allow third parties to inter-operate with the gatekeeper's own services in certain specific situations;
- Allow their business users to access the data that they generate in their use of the gatekeeper's platform;
- Provide companies advertising on their platform with the tools and information necessary for advertisers and publishers to carry out their own independent verification of their advertisements hosted by the gatekeeper;
- Allow their business users to promote their offer and conclude contracts with their customers outside the gatekeeper's platform.[64]

Further, gatekeepers shall not:

- Treat services and products offered by the gatekeeper itself more favourably in ranking than similar services or products offered by third parties on the gatekeeper's platform;
- Prevent consumers from linking up to businesses outside their platforms;
- Prevent users from un-installing any pre-installed software or app if they wish so;
- Track end users outside of the gatekeepers' core platform service for the purpose of targeted advertising, without effective consent having been granted.[65]

The DMA's obligations are accompanied with significant sanctions. Fines of up to 10% of the company's total worldwide annual turnover, or up to 20% in the event of repeated infringements, can be imposed (Article 30 of the DMA). Given that, for example, Alphabet's annual revenue for 2024 was approx. USD 350 billion, the max-

---

62 European Commission Website "Digital Markets Act (DMA) – Gatekeepers", available at https://digital-markets-act.ec.europa.eu/gatekeepers_en.

63 Cf. references at fn. 45–53.

64 See European Commission Website "Digital Markets Act (DMS) – About – What does this mean for gatekeepers?", available at https://digital-markets-act.ec.europa.eu/about-dma_en.

65 Ibid.

imum possible fine could be up to USD 70 billion. In addition, in case of systematic infringements of the DMA obligations by gatekeepers, additional remedies may be imposed, which could include behavioural and structural remedies, for instance even a divestiture of (parts of) a business (Article 18 of the DMA).

c) Impact of the DMA in its First Year

The DMA saw the first anniversary in March 2025 since its obligations started to apply.[66] The designated gatekeepers have just submitted their compliance reports shortly after, detailing on hundreds of pages the measure they have taken or are considering in order to comply with the DMA's obligations.[67] In parallel, the EC has already issued its first fines under the DMA against Meta and Apple in April 2025, totally EUR 700 million.[68] While significant, these fines are far below the legally possible maximum of 10% of global turnover.

A major point of criticism levied at the DMA is its rigidity – the obligations apply to all gatekeepers with little room for exemptions. Furthermore, potential defences are limited to privacy and security and subject to high evidentiary burden, with no room to take product quality of user-friendliness into account.[69] Google's changes to its Google search service may serve as a first glimpse into how difficult it will be to "get it right" under the DMA. In 2024, Google modified the display of search results by removing clickable maps in search results. This removes the advantage of having Google's mapping service only one click away from its search service as it forces users on Google Search to first search for a mapping service, enter it and then in the mapping service search again (or alternatively go directly to the mapping service of their choice).[70] Early research shows that so far, the change has not let to a statistically significant increase in the discovery or adoption of alternative mapping services, while appreciably increasing users' search costs.[71] One may suspect that Google might have chosen this specific design so as to prove its basic argument, namely that its dominant position stems from its business partners and users preferring its su-

66 Cf. European Commission Website "Fourth meeting of the Digital Markets Act High-Level Group on the DMA first anniversary", available at https://digital-markets-act.ec.europa.eu/fourth-meeting-digital-markets-act-high-level-group-dma-first-anniversary-2025-03-07_en.

67 See European Commission Website "Digital Markets Act (DMA) – Compliance reports", available at https://digital-markets-act-cases.ec.europa.eu/reports/compliance-reports.

68 EC, Press Release, 23 April 2025, available at https://ec.europa.eu/commission/presscorner/detail/en/ip_25_1085.

69 Cf. e.g. *Manne/Radic/Auer*, Regulate for What?, A Closer Look at the Rationale and Goals of Digital Competition Regulations, Berkeley Business Law Journal, Volume 22, No. 1 (2024), p. 62.

70 See Google help "Google Maps not being linked from Google Search results page", available at https://support.google.com/websearch/thread/261655134/google-maps-not-being-linked-from-google-search-results-page?hl=en.

71 *Pape/Rossi*, Is Competition Only One Click Away? The Digital Markets Act Impact on Google Maps, CESifo Working Papers 11226 (July 2024), available at https://www.cesifo.org/en/publications/2024/working-paper/competition-only-one-click-away-digital-markets-act-impact-google.

perior services rather than any abusive practices aimed at obstructing competing services.[72]

However that may be, it clearly raises the question whether *ex ante* regulation will indeed be more efficient than the traditional enforcement of Article 102 TFEU. While the catalogue of "do's & don'ts" under the DMA appears quite clear, it does not follow in all cases which exact measures each gatekeeper should adopt. This is especially true because the DMA purpose is "ensuring for all business, contestable and fair markets in the digital sector across the Union where gatekeepers are present, to the benefit of business users and end users" (Article 1(1) of the DMA). As Google is showing, measures that may make a market more contestable for competitors can have detrimental consequences for users, and it may be more difficult to hit upon the "right" solution than the authors of the DMA could have wished.

3. Smartphone Act (Japan)

a) Scope and Obligations of the SSCPA

The SSCPA follows the DMA in that its obligations are not of general application but require undertakings to be designated based on criteria defined by a separate Cabinet Order. As defined by Cabinet Order of 10 December 2024, the threshold for companies that can be designated under the SSCPA was set at a minimum of 40 million monthly active users.[73] Unlike the DMA, the designation under the SSCPA is based solely on quantitative criteria, which was expected to make for a smoother designation process.[74] The JFTC has designated Google (under all four categories: operating software, app store, browser and search engine), Apple (operating software, app store and browser) and iTunes (app store).[75] This had been widely expected given the SSCPA's scope is limited to providers of mobile operating software, app store or browser, or search service using a search engine (Article 3(1) in connection with Article 2(8) of the SSCPA).[76] Yahoo Japan, which offers search service, digital ads,

72 Cf. posts by Oliver *Bethell*, Google's Director of Competition EMEA on the effects of Google's changes in the first year under the DMA (available at https://www.linkedin.com/pulse/reflections-one-year-dma-oliver-bethell-o143e/?trackingId=Zl2RzWboI02%2Be%2FTPEU7v9g%3D%3D) and on a recent test by Google similarly concluding that making the changes some industry players request would harm users and businesses: *Bethell*, Google Blog "Sharing data on our DMA hotels test", available at https://blog.google/feed/sharing-data-on-our-dma-hotels-test/.

73 Cf. Appendix 1–1 to Cabinet Order of 10 December 2024, available at https://www.jftc.go.jp/houdou/pressrelease/2024/dec/241210_smartphone.html.

74 *Takamiya/Shiozaki*, A Comparative Analysis of Japan's Smartphone Focused Ex Ante Regulation and the DMA, Competition Policy International, 24 March 2025, available at https://www.pymnts.com/cpi-posts/a-comparative-analysis-of-japans-smartphone-focused-ex-ante-regulation-and-the-dma/#_ftn2.

75 *JFTC*, Designation of Specified Software Operators under the Act on Promotion of Competition for Specified Smartphone Software, 31 March 2025, available at https://www.jftc.go.jp/en/pressreleases/yearly-2025/March/250331.html.

76 See Interview with *Takizawa*, The View from Japan: A TOTM Q&A with Sayako Takizawa, available at https://truthonthemarket.com/2024/09/03/the-view-from-japan-a-totm-qa-with-sayako-takizawa/; *Vande Walle*, Is the EU's Digital Markets Act going global? How Japan

news, shopping, map and other services escaped designation because it has less than 40 million monthly active users in any of the regulated services, although it boasts a total of 85 million monthly active users for the entirety of its services.[77]

Once designated, a provider shall:

- Not use acquired data for proprietary services competing with third parties (Article 5 of the SSCPA);
- Not unjustly discriminate against or unfairly treating app developers in transactions or usage terms (Article 6 of the SSCPA);
- Neither prevent third-party providers from offering their proprietary app stores nor prevent users from using alternative services (Article 7 of the SSCPA);
- Not prevent app developers from using third-party billing systems, linking out to their own websites or using alternative browsers (Article 8 of the SSCPA);
- Not treat own services favourably compared to competitors' in search results (Article 9 of the SSCPA);
- Make it easy for users to change default settings and offer a choice screen for alternative browsers, search services, etc. (Article 12 of the SSCPA).[78]

Importantly, the obligations under Articles 7, 8 and 9 of the SSCPA are subject to "justifiable reasons". Actions deemed necessary for ensuring cybersecurity, protection of user data, youth protection, abnormal operation of smartphones (e. g. through significant delays) or criminal activities (e. g. gambling) may qualify as "justifiable reasons" for noncompliance if these objectives are difficult to achieve through other means that are less restrictive of competition.[79] This is materially different from the DMA, whose obligations apply irrespective of any effects a conduct may have.[80] In

is crafting its own version of digital regulation with the Smartphone Act, EU-Renew, 21 August 2024, available at https://eu-renew.eu/is-the-eus-digital-markets-act-going-global-how-japan-is-crafting-its-own-version-of-digital-regulation-with-the-smartphone-act.

77 *Sakamaki*, Apple, Google to be regulated by Japan's new smartphone competition law, MLex (1 April 2025), available at https://content.mlex.com/#/content/1642579/apple-google-to-be-regulated-by-japan-s-new-smartphone-competition-law?referrer=search_linkclick.

78 Cf. for an overview in English: JFTC, Outline of the Acton Promotion of Competition for Specified Smartphone Software, June 2024, available at https://www.japaneselawtranslation.go.jp/outline/154/905R644.pdf; cf. for a comparison of SSCPA and DMA obligations: *Ribera Martínez/Lee*, The Japanese Smartphone Act: Teaching Competition Law New Tricks, July 2024, available at https://competitionlawblog.kluwercompetitionlaw.com/2024/07/02/the-japanese-smartphone-act-teaching-competition-law-new-tricks/.

79 JFTC, Subordinate Legislations and Guidelines of the Act on the Promotion of Competition for Specified Smartphone Software (Mobile Software Competition Act (MSCA)), 29 July 2025, p. 25, available at https://www.jftc.go.jp/file/MSCA_Guidelines_tentative_translation.pdf; cf. also the overview at *Takamiya/Shiozaki* (fn. 74), table 3.

80 See Interview with *Takizawa* (fn. 76); *Ribera Martinez/Lee* (fn. 78). To the contrary, *Wakui* argues that the SSCPA does not require a showing of anticompetitive effects and its justifications are more limited than those usually admitted by the JFTC under the Antimonopoly Act, see *Wakui*, Japan's Enactment of the Smartphone Act, SCiDA Global Regulation Series (3 October 2024), available at https://scidaproject.com/2024/10/03/japans-enactment-of-the-smartphone-act/.

fact, the "no-effects approach" of the DMA is its distinguishing feature, making it possible for the EC to intervene irrespective of anti-competitive effects or other justifications.

The SSCPA provides for steep sanctions, in the form of a surcharge of 20% of the sales related to a prohibited act, without leeway to the JFTC to lower or increase the fine depending on the circumstances of a specific case.[81]

b) Does the SSCPA go beyond the Antimonopoly Act?

The SSCPA bears some clear resemblances to the DMA, in particular in terms of the designation system to define its personal scope of application as well as the types of conduct that are either required or prohibited of designated service providers. However, as shown above, the SSCPA materially differs from the DMA in both regards given its much narrower scope of application and qualifying its core obligations by allowing "justifiable reasons". It is the latter feature which has raised the question to what degree the SSCPA goes beyond what could have been achieved by simply applying the Antimonopoly Act.

One material difference between the SSCPA and the Antimonopoly Act lies in their respective objective: The SSCPA aims at improving people's lives and the sound development of the national economy (Article 1 of the SSCPA) instead of consumer welfare which is traditionally the purpose of competition law. This "safety first" approach[82] gives more leeway both to the designated undertakings to argue in favour of their conduct, as well as to the JFTC to apply the obligations under the SSCPA.

Furthermore, traditional competition law would require showing a dominant market position and its abuse. Although this seems straightforward given Apple's and Google's sheer size, recent case-law has shown that it is not: Epic Games' challenge of Apple's Appstore commission and anti-steering policies was unsuccessful in the U.S. because the Court defined the market as that for "digital mobile gaming transactions", in which Apple was found not to hold an illegal monopoly.[83] Given the SSCPA's obligations apply by virtue of the designation decision, it will not be necessary for the JFTC to first establish market power before examining whether conduct of the designated service provider falls within the prohibited categories under the SSCPA.[84]

The big question is: If the SSCPA's obligations are not directly based on market power, will they be interpreted in the same vein as traditional competition law principles, meaning that the JFTC would be expected to follow the case-law and decisional practice under the Antimonopoly Act? Or will the SSCPA's different systematic approach and legislative purpose mean that new theories of harm may apply?

81 *Vande Walle* (fn. 76).

82 See *Vande Walle* (fn. 76).

83 Epic Games, Inc. v. Apple Inc., 559 F. Supp. 3d 898 at 921 (N.D. Cal. 2021); cf. for this reference and further context *Schlaefli*, The App Store Dilemma: Revenue "Cuts," App Restrictions, and Payment Systems, Is There Unfair Competition?, 61 Hous. L. Rev. (2024) at fn. 21. The Court adopted neither Epic Games' very narrow market definition (Apple's App Store) nor Apple's wider one (games).

84 *Takamiya/Shiozaki* (fn. 74).

c) Chrystal-Ball-Gazing: What Impact May the SSCPA Have?

The SSCPA only applies to smartphone-related services and thus does not affect platforms for e-commerce or social media. This may make it easier to handle as the JFTC, which is tasked with enforcing the SSCPA, can focus on a narrower set of issues. As the first year of DMA enforcement has shown, several of its various obligations are complex to assess, both from a technical as well as from an economical perspective. For instance, it will be crucial to find the right balance between keeping markets contestable while maintaining the benefits and user-friendliness that users and business partners are accustomed to.

Google's modification of its search functionality should serve as a cautionary example: The JFTC will need high technical capabilities to understand the options and limits from a technological perspective, assess the consequences of proposed measures comprehensively, and verify the designated companies' arguments. Ultimately, it will be for the JFTC to weigh interests that may not align: enabling app developers to contest Google's and Apple's ecosystems or improving the service for business and individual users.[85]

As the first experience with the DMA has shown, it is not straightforward what the DMA's obligations require exactly. Where gatekeepers are engaging with the EC, the "regulatory dialogue" (Article 8 of the DMA) is time-consuming and resource-intensive, and nothing else applies where gatekeepers do not engage sufficiently and the EC has opened investigations. The SSCPA leaves even more grey areas due to the possibility of justification, and it seems doubtful whether its enforcement would be quicker or bolder than the JFTC's actions under the Antimonopoly Act. In fact, the threat of the automatic surcharge of 20% may serve as leverage for the JFTC to persuade designated providers to adopt similar measures as they are taking under the DMA in Europe rather than actually imposing sanctions, which would likely, as in AMA proceedings be a (presumably remote) *ultima ratio*.[86]

III. Legislation on Artificial Intelligence

1. Setting the Scene

AI, broadly speaking, refers to technologies programmed to analyse the world around them and take action to achieve specific goals.[87] AI is said to be the second big digital leap since the internet has become widely used. The hope is that the masses of data that are generated can be leveraged more effectively to free humans from cumbersome, repetitive tasks. The fear, in short, is that computers will operate outside of human control and without oversight, raising legal, ethical and societal questions.

85 Cf. in a similar vein *Takigawa*, Toshiaki, Reining in Smartphone Ecosystems and App Stores: A Critique of the Japanese Smartphone Act in Comparison to EU and US Regulatory Approaches, Antitrust Bulletin (forthcoming 2025).

86 Cf. *Takamiya/Shiozaki* (fn. 74); *Vande Walle* (fn. 76).

87 European Commission, "Artificial Intelligence", available at https://digital-strategy.ec.europa.eu/en/policies/artificial-intelligence.

Legislating AI is controversial. The main challenge in this respect is that regulation should be sufficiently adaptive to accommodate the technological progress, which is especially rapid in AI.[88]

The EU and Japan are aligned on the general principles of AI and its regulation. This was exemplified by Japan's signing the Council of Europe's AI Convention[89], having contributed to the drafting as the only observer state of the Council of Europe from Asia.[90] Japan is also influencing the development of AI standards at global level through the ongoing Hiroshima AI Process, kicked off at the G7 Hiroshima Summit in 2023.[91]

In 2019, both the EU[92] and Japan[93] adopted general principles on AI. The common principles are human agency and oversight; technical robustness and safety; privacy and data governance; fairness, accountability and transparency. While the Japanese guidelines also highlight education/literacy, fair competition and innovation, the EU guidelines add diversity as well as environmental and societal well-being.

The generality of the principles notwithstanding, this subtle difference foreshadows the development legislative efforts have taken in both jurisdictions: The EU (as so often) has adopted a more prescriptive approach with legally binding obligations carrying sanctions in case of non-compliance (see below 2.), whereas the Japanese lawmaker is expected to enact legislation promoting AI without sanctions, supplemented by non-binding guidelines (see below 3.).

2. Artificial Intelligence Act (EU)

As one of the last pieces of legislation adopted before the European elections of 2024, the EU Parliament adopted the Artificial Intelligence Act (EU AI Act).[94] While

---

88 Cf. *Clarke*, Sam/*Whittlestone*, Jess/*Maas*, Matthijs/*Belfield*, Haydn/*Hernández-Orallo*, José/*Ó hÉigeartaigh*, Seán, Submission of Feedback to the European Commission's Proposal for a Regulation laying down harmonised rules on artificial intelligence (2021), available at https://ec.europa.eu/info/law/better-regulation/have-your-say/initiatives/12527-Artificial-intelligence-ethical-and-legal-requirements/F2665626_en.

89 Council of Europe Framework Convention on Artificial Intelligence and Human Rights, Democracy and the Rule of Law (5 October 2024), available at https://rm.coe.int/1680afae3c.

90 See *Ministry of Foreign Affairs of Japan*, Press Release (11 February 2025), available at https://www.mofa.go.jp/press/release/pressite_000001_00983.html.

91 See *Ministry of Internal Affairs and Communications of Japan*, Hiroshima AI process, available at https://www.soumu.go.jp/hiroshimaaiprocess/en/index.html.

92 *Independent High-Level Expert Group on Artificial Intelligence*, Ethics Guidelines for Trustworthy AI (2019), available at https://digital-strategy.ec.europa.eu/en/library/ethics-guidelines-trustworthy-ai.

93 Social Principles of Human-Centric AI (2019), available at https://www.cas.go.jp/jp/seisaku/jinkouchinou/pdf/humancentricai.pdf.

94 Regulation (EU) 2024/1689 of the European Parliament and of the Council of 13 June 2024 laying down harmonised rules on artificial intelligence and amending Regulations (EC) No 300/2008, (EU) No 167/2013, (EU) No 168/2013, (EU) 2018/858, (EU) 2018/1139 and (EU) 2019/2144 and Directives 2014/90/EU, (EU) 2016/797 and (EU) 2020/1828 (Artificial Intelligence Act), available at https://eur-lex.europa.eu/legal-content/EN/TXT/?uri=CELEX%3A32024R1689.

it entered into force on 1 August 2024, its obligations are coming into effect over a staggered period of two years and the EU AI Act will apply fully from 2 August 2026 (Article 113 of the EU AI Act).

a) Risk-Based Approach

The EU AI Act is the first comprehensive legal framework on AI worldwide, with the aim to foster trustworthy AI in Europe (Article 1 of the EU AI Act). It follows a "risk-based approach", meaning that the rules and obligations imposed on AI systems are proportionate to the level of risk they can generate (Recitals 26–27 of the EU AI Act).

The only obligation that applies to all AI systems[95] is that of AI literacy (Article 4), requiring providers[96] and developers[97] of AI systems to ensure that their staff and other persons dealing with the operation and use of AI systems on their behalf have sufficient skills, knowledge and understanding to make an informed choice to deploy AI systems and are aware of the opportunities, risks and potential harm they entail (Article 3(56) of the EU AI Act).

Most AI systems are expected to fall into the low/minimal risk or limited risk categories.[98] Low/minimal risk AI systems do not face any obligations under the EU AI Act. AI systems that are intended to interact directly with natural persons face (only) transparency obligations (Article 50 of the EU AI Act): They shall be designed and developed in such a way that the user is informed that they are interacting with an AI system, for example when using chatbots, deepfakes or AI-created contents or emotion recognition/biometric categorisation systems.

Most obligations under the EU AI Act target AI systems that are classified as "high-risk". High-risk AI use cases include (cf. Article 6 and Annex III of the EU AI Act):

- AI safety components in critical infrastructures (e.g. transport), the failure of which could put the life and health of citizens at risk;

---

95 An "AI system" is defined as "a machine-based system that is designed to operate with varying levels of autonomy and that may exhibit adaptiveness after deployment, and that, for explicit or implicit objectives, infers, from the input it receives, how to generate outputs such as predictions, content, recommendations, or decisions that can influence physical or virtual environments" (Article 3(1) of the EU AI Act).

96 A "provider" is "a natural or legal person, public authority, agency or other body that develops an AI system or a general-purpose AI model or that has an AI system or a general-purpose AI model developed and places it on the market or puts the AI system into service under its own name or trademark, whether for payment or free of charge" (Article 3(3) of the EU AI Act).

97 A "deployer" is "a natural or legal person, public authority, agency or other body using an AI system under its authority except where the AI system is used in the course of a personal non-professional activity" (Article 3(4) of the EU AI Act).

98 A sample analysis found that around 62% of AI systems would fall into the "low risk" category, 28% in the "high-risk" category, and only 0.2% in the "unacceptable risk" category (the classification is unclear for the remaining approx. 10%), see *Klein* et al., Risk Classification Database (2024), available at https://www.appliedai-institute.de/assets/files/Risk-Classification-Database-September-2024_2024-09-24-100247_vnef.pdf.

- AI solutions used in education institutions, that may determine the access to education and course of someone's professional life (e. g. scoring of exams);
- AI-based safety components of products (e. g. AI application in robot-assisted surgery);
- AI tools for employment, management of workers and access to self-employment (e. g. CV-sorting software for recruitment);
- Certain AI use-cases utilised to give access to essential private and public services (e. g. credit scoring denying citizens opportunity to obtain a loan);
- AI systems used for remote biometric identification, emotion recognition and biometric categorisation (e. g. AI system to retroactively identify a shoplifter);
- AI use-cases in law enforcement that may interfere with people's fundamental rights (e. g. evaluation of the reliability of evidence);
- AI use-cases in migration, asylum and border control management (e. g. automated examination of visa applications);
- AI solutions used in the administration of justice and democratic processes (e. g. AI solutions to prepare court rulings).[99]

Where an AI system is considered to present a high-risk use case, various obligations apply, aiming at ensuring proper risk management, and human oversight over the design, development and operation of the AI system (cf. Articles 8–27 of the EU AI Act). These include:

- Adequate risk assessment and mitigation systems;
- High-quality of the datasets feeding the system to minimise risks of discriminatory outcomes;
- Logging of activity to ensure traceability of results;
- Detailed documentation providing all information necessary on the system and its purpose for authorities to assess its compliance;
- Clear and adequate information to the deployer;
- Appropriate human oversight measures;
- High level of robustness, cybersecurity and accuracy.[100]

b) First Interpretation Guidelines and Remaining Unclarity

One feature resulting from the novelty of the EU AI Act is that many aspects are still unclear. This can provoke two unintended reactions from addressees: either they do not comply due to lack of awareness of the new rules or, to err on the cautious side, they refrain from innovating or bringing novel tech on the market in the EU. In fact, uncertainty around the application of the General Data Protection Regulation

99 European Commission, "EU AI Act", available at https://digital-strategy.ec.europa.eu/en/policies/regulatory-framework-ai.

100 Ibid.

(GDPR) and recently also the DMA have been cited as reasons by tech companies why innovations were not (initially) made available to European users. To give but a few examples:

- Apple delayed the release of certain AI features, including Apple Intelligence, iPhone Mirroring, and SharePlay Screen Sharing, due to concerns over the DMA and its interoperability requirements;[101]
- Google postponed the launch of its AI chatbot, Bard in the EU after the Irish Data Protection Commission raised concerns about data protection and privacy;[102]
- OpenAI's ChatGPT was banned in Italy due to the local data protection authority's view that it did not comply with the GDPR;[103]
- Meta delayed the rollout of its AI Assistant in Europe for almost a year due to regulatory hurdles related to data privacy and compliance with the GDPR.[104]

To provide guidance on the first aspects of the EU AI Act that have started to apply from 2 February 2025, the EC has published guidelines on the definition of "AI systems",[105] on the AI systems that are prohibited due to posing unacceptable risks,[106] and a compilation of practices on AI literacy, followed by a webinar on 20 February 2025.[107]

---

101 *DW*, Apple delays release of new AI features in Europe (22 June 2024), available at https://www.dw.com/en/apple-delays-release-of-new-ai-features-in-europe/a-69444063; *Axios*, Apple says it won't roll out AI features in Europe due to regulatory concerns (21 June 2024), available at https://www.axios.com/2024/06/21/apple-ai-features-europe.

102 *Politico*, Google forced to postpone Bard chatbot's EU launch over privacy concerns (13 June 2023), available at https://www.politico.eu/article/google-postpone-bard-chatbot-eu-launch-privacy-concern/.

103 Cf. *Politico*, ChatGPT is entering a world of regulatory pain in Europe (10 April 2023), available at https://www.politico.eu/article/chatgpt-world-regulatory-pain-eu-privacy-data-protection-gdpr/; the European Data Protection Board (EDPB) investigated ChatGPT which eventually underwent adaptation to alley concerns and was made available to all users in the EU, cf. *EDPB*, Report of the work undertaken by the ChatGPT Taskforce (23 May 2024), available at https://www.edpb.europa.eu/system/files/2024-05/edpb_20240523_report_chatgpt_taskforce_en.pdf.

104 *The Verge*, Meta AI is rolling out in Europe after all (20 March 2025), available at https://www.theverge.com/news/632876/meta-ai-europe-whatsapp-facebook-instagram-rollout.

105 *EC*, The Commission publishes guidelines on AI system definition to facilitate the first EU AI Act's rules application, Guidelines available for download at https://digital-strategy.ec.europa.eu/en/library/commission-publishes-guidelines-ai-system-definition-facilitate-first-ai-acts-rules-application.

106 *EC*, Commission publishes the Guidelines on prohibited artificial intelligence (AI) practices, as defined by the EU AI Act, Guidelines available for download at https://digital-strategy.ec.europa.eu/en/library/commission-publishes-guidelines-prohibited-artificial-intelligence-ai-practices-defined-ai-act.

107 *EC*, Living repository to foster learning and exchange on AI literacy, available at https://digital-strategy.ec.europa.eu/en/library/living-repository-foster-learning-and-exchange-ai-literacy; *EC*, Third AI Pact webinar on AI literacy, available at https://digital-strategy.ec.europa.eu/en/events/third-ai-pact-webinar-ai-literacy.

Arguably the most uncertainty surrounds the classification of AI systems as "high-risk". While the abstract criteria appear clear and reasonable, the risk-based approach of the EU AI Act does not treat certain objectively prescribed AI systems as high-risk per se. Rather, the categorisation depends on the circumstances of the individual use case in which they are deployed. *Gikay et al.* give as example a delivery robot which can be operated in a controlled environment with few unpredictable variables, such as a warehouse, or in urban settings with heightened external obstacles and potential for misuse.[108] While the basic functions of the robot are the same, the complexity of the algorithms required for the different environments may transform the classification from a low risk to a high-risk system.[109]

It is expected that the EC will provide guidance on the classification as high-risk as well, ideally in good time to provide meaningful orientation before the obligations for high-risk AI systems start applying in August 2026. Looking at the guidance already issued, it is difficult to foresee how practically useful the high-risk guidance may be: The guidelines on defining AI systems are brief, high-level and mainly replicate the EU AI Act's provisions and recitals. Conversely, the guidelines on prohibited AI systems are extensive (135 pages) and contain at least some reference to research as well as examples, thus going beyond the content of the EU AI Act.

3. AI Promotion Act (Japan)

The legislative process and reactions to the EU's AI Act have been followed very closely by the government and practitioners in Japan. That said, the approach Japan is taking to AI regulation is touted as the "third way" between the EU's strict safety requirements and the unregulated environment in the U.S.[110]

a) Pivot Towards "Light Touch" Regulation

Japan is currently seen as favouring a "light touch" to avoid stifling innovation while still addressing potential risks. *Sakamaki*[111] analyses that the government's stance has undergone a marked shift: The Personal Information Protection Commission (PPC) was among the first in the world to caution OpenAI for using sensitive data scraped from the internet to train its generative AI system in 2023.[112] The establishment of a government panel on AI legislation in early 2024 was generally seen as

---

108 *Gikay/Lau/Sengul/Miron/Malin*, High-Risk Artificial Intelligence Systems under the European Union's Artificial Intelligence Act: Systemic Flaws and Practical Challenges, p. 18 (2023), available at https://bura.brunel.ac.uk/bitstream/2438/27608/1/Preprint.pdf.

109 Id.

110 *Kölling*, Martin, Japans Aufholjagd im Wettrennen um künstliche Intelligenz, Japanmarkt (1/2025), p. 13, available at https://my.page2flip.de/8600042/24086595/24086596/#/12.

111 See for the following *Sakamaki*, Sachiko, Japan's light-touch regulatory plans back 'most AI-friendly nation' ambitions, MLex (27 February 2025), available at https://content.mlex.com/#/content/1634614/japan-s-light-touch-regulatory-plans-back-most-ai-friendly-nation-ambitions?referrer=search_linkclick.

112 *Personal Information Protection Commission*, Warnings regarding the use of generative AI services (2 June 2023), available at https://www.ppc.go.jp/news/careful_information/230602_AI_utilize_alert/.

an indication that legislation, possibly akin to the EU AI Act, was on the horizon in Japan.[113]

However, the mood then shifted. Not least since the "DeepSeek shock" in February 2025, Japan has been eager to improve its competitiveness in the global race to market leadership in AI. The government has already successfully piloted the deployment of AI to maintain public services in an aging society and has committed staggering investment to building up the domestic chip production as well as developing the required energy resources.[114] Paradigmatic of the new light touch when it comes to regulating AI: The PPC is reportedly considering abandoning the requirement of prior consent when obtaining sensitive personal information for the development of artificial intelligence.[115]

b) Status Quo and "AI Promotion Act"

To date, Japan has issued non-binding guidelines for AI development and use. For example, the Ministry of Economy, Trade and Industry (METI) released the "AI Guidelines for Business Ver1.0" (AI Guidelines) in April 2024.[116] These guidelines provide recommendations for developing, providing and using AI responsibly. Similar in principle to the EU AI Act, the AI Guidelines favour a risk-based approach, without however spelling out which level of risk entails which measures. The measures recommended for advanced AI systems are broadly similar to the obligations that apply to high-risk AI systems under the EU AI Act, although due to the non-binding nature of the AI Guidelines, it is for the AI business actors to choose measures which they consider appropriate. The AI Guidelines specify that certain items apply only to "advanced AI systems", defined as "including the cutting-edge foundation models and generative AI systems" (see p. 10 and Section 2. D. of the AI Guidelines).

More formal regulations are being considered. Shortly after the AI Study Group published its Interim Report in February 2025,[117] the government tabled the Bill on the Promotion of Research, Development and Use of Artificial Intelligence-related Technology (AI Promotion Act) which has since been enacted.[118] The Interim Report

113 Cf. Also *GR Japan*, Japan's AI Governance: An Overview of Current Policies and Future Possible Regulations (2024), available at https://grjapan.com/insights/insights/shaping-future-japans-evolving-ai-governance-current-policies-and-future-possible.

114 Cf. *Mok*, Charles/*Tong*, Athena, Japan's Pragmatic Model for AI Governance, The Diplomat (13 February 2025), available at https://thediplomat.com/2025/02/japans-pragmatic-model-for-ai-governance/.

115 The Japan Times: Japan may ease privacy rules to aid AI development (23 February 2025), available at https://www.japantimes.co.jp/news/2025/02/23/japan/crime-legal/personal-info-law-revision-ai/.

116 *Ministry of Internal Affairs and Communications/Ministry of Economy, Trade and Industry*, AI Guidelines for Business Ver1.0 (2024), available at https://www.meti.go.jp/shingikai/mono_info_service/ai_shakai_jisso/pdf/20240419_9.pdf.

117 *AI Strategy Council/AI Institutional Study Group*, Interim Report (4 February 2025), available in English at https://www8.cao.go.jp/cstp/ai/interim_report_en.pdf.

118 Act on the Promotion of Research, Development, and Utilization of Artificial Intelligence-Related Technologies enacted on 28 May 2025, available at https://laws.e-gov.go.jp/law/507AC0000000053.

calls on the government to provide the recommended guidance for business operators through introducing legal systems, but proposes to rely on existing laws when it comes to governmental action against serious infringements.[119] Quite in line with these recommendations, the AI Promotion Act focuses on establishing the institutional framework for the governmental to study, supervise and guide the use of AI. This is in line with the government's stated objective to become "the country where developing and utilizing AI is easiest".[120]

The only obligation the AI Promotion Act puts on "business operators" (defined as any entity that intends to develop, provide or use AI-related technology) is that they "*shall actively strive* to improve the efficiency and sophistication of its business activities and create new industries through the active use of artificial intelligence-related technologies, and *shall cooperate* with the measures implemented by the national government" (Article 7 of the AI Promotion Act; emphasis added). While neither of these obligations are subject to penalties or fines, a failure to cooperate with the governments' future AI policy framework may entail administrative measures, such as guidance or a caution, against the business operator.[121] Measures the government is expected to take include surveys and research (Article 16 of the AI Promotion Act) and developing standards for the appropriate use of AI (Article 13 of the AI Promotion Act).[122]

Similar to the development the Japanese legislation on personal data protection has taken,[123] the legislator may start by introducing a basic framework, allowing the government to establish administrative procedures and business operators to become used to the new requirements, before (possibly) introducing tougher rules and eventually sanctions for non-compliance in a gradual way over time. The legislative development on AI regulation will likely be even more cautious, given the overarching goal of promoting rather than taming its development and use.

IV. In Conclusion: Plea for Less Politics in Competition Law

Both the EU and Japan are at a crossroads in regulating novel technological developments in sustainability and the digital sphere. As shown above, there is an intricate interplay between the evolving legal landscapes in the EU and Japan: While legisla-

---

119 Cf. *Habuka*, New Government Policy Shows Japan Favors a Light Tough for AI Regulation, CSIS Report (2025), available at https://www.csis.org/analysis/new-government-policy-shows-japan-favors-light-touch-ai-regulation; *Matsushita*, Roadmap for regulating artificial intelligence in Japan, Asia Business Law Journal (28 March 2025), available at https://law.asia/roadmap-regulating-artificial-intelligence-japan/.

120 See the Cabinet's overview of the AI Promotion Act, bottom box, available at https://www.cao.go.jp/houan/pdf/217/217gaiyou_2.pdf.

121 See *Tonomura/Komatsu*, Overview of Japan's "AI Law" Draft and Practical Points, NO&T Technology Law Update No. 59 (March 2025), available (in Japanese) at https://www.noandt.com/publications/publication20250306-1/.

122 Id.

123 Cf. for an overview of legal developments: *Personal Information Protection Commission Japan*, Topics, available at https://www.ppc.go.jp/en/.

tive developments in sustainability, digital market regulation, and AI in the EU have significantly influenced Japan's legal framework, Japan has adopted rules tailored to its national interest and legal tradition.

Competition law and its enforcement in Japan are traditionally less heavy-handed compared to the EU. Generally, Japan's regulatory approach, including the activities of the JFTC for competition law, relies more on guiding business operators towards desired outcomes rather than imposing penalties and adversary proceedings. This is exemplified by the active consultation process on sustainability agreements and the "light touch" approach to regulating AI. Overall, Japan does well to observe EU legislative experiments with caution to avoid unintended consequences, such as delayed availability of advanced technology. The "chilling effects" of EU law and enforcement on sustainability initiatives and the market launch of advanced technology are noticeable and a consequence that the Japanese government may want to avoid.

Even the EC is now emphasising the importance of AI in closing the "innovation gap" in its guiding objective to enhance competitiveness.[124] It remains to be seen how the enforcement of the AI Act will be affected by this new policy direction. There are also mixed messages around the enforcement of the DMA. While substantial fines have already been levied, officials have also emphasised the value of the regulatory dialogue in achieving compliance, and how resource-intensive the DMA's enforcement is.[125]

The overarching concern when looking at developments in sustainability, digital markets, and AI regulation both in the EU and Japan is the high political interest in these topics. Linked to this is a risk of a political agenda influencing enforcement decisions. While this is not in itself problematic – indeed, it is the legislator's prerogative to address novel issues by enacting new rules – the question is whether the current approach is entirely fit for purpose. It is indeed desirable that enforcement be based on precedent and guided by legal principles. Otherwise, decisions become unpredictable and stakeholders cannot adapt their behaviour appropriately.

This challenge is exemplified at the enforcement of digital market regulation. Both the EC and the JFTC have yet to show how they will employ their respective new powers and whether they will maintain the same degree of independence from political wishes. For instance, in response to the Trump administration's announcement to impose tariffs, some voices in Europe called for the DMA to be used to levy fines as "taxes" on U.S. digital companies. Any enforcement action by the EC could therefore be construed as acting upon this call to action, even if it is entirely unrelated and purely grounded in legal considerations. DG Competition has traditionally striven to

---

124 Cf. *EC*, EU Compass to regain competitiveness, January 2025, available at https://ec.europa.eu/commission/presscorner/detail/en/ip_25_339.

125 Cf. Olivier Guersent's statements at the Antitrust in Digital Economy, GCR conference on 1 April 2025 in Washington D.C., reported by MLex (https://content.mlex.com/#/content/1643427/big-tech-s-eu-antitrust-fines-are-no-benchmark-for-dma-sanctions-guersent-says?referrer=search_linkclick); Linsey McCallum's statements at the 7th W@Competition Conference, Women@, 13 March 2025 in Brussels, reported by MLex (https://content.mlex.com/#/content/1638495/regulatory-dialogue-preferred-over-dma-non-compliance-probes-says-eu-s-mccallum?referrer=search_linkclick).

counter any impression that its decisions were influenced by political or national interests. Still, *Schnitzer* and *Podszun* argue in favour of an independent EU enforcement agency to ensure the DMA is not (perceived as) being used as bargaining chip.[126]

In the field of sustainability, there is a clear divergence in approach: While the JFTC's Green Guidelines go beyond traditional competition law principles, DG Competition has previously resisted bending competition law principles to foster the "green agenda" of the EC. However, the task of the new Commissioner Ribera, who also oversees competition law, is to "to ensure that Europe stays on track for its goals set out in the European Green Deal, while driving the decarbonisation and industrialisation of our economy".[127] It remains to be seen whether this newly tailored portfolio will entail a shift in competition law policy towards actively promoting sustainability and decarbonisation.

On the other hand, for the regulation of AI both the EU and Japan are adopting new legislation and creating dedicated enforcement bodies rather than solely relying on existing frameworks, for instance for data protection or digital services. This adds a new layer of regulation for AI providers and deployers and has attracted criticism for stifling innovation. As the EU is trying to dial back overly bureaucratic regulation in general, it remains to be seen to what extend compliance measures under the AI Act can be integrated with those under existing regulations, for instance when it comes to documentation and reporting obligations, to ease the cost of compliance for businesses.

Literature

AI Strategy Council/AI Institutional Study Group: Interim Report (4 February 2025), available in English at https://www8.cao.go.jp/cstp/ai/interim_report_en.pdf.

Axios: Apple says it won't roll out AI features in Europe due to regulatory concerns (21 June 2024), available at https://www.axios.com/2024/06/21/apple-ai-features-europe.

Bethell, Oliver: Google Blog "Sharing data on our DMA hotels test", available at https://blog.google/feed/sharing-data-on-our-dma-hotels-test/.

Bethell, Oliver: On the effects of Google's changes in the first year under the DMA, available at https://www.linkedin.com/pulse/reflections-one-year-dma-oliver-bethell-o143e/?trackingId=Zl2RzWboI02%2Be%2FTPEU7v9g%3D%3D.

Cini, Michelle/*Czulno*, Patryk: The Origins of the Digital Markets Act. Explaining Policy Change, Vista Policy Paper (2/2022), available at https://fasos-research.nl/vista-jmn/files/2022/10/VISTA-Policy-Paper-02-Cini-and-Czulno-10-2022.pdf.

Clarke, Sam/*Whittlestone*, Jess/*Maas*, Matthijs/*Belfield*, Haydn/*Hernández-Orallo*, José/*Ó hÉigeartaigh*, Seán: Submission of Feedback to the European Commission's Proposal for

126 *Schnitzer/Podszun*, This is no big deal: Europe must stand strong on Big Tech, SCiDA blog (14 April 2025), available at https://scidaproject.com/2025/04/14/this-is-no-big-deal-europe-must-stand-strong-on-big-tech/.

127 EC: Teresa Ribera, Responsibilities, available at https://commission.europa.eu/about/organisation/college-commissioners/teresa-ribera_en.

a Regulation laying down harmonised rules on artificial intelligence (2021), available at https://ec.europa.eu/info/law/better-regulation/have-your-say/initiatives/12527-Artificial-intelligence-ethical-and-legal-requirements/F2665626_en.

DW: Apple delays release of new AI features in Europe (22 June 2024), available at https://www.dw.com/en/apple-delays-release-of-new-ai-features-in-europe/a-69444063.

European Data Protection Board: Report of the work undertaken by the ChatGPT Taskforce (23 May 2024), available at https://www.edpb.europa.eu/system/files/2024-05/edpb_20240523_report_chatgpt_taskforce_en.pdf.

Gikay, Asress Adimi/*Lau*, Pin Lean/*Sengul*, Cigdem/*Miron*, Alina/*Malin*, Ben: High-Risk Artificial Intelligence Systems under the European Union's Artificial Intelligence Act: Systemic Flaws and Practical Challenges (2023), p. 18, available at https://bura.brunel.ac.uk/bitstream/2438/27608/1/Preprint.pdf.

GR Japan: Japan's AI Governance: An Overview of Current Policies and Future Possible Regulations (2024), available at https://grjapan.com/insights/insights/shaping-future-japans-evolving-ai-governance-current-policies-and-future-possible.

Guersent, Olivier: Statements at the Antitrust in Digital Economy, GCR conference on 1 April 2025 in Washington D.C., reported by MLex (https://content.mlex.com/#/content/1643427/big-tech-s-eu-antitrust-fines-are-no-benchmark-for-dma-sanctions-guersent-says?referrer=search_linkclick).

Habuka, Hiroki: New Government Policy Shows Japan Favors a Light Tough for AI Regulation, CSIS Report (2025), available at https://www.csis.org/analysis/new-government-policy-shows-japan-favors-light-touch-ai-regulation.

International Chamber of Commerce: When Chilling Contributes to Warming. How Competition Policy Acts As a Barrier to Climate Action (2022), available at https://iccwbo.org/wp-content/uploads/sites/3/2022/11/when-chilling-contributes-to-warming-2.pdf.

Keidanren: Opinion on the "Draft Approach to the Antimonopoly Act on the activities of business operators and other entities toward the Realization of a Green Society" (13 February 2023), available at https://www.keidanren.or.jp/policy/2023/010.html.

Klein, Till et al.: Risk Classification Database (2024), available at https://www.appliedai-institute.de/assets/files/Risk-Classification-Database-September-2024_2024-09-24-100247_vnef.pdf.

Kölling, Martin: Japans Aufholjagd im Wettrennen um künstliche Intelligenz, Japanmarkt (1/2025), p. 13, available at https://my.page2flip.de/8600042/24086595/24086596/#/12.

Manne, Geoffrey/*Radic*, Lazar/*Auer*, Dirk: Regulate for What?, A Closer Look at the Rationale and Goals of Digital Competition Regulations, Berkeley Business Law Journal, Volume 22, No. 1 (2024), p. 62.

Matsushita, Yu: Roadmap for regulating artificial intelligence in Japan, Asia Business Law Journal (28 March 2025), available at https://law.asia/roadmap-regulating-artificial-intelligence-japan/.

McCallum, Linsey: Statements at the 7th W@Competition Conference, Women@, 13 March 2025 in Brussels, reported by MLex (https://content.mlex.com/#/content/1638495/regulatory-dialogue-preferred-over-dma-non-compliance-probes-says-eu-s-mccallum?referrer=search_linkclick).

Menkhaus, Heinrich: History of German-Japanese Scientific Relations in the Area of Legal Science, pp. 107 et seqq., in: Deutsche Gesellschaft des JSPS-Stipendiaten e. V. (ed.): 10th

Anniversary of the Deutsche Gesellschaft der JSPS-Stipendiaten e.V. (2005), available at https://www.jsps-club.de/fileadmin/veroeffentlichungen/Festschriften/Festschrift_10_Jahre_JSPS-Club.pdf.

Mok, Charles/*Tong*, Athena: Japan's Pragmatic Model for AI Governance, The Diplomat (13 February 2025), available at https://thediplomat.com/2025/02/japans-pragmatic-model-for-ai-governance/.

Nowag, Julian: Sustainability and Competition Law: An International Report, in: Kellezi, Pranvera/Kobel, Pierre/Kilpatrick, Bruce (eds.): Sustainability Objectives in Competition and Intellectual Property Law (2024), pp. 3–26, available at https://link.springer.com/chapter/10.1007/978-3-031-44869-0_1.

Pape, Louis-Daniel/*Rossi*, Michelangelo: Is Competition Only One Click Away? The Digital Markets Act Impact on Google Maps, CESifo Working Papers 11226, July 2024 (2024), available at https://www.cesifo.org/en/publications/2024/working-paper/competition-only-one-click-away-digital-markets-act-impact-google.

Podszun, Rupprecht (ed.): Digital Markets Act, 1st ed. (2024).

Politico: ChatGPT is entering a world of regulatory pain in Europe (10 April 2023), available at https://www.politico.eu/article/chatgpt-world-regulatory-pain-eu-privacy-data-protection-gdpr/.

Politico: Google forced to postpone Bard chatbot's EU launch over privacy concerns (13 June 2023), available at https://www.politico.eu/article/google-postpone-bard-chatbot-eu-launch-privacy-concern/.

Ribera Martínez, Alba/*Lee*, Sangyun: The Japanese Smartphone Act: Teaching Competition Law New Tricks, (July 2024), available at https://competitionlawblog.kluwercompetitionlaw.com/2024/07/02/the-japanese-smartphone-act-teaching-competition-law-new-tricks/.

Sakamaki, Sachiko: Apple, Google to be regulated by Japan's new smartphone competition law, MLex (1 April 2025), available at https://content.mlex.com/#/content/1642579/apple-google-to-be-regulated-by-japan-s-new-smartphone-competition-law?referrer=search_linkclick.

Sakamaki, Sachiko: Japan's light-touch regulatory plans back 'most AI-friendly nation' ambitions, MLex (27 February 2025), available at https://content.mlex.com/#/content/1634614/japan-s-light-touch-regulatory-plans-back-most-ai-friendly-nation-ambitions?referrer=search_linkclick.

Schlaefli, Pierre: The App Store Dilemma: Revenue "Cuts," App Restrictions, and Payment Systems, Is There Unfair Competition?, 61 Hous. L. Rev. (2024).

Schnitzer, Monika/*Podszun*, Robert: This is no big deal: Europe must stand strong on Big Tech, SCiDA blog (14 April 2025), available at https://scidaproject.com/2025/04/14/this-is-no-big-deal-europe-must-stand-strong-on-big-tech/.

Takamiya, Yusuke/*Shiozaki*, Kohei: A Comparative Analysis of Japan's Smartphone Focused Ex Ante Regulation and the DMA, Competition Policy International, 24 March 2025 (2025), available at https://www.pymnts.com/cpi-posts/a-comparative-analysis-of-japans-smartphone-focused-ex-ante-regulation-and-the-dma/#_ftn2.

Takamiya, Yusuke/*Shiozaki*, Kohei: Japan Fair Trade Commission publishes "Green Guidelines" (June 2023), available at https://awards.concurrences.com/IMG/pdf/jap.pdf?119382/96345e2b5e7b4104559e12f8d441e40d9640a1bab587e8bab64b74a4e34e0d85.

Takigawa, Toshiaki: Reining in Smartphone Ecosystems and App Stores: A Critique of the Japanese Smartphone Act in Comparison to EU and US Regulatory Approaches, Antitrust Bulletin (forthcoming 2025).

Takizawa, Sayako: The View from Japan: A TOTM Q&A with Sayako Takizawa, available at https://truthonthemarket.com/2024/09/03/the-view-from-japan-a-totm-qa-with-sayako-takizawa/.

The Japan Times: Japan may ease privacy rules to aid AI development (23 February 2025), available at https://www.japantimes.co.jp/news/2025/02/23/japan/crime-legal/personal-info-law-revision-ai/.

The Verge: Meta AI is rolling out in Europe after all (20 March 2025), available at https://www.theverge.com/news/632876/meta-ai-europe-whatsapp-facebook-instagram-rollout.

Tonomura, Keiji/*Komatsu*, Akira: Overview of Japan's "AI Law" Draft and Practical Points, NO&T Technology Law Update No. 59 (March 2025), available (in Japanese) at https://www.noandt.com/publications/publication20250306-1/.

Vande Walle, Simon: Is the EU's Digital Markets Act going global? How Japan is crafting its own version of digital regulation with the Smartphone Act, EU-Renew, 21 August 2024 (2024), available at https://eu-renew.eu/is-the-eus-digital-markets-act-going-global-how-japan-is-crafting-its-own-version-of-digital-regulation-with-the-smartphone-act.

Wakui, Masako: Japan's Enactment of the Smartphone Act, SCiDA Global Regulation Series (3 October 2024), available at https://scidaproject.com/2024/10/03/japans-enactment-of-the-smartphone-act/.

Unterschiede des deutschen und japanischen Arbeitsrechts und die Handhabung von Überstunden[1]

Von *Frank Becker*

Frank Becker ist Rechtsanwalt und Managing Partner der Atsumi & Sakai Europa GmbH in Frankfurt, das er 2015 als deutsches Büro der japanischen Kanzlei Atsumi & Sakai eröffnet hat. Er berät vor allem zu grenzüberschreitenden M&A-, Compliance- und Arbeitsrechtsthemen mit Fokus auf Japan. Studiert hat er in Saarbrücken und Sendai.

I. Einleitung

Im Westen hält sich ein sehr rigides Bild japanischer Arbeitskultur: Der frühmorgens im Zug schlafende *Salaryman*[2] auf dem Weg ins Büro, wo er auch bis spät in die Nacht bleiben wird – aus Loyalität zu einem Unternehmen, dem er sich lebenslang verschreibt.[3] Dieses Bild wurde maßgeblich durch Medienberichte im letzten Viertel des 20. Jahrhunderts geprägt.[4] Es ist ein Bild, das einer differenzierten Betrachtung nicht standhält, jedoch immer noch den Ausgangspunkt vieler Diskussionen über Arbeit in Japan bildet.

Meine erste intensive Auseinandersetzung mit diesem Themenkomplex verdanke ich Prof. Dr. Menkhaus, der meine Wahlstation an der Deutschen Industrie- und Handelskammer in Tokyo mit großer fachlicher Tiefe und menschlicher Wärme begleitete. Es ist seinem Engagement zu verdanken, dass ich nicht nur einen tiefen Einblick in die Strukturen des japanischen Arbeitsrechts erhalten habe, sondern auch Gelegenheit hatte, die kulturellen und praktischen Implikationen aus nächster Nähe zu erleben. Prof. Menkhaus beeindruckt nicht nur durch seine profunde Kenntnis des japanischen Rechts und seine wissenschaftliche Präzision, sondern auch durch seine Fä-

---

1 An dieser Stelle möchte ich mich bei meiner studentischen Mitarbeiterin Michelle Maurer für ihre großartige Unterstützung bei der Erstellung dieses Beitrags bedanken. Ohne ihren engagierten Einsatz hätte ich den Beitrag nicht rechtzeitig fertigstellen können.

2 Es handelt sich hier um eine stereotypische und übertriebene Darstellung eines japanischen Arbeitnehmers in Japan (der typischerweise als „*Salaryman*" bezeichnet wird), die die reale Situation in Japan nicht oder zumindest nicht mehr widerspiegelt.

3 Vgl. *Deutschmann/Weber*, Das Japanische Arbeitsbienen-Syndrom. Auswirkungen der Rundum-Nutzung der Arbeitskraft auf die Arbeitszeitpraxis am Beispiel Japans, in: PROKLA. Zeitschrift für Kritische Sozialwissenschaft, Band Nr. 17 (1987), S. 31.

4 *Shimada*, Das japanische Arbeitsrecht und seine Globalisiserung, in: Pécsi munkajogi közlemények, Band 2016, Heft Nr. 1 (2023), S. 4.

Duncker & Humblot · Berlin | https://doi.org/10.3790/978-3-428-59611-9.2025.418779

higkeit, junge Juristen[5] zu fördern und intellektuell herauszufordern. Seine ruhige, verbindliche und dabei stets klare Art, komplexe Sachverhalte zu vermitteln, hat meinen juristischen Blick nachhaltig geprägt.

Das Thema knüpft an einen Beitrag an, den ich Ende 1998 während meines Referendariats für die Mitgliederzeitschrift „Japan Markt“ der AHK Tokio verfasst habe. Auf Bitte von Prof. Dr. Menkhaus hatte ich damals über die Reform des japanischen Arbeitsstandardsgesetzes (労働基準法, *rōdō kijunhō*) (ASG) geschrieben. Sie stellte die erste umfassende Überarbeitung des ASG seit seiner Einführung im Jahr 1947 dar. Sie wurde im September 1998 vom japanischen Parlament verabschiedet.[6] Gegenstand der Reform war insbesondere die Begrenzung der jährlichen Überstunden auf maximal 360 Stunden. Ein weiterer wesentlicher Punkt war die Regelung ungleichmäßiger Arbeitsbelastungen: Bei einer Verteilung des Arbeitsanfalls über einen Zeitraum von mehr als drei Monaten durfte die tägliche Arbeitszeit zehn Stunden und die wöchentliche Arbeitszeit 52 Stunden nicht überschreiten. Diese Regelung zielte darauf ab, Spitzenbelastungen zu begrenzen und die Gesundheit der Arbeitnehmer zu schützen.

II. Rechtshistorische Grundlagen des Arbeitsrechts in Deutschland und Japan

1. Entwicklung des Arbeitsrechts in Deutschland

Das deutsche Arbeitsrecht geht auf die Konstruktion der Dienstmiete in den Pandekten zurück, die einen Austausch von Lohn gegen Arbeit vorsah. Mit dem Bürgerlichen Gesetzbuch (BGB) erfolgte ein Bruch mit der Vorstellung der Arbeitsleistung als Mietsache; der Arbeitsvertrag wurde als Dienstvertrag qualifiziert. Seit Inkrafttreten des BGB richtet sich das Arbeitsrecht teils nach den in §§ 611 ff. BGB kodifizierten Vorschriften über den Dienstvertrag, die noch keinen sozialen Ausgleich zwischen den Parteien vorsahen, sowie teils nach weiterhin anwendbarem Landesrecht.[7] Der BGB-Gesetzgeber verzichtete bewusst auf eine eigenständige Ausgestaltung des Arbeitsrechts, ging jedoch davon aus, dass diese Lücke in absehbarer Zeit durch eine einheitliche Regelung geschlossen würde.[8] Ein solche einheitliche Kodifikation wurde in der deutschen Rechtsgeschichte mehrmals angestrebt, ist im Ergebnis aber immer gescheitert.[9] Erst nach dem Ende des Ersten Weltkriegs begann das Arbeitsrecht

5 Sämtliche personenbezogene Bezeichnungen gelten im Beitrag gleichermaßen für alle Geschlechter; auf eine durchgängige geschlechterspezifische Differenzierung wurde im Interesse der Lesefreundlichkeit verzichtet.

6 Gesetz Nr. 112 vom 30.09.1998.

7 *Maties*, in: Gsell/Krüger/Lorenz/Reymann (Hrsg.), Beck-online.GROSSKOMMENTAR zum Zivilrecht, Stand 1. Februar 2015, § 611a BGB, Rn. 2017.

8 *Richardi*, Arbeitsvertragsgesetz und Privatautonomie, in: Neue Zeitschrift für Arbeitsrecht, Heft Nr. 17 (1992), S. 769.

9 So wurde dem Reichstag 1907 vom Reichsamt des Inneren eine solche Resolution vorgelegt, die aber vom Reichstag abgelehnt wurde. In der jüngeren Vergangenheit scheiterte der Entwurf der Arbeitsgesetzbuchkommission eines umfangreichen Arbeitsvertragsrechts 1977 noch vor Erreichen des eigentlich Gesetzgebungsverfahrens. Zuletzt schaffte es auch der

als eigenständigen Rechtsgebiet anerkannt und ausgearbeitet zu werden.[10] In der Rechtswissenschaft der damaligen Zeit fanden sich Diskussionen, das Arbeitsrecht aus dem BGB herauszulösen. Diese hatten zwar keinen Erfolg, schlugen sich aber darin nieder, dass der persönlichen Abhängigkeit des Arbeitnehmers als arbeitsrechtliches Problem stärkere Bedeutung zukam.[11] In der Folge wurde dem Bedürfnis nach Schutzvorschriften zunehmend entsprochen, was in der Unterschutzstellung der Arbeit in Art. 157 der Weimarer Reichsverfassung seinen Ausdruck fand.[12] Die Rückschritte während der Zeit des Nationalsozialismus auf dem Gebiet des Arbeitnehmerschutzes und der Arbeitnehmerfreiheit[13] wurden nach dem Zweiten Weltkrieg durch den Erlass von neuen Gesetzen zum Arbeitsrecht entgegengewirkt.[14] Seitdem erging – angepasst an die sich verändernden gesellschaftlichen Bedürfnisse in der Arbeitswelt – eine Vielzahl an Gesetzen zum Individualarbeitsrecht. Heute finden sich die einzelnen Vorschriften des Arbeitsrechts verstreut auf viele allgemeine Gesetze und arbeitsrechtliche Spezialgesetze.[15] Die Definition des Arbeitsvertrages in § 611a BGB wurde erst mit Wirkung zum 1. April 2017 in das BGB aufgenommen. Diese Zersplitterung des Arbeitsrechts führt einerseits zu einer erheblichen Unübersichtlichkeit, andererseits erschwert sie die Entwicklung einer einheitlichen Rechtsdogmatik.[16] Die neuzeitliche Entwicklung des Arbeitsrechts ist in weiten Teilen auf die höchstrichterliche Rechtsprechung zurückzuführen, die grundlegende arbeitsrechtliche Prinzipien geprägt hat, ohne dass diese immer Eingang in gesetzliche Regelungen gefunden hätten.[17] Darüber hinaus steht das deutsche Arbeitsrecht unter konstantem Einfluss des Europarechts, das seine Fortentwicklung maßgeblich mitbestimmt.[18]

Diskussionsentwurf eines Arbeitsvertragsgesetz von 2007 nicht, in den Rang einer Gesetzesinitiative erhoben zu werden. Vgl. hierzu *Richardi* (Anm. 8), S. 769; *Griese*, Die Gesetzentwürfe der Länder für ein Arbeitsvertragsgesetz, in: Neue Zeitschrift für Arbeitsrecht, Heft Nr. 15 (1996), S. 803 ff., *Maties*, in: BeckOGK (Anm. 7), § 611a BGB, Rn. 2040.

10 *Maties*, in: BeckOGK (Anm. 7), § 611a, Rn. 2022.

11 *Maties*, in: BeckOGK (Anm. 7), § 611a, Rn. 2029, 2031.

12 Bei den in die Weimarer Verfassung (WV) eingearbeiteten Regelungen zum Arbeitsrecht stellte Art. 157 Abs. 1 WV die Arbeit unter besonderen Schutz, während Abs. 2 einen Programmsatz an den Gesetzgeber vorsah, ein einheitliches Arbeitsrecht zu schaffen. Vgl. *Maties*, in: BeckOGK (Anm. 7), § 611a, Rn. 2023.

13 *Maties*, in: BeckOGK (Anm. 7), § 611a BGB, Rn. 2034 ff.; *Fischinger*, in: J. von Staudingers Kommentar zum Bürgerlichen Gesetzbuch, Vorbemerkungen zu § 611a BGB, Rn. 27.

14 *Maties*, in: BeckOGK (Anm. 7), § 611a BGB, Rn. 2038.

15 *Spinner*, in: Säcker/Rixecker/Oetker/Limperg/Schubert, Münchner Kommentar zum BGB, 9. Auflage (2023), § 611a BGB, Rn. 83.

16 *Löwisch*, Das Verhältnis von Arbeitsrecht und Zivilrecht in Japan und Deutschland, in: Düwell/Löwisch/Waltersmann/Wank (Hrsg.), Das Verhältnis von Arbeitsrecht und Zivilrecht in Japan, Bonner Schriften zum deutschen und europäischen Recht der Arbeit und der Sozialen Sicherheit, Band 15 (2013), S. 37.

17 *Spinner*, in: MüKo (Anm. 15), § 611a BGB, Rn. 83.

18 *Spinner*, in: MüKo (Anm. 15), § 611a BGB, Rn. 178 ff.

2. Entwicklung des Arbeitsrechts in Japan

Im Gegensatz zum deutschen „Flickenteppich“ an Arbeitsnormen arbeitete in Japan die *Kommission für Arbeitsgesetzgebung* nach dem Ende des Zweiten Weltkriegs einen einheitlichen Gesetzesentwurf aus. Mit Ausnahme des Fabrikgesetzes (工場法, *kōjōhō*) von 1911 zum Schutz von Fabrikarbeitern und Frauen gab es in Japan vor dem Zweiten Weltkrieg keine umfassenden Arbeitsgesetze.[19] Eine Ausnahme bildete insoweit der Bergbau, wo bereits Ende des 1900 Jahrhundert Arbeitsschutzvorschriften Eingang in das japanische Minengesetz (日本坑法, *nihon kōhō*) (1873) und die Bergbauindustrieverordnung (鉱業条例, *kōgyō jōrei*) (1890) fanden.[20]

Das japanische Arbeitsrecht basierte allein auf den Bestimmungen in Art. 623 ff. des japanischen Zivilgesetzes (民法, *minpō*) (ZivilG) über den Beschäftigungsvertrag[21], welche nach dem Vorbild des deutschen BGB geschaffen wurden, und entsprechend dem deutschen Vorbild einzig Parteiautonomie als Grundsatz kannten.[22]

Erst nach dem Zweiten Weltkrieg wurden die verfassungsrechtlichen Grundlagen des heutigen japanischen Arbeitsrechts geschaffen.[23] Dazu gehören das Recht auf Arbeit für jedermann gemäß Art. 27 Abs. 1 der japanischen Verfassung (日本国憲法, *nihonkoku kenpō*) (JV), die Verpflichtung des Gesetzgebers zur gesetzlichen Regelung von Löhnen, Arbeitszeiten, Ruhezeiten und sonstigen Arbeitsbedingungen nach Art. 27 Abs. 2 JV, das Recht auf Existenz als eines der Leitprinzipien des japanischen Arbeitsrechts gemäß Art. 25 JV, der Schutz vor Zwangsarbeit in Art. 18 JV sowie die Koalitionsfreiheit in Art. 28 JV.[24]

Die durch die besondere Situation der Nachkriegszeit bedingte Dringlichkeit führte dazu, dass sich die führenden Arbeitsrechtler in Japan bei der Ausarbeitung der nach Kriegsende erforderlichen grundlegenden Gesetzestexte auf das juristische Erbe der Vorkriegszeit stützten.[25] Die arbeitsrechtliche Theorie in Japan war dabei maßgeblich von deutschen Überlegungen geprägt. Insbesondere fanden die das so-

---

19 *Wada*, Einfluss fremder Rechtsordnungen auf das japanische Arbeitsrecht, in: Düwell/Haase (Hrsg.), Arbeit und Recht im gesellschaftlichen Wandel. 25 Jahre Gesellschaft für Arbeitsrecht in Deutschland und Japan. Festschrift zum 25. Geburtstag der Deutsch-Japanischen Gesellschaft für Arbeitsrecht e. V., (2023), S. 88.

20 *Marutschke*, Einführung in das japanische Recht (1999), S. 202.

21 Erst durch Einführung des ASG wurde der Vertragstyp umbenannt in den des Arbeitsvertrages.

22 *Nogawa*, Bürgerliches Recht und Arbeitsrecht – Einzelgesetze in Japan, in: Düwell/Löwisch/Waltersmann/Wank (Hrsg.), Das Verhältnis von Arbeitsrecht und Zivilrecht in Japan, Bonner Schriften zum deutschen und europäischen Recht der Arbeit und der Sozialen Sicherheit, Band 15 (2013), S. 41.

23 *Nishitani*, Bürgerliches Recht und Arbeitsrecht in Japan, in: Düwell/Löwisch/Waltersmann/Wank (Hrsg.), Das Verhältnis von Arbeitsrecht und Zivilrecht in Japan, Bonner Schriften zum deutschen und europäischen Recht der Arbeit und der Sozialen Sicherheit, Band 15 (2013), S. 8.

24 *Hanami/Komiya*, Labour Law in Japan, (2011), Abs. 76, S. 54.

25 *Wada* (Anm. 19), S. 88; *Nishitani*, Altes Europa – neues Amerika? Die Entwicklung des japanischen Arbeitsrechts und der Einfluss des deutschen und amerikanischen Rechts, in: Zeitschrift für Japanisches Recht, Heft Nr. 18 (2004), S. 133.

ziale Recht prägenden Gedanken, die bereits Einfluss auf die Weimarer Reichsverfassung genommen hatten, Eingang in das japanische Arbeitsrecht, etwa im Recht auf Existenz gemäß Art. 25 JV.[26] So wurde unter Zugrundelegung deutscher Arbeitsrechtsbegriffe und -systematik[27] eine auf Japan zugeschnittene Fassung des Rechts entwickelt.[28]

Im Zuge dieses Prozesses wurden zunächst 1947 das ASG und anschließend 1949 das Gewerkschaftsgesetz (労働組合法, *rōdō kumiai hō*) erlassen, das die in Art. 27 Abs. 2 JV geforderte Festlegung der Mindestanforderungen an die Arbeitsbedingungen verwirklichte und den Kern des japanischen Individualarbeitsrechts bildete.[29]

Obwohl das japanische Arbeitsrecht zunächst auf deutsche Grundlagen gestützt wurde, entwickelte es sich jedoch schnell eigenständig weiter. Anders als in der deutschen Rechtsordnung wurde in Japan die Auffassung vertreten, dass dem Arbeitsrecht aufgrund seines besonderen Regelungsinhalts eine Sonderstellung gegenüber dem allgemeinen Vertragsrecht zukomme und es vom Bürgerlichen Recht getrennt zu betrachten sei.[30] Bei der Auslegung von unbestimmten Rechtsbegriffen, dem Umgang mit Gesetzeslücken und der Rechtsfortbildung dieser Gesetze von Rechtsprechung und Lehre wird indes nicht direkt auf die allgemeinen Bestimmungen im ZivilG zum Arbeitsvertrag zurückgegriffen, sondern arbeitsrechtliche Auslegung im Lichte der Verfassung und nur der Generalklauseln des ZivilG[31] betrieben.[32] Die richterrechtliche Rechtsfortbildung des Arbeitsrecht wurde im Jahre 2007 durch das japanische Arbeitsvertragsgesetz (労働契約法, *rōdō keiyaku hō*) (JAVG) zum Teil kodifiziert.[33]

Bereits mit der Einführung des ASG wurde der Unterschied des Arbeitsvertrags zu anderen Vertragstypen klargestellt und von der Rechtsprechung bestätigt. Auch heute geht die japanische Rechtswissenschaft davon aus, dass dem Arbeitsrecht aufgrund seines besonderen Regelungscharakters[34] eine Sonderstellung gegenüber dem allge-

---

26 *Nishitani* (Anm. 25), S. 136.

27 *Knapp*, Ausgewählte Aspekte des japanischen Individualarbeitsrechts. Eine rechtsvergleichende Studie mit der österreichischen Arbeitsrechtsordnung (2017), aufrufbar unter https://unipub.uni-graz.at/obvugrhs/content/titleinfo/2324836?lang=de (zuletzt aufgerufen am 26. März 2025), S. 5.

28 *Wada* (Anm. 19), S. 93; *Nishitani* (Anm. 25), S. 134; *Wada*, Strukturelle Veränderungen in der japanischen Gesellschaft und im Arbeitsrecht, in: Düwell/Gallner/Haase/Wolmerath (Hrsg.), Auf dem Weg zu einem sozialen und inklusiven Rechtsstaat – Covid-19 als Herausforderung, Liber amicorum Franz Josef Düwell (2021), S. 227.

29 *Nishitani* (Anm. 25), S. 131 (136); *Nishitani* (Anm. 23), S. 8.

30 *Nishitani* (Anm. 23), S. 6 f.

31 So werden als Grundsätze für die Auslegung unter anderem Treu und Glauben, das Verbot des Rechtsmissbrauchs, sowie Sittenwidrigkeit herangezogen. Vgl. hierzu *Nogawa* (Anm. 22), S. 43.

32 *Nishitani* (Anm. 23), S. 8 f.

33 Hierin finden sich unter anderem Vorschriften zur Work-Life-Balance (Art. 3 Abs. 3 JAVG), Gleichberechtigung zwischen Arbeitgeber und -nehmer (Art. 3 Abs. 1 JAVG), gutem Glauben (Art. 3 Abs. 4 JAVG), sowie Rechtsmissbrauch (Art. 3 Abs. 5 JAVG).

34 Auf der Grundlage von Art. 25 JV und des darin normierten Rechts auf Existenz muss vor diesem Hintergrund die gewährte Teilhabe an den Früchten des wirtschaftlichen Wachstums

meinen Vertragsrecht zukommt und es als vom Bürgerlichen Recht eigenständig zu betrachten ist.

In den letzten Jahrzehnten wurde auch das japanische Arbeitsrecht immer komplexer. Neue Gesetzesnovellierungen[35] delegieren Detailregelungen verstärkt an die Exekutive, die Verordnungen zur Konkretisierung der Gesetze ohne parlamentarische Beratung erlassen kann. Zugleich werden die erlassenen Gesetze immer rechtstechnischer.[36] Zudem ist in der arbeitsrechtlichen Wissenschaft Japans eine Tendenz erkennbar, sich von der ursprünglich prägenden Vorstellung der abhängigen Arbeit und des durch ein Über-Unterordnungsverhältnis geprägten Arbeitsverhältnisses zu lösen und stärker das Recht des Arbeitnehmers auf Selbstbestimmung in den Vordergrund zu stellen.[37]

3. Vergleich

Die Arbeitsrechte beider Länder beruhen auf denselben rechtlichen Grundvorstellungen und teilen die fundamentalen Werte des Arbeitsschutzes. Ihre weitere Entwicklung wurde jedoch von unterschiedlichen kulturellen Wertvorstellungen und politischen Einflüssen geprägt. Im Folgenden sollen einige der daraus resultierenden Unterschiede im heutigen Arbeitsrecht aufgezeigt werden.

III. Die Arbeitsbeziehung als solche

1. Deutschland

Der Arbeitsvertrag ist in § 611a BGB als gegenseitiger Vertrag mit Hauptleistungspflichten ausgestaltet, bei dem Vergütung und Arbeitsleistung ausgetauscht werden. Er unterliegt damit den allgemeinen Regeln über Schuldverhältnisse.[38] Dennoch werden die Vertragspartner im Arbeitsrecht nicht gleichberechtigt behandelt. Dem deutschen Arbeitsrecht liegt das Verständnis zugrunde, dass der Arbeitnehmer dem Arbeitgeber strukturell unterlegen ist. Zwar steht beiden Parteien grundsätzlich die Vertragsautonomie zu, jedoch unterliegt der Arbeitnehmer faktisch dem Druck, das Arbeitsverhältnis aufrechtzuerhalten, um seinen Lebensunterhalt zu sichern.[39] Diese strukturelle Asymmetrie wird durch Einschränkungen der Vertragsfreiheit im Arbeitsrecht kompensiert, um eine weitgehende Waffengleichheit zwischen den

auch den Arbeitnehmern ermöglicht werden. Vgl. zum Recht auf Existenz *Nishihara*, Funktion der sozialen Grundrechte im japanischen Verfassungssystem, in: Zeitschrift für ausländisches öffentliches Recht und Völkerrecht (1990), S. 862.

35 In Art. 41-2 ASG werden bestimmte Fachkräfte vom Anwendungsbereich der Arbeitszeitregelung ausgeschlossen. Die Bestimmung der Voraussetzungen dieser Regelung, wie der Aufgabenbereich, die Höhe des Jahreslohns und das Verfahren für die Einführung, wird allerdings durch Verordnung der Regierung geregelt, vgl. *Wada* (Anm. 28), S. 224.

36 *Wada* (Anm. 28), S. 224.

37 *Wada* (Anm. 28), S. 227 f.

38 *Preis*, in: Erfurter Kommentar Müller-Glöge/Preis/Gallner/Schmidt, Erfurter Kommentar zum Arbeitsrecht, 25. Auflage (2025), § 611a BGB, Rn. 1.

39 *Schliemann*, Das Arbeitsrecht im BGB, 2. Auflage (2002), Rn. 23.

Parteien herzustellen.[40] Kritisch wird dabei insbesondere im Bereich des kollektiven Arbeitsrechts angemerkt, dass das Arbeitsrecht durch eine Vielzahl von Einzelgesetzen geprägt sei, was zu einer gewissen Unübersichtlichkeit führe.[41]

2. Japan

Wie in Deutschland wird auch in Japan das Verhältnis zwischen Arbeitgeber und Arbeitnehmer grundsätzlich als strukturell ungleich angesehen, woraus die Notwendigkeit eines besonderen Arbeitnehmerschutzes abgeleitet wird. Gleichwohl fehlt es in vielen Bereichen an entsprechenden Schutzvorschriften. So existieren in Japan weder eine gesetzliche Regelung zum Kündigungsschutz noch über die Lohnfortzahlung im Krankheitsfall.[42]

Dass das japanische Recht meist nur abstrakt einfachgesetzlich ausgestaltet ist,[43] ist Ausdruck des japanischen Verständnisses von Recht und Gerechtigkeit. Im Gegensatz zu Deutschland wird in Japan stärker auf die Idee der Gerechtigkeit selbst und auf verbindliche Grundsätze Wert gelegt als auf deren detaillierte gesetzliche Ausgestaltung. Historisch ergibt sich das im Westen durch Gesetze gesteuerte Verhalten in der japanischen Kultur vielmehr aus Traditionen und daraus erwachsenen sozialen Verhaltensregeln. Ein zentraler Bestandteil der japanischen Kultur ist etwa das Prinzip *giri* (義理), das die wechselseitige Verpflichtung einer Person gegenüber ihren verschiedenen sozialen Kreisen beschreibt, in denen insbesondere der Arbeitgeber eine herausragende Stellung einnimmt. Tatsächlich lässt sich das Verhältnis zwischen Arbeitgeber und Arbeitnehmer in Japan eher anhand dieses gesellschaftlich verpflichtenden Verhaltenskodex als auf Grundlage arbeitsrechtlicher Normen beschreiben. Die Arbeitsbeziehungen weisen eine Struktur auf, die familiären Verhältnissen ähnelt, und sind von vergleichbarem sozialem Druck und gegenseitiger Verantwortung geprägt.[44]

Die Arbeitsbeziehung in Japan wird nicht allein als vertragliche Verpflichtung zwischen Arbeitgeber und Arbeitnehmer verstanden, sondern zugleich als persönliche, auf Gegenseitigkeit beruhende Beziehung.[45] Der Arbeitsplatz gilt als integraler Bestandteil der eigenen Identität; die Wahl der beruflichen Tätigkeit beeinflusst nicht selten das gesamte weitere Leben.[46] Diese Sichtweise ist auch spirituell geprägt: Arbeit wird als etwas Ehrenhaftes betrachtet, und Fleiß gilt als Ausdruck persönlicher

---

40 *Sakowski*, Arbeitsrecht, 3. Auflage (2022), S. 1.

41 *Markmann*, 50 Jahre Arbeitsbeziehungen in Deutschland: eine Erfolgsgeschichte?, in: Industrielle Beziehungen, Heft Nr. 1 (1995), S. 98.

42 *Nishitani*, Flexibilisierung der Beschäftigung und des Arbeitsrechts in Japan, in: Zeitschrift für Japanisches Recht, Heft Nr. 10 (2000), S. 74.

43 *Knapp* (Anm. 27), S. 8.

44 *Yamamoto/Lloyd*, Ethical Considerations of Japanese Business Culture, in: Journal of Business Diversity, Heft Nr. 2 (2019), S. 117.

45 *Takami*, Current State of Working Hours and Overwork in Japan: Part II: Why do the Japanese Work Long Hours? in: Japan Labor Issues, Heft Nr. 18 (2019), S. 15.

46 *Shimada* (Anm. 4), S. 6.

Integrität und innerer Haltung. Die Tätigkeit selbst erhält dadurch eine fast ethische Qualität, die über die rein wirtschaftliche Dimension hinausreicht.

Zusammenfassend ähnelt sich der Charakter der Arbeitsbeziehung in Japan und Deutschland in rechtlicher Sicht sehr. Der über den Arbeitsvertrag hinausgehende psychologische Vertrag[47] zwischen den Parteien, der durch die Erwartungen an den jeweils anderen ausgefüllt wird, ist in Japan allerdings deutlich bestimmender. Dies ist wohl vor allem dem stärkeren gesellschaftlichen Druck geschuldet, sich konform zu den kulturell geprägten Arbeitsverhaltensnormen zu verhalten.

IV. Arbeitsvertragsgestaltung

Japans Arbeitswelt war lange dominiert von männlichen Arbeitnehmern, die in der Regel ein Leben lang angestellt waren und deren Gehalt sich jeweils auf Grundlage des Prinzips der Seniorität, also der Länge der Betriebszugehörigkeit, ergab. Aufgrund der traditionellen Gleichartigkeit des Arbeitsverhältnisses und der damit einhergehenden Gleichartigkeit der Arbeitsverträge war die Rolle des individuellen Arbeitsvertrags in Japan historisch gesehen nur sehr klein.[48] Statt individueller Ausgestaltung stand die kollektive Regelung im Vordergrund. Daraus ergibt sich eine Besonderheit des japanischen Arbeitsvertragsrechts: Nur wenige Punkte müssen im schriftlichen Arbeitsvertrag selbst geregelt sein. Während in Deutschland Arbeitsverträge regelmäßig detaillierte Regelungen zu Arbeitsbeginn, Arbeitszeit, Vergütung oder Überstunden enthalten, sind japanische Arbeitsverträge meist knapp und allgemein gehalten.

Die konkreten Arbeitsbedingungen werden in Japan regelmäßig in der sogenannten Arbeitsordnung (就業規則, *shūgyō kisoku*) festgelegt.[49] Diese ist ihrer Rechtsnatur nach Bestandteil des Arbeitsvertrags, kann jedoch einseitig durch den Arbeitgeber erlassen und geändert werden. Zwar ist der Arbeitgeber verpflichtet, die Arbeitsordnung unter Beteiligung der Gewerkschaft, die die Mehrheit der Arbeitnehmer repräsentiert, oder eines gewählten Arbeitnehmervertreters zu erstellen, jedoch besteht kein Einigungszwang im Sinne eines zweiseitigen Vertrags.[50] Die Mitwirkung der Arbeitnehmer beschränkt sich somit auf ein Beteiligungsrecht, nicht auf ein Vetorecht. Kommt es zu einer inhaltlichen Abweichung zwischen dem individuell mit dem Arbeitnehmer geschlossenen Arbeitsvertrag und der Arbeitsordnung, ist stets die für den Arbeitnehmer günstigere Regelung anzuwenden.[51]

Gemäß Art. 89 ASG sind Arbeitgeber, die mehr als zehn Arbeitnehmer beschäftigen, verpflichtet, eine Arbeitsordnung zu erstellen. Der Inhalt der Arbeitsordnung

---

47 Vgl. *Wehling*, in: Hirsch-Kreinsen/Minssen (Hrsg.), Lexikon der Arbeits- und Industriesoziologie, 2. Auflage (2017), S. 265.

48 *Yamakawa*, Overhaul After 50 Years: The Amendment of the Labour Standard Law, in: Japan Labor Bulletin, Heft Nr. 11 (1998), S. 8.

49 *Wada*, Die Regelung der Arbeitsbedingungen in japanischen Betrieben, in: Arbeit und Recht, Ausgabe 10 (2002), S. 372.

50 *Wada* (Anm. 49), S. 370.

51 *Hanami/Komiya*, (Anm. 24), Abs. 86, S. 58.

umfasst Regelungen zur Arbeitszeit, insbesondere zu Beginn und Ende der Arbeitszeit, Pausen, Ruhetagen und Urlaubszeiten sowie im Falle von Schichtarbeit zu den einzelnen Schichten (Art. 89 Nr. i ASG); Bestimmungen über die Festsetzung, Berechnung und Auszahlung der Löhne, einschließlich des Zeitpunkts der Lohnauszahlung sowie etwaiger Lohnerhöhungen (Art. 89 Nr. ii ASG); Regelungen zur Beendigung des Arbeitsverhältnisses sowie gegebenenfalls zu Ruhegeldern und Abfindungen (Art. 89 Nr. iii ASG); Vorschriften über die Auszahlung besonderer Lohnbestandteile (Art. 89 Nr. iv ASG); Bestimmungen über die Kostentragung für Verpflegung, Arbeitsmaterialien oder sonstige derartige Ausgaben (Art. 89 Nr. v ASG); gegebenenfalls Regelungen zur Sicherheit und zum Gesundheitsschutz am Arbeitsplatz (Art. 89 Nr. vi ASG); gegebenenfalls Bestimmungen zur Berufsausbildung (Art. 89 Nr. vii ASG); gegebenenfalls Vorschriften über Entschädigungen bei Verletzungen oder Krankheiten sowie Unterstützungsleistungen bei nicht berufsbedingten Verletzungen oder Erkrankungen (Art. 89 Nr. viii ASG); sowie gegebenenfalls Regelungen über die Gewährung, Art und Umfang von Boni oder Sanktionen (Art. 89 Nr. ix ASG). Art. 89 Nr. x ASG enthält schließlich eine Auffangklausel für sonstige Bestimmungen, die am Arbeitsplatz gelten sollen, jedoch nicht von den zuvor genannten Regelungsbereichen erfasst sind, d.h. weitere, durch Verordnung des Gesundheits-, Arbeits- und Wohlfahrtsministeriums festgelegte Punkte.

Vergleichend lässt sich konstatieren, dass im deutschen Arbeitsrecht dem individuellen Arbeitsvertrag eine größere Bedeutung zukommt als im japanischen Recht.[52] Zwar kennt auch das deutsche Recht kollektive Regelungsinstrumente in Form von Tarifverträgen und Betriebsvereinbarungen. Deren Regelungstiefe und -reichweite erreicht jedoch nicht das Ausmaß der japanischen Arbeitsordnung, die zentrale Arbeitsbedingungen – mit unmittelbarer Wirkung für alle Beschäftigten – auch einseitig durch den Arbeitgeber gestalten kann.

V. Arbeitszeit in Deutschland

1. Regelungen zur Arbeitszeit

Das deutsche Arbeitsrecht unterscheidet in seinen verschiedenen Arbeitsgesetzesquellen auch verschiedene Arbeitszeitbegriffe. Wenn von „Arbeitszeit" gesprochen wird, ist damit zumeist die tatsächliche mit der Arbeit verbrachte Zeit gemeint, also der arbeitsschutzrechtliche Arbeitszeitbegriff im Sinne des Arbeitszeitgesetzes (ArbZG).[53] Dieses verfolgt das Ziel, durch gesetzliche Höchstarbeitszeiten die Gesundheit der Arbeitnehmer zu schützen (§ 1 ArbZG). Für Fragen der Vergütung ist hingegen ein zivilrechtlicher Arbeitszeitbegriff maßgeblich, der sich nach der vertraglich geschuldeten Leistung richtet. Maßgebend für den arbeitsschutzrechtlichen Arbeitszeitbegriff sind die Vorschriften des ArbZG. Als Arbeitszeit versteht dieses

---

52 *Kiyono*, Chracteristics of and Differences between the Way of Working in Japan and Germany, in: Düwell/Gallner/Haase/Wolmerath (Hrsg.), Auf dem Weg zu einem sozialen und inklusiven Rechtsstaat – Covid-19 als Herausforderung, Liber amicorum Franz Josef Düwell (2021), S. 115f.

53 *Fuhlrott/Schmechel*, Ableistung und Vergütung von Überstunden, in: Arbeitsschutz in Recht und Praxis, Heft Nr. 1 (2024), S. 7.

die Zeit von Beginn bis Ende der Arbeit ohne die Ruhepausen (§ 2 Abs. 1 Hs. 1 ArbZG).

Grundsätzlich steht es den Arbeitsvertragsparteien frei, die Arbeitszeit im Rahmen ihrer Vertragsfreiheit zu bestimmen. Allerdings wird diese Freiheit durch das ArbZG insoweit beschränkt, als dass sich die Vereinbarung nur innerhalb der gesetzlichen Grenzen befinden darf.[54] In § 3 Satz 1 ArbZG wird die werktägliche[55] Höchstarbeitszeit auf acht Stunden festgesetzt. Damit liegt die wöchentliche Obergrenze bei 48 Stunden.[56] Solange die durchschnittliche Arbeitszeit innerhalb von sechs Monaten bzw. 24 Wochen diese Grenze nicht überschreitet, darf die tägliche Arbeitszeit gem. § 3 Satz 2 ArbZG bis zu zehn Stunden betragen. Weitere Ausnahmen bedürfen der Genehmigung der zuständigen Aufsichtsbehörde (§§ 14, 15 ArbZG).

Bei einer Arbeitszeit zwischen sechs und neun Stunden muss dem Arbeitnehmer nach spätestens sechs Stunden unterbrochener Arbeitszeit eine Pause von 30 Minuten gewährt werden. Ab einer Arbeitszeit von neun Stunden ist eine Ruhepause von 45 Minuten zu gewähren (§ 4 S. 1, 3 ArbZG). Nach Beendigung der täglichen Arbeitszeit ist eine ununterbrochene Ruhezeit von elf Stunden einzuhalten (§ 5 Abs. 1 ArbZG).

Die Beschäftigung an Sonn- und gesetzlichen Feiertagen ist grundsätzlich unzulässig (§ 9 Abs. 1 ArbZG). Ausnahmen hiervon sind in § 10 ArbZG geregelt, insbesondere für Beschäftigte in Krankenhäusern (§ 10 Abs. 1 Nr. 3), Gaststätten (§ 10 Abs. 1 Nr. 4) und Freizeiteinrichtungen (§ 10 Abs. 1 Nr. 7). Bei Inanspruchnahme einer solchen Ausnahme müssen mindestens 15 Sonntage pro Jahr beschäftigungsfrei bleiben (§ 11 Abs. 1 ArbZG). Zudem ist ein Ersatzruhetag zu gewähren (§ 11 Abs. 3 Satz 1, 2 ArbZG). Die wöchentliche Höchstarbeitszeit darf auch bei Sonn- oder Feiertagsarbeit nicht überschritten werden.

Durch Tarifvereinbarung kann von den Bestimmungen zur Höchstarbeitszeit, der Ruhepausen, der Ruhezeit, sowie von den Sonn- und Feiertagsregelungen abgewichen werden (vgl. §§ 7, 12 ArbZG).

Die Einhaltung der Vorschriften wird durch die zuständige Aufsichtsbehörde überwacht (§ 17 Abs. 1 ArbZG). Verstöße können gemäß §§ 22, 23 ArbZG mit Geldbußen bis zu 5.000 Euro oder, im Fall vorsätzlicher und wiederholter Zuwiderhandlung mit Gefährdung der Gesundheit des Arbeitnehmers, mit Freiheitsstrafe bis zu einem Jahr geahndet werden.

Vom persönlichen Anwendungsbereich des ArbZG ausgenommen sind gemäß § 18 Abs. 1 Nr. 1 leitende Angestellte, deren Arbeitszeit sich nicht in gleicher Weise steuern oder kontrollieren lässt und deren Tätigkeit wegen ihrer Leitungsfunktion eine besondere Eigenverantwortung erfordert.[57]

---

54 *Bayreuther*, Arbeitszeit zwischen unionsrechtlicher Grundrechtecharta und Vertrag, in: Recht der Arbeit, Heft Nr. 4 (2022), S. 290.

55 Werktage sind solche Tage, die weder Sonntage noch gesetzliche Feiertage sind, vgl. *Zerbe*, in: Tschöpe, Arbeitsrecht Handbuch, 6.A.VI., Rn. 27.

56 *Zerbe* (Anm. 55), 6.A.VI., Rn. 26.

57 U. a. auch ausgenommen sind Leiter von öffentlichen Dienststellen und deren Vertreter, sowie Arbeitnehmer, die zu selbständigen Entscheidungen in Personalangelegenheiten befugt

2. Überstunden

Unter den Begriff der Überstunden fällt diejenige Arbeitszeit, die über die vereinbarte Arbeitszeit hinaus geleistet wird.[58] Grundsätzlich besteht keine Verpflichtung des Arbeitnehmers, Überstunden zu leisten. Das dem Arbeitgeber nach § 106 GewO zustehende Weisungsrecht erstreckt sich nicht auf die Dauer der Arbeitsleistung.[59] Für einen entsprechenden Anspruch des Arbeitgebers auf das Ableisten von Überstunden durch den Arbeitnehmer ist – abgesehen von Notfällen (§ 14 ArbZG) – eine vertragliche Abrede nötig.[60] Eine solche ergibt sich meist aus Tarifvertrag.[61]

Selbst bei Vorliegen einer solchen Abrede dürfen Überstunden nur im Rahmen der gesetzlichen Höchstarbeitszeiten angeordnet werden.[62] § 3 ArbZG ist insoweit als Verbotsgesetz im Sinne von § 134 BGB zu qualifizieren.[63] Fehlt eine tarifvertragliche Regelung, die die Höchstarbeitszeit modifiziert, können Arbeitgeber Überstunden nur innerhalb der Grenzen von acht beziehungsweise zehn Stunden pro Tag anordnen.[64] Anders als im japanischen Arbeitszeitrecht sind die zulässigen Überstunden im deutschen Arbeitszeitgesetz bereits in die gesetzlichen Arbeitszeitgrenzen eingerechnet und können nicht zusätzlich geleistet werden.[65]

Die Vergütung von Überstunden ist im deutschen Arbeitsrecht gesetzlich nicht ausdrücklich normiert, sondern wurde bewusst der Regelung durch Arbeitsvertrag, Tarifvertrag oder Betriebsvereinbarung überlassen.[66] Dies bedeutet jedoch nicht, dass Überstunden bei Fehlen einer entsprechenden vertraglichen Vereinbarung generell unvergütet bleiben.

Zwar muss sich der Arbeitgeber eine Vergütungspflicht nicht aufdrängen lassen, allerdings ist er hierzu dann verpflichtet, wenn die Leistung der Überstunden durch ihn veranlasst wurde oder ihm diese zuzurechnen ist.[67] Eine Vergütungspflicht von Überstunden ergibt sich gem. § 612 Abs. 1 BGB dann,[68] wenn die Vergütung zu erwarten ist, also wenn sie bei Zugrundelegung eines objektiven Maßstabs und der Be-

---

sind (§ 18 Abs. 1 Nr. 2 ArbZG) und bestimmte Arbeitnehmer im Bereich der Pflege (§ 18 Abs. 1 Nr. 3 ArbZG).

58 *Vogelsang/Wensing*, Mehr Arbeit – mehr Geld, in: Recht der Arbeit, Heft Nr. 6 (2024), S. 317.

59 *Vogelsang/Wensing* (Anm. 58), S. 321.

60 *Pletke/Schrader/Siebert/Thoms/Klagges/Teubert*, Flexible Arbeit. Flexible Beschäftigungsverhältnisse, Personalanpassung, Vergütungssysteme, Arbeitszeitmodelle, Aufgabenänderung, 2. Auflage (2022), Rn. 468.

61 *Maschmann*, in: BeckOGK (Anm. 7), § 106 GewO, Rn. 181.

62 *Sakowski* (Anm. 40), S. 70.

63 Vgl. LAG Nürnberg, Urteil vom 19. Mai 2020, Az. 7 Sa 11/1, LS 1.

64 *Pletke/Schrader/Siebert/Thoms/Klagges/Teubert* (Anm. 60), Rn. 474.

65 *Kiyono* (Anm. 52), S. 118.

66 *Preis/Temming*, Arbeitsrecht. Individualarbeitsrecht, 7. Auflage (2024), Rn. 1279.

67 BAG, Urteil vom 10. April 2013, Az. 5 AZR 122/12, Rn. 13.

68 Eine Verpflichtung zur Vergütung gem. § 612 Abs. 1 BGB ergibt sich allerdings dann nicht, wenn die Vergütung der Überstunden wirksam vertraglich ausgeschlossen wurde, vgl. *Tautphäus*, FS Franz Josef Düwell, S. 661.

urteilung nach den Verkehrssitten, der Art, des Umfangs und der Dauer der Dienstleistung erwartet werden kann. Eine solche Vergütungserwartung kann sich auch aus der Üblichkeit in der jeweiligen Branche ergeben, etwa wenn einschlägige Tarifverträge in vergleichbaren Fällen eine Vergütung vorsehen.[69] In der arbeitsgerichtlichen Praxis wird dabei insbesondere auf die betriebliche Übung und die tatsächlichen Verhältnisse im Unternehmen sowie in der Branche abgestellt.

Hinsichtlich der Höhe der Vergütung ist § 612 Abs. 2 BGB einschlägig, wonach die übliche Vergütung zu zahlen ist. Allerdings muss diese nicht zwingend in Geld erfolgen, sondern dem Arbeitnehmer kann auch ein Ausgleich durch Freizeit eingeräumt werden.[70] Unter Freizeitausgleich ist die bezahlte Freistellung von der Arbeitspflicht zu verstehen.[71] Dies gilt im Übrigen auch dann, wenn die geleistete Arbeitszeit die gesetzlichen Höchstgrenzen überschreitet.[72] Voraussetzung für die Vergütung ist allerdings, dass die Arbeitsleistung vom Arbeitgeber explizit angeordnet, geduldet oder genehmigt wurde und diese im betrieblichen Interesse erforderlich war.[73] Eine über die Normalvergütung hinausgehende Pflicht zur Zahlung eines Überstundenzuschlags besteht gesetzlich nicht, kann aber individual- oder kollektivvertraglich vereinbart werden. In der Praxis sind Überstundenzuschläge weit verbreitet.[74]

Die Vereinbarung einer pauschalen Abgeltung von Überstunden ist grundsätzlich zulässig, solange sie den Arbeitnehmer nicht unangemessen benachteiligt.[75] Über die gesetzlichen Arbeitszeitgrenzen hinausgehende Überstunden können jedoch im Rahmen einer gesetzeskonformen Vertragsauslegung nicht von einer solchen Pauschalvergütung erfasst sein und sind gesondert zu vergüten.[76]

Keine Vergütungspflicht besteht bei sogenannten Diensten höherer Art, die besondere Fachkenntnisse, besondere künstlerische Fähigkeiten oder eine wissenschaftliche Ausbildung voraussetzen.[77] In diesen Fällen fehlt es regelmäßig an einer objektiven Erwartbarkeit der Vergütung. Nach der Rechtsprechung des Bundesarbeitsgerichts besteht insoweit kein allgemeiner Rechtsgrundsatz, wonach Arbeit über die vereinbarte Arbeitszeit hinaus automatisch zu vergüten wäre.[78] Eine Vergütungser-

---

69 BAG, Urteil vom 11. Oktober 2000, Az. AZR 122/99.

70 *Preis/Temming* (Anm. 66), Rn. 1280.

71 *Pletke/Schrader/Siebert/Thoms/Klagges/Teubert* (Anm. 60), Rn. 489.

72 LAG Rheinland-Pfalz, Urteil vom 16. Januar 2002, Az. 10 Sa 251/01.

73 *Sakowski* (Anm. 40), S. 87.

74 *Preis/Temming* (Anm. 66), Rn. 1281.

75 Eine unangemessene Benachteiligung des Arbeitnehmers durch Pauschalabreden liegt zum Beispiel dann vor, wenn ein pauschaler Ausschluss der Vergütung von Überstunden geregelt ist. Vgl. hierzu *Preis/Temming* (Anm. 66), Rn. 1284.

76 LAG Rheinland-Pfalz, Urteil vom 16. Januar 2002, Az. 10 Sa 251/01; *Zerbe* (Anm. 55), 6.A.VI., Rn. 82.

77 Zum Begriff der Dienste höherer Art BGH, Urteil vom 13. November 2014, Az. III ZR 101/14 in NJW-RR 2015, 686, Rn. 12.

78 BAG, Urteil vom 17. August 2011, Az. 5 AZR 406/20, LS. 2.

wartung entfällt zudem bei Arbeitnehmern mit besonders hohem Bruttojahresgehalt.[79]

VI. Arbeitszeit in Japan

1. Veränderung der Arbeitszeitregelung in Japan über die letzten Jahrzehnte

Bei der Einführung des ASG im Jahr 1947 war die Höchstarbeitszeit auf 48 Stunden pro Woche begrenzt.[80] Zweck des Gesetzes war primär der Schutz der Gesundheit der Arbeitnehmer; der Schutz des Familienlebens sowie kultureller oder sozialer Aktivitäten spielte keine Rolle. Dementsprechend enthielt das Gesetz keine Regelungen zur Begrenzung der Arbeit an Sonn- und Feiertagen.[81] Regelungen zur Begrenzung von Überstunden fanden sich in der ursprünglichen Fassung ebenso wenig.

Mit der Reform von 1987 wurden die gesetzliche Höchstarbeitszeit auf 40 Stunden pro Woche herabgesetzt, die Urlaubsansprüche der Arbeitnehmer erweitert und erstmals flexible Arbeitszeitsysteme gesetzlich anerkannt.[82] Zudem wurde dem Ministerium für Gesundheit, Arbeit und Soziales die Kompetenz eingeräumt, verbindliche Obergrenzen für Überstunden festzulegen. Zuvor konnte das Ministerium lediglich unverbindliche Empfehlungen aussprechen.[83] Die Richtlinien konnten jedoch durch eine Vereinbarung umgangen werden.[84]

Mit dem Gesetz zur Ausgestaltung der einschlägigen Gesetze zur Förderung der Arbeitsstil-Reform[85] wurde mit Geltung vom 1. April 2019 erstmals eine verbindliche Höchstgrenze für Überstunden direkt im Arbeitsgesetz implementiert. Darüber hinaus wurde die Verpflichtung des Arbeitgebers eingeführt, sicherzustellen, dass Arbeitnehmer mindestens fünf Urlaubstage pro Jahr tatsächlich in Anspruch nehmen, sowie die Gleichbehandlung von regulären und nicht-regulären Arbeitnehmern gesetzlich festgelegt.[86]

---

79 *Fuhlrott/Schmechel* (Anm. 53), S. 9; a. A. LAG Düsseldorf, Urteil vom 23. September 2020, Az. 14 Sa 296/20.

80 *Yamakawa* (Anm. 48), S. 7.

81 *Nishitani*, Vergleichende Einführung in das japanische Arbeitsrecht (2003), S. 201.

82 *Wada* (Anm. 28), S. 219.

83 *Yamakawa* (Anm. 48), S. 15.

84 *Takami*, Current State of Working Hours and Overwork in Japan: Part I: How Has It Changed Over the Years? in: Japan Labor Issues, Heft Nr. 16 (2019), S. 20; *Ishikawa/Schiebe*, The Japanese Work-Style Reform 2019, in: Zeitschrift für Japanisches Recht, Heft Nr. 47 (2019), S. 270.

85 Japanischer Titel des Gesetzes: 働き方改革を推進するための関係法律の整備に関する法律 (*hatarakikata kaikaku o suishin suru tame no kankei hōritsu no seibi ni kansuru hōritsu*).

86 *Takahashi/Kodama/Arita/Kazama/Sakai/Takeuchi/Owan*, Has Japan's worky style reform had the intended effect?, in: Applied Economics (2024), S. 1.

2. Arbeitszeitregelung in Japan

Arbeitszeit im Sinne des ASG ist definiert als jene Zeit, in der der Arbeitnehmer den Weisungen des Arbeitgebers unterliegt, abzüglich der Pausenzeiten.

Sämtliche Regelungen zur Arbeitszeit finden sich in den Art. 32 ff. ASG. Nach Art. 32 Abs. 1 und 2 ASG beträgt die zulässige Höchstarbeitszeit acht Stunden pro Tag und 40 Stunden pro Woche. Arbeitnehmern ist gemäß Art. 35 Abs. 1 ASG mindestens ein Ruhetag pro Woche zu gewähren. Bei einer täglichen Arbeitszeit von mehr als sechs Stunden ist eine Pause von mindestens 45 Minuten einzuräumen, bei mehr als acht Stunden eine Pause von mindestens einer Stunde (Art. 34 Abs. 1 ASG). Der Urlaubsanspruch beträgt je nach Dauer der Betriebszugehörigkeit zwischen zehn und zwanzig Tagen jährlich (Art. 39 Abs. 1, 2 ASG), wobei der Arbeitgeber verpflichtet ist, die tatsächliche Inanspruchnahme von mindestens fünf Urlaubstagen pro Jahr sicherzustellen (Art. 39 Abs. 7 ASG). Vom persönlichen Anwendungsbereich der Arbeitszeitregelungen ausdrücklich ausgenommen sind Arbeitnehmer in bestimmten Führungspositionen (Art. 41 Nr. ii ASG),[87] sowie Arbeitnehmer mit besonderen Fachkenntnissen, die hochqualifizierte und erfolgsorientierte Tätigkeiten verrichten (Art. 41-2 ASG).[88]

3. Ermessensarbeitszeit (*Discretionary Work System*)

Besonders problematisch ist die Ausnahmevorschrift für hochqualifizierte Tätigkeiten, die auf das System der Arbeit nach Ermessen (*Discretionary Work System*, 裁量労働制 (*sairyō rōdō sei*)) zurückgeht, geregelt in Art. 38-3 und 38-4 ASG. Dieses System erlaubt es Arbeitgebern und Arbeitnehmern, bei bestimmten Tätigkeiten – insbesondere bei hochqualifizierten Berufen wie Planern, Beratern oder Systemingenieuren – vertraglich zu vereinbaren, dass die tatsächlich geleistete Arbeitszeit unbeachtlich ist. Stattdessen wird eine bestimmte Zahl an Arbeitsstunden als erbracht fingiert, unabhängig von der real erbrachten Arbeitszeit.

Das *Discretionary Work System* unterliegt zwar formalen Anforderungen, etwa der Zustimmung eines Arbeitsmanagementausschusses sowie der individuellen Zustimmung des betroffenen Arbeitnehmers. In der Praxis wird das System jedoch häufig so eingesetzt, dass die gesetzlichen Arbeitszeitvorgaben – insbesondere hinsichtlich Höchstarbeitszeiten und Überstundenvergütung – faktisch ausgehöhlt werden. Ar-

---

87 Weiterhin sind vom persönlichen Anwendungsbereich Arbeitnehmer in Betrieben ausgeschlossen, die Land bewirtschaften oder urbar machen, Pflanzen anpflanzen, anbauen, ernten oder schneiden (Art. 41 lit. 1 ASG), Tiere züchten, Wassertiere oder -pflanzen ernten oder kultivieren oder ein anderes derartiges Viehzucht-, Serikultur- oder Fischereigeschäft betreiben (Art. 41 lit. iiii ASG), sowie Arbeitnehmer, die vertrauliche Vorgänge abwickelten (Art. 41 lit. i ASG).

88 Damit sind Arbeitnehmer gemeint, die in einem Bereich tätig sind, der ein hohes Maß fachlichen Wissens erfordert, in dem die geleistete Arbeit und das hieraus resultierende Ergebnis nicht zwingend korrelieren und deren Jahresgehalt den Schwellenwert von 10,75 Mio. JPY (ca. 66.350 EUR, April 2025) übersteigt, vgl. *Ishikawa/Schiebe* (Anm. 84), S. 272; *Hashimoto*, Arbeitsrecht in Japan, in: Recht der Internationalen Wirtschaft, Heft Nr. 9 (2018), S. 568.

beitnehmer leisten regelmäßig weit mehr Arbeitsstunden als fingiert, ohne dass dies zu einer entsprechenden Vergütung führt, während sich Arbeitgeber auf die vertraglich vereinbarte Arbeitszeit berufen.

Damit bildet das *Discretionary Work System* ein erhebliches Einfallstor zur Umgehung der arbeitszeitrechtlichen Schutzvorschriften und trägt wesentlich zur Problematik überlanger Arbeitszeiten in Japan bei. Zuletzt wurde mit einem am 1. April 2024 in Kraft getretenen Änderung die Arbeit nach Ermessen strenger geregelt, um zu verhindern, dass Arbeitgeber diese Form der Arbeit als Schlupfloch für unbezahlte Überstunden verwenden können.

4. Überstunden

Anders als im deutschen Recht können die Bestimmungen des ASG nicht durch Tarifvertrag (oder Arbeitsordnung) abbedungen werden.[89] Das ASG setzt zwingendes Recht, von dem grundsätzlich weder durch individuelle noch durch kollektive Vereinbarungen abgewichen werden kann. Allerdings enthält das Gesetz selbst zahlreiche Ausnahmetatbestände, die unter bestimmten Voraussetzungen Mehrarbeit über die in Art. 32 ASG festgelegten Höchstgrenzen hinaus zulassen.

a) Flexible Arbeitszeitregelungen

Das japanische Arbeitsrecht erlaubt eine flexible Gestaltung der Arbeitszeit. So gestatten Art. 32-2, 32-4 und 32-5 ASG die Einführung eines Arbeitssystems mit Zeitausgleich, während Art. 32-3 ASG die Einrichtung von Gleitzeitarbeitsmodellen ermöglicht. Daneben erlauben Art. 38-3 und 38-4 ASG die Gestaltung der Arbeitszeit nach Ermessen (*Discretionary Work System*). Innerhalb dieser Systeme dürfen Arbeitsstunden teilweise über die gesetzliche Tageshöchstgrenze hinausgehen, ohne als Überstunden im Sinne des Gesetzes zu gelten, solange die durchschnittliche Arbeitszeit innerhalb eines bestimmten Referenzzeitraums die gesetzlich vorgeschriebenen Grenzen nicht überschreitet.[90]

b) Überstunden zugunsten des öffentlichen Lebens

Eine weitere Ausnahme von den allgemeinen Arbeitszeitregelungen sieht Art. 40 Abs. 1 ASG vor. Danach ist das Ministerium für Gesundheit, Arbeit und Soziales befugt, für bestimmte Arten von Betrieben[91] Sonderregelungen hinsichtlich der Arbeitszeit zu erlassen, um Beeinträchtigungen des öffentlichen Lebens zu vermeiden.[92] Diese Sonderregelungen müssen sich gemäß Art. 40 Abs. 2 ASG jedoch an den allgemeinen arbeitszeitrechtlichen Grundsätzen orientieren und dürfen die Gesundheit der Arbeitnehmer nicht beeinträchtigen.

---

89 *Hashimoto* (Anm. 88), S. 564.

90 *Knapp* (Anm. 27), S. 54.

91 Beispielsweise Friseur-, Postauslieferungs- oder Passagiertransportbetriebe, sowie Betriebe im Gesundheits- oder Hygienebereich, vgl. Tabelle 1 im Anhang zum ASG.

92 *Nishitani* (Anm. 81), S. 205.

c) *Ausnahme im Katastrophenfall*

Gemäß Art. 33 Abs. 1 ASG ist der Arbeitgeber berechtigt, im Falle einer Naturkatastrophe oder eines sonstigen unabwendbaren Ereignisses die Arbeitszeitgrenzen zu überschreiten und Überstunden anzuordnen. Grundsätzlich bedarf eine solche Anordnung der Genehmigung durch die zuständige Regierungsbehörde. In dringenden Fällen kann der Arbeitgeber zunächst eigenständig handeln, muss die Anordnung jedoch unverzüglich nachträglich der Behörde melden. Die Vorschrift ist restriktiv auszulegen und findet auf rein betriebsbedingte Mehrarbeit keine Anwendung.[93] In der Praxis kommt der Ausnahmetatbestand des Art. 33 Abs. 1 ASG daher nur selten zur Anwendung.[94]

d) *Überstunden kraft betrieblicher Vereinbarung*

Die wohl am weitesten verbreitete und damit wichtigste Ausnahme von Art. 32 ASG findet sich in Art. 36 ASG, der die Zulässigkeit von Überstunden bei Vorliegen einer betrieblichen Vereinbarung regelt. Die Höchstgrenze für Überstunden, die aufgrund der üblichen, vorhersehbaren Arbeitsbelastung erforderlich sind (im Folgenden: gewöhnliche Überstunden), beträgt 45 Stunden im Monat und 360 Stunden im Jahr (Art. 36 Abs. 3, 4 ASG). Diese Obergrenzen wurden im Jahr 2019 erstmals in das ASG aufgenommen und sind vertraglich nicht disponibel.[95] Das Gesetz erlaubt jedoch unter bestimmten außergewöhnlichen Umständen eine Überschreitung dieser Grenzen. Bei einem normalerweise nicht vorhersehbaren erheblichen Anstieg der Arbeitsbelastung kann der Arbeitgeber vorübergehend bis zu 100 Überstunden pro Monat (Art. 36 Abs. 5, 6 Nr. ii ASG), 80 Überstunden im Monatsdurchschnitt über einen Zeitraum von zwei bis sechs Monaten (Art. 36 Abs. 5, 6 Nr. iii ASG) oder bis zu 720 Überstunden im Jahr (Art. 36 Abs. 5 ASG) anordnen. Eine Überschreitung der monatlichen Höchstgrenze von 45 Überstunden im Rahmen dieser Ausnahmeregelung ist allerdings nur in bis zu sechs Monaten pro Jahr zulässig (Art. 36 Abs. 5 Satz 2 ASG).

Voraussetzung für die Anordnung von Überstunden nach Art. 36 ASG ist der Abschluss einer sogenannten 36er-Vereinbarung サブロク協定 bzw. 36協定 (*saburoku kyōtei*) zwischen Arbeitgeber und Arbeitnehmervertretung.[96] Diese Vereinbarung muss bestimmte Mindestinhalte (*essentialia negotii*) aufweisen, nämlich: den Kreis der betroffenen Arbeitnehmer (Art. 36 Abs. 2 Nr. i ASG), den Geltungszeitraum, der maximal ein Jahr betragen darf (Art. 36 Abs. 2 Nr. ii ASG), die Gründe für die Anordnung von Überstunden (Art. 36 Abs. 2 Nr. iii ASG), die maximal zulässige Zahl der Überstunden pro Tag, Monat und Jahr (Art. 36 Abs. 2 Nr. iv ASG) sowie gege-

---

93 Vgl. Erklärung der Beratungsstelle für Beschäftigung des Ministeriums für Gesundheit, Arbeit und Soziales zu Arbeitsgesetzen, 2023, S. 95, aufrufbar unter https://kecc.mhlw.go.jp/pdf/explanations_of_labor_related_laws_en_2310.pdf.

94 *Hashimoto* (Anm. 88), S. 564.

95 *Ishikawa/Schiebe* (Anm. 84), S. 271.

96 *Nishitani* (Anm. 81), S. 226; die 36er Vereinbarungen wird auch als 3-6-Abkommen (so *Tanaka*, Recht kurz bitte (1). Überstunden und sogenannten 3-6-Abkommen, in: Japanmarkt (2010), S. 34 ff.) bezeichnet. Die Namensbezeichnung geht darauf zurück, dass sich die Pflicht zum Abschluss einer solchen Übereinkunft aus Art. 36 ASG ergibt.

benenfalls weitere durch Verordnung vorgeschriebene Angaben (Art. 36 Abs. 2 Nr. v ASG).

Für die Anordnung außergewöhnlicher Überstunden nach Art. 36 Abs. 5 ASG müssen zusätzlich die zulässige Zahl der Überstunden pro Monat sowie die zulässige Zahl der Monate, in denen die gewöhnlichen Überstunden überschritten werden dürfen, ausdrücklich in der Vereinbarung geregelt sein.

Die 36er-Vereinbarung begründet für sich genommen allerdings noch keinen schuldrechtlichen Anspruch des Arbeitgebers auf die Leistung von Überstunden. Sie bewirkt lediglich, dass Überstunden, die im Rahmen dieser Vereinbarung geleistet werden, nicht als gesetzeswidrig gelten. Der Arbeitgeber benötigt daher zusätzlich eine vertragliche Anspruchsgrundlage für die Anordnung von Überstunden, die regelmäßig in der Arbeitsordnung zu finden ist, welche – wie oben erläutert – Bestandteil des Arbeitsvertrages wird.[97]

e) Vergütung von Überstunden

Überstunden sind gemäß Art. 37 Abs. 1 ASG mit einem Prämienlohn zu vergüten. Für bis zu 60 Überstunden im Monat ist der Stundenlohn um einen Zuschlag zwischen 25 % und 50 % zu erhöhen. Überstunden, die diesen Schwellenwert überschreiten, sind mit einem Zuschlag von mindestens 50 %[98] auf den regulären Lohn zu vergüten.

Eine vertragliche Regelung, wonach bis zu 45 gewöhnliche Überstunden pauschal durch einen Überstundenzuschlag zusätzlich zum Basisgehalt abgegolten werden, ist grundsätzlich wirksam.[99] Übersteigen die tatsächlich geleisteten Überstunden jedoch die mit der Pauschale abgegoltene Zahl, sind die darüberhinausgehenden Überstunden gesondert zu vergüten. Dies folgt aus dem Zweck des Art. 37 ASG, der auf eine Begrenzung von Überstunden abzielt und dem Arbeitgeber zur Steuerung der Arbeitszeiten die Verpflichtung zur Zahlung von Prämienzuschlägen auferlegt.[100]

Anders als im deutschen Recht wird im japanischen Recht nicht zwischen arbeitsschutzrechtlichem und vergütungsrechtlichem Arbeitszeitbegriff unterschieden.[101] Die Berechnung der zu vergütenden Überstunden richtet sich einheitlich nach den Vorgaben der Art. 38 ff. ASG.

f) Rechtliche Konsequenzen der Nichteinhaltung der Überstundenregelung

Bei Verstößen gegen die gesetzlichen Arbeitszeitvorgaben drohen dem Arbeitgeber gemäß Art. 119 ASG strafrechtliche Sanktionen. Danach kann eine Geldbuße

---

97 *Wada* (Anm. 49), S. 372.

98 Zum 1. April 2023 wurde der Zuschlag auf Überstunden, die die 60-Stunden-Grenze überschritten haben, von 25 % auf 50 % erhöht.

99 *Müller*, Arbeitsrecht in Japan: Erhöhung der Zuschläge für Überstunden, aufrufbar unter https://www.cbbl-lawyers.de/news/arbeitsrecht-in-japan-erhoehung-der-zuschlaege-fuer-ueberstunden (zuletzt aufgerufen am 25. März 2025).

100 *Ikezoe*, On Payment or Non-payment of Premium Wages When Incorporated Into Annual Salary, in: Japan Labor Issues, Heft Nr. 10 (2018), S. 13.

101 *Hashimoto* (Anm. 88), S. 572.

von bis zu 300.000 Yen (etwa 1.850 Euro, April 2025) oder eine Freiheitsstrafe von bis zu sechs Monaten verhängt werden.

Die Sanktionierung erfolgt insbesondere dann, wenn der Arbeitgeber die gesetzlich festgelegten Höchstarbeitszeiten überschreitet, Überstunden ohne ordnungsgemäße Vereinbarung und Genehmigung leisten lässt – insbesondere ohne Abschluss oder ordnungsgemäße Einreichung der 36er-Vereinbarung – oder keine Überstundenvergütung zahlt. Die maximale Geldbuße gilt dabei nicht pro Einzelfall, sondern pro Täter.

Dies bedeutet, dass sowohl das Unternehmen als juristische Person als auch verantwortliche natürliche Personen wie etwa der Leiter der Personalabteilung jeweils mit bis zu 300.000 Yen belegt werden können. Der Ablauf von der Feststellung eines Verstoßes bis zur strafrechtlichen Sanktionierung ist dabei dreistufig ausgestaltet: Zunächst führt das zuständige Arbeitsinspektionsamt (労働基準監督署, *rōdō kijun kantokusho*) des japanischen Ministeriums für Gesundheit, Arbeit und Soziales (厚生労働省労働基準局, *kōsei rōdōshō rōdō kijunkyoku*) eine Untersuchung durch, wobei bereits die Verweigerung der Mitwirkung mit einer separaten Geldbuße geahndet werden kann. Wird im Rahmen der Untersuchung ein Verstoß festgestellt, so ergeht eine formelle Korrekturmaßnahme mit der Aufforderung, den Verstoß zu beseitigen. Erst wenn dieser Aufforderung nicht Folge geleistet wird, erfolgt die strafrechtliche Verfolgung. In der Praxis werden Bußgelder jedoch vergleichsweise selten verhängt.

Im Fiskaljahr 2023 wurden von den landesweit 139.215 durchgeführten regulären Arbeitsinspektionen in 96.831 Fällen (69,6 %) Verstöße gegen arbeitsrechtliche Vorschriften festgestellt[102], davon in 43.147 Fällen Verstöße im Zusammenhang mit Überstunden. Insgesamt kam es 2023 zu 799 strafrechtlichen Verweisungen an die Staatsanwaltschaft, wobei lediglich 57 davon Überstundenverstöße betrafen.[103] Selbst in diesen Fällen wurde lediglich in etwa 34 % der Fälle tatsächlich Anklage erhoben. Alle so geahndeten Fälle endeten mit der Verhängung von Geldbußen; es kam zu keinen Freiheitsstrafen oder Freisprüchen. In der Praxis bleibt die Strafverfolgung damit die Ausnahme, nicht zuletzt, weil viele Verstöße nicht angezeigt werden und Arbeitnehmer aufgrund sozialen oder betrieblichen Drucks von einer Beschwerde absehen.

Ergänzend können bei systematischer oder schwerwiegender Verletzung der Arbeitszeitvorschriften aufsichtsrechtliche Maßnahmen durch die Arbeitsinspektionsbehörden angeordnet werden, darunter Maßnahmen zur Verbesserung der Arbeitsbedingungen oder – bei Wiederholungsverstößen – sogar die vollständige oder teilweise Stilllegung des Betriebs.

---

102 *Labour Standards Bureau Ministry of Health, Labour and Welfare*, 2023 Annual Labour Standards Inspection Report (Vol. 76), S. 14.

103 Labour Standards Bureau Ministry of Health, Labour and Welfare (Anm. 102), S. 26.

5. Tatsächliche Handhabung von Überstunden und ihre kulturelle Einbettung

In den letzten Jahrzehnten ist die durchschnittliche Zahl der in Japan geleisteten Überstunden deutlich zurückgegangen.[104] Ursache hierfür sind unter anderem gesetzgeberische Maßnahmen der Regierung, die auf eine Reduzierung der Überstunden abzielen. Dennoch liegt die Zahl der Überstunden weiterhin auf einem hohen Niveau[105], insbesondere wenn man davon ausgeht, dass viele Überstunden gar nicht erfasst werden.[106] Im Folgenden werden die tatsächlichen Ursachen für Überstunden in Japan unter besonderer Berücksichtigung der kulturellen Einbettung des Arbeitsrechts in die japanische Gesellschaft näher untersucht.

a) Verhaltensnormen aufgrund des gemeinschaftlichen Charakters der Arbeit

Die japanische Kultur ist stark am Gemeinwohl orientiert und stellt dieses regelmäßig über die Belange des Einzelnen. Ausgangspunkt ist die Vorstellung, dass der Einzelne innerhalb einer harmonischen Gruppe aufgehen und sich entfalten kann, solange die Harmonie gewahrt bleibt.[107] Dieses Prinzip prägt auch die Arbeitsgemeinschaft, die durch ein stetes Streben nach Konfliktvermeidung und Aufrechterhaltung der Harmonie gekennzeichnet ist.[108] Die Interessen des Unternehmens und der Kollegschaft genießen dabei Vorrang vor den individuellen Interessen des einzelnen Arbeitnehmers.[109]

Wie oben bereits erläutert, besteht zwischen japanischen Arbeitnehmern und ihrem Arbeitgeber sowie ihren Kollegen ein besonderes soziales Verpflichtungsverhältnis. Das soziale Umfeld am Arbeitsplatz wird vielfach der Familie gleichgesetzt.[110] Arbeitnehmer empfinden es als Verpflichtung, niemandem zur Last zu fallen. Aus diesem kulturellen Hintergrund erklärt sich das in Japan verbreitete Phänomen der sogenannten Service-Überstunden (サービス残業, *sābisu zangyō*). Dabei handelt es sich um Überstunden, die zwar tatsächlich geleistet, aber nicht abgerechnet wer-

---

104 Während im Jahr 1987 die durchschnittliche geleistete Arbeitszeit pro Beschäftigtem in Stunden pro Jahr bei 2096 Stunden lag, sank die Anzahl 2023 auf 1611 Stunden, vgl. OECD, Average annual hours actually worked per worker, aufrufbar unter https://data-explorer.oecd.org/vis?lc=en&tm=hours%20worked&pg=0&snb=59&df[ds]=dsDisseminateFinalDMZ&df[id]=DSD_HW%40DF_AVG_ANN_HRS_WKD&df[ag]=OECD.ELS.SAE&df[vs]=1.0&dq= JPN%2BKOR%2BLVA%2BLTU%2BLUX%2BMEX%2BNLD%2BNZL%2BNOR%2BPOL%2BPRT%2BSVK%2BSVN%2BESP%2BSWE%2BCHE%2BTUR%2BGBR%2BUSA%2BOECD........_T....&pd=2010%2C&to[TIME_PERIOD]=false (zuletzt aufgerufen am 25. März 2025).

105 Im Jahr 2022 betrug die durchschnittliche monatliche Überstundenzeit in Japan 22,2 Stunden (1,4 Stunden höher als 2021), was hochgerechnet etwa 266,4 Stunden pro Jahr entspricht. Vgl. https://www.nippon.com/en/japan-data/h01577/ (zuletzt aufgerufen am 15. April 2025).

106 *Müller*, Karōshi und die Reaktion des Rechts, in: Zeitschrift für Japanisches Recht, Heft Nr. 51 (2021), S. 288 f.

107 *Yamamoto/Lloyd* (Anm. 44), S. 116.

108 *Kaspar/Schön*, Einführung in das japanische Recht, 2. Auflage (2024), § 2, S. 39.

109 *Takami* (Anm. 45), S. 16.

110 *Yamamoto/Lloyd* (Anm. 44), S. 117.

den.[111] Viele Arbeitnehmer arbeiten „freiwillig“ über die reguläre Arbeitszeit hinaus, ohne dies dem Arbeitgeber mitzuteilen,[112] etwa indem sie Arbeit mit nach Hause nehmen (持ち帰り残業, *mochikaeri zangyō*),[113] oder ihre Tätigkeit im Betrieb über das vorgesehene Maß hinaus fortsetzen.

Der soziale Druck, als fleißig und wertvoll für den Betrieb wahrgenommen zu werden, äußert sich zudem in der Praxis der sogenannten kollektiven Überstunden (付き合い残業, *tsukiai zangyō*). Arbeitnehmer verlassen den Arbeitsplatz häufig nicht, solange ihre Kollegen oder Vorgesetzten noch arbeiten, während auch Vorgesetzte ihrerseits nicht vor ihren Untergebenen das Büro verlassen möchten. Niemand will den Eindruck erwecken, weniger engagiert zu sein.[114] Fleiß (und Unterordnung) spielt bei der Bewertung für Beförderungen oft eine größere Rolle als die Qualität der tatsächlichen Arbeitsleistung.[115]

Ein weiteres Element des arbeitskulturellen Verhaltenskodex ist die Teilnahme an „freiwilligen“ betrieblichen Veranstaltungen außerhalb der Arbeitszeit.[116] Besonders bekannt sind die sogenannten *nomikai* (飲み会), Trinkzusammenkünfte nach Feierabend, die der Pflege beruflicher Beziehungen dienen sollen. Eine Nichtteilnahme wird von Kollegen häufig als unhöflich empfunden.

Zwar besteht arbeitsrechtlich grundsätzlich ein Vergütungsanspruch auch für freiwillig geleistete Überstunden, wenn der Arbeitgeber diese duldet, ohne dagegen Maßnahmen zu ergreifen.[117] Doch unter dem Einfluss des starken sozialen Zugehörigkeitsdrucks gilt vielfach das Prinzip: „Wo kein Kläger, da kein Richter“.

b) System der Lebenszeitanstellung

Das japanische Arbeitsrecht basiert auf der Grundannahme der Lebenszeitanstellung, also eines Eintritts ins Erwerbsleben unmittelbar nach Abschluss der Universität mit anschließender Beschäftigung bis zur Pensionierung.[118] Als Gegenleistung für die Loyalität und den Arbeitseinsatz des Arbeitnehmers gewährt der Arbeitgeber eine weitgehende Beschäftigungssicherheit. Aus diesem Verständnis heraus sieht das japanische Arbeitsrecht einen besonders starken Kündigungsschutz vor.[119] Zwar ent-

---

111 *Nishitani* (Anm. 81), S. 200.

112 *Shimada* (Anm. 4), S. 6.

113 *Takami* (Anm. 45), S. 16; *Deutschmann/Weber* (Anm. 3), S. 38.

114 *Ono*, Why Do the Japanese Work Long Hours? Sociological Perspectives on Long Working Hours in Japan, in: Japan Labor Issues, Heft Nr. 5 (2018), S. 41.

115 *Ono* (Anm. 114), 35 (39).

116 *Deutschmann/Weber* (Anm. 3), S. 38.

117 Vgl. Erklärung der Beratungsstelle für Beschäftigung des Ministeriums für Gesundheit, Arbeit und Soziales zu Arbeitsgesetzen (2023), S. 45, aufrufbar unter https://kecc.mhlw.go.jp/pdf/explanations_of_labor_related_laws_en_2310.pdf.

118 *Shimada* (Anm. 4), S. 6.

119 Dieses wurde vor allem durch richterliche Rechtsprechung geprägt. So ist entgegen § 627 Abs. 1 ZivilG eine Kündigung nicht einfach im Rahmen einer zweiwöchigen Kündigungsfrist möglich, sondern im Gegenteil nur dann wirksam, wenn „sie […] objektiv rational und nach herrschenden Gesellschaftsansichten […] angemessen ist“, vgl. *Nogawa* (Anm. 22), S. 44.

spricht die Vorstellung, das gesamte Berufsleben bei einem einzigen Arbeitgeber zu verbringen, längst nicht mehr der gelebten Realität, doch orientiert sich das Arbeitsrecht weiterhin an diesem Leitbild. Arbeitgeber sind daher gehalten, vorausschauend und langfristig mit ihren Arbeitnehmern zu planen.

Im Gegenzug wird von den Arbeitnehmern erwartet, in Phasen erhöhter Arbeitsbelastung zusätzliche Arbeit zu übernehmen und in wirtschaftlich schwierigen Zeiten Gehaltskürzungen hinzunehmen. Durch Mehrarbeit kann der Arbeitgeber auf Neueinstellungen verzichten, die in Zeiten wirtschaftlicher Flaute andernfalls entlassen werden müssten. Ebenso erübrigen sich betriebsbedingte Kündigungen, wenn das bestehende Personal kollektiv Einkommenseinbußen akzeptiert.[120]

c) Bestreitung des Lebensunterhalts

Da Arbeitnehmer in Japan Anspruch auf Zuschläge für geleistete Überstunden haben (vgl. Abschnitt VI.3.e)), kalkulieren viele diesen Mehrverdienst fest in ihre Lebensführung ein.[121] Dieser Anreiz wird zusätzlich dadurch verstärkt, dass es in Japan keine gesetzliche Lohnfortzahlung im Krankheitsfall gibt. Arbeitnehmer, die im Krankheitsfall nicht auf ein gesichertes Einkommen vertrauen können, neigen dazu, diese Unsicherheit durch Mehrarbeit zu kompensieren.

d) Unternehmensgewerkschaften

In Japan dominieren nicht Industriegewerkschaften, sondern Unternehmensgewerkschaften. Diese organisieren sich nicht branchenübergreifend nach Tätigkeitsfeldern, sondern bestehen jeweils auf Unternehmensebene und vertreten ausschließlich die Interessen der Arbeitnehmer eines einzelnen Unternehmens. Auch hier spiegelt sich das starke Harmoniebedürfnis innerhalb des Betriebs wider: Bei der Formulierung ihrer Forderungen berücksichtigen die Unternehmensgewerkschaften nicht nur die Interessen der Arbeitnehmer, sondern auch die wirtschaftlichen Möglichkeiten und die Situation des Arbeitgebers, um dessen Wettbewerbsfähigkeit nicht zu gefährden. In wirtschaftlich schwierigen Zeiten zeigt sich diese Haltung insbesondere im Zusammenspiel mit dem System der Lebenszeitanstellung, wenn Gewerkschaften Gehaltskürzungen akzeptieren, um Entlassungen zu vermeiden und die Belegschaft im Unternehmen zu halten.[122]

VII. Fazit

Die unterschiedlichen Regelungen und Praktiken im Umgang mit Überstunden in Deutschland und Japan sind sowohl auf arbeitsrechtliche Rahmenbedingungen als auch auf tief verankerte kulturell-soziale Kontexte zurückzuführen.

Das japanische Arbeitszeitrecht – insbesondere das Arbeitsstandardgesetz – enthält zahlreiche Ausnahmetatbestände, die die intendierte Begrenzung der Arbeitszeit

120 Vgl. *Takami* (Anm. 45), S. 15.

121 *Deutschmann/Weber* (Anm. 3), S. 40.

122 *Shimada* (Anm. 4), S. 8.

unterlaufen. Überstunden werden faktisch zusätzlich zur gesetzlichen Höchstarbeitszeit erbracht und unterliegen keiner effektiven Kontrolle. Die Gewerkschaften verfügen nur über begrenzte Durchsetzungskraft[123], und die zuständigen Aufsichtsbehörden sind oftmals strukturell und personell überlastet[124]. Besonders problematisch ist die Regelung des *Discretionary Work System*, das in der Praxis leicht zu einem Einfallstor für die Umgehung von Arbeitszeitschutzvorschriften werden kann.[125]

Gleichzeitig wirken gesellschaftliche Erwartungen, Normen und betriebliche Loyalitätsvorstellungen als erheblicher Verstärkungsfaktor für exzessive Arbeitszeiten. Die juristischen Regelungen können ohne Wandel in der sozialen Grundhaltung zur Arbeit nur begrenzt Wirkung entfalten.

Reformen unter Premierminister Abe – etwa durch die „*Work Style Reform Legislation*" – sowie jüngere Initiativen wie Kishidas „*New Form of Capitalism*" deuten auf einen vorsichtigen Paradigmenwechsel hin. Elemente wie flexible Arbeitszeitgestaltung und die Erosion des Senioritätsprinzips[126] markieren eine allmähliche Abkehr von traditionellen Strukturen.

Ob diese strukturellen Reformen jedoch auch einen Wandel der intrinsischen Arbeitshaltung und damit eine nachhaltige Reduktion von Überstunden bewirken, bleibt abzuwarten.

Literaturverzeichnis

Bayreuther, Frank: Arbeitszeit zwischen unionsrechtlicher Grundrechtecharta und Vertrag, in: Recht der Arbeit, Heft Nr. 4 (2022), S. 290 ff.

Bobke-von Camen, Manfred H.: Arbeitsbeziehungen und Arbeitsrecht in Japan, in: Arbeit und Recht, Ausgabe 4 (1990), S. 115 ff.

Deutschmann, Christoph/*Weber*, Claudia: Das Japanische Arbeitsbienen-Syndrom. Auswirkungen der Rundum-Nutzung der Arbeitskraft auf die Arbeitszeitpraxis am Beispiel Japans, in: PROKLA. Zeitschrift für Kritische Sozialwissenschaft, Band Nr. 17 (1987), S. 31 ff.

Employment Consultation Center, Ministry of Health, Labor and Welfare: Explanations of Labor-Related Laws (2023), aufrufbar unter https://kecc.mhlw.go.jp/pdf/explanations_of_labor_related_laws_en_2310.pdf (zuletzt aufgerufen am 27. März 2025).

Fuhlrott, Michael/*Schmechel*, Markus: Ableistung und Vergütung von Überstunden, in: Arbeitsschutz in Recht und Praxis, Heft Nr. 1 (2024), S. 7 ff.

Griese, Thomas: Die Gesetzentwürfe der Länder für ein Arbeitsvertragsgesetz, in: Neue Zeitschrift für Arbeitsrecht, Heft Nr. 15 (1996), S. 785 ff.

---

123 *Nishitani* (Anm. 81), S. 200.

124 *Ikeyama*, Examining Japan's Labor Standards Inspection Administration and Its Challenge from the Perspective of the Inspection Offices, in: Japan Labor Issues, Heft Nr. 42 (2023), S. 31.

125 *Wada* (Anm. 28), S. 228.

126 *Urata*, Japan's new labour market reforms need to go further, abrufbar unter https://eastasiaforum.org/2025/01/16/japans-new-labour-market-reforms-need-to-go-further/ (zuletzt aufgerufen am 27. März 2025).

Gsell, Beate/*Krüger*, Wolfgang/*Lorenz*, Stephan/*Reymann*, Christoph (Hrsg.): Beck-online.GROSSKOMMENTAR zum Zivilrecht, Stand 1. Februar 2015.

Hanami, Tadashi A./*Komiya*, Fumito: Labour Law in Japan (2011).

Hashimoto, Yoko: Arbeitsrecht in Japan, in: Recht der Internationalen Wirtschaft, Heft Nr. 9 (2018), S. 564 ff.

Hirsch-Kreinsen, Hartmut/*Minssen*, Heiner (Hrsg.): Lexikon der Arbeits- und Industriesoziologie, 2. Auflage (2017).

Ikeyama, Kiyoko: Examining Japan's Labor Standards Inspection Administration and Its Challenge from the Perspective of the Inspection Offices, in: Japan Labor Issues, Heft Nr. 42 (2023), S. 17 ff.

Ikezoe, Hirokuni: On Payment or Non-payment of Premium Wages When Incorporated Into Annual Salary, in: Japan Labor Issues, Heft Nr. 10 (2018), S. 12 ff.

Ishikawa, Keiko/*Schiebe*, Tobias: The Japanese Work-Style Reform 2019, in: Zeitschrift für Japanisches Recht, Heft Nr. 47 (2019), S. 269 ff.

Kaspar, Johannes/*Schön*, Oliver: Einführung in das japanische Recht, 2. Auflage (2024).

Kiyono, Kohei: Chracteristics of and Differences between the Way of Working in Japan and Germany, in: Düwell, Nora/Gallner, Inken/Haase, Karsten/Wolmerath, Martin (Hrsg.), Auf dem Weg zu einem sozialen und inklusiven Rechtsstaat – Covid-19 als Herausforderung, Liber amicorum Franz Josef Düwell (2021), S. 113 ff.

Knapp, Daniel: Ausgewählte Aspekte des japanischen Individualarbeitsrechts. Eine rechtsvergleichende Studie mit der österreichischen Arbeitsrechtsordnung (2017), aufrufbar unter https://unipub.uni-graz.at/obvugrhs/content/titleinfo/2324836?lang=de (zuletzt aufgerufen am 26. März 2025).

Labour Standards Bureau Ministry of Health, Labour and Welfare (厚生労働省労働基準局): 2023 Annual Labour Standards Inspection Report, (Vol. 76) 令和５年, 労働基準監督年報, 第76 回 (2023).

Löwisch, Manfred: Das Verhältnis von Arbeitsrecht und Zivilrecht in Japan und Deutschland, in: Düwell, Franz Josef/Löwisch, Manfred/Waltersmann, Raimund/Wank, Rolf (Hrsg.), Das Verhältnis von Arbeitsrecht und Zivilrecht in Japan, Bonner Schriften zum deutschen und europäischen Recht der Arbeit und der Sozialen Sicherheit, Band 15 (2013), S. 21 ff.

Markmann, Heinz: 50 Jahre Arbeitsbeziehungen in Deutschland: eine Erfolgsgeschichte?, in: Industrielle Beziehungen, Heft Nr. 1 (1995), S. 82 ff.

Marutschke, Hans Peter: Einführung in das japanische Recht (1999).

Maurer, Jürgen: Das Prinzip der Harmonie hat sich im Recht niedergeschlagen, Germany Trade and Invest, 18. Juli 2023, aufrufbar unter https://www.gtai.de/de/trade/japan/wirtschaftsumfeld/-das-prinzip-der-harmonie-hat-sich-im-recht-niedergeschlagen--1015198 (zuletzt aufgerufen am 27. März 2025).

Müller-Glöge, Rudi/*Preis*, Ulrich/*Gallner*, Inken/*Schmidt*, Ingrid: Erfurter Kommentar zum Arbeitsrecht, 25. Auflage (2025).

Müller, Matthias: Karōshi und die Reaktion des Rechts, in: Zeitschrift für Japanisches Recht, Heft Nr. 51 (2021), S. 273 ff.

Müller, Michael A.: Arbeitsrecht in Japan: Erhöhung der Zuschläge für Überstunden, 24. April 2024, aufrufbar unter https://www.cbbl-lawyers.de/news/arbeitsrecht-in-japan-erhoehung-der-zuschlaege-fuer-ueberstunden (zuletzt aufgerufen am 27. März 2025).

Nishihara, Hiroshi: Funktion der sozialen Grundrechte im japanischen Verfassungssystem, in: Zeitschrift für ausländisches öffentliches Recht und Völkerrecht (1990), S. 836 ff.

Nishitani, Satoshi: Altes Europa – neues Amerika? Die Entwicklung des japanischen Arbeitsrechts und der Einfluss des deutschen und amerikanischen Rechts, in: Zeitschrift für Japanisches Recht, Heft Nr. 18 (2004), S. 131 ff.

Nishitani, Satoshi: Bürgerliches Recht und Arbeitsrecht in Japan, in: Düwell, Franz Josef/Löwisch, Manfred/Waltersmann, Raimund/Wank, Rolf (Hrsg.), Das Verhältnis von Arbeitsrecht und Zivilrecht in Japan, Bonner Schriften zum deutschen und europäischen Recht der Arbeit und der Sozialen Sicherheit, Band 15 (2013), S. 5 ff.

Nishitani, Satoshi: Flexibilisierung der Beschäftigung und des Arbeitsrechts in Japan, in: Zeitschrift für Japanisches Recht, Heft Nr. 10 (2000), S. 73 ff.

Nishitani, Satoshi: Vergleichende Einführung in das japanische Arbeitsrecht (2003).

Nogawa, Shinobu: Bürgerliches Recht und Arbeitsrecht – Einzelgesetze in Japan, in: Düwell, Franz Josef/Löwisch, Manfred/Waltersmann, Raimund/Wank, Rolf (Hrsg.), Das Verhältnis von Arbeitsrecht und Zivilrecht in Japan, Bonner Schriften zum deutschen und europäischen Recht der Arbeit und der Sozialen Sicherheit, Band 15 (2013), S. 41 ff.

Ono, Hiroshi: Why Do the Japanese Work Long Hours? Sociological Perspectives on Long Working Hours in Japan, in: Japan Labor Issues, Heft Nr. 5 (2018), S. 35 ff.

Pletke, Matthias/*Schrader*, Peter/*Siebert*, Jens/*Thoms*, Tina/*Klagges*, Rhea-Christina/*Teubert*, René: Flexible Arbeit. Flexible Beschäftigungsverhältnisse, Personalanpassung, Vergütungssysteme, Arbeitszeitmodelle, Aufgabenänderung, 2. Auflage (2022).

Preis, Ulrich/*Temming*, Felipe: Arbeitsrecht. Individualarbeitsrecht, 7. Auflage (2024).

Richardi, Reinhard: Arbeitsvertragsgesetz und Privatautonomie, in: Neue Zeitschrift für Arbeitsrecht, Heft Nr. 17 (1992), S. 769 ff.

Säcker, Franz Jürgen/*Rixecker*, Roland/*Oetker*, Hartmut/*Limperg*, Bettina/*Schubert*, Claudia: Münchner Kommentar zum BGB, 9. Auflage (2023).

Sakowski, Klaus: Arbeitsrecht, 3. Auflage (2022).

Schliemann, Harald (Hrsg.): Das Arbeitsrecht im BGB, 2. Auflage (2002).

Shimada, Yuko: Das japanische Arbeitsrecht und seine Globalisiserung, in: Pécsi munkajogi közlemények, Band 2016, Heft Nr. 1 (2023), S. 5 ff.

Takahashi, Kohei/*Kodama*, Naomi/*Arita*, Kentaro/*Kazama*, Haruka/*Sakai*, Saisuke/*Takeuchi*, Masaya/*Owan*, Hideo: Has Japan's worky style reform had the intended effect?, in: Applied Economics (2024), S. 1 ff.

Takami, Tomohiro: Current State of Working Hours and Overwork in Japan: Part I: How Has It Changed Over the Years? in: Japan Labor Issues, Heft Nr. 16 (2019), S. 18 ff.

Takami, Tomohiro: Current State of Working Hours and Overwork in Japan: Part II: Why do the Japanese Work Long Hours?, in: Japan Labor Issues, Heft Nr. 18 (2019), S. 15 ff.

Takami, Tomohiro: Current State of Working Hours and Overwork in Japan: Part III: How Can We Prevent Overwork?, in: Japan Labor Issues, Heft Nr. 19 (2019), S. 25 ff.

Tanaka, Mikio: Recht kurz bitte (1). Überstunden und sogenannten 3-6-Abkommen, in: Japanmarkt (2010), S. 34 (https://www.city-yuwa.com/english/publication/pb_dealings/pdf/germany_36.pdf).

Tautphäus, Arno: Überstunden – Trotz Arbeit kein Lohn?, in: Düwell, Nora/Gallner, Inken/Haase, Karsten/Wolmerath, Martin (Hrsg.), Auf dem Weg zu einem sozialen und inklusiven Rechtsstaat – Covid-19 als Herausforderung, Liber amicorum Franz Josef Düwell (2021), S. 659 ff.

Tschöpe, Ulrich: Arbeitsrecht Handbuch, 14. Auflage (2025).

Urata, Shujiro: Japan's new labour reforms need to go further, East Asia Forum, 16. Januar 2025, aufrufbar unter https://eastasiaforum.org/2025/01/16/japans-new-labour-market-reforms-need-to-go-further/ (zuletzt aufgerufen am 27. März 2025).

Vogelsang, Hinrich/*Wensing*, Hans-Hubert: Mehr Arbeit – mehr Geld, in: Recht der Arbeit, Heft Nr. 6 (2024), S. 317 ff.

Wada, Hajime: Die Regelung der Arbeitsbedingungen in japanischen Betrieben, in: Arbeit und Recht, Ausgabe 10 (2002), S. 369 ff.

Wada, Hajime: Einfluss fremder Rechtsordnungen auf das japanische Arbeitsrecht, in: Düwell, Franz Josef/Haase, Karsten (Hrsg.), Arbeit und Recht im gesellschaftlichen Wandel. 25 Jahre Gesellschaft für Arbeitsrecht in Deutschland und Japan. Festschrift zum 25. Geburtstag der Deutsch-Japanischen Gesellschaft für Arbeitsrecht e. V. (2023).

Wada, Hajime: Strukturelle Veränderungen in der japanischen Gesellschaft und im Arbeitsrecht, in: Düwell, Nora/Gallner, Inken/Haase, Karsten/Wolmerath, Martin (Hrsg.), Auf dem Weg zu einem sozialen und inklusiven Rechtsstaat – Covid-19 als Herausforderung, Liber amicorum Franz Josef Düwell (2021), S. 217 ff.

Yamakawa, Ryuichi: Overhaul After 50 Years: The Amendment of the Labour Standard Law, in: Japan Labor Bulletin, Heft Nr. 11 (1998), S. 7 ff.

Yamamoto, Kat/*Lloyd*, Robert A: Ethical Considerations of Japanese Business Culture, in: Journal of Business Diversity, Heft Nr. 2 (2019), S. 113 ff.

Japan kopieren oder Japan kapieren?

Von *Manfred H. Bobke-von Camen*

Dr. Manfred Herbert Bobke-von Camen, ist Mitglied des Vorstands der Deutsch-Japanischen Gesellschaft für Arbeitsrecht. Nach seinem Studium der Rechtswissenschaften war er bis 1990 wissenschaftlicher Referent im Wirtschafts- und Sozialwissenschaftlichen Institut des DGB, mit einem Abstecher als Gastdozent an der Universität Chiba im Jahr 1985. Als Stellvertretender Generalsekretär des Europäischen Metallgewerkschaftsbundes begleitete er gemeinsame Forschungsvorhaben mit dem Japanischen Rat der Metallgewerkschaften im Internationalen Metall-Gewerkschaftsbund. Nach Jahren im Personalmanagement der Deutschen Bahn und der Deutschen Telekom war er bis 2020 Geschäftsführer bei der Flughafengesellschaft Berlin/Brandenburg.

I. Erinnerungen an eine Debatte zwischen Fordismus und Toyotismus

Als sich in der politischen Debatte und der ökonomischen Theorie etwa zu Anfang der 80er Jahre des vergangenen Jahrhunderts die Erkenntnis durchsetzte, dass „Made in Japan" nicht mehr für Billigprodukte und Imitate stand, sondern für technisch hoch entwickelte Kameras, Computer und vor allem Automobile, da war klar, dass sich Japan in der Weltwirtschaft zu einem ebenbürtigen Wettbewerber entwickelt hatte. Es fehlte nicht an Rufen, Japan durch Zollschranken und andere Handelsbeschränkungen auszubremsen, um die heimische Produktion zu schützen. Langsam setzte sich in Europa und Nordamerika aber die Einsicht durch, dass es nunmehr gelte, dem japanischen Erfolgsmodell auf die Spur zu kommen.

1. Beispielhafter Aufstieg der japanischen Automobilindustrie

Die japanische Automobilindustrie stieg Anfang der 1980er Jahre zum Weltmarktführer auf. Die japanische Firma Toyota hatte an dieser Entwicklung einen großen Anteil. Das Unternehmen steht noch heute an der Spitze der weltweiten Automobilproduktion, gefolgt vom Volkswagen-Konzern. Die heutige Debatte um Elektro-Antrieb und Computerisierung der Fahrzeuge, der Kampf um den chinesischen Markt und die Abschottungsversuche gegen chinesische Importe in den USA und der EU markieren eine neue Phase in der Geschichte der Automobilproduktion mit vielleicht noch größeren Folgen als bei der Ablösung des Fordismus, also der Fließbandproduktion (Assembly Line) mit Menschen als Anhängsel der Maschine, deren Muskelkraft gemessen und deren Körperbewegungen analysiert und optimiert wurden (Taylorismus) und deren Lehren nicht mehr zu Industrieroboter und Induktionsschleife passten. Die Fließbandproduktion auf Vorrat mit Zulieferprodukten auf der Halde

Duncker & Humblot · Berlin | https://doi.org/10.3790/978-3-428-59611-9.2025.418812

(Fordismus) wurde in den 80er Jahren des vorigen Jahrhunderts zunehmend weltweit durch postfordistische Produktionsstrukturen (Just-in-Time, on demand) abgelöst. Wegen der Vorreiterfunktion der Firma Toyota in diesen Produktionsstrukturen bürgerte sich hierfür die Bezeichnung Toyotismus ein.

Damals wie heute ging es um Wettbewerbsfähigkeit, Standortkonkurrenz und Arbeitsplatzabbau. An die Japanologie wurde die Frage gerichtet, ob es besondere kulturelle Merkmale gibt, die das japanische Wunder erklären. Die Politologie versuchte es mit einem Erklärungsansatz, der die koordinierende Rolle des MITI, des mächtigen japanischen Industrie- und Handelsministeriums sowie die jahrzehntelange dominierende Rolle der Liberaldemokratischen Partei hervorhob. In der Technik-Debatte häuften sich Berichte über die Fortschritte in der Mikroelektronik sowie die rasante Geschwindigkeit in der Anwendung neuer Erkenntnisse. Reisende berichteten von der Geldauszahlung am Bankautomaten, der Telefonkarte für das Telefonat in der Telefonzelle – bis dato unbekannt in Europa. Der superschnelle und dazu noch pünktliche Shinkansen, dessen Wagen im Bahnhof genau am vorbezeichneten Abschnitt halten – ein bis heute hierzulande unerreichtes Vorbild.

2. Rolle des Arbeitsrechts

Auch die Arbeitsrechtswissenschaft wurde gefragt, ob sie einen Beitrag zur Erklärung des rasanten Aufstiegs der japanischen Industrie leisten könne. Die Arbeitsgesetzgebung einschließlich der deutschen (Zivilrecht, Tarifvertragsrecht) und US-amerikanischen (unfair labor pratice) Einflüsse sowie der Rechtsprechung der arbeitsrechtlichen Kammern des Obersten Gerichtes (*saikōsai*) wurden analysiert. Hervorgehoben wurde die im internationalen Vergleich recht niedrige Zahl von vor Gericht ausgetragenen Konflikten sowie die Effizienz der zur Konfliktlösung herangezogenen Methoden Vermittlung, Ausgleich und Schlichtung.

Auch die Rechtswirklichkeit wurde beachtet. Einen Unterschied brachte Peter Hanau auf die griffige Fragestellung: „Deutschland, Weltmeister des Urlaubs – Japan, Weltmeister der Arbeit?"[1] Lag darin der Schlüssel des Erfolges? Ausufernde Mehrarbeit, vielleicht im schlimmsten Fall Tod durch Arbeit (*karōshi*)[2] und freie Tage nur an den Brückentagen der Golden Week statt „Samstags gehört Papi mir"-Mentalität und 6-Wochen Urlaub in Deutschland. Ein tatsächliches oder vermutetes Gefälle in puncto Arbeitsethos konnte allerdings nur bedingt zur Erklärung herangezogen werden.

---

1 *Hanau*, Deutschland, Weltmeister des Urlaubs – Japan, Weltmeister der Arbeit?, in: Hanau/Kimoto/Markmann/Tezuka, Die Arbeitswelt in Japan und in der Bundesrepublik Deutschland – ein Vergleich: Japanisch-Deutsches Symposium im Japanischen Kulturinstitut in Köln (1985), S. 47 ff.

2 Zu *karōshi* siehe *Kawahito*, When the Corporate Warrior Dies (1990).

a) Merkmale der japanischen Arbeitsbeziehungen

Zunehmend mehr versuchten die von der internationalen Diskussion überraschten japanischen Wissenschaftler, einem ausländischen Publikum die Merkmale der japanischen Arbeitsbeziehungen zu erläutern.[3]

Zu diesen Merkmalen zählte zum Beispiel

- die „lebenslange" Beschäftigung (d.h. bis zum Eintritt in das Rentenalter mit 55 Jahren) der Stammbelegschaften der Großindustrie,
- Unternehmens- und Betriebsgewerkschaften, die auf den ökonomischen Erfolg und damit die Konkurrenzstärke des Unternehmens als Voraussetzung erfolgreicher Gewerkschaftspolitik gerichtet sind,
- eine Spaltung der innerbetrieblichen Arbeitsmärkte durch formalisierte Trennung zwischen Stamm- und Randbelegschaften,
- die Einrichtung direkter Management-Belegschaftsbeziehungen unter Umgehung überbetrieblicher gewerkschaftlicher Vertretungsformen, teilweise gekoppelt an betriebliche Systeme individueller Lohn- und Karrieremuster,
- eine zumindest ab Mitte der 80er Jahre im internationalen Vergleich geringe Streikhäufigkeit. Dies galt aber erst nach Abebben der großen Streikwellen nach dem Zweiten Weltkrieg (besonders legendär: der große Mitsui-Miike Streik im Kohlebergbau) und der endgültigen Privatisierung der japanischen Staatsbahn und der daraufhin erfolgten Zurückdrängung der Gewerkschaft Kokuro, die zuvor die jährliche Frühlingsoffensive (*shuntō*) zur Eröffnung der Tarifverhandlungen landesweit organisiert hatte.

Zur Durchsetzung der für Japan typischen Teilung in Stamm- und Randbelegschaften war die Beseitigung einer rechtlichen Hürde erforderlich. Das Beschäftigungsstabilisierungsgesetz von 1947 (*shokugyō-hō*) hatte nämlich die gewerbsmäßige Arbeitnehmerüberlassung verboten. Verschiedene Lockerungen ab 1952 erlaubten den Einsatz von Fremdfirmen-Arbeitnehmern (*shagai-kō*) sowie Entsendungs-Arbeitnehmern (*haken-rōdōsha*). Gängige Praxis wurde die Befristung des Arbeitsverhältnisses der Leiharbeiter beim Verleiher sowie eine Ausweitung der Praxis, das Stammpersonal von Großbetrieben im Falle der Unterbeschäftigung an „befreundete Betriebe zu verleihen (*shukkō* Arbeitsverhältnis)" sowie die illegale Praxis der Entsendung durch Schein-Werkverträge.

Das 1985 verabschiedete „Gesetz für adäquate Verwaltung der Arbeitnehmer-Überlassungsunternehmen und Einordnung der Beschäftigungsbedingungen der Entsendungs-Arbeitnehmer" – so der sperrige Titel –legalisierte diese Praxis ab 1986.[4]

---

3 Vgl. zum Beispiel für viele: *Tokunaga*, Die japanischen Arbeitsbeziehungen, in: WSI-Mitteilungen 4/1986, S. 329 ff.

4 Vgl. *Kezuka*, Neue Entwicklung des Arbeitsrechts in Japan, in: WSI-Mitteilungen 4/1987, S. 218 ff.

b) Rolle der Gewerkschaften

Die Betriebs- und Unternehmensgewerkschaften der japanischen Großindustrie, unterstützten die unternehmerischen Anstrengungen zur Verbesserung der Produktivität.

Beispielhaft sei hier die Selbstdarstellung der Toyota-Gewerkschaften zitiert:

„1. Wir werden zum ökonomischen Wachstum der Nation beitragen, indem wir die Entwicklung der japanischen Automobilindustrie unterstützen.

2. Wir werden ein gegenseitiges Vertrauen als Basis für alle zukünftigen Arbeiter-Management-Beziehungen aufrecht erhalten.

3. Durch die aktive Vorantreibung des Produktivitätsfortschrittes können wir das Wohlergehen des Unternehmens erreichen und auch die Arbeitsbedingungen für die Beschäftigten erhalten oder sogar verbessern."

Zum Thema Flexibilität heißt es in einer gemeinsamen Deklaration mit dem Unternehmen:

„1. Die Nichtexistenz von Entlassungen begrenzt die Flexibilität, dies erkennt die Gewerkschaft und ist deshalb bereit, Überstunden zu arbeiten, und zwar nach der Arbeit oder an Feiertagen und auszuhelfen im Sinne von Versetzungen und Umsetzungen.

2. Um die Flexibilität zu erreichen, sind die Gewerkschaftsmitglieder bereit, ihre Hand auch zu geben, wenn unterhalb ihrer Qualifikation gearbeitet wird. Das müssen sie nicht, das tun sie aber."[5]

Das Japanische Produktivitätszentrum (Japanese Productivity Center = *nihon seisansei honbu*) förderte seit seiner Gründung im Jahre 1955 aktiv die Orientierung von Arbeitgebern und Gewerkschaften auf gemeinsame Produktivitätsziele – vor allem durch Untersuchungen und gemeinsame Studienreisen in viele Länder der Welt.

Auf der Ebene der Verbände formierten sich bereits Ende der 40er Jahre der Arbeitgeberverband Nikkeiren und der Industrieverband Keidanren. Ihnen stand eine zunächst kämpferische (*sanbetsu-kaigi*) sodann aber zersplitterte Gewerkschaftsbewegung gegenüber. Im Jahre 1987 wurde nach Auflösung der traditionellen Gewerkschaftszentralen Sohyo, Domei, Churitsuroren und Shin-Sanbetsu über das Zwischenstadium der Zusammenarbeit in Zenmin Rokyo der Gewerkschaftsdachverband Rengo gebildet, der zunächst viele Gewerkschaftzentralen der Privatindustrie vereinigte. In der Metall-Dachorganisation IMF-JC (seit 1964 aktiv) arbeiteten bereits der Stahl-Verband Tekkororen (Sohyo) der Automobil-Verband Jidosharoren (Domei) sowie der Elektro-Verband Denkiroren (Churitsuroren) zusammen. Im Jahre 1989 schlossen sich auch Gewerkschaftszentralen des öffentlichen Dienstes Rengo an. Rengo gilt heute als wichtigste Dachorganisation der Gewerkschaften. Die Basis der Gewerkschaftsbewegung bleibt die Betriebsorganisation.[6]

---

[5] Abgedruckt bei: *Bobke*, Flexibilisierung und Arbeitsbeziehungen in Japan, in: IG Metall (Hrsg.), Menschengerechte Arbeitszeiten – geschützte Arbeitsverhältnisse (1989), S. 177 ff.

[6] Vgl. *Kawanishi*, Enterprise Unionism in Japan (1992).

II. Japan kapieren

Auf der Suche nach dem Schlüssel der Erklärung für den Erfolg der japanischen Automobilindustrie sponsorten US-amerikanische Automobilfirmen mit circa 500.000 $ eine Studie des renommierten MIT die zu dem Ergebnis kam, dass Toyotas Produktionssystem allen anderen Systemen der Automobilproduktion überlegen war.[7] Dieses System, das seit den fünfziger Jahren des vorigen Jahrhunderts entwickelt worden war, umfasst Arbeitsorganisation, Förderung von Fertigkeiten, Zusammenfassung von Produktentwicklung und Fertigungstechnologie und die Beziehungen zum Lieferanten. Womack prägte den Begriff „Lean production" für das Toyota System. Die in Japan gebräuchlichen Worte Kaizen und Kanban fanden Eingang in die internationale Literatur. Dem Kaizen-Prinzip zur Folge können stetige kleine Verbesserungen zu Qualitätssprüngen führen während Kanban die Lieferketten optimiert und vom Ausgangspunkt der Bestellung des Kunden ohne überflüssige Lagerung alle erforderlichen Ressourcen zum richtigen Zeitpunkt bereitstellt. Muda und Kenbutsu gelangten ebenfalls in den Sprachgebrauch der Fachwelt, die Vermeidung von Verschwendung und die Einbeziehung der Lieferanten. Unter Verschwendung wird dabei auch die Nichtbeachtung der Vorschläge der Mitarbeitenden verstanden!

Missverständnisse und Fehlinterpretationen blieben dabei nicht aus. Ein Teil der Management-Lehre propagierte das japanische System zur Herstellung eines Konsenses der Führung im Umlaufverfahren (*ringi seido*) als vorbildlich.[8] Toyota beschritt den gegenteiligen Weg: Nach dem 3-Stempel-Prinzip sollte der Namensstempel (der in Japan die Unterschrift ersetzt) von lediglich drei Führungskräften zur Umsetzung von Maßnahmen ausreichend sein. Nach der gründlichen Umstrukturierung in der Produktion folgte in den 90er Jahren des vorigen Jahrhunderts ein beispielhafter Hierarchieabbau und eine dem entsprechende Kompetenzvermehrung für Produktionsarbeiter, deren Wissen und Erfahrung viel mehr zum Einsatz gelangen konnten.[9]

III. Japan kopieren?

Die Frage, wer wen kopiert oder kapiert, so schlagwortartig gestellt, lässt sich nicht beantworten. Der Autor des Standard-Werkes zum Toyota-Produktionssystem[10] verbeugt sich vor der historischen Leistung von Henry Ford, der Massenmotorisierung möglich gemacht und mit dem Spruch „Autos kaufen keine Autos" das Einkommen seiner Beschäftigten kräftig erhöht hat. Alle japanischen Unternehmen organisieren ihre Werke zunächst nach den Standards von Frederick Taylor und die ersten Vorschläge, Taylor zu überwinden, kamen nicht vom MIT, sondern vom britischen Ta-

---

7 Vgl. *Womack/Jones/Roos*, The machine that changed the world (1990).

8 *Rothlauf*, Interkulturelles Management, 2. Aufl. (2006), S. 426.

9 Vgl. dazu *Mori*, Einführung neuer Formen der Arbeitsorganisation bei Toyota Motor Corporation und Maßnahmen der Gewerkschaften, in: *Bobke/Kamada/Hammarström*, Lean Production, Neue Formen der Arbeitsorganisation (1996), S. 231 ff.

10 *Ohno*, Das Toyota Produktionssystem (1993), mittlerweile in 3. Aufl. (2013).

vistock Institut und stammen aus dem Jahre 1946.[11] Die japanischen Anstöße veränderten die Industrie radikal – trotzdem machten vor allem US-amerikanische Beratungsfirmen Umsatz und Gewinn mit der Formulierung und Standardisierung von Lehrsätzen zur Qualitätssicherung und just-in-time Produktion.

Die erneute Transition der Automobilproduktion steht bevor. Steigende Energiepreise, das Ende des Verbrennermotors und Einsatz künstlicher Intelligenz sind die Stichworte. Wird Tesla oder BYD Toyota an der Spitze der Tabelle ablösen, Volkswagen seine Position behaupten? Oder überrascht uns Toyota mit einer neuen Revolution im Automobilbau?

Literaturverzeichnis

Bobke, Manfred H.: Flexibilisierung und Arbeitsbeziehungen in Japan, in: IG Metall (Hrsg.), Menschengerechte Arbeitszeiten – geschützte Arbeitsverhältnisse (1989), S. 177 ff.

Hanau, Peter: Deutschland, Weltmeister des Urlaubs – Japan, Weltmeister der Arbeit?, in: Hanau, Peter/Kimoto, Saburo/Markmann, Heinz/Tezuka, Kazuaki, Die Arbeitswelt in Japan und in der Bundesrepublik Deutschland – ein Vergleich: Japanisch-Deutsches Symposium im Japanischen Kulturinstitut in Köln (1985), S. 47 ff.

Kawahito, Hiroshi: When the Corporate Warrior Dies (1990).

Kawanishi, Hirosuke: Enterprise Unionism in Japan (1992).

Kezuka, Katsutoshi: Neue Entwicklung des Arbeitsrechts in Japan, in: WSI-Mitteilungen 4/1987, S. 218 ff.

Mori, Toshio: Einführung neuer Formen der Arbeitsorganisation bei Toyota Motor Corporation und Maßnahmen der Gewerkschaften, in: Bobke, Manfred H./Kamada, Hiroshi/Hammarström, Olle, Lean Production, Neue Formen der Arbeitsorganisation (1996), S. 232 ff.

Ohno, Taiichi: Das Toyota Produktionssystem (1993).

Rothlauf, Jürgen: Interkulturelles Management, 2. Aufl. (2006).

Tokunaga, Shigeyoshi: Die japanischen Arbeitsbeziehungen, in: WSI-Mitteilungen 4/1986, S. 329 ff.

Trist, Eric/*Murray*, Hugh: The Social Engagement of Social Science (1993).

Womack, James P./*Jones*, Daniel T./*Roos*, Daniel: The machine that changed the world (1990).

---

11 Vgl. Trist/Murray, The Social Engagement of Social Science (1993).

Das Reflektieren gesellschaftsrechtlicher Vorgänge in Japan in deutschen Registern

Von *Meiko Dillmann*

Dr. Meiko Dillmann ist Partnerin der Sozietät ARQIS Partnerschaftsgesellschaft mbB am Standort München. Sie ist seit 15 Jahren als Mitglied des „Japan Desk" von ARQIS vornehmlich in der Beratung japanischer Unternehmen bei M&A Transaktionen und im Gesellschaftsrecht sowie als „Vertrauensanwältin" in allen weiteren Rechtsfragen tätig.

I. Einleitung[1]

Wenn ausländische Unternehmen in Deutschland tätig werden, stellen sich manchmal besondere Herausforderungen aufgrund unterschiedlicher formaler Anforderungen und rechtspraktischer Gepflogenheiten in den unterschiedlichen Ländern. Dies gilt insbesondere, wenn es darum gilt, strenge Formanforderungen gegenüber Handels- oder anderen Registern zu erfüllen, da abweichende formale Gepflogenheiten im Heimatland eine Erfüllung der deutschen Formanforderungen erschweren oder gar unmöglich machen können. Gerade bei Unternehmen aus Japan, einem Land, das in mancher Hinsicht von deutschen Vorstellungen abweichende Grundverständnisse im gesellschaftsrechtlichen Bereich aufweist,[2] stellen sich immer wieder Herausforderungen bei der Abbildung gesellschaftsrechtlicher Verhältnisse des Heimatlandes in deutschen Handels- und anderen Registern.

Im Folgenden sollen einige ausgewählte Probleme und Lösungsmöglichkeiten näher beleuchtet werden, die zum großen Teil auf Erfahrungen aus der täglichen Praxis

1 Ein großer Dank gilt meinen Kollegen Dr. Shigeo Yamaguchi (Rechtsanwalt) sowie Frau Miho Kuramochi (qualifiziert als japanische Rechtsanwältin) für wertvolle Anregungen und Diskussionen aus japanisch-rechtlicher Sicht und unserer gemeinsamen Praxis, sowie Herrn Maximilian Schröder (wissenschaftlicher Mitarbeiter) für die Unterstützung bei der Erstellung des Beitrags mit sorgfältigen Recherchen und kritischer Durchsicht.

2 Das japanische Gesellschaftsrecht war ursprünglich stark vom deutschen Gesellschaftsrecht beeinflusst, wurde jedoch nach dem Zweiten Weltkrieg „amerikanisiert" und danach mehrfach grundlegenden Reformen unterzogen, siehe etwa *Rodatz*, Einige Bemerkungen zu den Besonderheiten im japanischen Gesellschaftsrecht, in: Menkhaus, Das japanische im japanischen Recht (1994), S. 247 ff.; *Marutschke*, Einführung in das japanische Recht, 2. Auflage (2010), S. 245 ff.; *Menkhaus*, Allgemeines Gesellschaftsrecht in Japan, in: Menkhaus, Japanischer Brückenbauer zum deutschen Rechtskreis, Festschrift für Koresuke Yamauchi zum 60. Geburtstag (2006), S. 229, mit anschließenden tiefergehenden Erwägungen dazu, inwieweit sich noch deutschrechtliche dogmatische Vorstellungen im japanischen Gesellschaftsrecht finden; *Yamaguchi*, Abwehrmaßnahmen börsennotierter Aktiengesellschaften gegen feindliche Übernahmeangebote in Deutschland und Japan (2005), S. 9 m. w. N.

Duncker & Humblot · Berlin | https://doi.org/10.3790/978-3-428-59611-9.2025.418780

der Verfasserin bei der anwaltlichen Beratung japanischer Unternehmen in Deutschland beruhen. Aufgrund der Praxisrelevanz beziehen sich die meisten Ausführungen auf japanische Aktiengesellschaften,[3] die in Deutschland eine Tochtergesellschaft in Form einer GmbH oder eine Zweigniederlassung gründen, oder aus sonstigen Gründen Nachweise der japanischen Rechtslage in Deutschland erbringen müssen. Der Beitrag erhebt keinen Anspruch auf systematische Vollständigkeit, beruht aber auf jahrelanger Praxis und hofft daher, einen guten Querschnitt über die Probleme, die sich japanischen Unternehmen stellen (können), zu geben.

II. Nachweis der Existenz einer japanischen Aktiengesellschaft und Vertretungsbefugnis ihrer gesetzlichen Vertreter

1. Handelsregisterdokumente einer japanischen Aktiengesellschaft

Der Nachweis der Existenz einer japanischen Aktiengesellschaft erfolgt meist unproblematisch mit Hilfe eines Handelsregisterauszugs nebst beglaubigter Übersetzung in die deutsche Sprache.

Dabei ist jedoch zu beachten, dass es in Japan unterschiedliche Formen des Handelsregisterauszugs gibt, nämlich unter anderem die sogenannte „Bescheinigung über sämtliche gegenwärtigen Angaben" (現在事項全部証明書, *genzai jikō zenbu shōmeisho*), die „Bescheinigung über sämtliche historischen Angaben" (履歴事項全部証明書, *rireki jikō zenbu shōmeisho*) sowie die „Bescheinigung über Vertretungsverhältnisse" (代表者事項証明書, *daihyōsha jikō shōmeisho*). Außer der Besonderheit, dass auch eine „Bescheinigung über Vertretungsverhältnisse" erhältlich ist, die oftmals genügt, wenn nur die Vertretungsberechtigung von organschaftlichen Vertretern nachgewiesen werden muss, entspricht diese Situation dem deutschen Handelsregister mit der Möglichkeit, einen aktuellen oder chronologischen Handelsregisterauszug zu ziehen.

Ferner gibt es ein elektronisches Register. Dem Grundsatz nach müsste sich ein deutscher Notar gem. § 21 BNotO über die Existenz- und Vertretungsmacht auch durch eigene Einsichtnahme in das japanische elektronische Handelsregister überzeugen können, wenn das elektronische Register in Japan seiner rechtlichen Bedeutung nach dem deutschen Register entspricht. In der Praxis wird dies für viele Länder, insbesondere im europäischen oder englisch-sprachigen Raum, so gehandhabt; für Japan lässt sich hierzu jedoch keine Rechtsprechung finden, ob die deutsche Rechtspraxis das japanische elektronische Register als gleichwertig ansieht. Nach japanischem Verständnis bietet das elektronische Register allerdings nur eine Möglichkeit, mit den offiziellen Registern inhaltsgleiche Dokumente einzusehen. Den elektroni-

[3] Für einen Überblick über Gesellschaftsformen in Japan siehe etwa *Kansaku/Bälz*, in: Baum/Bälz (Hrsg.), Handbuch Japanisches Handels- und Gesellschaftsrecht (2011), S. 63 ff.; *Nukada/Shinjo*, in: Mayer-Sparenger/Jäckle (Hrsg.), Beck'sches M&A Handbuch, 2. Auflage (2022), § 104 Japan; *Burian/Shinkawa*, in: Wegen/Spahlinger/Barth (Hrsg.), Gesellschaftsrecht des Auslands, „Japan", Werkstand 9. Ergänzungslieferung (Oktober 2024).

schen Dokumenten selbst kommt allerdings kein Nachweiswert zu.[4] Daher könnten an der Gleichwertigkeit des Registers Zweifel bestehen. Die Relevanz dieser Frage ist aufgrund der sprachlichen Hürden gering; in der Praxis wird für einen formellen Nachweis ein „offizieller" Auszug in Papierform erforderlich, der vom japanischen Justizamt mit einer Richtigkeitsbestätigung versehen ausgestellt wird und für die Anerkennung in Deutschland mit einer Apostille versehen werden muss.

Vergleichbar mit dem deutschen Handelsregister ist auch, dass Löschungen von Angaben in einem japanischen Handelsregister erfolgen, indem die gelöschte Angabe unterstrichen wird. Der Auszug enthält zudem als Fußnote einen Vermerk, dass Unterstreichungen bedeuten, dass die Tatsache gelöscht ist. Der japanische Auszug ist so auch für deutsche Registergerichte oder Notare in dieser Hinsicht gut verständlich und intuitiv zugänglich.

Die Besonderheit beim japanischen elektronischen Register ist, dass es „Betriebszeiten" gibt. Außerhalb der „Betriebszeiten" oder an Schließtagen (hierzu gleich) ist das elektronische Register nicht einsehbar.

Ferner wird das japanische Handelsregister für mehrere Tage bzw. zum Teil mehrere Wochen „geblockt", während Änderungen eingetragen werden, d.h. in dieser Zeit ist weder das elektronische Register einsehbar noch können formelle Registerauszüge ausgestellt werden. Wird just in dieser Zeit eilig ein Registerauszug benötigt, muss dennoch die Freigabe des Registers abgewartet werden.

2. Insbesondere: Umfang und Nachweis der Vertretungsmacht der Direktoren (取締役, *torishimariyaku*)[5] einer japanischen Aktiengesellschaft

Etwas mehr Rücksicht auf die japanischen gesellschaftsrechtlichen Besonderheiten benötigt es beim Nachweis der Vertretungsbefugnis der gesetzlichen Vertreter einer japanischen Aktiengesellschaft.

4 Siehe etwa Immobilienregistrierung Information Center, Gemeinnützige Stiftung im Auftrag des japanischen Justizministeriums (公益財団法人不動産登記情報センター, *koeki zaidan hōjin fudōsan tōki jōhō sentā*) (ohne Datum): Informationsdienst zur Registrierung (登記情報提供サービス, *tōki jōhō teikyō sabisu*). Online verfügbar unter https://www1.touki.or.jp/service/index.html (abgerufen am 29. April 2025): „Die Registerinformationen, die dieser Service bereitstellt, entsprechen den Registerinformationen, die das Register zum Zeitpunkt der Informationsanforderung durch den Benutzer hält. Dieser Service ermöglicht jedoch nur eine ‚Betrachtung', und wird im Gegensatz zu einer Registerbescheinigung mit keinem Bestätigungsvermerk oder öffentlichem Siegel versehen."

5 In der einschlägigen Literatur wird der Begriff in der Regel als „Einzelverwaltungsrat" bzw. als „Verwaltungsratsmitglied" übersetzt, sofern die Gesellschaft über einen Verwaltungsrat (取締役会, *torishimariyakkai*) als Kollegialorgan verfügt, siehe etwa *Marutschke* (Anm. 2), S. 277 ff. und *Kansaku/Bälz* (Anm. 3), S. 109. Es gibt zudem die Rechtsformvariante der Aktiengesellschaft mit Nominierungsausschuss (etc.) (指名委員会等設置会社, *shimei iinkai tō secchi kaisha*), bei der nicht vertretungsberechtigte Direktoren, sondern vertretungsberechtigte Geschäftsführer (代表執行役, *daihyō shikkōyaku*) die Gesellschaft vertreten (Art. 420 GesG). Diese Variante ist jedoch in der Praxis selten.

a) Einzelvertretungs- vs. Gesamtvertretungsbefugnis

Im Gegensatz zur deutschen GmbH oder Aktiengesellschaft kennt die japanische Aktiengesellschaft keine Unterscheidung zwischen einzel- und gesamtvertretungsbefugten Direktoren. Gemäß Art. 349 Abs. 4 des japanischen Gesellschaftsgesetzes (会社法, *kaishahō*) sind vielmehr alle vertretungsbefugten Direktoren einzelvertretungsbefugt. Daneben gibt es Direktoren ohne Vertretungsbefugnis.

Dementsprechend unterscheidet der japanische Handelsregisterauszug zwischen „vertretungsbefugten Direktoren" (代表取締役, *daihyō torishimariyaku*) und (nicht-vertretungsbefugten) „Direktoren". Für die vertretungsberechtigten Direktoren ist allerdings nicht explizit vermerkt, dass sie einzelvertretungsbefugt sind. Bei Vorlage des Registerauszugs mit einer Übersetzung ins Deutsche vor einem deutschen Registergericht könnte sich dann das Problem stellen, dass die Einzelvertretungsbefugnis vom Registergericht in Zweifel gezogen wird.

Mittlerweile gibt es wiederholte Rechtsprechung, laut der bei einer Person, die in einem deutschen Handelsregister vergleichbaren ausländischen Register als „vertretungsberechtigt" eingetragen ist, grundsätzlich auch von einer Einzelvertretungsbefugnis ausgegangen werden kann. Auch explizit für die japanische Aktiengesellschaft findet sich entsprechende Rechtsprechung, die unter Heranziehung von Literaturnachweisen von einer Alleinvertretungsbefugnis der vertretungsberechtigten Direktoren ausgeht.[6]

Auf der anderen Seite zeigt das Vorhandensein von Rechtsprechung, dass die Vertretungsbefugnis dennoch in der Praxis ein Punkt sein kann, der in Zweifel gezogen wird. Eine zusätzliche Sicherheit kann es hier bieten, wenn die beglaubigte Übersetzung des Handelsregisterauszugs den Begriff des „*daihyō torishimariyaku*" gleich als „einzelvertretungsbefugtes Verwaltungsratsmitglied", „einzelvertretungsbefugter Direktor" oder „einzelvertretungsbefugtes Vorstandsmitglied" ausweist.[7]

b) Befugnis zur Vornahme von In-Sich-Geschäften

Demgegenüber besteht gemäß Art. 356, 365 des japanischen Gesellschaftsgesetzes keine pauschale Befugnis zur Vornahme von In-Sich-Geschäften allein aufgrund der organschaftlichen Stellung als vertretungsberechtigter Direktor. Vielmehr muss eine solche Befugnis im Einzelfall oder für bestimmte Arten von Geschäften durch Verwaltungsratsbeschluss erteilt werden. Daher gibt es – zu Recht – keine etablierte Praxis, die von der Befugnis zur Vornahme von In-Sich-Geschäften eines japanischen vertretungsbefugten Direktors ausgehen würde.

---

6 OLG München, Beschluss vom 9. März 2010, NZG 2010, S. 515 für eine japanische Aktiengesellschaft in einem registergerichtlichen Verfahren, sowie LG Düsseldorf, Urteil vom 19. November 2024, GRUR-RS 2024, 42952, Rn. 104 ff. für eine japanische Aktiengesellschaft in einem patentrechtlichen Zivilverfahren; BGH, Urteil vom 22. Februar 2022, GRUR 2022, S. 893, Rn. 14, 56. Dem folgend etwa auch *Schöner/Stöber*, Grundbuchrecht, 16. Auflage (2020), Rn. 3636 l.

7 Alternativ empfiehlt etwa Westhoff, eine Bestätigung eines japanischen Notars über die Alleinvertretungsberechtigung beizufügen, *Westhoff*, Vertretung japanischer Gesellschafter in deutschen Gesellschafterversammlungen – formale Probleme und kulturelle Hintergründe, in: DNotZ 2013, S. 6.

Soll ein vertretungsbefugter Direktor einer japanischen Aktiengesellschaft ein In-Sich-Geschäft im Sinne des § 181 BGB vornehmen (etwa wenn er sich zum Geschäftsführer bei der GmbH bestellt), müsste die Erteilung einer solchen Befugnis also gesondert nachgewiesen werden. Im Gegensatz zur Tatsache der Einzelvertretungsbefugnis wird es nicht möglich sein, dass die Übersetzung den „*daihyō torishimariyaku*" als „von den Beschränkungen des § 181 BGB befreit" ausweist, da dafür ein Verständnis der deutschen Rechtsvorschrift des § 181 BGB sowie der japanischen Rechtslage und rechtliche Subsumptionen und Wertungen im Rahmen der Übersetzung erforderlich wären.[8]

Einfacher als die Beibringung von Nachweisen der Befugnis zu In-Sich-Geschäften dürfte es in der Regel sein, die Situation eines In-Sich-Geschäfts zu vermeiden, indem man gerade nicht auf beiden Seiten einen vertretungsberechtigten Direktor (bzw. eine Person auf Basis einer von ihm erteilten Vollmacht) auftreten lässt.

c) Nachweis des Zeitpunkts des Amtsantritts

Als technische Besonderheit ist zu beachten, dass die Direktoren einer japanischen Aktiengesellschaft gemäß Art. 332 des japanischen Gesellschaftsgesetzes immer jeweils für maximal ein bis zwei Jahre bestellt und im Fall einer Verlängerung wiederbestellt werden. Bei einer solchen Wiederbestellung wird der Direktor in das Handelsregister jeweils neu als „wiederbestellt" mit dem Datum der Wiederwahl eingetragen. Daher ist aus der „Bescheinigung über sämtliche gegenwärtige Angaben" oder der „Bescheinigung über Vertretungsverhältnisse" für nach „Wiederbestellung" mehrjährig tätige Direktoren nicht erkennbar, seit wann die organschaftliche Stellung besteht. Wenn die Vertretungsbefugnis für einen vergangenen Zeitpunkt (z. B. den Zeitpunkt der Unterschrift einer Vollmacht oder eines anderen Dokuments) nachgewiesen werden muss, wird daher gegebenenfalls eine „Bescheinigung über sämtliche historische Angaben" benötigt, oder eine entsprechend ältere „Bescheinigung über sämtliche gegenwärtige Angaben".

III. Formale Anforderungen an eine Vollmacht

1. Augenzeugnis-Beglaubigung vs. „Vertretungs-Beglaubigung" durch japanische Notare

Eine Vollmacht bedarf in Deutschland grundsätzlich nicht der Form, die für das Rechtsgeschäft gilt, das mit Hilfe der Vollmacht vorgenommen wird, § 167 Abs. 2 BGB. Eine Ausnahme gilt etwa nach § 2 Abs. 2 GmbH für eine Vollmacht zur Grün-

---

8 *Krafka*, Registerrecht, 12. Aufl. (2024), Rn. 322 lehnt im Rahmen der Eintragung einer Zweigniederlassung die Eintragung von rechtlichen Vertretungsbeschränkungen, die denen des §181 BGB gleichkommen, und Befreiungen hiervon ab, „da sie allenfalls auf einer pseudojuristischen Parallelwertung beruhen können". Konkret lehnt auch die Rechtsprechung für den Fall einer englischen Limited entsprechende Eintragungen wegen „inhaltlicher und rechtssystematischer Unterschiede" ab, die zu einer Irreführung des Rechtsverkehrs führen und dem Zweck des Registers, die „tatsächlichen und rechtlichen Verhältnisse zuverlässig und vollständig darzustellen", widersprechen, siehe OLG Frankfurt a. M., FGPrax (2008), S. 165; OLG München, NZG (2005), S. 850; OLG Hamm FGPrax (2006), S. 276.

dung einer GmbH, die der Beglaubigung bedarf, sowie etwa auch für die Übernahmeerklärung im Rahmen einer Kapitalerhöhung, die ebenfalls zumindest nach herrschender Meinung und Praxis der Beglaubigung bedarf.[9]

Soll eine solche Beglaubigung in Japan stattfinden, besteht neben der Beglaubigung vor einer deutschen diplomatischen Vertretung die Möglichkeit der Beglaubigung durch einen japanischen Notar, wobei die notarielle Beglaubigung mit einer Apostille versehen werden muss.

Zur Beglaubigung einer Unterschrift vor dem japanischen Notar gibt es grundsätzlich zwei Möglichkeiten: Zum einen die Möglichkeit, dass der Unterzeichnende selbst vor dem Notar unterzeichnet und der Notar unter Feststellung der Identität des Unterzeichnenden beglaubigt, dass der Unterzeichnende in seiner Gegenwart unterzeichnet hat (sogenannte „Augenzeugnis-Beglaubigung" – 目撃認証, *mokugeki ninshō*) – dies entspricht einer Beglaubigung nach deutschem Verständnis. Zum anderen gibt es in Japan auch die Möglichkeit, dass der Unterzeichner nicht selbst den Notar aufsucht, sondern einen Vertreter zum Notar schickt, der dem Notar gegenüber bestätigt, dass der Unterzeichner die Unterschrift geleistet hat. Der Notar überzeugt sich nur von der Identität des Vertreters und beglaubigt aufgrund der Aussage des Vertreters, dass der Vertreter die Identität des Unterzeichners bestätigt hat (sogenannte „Vertretungs-Beglaubigung" – 代理認証, *dairi ninshō*).

Letztere genügt nicht den Anforderungen an eine deutsche Beglaubigung, nach der die Unterschrift „in Gegenwart des Notars" vollzogen oder anerkannt werden muss und eine Identitätsfeststellung des Unterzeichners durch den Notar stattfinden muss, §§ 40 Abs. 1, Abs. 4, 10 Abs. 1 BeurkG, was eine persönliche Anwesenheit des Unterzeichners vor dem Notar voraussetzt.[10]

In Japan ist die „Vertretungs-Beglaubigung" allerdings insbesondere bei vielbeschäftigen gesetzlichen Vertretern eines Unternehmens eine völlig selbstverständliche und übliche Praxis, und es ist in japanischen Unternehmen oft schwer zu vermitteln und durchzusetzen, dass sich eine solche „wichtige" Person höchstpersönlich zum Notar oder einer konsularischen Vertretung bemühen muss. In einigen Fällen aus der Praxis der Verfasserin bestanden Unternehmen darauf, nur mit einer „Vertretungs-Beglaubigung" vorzugehen. Sofern die Beglaubigung zwingend notwendig ist, wie etwa bei der Vollmacht zur Unterzeichnung einer Übernahmeerklärung bei Kapitalerhöhungen, wird dies von den Gerichten in aller Regel beanstandet. Daher kann ein Vorgehen über die „Vertretungs-Beglaubigung" jedenfalls nicht als rechtssicheres Vorgehen empfohlen werden.

---

9 BGH, Urteil vom 18. April 2005, II ZR 151/03 am Ende; *Ulmer/Casper*, in: Habersack/Casper/Löbbe (Hrsg.), GmbHG – Gesetz betreffend die Gesellschaften mit beschränkter Haftung – Großkommentar, 3. Aufl. (2021), GmbHG § 55 Rn. 75 m. w. N.; anderer Ansicht *Lieder*, in: Fleischer/Goette (Hrsg.), Münchener Kommentar zum Gesetz betreffend die Gesellschaften mit beschränkter Haftung, 5. Aufl. (2025), GmbHG § 55 Rn. 176.

10 BGH, Beschluss vom 10. August 1987, DNotZ (1988), S. 259; KG, Beschluss vom 3. März 2022, DNotZ (2022), S. 607, 610; OLG Karlsruhe, Beschluss vom 20. April 2022, Az. 1 W 25/22 (Wx).

2. Praktische Probleme bei der Beglaubigung durch japanische Notare

Der Theorie nach bescheinigt eine Beglaubigung auch durch den japanischen Notar nur, dass eine bestimmte Person die Unterschrift unter ein Dokument geleistet hat, nicht aber die inhaltliche Richtigkeit des Dokuments. Dennoch ist für die Praxis zu beachten, dass japanische Notare in weiterem Umfang auch den Inhalt eines beglaubigt zu unterzeichnenden Dokuments hinterfragen. So kann es vorkommen, dass der japanische Notar die Erforderlichkeit einer weiten Vollmacht hinterfragt, oder für die Unterzeichnung durch den Geschäftsführer einer GmbH in Gründung ein Handelsregistereintrag des Geschäftsführers verlangt. Hier kann nur versucht werden, im Einzelfall die Fragen des japanischen Notariats zu beantworten, und im Notfall auf andere Notariate auszuweichen.

3. Schreibweise der Unterschrift

Oft kommt von japanischer Seite die Frage auf, mit welcher Schreibweise die Unterschrift geleistet werden muss, insbesondere ob eine Unterzeichnung in japanischer Schreibweise möglich ist.

Grundsätzlich ist eine Unterschrift mit japanischen Schriftzeichen (wie auch anderen ausländischen Schriftzeichen) formwirksam.[11] Nach ständiger Rechtsprechung des BGH setzt eine „Unterschrift" nach Sprachgebrauch und Zweck der Formvorschrift des § 126 BGB „ein aus Buchstaben einer üblichen Schrift bestehendes Gebilde" voraus, „das nicht lesbar zu sein braucht". Es genügt das Vorliegen eines die Identität des Unterschreibenden ausreichend kennzeichnenden individuellen Schriftzuges, der einmalig ist, entsprechende charakteristische Merkmale aufweist, sich als Wiedergabe eines Namens darstellt und die Absicht einer vollen Unterschriftsleistung erkennen lässt.[12]

Völlig unproblematisch ist daher die Unterschrift nur in japanischen Zeichen, wenn sie beglaubigt wird, da hierbei die Identität durch den Notar festgestellt wird und auch für den europäischen Betrachter des Dokuments dann eindeutig erkennbar ist. Um Diskussionen oder Nachfragen zu vermeiden, kann es allerdings bei einfachschriftlicher Unterschrift in der Praxis empfehlenswert sein, (auch) in lateinischen Buchstaben zu unterzeichnen.

Selten wird bei lateinisch-schriftlicher Unterschrift von Unterzeichnern, die dies nicht gewohnt sind, mit Abkürzungen unterschrieben. Hier ist zu beachten, dass eine bewusste oder gewollte Namensabkürzung (Handzeichen, Paraphe) keine formgültige Unterschrift darstellt.[13] Ebenso genügt der Anfangsbuchstabe des Nachna-

11 VGH München NJW (1978), S. 510, 511 (für arabische Schrift); *Einsele*, in: Säcker/Rixecker/Oetker/Limperg/Schubert (Hrsg.), MüKoBGB 10. Aufl. (2025), BGB § 126 Rn. 18; *Hertel*, in: Staudinger (Begr.) BGB (2023), § 126, Rn. 108; *Litzenburger*, in: BeckOK BGB 73. Ed. 1. Februar 2025, BeurkG § 13 Rn. 15; *Kindler*, in: Heckschen/Herrler/Münch, Beck'sches Notar-Handbuch, 8. Aufl. (2024), § 31 Beurkundung. Rn. 285.

12 Z. B. BGH NJW (1985), S. 1227; BGH NJW (1987), S. 1333; BGH NJW (1994), S. 55.

13 BGH, NJW 1967, S. 2310; BGH NJW (1994), S. 55.

mens nicht zur Unterzeichnung eines notariell beurkundeten Kaufvertrags,[14] da bei einer notariellen Beurkundung gem. § 13 BeurkG eine ganze Unterschrift notwendig ist; bei einem bloßem Schrifterfordernis kommt ausnahmsweise ein notariell beglaubigtes Handzeichen in Betracht (§ 126 Abs. 1 Var. 2 BGB, § 40 Abs. 6 BeurkG).

IV. Besonderheiten bei der Gründung einer Tochtergesellschaft einer japanischen Aktiengesellschaft in Form einer GmbH

Werden die obigen Besonderheiten beachtet, insbesondere die Anforderungen an die Ausstellung einer gültigen Gründungs-Vollmacht und an den Nachweis der Existenz der Gesellschaft mittels eines Handelsregisterauszugs, ist die Gründung einer deutschen GmbH als Tochtergesellschaft einer japanischen Aktiengesellschaft in der Regel ein unkomplizierter und unproblematischer und mittlerweile praxiserprobter Vorgang, der selten Probleme mit den Registergerichten verursacht.

V. Besonderheiten bei Eintragung einer deutschen Zweigniederlassung einer japanischen Aktiengesellschaft

Etwas schwieriger bzw. aufwendiger sind die Anforderungen an die Eintragung einer Zweigniederlassung einer japanischen Aktiengesellschaft. Dies liegt daran, dass auch Tatsachen über die Aktiengesellschaft selbst einzutragen und Unterlagen der Aktiengesellschaft beizubringen sind.

Die meisten Anforderungen lassen sich problemlos erfüllen, allerdings gibt es im Wesentlichen zwei Vorgaben, die meist zu Diskussionen führen bzw. mit Unsicherheiten behaftet sind, bezüglich derer eine Beanstandung durch Registergerichte nicht ausgeschlossen werden kann:

1. Vorlage der Satzung in öffentlich beglaubigter Abschrift

Ein Punkt ist das Erfordernis der Vorlage einer Satzung in öffentlich beglaubigter Abschrift nebst beglaubigter Übersetzung in die deutsche Sprache gemäß § 13f Abs. 2 S. 1 HGB. Die Satzung einer japanischen Aktiengesellschaft wird nämlich zwar grundsätzlich einmalig bei der Gründung vom Notar beglaubigt und die Urfassung auch beim Notar verwahrt. Bei Änderungen wird allerdings die aktuelle Satzung nur gemäß Art. 31 des japanischen Gesellschaftsgesetzes in der Gesellschaft verwahrt, aber weder beim Notar noch beim Handelsregister hinterlegt, so dass dementsprechend keine öffentlich beglaubigte Abschrift davon erfolgen kann.

Sofern die Urschrift noch Geltung hat, könnte von der Möglichkeit gebraucht werden, von der beim Notar hinterlegten Satzung eine Abschrift zu erhalten, und diese vorgelegt werden.

---

14 OLG Stuttgart NZM (2002), S. 175.

Sofern die Urschrift aber nicht mehr gilt, kann über einen Umweg doch ein öffentlich beglaubigtes Dokument kreiert werden, das in der Praxis so auch von den meisten Registergerichten akzeptiert wird, indem eine Kopie der Satzung mit einer Erklärung eines vertretungsberechtigten Direktors der Gesellschaft versehen wird, der erklärt, dass die Satzung mit der derzeit gültigen Satzung übereinstimmt, und diese Erklärung des Direktors beglaubigt unterzeichnen zu lassen.

Bei einer späteren Änderung der Satzung der japanischen Aktiengesellschaft muss das entsprechende Prozedere dann wiederholt werden, um die hinterlegte Satzung gemäß § 13 f Abs. 4 HGB aktuell zu halten.

2. Angabe der Vertretungsregelung und Versicherungen durch die Direktoren

Zu einem erhöhten Aufwand führt auch das Erfordernis der Abgabe der Versicherungen nach § 37 Abs. 2 AktG durch „die Vorstandsmitglieder" der Aktiengesellschaft, insbesondere angesichts der bereits beschriebenen Hürden an die erforderliche beglaubigte Unterzeichnung der Versicherung. Die meisten Gerichte akzeptieren es zumindest, wenn nur die vertretungsberechtigten Direktoren eine Versicherung abgeben.

Zudem muss bei der Anmeldung der Zweigniederlassung gemäß § 13 f Abs. 2 S. 2 HGB i. V. m. § 37 Abs. 3 Nr. 2 AktG auch eine Angabe zur abstrakten Vertretungsregelung der Aktiengesellschaft angegeben werden. Das japanische Recht kennt jedoch grundsätzlich keine Unterscheidung in abstrakte und konkrete Vertretungsregelung, wie sie dem deutschen Recht geläufig ist. Vielmehr sind die vertretungsberechtigten Direktoren kraft Gesetzes stets einzelvertretungsberechtigt.[15] Meist lässt sich dies dem Gericht erklären und vermitteln, dass als abstrakte Vertretungsregelung „Jedes Vorstandsmitglied vertritt einzeln." einzutragen ist.

Insgesamt sind Zweigniederlassungen japanischer Unternehmen in der Praxis viel seltener als selbständige Tochtergesellschaften in Deutschland, so dass der Prozess auch insgesamt weniger standardisiert ist.

VI. Sonderfall: „Austausch" der Hauptniederlassung

Im Zusammenhang mit Zweigniederlassungen spannend ist auch folgende Konstellation:

Eine japanische Aktiengesellschaft A Ltd. („A Ltd. alt") hat in Deutschland eine Zweigniederlassung, die im deutschen Handelsregister eingetragen ist. A Ltd. alt wurde nun eine Holdinggesellschaft, die Anteile an ihren Tochtergesellschaften hält. Einer der Geschäftsbereiche der A Ltd. Alt (zu dem der gesamte Geschäftsbetrieb der deutschen Zweigniederlassung gehört) wurde auf eine andere japanische Aktiengesellschaft, die B Ltd. abgespalten, die eine Tochtergesellschaft der A Ltd. alt ist. Im Zuge dieser Abspaltung ging die deutsche Zweigniederlassung im Wege

[15] Siehe oben, Teil II.2.a).

der Universalsukzession auf die B Ltd. über. Nach der Abspaltung wurde die A Ltd. alt in A Holding Ltd. und die B Ltd. in A Ltd. („A Ltd. neu") umfirmiert.

Dabei stellten sich die beteiligten Gesellschaften die Frage, ob sie im deutschen Handelsregister die Zweigniederlassung der A Ltd. alt einfach stehenlassen lassen können, auch wenn die japanische A Ltd. neu nicht die gleiche juristische Person ist wie die japanische A Ltd. alt, oder nach der Abspaltung und Übertragung der Zweigniederlassung von der A Ltd. alt auf die A Ltd. neu eine neue Zweigniederlassung der A Ltd. neu im deutschen Handelsregister eintragen und die Zweigniederlassung der A Ltd. alt gelöscht werden muss.

Leider ist die Lösung hier eindeutig, dass nach Abspaltung unter anderem des Betriebs der Zweigniederlassung diese nicht mehr Zweigniederlassung des übertragenden Rechtsträgers (A Ltd. alt), sondern des übernehmenden Rechtsträgers (A Ltd. neu) ist. Die bisherige Zweigniederlassung war daher zu löschen in Verbindung mit der Anmeldung einer neuen Zweigniederlassung des übernehmenden Rechtsträgers (A Ltd. neu). Dass der übernehmende Rechtsträger sich anschließend in die Firma umfirmierte, die bislang der übertragende Rechtsträgers trug, änderte nichts daran, dass die Zweigniederlassung nunmehr zu einem anderen Rechtsträger gehörte.

VII. Zustimmungskataloge und „Management Rules" für deutsche Tochter-GmbHs einer japanischen Aktiengesellschaft

Oft besteht Bedarf, die internen Zustimmungsregeln des japanischen Headquarters auch für globale Tochtergesellschaften zu implementieren. Hier ist zu beachten, dass die in japanischen Aktiengesellschaften möglichen und üblichen Zustimmungsregeln/-mechanismen nicht unbedingt so in einer deutschen GmbH umsetzbar sind, insbesondere wegen der zwingenden Zuständigkeit der Gesellschafterversammlung für bestimmte Angelegenheiten. Insbesondere sehen japanisch geprägte Zustimmungskataloge oft eine Entscheidungskompetenz der Geschäftsführung zu Satzungsänderungen oder anderen Angelegenheiten, die nach deutschem GmbH-Recht zwingend in der Zuständigkeit der Gesellschafterversammlung liegen (für Satzungsänderungen: gemäß § 53 Abs. 1 GmbHG) vor. Hintergrund mag sein, dass auch in einer japanischen Aktiengesellschaft die Hauptversammlung nach Art. 466 Gesellschaftsgesetz über Satzungsänderungen entscheidet, aber gemäß Art. 298 Abs 1 Gesellschaftsgesetz in der Regel eine Entscheidung des Verwaltungsrats erforderlich ist, die Entscheidung über die Satzungsänderung zum Gegenstand der Hauptversammlung zu machen.

Die Zustimmungsregeln in Geschäftsordnungen für die Geschäftsführung enthalten nach der deutschen Praxis allerdings nur inhaltliche Entscheidungsbefugnisse, die hinsichtlich der zwingend der Gesellschafterversammlung vorbehaltenen Angelegenheiten in keiner Weise bei der Geschäftsführung liegen und daher in einem Zustimmungskatalog nicht der Entscheidung der Geschäftsführung zugewiesen werden können.[16]

---

16 Ausführliche Erörterung der grundsätzlich ausschließlichen Kompetenz der Gesellschafterversammlung siehe etwa *Harbart*, in: MüKoGmbHG (Anm. 9), GmbHG § 53 Rn. 58 ff.

VIII. Änderung nur des englischen Firmennamens eines japanischen Unternehmens

Gelegentlich ändern japanische Unternehmen die englische/lateinschriftliche Bezeichnung ihrer Firma, vornehmlich um ihr Image im internationalen Geschäftsverkehr zu ändern. Hier besteht das Problem, dass es keine offizielle Dokumentation für die Firmenänderung und damit für den Nachweis der Identität der Gesellschaft unter dem alten Namen und der Gesellschaft unter dem neuen Namen gibt.

Für das Handelsregister reicht es zunächst, dass die Geschäftsführer der deutschen Tochtergesellschaft in vertretungsberechtigter Anzahl eine neue Gesellschafterliste der deutschen Tochtergesellschaft unterzeichnen, die den neuen englischen Namen der Muttergesellschaft enthält, und diese zum Handelsregister einreichen. Weitere Nachweise sind nicht erforderlich. Dies ergibt sich daraus, dass § 40 Abs. 1 GmbHG grundsätzlich den Geschäftsführern die Pflicht auferlegt, Veränderungen in der Person des Gesellschafters „auf Mitteilung und Nachweis" in einer aktuellen Gesellschafterliste zu reflektieren. D. h. die Geschäftsführer prüfen die Richtigkeit der mitzuteilenden Änderung, und haften nach Abs. 3 für Schäden bei einem Verstoß gegen die Aktualisierungspflicht. Die Verantwortung für die Richtigkeit liegt damit bei der Geschäftsführung und eine Prüfung durch das Registergericht oder einen die Einreichung vermittelnden Notar findet nicht statt.[17]

IX. Änderung des Gesellschafters durch eine Verschmelzung nach japanischem Recht

„Einfach" zu lösen ist der Fall, dass sich durch eine Verschmelzung nach japanischem Recht der Gesellschafter einer deutschen GmbH ändert, weil z. B. die ursprüngliche Gesellschafterin, die japanische X Ltd., auf eine andere japanische Y Ltd. verschmolzen wird.[18] In diesem Fall können die Geschäftsführer der deutschen GmbH einfach eine neue Gesellschaferliste bei Gericht einreichen, ein Nachweis der Verschmelzung ist nicht erforderlich (siehe oben, Teil VIII.).

Zudem wäre auch der Nachweis der Verschmelzung nach japanischem Recht in der Regel unproblematisch möglich, da sowohl im Handelsregistereintrag der aufnehmenden Gesellschaft als auch im (dann gelöschten) Handelsregistereintrag der übertragenden Gesellschaft die Tatsache der Verschmelzung vermerkt wird. Für die gelöschte Gesellschaft ist ein Handelsregisterauszug nach der Löschung dann in

---

17 Bundestag-Drucksache 16/6140 vom 25. Juli 2007, S. 43 f.: „Nach Absatz 1 Satz 2 erfolgt die Änderung der Liste [...] auf Mitteilung und Nachweis. Den Geschäftsführern obliegt daher eine Prüfpflicht. Dadurch sollte im Regelfall die gebotene Sorgfalt bei Abgabe der Liste gewährleistet sein. Das Registergericht nimmt die Listen lediglich entgegen und hat keine inhaltliche Prüfpflicht."; OLG Frankfurt, Beschluss vom 22. 11. 2010 – 20 W 333/10. Aus der Erfahrung in der Praxis gibt es jedoch vereinzelt Notare, die hier einen Nachweis sehen möchten.

18 Generell zur Verschmelzung nach japanischem Recht, siehe etwa *Günal*, Die Verschmelzung im japanischen Gesellschaftsrecht (2014).

Form einer sogenannten „Bescheinigung über sämtliche gelöschte Angaben“ (抹消事項全部証明書, *masshō jikō zenbu shōmeisho*) erhältlich.

Wie eingangs erwähnt, erhebt der Beitrag keinen Anspruch, eine systematische Aufbereitung theoretisch denkbarer Probleme zu geben, sondern stellt praxisrelevante, und tatsächlich auch so vorkommende Probleme exemplarisch dar. Dennoch mögen diese Exempel verdeutlichen, wie spannend es sein kann, zwischen zwei Rechtsordnungen tätig zu werden und die unterschiedlichen Anforderungen und Traditionen der beiden Rechtsordnungen in Einklang zu bringen.

Literaturverzeichnis

Baum, Harald/*Bälz*, Moritz (Hrsg.): Handbuch Japanisches Handels- und Gesellschaftsrecht (2011).

Fleischer, Jürgen/*Goette*, Michael (Hrsg.): Münchener Kommentar zum Gesetz betreffend die Gesellschaften mit beschränkter Haftung (GmbHG), 5. Auflage (2025).

Günal, Deniz: Die Verschmelzung im japanischen Gesellschaftsrecht (2014).

Habersack, Mathias/*Casper*, Matthias/*Löbbe*, Marc (Hrsg.): GmbHG – Gesetz betreffend die Gesellschaften mit beschränkter Haftung – Großkommentar, Band 3, 3. Auflage (2021).

Hau, Wolfgang/*Poseck*, Roman (Hrsg.): BeckOK BGB, 73. Edition, Stand: 01.02.2025 (2025).

Heckschen, Bernd/*Herrler*, Jan/*Münch*, Andreas (Hrsg.): Beck'sches Notar-Handbuch, 8. Aufl. (2024).

Immobilienregistrierung Information Center, Gemeinnützige Stiftung im Auftrag des japanischen Justizministeriums (公益財団法人不動産登記情報センター, *koeki zaidan hōjin fudōsan tōki jōhō sentā*) (ohne Datum): Informationsdienst zur Registrierung (登記情報提供サービス, *tōki jōhō teikyō sabisu*). Online verfügbar unter https://www1.touki.or.jp/service/index.html (zuletzt abgerufen am 29. April 2025).

Krafka, Alexander: Registerrecht, 12. Auflage (2024).

Marutschke, Hans-Peter: Einführung in das japanische Recht, 2. Auflage (2010).

Mayer-Sparenberg, Wolfgang/*Jäckle*, Christof (Hrsg.): Beck'sches M&A Handbuch 2. Auflage (2022).

Menkhaus, Heinrich: Allgemeines Gesellschaftsrecht in Japan, in: Menkhaus, Heinrich/Sato, Fumihiko (Hrsg.): Japanischer Brückenbauer zum deutschen Rechtskreis, Festschrift für Koresuke Yamauchi zum 60. Geburtstag (2006).

Rodatz, Peter: Einige Bemerkungen zu den Besonderheiten im japanischen Gesellschaftsrecht, in: *Menkhaus*, Heinrich (Hrsg.): Das japanische im japanischen Recht (1994).

Säcker, Franz Jürgen/*Rixecker*, Roland/*Oetker*, Hartmut/*Limperg*, Bettina (Hrsg.): Münchener Kommentar zum Bürgerlichen Gesetzbuch, Band 1: Allgemeiner Teil §§ 1–240, AllgPersönlR, StiftRG, ProstG, AGG, 10. Auflage (2025).

Säcker, Franz Jürgen/*Rixecker*, Roland/*Oetker*, Hartmut/*Limperg*, Bettina (Hrsg.): Münchener Kommentar zum Bürgerlichen Gesetzbuch, Band 13: Internationales Privatrecht II (Art. 50–253 EGBGB), 9. Auflage (2025).

Staudinger, Julius von (Begr.): Kommentar zum Bürgerlichen Gesetzbuch mit Einführungsgesetz und Nebengesetzen, Neubearbeitung 2023 (2023).

Stöber, Kurt/*Schöner*, Hartmut: Grundbuchrecht, 16. Auflage (2020).

Wegen, Gerhard/*Spahlinger*, Andreas/*Barth*, Marcel: Gesellschaftsrecht des Auslands, München 2024. (Werkstand des Kapitels Japan: 9. Ergänzungslieferung Oktober 2024) (2024).

Westhoff, Michael: Vertretung japanischer Gesellschafter in deutschen Gesellschafterversammlungen – formale Probleme und kulturelle Hintergründe, in: DNotZ (2013), S. 4 ff.

Yamaguchi, Shigeo: Abwehrmaßnahmen börsennotierter Aktiengesellschaften gegen feindliche Übernahmeangebote in Deutschland und Japan (2005).

Allgemeine Arbeitsvertragsbedingungen

Historische Entwicklung und rechtliche Regelung in Deutschland

Von *Franz Josef Düwell*

Prof. Franz Josef Düwell, Honorarprofessor an der Universität Konstanz, war von 2001 bis 2011 Vorsitzender Richter des Neunten Senats des Bundesarbeitsgerichts. Er hat mehrfach als Schlichter in Arbeitskämpfen fungiert und wirkt seit Jahrzehnten als Herausgeber an zahlreichen arbeitsrechtlichen Kommentaren mit. Prof. Düwell ist Mitbegründer der Deutsch-Japanischen Gesellschaft für Arbeitsrecht e.V. und folgte dem Jubilar 2016 in der Rolle des Vorstandsvorsitzenden nach. Im Jahr 2007 verbrachte er einige Wochen in Tokyo, als Gastprofessor an der Chuo Universität. Prof. Düwell ist Träger des Bundesverdienstkreuzes am Bande.

I. Widmung

Ich widme diesen Beitrag dem von mir hochgeschätzten Emeritus Professor Dr. Heinrich Menkhaus. Ich habe ihn 1997 in Tokyo auf dem Gründungskongress der Japanisch-Deutschen Gesellschaft für Arbeitsrecht (DJGA) kennengelernt. Ich hielt damals in Vertretung des Präsidenten des Bundesarbeitsgerichts ein Referat über das am 1. Oktober 1997 in Kraft getretene Arbeitsrechtliche Gesetz zur Förderung von Wachstum und Beschäftigung. Durch Einschnitte in das gewachsene deutsche Arbeitsrecht sollten „Wachstumsbremsen" entfallen. Diese Deregulierung war das Hauptziel der Wirtschaftspolitik, die das 1994 gebildete fünfte Kabinett Kohl verfolgte, das von dem gefühlten Dauerkanzler Helmut Kohl im Rahmen einer Koalition des Christdemokraten mit dem freidemokratischen Vizekanzler Klaus Kinkel gebildet worden war. Heinrich Menkhaus war damals als Vertreter der in Tokyo ansässigen Deutschen Industrie- und Handelskammer bei dem Kongress anwesend. Wir sahen uns nur flüchtig. In den Folgejahren kam es jedoch zu einer engen Zusammenarbeit. Mit diesem Beitrag möchte ich einen Teil der Dankesschuld abtragen.

II. Rechtswissenschaftlicher Austausch Deutschland – Japan auf dem Gebiet des Arbeitsrechts

1997 war aus unterschiedlichen Gründen eine günstige Situation für die Vertiefung der deutsch-japanischen Beziehungen im Arbeitsrecht. In beiden Ländern war damals eine Umbruchstimmung.

In Deutschland waren die Intellektuellen der langen Kanzlerschaft Helmut Kohls überdrüssig. Es entstand eine Wechselstimmung zum Experiment rot-grün. Bei der

Duncker & Humblot · Berlin | https://doi.org/10.3790/978-3-428-59611-9.2025.424098

Bundestagswahl im September 1998 wurde zum ersten und bisher einzigen Mal eine Bundesregierung komplett abgelöst, während sich bei allen anderen Regierungswechseln lediglich einer der vorherigen Koalitionspartner änderte. Außerdem gewann mit der SPD erstmals eine Partei mehr als 20 Millionen Stimmen hinzu, so dass erstmals mit SPD und „Grüne“ zwei traditionell „links der Mitte“ eingestufte Parteien mehr als 50 Prozent der Sitze im Bundestag erhielten.

In Japan war ebenfalls ein Umdenken angesagt. Japans Waren- und Kapitalexporte waren in den 1980er Jahren unaufhörlich angestiegen und ließen das rohstoffarme Inselland zum weltgrößten Netto-Gläubiger der USA aufsteigen. Japans Anteil am „Welt-BIP“ betrug 1995 18 %. Das reine Netto-Auslandsvermögen Japans belief sich Ende 1995 auf 77 Bio. Yen.[1] 1989 wurde Tokyo die umsatzstärkste Börse der Welt. Nach Wiederanlage suchende Exportgewinne und billig geschöpftes Kreditgeld ließen die Aktien- und Immobilienpreise explodieren. Das Ende der „Luftblasenwirtschaft“ (Bubble Economy) war unausweichlich. Die Inflation von Vermögenswerten (Assets) koppelte allgemeines Wachstum und Einkommen der abhängig Beschäftigten ab. 1990 kam es in Bekämpfung der Inflation zur Erhöhung der Leitzinsen. Daraufhin kehrte sich die Preisspirale in eine länger andauernde Asset-Deflation um: Grundstückspreise und Kurse sackten ab. Das war der Beginn der wirtschaftlichen Stagnation. Zudem nahm die Lebenserwartung noch immer zu, während die Geburtenrate deutlich unter das Reproduktionsminimum sank, so dass das Durchschnittsalter der Erwerbstätigen stieg und der Anteil der aktiven Arbeitskräfte an der Bevölkerung fiel. So stand 1997 das bisherige Sozialmodell in Japan zur Debatte. Arbeitslosigkeit wurde erstmals in Japan ein Problem; denn die offizielle Arbeitslosenrate 1996 stieg mit 3,4 % auf den seit Erfassungsbeginn 1953 höchsten Wert. Premierminister Murayama Tomiichi von der Sozialistischen Partei Japans (SPJ), die sich 1996 in Sozialdemokratische Partei (SDP) umbenannte, trat ab. Ryūtarō Hashimoto von der Liberaldemokratischen Partei (LDP) übernahm. Als Gegenmittel stellten die Regierungspartei LDP und das Hashimoto-Kabinett Ende 1996 einen umfassenden Deregulierungskatalog auf. Kein Wunder, dass in dieser Situation, in der Fusion und Unternehmensverkäufe erleichtert, Beschäftigung sowie Entgelt der Kernbelegschaften flexibilisiert und differenziert wurden, das Interesse am deutschen Arbeitsrecht wuchs; denn dort hatte diese Rechtsentwicklung bereits 1972 mit dem Betriebsübergangsrecht in § 122 BetrVG und mit dem Arbeitnehmerüberlassungsgesetz eingesetzt. 1994 kam dann noch das die Spaltung von Rechtsträgern zulassende Umwandlungsgesetz hinzu.

Dieser historische Kairos führte 1997 sowohl zur Gründung der Deutsch-Japanischen Gesellschaft für Arbeitsrecht als auch zur Konstituierung der japanischen Schwestergesellschaft. In Deutschland war der 1980 einsetzende wirtschaftliche Aufstieg Japans aufmerksam registriert worden. Als ein Schlüssel für diesen Erfolg wurde in den 90er Jahren „Kaizen“ entdeckt. Anstelle von radikalen Umgestaltungen setzt diese japanische Methode auf beständige, schrittweise Fortschritte. Diese sind leichter zu implementieren, erhöhen die Motivation und stärken das Engagement der Beteiligten.

---

[1] *Berndt*, Sieger oder Verlierer, in: Blätter für deutsche und internationale Politik, 5/1997, S. 587 ff.

Nach den Gesellschaftsgründungen fand ein intensiver wissenschaftlicher Austausch statt. Es kam jährlich zu Begegnungen in Deutschland und Japan. An der Marburger Universität entstand zudem ein Japan-Zentrum und Heinrich Menkhaus erhielt Anfang der 2000er Jahre den Lehrstuhl für Japanisches Recht sowie die Leitung des Instituts für Privatrechtsvergleichung. Kurz darauf wurde er zum Vorstandsvorsitzenden der DJGA gewählt. Da ich dem erweiterten Vorstand angehörte, wurde unser persönlicher Kontakt intensiviert. Als Heinrich Menkhaus 2008 den Ruf an die Meiji Universität in Tokyo annahm, hat er mich bei allen Veranstaltungen stets mit großzügiger Gastfreundschaft an der Meiji-Universität empfangen. Er hat mir geduldig das mir fremde japanische Recht und auch den besonderen japanischen „way of life" nahegebracht. Als Nachfolger im Vorsitz der Deutsch-Japanischen Gesellschaft für Arbeitsrecht ist es mir auch eine Herzenssache, Heinrich Menkhaus für die jahrzehntelange Kärrnerarbeit zu danken, die er als Vereinsvorsitzender im Dienst der DJGA und damit zugleich zur Vertiefung der deutsch-japanischen Beziehungen in der Arbeitsrechtswissenschaft vollbracht hat. In Japan hat diese mühsame ehrenamtliche Tätigkeit die verdiente Anerkennung gefunden. Der japanische Kaiser hat Heinrich Menkhaus den „Orden der aufgehenden Sonne" verliehen. Ich durfte 2024 der Übereichung durch den japanischen Botschafter Yanagi im Rahmen eines glanzvollen Empfangs in der Botschaft von Japan in Berlin beiwohnen.

An den von den beiden Schwestergesellschaften erfolgreich initiierten wissenschaftlichen Austausch knüpfe ich an. Zum Thema meines Beitrags hat mich die hervorragende rechtsvergleichende Untersuchung „Arbeitsordnung und allgemeine Arbeitsbedingungen"[2] angeregt, die im Frühjahr 2025 in der Schriftenreihe der Deutsch-Japanischen Gesellschaft für Arbeitsrecht erschienen ist. Ich möchte aus deutscher Perspektive ergänzend dazu einige Aspekte beitragen, warum und in welcher Weise sich die deutsche Arbeitsrechtsordnung anders als die japanische entwickelt hat.

III. Arbeitsordnung

1. Das Arbeitgeberrecht, die Arbeitsbedingungen kollektiv zu regeln

a) Die Arbeitsordnung im Deutschen Kaiserreich

Die Reichsverfassung von 1871 erwähnt weder das Arbeitsrecht noch die Beteiligung der Arbeiter. Zur ersten gesetzlichen Regelung kam es, nachdem im „Dreikaiserjahr" 1888 der erst 29 Jahre alte Wilhelm II. die Regentschaft übernommen hatte. Unter dem Eindruck des großen Bergarbeiterstreiks vom Mai 1889 schlug der junge Kaiser zum Missfallen seines Reichskanzlers Bismarcks einen sozialpolitischen Reformkurs ein. Wie Wilhelm nach seiner Abdankung in seinen Erinnerungen beschrieb, wollte er damit „die Seele des deutschen Arbeiters gewinnen."[3] Mit der Novellierung der Reichsgewerbeordnung setzte sich der Kaiser durch. Das so genannte Arbeiterschutzgesetz[4] führte im Deutschen Reich eine erste Beteiligung der Arbeiter-

2 *Wank/Yoshida*, Arbeitsordnung und allgemeine Arbeitsbedingungen – Ein Vergleich der Entwicklung in Deutschland und in Japan (2025).

3 *Wilhelm II.*, Ereignisse und Gestalten (1922), S. 33.

4 RGBl. 1892, S. 261.

schaft an der Regelung von allgemeinen Arbeitsbedingungen ein. Bis dahin herrschte das Vorbild der Hausordnung: Der Arbeitgeber war Hausherr und konnte einseitig eine Arbeitsordnung erlassen. Zeitgenössische Arbeiter empfanden diese Ordnung häufig als „Zuchthausordnung". Es erfolgte eine Regulierung. Die Regeln über das Verhalten und die Ordnung mussten in Fabriken mit mindestens 20 Arbeitern in einer Arbeitsordnung schriftlich zusammengefasst werden (§§ 134a–g GewO). Zusätzlich wurde eine gesetzliche Grundlage für die fakultative Errichtung von ständigen Arbeiterausschüssen in diesen Fabriken geschaffen (§ 134h GewO). Der Erlass der Arbeitsordnung blieb zwar weiterhin in der alleinigen Befugnis des Arbeitgebers. Die Ausgestaltung des Verfahrens führte jedoch zu einer Inhaltskontrolle. Vor dem endgültigen Erlass der Arbeitsordnung musste der Fabrikherr sämtliche großjährigen Arbeiter oder den Arbeiterausschuss anhören. Die Arbeitsordnung musste danach der unteren Verwaltungsbehörde vorgelegt und dort einer Rechtmäßigkeitsprüfung unterzogen werden. Nach § 134b GewO waren zwingend aufzunehmen:

1. Regelungen über Anfang und Ende der regelmäßigen täglichen Arbeitszeit,
2. über die Pausen sowie
3. über den Zeitpunkt und die Art der Abrechnung der Lohnzahlung.

Diese Vorgaben hatten die Funktion, den Fabrikherrn zu einer bindenden und behördlich überprüfbaren Festlegung zu veranlassen. Eine Mitbestimmung durch den Arbeiterausschuss war nur erforderlich, soweit durch Vorschriften das Verhalten der Arbeitnehmer bei Inanspruchnahme der Wohlfahrtseinrichtungen geregelt werden sollte. Eine im Wesentlichen inhaltsgleiche Regelung wurde für den Bergbau mit dem Änderungsgesetz zum Allgemeinen Berggesetz für die preußischen Staaten vom 24. Juni 1892[5] in Kraft gesetzt. Die gesetzlich empfohlene Bildung freiwilliger Arbeiterausschüsse scheiterte in der Praxis am Unwillen der Ruhrindustriellen. Deren ablehnende Haltung hatte 1890 auf der Tagung des Vereins für Sozialpolitik Henri Axel Bueck, der Geschäftsführer des Centralverbandes deutscher Industrieller, deutlich zum Ausdruck gebracht. Arbeiterausschüsse würden „eine Gleichberechtigung und ein Selbstbestimmungsrecht in Aussicht stellen, welches absolut nicht mit unserer Wirtschafts- und Gesellschaftsordnung vereinbar ist."[6]

Nachdem es erneut 1905 zu Streiks mit bürgerkriegsähnlichen Auseinandersetzungen gekommen war, bemühte sich der Kaiser durch eine „versöhnende Arbeiterpolitik" die Verhältnisse zu befrieden. Deshalb wurde in § 80f Abs. 1 des Allgemeinen Berggesetzes idF des Änderungsgesetzes vom 14. Juli 1905[7] die obligatorische Bildung der Arbeiterausschüsse angeordnet. Die Haltung der Gewerkschaften war zunächst zurückhaltend. Erst als sich die christlichen Gewerkvereine um die Sitze in den Arbeiterausschüssen bewarben, nahm auch der zahlenmäßig stärkere Verband der Rheinisch-Westfälischen Bergleute, aus dem später die Industriegewerkschaft Bergbau hervorging, an den Wahlen teil.[8] Die Vertretung der Belegschaften durch

---

5 Preußische Gesetzsammlung (GS) 1892, S. 131.

6 Zitiert nach *Teuteberg*, Geschichte der industriellen Mitbestimmung (1961), S. 295.

7 Preußische GS (1905), S. 307.

8 Vgl. *Tenfelde/Tischler*, Bis vor die Stufen des Throns (1986), S. 390.

Arbeiterausschüsse war noch nicht flächendeckend. 1914 wurde erstmals ein Deckungsgrad von 10 vom Hundert erreicht.[9]

b) Die Einführung der Mitbestimmung im Rahmen der Kriegswirtschaft 1916

Einen Ausbau der Beteiligungsrechte brachte das unter dem Druck des Ersten Weltkriegs entstandene Gesetz über den vaterländischen Hilfsdienst vom 5. Dezember 1916.[10] § 2 Abs. 1 Hilfsdienstgesetz (HDG) verpflichtete alle nicht zum Militär einberufenen Männer zwischen dem vollendeten 17. und 60. Lebensjahr zur Arbeit „bei Behörden, behördlichen Einrichtungen, in der Kriegsindustrie, in der Land- und Forstwirtschaft, in der Krankenpflege, in kriegswirtschaftlichen Organisationen jeder Art oder in sonstigen Berufen oder Betrieben, die für Zwecke der Kriegsführung oder der Volksversorgung unmittelbar oder mittelbar Bedeutung haben." In § 11 Abs. 1 HDG war bestimmt:

„In allen für den vaterländischen Hilfsdienst tätigen Betrieben, für die Titel VII der Gewerbeordnung gilt und in denen in der Regel mindestens fünfzig Arbeiter beschäftigt werden, müssen ständige Arbeiterausschüsse bestehen."

Für die Bestellung der Mitglieder galt nach § 11 Abs. 2 Satz 2 HDG:

„Die Mitglieder dieser Arbeiterausschüsse werden von den volljährigen Arbeitern des Betriebs oder der Betriebsabteilung aus ihrer Mitte in unmittelbarer und geheimer Wahl nach den Grundsätzen der Verhältniswahl gewählt."

Nach § 12 HDG erhielten die Ausschüsse bei Streitigkeiten über die Arbeitsbedingungen das Recht, einen Schlichtungsausschuss anzurufen, den Vorläufer der heutigen in § 76 BetrVG geregelten Einigungsstelle.

c) Die Festigung der Mitbestimmung in der Weimarer Republik

Sofort nach dem Waffenstillstand im Ersten Weltkrieg wurde am 15. November 1918 in dem Abkommen der Zentralarbeitsgemeinschaft der Arbeitgeberverbände und der Gewerkschaften, so genanntes Stinnes-Legien-Abkommen, neben der gegenseitigen Anerkennung der Tariffähigkeit auch die obligatorische Errichtung von Arbeiter- und Angestelltenausschüssen für alle Betriebe mit mindestens 50 Beschäftigten bestimmt.[11] Die Verordnung über Tarifverträge, Arbeiter- und Angestelltenausschüsse und Schlichtung von Arbeitsstreitigkeiten (TVVO) vom 23. Dezember 1918[12] setzte die Ergebnisse des Abkommens mit Gesetzeskraft um.

Die Weimarer Reichsverfassung vom 11. August 1919[13] sah an sich eine umfassende Beteiligung der Arbeiter und Angestellten im Sinne einer Wirtschaftsdemokratie vor. Nach Art. 165 der Verfassung war eine gesetzliche Vertretung in nach Wirtschaftsgebieten gegliederten Bezirksarbeiterräten vorgesehen. Auf Reichsebene sollte der Reichsarbeiterrat im Zusammenwirken mit den Vertretungen der Unterneh-

---

9 *Bieber*, Zwischen Kasernenhof und Rätesystem (1999), S. 519.

10 RGBl. 1935 Teil I, S. 1333.

11 *Blanke*, Kollektives Arbeitsrecht (1975), S. 185; demnächst *Düwell*, Mitbestimmung und Betriebsräte, in: Dreyer (Hrsg.), Die Weimarer Reichsverfassung. Aufbruch und Innovation.

12 RGBl. 1918, S. 1456.

13 RGBl. 1919, S. 1383.

men den Reichswirtschaftsrat bilden. Dieses Modell einer Wirtschafts- und Rätedemokratie wurde jedoch nicht vollständig umgesetzt. Die Gesetzgebung zur Ausführung von Art. 165 der Verfassung beschränkte sich auf betrieblicher Ebene auf das Betriebsrätegesetz vom 4. Februar 1920[14] sowie das Gesetz über die Betriebsbilanz und die Betriebsgewinn- und Verlustrechnung vom 5. Februar 1921.[15]

Das Betriebsrätegesetz von 1920 schuf erstmals eine eigenständige und ausführliche Regelung der Beziehungen auf Betriebsebene. Danach waren Betriebsvertretungen durch Arbeiter- und Angestelltenräte in allen Betrieben, Geschäften und Verwaltungen des öffentlichen und privaten Rechts mit in der Regel mindestens 20 beschäftigten Arbeitnehmern obligatorisch. In Betrieben mit mindestens fünf wahlberechtigten Arbeitnehmern, von denen drei wählbar sein mussten, war nach § 2 ein Betriebsobmann zu wählen. Die Befugnisse der Betriebsräte beschränkten sich im Wesentlichen auf Überwachungs-, Unterrichtungs- und Anhörungsrechte. Mitwirkungsrechte bestanden u. a. bei der Bekämpfung von Unfall- und Gesundheitsgefahren und der Verwaltung betrieblicher Wohlfahrtseinrichtungen. Als fundamentales Mitbestimmungsrecht wurde aus dem Hilfsdienstgesetz übernommen, dass die Zustimmung der Betriebsvertretung vor Erlass oder Änderung der Arbeitsordnung erforderlich ist. Neu war in § 66 Nr. 5 Betriebsrätegesetz die Aufgabe des Betriebsrats aufgenommen „für die Arbeitnehmer gemeinsame Dienstvorschriften und Änderungen derselben im Rahmen der geltenden Tarifverträge nach Maßgabe des § 75 mit dem Arbeitgeber zu vereinbaren." In dem in Bezug genommenen § 75 Betriebsrätegesetz war geregelt:

> „Sollen [...] gemeinsame Dienstvorschriften vereinbart werden, so hat der Arbeitgeber den Entwurf, soweit die Bestimmungen nicht auf Tarifvertrag beruhen, dem Betriebsrat vorzulegen. Kommt über den Entwurf keine Einigung zustande, so können beide Teile den Schlichtungsausschuß anrufen, der eine bindende Entscheidung trifft. Die Verbindlichkeit der Entscheidung erstreckt sich nicht auf die Dauer der Arbeitszeit."

Mit dieser Regelung ist die Grundlage für die heute in § 87 Abs. 1 i. V. m. § 76 BetrVG geregelte Mitbestimmung in sozialen Angelegenheiten geschaffen worden, die das Bestimmungsrecht des Arbeitgebers in diesen Angelegenheiten unter den Zustimmungsvorbehalt des Betriebsrats stellt.

d) Die Abschaffung der Mitbestimmung unter dem NS-Regime

Mit dem Gesetz zur Ordnung der nationalen Arbeit (kurz: Arbeitsordnungsgesetz, AOG) vom 20. Januar 1934[16] und dem Gesetz zur Ordnung der Arbeit in öffentlichen Verwaltungen und Betrieben vom 23. März 1934[17] ist das Betriebsrätegesetz 1920 aufgehoben worden. Es wurde das nationalsozialistische Führerprinzip eingeführt. Danach entschied der Unternehmer als Führer des Betriebes. Ein Vertrauensrat, der aus dem Unternehmer als Vorsitzenden und den Vertrauensmännern der Gefolgschaft in Betrieben mit in der Regel mindestens 20 Beschäftigten gemeinsam gebildet wurde, hatte nur beratende Funktion. Die Vertrauensmänner wurden nicht gewählt,

---

14 RGBl. 1920, S. 147.

15 RGBl. 1921, S. 159.

16 RGBl. 1934 Teil I, S. 45.

17 RGBl. 1934 Teil I, S. 220.

sondern wurden aufgrund einer vom Führer des Betriebs im Einvernehmen mit dem Obmann der NS-Betriebszellenorganisation aufgestellten Einheitsliste bestellt.[18]

e) Die Wiederherstellung der Betriebsverfassung nach dem 2. Weltkrieg

Nach der Befreiung von dem NS-Regime wurden das AOG durch die Kontrollratsgesetze Nr. 40 vom 30. November 1946[19] und Nr. 56 vom 30. Juni 1947[20] aufgehoben. Ein Teil der in den Besatzungszonen gebildeten Länder schuf eigenständige Regelungen. Die 1949 gegründete Bundesrepublik hat mit dem Betriebsverfassungsgesetz vom 11. Oktober 1952[21] die Rechtszersplitterung beseitigt. § 88 Abs. 1 BetrVG 1952 nahm die Verwaltungen und Betriebe des öffentlichen Dienstes aus dem Geltungsbereich der Betriebsverfassung aus und behielt deren Verfassung einer besonderen Regelung vor. Das Personalvertretungsgesetz des Bundes vom 6. August 1955 traf diese Regelung für die Dienststellen des Bundes und gab für die entsprechenden Ländergesetze einen Rahmen vor. Seitdem unterscheiden sich Betriebs- und Dienststellenverfassung. Die Unterscheidung hat jedoch im Wesentlichen nur formale Bedeutung. Die materielle Mitbestimmung unterscheidet sich kaum. Die sozialliberale Koalition unter Kanzler Willy Brandt erweiterte 1972 die betriebliche Mitbestimmung[22] durch ein Reformgesetz vom 15. Januar 1972.[23] In dem heute geltenden § 87 Abs. 1 BetrVG ist der Katalog der zwingenden Mitbestimmungstatbestände in sozialen Angelegenheiten wie folgt festgelegt:

„Der Betriebsrat hat, soweit eine gesetzliche oder tarifliche Regelung nicht besteht, in folgenden Angelegenheiten mitzubestimmen:

1. Fragen der Ordnung des Betriebs und des Verhaltens der Arbeitnehmer im Betrieb;
2. Beginn und Ende der täglichen Arbeitszeit einschließlich der Pausen sowie Verteilung der Arbeitszeit auf die einzelnen Wochentage;
3. vorübergehende Verkürzung oder Verlängerung der betriebsüblichen Arbeitszeit;
4. Zeit, Ort und Art der Auszahlung der Arbeitsentgelte;
5. Aufstellung allgemeiner Urlaubsgrundsätze und des Urlaubsplans sowie die Festsetzung der zeitlichen Lage des Urlaubs für einzelne Arbeitnehmer, wenn zwischen dem Arbeitgeber und den beteiligten Arbeitnehmern kein Einverständnis erzielt wird;
6. Einführung und Anwendung von technischen Einrichtungen, die dazu bestimmt sind, das Verhalten oder die Leistung der Arbeitnehmer zu überwachen;
7. Regelungen über die Verhütung von Arbeitsunfällen und Berufskrankheiten sowie über den Gesundheitsschutz im Rahmen der gesetzlichen Vorschriften oder der Unfallverhütungsvorschriften;

---

18 *Hueck/Nipperdey/Dietz*, Gesetz zur Ordnung der nationalen Arbeit (1934), S. 97–115.

19 ABl. KR 1946, S. 229.

20 ABl. KR 1947, S. 287.

21 BGBl. 1952 Teil I, S. 681.

22 Dazu *Düwell*, Mehr Demokratie wagen! Betriebsverfassungsgesetz 1972 als Reformgesetz, in: Gün/Hopmann/Niemerg (Hrsg.), Gegenmacht statt Ohnmacht (2020), S. 113–123.

23 BGBl. 1972 Teil I, S. 13.

8. Form, Ausgestaltung und Verwaltung von Sozialeinrichtungen, deren Wirkungsbereich auf den Betrieb, das Unternehmen oder den Konzern beschränkt ist;
9. Zuweisung und Kündigung von Wohnräumen, die den Arbeitnehmern mit Rücksicht auf das Bestehen eines Arbeitsverhältnisses vermietet werden, sowie die allgemeine Festlegung der Nutzungsbedingungen;
10. Fragen der betrieblichen Lohngestaltung, insbesondere die Aufstellung von Entlohnungsgrundsätzen und die Einführung und Anwendung von neuen Entlohnungsmethoden sowie deren Änderung;
11. Festsetzung der Akkord- und Prämiensätze und vergleichbarer leistungsbezogener Entgelte, einschließlich der Geldfaktoren;
12. Grundsätze über das betriebliche Vorschlagswesen;
13. Grundsätze über die Durchführung von Gruppenarbeit; Gruppenarbeit im Sinne dieser Vorschrift liegt vor, wenn im Rahmen des betrieblichen Arbeitsablaufs eine Gruppe von Arbeitnehmern eine ihr übertragene Gesamtaufgabe im Wesentlichen eigenverantwortlich erledigt;
14. Ausgestaltung von mobiler Arbeit, die mittels Informations- und Kommunikationstechnik erbracht wird.“

2. Die heutige Mitbestimmung beim Ordnungsverhalten

Die Einschränkung des Bestimmungsrechts des Arbeitgebers durch den in § 87 Abs. 1 Nr. 1 BetrVG gegelten Mitbestimmungstatbestand wird in dem folgenden Beispielsfall „Radiohören“[24] deutlich:

Der Arbeitgeber betreibt einen geographischen Verlag, in dem Landkarten hergestellt werden. In der Abteilung Kartographie werden nach Vorlagen Karten gezeichnet und Schriften eingetragen. Hier war wegen der monotonen Arbeit das Radiohören seit mehr als 10 Jahren geduldet. Der Arbeitgeber will das nicht mehr dulden und verbietet das Radiohören. Der Betriebsrat wendet ein, die Arbeit könne auch während des Radiohörens erbracht werden.

Das Bundesarbeitsgericht hat entschieden: Das Verbot, Radio zu hören, gestalte die betriebliche Ordnung und betreffe das Verhalten der Arbeitnehmer im Betrieb. Das Verbot sei damit unwirksam, weil nach § 87 Abs. 1 Nr. 1 BetrVG der Betriebsrat in Fragen der Ordnung des Betriebs und des Verhaltens der Arbeitnehmer im Betrieb mitzubestimmen habe. Anders als das Landesarbeitsgericht angenommen habe, betreffe das Verbot, Radio zu hören, nicht die die dem Bestimmungsrecht des Arbeitsgebers vorbehaltene Frage, in welcher Weise bestimmte Arbeiten auszuführen seien.

---

24 Nachgebildet BAG, Urteil v. 14. Januar 1986 – 1 ABR 75/83, BAGE 50, 330.

IV. Allgemeine Arbeitsbedingungen

1. Unmittelbare Wirkung von Gesetz, Tarifvertrag und Betriebsvereinbarung

Es bestehen zwei Möglichkeiten, wie Allgemeine Arbeitsbedingungen Bedeutung für das individuelle Arbeitsverhältnis erhalten. Entweder sind sie von Dritten aufgestellt und wirken „von außen" auf den Individualvertrag ein, oder sie werden in den Vertrag integriert.[25] Eine Einwirkung von außen findet normativ qua lege bei Allgemeinen Arbeitsbedingungen statt, die in Gesetzen, Rechtsverordnungen und Satzungen aufgestellt sind. Sind sie in Tarifverträgen und Betriebsvereinbarungen geregelt, wirken sie ebenfalls unmittelbar und zwingend, ohne dass es einer vertraglichen Einbeziehungserklärung der Arbeitsvertragsparteien bedarf. Für die Bestimmungen des Tarifvertrags, die den Inhalt von Arbeitsverhältnissen ordnen, ist diese unmittelbar und zwingende Wirkung in § 4 Abs. 1 Satz 1 TVG für den Fall angeordnet, dass die Arbeitsvertragsparteien beiderseits Tarifgebundene sind, die unter den Geltungsbereich des Tarifvertrags fallen. Für Arbeitsvertragsparteien, die nicht diese Voraussetzungen erfüllen, hat die Rechtsprechung die vertragliche Inbezugnahme entwickelt. Mit der so genannten Gleichstellungsabrede soll vertragsrechtlich bewirkt werden, dass ein Arbeitnehmer tarifrechtlich so steht, als ob Tarifbindung bestünde.[26] Haben der Arbeitgeber und der Betriebsrat eine Betriebsvereinbarung über allgemeine Arbeitsbedingungen nach § 77 Abs. 1 BetrVG geschlossen, so hat dafür der Gesetzgeber in § 77 Abs. 4 Satz 1 BetrVG angeordnet:

„Betriebsvereinbarungen gelten unmittelbar und zwingend."

Ist z. B. die Zulässigkeit des Radiohörens in einer Betriebsvereinbarung geregelt, so kann der Arbeitgeber nur durch eine abändernde Betriebsvereinbarung zu einer anderen Regelung gelangen.

2. Vom Arbeitgeber vorformulierte allgemeine Bedingungen

Im Zuge des Vertriebs von Produkten aus der industriellen Massenproduktion kam es im 20. Jahrhundert weltweit zur Aufstellung von allgemeinen Geschäftsbedingungen (AGB), mit denen die Unternehmer gegenüber den Bestellern den Vertragsschluss durch ein vorformuliertes Klauselwerk vereinfachen, beschleunigen und standardisieren konnten. Diese einseitig aufgestellten AGB verändern in der Regel gegenüber dem Gesetz die dort vorgesehene Risikoverteilung und vor allem die Haftungsregelung zu Lasten des Bestellers. Die Gefahr eines unfairen Vertragsdiktats führte zu der Einsicht, es sei geboten, allgemeine Geschäftsbedingungen einer Kontrolle zu unterwerfen und bestimmten Klauseln die Rechtswirksamkeit zu versagen. 1976 wurde deshalb in Deutschland das Gesetz zur Regelung des Rechts der Allgemeinen Geschäftsbedingungen (AGB-Gesetz)[27] erlassen. Mit dem Gesetz zur Mo-

---

25 *Wank*, in: Wank/Yoshida (Hrsg.), Arbeitsordnung und allgemeine Arbeitsbedingungen – Ein Vergleich der Entwicklung in Deutschland und in Japan (2025), S. 59.

26 BAG, Urteil v. 25. September 2002 – 4 AZR 294/01, BAGE 103, 9, 14 = AP TVG § 1 Bezugnahme auf Tarifvertrag Nr. 26; BAG, Urteil v. 27. November 2002 – 4 AZR 663/01 = BAGE 104, 39, 42 = AP BGB § 611 Rotes Kreuz Nr. 18.

27 BGBl. 1976 Teil I, S. 3317.

dernisierung des Schuldrechts vom 26. November 2001 (SMG)[28] wurde der materiell-rechtliche Inhalt des AGB-Gesetzes mit kleineren Änderungen in das BGB verpflanzt. Diese Bestimmungen haben jetzt ihren Standort in §§ 305–310 BGB.

a) Einbeziehung des Arbeitsverhältnisses in das AGB-Recht

Die vor dem Inkrafttreten des SMG in § 23 Abs. 1 AGBG enthaltende Bereichsausnahme für das Arbeitsrecht wurde aufgehoben. Seit dem 1. Januar 2002 unterliegen damit auch Arbeitsverträge der AGB-Kontrolle. Bereits vor dem SMG unterzog die Rechtsprechung Arbeitsverträge einer „Inhaltskontrolle". Deren Rechtsgrundlage war der unbestimmte Rechtsbegriff „Treu und Glauben" aus § 242 BGB. Die Rechtsprechung war jedoch uneinheitlich. Das nahm der Gesetzgeber zum Anlass, die Bereichsausnahme für das Arbeitsrecht aufzugeben.[29]

b) Richterliche AGB-Kontrolle

Vom Arbeitgeber für eine Vielzahl von Arbeitsverhältnissen einseitig aufgestellte Vertragsbedingungen, gelten nach § 305 Abs. 1 Satz 1 BGB als AGB. Ab drei geplanten Verwendungen geht die Rechtsprechung von der erforderlichen Vielzahl aus.[30] Dann sind die in den AGB verwendeten Klauseln anhand der §§ 307, 308 und § 309 BGB auf ihre Angemessenheit zu prüfen.

Dabei gehen besondere Klauselverbote der allgemeinen Inhaltskontrolle vor. Bei Ausüben der richterlichen Kontrolle ist stets zu klären, ob gemäß § 310 Abs. 4 Satz 2 BGB die AGB-Normen wegen der Besonderheiten des Arbeitsrechts uneingeschränkt zur Anwendung gelangen können. Im Übrigen sind nach § 310 Abs. 4 Satz 1 BGB die Bestimmungen in Tarifverträgen, Betriebs- und Dienstvereinbarungen von der Anwendung der AGB-Normen ausgenommen.

aa) Prüfung der Klauselverbote

§ 309 BGB enthält Klauselverbote ohne Wertungsmöglichkeit. So ist nach § 307 Nr. 7 BGB ein Haftungsausschluss des Arbeitgebers oder eine Haftungsbegrenzung bei Schäden des Arbeitnehmers, die auf vorsätzlich oder grobfahrlässige Pflichtverletzung des Arbeitgebers, seines gesetzlichen Vertreters oder seiner Erfüllungsgehilfen beruhen, ausgeschlossen.

§ 308 BGB enthält Klauselverbote mit Wertungsmöglichkeit. So bestimmt § 308 Nr. 4 BGB, dass die Vereinbarung eines Rechts des Arbeitgebers, die dem Arbeitnehmer versprochene Leistung zu ändern oder von ihr abzuweichen, unwirksam ist, wenn nicht die Vereinbarung der Änderung oder Abweichung unter Berücksichtigung der Interessen des Verwenders für den anderen Vertragsteil zumutbar ist.

Beispielsfall Dienstwagen: Häufig entsteht Streit über die Rückgabe eines auch privat nutzbaren Dienstfahrzeugs während der Kündigungsfrist. Im Arbeitsvertrag lautet die vom Arbeitgeber verwandte Klausel:

---

28 BGBl. 2001 Teil I, S. 3138.

29 BT-Drs. 14/6857, S. 53 f.

30 BAG, Urteil v. 23. Januar 2007 – 9 AZR 482/06, NZA (2007), S. 748, Rn. 15 m. w. N.

„Die private Nutzung des Dienstfahrzeugs kann vom Arbeitgeber widerrufen werden, wenn das Arbeitsverhältnis gekündigt ist und der Arbeitgeber den Mitarbeiter berechtigt von seiner Verpflichtung zur Arbeitsleistung freigestellt oder suspendiert hat.“

Das BAG hat entschieden, die Regelung genüge den formellen Anforderungen von § 308 Nr. 4 BGB. Nach dem dort vorgesehenen Transparenzgebot müsse eine solche Klausel klar und verständlich gefasst sein und zumindest die Richtung angeben, aus der der Widerruf möglich sein soll. Das war hier der Fall, weil die Widerrufsklausel unter Berücksichtigung der Freistellung die dienstliche und private Nutzung in sachgerechter Weise verknüpft.[31]

bb) Richterliche Angemessenheitskontrolle

Ist keine der Klauselverbote-Sonderregelungen aus §§ 308, 309 BGB anwendbar, greift die in § 307 BGB geregelte richterliche Angemessenheitskontrolle ein. Gegenstand dieser Prüfung ist der objektive Inhalt der Regelung, der im Wege der Auslegung zu ermitteln ist. Dabei ist ein genereller, typisierender, vom Einzelfall losgelöster Maßstab anzulegen.[32] Vom Gericht sind die Interessen der Arbeitgeber- und der Arbeitnehmerseite zu berücksichtigen. Zugrunde gelegt wird die typische Interessenlage.[33]

§ 307 BGB enthält in Abs. 2 Nr. 1, 2 und Abs. 1 Satz 1 drei Konkretisierungen des Verbots der unangemessenen Benachteiligung:

1. wenn eine Bestimmung mit wesentlichen Grundgedanken der gesetzlichen Regelung, von der abgewichen wird, nicht zu vereinbaren ist oder
2. wesentliche Rechte oder Pflichten, die sich aus der Natur des Vertrags ergeben, so einschränkt, dass die Erreichung des Vertragszwecks gefährdet ist oder
3. wenn eine Bestimmung auf sonstige Weise den Vertragspartner des Verwenders entgegen den Geboten von Treu und Glauben unangemessen benachteiligt.

Die Anwendung des § 307 Abs. 2 Nr. 1 BGB kommt bei der Inhaltskontrolle arbeitsvertraglicher Regelungen häufig vor, da das Arbeitsrecht zu großen Teilen aus zwingendem Recht oder Richterrecht besteht. Auch richterrechtlich entwickelte Grundsätze werden von § 307 Abs. 2 Nr. 1 BGB erfasst.[34] Erforderlich ist eine Abweichung von wesentlichen Grundgedanken der gesetzlichen Regelung, d. h. der materielle Regelungsgehalt des gesetzlichen Leitbildes muss zulasten des Arbeitnehmers verändert worden sein. Zu differenzieren ist zwischen frei änderbaren Zweckmäßigkeitserwägungen und nicht abdingbaren Gerechtigkeitsgeboten.[35] Da es sich

---

31 BAG, Urteil v. 12. Februar 2025 – 5 AZR 171/24, NZA (2025), S. 646, Rn. 19.

32 BAG, Urteil v. 25. April 2018 – 7 AZR 520/16, NZA (2018), S. 1061, Rn. 33.

33 BAG, Urteil v. 22. Oktober 2024 – 3 AZR 23/24, NZA (2025), S. 640, Rn. 27; zustimmend: *Langohr-Plato*, Rechtskraft von Gerichtsurteilen im Kontext der betrieblichen Altersversorgung, in: jurisPR-ArbR 8/2025 Anm.1.

34 BAG, Urteil v. 24. Oktober 2002 – 6 AZR 623/00, NZA (2003), S. 668; BGH, Urteil v. 10. Dezember 1992 – I ZR 186/90, NJW (1993), S. 721.

35 BGH, Urteil v. 5. November 1989 – III ZR 95/97, NJW (1999), S. 635; BAG, Urteil v. 7. Dezember 2005 – 5 AZR 535/04, NZA (2006), S. 423.

bei § 307 Abs. 2 Nr. 1 BGB nur um eine Vermutungsregel handelt, entfällt die Unwirksamkeit, wenn die Gesamtwürdigung aller Umstände ergibt, dass die Klausel den Arbeitnehmer nicht unangemessen benachteiligt. So kann z. B. zugunsten des Arbeitgebers berücksichtigt werden, dass für die Überwälzung eines bestimmten Risikos auf den Arbeitnehmer ein angemessener Ausgleich gewährt wird.[36]

cc) Richterliche Transparenzkontrolle

§ 307 Abs. 1 Satz 2 BGB kodifiziert das sog. Transparenzgebot. Danach liegt eine unangemessene Benachteiligung auch dann vor, wenn die Regelung nicht hinreichend klar und verständlich ist. Übersteigerte Anforderungen an die Transparenz einzelner Regelungen dürfen jedoch nicht gestellt werden.[37] Auslegungsbedürftigkeit ist nicht mit Intransparenz gleichzusetzen.[38] Die verwendete Klausel muss die tatbestandlichen Voraussetzungen und Rechtsfolgen so genau beschreiben, dass für den Arbeitgeber keine ungerechtfertigten Beurteilungsspielräume entstehen.[39] Rechtsbegriffe aus der Gesetzessprache sowie unbestimmte und auslegungsbedürftige Rechtsbegriffe dürfen verwendet werden. Jedoch werden strengere Maßstäbe angelegt als bei Gesetzen; denn diese werden nur an der Verfassung und dem Gebot der Normenklarheit gemessen.[40] Deshalb kann bei AGB-Klauseln eine weitergehende Konkretisierung verlangt werden; zumal ein Branchenbezug möglich ist.[41] Ist die Rechtslage so missverständlich dargestellt, dass sie geeignet ist, den Arbeitnehmer von der Durchsetzung seiner Ansprüche abzuhalten, kann eine unangemessene Benachteiligung vorliegen. Deshalb muss der gesetzlich besonders vor Verfall und Verwirkung geschützte Mindestlohn zwingend aus der AGB-Verfallsklausel ausgenommen werden.[42] Enthält die Klausel selbst keine Rechtsfolgenanordnung, kann sich diese auch aus der Überschrift „Ausschlussfrist" und der zwingenden Anordnung einer Klageerhebung ergeben.[43] Die Zusage eines gewinn- und leistungsabhängigen Bonus, die in einer anderen Klausel einem Freiwilligkeitsvorbehalt unterstellt ist, verstößt gegen das Transparenzgebot.[44] Für die Beurteilung, ob eine Regelung intransparent ist, wird nicht auf den flüchtigen Betrachter, sondern auf den aufmerksamen und sorgfältigen Teilnehmer am Wirtschaftsverkehr abgestellt.[45]

---

36 *Roloff*, in: Henssler/Willemsen/Kalb (Hrsg.), Arbeitsrecht-Kommentar, 11. Aufl. (2024), § 307 BGB Rn. 10.

37 BAG, Urteil v. 31. August 2005 – 5 AZR 545/04, NZA (2006), S. 324.

38 BGH, Urteil v. 17. Dezember 1999 – VII ZR 243/97, NJW (1999), S. 942.

39 BAG, Urteil v. 31. August 2005 – 5 AZR 545/04, NZA (2006), S. 324.

40 BAG, Urteil v. 5. September 2023 – 9 AZR 350/22, NZA (2024), S. 325, Rn. 41.

41 BAG, Urteil v. 26. Januar 2017 – 6 AZR 671/15, NZA-RR (2017), S. 325, Rn. 27.

42 BAG, Urteil v. 18. September 2018 – 9 AZR 162/18, NZA (2018), S. 1619, Rn. 35, 48.

43 BAG, Urteil v. 25. Mai 2005 – 5 AZR 572/04, NZA (2005), S. 1111.

44 BAG, Urteil v. 24. Oktober 2007-10 AZR 825/06, NZA (2008), S. 40; für den Fall einer Weihnachtsgratifikation BAG, Urteil v. 20. Februar 2013 – 10 AZR 177/12, NZA (2013), S. 1015.

45 BAG, Urteil v. 23. Januar 2014 – 8 AZR 130/13, NZA (2014), S. 777.

dd) Grenze der richterlichen Angemessenheitskontrolle

Die Angemessenheitskontrolle gilt nach § 307 Abs. 3 Satz 1 BGB nicht für Klauseln, die den Umfang der von den Parteien geschuldeten Vertragsleistung festlegen; denn es ist nicht Aufgabe des Gerichts, über die §§ 305 ff. BGB den „gerechten Preis" für die zu leistende Arbeit zu ermitteln.[46] Allerdings gilt die Transparenzkontrolle.

Beispiel Überstundenvergütung: In dem vom Arbeitgeber für Einstellungen verwandten Vertragsformular ist ein festes Monatsentgelt für die tarifliche Regelarbeitszeit mit dem Zusatz vereinbart, die ersten zwanzig Überstunden im Monat seien „mit drin". Nach ständiger Rechtsprechung ist eine derart pauschal die Vergütung von Überstunden regelnde Klausel nur dann klar und verständlich, wenn sich aus dem Arbeitsvertrag selbst ergibt, welche Arbeitsleistungen in welchem zeitlichen Umfang von ihr erfasst werden sollen; denn der Arbeitnehmer muss bereits bei Vertragsabschluss erkennen können, was ggf. „auf ihn zukommt" und welche Leistungen er für die vereinbarte Vergütung maximal erbringen muss.[47] Gemessen daran hat das BAG die Klausel „im Monat mit drin", als hinreichend transparent beurteilt.[48] Eine Angemessenheitskontrolle findet nicht statt; denn die Festlegung der Entgelthöhe für eine Arbeitszeit, die bis zu 20 Stunden die monatliche tarifliche Arbeitszeit überschreiten kann, ist eine der Angemessenheitskontrolle entzogene Hauptleistungsabrede, weil sie nur die Gegenleistung des Arbeitgebers für die vom Arbeitnehmer erbrachte Arbeitsleistung betrifft.[49]

Literaturverzeichnis

Berndt, Enno: Sieger oder Verlierer, in: Blätter für deutsche und internationale Politik, 5/1997, S. 587 ff.

Bieber, Hans-Joachim: Zwischen Kasernenhof und Rätesystem (1999).

Blanke, Thomas: Kollektives Arbeitsrecht (1975).

Düwell, Franz Josef: Mehr Demokratie wagen! Betriebsverfassungsgesetz 1972 als Reformgesetz, in: Gün, Isaf/Hopmann, Benedikt/Niemerg, Reinhold (Hrsg.), Gegenmacht statt Ohnmacht (2020), S. 113–123.

Düwell, Franz Josef: Mitbestimmung und Betriebsräte, demnächst in: Dreyer, Michael (Hrsg.), Die Weimarer Reichsverfassung. Aufbruch und Innovation.

Henssler, Martin/*Willemsen*, Heinz Josef/*Kalb*, Heinz-Jürgen (Hrsg.): Arbeitsrecht Kommentar, 11. Aufl. (2024).

Hueck, Alfred/*Nipperdey*, Hans Carl/*Dietz*, Rolf: Gesetz zur Ordnung der nationalen Arbeit (1934), S. 97–115.

Langohr-Plato, Uwe: Rechtskraft von Gerichtsurteilen im Kontext der betrieblichen Altersversorgung, in: jurisPR-ArbR 8/2025 Anm. 1.

---

46 BAG. Urteil v. 31. August 2005 – 5 AZR 545/04 – zu II 3 a der Gründe, BAGE 115, S. 372.

47 BAG, Urteil v. 1. September 2010 – 5 AZR 517/09, BAGE 135, S. 250, Rn. 15; BAG, Urteil v. 17. August 2011 – 5 AZR 406/10, NZA (2011), S. 1335, Rn. 14.

48 BAG, Urteil v. 16. Mai 2012 – 5 AZR 331/11, NZA (2012), S. 908, Rn. 22.

49 BAG, Urteil v. 16. Mai 2012 – 5 AZR 331/11, NZA (2012), S. 908, Rn. 26.

Tenfelde, Klaus/*Tischler*, Helmuth: Bis vor die Stufen des Throns (1986).

Teuteberg, Hans Jürgen: Geschichte der industriellen Mitbestimmung (1961).

Wank, Rolf/*Yoshida*, Mariko: Arbeitsordnung und allgemeine Arbeitsbedingungen – Ein Vergleich der Entwicklung in Deutschland und in Japan (2025).

Wilhelm II.: Ereignisse und Gestalten (1922).

Japan und seine Beziehungen zu China und Korea vor und nach dem Zweiten Weltkrieg unter besonderer Berücksichtigung der Konferenzen während des Zweiten Weltkriegs

Von *Gilbert Gornig*

Professor Dr. iur. utr. Dr. h.c. mult. Gilbert Gornig, geboren 1950 in Deggendorf, Bayern, lehrte bis 2016 an der Philipps-Universität Marburg öffentliches Recht, Völkerrecht und Europarecht. Er war Direktor des Instituts für öffentliches Recht und Dekan des Fachbereichs Rechtswissenschaften. Seine Lehrtätigkeit umfasste das Staatsrecht, Verwaltungsrecht, Völkerrecht, Europarecht und die allgemeine Staatslehre. Er hat in seinen Fachgebieten über 600 Publikationen in zehn Sprachen vorgelegt. Er ist Inhaber mehrerer Gastprofessuren im Ausland, insbesondere in China. Zudem war er fast zehn Jahre Richter am Verwaltungsgerichtshof Kassel und erhielt das Bundesverdienstkreuz sowie den chilenischen Orden Bernardo O'Higgins.

Ist von den Konferenzen von Teheran, Jalta oder Potsdam die Rede, so denkt man in erster Linie an die dortigen Verhandlungen über das Schicksal des deutschen Staates. Blickt man jedoch in den Index der Konferenzprotokolle „Foreign Relations of the United States. Diplomatic Papers", die vom Department of State der Vereinigten Staaten herausgegeben wurden, so sieht man, dass die auf den Konferenzen versammelten Staatenvertreter auch über das Schicksal Japans, Chinas und Koreas verhandelt haben.

I. Japan und China

1. Kurzer Überblick über die Geschichte seit 1894

a) Erster Chinesisch-Japanischer Krieg

Im Jahre 1894, zur Zeit der Mandschu-Dynastie, brach der erste chinesisch-japanische Krieg von 1894 bis 1895 um den Einfluss in Korea aus.[1] Am 21. November 1894 eroberte Japan die Bucht von Lüshun. China unterlag im Krieg und hatte im Friedensvertrag von Shimonoseki[2] vom 17. April 1895 die Unabhängigkeit Koreas anzuer-

1 Dazu *Paine*, The Sino Japanese War of 1894–1895 – Perceptions, Power and Primacy (2003).

2 Text: *Strupp*, Urkunden zur Geschichte des Völkerrechts, Bd. II: Vom Berliner Kongress bis 1911 (1911), S. 124 ff. Ratifiziert wurde der Vertrag am 8. Mai 1895. *Liszt*, Das Völkerrecht, systematisch dargestellt, 11. Aufl. (1918), S. 28.

Duncker & Humblot · Berlin | https://doi.org/10.3790/978-3-428-59611-9.2025.418961

kennen sowie Taiwan (Formosa), die Pescadores-Inseln[3] und die Halbinsel Liaodong[4] in der Mandschurei an Japan abzutreten.[5] Der Vertrag bedeutete damit den Beginn der 50 Jahre dauernden japanischen Herrschaft über Taiwan. Obwohl Japan gehofft hatte, in der Mandschurei stärkeren Einfluss zu gewinnen, setzte sich das Russische Reich durch und erhielt die Konzession für die Mandschurische Eisenbahn sowie Port Arthur[6] als Pachthafen, was Japan nicht gefiel.[7]

b) Boxer-Aufstand

Im Jahr 1900 brach in China der sog. Boxer-Aufstand[8] aus. Die Aufständischen hatten das Ziel, die Selbständigkeit Chinas gegenüber Europa und Japan zu verwirklichen. Um den Aufstand niederzuschlagen, schickten die Weltmächte gemeinsam Truppen nach China. Nach der Zerschlagung des Aufstandes blieben die russischen Truppen in der Mandschurei. Angesichts dieses Verhaltens Russlands schlossen das Vereinigte Königreich und Japan am 30. Januar 1902 einen Allianzvertrag[9] gegen Russland. Darin vereinbarten sie, dass sie gegenseitig ihre Interessen in China bzw. in Korea respektierten.

c) Russisch-Japanischer Krieg

Japan war mit dem Ergebnis des Ersten Chinesisch-Japanischen Krieges nicht einverstanden, denn es wollte an die Bodenschätze der Mandschurei kommen. Mit einem Angriff Japans auf Port Arthur am 9. Februar 1904 brach der Russisch-Japani-

---

3 Die Pescadoren oder auch Penghu-Inseln sind eine Inselgruppe in der Straße von Taiwan. Im auf die Kapitulation Japans folgenden Friedensvertrag von San Francisco vom 28. April 1952 (vgl. unten II.) gab Japan 1951 seine Ansprüche auf Taiwan und die Penghu-Inseln auch formell auf.

4 Liaodong ragt in das Gelbe Meer hinein. Sie trennt die Koreabucht im Osten vom Golf von Bohai im Westen. Im Vertrag von Shimonoseki wurde die Halbinsel zunächst Japan zuerkannt. Nach der Intervention Russlands, Frankreichs und Deutschlands wurde dies wieder rückgängig gemacht. Convention for the Lease of the Liaotung Peninsula vom 27. März 1898, Text: abrufbar unter https://en.wikisource.org/wiki/Convention_for_the_Lease_of_the_Liaotung_Peninsula (zuletzt abgerufen am 16. Februar 2025).

5 Im Jahre 1898 musste China an Deutschland Kiautschou, an England Weihaiwei, an Frankreich Kuang-chou-Wan und an Russland Südliaodong verpachten. Vgl. *Gornig*, Hongkong, Von der britischen Kronkolonie zur chinesischen Sonderverwaltungszone (1998), S. 56 ff., 64 ff.

6 Der Ort war eine unbefestigte Fischersiedlung, als der Royal-Navy-Leutnant William C. Arthur mit dem Kanonenboot HMS Algerine den Naturhafen 1860 während des Zweiten Opiumkrieges (1856–1860) als Port Arthur sicherte. Heute heißt die Stadt Lüshunkou und ist ein Stadtteil der Hafenstadt Dalian der Halbinsel Liaodong im Nordosten Chinas.

7 Von 1905 bis 1945 pachtete das Japanische Kaiserreich den Hafen. Nach dem Zweiten Weltkrieg bis 1955 war die Stadt unter sowjetischer Verwaltung.

8 Bei den Boxern handelt es sich um die nordchinesische Gruppe I Ho Ch'uan. Sie wurde als Boxer bekannt, weil ihre Mitglieder sich nach der Ausführung rituellen Scheinboxens für unverwundbar hielten. Zum Boxer-Aufstand vgl. *Klein* (Hrsg.), The Boxer War. Media and Memory of an Imperialist Intervention (2020); *Kuß/Martin* (Hrsg.), Das Deutsche Reich und der Boxeraufstand (2002); *Kaminski*, Der Boxeraufstand – entlarvter Mythos (2000); *O'Connor*, Der Boxeraufstand. Gewalt und Tragödie (1980).

9 Text: *Fleischmann*, Völkerrechtsquellen in Auswahl, 1905, S. 320.

sche Krieg[10] aus, der vom 8. Februar 1904 bis 5. September 1905 dauerte. Als Japan in diesem Krieg siegte, einigten sich beide Staaten im Frieden von Portsmouth[11] vom 5. September 1905 auf eine Aufteilung der Interessensphären zu Lasten Chinas: Japan bekam Korea und die südliche Mandschurei, Russland erhielt die Kontrolle über die Mongolei und die nördliche Mandschurei.[12] Japan baute nun die Südmandschurische Eisenbahn[13], die Rohstoffe nach Korea transportieren sollte. Korea wurde 1905 japanisches Protektorat und 1910 annektiert.[14] Ferner kam die Hafenstadt Dalian von 1905 bis 1945 unter japanische Kontrolle und erhielt den Namen Dairen (japanisch 大連市, *Dairen-shi*).[15]

d) Republik China

Am 10. Oktober 1911 begann in Wuchang[16] am Yangtse die Revolution gegen das Kaisertum in China. In vielen Provinzen kam es zu Unruhen. Die Revolutionäre bildeten unter Sun Yat-Sen[17], dem Gründer der Kuomintang[18] (Nationale Volkspartei) und Führer der Opposition, in Nanjing (Südliche Hauptstadt) eine eigene Regierung. Am 1. Januar 1912 wurde China Republik[19], die Mandschu-Dynastie (Qing-Dynastie[20]) dankte ab, Tibet und die äußere Mongolei fielen von China ab. Sun Yat-sen wurde als Präsident der Republik vereidigt. Er rüstete, seit 1924 mit sowjetischer Hilfe, die 1912 gegründete Kuomingtang in Kanton militärisch aus, so dass ihre Streitkräfte unter Führung Chiang Kai-sheks die Einheit Chinas wieder herstellten.

---

10 Dazu *Bremm*, Russlands Desaster im Fernen Osten – Der Russisch-Japanische Krieg 1904/05, in: Österreichische Militärische Zeitschrift, Ausgabe 6 (2004), S. 699 ff.

11 Text: *Martens/Stoerk* (Hrsg.), Nouveau Recueil Général de Traités et Autres Actes Relatifs aux Rapports de Droit International, deuxième série, Bd. XXXIII, S. 1 ff.; *Strupp* (Anm. 2), S. 139 ff.

12 Vgl. Art. 2, 3, 4. Nach Art. 9 musste Russland an Japan die südliche Hälfte der Insel Sachalin und die angrenzenden Inseln abtreten. Vgl. auch das Russisch-japanische Mandschurei-Abkommen vom 21. Juni (julianisch)/10. Juli 1910 (gregorianisch), Text: *Martens/Triepel* (Hrsg.), Nouveau Recueil Général de Traités et Autres Actes Relatifs aux Rapports de Droit International, troisième série, Bd. III, S. 753 ff.; *Strupp* (Anm. 2), S. 149 ff.

13 Die Gesellschaft übernahm die zuvor von Russland erbaute Transmandschurische Eisenbahnstrecke von Harbin nach Port Arthur.

14 Vgl. unten II.

15 Dalian wurde 1899 von den Russen gegründet und gehörte 1905 bis 1945 zum japanischen Pachtgebiet. Nach dem Zweiten Weltkrieg wurde die Stadt zuerst von China und der Sowjetunion gemeinsam verwaltet und 1955 wieder an China zurückgegeben. 1950 wurde sie mit Lüshunkou (veraltet: Lüshun bzw. Port Arthur) und Jinzhou zu *Lǚdà* vereinigt, das 1981 wieder in Dalian umbenannt wurde.

16 Wuchang ist heute ein Stadtbezirk von Wuhan, der Hauptstadt der Provinz Hubei in der Volksrepublik China. Bis 1949 war Wuchang eine eigene Stadt, dann wurde Wuchang mit Hankou und Hanyang zur Stadt Wuhan fusioniert.

17 Dazu *Herrfahrdt*, Sun Yatsen. Der Vater des neuen China (1948).

18 Vgl. *Domes*, Kuomintang-Herrschaft in China (1970).

19 *Rowe*, Kleine Geschichte des modernen China (o. J.), S. 42 ff.; *Kaminski*, Chinesische Positionen zum Völkerrecht (1973), S. 128 ff.

20 Die Mandschu-Dynastie wurde 1616 begründet und herrschte ab 1644 im Kaiserreich China. Sie löste die Ming-Dynastie ab und endete nach der Xinhai-Revolution von 1911 mit der Ausrufung der Republik China am 1. Januar 1912.

e) Annexion der Mandschurei durch Japan

Am 18. September 1931 wurde die Mandschurei nach der sog. Mukden (Schenjang)-Schlacht[21] von Japan annektiert.[22] Die Japaner errangen den Sieg[23] und zwangen die russischen Truppen zum Rückzug. Seit der Gründung war Mandschukuo[24] ein von Japan errichtetes „Kaiserreich" in der Mandschurei. Am 1. März 1932 mit dem letzten Qing-Kaiser P'u Yi[25] an der Spitze war dieses Kaiserreich bis 1945 eine japanische Kolonie. Die Souveränität über Mandschukuo nach innen wie nach außen lag bei Japan.[26]

f) Zweiter Chinesisch-Japanischer Krieg

Im Jahre 1937 kam es zum Zweiten Chinesisch-Japanischen Krieg[27] vom 7. Juli 1937 bis 9. September 1945, der in Japan als Japanisch-Chinesischer Krieg (日中戦争) und in der Volksrepublik China und der Republik China als „Antijapanischer Krieg" (抗日戰爭 / 抗日战争) bezeichnet wird. In China wird auch vom „Krieg des Widerstands" bzw. „Widerstandskrieg" (抗戰 / 抗战) gesprochen.

Trotz der Zweckgemeinschaft von Roter Armee und Kuomintang[28] eroberten die Japaner die Städte Beijing (Nördliche Hauptstadt), Shanghai und Nanjing, die gesamte Küste sowie große Teile des östlichen China. Chiang Kai-shek musste die ganze Zeit einen Vier-Fronten-Krieg führen und zwar gegen die Japaner, gegen die Kommunisten, gegen die Rebellen, die durch die früheren Banditen und halb unabhängi-

---

21 Mukden, japanisch Schenjang, ist eine Stadt in der Mandschurei und war 1625 bis 1644 Hauptstadt des chinesischen Reiches. Von 1931 bis 1945 war Mukden von den Japanern besetzt.

22 Vgl. *Tung*, China and the Foreign Powers: The Impact of and Reaction to Unequal Treaties, (1970), S. 257 ff.; *Albrecht*, Der chinesisch-japanische Konflikt und das Völkerrecht (1933), S. 8 ff., 56 ff.

23 Mit über 600.000 kämpfenden Soldaten war die Schlacht von Mukden die größte Schlacht zwischen der Völkerschlacht bei Leipzig 1813 und dem Beginn des Ersten Weltkriegs 1914.

24 Es bestand bis zum 18. August 1945, wurde aber international nur von 23 Staaten anerkannt.

25 Aisin Gioro Pu Yi war von 1908 bis 1912 zwölfter und letzter Kaiser der Qing-Dynastie in China. Später kollaborierte Pu Yi mit Japan, das ihn zum Kaiser des Marionettenstaates (*puppet state*) Mandschukuo machte (1932/34 bis 1945). Er starb im Jahr 1967 als einfacher Bürger der Volksrepublik China. Vgl. zum Leben *Pu Yi*, Ich war Kaiser von China (1986). Zum Marionettenstaat vgl. *Gornig*, Völkerrecht (2023), § 14 Rn. 38.

26 Die Sowjetunion erkannte Mandschukuo am 13. April 1951 unter Verletzung des sinosowjetischen Vertrages vom 31. Mai 1924 (Text: American Journal of International Law Bd. 19 (1925), S. 53 ff.) und des sino-sowjetischen Nichtangriffsvertrages vom 21. August 1937 (Text: ZaöRV Bd. 7 (1937), S. 945 f.) im Austausch gegen die Anerkennung der äußeren Mongolei durch Japan an. Damit bestätigten sich Japan und die Sowjetunion gegenseitig ihren Raub, den bislang nur Japan zurückerstatten musste. Aufgrund der Stimson-Doktrin weigerten sich die USA diesen neuen Staat Mandschukuo anzuerkennen. Vgl. auch *Albrecht*, Der chinesisch-japanische Konflikt und das Völkerrecht (1933), S. 8 ff., 56 ff. Zur Stimson Doktrin vgl. *Gornig* (Anm. 25), § 48 Rn. 1.

27 Dazu *Mitter*, China's War with Japan, 1937–1945: The Struggle for Survival (2014); *Mitter*, Forgotten Ally: China's World War II, 1937–1945 (2014).

28 Die Einheitsfront von Kuomingtang und der kommunistischen Partei Chinas zerbrach, als die Alliierten 1945 die Japaner besiegt hatten.

gen Provinzgouverneure und Generäle verkörpert wurden, sowie gegen die westlichen „Imperialisten", vor allem das Vereinigte Königreich, das wie die Sowjetunion ein schwaches China wollte. Nach dem Angriff der Japaner auf Pearl Harbor am 7. Dezember 1941 erfolgte der Kriegseintritt der USA. Somit wurde der chinesisch-japanische Krieg ein Schauplatz des Pazifikkrieges und damit Teil des Zweiten Weltkrieges.

g) China und Japan als Gegenstand der Kriegskonferenzen

Das Schicksal Japans und Chinas war unter anderem auch Gegenstand der während des Zweiten Weltkriegs abgehaltenen großen Konferenzen der Großmächte, nämlich der Konferenzen in Kairo, Teheran, Jalta und Potsdam.[29] In Kairo war der chinesische Präsident selbst zugegen und konnte seine Vorschläge und Interessen präsentieren.

2. Konferenz von Kairo vom 22. bis 26. November 1943

a) Ablauf der Konferenz

Vom 22. bis 26. November 1943 trafen sich in Kairo die Präsidenten der USA und Chinas, Franklin D. Roosevelt und Generalissimus Chiang Kai-shek, sowie der britische Premierminister Winston S. Churchill.[30] Für die US-amerikanische Delegation und insbesondere Roosevelt hatte die Konferenz in Kairo in erster Linie das Ziel mit dem chinesischen Generalissimus Chiang Kai-shek zu sprechen.[31] Bei einem persönlichen Zusammentreffen Roosevelts mit Chiang Kai-shek am 23. November1943 in Abwesenheit des britischen Premierministers brachte der US-amerikanische Präsident zum Ausdruck, dass China seinen Platz als eine der vier Großmächte einnehmen und an allen Entscheidungen beteiligt werden sollte.

Im chinesischen Bericht[32] über die private Zusammenkunft des Generalissimus mit Präsident Roosevelt am 23. November 1943 finden sich auch Hinweise zur Frage der Beibehaltung oder Abschaffung der japanischen Monarchie. Der chinesische Generalissimus sprach sich dafür aus diese Entscheidung dem japanischen Volk selbst zu überlassen. Auch bei der von Roosevelt vorgesehenen führenden Beteiligung Chinas an der späteren militärischen Besetzung Japans neigte der chinesische Staatsmann zur Zurückhaltung. Allerdings waren sich beide Regierungschefs über die Reparationsverpflichtung Japans gegenüber China einig, die durch Lieferung industrieller Produkte, von Ausrüstungen und Schiffen erfüllt werden sollte. Schließlich stimmten Roosevelt und Chiang Kai-shek überein, dass die vier nordöstlichen Provinzen Chinas, Taiwan und die Pescadores-Inseln, die von Japan gewaltsam annektiert worden

---

29 Siehe *Gornig*, China und Korea als Gegenstand der Verhandlungen von Kairo, Teheran, Jalta und Potsdam, in: Meissner/Blumenwitz/Gornig (Hrsg.), Das Potsdamer Abkommen. III. Teil: Rückblick nach 50 Jahren (1996), S. 106 ff.

30 Vgl. United States Department of State, Foreign Relations of the United States. Diplomatic Papers. The Conferences at Cairo and Tehran 1943 (1961) (Department of State Publication 7187), S. 3 ff., 293 ff.

31 Vgl. *Churchill*, The Second World War, vol. 5: Closing the Ring (1951), S. 328.

32 Vgl. United States Department of State, Foreign Relations of the United States. Diplomatic Papers. The Conferences at Cairo and Tehran 1943 (1961) (Department of State Publication 7187), S. 323 ff.

waren[33], nach dem Krieg China zurückgegeben werden müssten.[34] Auch die Halbinsel Liaodong mit seinen zwei Häfen Lüshunkou (Port Arthur), heute ein Stadtbezirk der chinesischen Hafenstadt Dalian, (japanisch: *dairen-shi*, kurz: 連 / 连)[35], waren davon erfasst. Die Ryūkyū-Inseln[36] sollten eventuell gemeinsam besetzt und unter der Treuhandschaft einer internationalen Organisation gemeinsam verwaltet werden. Im Laufe der Konferenz wurde darüber hinaus der künftige rechtliche Status des Hafens Dairen, von Indochina, der äußeren Mongolei, von Tannu Tuwa[37] und von Taiwan behandelt.[38] Auch über die künftige Stellung der britischen Besitzungen, insbesondere Indien, Hong Kong, Burma und Malaysia, wurde bei diesem Gespräch diskutiert.

Am 25. November 1943 wurden mit den chinesischen Vertretern vor allem strategische Überlegungen angestellt.[39] Roosevelt traf gegen Abend noch einmal Chiang Kai-shek, den er mehr unterstützen wollte.[40] Er versprach dem Generalissimus eine groß angelegte amphibische Operation im Golf von Bengalen gegen die Japaner.[41] Die US-amerikanischen Militärs hatten allerdings eine Offensive in Burma befürwortet.[42]

b) Kairoer Erklärung vom 26. November 1943

aa) Inhalt

Am 26. November 1943 einigten sich Präsident Roosevelt, Premierminister Churchill und Präsident Chiang Kai-shek auf die sog. Kairoer Erklärung[43] über künftige militärische Operationen gegen Japan. Die Deklaration der drei Großmächte USA, Vereinigtes Königreich und China wurde erst nach Konferenzschluss veröffentlicht,

---

33 Dazu vgl. oben I.1.a).

34 Vgl. auch *Rowe* (Anm. 19), S. 83.

35 Vgl. oben I.1.c).

36 Die Ryūkyū-Inseln sind heute eine zu Japan gehörende Inselgruppe im Ostchinesischen Meer südwestlich von Japan, die sich über 1.200 km zwischen Kyūshū und Taiwan erstreckt. Dazu vgl. *Blumenwitz*, Potsdam und die russisch-japanischen Grenzregelung, in: Blumenwitz/Gornig/Meissner (Hrsg.), Potsdam – 50 Jahre danach (1996), S. 91 ff.

37 Tuwinische Volksrepublik, vgl. *Gornig* (Anm. 25), § 53 Rn. 1.

38 Vgl. auch *Zieger*, Die Teheran-Konferenz (1967), S. 71.

39 Vgl. United States Department of State, Foreign Relations of the United States. Diplomatic Papers. The Conferences at Cairo and Tehran 1943 (1961) (Department of State Publication 7187), S. 347 f.

40 Vgl. *Zieger* (Anm. 38), S. 66 f.

41 Vgl. United States Department of State, Foreign Relations of the United States. Diplomatic Papers. The Conferences of Cairo and Tehran 1943 (1961) (Department of State Publication 7187), S. 349 f.

42 *Churchill*, The Second World War, vol. 4: The Hinge of Fate (1950), S. 606, 702 ff.

43 Text: United States Department of State, Foreign Relations of the United States. Diplomatic Papers. The Conferences of Cairo and Tehran 1943 (1961) (Department of State Publication 7187), S. 448 f.

weil Roosevelt Wert darauflegte, vor der Publizierung die sowjetische Zustimmung einzuholen[44], obwohl sich Russland mit Japan nicht im Kriegszustand befand.[45]

In der Kairoer Erklärung vom 26. November 1943 kamen Präsident Roosevelt, Premierminister Churchill und Präsident Chiang Kai-shek überein: „All the territories Japan has stolen from the Chinese, such as Manchuria, Formosa, and the Pescadores, shall be restored to the Republic of China"[46]. Weiterhin ist in dem Kommuniqué die Absicht der Drei-Mächte zum Ausdruck gekommen Korea zu gegebener Zeit Freiheit und Unabhängigkeit zu gewähren.

Durch die Kairoer Erklärung erhielt China aber nicht die territoriale Souveränität[47] über diese Gebiete zurück. Aus der Kairoer Erklärung erwächst China wegen der „von Japan gestohlenen Gebiete" nur ein Anspruch gegen die Erklärungspartner Vereinigtes Königreich und die USA, alles zu unterlassen, was dem Erwerb oder der Beibehaltung der territorialen Souveränität Chinas über Formosa entgegenstünde, und alles zu tun, China die territoriale Souveränität zu verschaffen. Die Alliierten hätten die territoriale Souveränität im Jahre 1943 nicht übertragen können, da sie die Souveränität nicht besaßen.[48]

bb) Bindungswirkung der Kairoer Erklärung

Die Rechtsqualität der Kairoer Erklärung ist umstritten. Sie könnte völkerrechtlich bindend oder nur die unverbindliche Erklärung einer Absicht sein.

Für eine Absichtserklärung könnte der Wortlaut sprechen: Die Kairoer Erklärung sagt nämlich, „(e)s ist ihr Ziel", dass die von Japan gestohlenen Gebiete zurückkehren

44 Sie erfolgte auch: vgl. Memorandum des 63. Treffens des Pacific War Council am 12. Januar 1944 in Washington, Text: United States Department of State, Foreign Relations of the United States. Diplomatic Papers. The Conferences of Cairo and Tehran 1943 (1961) (Department of State Publication 7187), S. 869. Vgl. *Feis*, Churchill, Roosevelt, Stalin: The War They Waged and the Peace They Sought (1957), S. 253.

45 Offensichtlich konsultierte Roosevelt die Experten des Außenministeriums nicht vor der Konferenz von Kairo zu Ostasien, denn sie spielten bei der Abfassung der Deklaration von Kairo keine Rolle und lasen diese erst als sie am 1. Dezember 1943 veröffentlicht wurde. *Feis* (Anm. 44), S. 252; *Borton*, American Pre-Surrender Planning for Postwar Japan, Occasional Papers of the East Asian Institute (1967), S. 12; *Mattray*, The Reluctant Crusade: American Foreign Policy in Korea, 1941–1950, (1977), S. 54 f.

46 Die Erklärung besagt also: „Japan alle Inseln im Pazifik wegzunehmen, die es seit dem Beginn des Ersten Weltkriegs 1914 sich angeeignet oder in Besitz genommen hat, und der Republik China alle Gebiete zurückzugeben, die Japan den Chinesen gestohlen hat, wie die Mandschurei, Formosa und die Pescatores-Inseln." Deutscher Text: *Zieger* (Anm. 38), S. 186. Vgl. auch *Whiting*, Morality, Taiwan, and U.S. Policy, in: Cohen/Friedman/Hinton/Whiting (Hrsg.), Taiwan and American Policy. The Dilemma in U.S.-China Relations (1971), S. 82 ff.

47 Dazu *Gornig* (Anm. 25), § 66 Rn. 4 ff., davon zu unterscheiden ist die Gebietshoheit, vergleichbar dem Besitz.

48 George Kennan beschrieb die Entscheidung in Kairo, Formosa China zurückzugeben, als „thoughtless tossing to China of a heavily inhabitated and strategically important island which had not belonged to it in recent decades". Er wies darauf hin, dass der Schritt unternommen wurde, „before we had the idea of what the future China was going to be like, and without any consultation of the wishes of the inhabitants of the island (…)". *Kennan*, Russia and the West under Lenin and Stalin (1960), S. 377; vgl. auch *Blum*, The United States and China in World Affairs (1966), S. 247.

sollten. Sie ist vage und nicht in der für völkerrechtliche Verträge üblichen Form abgeschlossen, vor allem nicht ratifiziert worden. Überhaupt wird grundsätzlich der rechtlich verpflichtende Charakter von Kriegszielerklärungen bestritten.[49]

Der Völkerrechtler Hersch Lauterpacht hält jedoch Kriegszielerklärungen unter Umständen für verbindlich. Er brachte zum Ausdruck, dass offizielle Erklärungen in Form von Konferenzberichten, die von den Staats- oder Regierungschefs unterzeichnet wurden, in dem Maße als rechtlich bindend für die betreffenden Staaten angesehen werden können, als sie bestimmte Verhaltensmaßnahmen enthalten. Die Berichte der Konferenzen der Regierungschefs des Vereinigten Königreichs, der Vereinigten Staaten und Russlands auf der Krim und im Februar 1945 und im Potsdam im August desselben Jahres führt er als Beispiele an.[50]

Auch die britische Regierung wollte nicht die Bindungswirkung der Kairoer Erklärung ausschließen, als sie diese unterzeichnete. Der damalige Außenminister Anthony Eden sagte am 14. Dezember 1943 im Unterhaus in der Debatte über die Kairoer Erklärung,[51] London fühle sich an diese Erklärung gebunden.[52] Die Frage, ob er sich juristisch daran gebunden fühlte oder nur politisch, blieb unbeantwortet. Der spätere britische Außenminister Ernest Bevin meinte am 14. Dezember 1950, das Vereinigte Königreich habe keinen Grund, sein Wort zu brechen und die Kairoer Erklärung zu verleugnen.[53] Nur Churchill betonte am 1. Februar 1955 im Unterhaus, dass die Kairoer Erklärung nur eine Absichtserklärung gewesen sei mit dem Versprechen, die Gebiete nach Kriegsende China zurückzugeben oder China die Wiedererlangung der Souveränität zu ermöglichen.[54]

Der US-amerikanische Präsident Harry S. Truman führte in seiner Botschaft an den Kongress[55] am 5. Januar 1950 aus, dass in der gemeinsamen Erklärung von Kairo vom 26. November 1942 der Präsident der USA, der britische Premierminister und der Präsident Chinas ihre Absicht äußerten, dass China solche Gebiete zurückerhalten solle, die Japan ihnen gestohlen habe. Die USA seien auch einer der Unterzeichnerstaaten der Potsdamer Erklärung vom 26. Juli 1945, die bestimmt habe, dass die Bedingungen der Kairoer Erklärung ausgeführt werden sollten. Die Bedingungen dieser Erklärung seien von Japan im Zeitpunkt seiner Kapitulation angenommen worden. Gemäß diesen Erklärungen habe Japan Formosa dem Generalissimus

---

49 Vgl. *Heydte*, Glossen über Wesen und Funktion des Kriegs im Völkerrecht, in: Göttinger Arbeitskreis (Hrsg.), Mensch und Staat in Recht und Geschichte. Festschrift für Herbert Kraus (1954), S. 78ff.

50 *Lauterpacht*, The Contemporary Practice of the United Kingdom in the Field of International Law – Survey and Comment, International and Comparative Law Quarterly, Bd. 8 (1959), S. 187.

51 Er sagte dies nach dem Hinweis auf eine Bemerkung Churchills über einen eventuellen Kriegseintritt Japans kurz vor dessen Angriff auf den US-amerikanischen Stützpunkt Pearl Harbour am 8. Dezember 1941.

52 *Hansard*, Parliamentary Papers, H. C. (1943), Spalte 1427.

53 *Röper*, Die Formosa-Frage. Ein Beitrag zur Bestimmung der völkerrechtlichen Stellung der chinesischen Nationalregierung und des kommunistischen China (1966), S. 95.

54 *Hansard*, Parliamentary Papers, H. C. (1943), Spalte 602.

55 *Harry S. Truman*, The President's News Conference, January 5, 1950, www.truman library.gov (zuletzt abgerufen am 24. September 2025).

Chiang Kai-shek übergeben, und während der vergangenen vier Jahre hätten die USA und die anderen Alliierten Mächte die Ausübung der chinesischen Autorität über die Insel hingenommen. Auch wenn es diese Worte nicht wirklich deutlich machen, betrachteten die USA die Verpflichtungen aus der Kairoer Erklärung für rechtsverbindlich, weil sie mit Rechtsbindungswillen abgeschlossen worden seien.

Es ist naheliegend, die Kairoer Erklärung als ein aus US-amerikanischer Sicht *executive agreement* zu betrachten. *Executive agreements* werden vom Präsidenten allein abgeschlossen, entweder im Rahmen einer eigenen Kompetenz oder einer Ermächtigung durch die Legislative oder eines Staatsvertrages. So kann der US-amerikanische Präsident ein *executive agreement* sogar dann abschließen, wenn seine Zuständigkeit zu ihrem Abschluss innerstaatlich nicht ausdrücklich vorgesehen, aber auch nicht ausdrücklich ausgeschlossen ist.[56] Diese *executive agreements* können im Übrigen von der Gerichtsbarkeit inhaltlich nicht kontrolliert werden.[57]

c) Würdigung

Die Kairoer Erklärung kann also als ein echter zwischen Staats- bzw. Regierungschefs der USA, des Vereinigten Königreichs und Chinas abgeschlossener Vertrag in Form eines Regierungsabkommens qualifiziert werden, dem die übrigen gegen Japan kriegführenden Vereinten Nationen spätestens mit der Unterzeichnung der japanischen Kapitulationsurkunde[58] beigetreten sind. Die Vereinbarungen über Gestaltung und Grenzen Nachkriegsjapans und das Schicksal seiner Besitzungen, selbst wenn sie zunächst als Kriegszielerklärung gedacht waren, wurden in die Kapitulationsurkunde Japans geschrieben; diese nahm Japan an und versprach, die auf der Kairoer Erklärung basierende Potsdamer Erklärung[59] auszuführen. Die Alliierten wollten den Krieg fortsetzen, wenn Japan sich weigerte, u. a. die Mandschurei und Formosa (Taiwan) an China zurückzugeben. Die Kairoer Erklärung legte den USA und dem Vereinigten Königreich auch konkrete Pflichten auf, nämlich alles zu unterlassen, was China hinderte, die Souveränität über die Mandschurei und Formosa zurückzugewinnen, und die Souveränität anzuerkennen, sobald China sie erlangt habe.

Bei der Kairo-Konferenz bemühte sich Roosevelt, Chinas Stellung gegenüber Japan zu stärken und auch seine Vision von den Nachkriegs-Machtverhältnissen im ostasiatischen Raum umzusetzen. Ein stabiles, demokratisches pro-westliches China

---

56 So kann der US-amerikanische Präsident selbständig u. a. Gebietsänderungen regeln, Kriege und Blockaden, z. B. 1962 gegen Kuba, erklären. Der Koreakrieg wurde vom Kongress nie genehmigt („Mister Truman's War“) und die so wichtigen Monroe-, Truman und Eisenhower-Doktrinen, aufgrund derer es mehrfach, so z. B. 1958 im Libanon, zu militärischen Interventionen kam, sind dem Kongress nie vorgelegt worden. 1908 erklärten die USA und Japan die Unabhängigkeit, die Unverletzlichkeit und das Prinzip gleicher Chancen für Handel und Industrie aller Staaten in China zu unterstützen. 1940 tauschten die USA fünfzig noch aus dem Ersten Weltkrieg stammende Zerstörer gegen die zeitweilige Überlassung britischer Marine- und Luftbasen in der westlichen Hemisphäre ein. Im Jahre 1941 verpflichteten sich die USA, das damals zu Dänemark gehörende Island zu verteidigen. In all diesen Fällen liegt auf Seiten der USA nur ein „executive agreement“ vor.

57 United States v. Curtiss Wright Corp., 299 U.S. 304, 319, 320 (1936); United States v. Belmont 301 U.S. 324 (1937).

58 Text: *Röper* (Anm. 53), S. 241 f., Anlage 9.

59 Dazu vgl. unten 5.

war für ihn Grundvoraussetzung für ein stabiles friedliches Asien, allerdings müsste Japan demilitarisiert werden. Roosevelt erwartete von China, dass es in den meisten Nachkriegsdisputen für die USA Partei ergreifen werde, so dass die Vereinigten Staaten einen weiteren wichtigen Verbündeten hätten. Sollte China aber zu schwach sein, um eine Schlüsselrolle im Nachkriegsasien zu spielen, müssten die USA mehr Verantwortung übernehmen. Roosevelt hoffte, eine Einflussnahme Chinas im Nachkriegsasien insbesondere dadurch herbeiführen zu können, dass er China eine wichtige Rolle bei der Korea-Frage zudachte, auch wenn dies auf Kosten der koreanischen Unabhängigkeit geschehen sollte. In Kairo merkte er an, dass China Ansprüche auf die Mandschurei und Korea geltend mache.[60] Das Protokoll der Kairoer Konferenz zeigt allerdings, dass China seiner Hoffnung Ausdruck verliehen hatte, Korea möge nach dem Krieg unabhängig werden.[61]

Letztlich war die Kairoer Konferenz eine die Teheraner Hauptkonferenz vorbereitende Konferenz der Staats- und Regierungschefs. Roosevelt zeigte in der Kairoer Deklaration keinerlei Bedenken, territoriale Verschiebungen in Ostasien zu fordern, ohne die betroffenen Staaten daran zu beteiligen. Dieses Großmachtsgebaren, das seit über 80 Jahren als überwunden galt, wird heute zwischen Trump und Putin praktiziert.

3. Konferenz von Teheran vom 28. November 1943 bis 1. Dezember 1943

Dem US-amerikanischen Präsidenten ging es auf der Teheraner Konferenz[62] vom 28. November 1943 bis 1. Dezember 1943, bei der die USA, die UdSSR und das Vereinigte Königreich vertreten waren, vor allem um die Errichtung einer alle Mitglieder der Vereinten Nationen umfassenden Institution, die periodisch und an verschiedenen Orten zusammentreten und das Recht zu Empfehlungen besitzen sollte.

Ein gemeinsames Vorgehen gegenüber Japan war noch nicht gefunden. Dem Memorandum des 63. Treffens des Pacific War Council[63] am 12. Januar 1944 in Washington ist zu entnehmen, dass Marschall Stalin in Teheran zustimmte, die Mandschurei, Formosa (Taiwan) und die Pescadores-Inseln an China zurückgegeben. Stalin wies ferner darauf hin, dass Russland keinen eisfreien Hafen in Sibirien habe und

---

60 Vgl. auch United States Department of State, Foreign Relations of the United States. Diplomatic Papers. The Conferences at Cairo and Tehran (1961) (Department of State Publication 7187), S. 257, 334.

61 Vgl. das Gespräch Chiang Kai-sheks mit Roosevelt am 23. November und das Memorandum der chinesischen Regierung vom 24. November 1943, in: United States Department of State, Foreign Relations. Diplomatic Papers. The Conferences at Cairo and Tehran (1961) (Department of State Publication 7187), S. 325, 389.

62 Vgl. United States Department of State, Foreign Relations of the United States. Diplomatic Papers. The Conferences at Cairo and Tehran (1961) (Department of State Publication 7187), S. 459 ff.

63 Vgl. United States Department of State, Foreign Relations of the United States. Diplomatic Papers. The Conferences at Cairo and Tehran (1961) (Department of State Publication 7187), S. 869.

daher einen anstrebe. Er schlug vor Dalian (Dairen)[64] als Freihafen der ganzen Welt zur Verfügung zu stellen. Es könnten damit sibirische Exporte und Importe über diesen Hafen verschifft werden. Stalin wollte also die Nutzung der zur Zarenzeit gepachteten und nach dem Russisch-Japanischen Krieg an Japan abgetretenen Häfen Dairen und Port Arthur wiedererlangen. Die Waren könnten von und nach Sibirien mit der Mandschurischen Eisenbahn befördert werden,[65] die allerdings China gehören solle. China sollte die Territorien, die Japan von ihm erobert hatte, zurückerhalten und Korea sollte unabhängig werden. Der Sowjetunion wurden Südsachalin und die Kurilen zugesagt. Stalin betonte, China müsse aktiv in den Krieg eingreifen, um sich den Wiedergewinn seines Territoriums zu verdienen.[66]

4. Konferenz von Jalta vom 4. Februar bis 11. Februar 1945

a) Teilnehmer

Die Republik China nahm an der Konferenz in Jalta[67] vom 4. Februar bis 11. Februar 1945 zwischen den drei Großmächten USA, UdSSR und dem Vereinigten Königreich nicht teil. Gleichwohl wurde China auf dieser Konferenz schon als Großmacht betrachtet. Japan war unter anderem Gegenstand der Diskussionen.

b) Geheimabkommen von Jalta vom 11. Februar 1945

Im Geheimabkommen von Jalta[68] zwischen den USA, dem Vereinigten Königreich und der Sowjetunion vom 11. Februar 1945 über den Eintritt der Sowjetunion in den Krieg gegen Japan sahen die Großmächte zahlreiche einseitige Leistungen Chinas an die Sowjetunion vor. Es wurde nicht berücksichtigt, dass die Sowjetunion auf ihre Rechte aus den sog. Ungleichen Verträgen[69] zwischen China und den europäischen

---

64 Dalian ist heute eine Hafenstadt in der Provinz Liaoning, China; japanisch: *dairen-shi*, kurz: 連/连. Vgl. oben I.1.c).

65 Vgl. United States Department of State, Foreign Relations of the United States. Diplomatic Papers. The Conferences at Cairo and Tehran (1961) (Department of State Publication 7187), S. 567.

66 *Weinberg*, Eine Welt in Waffen. Die globale Geschichte des Zweiten Weltkriegs (1995), S. 668.

67 United States Department of State, Foreign Relations of the United States. Diplomatic Papers. The Conferences at Malta and Yalta 1945, (1955) (Department of State Publication 6199).

68 Text: *Kappe-Hardenberg* (Hrsg.), Die Jalta-Dokumente. Roosevelt, Churchill und Stalin auf der Krim-Konferenz im Februar 1945 (1987), S. 577 f. Vgl. auch *Fischer* (Hrsg.), Teheran, Jalta, Potsdam. Die sowjetischen Protokolle von den Kriegskonferenzen der „Großen Drei" (1968), S. 196; *Jacobsen*, Der Zweite Weltkrieg (1965), S. 411; auch *Röper* (Anm. 53), S. 232, Anlage 2.

69 Der Begriff der ungleichen Verträge wurde in der Zeit des Kolonialismus für Verträge verwendet, in denen die asiatischen und afrikanischen Länder übervorteilt wurden. Gemeinsam ist der Mehrheit der Definitionsversuche, dass ein ungleicher Vertrag folgende Merkmale aufweisen müsse: nicht unerhebliches Ungleichgewicht der gegenseitig vereinbarten Leistungen, Ausübung von Zwang oder Druck und Zuwiderlaufen den Interessen des benachteiligten Staates. Dem Völkerrecht ist jedoch ein Gebot der Ausgewogenheit vertraglicher Leistungen fremd geblieben. Es herrscht daher die Auffassung vor, dass die bloße Ungleichheit der vereinbarten Leistungen nicht die Wirksamkeit eines Vertrages beeinträchtigen könne, da

Mächten, Japan und den USA im 19. und beginnenden 20. Jahrhundert verzichtet hatte. Es sollte die Rechtsposition des zaristischen Russlands wiederhergestellt werden.[70]

Im Abkommen der drei Großmächte vom 11. Februar 1945 wurde in Punkt 2 festgelegt, dass die Rechte Russlands, „die durch den hinterlistigen Angriff Japans im Jahre 1904 verletzt wurden", wiederhergestellt werden sollten und zwar

- die Rückgabe des südlichen Teils der Insel Sachalin und aller vorgelagerten Inseln an die Sowjetunion,
- die Internationalisierung des Handelshafens Dalian (Dairen) unter Wahrung der besonderen Interessen der Sowjetunion an diesem Hafen,
- die Wiederherstellung des Pachtvertrags für Port Arthur als Flottenstützpunkt der UdSSR,
- die gemeinsame Nutzung der ostchinesischen und der südmandschurischen Eisenbahnlinie, die einen Zugang nach Dairen verschafft, auf der Basis einer gemischten sowjetisch-chinesischen Gesellschaft unter Wahrung der besonderen Interessen der Sowjetunion und unter Berücksichtigung dessen, dass China die volle Souveränität in der Mandschurei behält.

In Punkt 3 wurde vereinbart, dass die Kurilen[71] der Sowjetunion übergeben werden sollten. Die Regierungschefs waren sich einig, dass die Forderungen der Sowjetunion erfüllt werden müssten, sobald Japan besiegt sei. Die Sowjetunion drückte ihrerseits die Bereitschaft aus, mit der nationalchinesischen Regierung einen Freundschafts- und Bündnispakt abzuschließen, um China mit bewaffneten Streitkräften bei der Befreiung Chinas vom japanischen Joch beizustehen.

Japan und China sollten also zu Gunsten der Sowjetunion und mit Billigung der USA große territoriale und rechtliche Verluste hinnehmen, zu denen China vor allem von den USA unter Verletzung der Kairoer Erklärung gezwungen wurde.[72] Die Verabredung sollte durch einen sino-sowjetischen Freundschaftsvertrag gekrönt wer-

im Völkerrecht Vertragsfreiheit bestehe. Insgesamt wurde daher in der Völkerrechtslehre eine Unwirksamkeit ungleicher Verträge abgelehnt. Ausführlich *Gornig* (Anm. 25), § 35 Rn. 22 ff.

70 *Röper* (Anm. 53), S. 58 f.

71 In § 2 des Vertrags von Sankt Petersburg vom 7. Mai 1875 (Text: abrufbar unter https://ru.wikisource.org/wiki (zuletzt abgerufen am 22. Februar 2025)) wurden die (nördlichen) 18 Inseln zwischen Urup und Shumshu nördlich von Etorofu Japan zugesprochen; im Gegenzug wurde Sachalin vollständig an Russland abgetreten. Damit war damals der gesamte Kurilen-Archipel unter japanische Hoheit gefallen. Am 9. August 1945 begann der sowjetisch-japanische Krieg – am selben Tag wie der Atombombenabwurf auf Nagasaki. In der Folge besetzte die Rote Armee alle seit dem Vertrag von Portsmouth (1905) zu Japan gehörenden Kurileninseln sowie die Habomai-Inseln Shikotan, Kunashiri und Etorofu. Allein auf den nach 1945 von der Sowjetunion eroberten Südkurilen-Inseln Etorofu und Kunashiri und den zur Präfektur Hokkaidō gehörenden Shikotan und Habomai-Inseln lebten 1945 insgesamt ca. 17.300 Japaner. Dazu: *Hasegawa*, The Northern Territories Dispute and Russo-Japanese Relations (1998); *Rees*, The Soviet Seizure of the Kuriles (1985).

72 Vgl. *Röper* (Anm. 53), S. 57.

den.[73] Roosevelt kam es infolge einer Fehleinschätzung der militärischen Möglichkeiten Japans nur auf den Eintritt der Sowjetunion in den Krieg im Fernen Osten und ihren Beitritt zu der zu gründenden UNO an, und versprach daher die chinesische Regierung zur Annahme der Jalta-Bedingungen in einem noch abzuschließenden Freundschaftsvertrag zu nötigen.

Am 14. August 1945 wurde der Vertrag über Freundschaft und Bündnis[74] von der Nationalregierung der Republik China und der Regierung der Union der Sozialistischen Sowjetrepubliken unterzeichnet. Sowjetische und mongolische Truppen besetzten daraufhin die Innere Mongolei und die Mandschurei, nachdem sie diese von den Japanern erobert hatten. In einer im Zusammenhang mit dem Vertrag abgegebenen Erklärung akzeptierte China die Unabhängigkeit der Äußeren Mongolei innerhalb ihrer bisherigen Grenzen. Außerdem stellte die Sowjetunion ihre Unterstützung für die Chinesische Kommunistische Partei ein. China stellte jedoch fest, dass die Sowjetunion gleichwohl die Chinesische Kommunistische Partei und die Volksbefreiungsarmee, die sich der regierenden Kuomintang und der Regierung der Republik China widersetzten, heimlich und kontinuierlich unterstützte. Die Beziehung brach zusammen, nachdem die Kommunistische Partei Chinas am 1. Oktober 1949 in Peking die Volksrepublik China ausgerufen hatte, die von der Sowjetunion anerkannt wurde.[75]

c) Folge

Die Republik China nahm an der Konferenz in Jalta nicht teil und unterzeichnete erst recht nicht das Jaltaer Abkommen, war also daran nicht gebunden. Am 9. Juni 1945 wurde aber der chinesische Außenminister T. V. Soong durch den Präsidenten der USA Harry S. Truman von dem Geheimvertrag unterrichtet und mit Erfolg gedrängt die Abmachungen zu akzeptieren. Die Regierung Chiang Kai-sheks begann daraufhin Verhandlungen mit der Sowjetunion, die zur Unterzeichnung des sino-sowjetischen Freundschaftsvertrages am 14. August 1945 führten, in dem sich beide Staaten verpflichteten, die territoriale Souveränität des anderen zu respektieren.[76] Japan verlor durch die Vereinbarungen die eroberten Gebiete.

---

73 Vgl. *Röper* (Anm. 53), S. 58, S. 232, Anlage 2.

74 Text: *Röper* (Anm. 53), S. 256 ff., Anlage 22, 23.

75 Die UN-Generalversammlung verabschiedete am 1. Februar 1952 die Resolution 505 (Text: abrufbar unter https://www.worldlii.org/int/other/UNGA/1952/50.pdf, zuletzt abgerufen am 19. Februar 2025), in der bestätigt wurde, dass die Sowjetunion gegen die Vertragsbedingungen verstoßen hatte, indem sie die Kommunistische Partei Chinas während des chinesischen Bürgerkriegs unterstützte.

76 China war nun zwar geschwächt, aber als Großmacht anerkannt, nicht zuletzt durch den Konsens, dass China ständiges Mitglied des Sicherheitsrats der UNO unter Führung der Nationalregierung Chiang Kai-sheks werden solle. Vgl. zur Geschichte Chinas zwischen 1922 und 1972 *Gittings*, The World and China 1922–1972 (1974) S. 52 ff.

5. Konferenz von Potsdam vom 17. Juli bis 2. August 1945

Auf der Konferenz von Potsdam vom 17. Juli bis 2. August 1945 der drei Großmächte USA, UdSSR und Vereinigtes Königreich wurde diskutiert, wie die Nachkriegsordnung gestaltet werden könnte.[77]

In die Potsdamer Erklärung[78] des Präsidenten der USA, des Präsidenten der Nationalregierung Chinas und des Premierministers des Vereinigten Königreichs vom 26. Juli 1945, der die Sowjetunion am 8. August 1945 mit der Kriegserklärung an Japan beitrat, wurde die Kairoer Erklärung (Nr. 8) übernommen und Japan unter ausdrücklicher Berufung auf diese auf die Hauptinseln Honshu, Hokkaido, Kyushu und Shikoku sowie einige noch zu bestimmende kleinere Inseln beschränkt. Die USA versprachen damit dafür zu sorgen, dass China die von Japan gestohlenen Gebiete zurückerhält.

Am 10. August 1945 – die Atombomben wurden am 6. August auf Hiroshima und am 9. August 1945 auf Nagasaki geworfen – meldete Radio Tokyo, Japan habe China, den USA, dem Vereinigten Königreich und der Sowjetunion die Annahme der Bedingungen der Potsdamer Erklärung mitgeteilt, falls es das Kaiserhaus behalten könne.[79] Die Großmächte erklärten sich am 14. August 1945 mit der Bedingung einverstanden.[80] Am 14. August 1945 teilte Japan den Siegern abermals mit, die Bedingungen der Potsdamer Erklärung annehmen und die zur Durchführung nötigen Befehle erlassen zu wollen. Am gleichen Tage legte der Tenno in einer Rundfunkansprache, der ersten eines japanischen Kaisers, die Gründe für die Kapitulation dar und forderte das Volk auf Ruhe und Ordnung zu bewahren. Japan nahm im Waffenstillstandsvertrag die Bedingungen der Potsdamer Erklärung an, die auch Moskau zu erfüllen versprach, als es am 8. August 1945 Japan „getreu seinen Verpflichtungen gegenüber seinen Alliierten" den Krieg erklärte.[81]

Die Kapitulationsurkunde[82], die am 2. September 1945, 9.45 Uhr Tokioer Zeit, auf der USS Missouri unterzeichnet wurde, enthielt in Art. 6 den Passus, Japan nehme die Bedingungen der Potsdamer Erklärung an und werde die zur Durchführung nötigen Befehle erlassen. Dann besetzten die in den Erklärungen genannten Staaten die für sie vorgesehenen Gebiete, soweit das nicht schon geschehen war. China besetzte u. a. Formosa und richtete dort am 25. Oktober 1945 eine Zivilverwaltung mit General Chen Yi als Gouverneur ein und erhob es zur 34. Provinz.

---

[77] Vgl. z. B. *Deuerlein*, Potsdam 1945. Ende und Anfang (1970), S. 100 ff.

[78] Text: *Röper* (Anm. 53), S. 233 f., Anlage 3; ebenso *Deuerlein*, Potsdam 1945. Quellen zur Konferenz der „Großen Drei" (1963), S. 152 f.

[79] *Röper* (Anm. 53), S. 235, Anlage 4. Vgl. auch die Alliierte Antwortnote vom 11. August 1945, Text: *Röper* (Anm. 53) S. 236, Anlage 5; *Truman*, Memoiren, Bd. I (1955), S. 442.

[80] *Truman*, Memoiren, Bd. I (1955), S. 443.

[81] Text der Kriegserklärung: abrufbar unter https://avalon.law.yale.edu/wwii/s4.asp (zuletzt abgerufen am 9. März 2025).

[82] Text: *Röper* (Anm. 53), S. 241, Anlage 9; ferner: abrufbar unter https://www.diaoyudao.org.cn/de/2015-06/30/content_35947375.htm (zuletzt abgerufen am 22. Februar 2025).

6. Friedensvertrag von San Francisco vom 8. September 1951

Der Friedensvertrag von San Francisco[83] vom 8. September 1951 trat am 28. April 1952 in Kraft.[84] Der Vertrag bedeutet das Ende der US-amerikanischen Besatzungszeit in Japan nach dem Zweiten Weltkrieg. Mit dem Vertrag verzichtete Japan in Art. 2 beispielsweise auf Formosa, die Pescadores-Inseln, die Spratly-Inseln und die Paracel-Inseln, ohne diese Gebiete ausdrücklich China zuzusprechen. Man kann hier von Dereliktion[85] sprechen:

- „Japan recognizing the independence of Korea, renounces all right, title and claim to Korea, including the islands of Quelpart, Port Hamilton and Dagelet.
- Japan renounces all right, title and claim to Formosa and the Pescadores.
- Japan renounces all right, title and claim to the Kurile Islands, and to that portion of Sakhalin and the islands adjacent to it over which Japan acquired sovereignty as a consequence of the Treaty of Portsmouth of September 5, 1905.
- Japan renounces all right, title and claim in connection with the League of Nations Mandate System, and accepts the action of the United Nations Security Council of April 2, 1947, extending the trusteeship system to the Pacific Islands formerly under mandate to Japan.
- Japan renounces all claim to any right or title to or interest in connection with any part of the Antarctic area, whether deriving from the activities of Japanese nationals or otherwise.
- Japan renounces all right, title and claim to the Spratly Islands and to the Paracel Islands.“

Einige Fragen blieben nach dem Friedensvertrag von San Francisco ungeklärt wie etwa das Verhältnis zu China. Zwar hatte Japan am 28. April 1952, dem Tag des Inkrafttretens des Friedensvertrages von San Francisco, einen separaten Vertrag mit der Republik China[86] unterzeichnet, aber ohne die Beteiligung der Volksrepublik China[87], die damals noch nicht anerkannt war. In diesem Friedensvertrag wiederholte Japan den Verzicht, allerdings wiederum ohne China diese Gebiete ausdrücklich zu übertragen. Weiterhin akzeptierte Japan, dass alle zwischen China und Japan vor

---

83 Text: Europa-Archiv, Bd. VII (1952), S. 5267 ff.; ferner: abrufbar unter https://en.wikisource.org/wiki/Treaty_of_San_Francisco (zuletzt abgerufen am 19. Februar 2025).

84 Vgl. *Hasegawa*, Racing the Enemy: Stalin, Truman, and the Surrender of Japan (2006).

85 Dazu *Gornig* (Anm. 25), § 69 Rn. 58, § 66 Rn. 20.

86 Text: *Röper* (Anm. 53), S. 243, Anlage 10.

87 Der Friedens- und Freundschaftsvertrag zwischen Japan und der Volksrepublik China wurde erst am 12. August 1978 abgeschlossen. In Art. II heißt es: „The Contracting Parties declare that neither of them should seek hegemony in the Asia-Pacific region or in any other region and that each is opposed to efforts by any other country or group of countries to establish such hegemony.“; Text: abrufbar unter https://en.wikisource.org/wiki/Treaty_of_Peace_and_Friendship_between_Japan_and_the_People%27s_Republic_of_China (zuletzt abgerufen am 19. Februar 2025).

dem 9. Dezember 1941, dem Tag der Kriegserklärung Chinas an Japan[88], geschlossenen Verträge null und nichtig seien. Schließlich erkannte Japan auch die Unabhängigkeit Koreas an.[89]

Ebenso wie um die Kurilen gibt es bis heute Konflikte um die unbewohnten Senkaku-Inseln, die zwischen Japan und Taiwan liegen. Nach chinesischer Auffassung gehörten sie einst zum Kaiserreich China. Japan widerspricht und erkennt die von China angeführten Beweise nicht an. Im Jahr 1895 annektierte Japan die Senkaku-Inseln, kurz vor dem Ende des Ersten Chinesisch-Japanischen Krieges. Seinen Anspruch verlor Japan im Zuge des Friedensvertrages von San Francisco. Nach der Unterzeichnung eines Rückgabevertrages, gelangten die Inseln im Jahr 1972 durch die USA, die sie besetzt hatten, wieder zurück unter die japanische Verwaltung. Gleichwohl beanspruchen auch China und Taiwan die Inseln für sich. In jüngster Zeit kam es immer wieder zu Spannungen zwischen China und Japan wegen der Zugehörigkeit der Senkaku-Inseln.[90]

7. Resümee

Die Bezeichnung Formosas in der Kairoer Erklärung als durch Japan von China „gestohlenes" Gebiet war die moralische Verurteilung einer Gebietsübertragung, die seit 1895 auch als dem Völkerrecht widersprechend betrachtet wurde. Es wird dabei darauf Bezug genommen, dass nach dem Ersten Chinesisch-japanischen Krieg China aufgrund des Friedensvertrages von Shimonoseki vom 17. April 1895 am 2. Juni 1895 als Folge des von Japan siegreich geführten Angriffskrieges die Insel Formosa an Japan übertragen musste. Ein völkerrechtliches Kriegs- und Gewaltverbot hatte sich damals noch nicht durchgesetzt und stand daher weder dem Krieg noch der Annexion entgegen.[91] Bei der Kriegserklärung an Japan am 9. Dezember 1941 hatte China dann alle Verträge, Konventionen, Abmachungen und Übereinkommen über die Beziehungen zu Japan für null und nichtig erklärt, also auch den Friedensvertrag von Shimonoseki. Dies wurde durch Art. 4 des Friedensvertrags mit Japan vom 28. April 1952 bestätigt. Japan hatte somit Formosa 50 Jahre in Besitz gehabt. In der Kapitulationsurkunde, in der Japan die Bedingungen der Potsdamer Erklärung annahm, ist eine Abtretung der Gebiete zu sehen, die nicht mehr Japan gehören sollten, also aller Gebiete außer die Inseln Honshu, Hokkaido, Kyushu, Shikoku und einige kleinere Inseln. Japan unterzeichnete die Kapitulationsurkunde und zog in Erfüllung seine Truppen zurück. Dann gliederten China, aber auch die Sowjetunion, diese aufgegebenen Gebiete ihrem Staatsverband ein.[92]

---

88 Text: abrufbar unter https://www.jewishvirtuallibrary.org/china-s-declaration-of-war-against-japan-germany-and-italy-december-1941 (zuletzt abgerufen am 9. März 2025).

89 Dazu vgl. unten II.

90 Vgl. dazu *Gornig* (Anm. 25), § 81 Rn. 57. Ferner: *McCormack*, Much Ado over Small Islands: The Sino-Japanese Confrontation over Senkaku/Diaoyu, in: The Asia-Pacific Journal, Bd. 21 (2013), abrufbar unter https://lawexplores.com/much-ado-over-small-islands-the-sino-japanese-confrontation-over-senkakudiaoyu/ (zuletzt abgerufen am 19. Februar 2025).

91 *Gornig* (Anm. 25), §§ 11, 12, 45.

92 *Gornig* (Anm. 29), S. 118 f.

II. Japan und Korea

1. Japan und Korea in der Geschichte des 20. Jahrhunderts

Am 15. August 2025 begeht Korea den 80. Jahrestag der Befreiung von japanischer Kolonialherrschaft mit einem symbolischen Akt: an diesem Tag vor 80 Jahren begann der Abbruch des ehemaligen japanischen Gouverneurspalastes im Zentrum von Seoul. Koreanische Zeitungen bezeichneten diese Aktion als „Säuberung des Landes von kolonialen Überbleibseln". Nach den Worten von Staatspräsident Kim Young-sam sollte damit der Nationalgeist der Koreaner gestärkt werden.[93]

a) Chinesisch-Japanischer Krieg

Im Jahre 1637 musste der koreanische König die Oberhoheit der chinesischen Mandschu-Kaiser anerkennen, die 1644 die Qing-Dynastie in China begründeten. Bis 1894 blieb Korea ein Vasallenstaat Chinas. Im Jahre 1894 schickten China und Japan Truppen auf ein Hilfesuchen des koreanischen Königs nach Korea, um einen Aufstand niederzuschlagen.[94] Nach der Niederschlagung der Aufständischen blieben aber die Truppen beider Länder weiterhin in Korea und kämpften dort um die Vorherrschaft. Die Japaner siegten in diesem Krieg und China verzichtete im Friedensvertrag von Shimonoseki[95] am 17. April 1895 auf alle Rechte in Korea.[96]

b) Russisch-Japanischer Krieg

Nach dem Chinesisch-Japanischen Krieg 1894/95[97] kämpften Russland und Japan um die Vorherrschaft in Korea. Mit einem japanischen Angriff am 9. Februar 1904 auf Port Arthur brach der Russisch-Japanische Krieg aus.[98] Im Friedensvertrag von Portsmouth[99] zwischen Russland und Japan vom 5. September 1905 akzeptierte Russland, dass Korea dem japanischen Interessengebiet zugehöre. In Art. 2 verzichtete Russland auf seinen Einfluss in der Mandschurei und übergab seine Pachtgebiete und Rechte auf der Halbinsel Liaodong und die südmandschurische Eisenbahn an Japan. Am 14. Oktober ratifizierte der japanische Kaiser den Vertrag.[100] Japan erwarb weiterhin vom Vereinigten Königreich im zweiten Britisch-Japanischen Allianzver-

---

93 Zur Geschichte Koreas vgl. *Zöllner*, Geschichte der japanisch-koreanischen Beziehungen. Von den Anfängen bis zur Gegenwart (2017); *Eggert/Plassen*, Kleine Geschichte Koreas (2005); *Kim*, Koreanische Geschichte: Einführung in die koreanische Geschichte von der Vorgeschichte bis zur Moderne (2004).

94 Es war ein Aufstand der 1859 von Choc Che-u gegründeten Tonghak-Bewegung, den sog. Tonghangsan. Die Tonghak-Bewegung war extrem fremden- und japanfeindlich eingestellt.

95 Text: *Strupp* (Anm. 2), S. 124 ff.

96 Vgl. *Park*, Korea: A History (2022); *Peterson/Margulies*, A Brief History of Korea (2009), S. 104 ff., 141 ff.; *Pratt*, Everlasting Flower: A History of Korea (2007).

97 Vgl. oben I.1.a).

98 Vgl. oben I.1.c).

99 Text: *Martens/Stoerk* (Hrsg.), Nouveau Recueil Général de Traités et Autres Actes Relatifs aux Rapports de Droit International, deuxième série, Bd. XXXIII, S. 1 ff.

100 Vgl. *Bersihand*, Geschichte Japans von den Anfängen bis zur Gegenwart (1963), S. 384 f.; *Hu*, Le problème coréen (1953), S. 58 f.

trag[101] vom 12. August 1905 die eindeutige Zustimmung zu seiner alleinigen Herrschaft über Korea.[102] Die USA hatten durch einen geheimen Notenwechsel[103] zwischen dem japanischen Premierminister Count Taro Katsura und dem US-amerikanischen Präsidenten William Howard Taft[104] vom 29. Juli 1905 Japans Vorrechte in Korea akzeptiert.[105]

c) *Japanisches Protektorat*

Im Jahre 1905 wurde Korea japanisches Protektorat. Nachdem der König den Protektoratsvertrag ablehnte, bedrohte der japanische Bevollmächtigte in Abwesenheit des Königs während einer Kabinettssitzung die Regierungsmitglieder, nahm den Ministerpräsidenten fest und hielt ihn von der Kabinettssitzung fern, weil er gegen den Abschluss eines Protektoratsvertrages besonders heftigen Widerstand leistete. Die anderen Kabinettsmitglieder durften den Sitzungssaal nicht verlassen, bis der Vertrag unterzeichnet sein würde. Gleichwohl erhielt Japan keine Zustimmung des Kabinetts. Die fehlenden Unterschriften, besonders die des koreanischen Kaisers, veranlassen koreanische Historiker dazu, die Legalität des Vertrages zu bezweifeln. Allerdings war Itō Hirobumi[106] das Dekret Gojongs vom 3. August 1885 bekannt, wonach es bei Verträgen zwischen Groß-Korea und anderen Nationen ausreichte, wenn das Siegel des Außenministeriums auf dem Dokument vorhanden war. Dies tat Pak Jesun in seiner Funktion als Außenminister mittels des entsprechenden Siegels; der Vertrag trat daraufhin sofort in Kraft.[107] Es wird aber auch vertreten, dass der japanische Gesandte den Stempel des Außenministers rauben ließ und den Protektoratsvertrag selbst abstempelte, was den Vertrag nichtig machen würde.[108]

---

101 Text: *Martens/Stoerk* (Hrsg.), Nouveau Recueil Général de Traités et Autres Actes Relatifs aux Rapports de Droit International, deuxième série, Bd. XXXV, S. 402 ff. Die beiden Vertragsparteien sicherten sich im ersten Allianzvertrag vom 30. Januar 1902 die Unabhängigkeit und Unantastbarkeit des Staatsgebietes von China und Korea zu.

102 In Art. 3 des zweiten Allianzvertrages heißt es: „Japan possessing paramount political, military, and economic interests in Korea, Great Britain recognizes the right of Japan to take such measures of guidance, control and protection in Korea as she may deem proper and necessary to safeguard and advance those interests, provided always that such measures are not contrary to the principle of equal opportunities for the commerce and industry of all nations."

103 Text: abrufbar unter https://worldjpn.net/documents/texts/pw/19050729.O1E.html (zuletzt abgerufen am 9. März 2025).

104 Dazu *Lindsay/Shortridge*, TWE Remembers: The Taft-Katsura Memorandum, abrufbar unter https://www.cfr.org/blog/twe-remembers-taft-katsura-memorandum-0 (zuletzt abgerufen am 9. März 2025).

105 *Hu* (Anm. 100), S. 60.

106 Kōshaku Itō Hirobumi war ein Samurai und japanischer Politiker. Itō wurde im Jahr 1885 der erste Premierminister von Japan und bekleidete dieses Amt bis 1901 insgesamt viermal.

107 Dazu *Sakamoto*, The Validity of the Japan-Korea Protectorate Treaty, in: Kansai University Review of Law and Politics, Nr. 18 (1997), S. 59 ff.

108 Vgl. *Shin*, Die Geschichte der Außenpolitik in Ostasien (1978), zit. nach *Shin*, Die Übertragbarkeit der deutschen Wiedervereinigungsmodelle auf das geteilte Korea (1993), S. 22 f.

Nach Art. 1 des am 17. November 1905 abgeschlossenen Protektoratsvertrags[109] konnte Japan vollständig die Verantwortung für Koreas Außenpolitik übernehmen. In Art. 2 verpflichtete sich Japan alle noch gültigen Verträge Koreas mit ausländischen Mächten fortzuführen und gegebenenfalls durchzusetzen. Korea wiederum durfte keine weiteren Verträge mit ausländischen Mächten unterzeichnen. In Art. 3 wurde eine ständige Vertretung der japanischen Regierung am Kaiserhof Koreas ausgehandelt. Diese Vertretung, genannt *general-resident*, hatte die Aufgabe sich um diplomatische Angelegenheiten zu kümmern und zu dirigieren. In Art. 5 verpflichtete sich Japan das Wohl und die Würde des koreanischen Kaiserhauses zu erhalten. Zugleich wurden alle Handelsangelegenheiten, welche über koreanische Häfen liefen, unter japanische Aufsicht gestellt.[110]

Korea berichtete auf der zweiten Friedenskonferenz, die im Juli 1907 in Den Haag stattfand, über die Vorkommnisse und begründete die Nichtigkeit des Vertrages damit, dass das Siegel des Königs darauf fehle.[111] Japan beschuldigte daraufhin den koreanischen König, seinetwegen das Gesicht verloren zu haben und zwang ihn zurückzutreten.[112] Daraufhin übernahm der Kronprinz das Amt des Königs. Unter Fortführung der militärischen Bedrohung gegen den neuen König schloss Japan den neuen Korea-Japan-Vertrag[113] vom 24. Juli 1907 ab. Mit diesem Vertrag wurde Korea völlig unter japanische Herrschaft gestellt.[114]

d) Korea als Kolonie Japans

Korea wurde schließlich im Vertrag am 22. August 1910[115] von Japan annektiert und in eine japanische Kolonie umgewandelt. Nach Art. 1 vollzieht Seine Majestät, der Kaiser von Korea, die vollständige und permanente Abtretung aller Souveränitätsrechte über ganz Korea an seine Majestät, den Kaiser von Japan. Nach Art. 2 ak-

109 Vgl. Japanisch-Koreanisches Abkommen vom 17. November 1905, Text: *Martens/Stoerk* (Hrsg.) Nouveau Recueil Général de Traités et Autres Actes Relatifs aux Rapports de Droit International, deuxième série, Bd. XXXIV, S. 727 ff. Zu Zeiten des Abschlusses des Vertrages wurde der Vertrag in Japan Japanisch-Koreanischer Verhandlungsvertrag (日韓交渉条約) und in Korea Koreanisch-Japanischer Verhandlungsvertrag (한일 협상 조약) genannt.

110 Der Protektoratsvertrag von 1905 wurde ausdrücklich durch den Grundlagenvertrag zwischen Japan und der Republik Korea vom 22. Juni 1965 durch beide Vertragspartner in Art. II als null und nichtig deklariert: „It is confirmed that all treaties or agreements concluded between the Empire of Japan and the Empire of Korea on or before August 22, 1910 are already null and void.“; Text: abrufbar unter https://en.wikisource.org/wiki/Treaty_on_Basic_Relations_Between_Japan_and_the_Republic_of_Korea (zuletzt abgerufen am 22. Februar 2025).

111 *Hu* (Anm. 100), S. 61.

112 *Hu* (Anm. 100), S. 62; *Shin* (Anm. 108), S. 23 m. w. N.

113 Text: American Journal of International Law, Bd. 1 (1906), S. 397; *Strupp* (Anm. 2), S. 145; Weitere Informationen abrufbar unter https://en.wikipedia.org/wiki/Japan%E2%80%93Korea_Treaty_of_1907 (zuletzt abgerufen am 19. Februar 2022).

114 Durch den Vertrag wurden innenpolitische Angelegenheiten Koreas, wie etwa die Auflösung der koreanischen Truppen und Justiz und Gefängnisangelegenheiten von Japan übernommen. Der koreanische Königspalast wurde unter Bewachung japanischer Militärpolizei gestellt.

115 Text: *Martens/Triepel* (Hrsg.), Nouveau Recueil Général de Traités et Autres Actes Relatifs aux Rapports de Droit International, troisième série, Bd. IV, S. 24 ff.; *Strupp* (Anm. 2), S. 151 ff.

zeptiert Seine Majestät, der Kaiser von Japan, diese Abtretung und stimmt der vollständigen Annexion Koreas durch das Japanische Reich zu. Als Folge der Annexion übernimmt die japanische Regierung gemäß Art. 6 die gesamte Regierung und die Verwaltung Koreas und verpflichtet sich, unter der Einhaltung der dort geltenden Gesetze für den vollen Schutz der Menschen und des Eigentums der Koreaner und für die Förderung des Wohlstands aller zu sorgen. In diesem Vertrag übertrug somit der koreanische Kaiser auf ewig alle Staatsgewalt dem japanischen Kaiser. Seitdem verwaltete Japan durch einen japanischen Generalgouverneur[116] Korea als Kolonie[117].

Nach der Unabhängigkeitsbewegung vom 1. März 1919 – es war der Tag, an dem der letzte koreanische Kaiser bestattet wurde – erfolgte ein Protest gegen die japanische Kolonialmacht. Millionen Koreaner demonstrierten danach für das Recht auf nationale Selbstbestimmung, das aber damals noch kein Rechtssatz, sondern ein politisches Postulat war. Japan erklärte daher die Aufhebung des kolonialen Status' Koreas, die Beendigung der militärischen Verwaltung Koreas und die Beseitigung der Diskriminierung der Koreaner. Diese Erklärung wurde allerdings nie umgesetzt.[118]

2. Konferenz von Kairo vom 22. bis 26. November 1943

Auf der Konferenz in Kairo zwischen dem US-amerikanischen Präsidenten, dem britischen Premierminister und dem chinesischen Generalissimo Chiang Kai-shek im November 1943 hatte Stalin den Plan der Vereinigten Staaten, Korea bald frei und unabhängig von Japan werden zu lassen, ausdrücklich gutgeheißen.[119]

Nach einem US-amerikanischen Entwurf vom 24. November 1943 sollte Korea zum „frühestmöglichen Zeitpunkt" („earliest possible moment") seine Unabhängigkeit erhalten. Am nächsten Tag änderte Roosevelt diese Fassung dahingehend, dass es nun hieß, „im richtigen Zeitpunkt" („proper moment").[120]

---

116 Der Generalgouverneur übte seine Herrschaft mit militärischer Gewalt aus und war dem japanischen Kaiser direkt verantwortlich. Die 635.000 Japaner in Korea bildeten gegenüber den 25 Millionen Koreanern eine mit Privilegien versehene Oberschicht.

117 Vgl. auch die Japanische Proklamation betreffend die Annexion Koreas, das Kaiserlich japanische Reskript betreffend die Annexion Koreas und die Bekanntmachung des japanischen Außenministeriums, Texte: *Strupp* (Anm. 2), S. 152 ff.

118 Vielmehr versuchte Japan verstärkt den Koreanern die eigene Kultur aufzuzwingen. So mussten die Koreaner die japanische Religion (Shintoismus) übernehmen und ihre Namen nach japanischem Stil ändern.

119 Die USA entwarfen daher für Korea folgende Pläne: Einrichtung einer multilateralen Treuhand für Korea in den Jahren 1943 bis 1946 und Lösung des Korea-Problems mittels der Vereinten Nationen in den Jahren 1947 bis 1950. Korea sollte unter der Treuhand der Weltmächte stehen, solange es diese für richtig hielten. Die multilaterale Treuhand sollte einen unilateralen Kolonialismus ersetzen und die Kolonien, also auch Korea, auf die Unabhängigkeit vorbereiten. Vgl. *Cumings*, Introduction: The Course of Korean-American Relations, 1943–1953, in: Cumings (Hrsg.), Child of Conflict. The Korean-American Relationship, 1943–1953 (1983), S. 103. Das Treuhandmodell stieß von Anfang an in der internationalen Diskussion auf Widerstand, vgl. *Gornig* (Anm. 29), S. 124 f.

120 United States Department of State, Foreign Relations of the United States. Diplomatic Papers. Conferences at Cairo and Tehran (1961) (Department of State Publication 7187), S. 399–400.

Am 1. Dezember 1943 veröffentlichten die Teilnehmer der Konferenz von Kairo die sog. Kairoer Deklaration[121], in der zum ersten Mal deutlich die Forderung erhoben wurde, Korea unabhängig werden zu lassen, sobald Japan besiegt sei.

3. Konferenz von Teheran vom 28. November bis 1. Dezember 1943

Auf der Konferenz von Teheran stimmte Marschall Stalin zu, dass Korea unabhängig werden müsse. Er vertrat auch die Auffassung, dass die Koreaner noch nicht fähig seien, sich selbst zu regieren, und dass sie unter ein 40-jähriges Tutorium zu stellen seien, jedenfalls wenn der Krieg gegen Japan beendet sei. Die Unabhängigkeit Koreas galt damit als beschlossen.

4. Konferenz von Jalta vom 4. Februar 1945 bis 11. Februar 1945

Während informeller Diskussionen mit Stalin am 8. Februar 1945 auf der Konferenz von Jalta kam zum Ausdruck, dass Korea eine Treuhand von 20 oder 30 Jahren genießen sollte. Stalin erwiderte diesmal, je kürzer die Treuhandverwaltung sei, desto besser.[122]

Gleichwohl erklärte kurz vor dem Ende des Zweiten Weltkrieges am 1. April 1945 der japanische Kaiser in einer politischen Grundsatzrede, dass Korea nun Bestandteil des japanischen Mutterlandes sei. Dies ist ein Beweis dafür, dass Korea bis dahin von Japan nicht als Bestandteil Japans, sondern als Kolonie betrachtet wurde.[123]

5. Konferenz von Potsdam vom 17. Juli bis 1. August 1945

Zunächst wurde auf der Konferenz von Potsdam die Treuhandschaft der vier Hauptsiegermächte über Korea beschlossen, welche die spätere Unabhängigkeit der Halbinsel garantieren sollte. Später einigten sich aber die Sowjetunion und die USA auf zwei Besatzungszonen, in denen jede der beiden Mächte in eigener Verantwortung die japanischen Truppen entwaffnen und repatriieren sollte. Truman und Stalin waren sich einig, dass das Hauptproblem im Hinblick auf Korea darin liege, wie die japanische Übergabe in diesem Gebiet vorzunehmen sei. Die nächste US-amerikanische Armee stand auf Okinawa[124], also etwa 1.000 km von Korea entfernt, eine russische Armee dagegen befand sich unmittelbar an der koreanischen Grenze.

---

121 Vgl. oben I.2.b).

122 Vgl. *Gornig* (Anm. 29), S. 127 ff.

123 Vgl. *Langen*, Die Gebietsverluste Japans nach dem Zweiten Weltkrieg (1971), S. 140. Vgl. etwa auch *Dix*, Politische Geographie: Weltpolitisches Handbuch, 2. Aufl. (1923), S. 319, der Korea mit über 17 Millionen Einwohnern und 220.741 qkm selbstverständlich Japan zurechnet.

124 Die Inselgruppe Okinawa liegt im südlichen Teil von Japan. Sie besteht aus vier Hauptinseln und etwa 160 kleinen Inseln, die sich über eine Länge von fast 1.000 Kilometern nach Süden erstrecken.

Diese beiden Armeen hatten die Kapitulation der japanischen Truppen in Korea entgegenzunehmen.[125]

6. Folge

Am 8. August 1945 stießen 100.000 Russen unter General Iwan M. Tschistjakow über die koreanische Grenze und marschierten südwärts gegen den 38. Breitengrad. Von Okinawa aus stach das 24. US-amerikanische Corps unter General John Hodge einen Monat später nach Korea in See, um Korea südlich des 38. Breitengrades zu besetzen. Sie landeten am 8. September 1945 auf dem koreanischen Festland. Die als provisorisch vorgesehene und nur zu Besatzungszwecken gedachte Trennungslinie am 38. Breitengrad erwies sich in der weiteren politischen Entwicklung als entscheidender Faktor bei der Teilung der koreanischen Nation. Noch heute stellt der 38. Breitengrad die Trennungslinie zwischen der kommunistischen Volksrepublik Korea und der westlich orientierten Republik Korea dar.

III. Schluss

Auf den Konferenzen in Kairo, Teheran, Jalta und Potsdam wurden nicht allein Weichen für das Schicksal Deutschlands gestellt. Mit beispielloser Arroganz haben auf den Nachkriegskonferenzen Vertreter der USA, der UdSSR und des Vereinigten Königreichs nicht nur entscheidend die Teilung und Verkleinerung Deutschlands vorbereitet, sondern auch über das Schicksal Japans, Chinas und Koreas befunden. Dass sie damit auch das Schicksal von Millionen von Menschen beeinflussten, war den Staatsmännern selten bewusst. Dies wird beim Lesen der Konferenzdokumente in erschreckender Weise deutlich. Trump und Putin eifern den Siegern von damals bei der Behandlung des Angriffskrieg Russlands gegen die Ukraine nach. Sie haben aus der Geschichte also nichts gelernt, – aber wahrscheinlich kennen sie sie gar nicht.

Literaturverzeichnis

Albrecht, Dieter: Der chinesisch-japanische Konflikt und das Völkerrecht (1933).

Bersihand, Roger: Geschichte Japans von den Anfängen bis zur Gegenwart (1963).

Blum, Robert: The United States and China in World Affairs (1966).

Blumenwitz, Dieter: Potsdam und die russisch-japanischen Grenzregelung, in: Blumenwitz, Dieter/Gornig, Gilbert/Meissner, Boris (Hrsg.), Potsdam – 50 Jahre danach (1996), S. 91 ff.

Borton, Hugh: American Pre-Surrender Planning for Postwar Japan, Occasional Papers of the East Asian Institute (1967).

Bremm, Klaus-Jürgen: Russlands Desaster im Fernen Osten – Der Russisch-Japanische Krieg 1904/05, in: Österreichische Militärische Zeitschrift, Nr. 6 (2004), S. 699 ff.

Churchill, Winston S.: The Second World War, Vol. 4: The Hinge of Fate (1950).

---

[125] Vgl. *Gornig* (Anm. 29), S. 131 ff.

Churchill, Winston S.: The Second World War, Vol. 5: Closing the Ring (1951).

Cumings, Bruce: Introduction: The Course of Korean-American Relations, 1943–1953, in: Cumings, Bruce (Hrsg.), Child of Conflict. The Korean-American Relationship, 1943–1953 (1983), S. 103.

Deuerlein, Ernst: Potsdam 1945. Ende und Anfang (1970).

Deuerlein, Ernst: Potsdam 1945. Quellen zur Konferenz der „Großen Drei" (1963).

Dix, Arthur: Politische Geographie: Weltpolitisches Handbuch, 2. Aufl. (1923), S. 319.

Domes, Jürgen: Kuomintang-Herrschaft in China (1970).

Eggert, Marion/*Plassen*, Jörg: Kleine Geschichte Koreas (2005).

Feis, Herbert: Churchill, Roosevelt, Stalin: The War They Waged and the Peace They Sought (1957).

Gittings, John: The World and China 1922–1972 (1974).

Gornig, Gilbert: China und Korea als Gegenstand der Verhandlungen von Kairo, Teheran, Jalta und Potsdam, in: Meissner, Boris/Blumenwitz, Dieter/Gornig, Gilbert (Hrsg.), Das Potsdamer Abkommen. III. Teil: Rückblick nach 50 Jahren (1996), S. 103–134.

Gornig, Gilbert: Hongkong, Von der britischen Kronkolonie zur chinesischen Sonderverwaltungszone (1998).

Gornig, Gilbert: Völkerrecht. 1. Aufl. (2023).

Hasegawa, Tsuyoshi: The Northern Territories Dispute and Russo-Japanese Relations (1998).

Herrfahrdt, Heinrich: Sun Yatsen. Der Vater des neuen China (1948).

Heydte, Friedrich August Freiherr von der: Glossen über Wesen und Funktion des Kriegs im Völkerrecht, in: Göttinger Arbeitskreis (Hrsg.), Mensch und Staat in Recht und Geschichte. Festschrift für Herbert Kraus (1954), S. 73 ff.

Hu, Hung-Lick: Le problème coréen (1953).

Jacobsen, Hans-Adolf: Der Zweite Weltkrieg (1965).

Kaminski, Gerd: Chinesische Positionen zum Völkerrecht (1973).

Kaminski, Gerd: Der Boxeraufstand – entlarvter Mythos (2000).

Kim, Hiyoul: Koreanische Geschichte: Einführung in die koreanische Geschichte von der Vorgeschichte bis zur Moderne (2004).

Klein, Thoralf (Hrsg.): The Boxer War. Media and Memory of an Imperialist Intervention (2020).

Kuß, Susanne/*Martin*, Bernd (Hrsg.): Das Deutsche Reich und der Boxeraufstand (2002).

Langen, Benita: Die Gebietsverluste Japans nach dem Zweiten Weltkrieg (1971).

Lauterpacht, Hersh: The Contemporary Practice of the United Kingdom in the Field of International Law – Survey and Comment, in: International and Comparative Law Quarterly, Bd. 8 (1959), S. 168 ff.

Lindsay, James M./*Shortridge*, Anna: TWE Remembers: The Taft-Katsura Memorandum, in: Council on Foreign Relations (31. Juli 2020), abrufbar unter https://www.cfr.org/blog/twe-remembers-taft-katsura-memorandum-0 (zuletzt abgerufen am 9. März 2025).

Liszt, Franz von: Das Völkerrecht, systematisch dargestellt, 11. Aufl. (1918).

Mattray, James: The Reluctant Crusade: American Foreign Policy in Korea, 1941–1950 (1977).

McCormack, Gavan: Much Ado over Small Islands: The Sino-Japanese Confrontation over Senkaku/Diaoyu, in: The Asia-Pacific Journal, Bd. 21 (2013).

Mitter, Rana: China's War with Japan, 1937–1945: The Struggle for Survival (2014).

Mitter, Rana: Forgotten Ally: China's World War II, 1937–1945 (2014).

O'Connor, Richard: Der Boxeraufstand. Gewalt und Tragödie (1980).

Paine, S. C. M.: The Sino Japanese War of 1894–1895 – Perceptions, Power and Primacy (2003).

Park, Eugene Y.: Korea: A History (2022).

Peterson, Mark/*Margulies*, Phillip: A Brief History of Korea (2009).

Pratt, Keith: Everlasting Flower: A History of Korea (2007).

Pu Yi, Aisin Gioro: Ich war Kaiser von China (1986).

Rees, David: The Soviet Seizure of the Kuriles (1985).

Röper, Erich: Die Formosa-Frage. Ein Beitrag zur Bestimmung der völkerrechtlichen Stellung der chinesischen Nationalregierung und des kommunistischen China (1966).

Rowe, David N.: Kleine Geschichte des modernen China (o. J.).

Sakamoto, Shigeki: The Validity of the Japan-Korea Protectorate Treaty, in: Kansai University Review of Law and Politics, Nr. 18 (1997), S. 45–94.

Shin, Ki-Siuk: Die Geschichte der Außenpolitik in Ostasien (1978).

Shin, Yong-Ho: Die Übertragbarkeit der deutschen Wiedervereinigungsmodelle auf das geteilte Korea (1993).

Truman, Harry S.: Memoiren, Bd. I (1955).

Tung, William L.: China and the Foreign Powers: The Impact of and Reaction to Unequal Treaties (1970).

Weinberg, Gerhard L.: Eine Welt in Waffen. Die globale Geschichte des Zweiten Weltkriegs (1995).

Whiting, Allen S.: Morality, Taiwan, and U.S. Policy, in: Cohen, Jerome A./Friedman, Edward/Hinton, Harold C./Whiting, Allen S. (Hrsg.), Taiwan and American Policy. The Dilemma in U.S.-China Relations (1971), S. 82 ff.

Zieger, Gottfried: Die Teheran-Konferenz (1967).

Zöllner, Reinhard: Geschichte der japanisch-koreanischen Beziehungen. Von den Anfängen bis zur Gegenwart (2017).

Geschäftsführungsentscheidungen in der japanischen Aktiengesellschaft

Von *Deniz Günal*

Dr. Deniz Günal ist Syndikusrechtsanwalt bei der Volkswagen AG. Er studierte an der Universität zu Köln und der Keio Universität in Tokyo. Nach einem Forschungsaufenthalt an der Chuo Universität promovierte er an der Philipps-Universität Marburg. Sein Tätigkeits- und Interessenschwerpunkt liegt im Handels- und Gesellschaftsrecht.

Der Autor bedankt sich herzlich bei Prof. Heinrich Menkhaus, der ihm die Augen dafür geöffnet hat, wie weit sich das japanische Gesellschaftsrecht über die Grenzen des Gesellschaftsgesetzes (GesG)[1] hinaus erstreckt und wie tief das japanische und deutsche Recht auch heute noch verbunden sind.[2]

Dieser Beitrag geht aus Sicht des deutschen Rechts der Frage nach, wie die Kompetenz für Geschäftsführungsentscheidungen innerhalb der verschiedenen Erscheinungsformen der japanischen Aktiengesellschaft gesetzlich allokiert ist, inwieweit Unternehmen hiervon abweichen können und welche Risiken sich für die Geschäftsführung der Gesellschaft hierbei ergeben.

I. Gesetzliche Ausgangslage

Die Aktiengesellschaft (株式会社, *kabushiki kaisha*) ist mit Abstand die häufigste Gesellschaftsform in Japan und beliebt als Rechtsform sowohl für kleine inhabergeführte, wie für große börsennotierte Unternehmen. Diese Rolle erfüllt sie nicht zuletzt dadurch, dass das GesG Aktiengesellschaften einen hohen Grad an Flexibilität hinsichtlich ihrer Unternehmensverfassung bietet.[3] Das GesG ermöglicht sowohl eine dualistische Struktur, bei der die Geschäftsführung – also die Direktoren (取締役, *torishimariyaku*) oder ein aus Direktoren gebildeter Verwaltungsrat (取締役会, *torishimariyaku kai*) – durch gesellschaftsinterne Prüfer (監査役, *kansayaku*) bzw. ei-

---

1 Gesellschaftsgesetz (会社法, *kaishahō*), Gesetz Nr. 86/2005.

2 Vgl. etwa *Menkhaus*, Allgemeines Gesellschaftsrecht in Japan, in: Menkhaus, Japanischer Brückenbauer zum deutschen Rechtskreis, Festschrift für Koresuke Yamauchi zum 60. Geburtstag (2006), S. 229 ff.

3 Zu Geschichte und Struktur der japanischen Aktiengesellschaft vgl. etwa *Kansaku*, Hiruyuki/*Bälz*, Moritz, in: Baum, Harald/Bälz, Moritz (Hrsg.), Handbuch des Japanischen Handels- und Wirtschaftsrechts (2011), S. 83 ff. und *Meckel*, Verena, Die Corporate Governance im neuen japanischen Gesellschaftsrecht unter besonderer Berücksichtigung der Aufgaben von Verwaltungs- und Prüferrat, in: Zeitschrift für Japanisches Recht, Heft Nr. 29 (2019), S. 53 ff.

Duncker & Humblot · Berlin | https://doi.org/10.3790/978-3-428-59611-9.2025.418781

nen Prüferrat (監査役会, *kansayaku kai*) überwacht werden, als auch eine monistische Struktur, bei der Ausschüsse innerhalb des Verwaltungsrats diese Aufgabe übernehmen.

Das japanische Recht unterscheidet wie das deutsche zwischen Geschäftsführung (業務執行, *gyōmu shikkō*) und Vertretung (代表, *daihyō*). Eine Gesellschaft mit ausschließlich vinkulierten Aktien kann, sofern sie über keinen Prüferrat verfügt und es sich um keine Gesellschaft mit Ausschüssen (s. u.) handelt, auf einen Verwaltungsrat verzichten und die Geschäftsführung einem oder mehreren Direktoren anvertrauen (Art. 327 Abs. 1 GesG). Hat die Gesellschaft nur einen Direktor, führt dieser die Geschäfte allein. Hat sie mehrere, führen zwar alle die Geschäfte, doch werden Geschäftsführungsentscheidungen (業務執行の決定, *gyōmu shikkō no kettei*) im Kollegialprinzip mit einfacher Mehrheit der Stimmen aller Direktoren getroffen, sofern die Satzung nichts anderes bestimmt (Art. 348 Abs. 2 GesG).[4] Die Direktoren vertreten die Gesellschaft (einzeln) gegenüber Dritten, sofern die Hauptversammlung keine vertretungsberechtigten Direktoren (代表取締役, *daihyō torishimariyaku*) bestimmt (Art. 349 Abs. 1, Abs. 4 GesG). Die Hauptversammlung (株主総会, *kabunushi sōkai*) behält stets die Möglichkeit, im Innenverhältnis sämtliche Angelegenheiten im Zusammenhang mit der Gesellschaft zu entscheiden, einschließlich deren Organisation, Betrieb und Leitung (Art. 295 Abs. 1 GesG), mithin auch Einzelfragen der Geschäftsführung.[5] Diese Allzuständigkeit die Aktiengesellschaft macht die Aktiengesellschaft auch für kleinere Unternehmen mit festem Aktionärskreis attraktiv.

Sonstige Aktiengesellschaften verfügen über einen Verwaltungsrat, der aus mindestens drei Direktoren besteht (Art. 331 Abs. 5 GesG). Der Verwaltungsrat trifft Geschäftsführungsentscheidungen und zudem sämtliche sonstige Entscheidungen im Zusammenhang mit der Gesellschaft, die nicht durch Gesetz oder Satzung der Hauptversammlung zugewiesen sind (Art. 362 Abs. 2 Nr. 1, 295 Abs. 2 GesG). Die Hauptversammlung also ist anders als bei der Gesellschaft ohne Verwaltungsrat nur in abschließend normierten Fällen zuständig (Trennung von Eigentümerschaft und Kontrolle).

Dem Verwaltungsrat obliegt die Überwachung (監督, *kantoku*) der Arbeit der Direktoren[6] (Art. 362 Abs. 2 Nr. 2 GesG) und er beruft aus seiner Mitte einen oder mehrere vertretungsberechtigte Direktoren sowie ggf. geschäftsführende Direktoren (業務執行取締役, *gyōmu shikkō torishimariyaku*) (nachfolgend gemeinsam „geschäftsführende Direktoren"), die das Geschäft der Gesellschaft führen (Art. 362 Abs. 2, 363 GesG). Dies ist ein Unterschied zur deutschen Aktiengesellschaft, wo

---

4 Es wird diskutiert, dass ob das Mehrheitsprinzip auch gilt, wenn die Hauptversammlung einen oder mehrere vertretungsberechtigte Direktoren bestellt hat. Die Rechtsprechung hierzu ist nicht einheitlich. Vgl. *Egashira*, Kenjirō/*Nakamura*, Naoto, 論点会社法 (*ronten kaishahō*, Issues in Corporate Law), 2. Auflage (2021), Bd. 3, S. 91 m. w. N.

5 *Egashira/Nakamura* (Anm. 4), S. 90.

6 Dies ist vergleichbar mit der Rechtslage für die deutsche Aktiengesellschaft, bei der die Vorstandsmitglieder ebenfalls zur gegenseitigen Überwachung verpflichtet sind, vgl. etwa *Weber*, Markus, in: Hölters, Wolfgang/Weber, Markus (Hrsg.), AktG, 4. Auflage (2022), § 77 Rn. 34 ff.

grundsätzlich sämtliche Vorstandsmitglieder gemeinschaftlich zur Geschäftsführung befugt sind (§ 77 Abs. 1 Satz 1 AktG).

Beschlüsse des Verwaltungsrats werden in Sitzungen mit einfacher Mehrheit der anwesenden Direktoren bei einem Quorum von mehr als der Hälfte der konkret stimmberechtigen Direktoren getroffen, sofern die Satzung nicht höhere Voraussetzungen vorsieht (Art. 369 Abs. 1 GesG). Die Mehrheitserfordernisse sind also weniger streng als bei der Aktiengesellschaft ohne Verwaltungsrat, bei der die Stimmen aller Direktoren gezählt werden.

Zwei Sonderformen der Aktiengesellschaft mit Verwaltungsrat sind Gesellschaften mit Nominierungsausschuss (etc.) (指名委員会等設置会社, *shimei iinkai tō secchi kaisha*) und Gesellschaften mit Prüfungs- und Überwachungsausschuss (監査等委員会設置会社, *kansatō iinkai secchi kaisha*).[7] Beide Formen sind für große, kapitalmarktorientierte Unternehmen konzipiert und ihnen ist gemein, dass anstelle eines Prüferrats oder einzelner Prüfer ein verwaltungsratsinterner Prüfungsausschuss (監査委員会, *kansa iinkai*) bzw. ein Prüfungs- und Überwachungsausschuss (監査等委員会, *kansatō iinkai*) die pflichtgemäße Erfüllung der Aufgaben der Geschäftsführung und die Rechtmäßigkeit der Rechnungslegung prüft (Art. 404 Abs. 2/ Art. 399-2 Abs. 3 GesG).[8]

Die Gesellschaft mit Nominierungsausschuss hat mindestens drei Ausschüsse, nämlich einen Nominierungs-, Prüfungs- und einen Vergütungsausschuss. Bei dieser Gesellschaft führen nicht Direktoren, sondern Geschäftsführer (執行役, *shikkōyaku*) die Geschäfte (Art. 415, 418 Abs. 2 GesG) und vertreten die Gesellschaft auch gegenüber Dritten (Art. 420 GesG). Geschäftsführung und Geschäftsführungsentscheidungen sind also personell getrennt, wobei es möglich ist, dass ein Direktor gleichzeitig das Amt eines Geschäftsführers ausübt (Art. 402 Abs. 6 GesG).

Die Gesellschaft mit Prüfungs- und Überwachungsausschuss ist ein Hybrid aus einer regulären Aktiengesellschaft mit Verwaltungsrat und einer Gesellschaft mit No-

---

7 Die Aktiengesellschaft mit Nominierungsausschuss (etc.) wurde im Jahr 2003 als „Gesellschaft mit Ausschüssen etc." (委員等会設置会社, *iinkai tō secchi kaisha*) eingeführt. Die Gesellschaft mit Prüfungs- und Überwachungsausschuss wurde 2015 geschaffen, da nur sehr wenige Unternehmen die Gesellschaft mit Nominierungsausschuss (etc.) in Anspruch nahmen (weniger als 2 % der an der Tokyo Stock Exchange notierten Unternehmen im Jahr 2015). Als Grund galt in der Praxis insbesondere die Skepsis gegenüber externen Direktoren, welche in allen Ausschüssen die Mehrheit stellen müssen. Bei der Gesellschaft mit Prüfungs- und Überwachungsausschuss ist dies nur für einen Ausschuss nötig. Tatsächlich ist die Gesellschaft mit Prüfungs- und Überwachungsausschuss deutlich beliebter. Vgl. etwa *Nagashima Ohno & Tsunematsu*, NO&T Legal Update No. 1, May 2015 (2015), S. 2, https://www.noandt.com/wp-content/uploads/2019/09/japan_no01_1.pdf.

8 Der Prüfungs- und Überwachungsausschuss verfügt weitgehend über die gleichen Rechte und Pflichten wie der Prüfungsausschuss einer Gesellschaft mit Nominierungsausschuss, doch hat er eine etwas herausgehobenere Stellung. Da keine strukturelle Trennung zwischen Geschäftsführung und Überwachung besteht, ist das abstrakte Risiko von Interessenkonflikten innerhalb des Verwaltungsrats höher. Die Konstruktion des Ausschusses entspricht daher noch mehr einem Prüfungsrat. So werden seine Mitglieder direkt von der Hauptversammlung gesondert gewählt. Der Ausschuss berichtet direkt an die Hauptversammlung und reguläre Direktoren haben kein Recht, seine Protokolle einzusehen. Zu den Unterschieden vgl. etwa *Kanda*, Hideki, 会社法 (*kaishahō*, Gesellschaftsrecht), 26. Auflage (2024), S. 282 f.

minierungsausschuss. Sie hat einen Prüfungs- und Überwachungsausschuss, jedoch keine weiteren obligatorischen Ausschüsse. Wie in der typischen Aktiengesellschaft mit Verwaltungsrat führen geschäftsführende Direktoren die Geschäfte und der Verwaltungsrat überwacht diese (Art. 399-13 Abs. 1 GesG).

II. Möglichkeiten und Grenzen der Delegation von Entscheidungskompetenzen

1. Allgemeines

Wie dargestellt unterscheidet das GesG zwischen Geschäftsführungsentscheidungen und Geschäftsführung. Die geschäftsführenden Direktoren bzw. Geschäftsführer einer Gesellschaft mit Verwaltungsrat setzen also dessen Beschlüsse um und benötigen für wesentliche eigene Entscheidungen eine entsprechende Ermächtigung.[9]

Um eine effektive und effiziente Unternehmensführung zu gewährleisten, ist es daher in der Praxis üblich, geschäftsführenden Direktoren bzw. Geschäftsführern die Entscheidungskompetenz für bestimmte Geschäfte oder Arten von Geschäften zu übertragen und zu regeln, welche Maßnahmen sie dem Verwaltungsrat zur Entscheidung vorlegen müssen und über welche Maßnahmen sie nur zu berichten haben.[10] Größere Gesellschaften bilden zudem Ressorts und übertragen die Leitung bestimmter Bereiche auf Direktoren und leitende Angestellte (執行役員, *shikkō yakuin*), um die Arbeit des Verwaltungsrats zu entlasten.[11] Anders als in Deutschland ist es zulässig, hierbei einzelnen Direktoren die finale Entscheidungsgewalt zuzusprechen und so eine Hierarchie zwischen formell gleichberechtigten Direktoren zu schaffen.[12]

Auch bei der deutschen Aktiengesellschaft ist es möglich und auch üblich, durch Satzung oder Geschäftsordnung des Vorstands vom Prinzip der Gesamtgeschäftsführung abzuweichen (vgl. § 77 Abs. 1 Satz 2 AktG). Gebräuchlich ist das Mehrheitsprinzip, oft kombiniert mit einem Recht des Vorstandsvorsitzenden zu einem Stichentscheid, sowie eine Aufteilung in Ressorts und ggf. Ausschüsse.[13] Grenzen der Geschäftsverteilung ergeben sich jedoch insb. aus den Prinzipien der Gesamtleitung, der Gleichberechtigung und der Gesamtverantwortung des Vorstands. Nach dem Prinzip der Gesamtleitung darf die Leitung des Unternehmens nicht auf einzelne Vorstandsmitglieder, Gruppen oder Ausschüsse delegiert werden. Hierzu gehören neben den gesetzlich normierten Fällen vor allem die zentralen unternehmerischen Führungsaufgaben wie die Unternehmensplanung, -strukturierung und -kontrolle sowie die

---

9 Vgl. etwa *Kanda* (Anm. 8), S. 252.

10 Vgl. *Kanda* (Anm. 8), S. 239, 249 und beispielsweise Art. 5, 6 der Geschäftsordnung des Verwaltungsrats der Toyota Motor Corporation, https://www.sec.gov/Archives/edgar/data/1094517/000119312511172686/dex12.htm.

11 In der Praxis ist die Terminologie leider nicht einheitlich. Teilweise werden Direktoren als „執行役員 (*shikkō yakuin*)" oder „業務担当取締役 (*gyōmu tantō torishimariyaku*)" (Direktor zuständig für die Geschäftsführung) bezeichnet.

12 *Kanda* (Anm. 8), S. 252.

13 Vgl. *Spindler*, Gerald, in: Götte/Habersack/Kalss (Hrsg.), Münchener Kommentar zum Aktiengesetz, 6. Auflage (2023), § 77 AktG, Rn. 12.

Besetzung der wichtigsten Führungspositionen.[14] Der Grundsatz der Gleichberechtigung der Vorstandsmitglieder verbietet hierbei eine Hierarchie zwischen Vorstandsmitgliedern mit Mitgliedern erster und zweiter Klasse.[15] Schließlich trägt nach dem Prinzip der Gesamtverantwortung jedes Vorstandsmitglied die umfassende Verantwortung für die gesamte Geschäftsführung der Gesellschaft[16] und ist verpflichtet, die übrigen Mitglieder zu überwachen.[17]

2. Aktiengesellschaft ohne Verwaltungsrat

Angesichts der festen Aktionärsstruktur und des regelmäßig engen Vertrauensverhältnisses zwischen Aktionären und Direktoren hat eine Aktiengesellschaft ohne Verwaltungsrat vergleichsweise große Freiheiten, durch Satzung oder Beschluss der Direktoren Geschäftsführungentscheidungen an einzelne Direktoren zu übertragen.[18] Es ist sogar zulässig, Dritte mit Entscheidungskompetenzen auszustatten, etwa einen Beirat aus Aktionärsvertretern auf Basis eines Joint Venture Vertrages.[19] Entnommen wird diese Freiheit dem Wortlaut des eingangs erwähnten Art. 348 Abs. 2 GesG, wonach das Mehrheitsprinzip nur gilt, soweit die Satzung nichts anderes bestimmt.

Art. 348 Abs. 3 GesG verbietet es allerdings, die Entscheidung über folgende Maßnahmen an einzelne Direktoren zu delegieren: Berufung und Abberufung von Prokuristen (支配人, *shihainin*), Errichtung, Änderung und Abschaffung von Zweigniederlassungen, Einberufung der Hauptversammlung, Ausgabe von Anleihen, Einrichtung eines internen Kontrollsystems (mehr dazu unter 3. unten) sowie Haftungserlass für Direktoren.

Es ist streitig, ob dieses Verbot auch für den Fall einer Übertragung der Entscheidungsbefugnisse durch Satzung gilt.[20] Stimmen, die diese Frage verneinen, argumentieren, dass Art. 348 Abs. 2 GesG abweichende Bestimmungen zur Entscheidungsfindung ausdrücklich zulasse. Dem Gesetzgeber sei es nicht darauf angekommen, die genannten Maßnahmen nur durch mehrere Personen entscheiden zu lassen. So könne ein Einzeldirektor auch alleine entscheiden. Die wohl herrschende Meinung bejaht jedoch ein Verbot unter Verweis auf die Bedeutsamkeit der Maßnahmen sowie den Wortlaut und die systematische Stellung des Abs. 3.[21] Abs. 3 enthält anders als Abs. 2 auch keinen Satzungsvorbehalt.

---

14 *Weber* (Anm. 6), § 77 AktG, Rn. 29.

15 *Weber* (Anm. 6), § 77 AktG, Rn. 30.

16 *Weber* (Anm. 6), § 77 AktG, Rn. 31.

17 *Spindler* (Anm. 12), § 77 AktG, Rn. 62.

18 So auch *Egashira/Nakamura* (Anm. 4), S. 92 m. w. N.

19 *Egashira/Nakamura* (Anm. 4), S. 91.

20 Zum Meinungsstand vgl. *Egashira/Nakamura* (Anm. 4) S. 91 ff. m. w. N.

21 Vgl. *Egashira/Nakamura* (Anm. 4); im Ergebnis auch *Kondo*, Mitsuo, 最新株式会社法 (*saishin kabushiki kaishahō*, Aktuelles Recht der Aktiengesellschaften), 9. Auflage (2020), S. 265 und *Kanda* (Anm. 8), S. 287.

3. Aktiengesellschaft mit Verwaltungsrat

Ein Verwaltungsrat unterliegt strengeren Grenzen. Er darf generell keine Entscheidungen über wesentliche Geschäftsführungsmaßnahmen an einzelne Direktoren (oder sonstige Personen) delegieren, einschließlich Verfügung über und Annahme von wesentlichen Vermögenswerten, Aufnahme von Krediten in erheblichem Umfang, Berufung und Abberufung von Prokuristen und anderen wichtigen Mitarbeitern, Errichtung, Änderung und Abschaffung wichtiger Strukturen einschließlich Zweigniederlassungen, Ausgabe von Anleihen, Einrichtung eines internen Kontrollsystems und Haftungserlass für Direktoren (Art. 362 Abs. 4 GesG).

Sofern es sich um keine Gesellschaft mit Nominierungsausschuss handelt und sie mindestens sechs Direktoren hat, von denen mindestens eines ein sog. externer Direktor (社外取締役, *shagai torishimari yaku*)[22] ist, kann der Verwaltungsrat die genannten Entscheidungen über wesentliche Vermögenswerte und erhebliche Kredite einem Gremium von mindestens drei Direktoren überlassen (sog. Sonderdirektoren (特別取締役, *tokubetsu torishimari yaku*), Art. 373 Abs. 1 GesG). Ein Beschluss der Sonderdirektoren entfaltet die gleiche Wirkung wie ein Verwaltungsratsbeschluss. Um Transparenz zu gewährleisten, muss einer der Sonderdirektoren den Verwaltungsrat unverzüglich nach der Beschlussfassung über den Inhalt des Beschlusses informieren (Art. 373 Abs. 3 GesG).

4. Aktiengesellschaft mit Nominierungsausschuss (etc.)

Die Kernfunktion des Verwaltungsrats einer Aktiengesellschaft mit Nominierungsausschuss liegt in der Berufung, Abberufung und Überwachung der Arbeit der Geschäftsführer.[23] Er entscheidet zwar über grundlegende Prinzipien der Geschäftsführung, Kernpunkte der Arbeit des Prüfungsausschusses, das Verhältnis der Geschäftsführer untereinander (Aufgabenteilung, Befehlshierarchie etc.), Einzelheiten zur Einberufung von Sitzungen und die Einrichtung eines internen Kontrollsystems, doch kann er Geschäftsführungsentscheidungen weitgehend auf die Geschäftsführer übertragen und sich auf das Treffen von Grundsatzentscheidungen beschränken (sog. Monitoring-Modell[24]) (vgl. Art. 416 Abs. 1, Abs. 4 GesG). Eine Delegation dieser Entscheidungen an Direktoren ist hingegen nicht zulässig.

Folglich kann der Verwaltungsrat im Rahmen seiner Kompetenzen auch grundlegende Entscheidungen wie die Ausgabe neuer Aktien oder Anleihen an einen oder mehrere Geschäftsführer übertragen. Ausgenommen sind lediglich die in Art. 416 Abs. 4 GesG abschließend aufgeführten Grundlagengeschäfte. Dies sind etwa bestimmte Entscheidungen im Zusammenhang mit der Übertragung von Aktien und Bezugsrechten, Einberufung der Hauptversammlung und Vorschlag der Tagesordnung, Berufung und Abberufung der Ausschussmitglieder und Geschäftsführer, Haftungserlass für Geschäftsführer und Inhalt von Umwandlungsverträgen.

---

22 Art. 2 Nr. 15 GesG enthält eine komplexe Legaldefinition, die eine Unabhängigkeit der Personen vom Einfluss der übrigen Direktoren und einzelner Aktionäre sicherstellen soll.

23 Vgl. Art. 416 Abs. 1 Nr. 2 GesG und *Kanda* (Anm. 8), S. 240, 284.

24 Vgl. *Kanda* (Anm. 8), S. 200, 279, 285.

5. Aktiengesellschaft mit Prüfungs- und Überwachungsausschuss

Die Kompetenzen des Verwaltungsrats in Gesellschaften mit Prüfungs- und Überwachungsausschuss entsprechen im Wesentlichen denen in einer großen Aktiengesellschaft mit Verwaltungs- und Prüferrat.[25] Auch hier überwacht der Verwaltungsrat die Arbeit der Direktoren, beruft vertretungsberechtigte Direktoren und trifft Entscheidungen der Geschäftsführung, insb. über grundlegende Prinzipien der Geschäftsführung, Kernpunkte der Arbeit des Prüfungs- und Überwachungsausschusses sowie die Einrichtung eines internen Kontrollsystems (Art. 399-13 Abs. 1 GesG).

Der Verwaltungsrat ist nicht generell daran gehindert, Entscheidungen über wesentliche Geschäftsführungsmaßnahmen zu delegieren. Art. 399-13 Abs. 4 enthält jedoch einen mit Art. 362 Abs. 2 GesG nahezu identischen Katalog von Maßnahmen, die nicht an einzelne Direktoren übertragen werden dürfen.[26] Sofern die Mehrzahl der Direktoren jedoch extern sind, ist eine Übertragung dennoch in einem ähnlichen Umfang wie in einer Aktiengesellschaft mit Nominierungsausschuss zulässig. Art. 399-13 Abs. 5 GesG zeigt die Grenzen auf und schließt nahezu die gleichen Maßnahmen aus wie Art. 416 Abs. 4 GesG. Daneben besteht die Möglichkeit, in der Satzung den Verwaltungsrat zu ermächtigen, wesentliche Geschäftsführungsentscheidungen vollständig oder teilweise an einzelne Direktoren zu übertragen (Art. 399-13 Abs. 6 GesG).

Begründet wird die im Vergleich zu regulären Aktiengesellschaften mit Verwaltungsrat große Freiheit des Verwaltungsrats damit, dass die Kontrollmöglichkeiten durch Prüfungs- und Überwachungsausschuss und die Hauptversammlung besonders stark ausgeprägt sind.[27] So beträgt die Amtszeit der Direktoren maximal ein statt zwei Jahre, so dass ihre Bestellung durch die Hauptversammlung jährlich neu bestätigt werden muss (Art. 332 Abs. 1, Abs. 3 GesG). Der Prüfungs- und Überwachungsausschuss besteht überwiegend aus externen Direktoren und seine Mitglieder werden direkt von der Hauptversammlung getrennt von den übrigen Direktoren gewählt (Art. 329 Abs. 2, 331 Abs. 6 GesG). Schließlich hat der Ausschuss das Recht, der Hauptversammlung seine Auffassung zur Berufung, Abberufung, Amtsniederlegung und Vergütung der Direktoren mitzuteilen (Art. 399-2 Abs. 3 Nr. 3 i. V. m. 342-2 Abs. 4, 361 Abs. 6 GesG).

III. Sonstige Einschränkungen

Direktoren und Geschäftsführer haben die Gesellschaft mit der Sorgfalt eines gewissenhaften Beauftragten zu leiten (Art. 330/402 Abs. 2 GesG i. V. m. Art. 644 Zivilgesetz, ZivilG[28]). Nach der Rechtsprechung sind demnach unternehmerische Ent-

25 Vgl. *Kanda* (Anm. 8), S. 280.

26 Art. 399-13 ist *lex specialis* zu Art. 362 GesG, der somit nicht auf Aktiengesellschaften mit Prüfungsausschuss anwendbar ist. Vgl. *Egashira/Nakamura* (Anm. 4), S. 452.

27 Vgl. *Oka*, Nobuhiro, 株式会社法 (*kabushiki kaishahō*, Recht der Aktiengesellschaften), 2. Auflage (2023), S. 583.

28 民法 (*minpō*), Gesetz Nr. 89/1896.

scheidungen professionell, vorausschauend und strategisch zu treffen, wobei der Geschäftsführung ein gewisser Ermessenspielraum zukommt (経営判断原則, *keiei handan gensoku*, eine Variante der *business judgement rule*). Damit eine Handlung nicht als pflichtwidrig beurteilt wird, muss sie professionell beurteilt worden sein und weder das Verfahren zur Entscheidungsfindung noch der Inhalt der Entscheidung selbst darf grob unvernünftig (著しく不合理, *ichijirushiku fugōri*) sein.[29] Hieraus folgt, dass die geschäftsführenden Organe strategische Grundsatzentscheidungen und Kompetenzen für Maßnahmen mit absehbar hohem Risiko nicht unkontrolliert aus der Hand geben dürfen.

Große Gesellschaften[30] und Gesellschaften mit obligatorischen Ausschüssen haben zudem ein internes Kontrollsystem (内部統制システム, *naibu tōsei shisutemu*) einzurichten mit dem Ziel, dass die geschäftsführenden Direktoren bzw. Geschäftsführer das Unternehmen im Einklang mit Recht und Satzung leiten und dass die Geschäfte der Gesellschaft, der Tochtergesellschaften und der Unternehmensgruppe insgesamt angemessen geführt werden (Art. 348 Abs. 3 Nr. 4, Abs. 4/362 Abs. 4 Nr. 6, Abs. 5/399-13 Abs. 1 Nr. 3, Abs. 2/416 Abs. 1 Nr. 1 (e), Abs. 2 GesG).[31] Dieses Kontrollsystem muss ein im Hinblick auf das Geschäft adäquates Informations-, Risikomanagement- und Compliance-System beinhalten, das die Angemessenheit und Effizienz der Geschäftsführung sicherstellt (vgl. Art. 98, 100, 110-4, 112 Durchführungsverordnung zum Gesellschaftsgesetz[32]).

Im Falle einer schuldhaften Verletzung der genannten Pflichten haften Direktoren und Geschäftsführer der Gesellschaft für Schäden, die sie der Gesellschaft zufügen (Art. 423 Abs. 1 GesG). Darüber hinaus haften sie Dritten für Schäden durch vorsätzliche und grob fahrlässige Pflichtverstöße (Art. 429 Abs. 1 GesG).

IV. Ergebnis

Vor dem Hintergrund, dass das japanische Recht sowohl monistische wie dualistische Unternehmensverfassungen zulässt, besteht eine größere Flexibilität hinsichtlich der Verantwortlichkeiten der Direktoren als in einer deutschen Aktiengesellschaft. Es greift hierbei weder ein strenges Prinzip der Gesamtleitung durch den Verwaltungsrat, noch ein enger Grundsatz der Gleichberechtigung der Direktoren.

In allen Varianten der japanischen Aktiengesellschaft ist es möglich, die grundsätzlich bei sämtlichen Direktoren bzw. dem Verwaltungsrat liegende Kompetenz für Geschäftsführungsentscheidungen in einem gewissen Rahmen an einzelne Direktoren bzw. Geschäftsführer zu übertragen. Der Umfang unterscheiden sich je nach Rechtsformvariante, doch ist allen Aktiengesellschaften gemein, dass ein Kern an

29 Vgl. *Kanda* (Anm. 8), S. 253 ff. m. w. N.

30 *Dai kaisha*, also Gesellschaften, die nach der Bilanz des letzten Geschäftsjahres ein Stammkapital von mindestens JPY 500 Mio. oder Verbindlichkeiten von mindestens JPY 500 Mrd. aufweisen (Art. 2 Nr. 6 GesG).

31 Vgl. *Kanda* (Anm. 8), S. 256 sowie *Kondo* (Anm. 21), S. 288.

32 会社法施行規則 (*kaishahō shikō kisoku*), Verordnung des Justizministeriums Nr. 12/2006 v. 7. 2. 2006. Vgl. hierzu etwa *Oka* (Anm. 27), S. 423 ff.

Grundsatzentscheidungen bei sämtlichen Direktoren bzw. dem Gesamtverwaltungsrat verbleiben müssen.

Aktiengesellschaften ohne Verwaltungsrat sind besonders flexibel in der Gestaltung ihrer Corporate Governance. Entsprechend können Entscheidungskompetenzen an einzelne Direktoren und sogar Dritte übertragen werden. Lediglich eine Hand voll wesentlicher, abschließend gesetzlich normierter Geschäftsführungsentscheidungen sind nicht übertragbar.

Aktiengesellschaften mit Verwaltungsrat ohne obligatorische Ausschüsse sind stärker gebunden. Doch auch hier ist eine Delegation an einzelne Direktoren möglich, sofern wesentliche Geschäftsführungsentscheidungen beim Verwaltungsrat als Gesamtorgan verbleiben. Aktiengesellschaften mit Nominierungsausschuss oder mit Prüfungs- und Überwachungsausschuss verfügen hierbei über besonders große Freiheiten. Hintergrund ist eine ausdifferenzierte Corporate Governance mit externen Direktoren, bei der die Geschäftsführung durch ein obligatorisches internes Kontrollsystem gebunden ist und durch den Verwaltungsrat, seine Ausschüsse und die Hauptversammlung kontrolliert wird.

Unabhängig von der konkreten Rechtsformvariante werden Direktoren an ihrer allgemeinen Sorgfaltspflicht gemessen, wenn sie von der gesetzlich vorgesehenen Kompetenzverteilung abweichen. Gibt es ein internes Kontrollsystem, muss dieses den gesetzlichen Anforderungen genügen und es setzt gleichzeitig den Rahmen für die Delegation von Entscheidungen. Im Falle eines Verstoßes gegen die genannten Grundsätze kommt je nach Verschuldensgrad eine Haftung der Direktoren bzw. Geschäftsführer gegenüber der Gesellschaft und Dritte in Betracht.

Literaturverzeichnis

Baum, Harald/*Bälz*, Moritz (Hrsg.): Handbuch des Japanischen Handels- und Wirtschaftsrechts (2011).

Egashira, Kenjirō/*Nakamura*, Naoto: 論点会社法 *(ronten kaishahō*, Issues in Corporate Law), 2. Auflage (2021), Bd. 3.

Goette, Wulf/*Habersack*, Mathias/*Kalss*, Susanne (Hrsg.): Münchener Kommentar zum Aktiengesetz, 6. Auflage (2023).

Hölters, Wolfgang/*Weber*, Markus (Hrsg.): AktG, 4. Auflage (2022).

Kanda, Hideki: 会社法 (*kaishahō*, Gesellschaftsrecht), 26. Auflage (2024).

Kondo, Mitsuo, 最新株式会社法 (*saishin kabushiki kaishahō*, Aktuelles Recht der Aktiengesellschaften), 9. Auflage (2020).

Meckel, Verena: Die Corporate Governance im neuen japanischen Gesellschaftsrecht unter besonderer Berücksichtigung der Aufgaben von Verwaltungs- und Prüferrat, in: Zeitschrift für Japanisches Recht, Heft Nr. 29 (2019), S. 53 ff.

Menkhaus, Heinrich: Allgemeines Gesellschaftsrecht in Japan, in: Menkhaus, Heinrich/Sato, Fumihiko (Hrsg.): Japanischer Brückenbauer zum deutschen Rechtskreis, Festschrift für Koresuke Yamauchi zum 60. Geburtstag (2006).

Nagashima Ohno & Tsunematsu, NO&T Legal Update No. 1, May 2015 (2015), https://www.noandt.com/wp-content/uploads/2019/09/japan_no01_1.pdf.

Oka, Nobuhiro, 株式会社法 (*kabushiki kaishahō*, Recht der Aktiengesellschaften), 2. Auflage (2023).

Welche gesetzlichen Kündigungsfristen gelten für das Anstellungsverhältnis des Geschäftsführers einer GmbH?

Scire leges non hoc est verba earum tenere, sed vim ac potestatem.

Celsus, Dig. 1, 3, 17

Von *Karsten Haase*

Karsten Haase ist Rechtsanwalt und Fachanwalt für Arbeitsrecht in Düsseldorf. Neben seiner seit 2007 andauernden Tätigkeit als Lehrbeauftragter für Arbeits- und Wirtschaftsrecht (zuletzt an der Hochschule Düsseldorf) sowie als Referent auf nationalen und internationalen Tagungen ist er ebenso seit vielen Jahren publizistisch tätig, insbesondere zu arbeitsrechtlichen Themenstellungen sowie zu solchen des Rechts der GmbH und ihres Geschäftsführers. Als das geschäftsführende Mitglied des Vorstands der Deutsch-Japanischen Gesellschaft für Arbeitsrecht e. V. trägt er zudem seit 2016 regelmäßig auf Veranstaltungen in Deutschland und Japan vor und veröffentlicht zu rechtsvergleichenden Themen des deutschen und japanischen Arbeitsrechts.

I. Einleitung

Die jahrzehntelange Diskussion um den (arbeits-)rechtlichen Status des Geschäftsführers[1] ist Legende. Sie wird seit jeher kontrovers in Rechtsprechung und Literatur geführt – national und seit längerer Zeit auch unionsrechtlich.[2]

Eng mit dieser Diskussion war und ist die nicht minder kontrovers diskutierte Frage verbunden, ob sich der Geschäftsführer auch auf Arbeitnehmerschutzvorschriften berufen kann. Im Laufe der Jahre entwickelte sich hierzu in der Rechtsprechung des EuGH, des BAG und des BGH sowie in der Literatur jedenfalls im Hinblick auf das Anstellungsverhältnis des Fremdgeschäftsführers und des Minderheitsgesellschafter-Geschäftsführers ohne beherrschenden Einfluss auf die Gesellschafterversammlung ein umstrittener, dafür aber doch bunter Strauß an Kasuistik. Diese Kasu-

1 Gemeint ist immer der Geschäftsführer einer GmbH.

2 *Preis/Sagan*, Der GmbH-Geschäftsführer in der arbeits- und diskriminierungsrechtlichen Rechtsprechung des EuGH, BGH und BAG, in: ZGR (2013), S. 26, 27 ff.; *Junker*, Die Einflüsse des europäischen Rechts auf die personelle Reichweite des Arbeitnehmerschutzes – Der Arbeitnehmerbegriff in der Rechtsprechung des Europäischen Gerichtshofes, in: EuZA (2016), S. 184 ff.; *Boemke*, Aktuelles zum GmbH-Geschäftsführer aus arbeitsrechtlicher Sicht, in: RdA, (2018), S. 1 ff.; *Schubert*, Arbeitnehmerschutz für GmbH-Geschäftsführer, in: ZESAR (2013), S. 5, 7 ff.; *Altmeppen*, Der GmbH-Geschäftsführer als unabhängiger Treuhänder der Allgemeinheit, in: NJW (2022), S. 2785 ff.

Duncker & Humblot · Berlin | https://doi.org/10.3790/978-3-428-59611-9.2025.426870

istik reicht von der Anwendbarkeit der RL 92/85/EWG (Mutterschutzrichtrichtlinie)[3] auf die schwangere Fremdgeschäftsführerin[4] über die Anwendbarkeit der RL 98/59/EG (Massenentlassungsrichtlinie)[5] auf den Fremdgeschäftsführer[6], die Anwendbarkeit des BUrlG auf den Fremdgeschäftsführer[7] und weiter über die Anwendbarkeit des diskriminierungsrechtlichen Kündigungsschutzes nach dem AGG wegen des Lebensalters des Fremdgeschäftsführers,[8] die Anwendbarkeit des diskriminierungsrechtlichen Kündigungsschutzes nach dem AGG oder des besonderen Kündigungsschutzes nach dem SGB IX auf den (schwer-)behinderten Fremdgeschäftsführer,[9] bis hin zum Ausgleich für die vom Fremdgeschäftsführer geleistete Nachtarbeit in Form von Zuschlägen oder Freizeit.[10] Diese Spannbreite ist beachtlich.[11]

---

3 RL 92/85/EWG des Rates vom 19. Oktober 1992 über die Durchführung von Maßnahmen zur Verbesserung der Sicherheit und des Gesundheitsschutzes von schwangeren Arbeitnehmerinnen, Wöchnerinnen und stillenden Arbeitnehmerinnen am Arbeitsplatz, (Mutterschutzrichtlinie), ABl. Nr. L 348, 28. November 1992, 1 ff.

4 EuGH, Urteil v. 11. November 2000 – Danosa, C-232/09, ECLI:EU:C:2010:674.

5 RL 98/59/EG des Rates vom 20. Juli 1998 zur Angleichung der Rechtsvorschriften der Mitgliedsstaaten über Massenentlassungen, ABl. Nr. L 225, 12. August 1998, 16 ff.

6 EuGH, Urteil v. 9. Juli 2015 – Balkaya, C-229/14, ECLI:EU:C:2015:455.

7 BAG, Urteil v. 25. Juli 2023 – 9 AZR 43/22, NZA (2023), S. 1533 ff.: Anwendbarkeit des auf Art. 7 RL 2003/88/EG des Europäischen Parlaments und des Rates vom 4. November 2003 über bestimmte Aspekte der Arbeitszeitgestaltung, ABl. Nr. L 299, 18. November 2003 beruhenden BUrlG auf den Fremdgeschäftsführer, so z. B. bezüglich der Urlaubsabgeltung nach § 7 Abs. 4 BUrlG, der entsprechend richtlinienkonform auszulegen sei; vgl. hierzu auch *Werner*, Anwendung des Bundesurlaubsgesetzes auf den GmbH-Geschäftsführer, in: NZA (2025), S. 685 ff.; noch ohne Bezug auf das Unionsrecht *Haase*, Der Erholungsurlaub des Geschäftsführers einer GmbH aus rechtlicher Sicht, in: GmbHR (2005), S. 265 ff. und S. 338 ff.

8 BGH, Urteil v. 26. März 2019 – II ZR 244/17, NJW (2019), S. 2086, Rn. 17 ff. mit Anm. *Lunk*: Fremdgeschäftsführer bei europarechtskonformer Auslegung insoweit Arbeitnehmer im Sinne von § 6 Abs. 1 Nr. 1 AGG, wie bei einer Kündigung seines Geschäftsführeranstellungsverhältnisses der sachliche Anwendungsbereich des AGG über § 2 Abs. 1 Nr. 2 AGG eröffnet ist und somit der diskriminierungsrechtliche Kündigungsschutz zumindest wegen des Alters im Sinne von § 1 AGG.

9 Vgl. zur Anwendbarkeit des diskriminierungsrechtlichen Kündigungsschutzes nach dem AGG auf den (schwer-)behinderten Fremdgeschäftsführer eingehend *Haase*, Der diskriminierungsrechtliche Kündigungsschutz des (schwer-)behinderten oder einem solchen gleichgestellten Geschäftsführers einer GmbH nach dem AGG und dem SGB IX im Lichte der Rechtsprechung des EuGH, des BGH und des BAG, in: Düwell/Gallner/Haase/Wolmerath (Hrsg.), Auf dem Weg zu einem sozialen und inklusiven Rechtsstaat – Covid-19 als Herausforderung, Liber Amicorum Franz Josef Düwell (2021), S. 327 ff.; vgl. zur Anwendbarkeit des besonderen Kündigungsschutzes nach dem SGB IX auf den schwerbehinderten Fremdgeschäftsführer ausführlich *Haase*, Der besondere Kündigungsschutz eines schwerbehinderten Geschäftsführers einer GmbH i. S. d. §§ 168, 174 Abs. 1 SGB IX – Eine Bewertung nach deutschem und europäischem Recht unter Berücksichtigung der Milkova-Entscheidung des EuGH, in: GmbHR (2019), S. 980 ff.

10 *Günther-Gräff*, Der GmbH-Geschäftsführer und § 6 Abs. 5 ArbZG, in: Jacobs/Kiel/Oberthür/Oetker/Schubert (Hrsg.), Arbeitsrecht in Praxis und Wissenschaft, Festschrift für Stefan Lunk (2025), S. 141 ff.

11 Vgl. hierzu auch den Überblick über den aktuellen Stand der Diskussion zu den auf den Geschäftsführer anwendbaren Arbeitnehmerschutzvorschriften bei *Simon/Schulze/Brandhoff/Lücke*, in: Saenger/Inhester (Hrsg.), GmbHG, Handkommentar, 5. Aufl. (2024), § 35 GmbHG Rn. 63 f.; *Jaeger/Steinbrück*, in: Fleischer/Goette (Hrsg.), Münchener Kommentar zum Gesetz

II. Problemstellung

Gehören in diese Kasuistik an umstrittenen Arbeitnehmerschutzvorschriften zu Gunsten des Geschäftsführers auch die gesetzlichen Kündigungsfristen für Arbeitsverhältnisse, die analog § 622 BGB auf sein Anstellungsverhältnis zur Anwendung gelangen sollen? Oder doch die gesetzlichen Kündigungsfristen nach § 621 BGB, die für Dienstverhältnisse gelten, die keine Arbeitsverhältnisse im Sinne des § 622 BGB sind?

In der bisherigen Rechtsprechung des BGH und der ihm folgenden Literatur wird seit Jahrzehnten die Ansicht vertreten, dass aufgrund einer planwidrigen Gesetzeslücke die gesetzlichen Kündigungsfristen des für Arbeitsverhältnisse geltenden § 622 Abs. 1 und Abs. 2 BGB in analoger Heranziehung auf das Anstellungsverhältnis des Fremdgeschäftsführers oder Minderheitsgesellschafter-Geschäftsführers Anwendung finden.[12] Dies muss verwundern, wird doch nach ständiger Rechtsprechung gerade des BGH und der ihm folgenden Literatur eben dieses Anstellungsverhältnis als freies Dienstverhältnis mit Geschäftsbesorgungscharakter nach §§ 611, 675 BGB und nicht als Arbeitsverhältnis definiert.[13] Das BAG hingegen hat erstmals im Jahr 2020 Gelegenheit gehabt, zu dieser Frage Stellung zu nehmen und diese dahingehend beantwortet, dass für das Anstellungsverhältnis eines jeden Geschäftsführers, also auch für das des Fremdgeschäftsführers, die gesetzlichen Kündigungsfristen des § 621 BGB maßgeblich sein sollen, also die für Dienstverhältnisse, die keine Arbeitsverhältnisse im Sinne des § 622 BGB darstellen.[14]

Der Kern dieser Auseinandersetzung ist nicht – wie so oft – die Frage nach dem Status des Geschäftsführers. Arbeitnehmer nach nationalem Recht bzw. Unionsrecht oder freier Dienstnehmer? Eine Verkürzung auf die Formel „Arbeitsverhältnis dann § 622 BGB, freies Dienstverhältnis dann § 621 BGB“ wird der Problematik nicht gerecht. Denn Dreh- und Angelpunkt zur Klärung dieser Auseinandersetzung ist die Frage, ob die vom BGH propagierte planwidrige Gesetzeslücke existiert und wenn ja, im Rahmen welcher Analogie sie zu schließen ist.

Ausgangspunkt für die vorliegende Erörterung soll die erst kürzlich veröffentlichte Entscheidung des BGH vom 5. November 2024[15] sein, mit der der Zweite Zivilsenat

---

betreffend die Gesellschaften mit beschränkter Haftung, 4. Aufl. (2023), § 35 GmbHG Rn. 295 ff.

12 Zuletzt BGH, Urteil v. 5. November 2024 – II ZR 35/23, NZG (2025), S. 663 Rn. 45 f. m. w. N.

13 Vgl. III. 1. b) aa), Anm. 28 und 29.

14 BAG, Urteil v. 11. Juni 2020 – 2 AZR 374/19, NJW (2020), S. 2824 Rn. 35 ff.

15 BGH, Urteil v. 5. November 2024 – II ZR 35/23, AP BGB § 622 Nr. 80; vgl. hierzu *Haase*, Fristen für die außerordentliche sowie ordentliche Kündigung des Anstellungsverhältnisses eine GmbH-Geschäftsführers, in: LMK (2025), S. 810482; *Werner*, Die Fristen für die Kündigung des Geschäftsführers einer GmbH & Co. KG – zugleich Anmerkung zum Urteil des BGH vom 5. November 2024 – II ZR 35/23, in: BB (2025), S. 760 ff.; *Hackethal*, Kündigungsfrist von (Fremd-)Geschäftsführern – Anwendung von § 622 BGB, in: BB (2025), S. 703 f.; *Henssler*, Zur Frist für Kündigung des Anstellungsvertrages eines GmbH-Geschäftsführers, in: ZIP (2025), S. 562 f.; *Arnold*, Geltung der Kündigungsfristen nach § 622 Abs. 1, Abs. 2 BGB für Geschäftsführerverträge, in: FD-ArbR (2025), S. 802392; *Ante*, Fristen

des BGH in ausdrücklicher Abgrenzung zur Rechtsprechung des Zweiten Senats des BAG[16] erneut und in ständiger Rechtsprechung – aber erneut und in ständiger Rechtsprechung falsch und contra legem – die Meinung vertritt, dass auf Anstellungsverhältnisse „von Geschäftsführern, die keine Mehrheitsgesellschafter sind, die zum Nachteil des Geschäftsführers grundsätzlich nicht abdingbaren (§ 622 Abs. 4, 5 BGB) Kündigungsfristen für Arbeitsverhältnisse (§ 622 Abs. 1 und Abs. 1 BGB) entsprechend anzuwenden sind"[17] und nicht die – je nach Sachverhalt erheblich kürzeren – nach § 621 BGB, die für Dienstverhältnisse gelten, die keine Arbeitsverhältnisse im Sinne des § 622 BGB sind.[18]

III. Status des Geschäftsführers einer GmbH

Zum besseren Verständnis soll zunächst ein kurzer Überblick über die aktuelle Diskussion zum Status des Geschäftsführers gegeben werden. Bei der Bewertung des Status des Geschäftsführers und somit auch der Rechtsnatur seines Anstellungsverhältnisses ist zwischen dem nationalen Recht und dem Unionsrecht zu unterscheiden.

1. Status des Geschäftsführers einer GmbH nach nationalem Recht

Der Streit darüber, ob und unter welchen Bedingungen der Geschäftsführer persönlich abhängiger Arbeitnehmer in einem weisungsgebundenen Arbeitsverhältnis nach § 611a BGB oder doch selbständiger Dienstnehmer im Rahmen eines freien Dienstverhältnisses mit Geschäftsbesorgungscharakter nach §§ 611, 675 BGB ist, ist im deutschen Recht seit Jahrzehnten Gegenstand kontroverser Auseinandersetzungen in der höchstrichterlichen Rechtsprechung des BGH und BAG und den ihnen jeweils folgenden Teilen der Literatur.[19]

a) Begriff des Arbeitnehmers nach nationalem Recht

In ständiger Rechtsprechung definierte das BAG[20] und die ihm folgende Literatur[21] den gesetzlich nicht geregelten Begriff des Arbeitnehmers als eine natürliche Person,

für die Kündigung des Anstellungsvertrages eines GmbH-Geschäftsführers, in: GWR (2025), S. 14; *Jenne/Sprösser*, Kündigungsfristen für Geschäftsführer: Der BGH bleibt seiner Linie treu, in: BB (2025), S. 596; *Schirrmacher*, Zur Frist für die Kündigung des Anstellungsvertrags eines GmbH-Geschäftsführers – Anmerkung zu BGH v. 5. 11. 2024 – II ZR 35/23, in: GmbHR (2025), S. 299 ff.

16 BAG, Urteil v. 11. Juni 2020 – 2 AZR 374/19, NJW (2020), S. 2824 Rn. 35 ff.

17 BGH, Urteil v. 5. November 2024 – II ZR 35/23, NZG (2025), S. 663 Rn. 45 m. w. N.

18 So aber BAG, Urteil v. 11. Juni 2020 – 2 AZR 374/19, NJW (2020), S. 2824 Rn. 35 ff.

19 Vgl. den Überblick bei *Preis/Sagan* (Anm. 2), S. 27 ff.; *Boemke* (Anm. 2), S. 1 ff.; *Haase* (Anm. 9), S. 981 f.

20 Statt vieler BAG, Urteil v. 10. April 1991 – 4 AZR 467/90, NZA (1991), S. 856, 857; BAG, Beschluss v. 16. Februar 2000 – 5 AZB 71/99, NZA (2000), S. 385, 387; BAG, Beschluss v. 26. September 2002 – 5 AZB 19/01, NZA (2002), S. 1412, 1414.

21 Vgl. statt vieler nur *Spinner*, in: Henssler/Krüger (Redakteure), Münchener Kommentar zum Bürgerlichen Gesetzbuch, Band 5, 9. Aufl. (2023), § 611a BGB Rn. 88.

die aufgrund eines privatrechtlichen Vertrags in den Diensten eines anderen zur Leistung weisungsgebundener, fremdbestimmter Arbeit in persönlicher Abhängigkeit verpflichtet ist.

Der Gesetzgeber goss diese über Jahrzehnte gewachsene Definition sodann in die Kodifikation des § 611a Abs. 1 BGB, der zwar nur den Begriff des Arbeitsvertrages definiert, auf diese Weise jedoch zugleich auch implizit den des Arbeitnehmers. Der Gesetzgeber rekurrierte dabei auf die Kasuistik der Arbeitsrechtsprechung.[22] § 611a BGB, der am 1. April 2017 in Kraft getreten ist,[23] enthält daher nun die Legaldefinition des Begriffs des Arbeitsvertrages und damit zeitgleich implizit auch den des Begriffs des Arbeitnehmers.[24]

§ 611a BGB ist, wie Preis es zutreffend formuliert, „der Schlüssel für die Anwendung des Arbeitsrechts".[25] Der Zweck der Vorschrift ist, den abhängigen Arbeitsvertrag von dem freien Dienstvertrag abzugrenzen. Hinter dieser Abgrenzung steht, wie Preis es abermals zutreffend festhält, die „Globalmaxime der Schutzbedürftigkeit des Arbeitnehmers".[26]

b) Geschäftsführer einer GmbH als Arbeitnehmer nach nationalem Recht

Der BGH, das BAG und die ihnen jeweils folgenden Stimmen in der Literatur sind sich in der Bewertung des rechtlichen Status des Geschäftsführers weitestgehend einig, dass es sich bei diesem um einen freien Dienstnehmer und bei seinem Anstellungsverhältnis um ein freies Dienstverhältnis mit Geschäftsbesorgungscharakter nach §§ 611, 675 BGB handelt. Von dieser gemeinsamen Linie weicht das BAG in zwei seltenen Ausnahmesachverhalten ab.[27]

---

22 *Preis/Greiner*, in: Müller-Glöge/Preis/Gallner/Schmidt (Hrsg.), Erfurter Kommentar zum Arbeitsrecht, 25. Aufl. (2025), § 611a BGB Rn. 9; vgl. auch *Joussen*, in: Rolfs/Giesen/Meßling/Udsching (Hrsg.), BeckOK Arbeitsrecht, 76. Edition (2025), § 611a BGB Rn. 5.

23 Art. 2 des Gesetzes zur Änderung des Arbeitnehmerüberlassungsgesetzes und anderer Gesetze vom 21. Februar 2017, BGBl. 2017 Teil I, 258.

24 *Preis/Greiner* (Anm. 22), § 611a BGB Rn. 3 und 8; vgl. auch *Joussen* (Anm. 22), § 611a BGB Rn. 4 und 7; vgl. zur Kritik an § 611a BGB statt vieler *Preis/Greiner* (Anm. 22), § 611a BGB Rn. 9 ff.; aber auch *Preis*, § 611a BGB – Potenziale des Arbeitnehmerbegriffs, in: NZA (2018), S. 817 ff.

25 *Preis/Greiner* (Anm. 22), § 611a BGB Rn. 3.

26 *Preis/Greiner* (Anm. 22), § 611a BGB Rn. 3.

27 Soweit ersichtlich wird eine ältere arbeitsrechtlich geprägte Mindermeinung (vgl. die Hinweise bei *Wank/Maties*, Arbeitnehmer oder Gesellschaftsorgan oder Vereinsmitglied?, in: NZA (2007), S. 353, 354 m. w. N. in dortiger Fn. 9; *Preis/Sagan* (Anm. 2), S. 26, 27 m. w. N. in dortiger Fn. 1), die mit unterschiedlichen Begründungen davon ausging, dass das Anstellungsverhältnis eines Fremdgeschäftsführers bzw. das eines Minderheitsgesellschafter-Geschäftsführers ohne beherrschenden Einfluss auf die Gesellschafterversammlung ein Arbeitsverhältnis darstelle, nicht mehr vertreten. Im Kern hat diese Mindermeinung dahingehend argumentiert, dass solche Geschäftsführer aufgrund § 37 Abs. 1 GmbHG einem Arbeitnehmer vergleichbar den Weisungen der GmbH unterlägen und sie ähnlich einem Arbeitnehmer sozial schutzbedürftig seien.

aa) Gesellschaftsrechtlich orientierte Sichtweise des BGH und der ihm folgenden Literatur

Der BGH[28] und die ihm folgenden Stimmen in der Literatur[29] argumentieren, dass das Anstellungsverhältnis eines jeden Geschäftsführers ausnahmslos ein freies Dienstverhältnis mit Geschäftsbesorgungscharakter nach §§ 611, 675 BGB darstelle und der Geschäftsführer als freier Dienstnehmer zu bewerten sei. Der Geschäftsführer sei nach § 35 Abs. 1 GmbHG das Vertretungsorgan der GmbH. Aufgrund dieser Organstellung komme ihm die oberste arbeitsrechtliche Weisungsbefugnis innerhalb der GmbH zu, weshalb er auch sämtliche Pflichten der GmbH als Arbeitgeber i. S. d. Arbeits- und Sozialrechts für die GmbH wahrnehme. Dies schließe einen Status als Arbeitnehmer aus, der den Geschäftsführer ansonsten zum Adressaten arbeitsrechtlicher Weisungen werden ließe. Weisungen der GmbH nach § 37 Abs. 1 GmbHG konkretisierten lediglich seine Pflichten als deren Vertretungsorgan, ohne dass hierdurch ein Wechsel vom Status des Organvertreters hin zu dem eines Arbeitnehmers eintreten könne.

bb) Differenzierende Sichtweise des BAG und der ihm folgenden Literatur

In Übereinstimmung mit der Rechtsprechung des BGH und seiner Begründung gehen das BAG[30] und die ihm folgenden Stimmen in der Literatur[31] ebenfalls regelmäßig davon aus, dass das Anstellungsverhältnis des Geschäftsführers als ein freies Dienstverhältnis mit Geschäftsbesorgungscharakter nach §§ 611, 675 BGB zu bewerten sei, sodass der Geschäftsführer als freier Dienstnehmer tätig werde.

Von der Rechtsprechung des BGH unterscheidet sich die des BAG allerdings dadurch, dass das BAG zwei Situationen anerkennt, in denen das Anstellungsverhältnis

---

28 BGH, Urteil v. 9. November 1967 – II ZR 64/67, BGHZ 49, 30, 31 f.; BGH, Urteil v. 9. Februar 1978 – II ZR 189/76, NJW (1978), S. 1435, 1436; BGH, Urteil v. 29. Januar 1981 – II ZR 92/80, BGHZ 79, 291, 292 f.; BGH, Urteil v. 26. März 1984 – II ZR 220/82, BGHZ 91, 1, 3; BGH, Urteil v. 10. Mai 2010 – II ZR 70/09, Rn. 7; BGH, Urteil v. 26. März 2019 – II ZR 244/17, Rn. 27; s. auch OLG Düsseldorf, Urteil v. 18. Oktober 2012 – I-6 U 47/12, GmbHR (2012), S. 1347, 1349 ff.; OLG Hamm, Urteil v. 26. April 2007 – 27 U 7/07, GmbHR (2007), S. 820, 821 m. Komm. *Haase*; vgl. auch *Jaeger/Steinbrück* (Anm. 11), § 35 GmbHG Rn. 292 m. w. N.

29 *Jaeger/Steinbrück* (Anm. 11), § 35 GmbHG Rn. 278 f.; *Kleindiek*, in: Lutter/Hommelhoff (Hrsg.), GmbH-Gesetz, 21. Aufl. (2023), Anh. zu § 6 GmbHG Rn. 3a; *Lenz*, in: Michalski/Heidinger/Leible/Schmidt (Hrsg.), Kommentar zum Gesetz betreffend die Gesellschaften mit beschränkter Haftung (GmbH-Gesetz), 4. Aufl. (2023), § 35 GmbHG Rn. 120; *Beurskens*, in: Noack/Servatius/Haas (Hrsg.), Gesetz betreffend die Gesellschaften mit beschränkter Haftung, 24. Aufl. (2025), § 37 GmbHG Rn. 102 f.; *Oetker*, in: Henssler/Strohn (Hrsg.), Gesellschaftsrecht, 6. Aufl. (2024), § 35 GmbHG Rn. 103 f.; *Altmeppen*, in: Altmeppen, Gesetz betreffend die Gesellschaften mit beschränkter Haftung, 11. Aufl. (2023), § 6 GmbHG Rn. 79, 83; jedenfalls im Regelfall *Hohenstatt*, in: Scholz (Hrsg.), Kommentar zum GmbH-Gesetz, II. Band, 13. Aufl. (2024), § 35 GmbHG Rn. 264.

30 BAG, Urteil v. 26. Mai 1999 – 5 AZR 664/98, NZA (1999), S. 987, 989; BAG, Urteil v. 24. November 2005 – 2 AZR 614/04, NZA (2006), S. 366 Rn. 18; BAG, Beschluss v. 21. Januar 2019 – 9 AZB 23/18, Rn. 24, (LS) BB (2019), S. 1683 m. Komm. *Haase*; OLG München, Urteil v. 16. Mai 2007 – 14 U 399/04, NZA-RR (2007), S. 579, 580; vgl. auch *Jaeger/Steinbrück* (Anm. 11), § 35 GmbHG Rn. 293 m. w. N.

31 *Preis/Greiner* (Anm. 22), § 611a BGB Rn. 95; *Oetker* (Anm. 29), § 35 GmbHG Rn. 104; *Düwell*, in: Dau/Düwell/Joussen/Luik (Hrsg.), Sozialgesetzbuch IX, 6. Aufl. (2021), Rn. 5.

des Geschäftsführers als ein Arbeitsverhältnis im Sinne des § 611a BGB und der Geschäftsführer als ein persönlich abhängig und weisungsgebunden beschäftigter Arbeitnehmer zu charakterisieren sein soll:

Zum einen in extremen Ausnahmefällen dann, wenn abweichend von der Bezeichnung des Vertrages als Dienstvertrag aufgrund seiner tatsächlichen Durchführung kein Dienstverhältnis mit Geschäftsbesorgungscharakter nach § 611, § 675 BGB gegeben sei, sondern ein Arbeitsverhältnis nach § 611a BGB, das Geschäftsführeranstellungsverhältnis also tatsächlich als Arbeitsverhältnis gelebt werde und dann auch als solches zu bewerten sei. In solchen extremen Ausnahmefällen, an die hohe Anforderungen zu stellen seien, sei der Geschäftsführer dann Arbeitnehmer der GmbH, wenn der GmbH ihm gegenüber eine über ihr gesellschaftsrechtliches Weisungsrecht hinausgehende Weisungsbefugnis auch bzgl. der Umstände zukomme, unter denen der Geschäftsführer seine Leistung zu erbringen habe, und durch arbeitsbegleitende und verfahrensorientierte Weisungen – wie im Fall des § 106 GewO – die konkreten Modalitäten der Leistungserbringung bestimmen könne.[32]

Zum anderen soll nach Ansicht des BAG die Möglichkeit bestehen, dass als Grundlage für die Tätigkeit als Geschäftsführer auch ausdrücklich ein Arbeitsverhältnis vereinbart werden könne. Die Tätigkeit des Geschäftsführers als Vertretungsorgan der GmbH nach § 35 GmbHG beruhe dann auf diesem Arbeitsverhältnis, weshalb der Geschäftsführer in diesem Fall auch als Arbeitnehmer zu charakterisieren sei. Auf die tatsächliche Durchführung des Arbeitsverhältnisses komme es dann nicht (mehr) an. Dies folge aus der Privatautonomie der GmbH und ihres Geschäftsführers.[33] Denn Kraft der garantierten Vertragsfreiheit können die Parteien auch unter Geltung von § 611a BGB, obgleich die tatsächliche Vertragsdurchführung die Vereinbarung eines freien Dienstverhältnisses erlaubte, wirksam ein Arbeitsverhältnis begründen.[34]

2. Status des Geschäftsführers einer GmbH nach Unionsrecht

Die Diskussion um den rechtlichen Status des Geschäftsführers hat auf unionsrechtlicher Ebene seit den Danosa-, Balkaya- und Holterman-Judikaten des

32 BAG, Urteil v. 26. Mai 1999 – 5 AZR 664/98, NZA (1999), S. 987, 989; BAG, Urteil v. 24. November 2005 – 2 AZR 614/04, Rn. 18, GmbHR (2006), S. 592 m. Komm. *Haase*; BAG, Beschluss v. 21. Januar 2019 – 9 AZB 23/18, Rn. 24, (LS) BB (2019), S. 1683 m. Komm. *Haase*; BAG, Beschluss v. 8. Februar 2022 – 9 AZB 40/21, NZA (2022), S. 430; BAG, Urteil v. 20. 07. 2023 – 6 AZR 228/22, NZA (2023), S. 1457, 1459; vgl. auch OLG München, Urteil v. 16. Mai 2007 – 14 U 399/04, NZA – RR (2007), S. 579, 580; vgl. auch *Jaeger/Steinbrück* (Anm. 11), § 35 GmbHG Rn. 293; *Günther-Gräff* (Anm. 10), S. 141 f.

33 BAG, Urteil v. 17. Juni 2020 – 7 AZR 398/18, NZA (2020), S. 1470, 1471; BAG, Urteil v. 18. März 2014 – 9 AZR 740/13, BeckRS (2014), S. 70030; BAG, Beschluss vom 25. Januar 2007 – 5 AZB 49/06, NZA (2007), S. 580, Rn. 12; *Günther-Gräff* (Anm. 10), S. 141, 142.

34 BAG, Urteil v. 21. April 2005 – 2 AZR 125/04, AP KSchG 1969 § 1 Betriebsbedingte Kündigung Nr. 134; BAG, Beschluss v. 25. Januar 2007 – 5 AZB 49/06, NZA (2007), S. 580; *Spinner* (Anm. 21), § 611a BGB Rn. 90 m. w. N.; *Stoffels*, Statusvereinbarungen im Arbeitsrecht, in: NZA (2000), S. 690, 695.

EuGH[35] eine neue und bis dahin ungeahnte Dynamik erhalten.[36] Hat der EuGH in diesen Entscheidungen doch konstatiert, dass Fremd- und Minderheitsgesellschafter-Geschäftsführer ohne beherrschenden Einfluss auf die Gesellschafterversammlung unter Beachtung des autonomen unionsrechtlichen Arbeitnehmerbegriffs im Sinne des Art. 45 AEUV als unionsrechtliche Arbeitnehmer der GmbH qualifiziert werden können.

a) Unionsrechtlicher Arbeitnehmerbegriff

Ein einheitlicher unionsrechtlicher Begriff des Arbeitnehmers ist weder im Primär- noch im Sekundärrecht der EU existent.[37] Vielmehr wird in den jeweiligen Unionsrechtsakten zur Bestimmung des Personenkreises der Arbeitnehmer differenziert:[38] Der jeweilige Unionsrechtsakt, z. B. eine unionsrechtliche Richtlinie, kann zur Bestimmung des in ihm verwendeten Begriffs des Arbeitnehmers auf das jeweilige nationale Recht der Mitgliedsstaaten der EU verweisen, der Begriff des Arbeitnehmers für seinen Geltungsbereich selbst definieren oder aber auch diesen lediglich verwenden, ohne ihn selbst zu definieren oder zur Begriffsbestimmung auf das nationale Recht zu verweisen.[39] So ist anhand des jeweiligen Unionsrechtsakts zunächst zu ermitteln, von welchem Begriff des Arbeitnehmers er ausgeht, um sodann zu überprüfen, ob ein Geschäftsführer unter diesen subsumiert werden kann.

b) Primärrechtlicher autonomer Arbeitnehmerbegriff nach Art. 45 AEUV

Wird in einer Richtlinie der Begriff des Arbeitnehmers lediglich verwendet, ohne ihn selbst zu definieren oder zur Begriffsbestimmung auf das nationale Recht zu verweisen, so geht der EuGH davon aus, dass dieser sodann autonom zu bestimmen sei. Hierzu rekurriert er in seiner einschlägigen Rechtsprechung regelmäßig auf den Arbeitnehmerbegriff aus dem Recht der Arbeitnehmerfreizügigkeit nach Art. 45 AEUV[40], den er seit seinem richtungsweisenden Lawrie-Blum-Judikat[41] in ständiger Rechtsprechung geprägt hat. Bei diesem Arbeitnehmerbegriff handelt es sich um ei-

---

35 EuGH, Urteil v. 11. November 2010 – Danosa, C-232/09, ECLI:EU:C:2010:674; EuGH, Urteil v. 9. Juli 2015 – Balkaya, C-229/14, ECLI:EU:C:2015:455; EuGH, Urteil v. 10. September 2015 – Holterman, C-47/14, ECLI:EU:C:2015:574.

36 Vgl. nur *Preis/Sagan* (Anm. 2), S. 26 ff.; *Junker* (Anm. 2), S. 184 ff.; *Boemke* (Anm. 2), S. 1 ff.

37 Statt vieler *Schneider/Wunderlich*, in: Becker/Hatje/Schoo/Schwarze (Hrsg.), EU-Kommentar, 4. Aufl. (2019), Art. 45 AEUV Rn. 10.

38 OLG Düsseldorf, Urteil v. 16. Oktober 2012 – 6 U 47/12, BB (2013), S. 1403, 1405; *Jaeger/Steinbrück* (Anm. 11), § 35 GmbHG Rn. 294; *Hohenstatt* (Anm. 29), § 35 GmbHG Rn. 276; *Rebhahn*, Die Arbeitnehmerbegriffe des Unionsrechts in der neueren Judikatur des EuGH, in: EuZA (2012), S. 3, 5 ff.; *Vielmeier*, GmbH-Geschäftsführer als Arbeitnehmer im Rahmen der Massenentlassungsrichtlinie?, in: NJW (2014), S. 2678, 2679.

39 *Jaeger/Steinbrück* (Anm. 11), § 35 GmbHG Rn. 294; *Wank*, Die personellen Grenzen des Europäischen Arbeitsrechts: Arbeitsrecht für Nicht-Arbeitnehmer, in: EuZA (2008), S. 172, 183 ff. mit einem Überblick über die verschiedenen Arbeitnehmerbegriffe in den einzelnen Richtlinien der EU.

40 Vertrag über die Arbeitsweise der Europäischen Union in der Fassung des Vertrages von Lissabon v. 13. Dezember 2007, ABl. EU Nr. C 306 v. 17. Dezember 2007, S. 1 ff.

41 EuGH, Urteil v. 3. Juli 1986 – Lawrie-Blum, C-66/85; ECLI:EU:C:1986:284; vgl. hierzu *Junker* (Anm. 2), S. 184, 188 ff.

nen autonomen Begriff des Unionsrechts, der für alle Normbereiche, die mit der Arbeitnehmerfreizügigkeit einhergehen, einer einheitlichen unionsrechtlichen Auslegung unterliege.[42] Er sei weit auszulegen und anhand objektiver Kriterien autonom zu definieren, die das Arbeitsverhältnis im Hinblick auf die Rechte und Pflichten der betroffenen Personen kennzeichnen. Das wesentliche Merkmal des Arbeitsverhältnisses bestehe darin, „dass jemand während einer bestimmten Zeit für einen anderen nach dessen Weisung Leistungen erbringt, für die er als Gegenleistung eine Vergütung erhält."[43]

So soll immer dann, wenn ein Unionsrechtsakt in Bezug auf den Arbeitnehmerbegriff selbst keinen Verweis auf nationales Recht oder keine eigenständige Bestimmung des Begriffs des Arbeitnehmers aufweist, dieser primärrechtliche und autonom zu bestimmende unionsrechtliche Arbeitnehmerbegriff im Sinne des Art. 45 AEUV zum Zuge kommen.[44] Faktisch ist dieser Arbeitnehmerbegriff des Art. 45 AEUV zum Arbeitnehmerbegriff des Unionsrechts geworden.[45]

c) Geschäftsführer als unionsrechtlicher Arbeitnehmer

Der EuGH hat bislang in drei Entscheidungen zu der Frage Stellung genommen, ob ein Geschäftsführer unionsrechtlicher Arbeitnehmer sein kann: In seinem Danosa-Judikat[46] zur Anwendbarkeit der RL 92/85/EWG (Mutterschutzrichtlinie)[47] auf die schwangere Fremdgeschäftsführerin, in seinem Balkaya-Judikat[48] zur Anwendbarkeit der RL 98/59/EG (Massenentlassungsrichtlinie)[49] auf den Fremdgeschäftsführer und in seinem Holterman-Judikat[50] zur Anwendbarkeit der VO (EG) Nr. 44/2001 (gerichtliche Zuständigkeit und die Anerkennung und Vollstreckung von Entschei-

42 *Fuchs/Marhold*, Europäisches Arbeitsrecht, 4. Aufl., 2014, S. 55 ff.; *Preis/Greiner* (Anm. 22), § 611a BGB Rn. 18; *Steinmeyer*, in: Franzen/Gallner/Oetker (Hrsg.), Kommentar zum Europäischen Arbeitsrecht, 5. Aufl. (2024), Art. 45 AEUV Rn. 10.

43 EuGH, Urteil v. 3. Juli 1986 – Lawrie-Blum, C-66/85, ECLI:EU:C:1986:284, Rn. 16 f.; vgl. auch EuGH, Urteil v. 13. Januar 2004 – Allonby, C-256/01, ECLI:EU:C:2004:18, Rn. 67; EuGH, Urteil v. 20. September 2007 – Kiiski, C-116/06, ECLI:EU:C:2007:536, Rn. 25; *Schneider/Wunderlich* (Anm. 37), Art. 45 AEUV Rn. 10; *Steinmeyer* (Anm. 42), Art. 45 AEUV Rn. 11; *Epiney*, in: Vedder/Heintschel von Heinegg (Hrsg.), Europäisches Unionsrecht, 2. Aufl. (2018), Art. 45 AEUV Rn. 10; *Fuchs/Marhold* (Anm. 42), S. 55, 57.

44 EuGH, Urteil v. 3. Juli 1986 – Lawrie-Blum, Rs. C-66/85, ECLI:EU:C:1986:284, Rn. 16 f.; EuGH, Urteil v. 23. März 2004 – Collins, Rs. C-138/02, ECLI:EU:C:2004:172, Rn. 26; EuGH, Urteil v. 7. September 2004 – Trojani, C-456/02, ECLI:EU:C:2004:488, Rn. 15; EuGH, Beschluss v. 7. April 2011 – May, Rs. C-519/09, ECLI:EU:C:2011:221, Rn. 22; *Preis/Greiner* (Anm. 22), § 611a Rn. 18; *Hohenstatt* (Anm. 29), § 35 GmbHG Rn. 286 ff.

45 *Preis/Sagan* (Anm. 2), S. 26, 47.

46 EuGH, Urteil v. 11. November 2000 – Danosa, C-232/09, ECLI:EU:C:2010:674.

47 RL 92/85/EWG des Rates vom 19. Oktober 1992 über die Durchführung von Maßnahmen zur Verbesserung der Sicherheit und des Gesundheitsschutzes von schwangeren Arbeitnehmerinnen, Wöchnerinnen und stillenden Arbeitnehmerinnen am Arbeitsplatz, (Mutterschutzrichtlinie), ABl. Nr. L 348, 28. November 1992, 1 ff.

48 EuGH, Urteil v. 9. Juli 2015 – Balkaya, C-229/14, ECLI:EU:C:2015:455.

49 RL 98/59/EG des Rates vom 20. Juli 1998 zur Angleichung der Rechtsvorschriften der Mitgliedsstaaten über Massenentlassungen, ABl. Nr. L 225 vom 12. August 1998, 16 ff.

50 EuGH, Urteil v. 10. September 2015 – Holterman, C-47/14, ECLI:EU:C:2015:574.

dungen in Zivil- und Handelssachen[51]) in Zusammenhang mit einem Minderheitsgesellschafter-Geschäftsführer ohne beherrschenden Einfluss auf die Gesellschafterversammlung.

In allen drei Unionsrechtsakten findet sich in Bezug auf den Arbeitnehmerbegriff selbst weder ein Verweis auf nationales Recht noch eine eigenständige Bestimmung des Begriffs des Arbeitnehmers, sodass der EuGH in allen drei Entscheidungen auf den primärrechtlichen und autonomen unionsrechtlichen Arbeitnehmerbegriff im Sinne des Art. 45 AEUV zurückgriff und sowohl die Fremdgeschäftsführer als auch den Minderheitsgesellschafter-Geschäftsführer ohne beherrschenden Einfluss auf die Gesellschafterversammlung als unionsrechtliche Arbeitnehmer bewertete, sodass hinsichtlich dieser Typen von Geschäftsführern mittlerweile von einer ständigen und gesicherten Rechtsprechung des EuGH ausgegangen werden kann.

IV. Gesetzliche Kündigungsfristen für das Anstellungsverhältnis des Geschäftsführers einer GmbH: unmittelbar nach § 621 BGB oder analog § 622 BGB?

Haben die Parteien des Geschäftsführeranstellungsvertrags keine Kündigungsfristen vereinbart oder lediglich vereinbart, dass die „gesetzlichen Kündigungsfristen" gelten sollen, stellt sich die Frage, welche gesetzlichen Kündigungsfristen auf das Anstellungsverhältnis des Geschäftsführers Anwendung finden. Hierzu besteht in der höchstrichterlichen Rechtsprechung des BGH und des BAG und der ihnen jeweils folgenden Stimmen in der Literatur erheblicher Streit. Hiernach kommen für das BAG und die ihm folgende Literatur lediglich die gesetzlichen Kündigungsfristen nach § 621 BGB in Betracht, also die für Dienstverhältnisse, die keine Arbeitsverhältnisse im Sinne des § 622 BGB sind. Der BGH und die ihm folgende Literatur greifen hingegen auf die gesetzlichen Kündigungsfristen für Arbeitsverhältnisse in analoger Anwendung von § 622 BGB zurück.

1. Prinzipien der Bemessung der Kündigungsfristen nach § 621 BGB und § 622 BGB

Sowohl § 621 BGB als auch § 622 BGB regeln gesetzliche Kündigungsfristen. Deren Bemessung erfolgt jedoch nach unterschiedlichen Prinzipien.

§ 621 BGB regelt die gesetzlichen Kündigungsfristen für ein Dienstverhältnis, das kein Arbeitsverhältnis im Sinne des § 622 BGB ist. Die Dauer dieser Kündigungsfristen orientiert sich gemäß der Staffel des § 621 Nr. 1 bis Nr. 5 BGB in Abhängigkeit davon, nach welchem Zeitabschnitt die Vergütung bemessen ist. Unerheblich ist die Dauer des Dienstverhältnisses oder der Auszahlungsmodus der Vergütung.[52] Ist

---

51 Abl. L 12 v. 16. Januar 2001, 1 ff.; ersetzt durch die VO (EU) Nr. 1215/2012, Verordnung über die gerichtliche Zuständigkeit und die Anerkennung und Vollstreckung von Entscheidungen in Zivil- und Handelssachen, Abl. L 315 v. 20. Dezember 2012, 1 ff.

52 BAG, Urteil v. 11. Juni 2020 – 2 AZR 374/19, NJW (2020), S. 2824 Rn. 47; *Engshuber*, in: Henssler/Krüger (Redakteure), Münchener Kommentar zum Bürgerlichen Gesetzbuch,

z. B. nach § 621 Nr. 1 BGB die Vergütung nach Tagen bemessen, so ist die Kündigung zulässig an jedem Tag für den Ablauf des folgenden Tages. Ist hingegen die Vergütung bspw. nach Monaten bemessen, so ist die Kündigung nach § 621 Nr. 3 BGB spätestens am 15. eines Monats für den Schluss des Kalendermonats zulässig.

§ 622 BGB hingegen regelt die gesetzlichen Kündigungsfristen bei einem Arbeitsverhältnis. Hier knüpft das Gesetz an die Dauer des Arbeitsverhältnisses im Betrieb an, also an die hierdurch vermittelte Dauer der Betriebszugehörigkeit und des hierdurch verdienten sozialen Besitzstandes. Nach § 622 Abs. 1 BGB kann das Arbeitsverhältnis eines Arbeitnehmers in den ersten zwei Jahren des Arbeitsverhältnisses mit einer für beide Arbeitsvertragsparteien geltenden (Grundkündigungs-)Frist von vier Wochen zum Fünfzehnten oder zum Ende eines Kalendermonats gekündigt werden.[53] Für den Fall der Kündigung des Arbeitsverhältnisses durch den Arbeitgeber verlängern sich diese Kündigungsfristen nach Gesetz zugunsten des Arbeitnehmers mit zunehmender Dauer des Arbeitsverhältnisses gemäß der Staffel des § 622 Abs. 2 Nr. 1 bis Nr. 7 BGB von zunächst einem Monat zum Monatsende nach zweijährigem Bestand des Arbeitsverhältnisses auf maximal sieben Monate zum Monatsende nach zwanzigjährigem Bestand.[54] Der Gesetzgeber verfolgt mit § 622 BGB mithin eine soziale Schutzfunktion, insbesondere für ältere Arbeitnehmer, indem er die Kündigungsfristen entsprechend der Dauer des Arbeitsverhältnisses und der damit vom Arbeitnehmer gezeigten Betriebstreue als Teil seines sozialen Besitzstandes verlängert.[55] Für die durch den Arbeitnehmer erklärte Kündigung seines Arbeitsverhältnisses gelten diese verlängerten Kündigungsfristen nach § 622 Abs. 2 BGB nur dann, wenn dies gesondert mit ihm im Wege einer Gleichbehandlungsabrede, z. B. im Arbeitsvertrag, vereinbart wurde.[56]

2. Gesetzliche Kündigungsfristen für das Anstellungsverhältnis des Geschäftsführers einer GmbH und Unionsrecht

Weder die gesetzlichen Kündigungsfristen nach § 621 BGB noch die nach § 622 BGB beruhen auf Unionsrecht. Mit ihnen wird daher kein Unionsrecht in deutsches Recht umgesetzt. Sie sind unionsrechtlich nicht determiniert. Eine unionsrechtliche Regelung, die entsprechende Kündigungsfristen im Sinne des Unionsrechts für persönlich abhängige und weisungsgebundene Arbeitnehmer oder freie Dienstnehmer vorsieht, ist nicht existent. Auch sonst sind keine unionsrechtlichen Regelungen gegeben, die die Anwendung eines unionsrechtlichen Arbeitnehmerbegriffs, so z. B. des primärrechtlichen autonomen Arbeitnehmerbegriffs im Sinne des Art. 45 AEUV, rechtfertigen. Aufgrund dessen ist auch der unionsrechtliche Arbeitnehmerbegriff

Band 5, 9. Aufl. (2023), § 621 BGB Rn. 18; *Müller-Glöge* in: Müller-Glöge/Preis/Gallner/Schmidt (Hrsg.), Erfurter Kommentar zum Arbeitsrecht, 25. Aufl. (2025), § 621 BGB Rn. 6; *Boecken*, in: Boecken/Düwell/Diller/Hanau (Hrsg.), Gesamtes Arbeitsrecht, 2. Aufl. (2023), § 621 BGB Rn. 6 ff.

53 Vgl. statt vieler *Engshuber* (Anm. 52), § 622 BGB Rn. 23.

54 Vgl. statt vieler *Engshuber* (Anm. 52), § 622 BGB Rn. 24 ff.

55 *Müller-Glöge* (Anm. 52), § 622 BGB Rn. 2.

56 *Müller-Glöge* (Anm. 52), § 622 BGB Rn. 10b.

nicht relevant für die Klärung der Frage, ob die gesetzlichen Kündigungsfristen des § 621 BGB oder die des § 622 BGB auf das Anstellungsverhältnis eines Geschäftsführers anzuwenden sind.[57]

3. Gesetzliche Kündigungsfristen für das Anstellungsverhältnis des Geschäftsführers einer GmbH und nationales deutsches Recht

Für die Klärung der Frage, ob auf das Anstellungsverhältnis des Geschäftsführers die gesetzlichen Kündigungsfristen für Arbeitsverhältnisse unmittelbar oder analog nach § 622 BGB oder die für Dienstverhältnisse, die keine Arbeitsverhältnisse im Sinne des § 622 BGB sind, nach § 621 BGB anwendbar sind, ist somit allein das nationale deutsche Recht maßgeblich.

a) Gesetzliche Kündigungsfristen für Arbeitsverhältnisse analog § 622 BGB

Zwar gehen der BGH und die ihm folgende Literatur davon aus, dass der Geschäftsführer kein persönlich abhängiger und weisungsgebundener Arbeitnehmer, sondern ein freier Dienstnehmer in einem freien Dienstverhältnis mit Geschäftsbesorgungscharakter nach §§ 611, 675 BGB ist.[58] Gleichwohl stimmen der BGH[59] in ständiger Rechtsprechung und die ihm folgenden Stimmen in der Literatur[60] darin überein, dass auf Anstellungsverhältnisse von Geschäftsführern, die keine Mehrheitsgesellschafter bzw. keine beherrschenden Gesellschafter sind, aufgrund einer planwidrigen Regelungslücke die für Arbeitsverhältnisse geltenden gesetzlichen Kündigungsfristen in analoger Heranziehung des § 622 BGB anwendbar sein sollen.

Zur Begründung einer planwidrigen gesetzlichen Regelungslücke bezieht sich der BGH zunächst auf das Erste Arbeitsrechtsbereinigungsgesetz[61] aus dem Jahr 1969.[62]

---

57 Vgl. so auch *Müller-Glöge* (Anm. 52), § 622 BGB Rn. 7; *Boemke* (Anm. 2), S. 1, 20 für § 622 BGB.

58 Vgl. oben Ziffer III. 1. b) aa).

59 BGH, Urteil v. 29. Januar 1981 – II ZR 92/80, NJW (1981), S. 1270 f.; BGH, Urteil v. 26. März 1984 – II ZR 120/83, NJW (1984), S. 2528 f., BGH, Urteil v. 9. März 1987 – II ZR 132/86, NJW (1987), S. 2073, 2074; BGH, Urteil v. 5. November 2024 – II ZR 35/23, NZG (2025), S. 663 Rn. 45 f.; für das Mitglied des Vorstands einer AG BGH, Urteil v. 11. Mai 1981 – II ZR 126/80, NJW (1981), S. 2748, 2749 und BGH, Urteil v. 29. Mai 1989 – II ZR 220/88, NJW (1989), S. 2683, 2684.

60 Statt vieler *Kleindiek* (Anm. 29), Anh. zu § 6 GmbHG Rn. 53; *Jaeger/Steinbrück* (Anm. 11), § 35 GmbHG Rn. 434 f.; *Oetker* (Anm 29), § 35 GmbHG Rn. 178 f.; *Linck*, in: Ascheid/Preis/Schmidt (Hrsg.), Kündigungsrecht, , Großkommentar zum gesamten Recht der Beendigung von Arbeitsverhältnissen, 7. Aufl. (2024), § 622 BGB Rn. 12; *Spilger*, in: Bubach/Gallner/Heinkel (Hrsg.), KR Gemeinschaftskommentar zum Kündigungsschutzgesetz und zu sonstigen kündigungsrechtlichen Vorschriften, 14. Aufl. (2025), § 622 BGB Rn. 79; *Engshuber* (Anm. 52), § 622 BGB Rn. 10; *Müller-Glöge* (Anm. 52), § 622 Rn. 7.

61 Gesetz zur Änderung des Kündigungsrechtes und anderer arbeitsrechtlicher Vorschriften (Erstes Arbeitsrechtsbereinigungsgesetz) vom 14. August 1969, BGBl. 1969, Teil I, S. 1106; vgl. hierzu *Röhsler*, in: Schliemann (Hrsg.), Das Arbeitsrecht im BGB, 2. Aufl. (2002), § 622 BGB Rn. 2; *Engshuber* (Anm. 52), § 622 BGB Rn. 2; *Temming*, in: von Staudinger (Begr.), Kommentar zum Bürgerlichen Gesetzbuch mit Einführungsgesetz und Nebengesetzen (2022), § 621 BGB Rn. 2.

62 BGH, Urteil v. 29. Januar 1981 – II ZR 92/80, NJW (1981), S. 1270 f.

Nach der Rechtsprechung des BGH habe § 622 BGB in der bis zum Inkrafttreten des Ersten Arbeitsrechtsbereinigungsgesetzes geltenden Fassung am 1. September 1969 auch für Geschäftsführer als „zur Leistung von Diensten höherer Art Angestellten" gegolten.[63] Mit dem Ersten Arbeitsrechtsbereinigungsgesetz habe der Gesetzgeber jedoch nicht beabsichtigt, die bis dahin in § 622 BGB geregelten Anstellungsverhältnisse von Geschäftsführern anders zu werten und nunmehr dem § 621 BGB zu unterstellen.[64] Der Gesetzgeber habe mit dem Ersten Arbeitsrechtsbereinigungsgesetz lediglich das Ziel verfolgt, das Recht der Kündigungen von Arbeitsverhältnissen zu vereinheitlichen und zu bereinigen.[65] Er soll dabei davon ausgegangen sein, dass § 622 BGB in der bis zum Inkrafttreten des Ersten Arbeitsrechtsbereinigungsgesetzes für selbständige Dienstverhältnisse ohne Bedeutung gewesen sei.[66] Der Gesetzgeber habe dabei jedoch nicht bedacht, dass die höhere Dienste leistenden Geschäftsführer, die bisher als Angestellte unter den bis zum Inkrafttreten des Ersten Arbeitsrechtsbereinigungsgesetzes geltenden persönlichen Anwendungsbereich von § 622 BGB fielen, keine Arbeitnehmer gewesen seien.[67] Es liege daher keine bewusste Entscheidung des Gesetzgebers dazu vor, dass Anstellungsverhältnisse von Geschäftsführern nicht mehr unter § 622 BGB in der ab dem 1. September 1969 geltenden Fassung des Ersten Arbeitsrechtsbereinigungsgesetzes fallen sollen.[68] Vielmehr handele es sich hier um ein „Redaktionsversehen" des Gesetzgebers[69] – eine planwidrige Regelungslücke. Es bestehe daher kein Hindernis, die bis zum Inkrafttreten des Ersten Arbeitsrechtsbereinigungsgesetzes allgemein für höhere Angestellte und ab dem 1. September 1969, also mit Inkrafttreten des Ersten Arbeitsrechtsbereinigungsgesetzes, „für Arbeitnehmer geltende Wertung des Gesetzgebers auf das Anstellungsverhältnis des GmbH-Geschäftsführers als auch insoweit einzig sachgemäß zugrunde zu legen."[70]

Die planwidrige Regelungslücke in § 622 BGB bestehe nach Ansicht des BGH auch über die Reform des Kündigungsfristengesetzes (KündFG)[71] im Jahr 1993 hinaus, weil der Gesetzgeber anlässlich dieser Reform in „offenbarer Kenntnis" der bis 1993 ergangen Rechtsprechung des BGH die Frage der Kündigungsfristen für Or-

---

63 BGH, Urteil v. 29. Januar 1981 – II ZR 92/80, NJW (1981), S. 1270, 1271.

64 BGH, Urteil v. 29. Januar 1981 – II ZR 92/80, NJW (1981), S. 1270, 1271.

65 BGH, Urteil v. 29. Januar 1981 – II ZR 92/80, NJW (1981), S. 1270, 1271.

66 BGH, Urteil v. 29. Januar 1981 – II ZR 92/80, NJW (1981), S. 1270, 1271.

67 BGH, Urteil v. 29. Januar 1981 – II ZR 92/80, NJW (1981), S. 1270, 1271; *Engshuber* (Anm. 52), § 621 BGB Rn. 12.

68 BGH, Urteil v. 29. Januar 1981 – II ZR 92/80, NJW (1981), S. 1270, 1271; *Engshuber* (Anm. 52), § 621 BGB Rn. 12.

69 BGH, Urteil v. 29. Januar 1981 – II ZR 92/80, NJW (1981), S. 1270, 1271; *Engshuber* (Anm. 52), § 621 BGB Rn. 12.

70 BGH, Urteil v. 29. Januar 1981 – II ZR 92/80, NJW (1981), S. 1270, 1271.

71 Gesetz zur Vereinheitlichung der Kündigungsfristen von Arbeitern und Angestellten (Kündigungsfristengesetz – KündFG) vom 7. Oktober 1993, BGBl. 1993, Teil I, S. 1668; vgl. hierzu *Röhsler* (Anm. 61), § 622 BGB Rn. 4.

ganmitglieder weder ausdrücklich angesprochen noch korrigiert habe.[72] Sinn und Zweck des KündFG sei es in Vollziehung des Gesetzgebungsauftrages aufgrund des Beschlusses des BVerfG vom 30. Mai 1990[73] gewesen, ausschließlich die Kündigungsfristen für die ordentliche Kündigung für Arbeiter und Angestellte sowie die Rechtslage in den alten und den neuen Bundesländern anzupassen und zu vereinheitlichen.[74] Hieraus schlussfolgert der BGH, dass der Gesetzgeber die Rechtsprechung des BGH „offensichtlich gebilligt" habe, sodass eine bewusste Wertentscheidung des Gesetzgebers, den persönlichen Anwendungsbereich von § 622 BGB ausschließlich auf Arbeitsverhältnisse zu beschränken, nicht erkennbar sei.[75]

Um unter den persönlichen Anwendungsbereich von § 622 BGB zu fallen, müsse der Geschäftsführer jedoch mit einem Arbeitnehmer vergleichbar sein. Dies sei dann der Fall, wenn (auch) der Geschäftsführer seine Arbeitskraft vollständig oder hauptsächlich bzw. hauptberuflich[76] der GmbH in einem Dienstverhältnis mit festen Bezügen zur Verfügung stelle und mithin wirtschaftlich abhängig sei.[77] Der Gesetzgeber habe allein dies ausreichen lassen, um die Kündigungsfristen des bis zum Inkrafttreten des Ersten arbeitsrechtlichen Bereinigungsgesetzes am 1. September 1969 geltenden § 622 BGB anzuwenden.[78] Dass der Geschäftsführer gegenüber den Arbeitnehmern der GmbH die Arbeitgeberfunktionen wahrnehme, ändere hieran nichts. Denn im Verhältnis zur GmbH stehe er in einem Anstellungsverhältnis, das ihn zu Diensten verpflichte, das gekündigt werden könne und durch das er aufgrund seiner Bezüge von der GmbH „mehr oder weniger wirtschaftlich abhängig" sei.[79]

Damit der Geschäftsführer unter den persönlichen Anwendungsbereich von § 622 BGB fallen kann, müsse weiterhin zwischen dem Geschäftsführer und den Arbeitnehmern der GmbH auch eine vergleichbare Interessenlage bestehen, um die planwidrige Regelungslücke im Sinne einer Analogie zu § 622 BGB schließen zu können.[80] Der BGH geht dabei davon aus, dass der Geschäftsführer wie ein Arbeitneh-

---

72 BGH, Urteil v. 5. November 2024 – II ZR 35/23, NZG (2025), S. 663 Rn. 46; vgl. auch BGH, Urteil v. 29. Januar 1981 – II ZR 92/80, NJW (1981), S. 1270 f.; *Linck* (Anm. 60), § 622 BGB Rn. 12.

73 BVerfG, Beschluss v. 30. Mai 1990 – 1 BvL 2 /83 u. a., NJW (1990), S. 2246 ff.

74 BGH, Urteil v. 5. November 2024 – II ZR 35/23, NZG (2025), S. 663 Rn. 46; vgl. auch BGH, Urteil v. 29. Januar 1981 – II ZR 92/80, NJW (1981), S. 1270 f.

75 BGH, Urteil v. 5. November 2024 – II ZR 35/23, NZG (2025), S. 663 Rn. 46; vgl. auch BGH, Urteil v. 29. Januar 1981 – II ZR 92/80, NJW (1981), S. 1270 f.; *Engshuber* (Anm. 52), § 621 BGB Rn. 12; *Linck* (Anm. 60), § 622 BGB Rn. 12.

76 BGH, Urteil v. 26. März 1984 – II ZR 120/83, NJW (1984), S. 2528 f.; BGH, Urteil v. 9. März 1987 – II ZR 132/86, NJW (1987), S. 2073, 2074.

77 BGH, Urteil v. 29. Januar 1981 – II ZR 92/80, NJW (1981), S. 1270, 1271; *Engshuber* (Anm. 52), § 621 BGB Rn. 12; vgl. auch *Müller-Glöge* (Anm. 52), § 622 BGB Rn. 7; *Oetker* (Anm. 29), § 35 GmbHG Rn. 178; *Jaeger/Steinbrück* (Anm. 11), § 35 GmbHG Rn. 434.

78 BGH, Urteil v. 29. Januar 1981 – II ZR 92/80, NJW (1981), S. 1270, 1271; *Engshuber* (Anm. 52), § 621 BGB Rn. 12.

79 BGH, Urteil v. 29. Januar 1981 – II ZR 92/80, NJW (1981), S. 1270, 1271; BGH, Urteil v. 26. März 1984 – II ZR 120/83, NJW (1984), S. 2528 f.; BGH, Urteil v. 9. März 1987 – II ZR 132/86, NJW (1987), S. 2073, 2074.

80 BGH, Urteil v. 29. Januar 1981 – II ZR 92/80, NJW (1981), S. 1270, 1271.

mer mit seinem Verdienst seinen Lebensunterhalt als auch den seiner Familie verdiene. Hieraus resultiere auch, dass der Geschäftsführer wie ein Arbeitnehmer hinreichend Zeit für einen beruflichen Neuanfang bzw. Neuorientierung im Fall der Kündigung seines Anstellungsverhältnisses benötige. Die GmbH profitiere ebenso von einer längeren Kündigungsfrist als nach § 621 BGB, da sie eine genügende Zeitspanne benötige, um für den gekündigten Geschäftsführer einen qualifizierten Nachfolger zu suchen und einzustellen.[81]

Der BGH hat sich bislang nur dahingehend positioniert, dass die gesetzlichen Kündigungsfristen analog § 622 BGB auf das Anstellungsverhältnis des Geschäftsführers zur Anwendung gelangen, „soweit dieser nicht beherrschender Gesellschafter"[82] bzw. kein „Mehrheitsgesellschafter" ist.[83] In anderen Entscheidungen konnte der BGH die Frage dahinstehen lassen, „ob § 621 BGB dann zu gelten hat, wenn der Geschäftsführer zugleich als Gesellschafter an der GmbH maßgeblich beteiligt ist".[84] § 622 BGB soll hingegen analog auf den Geschäftsführer Anwendung finden, der „einen maßgeblichen Teil des Stammkapitals hält", was dann der Fall sein soll, wenn der Geschäftsführer ein Drittel des Stammkapitals der GmbH hält.[85] Anderseits hat der BGH aber auch entschieden, dass die Frage, ob sich die für das Anstellungsverhältnis eines „beherrschenden Gesellschafter-Geschäftsführers" maßgebliche gesetzliche Kündigungsfrist aus einer analogen Anwendung von § 622 BGB oder aus § 621 BGB herleite, „bedeutungslos" sei, „da dessen Anstellungsvertrag ohnehin nicht gegen seinen Willen gekündigt werden" könne.[86] Die dem BGH folgende Literatur jedenfalls zieht aus der Rechtsprechung des BGH den Umkehrschluss und geht von der Anwendbarkeit von § 621 BGB auf das Anstellungsverhältnis des „beherrschenden Gesellschafter-Geschäftsführers" beziehungsweise des „Mehrheitsgesellschafter"-Geschäftsführers aus.[87]

b) Gesetzliche Kündigungsfristen nach § 621 BGB für Dienstverhältnisse, die keine Arbeitsverhältnisse im Sinne des § 622 BGB sind

Das BAG und der ihm folgende Teil der Literatur stimmen mit dem BGH und dem ihm folgenden Teil der Wissenschaft darin überein, dass der Geschäftsführer – bis auf zwei seltene Ausnahmefälle – grundsätzlich nicht als persönlich abhängiger und weisungsgebundener Arbeitnehmer, sondern als freier Dienstnehmer in einem freien Dienstverhältnis mit Geschäftsbesorgungscharakter nach §§ 611, 675 BGB zu bewerten ist.[88] Aus diesem Grund gehen das BAG[89] und die ihm folgenden Stimmen

---

81 BGH, Urteil v. 29. Januar 1981 – II ZR 92/80, NJW (1981), S. 1270, 1271; BGH, Urteil v. 26. 3. 1984 – II ZR 120/83, NJW (1984), S. 2528 f.

82 BGH, Urteil v. 9. März 1987 – II ZR 132/86, NJW (1987), S. 2073, 2074.

83 BGH, Urteil v. 5. November 2024 – II ZR 35/23, NZG (2025), S. 663 Rn. 45.

84 BGH, Urteil v. 29. Januar 1981 – II ZR 92/80, NJW (1981), S. 1270, 1271.

85 BGH, Urteil v. 26. März 1984 – II ZR 120/83, NJW (1984), S. 2528, 2529.

86 BGH, Urteil v. 26. März 1984 – II ZR 120/83, NJW (1984), S. 2528, 2529.

87 *Jaeger/Steinbrück* (Anm. 11), § 35 GmbHG Rn. 435; *Müller-Glöge* (Anm. 52), § 622 BGB Rn. 7; *Engshuber* (Anm. 53), § 622 Rn. 12.

88 Vgl. III. 1. b) bb).

89 BAG, Urteil v. 11. Juni 2020 – 2 AZR 374/19, NJW (2020), S. 2824 Rn. 41.

in der Literatur[90] konsequenterweise in Abgrenzung zur vorgenannten Rechtsprechung des BGH davon aus, dass nach § 621 BGB auf das Anstellungsverhältnis eines jeden Geschäftsführers die gesetzlichen Kündigungsfristen für Dienstverhältnisse, die keine Arbeitsverhältnisse im Sinne des § 622 BGB sind, Anwendung finden. So führt das BAG aus, dass sich (auch) ein Geschäftsführer, „der nicht Mehrheitsgesellschafter der GmbH ist und zu ihr in keinem Arbeitsverhältnis steht, nicht auf die verlängerten Kündigungsfristen des § 622 Abs. 2 BGB berufen" könne.[91]

Mit Blick auf den Wortlaut von § 622 BGB sei diese Vorschrift nur auf die Kündigung eines Arbeitsverhältnisses anzuwenden. Mit § 621 BGB, der für freie Dienstverhältnisse gelte, fehle es an einer ausfüllungsbedürftigen planwidrigen Regelungslücke, die eine analoge Anwendung von § 622 Abs. 1 und Abs. 2 BGB auf die Kündigung eines Geschäftsführeranstellungsvertrages zuließe, wie dies aber vom BGH propagiert wird. Daher komme es auch nicht darauf an, dass die Kündigungsfristen nach § 622 Abs. 1 und Abs. 2 BGB für die Geschäftsführer, die nicht Mehrheitsgesellschafter der GmbH sind, interessengerechter seien.[92]

Das BAG untermauert seine Meinung zudem mit einem Hinweis zur Entstehungsgeschichte von § 622 BGB. Denn mit der seit dem 15. Oktober 1993 gemäß dem KündFG geltenden Neufassung des § 622 BGB[93] habe der Gesetzgeber die Anbindung der Kündigungsfristen nach § 622 BGB an Arbeitsverhältnisse betont. Es sei nichts dafür ersichtlich, dass der Gesetzgeber die für (Fremd-)Geschäftsführer geltenden Kündigungsfristen in § 622 BGB geregelt habe bzw. dort geregelt haben wollte. Anderenfalls hätte der Gesetzgeber im Rahmen der Neufassung des § 622 BGB die Rechtsauffassung des BGH klarstellend in eine gesetzliche Regelung übernommen.[94] Anzeichen für ein diesbezügliches „Redaktionsversehen" des Gesetzgebers seien nicht ersichtlich.[95]

Schließlich ergäben sich nach Ansicht des BAG ansonsten auch Wertungswidersprüche mit der Rechtsprechung des 9. Senats des BAG, wonach § 622 BGB nicht

---

90 *Altmeppen* (Anm. 29), § 6 GmbHG Rn. 137 ff.; *Beurskens* (Anm. 29), § 38 GmbHG Rn. 143; *Simon/Schulze/Brandhoff/Lücke* (Anm. 11), § 35 Rn. 117; *Spengler*, in: Gallner/Mestwerdt/Nägele-Berkner (Hrsg.), Kündigungsschutzrecht, 8. Aufl. (2025), § 622 BGB Rn. 3; *Boecken* (Anm. 52), § 622 BGB Rn. 4; *Pusch/Daub*, in: Boecken/Düwell/Diller/Hanau (Hrsg.), Gesamtes Arbeitsrecht, 2. Aufl. (2023), § 38 GmbHG Rn. 24; *Boemke* (Anm. 2), S. 1, 20 f.; *Hümmerich*, Grenzfall des Arbeitsrechts: Kündigung des GmbH-Geschäftsführers, in: NJW (1995), S. 1177, 1178 ff.; *Uffmann*, Interim Management in Zeiten nachhaltiger Unternehmensführung, in: ZGR (2013), S. 273, 298 ff.; *Uffmann*, Kündigungsfristen für Geschäftsführeranstellungsverträge Rechtsprechungsdivergenz zwischen BGH und BAG, in: NJW (2020), S. 3210, 3211 ff.

91 BAG, Urteil v. 11. Juni 2020 – 2 AZR 374/19, NJW (2020), S. 2824 Rn. 41.

92 BAG, Urteil v. 11. Juni 2020 – 2 AZR 374/19, NJW (2020), S. 2824 Rn. 42; *Beurskens* (Anm. 29), § 38 GmbHG Rn. 143.

93 Gesetz zur Vereinheitlichung der Kündigungsfristen von Arbeitern und Angestellten (Kündigungsfristengesetz – KündFG) vom 7. Oktober 1993, BGBl. 1993, Teil I, S. 1668; vgl. hierzu *Röhsler* (Anm. 61), § 622 BGB Rn. 4.

94 BAG, Urteil v. 11. Juni 2020 – 2 AZR 374/19, NJW (2020), S. 2824 Rn. 43; *Beurskens* (Anm. 29), § 38 GmbHG Rn. 143.

95 BAG, Urteil v. 11. Juni 2020 – 2 AZR 374/19, NJW (2020), S. 2824 Rn. 43; *Beurskens* (Anm. 29), § 38 GmbHG Rn. 143.

auf arbeitnehmerähnliche Personen anzuwenden sei.[96] Mit der Rechtsprechung des BGH,[97] § 622 Abs. 1 und Abs. 2 BGB auf Anstellungsverhältnisse von (Fremd-)Geschäftsführern analog anzuwenden, wäre dies nicht vereinbar, da die soziale Typik der von (Fremd-)Geschäftsführern geleisteten Dienstleistungen noch weniger mit der von Arbeitnehmern vergleichbar sei als die von arbeitnehmerähnlichen Personen.[98]

c) Abwägung

Der Kern der Abwägung beider vorgenannten Meinungen besteht in der Klärung der Frage, ob die vom BGH angenommene planwidrige Gesetzeslücke hinsichtlich der gesetzlichen Kündigungsfristen des Anstellungsverhältnisses des Geschäftsführers existiert und ob diese mit einer Analogie zu § 622 BGB zu schließen ist. Dabei hat man im Blick zu halten, ob nicht bereits mit § 621 BGB seit dem 1. September 1969, also seit dem Inkrafttreten des Ersten Arbeitsrechtsbereinigungsgesetzes, eine Regelung existiert, die nach dem gesetzgeberischen Willen die gesetzlichen Kündigungsfristen des Anstellungsverhältnisses des Geschäftsführers abschließend regelt, sodass es bereits an einer Regelungslücke im Gesetz mangelt und sich eine Analogie zu § 622 BGB gegen den gesetzgeberischen Willen als contra legem verbietet.

aa) Die Ausfüllung von Gesetzeslücken im Wege der Analogie

Im deutschen Recht existiert keine gesetzliche Regelung, wie Lücken in einem Gesetz zu schließen sind. Man bedient sich hierzu grundsätzlich der juristischen Methodenlehre, nach der die allgemein anerkannte Form der Schließung von Gesetzeslücken die Analogie darstellt.[99]

Eine Analogie setzt voraus, dass das Gesetz eine Regelungslücke enthält und der zu beurteilende Sachverhalt in rechtlicher Hinsicht soweit mit dem Tatbestand vergleichbar ist, den der Gesetzgeber geregelt hat, dass angenommen werden kann, der Gesetzgeber wäre bei einer Interessenabwägung, bei der er sich von den gleichen Grundsätzen hätte leiten lassen wie bei dem Erlass der herangezogenen Gesetzesvorschrift, zu dem gleichen Abwägungsergebnis gekommen.[100]

---

96 BAG, Urteil v. 8. Mai 2007 – 9 AZR 777/06, AP BGB § 611 Arbeitnehmerähnlichkeit Nr. 15 Rn. 13, 21, 25 ff. (m. Anm. *Schubert*); vgl. zur sozialen Typik der Dienstleistungen des Geschäftsführers in Abgrenzung zu denen einer arbeitnehmerähnlichen Person BAG, Beschluss v. 21. Januar 2019 – 9 AZB 23/18, NJW (2019), S. 1627 Rn. 39; *Uffmann* (Anm. 90), ZGR (2013), S. 273, 299 f.

97 BGH, Urteil v. 5. November 2024 – II ZR 35/23, NZG (2025), S. 663 Rn. 45 f.

98 BAG, Urteil v. 11. Juni 2020 – 2 AZR 374/19, NJW (2020), S. 2824 Rn. 43.

99 *Horn*, Einführung in die Rechtswissenschaft und Rechtsphilosophie, 5. Aufl., 2011, Rn. 187; *Larenz/Canaris*, Methodenlehre der Rechtswissenschaft, 3. Aufl. (1995), S. 202.

100 BGH, Urteil v. 14. Dezember 2006 – IX ZR 92/05, NJW (2007), S. 992 Rn. 15; BGH, Urteil v. 13. Juli 1988 – IV a 55/87, NJW (1988), S. 2734; BGH, Urteil v. 13. März 2003 – I ZR 290/00, NJW (2003), S. 1932, 1933; BGH, Urteil v. 16. Juli 2003 – VIII ZR 274/02, NJW (2003), S. 2601, 2603; vgl. auch *Larenz/Canaris* (Anm. 99), S. 202; *Schwacke*, Juristische Methodik, 5. Aufl. (2011), S. 130 ff.

Voraussetzung für eine Analogie als Instrument der Rechtsfortbildung ist eine planwidrige Unvollständigkeit bzw. Regelungslücke des Gesetzes.[101] Ob die Unvollständigkeit des Gesetzes planwidrig oder plangemäß ist, bemisst sich anhand der dem Gesetz zugrunde liegenden Regelungsabsicht, d. h. dem tatsächlichen oder mutmaßlichen Willen des Gesetzgebers.[102] Die dem Gesetz zu Grunde liegende Regelungsabsicht ist aus ihm selbst im Wege der Gesetzesauslegung, insbesondere der historischen und teleologischen Auslegung, zu erschließen. Dabei ist zu fragen, ob das Gesetz, gemessen an seiner eigenen Regelungsabsicht, planwidrig unvollständig ist.[103]

bb) Gesetzesauslegung von § 621 BGB und § 622 BGB

Ob in puncto der gesetzlichen Kündigungsfristen des Anstellungsverhältnisses des Geschäftsführers mit oder seit dem Inkrafttreten des Ersten Arbeitsrechtsbereinigungsgesetzes eine planwidrige Gesetzeslücke entstanden ist, die mittels einer Analogie zu § 622 BGB zu schließen ist, oder ob eine solche aufgrund desselben Ersten Arbeitsrechtsbereinigungsgesetzes gar nicht (erst) entstanden ist, da der Gesetzgeber bewusst und plangemäß diese gesetzlichen Kündigungsfristen für das Anstellungsverhältnis des Geschäftsführers durch eine unmittelbare Anwendung von § 621 BGB geregelt hat, ist im Wege der Gesetzesauslegung zu ermitteln.[104]

Die Gesetzesauslegung erfolgt vorliegend für § 621 BGB und § 622 BGB zusammen. Denn beide Normen wurden zusammen(-hängend) durch dasselbe Erste Arbeitsrechtsbereinigungsgesetz „aus einem Guss" zeitgleich und inhaltlich sowie (gesetzes-)systematisch und auch teleologisch aufeinander abgestimmt geändert und traten zeitgleich am 1. September 1969 durch das Erste Arbeitsrechtsbereinigungsgesetz neu geschaffen in Kraft.

(1) Auslegung nach dem Wortlaut

Das Ergebnis der Auslegung nach dem Wortlaut bzw. Wortsinn von § 621 BGB und § 622 BGB ist eindeutig: Die gesetzlichen Kündigungsfristen des Anstellungsverhältnisses des Geschäftsführers richten sich nach § 621 BGB. Die vom BGH und der ihm folgenden Literatur propagierte planwidrige Regelungslücke ist nicht existent. Eine Analogie zu § 622 BGB verbietet sich als contra legem.

Nach dem ausdrücklichen Wortlaut von § 622 BGB regelt dieser ausschließlich gesetzliche Kündigungsfristen von „Arbeitsverhältnissen" im Sinne des § 611a BGB. Aus dem Wortlaut des § 622 BGB kann nichts dafür hergeleitet werden, dass diese Vorschrift auch gesetzliche Kündigungsfristen von freien Dienstverhältnissen regelt. Das muss § 622 BGB auch nicht, denn die gesetzlichen Kündigungsfristen von

---

101 BGH, Urteil v. 14. Dezember 2006 – IX ZR 92/05, NJW (2007), S. 992 Rn. 15; *Larenz/Canaris* (Anm. 99), S. 194 ff.; *Canaris*, Die Feststellung von Lücken im Gesetz, 2. Aufl. (1983), S. 37; *Schwacke* (Anm. 100), S. 133.

102 *Larenz/Canaris* (Anm. 99), S. 194.

103 BGH, Urteil v. 14. Dezember 2006 – IX ZR 92/05, NJW (2007), S. 992 Rn. 15; BGH, Urteil v. 13. November 2001 – X ZR 134/00, GRUR (2002), S. 238, 241; ebenso *Schwacke* (Anm. 100), S. 12, jeweils unter Hinweis auf die systematische, historische und teleologische Auslegung.

104 Vgl. auch BGH, Urteil v. 28. Juni 1978 – IV ZR 47/77, NJW (1978), S. 1855 f.

Dienstverhältnissen, und somit auch die des Anstellungsverhältnisses des Geschäftsführers, richten sich unmittelbar nach § 621 BGB. Auch der Wortlaut von § 621 BGB ist unmissverständlich. § 621 BGB regelt ausdrücklich die gesetzlichen Kündigungsfristen bei einem „Dienstverhältnis", das „kein Arbeitsverhältnis im Sinne des § 622 BGB" ist.

Die vom BGH argumentierte planwidrige Regelungslücke hinsichtlich der gesetzlichen Kündigungsfristen des Anstellungsverhältnisses des Geschäftsführers existiert daher aufgrund dieses ausdrücklichen Wortlauts beider Normen nicht. Da der Geschäftsführer nach Meinung des BGH, des BAG und der ihnen jeweils folgenden Stimmen in der Literatur aber grds. kein persönlich abhängiger und weisungsgebundener Arbeitnehmer in einem Arbeitsverhältnis ist, sondern ein freier Dienstnehmer in einem freien Dienstverhältnis mit Geschäftsbesorgungscharakter nach §§ 611, 675 BGB,[105] ergeben sich die gesetzlichen Kündigungsfristen für das Anstellungsverhältnis des Geschäftsführers allein und unmittelbar aus § 621 BGB.[106]

(2) Historisch-teleologische Auslegung

Auch die historisch-teleologische Auslegung von § 621 BGB und § 622 BGB, also die sowohl gemäß ihrer Entstehungsgeschichte als auch gemäß ihrem vom Gesetzgeber gewollten Sinn und Zweck, kommt zu einem eindeutigen Ergebnis: Die gesetzlichen Kündigungsfristen des Anstellungsverhältnisses des Geschäftsführers richten sich auch hiernach in unmittelbarer Anwendung nach § 621 BGB und nicht analog § 622 BGB.

Die historische und die teleologische Auslegung sollen hier zusammen durchgeführt werden, da sich aus der historischen Auslegung der §§ 621, 622 BGB zugleich auch unmittelbar der Wille des Gesetzgebers in Bezug auf den Sinn und Zweck (ratio legis) beider Normen eindeutig und unmissverständlich ergibt.

(a) Ausgangssituation vor dem Inkrafttreten des Ersten Arbeitsrechtsbereinigungsgesetzes

Der Zeitraum vor dem Inkrafttreten des Ersten Arbeitsrechtsbereinigungsgesetzes, also vor dem 1. September 1969, war in Bezug auf die gesetzlichen Kündigungsfristen von Arbeits- und Dienstverhältnissen von Rechtszersplitterung gekennzeichnet. Ursprünglich waren die gesetzlichen Kündigungsfristen für Arbeiter und Angestellte unterschiedlich geregelt und über verschiedene (Sonder-)Gesetze verstreut. Für die wohl überwiegende Anzahl der Arbeitnehmer, also die gewerblichen und technischen Angestellten sowie für die Arbeiter waren die gesetzlichen Kündigungsfristen in den seinerzeitigen §§ 122, 133a GewO und für die kaufmännischen Angestellten, den Handlungsgehilfen, im seinerzeitigen § 66 HGB geregelt.[107] Weiterhin gab es

105 Vgl. III. 1. b) aa) und bb).

106 Vgl. auch BAG, Urteil v. 11. Juni 2020 – 2 AZR 374/19, NJW (2020), S. 2824 Rn. 42; auch *Uffmann* (Anm. 90), NJW (2020), S. 3210 Rn. 12; *Uffmann* (Anm. 90), ZGR (2013), S. 273, 298; *Boemke* (Anm. 2), S. 1, 21.

107 Zur Entstehungsgeschichte des § 621 BGB vgl. *Engshuber* (Anm. 52), § 621 BGB Rn. 3; *Temming* (Anm. 61), § 621 BGB Rn. 1 ff.; zur Entstehungsgeschichte des § 622 BGB vgl. *Engshuber* (Anm. 52), § 622 BGB Rn. 1 ff.; *Röhsler* (Anm. 61), § 622 BGB Rn. 1 ff.

u. a. verschiedene (Sonder-)Kündigungsvorschriften in der vorläufigen Landarbeitsordnung, für Arbeitnehmer nach dem Binnenschifffahrts- und dem Flößereigesetz sowie in den verschiedenen Berggesetzen der Bundesländer.[108]

§ 622 BGB in seiner ursprünglichen Erstfassung, die bis zum Inkrafttreten des Ersten Arbeitsrechtsbereinigungsgesetz am 1. September 1969 galt, regelte die ordentlichen Kündigungsfristen für Arbeitsverhältnisse und den dort tatbestandlich genannten Personenkreis:

> „§ 622
>
> Das Dienstverhältnis der mit festen Bezügen zur Leistung von Diensten höherer Art Angestellten, deren Erwerbstätigkeit durch das Dienstverhältnis vollständig oder hauptsächlich in Anspruch genommen wird, insbesondere der Lehrer, Erzieher, Privatbeamten, Gesellschafterinnen, kann nur für den Schluß eines Kalendervierteljahres und nur unter Einhaltung einer Kündigungsfrist von sechs Wochen gekündigt werden, auch wenn die Vergütung nach kürzeren Zeitabschnitten als Vierteljahren bemessen ist.“

Gemäß dem Wortlaut von § 621 BGB in der Fassung vor dem Inkrafttreten des Ersten Arbeitsrechtsbereinigungsgesetzes regelte dieser – vergleichbar mit § 621 BGB in seiner aktuellen heutigen Fassung – die Kündigungsfristen für Dienstverhältnisse gestaffelt unter Berücksichtigung der Bemessung der Vergütung nach Zeitabschnitten. § 623 BGB regelte zu diesem Zeitpunkt noch die Kündigungsfrist für Dienstverhältnisse für den Fall, dass die Vergütung nicht nach Zeitabschnitten bemessen wurde.

(b) Erstes Arbeitsrechtsbereinigungsgesetz

Das Erste Arbeitsrechtsbereinigungsgesetz ist das maßgebliche Gesetz zum Verständnis der Entstehungsgeschichte und des Willens des Gesetzgebers zu Sinn und Zweck von § 621 BGB und § 622 BGB und somit zur Auslegung beider Vorschriften.

(aa) Gang des Gesetzgebungsverfahrens

Angesichts der dargelegten Rechtszersplitterung im Bereich der Vorschriften über die gesetzlichen Kündigungsfristen für Arbeiter, gewerbliche und technische Angestellte, kaufmännische Angestellte sowie sonstiger Kündigungsvorschriften beabsichtigte der Gesetzgeber diese zu bereinigen und zu vereinheitlichen, was mit dem Ersten Arbeitsrechtsbereinigungsgesetz vom 14. August 1969[109] auch geschah. Zum Hauptanliegen dieses Gesetzes lässt sich der Begründung der Bundesregierung aus den Gesetzgebungsmaterialien entnehmen:

> „I. Allgemeines
>
> Das Hauptanliegen des Entwurfs ist eine Vereinheitlichung und Bereinigung des Rechts zur Kündigung von Arbeitsverhältnissen. Gegenwärtig ist dieses Recht der ordentlichen und außerordentlichen Kündigung für die einzelnen Arbeitnehmergruppen in verschiedenen Gesetzen und zum Teil ohne innere Rechtfertigung unterschiedlich geregelt. Diese unerfreuliche

---

108 *Temming* (Anm. 61), § 621 BGB Rn. 2.

109 Gesetz zur Änderung des Kündigungsrechtes und anderer arbeitsrechtlicher Vorschriften (Erstes Arbeitsrechtsbereinigungsgesetz) vom 14. August 1969, BGBl. 1969, Teil I, S. 1106.

Rechtszersplitterung auf einem Gebiete, das gerade im Arbeitsrecht von besonderer Bedeutung ist, soll durch eine für alle Arbeitnehmer geltende vereinheitlichende Regelung des allgemeinen Kündigungsrechts abgelöst werden. (…)"[110]

Daneben wurden zu einzelnen Vorschriften auch weitere Anliegen verfolgt, so auch zu § 621 BGB und § 622 BGB. Hierzu lässt sich der Begründung der Bundesregierung aus den Gesetzgebungsmaterialien zu Art. 2 Nr. 3 bis 5 des Ersten Arbeitsrechtsbereinigungsgesetzes, der die in §§ 621, 622 BGB vorzunehmenden Änderungen bzw. Ergänzungen betrifft, entnehmen:

„Zu Artikel 2 Nr. 3 bis 5

Die in den Nr. 3 bis 5 vorgesehene Änderung bzw. Ergänzung des Bürgerlichen Gesetzbuches sieht eine systematische Unterscheidung der ordentlichen Kündigung für Arbeitsverhältnisse einerseits sowie für sonstige Dienstverhältnisse, die keine Arbeitsverhältnisse sind, andererseits vor. (…)"[111]

Als Begründung zum neu zu regelnden § 621 BGB findet sich in der Begründung der Bundesregierung:

„Zu Artikel 2 Nr. 3 bis 5

(…) § 621 BGB soll künftig die umfassende Regelung der ordentlichen Kündigung für solche Dienstverhältnisse enthalten, die keine Arbeitsverhältnisse sind. Aus diesem Grund wird ihm als Absatz 5 der bisherige § 623 BGB angefügt. Der bisherige § 622 BGB ist für selbständige Dienstverhältnisse ohne praktische Bedeutung und deshalb nicht in § 621 BGB aufgenommen worden. (…)"[112]

So wurde – wie aus den Gesetzgebungsmaterialien ersichtlich – zunächst auch lediglich vorgeschlagen, in § 621 BGB den § 623 BGB mit unverändertem Wortlaut als neuen Absatz 5 anzufügen.[113]

Zu § 622 BGB findet sich in der Begründung der Bundesregierung:

„Zu Artikel 2 Nr. 3 bis 5

(…) Die Neufassung des § 622 BGB regelt unter Verdrängung des bisherigen § 622 die allgemeinen Kündigungsfristen für Arbeitsverhältnisse. (…)"[114]

Den Gesetzesmaterialien lässt sich des Weiteren aus der Stellungnahme des Bundesrates zum Ersten Arbeitsrechtsbereinigungsgesetz entnehmen, dass dieser mit dem Vorschlag der Bundesregierung zum Wortlaut des § 621 BGB nicht einverstanden war. Denn der Bundesrat empfahl der Bundesregierung zu § 621 BGB folgende Klarstellung:

„(…) Klarstellung, daß § 621 BGB künftig nur für solche Dienstverhältnisse gelten soll, die keine Arbeitsverhältnisse (§ 622 i. d. F. des Entwurfs) sind. Der vorgeschlagenen Fassung fügt sich dann in klarer Abhebung die neue Fassung des § 622 an, die eindeutig von Arbeits-

110 BT-Drs. V/3913 v. 24. Februar 1969, S. 8.

111 BT-Drs. V/3913 v. 24. Februar 1969, S. 10.

112 BT-Drs. V/3913 v. 24. Februar 1969, S. 10.

113 BT-Drs. V/3913 v. 24. Februar 1969, S. 3.

114 BT-Drs. V/3913 v. 24. Februar 1969, S. 10.

verhältnissen von Angestellten und Arbeitern, also von unselbständigen Dienstverhältnissen, spricht.“[115]

Dem wurde sodann auch im Gesetzgebungsverfahren durch die Bundesregierung wie folgt entsprochen:

„Der Anregung des Bundesrates, klarzustellen, daß 621 BGB künftig nur für Dienstverhältnisse gilt, die nicht Arbeitsverhältnisse sind, stimmt die Bundesregierung zu. Statt der vom Bundesrat vorgeschlagenen Fassung, sollte jedoch in Anlehnung an die Neufassung des § 565 BGB folgende Formulierung gewählt werden:

„§ 621

Bei einem Dienstverhältnis, das kein Arbeitsverhältnis ist, ist die Kündigung zulässig, (…)“.[116]

Das Erste Arbeitsrechtsbereinigungsgesetz trat sodann am 01. September 1969 in Kraft und mit ihm die neugefassten §§ 621, 622 BGB. § 621 BGB hatte folgende Fassung:

„3. § 621 erhält folgende Fassung:

§ 621

Bei einem Dienstverhältnis, das kein Arbeitsverhältnis im Sinne des § 622 ist, ist die Kündigung zulässig (…)“.[117]

Es folgt im Gesetzestext von § 621 Nr. 1 bis 5 BGB die Staffelung der Kündigungsfristen gemäß der nach Zeitabschnitten bemessenen Vergütung, in die der Text des bisherigen § 623 BGB als neue Nr. 5 aufgenommen wurde.[118]

§ 622 BGB wiederum wurde durch folgende neue Fassung ersetzt:

„4. § 622 wird durch folgenden § 622 ersetzt:

§ 622

Das Arbeitsverhältnis eines Angestellten kann unter Einhaltung einer Kündigungsfrist von sechs Wochen zum Schluß eines Kalendervierteljahres gekündigt werden. Eine kürzere Kündigungsfrist kann einzelvertraglich nur vereinbart werden, wenn sie einen Monat nicht unterschreitet und die Kündigung nur für den Schluß eines Kalendermonats zugelassen wird. (…)“.[119]

(bb) Sinn und Zweck von §§ 621, 622 BGB und der Wille des Gesetzgebers

Das Gesetzgebungsverfahren zu §§ 621, 622 BGB in der Fassung des Ersten Arbeitsrechtsbereinigungsgesetzes macht deutlich, dass die vom BGH unterstellte planwidrige Regelungslücke in Bezug auf die für das Anstellungsverhältnis eines Geschäftsführers geltenden gesetzlichen Kündigungsfristen nicht besteht, durch das Erste Arbeitsrechtsbereinigungsgesetz auch nicht entstanden ist. Vielmehr hat der

---

115 BT-Drs. V/3913 v. 24. Februar 1969, S. 14.

116 BT-Drs. V/3913 v. 24. Februar 1969, S. 15.

117 BGBl. 1969, Teil I, S. 1106, 1107.

118 BGBl. 1969, Teil I, S. 1106, 1107.

119 BGBl. 1969, Teil I, S. 1106, 1107.

Gesetzgeber bewusst und planvoll mit dem ersten Arbeitsrechtsbereinigungsgesetz die gesetzlichen Kündigungsfristen für Dienstverhältnisse, die keine Arbeitsverhältnisse im Sinne des § 622 BGB sind, ausschließlich dem Regelungsregime des § 621 BGB in unmittelbarer Anwendung unterworfen, was somit auch für das Anstellungsverhältnis des Geschäftsführers als Dienstverhältnis mit Geschäftsbesorgungscharakter nach §§ 611, 675 BGB gilt. Die für Arbeitsverhältnisse geltenden gesetzlichen Kündigungsfristen hat der Gesetzgeber hingegen zeitgleich mit dem Ersten Arbeitsrechtsbereinigungsgesetz bewusst und planvoll dem Regelungsregime des § 622 BGB unmittelbar unterworfen.

Der BGH irrt, wenn er die Ansicht vertritt, dass der Gesetzgeber mit dem Ersten Arbeitsrechtsbereinigungsgesetz nicht beabsichtigt habe, die bis dahin in § 622 BGB geregelten Anstellungsverhältnisse anders zu werten und nunmehr dem § 621 BGB zu unterstellen.[120] Der BGH geht ebenfalls fehl in der Annahme, wenn er ausführt, dass der Gesetzgeber mit dem Ersten Arbeitsrechtsbereinigungsgesetz lediglich das Ziel verfolgt habe, das Recht der Kündigungen von Arbeitsverhältnissen zu vereinheitlichen und zu bereinigen.[121] Richtig ist vielmehr, dass der Gesetzgeber insbesondere mit §§ 621, 622 BGB weitergehende Ziele verfolgt hat, als nur die Vereinheitlichung und Bereinigung des Kündigungsrechts. Denn der Gesetzgeber hat mit der Unterscheidung zwischen § 621 BGB und § 622 BGB ausdrücklich eine strenge „systematische Unterscheidung der ordentlichen Kündigung für Arbeitsverhältnisse einerseits sowie für sonstige Dienstverhältnisse die keine Arbeitsverhältnisse sind, andererseits" bezweckt.[122] Diese strenge „systematische Unterscheidung" soll nach dem Willen des Gesetzgebers in der Weise umgesetzt werden, dass § 621 BGB „künftig die umfassende Regelung der ordentlichen Kündigung für solche Dienstverhältnisse enthalten" soll, „die keine Arbeitsverhältnisse sind".[123] § 622 BGB hingegen soll „unter Verdrängung des bisherigen § 622 BGB die allgemeinen Kündigungsfristen für Arbeitsverhältnisse" regeln.[124] Mit dieser unmissverständlichen „systematischen Unterscheidung" hat der Gesetzgeber aber auch die Kündigungsfristen für das Anstellungsverhältnis des Geschäftsführers unter § 621 BGB gezogen, da es sich bei ihm grundsätzlich um ein freies Dienstverhältnis mit Geschäftsbesorgungscharakter nach §§ 611, 675 BGB handelt.[125] Anhaltspunkte dafür, dass ausgerechnet das Anstellungsverhältnis des Geschäftsführers von § 621 BGB ausgenommen sein soll, können den Gesetzmaterialien nicht entnommen werden. Dies würde auch nicht in das gesetzgeberische Konzept einer strengen „systematischen Unterscheidung" zwischen den Kündigungsfristen von Arbeitsverhältnissen und denen von freien Dienstverhältnissen passen. Eine entsprechende Ausnahme für das freie Dienstverhältnis eines Geschäftsführers wäre systemwidrig.

Wenn der Gesetzgeber ausdrücklich klarstellt, dass die Änderungen bei § 621 BGB und § 622 BGB eine „systematische Unterscheidung" der ordentlichen Kündigung

---

120 BGH, Urteil v. 29. Januar 1981 – II ZR 92/80, NJW (1981), S. 1270, 1271.

121 BGH, Urteil v. 29. Januar 1981 – II ZR 92/80, NJW (1981), S. 1270, 1271.

122 BT-Drs. V/3913 v. 24. Februar 1969, S. 10.

123 BT-Drs. V/3913 v. 24. Februar 1969, S. 10.

124 BT-Drs. V/3913 v. 24. Februar 1969, S. 14.

125 Vgl. III. 1. b) aa) und bb).

für „Arbeitsverhältnisse einerseits“ sowie für „sonstige Dienstverhältnisse“, die „keine Arbeitsverhältnisse sind“, andererseits bezwecken soll, so bedeutet dies mithin im Umkehrschluss: Eine solche strenge „systematische Unterscheidung“ hat es zuvor nicht gegeben, ansonsten wäre eine entsprechende Klarstellung in den Gesetzesmaterialien nicht notwendig gewesen. Dies gilt gerade auch für die Rechtsprechung des BGH in der Zeit vor dem Ersten Arbeitsrechtsbereinigungsgesetz, als der BGH die Kündigungsfristen der Anstellungsverhältnisse von Geschäftsführern aus § 622 BGB in der Fassung vor dem Ersten Arbeitsrechtsbereinigungsgesetz hergeleitet hat, der für Arbeitsverhältnisse galt, und nicht dogmatisch zutreffend aus § 621 BGB, der für die Kündigungsfristen freier Dienstverhältnisse maßgeblich war.[126] Der im Ersten Arbeitsrechtsbereinigungsgesetz zum Ausdruck gekommene Wille des Gesetzgebers zielte mithin klar und eindeutig daraufhin, planvoll und unmissverständlich zwischen unselbständigen Arbeitsverhältnissen und selbständigen bzw. freien Dienstverhältnissen zu differenzieren.

Der Gesetzgeber setzte diese strenge „systematische Unterscheidung“ auch bewusst und planvoll in der Weise um, dass § 622 BGB bis heute „unter Verdrängung des bisherigen § 622 die allgemeinen gesetzlichen Kündigungsfristen für Arbeitsverhältnisse“ regelt.[127] Für Dienstverhältnisse, die keine Arbeitsverhältnisse sind, regelt hingegen bis heute § 621 BGB die gesetzlichen Kündigungsfristen. Durch die Übernahme der vom Bundesrat empfohlenen Formulierung in den Gesetzestext wird dies noch deutlicher. Der Bundesrat stellte in seiner Stellungnahme zum Entwurf des Ersten Arbeitsrechtsbereinigungsgesetzes der Bundesregierung unmissverständlich klar, „daß § 621 BGB künftig nur für solche Dienstverhältnisse gelten soll, die keine Arbeitsverhältnisse (§ 622 i. d. F. des Entwurfs) sind.“ Im Umkehrschluss: Wenn § 621 BGB erst „künftig“ nur für solche Dienstverhältnisse gelten soll, die keine Arbeitsverhältnisse sind, dann galt dies bislang nicht, was z. B. durch die hier kritisierte Analogie-Rechtsprechung des BGH belegt wird. Da die freien Dienstverhältnisse von Geschäftsführern grundsätzlich keine Arbeitsverhältnisse sind, sind die für sie geltenden gesetzlichen Kündigungsfristen daher ab dem Inkrafttreten des Ersten Arbeitsrechtsbereinigungsgesetzes – und somit „künftig“ – nur noch aus § 621 BGB herzuleiten. Der Bundesrat führt sodann in seiner Stellungnahme weiter aus, dass sich der von ihm vorgeschlagenen Fassung des § 621 BGB dann „in klarer Abhebung die neue Fassung des § 622 BGB“ anfüge, „die eindeutig von Arbeitsverhältnissen von Angestellten und Arbeitern, also von unselbständigen Dienstverhältnissen spricht“.[128] Auch dies macht die vom Gesetzgeber bezweckte eindeutige Unterscheidung zwischen den gesetzlichen Kündigungsfristen von Arbeitsverhältnissen einerseits und denen von freien Dienstverhältnissen andererseits deutlich. Gegen diesen vom Gesetzgeber gewollten Zweck verstößt jedoch der BGH, wenn er auch heute noch die gesetzlichen Kündigungsfristen für das Anstellungsverhältnis des Geschäftsführers als freies Dienstverhältnis analog § 622 BGB aus denen für Arbeits-

126 BGH, Urteil v. 29. Januar 1981 – II ZR 92/08, S. 1270, 1271 mit Verweis auf BGH, Urteil v. 16. Dezember 1953 – II ZR 41/53, NJW (1953), S. 505.

127 BT-Drs. V/3913 v. 24. Februar 1969, S. 10.

128 BT-Drs. V/3913 v. 24. Februar 1969, S. 14.

verhältnisse geltenden Kündigungsfristen herleitet[129] und nicht dogmatisch und systematisch zutreffend aus § 621 BGB.

Bemerkenswert ist auch, dass der Gesetzgeber ausdrücklich klarstellt, dass nach seinem Willen § 621 BGB die „umfassende Regelung" der ordentlichen Kündigung für solche Dienstverhältnisse, die keine Arbeitsverhältnisse sind, enthalten soll.[130] Mit dieser kategorischen Formulierung wird ausdrücklich klargestellt, dass aufgrund dieser „umfassenden Regelung" sämtliche, also alle Dienstverhältnisse, die keine Arbeitsverhältnisse im Sinne des § 622 BGB sind, hinsichtlich ihrer gesetzlichen Kündigungsfristen abschließend unter § 621 BGB zu subsumieren sind. Aufgrund dieser kategorischen Formulierung muss dies dann aber auch für das Anstellungsverhältnis des Geschäftsführers gelten, dass grds. kein Arbeitsverhältnis ist, sondern ein freies Dienstverhältnis mit Geschäftsbesorgungscharakter nach §§ 611, 675 BGB.[131] Von einer planwidrigen Regelungslücke, die der BGH vermutet,[132] kann auch hier keine Rede sein.

Dass der Begründung der Bundesregierung zum Ersten Arbeitsrechtsbereinigungsgesetz zu entnehmen ist, dass der bisherige § 622 BGB „für selbständige Dienstverhältnisse ohne praktische Bedeutung" gewesen sei und deshalb bewusst nicht in § 621 BGB aufgenommen wurde, ändert an der hier vertretenen Ansicht nichts und schon gar nicht im Sinne des BGH, der diese Formulierung fälschlicherweise als Beleg für ein Redaktionsversehen des Gesetzgebers bewertet.[133] Diese Wertung des BGH ist wenig überzeugend.[134] Denn der Hinweis in den Gesetzesmaterialien, dass „der bisherige § 622 BGB" in der Fassung bis zum Inkrafttreten des Ersten Arbeitsrechtsbereinigungsgesetzes „für selbständige Dienstverhältnisse ohne praktische[135] Bedeutung" gewesen sei,[136] kann auch in anderer Weise interpretiert werden, als der BGH dies tut.[137] Denn zum einen bedeutet dieser Hinweis, dass dem Gesetzgeber sehr wohl bewusst war, dass § 622 BGB für selbständige Dienstverhältnisse, also auch für Anstellungsverhältnisse von Geschäftsführern, Bedeutung haben kann, wie dies auch die damalige Analogie-Rechtsprechung des BGH belegt.[138]

---

129 BGH, Urteil v. 5. November 2024 – II ZR 35/23, NZG (2025), S. 663 45 f.

130 BT-Drs. V/3913 v. 24. Februar 1969, S. 10.

131 Vgl. III. 1. b) aa) und bb); s. auch *Boemke* (Anm. 2), S. 1, 21.

132 BGH, Urteil v. 5. November 2024 – II ZR 35/*23*, NZG (2025), S. 663 Rn. 46.

133 So aber z. B. BGH, Urteil v. 29. Januar 1981 – II ZR 92/80, NJW (1981), S. 1270, 1271.

134 So auch *Uffmann* (Anm. 90), ZGR (2013), S. 273, 299; *Uffmann* (Anm. 90), NJW (2020), S. 3210 Rn. 15.

135 *Uffmann* (Anm. 90), ZGR (2013), S. 275, 299 in der dortigen Fn. 129; *Uffmann* (Anm. 90), NJW (2020), S. 3210 Rn. 14 f., weist zurecht darauf hin, dass in der einschlägigen Rechtsprechung des BGH dieser aus den Gesetzesmaterialien das Wort „praktische" bemerkenswerterweise nicht zitiert. So wird aus „ohne praktische Bedeutung" aus den Gesetzesmaterialien (BT-DRs V/3913 v. 24. Februar 1969, S. 10) für den BGH „ohne Bedeutung", so z. B. in BGH, Urteil v. 29. Januar 1981 – II ZR 92/80, NJW (1981), S. 1270, 1271.

136 BT-Drs. V/3913 v. 24. Februar 1969, S. 10.

137 *Uffmann* (Anm. 90), ZGR (2013), S. 273, 299; *Uffmann* (Anm. 90), NJW (2020), S. 3210 Rn. 15.

138 BGH, Urteil v. 29. Januar 1981 – II ZR 92/80 = NJW (1981), S. 1270, 1271.

Nur diese „Bedeutung“ war (halt) ohne „praktische“ Relevanz.[139] Zum anderen war § 622 BGB in seiner ursprünglichen Fassung dispositiv.[140] Dies bedeutet, dass die fehlende „praktische Bedeutung“ von § 622 BGB auch einfach damit begründet werden kann, dass die mangelnde praktische Relevanz von § 622 BGB auf vertraglich vereinbarten Kündigungsfristen oder Befristungsabreden beruhte,[141] was für Anstellungsverhältnisse mit Geschäftsführern weit verbreitet war und auch heute noch ist. Im Umkehrschluss: Hätte § 622 BGB in der Fassung bis zum Ersten Arbeitsrechtsbereinigungsgesetz eine „praktische Bedeutung“ für selbständige Dienstverhältnisse gehabt, so hätte der Gesetzgeber § 622 BGB, den der BGH bis dahin zur Ermittlung der Kündigungsfristen für Anstellungsverhältnisse von Geschäftsführern herangezogen hat, in § 621 BGB aufgenommen, der ab dem Inkrafttreten des Ersten Arbeitsrechtsbereinigungsgesetzes alleinig die gesetzlichen Kündigungsfristen für freie Dienstverhältnisse regelt, also auch die für Anstellungsverhältnisse von Geschäftsführern. Jedenfalls in dem Umfang, wie § 622 BGB bis zum Inkrafttreten des Ersten Arbeitsrechtsbereinigungsgesetzes auch für selbständige Dienstverhältnisse Geltung hatte. Dies ist jedoch nicht geschehen. Der Gesetzgeber hat daher bewusst und planvoll darauf verzichtet, § 622 BGB in der Fassung bis zum Inkrafttreten des Ersten Arbeitsrechtsbereinigungsgesetzes in § 621 BGB aufzunehmen. § 622 BGB in der Fassung bis zum Inkrafttreten des Ersten Arbeitsrechtsbereinigungsgesetzes wurde sodann von § 622 BGB in der Fassung ab dem Inkrafttreten des Ersten Arbeitsrechtsbereinigungsgesetzes „verdrängt“, der nach dem Plan des Gesetzgebers nur noch die gesetzlichen Kündigungsfristen für Arbeitsverhältnisse regelt. § 622 BGB in der Fassung bis zum ersten Arbeitsrechtsbereinigungsgesetz sowie sein bis dahin geltender Regelungsgehalt ist (ersatzlos) verdrängt worden, also auch für selbständige Dienstverhältnisse von Geschäftsführern. Anders als es der BGH vertritt,[142] hat es der Gesetzgeber daher sehr wohl beabsichtigt, die bisher unter § 622 BGB geregelten Anstellungsverhältnisse von Geschäftsführern anders zu werten und ab dem Inkrafttreten des Ersten Arbeitsrechtsbereinigungsgesetzes § 621 BGB zu unterstellen.[143] Dem BGH kann somit auch nicht gefolgt werden, wenn er die Meinung vertritt, dass der Gesetzgeber dabei nicht bedacht habe, dass die höhere Dienste leistenden Geschäftsführer, die bis zum Inkrafttreten des Ersten Arbeitsrechtsbereinigungsgesetzes als Angestellte unter den geltenden persönlichen Anwendungsbereich des bis dahin geltenden § 622 BGB vom BGH subsumiert wurden, keine Arbeitnehmer gewesen seien.[144] Denn abgesehen davon, dass die Gesetzesmaterialien hierfür nichts hergeben, hat der Gesetzgeber bewusst dahingehend entschieden, dass der bis zum Inkrafttreten des Ersten Arbeitsrechtsbereinigungsgesetz geltende § 622 BGB in dem Umfang, wie er nach der hier kritisierten Rechtsprechung des BGH für selbstän-

139 BT-Drs. V/3913 v. 24. Februar 1969, S. 10.

140 So *Uffmann* (Anm. 90), ZGR (2013), S. 273, 299; *Uffmann* (Anm. 90), NJW (2020), S. 3210 Rn. 15 m.w.N.

141 So *Uffmann* (Anm. 90), ZGR (2013), S. 273, 299; *Uffmann* (Anm. 90), NJW (2020), S. 3210 Rn. 15.

142 BGH, Urteil v. 29. Januar 1981 – II ZR 92/80, NJW (1981), S. 1270, 1271.

143 Anders aber BGH, Urteil v. 29. Januar 1981 – II ZR 92/80, NJW (1981), S. 1270, 1271.

144 BGH, Urteil v. 29. Januar 1981 – II ZR 92/80, NJW (1981), S. 1270, 1271; *Engshuber* (Anm. 52), § 621 BGB Rn. 12.

dige Dienstverhältnisse von Geschäftsführern galt, nicht von § 621 BGB aufgenommen werden, sondern ab dem Inkrafttreten des Ersten Arbeitsrechtsbereinigungsgesetz durch den neuen § 622 BGB verdrängt werden sollte.

Der BGH mag die analoge Anwendung von § 622 BGB auf das Anstellungsverhältnis des Geschäftsführers für sach- und interessengerechter halten als die von § 621 BGB mit in der Regel kürzeren Kündigungsfristen. Denn für den BGH habe der Geschäftsführer vergleichbar einem Arbeitnehmer als hauptberuflich Tätiger für sich und seine Familie den Lebensunterhalt zu bestreiten und benötige daher während des Laufs der Kündigungsfrist hinreichend Zeit zur beruflichen Neuorientierung.[145] Auf diese Erwägungen kommt es jedoch nicht an, sondern vielmehr nur auf den Willen des Gesetzgebers. Der Gesetzgeber hat es aber ausreichend sein lassen, den Geschäftsführer durch die Kündigungsfristen nach § 621 BGB abzusichern. Bei den Erwägungen des BGH handelt es sich lediglich um einen (subjektiven) rechts- bzw. gesellschaftspolitischen Wunsch. Ein solcher stellt jedoch weder eine Regelungslücke dar noch kann er eine solche kreieren.[146] Eine gleichwohl erfolgende Analogie zur Verfolgung eines solchen Wunsches verstößt gegen das Gesetz,[147] da sich der BGH hierdurch nicht nur über den gesetzgeberischen Willen hinwegsetzt, sondern sich verfassungswidrig auch an die Stelle des Gesetzgebers begibt.[148]

(c) Kündigungsfristengesetz

In seiner Entscheidung vom 5. November 2024[149] zieht der BGH zusätzlich auch das KündFG[150] zur historischen Begründung dafür heran, dass er die gesetzlichen Kündigungsfristen des Geschäftsführers nach wie vor wegen einer planwidrigen Regelungslücke aus einer analogen Anwendung des § 622 BGB herleitet. Der Sinn und Zweck des KündFG habe darin bestanden, in Vollziehung des Gesetzgebungsauftrages aufgrund des Beschlusses des BVerfG vom 30. Mai 1990[151] ausschließlich die Kündigungsfristen für die ordentliche Kündigung für Arbeiter und Angestellte sowie die Rechtslage in den alten und den neuen Bundesländern anzupassen und zu vereinheitlichen.[152] Aufgrund dessen habe er die Frage nach den gesetzlichen Kündigungsfristen für Organmitglieder weder ausdrücklich ansprechen noch korrigieren müs-

145 BGH, Urteil v. 29. Januar 1981 – II ZR 92/80, NJW (1981), S. 1270, 1271; BGH, Urteil v. 26. März 1984 – II ZR 120/83, NJW (1984), S. 2528 f.

146 Vgl. *Beaucamp/Treder*, Methoden und Technik der Rechtsanwendung, 3. Aufl. (2015), Rn. 276.

147 Vgl. *Schwacke* (Anm. 100), S. 126.

148 Vgl. auch *Hümmerich* (Anm. 90), S. 1177, 1180 f.

149 BGH, Urteil v. 5. November 2024 – II ZR 35/23, NZG (2025), S. 663 Rn. 46.

150 Gesetz zur Vereinheitlichung der Kündigungsfristen von Arbeitern und Angestellten (Kündigungsfristengesetz – KündFG) vom 7. Oktober 1993, BGBl. 1993, Teil I, S. 1668.

151 BVerfG, Beschluss v. 30. Mai 1990 – 1 BvL 2/83 u. a., NJW (1990), S. 2246 ff.

152 BGH, Urteil v. 5. November 2024 – II ZR 35/23, NZG (2025), S. 663 Rn. 46; vgl. auch BGH, Urteil v. 29. Januar 1981 – II ZR 92/80, NJW (1981), S. 1270 f.; vgl. auch *Röhsler* (Anm. 61), § 622 BGB Rn. 4.

sen.[153] Hieraus ergebe sich, dass der Gesetzgeber in „offenbarer Kenntnis" der bis 1993 ergangen Rechtsprechung des BGH diese „offensichtlich gebilligt" habe, sodass eine bewusste Wertentscheidung des Gesetzgebers, den persönlichen Anwendungsbereich von § 622 BGB ausschließlich auf Arbeitsverhältnisse zu beschränken, nicht erkennbar sei.[154] Auch diese Argumentation des BGH kann nicht überzeugen.

Zum einen geht der BGH fehl in der Annahme, dass mit dem KündFG eine „bewusste Wertentscheidung" des Gesetzgebers, den persönlichen Anwendungsbereich von § 622 BGB ausschließlich auf Arbeitsverhältnisse zu beschränken, nicht erkennbar gewesen sei. Denn einer solchen „bewussten Wertentscheidung" hatte es auch nicht mehr bedurft. Schließlich hatte der Gesetzgeber diese bereits im bzw. mit dem Ersten Arbeitsrechtsbereinigungsgesetz getroffen, als er eine klare „systematische Unterscheidung" zwischen der ordentlichen Kündigungsfrist für Arbeitsverhältnisse (§ 622 BGB) einerseits sowie der für sonstige Dienstverhältnisse, die keine Arbeitsverhältnisse sind (§ 621 BGB), andererseits, getroffen und in § 621 BGB eine „umfassende Regelung der ordentlichen Kündigung für solche Dienstverhältnisse" geschaffen hatte, „die keine Arbeitsverhältnisse sind."[155] Zum anderen geht das BAG zu Recht davon aus, dass der Gesetzgeber mit der ab dem 15. Oktober 1993 infolge des KündFG geltenden Neufassung von § 622 BGB lediglich die Anbindung der Kündigungsfristenregelung an Arbeitsverhältnisse betont habe.[156] Dafür, „dass er die Kündigungsfristenregelung für (Fremd-)Geschäftsführer dort verortet sehen wollte", ist aus den Gesetzesmaterialien jedoch nichts ersichtlich.[157] Hätte er dies gewollt, so hätte er das KündFG zum Anlass genommen, die bestehende Rechtsprechung des BGH, die sich der Krücke einer analogen Anwendung von § 622 BGB bedient, zwecks unmittelbarer und nicht nur analoger Anwendung von § 622 BGB in das Gesetz zu übernehmen, was aber nicht erfolgt ist.[158] Anzeichen bzw. Indizien für ein entsprechendes – weiteres – Redaktionsversehen des Gesetzgebers bestehen jedenfalls – zu Recht – nicht.[159]

Dafür, dass die bewusste Wertentscheidung des Gesetzgebers darin bestanden hat, den persönlichen Anwendungsbereich von § 622 BGB in der Fassung des KündFG ausschließlich auf Arbeitsverhältnisse zu beschränken, kann auch auf das Gesetzgebungsverfahren zum KündFG und die dortige Stellungnahme des Bundesrates zu

---

153 BGH, Urteil v. 5. November 2024 – II ZR 35/23, NZG (2025), S. 663 Rn. 46; vgl. auch BGH, Urteil v. 29. Januar 1981 – II ZR 92/80, NJW (1981), S. 1270 f.; *Linck* (Anm. 60), § 622 BGB Rn. 12.

154 BGH, Urteil v. 5. November 2024 – II ZR 35/23, NZG (2025), S. 663 Rn. 46; vgl. auch BGH, Urteil v. 29. Januar 1981 – II ZR 92/80, NJW (1981), S. 1270 f.; *Engshuber* (Anm. 52), § 621 BGB Rn. 12; *Linck* (Anm. 60), § 622 BGB Rn. 12.

155 Vgl. BT-Drs. V/3913 v. 24. Februar 1969, S. 10.

156 BAG, Urteil v. 11. Juni 2020 – 2 AZR 374/19, NJW (2020), S. 2824 Rn. 43; vgl. auch BT-Drs. 12/4902 v. 11. Mai 1993, S. 6, 8 f.

157 BAG, Urteil v. 11. Juni 2020 – 2 AZR 374/19, NJW (2020), S. 2824 Rn. 43.

158 BAG, Urteil v. 11. Juni 2020 – 2 AZR 374/19, NJW (2020), S. 2824 Rn. 43.

159 BAG, Urteil v. 11. Juni 2020 – 2 AZR 374/19, NJW (2020), S. 2824 Rn. 43.

Art. 1 KündFG und seinen Beschluss zu Art. 1 KündFG (§ 622 Abs. 1 BGB) verwiesen werden.[160] Dort heißt es:

> „In Art. 1 sind in § 622 Abs. 1 die Worte ‚eines Arbeiters oder eines Angestellten (Arbeitnehmers)' zu ersetzen durch die Worte ‚eines Arbeitnehmers'".[161]

Zur Begründung führt der Bundesrat aus:

> „Die Aufnahme der Begriffe ‚Arbeitnehmer und Angestellter' ist überflüssig, da der Begriff der Arbeitnehmer insoweit eindeutig ist. Der vorgelegte Gesetzesentwurf will gerade den Unterschied zwischen Arbeitern und Angestellten bei den Kündigungsfristen beseitigen."[162]

Im Gesetzgebungsverfahren war man sich daher durchaus darüber bewusst, den persönlichen Anwendungsbereich von § 622 BGB in der Fassung des KündFG ausschließlich auf Arbeitnehmer und deren Arbeitsverhältnisse zu beschränken.

Dass der BGH argumentiert, dass der Gesetzgeber beim Inkrafttreten des KündFG „in offenbarer Kenntnis der Rechtsprechung der Rechtsprechung des BGH" gehandelt habe,[163] ist ebenfalls nicht belegt und lediglich als Unterstellung des BGH zu werten. Jedenfalls argumentiert der BGH erneut geschickt: Nun habe der Gesetzgeber nicht mehr – wie noch beim Ersten Arbeitsrechtsbereinigungsgesetz – versehentlich eine planwidrige Regelungslücke geschaffen, sondern, indem er „die Frage der Kündigungsfristen für Organmitglieder weder ausdrücklich angesprochen noch korrigiert" habe, in offenbarer Kenntnis der Rechtsprechung des BGH diese „offensichtlich gebilligt",[164] also die seit dem Ersten Arbeitsrechtsbereinigungsgesetz vermeintlich bestehende planwidrige Regelungslücke geschlossen, ohne dies jedoch im KündFG in irgendeiner Weise zum Ausdruck zu bringen. Auch hierfür fehlt jeglicher Beleg in den Gesetzesmaterialien. Ansonsten hätte sich der BGH auch damit auseinandersetzen müssen, dass der Gesetzgeber die nach Auffassung des BGH bereits seit dem Ersten Arbeitsrechtsbereinigungsgesetz bestehende planwidrige Regelungslücke erneut unbewusst und planwidrig perpetuiert hat, also ein erneutes Redaktionsversehen gegeben ist. Von einem solchen erneuten Redaktionsversehen kann bei Inkrafttreten des KündFG, also nach über zwei Jahrzehnten seit dem Ersten Arbeitsrechtsbereinigungsgesetz, allen Ernstes nicht mehr ausgegangen werden.[165]

(d) Weitere § 622 BGB abändernde Gesetze

Seit dem maßgeblichen Ersten Arbeitsrechtsbereinigungsgesetz aus dem Jahr 1969 wurde § 622 BGB mehrfach geändert,[166] so z.B. durch das Arbeitsgerichts-Ände-

---

160 Vgl. auch ausführlich *Hümmerich* (Anm. 90), S. 1177, 1180.

161 Anlage (Beschluss) vom 18. Juni 1993 zur Stellungnahme des Bundesrats zum Entwurf eines Gesetzes zur Vereinheitlichung der Kündigungsfristen von Arbeitern und Angestellten (Kündigungsfristengesetz – KündFG) vom 7. Mai 1993, BR-Drs 310/93.

162 Anlage (Beschluss) vom 18. Juni 1993 zur Stellungnahme des Bundesrats zum Entwurf eines Gesetzes zur Vereinheitlichung der Kündigungsfristen von Arbeitern und Angestellten (Kündigungsfristengesetz – KündFG) vom 7. Mai 1993, BR-Drs 310/93.

163 BGH, Urteil v. 5. November 2024 – II ZR 35/23, NZG (2025), S. 663 Rn. 46.

164 BGH, Urteil v. 5. November 2024 – II ZR 35/23, NZG (2025), S. 663 Rn. 46.

165 Eingehend *Hümmerich* (Anm. 90), S. 1177, 1180.

166 Vgl. auch *Uffmann* (Anm. 90), ZGR (2013), S. 273, 299.

rungsgesetz,[167] das Kündigungsfristengesetz,[168] das Arbeitsrechtliche Beschäftigungsförderungsgesetz,[169] das Gesetz zu Korrekturen in der Sozialversicherung und zur Sicherung der Arbeitnehmerrechte[170] bis hin zum Qualifizierungschancengesetz.[171] Der Gesetzgeber hat jedoch keines dieser zahlreichen Gesetze zum Anlass genommen, die Kündigungsfristenregelung für das Anstellungsverhältnis des Geschäftsführers oder sonstiger freier Dienstverhältnisse in § 622 zu verorten oder sich in den entsprechenden Gesetzesmaterialien hierzu zumindest zu positionieren. Wäre es sein Wille gewesen, so hätten die zahlreichen Neuregelungen des § 622 BGB ihm zuhauf Anlass und Gelegenheit geboten, die Rechtsprechung des BGH zur analogen Anwendung von § 622 BGB in gesetzliche Regelungen zu gießen. Dies ist jedoch nicht geschehen. Selbst der BGH wird nicht behaupten wollen, dass es sich hierbei immer wieder und somit um permanente Redaktionsversehen des Gesetzgebers und somit um eine sich immer weiter perpetuierende planwidrige Regelungslücke in Bezug auf die gesetzlichen Kündigungsfristen für das Dienstverhältnis des Geschäftsführers handelt.

Vielmehr belegen auch diese zahlreichen Gesetze, mit denen § 622 BGB seit dem Ersten Arbeitsrechtsbereinigungsgesetz geändert wurde, dass der Gesetzgeber für Änderungen in § 622 BGB im Sinne der Analogie-Rechtsprechung des BGH deswegen keinerlei Veranlassung sah, weil er bereits mit dem Ersten Arbeitsrechtsbereinigungsgesetz eine klare „systematische Unterscheidung“ zwischen der ordentlichen Kündigung für Arbeitsverhältnisse nach § 622 BGB einerseits sowie andererseits für sonstige Dienstverhältnisse, die keine Arbeitsverhältnisse im Sinne des § 622 BGB sind, getroffen hatte. Denn mit § 621 BGB hatte er bereits im Ersten Arbeitsrechtsbereinigungsgesetz eine „umfassende Regelung der ordentlichen Kündigung für solche Dienstverhältnisse“, geschaffen, „die keine Arbeitsverhältnisse sind“.[172]

Dies wird noch deutlicher, wenn man sich vor Augen hält, dass seit dem Ersten Arbeitsrechtsbereinigungsgesetz im Jahr 1969 die mittlerweile legendären Danosa-, Balkaya- und Holterman-Judikate des EuGH zum unionsrechtlichen Arbeitnehmerstatus des Fremd- und Minderheits-Gesellschaftergeschäftsführers ohne beherrschenden Einfluss auf die Gesellschafterversammlung ergangen sind, die das nationale deutsche Arbeits- und auch Gesellschaftsrecht nahezu erschüttert haben.[173] Auch angesichts dieser Judikatur und der hierdurch ausgelösten intensiven Diskussi-

---

167 Gesetz zur Änderung des Arbeitsgerichtsgesetzes und anderer arbeitsrechtlicher Vorschriften (Arbeitsgerichts-Änderungsgesetz) vom 26. Juni 1990, BGBl. 1990, Teil I, S. 1206.

168 Gesetz zur Vereinheitlichung der Kündigungsfristen von Arbeitern und Angestellten (Kündigungsfristengesetz – KündFG) vom 7. Oktober 1993, BGBl. 1993, Teil I, S. 1668.

169 Arbeitsrechtliches Gesetz zur Förderung von Wachstum und Beschäftigung (Arbeitsrechtliches Beschäftigungsförderungsgesetz) vom 25. September 1996, BGBl. 1996, Teil I, S. 1476.

170 Gesetz zu Korrekturen in der Sozialversicherung und zur Sicherung der Arbeitnehmerrechte vom 19. Dezember 1998, BGBl. 1998, Teil I, S. 3843.

171 Gesetz zur Stärkung der Chancen für Qualifizierung und für mehr Schutz in der Arbeitslosenversicherung (Qualifizierungschancengesetz) vom 18. Dezember 2018, BGBl. 2018, Teil I, S. 2651.

172 Vgl. IV. 3. c) bb) (2) (b) sowie BT-Drs. V/3913 v. 24. Februar 1969, S. 10.

173 Vgl. III. 2. c).

on in der arbeits- und auch gesellschaftsrechtlichen Rechtsprechung und Literatur zum Status des Geschäftsführers nach nationalem Recht und Unionsrecht hat der Gesetzgeber, dem diese intensive Diskussion nicht entgangen ist, keinerlei Veranlassung gesehen, die streitige Rechtsprechung des BGH zur analogen Anwendung des ausschließlich für Arbeitsverhältnisse geltenden § 622 BGB auf das Anstellungsverhältnis des Geschäftsführers als freies Dienstverhältnis normativ zu vertypen.

Hingegen sah sich der Gesetzgeber aber beispielsweise veranlasst, auch in Konsequenz der Danosa-Judikatur des EuGH zur Anwendung der Mutterschutzrichtlinie der EU auf die Fremdgeschäftsführerin[174] im Rahmen einer grundlegenden Überarbeitung des MuSchG im Jahre 2017[175] auch der schwangeren (Fremd-)Geschäftsführerin als freien Dienstnehmerin und unionsrechtlichen Arbeitnehmerin nach § 1 Abs. 2 Satz 1 MuSchG den persönlichen Anwendungsbereich des MuSchG zu eröffnen, soweit diese nach § 7 Abs. 1 SGB IV Beschäftigte ist.[176] Zu § 622 BGB geschah seit dem Ersten Arbeitsrechtsbereinigungsgesetz trotz der hier kritisierten Analogie-Rechtsprechung des BGH jedoch nichts.

(3) Gesetzessystematische Auslegung

Auch die gesetzessystematische Auslegung der §§ 621, 622 BGB führt zu dem Ergebnis, dass die gesetzlichen Kündigungsfristen für das Anstellungsverhältnis des Geschäftsführers als einem freien Dienstverhältnis mit Geschäftsbesorgungscharakters nach §§ 611, 675 BGB nicht im Wege einer analogen Heranziehung von § 622 BGB herzuleiten sind, sondern sich unmittelbar aus § 621 BGB ergeben. Da die neue Gesetzessystematik zu §§ 621, 622 BGB durch das Erste Arbeitsrechtsbereinigungsgesetz und den darin zum Ausdruck gekommenen gesetzgeberischen Willen geschaffen und seit dem auch nicht mehr verändert wurde, ist die gesetzessystematische Auslegung von §§ 621, 622 BGB letztlich eine sich unmittelbar aus der historischen Auslegung ergebende Konsequenz. Die gesetzgeberische Systematik folgt ausdrücklich dem gesetzgeberischen Willen und stellt letztlich dessen Umsetzung dar.

So soll der Fokus erneut auf die Gesetzesmaterialien zum Ersten Arbeitsrechtsbereinigungsgesetz und den darin manifestierten Willen des Gesetzgebers gerichtet werden, wenn dort zu §§ 621, 622 BGB der ausdrückliche Wille des Gesetzgebers dahingehend zum Ausdruck gebracht wurde, dass die vorgesehene „Änderung bzw. Ergänzung“ in §§ 621, 622 BGB „eine systematische Unterscheidung der ordentlichen Kündigung für Arbeitsverhältnisse einerseits sowie für sonstige Dienstverhältnisse, die keine Arbeitsverhältnisse sind, andererseits“ vorsehe.[177] Dieser Wille des Gesetzgebers wurde sodann auch durch die Stellungnahme des Bundesrats, dem die Bundesregierung entsprach und die der Bundestag letztlich beschloss,

---

174 EuGH, Urteil v. 11. November 2000 – Danosa, C-232/09, ECLI:EU:C:2010:674.

175 Gesetz zur Neuregelung des Mutterschutzrechts vom 23. Mai 2017, BGBl. 2017, Teil I, S. 1228.

176 Vgl. hierzu näher *Rütz/Voigt*, Zentrale Fortentwicklungen des Mutterschutzes unter Berücksichtigung der Novelle des Mutterschutzgesetzes 2025, in: NJW (2025), S. 2505 Rn. 8 ff.

177 BT-Drs. V/3913 v. 24. Februar 1969, S. 10.

noch pointierter dahingehend herausgearbeitet, „daß § 621 BGB künftig nur für solche Dienstverhältnisse gelten soll, die keine Arbeitsverhältnisse (§ 622 i. d. F. des Entwurfs)“ sind.[178] So „fügt sich dann in klarer Abhebung die neue Fassung des § 622 an, die eindeutig von Arbeitsverhältnissen von Angestellten und Arbeitern, also von unselbständigen Dienstverhältnissen, spricht.“[179]

Diesem ausdrücklichen Willen des Gesetzgebers folgte dessen planvolle Umsetzung auch hinsichtlich der Gesetzessystematik in Gestalt einer strengen „systematischen Unterscheidung der ordentlichen Kündigung für Arbeitsverhältnisse einerseits sowie für sonstige Dienstverhältnisse, die keine Arbeitsverhältnisse sind, andererseits“[180]. § 611 BGB regelt den Dienstvertrag. Wird mit einem solchen Dienstvertrag ein Dienstverhältnis begründet, das kein Arbeitsverhältnis im Sinne des § 622 BGB ist, so regeln sich für dieses die gesetzlichen Kündigungsfristen nach § 621 BGB. § 611a BGB regelt hingegen den Arbeitsvertrag als Unterfall des Dienstvertrages,[181] und somit als lex specialis.[182] Wird mit einem solchen Arbeitsvertrag ein Arbeitsverhältnis begründet, so regeln sich für dieses die gesetzlichen Kündigungsfristen nach § 622 BGB. § 622 BGB folgt daher in „klarer Abhebung“ § 621 BGB.[183]

cc) Ergebnis

Die Auslegung der §§ 621, 622 BGB hat klar zu Tage gebracht, dass im Hinblick auf die gesetzlichen Kündigungsfristen des Geschäftsführers keine Regelungslücke besteht, und schon gar keine planwidrige. Im Gegenteil: Die gesetzlichen Kündigungsfristen für Dienstverhältnisse, die keine Arbeitsverhältnisse im Sinne des § 622 BGB sind, hat der Gesetzgeber willentlich, plangemäß und abschließend in § 621 BGB geregelt. Da das Anstellungsverhältnis des Geschäftsführers als ein solches Dienstverhältnis zu bewerten ist, regeln sich die gesetzlichen Kündigungsfristen für sein Anstellungsverhältnis nach § 621 BGB. Die planwidrige Regelungslücke, die der BGH zu erkennen glaubt, ist im Rahmen des Ersten Arbeitsrechtsbereinigungsgesetzes durch die Schaffung des § 621 BGB gar nicht erst entstanden. Mangels einer (planwidrigen) Regelungslücke muss daher eine Analogie ausscheiden, anderenfalls man im Fall einer erzwungenen Analogie das Gesetz gegen den Willen des Gesetzgebers und somit contra legem auslegen würde. Einer Erörterung der von beiden Seiten weiter vorgebrachten Argumente, so z. B. des Arguments des BAG auf den ansonsten entstehenden Wertungswiderspruch aufgrund der Anwendbarkeit von § 622 BGB auf Fremdgeschäftsführer bei dessen gleichzeitiger Nichtanwendbarkeit auf arbeitnehmerähnliche Personen,[184] bedarf es daher nicht mehr.

---

178 BT-Drs. V/3913 v. 24. Februar 1969, S. 14.

179 BT-Drs. V/3913 v. 24. Februar 1969, S. 14.

180 BT-Drs. V/3913 v. 24. Februar 1969, S. 10.

181 *Preis* (Anm. 22), § 611a BGB Rn. 1; *Thüsing*, in: Henssler/Willemsen/Kalb (Hrsg.), Arbeitsrecht Kommentar, 11. Aufl. (2024), § 611a BGB Rn. 18.

182 *Joussen* (Anm. 22), § 611a BGB Rn. 4.

183 BT-Drs. V/3913 v. 24. Februar 1969, S. 14.

184 BAG, Urteil v. 11. Juni 2020 – 2 AZR 374/19, NJW (2020), S. 2824 Rn. 44.

Nach alledem ist der Ansicht des BAG[185] zu folgen, nach der sich die gesetzlichen Kündigungsfristen für das Anstellungsverhältnis eines jeden Geschäftsführers aus § 621 BGB ergeben. Somit kann sich auch ein „Geschäftsführer, der nicht Mehrheitsgesellschafter der GmbH ist und zu ihr in keinem Arbeitsverhältnis steht, nicht auf die verlängerten gesetzlichen Kündigungsfristen des § 622 Abs. 2 BGB berufen."[186] Dies gilt somit auch für den Fremdgeschäftsführer ohne Beteiligung am Kapital der GmbH. Ein gewisser sozialer Schutz durch die gesetzlichen Kündigungsfristen des § 622 BGB entfällt. Lediglich dann, wenn das Anstellungsverhältnis des Geschäftsführers in seltenen Fällen ausnahmsweise als Arbeitsverhältnis und der Geschäftsführer als persönlich abhängiger und weisungsgebundener Arbeitnehmer zu charakterisieren sind,[187] sind die gesetzlichen Kündigungsfristen für das Anstellungsverhältnis des Geschäftsführers aus § 622 BGB herzuleiten.

Die Analogie-Rechtsprechung des BGH, die – wie aufgezeigt – konsequenterweise abzulehnen ist, bildet mit der des BAG, wenn überhaupt nur eine kleine Schnittmenge, nämlich für die beherrschenden Gesellschafter-Geschäftsführer. Denn der BGH wendet die gesetzlichen Kündigungsfristen analog § 622 BGB auf das Anstellungsverhältnis eines jeden Geschäftsführers an, „soweit dieser nicht beherrschender Gesellschafter" ist.[188] Zugleich hält der BGH die Frage, ob sich die gesetzlichen Kündigungsfristen des Anstellungsverhältnisses eines beherrschenden Gesellschafter-Geschäftsführers dann auch aus § 621 BGB herleiten, aber auch für „bedeutungslos", „da dessen Anstellungsverhältnis ohnehin nicht gegen seinen Willen gekündigt werden" könne.[189]

Nur der Vollständigkeit halber soll mit derselben Begründung wie für die Kündigung des Anstellungsverhältnisses des Geschäftsführers durch die GmbH erwähnt werden, dass für den Fall, dass vertraglich keine Kündigungsfristen vereinbart wurden, die gesetzlichen Kündigungsfristen nach § 621 BGB natürlich auch für die Eigenkündigung des Geschäftsführers gelten.[190]

V. Und nun?

Der BGH und das BAG sind aufgrund ihrer widerstreitenden Rechtsprechung ineinander verhakt. Zurzeit ist nicht ersichtlich, dass einer der beiden Kontrahenten von seinem Standpunkt abrücken und sich auf den anderen zubewegen wird, was auch für die ihnen jeweils folgenden Stimmen in der Literatur gelten dürfte. Dies führt im Rechtsverkehr zu Rechtsunsicherheit. Rechtsklarheit sucht man auch hier vergebens. Um dem zu entrinnen, bieten sich folgende Möglichkeiten:

---

185 BAG, Urteil v. 11. Juni 2020 – 2 AZR 374/19, NJW (2020), S. 2824 Rn. 35 ff.

186 BAG, Urteil v. 11. Juni 2020 – 2 AZR 374/19, NJW (2020), S. 2824 Rn. 41.

187 Vgl. III. 1. b) bb).

188 BGH, Urteil v. 9. März 1987 – II ZR 132/86, NJW (1987), S. 2073, 2074.

189 BGH, Urteil v. 26. März 1984 – II ZR 120/83, NJW (1984), S. 2528, 2529.

190 Vgl. *Jaeger/Steinbrück* (Anm. 11), § 35 GmbHG Rn. 436, allerdings für die gesetzlichen Kündigungsfristen für das Anstellungsverhältnis des Geschäftsführers analog § 622 BGB.

1. Gemeinsamer Senat der obersten Gerichtshöfe des Bundes

Der BGH und das BAG haben es als Kontrahenten selbst in der Hand, Klärung zu schaffen. Beide können als zwei der fünf obersten Gerichtshöfe des Bundes den Gemeinsamen Senat der obersten Gerichtshöfe des Bundes[191] anrufen, um klären zu lassen, ob sich die gesetzlichen Kündigungsfristen für das Anstellungsverhältnis des Geschäftsführers unmittelbar nach § 621 BGB richten oder sich aus einer analogen Anwendung von § 622 BGB ergeben.

a) Verfahren vor dem Gemeinsamen Senat der obersten Gerichtshöfe des Bundes

Der GmS-OGB ist eine Einrichtung zur Wahrung der Einheitlichkeit der Rechtsprechung der in Art. 95 Abs. 1 GG genannten obersten Gerichtshöfe des Bundes. Rechtsgrundlage für seine Errichtung ist Art. 95 Abs. 3 GG,[192] wonach der GmS-OGB aus den in Art. 95 Abs. 1 GG genannten obersten Gerichtshöfen des Bundes zu errichten ist. Alles weitere regelt ein Bundesgesetz, bei dem es sich um das RsprEinhG handelt.[193] Der Sitz des GmS-OGB ist nach § 1 Abs. 2 RsprEinhG Karlsruhe. Dort wurde er auch am 1. Januar 1969 errichtet.

Will ein oberster Gerichtshof des Bundes in einer Rechtsfrage von der Entscheidung eines anderen obersten Gerichtshofs oder des GmS-OGB abweichen, so hat er verpflichtend den GmS-OGB anzurufen, woraufhin dieser nach § 2 Abs. 1 RsprEinhG entscheidet. Der GmS-OGB entscheidet nach § 15 Abs. 1 Satz 1 RsprEinhG nur über die strittige Rechtsfrage und nur insoweit, als es im Einzelfall für die Ausräumung der Divergenz in der Rechtsprechung der obersten Gerichtshöfe des Bundes erforderlich ist. Schließt sich der Senat des obersten Gerichtshofs, von dessen Entscheidung abgewichen werden soll, innerhalb eines Monats durch Beschluss der Rechtsauffassung des vorlegenden Senats an, so ist das Vorlageverfahren nach § 14 Satz 1 RsprEinhG einzustellen. Ansonsten kommt es zur Sachentscheidung durch den GmS-OGB. Nach § 16 RsprEinhG ist seine Entscheidung in der vorliegenden Sache für das erkennende und vorlegende oberste Bundesgericht bindend. Der GmS-OGB ist gesetzlicher Richter im Sinne des Art. 101 Abs. 1 Satz 1 GG.[194]

b) Vertane Chance des BAG

In seiner Entscheidung vom 11. Juni 2020[195] hatte das BAG Gelegenheit, das obligatorische Vorlageverfahren beim GmS-OGB nach § 11 Abs. 3 RsprEinhG in Verbindung mit § 4 RsprEinhG einzuleiten. Denn mit seiner Entscheidung vom 11. Juni 2020 wich das BAG im Sinne von § 2 Abs. 1 RsprEinhG in der Rechtsfrage, ob auf das Anstellungsverhältnis des Geschäftsführers die gesetzlichen Kündigungsfristen nach § 621 BGB oder analog § 622 BGB Anwendung finden, von der Rechtspre-

191 Nachfolgend: GmS-OGB.

192 Sechzehntes Gesetz zur Änderung des Grundgesetzes vom 18. Juni 1968, Teil I, S. 657.

193 Gesetz zur Wahrung der Einheitlichkeit der Rechtsprechung der obersten Gerichtshöfe des Bundes vom 19. Juni 1968, BGBl. 1968, Teil I, S. 661.

194 *Temming* (Anm. 61), § 622 BGB Rn. 8a.

195 BAG, Urteil v. 11. Juni 2020 – 2 AZR 374/19, NJW (2020), S. 2824 Rn. 48 ff.

chung des BGH ab. Die Gelegenheit für ein Vorlageverfahren an den GmS-OGB ergriff das BAG jedoch bewusst nicht.[196]

Das BAG hat seine Entscheidung vom 11. Juni 2020 damit begründet, dass nach § 2 Abs. 1 RsprEinhG keine Vorlagepflicht bestanden habe. Denn eine Divergenz zur Rechtsprechung des BGH betreffend § 622 Abs. 1 BGB a. F. habe nicht vorgelegen, da diese Norm mit Wirkung ab dem 15. Oktober 1993 durch das KündFG grundlegend geändert worden sei. In der Zeit nach dieser Neufassung, also nach dem 15. Oktober 1993 seien jedoch zur neuen und durch das KündFG geschaffenen Rechtslage keinerlei Entscheidungen des BGH dokumentiert, „in denen er sich tragend zur gesetzlichen Kündigungsfrist für (Fremd-)Geschäftsführer einer GmbH geäußert" habe.[197] In seinem Urteil vom 19. September 2005 habe es der BGH ausdrücklich offengelassen, ob § 622 Abs. 6 BGB in der Fassung des KündFG auf das Anstellungsverhältnis eines Geschäftsführers entsprechende Anwendung finde.[198] Es fehle daher an einer abweichenden Entscheidung im Anwendungsbereich derselben Rechtsvorschrift im Sinne des § 2 Abs. 1 RsprEinhG.[199]

Die Entscheidung des BAG, den GmS-OGB nicht anzurufen, war unzutreffend.[200] Denn zum einen hat das BAG verkannt, dass der BGH sehr wohl in seiner Entscheidung vom 20. August 2019 an seiner Rechtsprechung zu § 622 BGB auch nach dem Inkrafttreten des KündFG festgehalten hat,[201] weshalb das BAG die nach wie vor bestehende Divergenz zur Rechtsprechung des BGH mit der Konsequenz hätte erkennen müssen, seiner Vorlagepflicht nach § 2 Abs. 1 RsprEinhG i. V. m. § 11 RsprEinhG an den GmS-OGB nachzukommen.[202] Zum anderen hätte das BAG aufgrund der in seiner Entscheidung vom 11. Juni 2020[203] selbst zitierten Entscheidung des BGH vom 19. September 2005[204] in Erwägung ziehen müssen, die strittige Rechtsfrage dem GmS-OGB nach § 2 Abs. 1 RsprEinhG i. V. m. § 11 RsprEinhG vorzulegen. Zwar hat der BGH in seiner Entscheidung vom 19. September 2005 die Anwendung des novellierten § 622 BGB offengelassen, was das BAG auch durchaus erkannt hat. Der BGH hat in dieser Entscheidung aber unter Nennung seiner bisherigen

---

196 BAG, Urteil v. 11. Juni 2020 – 2 AZR 374/19, NJW (2020), S. 2824 Rn. 49 f.; kritisch hierzu BGH, Urteil v. 5. November 2024 – II ZR 35/23, NZG (2025), S. 663 Rn. 46; *Uffmann* (Anm. 90), NJW (2020), S. 3210, Rn. 8; *Temming* (Anm. 61), § 622 BGB Rn. 8a.

197 BAG, Urteil v. 11. Juni 2020 – 2 AZR 374/19, NJW (2020), S. 2824 Rn. 50.

198 BGH, Urteil v. 19. September 2005 – II ZR 173/04, NJW (2005), S. 3641, 3643 mit Verweis auf seine vorherigen Urteile; BAG, Urteil v. 11. Juni 2020 – 2 AZR 374/19, NJW (2020), S. 2824 Rn. 50.

199 BAG, Urteil v. 11. Juni 2020 – 2 AZR 374/19, NJW (2020), S. 2824 Rn. 49 f.

200 So auch *Linck* (Anm. 60), § 622 BGB Rn. 12; *Temming* (Anm. 61), § 622 BGB Rn. 8a; *Uffmann* (Anm. 90), NJW 2020, 3210, Rn. 8.

201 BGH, Urteil v. 20. August 2019 – II ZR 121/16, NJW (2019), S. 3718 Rn. 34; vgl. auch BGH, Urteil v. 5. November 2024 – II ZR 35/23, AP BGB § 622 Nr. 80 Rn. 46.

202 So auch *Linck* (Anm. 60), § 622 BGB Rn. 12; *Temming* (Anm. 61), § 622 BGB Rn. 8a; *Uffmann* (Anm. 90), NJW 2020, 3210, Rn. 8.

203 BAG, Urteil v. 11. Juni 2020 – 2 AZR 374/19, NJW (2020), S. 2824 Rn. 50.

204 BGH, Urteil v. 19. September 2005 – II ZR 173/04, NJW (2005), S. 3641 ff.

Rechtsprechung zur analogen Anwendung von § 622 BGB auf das Anstellungsverhältnis des Geschäftsführers an dieser ausdrücklich festgehalten.[205]

Es bleibt daher zu hoffen, dass zukünftig entweder der BGH oder das BAG zur Klärung der Frage, ob auf das Anstellungsverhältnis des Geschäftsführers die gesetzlichen Kündigungsfristen nach § 621 BGB oder analog § 622 BGB Anwendung finden, den Weg zum GmS-OGB finden und diesen auch nicht scheuen. Die Rechtsansichten dieser beiden obersten Bundesgerichte liegen jedenfalls klar und eindeutig auf dem Tisch. Halten sie an ihnen in künftigen Entscheidungen fest, so weichen beide in dieser Rechtsfrage von der Entscheidung des jeweils anderen ab. Der Weg zum GmS-OGB als gesetzlichem Richter im Sinne des Art. 101 Abs. 1 Satz 1 GG ist dann nach § 2 Abs. 1 RsprEinhG eröffnet. Ein Unbehagen vor dem „verfassungsrechtlich ohnehin bedenklichen Rechtfertigungstopos" des „horror pleni" ist jedenfalls unbegründet.[206]

2. Vertragliche Vereinbarung der Kündigungsfristen zwischen GmbH und Geschäftsführer

Aber auch der Geschäftsführer und seine Dienstgeberin, die GmbH, haben es in der Hand, selbst für Abhilfe sowie Rechtssicherheit und -klarheit zu sorgen. Denn aufgrund ihrer Vertragshoheit kann ein jeder Geschäftsführer mit seiner Dienstgeberin die gesetzlichen Kündigungsfristen des § 622 BGB einvernehmlich vereinbaren.[207]

3. Ruf nach dem Gesetzgeber

Und zu guter Letzt bleibt auch hier der Ruf nach dem Gesetzgeber. Dieser hat es in der Hand, für Rechtssicherheit und -klarheit zu sorgen. Dies jedoch nur klarstellend, denn mit dem Ersten Arbeitsrechtsbereinigungsgesetz hat er im Jahr 1969 bereits Rechtssicherheit und -klarheit geschaffen, indem er das Anstellungsverhältnis des Geschäftsführers unter den Anwendungsbereich von § 621 BGB gezogen hat, also unter den für Dienstverhältnisse, die keine Arbeitsverhältnisse im Sinne des § 622 BGB sind. Ob der Gesetzgeber jedoch einem entsprechenden Ruf nach Klarstellung folgen wird, dürfte eher unwahrscheinlich sein.

VI. Schlusswort

Heinrich Menkhaus und ich kennen uns seit dem 18. März 2016. An diesem Tag wurde ich in Frankfurt am Main in Anwesenheit des Jubilars von der Mitgliederver-

---

205 BGH, Urteil v. 19. September 2005 – II ZR 173/04, NJW (2005), S. 3641, 3643 unter ausdrücklicher Nennung von BGH, Urteil v. 29. Januar 1981 – II ZR 92/80, NJW (1981), S. 1270 f.; BGH, Urteil v. 26. März 1984 – II ZR 120/83, NJW (1984), S. 2528 f.; BGH, Urteil v. 9. März 1987 – II ZR 132/86, NJW (1987), S. 2073 f.; vgl. wie hier auch *Uffmann* (Anm. 90), NJW (2020), S. 3210 Rn. 8.

206 So zutreffend *Temming* (Anm. 61), § 622 BGB Rn. 8a.

207 Statt vieler nur *Beurskens* (Anm. 29), § 38 GmbHG Rn. 144; vgl. auch *Altmeppen* (Anm. 29), § 6 GmbHG 135, 137.

sammlung der Deutsch-Japanischen Gesellschaft für Arbeitsrecht e. V. zum geschäftsführenden Mitglied ihres Vorstands gewählt.

Sieben Jahre – und so manche Tagung und auch persönliche Begegnung in Deutschland und Japan – später besuchte Heinrich Menkhaus mich in meiner Kanzlei, die nur einen Steinwurf entfernt von einer seiner ehemaligen Wirkungsstätten, der Rechtsanwaltskanzlei Bruckhaus Kreifels Winkhaus & Lieberknecht, gelegen ist, um mit mir von dort zu einem Empfang der japanischen Generalkonsulin in Düsseldorf aufzubrechen. Er berichtete mir bei dieser Gelegenheit von einer Festschrift zu Ehren seines siebzigsten Geburtstages und fragte mich, ob ich eventuell bereit wäre, einen Beitrag zu dieser Festschrift beizusteuern, was ich geehrt sofort und sehr gerne bejahte. Er sagte noch, dass es kein „typisch juristischer" Beitrag sein müsse. Es könne auch etwas „Deutsch-Japanisches" sein.

Und nun bin ich hier mit einem doch ganz typisch juristischen Beitrag. Immerhin: Ein Querschnittsthema aus den Bereichen des Arbeits- und Gesellschaftsrechts, zwei Rechtsbereichen in denen Heinrich Menkhaus seit jeher in Deutschland und auch in Japan zu Hause ist und gewirkt hat. Auch als langjähriger Vorsitzender der Deutsch-Japanischen Gesellschaft für Arbeitsrecht e. V.

Ich widme meinen Beitrag von Herzen gerne Heinrich Menkhaus zu seinem siebzigsten Geburtstag und hoffe, dass er ein wenig Gefallen an ihm findet. Sein grenzüberschreitendes Schaffen zwischen Deutschland und Japan erfährt nun mit seiner Emeritierung an der Meiji Universität in Tokyo eine Zäsur, aber ganz sicher kein Ende. Für sein langjähriges und enormes Schaffen für den akademisch-wissenschaftlichen, kulturellen und auch menschlichen Austausch zwischen Deutschland und Japan und sein Bemühen um Verständigung und gegenseitiges Verständnis zwischen beiden Staaten und ihren Kulturen gebührt ihm großer und nachhaltiger Dank. Ich bin mir sicher: Zwischen diesen Welten wird er auch weiterhin wandeln, wirken und helfen.

Ad multos annos!

Literaturverzeichnis

Altmeppen, Holger: Der GmbH-Geschäftsführer als unabhängiger Treuhänder der Allgemeinheit, in: NJW (2022), S. 2785 ff.

Altmeppen, Holger: Gesetz betreffend die Gesellschaften mit beschränkter Haftung, 11. Aufl. (2023).

Ante, Johann: Fristen für die Kündigung des Anstellungsvertrages eines GmbH-Geschäftsführers, in: GWR (2025), S. 114.

Arnold, Christian: Geltung der Kündigungsfristen nach § 622 Abs. 1, Abs. 2 BGB für Geschäftsführerverträge, in: FD-ArbR (2025), S. 802392.

Ascheid, Reiner/*Preis*, Ulrich/*Schmidt*, Ingrid: Kündigungsrecht, Großkommentar zum gesamten Recht der Beendigung von Arbeitsverhältnissen, 7. Aufl. (2024).

Beaucamp, Guy/*Treder*, Lutz: Methoden und Technik der Rechtsanwendung, 3. Aufl. (2015).

Becker, Ulrich/*Hatje*, Armin/*Schoo*, Johann/*Schwarze*, Jürgen (Hrsg.): EU-Kommentar, 4. Aufl. (2019).

Boecken, Winfried/*Düwell*, Franz Josef/*Diller*, Martin/*Hanau*, Hans (Hrsg.): Gesamtes Arbeitsrecht, 2. Aufl. (2023).

Boemke, Burkhard: Aktuelles zum GmbH-Geschäftsführer aus arbeitsrechtlicher Sicht, in: RdA (2018), S. 1 ff.

Bubach, Bettina/*Gallner*, Inken/*Heinkel*, Ronny: KR Gemeinschaftskommentar zum Kündigungsschutzgesetz und zu sonstigen kündigungsrechtlichen Vorschriften, 14. Aufl. (2025).

Canaris, Claus-Wilhelm: Die Feststellung von Lücken im Gesetz, 2. Aufl. (1983).

Dau, Dirk/*Düwell*, Franz Josef/*Joussen*, Jacob/*Luik*, Steffen (Hrsg.): Sozialgesetzbuch IX, 6. Aufl. (2021).

Fleischer, Holger/*Goette*, Wulf (Hrsg.): Münchener Kommentar zum Gesetz betreffend die Gesellschaften mit beschränkter Haftung, Band 2, 4. Aufl. (2023).

Franzen, Martin/*Gallner*, Inken/*Oetker*, Hartmut (Hrsg.): Kommentar zum Europäischen Arbeitsrecht, 5. Aufl. (2024).

Fuchs, Maximilian/*Marhold*, Franz: Europäisches Arbeitsrecht, 4. Aufl. (2014).

Gallner, Inken/*Mestwerdt*, Wilhelm/*Nägelke-Berkner*, Anja (Hrsg.): Kündigungsschutzrecht, 8. Aufl. (2025).

Günther-Gräff, Eva: Der GmbH-Geschäftsführer und § 6 Abs. 5 ArbZG, in: Jacobs, Matthias/Kiel, Heinrich/Oberthür, Nathalie/Oetker, Hartmut/Schubert, Claudia (Hrsg.): Arbeitsrecht in Praxis und Wissenschaft, Festschrift für Stefan Lunk (2025), S. 141 ff.

Haase, Karsten: Der besondere Kündigungsschutz eines schwerbehinderten Geschäftsführers einer GmbH i. S. d. §§ 168, 174 Abs. 1 SGB IX – Eine Bewertung nach deutschem und europäischem Recht unter Berücksichtigung der Milkova-Entscheidung des EuGH, in: GmbHR (2019), S. 980 ff.

Haase, Karsten: Der diskriminierungsrechtliche Kündigungsschutz des (schwer-)behinderten oder einem solchen gleichgestellten Geschäftsführers einer GmbH nach dem AGG und dem SGB IX im Lichte der Rechtsprechung des EuGH, des BGH und des BAG, in: Düwell, Nora/Gallner, Inken/Haase, Karsten/Wolmerath, Martin (Hrsg.): Auf dem Weg zu einem sozialen und inklusiven Rechtsstaat – Covid-19 als Herausforderung, Liber Amicorum Franz Josef Düwell (2021), S. 327 ff.

Haase, Karsten: Der Erholungsurlaub des Geschäftsführers einer GmbH aus rechtlicher Sicht, in: GmbHR (2005), S. 265 ff. und 338 ff.

Haase, Karsten: Fristen für die außerordentliche sowie ordentliche Kündigung des Anstellungsverhältnisses eine GmbH-Geschäftsführers, in: LMK (2025), S. 810482.

Hackethal, Philip: Kündigungsfrist von (Fremd-)Geschäftsführern – Anwendung von § 622 BGB, in: BB (2025), S. 703 f.

Henssler, Martin: Zur Frist für Kündigung des Anstellungsvertrages eines GmbH-Geschäftsführers, in: ZIP (2025), S. 562 f.

Henssler, Martin/*Krüger*, Wolfgang (Redakteure): Münchener Kommentar zum Bürgerlichen Gesetzbuch, Band 5, 9. Aufl. (2023).

Henssler, Martin/*Strohn*, Lutz (Hrsg.): Gesellschaftsrecht, 6. Aufl. (2024).

Henssler, Martin/*Willemsen*, Heinz Josef/*Kalb*, Heinz-Jürgen (Hrsg.): Arbeitsrecht Kommentar, 11. Aufl. (2024).

Horn, Norbert: Einführung in die Rechtswissenschaft und Rechtsphilosophie, 5. Aufl. (2011).

Hümmerich, Klaus: Grenzfall des Arbeitsrechts: Kündigung des GmbH-Geschäftsführers, in: NJW (1995), S. 1177 ff.

Jenne, Moritz/*Sprösser*, Etienne: Kündigungsfristen für Geschäftsführer: Der BGH bleibt seiner Linie treu, in: BB (2025), S. 596.

Junker, Abbo: Die Einflüsse des europäischen Rechts auf die personelle Reichweite des Arbeitnehmerschutzes – Der Arbeitnehmerbegriff in der Rechtsprechung des Europäischen Gerichtshofes, in: EuZA (2016), S. 184 ff.

Larenz, Karl/*Canaris*, Claus-Wilhelm: Methodenlehre der Rechtswissenschaft, 3. Aufl. (1995).

Lutter, Marcus/*Hommelhoff*, Peter: GmbH-Gesetz, 21. Aufl. (2023).

Michalski, Lutz/*Heidinger*, Andreas/*Leible*, Stefan/*Schmidt*, Jessica (Hrsg.): Kommentar zum Gesetz betreffend die Gesellschaften mit beschränkter Haftung (GmbHG-Gesetz), 4. Aufl. (2023).

Müller-Glöge, Rudi/*Preis*, Ulrich/*Gallner*, Inken/*Schmidt*, Ingrid (Hrsg.): Erfurter Kommentar zum Arbeitsrecht, 25. Aufl. (2025).

Noack, Ulrich/*Servatius*, Wolfgang/*Haas*, Ulrich: Gesetz betreffend die Gesellschaften mit beschränkter Haftung, 24. Aufl. (2025).

Preis, Ulrich: § 611a BGB – Potenziale des Arbeitnehmerbegriffs, in: NZA (2018), S. 817 ff.

Preis, Ulrich/*Sagan*, Adam: Der GmbH-Geschäftsführer in der arbeits- und diskriminierungsrechtlichen Rechtsprechung des EuGH, BGH und BAG, in: ZGR (2013), S. 26 ff.

Rebhahn, Robert: Die Arbeitnehmerbegriffe des Unionsrechts in der neueren Judikatur des EuGH, in: EuZA (2012), S. 3 ff.

Rolfs, Christian/*Giesen*, Richard/*Meßling*, Miriam/*Udsching*, Peter: BeckOK Arbeitsrecht, 76. Edition (2025).

Rütz, Eva Maria/*Voigt*, Jana Anna: Zentrale Fortentwicklungen des Mutterschutzes unter Berücksichtigung der Novelle des Mutterschutzgesetzes 2025, in: NJW (2025), S. 2505 ff.

Saenger, Ingo/*Inhester*, Michael (Hrsg.): Kommentar zum GmbH-Gesetz, 5. Aufl. (2024).

Schirrmacher, Paul: Zur Frist für die Kündigung des Anstellungsvertrags eines GmbH-Geschäftsführers – Anmerkung zu BGH v. 5.11.2024 – II ZR 35/23, in: GmbHR (2025), S. 299 ff.

Schliemann, Harald (Hrsg.): Das Arbeitsrecht im BGB, 2. Aufl. (2002).

Scholz, Franz (Hrsg.): Kommentar zum GmbH-Gesetz, II. Band, 13. Aufl. (2024).

Schubert, Claudia: Arbeitnehmerschutz für GmbH-Geschäftsführer, in: ZESAR (2013), S. 5 ff.

Schwacke, Peter: Juristische Methodik, 5. Aufl. (2011).

Staudinger, Julius von (Begr.): Kommentar zum Bürgerlichen Gesetzbuch mit Einführungsgesetzen und Nebengesetzen (2022).

Stoffels, Markus: Statusvereinbarungen im Arbeitsrecht, in: NZA (2000), S. 690 ff.

Uffmann, Katharina: Interim Management in Zeiten nachhaltiger Unternehmensführung, in: ZGR (2013), S. 273 ff.

Uffmann, Katharina: Kündigungsfristen für Geschäftsführeranstellungsverträge Rechtsprechungsdivergenz zwischen BGH und BAG, in: NJW (2020), S. 3210 ff.

Vedder, Christoph/*Heintschel von Heinegg*, Wolff (Hrsg.): Europäisches Unionsrecht, Handkommentar, 2. Aufl. (2018).

Vielmeier, Stephan: GmbH-Geschäftsführer als Arbeitnehmer im Rahmen der Massenentlassungsrichtlinie?, in: NJW (2014), S. 2678 ff.

Wank, Rolf: Die personellen Grenzen des Europäischen Arbeitsrechts: Arbeitsrecht für Nicht-Arbeitnehmer, in: EuZA (2008), S. 172 ff.

Wank, Rolf/*Maties*, Martin: Arbeitnehmer oder Gesellschaftsorgan oder Vereinsmitglied?, in: NZA (2007), S. 353 ff.

Werner, Rüdiger: Anwendung des Bundesurlaubsgesetzes auf den GmbH-Geschäftsführer, in: NZA (2025), S. 685 ff.

Werner, Rüdiger: Die Fristen für die Kündigung des Geschäftsführers einer GmbH & Co. KG – zugleich Anmerkung zum Urteil des BGH vom 5. November 2024 – II ZR 35/23, in: BB (2025), S. 760 ff.

"Chinese (Legal) History" or "The (Legal) History of China"?

The History of "Chinese States" seen from the Perspective of a Japanese College Classroom

By *Arnd Helmut Hafner*

Prof. Dr. Arnd Helmut Hafner ist Professor für Chinesische Rechtsgeschichte an der Juristischen Fakultät der Meiji-Universität. Er studierte Modernes Japanisches Recht und Rechtssoziologie, erwarb den Bachelor, Master und Doktor der Rechtswissenschaften an der Juristischen Fakultät und durchlief parallel dazu eine traditionelle Ausbildung in Chinesischer Geschichte an der Abteilung für Orientalistik im Institut für Humanwissenschaften, beides an der Universität Kyoto. Er studierte zudem Chinesische Paläographie am Institut für Chinesische Sprache und Literatur der Universität Peking.

I. The Modern Concept of "China"

Classes on "Chinese Legal History" at the School of Law of Meiji University in Tokyo regularly afford the author with the opportunity to reflect on what kind of history this subject is focusing on. While differing slightly in regard to the most common translation of "Legal History"[1], the Japanese and Chinese languages share the particularity that they hardly can distinguish "Chinese history" from the "history of China". In both cases, they put the noun "China" in front of the noun "history" without adding any clear morphological marker, creating a compound like "China history (*Chūgoku rekishi = Zhōngguó lìshǐ* 中國歷史 or *Chūgoku shi = Zhōngguó shǐ* 中國史)"[2]. The problem is that the denomination of "China" is a highly politicized issue. In Japan, "Oriental (Legal) History" is often used as a substitute to avoid direct reference to "China"[3].

---

1 *Hōseishi* 法制史 in Japanese, and *fǎlǜshǐ* 法律史 in Chinese.

2 To avoid redundancy, this paper uses traditional fonts that are virtually identical for Japanese and Chinese. Postwar Japan and the People's Republic of China both developed distinct simplified font sets. The traditional fonts are still in use in the Hong Kong Special Administrative Region 香港特別行政區 of the People's Republic of China and in Taiwan, which is claimed as the province of Taiwan 臺灣省 by the People's Republic of China, and considered as the Republic of China 中華民國 by its own governing body as well as about ten sovereign states in the world.

3 If the research really goes beyond the scope of Chinese history, researchers tend to use terms like "East-Eurasian" or "Central-Eurasian" history rather than "Oriental history". Or they directly refer to other national histories like "Mongolian history" etc.

Duncker & Humblot · Berlin | https://doi.org/10.3790/978-3-428-59611-9.2025.418782

Nowadays, the most common denomination of “China” is, in both languages, a compound of two characters that mean something like “middle” or “center” and “country” or “state”, respectively. As there are again no morphological features that could limit the exact syntax of the compound, it is difficult to determine its literal meaning. In European languages it is often translated as “The Middle Kingdom”. For convenience, this article will follow this common translation.

This denomination has often been said to have been invented in modern Chinese by the late Qing scholar and reformist politician Liáng Qǐchāo 梁啓超 (1873–1929). It also found relatively broad acceptance in Japan after the end of the Second World War, although some resistance can still be felt.[4] Liáng Qǐchāo also expressed some hesitation. He explained his motives for the introduction of the denomination in his “Outline of Chinese History (*Zhōngguó shǐ xùlùn* 中國史敍論)” in 1901 as follows[5]:

> There is nothing I am ashamed of more than for the fact that our country does not have a name. We are used to refer to “the Xia”, “the Han-people” or “the Tang-people”, (but) these (= Xia, Han, Tang) are dynasty names. Foreigners call (us) “Zhendan” or “Zhina”, (but) these are not our own denominations. Naming our history as “Xia”, “Han” or “Tang” would violate the principle of the people’s supremacy. Naming it “Zhendan” or “Zhina” would mean losing the right to self-definition. Calling (ourselves) the “Middle Kingdom” or the “Middle Glory[6]” might be criticized by others as arrogant.
>
> 吾人所最慚愧者, 莫如我國無國名之一事。尋常通稱, 或曰諸夏, 或曰漢人, 或曰唐人, 皆朝名也。外人所稱, 或曰震旦, 或曰支那, 皆非我所自命之名也。以夏漢唐等名吾史, 則戻尊重國民之宗旨; 以震旦、支那等名吾史, 則失名從主人之公理。曰中國、曰中華, 又未免自尊自大, 貽譏旁觀。

We need to keep in mind that the state in which Liáng Qǐchāo lived at that time had its own name. It called itself the “Qing 清” or the “Great Qing 大清”. The decision for this name was made by Abahai or Hong Taiji 皇太極 (1592–1643). In 1628, he succeeded his father Nurhaci as the Khan of the later Jin and changed the name of the state to “Qing” when he claimed the title emperor in 1636. To cite only very common legal history sources, this state edited its own history as the “Veritable Records of the Great Qing (*Dàqīng shílù* 大清實錄)”, finalizing a complete set of records after the

4 A relatively recent expression of discomfort can be found in *Kubo* 久保, Lecture: What Should “China” Be Called in Japanese? (*tokubetsu kōgi Shina to Chūgoku no yurai* 特別講義支那と中国の由来), in: Shikoku Gakuin University Treatises (*shikoku gakuin daigaku ronshū* 四国学院大学論集) No. 143 (2014).

5 *Liáng* 梁, Outline of Chinese History (*Zhōngguó shǐ xùlùn* 中國史敍論) (1901) (p. 253).

6 The literal meaning of this term is again difficult to determine. It is the Chinese equivalent of the word “China” in both “The People’s Republic of China 中華人民共和國” and “The Republic of China 中華民國”. It appears that the compound was established initially during the Eastern Jin (*dōngjìn* 東晉, 317–420 CE). This was a time when many Chinese speaking people fled their homelands in and around the “Middle Plains” and colonized the southern parts of modern China. *Huá* 華 refers to their Chinese civilization, and *zhōng* 中 most probably to the “Middle Plains”. The entire compound expresses their yearning for their lost homelands. S. also *Kojima* 小島, The History Perception Zhōnghuá: Centered on the Spring and Autumn School (*chūka no rekishi ninshiki: shunjūgaku wo chūshin ni* 中華の歴史認識—春秋学を中心に), in: Akita 秋田 et al. (ed.), The World History of “World History” (*“sekai shi” no sekai shi* 「世界史」の世界史) (2016).

death of each emperor. Comprehensive corpora of legal norms were also regularly compiled under the names "Comprehensive Canon of the Great Qing (*Dàqīng huìdiǎn* **大清會典**)" and "Detailed Rules and Regulations to the Comprehensive Canon of the Great Qing (*Dàqīng huìdiǎn zélì* **大清會典則例** or *Dàqīng huìdiǎn shílì* **大清會典事例**)"[7]. In addition, the periodical in which Liáng first published his "Outline of Chinese History" bears the name "The China Discussion (*Qīng yì bào* **清議報**)", rendering "China" as "Qīng". He was the editor of the periodical. In other words, Liáng Qǐchāo's argument that his country lacks a proper name, or that there were only some "dynasty names", must be taken with a grain of salt. It reflects his political views rather than historical reality.

Liáng Qǐchāo participated as a disciple of Kāng Yǒuwéi **康有爲** in the Hundred Days' Reform in 1898. After the suppression of the movement, Liáng Qǐchāo, along with Kāng Yǒuwéi, went into exile in Japan where he wrote, among other works, the "Outline of Chinese History". The reform movement led by Kāng Yǒuwéi aimed to restore the authority of the state by establishing a reformed constitutional monarchy in the European style, taking the Meiji Restoration in Japan as a role model to follow. Even in exile, Liáng Qǐchāo remained committed to his teacher's monarchist ideology, for which he has often been criticized by republican or democratic revolutionists.

However, the monarchy that was proposed to be restored was already completely different from the Manchu-led multiethnic empire as which the Qing state started its history. The actual political power in the monarchy was in the hands of regional governors in the Chinese speaking parts of the empire who developed into regional warlords during the dissolution of the empire. After his return to "China" in 1912, Liáng Qǐchāo himself served as justice minister and finance minister under Yuán Shìkǎi **袁世凱** (1859–1916) and Duàn Qíruì **段祺瑞** (1865–1936), two of the most powerful warlords after the republican revolution and the establishment of the Republic of China at the end of 1911. Yuán Shìkǎi usurped the political power in 1913 and attempted to establish himself as the emperor of a new "Chinese" monarchy in 1915[8].

Though many remnants of Manchu influence were still waiting to be swept away by the impending revolution, the main power constellation in the Qing state had already undergone a tremendous change before Liáng Qǐchāo participated in the Hundred Days' Reform. The originally multifaceted Manchu empire had been transformed into a very Chinese empire[9]. It was this very "Chinese" Qing Empire for

---

7 Since these comprehensive corpora entail the complete body of penal law, the common description as "corpus on administrative matters" can hardly be considered accurate.

8 It should be mentioned, however, that Liáng opposed Yuán's attempt.

9 A very vehement discussion about the "Chineseness" or "not-Chineseness" of the Qing state has been conducted between Evelyn S. Rawski (**羅友枝**) and Ping-ti Ho (**何炳棣**). Beside nationalistic emotions, their divergence could also be understood as a reflection of the change in basic characteristics of the Qing state over time. See *Ho* **何**, The Significance of The Ch'ing Period in Chinese History, in: Journal of Asian Studies 26(2) (1967); *Rawski*, Presidential Address: Reenvisioning the Qing: The Significance of the Qing Period in Chinese History, in: Journal of Asian Studies Vol. 55 No. 4 (1996); *Ho* **何**, In Defense of Sinicization: A Rebuttal of

which Liáng Qǐchāo invented the concept of "China" or "Middle Kingdom". It was also this new Chinese empire that attempted to compete with other modern empires for colonial control over neighboring territories, such as the Indochinese peninsula or the Korean peninsula, during the Sino-French War (1884–1885) and the First Sino-Japanese War (1894–1895).

In other words, the invention of "China" in modern Chinese envisaged the establishment of a Chinese nation within an imperialistic international order of nation states. Liáng Qǐchāo, and most probably many of his contemporaries, were very fast in adapting to and following European imperialism. This fact is exemplified by the racist explanation of the ethnic composition of his newly created national history:

> If we now count the races within the range of Chinese history, there are not less than several tens, however those well-known and with influence are six.
>
> First, the Miao people. This is the indigenous people of China, which is comparable to the red people in contemporary America and the black people in Australia. This people played a significant role in prehistoric times. However, the more the Han people developed, the more the Miao people was chased down, from the North to the South, so that nowadays it is barely surviving in small parts of Hunan, Guizhou, Yunnan and Guangxi. You also find them sometimes in Vietnam or Myanmar.
>
> Secondly, the Han people. This is us who are now distributed throughout the country, the progeny of civilization, the offspring of the Yellow Emperor. For thousands of years, the illustrious fame of the world, what is called civilization in Asia, all of that has been sown and harvested by us.
>
> ....
>
> 今考中國史範圍中之各人種, 不下數十, 而最著明有關係者, 蓋六種焉。
>
> 其一苗種　是中國之土族也,　猶今日阿美利加之紅人、澳大利亞之黑人也。其人在歷史以前曾占重要之地位。自漢族日漸發達, 苗種即日就窘迫, 由北而南, 今猶保残喘於湖南、貴州、雲南、廣西之間。其在安南、緬甸等地, 亦間有焉。
>
> 其二漢種　即我輩現時徧布於國中, 所謂文明之冑、黄帝之子孫, 是也。... (略) ...數千年来, 赫赫有聲於世界, 所謂亜細亜之文明者, 皆我種人自播之而自穫之者也。
>
> ... (略) ...[10]

This appears to be the yellow rendition of European notions of white supremacy. The "Yellow Emperor" is one of the legendary "Three Sovereigns and Five Emperors" who are said to have ruled before the Xia 夏, the allegedly first Chinese dynasty. Sources differ in the names and order of these eight heroic rulers. Among them, the Yellow Emperor is often said to be of rather late origin and seems to have a closer relation to the Taoist tradition rather than to Confucianism. Therefore, the arbitrary selection of the Yellow Emperor among so many different candidates also alludes to a fast internalization of European race theory.[11]

Evelyn Rawski's Reenvisioning the Qing, in: Journal of Asian Studies Vol. 57 No. 1 (1998). See also: *Rawski*, The Last Emperors: A Social History of Qing Imperial Institutions (1998).

10 *Liáng* (fn. 5) (pp. 285–286).

11 For the racist construction of the yellowness of Chinese people in 19th century Europe, s. *Demel*, Wie die Chinesen gelb wurden: Ein Beitrag zur Frühgeschichte der Rassentheorien, in:

Modern nation states are closely associated with clearly defined territories. Liáng Qǐchāo's short "Outline of Chinese History" did not forget to address this topic shortly, either:

> The jurisdiction of Chinese history can be divided into five major parts. First China proper, second Xinjiang, third Qinghai and Xizang (Tibet), fourth Mongolia, fifth Manchuria.
> …
> 中國史所轄之地域, 可分爲五大部。一中國本部, 二新疆, 三青海、西藏, 四蒙古, 五滿洲。… (略) …[12]

What catches our attention above all here is the expression "China proper"[13]. If the four other regions had been indivisible parts of a Chinese nation's territory, no part would have been considered even more "proper Chinese" than the others. This expression indirectly acknowledges that the envisaged Chinese nation state actually wasn't as Chinese as it claimed to be.

Modern nation states that have large geographical areas populated mainly by different ethnic groups often experience this phenomenon. The Japanese expression "Mainland Japan 日本本土" bears a striking resemblance to "China proper". The expression was used to discriminate against ethnically different populations in Taiwan and the Korean peninsula during the colonial rule. Nowadays, it is still used to draw a line between the insular prefecture of Okinawa and the rest of the Japanese archipelago, although the degree of discrimination may differ significantly.

II. The Search for "China" in "Chinese History"

In the previous section, we have seen numerous traces of European imperialism in Liáng Qǐchāo's adoption of the modern concept of "China". The context into which Liáng Qǐchāo puts it makes the Chinese and Japanese denomination "*Zhōngguó/Chūgoku* 中國 (≈ 'Middle Kingdom')" look like a translation of the European word "Chi-

Historische Zeitschrift Vol. 255 (1992). Cited from English version: "How the Chinese Became Yellow: A Contribution to the Early History of Race Theories", in: Brandt/Purdy (ed.), China in the German Enlightenment (2016). However, Demel supposes that there had been a traditional preference for the color yellow in traditional Chinese "colour mythology" (p. 39), which, according to him, eventually aligned with 19th century European race theory.

12 *Liáng* (fn. 5) (p. 283).

13 The translation renders the Chinese term "*Zhōngguó běnbù* 中國本部" as "China proper". The literal meaning of "*běnbù*" is "main or central part". However, what is left of China's territory after removing the other four parts is not the geographical center of China. To the contrary, the major cities of this part, such as Shanghai, Guangzhou or Tianjin, are located on the eastern or southern periphery. The only common feature of this part of China's territory that could be connected with "main" or "central" is that this is the part in which, traditionally, Chinese speaking people comprised the bulk of the population. In other words, "Chineseness" became the measure of centrality, "China proper" became the main part of "China". Of course, modern Chinese citizens who internalized Liáng's sinocentric view will surely criticize me for misunderstanding a purely geographical term, or, may be, an administrative term deriving from the late Qing.

na". In Japan, the denomination "*Shina* 支那"[14] was widely used just in that sense from the late Edo period until the end of WWII. It was used to refer to a country called "China" by Europeans and to distinguish the modern Chinese nation state from the countless historical Chinese states or "dynasties"[15].

Because of the disrespect toward the modern Chinese nation state, this denomination gradually acquired a discriminatory meaning. But the wording itself does not carry any negative connotations. Liáng's "Outline of Chinese History" referred to it as one of the foreign denominations for China. "*Shina* or *Zhina* 支那" originally is the Chinese counterpart for the Sanskrit "Cīna" in Chinese translations of Buddhist sutras. "Cīna" was transmitted to India via the old Iranian "Čin/Činistan" or Sogdian "Čynstn", which is derived from the self-denomination of an ancient Chinese state, the Qin 秦[16]. Even Liáng himself used this foreign denomination in the same way as he later used the "Middle Kingdom (*Zhōngguó/Chūgoku* 中國)", until shortly before publishing his "Outline of Chinese History"[17]. If we consider the denomination "Middle Kingdom (*Zhōngguó/Chūgoku* 中國)" and "*Shina* or *Zhina* 支那" as translations of the European word "China", could it then be that the modern "China" itself is nothing more than an invention of European imperialism?

This is certainly an untenable stance from the perspective of the modern nation state. National narratives commonly trace their origins to long-standing premodern traditions. This also has a significant impact on the academic discourse. One protagonist of a "China" that goes further back into pre-modern history is Professor Gě Zhaòguāng from Fudan University 復旦大學 in Shanghai. His book *Here in "China" I Dwell: Reconstructing the Historical Discourses of "China"*[18] tries to establish

14 This is the Japanese equivalent to the Chinese "*Zhina* 支那" which Liáng referred to in his "Outline of Chinese History".

15 S. *Wada* 和田, On the Original Meaning of the Terms "*Shina*" and "*Shinajin*" (*Shina oyobi Shinajin to iu go no hongi ni tsuite* 支那及び支那人という語の本義について), in: Wada 和田 (ed.), Treatises on Oriental History (*tō-a shi ronsō* 東亞史論藪) (1942). Take note that the author's strong defiance toward the territorial claims of the modern Chinese nation state is also reflected in his wording. This is the underlying cause of the discriminatory connotations.

16 *Pelliot* (author)/*Hambis* (ed.): Notes on Marco Polo I (1959) (pp. 264–278). It yet remains a disputed issue whether it derived from the so-called Qin dynasty, which "unified" the first Chinese empire in 221 BCE, or from the fore-running regional state of Qin, which lasted from the 8th century BCE until 205 BCE. The reason is that the Sanskrit word "Cīna" appears to have been in use long before the time of the First Emperor Yíng Zhèng of the Qin 秦始皇嬴政. See, for instance, *Ghosh*, Origin and Antiquity of the Sanskrit Word CĪNA as the name of China, in: Annals of the Bhandarkar Oriental Research Institute Vol. 42 No. 1–4 (1961).

17 For instance *Liáng* 梁, Treatise on Religious Reform in China (*lùn Zhīnà zōngjiào gǎigé* 論支那宗教改革), in: The China Discussion (*Qīng yì bào* 清議報) No. 19–20 (1899) and *Liáng* 梁, Treatise China's Momentum for Independence in Face of the Oriental Politics of Japan (*lùn Zhīnà dúlì zhī shìlì yǔ Rìběn dōngfāng zhèngcè* 論支那獨立之勢力與日本東方政策), in: The China Discussion (*Qīng yì bào* 清議報) No. 26 (1899).

18 *Gě* 葛, Here in "China" I Dwell: Reconstructing Historical Discourses of "China" for Our Time (*zhái zī Zhōngguó: chóngjiàn yǒuguān "Zhōngguó" de lìshǐ lùnshù* 宅兹中國：重建有關"中國"的歷史論述) (2011). This book has been translated into numerous languages and seems to have yielded significant influence. The German translation of its sequel – *Gě* 葛, The Inside and Outside of Historical China: A Reclarification of the Concept of China and its Borders (*lìshǐ Zhōngguó de nèi yǔ wài: yǒuguān "Zhōngguó" yǔ "zhōubiān" gàiniàn de zài*

a "Chinese stance" on this topic based on pre-modern historical sources. The problem is that by definition of the Chinese language, the "Chinese stance (*Zhōngguó lìchǎng* 中國立場)" that he intends to promote cannot be distinguished from the "stance of China (equally *Zhōngguó lìchǎng* 中國立場)[19]". So, if "China" is a creation of modern European imperialism, his endeavor is doomed to fail, since it hardly can be anything else than the projection of this modern nation state notion into history. Let's briefly review what he has to say.

First, in the title of his book, he uses a very symbolic expression from a Western Zhou (11th – 8th century BCE) bronze inscription. It contains the string "*Zhōngguó* 中國", which in the modern Chinese language conveys the meaning "China" or "Middle Kingdom". It is obvious that the title alludes to the possibility of "China" reaching far back into early history.

Gě Zhaòguāng acknowledges that he utilizes the phrase solely for symbolic purposes, and that the bronze inscription carries a completely different meaning with the same string. According to Gé, the "*Zhōngguó* 中國" here refers to the place Luòyáng 洛陽, which has been often called the "middle under heaven (*tiān zhī zhōng* 天之中)", and where the Western Zhou erected an eastern capital after defeating and destroying the Shang polity that had its political center in this region. Slightly different from Gé, I would take the string "*Zhōngguó* 中國" in this inscription in the plural form "middle lands", referring rather vaguely to the newly occupied region. In Japanese, the reading "*naka tsu kuni* (中つ國or中國)" would correspond to this meaning. The string reads like this in the expression "*Ashihara no naka tsu kuni* 葦原の中つ國", which is another denomination for Japan, representing the middle between the heavenly sphere of the gods (*Takama ga hara* 高天原) and the land of the dead (*yomi* 黄泉).

Second, while still alluding to numerous historical sources from earlier times, Gé openly argues that a clear national identity of "China" has been formed at latest during the Song dynasty. He points to works such as "Treatise on the Middle Kingdom (*Zhōngguó lùn* 中國論)" and "Treatise on Orthodoxy (*zhèngtǒng lùn* 正統論)" from Shí Jiè 石介 (1005–1045) and Ōuyáng Xiū 歐陽修 (1007–1072) which try to establish a tradition of a legitimate "Middle Kingdom" in contrast to the surrounding barbaric states and traditions. The "*Treatise on Orthodoxy*" explicitly draws up a historical line of orthodox dynasties in order to prove the legitimacy of the Northern Song state (960–1127) in contrast to the surrounding states. This view was ardently endorsed by intellectuals like Zhū Xī during the Southern Song (1127–1279).

The problem is that this line is anything but self-evident.

---

chéngqīng 歷史中國的內與外:有關"中國"與"周邊"概念的再澄清) (2017) – decorates the first translation cycle of the research project "China Übersetzen/Translating China" at the Max Planck Institute for Legal History and Legal Theory (https://www.lhlt.mpg.de/research-project/china-norms-ideas-practices, accessed on 5 May 2025).

19 This expression appears on about 10 occasions in the slightly more than 300 pages of the book. The first appearance can be found on page 4 in the preface.

III. Non-Chinese "Chinas" in History

Before we focus on the line of orthodox dynasties, let us cast a glance at a "Treatise on the Middle Kingdom" of a quite different provenance. The following is a part of the preface of the book containing the treatise:

> With all humility, I had only eyes for the classics of the outer dynasties, adoring their notabilities without recognizing the beauty of the lands of the civilization of the "Middle Glory" to which I have been born. Was it out of curiosity or a passion for the exotic? Or rather, do I need to admit my negligence and lack of principle? The water and soil of the "Middle Kingdom" are so outstanding among the international community of countries, and its notabilities so accomplished and elegant. … Now in the winterly eleventh month of the year, I arranged the true events of our imperial lineage, in order to make our children recite them.
>
> 愚生中華文明之土, 未知其美, 專嗜外朝之經典, 嘐嘐慕其人物。何其放心乎, 何其喪志乎?抑好奇乎, 將尚異乎?夫中國之水土, 卓爾於萬邦, 而人物精秀于八紘。… (略) …今歳冬十有一月, 編次皇統之實事, 令兒童誦焉[20]。

The author, commanding a refined Confucian vocabulary, shows his pride in being born in the civilization of the "Middle Glory". He argues that his country, the "Middle Kingdom", is one of the most outstanding in the world. However, neither is Chinese his mother tongue, nor is the soil on which he was born in any way Chinese. His name is Yamaga Sokō (山鹿素行, 1622–1685), born in Aizu, modern prefecture of Fukushima, Japan. As an ardent admirer turned critic of the Neo-Confucian school of Zhuzi (*Zhūzǐ xué = Shushi gaku* 朱子學), he has been exiled from Edo, modern Tokyo, for ten years because of his criticism against this school of thought in his book "The Summary Collection of the Holy Teachings (*seikyō yōroku* 聖教要録)", published in 1665. The book cited above, "The Facts of the Middle Court (*chūchō jijitsu* 中朝事實)", was written during his exile in the Akō Domain (*Akōhan* 赤穂藩), modern Hyōgo prefecture. The following expressions of its second chapter, "The Treatise on the Middle Kingdom", provide further proof for his identification of Japan with the "Middle Kingdom", or "China" if we follow modern translations:

> The Imperial Ancestor (Sumemi Oya), their Majesty the High Emperor (Takami) Musubi, wished to establish the Imperial Grandson (Sumemi Ma), their Majesty Amatsuhiko Hikoho no Ninigi as the Lord of the *Central Lands of Ashihara (Ashihara no Naka tsu Kuni)*[21].

---

20 Bureau for Social Education of the Japanese Ministry of Education (*monbushō shakai kyōiku kyoku* 文部省社會教育局), The Facts of the Middle Court (*chūchō jijitsu* 中朝事實), Japanese Thought Series Vol. 8 (*nihon sisō sōsho dai happen* 日本思想叢書第八編) (1933).

21 This is a quotation from Nihon Shoki (日本書記, 神代下天孫降迹章), one of the six official Japanese Chronicles. During translation, I referred to *Chor* (左), Nihon Shoki (日本書紀) Trilingual: Selections in the Original Classical Chinese (Kanbun) with English Translation based on the Iwanami Bunko edition (five volumes, 1994–1995), in: Libraries Staff Reports, University of Alberta Library (2018), available at: https://doi.org/10.7939/R35Q4S142, accessed on 5 May 2025, and *Aston*, Nihongi: Chronicles of Japan from the Earliest Times to A. D. 697, first published in Proceedings of Japan Society (1896), electronically published by Japanese Historical Text Initiative, University of California Berkeley (1996), available at: https://jhti.studentorg.berkeley.edu/Nihon%20shoki.html, accessed on 5 May 2025, but did not strictly follow their suggestions. The latter does not contain a literal translation of the said quotation.

I dare to contemplate carefully. This is a reference to our court as the "Middle Kingdom (Chūgoku)". Before this, the great god Amaterasu (Amaterasu no Ōmikami) said, "I heard that there is a God of Food Security (Ukemochi no Kami) in the "Central Lands of Ashihara (Ashihara no Naka tsu Kuni)". That shows that the denomination "Middle Kingdom (Chūgoku)" has existed since remote ancient times[22].

「皇祖高皇產靈尊, 遂欲立皇孫天津彥彥火瓊瓊杵尊, 以爲葦原中國之主」。

謹按, 是以本朝爲中國之謂也。先是, 天照大神在於天上曰：聞葦原中國有保食神, 然則中國之稱, 自往古旣有此也。... (略) ...

No doubt, claiming the title "Middle Kingdom" is a kind of defiance against the hegemony of the Qing state. In opposition to the Qing's "Great under the heaven", Japan made claims over a "small under the heaven (*shō tenka* = *xiǎo tiānxià* 小天下)" by domestic use of terms such as "heavenly court (*tenchō* = *tiāncháo* 天朝)" or "son of heaven (*tenshi* = *tiānzǐ* 天子)" in reference to the Japanese emperor and "under the heaven (*tenka* = *tiānxià* 天下)" in reference to the shogun. Concepts such as "small middle glory (so junghwa소중화= *xiǎo zhōnghuá* 小中華)" and "southern heaven (*nam thiên* = *nán tiān* 南天)" have been used in similar ways on the Korean and Indochinese peninsulas[23]. The neighbors of the Ming and Qing Empires could not help but adopt a combination of adaptation and defiance.

Gě Zhàoguāng takes this defiance as a sign of the dissolution of the common East-Asian culture. From his perspective of China, any disrespect toward the continental "Middle Kingdom" is considered a De-Sinification[24]. That is, of course, not true. Deep understanding of the Chinese language and incorporation of the cultural values conveyed by this language was the main drive for both adaptation and defiance. The whole rivalry was a project that was entirely Chinese. A further citation from the chapter "The treatise on the Middle Kingdom" might illuminate this:

Allow me some foolish contemplations. The movements of heaven and earth, the change of the four seasons, if they reach the balanced middle, then wind, rain, frost and heat will not go to extremes. Therefore, water and soil are fertile, and people are refined. That is what is called the "Middle Kingdom (Chūgoku)". Among the many countries, only our court and the outer court have reached the balanced middle. In addition, our court has been blessed by their Majesty the Heavenly Middle Lord (Ame no Minaka Nushi) since the Era of the Gods (Kamiyo/Jindai), and the two gods (Izanagi and Izanami) erected the pillar supporting the middle of the country. Without any doubt, it is the natural force of Heaven and Earth that makes our court the "Middle Kingdom (Chūgoku)".

---

22 That Yamaga intermingles two different usages and meanings of the string "*Zhōngguó/ Chūgoku* 中國" resembles the allusive use of a Western Zhou bronze inscription by Gě Zhàoguāng in his book title. Both should well be aware of the semantic differences, but could not resist the temptation to project their own concept of the "Middle Kingdom" back into very old times based on the equivalence in the superficial spelling of the string.

23 *Mitani* 三谷 et al., The World Seen by "Peripheral Countries": Japan, Korea, Vietnam (*"shūhen koku" no sekai zō* 「周辺国」の世界像一日本・朝鮮・ベトナム」), in: Akita 秋田 et al. (ed.), The World History of "World History" (*"sekai shi" no sekai shi* 「世界史」の世界史) (2016).

24 See, for instance, chapter 4 "Occident versus Orient or Orient versus Orient (*xīfāng yǔ dōngfāng, huòzhě dōngfāng yǔ dōngfāng* 西方與東方, 或者是東方與東方)" of *Gě* (fn. 16), pp. 151–168.

Only our court has found the correct path of Heaven and achieved the "Middle Kingdom (Chūgoku)" on Earth. … Not to mention that Kōrai (= Goryeo 고려), Shiragi (= Silla 신라) and Kudara (= Paekche 백제) are protectoral vassals of our court.

愚按, 天地之所運, 四時之所交, 得其中則風雨寒暑之會不偏。故水土沃而人物精。是乃可稱中國。萬邦之衆, 唯本朝及外朝得其中, 而本朝神代既有天御中主尊；二神建國中柱, 則本朝之爲中國, 天地自然之勢也。… (略) …

獨本朝中天之正道, 得地之中國, … (略) …況高麗[25]、新羅、百濟, 皆本朝之藩臣乎。

Nobody who is to any degree familiar with Chinese thought or Chinese historiography could deny that this description of a well-balanced, culturally superior "Middle Kingdom" is a very Chinese concept. Except for the reference to the Qing as the "outer court" and to the names of Japanese gods, the same wording could have been used under any of the numerous Chinese states or dynasties.

The last sentence of the citation reminds us that the Chinese way of conceptualizing is not necessarily more peace-oriented than modern nation state concepts. The "Middle Kingdom" is a claim for supremacy and domination over other states. That is the cause why Liáng Qǐchāo's anticipated criticism of arrogance against his translation of "China". It is also the reason why it is so easily translated into modern colonialistic narratives. For instance, Yamaga Sokō's *The Facts of the Central Court* has been repeatedly reprinted in modern imperial Japan by highly political figures like Nogi Maresuke (乃木希典, 1849–1912), a general well known for his very disputed victory in the siege of Lǚshùn (旅顺) during the Japanese-Russian war as well as his following the Emperor Meiji (Mutsuhito 睦仁, 1852–1912) to the grave, and by the Ministry for Education[26]. It was a perfect fit for the political propaganda of those times.

Modern Japan's drive for hegemony can be seen as the colonialistic extension of traditional concepts of cultural supremacy. The following words of Naitō Torajirō 内藤虎次郎 (1866–1934), better known as Naitō Konan 内藤湖南, who is commonly counted as one of the founders of the Kyoto School of Chinese or Oriental history, might leave no doubt about this trace of thought:

Our Power is increasing day by day. From the south, where Harada Magoshichirō and Yamada Nizaemon (tried to) establish a government, to the north, where Mamiya Rinzō first set foot, in the West reaching to the continent which His Serene Highness Toyotomi already put his hands on. Our glorious inspiration will descend on these areas within a little more than a decade. By replacing Europe, we can elevate the Orient and make it the new center of global civilization. That will happen within the turning of a hand.

吾の威力日に以て伸暢、南は原田孫七郎、山田仁左衛門が経略せる地より、北は間宮林蔵が跋渉せる処を極め、西豊公が指画せし大陸に及ぶ、我が風化を光被せ

25 *Takazawa* 高澤, The Facts of the Middle Court (*chūchō Jijitsu* 中朝事實) (1985), which claims to be based on a private reprint by Nogi Maresuke, changes *Kōrai* 高麗 (= *Goryeo*) to *Chōsen* 朝鮮 (=*Joseon*). The wording of Kawatani 川谷, Annotated Edition of the Facts of the Middle Court and the Summary Collection of the Holy Teachings (*chūchō jijitsu oyobi seikyō yōroku jutsugi* 中朝事及聖教要錄述義) (1936), is equal to *Bureau for Social Education of the Japanese Ministry of Education* (*monbushō shakai kyōiku kyoku* 文部省社會教育局) (fn. 18).

26 See for instance the editions mentioned in the previous note.

しめんこと、蓋し十数年内の事たらん。東方の新極致を成就し、以て欧州に代興して、新たに坤輿文明の中心たらんこと、反掌の間に在らざらんや[27]。

Harada Magoshichirō was a Japanese merchant who traded with the Philippines in the 16th century. He recommended Toyotomi Hideyoshi to invade and occupy the Luzon Island, the main island of the modern Republic of the Philippines. Toyotomi Hideyoshi had plans to move his government to Peking and rule the "Under the Heaven" from there during the early, yet successful stage of his invasion into the Korean Peninsula. Reference to these historical figures draws an indubitable line between modern Japanese claims to hegemony in at least East Asia and the fight for hegemony in the late 16th and early 17th century, which eventually was decided in favor of the Manchu ethnic group that erected the Qing Empire.

Liáng Qǐchāo shares the same thirst for hegemony in his "Outline of Chinese History", embracing again European supremacist racism:

The Great Eastern (= Oriental) history, that is what the Japanese call East Ocean (= Oriental) history. The driving force behind the Great East lies entirely in China. Therefore, the status of the Chinese people in the Great Eastern history is identical to that of the Arian people in World history.

泰東史者,日本人所稱東洋史也。泰東之主動力,全在中國。故泰東史中,中國民族之地位一如世界史中阿利揚民族之地位。[28]

IV. The Fluidity of "Chinese" Identity

Without any doubt, the "Middle Kingdom" is a highly political concept. Across time and space, it has been utilized for many political agendas, rewriting history time and again. One important rewriting project developed during the late stage of the Tang era and led to a sort of new national identity under the Song as depicted by Gě Zhàoguāng and many other scholars before him. Huángfǔ Shí 皇甫湜 (777–835) is an early exponent of this new perspective. His "Treatise on the Legitimacy of the Eastern Jin and the Northern Wei 東晉元魏正閏論"[29] exemplifies a fundamental change in the center of gravity in traditional Chinese historiography. As his

27 *Naitō* 内藤: Supplement: Geopolitical Speculations (*furoku: chisei okusetu* 附録「地勢臆説」), in: Treatise on History of Early Modern Humanities (*kinsei bungaku shi ron* 近世文学史論) (1897); cited from Collected Works of Naitō Konan Vol. 1 (*naitō konan zenshū dai ikkan* 内藤湖南全集第1巻) (1996). Interestingly, the Japanese original can be converted into classical Chinese without changing even one of the entailed Chinese characters. This also shows how deep-rooted in classical Chinese the formal Japanese of the Meiji-era was:

吾威力日以伸暢, 南自原田孫七郎、山田仁左衛門經略之地, 北極間宮林蔵跋渉之處, 西及豊公指畫之大陸,我風化將光被,蓋十数年内之事矣。成就東方新極致,以代興歐州,新爲坤輿文明之中心,不在於反掌之間乎。

This grave identification with Chinese culture by non-Chinese speakers and the stern incorporation of Chinese concepts into non-Chinese languages is probably difficult to understand for scholars that grew up under modern Chinese nationalism.

28 *Liáng* (fn. 5).

29 *Dǒng* 董 et al. (ed.): Collected Works of the Tang (*quán táng wén*全唐文, 兩淮鹽政 (1814), cited from reprint by Shanghai Ancient Books Publishing House 上海古籍出版社 (1990), Vol. 686.

narrative is quite complex, we will provide detailed explanations that are comprehensible even for readers who are not very familiar with Chinese history after the following quotation:

> Due to the political chaos created by Emperor Hui, numerous barbarians brought turmoil to the Glorious (Civilization). The Jin had to relocate to the South, and indeed established (Sīmǎ Ruì) as Emperor Yuan. That is, in regard to the actual affairs and their meaning, absolutely the same as Zuyi's destruction of Geng, Pangeng's resettlement to Bo, King You's dwelling in Zhi, and King Ping's avoidance of the Rong.
>
> But the Tuoba are actually Xiongnu people. They came from the regions of You (Northern Hebei) and Dai (Northern Shanxi) and established themselves in the homelands of our royal ancestors, demanding the rank and title of the "Middle Kingdom". If you call it (a replacement by) extinction, the Jin not yet have been completely replaced; if you call it a (legitimate) handover, there was nothing left to be passed on. Nevertheless, previous books gave the (Tuoba turned) Yuan the imperial title and recent recordings placed the (Eastern) Jin on a secondary position. This is a total mistake.
>
> Some argue that the place where the (Tuoba turned) Yuan were dwelling is the "Middle Kingdom".
>
> My answer is: It is the righteous rites that make (us) the "Middle Kingdom"; calling them barbarians is because of the lack of the rites. How can you connect it to geography.
>
> 惠帝無道, 群胡亂華, 晉之南遷, 實曰元帝, 與夫祖乙之圮耿, 盤庚之徙亳, 幽王之居彘, 平王之避戎, 其事同, 其義一矣。
>
> 而拓跋氏實匈奴, 來自幽代, 襲有先王之桑梓, 自爲中國之位號。謂之滅耶, 晉實未改, 謂之禪耶, 已無所傳。而往之著書者有帝元, 今之爲錄者, 皆閏晉, 可謂失之遠矣。
>
> 或曰: 元之所居中國也。
>
> 對曰: 所以爲中國者, 禮義也, 所謂夷狄者, 無禮義也。豈繫於地也。

Gě Zhaòguāng only quoted the last sentence of this text in his book. That might well fit into his "Chinese stance", putting the "Middle Kingdom" at the center of civilization. However, Huángfǔ's treatise reflects a much more complex issue. To understand it, it is crucial to be aware that, starting with Sīmǎ Qiān 司馬遷 (BCE 145/135?~?)'s *Records of the Grand Historian* 史記 (finished around BCE 91), traditional Chinese historiography revolves around ruling sovereigns, acknowledging only one legitimate ruler at one point of time. In other words, the official annals attempt to establish a single line of legitimate sovereigns, starting with the legendary times of the Three Sovereigns and Five Emperors (Sānhuáng Wǔdì 三皇五帝) and concluding with the contemporary emperor.[30] In this manner, the current emperor is depicted as the legitimate successor to thousands of years of legitimate rule[31]. The existence of a significant period of undeniable competition between numerous sovereign-like rulers leads to a legitimacy crisis in this type of historiography. The

30 Admittedly, Sīmǎ Qiān made a very individual choice by incorporating the short interim government by Liú Bāng's rival Xiàng Yǔ and dropping out Liú Bāng's son Liú Yíng 劉盈 (posthumously Emperor Huì 惠帝) who was under the control of his mother, Empress Lǚ 呂后. For Confucians, these are untenable deviations. Nevertheless, Sīmǎ established a clear line of always one ruler at a time.

31 Diminishing the diverse Chinese states into mere "dynasties", as Liáng Qǐchāo did in his "Outline of Chinese History", is also an essential part of this political discourse.

Warring States Period (453/403–221 BCE) and the Period of the Northern and Southern Dynasties (439–589 CE) were the two main causes for headaches. Huángfŭ's treatise is dedicated to the latter.

Emperor Huì 惠帝, who is mentioned at the beginning of the quotation, refers to Sīmă Zhōng 司馬衷 (259–306 CE, r. 290–306), the second emperor of the Western Jin Empire (265–316). During his reign, political interference by his in-laws led to the "Rebellion of the Eight Kings (*bawang zhi luan* 八王之亂, 291–306)", which was followed by a devastating rebellion of Non-Chinese military forces that had fought under the eight kings. This rebellion is known in Chinese historiography as the Rebellion of the Yongjia era (*yǒngjiā zhi luàn* 永嘉之亂, 307–313), which led to the collapse of the Jin state. Sīmă Ruì 司馬睿, at that time the King of Lángyá (Lángyá Wáng 琅邪王), who avoided the turmoil in the Northern areas and resided in Jiànkāng 建康, modern Nanking 南京, restored the state in 317 with a new capital in Jiànkāng. This restored Jin is commonly referred to as the Eastern Jin (317–420). It mainly governed the areas in the south of the Huai-River and the Yangtze-River, while pushing the frontier of Chinese colonization further to the South-East coastal areas. It was succeeded by the Southern states of the Sòng 宋 (420–479), the Qí 齊 (479–502), the Liáng 梁 (502–557) and the Chén 陳 (557–589).

From this time onward, the North China Plain (*Huáběi Píngyuán* 華北平原) was under the rule of Non-Chinese people for many centuries. If we count in the so-called conquering dynasties it became rather exceptional that governments could be established in these areas without at least significant assistance of non-Chinese armies until the end of the Qing state (1616–1912). During the first hundred years, numerous political entities of changing origin replaced each other in relatively short cycles. This period is known as the "Five Barbarians and Sixteen Countries (*Wǔhú Shíliùguó* 五胡十六國)" in Chinese historiography. At the end of this period, the Tuòbá 拓跋, a branch of the Xiānbēi 鮮卑 or Särbi people, one of the so-called Five Barbarians, succeeded in unifying the North China Plains and the Loess Plateau (*huángtǔ gāoyuán* 黃土高原). This is the beginning of the "Northern and Southern Dynasties" period, during which relatively stable ruling bodies competed against each other in the North and the South.

We should mention that the Five Barbarians were not barbarians. One of their first protagonists, Liú Yuān 劉淵 (?–310), proclaimed the restoration of the Han Empire (202 BCE-8 CE, 25–220 CE) in 304 CE, asserting his legitimate heir to both the chief of the Xiongnu (Chányú 單于) and the Han Emperors (Huángdì 皇帝), whom he worshipped as his maternal ancestors. He is said to have demonstrated excellence in academics and in martial arts. He had a strong connection with the high Jin court, being embraced by Sīmă Zhāo 司馬昭 (211–265, posthumously Emperor Wen 文帝) and Sīmă Yăn 司馬炎 (236–290, Emperor Wu 武帝), and being greatly feared by his political opponents. In modern terms, he was a migrant who had lived on Chinese dominated soil for generations. That made him acquainted with Chinese language and culture. Simultaneously, he was able to maintain his Xiongnu identity, since migration happened not individually but in greater social units like Jewish and other migrations in medieval Europe.

In other words, the Five Barbarians are not foreign invaders. At least their leading classes are mostly people with dual identities, deeply rooted in Chinese culture. Their rulers claim dual sovereign titles, the Chinese Emperor (Huángdì 皇帝) and the Xiongnu "Chanyu" or the Särbi, later Turkic-Mongolian, "Khan"[32]. This tradition was unwaveringly followed by early Tang emperors. Since the Tang state emerged out of the Särbi dominated ruling class that had been created by Yǔwén Tài 宇文泰 (505–556, effective founder of the Northern Zhou 北周) at the end of the Northern Wei, early Tang emperors were in no position to deny the legitimacy succession from the Northern Wei through Northern Zhou and Sui to themselves. The legitimacy of the Northern Wei must have been unquestioned for most early Tang people.

The second half of the Tang era, during which Huángfǔ wrote his treatise, saw a complete change. The main pillar of state power was no longer the close relationship with Central Asia and the Turkic-Mongolian world but rather the economic wealth of the South. This shift in gravity undoubtedly gave Southerners a new voice. The South was no longer a remote periphery like it was in earlier times. Economic success prompted the Southerners to claim that they were the true guardians of Chinese culture, which had been brought to the South by the Eastern Jin and continuously transmitted by the Southern states[33]. Therefore, it is no surprise that Huángfǔ, one of the early protagonists of a new line of succession of legitimacy, is himself a Southerner, coming from Mùzhōu 睦州 in the modern province Zhejiang. The Southern dominance in the economy, politics and culture became unshakable during the Song, causing a completely different identity to emerge.

Huángfǔ's rewriting of history shows a high resemblance to Liáng Qǐchāo's creation of a Chinese "China". As a natural result, some people might understand this new identity as the roots of modern Chinese national identity. In fact, it is based on the exclusion of elements that definitely would need to be included in the identity of modern nationalists' view on Chinese history. For instance, Gě Zhaòguāng cites Zhū Xī 朱熹's criticism of the contamination of even the royal house by barbarian culture and takes this as an early example of a "Chinese stance/stance of China". But what Zhū Xī is criticizing is the cultural heritage of the so-called Northern dynasties, including the early Tang dynasty, which we described earlier. He endeavors to establish lines of demarcation that are entirely different from nationalism in modern China.

---

32 The first proven instance is an epigraph found in the Oroqen Autonomous Banner in Inner Mongolia (内蒙古自治区鄂倫春旗嘎仙洞内石刻) in which Tuòbá Tāo 拓跋燾 (408–452 CE), the Emperor Tàiwǔ 太武帝 (r. 423–452), referred to his ancestors as "*kèhán* 可寒". Mǐ 米: A Preliminary Study of the Discovery of the Stone Cave of the Xianbei Nationality (*Xiānbēi shíkū de fāxiàn yǔ chūbù yánji* ū鮮卑石窟的發現與初步研究), in: Cultural Relics (Wén wù 文物) No. 297 (1981–2) (1981); Wang 王: Stone Inscription at the Western Cliff of Gaxiandong (*Gāxiāndòng xībì móyá kèshí* 嘎仙洞西壁摩崖刻石) (2003).

33 The ruling class of the southern states had themselves already developed an identity of the "Central Glory 中華" under heaven. Influence of southern culture can also be seen from early periods of the Tang, for example in the Correct Meaning of the Five Classics (*wǔ jīng zhèngyì* 五經正義), a comprehensive body of commentaries on the five Confucian classics compiled and finally published in 653 by imperial order.

In addition, as so often with regionalism and nationalism, the boundaries are vague and ambiguous. Huángfǔ's treatise refers to at least three different standards to establish a distinction between legitimate dynasties and others. That are ethnic background, geography, and degree of civilization. Huángfǔ's main argument against the legitimacy of the Tuoba's rule is their ethnic origin. According to him, their Xiongnu heritage prevents them from being legitimate rulers. The "Middle Kingdom", which some people argue that the (Tuòbá turned) Yuán[34] were dwelling in, refers to the "Central Plains" around Luòyáng 洛陽, which was the economic and cultural center until at least the Han era. This geographical argument is denied by Huángfǔ based on the difference in the degree of civilization embodied in the rites[35].

Interestingly, all of these standards can be interpreted quite flexibly. Huángfǔ admits that even the Xiongnu people could have been considered legitimate rulers if they had completely extinguished the Jin or if the Jin had handed over the throne to them. The latter alludes to the famous Shànràng 禪讓, the highly ceremonial inauguration of a new emperor by the last emperor of the old imperial house combined with his own abdication. Since neither extinction nor handover happened, Huángfǔ sticks to his ethnically motivated refusal.

That the Tuoba ruled over the traditional heartlands of the "Middle Kingdom", the "Central Plains" around Luòyáng 洛陽, would have hit Sīmǎ Ruì, the succeeding emperors of the Eastern Jin, and many of their subjects, much harder than Huángfǔ. They still dreamt about recovering their homelands and relocating back to there. For them, the "Middle Kingdom" had a very clear geographical range, different from their temporary place of refuge in the southern periphery. In contrast, Huángfǔ did not feel the weight of this argument. He easily pushed it away with the very evasive argument of a superior civilization based on rites.

V. The Path Back to a Chinese "Middle Kingdom"

The sense of superiority of Southern culture was shattered by other civilized Chinese states of diverse ethnicities. Centuries of rule by the Mongolian Chinese empire of the Yuán and the Manchu Chinese empire of the Qīng actually leave little room for rational assumptions about the continuity of a national identity. Therefore, the important question arises as to why the Manchu Qing Empire finally gave again birth to a Chinese "Middle Kingdom" or a Chinese "China" and not to a Mongolian or Tibetan

34 The ruling family of the Northern Wei, the Tuòbá, changed their family name to Yuán when relocating the capital from Píngchéng near modern Dàtóng, Shānxī province, to Luòyáng, modern Hénán province, in 493.

35 Interestingly, the argument of a higher degree of civilization based on rites was also used by the "Barbarians" to discriminate each other and position themselves as the "Middle Kingdom". When Fú Jiān, also Pú Jiān (苻堅, 317–355 CE), the Tibetan founder of the Former Qin, caught Tuòbá Shèyìqián 拓跋涉翼犍, the King of Dai 代王, a forerunner state of the Northern Wei, he made him study the rites at the national university. During a visit to the university, Fú Jiān told Shèyìqián that "in the Middle Kingdom, people learn to cultivate themselves 中國以學養性" (s. "The Records of Fú Jiān (Vol. 1) 載記·苻堅上", in: *Fáng*, Xuánlíng 房玄齡 et al.: The Book of the Jin (Jìn shū 晉書) (648), cited from the Zhōnghuá shūjú 中華書局 edition (1974), p. 2899).

one? In other words, why did the Manchu led multiethnic empire become dominated by the Chinese speaking population concentrated in the southeastern part of the empire.

Gě Zhaòguāng or Liáng Qǐchāo might like to believe in the superiority of Chinese culture, which will eventually assimilate all other cultures. For them, there was probably no other alternative. But the mere existence of Chinese looking empires that were established by Manchu, Mongolian, Khitai, Xianbei and other ethnic groups provides ample evidence for other alternatives.

Actually, the only Chinese state of which that can be proven to have achieved control over areas in the Northern half of modern China without reliance on the military power of Non-Chinese people after the collapse of the Han Empire is the Ming. Even in this case, shortly after the death of its founder, Zhū Yuánzhāng 朱元璋 (1328–1398, *hóngwǔ huángdì* 洪武皇帝), one of his sons, Zhū Dì 朱棣 (1360–1424), the King of Yan (*yānwáng* 燕王) and later Emperor Yongle (*yǒnglè huángdì* 永樂皇帝, r. 1402–1424), turned the power constellations within this empire upside down by defeating and pressing into suicide the legitimate heir of the throne with the help of Mongolian cavalry and forcefully moving the capital from Nanjing to Beijing. Obviously, the question of the reasons for a Chinese modern nation state requires a more comprehensive answer.

In my Japanese classroom, I usually ask my students to consider two facts regarding this question. One is the fact that silver was used as standard currency from the middle of the Ming Empire to the end of the Qing Empire. The other fact is the defeat of the Junggar Empire by the Qianlong emperor (*Aisin-Gioro Hung Li* = *Àixīn-juéluó Hónglì* 愛新覺羅弘曆, *qiānlóng huángdì* 乾隆皇帝, 1711–1799, r. 1735–1795) in 1759. What do these two facts tell us about world history and the position of the "Middle Kingdom" within it?

First, there has never been any significant production of silver in the territories of these two empires or within the geographical range of modern China. The Ming Empire adopted silver as standard currency in a very reluctant manner, which was tantamount to the loss of an autonomous monetary policy[36]. It could also be taken as the capitulation of the Ming in front of the overwhelming, in the beginning illegal, influx of silver.

That Japan and European colonies in South and Middle America provided the tremendous amounts of the precious metal that were necessary to satisfy the huge domestic market alludes to a Chinese dominance in the maritime trade at the time. In Guangzhou and other Chinese harbors, the Portuguese and Japanese economies were reduced to mere providers of natural resources. In other words, the global maritime trade that sustained British and US-American hegemony in the 19th and 20th century was not necessarily invented by Europe. But it was neither a deliberate invention of the Ming Empire. A fast growing, mainly Chinese speaking, highly mercantile

---

36 To assess the historical significance of this, the reader might just recall the shock waves that ran through the governing boards of central banks when Meta, then Facebook, announced the plan to issue their own digital currency. With billionaires in charge now, of course, the attitude has changed completely.

society forced the recognition of international trade on the probably most rigid moralistic Confucian state throughout the history of Chinese states.

Second, the Junggar, which were a threat to the Qing Empire for almost an entire century, turned out to be the last continental nomadic empire. Since wars are in most cases decided by the ability to throw resources into it, the defeat of the Junggar Empire and the subsequent entire eradication of its population symbolize the complete turn of the tide in the economic power that can be extracted from maritime and continental trade. Having positioned itself at the center of the international maritime trade during the 17th to 18th centuries, the Qing Empire easily obtained sufficient resources to prevail.

Nowadays, the term "landlocked" is emblematic for the indispensability of access to the sea in economic development. Continental nomadic economies have become symbols of economic backwardness. In the best case, they evoke sentimental romanticism. In the light of transportation costs for a cellular phone from China to Europe not exceeding several cents or several tens of cents, it is obvious that nowadays, continental trade cannot compete with maritime trade.[37]. However, it is important to remember that this was not the casFe all the time. For a long time, cultural exchange and economic interaction in landlocked Central Eurasia had been the catalyst for development, and nomadic people had often been the front-runners of progress. Chinese history is only one of the many beneficiaries of the continental trade and interchange.

The cradle of Chinese culture is located in a highly ecotonal area. The so-called "Central Plains" are a region where arid continental climate and monsoonal-dominated maritime climate meet. It is suitable for nomadic livestock farming as well as sedentary agriculture. Throughout history, different economic lifestyles have been adopted by different ethnic groups in this area.

From the Spring and Autumn Period to the Western Han, the areas around the "Central Plains", i.e. the North China Plain, the Loess Plateau, the Szechwan Basin (*Sichuan pendi* 四川盆地) and the Northern half of the Middle China Plains, seem to have been dominated politically, economically, and culturally by certain types of Chinese speaking people. With the Eastern Han, a long-term migration process started. Many Chinese speaking people moved to the South of the Yangtse River. By and by they drove out or assimilated indigenous people and colonized the areas in the southern half of modern China. It is a historical process similar to the colonization of the Americas by European people, only taking much longer. At the same time non-Chinese people from the North and Northwest infiltrated the northern areas, creating a situation in which, as already mentioned, political rule in the northern areas became almost impossible without the involvement of non-Chinese people.

The process eventually brought North-Chinese areas into the political and economic networks of central Eurasia, while the South-Chinese areas were integrated into the maritime networks of the Southern Sea. By the time, the difference between both ar-

---

37 It is true that the pandemic and political instability after it inflated prices of maritime transportation. It is also true that some elements of the Chinese Belt and Road Initiative aim to revive continental transportation infrastructure and trade networks. Whether this is sufficient to reverse the tide is yet to be proven by history.

eas became so great that foreign observers were completely unaware of any united entity in the fashion of modern China. Despite not being aware of the logical consequences, the editors of the 6th Volume of *The Cambridge History of China* also pointed out this fact:

> It is nevertheless remarkable that outside observers – Marco Polo is an example – did not realize the basic unity of China. For the fourteenth-century Europeans, Cathay – a name derived from the Khitan ethnic designation and meaning "northern China" – was a country different from Manzi (southern China), and only in the "age of discoveries" in the sixteenth century did Europeans become aware that Cathay and Manzi were in reality parts of that greater unity that we now call China.[38]

The important question is whether Cathay and Manzi were really parts of a greater unity. Could it not be that the contemporary observer proves our projection of modern China into history correctly as an anachronism?

The situation in the fourteenth century may not be as idiosyncratic as it seems. According to Paul Pelliot (1878–1945), "Taβɣač" had been the denomination used by central Asian foreigners to refer to the Tang Empire during the seventh and eighth centuries. This denomination is derived from the Xianbei grounder family of the Northern Wei (*Bei Wei* 北魏), the Tuòbá 拓跋 in modern Chinese. At the same time, the Arabic and Iranian denomination "Šīn" and "Čīn", the Sanskrit term "Cīna", and its Chinese translation "支那", which are all etymologically connected to the modern word "China", were only used in regard to the Kanton area or the Southern Sea. It was not before the sixteenth century that Portuguese sailors, based on the Malayan variation "Čīna", reinvented "China" in reference to a greater unity that we now still recognize in a similar way[39].

In contrast to the "discovery" of West India or the Americas, the "discovery of China" was willingly embraced by the objects of the discovery, the Chinese people. This "discovery" was not a wield phantasy but a sober observation of economic and political realities that developed out of maritime trade centered in Kanton. It also aligned well with the ambitions of Chinese revolutionary forces that thrived to take over the Manchu hegemony in East-Asia after the nineteenth century.

VI. What is a "Chinese State"?

In English, the meaning of the adjective "Chinese" is usually defined as "belonging to or relating to China, its people, or its language".[40] That is more or less true in daily conversation, but strictly speaking, the Chinese language is, of course, older than any Chinese state or even the Chinese script, not to mention the short history of the modern nation state China. In other words, the Chinese language is not the monopoly of the modern nation state China. It is highly anachronistic to define the Chineseness of diverse fragments of history in the context of a specific modern nation state.

---

38 *Franke/Twitchett*, The Cambridge History of China Volume 6 – Alien Regimes and Border States, 907–1368 (1994), p. 21.

39 *Pelliot* (fn. 14), pp. 217–229, 264–278.

40 *Cambridge University Press & Assessment (n. d.).*

In history, there have been many states run by speakers of a tongue different from Chinese who nevertheless utilized the Chinese language in order to establish legal institutions and create administrative documents as a main pillar of statecraft. The various states mentioned earlier that ruled the northern part of modern China for more than a millennium are just a few examples. In fact, the geographical range of this type of "Chinese state" extends far beyond the territory of modern China. We can easily find them on the Korean and Indochina peninsulas, as well as on the Japanese Archipelago. For instance, no knowledge of Korean or Japanese is required to read the legal norms or documents that the Ritsuryō-Kokka 律令国家 created during the Asuka era (end 6.c. – 710 CE) and the Nara era (710 – 784 CE) on modern Japanese soil, or that the Dae Joseon Guk (Daejoseonguk 대조선국大朝鮮國, better known as 李氏朝鮮 (Issi Joseon 이씨 조선 = *Lǐshì Cháoxiǎn* = *Rishi Chōsen*) in Japanese and Chinese, 1392 – 1897) created on modern Korean soil. The well-educated managers of these states wrote them in refined Chinese. On the contrary, modern Japanese or Koreans will be blocked from accessing them without a proper training in Chinese. We could refer to this type of state as "Chinese states" without any reference to modern China. Pertinent states are "Chinese states" established and run by non-Chinese people with the help of the Chinese language.[41]

As mentioned in the first section, the modern Japanese and modern Chinese languages lack any morphological features that could make the same difference. The "Chinese" of a "Chinese state" is always the same as "China". Fortunately, both languages offer additional methods for referring to both the language that is commonly used in modern China and the earlier variants of this language. One denomination is "*kango* 漢語" in Japanese. It refers mainly to written old Chinese. The same string is read "*hànyǔ*" in Chinese, mainly referring to spoken modern Chinese. The Chinese term "*hànwén* 漢文" carries a connotation similar to the Japanese word *kango.* In Japanese, this string is read Kanbun. It mainly refers to the traditional Japanese readings of classical Chinese. When teaching in Japanese classrooms or giving talks in Chinese, I utilize these language tools to create the new compounds "*kango kokka* 漢語國家" and "*hànwén guójiā* 漢文國家" respectively. These neologisms allow me to express exactly what I understand under "Chinese states", i. e. states whose insti-

[41] Here, the question arises: what are non-Chinese people, and what are Chinese people? I would like to refer to language again, i. e. the first or main language spoken by a group of people appears to me to be the best way to define their affiliation. Determining this language can be a bit of a challenge at times. For instance, I am always puzzled by the question of which language might have been the mother tongue of Lǐ Shìmín 李世民 (598/600 – 649 CE), the second emperor and the virtual founder of the Tang Empire (618 – 907 CE). He maintained a close connection with the military faction that originated from the Wǔchuān 武川 garrison on the northern border of the Xiānbēi or Särbi state of the Northern Wei. He was able to communicate effectively with the many Turkic-Mongolian leaders who often accompanied him on his excursions and hunts. At the same time, he managed to establish himself in an unshakeable position in Chinese historiography as the ideal of prudent rulership through the famous collection of discussions with his Chinese speaking ministers, the zhēn guān zhèng yào 貞觀政要. Although I am confident that his ancestors spoke a non-Chinese language, presumably a Särbi dialect, and that his successors on the throne ceased to use it entirely and became monolingual Chinese speakers, I cannot provide a definitive conclusion about his first language. This puzzle serves to me as a good reminder that race and ethnic affiliation are by far too elusive concepts as to take seriously as guidance for historical research.

tutions are established by Chinese language, independent of their geographical location or ethnic background.

To clarify the chronological order, I first developed the Japanese term "*kango kokka*" during my classes at Meiji University during the academic years 2021 and 2022. It was the outcome of overcoming the odds to circumvent the politically loaded denominations "Middle Kingdom" and "Orient". During a one-year visit to the University of Chicago from 2023 to 2024, I translated "*kango kokka*" into "Chinese states". I recognized that defining a state by the language it uses to establish its legal institutions is not as weird as it first sounded to me. We only need to abandon the simplistic understanding that "Chinese" is related to the modern nation state "China".[42] Finally, during a four month visit to Beijing University in 2024 and an even shorter trip to Taiwan for a series of lectures in 2025, I gained the confidence that the Chinese "*hànwén guójiā*" can convey almost the same connotation as the original Japanese neologism.

"Chinese states" can have completely different ethnic backgrounds. Following the example of the "Roman Empire of the German Nation", we could call the Northern Wei and its successors the "Chinese Empire(s) of the Xiānbēi or Särbi Nation" or the Qing Empire the "Chinese Empire of the Manchu Nation"[43]. The ethnic diversity of Chinese states also makes it easier to comprehend the fact that there have been so many cultural movements throughout Chinese history that resembled a renaissance. It is not because Chinese history was a history of stagnation for two millennia caused by Oriental despotism. Similar to the Carolingian Renaissance, history needed to be rewritten and classics needed to be reinterpreted as the cultural foundation of the new state, whenever the social or ethnic composition of the ruling class changed. The retrospective examination of Chinese classics was actually a sign of socio-political change.

The Xiānbēi or Särbi Renaissance laid the foundation for the legal institutions of the Tang Empire. These institutions were exported to other East-Asian states, and are, nowadays, often celebrated as the essence of Chinese statecraft during the alleged two thousand years of "imperial rule". Even Chinese speaking people conducted similar rewritings and reinterpretations when they came into power. The difference is that they are awarded their merits in modern nationalist Chinese narratives, while the Särbi, Cathay, Mongolian, Manchu and so on do not. In my view, reducing

42 I am grateful to the three Chinese students who attended that course, Lǚ Xuě yán 呂雪妍, Wú Fāng 吳方, and Yáng Qǐyǔ 楊起予, for their insightful discussions on the contents of this paper.

43 Admittedly, the former metaphor fits better than the later. At the institutional level, the northern Wei was still a purely Chinese empire, but the landscape was altered by the appearance of states with native scripts in the immediate vicinity of Chinese states, starting in the 8th century. The Liáo 遼 (907–1125) was the first state to have a bilingual institutional structure. The Qing developed a fully-fledged multilingual institutional framework. This indeed limits the validity of the "Chinese state" concept. However, the question remains as to why the Chinese language, unlike Latin in Europe, was able to outlast many vernacular languages. A comparison with modern English language imperialism could further illuminate this issue.

"the history of China" to a short period of several centuries in modern times might well open our eyes to a much more diverse and global history of "Chinese states"[44].

Literature

Aston, William G.: Nihongi: Chronicles of Japan from the Earliest Times to A. D. 697, first published in Proceedings of Japan Society (1896), electronically published by Japanese Historical Text Initiative, University of California Berkeley (1996), available at: https://jhti.studentorg.berkeley.edu/Nihon%20shoki.html, accessed on 5 May 2025.

Bureau for Social Education of the Japanese Ministry of Education (*monbushō shakai kyōiku kyoku* 文部省社會教育局): The Facts of the Middle Court (*chūchō jijitsu* 中朝事實), Japanese Thought Series Vol. 8 (*nihon shisō sōsho dai happen* 日本思想叢書第八編) (1933).

Cambridge University Press & Assessment (n. d.): "Chinese", in: Cambridge.org dictionary, retrieved on 15 May 2025, from https://dictionary.cambridge.org/dictionary/english/chinese?q=Chinese.

Chor, Louis W. Y. (左永業): Nihon Shoki (日本書紀) Trilingual: Selections in the Original Classical Chinese (Kanbun) with English Translation based on the Iwanami Bunko edition (five volumes, 1994–1995), in: Libraries Staff Reports, University of Alberta Library (2018), available at: https://doi.org/10.7939/R35Q4S142, accessed on 5 May 2025.

Demel, Walter: Wie die Chinesen gelb wurden: Ein Beitrag zur Frühgeschichte der Rassentheorien, in: Historische Zeitschrift Vol. 255 (1992). Cited from English version: "How the Chinese Became Yellow: A Contribution to the Early History of Race Theories", in: Brandt, Bettina/Purdy, Daniel L. (ed.), China in the German Enlightenment (2016).

Dǒng, Gào 董誥 et al. (ed.): Collected Works of the Tang (*quán táng wén* 全唐文) (1814), cited from reprint by Shanghai Ancient Books Publishing House 上海古籍出版社 (1990).

Fáng, Xuánlíng 房玄齡 et al.: The Book of the Jin (*Jìn shū* 晉書) (648), cited from the Zhōnghuá shūjú 中華書局 edition (1974).

Franke, Herbert/*Twitchett*, Denis: The Cambridge History of China Volume 6 – Alien Regimes and Border States, 907–1368 (1994).

Ge, Zhaoguang 葛兆光: Here in "China" I Dwell: Reconstructing Historical Discourses of "China" for Our Time (*zhái zī Zhōngguó: chóngjiàn yǒuguān "Zhōngguó" de lìshǐ lùnshù* 宅茲中國: 重建有關"中國"的歷史論述) (2011). Citations are based on the Chinese version. The page numbers etc. may be different in the English version.

Ge, Zhaoguang 葛兆光: The Inside and Outside of Historical China: A Reclarification of the Concept of China and its Borders (*lìshǐ Zhōngguó de nèi yǔ wài: yǒuguān "Zhōngguó" yǔ "zhōubiān" gàiniàn de zài chéngqīng* 歷史中國的内與外:有關"中國"與"周邊"概念的再澄清) (2017).

44 Rewriting Chinese legal history as the history of "Chinese states" does not go without a sympathy for postmodern deconstructions of modern nationalist narratives. These are often remarkable illuminations of the many unconscious adoptions of collective hallucinations that are embedded in our understandings of sex/gender, race or ethnicity etc. However, we must not throw the baby out with the bathwater. In full awareness that we have only access to a tiny fraction of linguistic realities in the history, the focus on language might well be a useful tool to avoid falling into nihilistic traps when deconstructing essentialist concepts of a never changing China.

Ghosh, Manomohan: Origin and Antiquity of the Sanskrit Word CĪNA as the name of China, in: Annals of the Bhandarkar Oriental Research Institute Vol. 42 No. 1–4 (1961).

Ho, Ping-ti 何炳棣: In Defense of Sinicization: A Rebuttal of Evelyn Rawski's Reenvisioning the Qing, in: Journal of Asian Studies Vol. 57 No. 1 (1998).

Ho, Ping-ti 何炳棣: The Significance of The Ch'ing Period in Chinese History, in: Journal of Asian Studies 26(2) (1967).

Kawatani, Tomohide 川谷致秀: Annotated Edition of the Facts of the Middle Court and the Summary Collection of the Holy Teachings (*chūchō jijitsu oyobi seikyō yōroku jutsugi* 中朝事及聖教要錄述義), (1936).

Kojima, Tsuyoshi 小島毅: The History Perception 'Zhōnghuá': Centered on the Spring and Autumn School (*chūka no rekishi ninshiki: shunjūgaku wo chūshin ni* 中華の歴史認識ー春秋学を中心に), in: Akita Shigeru 秋田茂 et al. (ed.), The World History of "World History" (*"sekai shi" no sekai shi* 「世界史」の世界史) (2016).

Kubo, Kōji 久保耕治: Lecture: What Should 'China' Be Called in Japanese? (*tokubetsu kōgi Shina to Chūgoku no yurai* 特別講義:支那と中国の由来), in: Shikoku Gakuin University Treatises (*Shikoku gakuin daigaku ronshū* 四国学院大学論集) No. 143 (2014).

Liang, Qichao 梁啓超: Outline of Chinese History (*Zhōngguó shǐ xùlùn* 中國史敍論), in: The China Discussion (*Qing Yi Bao* 清議報) No. 90–91 (1901); also in: *yǐnbīngshì wénjí lèibiān* (second volume) 飲氷室文集類編下册 (1904).

Liang, Qichao 梁啓超: Treatise China's Momentum for Independence in Face of the Oriental Politics of Japan (*lùn Zhōngguó dúlì zhī shìlì yǔ rìběn dōngfāng zhèngcè* 論支那獨立之勢力與日本東方政策), in: The China Discussion (*Qīng yì bào* 清議報) No. 26 (1899).

Liang, Qichao 梁啓超: Treatise on Religious Reform in China (*lùn Zhīnà zōngjiào gǎigé* 論支那宗教改革), in: The China Discussion (Qīng yì bào 清議報) No. 19–20 (1899); also in: *yǐnbīngshì wénjí lèibiān* (first volume) 飲氷室文集類編上册 (1904).

Mi, Wenping 米文平: A Preliminary Study of the Discovery of the Stone Cave of the Xianbei Nationality (*Xiānbēi shíkū de fāxiàn yǔ chūbù yánjiū* 鮮卑石窟的發現與初步研究), in: Cultural Relics (*Wén wù* 文物) No. 297 (1981–2) (1981).

Mitani, Hiroshi 三谷博/*Li*, Sonshi 李成市 (I Seongsi 이성시)/*Momoki*, Shirō 桃木至郎: The World Seen by "Peripheral Countries": Japan, Korea, Vietnam (*"shūhen koku" no sekai zō* 「周辺国」の世界像ー日本・朝鮮・ベトナム」), in: Akita Shigeru 秋田茂 et al. (ed.), The World History of "World History" (*"sekai shi" no sekai shi* 「世界史」の世界史) (2016).

Motegi, Toshio 茂木敏夫: Reconstructing Chinese Empire into 'Zhongguo' as a Nation-State (*shinmatsu ni okeru 'Chūgoku' no sōshutsu to Nihon* 清末における「中國」の創出と日本), in: China: Society and Culture (*Chūgoku: shakai to bunka* 中国ーー社会と文化) No. 10 (1995).

Naitō, Torajirō 内藤虎次郎: Supplement: Geopolitical Speculations (*furoku: chisei okusetu* 附録「地勢臆説」), in: Treatise on History of Early Modern Humanities (*kinsei bungaku shi ron* 近世文学史論) (1897); cited from Collected Works of Naitō Konan Vol. 1 (*naitō konan zenshū dai ikkan* 内藤湖南全集第1巻) (1996).

Pelliot, Paul (author)/*Hambis*, Louis (ed.): Notes on Marco Polo I (1959).

Rawski, Evelyn S. (羅友枝): Presidential Address: Reenvisioning the Qing: The Significance of the Qing Period in Chinese History, in: Journal of Asian Studies Vol. 55 No. 4 (1996).

Rawski, Evelyn S.: The Last Emperors: A Social History of Qing Imperial Institutions (1998).

Takazawa, Shinichirō 高澤信一郎編: The Facts of the Middle Court (*chūchō Jijitsu* 中朝事實), Association for Publication of the Facts of the Middle Court in Celebration of the 60th Year of Reign (*gozaii rokujū nen hōshuku zhūchō jijitsu kankō kai* 御在位六十年奉祝中朝事實刊行會) (1985).

Wada, Sei 和田清: On the Original Meaning of the Terms 'Shina' and 'Shinajin' (*Shina oyobi Shinajin to iu go no hongi ni tsuite* 支那及び支那人という語の本義について), in: Wada, Sei 和田清 (ed.), Treatises on Oriental History (*tō-a shi ronsō* 東亜史論藪) (1942).

Wang, Limin 王立民: Stone Inscription at the Western Cliff of Gaxiandong (Gāxiāndòng xībì móyá kèshí 嘎仙洞西壁摩崖刻石) (2003).

(English translations not included in original publications are tentative translations by the author of this article. Some original English translations of Japanese titles exhibit a significant difference from the literal meaning of the Japanese title. The author did not make any amendments to them).

Wege nach Japan: Von der Austauschschülerin in Okazaki zur Richterhospitantin

Ein persönlicher Erfahrungsbericht

Von Cornelia Hagedorn

Cornelia Hagedorn ist Richterin am Oberlandesgericht Schleswig. Sie absolvierte ein Studium der Rechtswissenschaften und des japanischen Rechts in Trier, Salamanca und Würzburg. Das Referendariat verbrachte sie in Bremen und arbeitete danach in einer Forschungsgruppe der Max-Planck-Gesellschaft. Sie promovierte an der Universität Heidelberg mit einer rechtsvergleichenden Arbeit. Seit 2010 ist sie Richterin in Schleswig-Holstein. Von 2017 bis 2019 arbeitete sie zudem als wissenschaftliche Mitarbeiterin am Bundesverfassungsgericht.

Die Faszination für Japan erfasst viele Menschen aus unterschiedlichen Gründen. Schon seit einiger Zeit sind es Anime und Manga, die vor allem junge Menschen in ihren Bann ziehen. Aber auch die zahlreichen Kampfsportarten, Zen-Meditation, die Ästhetik von Teezeremonie und Ikebana oder der vielbeschworene Kontrast zwischen Tradition und Moderne wecken seit Jahrzehnten in vielen eine Sehnsucht, dieses Land auf die eine oder andere Art näher kennen zu lernen.

Bei mir waren es jugendliche Abenteuerlust, jahrelanges Judotraining sowie die Ansage meines Vaters: „Wenn schon ein Jahr Ausland, dann Japan, denn wenn du Japanisch sprichst, findest du später mal einen guten Job", die mich als 17-Jährige in den 1990er Jahren für ein Jahr in eine japanische Gastfamilie in Okazaki, Aichi-ken, versetzten. Dies hat mein Leben nachhaltig geprägt.

Die grundsätzliche Japan-Faszination führt bei einigen Menschen dazu, dass sie ihr Leben dauerhaft auf Japan ausrichten, sodass dieses Land zu ihrer zweiten Heimat wird und sie selbst zu Förderern des interkulturellen Austauschs. Die Anzahl speziell der deutschen Juristen, die mit Japan befasst sind, ist naturgemäß im Verhältnis nochmals geringer. Wenn man jedoch in diese Kreise eintaucht, fällt auf, wie groß die Bandbreite und die Betätigungsfelder sind. Professor Menkhaus nimmt in dieser Gemeinschaft eine herausragende Stellung ein. Wer sich im deutschen Sprachraum mit dem japanischen Recht befasst, kommt um seine Schriften, insbesondere zum „Japanischen im japanischen Recht" nicht herum.

Meinen ganz persönlichen japanbezogenen Erfahrungsschatz, der mich von der Oberschule West-Okazaki (*okazaki nishi kōkō*) über das Jurastudium – auch des japanischen Rechts –, ein Anwaltspraktikum in Tokyo, eine rechtsvergleichende Dissertation zum Thema Rechtsetzung im Bereich der Biomedizin in Japan und zuletzt

Duncker & Humblot · Berlin | https://doi.org/10.3790/978-3-428-59611-9.2025.418932

durch eine Richterhospitation immer wieder in dieses Land führte, möchte ich in diesem Beitrag mit dem geneigten Leser teilen.

I. Nationale Grenzen überwinden, um in der Welt Heimat zu finden

Im Jahr 1995 nach Japan zu reisen, zumal nicht nach Tokyo, sondern in eine japanische „Kleinstadt" von 400.000 Einwohnern, war sicherlich eine Erfahrung, die man im Jahr 2025 nicht in vergleichbarer Weise machen kann.[1] Abgesehen von einem englischen „Liaison Teacher", genannt „Lee from Leeds", der als Sprachassistent die inoffizielle Aufgabe hatte, die Sprachkenntnisse der Englischlehrer an meiner Schule zu verbessern, war ich die einzige Ausländerin weit und breit. Es gab kein Internet, keine Handys, keine Übersetzungsapps. Telefonate waren so teuer, dass ich in der gesamten Zeit exakt zweimal mit meiner Familie in Husum telefonierte, an meinem Geburtstag und an Weihnachten. Sprachlich hatte ich mich auf mein Austauschjahr durch Selbststudium mit einem Langenscheidt-Kurs, der zur Schulung des Hörverständnisses Kassetten beinhaltete, vorbereitet. Vier Stunden pro Woche, konsequent ein Jahr lang durchgezogen.

Dieses Training hatte mich jedoch weder auf die am ersten Schultag von mir erwartete Selbstvorstellung noch auf den Ansturm meiner Mitschülerinnen und Mitschüler am Ende des ersten Unterrichtstages vorbereitet. Mein Gastvater hatte mir zum Glück ein paar Begrüßungsworte aufgeschrieben, die ich sicherheitshalber von Hiragana in Romaji übertrug, um sie vor der 1.200-köpfigen Schüler- und Lehrerschaft in der Schulturnhalle fehlerfrei vortragen zu können. Während im anschließenden Unterricht am ersten Schultag nach den Frühjahrsferien alle 45 Schülerinnen und Schüler in Schuluniform, streng nach Geschlechtern getrennt, brav und still dem Unterricht folgten und ich mich an Einzeltisch Nummer 46 zu fragen begann, ob ich je verstehen würde, worum es ging, brach pünktlich mit dem Abschlussläuten der Schulglocke das Chaos aus. Gefühlt alle 45 Schülerinnen und Schüler stürzten, mit ihren Englisch-Wörterbüchern bewaffnet, auf meinen Tisch zu und bestürmten mich mit Fragen auf Japanisch und Englisch in einer Mischung und Geschwindigkeit, die mich überwältigten. Zwei Mitschülerinnen luden mich im Anschluss zu einem Häagen Dasz-Eis ein, da sie aufgrund der von ihnen erkannten phonetischen Ähnlichkeit der Eismarke mit meinem Nachnamen meinten, das sei „mein" Eis.

Natürlich kehrte recht schnell Routine in mein Schulleben ein und die Mitschülerinnen und Mitschüler gewöhnten sich an mich und meine noch sehr beschränkten Kommunikationsfähigkeiten. Diese besserten sich jedoch schnell – auch dank des Einsatzes einiger Lehrerinnen und Lehrer, die mir in ihren Freistunden in der Schulbücherei, wo ich einige Unterrichtsstunden (etwa, wenn in meiner Klasse Altjapanisch unterrichtet wurde) verbringen durfte, individuellen Sprachunterricht erteilten. So habe ich etwa anhand des berühmten Zeichentrickfilms „Mein Nachbar Totoro" (*tonari no totoro*) Japanisch gelernt. Mit meinen zunehmenden sprachlichen Fähig-

[1] Die Austauschorganisation AFS (American Field Service), über die ich nach Japan kam, bot in den 1990er Jahren deutschlandweit fünf Plätze pro Jahr für einen Austausch nach Japan an; aktuell sind es mehr als 20. Weitere Informationen abrufbar unter: https://www.afs.de/ (zuletzt abgerufen am 1. Mai 2025).

keiten nutzten wir diese Stunden im Laufe des Jahres immer mehr zum lebhaften Austausch über die Besonderheiten von Deutschland und Japan. Einer der Lehrer spielte in diesen Stunden des Öfteren auf seiner Bambusflöte (*shakuhachi*), deren Töne wie aus einer fernen Zeit kommend durch die Schulflure klangen. Dieser Lehrer, Shibata-sensei, finanzierte mir das ganze Jahr lang Unterricht auf dem Koto (eine Art liegende Harfe – Wölbbrettzither – mit 13 Saiten). Das Leihinstrument zum Üben stellte er mir ebenfalls zur Verfügung, es fand seinen Platz in dem von meinem Gastgroßvater bewohnten Tatami-Zimmer im Haus meiner Gastfamilie. Mit dem täglichen Judotraining, das ich als Hobbygruppe (*bukatsu*) in der Schule gewählt hatte, den Übungen auf dem Koto, extra Judotraining im Nachbarort am Wochenende und allabendlichem Briefeschreiben an Freunde und Familie in der Heimat war ich von Anfang an gut beschäftigt. Und die Gastfreundschaft, die ich erlebte, war schier überwältigend. Neben dem Musikunterricht nahm mich Shibata sensei in den Sommerferien mit auf eine Wander-Exkursion auf meinen Traumgipfel, den Fuji-san. Die Musiklehrerin lud mich ein auf ein Ski-Wochenende ihrer Familie in Nagano-ken mit Übernachtung im Ryōkan, inklusive Kaiseki-Menü und langsamem Auftauen nach dem Skitag in der heißen Quelle im Garten (*rotenburo*) – davon träume ich heute noch…

Die Runde der Lehrer in der Schulbibliothek sollte es auch sein, die mich bei der Ausarbeitung einer Rede unterstützte, die ich bei einem Wettbewerb der Austauschschüler des ganzen Bezirks im letzten Drittel meines Austauschjahres halten wollte. Es ging um das Thema „Was ich durch meinen Austauschaufenthalt gelernt habe" (*ryūgaku de eta koto*) und ich wollte mich natürlich nicht darauf beschränken, meine Missgeschicke im Alltag zu schildern, wie das Betreten der Küche zum gemeinsamen Abendessen in Toilettenlatschen, der misslungene Versuch, vergorenen Sojabohnenquark (*natto*) zu essen oder der Umstand, dass es sich bei dem „*tomodachi*", den ich zum Judoverein mitnehmen wollte, nicht um eine Freundin, sondern um einen Mitschüler aus dem schulischen Judoclub handelte, was nach dem Verständnis meiner Gasteltern nicht ging (im Japanischen wird weder zwischen Geschlechtern noch zwischen Einzahl und Mehrzahl unterschieden). Vielmehr ging es mir in meiner Rede darum, meine Erkenntnis zu teilen, dass trotz aller kulturellen Unterschiede die Menschen doch alle im Herzen gleich seien und ich dafür plädierte, über nationale Grenzen hinweg die Welt als Heimat aller zu erleben. Trotz eines Maskottchens in Form des kleinen Totoro und des intensiven Trainings in der Schulbibliothek konnte ich die Jury nicht überzeugen, sondern verlor gegenüber einer Norwegerin, die in ihrer kurzweiligen Rede eben jene typischen Missgeschicke eines Ausländers in Japan zum Besten gab. Aber viel wichtiger waren mir das positive Feedback und die Unterstützung meiner engagierten Lehrer und Gastfamilie.

Ja, meine Gastfamilie – ohne sie hätte ich sicherlich nicht in gleichem Maße das Gefühl entwickelt, in Japan meine zweite Heimat zu haben, mich akzeptiert, wenn nicht gar geliebt, und rundum gut aufgehoben zu fühlen. Ich hatte vier Gastgeschwister und teilte mir mit den beiden jüngeren Schwestern ein Zimmer, in dem wir abends im Gleichtakt die Futons aus dem Schrank holten, nebeneinander ausrollten und jede für sich noch ein wenig lasen, bevor eine von uns „*denki wo kesu?*" fragte und das Oberlicht durch Ziehen an der daran befindlichen Schnur löschte. Meine beiden älteren Gastgeschwister hatten eigene Zimmer, in denen sie die wenige neben der

Ganztagsschule verbleibende Freizeit damit verbrachten, zu lernen. Insbesondere meinen Gastbruder Yoshihiro, der sich auf das Uni-Eintrittsexamen vorbereitete, bekam ich eigentlich nur bei dem gemeinsamen Abendessen zu Gesicht. Er durfte danach auch stets als erster das Bad (*ofuro*) nutzen, weil er im Anschluss immer noch bis tief in die Nacht lernte. Übrigens mit Erfolg: er schaffte das schwierigste Eintrittsexamen Japans und wurde zum Studium an der Tokyo Universität zugelassen.

Meine Gasteltern waren beide Lehrer, wobei meine Gastmutter (*okāsan*), anstatt in ihrem Beruf als Englischlehrerin zu arbeiten, den Tag damit verbrachte, sich um die Großfamilie zu kümmern, wozu auch noch der im Haus wohnende Großvater und ihre beiden etwas entfernt lebenden Eltern gehörten. Das hieß für sie: jeden Morgen um 6 Uhr aufstehen, um für acht Personen das Frühstück und für alle Schulkinder die Lunchbox (*obento*) zuzubereiten. Wenn alle das Haus verlassen hatten, wusch sie täglich Berge von Wäsche, erledigte Einkäufe und begann schon mit den Vorbereitungen für das Abendessen.

Gegen 20 Uhr versammelten wir uns alle in der Wohnküche am *kotatsu*, dem niedrigen Tisch (im Winter mit integrierter Heizdecke), der mit Köstlichkeiten aller Art beladen war. Wenn ich – aufgrund der damals in Deutschland vorherrschenden Vorstellung, die Japaner ernährten sich ausschließlich von Reis und rohem Fisch – jemals gehofft gehabt hatte, schlank und rank (und nicht etwa, wie der typische USA-Austauschschüler, zehn Kilo schwerer) in die Heimat zurückkehren zu können, so starb diese Hoffnung bereits in den ersten Tagen. Nie hätte ich mir vorstellen können, welch phantasievolle, überwältigende Vielfalt an Speisen mich in meinem Gastland erwartete! Heute mag das niemanden mehr überraschen, aber damals war das einzige japanische Gericht, von dem die meisten schon gehört hatten (aber nur in Theorie): Sushi. So freute ich mich an jedem Schultag aufs Neue auf das Überraschungspaket, das meine Lunchbox bieten würde, und zu meinem 18. Geburtstag gab es weder eine große Party noch den Führerschein oder einen ersten Alkoholexzess, sondern etwas viel Besseres: einen Sushi-cake! Ich habe noch immer ein schlechtes Gewissen, meiner Gastfamilie die Haare vom Kopf gegessen zu haben. Aber interkultureller Austausch geht wohl überall auch und vor allem durch den Magen, und da war ich eine dankbare Kandidatin, die immer brav ein ganzes Repertoire an Lieblingsspeisen aufzählte, wenn die stets gestellte Frage danach kam. Darunter übrigens an prominenter Stelle *korokke*, wobei mir (und sicher oft genauso wenig meinem Gegenüber) nicht bewusst war, dass es sich dabei um die aus den Niederlanden „importierten" Kroketten (japanischer Art) handelt.

Im Nachhinein denke ich, dass es vor allem der Wunsch meiner Gastmutter war, mich aufzunehmen, um Abwechslung in ihren anstrengenden und wohl auch etwas eintönigen Alltag zu bringen. Sie war noch nie im Ausland gewesen, sprach doch besser Englisch als mancher Fachlehrer an meiner Schule und war voller Neugier auf meine Erzählungen über das Alltagsleben in meiner Heimat. Ihrer Warmherzigkeit und ihrer Unterstützung verdanke ich unendlich viel. Aber auch der Rest der Familie empfing mich mit offenen Armen, wobei es sicher für meine Gastgeschwister nicht immer einfach war, wenn der Fokus allzu oft auf mir und meinen vielfältigen Aktivitäten lag.

Zum Glück konnte die ganze Familie (mit Ausnahme des Großvaters) im Sommer nach meiner Abreise ihre erste Auslandsreise unternehmen und mich in meiner nordfriesischen Heimat besuchen. Meine Eltern organisierten den Kleinbus des schulischen Rudervereins für Fahrten durch das ganze Bundesland und wir alle versuchten, meiner japanischen Familie in der kurzen Zeit ihres Aufenthalts ihre Gastfreundschaft so gut wie möglich zu erwidern.

II. Ein Sommer in Tokyo

Natürlich erlebte ich nach der Rückkehr nach Deutschland das typische Rückkehrerphänomen: mein Umfeld in der Heimat hatte sich nicht verändert, während ich innerlich zu einem neuen Menschen geworden war, was ich auch äußerlich durch Schwarzfärbung meiner (eigentlich blonden) Haare zum Ausdruck brachte. Es half nichts, die Routine des Alltags hatte mich schnell wieder im Griff und mir war klar, dass ich meine innere Entwicklung nur in einer neuen Umgebung mit anderen Menschen fortsetzen können würde. Da war der Schritt an die Universität Trier, wo man praktischerweise nicht nur Jura, sondern auch Japanologie und japanisches Recht studieren konnte, naheliegender, als die räumliche Distanz von 700 km vermuten lassen würde.

Zwar war mir bewusst, dass sich gerade die Rechtswissenschaft nicht optimal beruflich mit meinem Interesse an Japan würde verbinden lassen. Ich träumte zu jener Zeit allerdings von einer Karriere im Auswärtigen Amt. Außerdem gab es ja die Option, mit meinen Sprachkenntnissen in einer Großkanzlei mit Sitz in Japan arbeiten zu können. Zunächst einmal lernte ich in der fachspezifischen Fremdsprachenausbildung[2] japanische Vokabeln wie „Vertragsschluss“, „Schuldanerkenntnis“ und „deliktischer Schadensersatzanspruch“, wobei meine Kommilitonen überwiegend sprachlich noch nicht einmal dazu der Lage waren, eine Essensbestellung in einem japanischen Café vorzunehmen. Problematisch fand ich zudem den Umstand, dass wir vom ersten Semester an Einführungen in alle zentralen Rechtsgebiete des japanischen Rechts bekamen, wo wir doch das deutsche Rechtssystem kaum kannten bzw. uns dieses über mehrere Semester hinweg in viel langsamerer Geschwindigkeit vertraut machten. Einen Vergleich der Rechtssysteme oder auch nur eine vergleichende Einordnung des Gehörten hätte ich persönlich in späteren Studienjahren deutlich besser vornehmen können.

Die Ausbildung brachte jedoch die Möglichkeit mit sich, ein Stipendium des DAAD Tomo no kai (Freundeskreis ehemaliger Stipendiaten des DAAD) zu erlangen. So durfte ich den Sommer 1999 in Tokyo verbringen, wo ich zweimal wöchentlich einen Sprachkurs im Asahi Culture Center besuchte und als Praktikantin in der Rechtsanwaltskanzlei Dr. Neumann & Partner arbeitete. Die Kanzlei betreute unter

2 Die Fachspezifische Fremdsprachenausbildung im Rahmen des Jurastudiums wird von der Universität Trier schon seit über 30 Jahren angeboten und fortlaufend ausgebaut. Ab Herbst 2024 wird in diesem Rahmen erstmals ein Studiengang zum „International Legal Studies Bachelor“ angeboten.Weitere Informationen abrufbar unter: https://www.uni-trier.de/universitaet/fachbereiche-faecher/fachbereich-v/internationale-rechtsstudien-ffa/profil (zuletzt abgerufen am 1. Mai 2025).

anderem kleine und mittelständische europäische Unternehmen, die auf dem japanischen Markt Fuß fassen wollten. Die Arbeit reichte vom Sortieren der Visitenkarten-Kartei der Kanzlei – was nicht immer einfach ist, wenn diese auf Japanisch beschrieben sind – über das Verfassen von Schriftsätzen, Anfertigung von Übersetzungen bis hin zu Telefondiensten auf Deutsch, Englisch und Japanisch. Ich lernte, was „Feldenkrais“ ist, da ein Mandant diese alternativmedizinische Methode in Japan verbreiten wollte, bearbeitete Schriftverkehr in einem von Dr. Neumann betreuten internationalen Schlichtungsverfahren über eine Vertriebsvereinbarung und fertigte englischsprachige Vertragsentwürfe.

Untergebracht war ich auf Vermittlung des DAAD Tomo No Kai bei einer alleinstehenden japanischen Klavierlehrerin, die mir ihre Zweitwohnung, in der sich nicht viel mehr als ein großer Flügel für ihre Unterrichtsstunden befand, zur Verfügung stellte. Das Frühstück war inklusive, so dass ich jeden Morgen zwei Stockwerke zu ihrer Privatwohnung hinaufstieg und mich an den von ihr aufgetischten Köstlichkeiten labte. Die Freude wurde allerdings zunehmend dadurch getrübt, dass sie mir jeden Morgen gegenübersaß, und mir – ohne selbst etwas zu essen – Gesellschaft leistete. Zunächst machte mir die morgendliche Konversation noch Spaß. Jedoch spürte ich in ihrer Ausstrahlung eine zunehmende Missbilligung, und immer häufiger erzählte sie von meinen Vorgängern, die offenbar alle überaus fleißig gewesen waren und ihre freie Zeit in der Wohnung mit Sprachstudien und Zeitungslektüre verbracht hatten. Ich hingegen hatte verschiedene Kontakte in Tokyo, so dass ich die Abende und Wochenenden für Erkundungen der Stadt und Umgebung und natürlich auch diverse Feierlichkeiten nutzte, anstatt mich in die Wohnung zurückzuziehen. Mein Gastbruder aus Okazaki zeigte mir seine Universität und nahm mich mit zu ein paar studentischen Veranstaltungen. Meinen sprachlichen Fähigkeiten hat das sicher nicht geschadet – in der Wohnung hätte ich allenfalls ein paar Kanji mehr gelernt. Nur merkte meine Gastgeberin das nicht, da mich ihr zunehmend kritischer Ton und Fragestil so verunsicherte, dass ich beim Frühstück keinen geraden Satz mehr hervorbrachte und mir der Appetit verging.

Später bekam ich heraus, dass sie mich offenbar für eine Art Flittchen hielt, weil mehrfach verschiedene „Herren“ bei ihr angerufen hatten, um mich zu sprechen. Dass es sich dabei schlicht um Studienfreunde handelte, mit denen ich mich für Unternehmungen verabredet hatte, und die deshalb überwiegend männlich waren, weil dies den damaligen Mehrheitsverhältnissen unter den ausländischen Praktikanten in Tokyo entsprach, war ihr offensichtlich unklar. Dennoch bot sie an, eine Abschiedsparty für mich zu organisieren, da sie das bei allen meine Vorgänger auch so gemacht habe. Ich lud also alle meine Freunde und Kolleg:innen ein und meine Gastgeberin zeigte sich schlussendlich durchaus angetan von den freundlichen und wohlerzogenen Personen, mit denen ich verkehrte. So trennten sich nach zwei Monaten unsere Wege in versöhnlicher Stimmung.

In meinem anschließenden Urlaub bereiste ich das Land per Anhalter. Dies ermöglichte mir intensive Begegnungen mit mutigen Japanerinnen und Japaner, die sich trauten, eine mit einem Pappschild am Straßenrand stehende Ausländerin mitzunehmen, von der sie nicht wissen konnten, dass sie fließend Japanisch sprach. Eine Gruppe von Studierenden lud mich gleich über Nacht in ein Zimmer in ihr Wohnheim ein und testete meine Trinkfestigkeit anhand aller im örtlichen Supermarkt (*konbini*) verfügbaren Biersorten. Eine Seniorengruppe nahm mich mit zum Sightseeing in einem Landschaftspark bei Aizu Wakamatsu. Dennoch verbrachte ich teils lange Minuten und manchmal auch Stunden mit dem Warten an der Straße.

Viel einfacher wurde das Reisen, als ich die Strecke Tokyo – Okazaki auf dem Weg zu meiner Gastfamilie mit meinem Gastbruder gemeinsam per Anhalter bewältigte. Wir mussten nie länger als fünf Minuten warten, bevor uns jemand mitnahm und auf der Weiterfahrt neugierig über unsere Reise befragte. Mein Gastbruder war sehr erstaunt, wie schnell man die Strecke auch ohne Shinkansen bewältigen konnte.

III. Rechtsvergleichung

Das weitere Studium verbrachte ich in Salamanca und Würzburg und auch das Referendariat führte mich nicht zurück nach Japan, sondern nach New York und Speyer. Jedoch verlor ich nie ganz den Kontakt, sondern mühte mich mal mehr, mal weniger erfolgreich mit dem jährlichen Weihnachtsbrief an meine Gastfamilie, der stets ein Update über die aktuellen Entwicklungen in meinem Leben enthielt. Ehrensache, dass ich den Brief stets auf Japanisch verfasste und mich auch die technischen Arbeitserleichterungen wie Schreib- und Übersetzungsprogramme nicht davon abhielten, den Brief handschriftlich zu erstellen. Allerdings wurde mein Vokabular über die Jahre immer beschränkter und selbst die einfachsten Kanji kamen bei mir nicht mehr ohne Nachschlagen aufs Papier.

So war ich erfreut über eine am Max-Planck-Institut für ausländisches öffentliches Recht und Völkerrecht angesiedelte Promotionsstelle, die mir eine rechtsvergleichende Arbeit ermöglichte. Die fünfköpfige Forschungsgruppe der Max-Planck-Gesellschaft forschte unter der Leitung von Dr. Silja Vöneky zum Thema „Demokratische Legitimation ethischer Entscheidungen im Recht" und neben Arbeiten zum deutschen, Europa- und Völkerrecht sollte es eine rechtsvergleichende Publikation aus der Gruppe geben. Ich entschied mich für einen Vergleich von Japan und Großbritannien, die beide sehr unterschiedliche und aus deutscher Perspektive lehrreiche Ansätze bei der Rechtsetzung in ethisch umstrittenen Themengebieten verfolgen.[3]

Auch wenn ich in Heidelberg exzellente Forschungsbedingungen vorfand, war die Quellenlage zu meinen Forschungsfragen eher dünn, zumal was Japan anbelangt. Denn dieses Land führte am Heidelberger Institut als Forschungsgebiet zumindest damals eher ein Nischendasein (am Hamburger Max-Planck-Institut für ausländisches und internationales Privatrecht sieht das natürlich ganz anders aus, aber ich war ja im öffentlichen Recht unterwegs). Ein Forschungsaufenthalt musste also her. Auf einer Tagung zur Rechtsphilosophie in Würzburg kam ich mit einem der

---

3 Die Ergebnisse sind nachzulesen in folgenden Publikationen: *Hagedorn*, Bioethik und Recht in Japan – Die demokratische Legitimität der Rechtsetzung im Bereich der Biomedizin, in: ZJapanR, Bd. 13 Nr. 25 (2008), S. 27–62; *Hagedorn*, Dissensbewältigung durch Expertenkonsens?, in: Vöneky/Hagedorn/Clados/von Achenbach (Hrsg.), Legitimation ethischer Entscheidungen im Recht – Interdisziplinäre Untersuchungen (2009), S. 234–253; *Hagedorn*, Legitime Strategien der Dissensbewältigung in demokratischen Staaten – Ein Vergleich von Rechtsetzungsverfahren im Bereich der Biomedizin in Japan und Großbritannien (2013).

dort anwesenden japanischen Wissenschaftler ins Gespräch. Es stellte sich heraus, dass Professor Takahiro Hattori von der Kyoto Universität kam und es mir tatsächlich ermöglichte, als Gastwissenschaftlerin dorthin zu reisen. Über die Max-Planck-Gesellschaft ließ sich auch finanziell und organisatorisch alles regeln, so dass ich im Frühling 2007 (endlich!) wieder die Koffer packte für einen zweimonatigen Aufenthalt in Kyoto. Vorher absolvierte ich allerdings noch einen zweiwöchigen Intensivsprachkurs an der Universität München, um mein etwas eingerostetes „Oberschüler-Japanisch" (*kōkōsei no kotoba*) aufzumöbeln und mich insbesondere in Sachen Höflichkeitssprache (*keigo*) nicht völlig zu blamieren.

Der Plan war folgender: Da ich aufgrund begrenzter Kanji-Kenntnisse nicht in der Lage war, ganze Monographien zu evaluieren, wollte ich meine Forschungsfragen durch Experteninterviews klären und die durch Quellenstudium in Deutschland gewonnenen Erkenntnisse einem Realitätscheck unterziehen. Dabei war mir Professor Hattori von unermesslicher Hilfe: er schaffte es, mir durch zahlreiche wohlformulierte Email-Anfragen insgesamt zehn Interviewpartner zu organisieren. Für die Treffen war ich viel unterwegs, nach Tokyo, Kobe, Osaka. Neben Professoren der Universitäten Kyoto, Tokyo, Sophia, Waseda und Osaka Präfektur sprach ich mit einem Wissenschaftler des Riken Center for Developmental Biology und einem Mitarbeiter des Wissenschaftsministeriums. Und natürlich verbrachte ich auch lange (und einsame) Stunden in meinem komplett leeren Mitarbeiterbüro mit der Lektüre ausgewählter Texte und Publikationen meiner Interviewpartner. Ich wohnte im „Haus der Begegnung"[4] in fußläufiger Nähe zu meiner Forschungsstätte und hatte dort in internationaler Atmosphäre auch Gelegenheit zum Austausch mit Studierenden und anderen Gastwissenschaftlern. Außerdem begleitete mich teilweise eine Doktorandin von Professor Hattori auf meinen Reisen. Die Bemühungen Professor Hattoris, mir Kontakt zu den (ausnahmslos männlichen) Promotionsstudenten der Rechtsphilosophie zu vermitteln, mündete in einer extrem verkrampften Konversation und der Aufnahme zweier Fotos, wonach es keinen weiteren Austausch mehr gab. Waren sie allesamt so schüchtern oder ich zu angsteinflößend? Irgendjemand erklärte mir, dass Studierende an Traditionsuniversitäten, vor allem aber der Universität Kyoto, im Schnitt deutlich zurückhaltender seien als Studierende und Postgraduierte an „normaleren" Universitäten. Ich nahm diese Information dankbar an als Erklärung für meine Schwierigkeiten, Kontakte zu knüpfen. Vielleicht war das aber auch meiner exotischen Stellung als Gastwissenschaftlerin geschuldet, dass ich zu keiner Gruppe dazu gehörte. Auch in den (wenigen) Vorlesungen, die ich interessehalber besuchte, blieb ich alleine. Umso dankbarer dachte ich nun zurück an das Jahr in Okazaki, wo Einsamkeit ein Fremdwort für mich gewesen war.

IV. Richterhospitation

Wieder sollten sieben Jahre vergehen, bis sich mir erneut berufliche Anknüpfungspunkte nach Japan boten. Meine Entscheidung für den Richterberuf führte dazu, dass ich jahrelang ausschließlich mit dem deutschen Recht befasst war und mein Interesse

4 Informationen zur Unterkunft abrufbar unter: https://hdbkyoto.jp/ (zuletzt abgerufen am 1. Mai 2025).

an weiterem Austausch mit Japan unerfüllt blieb. Immerhin fand im Jahr 2012 eine Tagung der Deutschen Richterakademie zum Japanischen Recht statt, auf der ich endlich von einer Möglichkeit der erneuten Befassung mit Japan und dem japanischen Recht erfuhr: die jährlich stattfindende Hospitation deutscher Richter:innen und Staatsanwält:innen in der japanischen Justiz!

Eine Kooperation des Bundesministeriums der Justiz mit dem japanischen Justizministerium und dem Obersten Gerichtshof von Japan ermöglicht seit 1981 einen deutsch-japanischen Juristenaustausch. Jedes Jahr entsendet das Bundesministerium der Justiz eine Richterin bzw. einen Richter oder eine Staatsanwältin bzw. einen Staatsanwalt aus Deutschland für einen zweimonatigen Studienaufenthalt in die japanische Justiz, während im – etwas ungleichgewichtigen – Gegenzug jeweils zwei bis drei japanische Juristinnen und Juristen für ein Jahr an deutschen Gerichten und Staatsanwaltschaften hospitieren. Das Programm wird vom Bundesjustizministerium finanziert und die Reise wurde von meinem Bundesland als Dienstreise genehmigt.

Im Oktober 2014 ging es los. Im Vorfeld hatte das japanische Justizministerium angefragt, welche Interessengebiete ich hätte, und welche Gerichte außerhalb von Tokyo ich besuchen wollte. Entsprechend war ein detaillierter Plan für mich erstellt worden, der Stationen in Tokyo, Kyoto, Osaka und Morioka beinhaltete. In Tokyo besuchte ich zum Teil mehrere Tage hintereinander den Obersten Gerichtshof, das Obergericht für geistiges Eigentum, Oberlandesgericht, Landgericht, Familiengericht und Amtsgericht. Außerdem unter anderem für jeweils (nur) einen halben Tag Staatsanwaltschaft, Rechtsanwaltskammer, Justizministerium, Juristenausbildungszentrum, Gefängnisse, Jugenduntersuchungsanstalt.

Meist verliefen die Besuche nach dem gleichen Schema: nach einem „Höflichkeitsbesuch" bei dem Gerichtspräsidenten oder Leiter der Institution bekam ich von einem für mich abgestellten Mitarbeiter einige Erläuterungen zu der besuchten Institution anhand von PowerPoint-Präsentationen und anderen Materialien auf Japanisch oder Englisch, manchmal sogar auf Deutsch, wenn es sich um Kolleginnen oder Kollegen handelte, die bereits eine Hospitation in Deutschland verbracht hatten. Es folgte eine Führung durch die Institution. An den Gerichten, wo ich zum Teil mehrere Tage hospitierte, bekam ich Gelegenheit zur Teilnahme an Verhandlungen und zum Aktenstudium. Dies ermöglichte mir spannende Einblicke in den Justizalltag, was vor allem deshalb interessant war, weil ich es unmittelbar mit meinen eigenen beruflichen Erfahrungen in Deutschland vergleichen konnte.[5]

Ich wohnte im Azabu Court Residential Hotel in Hiroo, von wo aus ich sehr gut das Gerichtszentrum Tokyos an der Station Kasumigaseki erreichen konnte. Außerdem konnte ich dort vorübergehend ein größeres Appartement anmieten, als nämlich mein Mann mit unseren beiden damals drei und fünf Jahre alten Kindern für zwei Wochen zu Besuch kam. Auch diese Besonderheit hatte die überaus zuvorkommende

[5] Es würde den Rahmen und die Zielrichtung des vorliegenden Berichts sprengen, meine Beobachtungen im Detail wiederzugeben und mit Fakten zu belegen, weshalb ich mich hier – dem bisherigen Stil dieses Beitrags treu bleibend – auf eine rein subjektive und damit bewusst unwissenschaftliche Schilderung meiner Eindrücke beschränke. Auf Anfrage übersende ich gerne einen (unveröffentlichten) Bericht über das von mir absolvierte Programm.

Mitarbeiterin des Obersten Gerichtshofs (*saikō saibansho*), die das Programm für mich entworfen hatte, bei der Planung berücksichtigt, so dass ich in den Zeiten vor und nach dem Familienbesuch deutlich mehr Termine als meine Vorgänger hatte, jedoch in den zwei Wochen nur einige wenige Veranstaltungen besuchte. Die deutsche Botschaft veranstaltete sogar einen Empfang für mich, zu dem neben zahlreichen Richterkolleg:innen auch alte Bekannte – wie mein ehemaliger Praktikumschef Rechtsanwalt Dr. Neumann – eingeladen wurden.

In den ersten Tagen bekam ich am Obersten Gerichtshof Einführungen in das japanische Gerichtssystem, Zivilprozessrecht, Straf-, Familien-, Patent- und Verwaltungsrecht. So gerüstet, erlebte ich den Arbeitsalltag der größten Zivilkammer des Landgerichts Tokyo (*chihōsaibansho*). Sie ist (bzw. war im Jahr 2014, alle Angaben beziehen sich auf diesen Zeitraum) mit zwei Vorsitzenden und acht Beisitzern besetzt, die gemeinsam in einem Großraumbüro im 12. Stock des riesigen, kastenartigen Gerichtsgebäudes arbeiteten. Zu den Verhandlungsterminen gelangte man mit einem speziellen, dem Gerichtspersonal vorbehaltenen Aufzug. Interessanterweise gibt es in Japan – so wurde mir gesagt – keinen einzigen Gerichtssaal mit Fenstern. Dies soll zum einen die Flucht von Angeklagten, zum anderen aber jegliche Ablenkung der Anwesenden verhindern.

Japanische Richter tragen recht simple Roben, die über den meist schwarzen Anzügen kaum auffallen. Anwälte tragen keine Roben und waren von den Parteien für mich nur zu unterscheiden, wenn sie einen Anstecker im Revers trugen. Die Sitzungen laufen streng formal ab. Der Saaldiener ruft „*kiritsu kudasai*" (immerhin eine höfliche Aufforderung, aufzustehen), bevor die Richter eintreten und alle stehen auf und verbeugen sich (auch die Richter), bevor sie sich hinsetzen. Zudem ist immer auch ein Rechtspfleger anwesend, der das Protokoll führt und Schriftstücke weiterreicht. Die Verhandlungen im Zivilrecht waren überwiegend sehr kurz, es wurden Schriftstücke ausgetauscht, Beweismittel im Original eingesehen und von den Richtern und der Gegenseite geprüft. Der Vorsitzende Richter gab Hinweise, manchmal erwiderten die Rechtsanwälte etwas. Dann wurden in der Regel neue Termine vereinbart, wofür alle ihre Terminkalender zückten und alles eintrugen. Für Vergleichsgespräche wurde in einen gesonderten Raum mit einem runden Tisch gewechselt. Interessant war etwa ein kurzes Vergleichsgespräch in einer Einzelrichtersache, in der es um die Schadensersatzklage einer betrogenen Ehefrau gegen die neue Partnerin ihres Ehemannes ging. Sie wollte Schmerzensgeld in Höhe von 5,5 Mio. Yen. Da die Beklagte wenig Geld hatte, sollte nun ein Vergleich über 1 Mio. Yen zustande kommen. Derartige Klagen sind in Japan nach Aussage des zuständigen Richters recht häufig, da Ehebruch als Grundlage für einen Schadensersatzanspruch durch die Rechtsprechung des Obersten Gerichtshofs anerkannt wird.

Interessant war auch der Besuch des Obergerichts für Geistiges Eigentum. Dieses 2005 gegründete Gericht ist das einzige Fachgericht in Japan. Da die Verfassung die Einrichtung von Fachgerichtszweigen verbietet, gilt das Gericht trotz seines eigenen Präsidenten und der ausschließlichen Zuständigkeit für gewerblichen Rechtsschutz organisatorisch als Abteilung des Oberlandesgerichts.

In der Ermittlungsrichterabteilung des Landgerichts herrschte Hochbetrieb. Die acht Richter der Ermittlungskammer führten in wechselnden Schichten im Zehn-Minuten-Takt 30–60 Anhörungen in Untersuchungshaftfällen pro Tag durch. Bei der Anhörung sind Verteidiger nicht zugelassen. Es kommt nach Angaben der mich betreuenden Richterin nur in 4–5 % der Fälle vor, dass die beantragte Untersuchungshaft nicht angeordnet wird.

Am Familiengericht Tokyo (*katei saibansho*) gibt es 40 Richter:innen und ca. 120 Untersuchungsbeamte (*chōsakan*), die die Richter bei ihrer Arbeit unterstützen und Familienanhörungen, -besuche etc. durchführen. Das Gericht ist zuständig für Nachlass-, Familien-, Jugend- und Betreuungssachen. Es gibt im Familiengericht 83 Schlichtungsräume, die stets besetzt sind. Das liegt daran, dass die Durchführung einer Schlichtung in streitigen Scheidungsverfahren obligatorisch ist. Die zuständige Richterin war nur bei der Vorbesprechung mit den Schlichtern anwesend, den Rest erledigen in der Regel die Schlichter ohne Richterbeteiligung. Die Amtszeit für Schlichter (*chōtei in*) beträgt zwei Jahre, kann aber verlängert werden. Es gibt sehr viele Bewerber, darunter viele bereits pensionierte ältere Menschen, von denen nur jeder dritte ausgewählt wird. Sie haben den Status von „Beamten auf Zeit", bekommen als Entlohnung Tagegeld und sind zum Teil fast täglich (immer mit anderen „Mitschlichtern") am Gericht tätig. An den Landgerichten gibt es auch beruflich spezialisierte Schlichter, etwa Architekten oder Ingenieure in der Baukammer. Mitglied der Kammer für Steuerstrafrecht war ein Beamter der Steuerbehörde als „Experte". Auch die Rechtspfleger übernehmen in Japan vielfältigere Aufgaben als ihre deutschen Kollegen. So sind als Richter an den Amtsgerichten (*kan'i saibansho*) zum Teil bereits pensionierte Richter und Richterinnen (da die Pensionsgrenze in der Justiz allgemein bei 65 Jahren liegt, an den Amtsgerichten – sowie am Obersten Gerichtshof – jedoch bei 70 Jahren), überwiegend aber erfahrene Rechtspfleger tätig. An den Landgerichten übernehmen die Rechtspfleger viele Tätigkeiten, die in Deutschland Richtern vorbehalten sind, wie die Zulässigkeits- und Schlüssigkeitsprüfung der Neueingänge, die Organisation des Verfahrensablaufs, die Vorbereitung von einfacheren Entscheidungen und Vergleichsvorschlägen, die Gewährung von Akteneinsicht, Fristenkontrollen etc.

Das ist sicher – neben den auf verschiedenen Gründen beruhenden erheblich geringeren Verfahrenszahlen – ein Grund dafür, warum es in Japan bei einer Bevölkerung von 124 Millionen nur rund 4.000 Richter gibt.[6] Die Richterschaft wies 2014 einen Frauenanteil von 25 % auf. Dieser geringe Frauenanteil ist zum Teil sicherlich begründet durch die fehlende Möglichkeit zur Teilzeitbeschäftigung, die sich aus der japanischen Verfassung ableiten soll. Hinzu kommt, dass alle Richter in Japan unabhängig von ihrer Stellung bis zur Pensionierung alle drei Jahre im gesamten Landesgebiet versetzt werden. Dies entspricht dem japanischen Verständnis von richterlicher Unabhängigkeit. Durch die häufigen Versetzungen – bei denen, wie mir versichert wurde, auf familiäre Belange durchaus Rücksicht genommen wird – soll zum

6 Ein Überblick zum Gerichtssystem in Japan findet sich auf der Webseite des Obersten Gerichtshofs, abrufbar unter: https://www.courts.go.jp/english/vc-files/courts-en/file/2020_Courts_in_Japan.pdf. In Deutschland mit einer Bevölkerung von 83 Millionen waren im Jahr 2022 insgesamt rund 22.000 Richter und Richterinnen tätig, vgl. Bundesamt für Justiz, Richterstatistik 2022 (Stand 2. April 2024), abrufbar unter: https://www.bundesjustizamt.de/SharedDocs/Downloads/DE/Justizstatistiken/Richterstatistik_2022.pdf?__blob=publicationFile&v=4 (zuletzt abgerufen am 1. Mai 2025).

einen eine einheitliche Rechtsprechung in ganz Japan gewährleistet, zum anderen verhindert werden, dass die Richter enge Bindungen in die Bevölkerung der jeweiligen Stadt entwickeln und dadurch die Gefahr von Korruption und Befangenheit entsteht. Die richterliche Unabhängigkeit wird also eher im Sinne einer Unabhängigkeit von der Gesellschaft verstanden denn – wie bei uns – als Unabhängigkeit von der Exekutive. Es gibt auch kaum eine Möglichkeit der Spezialisierung, weil es keine unterschiedlichen Fachgerichtsbarkeiten gibt, und die Richter mit der Versetzung regelmäßig auch das Rechtsgebiet, in dem sie tätig sind, wechseln. Dieses System bedingt nach meinen Beobachtungen zwar einen engen Zusammenhalt innerhalb der Richterschaft, aber auch eine erhebliche Distanz zur restlichen Bevölkerung und damit eine Elitenbildung. So hat meine ehemalige Gastfamilie nach meinem Eindruck bis heute keine genaue Vorstellung davon, wie der Berufsalltag eines Richters aussieht, sondern scheint diese Thematik mit einer gewissen Ehrfurcht zu betrachten.

Die mehrtägigen Außenstationen in den von mir gewählten Städten Kyoto und Morioka ermöglichten mir einen Vergleich zu dem in den Tokyoter Gerichten Erlebten. Wenig überraschend machte der Arbeitsalltag der in Kyoto und Morioka tätigen Kollegen einen ruhigeren Eindruck als die Abläufe in den verschiedenen Gerichten Tokyos.

Ein Kollege in Kyoto erläuterte mir die Methodik der Strafzumessung, wofür die japanischen Richter ein Nachschlagewerk (*kensaku seido*) nutzen. Dabei handelt es sich um ein Computerprogramm, das eine Art Diagramm zur Strafzumessung erstellt, wenn man verschiedene Faktoren wie Vorstrafen, Tatumstände oder Nachtatverhalten zu dem jeweiligen Fall in eine Datenbank eingibt – je genauer die Angaben, desto aussagekräftiger das Diagramm. Dieses System wird auch bei der Urteilsberatung mit den Schöffen angewandt. Erklärtes Ziel ist es, eine einheitliche Rechtsprechung in ganz Japan zu gewährleisten. Zum Teil wird auch mit Verteidiger und Staatsanwaltschaft die Anwendung eines bestimmten Diagramms auf den jeweiligen Fall vereinbart, was dann eine Art Deal darstellt.

In den japanischen Gefängnissen gibt es kein Gewaltproblem, sondern das Problem der Zunahme älterer Insassen. So waren 2013 17,4 % der Insassen über 60 und nur 14,9 % 20–29 Jahre alt. Auch der Frauenanteil nimmt zu und lag 2013 bei 9,3 %. 82,2 % der weiblichen, über 60-jährigen Insassen sind wegen Diebstahls zu Freiheitsstrafen verurteilt, bei den unter 60-jährigen liegt dieser Prozentsatz bei 30,8 %, während in dieser Altersgruppe 47,6 % der Frauen wegen Drogenmissbrauchs einsitzen. Ein Grund für diesen Anstieg ist den Angaben japanischer Kollegen zufolge die zunehmende Altersarmut, die manch Senioren dazu verleitet, sich durch kleine Diebstähle für den Winter in einem Gefängnis ein Dach über dem Kopf zu sichern.

Beeindruckend war der Besuch der Jugenduntersuchungsanstalt (*kanbetsusho*) in Kyoto, die ganz idyllisch am Kamogawa (Fluss) gelegen ist. Das Innere war allerdings alles andere als idyllisch. Der Anstaltsleiter erläuterte zunächst anhand einer PowerPoint-Präsentation ausführlich und mit Stolz das System und die Statistik. Pro Jahr kommen ca. 260 verhaltensauffällige Jugendliche aufgrund richterlichen Beschlusses zu Untersuchungszwecken in diese Anstalt und bleiben zwei bis acht Wochen dort, wobei es sich um eine familiengerichtliche Maßnahme und nicht etwa um die Verbüßung einer Strafe handelt. Die Führung durch die Anlage war sehr eindrucksvoll, wobei keine Rücksicht auf die Privatsphäre der Insassen genommen wurde. Mir wurde nahezu jeder Raum gezeigt: das Aufnahmezimmer, wo sich die Jugendlichen entkleiden müssen, untersucht werden und sodann Anstaltskleidung bekommen, die Gesprächs- und Untersuchungszimmer (ein Arzt war gerade dabei, einen Jugendlichen zu untersuchen), die engen Gesprächszimmer, in denen Familienangehörige ihr Kind pro Tag 30 Minuten lang sprechen können, die Sporthalle und schließlich die kleinen Einzel- und Gruppenzellen, jeweils mit Fernseher (nur ausgewählte Programme), Toilette und vergittertem Fenster zum Flur hin – so haben die Mitarbeiter jeden Jugendlichen stets im Blick. Zum Teil waren die Jugendlichen in ihren Zellen, was uns nicht hinderte, diese anzusehen. In den gemeinschaftlichen Waschräumen wird zweimal pro Woche gebadet oder geduscht. Sämtliche Mahlzeiten werden allein in den Zellen eingenommen. Am Wochenende, wenn die Mehrheit der Mitarbeiter frei hat, ist 48 Stunden Volleinschluss.

In Morioka erlebte ich die Verhandlung einer Schadensersatzklage wegen der Tsunami-Katastrophe, mit der Angehörige zweier durch den Tsunami getöteter Frauen Schadensersatz von der Stadt begehrten, da deren Notunterkünfte keinen Schutz geboten hatten. Am Wochenende unternahm ich mit zwei japanischen Kollegen eine Tour in das von der Flutkatastrophe betroffene Küstengebiet. Drei Jahre nach der Katastrophe waren in der Stadt Kamai-shi schon viele Gebäude wieder aufgebaut, erst bei näherem Hinsehen merkte man, dass sie alle neu sind. Überall waren riesige Baustellen und es herrschte großer Baulärm. Im Anschluss ging es weiter die Küste hinauf gen Norden, über Yamada nach Miyako. Die wunderschöne Küste war früher ein beliebtes Feriengebiet, jetzt waren die Städte dort größtenteils dem Erdboden gleich gemacht. Der Aufbau kam vor allem in Yamada nur langsam voran, man sah dort nichts mehr von der früher vorhandenen Stadt. Vom zentral gelegenen ehemaligen Bahnhof war nichts als ein paar verbogene Schienen übrig geblieben.

Ich denke, in diesen zwei Monaten habe ich einen sehr breiten Überblick über nahezu die gesamte japanische Justiz gewonnen. Tiefere Einblicke blieben mir jedoch wegen des straffen Zeitplans weitgehend verwehrt. Dabei habe ich die Stationen, an denen ich nicht nur einen oder gar einen halben, sondern zwei Tage verbringen konnte, als besonders gewinnbringend erlebt. Ich hätte mich über einen konkreten Forschungsauftrag seitens der entsendenden Behörde gefreut (wonach ich von den japanischen Kollegen auch häufig gefragt wurde). Denn ich halte die Rechtsvergleichung in beide Richtungen für sinnvoll, gerade in Bezug auf aktuelle, im Bundesjustizministerium laufende Reformvorhaben. Diese Erkenntnismöglichkeit wird von Seiten Japans auch im Rahmen des Hospitationsprogramms seit langem genutzt. So wurden vor Einführung des Schöffensystems im Jahr 2009 eine Vielzahl japanischer Richter an amerikanische und deutsche Gerichte entsandt, um die jeweilige Praxis der Laienbeteiligung im Strafprozess zu erforschen. Ihre Erkenntnisse sind in das erfolgreich eingeführte japanische Schöffensystem eingeflossen. Ich denke, auch Deutschland könnte davon profitieren, das Hospitationsprogramm weniger als diplomatischen Selbstzweck zu führen, sondern mit dem Ziel, durch Rechtsvergleichung Anregungen im Bereich der Rechtsfortbildung zu gewinnen.

V. Und seither…

Leider war die Richterhospitation – über die ich in der Folge im Kollegenumfeld noch mehrere Vorträge halten durfte – mein bislang letzter beruflicher Berührungspunkt mit Japan. Ich habe jedoch im Jahr 2024 mit meiner Familie erstmals eine rein private Reise dorthin unternommen, die natürlich Treffen mit sämtlichen Mitgliedern meiner (inzwischen sehr gewachsenen) ehemaligen Gastfamilie beinhaltete. Eine Richterkollegin, die 2005 ein Jahr am Landgericht Lübeck hospitiert hatte, trafen wir in Kyoto. Jedoch blieb der familiäre Austausch trotz des zahlreichen Nachwuchses meiner Gastgeschwister bislang einseitig.

Um das zu ändern, haben wir seit Januar 2025 – und damit exakt 30 Jahre nach meinem Aufenthalt in Okazaki – eine japanische Austauschschülerin aus Otaru, Hokkaido für ein halbes Jahr zu Gast, die unseren Alltag teilt, die Schule meiner Söhne besucht und in Schulchor und Ruderclub mitmacht. Ich bemühe mich, ihr eine ähnlich prägende Erfahrung zu ermöglichen, wie ich sie damals machen durfte. So schließt sich für mich der Kreis.

Literaturverzeichnis

Bundesamt für Justiz: Richterstatistik 2022 (Stand 2. April 2024), abrufbar unter: https://www.bundesjustizamt.de/SharedDocs/Downloads/DE/Justizstatistiken/Richterstatistik_2022.pdf?__blob=publicationFile&v=4 (zuletzt abgerufen am 1. Mai 2025).

Hagedorn, Cornelia: Bioethik und Recht in Japan – Die demokratische Legitimität der Rechtsetzung im Bereich der Biomedizin, in: ZJapanR, Bd. 13 Nr. 25 (2008), S. 27–62.

Hagedorn, Cornelia: Dissensbewältigung durch Expertenkonsens?, in: Vöneky, Silja/Hagedorn, Cornelia/Clados, Miriam/von Achenbach, Jelena (Hrsg.), Legitimation ethischer Entscheidungen im Recht – Interdisziplinäre Untersuchungen (2009), S. 234–253.

Hagedorn, Cornelia: Legitime Strategien der Dissensbewältigung in demokratischen Staaten – Ein Vergleich von Rechtsetzungsverfahren im Bereich der Biomedizin in Japan und Großbritannien (2013).

Supreme Court of Japan: Courts in Japan, abrufbar unter: https://www.courts.go.jp/english/vc-files/courts-en/file/2020_Courts_in_Japan.pdf (zuletzt abgerufen am 1. Mai 2025).

Zur Fortbildungspflicht der Richterinnen und Richter in Deutschland und Japan[1]

Von *Rüdiger Henning*

Rüdiger Henning, Inhaber der Kanzlei Henning & Kollegen, hat Japan erstmals 1975 mit einer Judomannschaft bereist und dort seine Ehefrau kennengelernt. 1982 hat er seine Referendar-Wahlstation in Tokio absolviert. Während dieses Aufenthalts hat er den Jubilar kennengelernt, mit dem ihn seitdem eine enge Freundschaft verbindet. 2003 ist der Jubilar Mitglied der Kanzlei Henning & Kollegen geworden. Herr Henning war 23 Jahre Rechtsberater der Japanischen Internationalen Schule in Düsseldorf, 9 Jahre Vorsitzender des Rechtsausschusses des Deutschen Dan-Kollegiums e. V. und 14 Jahre gemeinsam mit dem Jubilar Vorstandsmitglied der Deutsch-Japanischen Gesellschaft für Arbeitsrecht e. V. Der Autor wünscht dem Jubilar noch viele Jahre der Schaffens- und Beitragskraft im Deutsch-Japanischen Rechtsbereich.

I. Ausbildung für die Befähigung zum Richteramt

1. Ausbildung in Deutschland

Wer sich in Deutschland für den Richterdienst bewirbt, bedarf der Befähigung zum Richteramt. Er muss ein Jurastudium an einer deutschen Hochschule absolviert haben, das je nach Befähigung dreieinhalb bis fünf Jahre dauert. An die universitäre Ausbildung schließt sich die Referendarzeit von 2 Jahren an, die im Rahmen eines Rotationsprinzips derzeit mit vier Pflichtstationen und einer Wahlstation ein erstes Tätigwerden in unterschiedlichen Bereichen juristischer Tätigkeiten bei Gerichten, Staatsanwaltschaften, Verwaltungen, Rechtsanwälten etc. ermöglicht und mit dem zweiten Staatsexamen beendet wird.

Nur diejenigen, die diese Ausbildungsabschnitte mit besonderer Qualifikation abgeschlossen haben, können in den Richterdienst berufen werden. Derzeit variieren die Einstellungsvoraussetzungen hinsichtlich der Ergebnisse der Examina von Bundesland zu Bundesland. Während in Nordrhein-Westfalen von Bewerberinnen und Bewerbern unter Verweis auf die Bestenauslese gemäß Art. 33 Abs. 2 GG ein Prädikat im zweiten Staatsexamen und bei weniger als 9 Punkten, mindestens aber 7,76 Punkten, besondere persönliche Eigenschaften erwartet werden, liegen die Anforderungen beispielsweise in Bayern bei 8 Punkten im zweiten bayerischen Staats-

[1] Für die Informationen dieses Beitrags zum japanischen Recht danke ich sehr herzlich Herrn *Professor Masahiko Tashiro* von der Universität Aichi, der nach Ablegung des Staatsexamens 1986 und Absolvierung der Referendarzeit 1988 von 1990 bis 2024 Richter und zuletzt Vorsitzender Richter am Landgericht Chiba, Außenstelle Matsudo war.

Duncker & Humblot · Berlin | https://doi.org/10.3790/978-3-428-59611-9.2025.423783

examen und in Sachsen bei mindestens sieben Punkten im zweiten Staatsexamen und mindestens 14 Punkten in beiden Examina zusammen.[2]

Ob diese Anforderungen in Zukunft aufrechterhalten bleiben können, scheint angesichts des demographischen Wandels, der auch vor den Gerichten nicht Halt macht, zweifelhaft. So werden bis zum Jahre 2030 in Sachsen nahezu 50 % der aktuell tätigen Richter pensioniert werden.[3] In Brandenburg werden es ca. 25 % sein.[4]

Da nicht ersichtlich ist, wie der hohe Bedarf an jungen Richterinnen und Richtern bei Aufrechterhaltung der aktuellen Qualifikationsanforderungen gedeckt werden soll, dürfte es zwangsläufig zu einer Absenkung der Einstellungsvoraussetzungen und damit möglicherweise zu einer Absenkung des Ausbildungsniveaus junger Richterinnen und Richter kommen.

2. Ausbildung in Japan

In Japan, das kein einheitliches Ausbildungssystem der Rechtsberufe kennt, erfolgt die Einstellung in den Richterdienst zunächst als Assistenzrichter. Die Einstellung setzt gemäß § 43 Japanisches Gerichtsgesetz voraus, dass der Bewerber das zweite Staatsexamen absolviert hat, ohne dass es klare Kriterien für die Anforderungen an die Prüfungsergebnisse und die weiteren Voraussetzungen einer Einstellung gibt. Denn neben den Prüfungsergebnissen der zweiten Staatsprüfung, die nicht allein entscheidend für die Einstellung sind, sind die persönliche Eignung und allgemeine Eigenschaften und Fähigkeiten, die bereits während der Referendarzeit beurteilt werden, von besonderer Bedeutung. Hierzu gehören eine umfassende Ausbildung und Allgemeinbildung, Menschenkenntnis, Integrität, Fairness, Ausdauer und Selbstbeherrschung.

Das zweite Staatsexamen, das nur derjenige absolvieren kann, der das im Jahre 2006 eingeführte erste Staatsexamen und die Referendarzeit absolviert hat, stellt allerdings so hohe Anforderungen an die Absolventinnen und Absolventen, dass nur eine äußerst geringe, lange Zeit im unteren zweistelligen Bereich liegende Prozentzahl der Prüfungskandidatinnen und -kandidaten das zweite Staatsexamen besteht.

Voraussetzung für die Ernennung zur Richterin bzw. zum Richter ist gemäß § 42 Abs. 1 JGG, dass die Bewerberin bzw. der Bewerber mindestens zehn Jahre lang als Assistenzrichter, Richter am Amtsgericht, Staatsanwalt, Rechtsanwalt oder Professor bzw. Assistenzprofessor an der juristischen Fakultät einer Universität gearbeitet hat.

---

2 https://www.justiz-karriere.nrw./berufe/staatsanwaltschaften-und-gerichte/richter, https://www.justiz.bayern.de/berufe-und-stellen/richter-und-staatsanwaelte, https://www.justiz.sachsen.de/content/1032htm.

3 dpa Meldung vom 03. April 2023 (Autorin *Kross*), Sächsischer Richterverein befürchtet Mangel an Juristen (vgl. https://www.sachsen-fernsehen.de/saechsischer-richterverein-befuerchtet-mangel-an-juristen-1295322/).

4 Legal Tribune Online vom 03. April 2023, Richtervereinigungen warnen vor Personalmangel im Osten (vgl. https://www.lto.de/recht/justiz/j/justiz-personal-engpass-pensionierungswelle-ostdeutschland-brandenburg-sachsen-richter-staatsanwaelte-referendariat-jobs-karriere).

Richter an Amtsgerichten brauchen anders als Assistenzrichter keine Volljuristen zu sein.

Auch in Japan zeichnet sich ab, dass der demographische Wandel die Gerichte erfasst. Die japanische Wirtschaftszeitung Nihon Keizai Shimbun hat am 13. April 2025 in einem Artikel über das „Geheimnis des Richtermangels“ davon berichtet, dass die Zahl der Assistenzrichter in den letzten zehn Jahren um 20 % gesunken sei, während die Anwaltschaft und andere Rechtsberufe um ca. 30 % gewachsen seien. Die Nihon Keizai Shimbun macht hierfür den Elitismus bei der Richterauswahl, die Praxis der häufigen Richterversetzungen an weit entfernte Gerichte, den Konkurrenzdruck durch Anwaltskanzleien und insbesondere die Großkanzleien verantwortlich und sieht das Risiko einer „massiven Erschütterung der Grundfesten der Justiz“. Auch in Japan zeichnet sich deshalb eine Absenkung der Examensanforderungen und der Einstellungsvoraussetzungen für junge Richterinnen und Richter ab.

II. Fortbildung zur Ausbildungserhaltung und Fortentwicklung der Kenntnisse und Fähigkeiten

1. Jede Fortbildung fußt bekanntermaßen auf der Qualität der Ausbildung

Die einmal erreichte Stufe der Ausbildung bleibt gerade im juristischen Bereich angesichts der ständigen Veränderung der Gesetzeslage und der Rechtsprechung allerdings nicht fortwährend erhalten. Zudem nimmt das europäische Recht immer größeren Einfluss auf das deutsche Rechtssystem. Mechthild Dyckmanns war eine der ersten, die die Frage nach der Fortbildungspflicht für Richterinnen und Richter aufwarf und darauf hinwies, dass es, soweit es um das Fachwissen der Richterinnen und Richter gehe, nicht ausreiche, sich bei der Einstellung um Juristinnen und Juristen mit guten Examensnoten zu bemühen, zumal der öffentliche Dienst gegenüber der Wirtschaft und insbesondere großen Anwaltskanzleien ohnehin wegen der Beschäftigungsbedingungen ins Hintertreffen gerate.[5] Veränderungen der Gesetze, eine immer komplexer werdende Rechtsprechung und Rechtsentwicklung sowie die Europäisierung und Internationalisierung des Rechtes bedürfe der ständigen Fort- und Weiterbildung von Richterinnen und Richtern, die ihrer Auffassung nach allerdings keiner gesetzlichen Regelung bedürfe, wie diese schon auf der 76. Justizministerkonferenz 2005 beschlossen worden sei und als konkrete Regelung in § 43a DiRG-E vorgesehen worden sei. Denn, wenn auch im Hinblick auf die Notwendigkeit der Fortbildung Einigkeit bestehe, bedürfe es hierzu mehr, als nur einen Satz ins Gesetz zu schreiben. So wie es für den freien Beruf des Rechtsanwalts zur freien Entscheidung gehöre, über die eigene Fortbildung zu befinden, so gelte dies ebenso für den unabhängigen Richter.

Das bayerische Richter- und Staatsanwaltsgesetz formuliert deshalb zu Recht zwischen Ausbildung und Fortbildung differenzierend in Art. 6 ähnlich wie § 3b des Hamburgischen Richtergesetzes, dass „Richter und Richterinnen … sich zur Erhaltung und Fortentwicklung ihrer Kenntnisse und Fähigkeiten fortzubilden haben“.

---

5 *Dyckmanns*, Fortbildungspflicht für Richter, in: DRiZ (2008), S. 149.

III. Fortbildungsmöglichkeiten für Richterinnen und Richter in Deutschland

1. Fortbildung durch „Learning on the Job“

Eine Verpflichtung zur dienstlichen Fortbildung setzt zwingend voraus, dass der Dienstherr diese durch geeignete Maßnahmen fördert, weshalb sich in allen Landesrichter- und Staatsanwältegesetzen, die eine dienstliche Fortbildungspflicht vorsehen, die ausdrücklich normierte Verpflichtung des Dienstherrn findet, die dienstliche Fortbildung durch geeignete Maßnahmen zu fördern und darüber hinaus auch weitere Bereiche, so etwa gemäß Art. 6 Bayerisches Richter- und Staatsanwaltsgesetz die ethischen und sozialen Grundlagen für die berufliche Praxis, einzubeziehen.

Die Förderung kann dabei durch die konkrete Tätigkeit begleitende Maßnahmen erfolgen, die eine Fortbildung bei „Learning on the Job“, d. h. ein Lernen neuer Kompetenzen und Fähigkeiten für eine spezielle Tätigkeit am aktuellen Arbeitsort, ermöglichen. Diese gerade in Japan in allen Berufssparten sehr geschätzte und verbreitete Art der Erhaltung und Fortentwicklung von Kenntnissen und Fähigkeiten wird im Bereich des Richterdienstes in Deutschland etwa dadurch praktiziert, dass junge Proberichterinnen und Proberichter zunächst einer Kammer zugeordnet werden, in der sie unter Anleitung erfahrener Kolleginnen und Kollegen die Einbindung in das System erfahren sowie das Zusammenwirken mit den Mitarbeiterinnen und Mitarbeitern der Geschäftsstellen und den Rechtspflegerinnen und den Rechtspflegern erlernen und mit den digitalen Systemen der Justiz und insbesondere der Abwicklung der Alltagsgeschäfte vertraut gemacht werden, aber auch Unterstützung und Anleitung bei der Entscheidungsfindung erhalten.

Die dienstliche Fortbildung durch „Learning on the Job“ beschränkt sich aber keineswegs auf die jeweilige Entscheidungseinheit. Sie wird im Bereich der ordentlichen Gerichtsbarkeit in Nordrhein-Westfalen in den ersten sechs Monaten durch die Teilnahme an der „Jungrichterstaffel“ in der Justizakademie Recklinghausen ergänzt. Die Teilnahme ist nicht verpflichtend, das Angebot wird faktisch allerdings von jeder Berufseinsteigerin und jedem Berufseinsteiger wahrgenommen.

2. Fortbildung durch institutionelle Einrichtungen

a) Die Deutsche Richterakademie

Die Deutsche Richterakademie ist eine überregionale Einrichtung mit föderalem Charakter. Sie wird von Bund und Ländern gemeinsam getragen. Grundlage für die Arbeit der Deutschen Richterakademie ist die zwischen dem Bund und den Ländern geschlossene „Verwaltungsvereinbarung über die Deutsche Richterakademie“.

Die Deutsche Richterakademie verfügt über zwei Tagungsstätten, und zwar in Trier seit 1973 und in Wustrau seit 1993. Die Fortbildungen der Deutschen Richterakademie stehen allen ca. 22.000 Richterinnen und Richtern der Bundesrepublik Deutschland offen.

Die Deutsche Richterakademie richtet sich mit ihrem Angebot an Richterinnen und Richter aller Zweige der Gerichtsbarkeit und alle Staatsanwältinnen und Staatsanwälte in Deutschland, aber auch an interessierte Berufsträger und Berufsträgerinnen aus dem Ausland, weshalb bei geeigneten Themenstellungen auch eine Ausschreibung im Rahmen des europäischen Fortbildungsnetzwerkes EJTN (European Judical Training Network) stattfindet.

Das jährliche Fortbildungsprogramm der Deutschen Richterakademie wird von der Programmkonferenz gestaltet, der die Aufgabe obliegt, das Fortbildungsprogramm der Deutschen Richterakademie zu entwickeln. Neben dem Direktor der Deutschen Richterakademie gehören der Programmkonferenz die Fortbildungsverantwortlichen des Bundes und der Länder an, bei denen es sich überwiegend um abgeordnete Richterinnen und Richter, Staatsanwältinnen und Staatsanwälte handelt, die für 2–3 Jahre an das entsprechende Justizministerium abgeordnet sind.

Im Kalenderjahr 2025 bietet die Deutsche Richterakademie in insgesamt 10 Themengebieten, die vom Völkerrecht über das Europarecht, das Zivilrecht und Strafrecht sowie die Fachgerichtsrechtsbereiche reichen, Fachtagungen, interdisziplinäre Tagungen, verhaltensorientierte Tagungen und sonstige Tagungen und Fortbildungsveranstaltungen an.

b) Die Europäische Rechtsakademie

Die Europäische Rechtsakademie ist eine öffentliche Stiftung bürgerlichen Rechts mit Sitz in Trier. Zu ihren Stiftern gehören die meisten EU-Mitgliedstaaten, die Bundesländer, die Stadt Trier und andere, die die Europäische Rechtsakademie auch finanziell unterstützen. Sie organisiert Tagungen und Seminare in ganz Europa und vermittelt darüber hinaus Wissen über die vierteljährliche Zeitschrift ERA Forum und bietet seit geraumer Zeit eine Auswahl an E-Learning-Produkten an.

c) Das European Judical Training Network

Das European Judical Training Network (EJTN) ist eine internationale non-profit Vereinigung nach den Bestimmungen belgischen Rechts, die im Jahre 2000 gegründet wurde und die juristische Ausbildungsinstitutionen aller EU-Mitgliedsstaaten zusammenbringen soll, um die Aus- und Fortbildung von Angehörigen der Justiz der EU-Mitgliedstaaten zu implementieren und zu fördern.

Das Bundesministerium der Justiz und für Verbraucherschutz ist für Deutschland Mitglied im European Judical Training Network. Die Bundesregierung hat auf eine Anfrage einzelner Abgeordneter und der Fraktion Bündnis 90/Die GRÜNEN mit der Drucksache 19/16307 vom 03. Januar 2020 mitgeteilt, dass im Jahre 2018 500 Richterinnen und Richter, Staatsanwältinnen und Staatsanwälte aus Deutschland an Veranstaltungen des EJTN teilgenommen haben, die mit erheblichen Mitteln der EU-Kommission gefördert werden.[6]

---

6 *Bundesregierung*, Antwort der Bundesregierung auf die Kleine Anfrage der Abgeordneten Katja Keul, Luise Amtsberg, Canan Bayram, weiterer Abgeordneter und der Fraktion BÜNDNIS 90/DIE GRÜNEN – Qualität der Justiz und bundeseinheitliches Fortbildungsrecht und bundeseinheitliche Fortbildungspflicht für Richterinnen und Richter, Drucksache 19/16307 vom 03. Januar 2020 (2020), S. 4.

d) Landeseigene Fortbildungsinstitutionen

Das Land Nordrhein-Westfalen betreibt bereits seit 1988 die Justizakademie in Recklinghausen, die mit einem umfangreichen Fortbildungsprogramm unter anderem auch Richterinnen und Richtern als überregionale Ausbildungsstätte zur Verfügung steht.

Entsprechende Einrichtungen gibt es beispielsweise in Hessen sowie in den nördlichen Bundesländern im sogenannten Nordverbund.

3. Fortbildung im Rahmen nicht institutioneller Fortbildungsmöglichkeiten

Neben den zuvor genannten institutionellen Fortbildungsmöglichkeiten gibt es auch nicht institutionelle Fortbildungsangebote der Landesministerien und der Obergerichte. Nach Nöhre und Meller-Hannich soll das Angebot schon weitgehend auf den Einsatz in bestimmten Rechtsgebieten abgestimmt sein und deutlich über das Programm der Richterakademie hinausgehen.[7]

IV. Fortbildungsmöglichkeiten für Richterinnen und Richter in Japan

In Japan bietet das Institut für juristische Ausbildung und Forschung (*Shihō kenshūjo*) Richterfortbildungen an. Diese sind teils obligatorisch, teils freiwillig.

Im ersten und dritten Jahr nach der Ernennung zur Assistenzrichterin bzw. zum Assistenzrichter und im ersten Jahr nach der Ernennung zur Richterin bzw. zum Richter finden jeweils Gruppenschulungen statt, in der die Teilnehmerinnen und Teilnehmer in die Organisation und die Verwaltung der Gerichte eingeführt werden sowie die Fallbearbeitung erlernen. Die Schulungen sind obligatorisch und gehören zur Dienstpflicht.

Wenn die Teilnehmerinnen und Teilnehmer im weiteren Verlauf ihrer Karriere zu Leitenden Richterinnen bzw. Leitenden Richtern an Landgerichten oder Vorsitzenden Richterinnen bzw. Vorsitzenden Richtern ernannt werden, finden erneut Schulungen gleicher Art statt. Auch diese Schulungen sind obligatorisch und gehören deshalb zu Dienstpflicht.

Darüber hinaus werden mehrmals im Jahr Fortbildungsveranstaltungen zu speziellen Themen angeboten. Die Teilnahme an diesen Veranstaltungen ist freiwillig.

Die Dozentinnen und Dozenten am Institut für juristische Ausbildung und Forschung sind Richterinnen und Richter der Abteilung für Richterausbildung. Professorinnen und Professoren, Rechtsanwältinnen und Rechtsanwälte sowie Staatsanwältinnen und Staatsanwälte werden je nach Thema als externe Dozentinnen und Dozenten hinzugezogen.

---

7 *Nöhre/Meller-Hannich*, Anwaltsspezialist trifft Richtergeneralist – Plädoyer für mehr Spezialisierung auf der Richterbank, in: NJW (2023), S. 2701, 2705.

V. Fortbildungspflicht für Richterinnen und Richter in Deutschland

1. Gesetzeslage und Gesetzgebungskompetenz

Im Gegensatz zu der in § 43 Abs. 6 BRAO und der in § 15 Fachanwaltsordnung festgelegten Fortbildungspflicht für Rechts- und Fachanwältinnen und Rechts- und Fachanwälte ist eine Pflicht für Richterinnen und Richter, sich fortzubilden, gesetzlich weitgehend nicht normiert.

Die Bundesregierung hat in ihrer Antwort vom 03. Januar 2020 auf eine kleine Anfrage einzelner Abgeordneter und der Fraktion Bündnis 90/Die GRÜNEN mitgeteilt, dass für Richterinnen und Richter in Bund und Ländern nach allgemeinem Verständnis in der Ausgestaltung des Richterdienstverhältnisses eine immanente Fortbildungspflicht bestehe.[8]

Nach geltendem Recht sei diese Fortbildungspflicht im Deutschen Richtergesetz (DRiG) und in den überwiegenden Richtergesetzen der Länder nicht ausdrücklich geregelt. So verweise das Deutsche Richtergesetz für Richterinnen und Richter des Bundes auf die einschlägigen Laufbahnvorschriften für Beamte, vgl. für Richterinnen und Richter des Bundes § 46 DRiG in Verbindung mit § 61 Abs. 2 des Bundesbeamtengesetzes.

Die Bundesregierung verweist in ihrer Antwort vom 03. Januar 2020 zudem darauf, dass, wenn einzelne Landesrichtergesetze etwa in Baden-Württemberg (§ 8a LRiStAG), Bayern (Art. 6 BayRiStaG), Nordrhein-Westfalen (§ 13 LRiStaG), Thüringen (§ 9 RiStaG) und Sachsen-Anhalt (§ 7 LRiG) die Fortbildungspflicht in einer eigenständigen Regelung normieren, die Fortbildungspflicht dadurch nur stärker sichtbar gemacht werde. In allen Fällen sei sie als eine allgemeine Pflicht zur dienstlichen Bildung formuliert, die durch eine an den Dienstherrn gerichtete allgemeine Pflicht, die Fortbildung durch geeignete Maßnahmen zu fördern, ergänzt werde.

Der Bund besitze seit der Föderalismusreform von 2006 auf dem Gebiet der Statusrechte und -pflichten der Richterinnen und Richter in den Ländern mit Ausnahme der Laufbahnen, Besoldung und Versorgung keine Gesetzgebungszuständigkeit. Er besitze daher keine Gesetzgebungskompetenz, Fragen der Fortbildung für die Richterinnen und Richter im Landesdienst zu regeln. Denn die Fortbildungspflicht sei keine Statuspflicht, weil sie den aktuellen Status nicht präge. Die Fortbildungspflicht könne sich mittelbar auf einen zukünftigen, jedoch ungewissen höheren Status insoweit auswirken, als sie mit Blick auf den Grundsatz der Bestenauslese gemäß Art. 33 Abs. 2 des Grundgesetzes geeignet sei, Eignung, Befähigung und fachliche Leistung nach Abschluss der Fortbildung positiv zu beeinflussen.

Auffallend ist, dass die jeweiligen Landesgesetze eine Fortbildungspflicht erst in der letzten Dekade aufgenommen haben. Aus diesem Umstand lässt sich nun allerdings nicht ableiten, dass zuvor die allgemeine Auffassung bestanden habe, dass Richterinnen und Richter nicht zur dienstlichen Fortbildung verpflichtet seien. So hat der Sachverständige Joachim Lüblinghoff anlässlich einer öffentlichen Sachverständigen-Anhörung des Ausschusses für Recht und Verbraucherschutz am 25. Sep-

---

8 *Bundesregierung*, Deutscher Bundestag, Drucksache 19/16307 vom 03.01.2020, S. 2.

tember 2019 zur Verbesserung der Qualität familienrechtlicher Verfahren die These vertreten, dass es eindeutig eine Fortbildungspflicht für Richterinnen und Richter gebe und diese nicht gesetzlich geregelt werden müsse. Denn diese Pflicht lasse sich den richterlichen Eidesnormen entnehmen. Klarer als in der Formel, wonach ein Richter sein Amt nach bestem Wissen und Gewissen ausüben werde, könne eine Fortbildungspflicht kaum normiert werden.

2. Normierungsbedarf und -kritik

Die Frage, ob es erforderlich ist, aufgrund zunehmender Globalisierung und immer komplizierterer Normen und Gerichtsverfahren eine Fortbildungspflicht für Richterinnen und Richter gesetzlich zu regeln, ist seit langem kontrovers diskutiert worden.

Die Diskussion über die Frage der Notwendigkeit einer gesetzlichen Regelung richterlicher Fortbildungspflichten betraf und betrifft im Kern vor allem die Frage, ob hierdurch nicht die richterliche Unabhängigkeit und die Berufsfreiheit in unzulässiger Weise eingeschränkt werden.

Recht früh konnte Einigkeit erzielt werden, dass es richterliche Tätigkeiten gibt, die ganz essenziell ein Wissen benötigen, das deutlich über die Gesetzeskenntnis und -anwendung hinausgeht und beispielsweise ökonomisches oder technisches Wissen verlangt.

Die Antworten auf diese Erkenntnis waren unterschiedlich und reichten von der Einrichtung von Spezialkammern etwa in Bausachen bis zur Normierung von Fortbildungspflichten für die speziellen richterlichen Tätigkeiten der Insolvenz- und Restrukturierungsrichterinnen und -richter.

Später gaben aufsehenerregende Prozesse im Zusammenhang mit dem sexuellen Missbrauch von Kindern den Anstoß für die Schaffung von Fortbildungspflichten von Familienrichterinnen und -richtern sowie Strafrichterinnen und -strafrichtern.

3. Fortbildungspflichten spezieller Richtergruppen

Schon seit geraumer Zeit gibt es deshalb spezielle Fortbildungspflichten für die vorgenannten Richtergruppen, die wie folgt normiert wurden:

a) Fortbildungspflicht für Insolvenz- und Restrukturierungsrichterinnen und -richter

§ 22 Abs. 6 S. 2 GVG normiert seit dem 01. Januar 2013 für Insolvenzrichterinnen und -richter sowie Restrukturierungsrichterinnen und -richter besondere Qualifikationsvoraussetzungen.

Die Bestimmung lautet:

> „Ein Richter auf Probe darf im ersten Jahr nach seiner Ernennung Geschäfte in Insolvenz- und Restrukturierungssachen nicht wahrnehmen. Richter in Insolvenz- und Restrukturierungssachen sollen, soweit dies zur Erfüllung der jeweiligen Richtergeschäftsaufgabe erforderlich ist, über belegbare Kenntnisse auf den Gebieten des Insolvenzrechts, des Restrukturierungsrechts, des Handels- und Gesellschaftsrechts sowie über Grundkenntnisse der für

das Insolvenz- und Restrukturierungsverfahren notwendigen Teile des Arbeits-, Sozial- und Steuerrechts und des Rechnungswesens verfügen. Einem Richter, dessen Kenntnisse auf diesen Gebieten nicht belegt sind, dürfen die Aufgaben eines Insolvenz- oder Restrukturierungsrichters nur zugewiesen werden, wenn der Erwerb der Kenntnisse alsbald zu erwarten ist."

b) Fortbildungspflicht für Familienrichterinnen und -richter

Die Fortbildungspflicht für Familienrichter ist durch das Gesetz zur Bekämpfung sexualisierter Gewalt gegen Kinder vom 16. Juni 2021 im Wege einer Änderung des § 23b Abs. 3 GVG mit Wirkung ab dem 01. Januar 2022 präzisiert worden, indem dieser Bestimmung folgende Sätze angefügt worden sind:

„Richter in Familiensachen sollen über belegbare Kenntnisse auf den Gebieten des Familienrechts, insbesondere des Kindschaftsrechts, des Familienverfahrensrechts und der für das Verfahren in Familiensachen notwendigen Teile des Kinder- und Jugendhilferechts sowie über belegbare Grundkenntnisse der Psychologie, insbesondere der Entwicklungspsychologie des Kindes, und der Kommunikation mit Kindern verfügen. Einem Richter, dessen Kenntnisse auf diesen Gebieten nicht belegt sind, dürfen die Aufgaben eines Familienrichters nur zugewiesen werden, wenn der Erwerb der Kenntnisse alsbald zu erwarten ist. Von den Anforderungen nach den Sätzen 3 und 4 kann bei Richtern, die nur im Rahmen eines Bereitschaftsdiensts mit der Wahrnehmung familienrechtlicher Aufgaben befasst sind, abgewichen werden, wenn anderenfalls ein ordnungsgemäßer und den betroffenen Richtern zumutbarer Betrieb des Bereitschaftsdienstes nicht gewährleistet wäre".

Die Deutsche Richterakademie bietet hierzu in jedem Jahr jeweils mehrtägige Veranstaltungen an, die sich etwa mit den Qualitätsstandards inhaltlicher und formaler Kriterien für rechtspsychologische Gutachten und Vorgehensweisen im Familienrecht, mit der Einführung in die Testpsychologie, psychologischen Grundkenntnissen, den Grundkenntnissen über kindliche Entwicklungsstufen und entsprechende Implikationen für Kindesanhörungen und aktuellen Entwicklungen im internationalen Kindschaftsrecht befassen oder psychologische Kompetenzen für eine entwicklungsgerechte, vollständige und suggestionsfreie Kindesanhörung vermitteln.

c) Fortbildungspflicht für Strafrichterinnen und -richter in Jugendstrafsachen

Die Fortbildungspflicht für Strafrichter ist ebenfalls durch das Gesetz zur Bekämpfung sexualisierter Gewalt gegen Kinder vom 16. Juni 2021 durch eine Neuregelung des § 37 JGG entsprechend der Fortbildungspflicht der Familienrichter normiert worden. Nach § 37 JGG n.F. gilt:

„(1) Die Richter bei den Jugendgerichten und die Jugendstaatsanwälte sollen erzieherisch befähigt und in der Jugenderziehung erfahren sein. Sie sollen über Kenntnisse auf den Gebieten der Kriminologie, Pädagogik und Sozialpädagogik sowie der Jugendpsychologie verfügen. Einem Richter oder Staatsanwalt, dessen Kenntnisse auf diesem Gebiet nicht belegt sind, sollen die Aufgaben eines Jugendrichters oder Jugendstaatsanwalts erstmals nur zugewiesen werden, wenn der Erwerb der Kenntnisse durch die Wahrnehmung von einschlägigen Fortbildungsangeboten oder eine anderweitige einschlägige Weiterqualifizierung alsbald zu erwarten ist.

(2) Von den Anforderungen des Abs. 1 kann bei Richtern und Staatsanwälten, die nur im Bereitschaftsdienst zur Wahrnehmung jugendgerichtlicher oder jugendstaatsanwaltschaftlicher Aufgaben eingesetzt werden, abgewichen werden, wenn anderenfalls ein ordnungsge-

mäßer und den betroffenen Richtern und Staatsanwälten zumutbarer Betrieb des Bereitschaftsdienstes nicht gewährleistet wäre."

4. Fortbildungspflicht versus richterliche Unabhängigkeit

Während für die Vereinigung von Fachwissen und Berufserfahrung in Spezialkammern und die Schaffung einer Fortbildungspflicht für die vorgenannten Richtergruppen Mehrheiten für eine gesetzliche Normierung gefunden werden konnten, begegnet die Normierung einer allgemeinen Fortbildungspflicht für alle Richterinnen und Richter im Deutschen Richtergesetz und den Richtergesetzen der Länder nach wie vor Bedenken.

Die Diskussion über die Frage der Notwendigkeit einer gesetzlichen Regelung richterlicher Fortbildungspflicht betrifft im Kern vor allem die Frage, ob hierdurch nicht die richterliche Unabhängigkeit in unzulässiger Weise eingeschränkt wird.

Das Grundgesetz formuliert in Art. 97 GG die richterliche Unabhängigkeit wie folgt:

„(1) Die Richter sind unabhängig und nur dem Gesetz unterworfen.

(2) Die hauptamtlich und planmäßig endgültig angestellten Richter können wider ihren Willen nur kraft richterlicher Entscheidung und nur aus Gründen und unter den Formen, welche die Gesetze bestimmen, vor Ablauf ihrer Amtszeit entlassen oder dauernd oder zeitweise ihres Amtes enthoben oder an eine andere Stelle oder in den Ruhestand versetzt werden. Die Gesetzgebung kann Altersgrenzen festsetzen, bei deren Erreichung auf Lebenszeit angestellte Richter in den Ruhestand treten. Bei Veränderung der Einrichtung der Gerichte oder ihrer Bezirke können Richter an ein anderes Gericht versetzt oder aus dem Amt entfernt werden, jedoch nur unter Belassung des vollen Gehaltes."

Schutzbereich und Kern des Art. 97 Abs. 1 GG ist der Schutz der Richterinnen und der Richter vor Weisungen, die in ihre sachliche und persönliche Unabhängigkeit eingreifen. Kein Dienstbefehl kann und soll dem Richter vorschreiben, wie er zu urteilen hat. Der Entscheidungsprozess und die Entscheidungsfindung selbst müssen deshalb von Einwirkungen anderer frei bleiben und allein der richterlichen Abwicklung und Entscheidungshoheit unterliegen.

Deshalb dürfen weder Bundes- noch Landesregierungen noch die Verwaltungen den Richterinnen und Richtern in Form von Verwaltungsvorschriften Leitlinien für deren rechtsprechende Tätigkeit geben. Gerade die jüngsten politischen Entwicklungen im Hinblick auf die Besetzung von Richterstellen machen deutlich, welche Bedeutung die Unabhängigkeit der Justiz und der Richter in der heutigen Zeit wieder gewinnt.

Die gesetzliche Normierung allgemeiner oder besonderer Fortbildungspflichten für Richterinnen und Richter auf Bundes- oder Landesebene greift nicht per se in den Schutzbereich der grundgesetzlich geschützten sachlichen und persönlichen Unabhängigkeit der Richterinnen und Richter ein.

Sie greift auch nicht in die einfachgesetzliche Regelung des § 25 DRiG ein, die beinhaltet, dass jede Richterin und jeder Richter unabhängig und nur dem Gesetz unterworfen ist.

Nach Nöhre und Meller-Hannich sollte die berufliche Entwicklung auf Seiten der Richterschaft von einer kontinuierlichen, letztlich verpflichtenden Fortbildung begleitet werden, die Richterinnen und Richter nicht als Eingriff in ihre verfassungsrechtliche Unabhängigkeit, sondern als Chance für eine Aufwertung ihres Berufsstandes in den Augen der übrigen Akteure des Gerichts verstehen sollten.[9] Nöhre und Meller-Hannich führen etwa den seit mehr als 20 Jahren anhaltenden starken Rückgang der Klageeingangszahlen in Zivilsachen von 25–30 % unter anderem auf das Missverhältnis der fehlenden Spezialisierung in der Richterschaft zu der deutlich intensiveren Spezialisierung der Anwaltschaft zurück.[10] Die fehlende Spezialisierung der einzelnen Richter sei weder durch die Einrichtung von Spezialspruchkörpern bei den Gerichten noch einen vermehrten Einsatz von Sachverständigen auszugleichen.[11]

Dass die Aus- und Fortbildung der Richter nicht als Eingriff in die richterliche Unabhängigkeit gesehen werden muss, sondern im Gegenteil der Förderung der richterlichen Unabhängigkeit dient, hat der Beirat europäischer Richterinnen und Richter (CCJE) bereits im Jahre 2010 gesehen und in der Magna Carta of Judges wie folgt formuliert:

> „Aus- und Fortbildung ist ein wichtiges Element zur Wahrung der Unabhängigkeit der Richter".

Besondere Aufmerksamkeit ist allerdings einer inhaltlichen Einflussnahme auf die Fortbildungsmöglichkeiten und Inhalte zu schenken. So muss eine inhaltliche Einflussnahme im Wege der Fortbildung, die eine bestimmte Rechtsprechungslinie nahelegt oder vorgibt, ausgeschlossen werden. In gleicher Weise muss ausgeschlossen werden, dass Richterinnen und Richter kurzfristig zu zeitlich und örtlich derart gebunden Fortbildungsmaßnahmen verpflichtet werden, dass sie gezielt an der Ausübung ihrer Rechtsprechungstätigkeit gehindert werden.

Besondere Aufmerksamkeit ist auch den Institutionen und den für sie handelnden Personen zu widmen, die für die dienstliche Fortbildung ausgesucht und eingesetzt werden.

5. Fortbildungspflicht versus Berufsfreiheit

Art. 12 Abs. 1 GG formuliert den grundgesetzlichen Schutz der Berufsfreiheit wie folgt:

> „Alle Deutschen haben das Recht, Beruf, Arbeitsplatz und Ausbildungsstätte frei zu wählen".

Dass eine dienstliche Fortbildungspflicht in die Berufsfreiheit eingreift, und zwar als Regelung zur Berufsausübung, dürfte unstreitig sein.

---

9 *Nöhre/Meller-Hannich* (Anm. 7) S. 2705.

10 *Nöhre*, Der Rückgang der Zivilklagen ist massiv – Die Forschungsergebnisse, in: Anwaltsblatt (2023), S. 472.

11 *Meller-Hannich/Nöhre/Höland*, Abschlussbericht zum Forschungsvorhaben „Erforschung der Ursachen des Rückgangs der Eingangszahlen bei den Zivilgerichten" vom 21. April 2023 (2023), S. 153.

Ein solcher Eingriff lässt sich nach der Rechtsprechung des Bundesverfassungsgerichts allerdings durch jede vernünftige Erwägung des Gemeinwohls rechtfertigen. Deshalb entspricht die Normierung einer allgemeinen oder besonderen dienstlichen Fortbildungspflicht ohne Weiteres dem Gemeinwohl, weil Bund und Länder die Qualität und Effizienz der Rechtspflege im Interesse aller Bürger sicherzustellen haben.

Bund und Länder einerseits und Richterinnen und Richter andererseits müssen gemeinsam bestrebt sein, richterliche Entscheidungen mit höchstmöglicher Qualität zu ermöglichen und zu erzielen. Für Bund und Länder bedeutet dies, dass sie Einrichtungen schaffen müssen, die diesem Zweck dienlich sind und durch eine geeignete Programm- und Themenauswahl Förderanreize schaffen, die zu einer freiwilligen Inanspruchnahme von Fortbildungsangeboten einladen. Zur Erreichung dieser Ziele müssen sowohl institutionelle als auch nicht institutionelle Einrichtungen geschaffen und unterhalten werden, die vollständig kostenfrei zur Verfügung gestellt werden sollten. Für Richterinnen und Richter bedeutet dies, dass sie sich des Umstands bewusst sein müssen, dass das Richteramt seine Legitimation nur unter der Herausforderung des lebenslangen Lernens bewahrt.

Christoph Conrad Henke weist in seinem Aufsatz „Legitimität und richterliche Entscheidung" zurecht daraufhin, dass Quantität, Qualität und Legitimität richterlicher Entscheidungen gleichermaßen von Bedeutung sind. Er weist zudem in Anknüpfung an Habermas darauf hin, dass bei der Legitimität die Anerkennungswürdigkeit der Entscheidungen im Mittelpunkt stehe. Ein Richter solle deshalb die Anerkennungswürdigkeit seiner Entscheidungen stets zum Ziel haben. Für das Legitimitätsniveau richterlicher Entscheidungen seien alle Umstände von Bedeutung, die deren Anerkennungswürdigkeit erhöhen oder senken. Der Sachkenntnis der Richterinnen und Richter komme hierbei im Anschluss an Tschentscher eine ebenso wichtige Rolle zu, wie der effektiven richterlichen Unabhängigkeit nach innen und außen.[12]

Eine Fortbildungspflicht für Richterinnen und Richter, sei sie nun gesetzlich verankert oder nicht, dient deshalb der Erreichung des notwendigen Legitimationsniveaus, das bei jedem staatlichen Handeln mit Entscheidungscharakter erforderlich ist, wie das Bundesverfassungsgericht dies im Beschluss vom 24. Mai 1995 – 2 BvF 1/92 bereits zum Ausdruck gebracht hat.

Wenn dem entgegengehalten wird, dass Richterinnen und Richter aufgrund ihrer permanenten Entscheidungsverpflichtung ohnehin gehalten sind, ständig und nicht nur sporadisch Literatur und Rechtsprechung zu überprüfen, zur Kenntnis zu nehmen und anzuwenden, mag dies die Berechtigung einer strukturierten, überregionalen und inzwischen internationalen Aus- und Fortbildung ebenso wenig zu ersetzen, wie fachübergreifende Aus- und Fortbildungen. Denn zum einen hat der Bundesgerichtshof in Bezug auf die Fortbildungspflicht von Fachanwältinnen und Fachanwälten entschieden, dass die Lektüre von Fachzeitschriften und Urteilen und selbst eigenen Publikationen in Fachzeitschriften die Fortbildung ebenso wenig wie das Fertigen von Schriftsätzen, die eine umfangreiche Recherche und einen hohen zeitlichen

---

12 Siehe insgesamt *Henke*, Legitimität und richterliche Entscheidung – Weshalb eine behutsame Fortentwicklung der traditionellen juristischen Methode zweckmäßig ist, in: ZIS (2015), S. 110f.

und gedanklichen Aufwand erfordern, ersetzen können. Entsprechendes dürfte für die Tätigkeit der Richterinnen und Richter gelten.

Nimmt man zum anderen hinzu, dass spezialisierte Anwälte und Fachanwälte Entscheidungen der nationalen Obergerichte binnen 4–6 Wochen und Entscheidungen des Europäischen Gerichtshofs binnen drei Monaten nicht nur zur Kenntnis nehmen müssen, sondern ihre Beratungs- und Vertretungstätigkeit entsprechend anpassen müssen, um einer Haftung zu entgehen, wird deutlich, welchen Maßstab Richterinnen und Richter für sich selbst gelten lassen müssen.

VI. Fortbildungspflicht in Japan

Die Pflicht zur Fortbildung hat für Richterinnen und Richter in Japan wie unter Ziffer I. 2. bereits dargestellt eine andere Basis als in Deutschland.

In Japan ist die Unabhängigkeit der Richterinnen und Richter in Art. 76 Abs. 3 der Verfassung geregelt. Dieser lautet:

> „Alle Richter üben ihr Amt unabhängig und nur nach ihrem Gewissen aus und sind nur an diese Verfassung und das Gesetz gebunden."

Das japanische Gerichtsgesetz regelt die Aufgaben der Richter und die Organisation der Gerichte im Einzelnen.

Da das japanische Institut für Ausbildung und Forschung eine dem Obersten Gerichtshof unterstellte Organisation ist, fällt es in dessen Schutzbereich, unterliegt keinen Weisungen und Einflussnahmen Dritter und steht somit auch unter keinem politischen Druck.

Eine mögliche Kollision zwischen Aus- und Fortbildungsmaßnahmen jeglicher Art, auch, soweit sie obligatorisch sind, und der richterlichen Unabhängigkeit wird deshalb nicht diskutiert.

Andererseits werden in Japan zusätzliche Qualifikationen der Richter überwiegend nicht für erforderlich gehalten. Wenn besondere Kenntnisse erforderlich sind, kann jederzeit ein Gerichtsangestellter (*saibansho-chōsakan* – judicial research officials) hinzugezogen werden, so etwa, wenn es um das Recht des geistigen Eigentums oder das Steuerrecht geht. Dieser übernimmt die für die Verhandlung und Entscheidung erforderlichen Recherchen und andere gesetzlich vorgesehene Aufgaben entsprechend der Anordnung des Gerichts, § 57 Abs. 2 JGG.

Darüber hinaus kann das Gericht technische Berater (*senmon-iin*) in das Verfahren einbeziehen, wenn es feststellt, dass es einen technischen Berater benötigt. Dieser kann sowohl im Zusammenhang mit der Beratung über die Anordnung und Formulierung von Beweisfragen hinzugezogen werden als auch zur Beratung über die Schaffung eines Rahmens für einen reibungslosen Ablauf des Gerichtsverfahrens. Die Vorsitzende Richterin bzw. der Vorsitzende Richter haben hierzu die Parteien anzuhören, die Hinzuziehung des technischen Beraters zu beschließen und dessen schriftliche oder mündliche Stellungnahme einzuholen, § 92–2 Abs. 1 JZPO.

In japanischen Gerichten werden Richterinnen und Richter häufig alle 2 bis 3 Jahre versetzt und bleiben selten in derselben Abteilung. Es fehlt ihnen daher im Vergleich zu japanischen Rechtsanwältinnen und Rechtsanwälten, die sich auf bestimmte Bereiche, wie beispielsweise Arzthaftung oder Bauprozesse, spezialisiert haben, an Fachwissen, das sie durch den Einsatz technischer Berater zu kompensieren versuchen. Die japanischen Rechtsanwältinnen und Rechtsanwälte versuchen den Einsatz technischer Berater aber häufig zu verhindern, weil sie glauben, dass die Hinzuziehung eines technischen Beraters zu einer inquisitorischen Verfahrensstruktur führt, die vom Gericht gesteuert wird.

VII. Fazit

1.

Es dürfte sich, soweit noch nicht geschehen, in Anlehnung an die Magna Carta of Judges empfehlen, in das Deutsche Richtergesetz und die Landesrichtergesetze aufzunehmen, dass die Richterin und der Richter die Pflicht und das Recht zur Aus- und Fortbildung haben. Die Richterin und der Richter sollten demgemäß zur Sicherung ihrer grundgesetzlich garantierten Unabhängigkeit eine Aus- und Fortbildung auch einfordern können.

2.

Soweit gegen die Normierung einer Aus- und Fortbildungspflicht eingewandt wird, dass jede Pflicht der Kontrolle und ihre Nichteinhaltung der Sanktion bedarf, damit sie Wirkung entfaltet, dürfte dieser Einwand durch den Erfolg und den Nutzungsgrad der institutionellen und nicht institutionellen Aus- und Fortbildungseinrichtungen bereits widerlegt sein. Die Erfahrung zeigt, dass die überwiegende Anzahl der Richterinnen und Richtern in ihrer dienstlichen Tätigkeit von Bildungsinteresse, Neugier und Verantwortungsbewusstsein für das Amt getragen ist. Ausreißer können die Regel nicht bestimmen.

Die Annahme, dass jede Nichteinhaltung einer Pflicht sanktioniert werden müsse, wird nicht geteilt. Denn wo genügend Aus- und Fortbildungsanreize geschaffen werden und Hemmnisse, wie etwa die Entstehung von Kosten wie Reisekosten, beseitigt werden, bedarf es keiner Sanktionen, die zur Wahrnehmung der Pflicht anhalten. Zudem kann jeder Bestrafungsgedanke leicht durch einen Belohnungsgedanken ersetzt werden, indem etwa die Bereitschaft zur eigenen Aus- und Fortbildung und die daran anschließende Umsetzung dieser Bereitschaft positiv in dienstliche Beurteilungen einfließt.

3.

Mit der Pflicht und dem Recht der Richterinnen und Richter zur bzw. auf Aus- und Fortbildung muss die Verpflichtung des Dienstherrn korrespondieren, beide in angemessener und ausreichender Weise zu fördern. Dabei bedarf es einer gewissen Kunst und Weitsicht, die breite Streuung unterschiedlichen Bedarfs und unterschiedlicher

Interessen von Richterinnen und Richtern unterschiedlicher Gerichte, Instanzen und Zuständigkeiten zu erfassen und abzudecken.

4.

Es dürfte sich des Weiteren mit Rücksicht auf aktuelle Entwicklungen in Bezug auf die Richterbesetzung oberster Gerichte, wie etwa des Bundesverfassungsgerichtes, aber auch die Besetzung von Richterstellen in den Ländern empfehlen, dem Dienstherrn aufzuerlegen, dass die Aus- und Weiterbildung politisch neutral zu erfolgen hat. Zwar sehen die entsprechenden Beamtengesetze ohnehin vor, dass Richterinnen und Richter sich bei Wahrnehmung ihrer Tätigkeit mit gebotener Zurückhaltung und politisch neutral verhalten sollen. Es darf aber in Erinnerung gerufen werden, dass bei der Schaffung des Grundgesetzes intendiert war, deutlich zu machen, dass Richterinnen und Richter als die die dritte Gewalt ausfüllenden Subjekte keine Beamten sind. Eine tatsächlich scharfe Trennung ist allerdings aufgrund der Tatsache, dass das Richteramt auch ein Beschäftigungsverhältnis ist, nicht möglich gewesen.

Möglicherweise lässt sich die politische Neutralität am ehesten dadurch gewährleisten, dass die Ausbildungsinstitute wie in Japan an ein oberstes Landes- oder Bundesgericht angegliedert werden.

5.

Die Justiz ist als dritte Gewalt ebenso wie alle anderen derzeit großen Disruptionen, wohl den größten seit mehreren Jahrzehnten, ausgesetzt und dies gleichzeitig. Die Justiz hat der demographische Wandel ebenso erreicht wie die Digitalisierung und KI. Alles gleichzeitig zu einem sachgerechten und angemessenen Ergebnis zu führen, ist eine der größten Herausforderungen der Zeit.

Bei dem unvermeidbaren Eindringen von KI in die Gerichte und deren Arbeit, der Erprobung vom Online-Klagen für jeden Bürger, den Überlegungen zur Einführung von strukturiertem Vortrag und Basisakten darf nicht übersehen werden, dass bei allen Akteuren vor Gericht der Mensch in seiner Gesamtheit nicht verloren gehen darf.

Denn hinter jedem der Prüfung durch ein Gericht zugeführten Sachverhalt stehen Menschen, die in ihrer Gesamtheit den Sachverhalt prägen. Wer die Einführung und Verbreitung von Videoverhandlungen miterlebt hat, wird festgestellt haben, dass es Licht und Schatten gibt. Licht insoweit, als Zeit und Kosten erspart werden können. Schatten insoweit, als die Interaktion zwischen Menschen nicht nur aus der Übermittlung von Bild und Ton besteht, weshalb bei Videoverhandlungen manch Menschliches verloren geht. Andreas Voßkuhle weist deshalb zu Recht darauf hin, dass im Mittelpunkt der Juristerei der konkrete Mensch mit all seinen vielfältigen Eigenschaften, Möglichkeiten und Fehlern stehe und jede Juristin und jeder Jurist ohne ernsthafte Liebe zum Menschen letztlich zu einer Art „Jurazomie“ werde, weil nur der, der den konkreten Menschen verstehe, diesem auch gerecht werde.[13]

13 *Voßkuhle*, Ohne Menschenliebe und Demut geht es nicht, in: NJW-aktuell 46/2025, S. 17.

Radke hat deshalb auf dem EDV-Gerichtstag 2024 in Bezug auf die Arbeit der Richterinnen und Richter zurecht darauf hingewiesen, dass richterliche Entscheidungen nicht durch Ergebnisse ersetzt werden dürfen, die Maschinen und Software auf noch so intelligente Weise liefern. Entscheider müsse immer der Mensch, soll heißen die Richterin oder der Richter, bleiben. Die richterliche Unabhängigkeit dürfe auch durch den KI-Einsatz in der Justiz nicht gefährdet werden.[14] KI muss deshalb im gerichtlichen Bereich ein Hilfsmittel der Richterinnen und Richter bleiben. Diese dürfen nicht zu Assistenten von KI werden.

KI wird auch auf die Aus- und Fortbildung von Richterinnen und Richtern einen erheblichen Einfluss nehmen. Manche Aus- und Fortbildung dürfte in Zukunft in erheblichem Umfang von KI gesteuert sein und vieles abkürzen und erleichtern. KI wird allerdings Berufserfahrung, fachübergreifenden Austausch und menschliche Interaktionen, die ebenfalls vermittelt werden müssen, nicht ersetzen können.

Literaturverzeichnis

Bundesregierung, Antwort der Bundesregierung auf die Kleine Anfrage der Abgeordneten Katja Keul, Luise Amtsberg, Canan Bayram, weiterer Abgeordneter und der Fraktion BÜNDNIS 90/DIE GRÜNEN – Qualität der Justiz und bundeseinheitliches Fortbildungsrecht und bundeseinheitliche Fortbildungspflicht für Richterinnen und Richter, Drucksache 19/16307 vom 03. Januar 2020 (2020).

Dyckmanns, Mechthild: Fortbildungspflicht für Richter, in: DRiZ (2008), S. 149 ff.

Henke, Christoph Conrad: Legitimität und richterliche Entscheidung – Weshalb eine behutsame Fortentwicklung der traditionellen juristischen Methode zweckmäßig ist, in: ZIS (2015), S. 110 f.

Meller-Hannich, Caroline/*Höland*, Armin/*Nöhre*, Monika: Abschlussbericht zum Forschungsvorhaben „Erforschung der Ursachen des Rückgangs der Eingangszahlen bei den Zivilgerichten" vom 21. April 2023 (2023).

Nöhre, Monika: Der Rückgang der Zivilklagen ist massiv – Die Forschungsergebnisse, in: Anwaltsblatt (2023), S. 472 ff.

Nöhre Monika/*Meller-Hannich*, Caroline: Anwaltsspezialist trifft Richtergeneralist – Plädoyer für mehr Spezialisierung auf der Richterbank, in: NJW (2023), S. 2701 ff.

Radke, Henning: Rechtsstaat im digitalen Zeitalter, Vortrag auf dem EDV-Gerichtstags am 12. September 2024.

Rath, Christian: Von Avataren als Zeugen und KI-Vergleichsvorschlägen, Legal Tribune Online vom 13. 09. 2024 (2024).

Voßkuhle, Andreas: Ohne Menschenliebe und Demut geht es nicht, in: NJW-aktuell 46/2025 (2025), S. 17.

---

14 *Radke*, Rechtsstaat im digitalen Zeitalter, Vortrag auf dem EDV-Gerichtstag am 12. September 2024, Bericht von *Rath*, Von Avataren als Zeugen und KI-Vergleichsvorschlägen, Legal Tribune Online vom 13. 09. 2024 (2024).

Begegnungen

Persönliche Erfahrungen mit dem Unternehmensrecht in Deutschland und Japan

Von *Michael Kling*

Prof. Dr. Michael Kling absolvierte sein Studium (1993–1998) und den Referendardienst (1999–2001) in Mainz. Promotion (2000) und Habilitation (2008) bei Prof. Dr. Meinrad Dreher, LL.M. an der Johannes Gutenberg-Universität in Mainz. Seit 2009 ist er Inhaber des Lehrstuhls für Bürgerliches Recht, Handels- und Wirtschaftsrecht, Europarecht sowie Gewerblichen Rechtsschutz an der Philipps-Universität Marburg. Seine Arbeitsschwerpunkte sind: Bürgerliches Recht, Wettbewerbs- und Kartellrecht, Vergaberecht, Handels- und Wirtschaftsrecht sowie Internationales Wirtschaftsrecht. Er ist Mitverfasser mehrerer Lehrbücher zum Wettbewerbs- und Kartellrecht, ferner Mitherausgeber der Schriften zum Handels- und Wirtschaftsrecht im Peter Lang Verlag und der Beiträge zum Kartellrecht (BtrKR) im Mohr Siebeck Verlag.

I. Einleitung

Die erste „Begegnung“ mit dem Jubilar fand vor rund 25 Jahren gänzlich ohne den Jubilar statt. Ich war damals Wissenschaftlicher Assistent an der Johannes Gutenberg-Universität in Mainz. Dort traf ich im Fakultätsgebäude regelmäßig auf den später namhaften japanischen Zivilprozessrechtler O, der ein Forschungsjahr in Mainz verbrachte und der in dem ihm zugewiesenen Büro, das dem meinen benachbart war, intensiv an einer Monographie arbeitete. Eines Tages bedeutete mir O, er fahre nach Marburg, um das dortige Japanzentrum aufzusuchen. Dieses Institut sei „sehr berühmt in Japan“. Sein Leiter sei ein deutscher Professor namens Menkhaus, er lehre japanisches Recht auf Japanisch. O wolle ihn in Marburg treffen.

Zu diesem Zeitpunkt hatte ich Marburg selbst noch nicht besucht. Ich wusste freilich um die Existenz von Stadt und Universität, allerdings lediglich von einer 1927 erschienenen silbernen 3-Mark-Sammlermünze, die anlässlich der 450-Jahr-Feier der Philipps-Universität verausgabt wurde und die sich in meiner Sammlung befand. Damals war weder absehbar, dass ich einmal Professor an der Philipps-Universität werden würde, noch dass das dortige Japaninstitut – offensichtlich ein bedeutender Brückenpfeiler des deutsch-japanischen Juristenaustauschs – vor meiner Ankunft zum Wintersemester 2008/09 bereits abgewickelt sein würde. Kaum zu vermuten gewesen war vor diesem Hintergrund, dass ich dem Jubilar einmal persönlich begegnen und dass sich aus dieser Begegnung sehr bald eine fruchtbare fachliche Beziehung und später eine wertvolle Freundschaft entwickeln würde. Auch dafür war ein Forschungsjahr maßgeblich. Der Jubilar brachte dieses – seiner vormaligen Büroräume

Duncker & Humblot · Berlin | https://doi.org/10.3790/978-3-428-59611-9.2025.418960

beraubt – in einem vakanten Büro des damaligen Dekans der Marburger Juristenfakultät zu, der gelegentlich eine abendliche illustre Runde bei sich zu versammeln pflegte. Diese Zusammenkünfte erwiesen sich in fachlicher wie persönlicher Hinsicht als sehr fruchtbringend. Sie führten dazu, dass ich die ehrenvolle Aufgabe erhielt, als Zweitgutachter bei den Promotionsverfahren zweier Herausgeber dieser Festschrift fungieren zu dürfen. Später sollte ich, der bereits Korea und Taiwan kennengelernt hatte, auf Einladung des Jubilars zweimal im Abstand von 10 Jahren – 2014 und 2024 – die Meiji-Universität in Tokio besuchen, um dort Vorträge zu halten und an juristischen Fachveranstaltungen teilzunehmen. Diese Reisen und der Austausch vor Ort haben mir unvergessliche Erinnerungen beschert, die weit über die juristischen Erkenntnisse hinausgehen. So habe ich in Japan Land und Leute sowie die japanische Kultur und Geschichte sehr schätzen gelernt. Die Erfahrungen, die ich dort – gerade auch dank des Jubilars und in seiner Begleitung – machen durfte, möchte ich in meinem Leben nicht missen. Bekanntlich übt Japan seit langer Zeit große Faszination auf Europäer aus. Lafcadio Hearns Bücher aus dem späten 19. und frühen 20. Jahrhundert geben ein beredtes Zeugnis davon: *„The first charm of Japan is intangible and volatile as a perfume.“*[1] Mir ging es mehr als 100 Jahre später nicht anders als vielen unserer Vorfahren.

Mein erster Japanaufenthalt liegt inzwischen schon mehr als 10 Jahre zurück und die Erinnerungen daran sind schon etwas verblasst. Einer ordentlichen Aktenführung und einer umfassenden Fotodokumentation verdanke ich jedoch die Information, dass der Dekan und ich am 2. Oktober 2014 auf Einladung des Jubilars an der Meiji-Universität öffentliche Vorträge gehalten haben. Ich sprach damals zum Thema „Die Rechtskontrolle von Netzentgelten im Energiesektor nach Kartellrecht, Energierecht und Zivilrecht“. Fast zehn Jahre später, am 20. März 2024, konnte ich an fast derselben Stelle zu einem vergaberechtlichen Thema sprechen. Der Vortragstitel lautete diesmal: „EU and German Public Procurement Law Economic Background & Main Procurement Law Principles“.

Das Sprichwort sagt: „Aller guten Dinge sind drei“, und so darf ich hoffen, dass sich meinen beiden Japanreisen in den Jahren 2014 und 2024 in absehbarer Zeit ein dritter (aber hoffentlich nicht letzter) Aufenthalt in Begleitung meines lieben Kollegen und Freundes Prof. Dr. Heinrich Menkhaus hinzugesellen wird.

II. Einige persönliche Erfahrungen mit dem japanischen Recht

1. Vorbemerkungen

In den vergangenen 15 Jahren hatte ich immer wieder die Gelegenheit zur Kooperation mit dem Jubilar auf rechtlicher Ebene. Die betroffenen Rechtsgebiete und Zusammenhänge waren dabei denkbar unterschiedlich. Der Schwerpunkt meiner wissenschaftlichen Interessen liegt zwar im Wettbewerbs-, Kartell- und Vergaberecht, aber auch im Gesellschaftsrecht haben sich unsere Wege gekreuzt. Vor dem Hintergrund, dass das Gesellschaftsrecht in meiner Mainzer Assistenzzeit zu meinen bevorzugten Rechtsgebieten zählte, war es mehr eine Freude denn eine Last, bekannten

[1] *Hearn*, Glimpses of Unfamiliar Japan, Band 1 (1903), S. 1.

Stoff aufzugreifen und an der mir bis dato unbekannten Rechtslage in Japan zu spiegeln.

2. Entwicklung der Kooperation japanischer und deutscher Juristen

Die Länder Asiens haben bekanntlich schon sehr frühzeitig Studien zum Recht europäischer Länder, namentlich der Rechtsordnungen von Deutschland und Frankreich, unternommen. Ein bemerkenswertes Ergebnis dieser frühen Beschäftigung mit Deutschland ist die Erfindung des deutschen Wortes „Dunkelziffer" durch den japanischen Juristen Shigema Oba im Jahr 1908, der diesen Begriff in seiner Erlanger Dissertation prägte.[2]

Anfang des letzten Jahrhunderts stand zunächst das Zivilrecht im Fokus, d. h. das seinerzeit neue BGB. In den Jahrzehnten darauf sollte das Verwaltungsrecht folgen. Der Jubilar hat die wissenschaftlichen Beziehungen der deutschen und japanischen Verwaltungsjuristen in der ersten Hälfte des 20. Jahrhunderts eingehend studiert und ist ein wahrhaft profunder Kenner dieses Beziehungsgeflechts, welches auch die Philipps-Universität einschließt. Schließlich wurde ab den 1980er Jahren das Kartellrecht zum Gegenstand der Bemühungen und zuletzt das WTO- und EU-Vergaberecht, welches im letzten Jahr Gegenstand eines gemeinsamen Seminars mit Herrn Kollegen Shigeki Kusunoki war.

Auf der Grundlage ihrer intensiven Vorarbeiten haben die Länder Asiens eigenständige Rechtsordnungen und Kodifikationen geschaffen. Dadurch, dass die Wurzeln unseres Rechts sich teilweise gleichen, haben wir die Möglichkeit zu einer fruchtbaren Rechtsvergleichung. Das Kartellrecht etwa, das seinen Ursprung im US-amerikanischen Recht hat, ist heute eine Materie, über die weltweit qualifiziert gesprochen werden kann, weil das Ideengut zumindest im Kern identisch ist. Es ist deshalb für uns Rechtswissenschaftler gewinnbringend, den fachlichen Austausch über die Kontinente hinweg zu suchen.

3. Umfang und Grenzen der Rechtsvergleichung

Dabei ist es allerdings notwendig, sich über die Grenzen einer solchen fachlichen Kommunikation klarzuwerden. Es geht keineswegs nur um sprachliche Hindernisse, die man mit Hilfe von Übersetzungstools oder einer Kommunikation in der Weltsprache Englisch notfalls überwinden oder zumindest abmildern kann. Vielmehr ist die Rechtswissenschaft eine Kulturwissenschaft. Der Jubilar hat – etwa im Vorspann an seinen Erstgutachten – immer wieder darauf hingewiesen, dass das Recht nach wie vor und ganz überwiegend ein „nationales Kulturphänomen" sei. Promovenden neigten dazu, den Aufwand für die Abfassung einer Dissertation zu unterschätzen. Für sie sei neben der weitreichenden Beherrschung der fremden Sprache in Wort und Schrift zudem eine weitgehende Kenntnis der fremden Kultur erforderlich. Das gelte insbesondere für den Inselstaat Japan. Nicht ausreichend sei demgegenüber

---

2 *Heine/Sahler*, Dieser Japaner erfand die „Dunkelziffer", in: Die Welt online (30. März 2016), abrufbar unter: https://www.welt.de/print/die_welt/kultur/article153790501/Dieser-Japaner-erfand-die-Dunkelziffer.html (zuletzt abgerufen am 7. Oktober 2025).

die Berücksichtigung von in fremden Sprachen veröffentlichter Literatur über ein ausländisches Rechtsgebiet, die zu Missverständnissen und fehlerhaften Interpretationen führen könne. So entstehe die Gefahr, dass ein völlig abwegiges Bild vermittelt werde.

Diese für Promovenden identifizierten Gefahren bestehen erst recht für Wissenschaftler aus dem Ausland, die nie in Japan gelebt und gearbeitet haben und die der Landessprache nicht mächtig sind. Für solche Personen – zu denen der Verfasser zu rechnen ist – beschränkt sich die Tätigkeit auf das wechselseitige Geben und Aufnehmen von Anregungen zum Weiterdenken durch die Adressaten in der jeweiligen Heimatrechtsordnung. Im Folgenden sollen vor diesem Hintergrund einige Anregungen festgehalten werden, die ich durch die Kooperation mit dem Jubilar erhalten habe.

III. Einzelheiten

1. Vereins- und Stiftungsrecht sowie gemeinnützige Rechtsträger

Im Jahr 2013 hat man mich zu einem von insgesamt drei Gutachtern der Dissertation von Frau Sandra Schuh bestellt. Damit wurde ich beruflich zum ersten Mal mit den neueren Entwicklungen in der japanischen Gesellschaft und dem japanischen Recht konfrontiert.[3] Ein wichtiges Thema war seinerzeit die Entwicklung Japans hin zu einer Zivilgesellschaft, die mit der Machtverlagerung von der in Japan traditionell starken Exekutive des Staates auf eine eigenverantwortlich handelnde Bürgerschaft einherging. Insofern konnte ich der Dissertation der Autorin entnehmen, dass das Erdbeben von Kobe im Jahr 1995 einen politischen Wendepunkt markiert, der eine Zäsur auch für das japanische Recht darstellt und wesentliche Auswirkungen auf das japanische Vereins- und Stiftungsrecht hat.

Private Initiativen waren in Japan dem Konzessionssystem unterworfen. Demgegenüber wurde das Konzessionssystem in Deutschland bereits durch die Aktienrechtsnovelle von 1870 abgeschafft und durch das bis heute gültige System der Normativbedingungen ersetzt.[4] Bürgerliches Engagement im Vereinsrecht war für die deutsche Gesellschaft über viele Jahrzehnte prägend; das gilt heute wohl nur noch mit abnehmender Tendenz. Der deutsche Gesetzgeber hat allerdings mit dem Ehrenamtsstärkungsgesetz von 2013[5] und mit dem Referentenentwurf eines Gesetzes zur Stärkung der genossenschaftlichen Rechtsform von 2024[6] Maßnahmen zur Stärkung des bürgerschaftlichen Engagements ergriffen, sodass gewisse Parallelen zu der Entwicklung in Japan zu verzeichnen waren bzw. sind.

---

3 *Schuh*, Gemeinnützige Rechtsträger in Japan und Deutschland (2014).

4 *Schubert*, Die Abschaffung des Konzessionssystems durch die Aktienrechtsnovelle von 1870, in: ZGR (1981), S. 285 ff.

5 BGBl. 2013 Teil I S. 556 v. 20. März 2013.

6 Referentenentwurf eines Gesetzes zur Stärkung der genossenschaftlichen Rechtsform vom 25. Juni 2025, abrufbar unter: https://www.bmj.de/SharedDocs/Gesetzgebungsverfahren/DE/2024_Genossenschaftsrecht.html (zuletzt abgerufen am 7. Oktober 2025).

Gänzlich neu war für mich das Phänomen des *amakudari*, d.h. die Vergabe von hochrangigen Versorgungsposten an pensionierte Angehörige des öffentlichen Dienstes.[7] Die wörtliche Übersetzung, nämlich: „vom Himmel herabsteigen", klingt zwar eher amüsant, führte aber zu nicht sachgerechten Handlungsweisen bei der Bewältigung der Folgen des Erdbebens von Kobe 1995 und nachfolgend zu Bestrebungen zur Förderung privater Initiative und dem oben angesprochenen Wandel Japans zu einer „Bürgergesellschaft". Mit der NPO (Non-Profit-Organisation) wurde damals ein neuer Rechtsträger für gemeinnützige Organisationen geschaffen, der später in das Vereins- und Stiftungsgesetz des Jahres 2006 einging, welches die Autorin umfassend analysiert hat.[8] Erdbeben sind für Japaner zwar etwas ganz Alltägliches, während sie in Europa nahezu unbekannt sind, aber selbst für ein Land wie Japan dürfte es eine Besonderheit darstellen, dass ein großes Erdbeben wie jenes von Kobe im Jahr 1995 unmittelbar in die Schaffung einer eigenständigen Gesellschaftsform einmündet. Ein wesentlicher Ertrag der Dissertation lag darin, die rechtlichen Entwicklungen in Japan sehr sorgfältig nachgezeichnet und diese als Ausdruck bestimmter gesellschaftlicher Veränderungen gekennzeichnet zu haben. Sie ist damit ein bemerkenswertes Beispiel für das Verständnis der Rechtswissenschaft als Kulturwissenschaft, wie es der Jubilar zu Recht einfordert.

2. Exkurs zur *business judgment rule* im Kapitalgesellschaftsrecht

An dieser Stelle sei zur Klarstellung noch auf Folgendes hingewiesen: Auch in Deutschland gab es jahrzehntelang das Phänomen, dass bestimmte zentrale Posten im Unternehmen an verdiente Personen und nicht an solche mit der besten fachlichen Eignung vergeben wurden. Eugen Schmalenbach hat diese für den Aufsichtsrat in der Aktiengesellschaft vor sehr langer Zeit einmal als „Sinekuren" bezeichnet.[9] Heute würde man dafür wohl die Bezeichnung „Ehrenposten" gebrauchen. Ich glaube nicht, dass man – ungeachtet bestehender Mängel bei der Ausübung der Kontrolle im Einzelfall – Aufsichtsratsposten in werbenden Unternehmen heute noch so bezeichnen darf. Grund dafür ist die *business judgment rule*, die heute sowohl die Tätigkeit der Vorstandsmitglieder als auch die der Aufsichtsratsmitglieder prägt. Der Wandel der Aufsichtsratstätigkeit ist bemerkenswert. Die Frequenz der Aufsichtsratssitzungen ist selbst bei mittelgroßen Unternehmen heute deutlich höher als die in § 110 Abs. 3 AktG vorgeschriebene Mindestzahl von zwei Aufsichtsratssitzungen. Zudem hat eine Professionalisierung der Aufsichtsratsmitglieder durch Qualifizierungsmaßnahmen stattgefunden, zu der in Deutschland etwa im Bereich des Bank- und Versi-

---

7 *Schuh* (Anm. 3), S. 3, 25.

8 Zum Reformverlauf *Schuh* (Anm. 3), S. 25 ff.

9 *Schmalenbach*, Die Überwachungspflicht des Aufsichtsrats, in: ZfHF (1910/1911), S. 275: „Wenn die Praxis der Vorschrift des Gesetzes nachlebte, würden die Wahlen zum Aufsichtsrat beherrscht werden von der Frage: Welche Personen sind besonders fähig, die Überwachung der Gesellschaft vorzunehmen? Man würde vielleicht auch andere Qualitäten verlangen, aber die Qualität für die Ausübung der Überwachungspflicht ist, wie schon der Name des Organs sagt, die wichtigste. Werden die Aufsichtsräte wirklich in diesem Sinne ausgewählt? Man braucht die Antwort nicht zu geben; jedes Kind weiß, dass es ganz anders ist. Aufsichtsratsstellen sind auch heute noch in allererster Linie Sinekuren."

cherungsrechts jedenfalls auch die Strenge des unionsrechtlich determinierten Regulierungsrechts maßgeblich beigetragen hat.

In Japan wurde die *business judgment rule* nach US-amerikanischem Vorbild etabliert. Maßgeblich ist danach die Forderung nach sog. „informierten Entscheidungen". Auch das deutsche Kapitalgesellschaftsrecht verlangt von den Geschäftsleitern die Entscheidungsfindung aufgrund „angemessener Information". Zu Informationspflichten von Vorstandsmitgliedern der Aktiengesellschaft wurde diesbezüglich von einem Strafsenat des BGH entschieden,

> „(...) dass sie grundsätzlich in der konkreten Entscheidungssituation die Ausschöpfung aller verfügbaren Informationsquellen tatsächlicher und rechtlicher Art verlangen, um auf dieser Grundlage die Vor- und Nachteile der bestehenden Handlungsoptionen sorgfältig abzuschätzen und den erkennbaren Risiken Rechnung zu tragen. Die konkrete Entscheidungssituation ist danach der Bezugsrahmen des Ausmaßes der Informationspflichten. Dementsprechend ist es notwendig, aber auch ausreichend, dass sich der Vorstand eine unter Berücksichtigung des Faktors Zeit und unter Abwägung der Kosten und Nutzen weiterer Informationsgewinnung ‚angemessene' Tatsachenbasis verschafft; je nach Bedeutung der Entscheidung ist eine breitere Informationsbasis rechtlich zu fordern. Dem Vorstand steht danach letztlich ein dem konkreten Einzelfall angepasster Spielraum zu, den Informationsbedarf zur Vorbereitung seiner unternehmerischen Entscheidung selbst abzuwägen. Ausschlaggebend ist dabei nicht, ob die Entscheidung tatsächlich auf der Basis angemessener Informationen getroffen wurde und dem Wohle der Gesellschaft diente, sondern es reicht aus, dass der Vorstand dies vernünftigerweise annehmen durfte. Die Beurteilung des Vorstands im Zeitpunkt der Entscheidungsfindung muss aus der Sicht eines ordentlichen Geschäftsleiters vertretbar erscheinen."[10]

Diese Pflicht zur angemessenen Information basiert letztlich auf der deutschen *business judgment rule*, die in § 93 Abs. 1 Satz 2 AktG kodifiziert ist und im Jahr 2005 durch das „Gesetz zur Unternehmensintegrität und Modernisierung des Aktienrechts" („UMAG")[11] kodifiziert wurde. Der Sache nach war sie vorher bereits höchstrichterlich anerkannt.[12]

Nach der höchstrichterlichen Rechtsprechung[13] definiert § 93 Abs. 1 Satz 2 AktG einen sog. „sicheren Hafen". Die Einhaltung seiner Voraussetzungen schließt eine Pflichtverletzung aus. Umgekehrt begründet die Überschreitung seiner Grenzen durch einen Verstoß gegen Informationspflichten für sich betrachtet noch keine Pflichtverletzung, sondern es ist auch dann noch pflichtgemäßes Handeln nach § 93 Abs. 1 Satz 1 AktG möglich. Allerdings indiziert der Verstoß gegen § 93 Abs. 1 Satz 2 AktG eine Pflichtverletzung. Letztlich ist eine Verletzung der Sorgfaltspflichten aus § 93 Abs. 1 Satz 1 AktG immer nur dann zu bejahen, wenn ein

---

10 BGH, Urteil v. 10. Februar 2022 – 3 StR 329/21, NZG (2022), S. 1294 Rn. 14 = ZIP (2022), S. 2435; siehe auch BGH, Urteil v. 12. Oktober 2016 – 5 StR 134/15, ZIP (2016), S. 2467 m. Anm. *Baur/Holle*, ZIP (2017), S. 555 = NJW (2017), S. 578 Rn. 34 m. w. N. m. Anm. *Brand* = EWiR (2017), S. 103 m. Anm. *Scholl.*

11 Gesetz v. 22. September 2005, BGBl. I S. 2802.

12 BGH, Urteil v. 21. April 1997 – II ZR 175/95, BGHZ 135, S. 244 = NJW (1997), S. 1926 – ARAG/Garmenbeck.

13 BGH, Urteil v. 12. Oktober 2016 – 5 StR 134/15, ZIP (2016), S. 2467, 2. red. Leitsatz.

schlechthin unvertretbares Vorstandshandeln vorliegt; d. h. der Leitungsfehler muss sich auch einem Außenstehenden förmlich aufdrängen.[14]

Die Wahrnehmung der Kontrollfunktion durch den Aufsichtsrat der AG setzt ebenfalls eine angemessene Informationsgrundlage voraus. Insoweit gilt also für die Haftung des Aufsichtsrats nach § 116 Satz 1 i.V.m. § 93 Abs. 2 AktG nichts anderes als für die Vorstandshaftung gemäß § 93 Abs. 2 AktG. Zu der Überwachungspflicht des Aufsichtsrats gehört es beispielsweise, „dass er sich über erhebliche Risiken, die der Vorstand mit Geschäften eingeht, kundig macht und ihr Ausmaß unabhängig vom Vorstand selbständig abschätzt".[15] Mit Blick auf Krisensituationen und das nur den Vorstand treffende Zahlungsverbot gemäß § 92 Abs. 2 Satz 1 AktG wurde vom Gesellschaftsrechtssenat des BGH Folgendes entschieden:

> „Den Aufsichtsrat treffen aber Informations-, Beratungs- und Überwachungspflichten. Er muss sich ein genaues Bild von der wirtschaftlichen Situation der Gesellschaft verschaffen und insbesondere in einer Krisensituation alle ihm nach §§ 90 Abs. 3, 111 Abs. 2 AktG zur Verfügung stehenden Erkenntnisquellen ausschöpfen (…)."[16]

Die strukturelle Parallelität der Entwicklungen in Japan und Deutschland wird anhand der Entwicklungen um die *business judgment rule* augenfällig. Die gestiegenen Anforderungen im Zusammenhang mit den Aufgaben der Unternehmensführung und ihrer Kontrolle, namentlich die Pflicht zur Entscheidung auf angemessener Informationsgrundlage, haben dazu geführt, dass sog. „Frühstücksdirektoren", die im Unternehmen reine Ehrenposten wahrnehmen, der Vergangenheit angehören dürften.

3. Weitere Entwicklungen im Gesellschafts- und Umwandlungsrecht

Das Gesellschafts- und Umwandlungsrecht wurde mir im Zusammenhang mit der Zweitbegutachtung der Dissertation von Herrn Deniz Günal, einem weiteren Mitherausgeber dieser Festschrift, nahegebracht.[17] Zunächst wurde ich davon überrascht, dass in Japan über lange Zeit keine einheitliche Normierung des Gesellschaftsrechts im Gesetz erfolgt ist und dass man sogar bei der sprachlichen Neufassung des Zivilgesetzes von 2004 einige für das Verständnis des allgemeinen Gesellschaftsrechts zentrale Begriffe ersatzlos gestrichen hatte.[18] Durch das Gesellschaftsrechtsgesetz von 2006 hat der japanische Gesetzgeber dann erstmals einen Teil des Gesellschaftsrechts in einer Kodifikation zusammengefasst.[19]

Für den Begriff der Gesellschaft i. S. einer „durch Rechtsgeschäft gegründeten Personenvereinigung des Privatrechts zur Erreichung eines bestimmten Zwecks" gibt es

---

14 BGH, Urteil v. 12. Oktober 2016 – 5 StR 134/15, ZIP (2016), S. 2467, 2. red. Leitsatz.

15 BGH, Beschluss v. 06. November 2012 – II ZR 111/12, NZG (2013), S. 339 f. = ZIP (2012), S. 2438.

16 BGH, Urteil v. 16. März 2009 – II ZR 280/07, NZG (2009), S. 551 Rn. 15 = ZIP (2009), S. 860, siehe auch BGH, Urteil v. 1. Dezember 2008 – II ZR 102/07, ZIP (2009), S. 70 Rn. 14 – MPS.

17 *Günal*, Die Verschmelzung im japanischen Gesellschaftsrecht (2014).

18 *Günal* (Anm. 17), S. 11.

19 *Günal* (Anm. 17), S. 1.

in der japanischen Sprache offensichtlich keine Entsprechung.[20] Auch ein Wort für den deutschen Begriff Gesellschaftsrecht existiert im Japanischen nach Angaben des Jubilars nicht.[21] Allerdings unterscheidet man auch in Japan zwischen personalistisch und körperschaftlich verfassten Rechtsträgern, allerdings offenbar weniger klar als im deutschen Recht.[22]

Für das Umwandlungsrecht gibt es ebenfalls keinen übergreifenden Begriff. Allerdings hat sich der (dem Wortlaut nach zu enge) Ausdruck *soshiki saihen* (Strukturänderung) dafür eingebürgert.[23]

In Deutschland hat man mit dem Umwandlungsgesetz von 1994 schon recht früh eine entsprechende Kodifikation geschaffen, während das Umwandlungsrecht in Japan im fünften Buch des Gesellschaftsgesetzes von 2006 geregelt wurde. Ich erinnere mich an die Warnung einer meiner Gesellschaftsrechtsprofessoren in Mainz, Professor T, bitte ja nicht das deutsche Umwandlungsgesetz von 1994 zu lesen, da es so unverständlich abgefasst worden sei, dass man es als Student unmöglich verstehen könne. Eine vergleichbare Warnung vor dem Gesetzestext habe ich später nie wieder gehört.

Eine weitere Überraschung lieferte der Befund, dass im japanischen Recht der Verein der Aktiengesellschaft nachempfunden wurde und nicht wie in Deutschland umgekehrt.[24]

Bei allen Unterschieden zwischen der Rechtslage in Deutschland und Japan sind mir zumindest zwei bekannte Phänomene begegnet. Das erste hängt zusammen mit dem vom Jubilar so bezeichneten „umgekehrten Maßgeblichkeitsprinzip“, nämlich der Tatsache, dass das Steuerrecht als maßgeblicher Faktor für das Gesellschafts-

---

20 Zum Begriff der Gesellschaft und dem in Japan gebräuchlichen, auf den Reformer *Yūkichi Fukuzawa* zurückgehenden Begriff *kaisha* siehe *Menkhaus*, Allgemeines Gesellschaftsrecht in Japan, in: Menkhaus/Sato (Hrsg.), Japanischer Brückenbauer zum deutschen Rechtskreis, Festschrift für Koresuke Yamauchi zum 60. Geburtstag (2006), S. 229 ff. mit dem Zwischenfazit: „Im Ergebnis kann also der Begriff *kaisha* auch nicht mit gutem Gewissen mit Handelsgesellschaft ins Deutsche übersetzt werden. Entsprechend kann das neue Gesetz über *kaisha* auch nicht als Handelsgesellschaftsgesetz übersetzt werden. Vielmehr ist festzustellen, dass es einen alle Gesellschaftsformen umfassenden Oberbegriff, der dem deutschen juristischen Fachbegriff Gesellschaft entspricht, in Japan ebenso wenig gibt, wie einen alle Handelsgesellschaften erfassenden einheitlichen Oberbegriff.“; siehe außerdem *Menkhaus*, a. a. O., S. 252: „Ein Oberbegriff für Gesellschaft etwa fehlt.“

21 *Menkhaus* (Anm. 20), S. 249 (236): „Fehlt schon ein japanischer Begriff für das deutsche Wort Gesellschaft, verwundert es nicht, dass es auch keine Legaldefinition des Begriffs Gesellschaftsrecht gibt. Auch das neue Gesetz über *kaisha* enthält diese nicht.“ Auch im deutschen Gesellschaftsrecht fehlt eine Legaldefinition des Begriffs Gesellschaftsrecht. Menkhaus stellt insoweit zu Recht auf die von der Rechtswissenschaft entwickelte Definition ab: „Danach ist das Gesellschaftsrecht das Recht der Personenvereinigungen des Privatrechts, die zur Erreichung eines bestimmten Zwecks durch Rechtsgeschäft begründet werden.“ (ebd.).

22 *Günal* (Anm. 17), S. 11, 13; siehe dazu aber auch *Menkhaus* (Anm. 20), S. 249 (242): „Obwohl man, soweit ersichtlich, zu Zeiten des alten Zivil- und alten Handelsgesetzes noch gar nicht deutlich zwischen personalistisch und körperschaftlich strukturierten Gesellschaften unterschied (…)“.

23 *Günal* (Anm. 17), S. 14.

24 *Günal* (Anm. 17), S. 95.

recht zu betrachten ist. In Deutschland ist beispielsweise die Existenz der GmbH & Co. KG eine Folge dieses Prinzips.

Das zweite Beispiel betrifft das Phänomen der Bekämpfung feindlicher Übernahmen, das in beiden Jurisdiktionen bekannt ist. Instruktiv ist insoweit die Darstellung des grundlegenden „Livedoor"-Falls durch den Verfasser.[25] Hier wie dort dürften feindliche Übernahmen als „Angriffe auf das Establishment" verstanden werden.

In methodischer Hinsicht hat mich die Dissertation von Herrn Günal vor allem deshalb überzeugt, weil er die Funktionalität als das methodische Grundprinzip des Rechtsvergleichs ansieht.[26] Das sollte zwar eine Selbstverständlichkeit sein; gleichwohl gibt es das Phänomen, dass rechtsvergleichende Arbeiten sich in Länderberichten mit einem anschließenden Rechtsvergleich erschöpfen, auch weiterhin. Typischerweise bringen solche Arbeiten weniger Erkenntnisgewinn als jene, denen das Funktionalitätsprinzip zugrundeliegt.

4. Kartellrecht

Im Bereich des Kartellrechts – einem Schwerpunktbereich meiner wissenschaftlichen Beschäftigung – bin ich in Forschung und Lehre immer wieder auf Bezüge zu Japan gestoßen. Auf den ersten Blick scheint eine Verbindung nicht bestehen zu können, da unterschiedliche Kontinente und unterschiedliche Märkte betroffen sind. Hinzu kommt, dass nach dem völkerrechtlichen Nichteinmischungsgebot an sich zu vermuten wäre, dass Kartellrechtsverstöße nur innerhalb der jeweiligen Jurisdiktion geahndet werden können. Tatsächlich aber ist das nicht der Fall. Vielmehr hat das Kartellrecht eine „internationale Dimension".[27] Das heißt, dass die Wettbewerbsregeln der Europäischen Union für Unternehmen aus Drittstaaten ebenso relevant werden können wie umgekehrt das Kartellrecht von Drittstaaten für Unternehmen mit Sitz in Europa. Bemerkenswert früh, nämlich im Jahr 1972, hat die Europäische Kommission mit Blick auf Unternehmen aus Japan eine Mitteilung verfasst, in der diese zur Beachtung des europäischen Kartellverbots (damals geregelt in Art. 85 EWGV, heute in Art. 101 AEUV) aufgefordert wurden.[28] Die genannte Mitteilung bezog sich auf Fälle, in denen japanische Industrien, zum Teil in autonomer Weise, zum Teil nach Abstimmung mit den entsprechenden europäischen Industrien, die Einfuhren von japanischen Erzeugnissen in die Gemeinschaft beschränken oder auf andere Weise in quantitativer, preislicher, qualitativer oder ähnlicher Hinsicht regeln sollten. Man kann somit feststellen, dass die Sanktionierung internationaler Kartelle durch die europäische Kartellbehörde kein neues Phänomen ist.[29]

---

25 *Günal* (Anm. 17), S. 38 ff.

26 *Günal* (Anm. 17), S. 7; insoweit *Kötz/Zweigert*, Einführung in die Rechtsvergleichung 3. Auflage (1996), S. 33 folgend.

27 *Kling*, Die internationale Dimension des Europäischen Kartellrechts, in: RIW (2020), S. 245 ff.

28 ABl. EG Nr. C 111, S. 13 v. 21. Oktober 1972.

29 *Kling* (Anm. 27), S. 251.

Dreh- und Angelpunkt für die Anwendung des jeweils eigenen Kartellrechts ist das sog. Auswirkungsprinzip, das sich gleichsam als kartellrechtliche „Allzweckwaffe" erwiesen hat. Sofern der Wettbewerb auf den heimischen Märkten durch Absprachen verfälscht wird, wird die zuständige Kartellbehörde nicht zögern, gegenüber Unternehmen aus Drittstaaten Untersagungsverfügungen zu erlassen und Bußgelder zu verhängen. Besonders spektakulär ist in dieser Hinsicht ein Fall, über den ich in meinem Beitrag in der Festschrift für Koresuke Yamauchi zum 70. Geburtstag berichten durfte.[30] Der Fall „Toshiba Corporation/Kommission" betraf ein internationales Kartell zwischen europäischen und japanischen Herstellern in Form eines *gentlemen's agreement*, das zum Inhalt hatte, die Märkte im Gebiet jeder dieser beiden Gruppen von Transformatorenherstellern zu respektieren und auf den Verkauf auf diesen Märkten zu verzichten. Die an dem *gentlemen's agreement* beteiligten Unternehmen waren über einen Zeitraum von vier Jahren ein- bis zweimal jährlich zusammengetroffen. Diese Treffen dienten nach Einschätzung der Kommission und der Rechtsprechung dazu, das streitgegenständliche *gentlemen's agreement* jeweils zu bestätigen.[31] Ausgehend davon, dass potentieller Wettbewerb zwischen den beteiligten Unternehmen bestand, wurde es als eine nach Art. 101 AEUV und Art. 53 des EWR-Abkommens verbotene bezweckte Wettbewerbsbeschränkung qualifiziert.[32] Auf die Feststellung tatsächlicher negativer Effekte für den Wettbewerb kam es nicht an.

Es verdient noch der Erwähnung, dass die Festschrift Herrn Kollegen Yamauchi am 14. Mai 2017 in Münster verliehen wurde und ich als seinerzeitiger Dekan des Fachbereichs Rechtswissenschaften der Philipps-Universität Marburg an der Verleihung als Gratulant mit einem Redebeitrag mitwirken durfte. Darin führte ich aus, dass die Philipps-Universität Marburg traditionell sehr enge Verbindungen nach Japan aufwies. So wurde die erste akademische Vorlesung über Japan an einer deutschen Universität im Jahre 1878 in Marburg gehalten, und zwar von Johannes Justus Rein (1835–1918), einem „Stammvater der Japanwissenschaften" in Deutschland. Rein hatte sich im Auftrag der preußischen Regierung von Dezember 1873 bis September 1875 in Japan aufgehalten. Im Jahr 1878 sprach er als erster Ordinarius für Geographie an der Philipps-Universität (1876–1883) über die Geographie und Naturgeschichte Japans.

Marburg war außerdem die erste Universität, die im Jahr 1988 ein interdisziplinäres wissenschaftliches Zentrum für Japanwissenschaften einrichtete. Dieses Zentrum, das von den Fachbereichen der Universität unabhängig war, wurde mit vier

---

30 *Kling*, Japanische Unternehmen vor dem EuGH? Die Verantwortlichkeit japanischer Unternehmen für Kartellverstöße nach Europäischem Kartellrecht, in: Menkhaus/Narazaki (Hrsg.), Japanischer Vorkämpfer für die Rechtsordnung des 21. Jahrhunderts, Festschrift für Koresuke Yamauchi zum 70. Geburtstag (2017), S. 243 ff.

31 Kommission, Entscheidung v. 7. Oktober 2009 – COMP/39.129, C (2009) 7601 final Tz. 129 ff., ABl. EU 2009 Nr. C 296, S. 21 – Leistungstransformatoren; siehe auch EuGH, Urteil v. 20. Januar 2016 – Rs. C-373/14 P, ECLI:EU:C:2016:26 Tz. 13 = WuW 2016, 176 = NZKart 2016, 131 – Toshiba Corporation/Kommission.

32 Kommission, Entscheidung v. 7. Oktober 2009 – COMP/39.129, C (2009) 7601 final Tz. 163 f., ABl. EU 2009 Nr. C 296, S. 21 – Leistungstransformatoren; EuG, Urteil v. 21. Mai 2014 – Rs. T-519/09, ECLI:EU:T:2014:263 Tz. 228 ff. – Toshiba Corporation/Kommission; EuGH, Urteil v. 20. Januar 2016 – Rs. C-373/14 P, ECLI:EU:C:2016:26 Tz. 60 ff. = WuW 2016, 176 = NZKart 2016, 23 ff. – Toshiba Corporation/Kommission.

Professuren – Geschichte, Religion, Wirtschaft und Recht – besetzt; es besaß vor allem die erste Professur für japanisches Recht im deutschen Sprachraum. Die Entscheidung, hier nicht allein die Sprachwissenschaft und Philologie zu berücksichtigen, war richtungsweisend. Heute wird die interdisziplinäre Forschung und Lehre von Seiten der Universitätsleitungen und der Politik allenthalben begrüßt, ja sogar aktiv eingefordert. Leider erfolgte die Aufgabe dieses innovativen und zukunftsweisenden Konzeptes für die Marburger Japanwissenschaften durch das Verbot der Neuaufnahme von Studierenden im Jahre 2005. Der Grund dafür war die sog. Zentrenbildung für Regionalstudien im Bundesland Hessen, die letztlich die endgültige Schließung des Japanzentrums durch Examinierung aller verbliebenen Studierenden im Jahre 2013 zur Folge hatte. Die Philipps-Universität Marburg hat dadurch nicht nur ein japanwissenschaftliches Zentrum, sondern auch ihre Reputation und Tradition in den Japanwissenschaften eingebüßt. Ich halte das für einen unverzeihlichen Fehler der damaligen Entscheidungsträger.

5. Vergaberecht

Zuletzt durfte ich mir im Frühjahr 2024 einen langgehegten Wunsch erfüllen und zum zweiten Mal nach Japan reisen. Der Jubilar und ich hatten schon länger das gemeinsame Projekt verfolgt, ein Seminar zum Vergaberecht in Japan und Deutschland zu veranstalten. Der „Workshop for Comparative Studies of Public Procurement Laws and Practices between Japan and Germany/EU“ konnte nach mehrjähriger Verzögerung durch die Coronapandemie endlich am 20. März 2024 an der Meiji-Universität unter Beteiligung renommierter Fachleute aus dem In- und Ausland stattfinden. Zu diesem Anlass habe ich einen selbständigen Text zum Thema „*A general Overview of the Legal Situation in Germany & the European Union*“ verfasst, der – wie die Beiträge der anderen Vortragenden – gegenwärtig noch der Publikation harrt, sodass an dieser Stelle dazu noch kein Zitat erfolgen kann.

Ich habe den Workshop in bester Erinnerung. Es würde an dieser Stelle zu weitgehen, auf die einzelnen vergaberechtlichen Details einzugehen. Jedenfalls wurde ich davon überrascht, dass man in Japan mit den Grundlagen des WTO-Vergaberechts (d. h. des GPA 2012) und mit den europäischen Vergaberichtlinien von 2014 bestens vertraut ist. Die Analysen dieser Materien könnten dazu beitragen, in Japan eine eigenständige Kodifikation des japanischen Vergaberechts anzuregen, die bislang noch fehlt. Diese sollte sich an den in Art. 15 GPA geregelten Grundsätzen der „*fairness and impartiality of the procurement process*“ orientieren, in etwa vergleichbar den „Fairness-Grundsätzen“ des deutschen Kartellvergaberechts, nämlich Wettbewerb, Transparenz und Gleichbehandlung (§ 97 Abs. 1, 2 GWB). Zudem sollte der Zuschlag nicht auf das billigste Angebot, sondern auf das Angebot mit dem besten Preis-Leistungs-Verhältnis (§ 127 Abs. 1 GWB) erfolgen. Von der „Aufladung“ der öffentlichen Auftragsvergabe mit politischen Zielsetzungen sollte möglichst abgesehen werden.

IV. Schluss

Der Jubilar hat sich als Brückenbauer zwischen Deutschland und Japan in hervorragender Weise verdient gemacht. Zuletzt wurde ihm aus diesem Grund im Sommer 2024 in Berlin der „Orden der Aufgehenden Sonne, goldene Strahlen mit Rosette" des japanischen Kaiserhauses verliehen. Es handelt sich um eine außergewöhnliche Ehre für einen ausländischen Staatsbürger. Mit der vorliegenden Festschrift gedenken wir nunmehr einerseits des Rechtswissenschaftlers Prof. Dr. Heinrich Menkhaus, andererseits aber auch eines langjährigen Weggefährten und Freundes. Es war mir eine Freude, den Jubilar seit meinem Dienstantritt am Fachbereich Rechtswissenschaften der Philipps-Universität Marburg zum Wintersemester 2008/09 ein Stück weit bis hierher begleiten zu dürfen, und ich verbinde dies mit der Hoffnung auf viele weitere gemeinsame Spaziergänge geistiger und physischer Art, sei es in Deutschland oder in Japan.

Literaturverzeichnis

Günal, Deniz: Die Verschmelzung im japanischen Gesellschaftsrecht (2014).

Hearn, Lafcadio: Glimpses of Unfamiliar Japan, Band 1 (1903).

Heine, Matthias/*Sahler*, Anne: Dieser Japaner erfand die „Dunkelziffer", in: Die Welt online (30. Juni 2016), abrufbar unter: https://www.welt.de/print/die_welt/kultur/article153790501/Dieser-Japaner-erfand-die-Dunkelziffer.html (zuletzt abgerufen am 7. Oktober 2025).

Kling, Michael: Die internationale Dimension des Europäischen Kartellrechts, in: RIW (2020), S. 245–252.

Kling, Michael: Japanische Unternehmen vor dem EuGH? Die Verantwortlichkeit japanischer Unternehmen für Kartellverstöße nach Europäischem Kartellrecht, in: Menkhaus, Heinrich/Narazaki, Midori (Hrsg.), Japanischer Vorkämpfer für die Rechtsordnung des 21. Jahrhunderts, Festschrift für Koresuke Yamauchi zum 70. Geburtstag (2017), S. 243–271.

Kötz, Hein/*Zweigert*, Konrad: Einführung in die Rechtsvergleichung, 3. Auflage (1996).

Menkhaus, Heinrich: Allgemeines Gesellschaftsrecht in Japan, in: Menkhaus, Heinrich/Sato, Fumihiko (Hrsg.), Japanischer Brückenbauer zum deutschen Rechtskreis, Festschrift für Koresuke Yamauchi zum 60. Geburtstag (2006), S. 229–252.

Schmalenbach, Eugen: Die Überwachungspflicht des Aufsichtsrats, in: ZfHF (1910/1911), S. 271–283.

Schubert, Werner: Die Abschaffung des Konzessionssystems durch die Aktienrechtsnovelle von 1870, in: ZGR (1981), S. 285–317.

Schuh, Sandra: Gemeinnützige Rechtsträger in Japan und Deutschland (2014).

Der Schutz von Ausländern im japanischen Verfassungsrecht

Von *Mika Knör*

Mika Knör ist Doktorand an der Graduate School of Law der Universität Nagoya und Stipendiat des japanischen Bildungsministeriums (MEXT-Stipendium). Sein Forschungsschwerpunkt liegt im japanischen Verfassungsrecht, insbesondere im Grundrechtsschutz von Ausländern und weiteren gesellschaftlichen Minderheiten.

I. Vorbemerkungen

Ein Studium des japanischen Rechts mag für die meisten Jura-Studierenden in Deutschland in Anbetracht des bereits durch den Pflichtstoff geforderten Arbeitspensums so fernliegen wie Japan selbst. Im Vergleich zu „klassischen" juristischen Disziplinen ist es deshalb als rechtsvergleichend-interessierter Student mit Japanbezug leider oftmals schwierig, wissenschaftliche Kontakte zu knüpfen. Umso mehr bin ich daher dankbar für die Gelegenheit, die sich mir durch die Begegnung mit Professor Menkhaus und die Autorenschaft in dieser Festschrift bietet. Den Jubilar lernte ich zunächst während des Auswahlgesprächs meines Stipendiums kennen, und später während seiner Gastvorträge an der Universität Nagoya umso mehr als Mentor und Kollegen zu schätzen. Ich freue mich auf die weitere Zusammenarbeit und darauf, in meiner eigenen wissenschaftlichen Laufbahn die von Ihm angelegten Pfade ins japanische Recht weiter zu erforschen und auszubauen.

Als studentischer Vertreter in dieser Festschrift möchte ich zunächst ein paar einleitende Bemerkungen zum Studium des japanischen Rechts abgeben. Zunächst zur wohl grundlegendsten Frage: „Warum japanisches Recht?" – In der Tat mag Japan als Studienziel und juristisches Forschungsgebiet exotisch erscheinen. Wer sich mit dem japanischen Recht beschäftigt, wird jedoch schnell feststellen, dass gerade aus deutscher Perspektive hier viele inhaltliche Überschneidungen bestehen. Nicht zuletzt ist das moderne japanische Rechtssystem während der Staatsmodernisierung in der Meiji-Restauration ab 1865 zu großen Teilen nach dem Vorbild des deutschen (bzw. preußischen) Rechts entstanden. So basiert auch das moderne japanische Zivil- und (materielle) Strafrecht zu großen Teilen auf dem deutschen BGB bzw. StGB.[1] Die Verfassung des japanischen Kaiserreichs von 1889 nahm sich wiederum ein Vor-

1 Zum Zivilrecht: *Schröder/Morinaga*, Zum Einfluß des BGB auf das japanische Zivilrecht, in Berger (Hrsg.), Rechtstransfer durch Zivilgesetzbücher, Beiträge Liechtenstein-Institut 29 (2005), S. 38; Zum Strafrecht: *Takayanagi*, A Century of Innovation: The Development of Japanese Law, 1868–1961, in Mehren (Hrsg.), Law in Japan (1963), S. 15.

Duncker & Humblot · Berlin | https://doi.org/10.3790/978-3-428-59611-9.2025.418783

bild an der preußischen Verfassung von 1848 und der Verfassung des deutschen Kaiserreichs von 1871.[2] Die Gemeinsamkeiten sind jedoch nicht nur historischer Natur. Auch heute begegnet man in der japanischen Rechtswissenschaft weiterhin deutschen Rechtsbegriffen.[3] Zumindest inhaltlich mag das Studium des japanischen Rechts somit näher liegen als zunächst gedacht.

Selbst in den Urteilen des japanischen Obersten Gerichtshofes (OGH) finden sich hin und wieder Verweise auf das deutsche Recht. So prüfte eine Entscheidung von 1975 zur Standortregulierung von Apotheken die Verletzung der Berufsfreiheit in beeindruckender Ähnlichkeit zum Bahnhofsapotheken-Urteil des Bundesverfassungsgerichts.[4] In einer neueren Entscheidung von 2023 zur Verfassungsmäßigkeit des japanischen Transsexuellengesetzes (特例法, *tokurei-hō*),[5] welches zur rechtswirksamen Änderung des eingetragenen Geschlechts die vorherige Sterilisation sowie operative Angleichung der äußeren Geschlechtsmerkmale forderte, zitierte Richter Uga Katsuya in seinem abweichenden Votum einen Beschluss des Bundesverfassungsgerichts von 2011 zur Verfassungswidrigkeit des Transsexuellengesetzes, um für eine weiterreichende Verfassungswidrigkeit der japanischen Bestimmungen zu argumentieren.[6] Als Kenner der deutschen Rechtsordnung wird man beim Studium des japanischen Rechts somit auch stetig aus einem neuen Blickwinkel mit der eigenen Rechtsordnung konfrontiert. Nicht nur fällt es hierdurch leichter, das japanische Rechtsdenken zu verstehen, es führt auch zu einem kritischen Umgang mit dem eigenen juristischen Hintergrund.

Letztlich ist das japanische Recht ein Musterbeispiel der Rechtsrezeption, welches aus einer Kombination fremder Rechtssysteme mit einem eigenen, japanischen Rechtsdenken geformt wurde.[7] Gerade diese Charakterisierung macht das verfassungsvergleichende Studium in Japan spannend und aufschlussreich. Zusätzlich hilft das große Interesse in der japanischen Rechtswissenschaft am deutschen Recht dabei, dass auch das eigene juristische Hintergrundwissen nicht in Vergessenheit gerät. Rechtsvergleichend interessierte Studierende möchte ich deshalb nur ermutigen, den Weg in das japanische Recht zu suchen und zum juristischen Dialog mit Japan beizutragen.

---

2 *Ando*, Die Entstehung der Meiji-Verfassung: zur Rolle des deutschen Konstitutionalismus im modernen japanischen Staatswesen (2000).

3 Als Anekdote: Während einer Vorlesung zum japanischen Verwaltungsrecht an der Universität Nagoya referierte der Professor zunächst ausgiebig über die Lehren Otto Mayers und die Aspekte eines Verwaltungsaktes.

4 OGH Japan, Urteil v. 30. April 1975, 1968 (gyō-tsu) 120; BVerfGE 7, S. 377.

5 Gesetz über besondere Bestimmungen zur Handhabung des Geschlechts von Personen mit Geschlechtsidentitätsstörung (性同一性障害者の性別の取扱いの特例に関する法律, *seidōitsushōgaisha no seibetsu no toriatsukai no tokurei ni kansuru hōritsu*), Gesetz Nr. 111 (2003), zul. geändert am 1. April 2022.

6 OGH Japan, Grand Bench, 25. Oktober 2023, Reiwa 2 (ku) No. 993, abweichende Meinung von Richter Uga.

7 *Ishikawa*, Codification, Decodification, and Recodification of the Japanese Civil Code, in Rivera (Hrsg.), The Scope and Structure of Civil Codes (2013), S. 267–285; *Rahn*, Rechtsdenken und Rechtsauffassung in Japan: dargestellt an der Entwicklung der modernen japanischen Zivilrechtsmethodik (1990).

Abschließend, und als allmählicher Übergang zum fachlichen Teil, soll nicht nur für das Studium des japanischen Rechts, sondern speziell des japanischen Verfassungsrechts geworben werden. Ein summarischer Überblick über die vorhandene deutschsprachige Literatur zum japanischen Recht zeigt leider immer noch ein klares Defizit im verfassungsrechtlichen Bereich.[8] Nun liegt es möglicherweise in der Natur des Verfassungsrechts, dass dieses vor allem aus nationaler Perspektive betrachtet wird, jedenfalls verglichen mit anderen, stärker international eingebundenen Rechtsgebieten (man denke hier zum Beispiel an das Wettbewerbsrecht oder Handels- und Gesellschaftsrecht). Betrachtet man die in den Verfassungen der Welt verankerten Grundrechte jedoch als unveräußerliche Menschenrechte, welche ungeachtet von nationalen Grenzen jedem Menschen von Geburt an zustehen, so entfalten diese schließlich auch internationale Bedeutung. Ebenso lassen sich durch den Vergleich mit anderen Ländern und Verfassungen auch Schutzdefizite im eigenen Land besser einordnen. Das Einstehen für den Schutz universeller Menschenrechte erfordert somit auch den Blick über den eigenen juristischen Tellerrand. Gerade in Zeiten demokratischer Rückschritte weltweit gilt es umso mehr, den Schutz der Grundrechte auch in der Rechtswissenschaft nicht nur als nationale Aufgabe zu verstehen.

II. Einleitung

Japan und Deutschland verbindet, dass beide Länder nach dem Ende des zweiten Weltkrieges mit der Aufgabe einer tiefgreifenden Demokratisierung und Umwälzung des Staates konfrontiert waren. Während Deutschland zumindest mit der Weimarer Republik auf ein Stück demokratischer Staatsgeschichte zurückschauen konnte, erhielt Japan 1947 zum ersten Mal in seiner Geschichte überhaupt eine liberale, demokratische Verfassung. Anders als in Deutschland war die neue „Verfassung des Staates Japan“[9] (im Folgenden als „Verfassung“ abgekürzt) auch kein Produkt eines nationalen Verfassungskonvents, sondern wurde in nicht mehr als sechs Tagen von Vertretern der amerikanischen Militärverwaltung ausgearbeitet und anschließend über wenige Wochen in Beratungen mit der japanischen Regierung fertiggestellt.[10]

Aufgrund dieser Geschichte wird die japanische Verfassung häufig voreilig als „aufoktroyierte“ Verfassung beschrieben.[11] Ohne an dieser Stelle zu tief in die Entstehungsgeschichte der japanischen Verfassung einzugehen, gilt es zunächst anzumerken, dass Vertreter der japanischen Regierung durchaus signifikanten Einfluss auf den Inhalt des finalen Verfassungstextes nahmen. Dies wird vor allem im Bereich der Ausländerrechte sichtbar. Während die amerikanische Militärverwaltung zunächst eine explizite Anerkennung der rechtlichen Gleichstellung von Ausländern

---

8 Man schaue bspw. auf die Beiträge in der größten deutschsprachigen Fachzeitschrift zum japanischen Recht, der „Zeitschrift für Japanisches Recht“. Zumindest in jüngeren Jahren ist dank der Arbeit von Prof. Tomoaki Kurishima von der Universität Saitama ein leichter Anstieg bei den Beiträgen zum Öffentlichen Recht zu verzeichnen.

9 Verkündet am 3. November 1946, in Kraft getreten am 3. Mai 1947.

10 *Goodman*, The Rule of Law in Japan. A Comparative Analysis (2017), S. 33.

11 Krit. hierzu: *Law*, The Myth of the Imposed Constitution, in Galligan/Versteeg (Hrsg.), Social and Political Foundations of Constitutions (2013), S. 239.

im Verfassungstext forderte, verschwand der entsprechende Artikel nach und nach aus den weiteren Entwürfen.[12]

Folge dieses Prozesses ist, dass die japanische Verfassung von 1947 zum Schutz ausländischer Staatsbürger zunächst schweigt. Anders als in Deutschland, wo die Unterscheidung zwischen „Jedermanns-Grundrechten“ und „Deutschen-Grundrechten“ bewusst von Beginn an im Grundgesetz angelegt wurde, blieb die Frage des Grundrechtsschutzes für Ausländer in Japan somit zunächst offen.[13] Es dauerte bis ins Jahr 1978, bis der japanische OHG eine Grundsatzentscheidung zum Grundrechtsstatus ausländischer Staatsbürger fällte. Die sogenannte „McLean“-Entscheidung stellte Ausländer zwar grundsätzlich in den Schutz der Verfassung, schränkte jedoch zugleich ein, dass hierdurch nicht der Ermessensspielraum der Einwanderungs- bzw. Ausländerbehörden in Aufenthaltsfragen eingeschränkt wird.[14] Bis heute prägt das Urteil den verfassungsrechtlichen Schutzumfang von ausländischen Staatsbürgern in Japan maßgeblich.

Nichtsdestotrotz sind Ausländer in Japan nicht gänzlich schutzlos gestellt. Gerade im Bereich des Grundrechtsschutzes gegenüber Privaten lassen sich klare Tendenzen seitens der Gerichte erkennen, ausländischen Staatsbürgern und ethnischen Minderheiten effektiven Schutz vor Diskriminierung im Zivilrechtsverkehr zu gewähren.[15] Zwar spielt hier auch das Völkerrecht, wie z. B. die UN-Konvention zur Beseitigung jeder Form von Rassendiskriminierung (ICERD) eine ausgeprägte Rolle, jedoch berufen sich die Gerichte zugleich auch auf verfassungsrechtliche Schutzvorschriften.[16] Auch wenn sich diese progressiven Trends noch nicht auf den Schutz vor staatlichen Grundrechtsverletzungen übertragen lassen, so sind auch hier vorsichtige Entwicklungslinien erkennbar, welche die strengen Leitlinien der McLean-Entscheidung möglicherweise aufweichen können.[17]

Ziel des folgenden Beitrages ist es, einen Überblick über die grundrechtliche Stellung ausländischer Staatsbürger im japanischen Verfassungsrecht zu geben. Als Hintergrund wird hier zunächst kurz die historische Position ausländischer Staatsbürger in der modernen japanischen Staatsgeschichte erläutert. Anschließend wird die verfassungsrechtliche Stellung der Ausländer in der heutigen japanischen Verfassung genauer erläutert, sowie notwendige Querbezüge zu anderen relevanten Rechtsvor-

---

12 *Webster*, Legal Excisions Omissions Are Not Accidents, in: Cornell International Law Journal 39, Nr. 2 (2006), S. 440 ff.; *Fisher*, „We the kokumin“: the Constitution, International Law and the Rights of Foreigners in Japan, in: Zeitschrift für Japanisches Recht, Nr. 39 (2015), S. 119 ff.

13 Zum Hintergrund des Grundgesetzes *Bäcker*, § 58 Historische und ideengeschichtliche Grundlagen der Grundrechte, in Stern/Sodan/Möstl (Hrsg.), Das Staatsrecht der Bundesrepublik Deutschland im europäischen Staatenverbund, Bd. 3 (2022), Rn. 47.

14 OGH Japan, Grand Bench, 4. Oktober 1978, Minshū 32 No. 7, 1223.

15 Näheres hierzu unter IV.

16 Zur Anwendbarkeit von Artikel 14 u. a.: Bezirksgericht Sapporo, 11. November 2002, 1806 Hanji 84; Hoher Gerichtshof Nagoya, 27. Oktober 2022, Reiwa 5 (ne) Nr. 487; zur Anwendbarkeit von Artikel 13 in Hassrede-Fällen: Hoher Gerichtshof Osaka, 8. Juli 2014, Heisei 25 (ne) Nr. 3235, 2232.

17 So z. B. im Fall der nachträglich für rechtswidrig erklärten Abschiebung zweier srilankischer Staatsbürger, Hoher Gerichtshof Tokio, 22. September 2021, Reiwa 2 (ne) 1423.

schriften vorgenommen. Sodann wird die Rechtslage zum Schutzumfang der japanischen Verfassung für Ausländer jeweils gegenüber dem Staat, sowie gegenüber Privaten anhand von bedeutsamen Gerichtsentscheidungen erklärt. Die Bewertung dieser beiden Themengebiete wird schließlich einen vorsichtigen Ausblick wagen, welche Entwicklungen zukünftig im Bereich des japanischen Verfassungsrechts für Ausländer erwartet werden können.

III. Ausländer in Japan und ihre Stellung in der japanischen Nachkriegsverfassung

Mit Blick auf die Geschichte Japans lässt sich die Beziehung des Landes zu ausländischer Migration als über lange Zeit ambivalent charakterisieren. Einerseits hat der kulturelle Austausch mit China schon früh tiefgreifenden Einfluss auf die Entwicklung der japanischen Kultur ausgeübt und ist noch heute in der Sprache (*Kanji-Schriftzeichen sowie Vokabular*), Philosophie (*Konfuzianismus*) und Religion (*Buddhismus*) des Landes sichtbar.[18] Von der westlichen Welt blieb Japan im Gegensatz hierzu jedoch bis in das 19. Jahrhundert hinein weitgehend isoliert. Der erste Kontakt mit dem Westen fand so tatsächlich erst in der Mitte des 16. Jahrhunderts statt, mit einer kleinen Gruppe portugiesischer Händler und Missionare. Wachsendes Misstrauen seitens der japanischen Bevölkerung und des Daimyōs Toyotomi Hideyoshi gegenüber den christlichen Missionaren und Ihren Bestrebungen in Japan führten jedoch schon im Jahr 1597 zur Hinrichtung von 26 Missionaren und Gläubigen in Nagasaki (heute bekannt als die Märtyrer von Nagasaki). Letztlich führte die Teilnahme christlicher Gläubiger an der Shimabara-Rebellion von 1637 gegen das Tokugawa-Shogunat zu einem kompletten Verbot des christlichen Glaubens und der Verbannung aller Portugiesen aus Japan.[19] In den folgenden zwei Jahrhunderten schloss Japan seine Grenzen nach außen nahezu vollständig. Einzig die Niederlande durften, auch begünstigt durch den dort vorherrschenden Protestantismus, Handelsbeziehungen mit Japan aufrechterhalten. Auch die Niederlande mussten Ihre Repräsentanz jedoch auf eine kleine künstliche Insel in der Bucht von Nagasaki (出島, *Dejima*) beschränken und waren strenger Überwachung ausgesetzt.[20]

Diese über 200 Jahre andauernde Periode der japanischen Isolation nach außen, bekannt als „*sakoku*" (鎖国, geschlossenes Land), endete erst im Jahr 1853, als eine Expedition der United States Navy unter dem Kommando von Commodore Matthew C. Perry Japan dazu zwang, seine Häfen für amerikanische Schiffe zu öffnen. Dies geschah zum einen zu Handelszwecken, aber auch um dort die Versorgung und Betankung US-amerikanischer Schiffe zu ermöglichen. Um eine Unterwerfung durch Gewalt zu verhindern, blieb dem Tokugawa-Shogunat angesichts der techno-

---

18 *Beasley*, The Rise of Modern Japan (1990), S. 15.

19 *Meyer*, Japan: A Concise History (2012), S. 98–99; *Elisonas*, Christianity and the Daimyo, in Hall (Hrsg.), The Cambridge History of Japan, Bd. 4 (1991), S. 368–372.

20 *Goodman*, Japan: The Dutch Experience (1986), S. 18.

logischen Überlegenheit der amerikanischen Kanonenboote wenig anderes übrig, als das Land wieder nach außen zu öffnen.[21]

Diese Öffnung des Landes für den Außenhandel erforderte schließlich auch eine Modernisierung des japanischen Rechtssystems. Die USA – sowie kurze Zeit später auch europäische Staaten – hatten das japanische Rechtssystem zuvor als unzuverlässig zur Sicherung Ihrer Wirtschaftsinteressen identifiziert, und zwangen Japan deshalb, eine Serie an ungleichen Verträgen abzuschließen.[22] Ausländische Unternehmen in Japan wurden hierdurch einseitig bevorzugt; ausländischen Gesandten wurde juristische Extraterritorialität zugesichert. Im Gegensatz zu den Portugiesen und später den niederländischen Händlern der Sakoku-Ära genossen Ausländer im Japan des späten 19. Jahrhunderts nun eine Position des Privilegs. Für japanische Nationalisten jener Zeit stellte dieses Privileg die Souveränität des Landes grundsätzlich infrage. Folglich war die Modernisierung des japanischen Rechtssystems (und der Wirtschaft) auch eine Frage der Wahrung oder Wiederherstellung der eigenen Staatssouveränität.[23]

Mit Beginn des 20. Jahrhunderts verfiel Japan mehr und mehr dem Autoritarismus. Gleichzeitig betrieb das Land im asiatischen Raum eine zunehmend aggressive und expansionistische Eroberungspolitik. Nach der Annexion Koreas im Jahr 1910 und der Mandschurei 1931, der umfassenden Invasion Chinas 1937 und der Expansion nach Südostasien während des Zweiten Weltkriegs erstreckte sich die japanische Kolonialsphäre in ihrer größten Ausdehnung von Südsachalin im Norden bis Indochina und Neuguinea im Süden.[24] Einher mit dieser Expansion gingen Gewalt und Ausbeutung der lokalen Bevölkerung. Während die genauen Zahlen umstritten sind, schätzen Historiker die Gesamtzahl der Todesopfer des japanischen Kolonialismus in Asien auf zwischen 10 und 30 Millionen Menschen.[25]

Im Rahmen seiner Kolonialherrschaft rekrutierte das Japanische Kaiserreich große Teile der lokalen Bevölkerung als Arbeiter, oftmals unter Anwendung von Zwang. Im heutigen Indonesien allein wurden zwischen vier und zehn Millionen sogenannte *rōmusha* (労務者, in etwa „Arbeitskraft“) zur Arbeit für die japanische Besatzung gezwungen, während in Korea etwa sieben Millionen Menschen unter dem Gesetz zur nationalen Mobilisierung als Arbeitskräfte eingezogen wurden.[26] Etwa 800.000

21 *Meyer* (Anm. 19), S. 128.

22 Ein Vertrag zwischen Preußen und Japan kam bspw. im Jahre 1861 zustande, s. hierzu *Menkhaus*, Der Japanisch-Preußische Freundschafts-, Schiffahrts- und Handelsvertrag von 1861 – Eine juristische Analyse anläßlich der offiziellen Feier des 160. Jubiläums des Beginns der japanisch-deutschen diplomatischen Beziehungen: Teil 1–, in: Meiji Law Journal 28 (2021), S. 35.

23 *Goodman* (Anm. 10), S. 18–21.

24 *Tanaka*, Hidden Horrors: Japanese War Crimes in World War II (2018), S. 3–9.

25 *Rummel*, Statistics of democide: genocide and mass murder since 1900 (1998), S. 32; *Rigg*, Bryan Mark, Japan’s Holocaust: History of Imperial Japan’s Mass Murder and Rape During World War II (2024), S. 225.

26 *NIOD Institute for War, Holocaust and Genocide Studies*, The Japanese Occupation and Pacific War (in numbers), abgerufen am 14. November 2024; *Park*, The politics of remembrance: the case of Korean forced laborers in the Second World War, in Shin/Park/Yang

Koreaner wurden als Zwangsarbeiter nach Japan gebracht, von denen etwa zehn Prozent infolge der harten Arbeitsbedingungen starben.[27] Bis heute beschäftigt diese Geschichte und damit einhergehende Fragen der Entschädigung die Rechtsprechung und Politik beider Länder. Hierbei steht insbesondere die Streitfrage im Mittelpunkt, ob die damalige Rekrutierung koreanischer Arbeiter tatsächlich unter den Begriff Zwangsarbeit (強制労働, *kyōsei rōdō*) fiel oder, wie die japanische Regierung insistiert, lediglich eine Maßnahme allgemeiner Kriegsmobilisierung (徴用, *chōyō*) gewesen sei, welche Koreaner als imperiale Subjekte in gleichem Maße betraf wie Japaner.[28]

Nach dem Ende des Zweiten Weltkriegs betrug die Gesamtzahl der Koreaner in Japan etwa 2,3 Millionen Menschen. Während viele kurz darauf in ihre Heimat zurückkehrten, entschieden sich etwa 600.000 Koreaner, dauerhaft in Japan zu bleiben.[29] Diese Gruppe bildete schließlich die Grundlage für die heutige koreanischer Minderheit in Japan („Zainichi-Koreaner"), die 2023 mit über 410.000 Menschen die drittgrößte ausländische Minderheit in Japan bildeten (Chinesen: 821.838, Vietnamesen: 565.026).[30] Ein Blick auf diese Zahlen verdeutlicht, dass die koloniale Geschichte Japans auch heute noch immer in der Demographie des Landes sichtbar bleibt. Hieraus ergibt sich, dass historische Aspekte auch bei der Untersuchung der aktuellen rechtlichen Situation von Ausländern und ethnischen Minderheiten berücksichtigt werden sollten.

Zusammenfassend zeigt die frühe Geschichte der Ausländer in Japan die komplexe Beziehung des Landes zur ausländischen Migration. Von Skepsis und Verfolgung während der kurzen Episode christlicher Missionierung im 16. Jahrhundert, über nahezu vollständige Isolation zur Zeit der *Sakoku*-Ära, bis hin zur Kolonisierung und Ausbeutung von Nachbarsstaaten während der ersten Hälfte des 20. Jahrhunderts lässt sich sagen, dass jedenfalls die Geschichte Japans keine inklusive Haltung gegenüber Ausländern offenbart. Auch heute zeigen Diskriminierungserfahrungen von Ausländern und ethnischen Minderheiten in Japan, dass diese historischen Auffassungen bis zu einem gewissen Grad auch nach der Demokratisierung des Landes

---

(Hrsg.), Rethinking Historical Injustice and Reconciliation in Northeast Asia: The Korean experience (2017), S. 55 (56).

27 *Park* (Anm. 26), S. 56; Duró/Palmer, Japan's Forgotten Korean Forced Laborers: The Search for Hidden Wartime Graves in Hokkaido, in: International Labor and Working-Class History (2. April 2024), S. 1–3.

28 Premierminister Suga, Kabinettsdokument Nr. 204, Frage Nr. 98 (Shūgiin, 27. April 2021); *Webster*, South Korea Shatters the Paradigm: Corporate Liability, Historical Accountability, and the Second World War, in: UCLA Journal of International Law and Foreign Affairs 26 (2022), S. 123.

29 *Tsunemoto*, Rights and Identifications of Ethnic Minorities in Japan: Indigenous Ainu and Resident Koreans, in: Asia-Pacific Journal on Human Rights and the Law 2, Nr. 1 (2001), S. 131–133.

30 *Japan Immigration Services Agency* (Einwanderungsbehörde Japans), 令和５年末現在における在留外国人数について, *reiwa 5-nenmatsu genzai ni okeru zairyū gaikokujinsū ni tsuite* (Zur Gesamtanzahl wohnhafter ausländischer Staatsbürger zum Jahresende 2023), Pressemitteilung (22. März 2024).

noch präsent sind.[31] Aus diesem Grund liefert die japanische Geschichte wichtige Hintergrunderkenntnisse, um die Rechtsstellung der Ausländer im japanischen Recht auch im Hier-und-Jetzt zu bewerten. Im Folgenden soll zunächst der Schutz von Ausländern gegen staatliche Grundrechtseingriffe unter der japanischen Nachkriegsverfassung von 1947 analysiert werden. Hierzu wird zunächst dargestellt, welche Rolle die Frage der Ausländerrechte in den Verfassungsberatungen zwischen der amerikanischen Militärverwaltung und der japanischen Regierung spielte. Sodann wird die aktuelle Rechtslage anhand des für Ausländerrechte in Japan bedeutenden McLean-Urteils des japanischen OGH kritisch erläutert, bevor auf neuere Entwicklungen in der Rechtsprechung eingegangen wird.

1. Die Frage der Ausländerrechte in den Verfassungsberatungen

Nach dem Zweiten Weltkrieg war der Schutz von Ausländern für die amerikanische Militärverwaltung ein zentrales Anliegen bei der Ausarbeitung der neuen japanischen Verfassung. Ein erster Sechs-Punkte-Plan vom 7. Januar 1946 zur Reform des japanischen Regierungssystems, entworfen vom „Koordinierungskomitee von Staat, Krieg und Marine“ (SWNCC), forderte ausdrücklich die Gewährleistung elementarer Grundrechte für „japanische Staatsbürger und alle Personen unter japanischer Gerichtsbarkeit.“[32] Im ersten Verfassungsentwurf vorgelegt am 13. Februar 1946 von General Douglas MacArthur fand dieses Grundprinzip Ausdruck in Artikel 13 („Alle natürlichen Personen sind vor dem Gesetz gleich.“), sowie Artikel 16 („Ausländer haben Anspruch auf den gleichen Schutz durch das Gesetz.“).[33] Die ausdrückliche Regelung der Gleichheit ausländischer Staatsbürger vor dem Gesetz zeigt, welche Bedeutung die amerikanischen Besatzungsbehörden der Frage des verfassungsrechtlichen Schutzes von Ausländern beimaßen.

Wie jedoch in der Literatur beispielsweise von Webster und Fisher beschrieben, wurden diese expliziten Bestimmungen zu den verfassungsmäßigen Rechten von Ausländern schrittweise durch nuancierte Änderungen und Übersetzungen der englischen Entwürfe ins Japanische aus dem Verfassungstext entfernt.[34] Der oben genannte Artikel 16 des Verfassungsentwurfes, welcher Ausländern expliziten Grundrechtsschutz gewähren sollte, verschwand vollständig. Vordergründig wurde die Streichung von der japanischen Seite damit begründet, dass der Schutz von Ausländern schon durch die allgemeine Gleichheitsklausel der Verfassung, sowie dem Verbot der Diskriminierung aufgrund der Rasse in Artikel 14 des finalen Verfassungstextes ausreichend gewährleistet, und eine explizite Erwähnung ausländischer Staats-

---

31 Zu fremdenfeindlicher Diskriminierung in Japan: *Pence*, Japanese Only: Xenophobic Exclusion in Japan's Private Sphere, in: New York International Law Review 20, Nr. 2 (Summer 2007), S. 101.

32 Dokumente der japanischen Parlamentsbibliothek, Documents with Commentaries Part 3 Formulation of the GHQ Draft and Response of the Japanese Government, 3–2 Reform of the Japanese Governmental System (SWNCC 228), National Diet Library.

33 Dokumente der japanischen Parlamentsbibliothek, Documents with Commentaries Part 3 Formulation of the GHQ Draft and Response of the Japanese Government, 3–15 GHQ Draft, February 13, 1946, National Diet Library.

34 *Fisher* (Anm. 12), S. 109; *Webster* (Anm. 12), S. 435.

bürger deshalb nichtmehr erforderlich sei. Jedoch merken Webster und Fisher zurecht an, dass die finale Version des Artikels 14 nicht das gleiche Schutzniveau gewährleisten könne, wie seine Vorgänger in Artikel 13 und 16 der früheren Verfassungsentwürfe.[35]

Dies ist nicht zuletzt dadurch bedingt, dass auch die allgemeine Gleichheitsklausel der Verfassung (in den Entwürfen zunächst Artikel 13, heute Artikel 14) essenziellen Veränderungen unterzogen wurde. So verschwand eine frühere Erwähnung der Staatsbürgerschaft als verbotenes Anknüpfungsmerkmal in den speziellen Diskriminierungsverboten des Gleichheitssatzes. Schließlich wurde auch die Formulierung „Alle natürlichen Personen (自然人, *shizen-jin*) sind vor dem Gesetz gleich" geändert zu „Alle Staatsbürger (国民, *kokumin*) sind vor dem Gesetz gleich".[36] Von besonderer Wichtigkeit ist hier der Blick auf den Wechsel im japanischen Wortlaut. Die finale Formulierung „*kokumin*" lässt sich heute am ehesten mit *Staatsbürger* übersetzen und läuft der universellen Formulierung des ersten Entwurfes somit diametral entgegen.[37] Obwohl es semantisch nicht ausgeschlossen gewesen wäre, auch Ausländer unter diesen Begriff zu fassen, ließ Artikel 10 des endgültigen Verfassungsentwurfs keinen Zweifel daran, dass „*kokumin*" als „Staatsbürger" zu verstehen sei. Artikel 10 legt fest, dass die Bedingungen zum Erwerb des Status als „*kokumin*" durch das Gesetz geregelt werden. Zu diesem Zweck wurde später das japanische Staatsangehörigkeitsgesetz verabschiedet, welches dem Abstammungsprinzip (*ius sanguinis*) folgt.[38] In diesem Zusammenhang kann das dritte Kapitel der Verfassung, das den Titel „Rechte und Pflichten der *kokumin*" trägt, letztlich nur als „Rechte und Pflichten der Staatsbürger" verstanden werden. Die unmissverständliche Anerkennung des Grundrechtsschutzes für Ausländer in der japanischen Nachkriegsverfassung, welche anfangs von General MacArthur explizit gefordert wurde, war somit am Ende der Entwurfsberatungen gänzlich aus dem Verfassungstext verschwunden.

Es wäre einfach, dieses Ergebnis auf sprachliche und semantische Unterschiede zurückzuführen. Wie Fisher jedoch argumentiert, ist das Verschwinden der expliziten Erwähnung von Ausländern in der japanischen Verfassung nicht einfach ein Fall von „lost in translation"[39]. Vielmehr sei der Ausschluss von Ausländern durch schrittweises methodisches Vorgehen der japanischen Vertreter in den Beratungen zur Verfassungsausarbeitung erfolgt, welche es ablehnten, Ausländern den gleichen Schutz unter der Verfassung zu gewähren.[40] Es ist schwer nachzuvollziehen, warum die US-Amerikanischen Vertreter derart bereitwillig einer so drastischen Verzerrung ihrer ursprünglichen verfassungsrechtlichen Vision zustimmten. Ob dies aufgrund von sprachlichen Missverständnissen, Zeitdruck, Überredung oder schlicht Naivität geschah, kann nicht abschließend beantwortet werden. Das Ergebnis ist jedoch eine Verfassung, die Ausländer weder explizit noch implizit einbezieht, wodurch die Fra-

35 *Fisher* (Anm. 12), S. 109 (123); *Webster* (Anm. 12), S. 444.

36 *Webster* (Anm. 12), S. 444.

37 Ausführlich zur Wortwahl *Webster* (Anm. 12), S. 445 ff.

38 Staatsbürgerschaftsgesetz (国籍法, *kokuseki-hō*), Gesetz Nr. 147 aus dem Jahr 1950, zul. geändert am 1. April 2024; s. auch *Webster* (Anm. 12), S. 44).

39 So auch *Fisher* (Anm. 12), S. 121.

40 *Webster* (Anm. 12), S. 445.

ge der Rechte von Ausländern und deren Schutz vollständig den Gerichten und der Verfassungsinterpretation überlassen wird.

2. Das „McLean"-Urteil des OGH als Grundsatzentscheidung

Im Jahr 1978 beantwortete der japanische OGH die Frage nach dem Einbezug ausländischer Staatsbürger in den Schutz der Verfassung in einem wegweisenden Urteil, welches heute allgemein unter Bezug auf den Namen des Klägers als „McLean"-Urteil bekannt ist.[41] McLean war ein US-amerikanischer Staatsbürger, welcher im Oktober 1969 zunächst mit einem Ein-Jahres Visum als Englischlehrer nach Japan gekommen war, während seines Aufenthalts jedoch auch zunehmend politisch aktiv wurde. So beteiligte er sich unter anderem an Demonstrationen gegen den Vietnamkrieg, gegen den 1960 zwischen Japan und den USA unterzeichneten gegenseitigen Sicherheitsvertrag,[42] sowie gegen die japanische Einwanderungs- bzw. Aufenthaltspolitik. Als McLean nun kurz vor Ablauf seines Visums dessen Verlängerung um ein weiteres Jahr beantragte, wurde sein Antrag vom Justizministerium als zuständiger Behörde auf Grundlage des japanischen Einwanderungsgesetzes[43] abgelehnt. Artikel 21 Abs. 3 des Einwanderungsgesetzes stellt die Visumsverlängerung in das Ermessen der Behörde, und schreibt fest, dass diese den Antrag auf Verlängerung nur dann genehmigen *kann*, „wenn die Behörde aufgrund der vom Antragssteller eingereichten Dokumente einen triftigen Grund dafür erkennt, dass eine Verlängerung des Aufenthaltszeitraums angemessen erscheint."[44]

Das Justizministerium begründete die Ablehnung zum einen damit, dass McLean es zuvor versäumt hatte, die Einwanderungsbehörden über einen kurz nach seiner Einreise erfolgten Wechsel des Arbeitsplatzes zu informieren. Weitaus schwerer wogen in der Ablehnungsentscheidung jedoch die politischen Aktivitäten McLeans. Für das Justizministerium stand fest, dass derartige politische Betätigungen von Ausländern dazu geeignet seien, zum einen die Beziehungen Japans mit seinen Partnerländern (wie hier den USA) zu beschädigen, und darüber hinaus auch befürchtet werden müsse, dass hierdurch in unerwünschter Weise Einfluss auf die politische Willensbildung des japanischen Volkes genommen werden könne.[45]

McLean klagte gegen den Ablehnungsbescheid und bekam vor dem Bezirksgericht Tokio zunächst Recht, woraufhin das Justizministerium Berufung einlegte und vor dem Hohen Gerichtshof Tokio die Aufhebung des erstinstanzlichen Urteils erringen

41 OGH Japan, Grand Bench, 4. Oktober 1978, Minshū 32 No. 7 1223.

42 Vertrag über gegenseitige Kooperation und Sicherheit zwischen Japan und den Vereinigten Staaten vom 19. Januar 1960.

43 Gesetz zur Einwanderungskontrolle und Anerkennung von Flüchtlingen (出入国管理及び難民認定法, *shutsunyūkoku kanri oyobi nanmin nintei hō*), Kabinettsbeschluss Nr. 319, 4. Oktober 1951, zul. geändert am 12. Dezember 2024, im Folgenden „Einwanderungsgesetz".

44 Art. 21 Abs. 3 Einwanderungsgesetz, Übersetzung aus dem Japanischen durch den Autor.

45 Aus den Ausführungen im Urteil, OGH Japan, Grand Bench, 4. Oktober 1978, Minshū 32 No. 7, 1223.

konnte.[46] In letzter Instanz bestätigte der japanische OGH das Berufungsurteil mit Entscheidung vom 4. Oktober 1978, womit McLean endgültig seinen Aufenthaltstitel verlor.

Zur Begründung führte der OGH mehrere Argumente an. Zum einen stellte der Gerichtshof klar, dass Artikel 22 der Verfassung, welcher die Bewegungsfreiheit schützt, keine Regelungen über die Einreise *nach* Japan enthalte und deshalb für Ausländer auch kein subjektives Recht auf Einreise gewähre. Darüber hinaus bestünde auch nach dem Völkergewohnheitsrecht in Abwesenheit spezieller Verträge keine Pflicht für Staaten, Ausländern die Einreise auf ihr Staatsgebiet zu gewähren. Aus diesem Grund sei es der freien Entscheidung des Staates überlassen, wem zu welchen Bedingungen die Einreise gewährt werden soll. Nach Ansicht des Gerichts folge hieraus auch, dass für Ausländer nicht nur kein Recht auf Einreise, sondern auch kein Recht auf Aufenthalt allgemein bestehe. Demnach sei auch die Verlängerung einer Aufenthaltsgenehmigung in das freie Ermessen der zuständigen Behörde, hier des Justizministeriums, gestellt. In diese Ermessensentscheidung könne das Justizministerium schließlich auch politische Fragen einstellen, wie bspw. die Auswirkungen der politischen Betätigung ausländischer Staatsbürger auf die japanische Gesellschaft oder auf die Beziehungen Japans zu anderen Staaten. Ausnahmen würden sich nur in äußerst eng umschriebenen Fällen ergeben, in denen die Entscheidung offensichtlich jeder faktischen Grundlage entbehre, oder in denen die Entscheidung nach vorherrschenden gesellschaftlichen Normen als eindeutig grob unangemessen anzusehen sei.

Auch wenn diese schier grenzenlose Ausweitung des behördlichen Ermessensspielraums in Einwanderungsfragen des Urteils aus rechtsstaatlichen Gesichtspunkten Fragen aufwirft, darf zugleich nicht übersehen werden, dass das Urteil erstmals eine höchstrichterliche Klarstellung zur Frage nach dem Einbezug ausländischer Staatsbürger in den Schutz der japanischen Verfassung lieferte. So stellte das Gericht bezüglich der grundsätzlichen Frage nach der Grundrechtsträgerschaft von Ausländern klar, dass die Grundrechte des dritten Kapitels der Verfassung auch ausländische Staatsbürger schützen. Ausnahme hiervon seien lediglich diejenigen Grundrechte, welche ihrem Wesen nach nur an japanische Staatsbürger gerichtet sind.[47]

Das McLean-Urteil beantwortete somit endlich die Fragen, welche durch das „Herausschreiben"[48] der Ausländerrechte aus der Verfassung während der Entwurfsverhandlungen offengeblieben waren. Zuvor gab es in dieser Frage lediglich einen Theorienstreit in der japanischen Rechtswissenschaft, hauptsächlich zwischen der sogenannten „Wortlauttheorie (文言説, *mongon-setsu*)" und der „Eigenschaftstheorie (性質説, *seishitsu-setsu*)."[49] Die Erstere argumentiert mit Blick auf den Wortlaut

46 Bezirksgericht Tokio, 2. Zivilkammer, 27. März 1973; Hoher Gerichtshof Tokio, 2. Zivilkammer, 25. September 1975.

47 Vor allem politische Rechte, wie bspw. das Wahlrecht in Artikel 15.

48 *Webster* (Anm. 12), S. 444, Übersetzung aus dem Englischen durch den Autor.

49 Ein Überblick findet sich (auf Japanisch) bei: *Muramatsu*, 外国人の政治的権利と主権—政治的権利を巡って (*gaikokujin no seijitekikenri to shuken – seijitekikenri wo megutte* = Zu den politischen Rechten von Ausländern und Souveränität – ein Überblick über die politischen Rechte), Kenpō Kenkyū 52 (2020), S. 118 ff.

der Verfassung ähnlich zur Typisierung im Deutschen Grundgesetz für eine Kategorisierung der japanischen Grundrechte in Staatsbürgerrechte und Menschenrechte. Tatsächlich gibt es auch in der japanischen Verfassung sprachliche Unterschiede zwischen den verschiedenen Grundrechten. Während sich beispielsweise der Gleichheitssatz in Artikel 14 explizit nur auf Staatsbürger (*kokumin*) bezieht („Alle Staatsbürger (すべて国民, *subete kokumin*) sind vor dem Gesetz gleich"), spricht die Berufs- sowie Bewegungsfreiheit in Artikel 22 von „allen Menschen (何人も, *nanbito mo*)".[50] Jedoch wird der Wortlauttheorie entgegengehalten, dass die Verfassung von 1947 trotz oberflächlicher Differenzierung im Wortlaut eben keine scharfe Trennung in Staatsbürgerrechte und Jedermannrechte vornimmt. So spreche z. B. das Recht auf Aufgabe der eigenen Staatsbürgerschaft in Artikel 22 Abs. 2 von „allen Menschen", jedoch ergebe sich schon aus Logikgründen, dass diese Vorschrift nur an japanische Staatsbürger adressiert sein könne.[51] Herrschende Lehre war und ist mithin die Eigenschaftstheorie, wie sie auch von Nobuyoshi Ashibe, dem wohl herausragendsten Verfassungsrechtler Japans vertreten wurde.[52]

Mit seiner Entscheidung im McLean-Urteil stellte sich nun schließlich auch der japanische OGH auf die Seite der Eigenschaftstheorie. Zur Erinnerung: Nach Auffassung des Gerichts schützen die Grundrechte der Verfassung auch ausländische Staatsbürger, mit Ausnahme derjenigen Grundrechte, welche ihrem Wesen (ihrer Eigenschaft) nach nur an japanische Staatsbürger gerichtet sein können. Dieser Einbezug in den Schutz der Verfassung war jedoch gewissermaßen ein Pyrrhus-Sieg für Ausländer in Japan. Das Urteil schränkte nämlich sogleich ein, dass es für Ausländer eben kein Recht auf Einreise oder Aufenthalt in Japan gäbe und der Schutz der Grundrechte somit lediglich innerhalb des gesetzlichen bzw. administrativen Rahmens des Einwanderungssystems gewährt sei. Den an der Entscheidung über eine Verlängerung der Aufenthaltserlaubnis beteiligten Behörden stehe es deshalb frei, die Ausübung der Grundrechte durch Ausländer als negatives Kriterium in ihre Ermessensausübung einzustellen, wie im Falle von McLean und seinen politischen Aktivitäten, welche nach Ansicht des Gerichtes grundsätzlich von der Rede- und Versammlungsfreiheit in Artikel 21 geschützt gewesen seien.

Im Ergebnis läuft der Grundrechtsschutz für Ausländer gegenüber dem Staat somit leer. Neben der grundsätzlichen Frage nach der Schlüssigkeit der Argumentation des Gerichts stellt sich die Frage, welchen Wert der Einbezug von Ausländern in den Schutz der Verfassung überhaupt hat, wenn die Ausübung dieser Grundrechte ohne Probleme zum Verlust der Aufenthaltsgenehmigung führen könne. Wenig überraschend sieht sich das Urteil regelmäßiger Kritik seitens der Medien und rechtswissenschaftlichen Literatur ausgesetzt. Ein Teil dieser Kritik fokussiert sich hierbei auf den Verweis des OGH auf das Völkerrecht. Schließlich betone das Gericht in seiner Urteilsbegründung, dass auch nach dem Völkergewohnheitsrecht in Abwesenheit

50 Artikel 14, 22 Verfassung des Staates Japan, Übersetzung durch den Autor.

51 *Takanori*, 外国人の公務就任権に関する予備的考察：外国人の人権享有主体性についての一試論 (*gaikokujin no kōmu shūnin ken ni kansuru yobiteki kōsatsu: Gaikokujin no jinken kyōyu shutaisei ni tsuite no ichi shiron* = Vorläufige Überlegungen zum Recht von Ausländern, öffentliche Ämter zu bekleiden: Ein Beitrag zur Grundrechtsträgerschaft von Ausländern). Takaoka Hōgaku 31 (März 2013), S. 75.

52 *Ashibe*, 憲法, (*kenpō* = Verfassungsrecht), 8. Auflage (2023), S. 94 ff.

spezieller Verträge keine Pflicht für Staaten bestehe, Ausländern die Einreise auf ihr Staatsgebiet zu gewähren. Kondō Atsushi verweist deshalb zurecht darauf, dass nach aktueller Rechtslage für Staaten durchaus auch auf völkerrechtlicher Ebene Verpflichtungen bestehen können, Ausländern die Einreise bzw. den Aufenthalt zu gewähren.[53] Diese können sich etwa aus dem völkerrechtliche Willkürverbot, dem non-refoulement Prinzip, oder auch dem völkerrechtlichen Recht auf Achtung des Familienlebens bzw. Einheit der Familie ergeben.[54] Die Folgen der McLean-Doktrin gerade für Familien, die aus einem japanischen und einem nicht-japanischen Elternteil bestehen, wurde auch von Izumi Tokuji, ehemaliger Richter am OGH, in einem Zeitungsinterview herausgehoben, in welchem er die Aufrechterhaltung des McLean-Urteils seitens der Judikative als „fahrlässig" bezeichnete.[55] Während das Vorhandensein eigener Kinder mit einem japanischen Partner auch Ausländern einen Aufenthaltsanspruch geben könne, stünden diese nach dem geltenden Recht ohne Schutz, wenn der japanische Teil lediglich Kinder aus einer vorherigen Beziehung mit in die neue Familie einbringe.

Zusätzlich zu der Kritik aus völkerrechtlicher Sicht muss festgehalten werden, dass das McLean-Urteil eine zweifelhafte Umkehr der traditionellen Normenhierarchie vornimmt. Schließlich stellt auch die Verfassung selbst in Artikel 98 klar, dass die Verfassung die „höchste Rechtsnorm des Landes"[56] ist. Nicht gesetzgeberische bzw. administrative Entscheidungen im Rahmen der Einwanderungspolitik sollten dem Grundrechtsschutz für Ausländer Schranken auferlegen, sondern der durch die Grundrechte gewährte Schutz sollte eben diesen Entscheidungen Grenzen aufzeigen.[57] Die Machtlosigkeit ausländischer Staatsbürger in Aufenthaltsfragen, selbst von solchen, welche sich seit Jahren bis Jahrzehnten in Japan aufhalten, zeigte sich jedoch erneut während der mehr als zwei Jahre andauernden Grenzschließungen Japans während der Corona-Pandemie.[58] Im Rahmen der rigiden Einreisesperren machte es keinen Unterschied, ob sich jemand erst wenige Monate oder mehrere Jahrzehnte im Land aufhielt; wer einmal ausgereist war, kam nicht wieder herein. Dagegen stellte der Menschenrechtsausschuss der Vereinten Nationen bezüglich der Umsetzung des ICCPR in Japan bereits im Jahr 1998 fest, dass das Recht auf Rückkehr in das eigene Land aus Artikel 12 Abs. 4 des Vertrages nicht so auszulegen sei,

---

53 *Kondō*, マクリーン事件判決の抜本的な見直し (*makurīn jiken hanketsu no bapponteki na minaoshi* = Eine Grundsätzliche Neubewertung des McLean-Urteils), in: Meijō Hougaku/Meijo Daigaku Hougakkai 70, Nr. 4 (2021), S. 1.

54 *Kondō* (Anm. 53), S. 7 ff.

55 *Ikeo*, Shinichi, 家族を引き裂く非人道的な入管行政…いまだに46年前の「マクリーン判決」が根拠このままでいいの? (*kazoku wo hikisaku hijindōteki na nyūkan gyōsei… imada ni 46 nen mae no „Makurīn hanketsu" ga konkyo – kono mama de ii no?* = Unmenschliche Einwanderungspolitik zerreißt Familien… immer noch stellt die McLean Entscheidung von vor 46 Jahren die Grundlage – kann es hierbei wirklich bleiben?), Tokyo Shimbun (21. Januar 2024).

56 Artikel 98 Verfassung des Staates Japan, Übersetzung durch den Autor.

57 Krit. *Jones*, Japan's Constitution won't protect revolting foreigners, The Japan Times (11. Oktober 2015).

58 *Knör*, Verfassungsblog, 30. Juni 2020.

dass hiermit nur das Land der eigenen Staatsbürgerschaft gemeint sei.[59] Leider gab es gegen die pandemiebedingten Einreiseverbote keine einzige Klage, weshalb unklar bleibt, ob der OGH seine Rechtsprechung in der heutigen Zeit aufrecht gehalten hätte. Jedenfalls bei den unteren Gerichten scheint sich jedoch eine, wenn auch sehr vorsichtige, Lockerung der McLean-Doktrin zu zeigen, was im Folgende näher beschrieben werden soll.

3. Neuere Entwicklungen – Das Recht auf rechtliches Gehör als Ausnahme?

Der japanische OGH hielt auch nach seiner Entscheidung im McLean-Fall an seiner dort entwickelten Dogmatik fest. So entschied das Gericht im Jahr 1998, dass der Verlust der unbefristeten Aufenthaltsgenehmigung für eine Zainichi-Koreanerin aufgrund ihrer Weigerung im Rahmen des Antrags auf eine Wiedereinreisegenehmigung Fingerabdrücke abzugeben, rechtmäßig gewesen sei.[60] Auch der Ausschluss ausländischer Staatbürger von bestimmten staatlichen Sozialleistungen wurde in einem Urteil von 2014 aufrechterhalten.[61] Somit bleibt zumindest auf höchstrichterlicher Ebene festzuhalten, dass die 1978 im McLean-Urteil entwickelte Dogmatik auch weiterhin Bestand hat.

Ein Urteil des Hohen Gerichtshofs Tokio von 2021[62] deutet jedoch an, dass zumindest bei den unteren Gerichten hier womöglich der Beginn einer Trendwende zu erkennen sein könnte. Kläger in dem Fall waren 2 sri-lankische Staatsbürger, welche zunächst in Japan Asyl beantragt hatten. Nachdem ihr Asylantrag abgelehnt wurde, legten die beiden Kläger zunächst Einspruch gegen den Ablehnungsbescheid ein. Als die Kläger jedoch im Dezember 2014 die Einwanderungsbehörde in Tokio aufsuchten, um eine Verlängerung ihrer Befreiung aus der sonst für alle Asylbewerber obligatorischen Ingewahrsamnahme zu beantragen, wurde ihnen plötzlich mitgeteilt, dass ihr Einspruch abgelehnt wurde. Die Kläger wurden daraufhin in Gewahrsam genommen und nicht einmal 24 Stunden später nach Sri Lanka abgeschoben. Durch diesen überaus kurzen Zeitraum zwischen der Belehrung über die Ablehnung ihres Einspruches und der Abschiebung am nächsten Tag gab es für sie keine Möglichkeit, Klage gegen die Entscheidung der Einwanderungsbehörde einzulegen. Der Hohe Gerichtshof Tokio sah hierin eine Verletzung ihrer verfassungsmäßigen Rechte auf rechtliches Gehör (Artikel 32), auf rechtmäßiges Verfahren (Artikel 31), sowie des Rechtes auf Achtung ihrer Person und ihrer Freiheit (Artikel 13), wobei der Schwerpunkt auf dem Recht auf rechtliches Gehör lag.

Besonders schwer wog für das Gericht, dass die Behörde laut den Verfahrensunterlagen wohl schon im Januar, bzw. für den zweiten Kläger im Oktober 2014 intern entschieden hatte, den Einspruch gegen die Ablehnung ihres Antrages auf Asyl abzulehnen. Obwohl die Kläger in der Zwischenzeit schon einmal bei der Einwanderungsbe-

---

59 *Ausschuss der Vereinten Nationen zur Beseitigung von Rassendiskriminierung*, Abschließende Bemerkungen des UN-Menschenrechtsausschusses zum vierten regelmäßigen Bericht zu Japan, 19/11/98. CCPR/C/79/Add.102, S. 19. November 1998.

60 OGH Japan, Zweiter Senat, 10. April 1998, Heisei 6 (gyō-tsu) 153.

61 OGH Japan, Zweiter Senat, 18. Juli 2014, Heisei 24 (gyō-hi) 45.

62 Hoher Gerichtshof Tokio, 22. September 2021, Reiwa 2 (ne) 1423.

hörde in Tokio erschienen waren, wurde ihnen die Ablehnung erst im Dezember mitgeteilt, bevor sie bereits am nächsten Tag abgeschoben wurden. Das Gericht sah hierin einen Beleg dafür, dass die Behörde gerade wollte, dass den Antragsstellern keine Gelegenheit zur Einreichung einer Klage bleiben würde, weshalb gar eine vorsätzliche Verletzung der Rechte der Kläger vorlag. Schließlich äußerte zumindest einer der Kläger auch direkt seinen Wunsch, Klage gegen die Entscheidung der Behörde einzulegen. Auch wenn das Einwanderungsgesetz grundsätzlich keine Bestimmungen enthalte, welche die Aussetzung des Vollzugs im Falle einer Klageerhebung vorsieht, so bestünde dennoch eine Verwaltungspraxis, wonach die Abschiebung für die Dauer des Verfahrens aufgeschoben wird (anderes gilt bei der vorherigen Erhebung des Widerspruchs, welcher gemäß Artikel 61–2–9 Abs. 3 (zum Zeitpunkt des Verfahrens 61–2–6 Abs. 3) zur Aussetzung der Abschiebung führt).[63] In jedem Fall sah das Gericht hier eine vorsätzliche Verletzung der prozessualen Rechte der Kläger aus Artikel 31 und 32 der Verfassung, weshalb es auf das Bestehen einer speziellen gesetzlichen Regelung letztlich nicht ankam.

Für eine Bewertung der Fortwirkung des McLean-Urteils bedeutet das Urteil des Hohen Gerichtshofs Tokio, dass zumindest bezüglich der Gewähr rechtlichen Gehörs eine vorsichtige Einschränkung des behördlichen Spielraums zu erwarten sein könnte. Ob sich jedoch auch der japanische OGH solchen Vorstößen anschließen würde, bleibt abzuwarten. Da die beklagte Behörde im vorliegenden Fall auf das Einlegen einer Revision zum höchsten Gericht des Landes verzichtete, bleibt trotz der im Vergleich zu 1978 stark gestiegenen Einwanderungszahlen und der damit einhergehenden wachsenden Bedeutung des Rechtsschutzes für Ausländer in Japan unklar, ob die im McLean-Urteil entwickelte Doktrin auch heute weiterhin uneingeschränkte Unterstützung seitens des Gerichts erfahren würde.[64]

4. Zwischenfazit

Ein Blick auf die Rechtsprechung zeigt, dass Ausländer in Japan trotz des grundsätzlichen Einbezugs in den Schutz der Grundrechte der japanischen Verfassung oftmals in der Realität schutzlos gestellt sind. Jedenfalls in aufenthalts- und einwanderungsrechtlichen Fragen stellt die grenzenlose Ausweitung des behördlichen Ermessensspielraums, wie sie vom OGH in seiner McLean-Entscheidung begründet wurde, ein oftmals unüberwindbares Hindernis bei der Anfechtung von Verwaltungsentscheidungen dar. Aber auch in anderen Fragen mit Staatsbezug, wie beispielsweise der Auszahlung staatlicher Sozialleistungen, oder gar der Gewähr des Wahlrechts auf lokaler Ebene, beruft sich die Rechtsprechung durchweg auf den Vorrang der ge-

63 Hanrei Taimuzu Nr. 1502, S. 57.

64 So ist die Anzahl ausländischer Staatsbürger an der japanischen Gesamtbevölkerung von 1990 bis 2024 von 0,85 % auf 2,7 % gestiegen, Zahlen aus: Japanisches Ministerium für Innere Angelegenheiten und Kommunikation, 住民基本台帳に基づく人口、人口動態及び世帯数 (*jūmin kihon daichō ni motozuku jinkō, jinkō dōtai oyobi setaisū* = Bevölkerung, Demografische Trends und Anzahl der Haushalte basierend auf dem Einwohnerregister), 1. Januar 2024.

setzgeberischen Einschätzungsprärogative.[65] Wenn auch die Gerichte hierdurch ausländische Staatsbürger von den genannten Bereichen nicht gänzlich ausschließen und die Möglichkeit einer entsprechenden gesetzlichen Regelung offen lassen, so bleibt es doch mit Blick auf die fast ununterbrochene Regierungszeit der konservativen Liberaldemokratischen Partei LDP zweifelhaft, ob eine solche Gesetzesinitiative zum besseren Schutz von Ausländern, gerade in Aufenthaltsfragen, erwartet werden kann. Immerhin geben Entscheidungen wie das Urteil des Hohen Gerichtshofs Tokio zum Recht auf rechtliches Gehör Hoffnung, dass in naher Zukunft ein Update auch seitens des OGH zu seiner im McLean-Urteil festgelegten Dogmatik zu erwarten sein könnte.

IV. Grundrechtsschutz für Ausländer gegenüber Privaten

Anders als bei Grundrechtsverletzungen durch staatliches Handeln, sind die Erfolgsaussichten von Klagen gegen Grundrechtsverletzungen durch Private für ausländische Staatsbürger in Japan deutlich höher. Dies mag zunächst verwundern, wenn man bedenkt, dass es in Japan bis heute keine umfassende Antidiskriminierungsgesetzgebung gibt. Im Folgenden soll daher aufgezeigt werden, wie die japanischen Gerichte in Anbetracht des Fehlens eines solchen gesetzlichen Diskriminierungsverbots durch Anwendung verfassungsrechtlicher sowie völkerrechtlicher Schutzvorschriften trotzdem effektiven Schutz vor Diskriminierung gewähren.

1. (Fehlende) Antidiskriminierungsgesetzgebung

Wie bereits erwähnt kennt das japanische Recht kein allgemeines Anti-Diskriminierungsgesetz wie etwa das deutsche Allgemeine Gleichbehandlungsgesetz (AGG) oder den US-amerikanischen Civil Rights Act.[66] Lediglich im Bereich der Hassrede wurde 2016 mit dem Gesetz zur Beseitigung von Hassrede[67] zum ersten Mal ein Gesetz erlassen, welches sich diskriminierenden Äußerungen mit Bezug zur ethnischen Herkunft widmet. Für die Betrachtung der rechtlichen Lage im Verhältnis von Ausländern zu privaten Akteuren bietet es sich daher zunächst an, zwischen Diskriminierung im allgemeinen Zivilrechtsverkehr und Hassrede zu unterscheiden.

Während es für den *allgemeinen Zivilrechtsverkehr* tatsächlich keine einfachgesetzliche Regelung im japanischen Recht gibt, welche Benachteiligung aufgrund be-

---

65 Zu Sozialleistungen OGH Japan, Zweiter Senat, 18. Juli 2014, Heisei 24 (gyō-hi) 45; Zum Wahlrecht auf lokaler Ebene OGH Japan, Zweiter Senat, 28. Februar 1995, Heisei 5 (gyō-tsu) 163.

66 Rechtsvergleichend *Kondō*, Hate Speech Regulation and Anti-discrimination in Japan, in Higaki/Nasu (Hrsg.), Hate Speech in Japan (2021), S. 17.

67 Gesetz zur Förderung von Maßnahmen zur Beseitigung von ungerechtfertigten diskriminierenden Äußerungen gegenüber Menschen von außerhalb Japans (本邦外出身者に対する不当な差別的言動の解消に向けた取組の推進に関する法律, *honpōgai-shusshinsha ni taisuru futō na sabetsuteki gendō no kaishō ni muketa torikumi no suishin ni kansuru hōritsu*), Gesetz Nr. 68, 2016, auch bekannt als „Gesetz zur Beseitigung von Hassrede (ヘイトスピーチ解消法, *heito supīchi kaishōhō*)“.

stimmter Merkmale wie etwa Herkunft oder ethnischer Abstammung verbietet, erlangen hier die in der japanischen Verfassung verankerte Gleichheit vor dem Gesetz (Artikel 14) und der Respekt vor dem Individuum (Art. 13), sowie die UN-Anti-Rassismus Konvention ICERD rechtliche Bedeutung. Obwohl, wie oben beschrieben, das Merkmal der Staatsbürgerschaft aus den verbotenen Diskriminierungsmerkmalen in Artikel 14 verschwand, stellte der japanische OGH bereits im Jahr 1950 klar, dass diese im verfassungsrechtlichen Gleichheitssatz enthaltene Aufzählung nicht als abschließend zu verstehen sei, sondern vielmehr Ausdruck des allgemeinen Verfassungsprinzips der Gleichheit vor dem Gesetz sei.[68] Somit ließe sich letzten Endes auch die Diskriminierung aufgrund der Staatsbürgerschaft unter das Diskriminierungsverbot in Artikel 14 subsumieren.[69] Basierend auf der Rechtsprechung des OGH in der McLean-Entscheidung ist somit wohl letztlich auch die Einbeziehung von Ausländern in Artikel 13, welcher als verfassungsrechtliche Auffangklausel fungiert, weniger problematisch, da in Fällen der Grundrechtsverletzung durch Private eben kein Konflikt mit staatlichen Entscheidungen im Bereich der Einwanderungspolitik besteht.[70] Letztlich erlangt für die japanischen Gerichte auch die UN-Anti-Rassismus Konvention ICERD als völkerrechtliche Grundlage Bedeutung in Diskriminierungsfällen.[71] Die Konvention, welche von Japan im Jahr 1995 ratifiziert wurde, verlangt von den Vertragsstaaten, Rassendiskriminierung zu verurteilen und „mit allen geeigneten Mitteln unverzüglich eine Politik der Beseitigung der Rassendiskriminierung in jeder Form und der Förderung des Verständnisses unter allen Rassen zu verfolgen" (Artikel 2 Abs. 1). Für die Gerichte besonders relevant ist auch Artikel 6 der Konvention, welcher von den Vertragsstaaten fordert, effektiven Rechtsschutz in Diskriminierungsfällen sicherzustellen.[72]

Auch im Bereich der *Hassrede* berufen sich die Gerichte auf die oben genannten Vorschriften der UN-Anti-Rassismus Konvention. Jedoch besteht hier mit dem Gesetz zur Beseitigung von Hassrede seit 2016 auch auf einfachgesetzlicher Ebene eine Vorschrift, welche rassistische Hassrede zumindest verurteilt, wenngleich das Gesetz nur von proklamatorischer Natur ist. Das Gesetz verurteilt zwar Hassrede aufgrund der Herkunft, sieht jedoch keine Sanktionsvorschriften jedweder Art vor. Darüber hinaus ist das Gesetz in seiner Definition von Hassrede überaus restriktiv, da Hassrede im Sinne des Gesetzes beschränkt ist, auf

68 OGH Japan, 11. Oktober 1950, Shōwa 25 (a) 292.

69 OGH Japan, Großer Senat, 26. Januar 2005, Heisei 10 (gyō-tsu) 93.

70 Zur Artikel 13 und Hassrede: Hoher Gerichtshof Osaka, 8. Juli 2014, Heisei 25 (ne) Nr. 3235, 2232.

71 Internationales Übereinkommen zur Beseitigung jeder Form von Rassendiskriminierung, 21. Dezember 1965, Resolution 2106 A (XX) der Generalversammlung der Vereinten Nationen, in Kraft getreten am 4. Januar 1969, von Japan ratifiziert am 15. Dezember 1995.

72 Artikel 6 ICERD: „Die Vertragsstaaten gewährleisten jeder Person in ihrem Hoheitsbereich einen wirksamen Schutz und wirksame Rechtsbehelfe durch die zuständigen nationalen Gerichte und sonstigen staatlichen Einrichtungen gegen alle rassisch diskriminierenden Handlungen, (…), sowie das Recht, bei diesen Gerichten eine gerechte und angemessene Entschädigung (…) für jeden infolge von Rassendiskriminierung erlittenen Schaden zu verlangen.", Deutscher Text unter: https://www.institut-fuer-menschenrechte.de/fileadmin/Redaktion/PDF/DB_Menschenrechtsschutz/ICERD/ICERD_Konvention.pdf.

„unfaire diskriminierende Äußerungen und Verhaltensweisen gegenüber Personen mit Herkunftsländern außerhalb Japans (...), die zur Ausgrenzung von Personen anstiften, die aus Ländern oder Regionen außerhalb Japans stammen oder deren Nachkommen sind und die rechtmäßig in Japan leben (...), welche darauf abzielen, die betreffenden Personen aufgrund Ihrer Herkunft von außerhalb Japans aus der lokalen Gemeinschaft auszuschließen."

Das Gesetz beschränkt sich somit nur auf die Diskriminierung von Menschen mit Migrationshintergrund mit legalem Aufenthaltstitel. Nationale Minderheiten, sowie Personen, welche sich illegal in Japan aufhalten, fallen somit nicht unter die Definition des Gesetzes.[73] Es scheint jedoch fraglich, weshalb rassistische Beleidigungen gegen Ausländer, welche sich jenseits der Gültigkeit ihres Visums in Japan aufhalten, weniger zu verurteilen sei als rassistische Beleidigungen gegen Ausländer mit gültiger Aufenthaltserlaubnis.

Das Fehlen effektiver Anti-Diskriminierungsgesetzgebung bzw. die Ineffektivität von Vorschriften wie dem Gesetz zur Beseitigung von Hassrede werden demnach auch seitens der Literatur, sowie der Vereinten Nationen im Rahmen der Überwachung von ICERD regelmäßig kritisiert. Auf UN-Ebene drängte der zuständige Ausschuss für die Beseitigung von Rassendiskriminierung zuletzt im Jahr 2018, dass Japan „im Einklang mit Artikel 1 und 2 des Vertrages spezifische und umfangreiche Gesetzgebung zum Verbot direkter und indirekter Diskriminierung"[74] erlassen solle. Im Bereich der Hassrede lobte der Ausschuss zwar die Bemühungen Japans in Gestalt des 2016 erlassenen Gesetzes, kritisierte jedoch zugleich dessen enge Definition von Hassrede und das Fehlen von Sanktionsvorschriften.[75] In der Literatur wird darüber hinaus betont, dass die Berufung auf verfassungs- bzw. völkerrechtliche Normen in einzelnen positiven Gerichtsentscheidungen nicht die gleiche Wirkung entfalten könne wie ein klar sanktionierendes Gesetz. Ohne das Bestehen einer gesetzlichen Grundlage seien Diskriminierungsklagen somit zudem mit einem hohen finanziellen Risiko verbunden.[76] Schließlich prüften die Gerichte eine diskriminierende Behandlung zunächst auf deren Angemessenheit, weshalb Opfer von Diskriminierung nicht gänzlich sicher sein können, dass auch ihr spezifischer Fall von den Gerichten positiv entschieden würde.[77] Wie Beispiele aus der Rechtsprechung zeigen werden, besteht in der Tat zunächst einmal das Risiko einer Niederlage vor den unteren Instanzen, verbunden mit dem zusätzlichen Kostenaufwand durch den Zug durch die Instanzen. Zunächst soll jedoch im folgenden Abschnitt das Vorgehen der Gerichte in Diskriminierungsfragen näher erörtert werden.

---

73 *Martin*, Striking the Right Balance: Hate Speech Laws in Japan, the United States, and Canada, in: Hastings Const. L.Q. 45, Nr. 3 (Spring 2018), S. 468.

74 Ausschuss der Vereinten Nationen zur Beseitigung von Rassendiskriminierung, „Abschließende Bemerkungen zum 10. und 11. regelmäßigen Berichts zu Japan (CERD/C/JPN/CO/10-11)", 26. September 2018, unter 8.

75 A. a. O., unter 13 und 14.

76 *Pence* (Anm. 31), S. 154 ff.

77 *Myslinska*, Racist Racism: Complicating Whiteness through the Privilege and Discrimination of Westerners in Japan, in: UMKC Law Rev. 83, Nr. 1 (2014), S. 19 ff.

2. Die Theorie der indirekten Anwendung der Grundrechte (間接適用説, *kansetsu tekiyō-setsu*)

Wie bereits erwähnt, lösen die japanischen Gerichte Diskriminierungsfälle in Anbetracht des Fehlens spezieller Antidiskriminierungsgesetzgebung durch Auslegung von Verfassungsrecht und Völkerrecht (ICERD). Bei der Entwicklung dieser Dogmatik standen die Gerichte jedoch zunächst vor der Aufgabe, die grundsätzliche Anwendbarkeit dieser Vorschriften auf Rechtsstreitigkeiten zwischen Privaten zu begründen, da die Grundrechte zunächst als „Abwehrrechte" im Verhältnis zwischen dem Bürger und dem Staat, und Regelungen des Völkerrechts zunächst lediglich als die Vertragsstaaten bindende Vorschriften verstanden wurden.[78] Hierzu entwickelten die Gerichte eine Rechtsfigur, welche zumindest oberflächlich Ähnlichkeiten mit der mittelbaren Drittwirkung im deutschen Verfassungsrecht aufweist.

Nach der „Theorie der indirekten Anwendung" finden verfassungsrechtliche Vorgaben, sowie völkerrechtliche Vorschriften durch Interpretation zivilrechtlicher Generalklauseln indirekten Eingang in die gerichtliche Entscheidung privater Dispute.[79] Von zentraler Bedeutung sind hier Artikel 1 und 90 des japanischen Zivilgesetzes[80] (ZivilG) als allgemeine Vorschriften, sowie Artikel 709 im Bereich des Deliktsrechts. Artikel 1 ZivilG stellt bürgerliche Rechte und deren Ausübung unter den Vorbehalt des öffentlichen Wohls, sowie guten Glaubens. Artikel 90 wiederum erklärt juristische Handlungen, welche gutem Glauben zuwiderlaufen für nichtig. Schließlich verleiht Artikel 709 ZivilG als deliktsrechtliche Vorschrift das Recht, im Falle einer Verletzung eines geschützten Rechts Schadensersatz zu verlangen. Für die japanischen Gerichte fungieren diese Generalklauseln als Einfallstor für die Anwendung verfassungs- bzw. völkerrechtlicher Vorschriften.[81] Schließlich könne die Auslegung solcher Vorschriften durch die Gerichte nicht im luftleeren Raum erfolgen. Vielmehr müsse die Verfassung als „höchstes Gesetz des Landes" (Artikel 98 der Verfassung) erste Anlaufstelle bei der Interpretation uneindeutiger Rechtsvorschriften sein.[82]

Zumindest an der Oberfläche erinnert die Theorie der indirekten Anwendung in Japan an die Theorie der mittelbaren Drittwirkung der Grundrechte in Deutschland. Die Unterschiede liegen hier jedoch im Detail. Während das Bundesverfassungsgericht in seinem Lüth-Urteil die Verfassung zum „Ausdruck einer objektiven Werteordnung" erhob, beschränken sich die japanischen Gerichte lediglich auf die Entscheidung von Einzelfällen durch fallgerechte Anwendung individueller Verfassungsvorschriften. Das japanische Recht bleibt somit ein Stück weit hinter dem Pathos des Bundesverfassungsgerichts zurück und versteht die Grundrechte weiterhin als Ab-

---

78 OGH Japan, Großer Senat, 12. Dezember 1973, 27 Minshū 11, 1536; Hoher Gerichtshof Osaka, 8. Juli 2014, Heisei 25 (ne) Nr. 3235, 2232; *Ashibe* (Anm. 52), S. 113.

79 *Ashibe* (Anm. 52), S. 115 ff.

80 Japanisches Zivilgesetz (民法, *minpō*, Gesetz Nr. 89 aus dem Jahr 1896, zul. geändert am 24. Mai 2024.

81 Mehr hierzu unter 3.

82 *Martin*, Glimmers of Hope: The Evolution of Equality Rights Doctrine in Japanese Courts From a Comparative Perspective, in: Duke J. Comp. & Int'l L. 20, Nr. 167 (2010), S. 174.

wehrrechte des Bürgers gegen den Staat, welche nur in Einzelfällen durch verfassungskonforme Auslegung zivilrechtlicher Generalklauseln in Privatstreitigkeiten zur Anwendung kommen. Im Folgenden werden einige wichtige Gerichtsentscheidungen die Entwicklung sowie praktische Relevanz der Theorie der indirekten Anwendung verdeutlichen.

3. Gerichtsentscheidungen

Die erste, wegweisende Entscheidung eines japanischen Gerichts, welche sich mit der Diskriminierung von Ausländern im Geschäftsverkehr beschäftigte, war ein Urteil des Bezirksgerichts Shizuoka von 1999 zum Ausschluss einer brasilianischen Staatsbürgern aus einem Juweliergeschäft in der Stadt Hamamatsu (im Folgenden „Hamamatsu-Juwelier-Fall").[83] Der Ladeninhaber hatte die Klägerin aufgrund Ihrer Herkunft des Ladens verwiesen und sich dabei auf einen Anstieg von Ladendiebstählen durch Ausländer, insbesondere brasilianischer Herkunft berufen. Das Gericht erkannte in dem Ausschluss eine unzulässige Diskriminierung aufgrund der Herkunft und verurteilte den Ladeninhaber zu einer Schadensersatzzahlung in Höhe von 1,5 Millionen Yen.

Die Entscheidung war aus zwei Gründen von herausragender Bedeutung. Erstens kam das Urteil kurz nachdem Japan 1995 das Internationale Übereinkommen zur Beseitigung jeder Form von Rassendiskriminierung (ICERD) ratifiziert hatte. In einem damals revolutionären Ansatz verwendete das Gericht ICERD als Interpretationsgrundlage bei der Auslegung allgemeiner Bestimmungen des japanischen Deliktsrechts (Artikel 709 ZivilG). In Anbetracht des Fehlens von spezifischer Antidiskriminierungsgesetzgebung, argumentierte das Gericht, dass die Pflicht zur Gewährleistung wirksamen Rechtsschutzes in Artikel 6 ICERD von den Vertragsstaaten zumindest verlangt, dass Opfern von rassenbezogener Diskriminierung die Möglichkeit gegeben wird, vor Gericht Schadensersatz zu verlangen. Hierauf aufbauend verwendete das Gericht die Verpflichtung zur Beseitigung rassenbezogener Diskriminierung in jeder Form aus Artikel 2 ICERD als interpretativen Maßstab, um die Frage der Illegalität einer rechtlichen Handlung (hier die Aufforderung, das Geschäft zu verlassen) gemäß Artikel 709 ZivilG zu entscheiden.

Noch bemerkenswerter ist jedoch, wie der vorsitzende Richter seine Argumentation durch eine detaillierte historische und philosophische Ausarbeitung der Bedeutung der Menschenrechte und der Menschenwürde entwickelte:

> „Menschen sind kleine individuelle Universen für sich, jeder mit einem unverwechselbaren Wert. Diese Vorstellung, dass alle Menschen einen unverwechselbaren Wert haben, bedeutet zugleich, dass alle Menschen frei und gleich sind. Alle Menschen teilen gleichermaßen das Recht auf Leben und das Recht, sich durch ihre eigene Kreativität und ihre eigenen Entscheidungen zu verwirklichen. (…) Indem man Wertgegensätze wie gut und schlecht überwindet und absolute Barmherzigkeit sowie allumfassende, absolute Liebe als seine Religion annimmt, erscheint der wahre Mensch als ein unersetzbares Wesen. Mit anderen Worten, Men-

83 Bezirksgericht Shizuoka, 12. Oktober 1999, 1718 Hanji 92; englische Übersetzung in: *Webster*, Bortz v. Suzuki, Judgment of October 12, 1999, Hamamatsu Branch, Shizuoka District Court, in: Pacific Rim Law & Policy Journal 16, Nr. 3 (2007), S. 631.

schen sind unabhängige, unverwechselbare Wesen, die nicht ersetzt werden können, einschließlich des privaten Aspekts, den wir in einem Lebensgefährten finden mögen. Dies erstreckt sich auf die Vereinigung eines Wesens mit einem anderen, wobei Menschen sich gegenseitig als unverwechselbare Entitäten begegnen. (…) Menschen werden den Wert sowohl von Ausländern als auch von Japanern erkennen, wenn sie sich daran erinnern, dass alle Menschen unverwechselbare Grundrechte genießen, dass alle Menschen tiefe Gefühle der Empathie für Andere hegen und dies dann in der täglichen Praxis durch den Respekt vor anderen umsetzen. (…) Wie oben erwähnt, sollten wir, insofern wir erkennen, dass Freiheit und Gleichheit aus dem Respekt vor anderen Menschen und dem Respekt vor den Grundrechten eines anderen Menschen hervorgehen, Freiheit und Gleichheit als Begleiter von Verantwortung verstehen. Wenn wir dies nicht anerkennen und keine Verantwortung übernehmen, wird nur die frivolste Form von Freiheit und Gleichheit bestehen."[84]

Dieses Zitat zeigt nur einen kleinen Teil der Ausführungen, die sich von der antiken griechischen Philosophie über die christliche Reformation, die deutschen und japanischen Verbrechen gegen die Menschlichkeit während des Zweiten Weltkriegs, bis hin zu den Gefahren moderner Technologie für zwischenmenschliche Beziehungen, der modernen japanischen Gesellschaft und ihrer Sichtweise auf die Grundrechte und letztlich der Natur der Demokratie selbst erstrecken. Im japanischen Rechtssystem, in dem Urteile normalerweise nah an den Argumenten der Parteien bleiben und Richter meist von allgemeinen theoretischen Ausführungen absehen, scheint diese philosophische Herleitung der Bedeutung der Menschenrechte außergewöhnlich, wenn nicht gar fehl am Platz. Indem das Urteil jedoch gerade erklärt, *warum* Gleichheit wichtig ist und wie sie im Kern mit der Menschenwürde selbst verbunden ist, geht die Errungenschaft des Urteils über die Schaffung von bloßer Gerechtigkeit für die beteiligten Parteien hinaus, indem es auch dazu beiträgt, das Bewusstsein für die Bedeutung der Menschenrechte, der Gleichheit und der liberalen Demokratie in Japan zu schärfen.

Die im Hamamatsu-Juwelier-Fall etablierte Doktrin der interpretatorischen Anwendung völker- sowie verfassungsrechtlicher Normen bei der Entscheidung zivilrechtlicher Diskriminierungsfälle kam im Jahr 2002 erneut zur Anwendung, als das Bezirksgericht Sapporo gegen ein öffentliches Badehaus in der Stadt Otaru („Otaru-Onsen-Fall") entschied, welches allen Ausländern und sogar einem in den USA geborenen, und später in Japan eingebürgerten Gast wegen seines westlichen Aussehens den Zutritt verweigerte.[85] Der eingebürgerte Kläger in diesem Fall, Arudou Debito, ist ein bekannter Menschenrechtsaktivist, welcher sich insbesondere im Kampf gegen fremdenfeindliche Diskriminierung in Japan einsetzte. Mit seiner Klage wollte Arudou nicht nur die diskriminierende Praxis des Badehauses anfechten, sondern auch die Stadt Otaru dazu zwingen, wirksame Antidiskriminierungsmaßnahmen zu erlassen. Obwohl das Gericht diese zweite Forderung nicht unterstützte, gab das Gericht Arudou insoweit Recht, als dass es feststellte, dass die Zutrittsverweigerung für alle Ausländer und sogar für eingebürgerte Staatsbürger aufgrund ihres Aus-

---

84 Bezirksgericht Shizuoka, 12. Oktober 1999, 1718 Hanji 92; Übersetzung ins Deutsche durch den Autor aus der englischen Übersetzung in *Webster* (Anm. 83), S. 655 ff.

85 Bezirksgericht Sapporo, 11. November 2002, 1806 Hanji 84; englische Übersetzung in: *Webster*, Arudou v. Earth Cure: Judgment of November 11, 2002 Sapporo District Court. Asian-Pacific Law & Policy Journal 9, Nr. 2 (2008), S. 297.

sehens rechtswidrige rassistische Diskriminierung darstellte. Hierdurch wurde nicht nur die gerichtliche Antidiskriminierungsdoktrin aus dem Hamamatsu-Juwelier-Fall gefestigt. Zusätzlich brachte der Prozess das Thema fremdenfeindlicher Diskriminierung in Japan in den Fokus der öffentlichen Aufmerksamkeit, was sogar dazu führte, dass das deutsche Generalkonsulat in Japan einen Protestbrief an den Bürgermeister von Otaru sandte.[86] Obwohl der Fall nicht zum Erlass strikter Antidiskriminierungsvorschriften führte, brachte Arudou durch seine Klage das Thema unaufhaltsam in das öffentliche Bewusstsein und schuf einen zusätzlichen Präzedenzfall im japanischen Antidiskriminierungsrecht.

Im Bereich der Hassrede fällte das Bezirksgericht Kyoto im Jahr 2013 ein wegweisendes Urteil gegen Mitglieder der bekannten rechtsextremistischen Organisation *Zaitoku-kai*[87] („Kyoto-Korean-School-Fall").[88] Mitglieder von *Zaitoku-kai* und anderen fremdenfeindlichen Gruppen hatten sich im Zeitraum zwischen 2009 und 2010 regelmäßig in der Nähe einer Grundschule für Kinder koreanischer Abstammung in Kyoto versammelt. Dort riefen die Beklagten rassistische Beleidigungen und beschädigten Schuleigentum, wodurch die Schule sich auch dazu gezwungen sah, bestimmte Schulaktivitäten abzusagen beziehungsweise zu verlegen. Das Bezirksgericht Kyoto entschied nun als erstes Gericht in Japan, dass derartige Handlungen rassistische Diskriminierung darstellen können, indem es sich auf ICERD als völkerrechtliche Grundlage stützte. Nach der Argumentation des Bezirksgerichts verpflichte ICERD nicht nur die Vertragsstaaten, gegen rassistische Diskriminierung vorzugehen. Vielmehr schloss das Urteil, dass Artikel 6 des Übereinkommens, welcher die Vertragsstaaten dazu verpflichtet, Rechtsschutzmöglichkeiten für Opfer von Diskriminierung zu schaffen, die nationalen Gerichte sogar direkt bindet. Der Hohe Gerichtshof Osaka wies jedoch im Berufungsurteil 2014 eine solche direkte Bindung durch ICERD zurück, auch wenn das Gericht ansonsten im Ergebnis dem erstinstanzlichen Urteil folgte.[89] Nach Ansicht des Berufungsgerichts sollten die Gerichte völkerrechtliche Bestimmungen zusammen mit verfassungsrechtlichen Vorschriften lediglich als interpretative Leitlinie bei der Anwendung allgemeiner Bestimmungen des Deliktsrechts verwenden, womit sich das Berufungsgericht wieder in die bestehende Rechtsprechungspraxis aus dem Hamamatsu-Juwelier-Fall und dem Otaru-Onsen-Fall eingliederte. 2014 bestätigte auch der japanische OGH das Urteil.[90]

Ein jüngeres Beispiel aus der Rechtsprechung ist eine Entscheidung des Hohen Gerichtshofes Nagoya von 2023, die sich mit der Ablehnung des Antrags zur Aufnahme der Mitgliedschaft in einem Golfclub für einen Mann koreanischer Abstammung befasste (Golfclub-Entscheidung).[91] Obwohl der Kläger 2018 die japanische Staatsbürgerschaft durch Einbürgerung erlangte, verweigerte der Golfclub die Aufnahme mit Verweis auf den früheren Besitz einer ausländischen Staatsbürgerschaft. Unter Beru-

86 *Webster*, Timothy (Anm. 85), S. 315.

87 Vereinigung von Bürgern gegen Sonderrechte für ethnische Koreaner in Japan (在日特権を許さない市民の会, *zainichi tokken wo yurusanai shimin no kai*).

88 Bezirksgericht Kyoto, 7. Oktober 2013, Heisei 22 (wa) No. 2655.

89 Hoher Gerichtshof Osaka, 8. Juli 2014, Heisei 25 (ne) Nr. 3235, 2232.

90 OGH Japan, 3. Kleiner Senat, 9. Dezember 2014.

91 Hoher Gerichtshof Nagoya, 27. Oktober 2022, Reiwa 5 (ne) Nr. 487.

fung auf das völkerrechtliche Verbot der Rassendiskriminierung unter ICERD klagte der Mann auf Entschädigung in Höhe von 3,3 Millionen Yen für erlittenes seelisches Leid.

Das Gericht erster Instanz wies die Klage des Klägers noch ab und erklärte, dass Entscheidungen über Mitgliedschaften im Ermessen des Golfclubs lägen, wie es durch die Vereinigungsfreiheit in Artikel 21 der Verfassung garantiert sei.[92] Zur Anwendung von Völkerrecht bzw. Verfassungsrecht argumentierte das erstinstanzliche Gericht, dass die Grundrechte der Verfassung sowie Rechte aus internationalen Verträgen direkt nur in Konflikten mit dem Staat anwendbar seien. Streitigkeiten zwischen zwei privaten Parteien sollten jedoch der Autonomie der beteiligten Parteien überlassen werden, wobei die Gerichte nur in schweren Fällen eingreifen sollten, wenn der gesellschaftlich akzeptable Rahmen der Privatautonomie überschritten wird. Das Gericht sah im vorliegenden Fall keine solchen außergewöhnlichen Faktoren und argumentierte, dass Golfspielen schließlich nicht wesentlich für die soziale Teilhabe sei und dass der Kläger darüber hinaus auch die Mitgliedschaft in anderen Golfclubs besitze.

Der Hohe Gerichtshof Nagoya hob das Urteil jedoch zugunsten des Klägers auf. Der Gerichtshof konkretisierte zunächst den Prüfungsmaßstab und erklärte, dass Verpflichtungen aus dem internationalen Recht nicht direkt auf private Streitigkeiten anwendbar seien. Doch ähnlich wie im Hamamatsu-Juwelier-Fall stellte das Urteil fest, dass die Entscheidung, ob eine diskriminierende Handlung eines privaten Akteurs eine illegale Handlung nach Deliktsrecht darstellt, unter Berücksichtigung von Artikel 14 Absatz 1 der Verfassung, Artikel 26 ICCPR[93] und dem Verbot rassistischer Diskriminierung in ICERD getroffen werden sollte. Unter Würdigung des Geistes dieser Regelungen sollten die Gerichte prüfen, ob eine private Handlung den sozial akzeptablen Rahmen der Privatautonomie überschreitet.

Obwohl der in diesem Fall entwickelte Prüfungsmaßstab weitgehend mit der bestehenden Rechtsprechung übereinstimmt, unterschied er sich von den Urteilen in Hamamatsu und Otaru dahingehend, dass das Gericht weitere Ausführungen zu den genauen Anforderungen der Gleichbehandlung für Unternehmen und dem jeweiligen Umfang ihrer vertraglichen Autonomie vornahm. Das Berufungsgericht erklärte hier, dass erstens der betroffene Club über eine beträchtliche Mitgliederzahl von etwa 1.500 Mitgliedern verfüge und dass zweitens Golfspielen ein Freizeitvergnügen sei, welches von großen Teilen der Gesellschaft ausgeübt werde. Daher besäße der Golfclub, wie das Gericht es nannte, „eine soziale Natur von gewissem Umfang/eine gewisse soziale Bedeutung (一定の社会性, *ittei no shakaisei*)“.[94] Mit anderen Worten bot der Club seine Dienste einer unbestimmten, großen Gruppe von Menschen an, für welche die Inanspruchnahme dieser Dienste von gewisser Bedeutung für ihre Teilnahme am sozialen Leben ist. Nach Ansicht des Gerichts würden die Dienstleistungen des Clubs somit unter den Begriff „öffentliches Leben“ in Artikel 1

92 Bezirksgericht Tsu, 19. April 2023, Reiwa 4 (wa) Nr. 138.

93 Internationaler Pakt über bürgerliche und politische Rechte (kurz *ICCPR*), 16. Dezember 1966, Resolution 2200 A (XXI) der Generalversammlung der Vereinten Nationen, in Kraft getreten am 23. März 1976, von Japan ratifiziert am 21. Juni 1979.

94 Hoher Gerichtshof Nagoya, 27. Oktober 2022, Reiwa 5 (ne) Nr. 487.

(1) ICERD fallen, in dessen Bereich der Vertrag alle Formen rassistischer Diskriminierung verbietet.[95] Nach dieser Doktrin könnten wohl große Einrichtungen, die ihre Dienste einem breiten Publikum anbieten, vergleichsweise strengen Gleichbehandlungserfordernissen unterliegen, während es unklar bleibt, welche Standards hier für kleinere Einrichtungen wie einzelne Bars oder Restaurants gelten würden.

Für deutsche Juristinnen und Juristen erinnert diese Argumentation stark an die Stadionverbot-Entscheidung des Bundesverfassungsgerichts von 2018 und die dort entwickelten „spezifischen Konstellationen", in denen sich verfassungsrechtliche Gleichbehandlungserfordernisse auch für das Verhältnis zwischen Privaten ergeben können.[96] Zur Erinnerung: das Bundesverfassungsgericht definierte diese Konstellationen als „Veranstaltungen, die aufgrund eigener Entscheidung der Veranstalter einem großen Publikum ohne Ansehen der Person geöffnet werden und [die] für die Betroffenen in erheblichem Umfang über die Teilnahme am gesellschaftlichen Leben entscheide[n]"[97]. Ob und inwieweit sich der Hohe Gerichtshof Nagoya bei seiner Urteilsfindung im Jahr 2023 hiervon inspirieren ließ, lässt sich jedoch nur mutmaßen.

Bei der Interessensabwägung stimmte das Berufungsgericht schließlich mit der ersten Instanz dahingehend überein, als dass es dem Golfclub im Rahmen des Prinzips der Privatautonomie und der Vereinigungsfreiheit ein weites Ermessen in Geschäftsentscheidungen zugestand. In diesem Fall argumentierte der Golfclub, dass eine Zunahme von ausländischen bzw. ausländisch-stämmigen Mitgliedern das Clubklima aufgrund von Unterschieden im Verhalten und Benehmen negativ beeinflussen würde. Das Berufungsgericht stellte jedoch die Legitimität dieses Arguments unter modernen gesellschaftlichen Werten bereits grundsätzlich infrage und entschied letztlich, dass zumindest für den Kläger, der in Japan geboren und aufgewachsen ist, dort sein ganzes Leben verbracht hat und sogar die japanische Staatsbürgerschaft angenommen hat, die Argumentation des Golfclubs keine Relevanz besitze.

Tatsächlich war der hier diskutierte Fall nicht der erste seiner Art. Bereits 2002, vor dem wegweisenden Urteil im Hamamatsu-Juwelier-Fall, akzeptierte der Hohe Gerichtshof Tokio die Entscheidung eines Golfclubs, einem Zainichi-Koreaner die Mitgliedschaft zu verweigern, als von der Privatautonomie des Golfclubs gedeckt.[98] Im Gegensatz dazu entschied das Bezirksgericht Tokio 1995 – noch vor der Ratifikation von ICERD durch Japan im selben Jahr –, dass die Weigerung eines Golfclubs, einem Zainichi-Koreaner vollständige Mitgliedschaftsrechte zu gewähren, gegen die Gleichheitsklausel in Artikel 14 der Verfassung verstoße.[99] Im Fall von 2023 klagte der Hohe Gerichtshof Nagoya nun ausdrücklich an, dass viele Golfclubs sich noch immer weigern, ausländische Staatsbürger als Mitglieder aufzunehmen. In gewisser Weise dienen die Golfclub-Fälle somit als ein Beispiel für die auch heute noch stattfindende Diskriminierung der koreanischen Minderheit in Japan. Obwohl Zainichi-Koreaner in Japan geboren und aufgewachsen sind und Japanisch ebenso gut spre-

---

95 Hoher Gerichtshof Nagoya, 27. Oktober 2022, Reiwa 5 (ne) Nr. 487.

96 BVerfGE 148, 267 – Stadionverbot.

97 BVerfGE 148, 267 – Stadionverbot, Rn. 41.

98 Hoher Gerichtshof Tokio, 23. Januar 2002, Heisei 13 (ne) 3550.

99 Bezirksgericht Tokio, 23. März 1995, Heiwa 4 (wa) 21675.

chen wie japanische Staatsbürger, werden sie noch immer aufgrund ihrer Herkunft aus bestimmten sozialen Räumen ausgeschlossen, selbst, wenn sie die japanische Staatsbürgerschaft angenommen haben.

In Bezug auf diese Diskriminierungserfahrungen betonte der Hohe Gerichtshof Nagoya in seinem Urteil von 2023, dass die Verweigerung der Mitgliedschaft dem Kläger nicht nur die Möglichkeit verwehrte, auf dem Gelände des Clubs Golf zu spielen und an Turnieren teilzunehmen. Vielmehr verletze eine solche Ablehnung für Mitglieder der koreanischen Minderheit in Japan, die während ihres Lebens häufig verschiedene Formen der Diskriminierung erfahren müssen, auch ihre Persönlichkeitsrechte und ihren Wert als Individuum. Obwohl es nur ein Satz des Urteils ist, kann eine solche explizite Anerkennung der Diskriminierungserfahrungen von ethnischen Koreanern in Japan ein wichtiges Signal der Minderheitenanerkennung in Japan darstellen und für diese, wie zuvor schon das Urteil des Bezirksgerichts Kyoto im Kyoto-Korean-School-Fall, zumindest ein gewisses Maß an Versöhnung bieten.

4. Zwischenfazit

Anders als im Falle von Grundrechtsverletzungen durch staatliches Handeln, lässt sich feststellen, dass die Gerichte in Japan Ausländer zumindest in einem gewissen Umfang vor Diskriminierung durch private Akteure schützen. In Ermangelung von gesetzlichen Regelungen gegen rassistische Diskriminierung zeigt hier die Anwendung von ICERD in Fällen von Diskriminierung und Hassrede die zentrale Rolle des Völkerrechts für die Rechte von Ausländern in Japan. In gewisser Weise füllen die japanischen Gerichte durch die Anwendung von Völkerrecht (und Verfassungsrecht) die Lücke, die von der Gesetzgebung durch ihre Weigerung, strenge Antidiskriminierungsgesetze zu erlassen, hinterlassen wurde.

Die explizite Anerkennung universeller Menschenrechte und von Diskriminierungserfahrungen ausländischer Staatsbürger und ethnischer Minderheiten in Japan in Urteilen wie dem Hamamatsu-Juwelier-Fall oder dem Golf-Club-Urteil von 2023 lässt darüber hinaus hoffen, dass die Gerichte sich auch der elementaren Bedeutung der Grundrechte in Diskriminierungsstreitigkeiten bewusst sind. Eine solche explizite Anerkennung von Minderheiten und Ihren alltäglichen Diskriminierungserfahrungen könnte für Gruppen wie die Zainichi-Koreaner mit Blick auf die japanische Geschichte sogar eine Chance auf Versöhnung mit dem japanischen Staat bieten. Trotz dieser positiven Signale im Bereich privater Diskriminierung bleibt jedoch unklar, wie japanische Gerichte auf rassistische Diskriminierung durch staatliche Akteure, wie z. B. Polizeibehörden, reagieren werden. Mit Blick auf eine 2024 eingereichte Klage gegen die Anwendung von Racial Profiling seitens der japanischen Polizei dürfte dieses Thema in Zukunft an Aufmerksamkeit gewinnen.[100]

Bei aller Positivität zeigt das Fehlen von Antidiskriminierungsgesetzen dennoch einen erheblichen Mangel an Anerkennung von Ausländern als vulnerabler Gruppe in der japanischen Gesellschaft. Insbesondere der Verweis der japanischen Regie-

---

100 *AP*, Testimony begins in lawsuit accusing Japanese police of racial profiling, *The Asahi Shimbun* (15. April 2024).

rung auf eine angeblich geringe Prävalenz von rassistischer Diskriminierung in Japan als Begründung für ihre Weigerung, strenge Antidiskriminierungsgesetze zu erlassen, widerspricht den Erfahrungen von Ausländern und ethnischen Minderheiten in Japan, wie sie sich in den oben beschriebenen Gerichtsverfahren widerspiegeln.[101] In Anbetracht derartiger Äußerungen seitens der japanischen Politik scheint es, als dass der japanische Staat die Erfahrungen von Opfern rassistischer Diskriminierung nicht wirklich ernst nimmt und jedenfalls keine Notwendigkeit für die gesetzliche Bekämpfung rassistischer Diskriminierung sieht. Im Gegensatz hierzu zeigt die entschlossene Haltung der japanischen Justiz eine positive Entwicklung hin zu einem effektiven Schutz von Ausländern und Minderheiten. Der Schutz durch die Gerichte kann hier jedoch nicht dasselbe Maß an staatlicher Anerkennung liefern, wie eine umfassende Antidiskriminierungsgesetzgebung.

V. Gesamtbewertung und Ausblick

Mit einem prozentualen Anteil von 2,7 % an der Gesamtbevölkerung Japans bilden ausländische Staatsbürger noch immer eine verschwindend geringe Minderheit in der japanischen Gesellschaft. Aus diesem Grund erscheint es angemessen, die Frage nach dem Umfang des Schutzes von Ausländern im japanischen Recht auch aus dem Blickwinkel des Schutzes vulnerabler Minderheiten zu betrachten. Schließlich kann nicht nur ihre im Vergleich zu multikulturellen Gesellschaften westlicher Demokratien geringe Anzahl Hindernisse dabei bereiten, Aufmerksamkeit für die spezifischen Anliegen nicht-japanischer Einwohner zu generieren. Zusätzlich ist Vorsicht geboten, dass durch die wichtige Arbeit im Kampf gegen die Diskriminierung „traditioneller" Minderheiten, wie der Zainichi-Koreaner, nicht der Blick für das Ganze verloren geht. So divers wie die ausländische Bevölkerung Japans ist, so unterschiedlich sind auch die unterschiedlichen Erfahrungen in der Behandlung durch den japanischen Staat, aber auch mit Diskriminierung im Alltag. Dass hier noch Aufklärungsbedarf besteht, zeigt anekdotisch auch ein Beitrag eines großen japanischen Fernsehsenders während der Corona-Pandemie, welcher die angeblich feuchte Aussprache der englischen Sprache mit einer erhöhten Ansteckungsgefahr durch englischsprachige Ausländer in Verbindung zu bringen versuchte.[102]

Gleichzeitig projizieren aktuelle Vorhersagen zur Bevölkerungsentwicklung in Japan, dass Ausländer im Jahr 2070 mehr als zehn Prozent der Bevölkerung stellen werden.[103] Es kann also erwartet werden, dass durch die zunehmende Sichtbarkeit von Ausländern im japanischen Alltag auch die Frage nach Ihrem Schutz vor Diskriminierung und staatlicher Willkür an Dringlichkeit gewinnen wird. Die japanische Gesellschaft und Politik, aber auch das japanische Recht, werden auf diese Entwicklung

---

[101] zur Haltung der japanischen Regierung s. *Kotani*, Proceed with Caution: Hate Speech Regulation in Japan, in: Hastings Constitutional Law Quarterly 45, Nr. 3 (Spring 2018), S. 607.

[102] *St. Michel*, „This is a pen": Taking a preposterous COVID-19 hypothesis to another level on social media, The Japan Times (6. Juni 2020).

[103] National Institute of Population and Social Security Research Tokyo, Japan, Population Projections for Japan: 2021–2070 (With long-range Population Projections: 2071–2120), in: Population Research Series, No. 347 (31. August 2023).

reagieren müssen, zum einen, um Japan fit zu machen für die Diversifizierung seiner Gesellschaft, aber auch, um Spannungen in der Bevölkerung zu vermeiden, und Konflikte frühzeitig zu lösen.

Vor diesem Hintergrund scheint es mit Blick auf noch immer von Ausländern erfahrene Alltagsdiskriminierung zunächst einmal fraglich, ob der derzeitige Ansatz einer Fall-zu-Fall Lösung von Diskriminierungsfällen durch die japanischen Gerichte wirklich ausreichen kann, um liberal-demokratische Anforderungen an den Schutz vulnerabler Minderheiten zu erfüllen. Während derartige Gerichtsentscheidungen für Einzelfallgerechtigkeit sorgen und individuelle Räume, wie Läden, Badehäuser oder Golfclubs öffnen können, so können sie nicht, jedenfalls nicht allein, die japanische Gesellschaft im Ganzen öffnen und für Inklusion in einem weiteren Kontext sorgen. Schließlich bedarf es zur gesellschaftlichen Inklusion von Ausländern zunächst einmal deren Anerkennung in der japanischen Gesellschaft. Ein starkes Antidiskriminierungsgesetz könnte hier ein wichtiges Signal setzen, dass die japanische Politik die Anliegen ausländischer Staatsbürger und ethnischer Minderheiten tatsächlich ernst nimmt. Es bleibt zu hoffen, dass das 2016 erlassene Gesetz zur Beseitigung von Hassrede hier nur ein erster Schritt von vielen bleibt.

Gerade im Hinblick auf Grundrechtseingriffe durch den japanischen Staat zeigt sich jedoch ein ernüchterndes Bild. Auch wenn Vorstöße unterer Gerichte, wie das Urteil des Hohen Gerichtshofes Tokio zur Verletzung des Rechts auf rechtliches Gehör hier Hoffnung auf eine baldige Äußerung auch des OGH geben kann, bleibt es schwer vorherzusagen, ob und inwieweit das höchste Gericht des Landes selbst heute von seiner im McLean-Urteil etablierten Rechtsprechung abrücken würde. Zu hoch könnte möglicherweise die Hürde sein, die durch die Betonung des Gerichts der staatlichen Souveränität in McLean und weiteren Urteilen mit Ausländerbezug aufgebaut wurde.

Aus deutscher Perspektive erscheint die auch heute noch aufrechterhaltene Gewährung grundrechtlichen Schutzes für Ausländer nur unter Vorbehalt staatlicher Entscheidungen im Bereich der Einwanderungspolitik aus dem McLean Urteil fast schon als Anachronismus, wenn zum Vergleich das Urteil des Bundesverfassungsgerichts zur Ausland-Ausland-Fernmeldeaufklärung herangezogen wird. Immerhin stellte das Gericht hier klar, dass die deutsche Staatsgewalt selbst im Ausland gegenüber Ausländern umfassend durch die Grundrechte des Grundgesetzes gebunden wird.[104] Die Erwartung einer derart egalitären Anwendung der Grundrechte der japanischen Verfassung durch den OGH scheint in naher Zukunft in der Tat eher unrealistisch. Für einen liberalen demokratischen Staat wie Japan sollte jedoch die Schaffung einer auf Gleichberechtigung und Ebenbürtigkeit basierenden Beziehung nicht nur zwischen Ausländern und Japanern, sondern auch zwischen Ausländern und dem japanischen Staat von essenzieller Bedeutung sein. Eine Stärkung der Rechtsposition von ausländischen Staatsbürgern gerade auch im Falle staatlicher Grundrechtseingriffe könnte schließlich auch dazu beitragen, Vertrauen, das durch die rigiden Einreisesperren Japans während der Corona-Pandemie in der ausländischen Bevölkerung verloren gegangen ist, wiederherzustellen.

---

104 BVerfGE 154, 152.

Zugleich würde die Rechtsstellung der Ausländer in Japan jedoch auch profitieren, wenn mehr ausländische Juristinnen und Juristen die Auseinandersetzung mit dem japanischen Recht, insbesondere auch dem japanischen Verfassungsrecht wagen würden. Um auf einer positiven Note zu enden, bleibt daher zu hoffen, dass durch das Wachstum der ausländischen Bevölkerung in Japan in Zukunft auch ein wachsendes Interesse am japanischen Recht in der rechtsvergleichenden Forschung erwartet werden kann.

Literaturverzeichnis

Ando, Junko: Die Entstehung der Meiji-Verfassung: zur Rolle des deutschen Konstitutionalismus im modernen japanischen Staatswesen. Monographien aus dem Deutschen Institut für Japanstudien der Philipp-Franz-von-Siebold-Stiftung, Band 27 (2000).

AP: Testimony begins in lawsuit accusing Japanese police of racial profiling, in: The Asahi Shimbun, 15. April 2024. https://www.asahi.com/ajw/articles/15230278.

Ashibe, Nobuyoshi: 憲法, (*kenpō* = Verfassungsrecht). 8. Auflage (2023).

Ausschuss der Vereinten Nationen zur Beseitigung von Rassendiskriminierung: Abschließende Bemerkungen des UN-Menschenrechtsausschusses zum vierten regelmäßigen Bericht zu Japan, 19/11/98. CCPR/C/79/Add.102, 19. November 1998.

Ausschuss der Vereinten Nationen zur Beseitigung von Rassendiskriminierung: Abschließende Bemerkungen zum 10. und 11. regelmäßigen Berichts zu Japan (CERD/C/JPN/CO/10-11), 26. September 2018.

Bäcker, Carsten: § 58 Historische und ideengeschichtliche Grundlagen der Grundrechte, in: Stern, Klaus/Sodan, Helge/Möstl, Markus (Hrsg.), Allgemeine Lehren der Grundrechte, 2., vollständig neu verfasste Auflage des von Klaus Stern begründeten Werks. Das Staatsrecht der Bundesrepublik Deutschland im europäischen Staatenverbund, Band 3 (2022).

Beasley, W. G.: The Rise of Modern Japan (1990).

Dokumente der japanischen Parlamentsbibliothek: Documents with Commentaries Part 3 Formulation of the GHQ Draft and Response of the Japanese Government, 3–2 Reform of the Japanese Governmental System (SWNCC 228). National Diet Library (o. J.), https://www.ndl.go.jp/constitution/e/shiryo/03/059shoshi.html.

Dokumente der japanischen Parlamentsbibliothek: Documents with Commentaries Part 3 Formulation of the GHQ Draft and Response of the Japanese Government, 3–15 GHQ Draft, February 13, 1946. National Diet Library (o. J.), https://www.ndl.go.jp/constitution/e/shiryo/03/076shoshi.html.

Duró, Ágota/*Palmer*, David: Japan's Forgotten Korean Forced Laborers: The Search for Hidden Wartime Graves in Hokkaido, in: International Labor and Working-Class History (2. April 2024), S. 1–20.

Elisonas, Jurgis: Christianity and the Daimyo, in: Hall, John Whitney (Hrsg.), The Cambridge History of Japan, 4:301–73 (1991).

Fisher, James C.: „We the kokumin": the Constitution, International Law and the Rights of Foreigners in Japan, in: Zeitschrift für Japanisches Recht, Nr. 39 (2015), S. 109–135.

Goodman, Carl F.: The Rule of Law in Japan. A Comparative Analysis. 4. Auflage (2017).

Goodman, Grant Kohn: Japan: The Dutch Experience. Rev. ed. London (1986).

Ikeo, Shinichi: 家族を引き裂く非人道的な入管行政…いまだに46年前の「マクリーン判決」が根拠このままでいいの?, *kazoku wo hikisaku hijindōteki na nyūkan gyōsei… imada ni 46 nen mae no „Makurīn hanketsu" ga konkyo – kono mama de ii no?* (Unmenschliche Einwanderungspolitik zerreißt Familien… immer noch stellt die McLean Entscheidung von vor 46 Jahren die Grundlage – kann es hierbei wirklich bleiben?), in: Tokyo Shimbun (21. Januar 2024). https://www.tokyo-np.co.jp/article/304154.

Ishikawa, Hiroyasu: Codification, Decodification, and Recodification of the Japanese Civil Code, in: Rivera, Julio César (Hrsg.), In The Scope and Structure of Civil Codes, 32:267–85. Ius Gentium: Comparative Perspectives on Law and Justice (2013).

Japan Immigration Services Agency (Einwanderungsbehörde Japans): 令和５年末現在における在留外国人数について, *reiwa 5-nenmatsu genzai ni okeru zairyū gaikokujinsū ni tsuite* (Zur Gesamtanzahl wohnhafter ausländischer Staatsbürger zum Jahresende 2023). Pressemitteilung (22. März 2024), https://www.moj.go.jp/isa/publications/press/13_00040.html.

Japanisches Ministerium für Innere Angelegenheiten und Kommunikation: 住民基本台帳に基づく人口、人口動態及び世帯数, *jūmin kihon daichō ni motozuku jinkō, jinkō dōtai oyobi setaisū* (Bevölkerung, Demografische Trends und Anzahl der Haushalte basierend auf dem Einwohnerregister) (1. Januar 2024), https://www.soumu.go.jp/main_sosiki/jichi_gyousei/daityo/jinkou_jinkoudoutai-setaisuu.html.

Jones, Colin P. A.: Japan's Constitution won't protect revolting foreigners, in: The Japan Times (11. Oktober 2015), https://www.japantimes.co.jp/community/2015/10/11/issues/japans-constitution-wont-protect-revolting-foreigners/.

Knör, Mika: New Salt into an Open Wound. Verfassungsblog: On Matters Constitutional (30. Juni 2020), https://verfassungsblog.de/new-salt-into-an-open-wound/.

Kondō, Atsushi: Hate Speech Regulation and Anti-discrimination in Japan, in: Higaki, Shinji/ Nasu, Yuji (Hrsg.), Hate Speech in Japan, 1. Aufl. (2021), S. 17–34.

Kondō, Atsushi: マクリーン事件判決の抜本的な見直し, *makurīn jiken hanketsu no bapponteki na minaoshi* (Eine grundsätzliche Neubewertung des McLean-Urteils), in: Meijo Hougaku/Meijo Daigaku Hougakkai 70, Nr. 4 (2021), S. 1–22.

Kotani, Junko: Proceed with Caution: Hate Speech Regulation in Japan, in: Hastings Constitutional Law Quarterly 45, Nr. 3 (Spring 2018), S. 603–22.

Law, David S.: The Myth of the Imposed Constitution, in: Galligan, Denis J./Versteeg, Mila (Hrsg.), Social and Political Foundations of Constitutions, 1. Aufl. (2013), S. 239–68.

Martin, Craig: Glimmers of Hope: The Evolution of Equality Rights Doctrine in Japanese Courts From a Comparative Perspective, in: Duke Journal of Comparative & International Law 20, Nr. 167 (2010), S. 167–246.

Martin, Craig: Striking the Right Balance: Hate Speech Laws in Japan, the United States, and Canada, in: Hastings Constitutional Law Quarterly 45, Nr. 3 (Spring 2018), S. 455–532.

Menkhaus, Heinrich: Der Japanisch-Preußische Freundschafts-, Schiffahrts- und Handelsvertrag von 1861 – Eine juristische Analyse anläßlich der offiziellen Feier des 160. Jubiläums des Beginns der japanisch-deutschen diplomatischen Beziehungen: Teil 1, in: Meiji Law Journal 28 (2021), S. 35–44.

Meyer, Milton W.: Japan: A Concise History. 4th ed. Lanham: Rowman & Littlefield Publishers (2012).

Muramatsu, Shinji: 外国人の政治的権利と主権 — 政治的権利を巡って, *gaikokujin no seijitekikenri to shuken – seijitekikenri wo megutte* (Zu den politischen Rechten von Ausländern und Souveränität – ein Überblick über die politischen Rechte), in: Kenpō Kenkyū 52 (2020), S. 117–145.

Myslinska, Dagmar Rita: Racist Racism: Complicating Whiteness through the Privilege and Discrimination of Westerners in Japan, in: UMKC Law Review 83, Nr. 1 (2014), S. 1–56.

National Institute of Population and Social Security Research Tokyo, Japan: Population Projections for Japan: 2021–2070 (With long-range Population Projections: 2071–2120). Population Research Series No. 347 (31. August 2023), https://www.ipss.go.jp/pp-zenkoku/j/zenkoku2023/pp2023_ReportALLc.pdf.

NIOD Institute for War, Holocaust and Genocide Studies: The Japanese Occupation and Pacific War (in numbers), abgerufen am (14. November 2024), https://www.niod.nl/en/frequently-asked-questions/japanese-occupation-and-pacific-war-numbers.

Park, Soon-Won: The politics of remembrance: the case of Korean forced laborers in the Second World War, in: Shin, Gi-Wook/Park, Soon-Won/Yang, Daqing (Hrsg.), Rethinking Historical Injustice and Reconciliation in Northeast Asia: The Korean experience (2007).

Pence, Canon: Japanese Only: Xenophobic Exclusion in Japan's Private Sphere, in: New York International Law Review 20, Nr. 2 (Summer 2007), S. 101–59.

Premierminister Yoshihide Suga: Cabinet Document No. 204, Question No. 98. Shūgiin (27. April 2021). https://www.shugiin.go.jp/internet/itdb_shitsumon.nsf/html/shitsumon/b204098.htm.

Rahn, Guntram: Rechtsdenken und Rechtsauffassung in Japan: dargestellt an der Entwicklung der modernen japanischen Zivilrechtsmethodik, 1990.

Rigg, Bryan Mark: Japan's Holocaust: History of Imperial Japan's Mass Murder and Rape During World War II. 1st ed. (2024).

Rummel, R. J.: Statistics of democide: genocide and mass murder since 1900, in: Macht und Gesellschaft, Bd. 2 (1998).

Schröder, Jan/*Morinaga*, Yoshiko: Zum Einfluß des BGB auf das japanische Zivilrecht, in: Berger, Elisabeth (Hrsg.), Rechtstransfer durch Zivilgesetzbücher, S. 38–44. Beiträge Liechtenstein-Institut 29 (2005).

St. Michel, Patrick: 'This is a pen': Taking a preposterous COVID-19 hypothesis to another level on social media, in: The Japan Times (6. Juni 2020), https://www.japantimes.co.jp/news/2020/06/06/national/media-national/pen-coronavirus-theories/.

Takanori, Tomoyuki: 外国人の公務就任権に関する予備的考察：外国人の人権享有主体性についての一試論, *gaikokujin no kōmu shūnin ken ni kansuru yobiteki kōsatsu: Gaikokujin no jinken kyōyu shutaisei ni tsuite no ichi shiron* (Vorläufige Überlegungen zum Recht von Ausländern, öffentliche Ämter zu bekleiden: Ein Beitrag zur Grundrechtsträgerschaft von Ausländern), in: Takaoka Hōgaku 31 (März 2013), S. 67–88.

Takayanagi, Kenzo: A Century of Innovation: The Development of Japanese Law, 1868–1961, in: Mehren, Arthus Taylor von (Hrsg.), Law in Japan (1963), S. 5–40.

Tanaka, Toshiyuki: Hidden Horrors: Japanese War Crimes in World War II. Second edition (2018).

Tsunemoto, Teruki: Rights and Identifications of Ethnic Minorities in Japan: Indigenous Ainu and Resident Koreans, in: Asia-Pacific Journal on Human Rights and the Law 2, Nr. 1 (2001), S. 119–142.

Webster, Timothy: Bortz v. Suzuki, Judgment of October 12, 1999, Hamamatsu Branch, Shizuoka District Court, in: Pacific Rim Law & Policy Journal 16, Nr. 3 (2007), S. 631–667.

Webster, Timothy: Legal Excisions Omissions Are Not Accidents. Cornell International Law Journal 39, Nr. 2 (2006), S. 435–455.

Webster, Timothy: South Korea Shatters the Paradigm: Corporate Liability, Historical Accountability, and the Second World War, in: UCLA Journal of International Law and Foreign Affairs 26 (2022), S. 123–149.

Webster, Timothy: Arudou v. Earth Cure: Judgment of November 11, 2002 Sapporo District Court. Asian-Pacific Law & Policy Journal 9, Nr. 2 (2008), S. 297–321.

Unterschiede zwischen dem deutschen und japanischen Kartellrecht am Beispiel der Fusionskontrolle bei „Killer-Akquisitionen“ und dem kartellrechtlichen Zuliefererschutz

Wo können Deutschland und Japan voneinander lernen?

Von *Florian Kotman*

Dr. Florian Kotman ist Counsel (Rechtsanwalt) bei Baker McKenzie in der Praxisgruppe „Antitrust & Competition“. Sein Arbeitsschwerpunkt liegt auf dem deutschen und europäischen Kartellrecht. Er ist daneben wissenschaftlicher Korrespondent für arbeits- und sozialrechtliche Fragen des Japan Institute for Labour Policy and Training (JILPT). Seine Dissertation erwarb er an der Universität Marburg und seinen Legum Magister an der Meiji Universität (Tokyo), jeweils mit Schwerpunkt auf deutsch-japanisches Arbeitsrecht.

Untersuchungen zum japanischen Recht erfreuen sich anhaltender Popularität. Die Anfang der 70er Jahre begründete und mittlerweile mehr als 50 Bände umfassende Schriftenreihe „Japanisches Recht“ sowie die noch junge, im Jahr 2015 begründete Schriftenreihe „Schriften zum Ostasiatischen Privatrecht“ beweisen, wie groß das Interesse an japanisch-rechtlichen Themen in Deutschland ist. In bedauerlicher Weise bemerkenswert ist jedoch, dass beide Schriftenreihen lediglich eine einzelne Untersuchung zum japanischen Kartellrecht beinhalten: eine Dissertation aus dem Jahr 1980 mit dem Titel „Gyoseishido und das Antimonopolgesetz in Japan“ von Herrn Dr. Wolfgang Pape. Generell sind deutschsprachige Arbeiten zum japanischen Kartellrecht rar. Die vorgenannte Dissertation scheint insgesamt die aktuellste deutschsprachige Arbeit zum japanischen Kartellrecht zu sein.

Dies ist insofern bedauerlich, als dass sich Unternehmen täglich mit dem Kartellrecht auseinandersetzen müssen. Kartellrechtliche Themen haben in dieser Hinsicht eine erhebliche praktische Bedeutung für das Wirtschaftsleben. Im Falle von Japan kommen eine mit Deutschland vergleichbare wirtschaftliche Entwicklung sowie ähnliche kartellrechtliche Probleme hinzu. Rechtsvergleichende Untersuchungen zum japanischen Kartellrecht drängen sich daher geradezu auf.

Die vorliegende Arbeit untersucht vor diesem Hintergrund zwei Themenkomplexe, die gleichsam aktuell wie kontrovers sind: Die Behandlung von „Killer-Akquisitionen“ im Rahmen der formellen Fusionskontrolle (hierzu nachfolgend unter I.) und den kartellrechtlichen Schutz von Zulieferern nach materiellem Kartellrecht (hierzu nachfolgend unter II.).

Duncker & Humblot · Berlin | https://doi.org/10.3790/978-3-428-59611-9.2025.418784

Die nachfolgenden Ausführungen sind nur als erste Schritte einer rechtsvergleichenden Untersuchung zu verstehen – in der Hoffnung, dass weitere Untersuchungen folgen werden.

I. Teil 1: „Killer-Akquisitionen" und Fusionskontrolle

Der Erwerb kleiner innovativer Unternehmen (wie Start-ups) durch große etablierte Unternehmen ist ein ubiquitäres Phänomen. Marktmächtige Unternehmen können so ihre bereits starken Marktpositionen weiter absichern und ausbauen sowie etwaigen Wettbewerbsdruck, der andernfalls durch das erworbene Unternehmen entstanden wäre, neutralisieren.[1] Die Gefahr transaktionsbedingter wettbewerbsdämpfender Effekte ist seit einigen Jahren im Fokus von Wettbewerbsbehörden und nationalen Gesetzgebern.[2]

Dies gilt auch für Deutschland und Japan. Beide Länder reagierten allerdings mit unterschiedlichen Maßnahmen: Der deutsche Gesetzgeber hat im Jahr 2017 mit § 35 Abs. 1a GWB die sog. Transaktionswertschwelle eingeführt, damit der Erwerb auch kleiner innovativer Unternehmen fusionskontrollrechtlich geprüft werden kann. Der japanische Gesetzgeber hat dagegen der japanischen Kommission für fairen Handel (公正取引委員会, *kōsei torihiki iinkai*) – abgekürzt im Folgenden mit JFTC (Japan Fair Trade Commission) – auferlegt, sich dem Thema anzunehmen. Die JFTC hat im Jahr 2019 überarbeitete fusionskontrollrechtliche Richtlinien[3] veröffentlicht, um Unternehmen anzuhalten, den Erwerb kleinerer Unternehmen mit der JFTC zu konsultieren und ggf. anschließend fusionskontrollrechtlich anzumelden.

Im Folgenden wird untersucht, ob und, wenn ja, inwiefern sich die beiden Ansätze gleichen bzw. unterscheiden und in der Praxis bewährt haben.

1. Zur Rechtslage in Deutschland

Das deutsche Fusionskontrollrecht fußt auf zwei Anmeldeschwellen: Eine rein umsatzbasierte Anmeldeschwelle (§ 35 Abs. 1 GWB) und die sog. Transaktionswertschwelle (§ 35 Abs. 1a GWB). Letztere wurde als Antwort auf die zunehmend grassierende Angst vor sog. „Killer-Akquisitionen" eingeführt. Ihre Funktion erklärt sich vor dem Hintergrund vermeintlicher Lücken der rein umsatzbasierten Anmeldeschwelle.

Gemäß der rein umsatzbasierten Anmeldeschwelle (§ 35 Abs. 1 GWB) ist ein Zusammenschlussvorhaben bei dem in Deutschland für Fusionskontrollprüfungen zuständigen Bundeskartellamt anzumelden, wenn im letzten Geschäftsjahr vor dem Zusammenschluss (i) die beteiligten Unternehmen insgesamt weltweit Umsatzerlöse

---

1 So beispielsweise *OECD Sekretariat*, Start-ups, Killer Acquisitions and Merger Control – Background Note, 12. Mai 2020 (DAF/COMP(2020)5), S. 23 ff.

2 Siehe hierzu u. a. *Europäische Kommission*, Evaluation of procedural and jurisdictional aspects of EU merger control, 26. März 2021 ({SEC(2021) 156 final} – {SWD(2021) 67 final}); *OECD Sekretariat* (Anm. 1), jeweils m. w. N.

3 Siehe hierzu näher die nachfolgenden Ausführungen in Abschnitt 2 des ersten Teils.

von mehr als 500 Mio. EUR erzielt haben, (ii) im Inland mindestens ein beteiligtes Unternehmen Umsatzerlöse von mehr als 50 Mio. EUR sowie (iii) ein anderes beteiligtes Unternehmen Umsatzerlöse von mehr als 17,5 Mio. EUR erzielt haben.

Rechtsklarheit, Rechtssicherheit und Transaktionssicherheit sprechen für umsatzbasierte Anmeldeschwellen: In der Praxis lässt sich üblicherweise schnell und einfach bestimmen, ob ein Zusammenschlussvorhaben anmeldepflichtig ist. Andererseits drohen bei starren umsatzbasierten Anmeldeschwellen Zusammenschlussvorhaben durch das Netz der Fusionskontrolle zu fallen, deren wettbewerbliche Auswirkungen eine fusionskontrollrechtliche Prüfung gegebenenfalls gerechtfertigt hätten. Hierzu gehören unter anderem die eingangs erwähnten „Killer-Akquisitionen".

Um diese Lücke im System der Fusionskontrolle zu schließen, führte der deutsche Gesetzgeber im Jahr 2017 mit § 35 Abs. 1a GWB ergänzend die sog. Transaktionswertschwelle ein.[4] Zusammenschlussvorhaben sind danach unter folgenden Voraussetzungen anmeldepflichtig:

1. die beteiligten Unternehmen haben im letzten Geschäftsjahr vor dem Zusammenschluss insgesamt weltweit Umsatzerlöse von mehr als 500 Mio. EUR erzielt,
2. im Inland im letzten Geschäftsjahr vor dem Zusammenschluss hat a) ein beteiligtes Unternehmen[5] Umsatzerlöse von mehr als 50 Mio. EUR erzielt und b) weder das zu erwerbende noch ein anderes beteiligtes Unternehmen haben Umsatzerlöse von jeweils mehr als 17,5 Mio. EUR erzielt,
3. der Wert der Gegenleistung für den Zusammenschluss beträgt mehr als 400 Mio. EUR und
4. das zu erwerbende Unternehmen nach Nummer 2 ist in erheblichem Umfang im Inland tätig.

Für die Praxis gestaltet sich insbesondere die Anwendung von § 35 Abs. 1a Nr. 4 GWB schwierig. wonach das Zielunternehmen „in erheblichem Umfang im Inland tätig" sein muss.[6] Zur besseren Handhabbarkeit der Transaktionswertschwelle hat das Bundeskartellamt am 1. Januar 2022 gemeinsam mit der österreichischen Bundeswettbewerbsbehörde – in Österreich existiert mit § 9 Abs. 4 KartG ein ähnlicher Anmeldetatbestand – einen Leitfaden veröffentlicht.[7] Dieser listet unter anderem Indikatoren zur Ermittlung der Erheblichkeit der Inlandstätigkeit auf. Hierzu gehören beispielsweise im Bereich der digitalen Wirtschaft die Nutzerzahl, der Umfang etwaiger Forschungs- und Entwicklungstätigkeiten im Inland und die Anzahl relevan-

---

4 Entwurf eines Neunten Gesetzes zur Änderung des Gesetzes gegen Wettbewerbsbeschränkungen, 7. November 2016, BT-Drs. 18/10207, S. 70 f.

5 Gemeint ist *nicht* das Zielunternehmen; siehe hierzu *Wessely*, in: Säcker/Bien/Meier-Beck/Montag (Hrsg.): Münchener Kommentar zum Wettbewerbsrecht, Band 2 Gesetz gegen Wettbewerbsbeschränkungen (GWB) §§ 1–96, 185, 186, 4. Aufl. (2022), GWB § 35, Rn. 38.

6 Mit dieser Voraussetzung wird dem völkerrechtlichen Auswirkungsgrundsatz Rechnung getragen, welcher einen hinreichenden Konnex zwischen den Auswirkungen des Zusammenschlussvorhabens und dem Wettbewerb in Deutschland voraussetzt; siehe BT-Drs. 18/10207 (Anm. 4), S. 72; *BKartA/BWB*, Leitfaden Transaktionswertschwelle, Stand: Januar 2022, Rn. 64.

7 *BKartA/BWB* (Anm. 6).

ter Patente für den inländischen Markt.[8] Im Einzelnen bleibt jedoch Vieles unklar: Welcher Umfang an inländischen Forschungs- und Entwicklungstätigkeiten ist erforderlich, um von einer erheblichen Inlandstätigkeit auszugehen? Unter welchen Voraussetzungen stellen die Umsatzerlöse einen angemessenen Gradmesser zur Ermittlung der Marktposition dar, so dass eine Anmeldepflicht alleine aufgrund geringer Umsätze des Zielunternehmens abgelehnt werden kann? Welche Bedeutung hat ein sich erst in einigen Jahren realisierendes Wettbewerbspotenzial auf die Prüfung der Erheblichkeit der Inlandstätigkeit?

Eine Konsultation mit dem Bundeskartellamt ist in der Praxis eher selten erfolgversprechend. Regelmäßig verweist das Bundeskartellamt auf das Prinzip der Selbsteinschätzung und rät dazu, im Zweifelsfalle das konsultierte Vorhaben vorsorglich anzumelden. Sollte sich im Nachgang einer vorsorglichen Anmeldung herausstellen, dass das Zusammenschlussvorhaben doch nicht anmeldepflichtig ist, können die Parteien – wie auch das Bundeskartellamt rät – ihre Anmeldung zurückzunehmen.[9] In der Praxis prüft das Bundeskartellamt – von wenigen Ausnahmen abgesehen – rein vorsorglich angemeldete Zusammenschlussvorhaben wie anmeldepflichtige Vorhaben. Die Frage, ob das vorsorglich angemeldete Vorhaben tatsächlich anmeldepflichtig war, bleibt offen. Für die Rechtssicherheit und Rechtsklarheit ist diese Verwaltungspraxis nicht förderlich, gerade mit Blick auf zukünftige Transaktionen.

Angeheizt wurden Diskussionen zum Anwendungsbereich der Transaktionswertschwelle zuletzt auch von Vertretern des Bundeskartellamts, die sich für eine Herabsetzung der Anmeldevoraussetzungen nach § 35 Abs. 1a GWB aussprechen. Die Vorschläge reichen von einer Streichung des Erfordernisses der Inlandstätigkeit[10] über das Abstellen auf die „Inlandsauswirkungen“[11] bis hin zur Erweiterung des Anwendungsbereichs auf „voraussichtliche Inlandstätigkeiten“[12]. Damit sollen auch solche Zusammenschlussvorhaben fusionskontrollrechtlich geprüft werden können, die sich erst zukünftig (etwa nach einigen Jahren) in Deutschland auswirken. Mit Blick auf Rechtssicherheit, Rechtsklarheit und Transaktionssicherheit ist keiner der diskutierten Vorschläge zu befürworten.[13]

Kritik zum Anwendungsbereich der Transaktionswertschwelle erklärt sich vor dem Hintergrund einiger Zusammenschlüsse, die aus Sicht des Bundeskartellamts von der Transaktionswertschwelle eigentlich hätten erfasst werden sollen, dies mangels erheblicher Inlandstätigkeit aber nicht wurden: Beim Zusammenschlussvorha-

---

8 *BKartA/BWB* (Anm. 6), Rn. 67, 105.

9 Die Rücknahme hat die Halbierung der Anmeldegebühren zur Folge (§ 62 Abs. 5 GWB).

10 *Monopolkommission*, Hauptgutachten XXIV, Wettbewerb 2022, Rn. 245 f.; *Monopolkommission*, Hauptgutachten XXI, Wettbewerb 2016, Rn. 19, mit Verweis auf § 35 Abs. 1a Nr. 2 lit. a GWB und § 185 Abs. 2 GWB, welche dem Auswirkungsgrundsatz ausreichend Rechnung tragen würden.

11 So *Göbel*, „Gotta catch ’em all?“ – Instrumente zum Aufgreifen von „Gap cases“ in der formellen Fusionskontrolle, in: ZWeR (2024), S. 51.

12 *Monopolkommission*, Hauptgutachten XXIV, Wettbewerb 2022, Rn. 246; *Käseberg*, Ein „Inflection“ – Punkt für die Fusionskontrolle?, in: NZKart (2025), S. 2.

13 Kritisch auch *Kresken/Wille*, „Make hard cases bad law?“ – Die angedachte Erweiterung der Transaktionswertschwelle, in: NZKart (2025), S. 195.

ben Meta/Kustomer (2021) sah das Bundeskartellamt die Voraussetzung der erheblichen Inlandstätigkeit mit Verweis auf die auch in Deutschland ansässigen Endkunden, den Ort der Datenverarbeitung, der sich auch in Deutschland befinde, und das erhebliche wettbewerbliche Potenzial von Kustomer als erfüllt an.[14] Dem widersprach das OLG Düsseldorf im Jahr 2022 auf Beschwerde von Meta: Das Zusammenschlussvorhaben sei mangels erheblicher Inlandstätigkeit nicht anmeldepflichtig gewesen.[15] Der Bundesgerichtshof gab dagegen mit Beschluss vom 17. Juni 2025 dem Bundeskartellamt recht: Der Zusammenschluss sei gemäß § 39 Abs. 1a Nr. 4 GWB anmeldepflichtig gewesen.[16]

Es folgte eine Reihe von Zusammenschlussvorhaben, bei denen das Bundeskartellamt eine Anmeldepflicht mangels erheblicher Inlandstätigkeit des Zielunternehmens ablehnte. Hierzu gehören die Zusammenschlussvorhaben Illumina/Grail (2022),[17] Microsoft/OpenAI (2023)[18] und Microsoft/Inflection (2024).[19]

Thorsten Käseberg[20] bezeichnete die Voraussetzung der erheblichen Inlandstätigkeit vor diesem Hintergrund als „korrekturbedürftige[n] Schwachpunkt“[21]. Ähnlich argumentiert Martin Göbel, Referent in der Abteilung Prozessführung und Recht des Bundeskartellamts, für den die Voraussetzung ein „Geburtsfehler“[22] ist.

Mit Blick auf die vorgenannten Fälle geht es dem Bundeskartellamt ersichtlich darum, den Erwerb (vermeintlich) innovativer Unternehmen fusionskontrollrechtlich prüfen zu können – idealerweise, ohne eine erhebliche Inlandstätigkeit nachweisen zu müssen. Rechtssicherheit, Rechtsklarheit und Transaktionssicherheit stehen dem entgegen. Insofern ist dem OLG Düsseldorf zuzustimmen, dass „[…] es dem Gesetzgeber bei der Einführung des Tatbestandsmerkmals der erheblichen Inlandstätigkeit auch gerade darum [ging], ein für die Zusammenschlussbeteiligten mit wenig Schwierigkeiten zu beurteilendes Kriterium zu bestimmen […], was im Sinne der

---

14 BKartA, Beschluss v. 9. Februar 2021, B6-37/21 – *Meta (Facebook)/Kustomer*, Rn. 19.

15 OLG Düsseldorf, Beschluss v. 23. November 2022 – Kart 11/21 (V) – *Meta (Facebook)/Kustomer*, NZKart (2023), S. 35. Das Bundeskartellamt gab das Zusammenschlussvorhaben nach Prüfung frei. Meta erwirkte jedoch eine gerichtliche Entscheidung durch Beschwerde gegen den Kostenfestsetzungsbeschluss.

16 BGH, Beschluss v. 17. Juni 2025 – KVR 77/22, *Meta/Kustomer*.

17 *Monopolkommission*, Hauptgutachten XXIV, Wettbewerb 2022, Rn. 242.

18 *BKartA*, Pressemitteilung v. 15. November 2023 zu Microsoft/OpenAI. OpenAI werde allenfalls etwa zwei Jahre nach Vollzug des Zusammenschlussvorhabens erheblich in Deutschland aktiv sein – jedenfalls aber noch nicht zum Vollzugszeitpunkt.

19 *BKartA*, Pressemitteilung v. 29. November 2024 zu Microsoft/Inflection. Die Zahl deutscher Nutzer des Chatbots Pi von Inflection war schlicht zu gering, als dass von einer erheblichen Inlandstätigkeit ausgegangen werden könnte.

20 Leiter des Referats „Grundsatzfragen der Wettbewerbspolitik, Kartellrecht, wettbewerbspolitische Fragen der Digitalisierung“ im Bundesministerium für Wirtschaft und Energie.

21 *Käseberg* (Anm. 12), S. 1.

22 *Göbel* (Anm. 11), S. 50.

Rechtssicherheit für die beteiligten Unternehmen, die sich durch die bußgeldbewehrte Anmeldepflicht einem staatlichen Eingriff ausgesetzt sehen, auch geboten ist“[23].

Ob derartigen Zusammenschlüssen tatsächlich ein statistisch belastbar erhöhtes Risiko einer erheblichen Behinderung wirksamen Wettbewerbs immanent ist (vgl. § 36 Abs. 1 S. 1 GWB), darf zumindest bezweifelt werden. Soweit ersichtlich, gibt es bisher lediglich ein Zusammenschlussvorhaben, das auf Grundlage der Transaktionswertschwelle anmeldepflichtig und Gegenstand eines Hauptprüfverfahrens[24] war: Thermo Fischer/Olink (2024). Das Hauptprüfverfahren wurde allerdings weniger aufgrund wettbewerblicher Bedenken eingeleitet, sondern vielmehr, um die komplexen betroffenen (Proteomik-)Märkte besser verstehen und abgrenzen zu können.[25] Hintergrund waren teils widersprüchlicher Rückmeldungen im Rahmen der bereits in der Vorprüfung, d.h. vor Einleitung des Hauptprüfverfahrens, durchgeführten Marktbefragung. Letztlich wurde das Zusammenschlussvorhaben am 17. Juni 2024 ohne Auflagen freigegeben.[26]

Eine andere Herangehensweise, um das Netz der Fusionskontrolle möglichst weit zu ziehen, haben einige nationale Gesetzgeber gewählt, indem sie ihre Wettbewerbsbehörden befähigten, die fusionskontrollrechtliche Prüfung von gegebenenfalls wettbewerblich problematischen Zusammenschlussvorhaben nach eigenem Ermessen zu initiieren (sog. Call-in Rechte). Call-in Rechte knüpfen insbesondere nicht an die Inlandsumsätze der beteiligten Unternehmen an. Europäische Wettbewerbsbehörden, die mit entsprechenden Befugnissen ausgestattet wurden, finden sich unter anderem in Dänemark, Irland und Italien.

Auch die Europäische Kommission vertrat im Jahr 2021 noch die Ansicht, Zusammenschlussvorhaben prüfen zu können, die gemäß der europäischen Fusionskontrollverordnung zwar nicht anmeldepflichtig sind, aber zur fusionskontrollrechtlichen Prüfung von einer oder mehreren nationalen Wettbewerbsbehörden an die Europäische Kommission verwiesen wurden. Dies galt nach der mittlerweile überholten Ansicht der Europäischen Kommission unabhängig davon, ob das Zusammenschlussvorhaben nach dem Wettbewerbsrecht der verweisenden Behörde fusionskontrollrechtlich anmeldepflichtig ist.[27] Dieser Ansicht widersprach der Europäische

---

23 OLG Düsseldorf, Beschluss v. 23. November 2022 – Kart 11/21 (V) – *Meta (Facebook)/Kustomer*, NZKart (2023), S. 35, Rn. 58.

24 Das Bundeskartellamt leitet nur selten Hauptprüfverfahren ein. Voraussetzung ist, dass das Zusammenschlussvorhaben aufgrund einer summarischen Prüfung nicht innerhalb der einmonatigen Frist des Vorprüfverfahrens freigegeben werden kann. Charakteristisch für Hauptprüfverfahren sind offene Fragen bei schwieriger Sachverhaltsaufklärung; vgl. *Dubberstein*, in: Säcker/Bien/Meier-Beck/Montag (Anm. 5), GWB § 40, Rn. 20.

25 Der Verfasser war als Berater von Olink unmittelbar am Verfahren beteiligt.

26 Siehe hierzu die Freigabeentscheidung des Bundeskartellamts v. 17. Juni 2024 – B3 – 25/24 (abrufbar unter: https://www.bundeskartellamt.de/SharedDocs/Entscheidung/DE/Entscheidungen/Fusionskontrolle/2024/B3-25-24.pdf?__blob=publicationFile&v=4 (zuletzt abgerufen am 12. Mai 2025)).

27 Rechtsgrundlage bildete nach Auffassung der Europäischen Kommission Art. 22 der Fusionskontrollverordnung, vgl. *Europäische Kommission*, Leitfaden zur Anwendung des Verweisungssystems nach Artikel 22 der Fusionskontrollverordnung auf bestimmte Kategorien von Vorhaben, 2021/C 113/01, Rn. 6.

Gerichtshof in seinem Urteil vom 3. September 2024 in Sachen Illumina/Grail: Eine Verweisung an die Europäische Kommission sei jedenfalls dann ausgeschlossen, wenn die verweisende Behörde nicht befugt ist, das Zusammenschlussvorhaben nach nationalem Fusionskontrollrecht zu prüfen.[28]

Nachdem nun ein Überblick über die aktuelle Rechtslage und den derzeitigen Diskussionsstand in Deutschland (und auf Ebene der Europäischen Union) gegeben wurde, wird der Blick auf Japan gelenkt: Wie geht das japanische Recht mit Zusammenschlussvorhaben um, die kleine innovative Unternehmen zum Gegenstand haben?

2. Zur Rechtslage in Japan

Das japanische Kartellrecht fußt auf dem Gesetz über das Verbot von privaten Monopolen und die Sicherstellung von lauterem Handel (私的独占の禁止及び公正取引の確保に関する法律, *shiteki dokusen no kinshi oyobi kōsei torihiki no kakuho ni kansuru hōritsu*) – nachfolgend Antimonopolgesetz (独占禁止法, *dokusen kinshi hō*) genannt.

Das Antimonopolgesetz umfasst neben dem „klassischen" Kartellrecht auch das Fusionskontrollrecht. Anmeldepflichten richten sich dabei nach den Umsätzen der am Zusammenschluss beteiligten Unternehmen. Anders als das deutsche Recht (mit § 35 Abs. 1 GWB) unterscheiden sich die umsatzbasierten Anmeldeschwellen nach der Art des Zusammenschlussvorhabens (Anteilserwerb, Vermögensübertragung, Verschmelzung, etc.).[29] Den in der Transaktionspraxis wichtigsten Zusammenschlusstatbestand stellt der Anteilserwerb dar: Ein Zusammenschlussvorhaben, bei dem mehr als 20 Prozent der Anteile an einer Zielgesellschaft erworben werden, ist dann anzumelden, wenn im letzten abgeschlossenen Geschäftsjahr der Erwerber in Japan einen Umsatz von mehr als 20 Mrd. JPY (d. h. etwa 120 Mio. EUR) und die Zielgesellschaft in Japan einen Umsatz von mehr als 5 Mrd. JPY (d. h. etwa 30 Mio. EUR) erzielt haben (Art. 10 Abs. 2 des Antimonopolgesetzes).

Die umsatzbasierten Anmeldeschwellen liegen damit erheblich über denen des deutschen Fusionskontrollrechts. Das Risiko, wettbewerbsverzerrende Zusammenschlussvorhaben nicht fusionskontrollrechtlich prüfen zu können, erscheint in Japan daher ungemein größer als in Deutschland.

Bezugnehmend unter anderem auf die deutsche Transaktionswertschwelle[30] hat die JFTC im Jahr 2019 ihre Richtlinien zum fusionskontrollrechtlichen Prüfverfah-

---

28 EuGH, Urteil v. 3. September 2024 – C–611/22 P und C–625/22 P, ECLI:EU:C:2024:677 – *Illumina/Grail*, NZKart (2024), S. 571.

29 Siehe Art. 9 ff. des Antimonopolgesetzes.

30 Siehe *JFTC*, Übersicht zu den Ansichten und Gedanken zu den Vorschlägen zur Anwendungsrichtlinie zur Fusionskontrolle des Antimonopolgesetzes sowie zur Anpassungsrichtlinie zum fusionskontrollrechtlichen Prüfverfahren (「企業結合審査に関する独占禁止法の運用指針」（案）及び「企業結合審査の手続に関する対応方針」（案）に対する意見の概要及びそれに対する考え方, *„kigyō ketsugō shinsa ni kansuru dokusen kinshi hō no un'yō shishin" (an) oyobi „kigyō ketsugō shinsa no tetsuzuki ni kansuru taiō hōshin" (an) ni taisuru iken no gaiyō oyobi sore ni taisuru kangaekata*) (2019), Antwort Nr. 16 zum Themenkomplex in Ziff. 2.

ren (企業結合審査の手続に関する対応方針, *kigyō ketsugō shinsa no tetsuzuki ni kansuru taiō hōshin*) umfassend überarbeitet.[31] Die am 17. Dezember 2019 veröffentlichten überarbeiteten Richtlinien empfehlen unter anderem, nicht anmeldepflichtige Zusammenschlussvorhaben unter bestimmten, nachfolgend näher dargestellten Voraussetzungen mit der JFTC zu konsultieren.[32] Die Empfehlung stützt sich auf Art. 10 Abs. 1 des Antimonopolgesetzes.[33] Danach darf ein Anteils- oder Vermögenserwerb nicht vollzogen werden, wenn dadurch der Wettbewerb in Japan substanziell beeinträchtigt wird (競争を実質的に制限, *kyōsō o jisshitsuteki ni seigen*).[34] Ergänzend dazu kann gemäß Art. 17–2 des Antimonopolgesetzes ein entgegen Art. 10 Abs. 1 des Antimonopolgesetzes vollzogenes Zusammenschlussvorhaben entflechtet werden.

Die überarbeiteten Richtlinien empfehlen die Konsultation bei Zusammenschlussvorhaben, deren Wert 40 Mrd. JPY (d. h. etwa 245 Mio. EUR) übersteigt und die sich auf Nachfrager in Japan auswirken werden. Dies sei jedenfalls dann der Fall, wenn eines der folgenden Regelbeispiele erfüllt ist:

1. das Zielunternehmen hat einen Geschäftsstandort (事業拠点, *jigyō kyoten*), einen Forschungs- und Entwicklungsstandort (研究開発拠点, *kenkyū kaihatsu kyoten*) oder einen vergleichbaren Standort in Japan;
2. Verkaufsaktivitäten des Zielunternehmens zielen auf japanische Kunden ab, beispielsweise durch die Nutzung einer japanischen Webseite oder japanischer Pamphlete; oder
3. der Gesamtumsatz des Zielunternehmens in Japan übersteigt 100 Mio. JPY (d. h. etwa 600.000 EUR).

Die Richtlinien der JFTC bezeichnen derartige Zusammenschlussvorhaben als „nicht anmeldepflichtige Zusammenschlussvorhaben" (届出不要企業結合計画, *todokede fuyō kigyō ketsugō keikaku*). Dies erscheint insofern irreführend, als dass das Ergebnis einer Konsultation eine zumindest faktische Anmeldepflicht nach sich ziehen kann. Sollten sich die am Zusammenschlussvorhaben beteiligten Parteien gegen eine Konsultation entscheiden, kann die JFTC die Parteien auf eigene Initiative zur fusionskontrollrechtlichen Anmeldung auffordern. Die JFTC sichtet zu diesem Zweck Veröffentlichungen zu Transaktionen unter anderem im Internet.[35]

---

31 Die überarbeiteten Richtlinien vom 17. Dezember 2019 sind abrufbar unter: https://www.jftc.go.jp/dk/kiketsu/guideline/guideline/taiouhoushin.html (zuletzt abgerufen am 12. Mai 2025).

32 Ibid.

33 *JFTC* (Anm. 30), Antwort Nr. 3 zum Themenkomplex in Ziff. 2.

34 Der Begriff der substanziellen Beeinträchtigung ist ein wesentliches Konzept des japanischen Kartellrechts. Eine substanzielle Beeinträchtigung liegt vor, wenn ein oder mehrere Unternehmen gemeinsam in der Lage sind, den Preis, die Qualität, die Produktionsmenge oder andere Marktkonditionen zu bestimmen, d. h. Marktmacht haben; siehe hierzu *Vande Walle/Shiraishi*, Competition Law in Japan, Comparative Competition Law (Juli 2015), S. 4 f. m. w. N. aus der Rechtsprechung.

35 *Ōnoki*, Zur Wirksamkeit von Abhilfemaßnahmen in der Fusionskontrolle (企業結合規制における問題解消措置の実効性について, *kigyō ketsugō kisei ni okeru mondai kaishō sochi no jikkōsei ni tsuite*) (2024), S. 68.

Ergänzend behält sich die JFTC das Recht vor, auch solche Zusammenschlussvorhaben fusionskontrollrechtlich zu prüfen, bei denen der Transaktionswert unter 40 Mrd. JPY liegt bzw. bei denen keines der zuvor genannten Regelbeispiele erfüllt ist – ein mit Blick auf Rechts- und Transaktionssicherheit kritikwürdiger Vorbehalt.

Vor diesem Hintergrund erscheint die Empfehlung, „nicht anmeldepflichtige Zusammenschlussvorhaben“ mit der JFTC zu konsultieren, wie eine faktische Verpflichtung zur Konsultation.

3. Zu den wesentlichen Unterschieden zur deutschen Transaktionswertschwelle

Die von den überarbeiteten Richtlinien der JFTC erfassten Zusammenschlussvorhaben unterscheiden sich in zwei wesentlichen Aspekten von Zusammenschlussvorhaben, die unter die deutsche Transaktionswertschwelle (§ 35 Abs. 1a GWB) fallen: (a) dem Transaktionswert sowie (b) dem Grad der erforderlichen Inlandsauswirkungen.

a) Zum Transaktionswert

Während die deutsche Transaktionswertschwelle nur Zusammenschlussvorhaben mit einem Transaktionswert von mehr als 400 Mio. EUR (§ 35 Abs. 1a Nr. 3 GWB) erfasst, zielen die Richtlinien der JFTC auf Zusammenschlussvorhaben mit einem Transaktionswert von lediglich 40 Mrd. JPY (d.h. etwa 245 Mio. EUR) ab. Dieser niedrige Transaktionswert wurde bereits im Rahmen des Konsultationsprozesses zur Überarbeitung der fusionskontrollrechtlichen Richtlinien kritisiert: Er führt auch mit Blick auf die Regelbeispiele dazu, dass annähernd jedes Zusammenschlussvorhaben mit der JFTC zu konsultieren ist. Dies widerspreche dem Zweck der Richtlinien, so die Kritik, die Anwendung des Antimonopolgesetzes bei Zusammenschlussvorhaben für Unternehmen zu erleichtern.[36] Die JFTC rechtfertigte den niedrigen Transaktionswert damit, dass bereits zuvor bei praktisch allen Zusammenschlussvorhaben, die aufgrund der umsatzbasierten Anmeldeschwellen (Art. 10ff. des Antimonopolgesetzes) angemeldet wurden, Kaufpreise von mindestens 40 Mrd. JPY gezahlt worden seien.[37] Ergänzend verwies die JFTC auf die Existenz transaktionswertbezogener Anmeldeschwellen in anderen Ländern, namentlich Deutschland und den Vereinigten Staaten von Amerika.[38] Unklar ist, wieso die JFTC nicht auch auf die Transaktionswertschwelle des österreichischen Kartellgesetzes verwies. Der in Österreich vorausgesetzte Transaktionswert von 200 Mio. EUR liegt deutlich unter den Schwellen der deutschen und US-amerikanischen Fusionskontrollregime und zudem unter dem japanischen Schwellenwert von 40 Mrd. JPY.

b) Zu den erforderlichen Inlandsauswirkungen

Der zweite wesentliche Unterschied zwischen beiden Fusionskontrollregimen liegt im Grad der zur Begründung einer Anmeldepflicht erforderlichen Inlandstätigkeit des Zielunternehmens.

---

36 *JFTC* (Anm. 30), Frage Nr. 9 zum Themenkomplex in Ziff. 2.

37 Zur Kritik: Ibid., Antwort Nr. 9 zum Themenkomplex in Ziff. 2.

38 Ibid., Antwort Nr. 16 zum Themenkomplex in Ziff. 2.

Während § 35 Abs. 1a Nr. 4 GWB eine Inlandstätigkeit „in erheblichem Umfang“ voraussetzt, empfehlen die überarbeiteten Richtlinien der JFTC eine Konsultation bei nahezu jeder inländischen Geschäftstätigkeit des Zielunternehmens. Dies zeigt sich insbesondere im zweiten Regelbeispiel. Danach kann alleine die Nutzung einer japanischen Webseite durch das Zielunternehmen eine Konsultation mit der JFTC erforderlich machen. Insofern erfassen die überarbeiteten Richtlinien der JFTC weit mehr Zusammenschlussvorhaben als die deutsche Transaktionswertschwelle.

Die vergleichsweise weit gefasste Konsultationsempfehlung lässt sich teils damit erklären, dass die JFTC insbesondere auch den Erwerb von Start-ups fusionskontrollrechtlich prüfen möchte.[39] Die Richtlinien spannen dazu ein weites Netz. Eine Anmeldepflicht ergibt sich daraus aber nicht zwingend. Das zeigt auch die Praxis: Zusammenschlussvorhaben, die Zielunternehmen mit nur geringen Inlandsumsätzen zum Gegenstand haben, werden grundsätzlich nicht konsultiert – auch wenn der Kaufpreis deutlich über 40 Mrd. JPY liegt. Vielmehr entscheiden sich die Parteien eines Zusammenschlussvorhabens häufig dazu, nur solche Vorhaben zu konsultieren, denen ein erheblicher Inlandsbezug immanent ist, beispielsweise in Form hinreichend wahrscheinlicher nachteiliger Wettbewerbseffekte. In den Statistiken der JFTC spiegelt sich diese Praxis eindrucksvoll wider.

4. Ein Blick auf die Statistiken

Laut einer Statistik der JFTC wurden im Zeitraum vom 1. Januar 2021 bis zum 31. Dezember 2023 jährlich durchschnittlich 330 Zusammenschlussvorhaben bei der JFTC zur fusionskontrollrechtlichen Prüfung angemeldet und geprüft. Durchschnittlich 14 Zusammenschlussvorhaben pro Jahr entfielen auf konsultierte Anmeldungen.[40] Damit gehen lediglich etwa 4 Prozent aller angemeldeten Zusammenschlussvorhaben auf Konsultationen zurück. Dieser niedrige Anteil legt nahe, dass die JFTC letztlich nur bei besonders gelagerten „nicht anmeldepflichtigen Zusammenschlussvorhaben“ zur Anmeldung rät bzw. „nicht anmeldepflichtige Zusammenschlussvorhaben“ schon grundsätzlich kaum konsultiert werden.[41]

Bedauerlicherweise sah die JFTC, soweit ersichtlich, bislang davon ab, offenzulegen, welche Besonderheiten eines Zusammenschlussvorhabens maßgeblich für eine fusionskontrollrechtliche Anmeldepflicht infolge einer Konsultation sind. Die JFTC bleibt auch in einschlägigen Pressemitteilungen äußerst vage: So wurde in einer Pressemitteilung aus dem Jahr 2023 die Anmeldung des Erwerbs von Figma durch Adobe, zwei US-amerikanische Unternehmen, schlicht mit dem hohen Transaktionswert und den zu erwartenden Inlandsauswirkungen begründet, ohne aber auf beide Ele-

---

39 Ibid., Antwort Nr. 4 zum Themenkomplex in Ziff. 2; siehe auch *Ōnoki* (Anm. 35), S. 67 m. w. N.

40 *JFTC*, Stand der fusionskontrollrechtlichen Anmeldungen im Jahr 2023 (令和５年度における企業結合関係届出の状況, *reiwa 5-nendo ni okeru kigyō ketsugō kankei todokede no jōkyō*) (5. Juli 2024).

41 Eine Statistik zur Anzahl der Konsultationen von „nicht anmeldepflichtigen Zusammenschlussvorhaben“ gibt es, soweit ersichtlich, nicht.

mente näher einzugehen.[42] Dass das Zusammenschlussvorhaben trotz Figmas' geringer inländischer Umsätze auch in Japan anzumelden war, ist insofern nicht überraschend, als dass der Zusammenschluss nach Ansicht der Europäischen Kommission zu einer erheblichen Behinderung des Wettbewerbs auf einigen weltweiten Märkten geführt hätte.[43] Es lässt sich somit schwerlich argumentieren, dass das Zusammenschlussvorhaben nicht auch in Japan hätte angemeldet werden müssen – auch wenn das Zielunternehmen die umsatzbasierten Schwellenwerte (Art. 10 Abs. 2 des Antimonopolgesetzes) nicht erfüllte.

Für Deutschland zeigt sich ein statistisch vergleichbares Bild: Im Zeitraum vom 9. Juni 2017, d.h. dem Tag des Inkrafttretens der Transaktionswertschwelle, bis Ende des Jahres 2020 wurden durchschnittlich weniger als ein Prozent aller angemeldeten Zusammenschlussvorhaben auf Grundlage der Transaktionswertschwelle angemeldet.[44] Im Jahr 2021 und im Jahr 2022 stieg dieser Anteil auf insgesamt vier Prozent.[45] Ursächlich dürfte die mit der 10. GWB Novelle ab dem 19. Januar 2021 erfolgte Anhebung der umsatzbasierten Anmeldeschwellen (§ 35 Abs. 1 GWB) von vormals 5 Mio. EUR auf 17,5 Mio. EUR und von 25 Mio. EUR auf 50 Mio. EUR gewesen sein. Der Anteil der transaktionswertbasierten Anmeldungen liegt damit auf einem vergleichbaren Niveau wie der Anteil der Zusammenschussvorhaben, die in Japan infolge einer Konsultation angemeldet wurden (jeweils an der Anzahl aller fusionskontrollrechtlichen Anmeldungen). Umso bemerkenswerter ist dies vor dem Hintergrund, dass die Voraussetzungen einer umsatzbasierten Anmeldepflicht in Deutschland, wie zuvor dargestellt, deutlich strenger sind als die Vorgaben der überarbeiteten Richtlinien, aufgrund derer eine Konsultation empfohlen

42 Siehe hierzu die Pressemitteilung der JFTC v. 21. Dezember 2023 (abrufbar unter: https://www.jftc.go.jp/houdou/pressrelease/2023/dec/kiketsu_231221.pdf (zuletzt abgerufen am 12. Mai 2025)).

43 Siehe zu wettbewerblichen Bedenken: Europäischen Kommission, Pressemitteilung v. 17. November 2023 (abrufbar unter: https://ec.europa.eu/commission/presscorner/detail/en/ip_23_5778 (zuletzt abgerufen am 12. Mai 2025)). Bemerkenswert ist, dass das Zusammenschlussvorhaben überhaupt nur deshalb von der Europäischen Kommission geprüft wurde, weil es unter die deutsche und österreichische Transaktionswertschwelle fiel. Die österreichische Bundeswettbewerbsbehörde stellte infolgedessen einen Verweisungsantrag an die Europäische Kommission, dem sich das Bundeskartellamt anschloss; siehe hierzu Europäische Kommission, Entscheidung v. 14. Februar 2023, Case M.11033 – *ADOBE/FIGMA*.

44 Im Jahr 2017 waren dies acht Zusammenschlussvorhaben, d.h. weniger 1 Prozent der insgesamt 1.303 angemeldeten Vorhaben, im Jahr 2018 zehn Zusammenschlussvorhaben, d.h. weniger als 1 Prozent der insgesamt 1.383 angemeldeten Vorhaben, im Jahr 2019 zehn Zusammenschlussvorhaben, d.h. weniger als 1 Prozent der insgesamt 1.433 angemeldeten Vorhaben und im Jahr 2020 drei Zusammenschlussvorhaben, d.h. weniger als 1 Prozent der insgesamt 1.236 angemeldeten Vorhaben. Siehe hierzu: *Bundesregierung*, BT-Drs. 19/26136, S. 4; *BKartA*, BT-Drs. 19/10900, S. 23; *BKartA*, BT-Drs. 19/30775, S. 29. Dies entspricht etwa den drei zusätzlichen Zusammenschlussvorhaben, die dem Gesetzesentwurf zur Transaktionswertschwelle als Annahme zugrunde gelegt wurden (siehe BT-Drs 18/10207 (Anm. 4), S. 2).

45 Im Jahr 2021 und im Jahr 2022 wurden insgesamt 75 Zusammenschlussvorhaben, d.h. etwa 4 Prozent der insgesamt 1.860 angemeldeten Vorhaben, auf Grundlage der Transaktionswertschwelle angemeldet. Siehe hierzu *BKartA*, BT-Drs. 20/7300, S. 25; fusionskontrollrechtliche Statistiken für die Jahre 2023 und 2024 lagen zum Zeitpunkt der Erstellung dieses Artikels noch nicht vor.

wird. Insofern wäre zu erwarten gewesen, dass der Anteil der Zusammenschussvorhaben, die infolge einer Konsultation angemeldet wurden, in Japan deutlich höher ist als der Anteil der transaktionswertbasierten Anmeldungen in Deutschland (jeweils an der Anzahl aller Anmeldungen).

Für Deutschland drängt sich somit die Frage auf, ob die Ausweitung des Anwendungsbereichs der Transaktionswertschwelle tatsächlich zu einer merklichen Zunahme fusionskontrollrechtlicher Anmeldungen führen würde und der verfolgte Zweck durch eine Anhebung überhaupt erreicht werden würde.

5. Schlussfolgerungen für eine Novellierung der Transaktionswertschwelle

Wie eingangs erwähnt, sprechen sich insbesondere Vertreter des Bundeskartellamts und der Monopolkommission dafür aus, die in § 35 Abs. 1a Nr. 4 GWB angelegte Voraussetzung der erheblichen Inlandstätigkeit anzupassen, um auch künftige Inlandsauswirkungen berücksichtigen zu können. Argumentiert wird mit dem Risiko, den Wettbewerb vor Verfälschungen zu schützen, die sich erst nach einiger Zeit manifestieren. Gegenargumente bilden Rechtssicherheit, Rechtsklarheit und Transaktionssicherheit.

Der Blick auf Japan lässt vermuten, dass die Herabsetzung der Voraussetzungen einer Anmeldepflicht nicht zwingend zu einer höheren Anzahl von Anmeldungen führen muss. Insofern deutet sich der Grundsatz an, dass je vager die Voraussetzungen einer Anmeldepflicht formuliert sind, desto eher neigen die Parteien eines Zusammenschlussvorhabens zu einer möglichst pragmatischen Interpretation der Anmeldevoraussetzungen. Die einer solchen Interpretation zugrundeliegende risikobasierte Entscheidung erscheint auch insofern vertretbar, als dass es nicht zuletzt mit Blick auf § 36 Abs. 1 S. 1 GWB[46] schwerlich das Ziel des Bundeskartellamts sein kann, Zusammenschlussvorhaben einer fusionskontrollrechtlichen Prüfung zu unterwerfen, die nach gebotener Selbsteinschätzung lediglich mäßige wettbewerbliche Auswirkungen im Inland haben werden.

Nicht zuletzt aus rechtspolitischer Sicht wäre schließlich interessant zu sehen, ob sich das im Rahmen dieser Untersuchung angedeutete Ergebnis durch weitere rechtsvergleichende Analysen stützen lässt. Der Gesetzgeber ist in jedem Falle aber gut darin beraten, die Reichweite der transaktionswertbedingten Anmeldepflicht nicht zu überdehnen.

II. Teil 2: Zum kartellrechtlichen Schutz von Zulieferern

Der zweite Teil dieses Artikels beleuchtet den Schutz von Zulieferern nach deutschem und japanischem Kartellrecht. Häufig gibt es ein erhebliches Machtgefälle zwischen den (kleineren) Zulieferern und den (größeren) Abnehmern. Exemplarisch ist das Verhältnis zwischen Automobilzulieferern und Automobilherstellern. Derar-

---

46 Danach sind nur solche Zusammenschlüsse zu untersagen, durch die der wirksame Wettbewerb erheblich behindert wird, insbesondere solche, von denen zu erwarten ist, dass sie eine marktbeherrschende Stellung begründen oder verstärken.

tige Machtgefälle bergen erhebliche wirtschaftliche Risiken für Zulieferer etwa in Form benachteiligender Geschäftsbedingungen. Fragen zum Umfang des kartellrechtlichen Zuliefererschutzes werden vor diesem Hintergrund sowohl in Deutschland als auch in Japan virulent.

Im Folgenden wird zunächst das deutsche und sodann das japanische Kartellrecht beleuchtet. Dabei werden Gemeinsamkeiten und Unterschiede aufgezeigt.

1. Zur Rechtslage in Deutschland

In Deutschland erstreckt sich der kartellrechtliche Schutz von Zulieferern entlang der Vorschriften des GWB. Wesentlich ist ein Missverhältnis der Verhandlungsmacht zwischen Zulieferer und Abnehmer. Der Zuliefererschutz ist daher Aufgabe der kartellrechtlichen Marktmachtmissbrauchsvorschriften (§§ 18 ff. GWB).

Der Schutz des Zulieferers, etwa vor unangemessenen Geschäftsbedingungen, setzt folglich eine marktbeherrschende (i. S. v. § 18 Abs. 1 GWB) oder zumindest sog. relativ marktmächtige (§ 20 Abs. 1 S. 1 GWB) Stellung des Abnehmers voraus.

Eine marktbeherrschende Stellung liegt vor, wenn der Abnehmer auf dem sachlich und räumlich relevanten Nachfragemarkt ohne Wettbewerber ist, keinem wesentlichen Wettbewerb ausgesetzt ist oder eine im Verhältnis zu seinen Wettbewerbern überragende Marktstellung hat (§ 18 Abs. 1 GWB). Es gilt die Vermutung, dass ein Unternehmen marktbeherrschend ist, wenn es einen Marktanteil von mindestens 40 Prozent hat (§ 18 Abs. 4 GWB). Soweit ersichtlich, gab es in den letzten fünf Jahren lediglich zwei behördliche bzw. gerichtliche Entscheidungen, in denen eine marktbeherrschende Stellung des Abnehmers angenommen wurde. Beide Entscheidungen betrafen Nachfragemärkte im digitalen Bereich.[47] Die geringe Anzahl einschlägiger Entscheidungen dürfte darauf zurückzuführen sein, dass zum einen eine abnehmerseitige marktbeherrschende Stellung nur ausnahmsweise, d.h. etwa auf Nachfragemärkten für Nischenprodukte, denkbar ist und zum anderen der Nachweis einer sog. relativen Marktmacht deutlich einfacher zu erbringen ist.

Relative Marktmacht liegt vor, wenn der Zulieferer hinsichtlich der Art der gelieferten Waren in der Weise vom Abnehmer abhängig ist, dass ausreichende und zumutbare Möglichkeiten, auf andere Abnehmer auszuweichen, nicht bestehen und somit ein deutliches Ungleichgewicht zur Gegenmacht des Abnehmers besteht (§ 20 Abs. 1 S. 1 GWB). Gemeinhin wird zwischen der sortimentsbedingten Abhängigkeit, der Spitzenstellungsabhängigkeit, der unternehmensbedingten Abhängigkeit und der mangelbedingten Abhängigkeit differenziert.[48] Im Zuliefererkontext ist insbesondere die unternehmensbedingte Abhängigkeit relevant.[49] Diese liegt vor, wenn

---

47 LG Düsseldorf, Urteil v. 18. April 2024 – 14d O 1/23, in dem von einer marktbeherrschenden Stellung von Facebook auf einem Nachfragemarkt für soziale Netzwerke ausgegangen wurde, sowie BGH, Urteil v. 6. Juli 2021 – KZR 11/18 – wilhelm.tel, wo der Nachfragemarkt der Übertragung von Programmsignalen über Breitbandkabel betroffen war.

48 Siehe hierzu *Bosch*, in: Bechtold/Bosch: GWB, Gesetz gegen Wettbewerbsbeschränkungen, §§ 1–96, 185, 186–187, 11. Aufl. (2025), GWB § 20, Rn. 12 ff. m. w. N.

49 So auch *Bosch* (Anm. 47), GWB § 20, Rn. 16 f.

einem Zulieferer das Ausweichen auf andere Abnehmer unzumutbar ist, etwa weil er in eine existenzielle Abhängigkeit zum Abnehmer geraten ist.[50] Eine derartige Abhängigkeit kann vorliegen, wenn der Zulieferer einen wirtschaftlich substanziellen Teil seiner Produktion auf Teile ausgerichtet hat, die er nur an einen Abnehmer liefert. Vertreten wird, dass ein Zulieferer, der zehn Prozent der produzierten Waren an einen großen Abnehmer liefert, bereits in eine unternehmensbedingte Abhängigkeit geraten kann, soweit Ausweichmöglichkeiten nicht existieren und der Verlust des durch diesen Produktionsanteil erzielten Deckungsbeitrages die wirtschaftliche Grundlage des Unternehmens gefährdet.[51]

Relative Marktmacht ist somit grundsätzlich deutlich einfacher nachweisbar als eine marktbeherrschende Stellung. Dennoch gibt es, soweit ersichtlich, nur wenige behördliche und gerichtliche Entscheidungen, welche die relative Marktmacht des Abnehmers gegenüber seinem Zulieferer zum Gegenstand haben.[52] In den letzten fünf Jahren findet sich, soweit ersichtlich, keine einschlägige Entscheidung.[53]

Festhalten lässt sich, dass es in Deutschland nur wenige Entscheidungen gibt, in denen die Marktmachtmissbrauchsvorschriften zum Schutz von Zulieferern herangezogen wurden.

a) Kontrahierungszwang bzw. Pflicht zur Aufrechterhaltung einer Geschäftsbeziehung

Sowohl die Verweigerung als auch der Abbruch einer Lieferbeziehung können für Zulieferer mit erheblichen finanziellen Nachteilen verbunden sein. Insofern drängt sich die Frage auf, unter welchen Voraussetzungen marktbeherrschenden bzw. relativ marktmächtigen Abnehmern ein Kontrahierungszwang auferlegt werden kann.

Ausgangspunkt bildet § 19 Abs. 2 Nr. 1 Var. 1 GWB. Danach liegt missbräuchliches Verhalten vor, wenn ein marktbeherrschendes bzw. (i. V. m. § 20 Abs. 1 S. 1 GWB) relativ marktmächtiges Unternehmen u. a. als Nachfrager einer bestimmten Art von Waren oder gewerblichen Leistungen ein anderes Unternehmen unmittelbar oder mittelbar unbillig behindert. Behinderung meint jede in einem rein objektiven Sinne zu verstehende Beeinträchtigung der Betätigungsmöglichkeiten im Wettbewerb, gleichgültig, ob „wettbewerbsfremde" oder in sonstiger Weise anfechtbare Mittel angewendet werden.[54]

§ 19 Abs. 2 Nr. 1 Var. 1 GWB erfasst demnach Fälle, in denen sich ein marktbeherrschender oder relativ marktmächtiger Abnehmer ohne sachlich rechtfertigenden Grund weigert, eine Geschäftsbeziehung mit einem Zulieferer einzugehen oder fort-

---

50 *Bosch* (Anm. 47), GWB § 20, Rn. 16.

51 *Bosch* (Anm. 47), GWB § 20, Rn. 17.

52 Siehe bspw. OLG Karlsruhe, Urteil v. 14. November 2007 – 6 U 57/06 – *Versandbuchhändler.* Siehe auch die zitierten Rechtsprechung sowie Entscheidungen des Bundeskartellamts in *Markert/Podszun*, in: Immenga/Mestmäcker (Hrsg.), Wettbewerbsrecht, Band 2 GWB, 7. Aufl. (2024), GWB § 20, Rn. 43–48.

53 Offengelassen in: OLG Düsseldorf, Urteil v. 5. Februar 2020 – U (Kart) 4/19 – *MQB-Hintersitzlehnen II.*

54 *Fuchs*, in: Immenga/Mestmäcker (Anm. 51), GWB § 19, Rn. 84.

zuführen.[55] Entscheidend ist, ob das Interesse des Anbieters an dem Abschluss bzw. der Aufrechterhaltung der Geschäftsbeziehung das Interesse des Abnehmers (als Normadressat) an der Vertragsabschlussfreiheit so sehr überwiegt, dass ein Kontrahierungszwang angezeigt ist.[56] Die Interessenabwägung richtet sich nach der Marktstellung des Abnehmers, dem Grad der Abhängigkeit des Zulieferers zum Abnehmer und der Möglichkeit des Zulieferers, Geschäftsbeziehungen mit anderen Abnehmern einzugehen.[57] Berücksichtigt werden dabei sowohl das Interesse des Abnehmers, nicht mehr Produkte abnehmen zu müssen als benötigt werden, als auch die Interessen anderer Zulieferer, denselben Abnehmer beliefern zu können.[58]

Im Ergebnis führt die Interessenabwägung nur ausnahmsweise zu einem Kontrahierungszwang. Dem liegt das Bestreben zugrunde, auch Unternehmen mit einer besonders starken Marktstellung einen möglichst großen Verhaltensspielraum zu gewähren.[59] Die Pflicht zur Rücksichtnahme auf die wettbewerblichen Betätigungsmöglichkeiten anderer Unternehmen kommt daher letztlich nur als „*ultima ratio*" in Betracht, demnach nur, wenn mildere, „d. h. die rechtliche und wirtschaftliche Entscheidungsfreiheit des Normadressaten weniger beschränkende Verhaltenspflichten nicht in Betracht komme[n] […]".[60]

Es erscheint somit wenig überraschend, dass Kontrahierungszwänge zugunsten von Zulieferern, soweit ersichtlich, bislang kaum Gegenstand behördlicher und gerichtlicher Entscheidungen waren.[61]

b) Schutz vor unangemessenen Geschäftsbedingungen und Diskriminierung

Auch benachteiligende und ggf. diskriminierende Geschäftsbedingungen können die finanziellen Interessen von Zulieferern nachhaltig beeinträchtigen. Der kartell-

55 Siehe etwa *Westermann*, in Säcker/Bien/Meier-Beck/Montag (Anm. 5), GWB § 19, Rn. 52 ff. m. w. N.

56 *Westermann*, in Säcker/Bien/Meier-Beck/Montag (Anm. 5), GWB § 19, Rn. 53.

57 BGH, Urteil v. 30. September 1971 – KZR 12/70 – *Vermittlungsprovision für Flugpassagen*, WuW/E BGH, S. 1203; BGH, Urteil v. 10. Februar 1987 – KZR 6/86 – *Freundschaftswerbung*, WuW/E BGH, S. 2363; BGH, Urteil v. 19. März 1996 – KZR 1/95 – WuW/E BGH, S. 3063 – *Pay-TV-Durchleitung*; OLG Karlsruhe, Urteil v. 27. August 1997, 6 U 4/97 (Kart) – *Feuerwehr-Drehleitern*, WuW/E DE–R, S. 82.

58 In diese Richtung auch BGH, Urteil v. 13. November 1990 – KZR 25/89 (Celle).

59 *Westermann*, in Säcker/Bien/Meier-Beck/Montag (Anm. 5), GWB § 19, Rn. 49 m. w. N. Siehe auch *Fuchs*, in: Immenga/Mestmäcker (Anm. 51), GWB § 19, Rn. 187 mit Verweis auf BGH, Urteil v. 13. November 1990 – KZR 25/89, WuW/E BGH, S. 2686 f. (zur Abnahmepflicht von Zuckerrüben); BVerfG, Nichtannahmebeschluss v. 9. Oktober 2000 – 1 BvR 1627/95, WuW/E DE – R S. 557; BGH, Urteil v. 2. Juli 1996 – KZR 31/95, WuW/E BGH, S. 3075 f. (zur Abnahmepflicht im Arzneimittelvertrieb unter bestimmten Voraussetzungen); ebenso BGH, Urteil v. 26. Mai 1987 – KZR 13/85 (Celle), wonach „Anbieter und Nachfrager – auch wenn sie eine marktbeherrschende oder marktstarke Stellung haben – ihre Vertriebs- und Bezugswege [grundsätzlich] nach eigener kaufmännischer Entscheidung bestimmen [können]. Ein Kontrahierungszwang kann nur ausnahmsweise unter den Voraussetzungen des § 26 II GWB [a. F.] in Frage kommen."

60 So bereits BGH, Urteil v. 13. November 1990 – KZR 25/89 (Celle).

61 Siehe hierzu die vorgenannten Entscheidungen.

rechtliche Schutz vor derartigen Maßnahmen wird in drei Vorschriften adressiert: § 19 Abs. 2 Nr. 2 GWB, § 19 Abs. 2 Nr. 5 GWB und § 19 Abs. 2 Nr. 1 Var. 2 GWB.

§ 19 Abs. 2 Nr. 2 GWB verbietet es marktbeherrschenden Unternehmen, Entgelte oder sonstige Geschäftsbedingungen zu fordern, die von denjenigen abweichen, die sich bei wirksamem Wettbewerb mit hoher Wahrscheinlichkeit ergeben würden. Geschäftspartner werden somit vor unangemessenen Geschäftsbedingungen geschützt.

§ 19 Abs. 2 Nr. 5 GWB, dessen Schutzbereich sich mit § 19 Abs. 2 Nr. 2 GWB überschneidet[62], verbietet es marktbeherrschenden oder (i. V. m. § 20 Abs. 2 GWB) relativ marktmächtigen Unternehmen ohne sachlich gerechtfertigten Grund Geschäftspartner aufzufordern, Vorteile zu gewähren.

Beide Vorschriften erfassen eine Vielzahl von Missbrauchshandlungen wie die Forderung exzessiv geringer Preise,[63] die Bindung des Zulieferers durch langfristige exklusive Lieferverpflichtungen und die Änderung der Geschäftsbedingungen in Dauerschuldverhältnissen zum Nachteil des Zulieferers.[64]

Flankiert wird der Schutz des Zulieferers durch das Verbot der Diskriminierung (§ 19 Abs. 2 Nr. 1 Var. 2 GWB). Danach liegt ein missbräuchliches Verhalten vor, wenn ein marktbeherrschendes oder (i. V. m. § 20 Abs. 1 GWB) relativ marktmächtiges Unternehmen ein anderes Unternehmen ohne sachlich gerechtfertigten Grund unmittelbar oder mittelbar anders behandelt als gleichartige Unternehmen.

Ob eine Diskriminierung vorliegt, ist auf Grundlage einer „Interessenabwägung unter Berücksichtigung der auf die Freiheit des Wettbewerbs gerichteten Zielsetzung des Gesetzes gegen Wettbewerbsbeschränkungen […]“[65] zu beantworten. Da auch marktbeherrschenden bzw. relativ marktmächtigen Abnehmern erhebliche unternehmerische Ermessensspielräume zugebilligt werden,[66] gelten für das Vorliegen einer sachlich nicht gerechtfertigten Ungleichbehandlung strenge Anforderungen.[67]

---

62 So auch *Wolf*, in Säcker/Bien/Meier-Beck/Montag (Anm. 5), § 19, Rn. 124 m. w. N.

63 Missbräuchlich kann sein, wenn vom Zulieferer ein Preis gefordert wird, der von demjenigen abweicht, der sich bei wirksamem Wettbewerb mit hoher Wahrscheinlichkeit ergeben würde. Die Angemessenheit des Preises richtet sich maßgeblich nach dem Vergleichsmarktkonzept. Das Konzept findet dort seine Grenze, wo sich aufgrund des hohen Spezialisierungsgrads des Zulieferers ein vergleichbarer Markt nicht identifizieren lässt. In jedem Fall kommt die Preisaufsicht nur als „*ultima ratio*“ in Betracht. Das Missbrauchsverbot dient nicht dazu, Anbietern ihre Existenz und ein auskömmliches Einkommen zu garantieren; siehe *BKartA*, BT-Drs. 8/2980, S. 34 f.; *Köhler*, Wettbewerbs- und kartellrechtliche Kontrolle der Nachfragemacht (1979), S. 54. Siehe auch *Fuchs*, in: Immenga/Mestmäcker (Anm. 51), GWB § 19, Rn. 242, wonach „[…] die Aufsicht über missbräuchlich zu niedrige Preise marktbeherrschender Nachfrager noch mehr ein letzter Notbehelf sein [dürfte], als dies für die Preiskontrolle bei Anbietermacht zutrifft.“

64 Siehe generell die Fallbeispiele in *Wolf*, in: Säcker/Bien/Meier-Beck/Montag (Anm. 5), § 19, Rn. 124.

65 BGH, Beschluss v. 21. Februar 1995 – KVR 10/94 (KG).

66 *Bosch* (Anm. 47), GWB § 19, Rn. 51; *Klumpe*, in: Kersting/Meyer-Lindemann/Podszun, Kartellrecht, Kommentar zum Deutschen und Europäischen Recht, 5. Aufl. (2025), GWB § 19, Rn. 151.

67 Hinzu kommt, dass für die sachliche Rechtfertigung einer unterschiedlichen Behandlung der Diskriminierende darlegungs- und beweispflichtig ist; ständige Rspr., vgl. BGH, Urteil v.

Festhalten lässt sich, dass das deutsche Kartellrecht einerseits ein grundsätzlich großes Spektrum an benachteiligenden Geschäftshandlungen erfasst, der kartellrechtliche Schutz von Zulieferern andererseits aber nur ausnahmsweise in Betracht kommt. Dies zeigt sich zum einen an der, soweit ersichtlich, nur geringen Anzahl behördlicher und gerichtlicher Entscheidungen, in denen ein Abnehmer als marktbeherrschend bzw. relativ marktmächtig angesehen wurde. Zum anderen werden an das Vorliegen vieler, für Zulieferer relevanter Missbrauchshandlungen hohe Anforderungen gestellt, um Eingriffe in die unternehmerische Betätigungsfreiheit möglichst gering zu halten. Vor diesem Hintergrund wird nunmehr der Blick auf Japan gelenkt.

2. Zur Rechtslage in Japan

Der kartellrechtliche Schutz von Zulieferern basiert in Japan im Wesentlichen auf zwei Gesetzen: (a) Dem Antimonopolgesetz und (b) dem Gesetz zur Verhinderung unter anderem von Zahlungsverzögerungen in Zulieferersituationen (下請代金支払遅延等防止法, *shitauke daikin shiharai chien-tō bōshi hō*), Gesetz Nr. 120/1956 – nachfolgend Zulieferergesetz (下請法, *shitauke hō*) genannt.

Beide Gesetze werden im Folgenden näher beleuchtet.

a) Antimonopolgesetz – Schutz vor unfairen Geschäftspraktiken

Das Antimonopolgesetz lässt sich strukturell in vier Bereiche teilen:

1. Das Verbot unbilliger Handelsbeschränkungen (不当な取引制限, *futōna torihiki seigen*), das auf (horizontale) Vereinbarungen zwischen Wettbewerbern Anwendung findet (Art. 3 i. V. m. Art. 2 Abs. 6 des Antimonopolgesetzes),
2. das Verbot privater Monopole (私的独占, *shiteki dokusen*), das auf den Schutz von Wettbewerbern vor Ausbeutungs- und Behinderungsmissbrauch abzielt (Art. 3 i. V. m. Art. 2 Abs. 5 des Antimonopolgesetzes),
3. das Verbot von unfairen Geschäftspraktiken (不公正な取引方法, *fukōseina torihiki hōhō*), das diverse, zumeist vertikale Beschränkungen des Wettbewerbs betrifft (Art. 19 des Antimonopolgesetzes), und
4. die Fusionskontrolle (Art. 9 ff. des Antimonopolgesetzes).[68]

Grundlage des kartellrechtlichen Zuliefererschutzes bildet Art. 19 des Antimonopolgesetzes, der unfaire Geschäftspraktiken verbietet. Art. 2 Abs. 9 des Antimonopolgesetzes definiert den Begriff der unfairen Geschäftspraktiken in Form einer enumerativen Liste konkreter Geschäftshandlungen. Erfasst sind unter anderem ungerechtfertigte Absprachen zwischen Wettbewerbern zur Nichtbelieferung von Unternehmen (Art. 2 Abs. 9 Nr. 1 des Antimonopolgesetzes), ungerechtfertigte Kampfreisangebote (Art. 2 Abs. 9 Nr. 3 des Antimonopolgesetzes), der Missbrauch

24. März 1981 – KZR 2/80, WuW/E BGH, S. 1797; BGH, Urteil v. 30. Juni 1981 – KZR 11/80 – *Allkauf-Saba*, WuW/E BGH, S. 1819; OLG Hamburg, Urteil v. 4. Juni 2009 – 3 U 203/08 – *CRS-Betreiber/Lufthansa*, WuW/E DE–R, S. 2840; *Bosch* (Anm. 47), GWB § 19, Rn. 44.

68 Siehe zu einem Überblick auf: *Vande Walle/Shiraishi* (Anm. 33).

einer überragenden Stellung (優越的位置, *yūetsuteki ichi*) (Art. 2 Abs. 9 Nr. 5 des Antimonopolgesetzes – dazu sogleich) sowie die unbillige Ungleichbehandlung von Unternehmen (Art. 2 Abs. 9 Nr. 6 lit. a) des Antimonopolgesetzes).

Das von Art. 19 i. V. m. Art. 2 Abs. 9 des Antimonopolgesetzes erfasste missbräuchliche Verhalten fällt in Deutschland teils unter das kartellrechtliche Verbot wettbewerbsbeschränkender Vereinbarungen (§ 1 GWB), teils unter den unlauterkeitsrechtlichen Mitbewerberschutz (§ 5 UWG) sowie teils unter die Verbotsvorschriften zum Marktmachtmissbrauch (§§ 19 f. GWB).

Soweit ersichtlich, wird der kartellrechtliche Zuliefererschutz ausschließlich im Kontext des Missbrauchs einer überragenden Stellung diskutiert. Gemäß Art. 2 Abs. 9 Nr. 5 des Antimonopolgesetzes stellen folgende Handlungen unfaire Geschäftspraktiken dar, soweit sie im Lichte des Handelsbrauchs unbillig (正常な商慣習に照らして不当に, *seijō na shōkanshū ni terashite futō ni*) und Ausdruck einer überragenden Stellung gegenüber dem Geschäftspartner sind:

- den Geschäftspartner im Rahmen einer fortdauernden Geschäftsbeziehung zu veranlassen, Waren oder Dienstleistungen ohne Bezug zur Geschäftsbeziehung zu erwerben (Art. 2 Abs. 9 Nr. 5 lit. a) des Antimonopolgesetzes),
- den Geschäftspartner im Rahmen einer fortdauernden Geschäftsbeziehung zu veranlassen, Geld, Dienstleistungen oder andere wirtschaftliche Vorteile zu gewähren (Art. 2 Abs. 9 Nr. 5 lit. b) des Antimonopolgesetzes) und
- bestellte Waren nicht anzunehmen, erhaltene Waren zurückzugeben, die Zahlung des Kaufpreises zu verzögern oder den Kaufpreis zu reduzieren sowie Geschäftsbedingungen zum Nachteil des Geschäftspartners zu vereinbaren oder zu ändern (Art. 2 Abs. 9 Nr. 5 lit. c) des Antimonopolgesetzes).

Der Schutzumfang von Art. 19 i. V. m. Art. 2 Abs. 9 Nr. 5 des Antimonopolgesetzes bleibt aufgrund des zugrundeliegenden Enumerationsprinzips partiell hinter dem Schutzumfang der §§ 18 ff. GWB zurück. Dies zeigt sich unter anderem daran, dass die Verweigerung bzw. der Abbruch einer Lieferbeziehung durch einen Abnehmer, soweit ersichtlich, weder in der japanischen Rechtsprechung noch in der Literatur als kartellrechtliches Problem diskutiert wird.[69] Derartige Diskussionen betreffen lediglich abgestimmte Verhaltensweisen zwischen Wettbewerbern (Art. 9 Abs. 1 Nr. 1

---

69 Unabhängig davon wird vertreten, dass der Geschädigte jedenfalls keinen Unterlassungs- oder Beseitigungsanspruch (差止請求 – *sashitome seikyū*), der auf Belieferung gerichtet ist, nach Art. 24 des Antimonopolgesetzes geltend machen kann. Ein schützenswertes Interesse liege aufgrund der nichtvorhandenen Vertragsbeziehung zum Anspruchszeitpunkt nicht vor; siehe *Nemoto*, Hisanori, Zur Möglichkeit eines Kontrahierungszwangs durch Unterlassungsansprüche – Eine Untersuchung zu den Wechselbeziehungen zwischen dem System der Unterlassungsansprüche und dem Vertragsrecht (差止請求権による『取引』強制の可否 – 差止請求権制度と契約法との相互関係に関する考察をも兼ねて, *sashitome seikyūken ni yoru „torihiki" kyōsei no kahi – sashitome seikyūken seido to keiyakuhō to no sōgokankei ni kansuru kōsatsu o mo kanete*), in: Wada/Takashima/Ishibashi/Ōsaka/Ōzawa, Die Rolle des Rechts in der modernen Zivilgesellschaft – Festschrift zum 70. Geburtstag von Professor Ryōichi Yoshimura (現代市民社会における法の役割 吉村良一先生古稀記念論集, *gendai shimin shakai ni okeru hō no yakuwari Yoshimura Ryōichi sensei koki kinen ronshū*), (2020), S. 367.

des Antimonopolgesetzes) und Lieferverweigerungen gegenüber (potenziellen) Wettbewerbern, etwa um deren Markteintritt zu verhindern.[70] Kontrahierungszwänge werden ansonsten, soweit ersichtlich, nur im Kontext des allgemeinen Zivilrechts[71] oder als Handlungsempfehlungen[72] diskutiert.

Bei Handlungen, die von Art. 2 Abs. 9 Nr. 5 des Antimonopolgesetzes erfasst sind, stellt sich die Frage, ob der sich ggf. missbräuchlich verhaltende Abnehmer eine überragende Stellung gegenüber seinem Zulieferer ausgenutzt hat.[73] In der Entscheidungspraxis der JFTC und der japanischen Literatur haben sich dazu im Wesentlichen vier Faktoren herausgebildet: der Grad der geschäftlichen Abhängigkeit, die Marktposition des Abnehmers, die Ausweichmöglichkeit des Zulieferers und die Bedeutung des Fortlaufens der Geschäftsbeziehung.[74]

Anders als in Deutschland finden sich in Japan mehrere behördliche Entscheidungen, in denen Abnehmern der Missbrauch einer überragenden Stellung gegenüber einer Vielzahl von Zulieferern vorgeworfen wird.[75]

Bereits in der ersten Entscheidung, die zum Missbrauch einer überragenden Stellung erging, der sog. San'yō Marunaka-Entscheidung vom 22. Juni 2011[76], stellte die JFTC fest, dass das Unternehmen San'yō Marunaka als Abnehmer eine überragende Stellung gegenüber 38 Zulieferern gehabt hat. Verpflichtungen dieser Zulieferer, unter anderem Arbeitnehmer zur Remodellierung der Geschäfte von San'yō Marunaka zu entsenden, Veranstaltungen von San'yō Marunaka ohne wirtschaftliche Gegenleistung zu finanzieren und bereits gelieferte Waren unverschuldet zurückzunehmen,

70 Siehe u. a. *Murakami*, Antimonopolgesetz (独占禁止法, *dokusen kinshi hō*), 9. Auflage (2019), S. 203 ff. sowie die dort zitierte Rechtsprechung.

71 Siehe hierzu bereits: DG Tōkyō, Urteil v. 16. Dezember 1987, *Hanreijiō* 1289, S. 68; DG Tōkyō, Urteil v. 28. August 1987, *Hanreijiō* 1274, S. 98; sowie DG Fukuoka (Kokura), Urteil v. 24. Dezember 1981, *Hanreijiō* 1050, S. 105.

72 Vgl. die Handlungsempfehlungen zu Art. 3 des Gesetzes zur Förderung kleinerer und mittlerer Zulieferer (中小企業支援法, *chūshō kigyō shien hō*), wonach ein Vertrag mit einem Zulieferer nur mit angemessener Vorlaufzeit und nur dann beendet werden soll, wenn berücksichtigt wurde, dass eine Vertragsbeendigung erhebliche wirtschaftliche Auswirkungen auf den Zulieferer haben kann.

73 Siehe zum Erfordernis der im Lichte des Handelsbrauchs festzustellenden Unbilligkeit (正常な商慣習に照らして不当に, *seijō na shōkanshū ni terashite futō ni*), *Murakami* (Anm. 69), S. 410. Diese Voraussetzung erscheint lediglich von untergeordneter Bedeutung.

74 Vgl. *Watanabe*, in: Watanabe/Usami (Hrsg.), Q&A – Praktischer Leitfaden zum novellierten Antimonopolgesetz (Q&A 改正独占禁止法実務入門, *Q&A Kaisei dokusen kinshi hō jitsumu nyūmon*) (2022), S. 26; *Murakami* (Anm. 69), S. 399; in diese Richtung JFTC, Entscheidung v. 22. Juni 2011 – JFTC-Entscheidungssammlung-Buch 58, Band 1, S. 193 bzw. S. 312. Siehe hierzu auch die Erwägungen der JFTC zum Missbrauch einer überragenden Stellung nach dem Antimonopolgesetz (優越的地位の濫用に関する独占禁止法上の考え方, *yūetsuteki chi'i no ran'yō ni kansuru dokusen kinshi hōjō no kangaekata*) v. 30. November 2010.

75 Zudem ergingen die bisher einzigen Bußgelder (Stand: 2022) aufgrund unfairer Geschäftspraktiken im Kontext des Missbrauchs einer überragenden Stellung, siehe *Watanabe* (Anm. 73), S. 26.

76 Siehe Buch 58, Band 1, S. 193 bzw. S. 312 der Entscheidungssammlung der JFTC.

stellten demnach unfaire Geschäftspraktiken dar, die mit einem Bußgeld von mehr als 222,16 Mio. JPY (etwa 2 Mio. EUR (2011)) geahndet wurden.

Noch im selben Jahr, namentlich in der Entscheidung vom 13. Dezember 2011 (modifiziert durch die Revisionsentscheidung vom 4. Juni 2015)[77], stellte die JFTC eine überragende Stellung des Unternehmens Toys 'R' Us gegenüber mehr als 70 Zulieferern fest. Daran anknüpfend verhängte die JFTC ein Bußgeld in Höhe von 222,18 Mio. JPY (etwa 1,6 Mio. EUR (2015)), da Toys 'R' Us einen Teil der Zulieferer dazu verpflichtet hatte, bereits gelieferte Waren unverschuldet zurückzunehmen und den Kaufpreis der Waren teils unberechtigterweise reduziert hatte.

Es folgten drei weitere Entscheidungen in den Jahren 2012 bis 2014 zu ähnlich gelagerten Sachverhalten.[78]

Die JFTC scheint an die Voraussetzung einer überragenden Stellung somit deutlich geringere Anforderungen zu stellen als das Bundeskartellamt an die Voraussetzungen der relativen Marktmacht. Dafür sprechen nicht nur die größere Anzahl einschlägiger Entscheidungen, sondern auch, dass die Faktoren, aufgrund derer das Vorliegen einer überragenden Stellung beurteilt wird (wie beispielsweise der Grad der geschäftlichen Abhängigkeit), mehr argumentativen Spielraum zu ermöglichen scheinen (oder zumindest mehr argumentativer Spielraum gewährt wird) als die deutschrechtliche Voraussetzung des Fehlens einer ausreichenden und zumutbaren Ausweichmöglichkeit. Insofern erscheint das Verbot des Missbrauchs einer überragenden Stellung als eine Besonderheit des japanischen Kartellrechts.[79] Festhalten lässt sich damit, dass der Schutzumfang des Antimonopolgesetzes für Zulieferer zwar kleiner ist als der Schutzumfang des GWB. Dieser kleinere Schutzumfang wird allerdings durch die verhältnismäßig niedrigeren Voraussetzungen, die an das Vorliegen einer überragenden Stellung gestellt werden, kompensiert.

b) Zulieferergesetz (下請法, shitauke hō)

Flankiert wird das Antimonopolgesetz durch das am 1. Juni 1956 in Kraft getretene Zulieferergesetz. Ziel des Gesetzes ist die Verhinderung unter anderem von Zahlungsverzögerungen, die Sicherstellung fairer Geschäftsbeziehungen zwischen Zulieferern und Abnehmern und der Schutz der Interessen von Zulieferern und damit die Förderung einer gesunden Entwicklung der japanischen Volkswirtschaft (siehe Art. 1 des Zulieferergesetzes).

Das Zulieferergesetz knüpft an das Verbot des Missbrauchs einer überragenden Stellung an, weist jedoch einige Besonderheiten auf. Zum einen ist der Nachweis einer überragenden Stellung des Abnehmers keine Voraussetzung für die Eröffnung

77 Siehe Buch 62, S. 119 der Entscheidungssammlung der JFTC.

78 Vgl. *Vande Walle/Shiraishi* (Anm. 33), S. 14 f.

79 In diese Richtung auch *Murakami* (Anm. 69), S. 399, wonach die Konzeption des Verbots des Missbrauchs einer überragenden Stellung als Besonderheit der japanischen Rechtsordnung zu verstehen ist. Kritisch dagegen mit Verweis ähnliche Vorschriften in anderen Jurisdiktionen, *Vande Walle/Shiraishi* (Anm. 33), S. 15.

des Anwendungsbereichs.[80] Voraussetzung ist stattdessen, dass das Stammkapital des Auftraggebers und das Stammkapital des Auftragnehmers bestimmte Schwellenwerte jeweils nicht über- oder unterschreiten[81], dass ein Auftragsgeschäft (委託取引, *itaku torihiki*)[82] vereinbart wurde und, dass eine der in Art. 2 Abs. 1 – 4 des Zulieferergesetzes genannten Arbeitsleistungen[83] geschuldet ist.

Der Anwendungsbereich des Zulieferergesetzes erfasst damit eine Vielzahl von Sachverhalten. Indiziell hierfür ist eine Statistik der JFTC, wonach alleine für das Jahr 2019 insgesamt 10.277 Fälle von Konsultationen zum Zulieferergesetz registriert wurden.[84]

Grund dafür dürfte auch sein, dass das Zulieferergesetz Abnehmern ein detailliertes Handlungsprogramm aus vier Pflichten[85] und elf Verboten[86] aufgibt. Die Vorga-

---

80 Dem entspricht die Ratio des Zulieferergesetzes, wonach sich Zulieferer üblicherweise in einer schwachen Verhandlungsposition gegenüber Abnehmern befinden und daher erwartungsgemäß davon absehen, gegen etwaige Rechtsverstöße des Abnehmers zivilrechtlich vorzugehen; vgl. *Murakami* (Anm. 69), S. 423.

81 So muss im Falle einer Auftragsfertigung (製造委託, *seizō itaku*; siehe hierzu näher Anm. 82) entweder (a) das Grundkapital des Auftraggebers 300 Mio. JPY (d.h. etwa 1,8 Mio. EUR (2024)) übersteigen und das Grundkapital des Auftragnehmers bei unter 300 Mio. JPY liegen oder (b) das Grundkapital des Auftraggebers zwischen 10 Mio. JPY (d.h. etwa 61 tausend EUR (2024)) und 300 Mio. JPY liegen, während das Grundkapital des Auftragnehmers bei unter 10 Mio. JPY liegen muss (Art. 2 Abs. 7 des Zulieferergesetzes).

82 Gemeint ist die Beauftragung eines anderen Unternehmens zur Bereitstellung von nach Vorgabe zu produzierenden bzw. zu reparierenden Waren oder Dienstleistungen (Art. 2 des Zulieferergesetzes); vgl. *Murakami* (Anm. 69), S. 424 f.

83 Hierzu gehört die Auftragsfertigung. Das Zulieferergesetz versteht darunter die Beauftragung eines anderen Unternehmens zur Herstellung von Waren, die zum Verkauf, zur Auftragsfertigung, zur Reparatur, zur eigenen Verwendung oder zum Verbrauch bestimmt sind, oder zur Herstellung diesbezüglicher Halbwaren, Teile, Zubehör oder Rohstoffe oder zur Herstellung von (Gieß-)Formen, die zur Herstellung derartiger Waren verwendet werden (siehe Art. 2 Abs. 1 des Zulieferergesetzes). Als weitere Arbeitsleistungen sind genannt: die Auftragsreparatur (修理委託, *shūri itaku*), die Beauftragung zur Herstellung informationsbasierter Produkte (情報成果物作成委託, *jōhō seikabutsu sakusei itaku*) und die Beauftragung zur Erbringung von Dienstleistungen (役務提供委託, *ekimuteikyō itaku*) (siehe Art. 2 Abs. 2–4 des Zulieferergesetzes).

84 Die referenzierte Statistik ist abrufbar unter: https://www.jftc.go.jp/houdou/pressrelease/2020/may/200527.html (zuletzt abgerufen am 12. Mai 2025).

85 (1) Die Pflicht, Zulieferern die Geschäftsbedingungen in schriftlicher Form zur Verfügung zu stellen (Art. 3 des Zulieferergesetzes), (2) die Pflicht, das Zahlungsdatum zu spezifizieren (Art. 2–2 des Zulieferergesetzes), (3) die Pflicht, Verzugszinsen in Höhe von 14,6 Prozent des ausstehenden Betrags beginnend mit dem 61ten Tag nach Erhalt der Auftragsleistung zu zahlen (Art. 4–2 des Zulieferergesetzes) und (4) die Pflicht, wesentliche Vertragsbedingungen zu verschriftlichen und aufzubewahren (Art. 5 des Zulieferergesetzes).

86 (1) Das Verbot, bestellte Waren oder Dienstleistungen trotz Nichtverschulden des Zulieferers nicht abzunehmen (Art. 4 Abs. 1 Nr. 1 des Zulieferergesetzes), (2) das Verbot der verspäteten Entgeltzahlung (Art. 4 Abs. 1 Nr. 2 des Zulieferergesetzes), (3) das Verbot, das vereinbarte Entgelt trotz Nichtverschulden des Zulieferers zu reduzieren (Art. 4 Abs. 1 Nr. 3 des Zulieferergesetzes), (4) das Verbot, eine erhaltene Ware trotz Nichtverschulden des Zulieferers zurückzugeben (Art. 4 Abs. 1 Nr. 4 des Zulieferergesetzes), (5) das Verbot, ein Entgelt, das erheblich unter dem liegt, was für vergleichbare Waren oder Dienstleistungen gezahlt wird, in unbilliger Weise zu vereinbaren (Art. 4 Abs. 1 Nr. 5 des Zulieferergesetzes), (6) das Verbot, den Zulieferer ohne sachlichen Grund zu verpflichten, bestimmte Waren oder Dienstleistungen

ben des Zulieferergesetzes sind zwingendes Recht und damit auch im Einvernehmen mit Zulieferern nicht abdingbar.[87]

Das Zulieferergesetz entfaltet seine disziplinierende Wirkung allerdings weniger durch Bußgeldvorschriften[88] als vielmehr durch das Konzept behördlicher Empfehlung (勧告, *kankoku*). Danach ist die JFTC befugt, eine Empfehlung zur Abhilfe des Verstoßes auszusprechen (Art. 7 des Zulieferergesetzes). Abhilfe kann je nach Einzelfall etwa durch die Abnahme der bestellten Ware, durch die vollständige Zahlung des Kaufpreises oder durch die Zahlung von Verzugszinsen erfolgen. Die Empfehlungen, die auch veröffentlicht werden können,[89] sind als bloße Verwaltungsanweisungen (行政指導, *gyōsei shidō*) nicht verpflichtend.[90] In der Praxis folgen betroffene Abnehmer den Empfehlungen der JFTC dennoch – sei es auch aus dem Grund, dass deren Umsetzung zu Folge hat, dass eine behördliche Verfolgung auf Grundlage des Antimonopolgesetzes in diesem Umfang ausgeschlossen wird (Art. 8 des Zulieferergesetzes).[91]

3. Schlussfolgerungen und abschließende Bemerkungen

Beim Schutz von Zulieferern unterscheidet sich das deutsche Kartellrecht somit substanziell vom japanischen Kartellrecht: Während das deutsche Kartellrecht den Schutzumfang auf Rechtsfolgenebene weit zieht, diesen aber auf Tatbestandsebene von verhältnismäßig strengen Voraussetzungen abhängig macht, ist der Zuliefererschutz im japanischen Kartellrecht eher eng, da enumerativ konzipiert, steht dafür

---

zu beziehen (Art. 4 Abs. 1 Nr. 6 des Zulieferergesetzes), (7) das Verbot, einen Zulieferer zu benachteiligen, weil dieser die JFTC oder den Leiter der Behörde für Klein- und Mittelbetriebe (中小企業庁長官, *chūshō kigyō-chō chōkan*) über einen Verstoß gegen Art. 4 Abs. 1 Nr. 1 – 5 des Zulieferergesetzes informiert hat (Art. 4 Abs. 1 Nr. 7 des Zulieferergesetzes), (8) das Verbot, einen Zahlungsanspruch des Abnehmers, der auf dem Kauf des Zulieferers von Materialien vom Abnehmer beruht, gegen einen nicht fälligen Zahlungsanspruch des Zulieferers trotz Nichtverschulden aufzurechnen bzw. dessen Zahlung zu verlangen (Art. 4 Abs. 2 Nr. 1 des Zulieferergesetzes), (9) das Verbot der (teilweisen) Zahlung mit einem Wechsel (手形, *tegata*), der bis zum Fälligkeitszeitpunkt bei einem üblichen Finanzinstitut nur schwerlich eingelöst werden kann (Art. 4 Abs. 2 Nr. 2 des Zulieferergesetzes), (10) das Verbot, den Zulieferer zu veranlassen, Geld, Dienstleistungen oder andere geldwerte Vorteile zu gewähren (Art. 4 Abs. 2 Nr. 3 des Zulieferergesetzes) und (11) das Verbot, den Inhalt des Auftragsgeschäfts zu ändern oder eine Nachbesserung der geschuldeten Leistung zu fordern, ohne dass dem Zulieferer ein Verschulden trifft (Art. 4 Abs. 2 Nr. 4 des Zulieferergesetzes).

87 *Murakami* (Anm. 69), S. 428.

88 Ein bußgeldbewehrter Verstoß liegt zum einen vor, wenn Zulieferern die Geschäftsbedingungen nicht in schriftlicher Form zur Verfügung gestellt wurden (Art. 10 Nr. 1 des Zulieferergesetzes) sowie zum anderen, wenn wesentliche Vertragsbedingungen entgegen Art. 5 des Zulieferergesetzes nicht verschriftlich oder nicht aufbewahrt wurden bzw. ein inhaltlich falsches Dokument angefertigt wurde (Art. 10 Nr. 2 des Zulieferergesetzes). Das Bußgeld trifft natürliche Personen (beispielsweise geschäftliche Vertreter) und kann bis zu 500.000 JPY (etwa 3.000 EUR) betragen.

89 Vgl. *Murakami* (Anm. 69), S. 429.

90 Den Betroffenen steht daher kein Rechtsschutz gegen die Empfehlungen der JFTC zur Verfügung; vgl. *Murakami* (Anm. 69), S. 428.

91 *Murakami* (Anm. 69), S. 428, 430.

aber unter weniger strengen Voraussetzungen. Dies zeigt sich insbesondere in der Entscheidungspraxis der JFTC zu den Voraussetzungen einer überragenden Stellung sowie den Voraussetzungen des Anwendungsbereichs des Zulieferergesetzes.

Daran anknüpfend stellen sich aus Sicht des Verfassers insbesondere zwei Fragen: Lässt sich das vorläufige Ergebnis, dass die JFTC den kartellrechtlichen Schutz von Zulieferern eher bejaht als das Bundeskartellamt, durch eine umfassende Analyse der Entscheidungspraxis beider Behörden bestätigen? Wenn dem so sein sollte, inwiefern wirken sich die Unterschiede zwischen dem deutschen und japanischen Recht auf die Geschäftswirklichkeit aus – sind Zuliefererbeziehungen in Japan beispielsweise beständiger und konfliktärmer als in Deutschland?

Wie eingangs erwähnt, lässt sich über den Vergleich des deutschen und japanischen Kartellrechts eine Fülle an Fragestellungen herausarbeiten, deren Beantwortung aus rechtswissenschaftlicher wie wirtschaftspolitischer Sicht von erheblicher praktischer Bedeutung ist. Dies gilt gleichermaßen für Deutschland wie für Japan. Insofern ist abschließend erneut zu betonen, dass eine Zunahme rechtsvergleichender Untersuchungen gerade im Bereich des Kartellrechts überaus begrüßenswert wäre.

Literaturverzeichnis

Bechtold, Rainer/*Bosch*, Wolfgang: GWB, Gesetz gegen Wettbewerbsbeschränkungen, §§ 1–96, 185, 186–187, 11. Auflage (2025).

Bundeskartellamt: Bericht des Bundeskartellamtes über seine Tätigkeit im Jahre 1978 sowie über Lage und Entwicklung auf seinem Aufgabengebiet (§ 50 GWB), 1. Juni 1979, BT-Drs. 8/2980.

Bundeskartellamt/Bundesregierung: Bericht des Bundeskartellamtes über seine Tätigkeit in den Jahren 2017/2018 sowie über die Lage und Entwicklung auf seinem Aufgabengebiet und Stellungnahme der Bundesregierung, 19. Juni 2019, BT-Drs. 19/10900.

Bundeskartellamt/Bundesregierung: Bericht des Bundeskartellamtes über seine Tätigkeit in den Jahren 2019/2020 sowie über die Lage und Entwicklung auf seinem Aufgabengebiet und Stellungnahme der Bundesregierung, 16. Juni 2021, BT-Drs. 19/30775.

Bundeskartellamt/Bundesregierung: Bericht des Bundeskartellamtes über seine Tätigkeit in den Jahren 2021/2022 sowie über die Lage und Entwicklung auf seinem Aufgabengebiet und Stellungnahme der Bundesregierung, 26. Juli 2023, BT-Drs. 20/7300.

Bundeskartellamt/Bundeswettbewerbsbehörde: Leitfaden Transaktionswertschwelle, Stand: Januar 2022, abrufbar unter: https://www.bundeskartellamt.de/SharedDocs/Publikation/DE/Leitfaden/Leitfaden_Transaktionsschwelle.html (zuletzt abgerufen am 12. Mai 2025).

Bundesregierung: Bericht gemäß § 18 Absatz 8 und § 43a des Gesetzes gegen Wettbewerbsbeschränkungen, 15. Januar 2021, BT-Drs. 19/26136.

Bundesregierung: Entwurf eines Neunten Gesetzes zur Änderung des Gesetzes gegen Wettbewerbsbeschränkungen, 7. November 2016, BT-Drs. 18/10207.

Europäische Kommission: Evaluation of procedural and jurisdictional aspects of EU merger control, 26. März 2021 ({SEC(2021) 156 final} – {SWD(2021) 67 final}).

Europäische Kommission: Leitfaden zur Anwendung des Verweisungssystems nach Artikel 22 der Fusionskontrollverordnung auf bestimmte Kategorien von Vorhaben, 2021/C 113/01.

Göbel, Martin: „Gotta catch 'em all?" – Instrumente zum Aufgreifen von „Gap cases" in der formellen Fusionskontrolle, ZWeR (2024), S. 37 ff.

Immenga, Ulrich/*Mestmäcker*, Ernst-Joachim (Hrsg.): Wettbewerbsrecht, Band 2 GWB, 7. Auflage (2024).

JFTC: Stand der fusionskontrollrechtlichen Anmeldungen im Jahr 2023 (令和５年度における企業結合関係届出の状況 – *Reiwa 5-nendo ni okeru kigyō ketsugō kankei todokede no jōkyō*) (5. Juli 2024), abrufbar unter: https://www.jftc.go.jp/dk/kiketsu/toukeishiryo/joukou_files/R5doukoukiketsu.pdf (zuletzt abgerufen am 12. Mai 2025).

JFTC: Übersicht zu den Ansichten und Gedanken zu den Vorschlägen zur Anwendungsrichtlinie zur Fusionskontrolle des Antimonopolgesetzes sowie zur Anpassungsrichtlinie zum fusionskontrollrechtlichen Prüfverfahren (「企業結合審査に関する独占禁止法の運用指針」（案）及び「企業結合審査の手続に関する対応方針」（案）に対する意見の概要及びそれに対する考え方 – *„Kigyō ketsugō shinsa ni kansuru dokusen kinshi hō no un'yō shishin" (an) oyobi „kigyō ketsugō shinsa no tetsuzuki ni kansuru taiō hōshin" (an) ni taisuru iken no gaiyō oyobi sore ni taisuru kangaekata*) (2019), abrufbar unter: https://www.jftc.go.jp/houdou/pressrelease/2019/dec/kiketu/attachment3.pdf (zuletzt abgerufen am 12. Mai 2025).

Käseberg, Thorsten: Ein „Inflection"-Punkt für die Fusionskontrolle?, NZKart (2025), S. 1 f.

Kersting, Christian/*Meyer-Lindemann*, Hans Jürgen/*Podszun*, Rupprecht (Hrsg.): Kartellrecht, Kommentar zum Deutschen und Europäischen Recht, 5. Auflage (2025).

Köhler, Helmut: Wettbewerbs- und kartellrechtliche Kontrolle der Nachfragemacht, Handelsrecht und Wirtschaftsrecht 49, Heidelberg (1979).

Kresken, Jan/*Wille*, Christian: „Make hard cases bad law?" – Die angedachte Erweiterung der Transaktionswertschwelle, NZKart (2025), S. 193 ff.

Monopolkommission: Hauptgutachten XXI, Wettbewerb 2016.

Monopolkommission: Hauptgutachten XXIV, Wettbewerb 2022.

Murakami, Masahiro (村上政博): Antimonopolgesetz (独占禁止法 – *dokusen kinshi hō*), 9. Auflage 2019.

Nemoto, Hisanori (根本尚徳): Zur Möglichkeit eines Kontrahierungszwangs durch Unterlassungsansprüche – Eine Untersuchung zu den Wechselbeziehungen zwischen dem System der Unterlassungsansprüche und dem Vertragsrecht (差止請求権による『取引』強制の可否 — 差止請求権制度と契約法との相互関係に関する考察をも兼ねて – *sashitome seikyūken ni yoru „torihiki" kyōsei no kahi – sashitome seikyūken seido to keiyakuhō to no sōgokankei ni kansuru kōsatsu o mo kanete*), in: Wada, Shinichi (和田真一)/Takashima, Hidehiro (高嶌英弘)/Ishibashi, Hideki (石橋秀起)/Ōsaka, Eri (大坂・恵里)/Ōzawa, Ryūichi (小沢隆一), Die Rolle des Rechts in der modernen Zivilgesellschaft – Festschrift zum 70. Geburtstag von Professor Ryōichi Yoshimura (現代市民社会における法の役割 吉村良一先生古稀記念論集 – *gendai shimin shakai ni okeru hō no yakuwari Yoshimura Ryōichi sensei koki kinen ronshū*) (2020), S. 335 ff.

OECD Sekretariat: Start-ups, Killer Acquisitions and Merger Control – Background Note, 12. Mai 2020 (DAF/COMP(2020)5).

Ōnoki, Takako (大軒敬子): Zur Wirksamkeit von Abhilfemaßnahmen in der Fusionskontrolle (企業結合規制における問題解消措置の実効性について – *kigyō ketsugō kisei ni okeru mondai kaishō sochi no jikkōsei ni tsuite*) (2024).

Säcker, Franz Jürgen/*Bien*, Florian/*Meier-Beck*, Peter/*Montag*, Frank (Hrsg.): Münchener Kommentar zum Wettbewerbsrecht, Band 2 Gesetz gegen Wettbewerbsbeschränkungen (GWB) §§ 1–96, 185, 186, 4. Auflage (2022).

Vande Walle, Simon/*Shiraishi*, Tadashi: Competition Law in Japan, Comparative Competition Law (Juli 2015).

Watanabe, Shinya (渡邉新矢)/*Usami*, Yoshiya (宇佐美善哉] (Hrsg.): Q&A – Praktischer Leitfaden zum novellierten Antimonopolgesetz (Q&A 改正独占禁止法実務入門 – *Q&A kaisei dokusen kinshi hō jitsumu nyūmon*) (2022).

Persönliche Eindrücke und Erfahrungen zu Japan und dem Leben als Deutsche in Japan

Von *Sabine Sauer-Tada*

Sabine Sauer-Tada, geboren am 20. 07. 1965 in Göttingen, hat Rechtswissenschaften an der Georg-August-Universität Göttingen und Japanisches Recht an der Fernuniversität Hagen studiert. Teile Ihres Referendariats absolvierte sie in Tokyo, wo sie von 1995 bis 1996 mit ihrer Familie lebte. Von 1998 bis 2011 leitete Frau Sauer-Tada die Abteilung Allgemeine Verwaltung bei der Kassenärztlichen Vereinigung Niedersachsen – Bezirksstelle Göttingen. Im Anschluss daran war sie als Rechtsanwältin mit dem Tätigkeitsschwerpunkt Vertragsarztrecht tätig und wechselte 2014 zum Bundesverwaltungsamt am Standort Friedland. Eines ihrer Hobbys ist Aikido.

Im letzten Herbst erhielt ich eine Mail, die für mich völlig überraschend kam.

Zum Anlass des siebzigsten Geburtstags von Prof. Dr. Menkhaus solle es eine Festschrift geben, für die Beiträge gewünscht seien. Sofort habe ich mich an meine Referendariatszeit bei Prof. Dr. Menkhaus am Deutschen Institut für Japanstudien vom Herbst 1992 bis Frühjahr 1993 erinnert gefühlt, die mir unvergesslich geblieben ist.

Der folgende kleine Beitrag für diese Festschrift bezieht sich nicht auf wissenschaftliche Aspekte des japanischen Rechts, sondern schildert rein subjektiv gesehen einige meiner Eindrücke und Erfahrungen im Zusammenhang mit Japan und der dortigen Gesellschaft.

Als Kind und Jugendliche in den 70er und beginnenden 80er Jahren beschränkte sich mein Weltbild auf Deutschland und die unmittelbar angrenzenden Nachbarländer. Asien und damit Japan war weit entfernt. Ab und zu habe ich japanische oder koreanische Studenten/innen in meiner Heimatstadt gesehen, die zumeist an der Universität studiert haben. Außerhalb der universitären Kreise gab es kaum Berührungspunkte mit der „Bürgerlichen Bevölkerung".

Allerdings ist bereits in meiner Kindheit der Slogan „Made in Japan" stark präsent gewesen. Auch bei den deutschen „Ottonormal-Bürger/innen" betrachtete man die japanische Wirtschaft mit Bewunderung und Hochachtung. Die Entwicklung der Automobilindustrie und der technischen Geräte stand dabei im Fokus. In den deutschen Familien entbrannte die Diskussion, ob die bekannten deutschen Marken oder die Japanischen zu bevorzugen seien. Besonders bei den Haushaltsgeräten entschieden sich viele häufig für die billigeren japanischen Anbieter. Dabei wurde hervorgehoben, diese hätten ja auch „fast" deutsche Qualität.

Duncker & Humblot · Berlin | https://doi.org/10.3790/978-3-428-59611-9.2025.423785

Von Beginn der 60er Jahre bis zur ersten Ölkrise 1973 erlebte Japan eine Phase des Hochwachstums. Dieser sogenannte „Nachkriegsboom“ war durchaus vergleichbar mit dem in Deutschland.

Beide Länder hatten den zweiten Weltkrieg verloren. Viele Städte waren zerstört, die Industrie und Wirtschaft lagen am Boden. Dennoch gelangen sowohl Japan als auch Deutschland der schnelle wirtschaftliche Wiederaufbau. Mit vereinten Kräften des überwiegenden Teils der Bevölkerungen stieg Japan zur dritt- und Westdeutschland zur viertgrößten Wirtschaftsmacht auf.[1] Die Gräueltaten des zweiten Weltkriegs wurden dabei größtenteils verdrängt. In der Regel sprach man bis weit in die 70er Jahre in der Bundesrepublik Deutschland in der Öffentlichkeit nicht darüber.

Aus meiner Sicht gibt es viele Parallelen sowohl in der historischen Entwicklung als auch in den „Charaktereigenschaften“ und Wertvorstellungen, welche in Japan und Deutschland für wichtig gehalten werden. Für den wirtschaftlichen Erfolg in beiden Ländern waren insbesondere Eigenschaften wie Disziplin, Ordnung, Sauberkeit, Obrigkeitsdenken, das Zugehörigkeitsgefühl und die Loyalität zum Arbeitgeber, der Ausbau von Zuliefererketten durch Kleinunternehmer und technische Innovationen mitentscheidend. Dies führte dazu, dass sich zumindest in den älteren Generationen Japaner/innen und Deutsche in der Regel freundlich gesonnen und mit gegenseitiger Achtung begegneten.

Oftmals werde ich gefragt, wie ich dazu kam, nach Japan zu gehen und was wichtig sei, wenn man dort eine Zeit lang leben oder arbeiten möchte.

Die erste Frage ist leicht zu beantworten. Zu Beginn meines Studiums lernte ich Mitte der achtziger Jahre meinen späteren Ehemann, einen Japaner kennen. So bin ich nach dem ersten juristischen Staatsexamen nach Japan gereist, um zu entscheiden, ob ich mir vorstellen kann, dort dauerhaft zu leben.

Mir war damals klar, dass die meisten japanischen Männer, die im Ausland studiert oder dort einige Jahre gearbeitet haben, anschließend wieder in ihr Heimatland zurückkehren. Mein Mann hatte mir sogar erzählt, er habe ein Papier unterschreiben müssen, nach seinem Studium wieder zurück nach Japan zu gehen und seine im Ausland erworbenen Kenntnisse zur Verfügung zu stellen. Eine Ehe hatte deshalb nur dann eine Chance, wenn ich bereit war, dorthin auszusiedeln.

In Japan galt noch das klassische Rollenbild, dass eine Frau dem Mann folgt. Daher sind die meisten japanischen Frauen nach ihrer Eheschließung mit einem Deutschen anschließend auch hier leben geblieben.

Während meines ersten Aufenthaltes lernte ich meine japanische Familie in der Provinz kennen. Das Leben auf dem Dorf war von der Landwirtschaft und in der Nähe der Küste immer noch vom Fischfang geprägt. Innerhalb der Familie tauschte man Gemüse und Obst aus und besorgte die restlichen Lebensmittel auf dem Wochenmarkt oder in Supermärkten. Warm gekocht wurde dreimal am Tag, eingekauft

---

1 Vgl. Liste der Länder nach historischer Entwicklung des Bruttoinlandsprodukts (BIP), die auf Schätzungen der Weltbank, des Internationalen Währungsfonds und den Vereinten Nationen beruht, abrufbar unter https://de.wikipedia.org/wiki/Liste_der_L%C3%A4nder_nach_historischer_Entwicklung_des_Bruttoinlandsprodukts.

fast täglich. So drehten sich die Gespräche der Frauen sehr viel darum, was es als nächstes Leckeres zum Essen gibt.

Für mich war das Leben dort anfangs sehr ungewohnt. Es gab einen festgelegten Tagesrhythmus und wenig Abwechslung. Als Beispiel: Um halb sechs abends erklang eine Melodie über Lautsprecher, welche als Zeichen galt, nach Hause zu gehen und zu essen. Das sehr warme Badewasser war bereits eingelassen. Gebadet wurde nach der Mahlzeit nach einer strikten Reihenfolge. Der Gast, das Familienoberhaupt und anschließend der Rest der Familie. Alles in allem war es ein sehr geruhsames Leben.

Ganz anders in den großen Städten. Die Menschenmengen, die Hochhäuser und die Hektik waren häufig sehr anstrengend für mich.

Inmitten der großen Städte gibt es jedoch auch Parks, japanische Gärten, Tempel oder Schreine, bei deren Besuch ich große Ruhe und Schönheit empfand. Das Moderne und das Traditionelle sind oft auf engem Raum miteinander verbunden und stehen dabei in einem viel größerem Kontrast, als ich das in Deutschland empfunden habe.

Bei meinem ersten Japanbesuch hatte ich keinerlei Sprachkenntnisse und meine Schwiegereltern und Schwägerin auf dem Land sprachen ausschließlich den örtlichen Dialekt. Die Frauen der Familie waren sehr freundlich zu mir und versuchten so lange auf mich einzureden, bis ich ahnte, was sie mir sagen wollten. Ich war die erste Ausländerin, die Anfang der 90er Jahre dort heiratete. In dem kleinen Ort der Provinz kannte jeder jeden und so waren die anderen Dorfbewohner/innen und entfernteren Familienangehörigen neugierig, aber gleichzeitig auch skeptisch.

Zurückgekehrt nach Deutschland beschloss ich, das nächste Mal nicht so unvorbereitet nach Japan zu reisen. Zweimal die Woche traf ich mich mit einer japanischen Juristin zum „Tandem". Ihr Deutsch war bereits fantastisch, mein Japanisch leider ganz am Anfang. So lernte ich einige Basissätze – zum Beispiel Begrüßungen und Verabschiedungen, sich nach der Gesundheit erkundigen oder über das Wetter und das Essen sprechen.

Ich schrieb mich in dem Studienfach Japanisches Recht an der Universität Hagen ein und erhielt sehr gut aufbereitete Skripte. Das Studium war damals schon problemlos von zu Hause aus möglich.

Bereits in Deutschland bauten mein Mann und ich uns ein Beziehungsgeflecht mit Japanern/innen auf. Zum Beispiel gab ich zwei Jungen Deutschunterricht, zeigte Gastprofessoren und Studenten/innen schöne Orte und Sehenswürdigkeiten meiner Heimat und lud sie zu uns nach Hause ein. Häufig waren wir auch zu Gast bei den in Deutschland lebenden japanischen Familien oder trafen uns im Restaurant. Ab und zu halfen wir bei der Organisation von japanischen Kulturveranstaltungen mit. Dieses Netzwerk half mir in späteren Zeiten sehr – sogar, wenn ich Japaner/innen jahrelang nicht gesehen hatte, standen sie mir in Notsituationen bei.

Umgekehrt ist es natürlich ebenso wichtig, dass man selbst bereit ist zu helfen, dieses anbietet und hierzu auch zur Verfügung steht. Es kam beispielsweise des Öfteren vor, dass sich Freunde und Bekannte bei mir meldeten, wenn sie seit langer Zeit einmal wieder in Deutschland waren und wir gemeinsam etwas zusammen unternahmen. Oder ich habe erlebt, dass mich japanische Professoren später darum baten, ihre/n Studenten/in etwas zu unterstützen, die in meiner Heimatstadt in Deutschland eine Zeit lang studierten. Unabhängig vom Zeitpunkt im Leben ist es ein Geben und Nehmen. Shiriai (Bekanntschaft) bedeutet für Japaner/innen nicht selten eine das Leben andauernde Bekanntschaft, wir würden das in Deutschland wohl Freundschaft nennen.

Aufgrund unserer bereits in Deutschland aufgebauten Beziehungen sind wir in Japan oft eingeladen worden. Meistens trafen wir uns aufgrund der dort oft beengten Lebensverhältnisse im Restaurant zum Essen. Nur bei Verwandten oder sehr guten Freunden sind Besuche zu Hause ebenfalls üblich.

In der Zeit, in der ich in Japan gelebt habe, beschwerten sich des Öfteren Deutsche bei mir. Obwohl sie bereits etliche Jahre in Japan lebten, hätten sie außerhalb der Geschäftsbeziehungen keine japanischen Bekannten und schon gar keine Einladungen von Japanern in ihr Haus erhalten. Meines Erachtens lag dieses zum einen daran, dass viele der Deutschen unter sich blieben oder sich in ihrer Freizeit allenfalls mit anderen Europäern oder Amerikanern trafen. Zum anderen lag es aber auch oft an mangelnden japanischen Sprachkenntnissen, die ein gegenseitiges Kennenlernen stark erschwerten.

Für das Verständnis von der Bevölkerung und der Kultur eines Landes sowie der Integration ist das Erlernen der Landessprache unabdingbar. Wie bereits erwähnt, ist es ohne Japanisch Kenntnisse in den ländlichen Bereichen sehr schwierig, eigenständig zurechtzukommen. In größeren Städten ist heutzutage mit Glück eine Verständigung auf Englisch möglich. Vieles von Land und Leuten erfährt man ohne fremde Hilfe jedoch meiner Erfahrung nach nicht.

Wertvolle Unterstützung bekam ich von meinem japanischen Ehemann, seiner Familie und von Freunden, auf die jederzeit Verlass war – ein unschätzbarer Vorteil.

Während meiner Referendariatszeit heiratete ich und beschloss, meinem Mann nach Tokyo zu folgen. Für den ersten Teil der Wahlstation bewarb ich mich bei der deutschen Botschaft, der Industrie- und Handelskammer und beim Deutschen Institut für Japanstudien, welches vom Bundesministerium für Forschung und Bildung mitfinanziert wird.[2] Ich beantragte die Verlängerung dieses Ausbildungsabschnitts von drei auf sechs Monate, was von der Präsidentin des für mich zuständigen Oberlandesgerichts unproblematisch durch Zuweisungsverfügung genehmigt wurde. Ich erhielt sogar einen sogenannten „Kaufkraftausgleich“, eine Erhöhung des normalen Referendariatsgehaltes um 80 %. Dieser diente dazu, das wesentlich teurere Leben in Japan bezahlen zu können.

So kam es, dass ich von Anfang November 1992 bis Ende April 1993 einen Teil meiner Referendariatsausbildung in Tokyo verbrachte, Herr Prof. Dr. Menkhaus arbeitete damals als Wissenschaftlicher Mitarbeiter am Deutschen Institut für Japanstudien, sagte mir sofort zu und eröffnete mir damit eine einmalige Chance. Hierfür bin ich ihm noch heute sehr dankbar.

---

2 Seit dem 1. September 2002 ist das Deutsche Institut für Japanstudien der Max Weber Stiftung, Deutsche Geisteswissenschaftliche Institute im Ausland, beigetreten.

Inhaltlich ging es bei meiner Tätigkeit primär um die Aufbereitung einer Bibliographie zum japanischen Finanzrecht in europäischen Sprachen. Im Mittelpunkt stand dabei die sogenannte „*baburu-keiki*" (Deutsch: Blasenhochkonjunktur) des japanischen Aktien- und Immobilienmarktes der zweiten Hälfte der 1980er Jahre.

Als japanische Banken Ende der 80er Jahre begannen, Kredite auszugeben, die durch überbewertete Immobilien abgesichert sein sollten (d.h. dem Immobilienkauf dienten), platze die Blase 1990. Der Wert der Immobilien sank innerhalb kurzer Zeit auf ein Viertel zurück, der Aktienmarkt implodierte. Die Banken blieben deshalb auf den „faulen Krediten" sitzen, was zum Konkurs von einigen japanischen Banken und Lebensversicherern führte. Andere Banken wurden vom Staat gerettet, was den Steuerzahler viel Geld kostete. Diese Zeit wurde auch als „verlorene Dekade" bezeichnet und war von Stagnation geprägt.[3]

Die japanische Wirtschaft benötigte mehrere Jahre, um sich zu regenerieren, der Bankensektor musste saniert werden und die Staatsverschuldung stieg auf über 150 Prozent des BIP. Das führte unter anderem zu hohen Mieten, Kapitalverlust sowie einer Erhöhung der Lebenshaltungskosten und hatte damit auch Einfluss auf weite Teile der Bevölkerung.

Im Rahmen der damaligen Recherche wurde ich von Prof. Dr. Menkhaus zu japanischen Banken und Bibliotheken mitgenommen und erhielt außerdem Einblicke in die japanische Referendariatsausbildung sowie das Gerichtssystem Japans. Er lud mich weiterhin zu seiner Lehrveranstaltung über die Bundesrepublik Deutschland an der Chūō Universität ein. Dadurch konnte ich juristische Studenten/innen und Professoren kennenlernen, die mich am Semesterende zu einer Seminarabschlussparty einluden.

Das Deutsche Institut für Japanstudien hatte damals lediglich 19 Mitarbeitende, davon 10 Wissenschaftler/innen aus unterschiedlichen Fachbereichen. Ich war dort von Beginn an willkommen und integriert. Wir sind fast täglich zusammen zum Mittagessen gegangen und haben uns ab und zu abends noch in einer Bar getroffen. Auch privat gab es gemeinsame Treffen beim Karaoke, zu kleineren Ausflügen oder privaten Feiern. Es waren für mich unvergessliche Monate, für die ich sehr dankbar bin!

Nach Feierabend gemeinsam mit den Kollegen/innen bei einer Izakaya oder Nomiya-san Bier und Sake zu konsumieren und einige Kleinigkeiten dabei zu essen war beliebt. Die Bars in den Städten waren zumeist gut gefüllt. In Tokyo galt es, den letzten Vorortzug nach Hause nicht zu verpassen, damit man nicht in einer Schlafröhre oder Ähnlichem übernachten musste.

In Japan ist es meiner Erfahrung nach nicht üblich, in der Öffentlichkeit eine eigene Meinung zu vertreten, offene Kritik oder negative Äußerungen anderen gegenüber gelten als „No-Go". Wichtig ist es, darauf zu achten, jemanden nicht „das Gesicht zu nehmen", d.h. ihn nicht bloßzustellen. Beim abendlichen Trinken ist die Atmosphäre wesentlich lockerer und mit steigendem Alkoholkonsum werden Probleme bei der Arbeit ebenfalls leichter einmal angesprochen. Dabei gilt in Japan die Regel:

---

3 Einen Kurzüberblick hierzu mit weiteren Hinweisen bietet der Wikipedia Artikel zu dem Stichwort Ushinawareta Nijūnen „Zwei verlorene Dekaden", abrufbar unter https://de.wikipedia.org/wiki/Ushinawareta_Nij%C5%ABnen.

was man unter Alkoholeinfluss äußert, ist am nächsten Tag dem anderen gegenüber nicht übelzunehmen.

Ich habe gelesen, dass die Corona-Zeit die Trinkgewohnheiten der Japaner/innen inzwischen verändert hat und viele Trinkstuben bereits ab 20 Uhr geschlossen sein sollen.[4] Sicherlich führt dies in den größeren Städten auch zu einer gesellschaftlichen Veränderung.

Früher war das gemeinsame Ausgehen immer eine gute Gelegenheit, sich im Privaten näher kennenzulernen und dabei eine/n feste/n Partner/in zu finden. Heutzutage hat laut einer Studie einer von vier verheirateten Erwachsenen unter 40 Jahren in Japan seine/n Partner/in über eine Singlebörse gefunden.[5] Der Anteil der jüngeren Singles nimmt stetig zu.

Auch hier lässt sich ein gesellschaftlicher Wandel erkennen. Als ich meinen Mann in den 80er Jahren kennenlernte, war es in Japan nicht selten, Ehen zu arrangieren. Wer mit Mitte 20 noch nicht verheiratet war, den/die versuchten Verwandte oder Freunde entsprechend dem sozialen Status zu „vermitteln". Hierzu gab es einen Fragebogen mit Fotos und Werdegang, die einem/r potentiellen Partner/in gegeben wurden. Dieses scheinen die Internetportale und die Singlebörsen nunmehr übernommen zu haben. Insgesamt sind die Japaner/innen allerdings pragmatisch, was die Partnersuche angeht – es geht weniger um die große Liebe als darum, dass man denkt, sich gemeinsam ein „gutes Leben" aufbauen zu können.

Während der eigenen Studienzeit besteht die Möglichkeit, sich für ein Auslandsstudium in Japan zu bewerben und dort ein oder zwei Semester zu verbringen.[6] Das Studium in Japan dauert üblicherweise ca. drei bis vier Jahre. An vielen Universitäten gibt es ein sehr breites Sport- und Kulturangebot, welches in der Regel über Studentenklubs organisiert ist, denen man sich anschließen kann. Allerdings wird häufig erwartet, regelmäßig zu den Klubs zu kommen und nicht nur sporadisch. Sucht man dort gute Freundschaften, sollten möglichst sehr gute Sprachkenntnisse vorhanden sein, da die Japaner/innen aufgrund der bestehenden Sprachbarriere in Kombination mit dem Mehraufwand, eine/n Fremde/n kulturell zu integrieren, oftmals reserviert bleiben.

In den Studentenwohnheimen oder während der Vorlesungen/Seminare lassen sich viele internationale Kontakte knüpfen, die Umgangssprache ist meistens Englisch.

---

4 Trinkkultur in Japan: Zum Wohl – der Staatskasse, Tagesschaubericht vom 30. August 2022, verfügbar unter https://web.archive.org/web/20220831104524/https://www.tagesschau.de/ausland/asien/japan-alkohol-101.html; Alkohol in Japan: Alter, Regeln und Trinkkultur, Artikel vom 05. Juli 2023, verfügbar unter https://www.japanwelt.de.

5 In Japan finden immer mehr Menschen ihren Partner über Singlebörsen, Artikel im Sumikai Magazin rund um Japan vom 17. September 2024, mit Hinweis auf eine landesweite Online-Umfrage in Japan, verfügbar unter https://sumikai.com/nachrichten-aus-japan/in-japan-finden-immer-mehr-menschen-ihren-partner-ueber-singleboersen-346337/.

6 Einen Überblick über das Auslandsstudium gibt es unter https://www.daad.de, Japan: Bildung und Wissenschaft-DAAD, der DAAD ist in Japan mit einer Außenstelle in Tokyo vertreten, auf dieser Seite gibt es auch einen Link zum Beratungsangebot und nähere Hinweise zum Thema Studieren und Leben in Japan.

Einige der deutschen Universitäten haben Austauschuniversitäten in Japan, in denen Direktstipendien vergeben werden. Das bedeutet, dass man die zum Teil teuren japanischen Studiengebühren nicht bezahlen muss und in der Regel die Möglichkeit der Unterbringung in einem Studentenwohnheim hat. Möchte man an japanischen Vorlesungen teilnehmen, sind oft mindestens C1 Kenntnisse erforderlich, was wenige deutsche Studenten/innen außerhalb der Japanologie schaffen. Allerdings gibt es auch internationale Programme, die primär dem Lernen der Sprache und Kultur dienen und bei denen die Eingangshürden sehr viel niedriger sind.

In der Regel sind auch Empfehlungsschreiben von deutschen Professoren/innen erforderlich, um solche Chancen zu erhalten.

Meiner Erfahrung nach ist das Leben in Japan viel leichter, wenn man versucht sich anzupassen. Das hieß für mich beispielsweise, bei einem etwas längerem Aufenthalt möglichst nicht ins Wohnheim zu ziehen, sondern in eine japanisch-sprachige Umgebung und ab und zu mit den Nachbarn Smalltalk zu halten. Insbesondere mit den älteren Frauen, die Zeit haben, ist das einfach. Tendenziell sind sie neugierig etwas Neues zu erfahren. Auch wenn man nur über das Wetter, die Gesundheit, das Essen oder die Qualität der nächstgelegenen Essstuben redet, ist der erste Schritt getan.

Außerhalb von studentischen und universitären Kreisen empfiehlt es sich ebenfalls in einen Verein einzutreten. Optimal ist es dabei natürlich, wenn man von einer/m Bekannten mitgenommen und dort vorgestellt wird.

Um Einblick in die traditionelle japanische Gesellschaft zu erhalten, bieten sich Möglichkeiten wie das Erlernen der Teezeremonie (*sadō*), des Blumenarrangements (*ikebana*), der Kalligraphie (*shodō*) oder von Kampfsportarten (*budō*) an. In einigen dieser Bereiche gibt es auch Workshops oder Ausstellungen. Die Lehrer/innen (*sensei*) bilden sich häufig lebenslang weiter und haben persönlich ein hohes Interesse an der Weitergabe dieser traditionellen Künste. Es gibt Vorführungen, Erklärungen und zum Teil erhält man die Gelegenheit, sich selbst in diesen Künsten zu üben. Dabei erfährt man immer viel Neues und ich erinnere mich an viele schöne Erlebnisse.

Leider gibt es heutzutage auch in Japan Nachwuchsprobleme. Die zumeist älteren Lehrer/innen beklagen sich, ihre Künste nicht mehr in angemessener Weise an Nachfolger/innen weitergeben zu können. Die japanischen Werte, die durch die Zen Künste stark mitgeprägt worden sind, würden langsam im Vergessenheit geraten. Immer weniger jüngere Menschen hätten Interesse daran. Daher freuen sie sich umso mehr, wenn Ausländer/innen Interesse an ihrer Kunst zeigen und diese lernen wollen.

Japanische traditionelle Künste basieren oftmals auf der Vorstellung, dass der Weg (*dō*) zu einer Verbesserung der eigenen Fertigkeiten lebenslang beschritten wird. Dieses erfordert Ruhe, Ernsthaftigkeit, Beharrlichkeit und Disziplin, Eigenschaften, die in unserer schnelllebigen Zeit oftmals verloren gehen. Gleichzeitig erfährt man vieles über sich selbst und wird in Achtsamkeit gegenüber den Mitmenschen geschult.

Möchte man in Japan gut zurechtkommen, empfiehlt es sich nach meiner Erfahrung folgende Dinge zu beachten:

Das Verhalten in der Öffentlichkeit ist dem sozialen Kontext angepasst. Teil hiervon sind Höflichkeitsabstufungen in der Sprache und auch bei den Verbeugungen.

Insbesondere bei Begrüßungen und Verabschiedungen gibt es große Unterschiede, beispielsweise verbeugt man sich tiefer einer/m Vorgesetzten oder Lehrer/in gegenüber und beachtet dabei das Hierarchiegefälle. Als Ausländer/in wird einem die Unkenntnis darüber zwar nie zum Vorwurf gemacht, das richtige Verhalten hilft aber ungemein bei der Integration und dabei, dass der/die andere sich wohl fühlt.

Sich für vieles auch prophylaktisch zu entschuldigen, ist oftmals üblich. Die häufigste Form hierfür ist das „*suminasen*". Je nach Kontext dient dieses von „Verzeihung, dass ich Sie belästige" bis hin zum Dankbarkeitsausdruck im Sinne „das wäre doch nicht nötig gewesen". Kennt man als Ausländer/in auch einige andere der Entschuldigungsformen/Ausdrücke und wendet sie richtig an, kommt dieses gesellschaftlich sehr gut an. Gleiches gilt für das Bedanken (einfachste Form „*arigato*"), für die es verschiedene Höflichkeitsformen und Ausdrücke zu speziellen Anlässen gibt.[7]

Zum guten Ton gehört es, zu jeglichen Anlässen kleinere Geschenke mitzubringen und möglichst schön verpackt zu übergeben. Zum Beispiel werden von einer Reise immer kleine Süßigkeiten oder Spezialitäten der Region (*omiyage*) mitgebracht und zu Neujahr werden sowohl an Geschäftsleute als auch im Privaten viele Geschenkpakete verschickt, um sich das gegenseitige Wohlwollen zu sichern.

Die Japaner/innen sind darauf geschult, mitzudenken, was der andere meinen könnte und das setzt voraus, die Gedanken des anderen zu erkennen. Ein „ja" bedeutet nicht unbedingt Zustimmung, sondern wird häufig auch der Höflichkeit halber oder aus Achtung seinem Gesprächspartner gegenüber geäußert. Dieses liegt daran, dass in Japan üblich ist, die Harmonie (*wa*) und die Einigkeit zu wahren. Das ist für Ausländer/innen schwierig einzuschätzen und führt nicht selten zu Missverständnissen im Privaten als auch bei Geschäftsbeziehungen. Mir hat es geholfen, darauf zu achten, in welchem Gesprächskontext das „ja" gesagt wird sowie die Körpersprache des Gesprächspartners genau zu beobachten. Das wahre Selbst (*honne*, zu Deutsch ungefähr der wahre Ton) zeigt man nur der Familie und guten Freunden gegenüber. So äußerten sich meine Schwiegereltern zum Beispiel mir gegenüber immer sehr direkt.

Wichtig ist es ebenfalls, sich sauber zu kleiden und eine gute Körperhygiene zu haben. In den öffentlichen Verkehrsmitteln der großen Städte werden Menschen, die riechen, leicht zur Belästigung. Das bereits erwähnte tägliche Baden ist deshalb fester Gegenstand des Tagesablaufes. Bei dem Besuch in einem Onsen oder einem öffentlichen Badehaus ist strikt darauf zu achten sich gründlichst mit Seife zu reinigen, bevor man ins Wasser steigt. Als Ausländerin bin ich von Japanerinnen oftmals im Stillen beobachtet worden, ob ich das auch wirklich tue. Bei Befolgen der Reinigungsrituale wurde ich mit Smalltalk oder zustimmenden Nicken belohnt.

Bekannte haben mich oft gefragt, ob ich keinen „Kulturschock" in Japan erlitten habe. Das Leben sei dort doch schließlich so anders. Anders als erwartet hatte ich die-

---

7 Vgl. hierzu hilfreiche Hinweise auf https://www.japanwelt.de: JapanweltBlog 13. November 2018, Sumimasen&Arigato: Zwei große Pfeiler der japanischen Sprache, JapanweltBlog 18. Dezember 2020, Ojigi – Verbeugen auf Japanisch, JapanweltBlog 03. Mai 2022, Arten für Entschuldigung auf Japanisch.

sen Kulturschock bei meiner Rückkehr nach Deutschland. Ich vermisste die japanische Höflichkeit, die Zuvorkommenheit und den Servicegedanken in den Geschäften.

Einiges war für mich jedoch schwierig zu verstehen, beispielsweise die innere Einstellung und Haltung von den Japanern/innen zu Dingen, auf die man keinen Einfluss haben kann oder vermeintlich nicht hat. Vieles wird mit der Redewendung „*shikata ga nai*" bedacht, was so viel bedeutet wie „da kann man nichts machen". Ist ein naher Angehöriger krank oder stirbt, trifft ein Erdbeben oder Tsunami oder eine andere Katastrophe Japan, ist die Politik oder die Wirtschaft schlecht, verhält sich jemand ungerecht einer anderen Person gegenüber, es ist *shikata ga nai.* Dieses Ertragen von Leiden ist meines Erachtens tief im Bewusstsein der Menschen verankert.

Während der Jahre, die ich in Japan verbracht habe, hatte ich privat zwei oder dreimal die Woche Japanischunterricht. Ein früherer Grundschuldirektor unterrichtete mich unentgeltlich in seinem Haus und betrachtete es als „*shumi*" (Hobby, Neigung, Interesse) und als seinen gesellschaftlichen Beitrag jungen Frauen aus dem Ausland Japanisch beizubringen. Er wurde hierfür von den Japanern/innen sehr bewundert.

Außerdem traf ich mich regelmäßig mit einer Dame aus den gehobenen Kreisen. Wir unterhielten uns überwiegend auf Japanisch und ich brachte ihr mit der Zeit auch einige deutsche Ausdrücke und Gepflogenheiten bei. Das Oberschichtjapanisch unterschied sich komplett von dem in der Provinz. So eckte ich mehrfach mit meiner Schwiegermutter an, die meinte, ich solle mal „normal" mit ihr sprechen, sie sei doch schließlich Familie.

Meinem Lehrer und meiner Lehrerin bin ich noch heute dankbar für die vielen Dinge, die sie mir beigebracht haben und die ich sicherlich auf keiner Sprachschule so intensiv vermittelt bekommen hätte. An den Wochenenden luden sie mich ab und an ein und zeigten mir viele schöne Orte in Tokyo und Umgebung, wir gingen gemeinsam zu Ausstellungen und Konzerten.

In Japan laden nach meiner Erfahrung die Älteren die Jüngeren ein, Gegeneinladungen werden dabei nicht erwartet. Ist man selbst bereits älter geworden, gehört es gesellschaftlich zum guten Ton dieses zurückzugeben, seinerseits die Jüngeren einzuladen und damit etwas Gutes an die folgende Generation weiterzugeben.

Viele Japaner/innen der gehobeneren Kreise und an den Universtäten sind sehr wissbegierig. Oftmals wurde ich über Entwicklungen in Europa und Amerika und zu meiner Meinung hierzu befragt. Zudem war es äußerst hilfreich, sich in der klassischen Musik und der Kunst auszukennen.

Bei meinen Schwiegereltern auf dem Dorf verliefen meine Aufenthalte natürlich ganz anders. Ich versuchte, beim Pflanzen und Ernten des Gemüses, bei den Essenszubereitungen, Waschen und Putzen zu helfen. Alles, was im täglichen Leben anfiel. Das freute meine Familie und auch die Nachbarn, die dieses ebenfalls sehr genau beobachteten. Aus der anfänglichen Skepsis entwickelte sich im Lauf der Jahre Anerkennung und die Zugehörigkeit zur japanischen Familie. Hierzu gehörten auch die regelmäßigen Besuche später mit meiner Tochter, der während ihrer Aufenthalte japanische Gepflogenheiten und Traditionen vermittelt worden sind. Letztere sind auf dem Land meiner Einschätzung nach oftmals präsenter als in den Großstädten.

Besonders kleinere Kinder werden nach Möglichkeit von den Großmüttern mitbetreut, wenn dieses erforderlich ist. Die ältere Generation unterstützt Kinder und Enkelkinder finanziell in nicht selten erheblichem Maße, um die teuren Lebenshaltungs- und Bildungskosten mittragen zu können. Als mein Schwiegervater erfuhr, dass ich schwanger bin, pachtete er noch mit Mitte 60 einige Reisfelder dazu, um die wachsende Familie unproblematisch ernähren zu können. Die Tätigkeit meines Ehemannes an der Universität war für ihn nicht greifbar genug und deshalb traute er der dortigen finanziellen Absicherung nicht so recht. Ich denke, dieses Verhalten war tief verwurzelt und basierte letztlich auch auf seinen Erfahrungen im zweiten Weltkrieg und der Gefahr der Naturkatastrophen, die Japan regelmäßig treffen können.

Direkt nach dem verheerenden Erdbeben von Kōbe im Jahr 1995, lud er mehrfach seinen kleinen Laster voll und verteilte dort Reis und Gemüse an die notleidende Bevölkerung. Dieses Verhalten, gerade in Notsituationen zur Stelle zu sein, habe ich besonders bei den älteren Japanern/innen häufig beobachtet. So fuhr mein japanischer Aikido Sensei aus Deutschland nach dem verehrenden Erdbeben und Tsunami in Fukushima im Frühjahr 2011 in die Region, um seine moralische und auch praktische Hilfe anzubieten.

Diese Hilfsbereitschaft kam mir oftmals im täglichen Leben zugute. Wenn ich als Ausländerin mal wieder ratlos den Weg nicht wusste oder welchen Preis das richtige Zugticket kostete, weil alles nur auf Kanji geschrieben war, erhielt ich selbst in Großstädten wie Tokyo von Fremden Hilfe. Die damit verbundene Freundlichkeit hat mich sehr beeindruckt.

Wenn ich heutzutage nach Japan reise, stelle ich fest, dass die „Amerikanisierung“ weiter vorangeschritten ist. Die Lebensweise der Amerikaner ist vielen jüngeren Leuten ein Vorbild. Sie steht für mehr Leichtigkeit und Spaß. Fastfoodketten haben sich verbreitet, die Ernährungsgewohnheiten verändern sich leider ebenfalls langsam, Baseball und Football sind zum Volkssport geworden und haben einen gleichen Stellenwert wie Sumo erhalten. Amerikanische sowie europäische Namen und Ausdrücke finden zunehmend Einzug im täglichen Sprachgebrauch, was man bereits den Katakana Zeichen auf den allgegenwärtigen Schrifttafeln und Leuchtreklamen entnehmen kann.

Weiterhin fällt mir der hohe Altersdurchschnitt in Japan auf. In der Provinz sehe ich mittlerweile fast nur noch Menschen, die über 70 Jahre alt sind und noch im hohen Alter ihr Land bestellen. Sehr viele von ihnen versuchen so lange wie möglich zu Hause wohnen zu bleiben. Es ist schwierig, geeignete Pflegeeinrichtungen oder Pflegekräfte zu finden und dieses ist natürlich mit sehr hohen Kosten verbunden.

Wenn in der Regel eine Tochter der Familie die Pflege übernimmt, hört sie häufig früher mit ihrer Arbeit auf, was wiederum zu späteren finanziellen Problemen führt. Dieses stellt ein nationales Problem dar.

Die geburtenstarken Jahrgänge („Babyboom-Jahre“) waren in Japan bereits Mitte der 50iger Jahre und damit ca. zehn Jahre vor denen in Deutschland. Hinzu kommen eine sehr hohe Lebenserwartung und eine niedrige Geburtenrate, die dazu führen, dass der demografische Wandel in Japan bereits stark fortgeschritten ist.[8]

In Deutschland hatten und haben wir eine starke Zuwanderung, die zumindest teilweise auch dazu führt, dass jüngere Arbeitskräfte zur Verfügung stehen. In Japan hingegen werden auch heute noch kaum Arbeitskräfte ins Land gelassen. Viele Gastarbeiter werden nur zeitweise geduldet, um beispielsweise auf dem Bau oder bei Pflegediensten zu arbeiten, erhalten aber keinen längerfristigen Aufenthaltstitel. Probleme werden mittel- und längerfristig sicherlich nur durch eine weitere Öffnung des Landes mit der Genehmigung dauerhafter Beschäftigungsverhältnisse für ausländische Arbeitskräfte zu lösen sein.

Zum Abschluss dieses kleinen Berichtes möchte ich auf die Stellung der Frauen in Japan eingehen, da mir dieses Thema sehr am Herzen liegt.

Viele Frauen gehen nach der Schule drei bis vier Jahre auf eine Universität und arbeiten dann für einige Jahre. Anschließend – mit Mitte 20 bis 30 Jahren – beginnt die Familienphase. Werden Kinder geboren, bleiben sie oftmals zu Hause oder arbeiten in Teilzeit. In der Regel verdienen die Männer das Geld und sind an den Wochentagen sehr lange bei der Arbeit.

Die Hauptlast der Kindererziehung liegt bei den Japanerinnen, die dafür verantwortlich sind, dass die nächste Generation eine gehobene Position in der Gesellschaft einnehmen kann. Der Nachwuchs soll möglichst auf gute Kindergärten, Schulen und anschließend Universitäten – dabei oftmals auch auf private Institutionen – gehen. Früh gilt es, Kinder darauf vorzubereiten und intensiv mit ihnen zu lernen. Der „Bildungsstress" wird damit auch zur Belastung für die Mütter.

Ein kleines Beispiel: Als ich schwanger war, wurde ich von einer in etwa im gleichen Monat schwangeren Mutter in Tokyo auf dem Spielplatz angesprochen, ob ich englisch sprechen könne. Nach unseren Entbindungen könnten wir uns ja mal regelmäßig treffen und englisch miteinander sprechen. Sie habe gelesen, dass es in Amerika einen berühmten japanischen Wissenschaftler gäbe, der einen Nobelpreis erhalten habe und von klein auf zweisprachig aufgewachsen sei. Außerdem habe sie vor, dass ihre Kinder früh Klavier oder Geige lernen. Das fördere die Verbindungen im Gehirn. Ich stand sprachlos daneben, soweit hatte ich nie gedacht.

Mütter bleiben in der Regel länger als in Deutschland zu Hause und halten dem Mann bei allen außerhalb der Arbeit liegenden Dingen den Rücken frei. Dieses bezieht sich insbesondere auf den Haushalt und die Pflege gesellschaftlicher und familiärer Beziehungen. Die damit verbundene klassische Rollenteilung verstärkt die finanzielle Abhängigkeit vom Ehemann. Frauen sind dennoch häufig die „Finanzmi-

---

8 Zur „Überalterung" der Bevölkerung trägt der Altersdurchschnitt bei, der in Japan für die Jahre 2021 bis 2024 weltweit der höchste mit 49,9 Jahren war, https://www.laenderdaten.info, die Lebenserwartung bei Frauen liegt bei 87 Jahren und bei Männern bei 81 Jahren, vgl. https://www.oecdbetterlifeindex,org; Hinzu kommt eine niedrige Geburtenrate, prognostizierter Wert im Jahr 2024 sind 1,22 Kinder pro Paar, siehe https://de.statistacom, unter Japan: Fertilitätsrate von 1950 bis 2023 und Prognosen bis 2050; Artikel von Michael Ziegler vom 25. Januar 2025 Japans Geburtenrate wird 2024 einen neuen Rekord-Tiefstand erreichen unter https://sumikai.com.

nister“ der Familien. Es ist dringend notwendig, das Geld gut einzuteilen. Der Lebensunterhalt in Japan ist wie bereits erwähnt teuer.

Sind die Kinder aus dem Haus, gehen viele Japanerinnen aus finanziellen Gründen wieder arbeiten. Da sie zwischenzeitlich lange zu Hause geblieben sind, ist dann jedoch oftmals nur noch eine Tätigkeit weit unterhalb ihres Ausbildungsniveaus möglich.[9]

Hat der Ehemann den beruflichen Aufstieg geschafft oder ist die Familie vermögend, stehen den Frauen die Türen für ein angenehmes Leben offen. So teilte mir eine Freundin mit: „Ein guter Mann ist kaum zu Hause und bringt viel Geld mit“. Aus ihrer Sicht verständlich.

Heutzutage ist in der jüngeren Generation eine schrittweise Gegenentwicklung zu beobachten. Der steigende Singleanteil führt zu einer Verringerung des familienbedingten „Karriereknicks“. Auch in Japan gibt es bereits einige fortschrittliche Paare, welche sich die Erziehung der Kinder teilen.

Auf dem japanischen Arbeitsmarkt gibt es meiner Einschätzung nach jedoch immer noch eine wesentlich niedrigere Chancengleichheit für Frauen als in Deutschland. Deshalb gehen auch viele Japanerinnen, die ich kennenlernte und die im Ausland studiert haben, anschließend nicht wieder zurück in ihr Heimatland. Vor allen Dingen Frauen, die bereits Karriere gemacht hatten, teilten mir mit, in Japan würden keine vergleichbaren Berufsmöglichkeiten für sie bestehen und auch gesellschaftlich hätten sie im Ausland größere Freiheiten.

Von diesen Schwierigkeiten war ich selbst damals in Japan nicht betroffen. Ohne direkte Bewerbungen erhielt ich Arbeitsangebote, mit denen ich nicht im Entferntesten gerechnet hatte. So boten mir Universitäten an, deutsches Recht oder Deutsch als Fremdsprache zu unterrichten. Bei Anfragen von japanischen Firmen ging es primär nicht um juristische Inhalte, sondern um die Aufrechterhaltung und Vermittlung von Geschäftsbeziehungen zu deutschen Firmen. Während meiner Referendariatszeit habe ich zusammen mit meinem Mann gut Geld mit der Tätigkeit verdient, technische/maschinenbauliche Texte oder Gebrauchsanleitungen vom Japanischen ins Deutsche zu übersetzen. Er war dabei für den technischen und ich für den sprachlichen Teil verantwortlich. Wenn man flexibel ist, ergeben sich als Ausländer/in neben dem erlernten Beruf in Japan viele Möglichkeiten, den Lebensunterhalt zu bestreiten.

In Deutschland habe ich nicht für eine japanische oder eine deutsche Firma gearbeitet. Ich kann mir aber gut vorstellen, dass es im Rahmen der internationalen Geschäftsbeziehungen etliche Chancen gibt, zumindest wenn man über gute englische und japanische Sprachkenntnisse verfügt.

Die Zeit, die ich im Verlauf meines Lebens in Japan verbringen durfte, hat mich sehr geprägt. Nicht zuletzt eröffnete mir der Blick vom Ausland aus ebenfalls eine neue Sichtweise auf Deutschland, insbesondere auf meine Identität als „Deutsche“,

---

9 Laut einer Studie der Weltbank belegte Japan bei der Gleichstellung der Geschlechter (gender equality) im Jahr 2023 Platz 104, den letzten von einem OECD Land belegten Platz, Woman Business and the Law 2023, Index Japan 78,8, Index Deutschland 100.

über die ich mir früher keine Gedanken gemacht hatte. Ich erfuhr Internationalität und wurde dabei weltoffener.

Ich wünsche mir für die Zukunft ein weiterhin bestehendes gutes Verhältnis zwischen Deutschland und Japan. Wir können alle mit unseren Erfahrungen und mit Achtsamkeit dazu beitragen.

Masterstudium an der Tohoku-Universität, Sendai

Von *Roger Schaack*

Dr. Roger Schaack ist Rechtsanwalt und seit über 30 Jahren Sozius der Rechtsanwaltssozietät Krömer | Steger | Westhoff. Er hat Rechtswissenschaften an den Universitäten Tübingen und München studiert und sein Referendariat am OLG Düsseldorf absolviert. Nach seiner Promotion an der Universität Tübingen hat er ein Magisterstudium an der Tohoku Universität in Sendai abgeschlossen.

Schon während meines Studiums der Rechtswissenschaften an der Eberhard Karls Universität Tübingen zu Beginn der 80er Jahre des vorherigen Jahrhunderts reifte in mir der Gedanke, auch einmal in Japan eine Universität zu besuchen. Ein drei Monate dauernder Aufenthalt zuvor in Japan hatte mich auf den Geschmack gebracht. Allerdings war der Gedanke an ein Studium in Japan erst einmal recht unspezifisch. Neben den Vorlesungen der rechtswissenschaftlichen Fakultät in Tübingen besuchte ich auch Kurse in Japanologie. Ich brachte aber nicht die erforderliche Konzentration auf, um mich ausreichend dem Erlernen der japanischen Sprache zu widmen. Der Gedanke an Japan rückte wieder in die Ferne.

Nach Abschluss der Referendarzeit und zu Beginn meiner anwaltlichen Tätigkeiten trat der Wunsch nach etwas anderem aber wieder deutlich hervor und ich sagte mir „jetzt oder nie“. Ich wollte nicht nur als Gasthörer einer Universität Vorlesungen besuchen und an Kursen teilnehmen, sondern einen akademischen Titel erwerben. Sich ein solches Ziel zu setzen, empfand ich als zwingend, um die anstehenden, insbesondere sprachliche Herausforderungen zu meistern. Ein Aufgeben sollte es nicht geben.

Ich erkundigte mich nach Masterprogrammen japanischer Universitäten. Deren Dauer von 2 Jahren reizte mich. Es war ein Zeitraum, der einem Heimischwerden in der japanischen Welt sicherlich förderlich war. Andererseits bedingte er auch die Suche nach einem Stipendium. 2 Jahre in Japan waren nicht billig. Ich erfuhr, dass das *Monbushō* (das damalige japanische Kulturministerium[1]) weltweit Stipendien vergab. Neben den Gebühren der Universität trug das *Monbushō* damals auch etwas über 2.000,00 DM monatlich zu den Lebenshaltungskosten bei. Die Flugkosten werden auch übernommen.

Damit ein Bewerber bei der Stipendienvergabe überhaupt eine Chance hatte, musste er vorher Kontakt zu einem Professor bzw. einer Professorin herstellen, der bzw. die sich bereit erklärten, den Bewerber zu betreuen. Internetrecherchen waren damals noch nicht möglich. Wie also Professoren/Professorinnen finden? Es gab ein Verzeichnis ehemaliger japanischer DAAD-Stipendiaten, die in Deutschland studiert

1 Offizielle englische Übersetzung: Ministry of Education, Science, Sports and Culture. Heute: *Monbu-kagaku-shō* (Ministry of Education, Culture, Sports, Science and Technology).

Duncker & Humblot · Berlin | https://doi.org/10.3790/978-3-428-59611-9.2025.418785

hatten. Es war daraus auch ersichtlich, an welcher Universität in Japan diese dann später tätig geworden sind. Dass das *Monbushō* Stipendien nur für ein Studium an einer staatlichen Universität vergab, schränkte die Auswahl ein wenig ein. Ich schrieb an Professoren/Professorinnen der Universität Tokyo, der Universität Kyoto und der Tohoku-Universität in Sendai. Letztere Universität sowie die Stadt Sendai waren mir zum damaligen Zeitpunkt völlig unbekannt. Ich beschrieb den Schwerpunkt meines beabsichtigten Studiums, nämlich im Bereich des Handels- und Gesellschaftsrechts und meine Absicht des Erwerbs des Mastertitels.

Aus Tokyo oder Kyoto habe ich nie eine Reaktion erhalten. Aus Sendai dagegen eine sehr herzliche und dies wurde für mich ein Glücksfall. Herr Prof. Aoi Hideo, damals Professor für Rechtstheorie und Rechtsphilosophie an der Tohoku-Universität in Sendai meldete sich und stellte Kontakt zu Herrn Prof. Seki Toshihiki, Professor für Handelsrecht ebenfalls an der Tohoku-Universität her. Er sei bereits hier erwähnt, dass nach dem japanischen Verständnis Gesellschaftsrecht traditionell Teil des Handelsrechts ist. Ein Blick in das deutsche HGB spricht nicht dagegen. Zumindest die Personengesellschaften sind dort geregelt. Mit Hilfe der Zusage von Herrn Prof. Seki bewarb ich mich um das Stipendium des *Monbushō*. Da ich die luxemburgische Staatsbürgerschaft besitze, erfolgte das Interview mit dem japanischen Botschafter in Luxemburg. Wir diskutierten über die japanische Einzigartigkeit. Ich muss gestehen, dass meine Kenntnisse über japanische Kultur und Philosophie sehr oberflächlich waren und ich deshalb in dem Interview auch überfordert war. Nichtdestotrotz bekam ich das Stipendium.

Im April 1990 startete ich mein Unterfangen, rechtzeitig zu Beginn des Studienjahres in Japan. Die Tohoku-Universität zählt zu den kaiserlichen Universitäten Japans und erscheint mittlerweile in Rankings teilweise vor den traditionell höher bewerteten Universitäten in Tokyo und Kyoto. Der juristische Campus der Universität liegt etwas erhöht über der Stadt und in der Nähe der Überreste einer Burganlage (*Aoba-jō*), die zu Beginn des 17. Jahrhunderts von der noch heute wohl bekanntesten Persönlichkeit Sendais, dem Fürsten (*daimyō*) Date Masamune gegründet wurde, aber später verfiel. In Sendai angekommen kümmerte sich sofort ein Tutor um mich, mit dem ich auch ein Studierzimmer teilte. Jedem – auch angehenden – Masterstudenten und Doktoranten wurde ein Studierzimmer im Gebäude der juristischen Fakultät zugewiesen, dass er mit einem oder zwei weiteren Mitstudenten teilte. Für Anschluss war somit gesorgt. Insgesamt belegten ca. 40 Personen die Studienzimmer. Die Tohoku-Universität hatte damals insgesamt ca. 500 ausländische Studenten. Der größte Teil kam aus dem ostasiatischen Raum, insbesondere aus China und Südkorea. Auch Studenten aus Südamerika waren nicht wenige, zumeist stammten sie von japanischen Immigranten ab. Europäische Studenten gab es fünf. Unter den Juristen war ich der einzige.

Die Universität bot Sprachkurse für die ausländischen Studenten an, die ich fleißig besuchte. Hier machten sich die unterschiedlichen Ausgangspositionen bemerkbar. Die chinesischen Studenten hatten keine Schwierigkeiten mit den Schriftzeichen. Warum auch – stammen die japanischen doch von den chinesischen ab. Dagegen hatten sie größere Schwierigkeiten mit der japanischen Grammatik. Diese zu durchdringen, gelang uns Europäern besser, während natürlich die Schriftzeichen eine Herausforderung waren. Da Juristerei nun mal viel aus Lesen besteht, wollte ich diese Fähigkeit, soweit wie nötig und so schnell wie möglich, in den Griff bekommen. Ich lernte jeden Morgen Schriftzeichen, ca. 1.800 insgesamt mit ihren verschiedenen Aussprachen („Lesungen"). Eine Systematik im Aufbau, Zusammensetzung und Lesung wurde erkennbar, was das Erlernen erleichterte.

Parallel besuchte ich Vorlesungen und Kurse im Handelsrecht, Zivil- und Zivilprozessrecht. Das Handelsrecht war aus unserer Sicht Gesellschaftsrecht und Gesellschaftsrecht war im Grunde Aktienrecht. Alles andere als Aktiengesellschaften spielte damals im Wirtschaftsleben so gut wie keine Rolle. Im Zivilrecht beuchte ich Vorlesungen über das Sachenrecht und belegte einen Kurs zum internationalen Prozessrecht.

Auffällig war im Zivilrecht die Nähe zur europäischen Rechtsordnung und im Handelsrecht die Orientierung an dem amerikanischen Recht. Dies ermöglichte insbesondere das sprachliche Verständnis. Hatte man im Sachenrecht verstanden, dass gerade über ein bestimmtes Thema gesprochen wurde, ließ sich erahnen, was im Anschluss Gegenstand des Vortrags der Professoren war. Da die Vorlesung sich auch weitgehend an ein Lehrbuch hielt, konnte ich parallel im Lehrbuch die Thematik verfolgen und mir so die Bedeutung der Schriftzeichen erschließen.

Andererseits erzeugte die Nähe der ausländischen Rechtsordnungen auf den ersten Blick eine gewisse Enttäuschung. Man glaubte schon alles zu kennen. Auch schien mir die japanische Rechtswissenschaft eine ausgesprochene Vorliebe für Theorien zu haben. Es gab zu Auslegungsfragen oft mindestens drei Theorien: eine Theorie A, eine der Theorie A widersprechende Theorie B und schließlich eine zwischen den Theorien A und B vermittelnde Theorie C. Die Rechtsprechung andererseits ließ kaum erkennen, welche Theorie gelten sollte. Hinweise auf akademisches Schrifttum gab es in Urteilen nicht zu finden.

Dies war aber nur der erste Blick. Je besser der Einstieg in die japanische Sprache und damit die japanische Rechtswissenschaft gelangte, umso deutlicher reifte in mir eine Vorstellung darüber, was die japanische Rechtskultur so besonders macht. Ich habe meine Schlüsse wissenschaftlich nicht näher untersucht – vielleicht sind sie auch nicht haltbar. Aber der Unterschied zwischen dem deutschen und dem japanischen Recht besteht für mich in der Denkweise. Die deutschen Juristen denken digital, die japanischen Juristen hingegen analog. Hier in Deutschland bilden wir Obersätze und subsummieren unter jedes Tatbestandsmerkmal. In jedem Schritt ist eine Entscheidung zwischen Ja und Nein zu treffen, deren Ergebnis dann den weiteren Prüfungsablauf bestimmt. Einprägsam hatte dies zu meiner Studienzeit in Tübingen im Zivilrecht Herr Prof. Dr. Gernhuber in seinem aus 50 Übersichten bestehenden „Systematischen Leitfaden zum Bürgerlichen Recht" und im Strafrecht Herr Prof. Dr. Fritjof Haft in seinen Lehrbüchern zum Allgemeinen und Besonderen Teil des Strafrechts beschrieben. Die analoge Denkweise der Japaner vergleicht dagegen Fälle, sucht nach Gemeinsamkeiten oder Unterschieden zwischen diesen, gewichtet die Gemeinsamkeit und die Unterschiede, um dann zu einer Entscheidung zu gelangen. Sind die Unterschiede nicht zu gewichtig, werden die Fälle gleichbehandelt, andernfalls unterschiedlich beurteilt. Das Gesetz wird dann ein Leitfaden, kein allein bestimmender Maßstab. Diese Denkweise, die weniger auf einer aus dem Sollen abgeleitete Begrifflichkeit als einer dem Sein entnommenen Wahrnehmung beruht, lässt die Grenzen der Dogmatik zerfließen. Das, was die DNA des deutschen Juristen ausmacht, wurde bei mir getroffen. Mühen wir uns in Deutschland ab, eine klare begriffliche Trennung zwischen einem die Anfechtung rechtfertigenden Inhaltsirrtum und rechtlich unbeabsichtigten Motivirrtum zu definieren, werfen die japanischen Juristen den Ballast ab und fragen sich schlicht, wann eine Situation so zu bewerten ist, dass eine Anfechtung gerechtfertigt ist und wann nicht. Diese Unbefangenheit gegenüber der Dogmatik spürte ich auch in einem für unsere Vorstellung krassen Fall. Das japanische Zivilrecht hat unter anderem den französischen Code Civil rezipiert. Dies hielt – wenn auch zeitlich schon deutlich vor meinem Studium in Sendai in den 90er Jahren liegend – einen Teil der japanischen Rechtswissenschaft nicht davon ab, darüber zu philosophieren, ob das deutsche Abstraktionsprinzip also die Trennung von schuldrechtlicher Verpflichtung und dinglichem Übergang – sich nicht in das japanische Recht integrieren ließ.

Sicherlich kann man sich fragen, inwieweit der – jedenfalls nach meinem Verständnis bestehende – analoge Ansatz durch die Unterschiede in der Sprache geprägt sind. Sprache bestimmt das Denken und das Denken bestimmt die Sprache. Jedenfalls die japanische Schrift ist konkret. Die Schriftzeichen haben einen bildlichen Ursprung und ihre Zusammensetzung folgt in einem gewissen Umfang der Bedeutung ihrer Bestandteile. Dies schärft den Blick für das Konkrete.

Im 2. Jahr meines Studiums wurde ich offiziell Masterstudent. Wesentlicher Schritt für den Mastertitel war das Abfassen der Masterarbeit. Ich widmete mich einem rechtsvergleichenden Thema, der Ermittlung von Abfindungen für Minderheitsgesellschafter, die aus einer Aktiengesellschaft ausgeschlossen werden, im japanischen und deutschen Recht. Zum damaligen Zeitpunkt ging es im deutschen Recht darum, den „wirklichen" Unternehmenswert zu ermitteln. Die Abfindung des ausgeschlossenen Gesellschafters sollte den Anteil an diesem Wert repräsentieren, unabhängig davon ob der Gesellschafter diesen an einem Markt durchsetzen konnte oder nicht. Der Gesellschafter war Teilhaber eines Unternehmens. Dagegen wurde er kaum gesehen als Teilnehmer eines Marktes, der mit Anteilen von Unternehmen handelte. Anders war es dagegen in Japan. Der Minderheitsgesellschafter wurde nicht idealisiert, sondern als das angesehen, was er grundsätzlich war, nämlich ein Anleger. Natürlich gibt es Fälle der Kursmanipulation. Diese Fälle behandelte das japanische Recht aber als Ausnahme, nicht als Regel. Mittlerweile setzt sich dieser pragmatische, auf den Börsenkurs abstellenden Ansatz auch in Deutschland mehr und mehr durch.

Das Studium in Japan vermittelte nicht nur in fachlicher Hinsicht einen neuen, zusätzlichen Blick auf juristische Begrifflichkeiten und juristische Argumentation. Auch persönlich war es eine Bereicherung. Werden Japaner weitläufig als zurückhaltend und kühl beschrieben, so empfand ich die japanische Gesellschaft als warm. Die japanische Höflichkeit erachte ich als wohltuend. Sie ließ mich als Teil meines sozialen Umfeldes empfinden. Niemals hatte ich das Gefühl abseits der anderen Studenten zu stehen. Auch wenn man als Europäer damals in Sendai exotisch wirkte, kam mir nie das Gefühl, ein Fremder zu sein. Das Exotische verhalf mir zu vielfältigen Begegnungen. Ich erhielt Einladungen, Vorträge über meine Eindrücke zu halten. Beispielsweise sprach ich in einer Kleinstadt am Rande von Sendai mit ca. 20 Jugendlichen über Jugend in Deutschland und Japan. Im Anschluss gab es ein Abendessen mit dem Bürgermeister und den sonstigen Honorationen der Stadt. Es gab nicht nur viel Fisch, sondern auch Nihonshu.

Die Zeit in Japan war eine sehr aufschlussreiche. Ich wünsche eine solche Zeit jedem, der sich die Chance eines Studiums in Japan nicht entgehen lässt.

Aufbau und Testfragen der japanischen Sozialarbeiterprüfung

Von *Andreas Scheller*

Dr. Andreas Scheller studierte Rechtswissenschaft an der Osaka Universität und promovierte zum Thema Sport und Recht. Nach Tätigkeiten als außerordentlicher Dozent, unter anderem an der Osaka Universität, lehrt er seit 2006 auf Japanisch als Associate Professor an der Hiroshima International University über die Grundlagen des japanischen Rechts. Sein Forschungsschwerpunkt liegt heute im japanischen Betreuungsrecht. Seit Jahren engagiert er sich regelmäßig aktiv als freiwilliger Helfer im Alten- und Behindertensport.

Anfang der 1980er Jahre hatte meine Schwester Martina zirka drei Jahre in Hiroshima verbracht, um verschiedenes Material für ihre Doktorarbeit über die Geschichte der Hafenstädte im Raum Inlandsee während der Tokugawa-Zeit zu sammeln. Der Forschungsaufenthalt an der Hiroshima Universität wurde von einem DAAD-Stipendium unterstützt, das ihr nicht nur den mehrmaligen direkten Besuch der Hafenstädte, sondern auch die korrekte Übersetzung und wissenschaftliche Analyse der teilweise jahrhundertealten Texte ermöglichte.

Als Gymnasiastin hatte sie zufällig an einem schwarzen Brett ihres Gymnasiums einen Aushang entdeckt, in dem ausländische Oberschüler Brieffreunde in Deutschland suchten. Eine Brieffreundschaft mit einem Oberschüler aus Japan führte dann dazu, dass sie ein Studium der japanischen Geschichte an der Philosophischen Fakultät der Universität Bonn begann. Nach Auswertung und Analyse der während des Studienaufenthaltes in Japan gesammelten Materialien konnte sie dann 1990 ihre Doktorarbeit über einen sehr interessanten Aspekt der japanischen Geschichte einreichen.[1]

Nachdem ein Kurzbesuch bei meiner Schwester während ihres Studienaufenthaltes in Hiroshima auch bei mir das Interesse an Japan geweckt hatte, begann ich 1992 ebenfalls einen Forschungsaufenthalt an der Universität Hiroshima. Professor Dr. Takenori Murakami der Juristischen Fakultät hatte mich eingeladen, um mit ihm als Gastforscher diverse deutsche bzw. japanische verwaltungsrechtliche Probleme zu analysieren und einige Aufsätze zu veröffentlichen.[2] Um meine Kenntnisse des ja-

1 *Scheller*, Versuch einer Typisierung von Hafenstädten im Raum Inlandsee während der Tokugawa-Zeit – Einflüsse von Handel und Verkehr auf die Entwicklung von sieben Hafenstädten (1990).

2 *Murakami/Scheller*, Der Weg zum Rechtsstaat (1992); *Murakami/Scheller*, Japans Wiederaufrüstung und die Entsendung japanischer Truppen für die UNO Friedensmission (PKO) (1993); *Murakami/Scheller*, Die neuartige Nutzung der Meeresoberfläche und die Seeverwaltungssatzung der Hiroshima Präfektur von 1991 (1993); *Murakami/Scheller*, Die Rechtsprobleme der Aufsicht der japanischen Verwaltungstätigkeit (1993).

Duncker & Humblot · Berlin | https://doi.org/10.3790/978-3-428-59611-9.2025.418813

panischen Rechts zu vertiefen, schloss ich dann im Jahre 2000 einen Magister- bzw. einen anschließenden Doktorkurs an der Juristischen Fakultät der Universität Osaka ab.[3] Nach Lehrtätigkeiten an der Osaka- sowie an der Hiroshima Universität, bin ich seit 2006 an der Hiroshima International University beschäftigt, die besonders Studenten ausbildet, die nach dem Abschluss im medizinischen, gesundheitstechnischen oder sozialen Bereich arbeiten.

Die meisten Studenten meiner Fakultät (Department of Social Welfare) bereiten sich vier Jahre lang auf die staatliche Sozialarbeiterprüfung vor. Obwohl man auch ohne diese Qualifikation in verschiedenen sozialen Bereichen berufstätig sein könnte, hat das Bestehen dieser Prüfung mehrere Vorteile, auf die ich später eingehen möchte.

Meine Aufgabe an der Fakultät besteht vornehmlich darin, die Vorlesungen der Fächer zu halten, die sich besonders mit rechtlichen Fragen beschäftigen. Für die Studenten ist es unabdingbar, grundlegende Begriffe des japanischen Rechts zu verstehen, um als Sozialarbeiter ihre Klienten professionell unterstützen bzw. beraten zu können.

Die folgenden Erklärungen bezüglich der universitären Ausbildung zum Sozialarbeiter bzw. der Vorbereitung zur staatlichen Sozialarbeiterprüfung beruhen im Wesentlichen auf meine bald zwanzigjährige Erfahrung als Lehrkraft der Hiroshima International University. An anderen Universitäten bzw. Fakultäten bestehen sicherlich marginal unterschiedliche Lehrpläne sowie Ausbildungsinhalte. Da der Inhalt der Sozialarbeiterprüfung jedoch für alle Prüflinge gleich ist, sind die folgenden Erläuterungen zur Vorbereitung der Prüfung auf die meisten anderen Universitäten übertragbar.

I. Notwendigkeit der Sozialarbeit in Japan

1. Der Begriff Soziale Arbeit

Bevor ich auf die Aufgabenbereiche von japanischen Sozialarbeitern eingehen werde, ist es kurz notwendig, den Begriff Soziale Arbeit zu erläutern, da grundsätzlich die Schwierigkeit besteht, den Gegenstand „Soziale Arbeit" genauer zu bestimmen und abzugrenzen. Es sollte die Frage beantwortet werden, welche Praxisfelder, Einrichtungen, Dienste und Berufe überhaupt zur Sozialen Arbeit gehören. Wenn man den Versuch unternimmt, allein vom Begriff „Sozialarbeit" auszugehen und dadurch Anhaltspunkte für die notwendige Eingrenzung zu gewinnen, wird man erkennen, dass der Terminus „Sozialarbeit" weder eindeutig ist, noch einhellig gebraucht wird und überdies den Gegenstand nur unscharf markiert.

Es existieren unterschiedliche Begriffe und Umschreibungen, mit denen das Feld der sozialen Arbeit bezeichnet wird: Früher sprach man von Fürsorge oder Wohlfahrtspflege, heute gebraucht man unterschiedliche Begriffe wie Soziale Arbeit, Sozialarbeit, Sozialpädagogik, Sozialarbeit/Sozialpädagogik, Kinder-, Jugend- und Fa-

---

[3] *Scheller, Doitsu ni okeru supo-tsu to hōsō no tanjikannyu-suhōdōken wo meguru hōritsumondai* [Rechtliche Probleme bezüglich der Kurzberichterstattung des Sportes in Deutschland] (1999).

milienhilfe, soziale Dienste, soziale Praxis, soziale Hilfsarbeit, sozialpflegerischer Bereich, psycho-soziale Hilfen, (Soziale-)Fürsorge, Sozialwesen und andere mehr. Alle diese Benennungen beziehen sich auf das Feld sozialer Arbeit; sie sind aber nicht völlig kongruent, sondern betonen verschiedene Aspekte oder Bereiche. Dies macht darauf aufmerksam, dass das Feld der Sozialen Arbeit kein einheitlich oder systematisch strukturierter Bereich ist, der sich eindeutig und trennscharf von anderen Bereichen abgrenzen lässt. Vielmehr ist er in sich völlig ausgestaltet und in seinen Rändern und Übergängen unscharf. Unscharfe Grenzziehungen bestehen insbesondere im Übergang zum Sozialhilfesystem, zum psychotherapeutischen Bereich, zum Strafvollzugs- und Justizwesen, zur Kinder- und Jugendpsychiatrie, zur Arbeitsverwaltung, zur Schule und dem Bildungswesen und zur Selbsthilfe- und Initiativgruppenbewegung.[4]

Ich werde später darauf eingehen, in welchen Bereichen japanische Sozialarbeiter besonders tätig sind und wie das Feld der Sozialen Arbeit eingegrenzt werden kann.

2. Gesellschaftliche Herausforderungen für Sozialarbeiter in Japan

Für Japan stellt der Geburtenrückgang und die alternde Gesellschaft ein drängendes Problem dar. 2024 lag der Anteil der über 65-Jährigen an der Gesamtbevölkerung bei zirka 30 %. Zugleich stagniert die Geburtenrate bei etwa 1,2, sodass die Situation weiterhin kritisch ist. Der Geburtenrückgang und der Prozess der alternden Gesellschaft wird voraussichtlich weiter voranschreiten, und dieser demografische Wandel wird für Japans Wirtschaft, Gesellschaft und die Sozialsysteme eine große Herausforderung bedeuten. Sozialarbeiter spielen in dieser Zeit der gesellschaftlichen Veränderungen in verschiedenen Bereichen eine äußerst wichtige Rolle, um das Wohl der Gemeinschaft zu erhalten und die Bevölkerung mit wichtigen Informationen zu versorgen.

a) Überalterung der Gesellschaft

Japan ist das Land mit der ältesten Bevölkerung der Welt. Dafür gibt es verschiedene Maßstäbe. Am häufigsten vergleicht man die Lebenserwartung bei Geburt. Hier steht Japan nach Zahlen von 2024 mit einer durchschnittlichen Lebenserwartung für beide Geschlechter von etwa 85 Jahren an der Weltspitze. Dabei überleben die Japanerinnen (88) die Männer (82) um etwa sechs Jahre. Bis zum Jahr 2050 soll die Lebenserwartung auf durchschnittlich rund 89 Jahre steigen.[5]

Ein anderer Indikator für die Bevölkerungsalterung ist die Anzahl der Hochbetagten. Jedes Jahr im September am Tag des Respekts vor dem Alter veröffentlicht die japanische Regierung diesbezügliche Zahlen. Danach lebten 2024 im ganzen Land zirka 95.000 Personen, die 100 Jahre alt oder älter waren. 1963, als diese Statistik

---

4 *Hering/Münchmeier*, Geschichte der Sozialen Arbeit, 3. Aufl. (2005), S. 11–12; über den Begriff Sozialarbeit in Japan siehe: *Ōta, So-sharuwa-ku jissen to shienkagaku* [Soziale Arbeit – Praxis und Unterstützung], 1. Aufl. (2008).

5 *Coulmas/Stalpers*, Japan, 1. Aufl. (2011), S. 64–66, mit neuen Daten von 2024.

zum ersten Mal erhoben wurde, gab es 163 Hundertjährige. Bis Mitte des 21. Jahrhunderts wird sich die Zahl nach einer Schätzung 500.000 nähern.[6]

Japans Alterung in einem relativ kurzen Zeitraum ist einerseits spektakulär und insgesamt ein Beweis einer erfolgreichen Gesellschaft. Andererseits stellt sie das Land vor neue Herausforderungen, die in der nahen Zukunft dringend Lösungsansätze erforderlich machen.

b) Sinkende Geburtenrate

Nach einer Hochrechnung wird die letzte Person in Japan vermutlich etwa im Jahre 3300 geboren werden. Keine Hochrechnung über eine solche Zeitspanne könnte den Anspruch erheben, eine realistische Prognose zu sein. Die Veröffentlichung dieser Voraussage akzentuierte aber die große Herausforderung, der Japan sich stellen muss und in vieler Hinsicht stellt: Seit 2005 schrumpft die Bevölkerung. Im ersten Jahr des negativen Wachstums ging die Bevölkerung nur um ein paar Tausend zurück, aber 2009 war diese Zahl bereits auf ein Minus von 183.000 angewachsen, ein Negativwachstum von 0,14 %. Im Jahre 2024 ist die Bevölkerungszahl jedoch schon um zirka 600.000 zurückgegangen. Verschiedene Daten lassen vermuten, dass ein weiterer Bevölkerungsrückgang unvermeidlich ist. Die Frage, die Wissenschaft und Regierung beschäftigt, ist allein, welches Ausmaß die Schrumpfung haben wird. Wegen der verschiedenen Faktoren, die auf die Gesamtbevölkerung einwirken, sind Prognosen außerordentlich schwierig. Geburtenrate, Sterberate und Wanderung sind zusammengenommen schon komplex genug, wenn nicht noch Epidemien, Naturkatastrophen oder Kriege dazukommen.[7]

Die auch in anderen Industriestaaten wahrnehmbare Tendenz des Geburtenrückgangs ist in Japan besonders ausgeprägt. Nach dem kurzlebigen Babyboom unmittelbar nach dem Zweiten Weltkrieg ist die Geburtenrate fast stetig gesunken. Allein in dem Jahrzehnt zwischen 1947 und 1957 fiel die Gesamtfertilitätsrate – die Zahl der Kinder, die eine Frau in ihrem Leben zur Welt bringt – von 4,54 auf weniger als die Hälfte: 2,04. Und sie fiel weiter. 1989 brachte den „1,57“ Schock, eine Fruchtbarkeitsrate, die so weit unter der Reproduktionsrate von etwas mehr als 2 liegt, dass sich die japanische Regierung gezwungen fühlte, mit Maßnahmen wie Steuererleichterungen und Kindergeld zu reagieren.[8] Der Trend wurde dadurch jedoch nicht auf-

6 *Coulmas/Stalpers* (Anm. 5), S. 64–66.

7 *Coulmas/Stalpers* (Anm. 5), S. 64–66.

8 Der 1,57 Schock hat noch einen anderen Hintergrund, der einen sehr aktuellen Bezug zur näheren Zukunft besitzt. Vom Ende des Zweiten Weltkrieges bis zu den 1980er Jahren konnten verschiedene Schwankungen der japanischen Geburtenrate festgestellt werden, die im gleichen Zeitraum oftmals auch in anderen Industrieländern bemerkt wurden. Das Jahr 1966 stellte jedoch eine Ausnahme dar, da in diesem Jahr die Geburtenrate nur bei 1,58 lag, was weit unter der Rate von den Vorjahren bzw. auch den danach folgenden Jahren lag. 1966 war das sogenannte Hinoeuma-Jahr. Der Begriff bezieht sich auf das Jahr des Feuerpferdes im chinesischen Kalender. Nach einem alten Aberglauben gelten in diesem Jahr geborene Frauen als besonders temperamentvoll und möglicherweise unglücksbringend für ihre zukünftigen Ehepartner, was zu einem bedeutenden Rückgang der Geburtenrate im Jahre 1966 führte. 1989 lag die Geburtenrate nun noch sogar unter der des Jahres 1966, obwohl es kein nach dem chinesischen Kalender unglücksverheißendes Jahr war. Das nächste Hinoeuma-Jahr wird 2026 sein, und es bleibt abzuwarten, ob der Aberglauben wie vor 60 Jahren auch diesmal einen Einfluss auf die Geburtenrate haben wird.

gehalten. Seit 2005 gehört die Fertilitätsrate mit 1,25 bzw. 1,3 zu den niedrigsten der Welt. 2024 lag diese Rate bei 1,2, im Großraum Tokio waren es sogar nur 0,99.

Das Japanische Institut für Bevölkerung und Soziale Sicherheit hält gegenwärtig verschiedene Szenarien vor, die realistisch erscheinen und ständig auf der Grundlage neuer Daten modifiziert werden. Bis 2070 rechnet es bei niedriger Sterberate und hoher Geburtenrate mit einer Gesamtbevölkerung von 99 Mio., eine niedrige Sterberate in Verbindung mit einer mittleren Geburtenrate resultiert in 91 Mio. und bei niedriger Sterberate und niedriger Geburtenrate wird die Zahl noch geringer sein: 87 Mio. In jedem Fall müssen sich staatliche Institutionen und Privatwirtschaft auf eine um ein Fünftel bis ein Drittel kleinere Bevölkerung einstellen. Dieser Rückgang der Erwerbsbevölkerung dürfte das Renten- und Gesundheitssystem vor schwer vorhersehbare Herausforderungen stellen.

Pessimisten halten es für möglich, dass die Rentenkassen zahlungsunfähig und der Altersquotient – das Verhältnis der Alten zu der erwerbstätigen Bevölkerung – so ungünstig werden könnten, dass Japans hoher Lebensstandard starke Einbußen erleiden wird. Was dafür getan werden kann, ist heute zweifellos eine der für Japans Zukunft wichtigsten Fragen.[9]

c) Weitere soziale Herausforderungen

Obwohl der Lebensstandard nach wie vor auf einem hohen Niveau liegt, existieren erhebliche Ungleichheiten bezüglich des Einkommens. Alleinerziehende Mütter, ältere Menschen und Behinderte sind davon besonders betroffen. Im Vergleich zu anderen Industrienationen ist das Rentenniveau relativ niedrig, sodass Altersarmut ein nicht zu unterschätzendes gesellschaftliches Problem darstellt. Ältere Menschen, Behinderte und Alleinerziehende sind auch nicht selten von sozialer Isolation betroffen.

Japanische Schulen kämpfen seit langem mit diversen Problemen. Überlastung der Lehrkräfte, Gewalt und Mobbing zwischen den Schülern sowie Schulverweigerung, um nur einige Probleme zu nennen, sind eine hohe Belastung für das Bildungssystem.

Der relativ hohe soziale Druck, diversen familiären sowie gesellschaftlichen Erwartungen zu entsprechen, führt oftmals zu Problemen wie Überarbeitung oder Mobbing am Arbeitsplatz. Solche Überlastungen im Beruf bzw. am Arbeitsplatz führen oft zu einem Anstieg von psychischen Gesundheitsproblemen, einschließlich Depression und hoher Selbstmordraten.[10]

II. Aufgabenbereich des staatlich anerkannten Sozialarbeiters

Ein staatlich anerkannter Sozialarbeiter ist eine Person, die Beratungen und andere Formen der Unterstützung für Menschen anbietet, die aufgrund von Behinderungen, Krankheiten oder Einflüssen der Umwelt Schwierigkeiten im Leben haben. Sozialarbeiter haben diverse Aufgaben, die darauf abzielen, das Wohl der Gemeinschaft zu fördern sowie Einzelpersonen und deren Familien zu beraten bzw. zu unterstützen.

---

9 *Coulmas/Stalpers* (Anm. 5), S. 64–66.

10 *Coulmas/Stalpers* (Anm. 5), S. 82.

In dem Gesetz über staatlich anerkannte Sozialarbeiter und Pflegekräfte werden sie als „Personen, die mit sozialarbeiterischen Kenntnissen und Fähigkeiten Beratung, Betreuung, Unterstützung und andere Dienste für Menschen anbieten, die körperlich oder geistig behindert sind oder aus Umweltgründen ihr tägliches Leben nicht bewältigen können" bezeichnet.[11] Die Qualifikation des zertifizierten Sozialarbeiters wird landesweit anerkannt.

Sozialarbeiter erbringen soziale Dienste auf der Grundlage des Ethikkodex für Sozialarbeit, der die Grundsätze festlegt, nach denen die professionellen Sozialarbeiter handeln sollten: den Klienten ausreichend zuhören, ihre Denkweisen und Ansichten respektieren sowie die Vertraulichkeit der Informationen bewahren.[12]

Staatlich anerkannte Sozialarbeiter unterstützen und beraten Menschen aller Altersgruppen bei der Lösung ihrer Probleme in ganz unterschiedlichen Bereichen:

Ältere Personen werden von Sozialarbeitern beraten und unterstützt, um ihren Alltag selbstständig führen bzw. unabhängig bewältigen zu können. Hilfe bei der Organisation von Pflegeleistungen sowie auch emotionale Unterstützung für ältere Menschen und ihre Familien gehören ebenfalls zu ihren Aufgaben.

Menschen mit körperlichen, geistigen oder psychischen Behinderungen werden entsprechend ihrer individuellen Behinderung gefördert, um den Alltag selbstständig bewältigen und am gesellschaftlichen Leben teilnehmen zu können.

Sozialarbeiter schützen die Rechte von Kindern bzw. Minderjährigen. Probleme der Jugendkriminalität, des Missbrauchs oder der Gewalt bedürfen individueller Lösungsansätze. In Kinderberatungszentren und Jugendschutzeinrichtungen helfen Sozialarbeiter bei der Betreuung und Unterstützung von vernachlässigten oder missbrauchten Kindern und Jugendlichen.

Menschen mit wirtschaftlichen Problemen oder in schwierigen Lebenssituationen, einschließlich Arbeitslosigkeit oder psychischer Gesundheitsprobleme, werden individuell beraten, um am gesellschaftlichen Leben besser teilnehmen zu können. Sozialarbeiter helfen den Betroffenen, Zugang zu notwendigen Ressourcen und Dienstleistungen zu erhalten.

In Krankenhäusern unterstützen sogenannte Medical-Social-Worker (MSW) Patienten bei der Navigation durch das Gesundheitssystem sowie bei der Vorbereitung auf das Leben nach einem längeren Krankenhausaufenthalt. Sie sind oftmals ein Bindeglied zwischen Patienten, medizinischem Personal und sozialen Diensten.

Auch in Einrichtungen des Strafvollzugs oder bei der Wiedereingliederung ehemaliger Straftäter in die Gesellschaft spielen Sozialarbeiter als Berater eine wichtige Funktion. Sie beraten Insassen von Strafvollzugsanstalten individuell, um ihnen bei persönlichen oder sozialen Problemen beizustehen. Um ein straffreies Leben nach der Entlassung zu ermöglichen, entwickeln sie individuelle Programme, in denen besonders die Unterstützung bei der Wohnraum- sowie Arbeitssuche im Vordergrund stehen.

---

11 *Shakaifukushishi oyobi Kaigofukushishihō* [Gesetz für Sozialarbeiter und Pflegekräfte] (Art. 2).

12 *Shakaifukushishi Rinriyōryō* [Ethikregeln für Sozialarbeiter].

In Gemeinden verbessern Sozialarbeiter das Gemeinwohl, indem sie zum Beispiel die Vernetzung von Einzelpersonen mit Freiwilligengruppen fördern. Sie arbeiten oftmals mit lokalen Organisationen und Behörden zusammen, um Programme und Dienstleistungen zu entwickeln, die den Bedürfnissen der Gemeinschaft entsprechen.

Die oben genannten Aufgaben erfordern einerseits von den Sozialarbeitern ein sehr breit gefächertes Wissen und tiefgreifende Erfahrung. Andererseits besteht für eine erfolgreiche Sozialarbeit auch oftmals die Notwendigkeit, Mitgefühl, Emotionen und Verständnis zu zeigen. Für den Zusammenhalt der Gesellschaft, für die Stärkung des sozialen Gefüges Japans sowie für die Linderung der Not von vielen Einzelpersonen spielen die Sozialarbeiter eine nicht zu unterschätzende Rolle.[13]

III. Staatliche Prüfung zum Sozialarbeiter

1. Prüfungsgeschichte

Während der Modernisierung Japans zur Meiji-Zeit Ende des 19. bzw. Anfang des 20. Jahrhunderts spielten verschiedene europäische Nationen, darunter auch das damalige Deutschland, eine wichtige Vorbildfunktion. Ob bei den Rechtswissenschaften, der Medizin, den Naturwissenschaften oder den Künsten – Japan orientierte sich auf verschiedenen Gebieten an dem damaligen Deutschen Reich. Die unter Bismarck in den 1880er Jahren erlassenen Sozialgesetze bildeten auch für Japan ein grundlegendes Modell für die Einführung einer Sozialversicherung.[14]

In dem Bereich der sozialen Sicherheit, der Gesundheit und der Sozialversicherung sind beide Länder bis in die Gegenwart miteinander verbunden. Bezüglich der von beiden Ländern gegen Ende des 20. Jahrhunderts fast gleichzeitig eingeführten Pflegeversicherung besteht auch nach über 25 Jahren ein reger wissenschaftlicher Austausch, da die demografische Entwicklung beider Staaten Gemeinsamkeiten zeigt und sich sowohl Japan als auch Deutschland mit ähnlichen Herausforderungen für die Zukunft konfrontiert sehen.

Die formale Sozialarbeiterausbildung entwickelte sich in Japan ursprünglich in den 20er Jahren des 20. Jahrhunderts. Nach dem Zweiten Weltkrieg wurden umfassende Reformen durchgeführt, um ein modernes Sozialsystem aufzubauen. Besonders der Artikel 25 der 1947 eingeführten Verfassung bildete die Grundlage für die soziale Sicherheit und Wohlfahrt[15]. Gleichzeitig wurde das Bildungssystem reformiert und ein modernes Hochschulsystem etabliert.

Während des wirtschaftlichen Aufschwungs wurde das soziale System weiter ausgebaut, um neue gesellschaftliche Herausforderungen zu bewältigen. Der demogra-

13 *Tanaka*, *So-sharuwa-ku to kenriyōgo* [Soziale Arbeit und Rechtsschutz], 1. Aufl. (2008).

14 *Aymans*, Japan, 1. Aufl. (1985), S. 42–43.

15 Art. 25: All people shall have the right to maintain the minimum standards of wholesome and cultured living. In all spheres of life, the State shall use its endeavors for the promotion and extension of social welfare and security, and of public health; Text: *Satō*, Japanese Text and English Translation of The Constitution of Japan, 2. Aufl. (2012).

fische Wandel machte dann schon vor der Jahrtausendwende eine neuerliche Anpassung der Sozialsysteme erforderlich, um neue Lösungsansätze für soziale Ungleichheiten zu finden.

Die Vorgängerorganisation der heutigen Japan Association for Social Work Education wurde 1955 von 17 Schulen als freiwillige Organisation gegründet. Als Reaktion auf die alternde Gesellschaft trat 1987 das Gesetz für zertifizierte Sozialarbeiter und zertifizierte Pflegekräfte in Kraft. Die Vereinigung wurde immer grösser und umfasste im Jahre 2023 zirka 250 Ausbildungseinrichtungen. Darüber hinaus existieren noch weitere Organisationen, die ebenfalls Einrichtungen anbieten, um eine Ausbildung zum Sozialarbeiter zu absolvieren. Was das Ergebnis all dieser Bildungsgänge betrifft, gab es 2023 etwa 280.000 zertifizierte Sozialarbeiter.[16]

2. Inhalte der Prüfung zum zertifizierten Sozialarbeiter

Es bestehen zirka ein Dutzend Möglichkeiten, um für die Prüfung zugelassen zu werden. Zwei oder drei Jahre lernen (plus Praktikum) an einer speziellen Fachschule berechtigen ebenso zu einer Prüfungsteilnahme wie vier Jahre studieren an einer Universität, die die für die Prüfung erforderlichen Fächer anbietet. Aber auch Personen, die mindestens vier Jahre Erfahrung in einem sozialen Beruf haben, besitzen die Chance, sich für die Prüfung anzumelden.

Um ein staatlich anerkannter Sozialarbeiter zu werden, müssen Bewerber an Hochschulen oder anderen Institutionen verschiedene Fächer im Bereich Soziales studieren, die vom Ministerium für Gesundheit, Arbeit und Soziales festgelegt wurden. Nach dem Abschluss des Studiums ist es dann notwendig, die staatliche Prüfung für zertifizierte Sozialarbeiter zu bestehen. Diese Prüfung deckt ein breites Spektrum an Bereichen ab und ist eine relativ schwierige staatliche Prüfung. Sie findet einmal pro Jahr Anfang Februar statt. Wenn man die Prüfung nicht besteht, kann man den Test erst im nächsten Jahr wieder absolvieren.[17]

Die Prüfung umfasst folgende 19 Fächer:

1. Struktur und Funktion des menschlichen Körpers und Krankheiten (7 Fragen)
2. Theorie der Psychologie und psychologische Unterstützung (7 Fragen)
3. Sozialtheorie und soziale Systeme (7 Fragen)
4. Moderne Gesellschaft und Wohlfahrt (10 Fragen)
5. Grundlagen der Sozialforschung (7 Fragen)
6. Grundlagen der Beratungsunterstützung und Beruf (7 Fragen)
7. Theorie und Methoden der Beratungsunterstützung 1
8. Theorie und Methoden der Beratungsunterstützung 2 (zusammen 21 Fragen)
9. Theorie und Methoden des Gemeinwohls (10 Fragen)

---

16 *So-sharuwa-ku kyōiku Gakkōrenmei, Shakaifukushishi kokkashiken* [Staatliche Prüfung zum Sozialarbeiter], 1. Aufl. (2024).

17 So-sharuwa-ku kyōiku Gakkōrenmei (Anm. 16).

10. Sozialverwaltung, Finanzen und Planung (7 Fragen)
11. Sozialversicherung (7 Fragen)
12. Altenhilfe und Pflegeversicherung (10 Fragen)
13. Unterstützung und Dienstleistungen für die Unabhängigkeit von Behinderten (7 Fragen)
14. Unterstützung und Wohlergehen von Kindern und Familien (7 Fragen)
15. Unterstützung für Menschen mit niedrigem Einkommen und Sozialhilfesystem (7 Fragen)
16. Gesundheit und medizinische Dienstleistungen (7 Fragen)
17. Beschäftigungsunterstützende Dienstleistungen (4 Fragen)
18. Rechtsschutz und Betreuung für Erwachsene (7 Fragen)
19. Resozialisierung von Straftätern (4 Fragen)[18]

Schon anhand dieser Fächerliste ist erkennbar, dass die durch die Prüfung abgedeckten Bereiche sehr breit gefächert sind. Um diese Prüfung erfolgreich zu bestehen, ist es unbedingt notwendig, Schwachstellen in einigen Fächern zu vermeiden. Wenn man in einem Fach überhaupt keine Frage richtig beantworten würde, fiele man automatisch durch die gesamte Prüfung.

IV. Lehrpläne der Universitäten

1. Herausforderungen im 21. Jahrhundert

Die Soziale Wohlfahrt des 21. Jahrhunderts sollte die Bedürfnisse ganz unterschiedlicher Personen präzise erfüllen können und dabei gleichzeitig die Menschenwürde des Einzelnen respektieren. Die Ausbildung an den Universitäten zielt darauf ab, interessierte und talentierte junge Menschen zu fördern, die in der Zukunft über Fachwissen und Techniken verfügen, um flexibel auf verschiedene Bedürfnisse zu reagieren und die Menschenwürde des Einzelnen achten zu können. Um konkrete Lösungen für Probleme des täglichen Lebens zu finden, sollten sie in der Lage sein, hochqualifizierte Beratungen und Hilfstätigkeiten durchzuführen. Außerdem benötigen sie Kenntnisse des Verwaltungs- und Betriebsmanagements der diversen Wohlfahrtsbereiche.[19]

An vielen Universitäten arbeiten deshalb Dozenten mit umfassender Praxiserfahrung im Sozialbereich. Außerdem werden oftmals diverse spezielle Vorbereitungsseminare für die staatliche Prüfung angeboten, um Ergebnisse zu erzielen, die sich mit anderen Ausbildungseinrichtungen messen lassen oder sie sogar übertreffen. Eine hohe Erfolgsquote bei der Prüfung ist für alle Ausbildungseinrichtungen ein Zeichen für eine erfolgreiche Ausbildung der Prüflinge. Diese Erfolgsquote wird oftmals für

---

18 *Itō Sōken Shikakushutoku shiensenta-, Shakaifukushishi kokushinabi* [Navigation zur staatlichen Sozialarbeiterprüfung], 1. Aufl. (2023).

19 *Ōta* (Anm. 4).

Werbezwecke verwendet, um die Attraktivität der Ausbildung zum Sozialarbeiter zu erhöhen und Interessenten anzuwerben.

Darüber hinaus haben viele Universitäten ein dichtes Netzwerk mit den Absolventen aufgebaut, die nach dem Universitätsabschluss im Bereich der sozialen Wohlfahrt arbeiten. Dieses Netzwerk zwischen Universität und den Alumni bildet oftmals eine nicht zu unterschätzende Ermutigung für die Studenten, die schwere Vorbereitung auf die Prüfung noch gewissenhafter anzugehen, da die Absolventen Ihr Wissen und Ihre Erfahrungen den Studenten in Sondervorlesungen oder besonderen Prüfungsvorbereitungskursen weitergeben.

2. Inhalte der Lehrpläne

Die Lehrpläne an den Universitäten werden durch diese staatliche Prüfung beeinflusst, und die oben genannten Prüfungsfächer sind in den Bildungseinrichtungen zum Standard geworden. Bewerber dieser Prüfung müssen außerdem 180 Stunden Praktikum in einem bestimmten Bereich der Sozialarbeit absolvieren, um für die Prüfung zugelassen zu werden.[20]

Der Lehrplan an den Universitäten wird regelmäßig den Erfordernissen der Prüfung angepasst, um den Studenten eine allgemeine Grundausbildung sowie eine professionelle Ausbildung in diversen Fachgebieten zu bieten.

Besonders in dem ersten Jahr an der Universität werden Kenntnisse in grundlegenden pädagogischen Fächern erworben, um die Grundlagen der Gesellschaft zu erfassen. Die Studierenden erhalten die Möglichkeit, diverse Gesellschaftsprobleme aus verschiedenen Perspektiven zu betrachten und ein ausgeprägtes Gefühl für Toleranz und Menschlichkeit zu entwickeln. Viele Studenten sind auch schon kurz nach dem Beginn des Studiums bemüht, Erfahrungen als freiwillige Helfer in Alters-, Behinderten- oder Kinderheimen sowie bei lokalen Festen oder Sportveranstaltungen zu sammeln.

Im zweiten und dritten Jahr werden die Studenten mit den Fächern vertraut gemacht, die für Sozialarbeiter erforderlich sind. Sie erlernen Fachwissen in verschiedenen Bereichen der sozialen Wohlfahrt sowie die in der Sozialarbeit notwendigen Techniken. Japanische sowie ausländische Sozialsysteme werden analysiert, um Fachwissen und Techniken zu erlernen, die bei der zukünftigen Beratung von essenzieller Bedeutung sind.

Im dritten Jahr findet grundsätzlich auch das Praktikum statt, das ebenfalls eine Bedingung für die Teilnahme an der Prüfung für Sozialarbeiter darstellt. Bei der Auswahl des Praktikums haben die Studierenden eine gewisse Auswahlmöglichkeit. In der Regel werden die Praktika in Einrichtungen der sozialen Wohlfahrt abgelegt. Viele wählen eine Einrichtung, die ihrem möglichen zukünftigen Arbeitsbereich entspricht. Für die meisten Einrichtungen sind diese Praktikanten natürlich eine willkommene Unterstützung bei der Betreuung von Alten, Behinderten, Kindern oder sozial benachteiligten Personen. Obwohl die meisten Studenten während des Praktikums ihre an der Universität erlernten Kenntnisse und Techniken schon in begrenztem Maße anwenden, be-

20 So-sharuwa-ku kyōiku Gakkōrenmei (Anm. 16).

zahlen die Universitäten in der Regel eine Gebühr an die Einrichtungen, um die Praktikanten Erfahrungen sammeln zu lassen. Die Praktikanten selbst, die oftmals unter hoher psychischer Belastung mehrere Wochen lang mit Ausdauer und Hingabe alte oder behinderte Personen in diesen Einrichtungen unterstützen, erhalten während des Praktikums grundsätzlich keinerlei finanzielle Zuwendungen.

Im dritten und vierten Studienjahr haben die Studenten auch die Möglichkeit, sich für einen Sozialbereich zu entscheiden, der ebenfalls möglicherweise ihrem Arbeitsbereich in der Zukunft entspricht. Sie können zum Beispiel zwischen Kursen der Kinder-, Behinderten- oder Altenhilfe wählen. Außerdem finden im vierten Studienjahr oftmals die oben erwähnten Sondervorlesungen oder besonderen Prüfungsvorbereitungskurse statt, die die Prüflinge sowohl auf den Inhalt als auch auf die besondere Stresssituation der unmittelbar bevorstehenden Prüfung vorbereiten.[21]

Diese besondere Stresssituation ist oftmals ein Hauptgrund für die relativ niedrige Erfolgsquote der Prüfung. Da die Prüfung jedes Jahr grundsätzlich Anfang Februar stattfindet und somit zirka vier bis fünf Wochen bevor die Studierenden die Universität beenden (etwa Mitte März), haben fast alle Prüflinge schon eine Art Vorvertrag in der Tasche, der sie dazu berechtigt, ab Anfang April als Festangestellter in einer sozialen Einrichtung zu arbeiten. Wie oben schon erwähnt wurde, ist das Bestehen der Sozialarbeiterprüfung in den meisten Einrichtungen keine absolute Bedingung für eine Anstellung im Wohlfahrtsbereich. Die Qualifikation als staatlich anerkannter Sozialarbeiter wird jedoch von vielen sozialen Einrichtungen mit Beginn der Anstellung mit einem erhöhten Gehalt belohnt. Außerdem werden Besitzer dieser Qualifikation von Anfang an innerhalb des Betriebes mit verantwortungsreichen Aufgaben betreut, und es besteht eine erhöhte Wahrscheinlichkeit, in relativ kurzer Zeit befördert zu werden.

Den Prüflingen ist also vor und während der Prüfung bewusst, dass ein Bestehen des Testes bzw. das Besitzen der Qualifikation ihren weiteren beruflichen Weg entscheidend beeinflussen könnte. Für einige Prüflinge, die zum Beispiel den oben erwähnten Berufszweig Medical-Social-Worker anstreben, um in Krankenhäusern Patienten für ein Leben nach dem Krankenhausaufenthalt zu beraten, ist das Besitzen der Qualifikation sogar eine Voraussetzung. Falls sie die Prüfung nicht bestehen, wird der oben genannte Vorvertrag in vielen Fällen aufgelöst. Das führt dann dazu, dass sie innerhalb kürzester Zeit versuchen müssen, noch bis Anfang April eine neue Anstellung bei einem anderen Arbeitgeber zu finden, bei dem der Besitz der Qualifikation keine Bedingung darstellen würde. Das Ergebnis der Prüfung wird in der Regel etwa Anfang März veröffentlicht, also etwa zwei Wochen vor dem Verlassen der Uni Mitte März und nur zirka drei bis vier Wochen vor dem angestrebten Arbeitsbeginn Anfang April.

3. Erfolgsquote der Prüfung

Um als zertifizierter Sozialarbeiter zu arbeiten, besteht die Notwendigkeit, die staatliche Prüfung zu bestehen. Diese Prüfung findet einmal pro Jahr statt – grundsätzlich am ersten Wochenende des Februars. Die Prüfung wird mit 150 Punkten bewertet, wobei pro Frage ein Punkt vergeben wird. Etwa 60 % der Fragen müssen richtig beantwor-

21 So-sharuwa-ku kyōiku Gakkōrenmei (Anm. 16).

tet werden, sodass eine Punktzahl von etwa 90 Punkten oder mehr erforderlich ist, um die Prüfung erfolgreich zu absolvieren. Allerdings variiert jedes Jahr die Punktzahl zum Bestehen der Prüfung – je nach Schwierigkeitsgrad der Prüfungsfragen. Es kann also sein, dass in einem Jahr zirka 90 Punkte ausreichen, um die Prüfung zu bestehen. Im nächsten Jahr sind dann aber vielleicht mehr als 100 Punkte notwendig, um die Prüfung mit Erfolg abzuschließen. Darüber hinaus ist es für alle Prüflinge unabdingbar, alle Prüfungsfächer etwa gleichmäßig vorzubereiten, da man in allen Fächern mindestens einen Punkt erreichen muss, um Erfolg zu haben. Wenn ein Prüfling zum Beispiel weit über 60 % der Fragen richtig beantworten würde, jedoch in einem Prüfungsfach nur null Punkte hätte, müsste er die Prüfung im nächsten Jahr oder später wiederholen.

Die Erfolgsquote der staatlichen Prüfung ist in den letzten Jahren deutlich gestiegen. In den Jahren 2020 bzw. 2021 hatten von zirka 40.000 Prüflingen 10 – 12.000 Personen bestanden. Die Erfolgsquote lag also etwa bei 30 %. Im Jahre 2024 war die Erfolgsquote 58,1 %, da von knapp 35.000 Prüflingen über 20.000 bestanden hatten.[22]

V. Prüfungsfächer mit direktem Kontext zur Rechtswissenschaft

Wie oben erwähnt wurde, umfasst die Prüfung zum zertifizierten Sozialarbeiter 19 verschiedene Fächer. In den meisten Fächern gibt es natürlich Prüfungsfragen, die sich oftmals indirekt mit Gesetzen oder rechtlichen Problemen befassen. Die folgenden zwei Prüfungsfächer behandeln jedoch im wesentlichen Bereiche des japanischen Rechts bzw. der japanischen Rechtsprechung: „Rechtsschutz und Betreuung für Erwachsene“ sowie „Rehabilitation von Straftätern“.

Für die Mehrheit der Prüflinge stellen diese beiden Prüfungsfächer besonders hohe Hürden zum Bestehen der Prüfung dar. Grundsätzlich gehören sie zu den Prüfungsfächern, in denen die wenigsten Durchschnittspunkte erreicht werden. Diese Tendenz kann man nicht nur in der alljährlichen Hauptprüfung, sondern auch in den diversen Vorbereitungsprüfungen feststellen, die jedes Jahr besonders im Sommer und Herbst durchgeführt werden, also etwa ein halbes Jahr vor der eigentlichen Prüfung im Februar.

Selbst für Angestellte sozialer Einrichtungen mit langjähriger Berufserfahrung erweisen sich diese Prüfungsfragen mit rechtlichem Hintergrund oft als schwer überwindbare Hindernisse auf dem Weg zu einer erfolgreichen Bewältigung der Prüfung. Für Studenten an den Universitäten oder ähnlichen Ausbildungsstätten, die in den meisten Fällen das Studium mit dem hehren Ziel begonnen haben, Menschen in Not irgendwie zu helfen, ist es unbedingt erforderlich, diese Prüfungsfragen mit besonderer Intensität vorzubereiten. Während die anderen Prüfungsfächer oft einen erkennbaren direkten Bezug zur Praxis bzw. zur Aufgabe eines Sozialarbeiters besitzen, erfordern diese beiden Fächer sowohl das Erlernen theoretischer als auch teilweise abstrakter Grundkenntnisse, die oftmals nur eine indirekte Verbindung mit der Praxis haben.

Die Vorbereitung auf diese zwei Prüfungsfächer stellt auch für die Studenten meiner Fakultät ein äußerst schwieriges Unterfangen dar, da sie als Mittel- oder Oberschüler

22 Itō Sōken Shikakushutoku Shiensenta- (Anm. 18).

nur wenig Möglichkeiten hatten, Grundbegriffe des Rechts zu erlernen. Außerdem müssen sie in den vier Jahren an der Fakultät natürlich in erster Linie das Wesen und die Technik der Sozialarbeit erfassen, sodass für das Erlernen von Rechtsbegriffen oft weder die nötige Zeit noch die notwendige Motivation besteht.

Am Ende dieses Kapitels möchte ich meine Unterrichtsmethoden erläutern, um die Studenten während der kurzen Studienzeit auf diese beiden Prüfungsfächer vorzubereiten.

1. Prüfungsinhalt von dem Fach Rechtsschutz und Betreuung für Erwachsene

Dieses Prüfungsfach erfordert Grundlagenkenntnisse in den folgenden vier Bereichen:[23]

- Grundlagen und Gemeinsamkeiten der Gesetze allgemein. Grundlagen der Verfassung, des Zivilrechts und des Verwaltungsrechts.
- Bedeutung des Rechtsschutzes und die ihn unterstützenden Mechanismen.
- Interessenvertretung von Personen, deren Rechte verletzt wurden oder die in ihrem täglichen Leben Unterstützung benötigen.
- Grundlagen des Betreuungsrechts: In den letzten Jahren hatten grundsätzlich zirka drei oder vier der insgesamt sieben Fragen dieses Faches einen direkten Bezug zum japanischen Betreuungsrecht. Das Betreuungsrecht wurde im Jahre 2000, also fast zeitgleich mit der Einführung der Pflegeversicherung, nach über 100 Jahren von Grund auf neu geregelt, um das Betreuungssystem auf die Anforderungen des 21. Jahrhunderts vorzubereiten. Noch bis zum Ende des 20. Jahrhunderts wurden ältere Familienmitglieder traditionell von der Familie versorgt bzw. gepflegt. Mit dem ständig anwachsenden Anteil von Älteren an der Bevölkerung sowie der Zunahme von Demenzerkrankungen, war es für die Familien immer schwieriger geworden, ältere Familienmitglieder selbst zu versorgen. Das vor zirka 25 Jahren neu eingeführte Betreuungsrecht besitzt das vornehmliche Ziel, den betroffenen Personen ein eigenständiges Leben zu ermöglichen und notwendige Beratung und Unterstützung anzubieten, ohne ihre rechtlichen Fähigkeiten sowie alltäglichen Freiheiten zu stark zu beschränken, wie es das schon im 19. Jahrhundert eingeführte alte System institutionalisiert hatte. Kernpunkte des Betreuungssystems sind deshalb der Schutz des alltäglichen Lebens, was sowohl den Schutz des Vermögens als auch eine praktische Unterstützung des Lebensalltags beinhaltet. Das Betreuungsrecht besteht aus zwei Bereichen: die gesetzliche Betreuung sowie die freiwillige Betreuung, die einer Vorsorgevollmacht ähnelt und durch einen Vertrag geregelt wird, der durch einen Notar aufgesetzt und beglaubigt wird. Das gesetzliche Betreuungssystem greift bei schwerer Beeinträchtigung der Geschäftsfähigkeit. Es wurde entwickelt, um Menschen zu beraten bzw. zu unterstützen, die aufgrund von körperlichen oder geistigen Einschränkungen nicht in der Lage sind, ihre Angelegenheiten eigenständig zu regeln. Wie oben schon erwähnt wurde, zielt dieses System vorrangig darauf ab, die Rechte und Würde der betreuten Personen zu schützen und es ihnen zu ermöglichen,

23 So-sharuwa-ku kyōiku Gakkōrenmei (Anm. 16).

ein möglichst selbstbestimmtes Leben führen zu können.[24] Die meisten Prüfungsfragen mit einem Kontext zum Betreuungssystem behandeln die gesetzliche Betreuung.

Um die Prüfungsaufgaben des Faches Rechtsschutz und Betreuung für Erwachsene zu bestehen, ist es notwendig, die folgenden Themen vorzubereiten.[25]

a) Grundlagen des Rechts

- Gesetze und Normen (Rechtsnormen, Beziehung zwischen Recht und Moral)
- Systeme, Arten und Funktionen des Rechts (Geschriebenes und ungeschriebenes Recht, Öffentliches Recht und Privatrecht, Materielles Recht und Verfahrensrecht, Merkmale und Funktionen von Rechtsnormen)
- Grundkenntnisse des Rechts und der Rechtsauslegung (Struktur der gesetzlichen Bestimmungen, Standards und Methoden der Rechtsauslegung)
- Studium des Gerichtssystems und der Präzedenzfälle (Art der Verfahren und der Urteile, Präzedenzfälle)

b) Zusammenhang von Sozialarbeit und Recht

- Verfassung (Grundprinzipien der Japanischen Verfassung, Grundlegende Menschenrechte, Menschenrecht und öffentliche Wohlfahrt, Gleichheit, Soziale Rechte)
- Zivilrecht (Allgemeine Bestimmungen des Zivilrechts, Vertragsrecht, Schadensersatz, Grundlagen des Familienrechts, Grundlagen des Erbschaftsrechts)
- Verwaltungsrecht (Staatliche und lokale Verwaltungsorganisationen, Beamtensystem, Formen des Verwaltungsakts, Verwaltungsstreitigkeiten, Staatliche Entschädigung, Lokale Selbstverwaltung)

c) Bedeutung des Rechtsschutzes und die ihn unterstützenden Mechanismen

- Bedeutung des Rechtsschutzes
- Angemessene Nutzung von Sozialleistungen
- Beschwerden
- Prävention und Gesetze bezüglich Misshandlung (Gesetz zur Verhinderung von Misshandlungen älterer Menschen, Gesetz zur Verhinderung von Kindesmisshandlungen, Gesetz zur Verhinderung von Misshandlungen Behinderter)
- Grundlagen des Antidiskriminierungsrechts (Gesetz zur Beseitigung der Diskriminierung Behinderter)

---

[24] *Fukuda/Mori, Kenriyōgo to seinenkōkenseido* [Rechtsschutz und Betreuungssystem], 4. Aufl. (2018).

[25] *Nihon So-sharuwa-ku kyōiku Gakkōrenmei, Kenriyōgo wo sasaeru hōseido* [Rechtsschutz und Rechtssystem], 2. Aufl. (2025); *Iryōjōhō Kagaku Kenkyūsho, Shakaifukushishi* [Sozialarbeiter], 1. Aufl. (2024).

– Richtlinien zur Unterstützung der Willensentscheidung (Leitlinien zur Entscheidungsunterstützung in Bezug auf die Bereitstellung von Diensten der Behindertenfürsorge, Leitlinien für den medizinischen und pflegerischen Entscheidungsprozess in der letzten Lebensphase, Leitlinien zur Unterstützung der Entscheidungsfindung im sozialen Leben von Menschen mit Demenz)

d) Rechtliche Probleme, die bei der Interessenvertretung von Personen auftreten können, deren Rechte verletzt wurden oder die in ihrem täglichen Leben Unterstützung benötigen.

– Einverständniserklärung (Rechtskonzept der Informierten Einwilligung, Rechtsprechung bezüglich der Informierten Einwilligung)

– Persönliche Daten und Datenschutz (Datenschutzsystem, Privatsphäre, Geheimnispflicht)

– Organisationen, Gruppen und Fachleute, die sich mit dem Schutz von Rechten befassen (Rolle der Organisationen und Gruppen, die sich mit dem Schutz von Rechten befassen, Familiengericht, Büro für Rechtsangelegenheiten, Rechtsanwalt, Notar)

e) Betreuung

– Grundlagen des Betreuungssystems (Gesetzliche Betreuung, Freiwillige Betreuung, Professionelle Betreuer)

– Details der Gesetzlichen Betreuung (Handlungsfähigkeit, Formalitäten)

– Details der Freiwilligen Betreuung (Handlungsfähigkeit, Formalitäten)

– Aktuelle Trends und Daten des Betreuungssystems (Projekt zur Förderung der Nutzung des Betreuungssystems)

f) Einige ausgewählte Testfragen des Fachs „Rechtsschutz und Betreuung für Erwachsene“[26]

Frage 36-77 (Februar 2024)

Wählen Sie zwei Rechte aus, die als soziale Rechte der Japanischen Verfassung gelten.

1 Eigentumsrecht

2 Recht am eigenen Bild (Porträtrecht)

3 Recht auf Bildung

4 Recht auf kollektive Tarifverhandlungen

5 Recht auf Selbstbestimmung

(richtige Antwort: 3, 4)

---

26 *So-sharuwa-ku kyōiku Gakkōrenmei* (Anm. 16).

Frage 36-82 (Februar 2024)

Wählen Sie aus der Liste die Person aus, die am häufigsten zum Betreuer bestellt wird.

1 Verwandter

2 Rechtsanwalt (*Bengoshi*)

3 Rechtsschreiber (*Shihōshoshi*)

4 Sozialarbeiter

5 Ehrenamtlicher Betreuer

(richtige Antwort: 3)

Frage 35-82 (Februar 2023)

Wählen Sie eine richtige Aussage zum Familiengericht aus.

1 Das Familiengericht behandelt Verfahren des Nachbarschaftsstreits

2 Das Familiengericht behandelt Schutzanordnungen bei häuslicher Gewalt

3 Das Familiengericht behandelt Verfahren der Anerkennung unehelicher Kinder

4 Das Familiengericht behandelt arbeitsrechtliche Verfahren

5 Das Familiengericht behandelt Verfahren der Schuldenkonsolidierung

(richtige Antwort: 3)

Frage 36-78 (2022)

Lesen Sie den Fall, und wählen Sie dann eine richtige Aussage, die zum gesetzlichen Erbanteil am Erbe von H passt.

H hinterließ bei seinem Tod sehr viel Eigentum. H.s Erben sind insgesamt 6 Personen: Ehepartner J, Kinder K, L und M sowie B und C, die Kinder von A sind, der vor H verstorben ist (H.s Enkelkinder). Beachten Sie, dass L ein adoptiertes und M ein uneheliches Kind ist.

1 Der gesetzliche Erbanteil von Ehegatte J beträgt ein Drittel

2 Der gesetzliche Erbanteil von Kind K beträgt ein Sechstel

3 Der gesetzliche Erbanteil des adoptierten Kindes L beträgt ein Siebtel

4 Der gesetzliche Erbanteil des unehelichen Kindes M beträgt ein Achtel

5 Der gesetzliche Erbanteil von Enkel B beträgt ein Siebtel

(richtige Antwort: 4)

2. Prüfungsinhalt von dem Fach Rehabilitation von Straftätern

Dieses Prüfungsfach erfordert Grundlagenkenntnisse in den folgenden vier Bereichen:[27]

- Strafrecht und Struktur des Strafjustizsystems
- Organisationen, die am Strafjustizsystem beteiligt sind
- Die Rolle von Sozialarbeitern in der Strafjustiz
- Unterstützung für Opfer von Straftaten

Um die Prüfungsaufgaben des Faches Rehabilitation von Straftätern zu bestehen, ist es notwendig, die folgenden Themen vorzubereiten.[28]

a) Soziales Umfeld (Initiativen zur Wiedereingliederung, Rückfallprävention, Maßnahmen für Beschäftigungsförderung von ehemaligen Strafgefangenen, Unterstützung für ältere Menschen und Behinderte)
b) Rolle der Sozialarbeiter in der Strafjustiz (Sozialarbeiter in Justizvollzugsanstalten, Sozialarbeiter und Bewährungssystem, Sozialarbeiter und kommunale Lebenshilfezentren)
c) Strafjustizsystem (Grundlagen des Strafrechts, Besonderheiten des Jugendstrafrechts)
d) Rehabilitationssystem (Grundzüge der Rehabilitation, Zusammenarbeit mit unterstützenden Organisationen, Grundlagen des Bewährungssystems, Bewährungshelfer, Big Brother and Sister Movement, kooperierende Arbeitgeber, Begnadigung, Aktivitäten zur Kriminalprävention)
e) Behandlung psychisch Kranker, die anderen Personen schwere Schäden zugefügt haben (Grundzüge des medizinischen Beobachtungssystems, Behandlung und Wiedereingliederung)
f) Unterstützung für Opfer von Straftaten (Gesetze für den Opferschutz)
g) Einige ausgewählte Testfragen des Fachs „Rehabilitation von Straftätern“[29]

---

27 *So-sharuwa-ku kyōiku Gakkōrenmei* (Anm. 16).

28 *Nihon So-sharuwa-ku kyōiku Gakkōrenmei* (Anm. 25).

29 *So-sharuwa-ku kyōiku Gakkōrenmei* (Anm. 16).

Frage 35-149 (Februar 2023)

Wählen Sie eine richtige Aussage zur Resozialisierung von Straftätern aus

1 Das Bewährungshelferbüro vermittelt einen neuen Arbeitsplatz

2 Die Bewährungsauflagen verpflichten den auf Bewährung Freigelassenen, Beratungsunterstützung des Arbeitsamtes anzunehmen

3 Das Arbeitsamt kann Arbeitgeber dazu verpflichten, auf Bewährung Freigelassene anzustellen

4 Das Bewährungshelferbüro kann Arbeitgeber dazu verpflichten, ausschließlich ehemalige Strafgefangene anzustellen

5 Das Arbeitsamt versorgt auf Bewährung Freigelassene mit allgemeinen Informationen zu freien Stellen und unterstützt sie bei der Arbeitssuche

(richtige Antwort: 5)

Frage 34-147 (Februar 2022)

Wählen Sie eine richtige Aussage zum Resozialisierungssystem aus

1 Das Resozialisierungssystem beinhaltet Aktivitäten zur Kriminalprävention

2 Das Resozialisierungssystem beinhaltet keinerlei Aktivitäten zur Kriminalprävention

3 Im Resozialisierungssystem werden vornehmlich Fälle innerhalb der Justizvollzugsanstalten behandelt

4 Das Resozialisierungssystem basiert auf dem Strafvollzugsgesetz

5 Die zuständige Behörde des Resozialisierungssystems ist das Ministerium für Gesundheit, Arbeit und Wohlfahrt

(richtige Antwort: 1)

Frage 36-148 (Februar 2024)

Wählen Sie eine richtige Aussage zu ehrenamtlichen Bewährungshelfern aus.

1 Sie arbeiten im Auftrag des Justizministeriums

2 Sie unterliegen der Anleitung und Aufsicht des Staatsanwalts

3 Sie haben keine Befugnis, als Bewährungsaufsicht zu agieren

4 Ein Gehalt wird abhängig von der Art des Bewährungsfalls gezahlt

5 Besuche bei Insassen der Justizvollzugsanstalt sind untersagt

(richtige Antwort: 1)

3. Methoden der Prüfungsvorbereitung

Wie am Anfang dieses Kapitels erwähnt wurde, stellen die Fragen der beiden Fächer mit direktem rechtswissenschaftlichen Kontext „Rechtsschutz und Betreuung für Erwachsene“ sowie „Rehabilitation von Straftätern“ sowohl für Universitätsstudenten als auch für in sozialen Berufen beschäftigten Personen schwer überwindbare Hindernisse auf dem Weg zu einem erfolgreichen Abschluss der Prüfung dar.

Hier möchte ich nun einige Methoden vorstellen, die es unseren Studenten ermöglichen sollen, im Unterricht der beiden oben genannten Fächer grundlegende rechtswissenschaftliche Begriffe zu erfassen, um eine Basis zu haben, in der staatlichen Prüfung zum Sozialarbeiter Fragen mit rechtswissenschaftlichem Kontext richtig zu beantworten. Der Unterricht zu den beiden Fächern findet grundsätzlich im dritten Jahr des Studiums statt. Da in den Semesterferien des dritten Jahres auch in den meisten Fällen das Praktikum stattfindet und sich viele Studenten außerdem vermehrt Gedanken über ihre berufliche Zukunft machen, steigt nach und nach das Bewusstsein für eine konzentrierte Vorbereitung auf die Prüfung.

Die folgenden Methoden basieren sowohl auf meiner persönlichen Erfahrung als auch auf den Erkenntnissen meiner Kollegen. Nicht nur an meiner Universität ist es seit einigen Jahren Standard, sich in sogenannten Faculty Development (FD) Kursen regelmäßig über verschiedene Unterrichtsmethoden auszutauschen, um das Lehrniveau zu erhöhen und die Studenten mit erfolgversprechenden Lehrmethoden zu unterrichten.

Ich möchte die folgenden persönlichen Unterrichtsmethoden in die beiden Stichwörter Motivation und Unterrichtsablauf unterteilen und etwas verkürzt bzw. vereinfacht darstellen:

a) Motivation

Sowohl am Anfang als auch während des Semesters wende ich folgende Methoden an, um die Motivation für eine konzentrierte Vorbereitung sowie ein erfolgreiches Bestehen der Prüfung zum Sozialarbeiter zu erhöhen:

- ich stelle Absolventen meiner Fakultät vor, die langjährige Erfahrung als Sozialarbeiter besitzen und mit Leidenschaft und Wissen ihre Klienten und deren Familien beraten und mit detaillierten Informationen versorgen, die oftmals deren Lebensqualität entscheidend verbessern
- ich erkläre die wichtige Rolle von Sozialarbeitern in der modernen Gesellschaft
- ich mache wiederholt die Wichtigkeit einer beruflichen Qualifikation verständlich
- ich erkläre die teilweise erheblichen Einkommensunterschiede zwischen Personen mit und ohne Qualifikation
- ich stelle die diversen Lernmethoden einiger ehemaliger Seminarstudenten vor, die erfolgreich die Prüfung vorbereitet und bestanden haben

b) Unterrichtsablauf

Die Vorlesungen finden während des Semesters insgesamt 16 Mal statt, jeweils für 90 Minuten. Um den oftmals schwierigen Inhalt verständlich darzustellen, wende ich die folgenden Methoden an:

- am Anfang des Unterrichtes schreibe ich die Stichwörter des heutigen Unterrichtes an die Tafel, um einen ersten Blick auf den Inhalt zu ermöglichen

- danach stelle ich anhand der Stichwörter dar, warum sowohl für einen zukünftigen Sozialarbeiter als auch für nicht im sozialen Bereich tätigen Personen das Erlernen dieser rechtlichen Grundbegriffe von Bedeutung ist
- grundsätzlich werden von mir ebenfalls am Unterrichtsanfang für zirka fünf bis zehn Minuten nochmals die Hauptinhalte des vorigen Unterrichtes zusammenfassend dargestellt
- für alle Fächer der Prüfung zum Sozialarbeiter gibt es Lehrbücher von verschiedenen Verlagen, die regelmäßig aktualisiert werden. Obwohl die Studenten die Lehrbücher in den Unterricht mitbringen, werden von mir zusätzlich für jeden Unterricht selbstangefertigte Papiere verteilt, um die wichtigsten Unterrichtsinhalte noch verständlicher darzustellen. In den Lehrbüchern werden teilweise nur Inhalte von Gesetzestexten wiedergegeben, die ohne Erklärung oftmals unverständlich sind
- in den von mir verteilten Papieren gibt es an vielen Stellen sogenannte Leerstellen, in die die Studenten besonders wichtige einzelne Fachbegriffe oder ganze Sätze selbst handschriftlich hineinschreiben müssen, da das handschriftliche Schreiben japanischer Begriffe in der Regel dazu führt, den Inhalt der Begriffe besser zu erfassen beziehungsweise im Gedächtnis zu behalten
- grundsätzlich erkläre ich diese wichtigen Begriffe nicht nur mündlich, sondern schreibe sie außerdem an die Tafel, um den Studenten die korrekte Schreibweise darzustellen, da viele gleichlautende japanische Begriffe mit verschiedenen Schriftzeichen geschrieben werden
- am Ende des Unterrichtes werden nochmals die wichtigsten Inhalte der heutigen Vorlesung zusammenfassend erklärt, und ich weise nochmals auf bestimmte Stichwörter hin, die in der staatlichen Prüfung zum Sozialarbeiter eine große Rolle spielen
- zum Schluss werden die Themen der folgenden Unterrichte erwähnt und die wesentlichen Punkte der nächsten Vorlesung vorgestellt, um den Studenten die Möglichkeit zu geben, Vorbereitungen zu treffen
- oftmals werden von mir auch vor dem Unterrichtsende Zettel verteilt und wieder eingesammelt, auf denen die Studenten einerseits von mir gestellte Fragen beantworten müssen und andererseits, falls notwendig, inhaltliche Fragen stellen können. Das ermöglicht mir, den Wissensstand der Teilnehmer festzustellen und auf Fragen einzugehen
- nach den Unterrichten oder zu sogenannten Sprechstunden der Lehrkräfte haben die Studenten außerdem die Möglichkeit, direkt Fragen zu stellen. Mit E-Mails bzw. Chat-Mails werden ebenfalls inhaltliche Fragen beantwortet. Wenn notwendig, werden Studenten mit Lernschwierigkeiten oder Behinderungen in den Seminarräumen der Lehrkräfte zusätzlich einzeln unterrichtet, um ihnen die Chance zu geben, schwer verständliche Inhalte auch außerhalb der normalen Vorlesung zu erlernen

VI. Überarbeitete Prüfung ab dem Jahre 2025

Die Regierung hatte 2023 beschlossen, die staatliche Prüfungsordnung für die Zertifizierung von Sozialarbeitern zu modifizieren, um das Prüfungssystem an die neuen Herausforderungen der Gesellschaft anzupassen. Die Neuregelung sieht eine Aufteilung in sechs Teile vor, sodass Wiederholungskandidaten nur die Prüfungsteile wiederholen müssen, die sie beim ersten Mal nicht bestanden haben. Mit der Überarbeitung soll es auch bereits im sozialen Bereich tätigen Angestellten leichter gemacht werden, die Qualifikation berufsbegleitend zu erwerben. Auf diese Weise soll sichergestellt werden, dass es schon vor der Mitte des 21. Jahrhunderts, wenn die Zahl der älteren Menschen in Japan voraussichtlich ihren Höhepunkt erreichen wird, mehr Fachkräfte gibt.

Diese neue überarbeitete Prüfung wurde erstmals im Februar 2025 durchgeführt. Der computergestützte Multiple-Choice-Test wird nach wie vor einmal pro Jahr stattfinden. Wie oben erwähnt, werden die bisherigen 19 Fächer in sechs Bereiche aufgeteilt, und die Prüflinge werden dann, bei einem möglichen zweiten oder dritten Versuch, von den bisher schon bestandenen Bereichen befreit. Dadurch entsteht die Möglichkeit, sich ausschließlich auf die noch nicht bestandenen Fächer vorzubereiten.[30]

Auch die neue Prüfung ist eine wichtige Qualifikation für diejenigen, die im Bereich der Sozialarbeit tätig sein möchten. Die Vorbereitung auf die Prüfung erfordert weiterhin ein umfassendes Studium der relevanten Themen und oft auch die Teilnahme an speziellen Vorbereitungskursen. Wenn auch der Inhalt der neuen Prüfung viele Gemeinsamkeiten mit der bisherigen Prüfung erkennen lässt, so wurden doch einige Änderungen und Aktualisierungen vorgenommen, um den aktuellen Anforderungen gerecht zu werden und sich den verändernden sozialen Bedürfnissen der Gesellschaft anzupassen. Für die Lehrkräfte in den Ausbildungseinrichtungen bedeutet das natürlich, die nach dem neuen System durchgeführten Prüfungen zu analysieren und die Prüflinge auf die Unterschiede zu den bisherigen Tests hinzuweisen.

VII. Nachwort

Die größten Probleme, mit denen sowohl Japan als auch viele andere Industrieländer konfrontiert sind – Überalterung der Gesellschaft, sinkende Geburtenrate, Vermögensungleichheit, weit verbreitete psychische Probleme, Kindesmissbrauch, Armut alleinerziehender Frauen usw. – stellen eine überwältigende Herausforderung dar. Viele Alumni unserer Fakultät kämpfen als Sozialarbeiter mit psychischen Anforderungen sowie einer immensen Arbeitsbelastung, auf die sie während der relativ kurzen Ausbildungszeit nur bedingt vorbereitet werden können. Besonders die diversen Praktiken während der Studienzeit in Behinderteneinrichtungen, Altersheimen oder Krankenhäusern sind für die Studenten eine unschätzbare Gelegenheit, den Alltag eines Sozialarbeiters in der Praxis kennenzulernen. Um die Studenten auf die zu-

---

30 *Iryōjōhō Kagaku Kenkyūsho* (Anm. 25).

künftigen Belastungen im Berufsalltag vorzubereiten, ist es meiner Meinung nach erforderlich, den Praxisbezug auch weiterhin in das Zentrum der Ausbildung zu stellen.

Meines Erachtens ist es auch zukünftig notwendig, den Studenten einen regen Austausch mit den Absolventen der Fakultät zu ermöglichen, die ihre als Sozialarbeiter erworbenen Erfahrungen an die Studenten weitergeben können. Der Informationsaustausch mit den Alumni erweitert nicht nur den Erfahrungshorizont der Studenten, sondern fördert auch ihre Motivation, das an der Universität erlangte Wissen als Sozialarbeiter vielen Menschen zur Verfügung zu stellen.

Wenn vor zirka 50 Jahren die Bitte eines japanischen Schülers um eine internationale Brieffreundschaft am schwarzen Brett des Gymnasiums von meiner Schwester übersehen bzw. ignoriert worden wäre, hätte sich der Inhalt ihrer Forschung vermutlich nicht auf die japanische Geschichte konzentriert. Ebenfalls ist es sehr unwahrscheinlich, dass es ohne ihren Einfluss zu meinem jetzigen Wirken an einer japanischen Universität gekommen wäre.

Einem flüchtigen Blick auf ein schwarzes Brett vor zirka einem halben Jahrhundert ist es zu verdanken, dass ich seit mehr als 30 Jahren als Gast in Japan leben und einen kleinen Beitrag zur Freundschaft und Verständigung zwischen Japan und Deutschland leisten darf.

Literaturverzeichnis

Aymans, Gerhard: Japan, 1. Aufl. (1985).

Coulmas, Florian/*Stalpers*, Judith: Japan, 1. Aufl. (2011).

Fukuda, Sachio/*Mori*, Nagahide: Kenriyōgo to seinenkōkenseido, 4. Aufl. (2018).

Hering, Sabine/*Münchmeier*, Richard: Geschichte der Sozialen Arbeit, 3. Aufl. (2005).

Iryōjōhō Kagaku Kenkyūsho: Shakaifukushishi, 1. Aufl. (2024).

Itō Sōken Shikakushutoku shiensenta-: Shakaifukushishi kokushinabi, 1. Aufl. (2023).

Murakami, Takenori/*Scheller*, Andreas: Der Weg zum Rechtsstaat (1992).

Murakami, Takenori/*Scheller*, Andreas: Die neuartige Nutzung der Meeresoberfläche und die Seeverwaltungssatzung der Hiroshima Präfektur von 1991 (1993).

Murakami, Takenori/*Scheller*, Andreas: Die Rechtsprobleme der Aufsicht der japanischen Verwaltungstätigkeit (1993).

Murakami, Takenori/*Scheller*, Andreas: Japans Wiederaufrüstung und die Entsendung japanischer Truppen für die UNO Friedensmission (PKO) (1993).

Nihon So-sharuwa-ku kyōiku Gakkōrenmei: Kenriyōgo wo sasaeru hōseido, 2. Aufl. (2025).

Ōta, Yoshihiro: So-sharuwa-ku jissen to shienkagaku, 1. Aufl. (2008).

Scheller, Andreas: Doitsu ni okeru supo-tsu to hōsō no tanjikannyu-suhōdōken wo meguru hōritsumondai (1999).

Scheller, Martina: Versuch einer Typisierung von Hafenstädten im Raum Inlandsee während der Tokugawa-Zeit – Einflüsse von Handel und Verkehr auf die Entwicklung von sieben Hafenstädten (1990).

So-sharuwa-ku kyōiku Gakkōrenmei: Shakaifukushishi kokkashiken, 1. Aufl. (2024).

Tanaka, Kōtarō: So-sharuwa-ku to kenriyōgo, 1. Aufl. (2008).

Die rechtliche Qualifizierung von Profisportlern in Japan

Eine Analyse am Beispiel des Sumō

Von *Tobias Schiebe*

Dr. Tobias Schiebe, LL.M. (Wellington) ist deutscher Rechtsanwalt und als registrierter ausländischer Anwalt in Japan bei der Kanzlei ARQIS in Tokio tätig. Zu seinem Praxisschwerpunkt zählt das Arbeitsrecht. Das Studium der Rechtswissenschaften absolvierte er in Kiel, gefolgt von einem Postgraduiertenstudium in Wellington, Neuseeland sowie anschließender Promotion im Bereich des Arbeitsrechts in Kiel. Sein Referendariat absolvierte er in Hamburg und Tokio.

I. Einleitung

Die Qualifizierung von Arbeitsverhältnissen stellt in Theorie und Praxis des Arbeitsrechts seit jeher ein zentrales und wiederkehrendes Thema dar. Während die entwickelten Kriterien zur Abgrenzung von abhängigen Arbeitnehmern im Vergleich zu selbstständigen Dienstnehmern ursprünglich stark von industriellen Arbeitsmodellen und später klassischen Angestelltenverhältnissen geprägt waren, sieht sich das moderne Arbeitsrecht zunehmend mit der Herausforderung konfrontiert, neuartige Beschäftigungsformen wie Crowdworking, plattformbasierte Arbeit (z.B. bei Fahr- oder Lieferdiensten) und Gig Economy-Modelle anhand etablierter Kriterien einzuordnen. Diese Entwicklung stellt sowohl in Deutschland als auch in Japan, wo vergleichbare Phänomene zu beobachten sind, die rechtliche Abgrenzung zwischen abhängiger Beschäftigung und selbstständiger Tätigkeit vor Herausforderungen.

Doch nicht nur im Rahmen innovativer Arbeitsmodelle stellen sich Fragen der arbeitsrechtlichen Einordnung der Beschäftigten. Auch traditionelle oder spezifische Beschäftigungsverhältnisse, deren Struktur sich von den klassischen Modellen unterscheiden, können Anlass zu komplexen rechtlichen Einordnungsfragen geben. Eine relevante Kategorie in diesem Zusammenhang sind beispielsweise Profisportler, deren vertragliche Bindungen oft spezielle, leistungsbezogene und von Verbandsregeln geprägte Elemente aufweisen, die eine einfache Qualifizierung unter den Abgrenzungskriterien erschweren können. Eine besonders tief in der Tradition Japans verwurzelte „Beschäftigung“ an der Schnittstelle zwischen Kulturinstitution und Profisport stellt der Sumō dar. Die von strengen Regeln geprägte Beziehung der Sumō-Ringer mit dem Sumō-Verband wirft Fragen hinsichtlich der rechtlichen Natur der Vertragsbeziehung auf und war Gegenstand eingehender gerichtlicher Auseinandersetzungen in Japan.

Duncker & Humblot · Berlin | https://doi.org/10.3790/978-3-428-59611-9.2025.418786

Der nachfolgende Artikel untersucht die Kriterien zur Abgrenzung von Arbeitsverhältnissen von Profisportlern in Japan und Deutschland und beleuchtet dabei insbesondere die rechtliche Einordnung von Sumō-Ringern anhand der Entscheidung des Bezirksgerichts Tokio vom 25. März 2013.

II. Die arbeitsrechtliche Klassifizierung von Profisportlern

1. Deutschland

In der deutschen Rechtsprechung bildeten Profisportler wiederholt den Gegenstand grundlegender rechtlicher Entscheidungen von Arbeits-, Sozial- und Finanzgerichten.[1] Ausgangspunkt für die arbeitsrechtliche Einordnung ist § 611a BGB. Hiernach ist Arbeitnehmer, wer durch den Arbeitsvertrag „im Dienste eines anderen zur Leistung *weisungsgebundener*, *fremdbestimmter* Arbeit in *persönlicher Abhängigkeit* verpflichtet" ist. Die Vorschrift führt weiter aus, dass das Weisungsrecht „Inhalt, Durchführung, Zeit und Ort" umfassen kann. Weisungsgebunden ist, wer seine Tätigkeit *nicht im Wesentlichen frei* gestalten und seine Arbeitszeit nicht selbst *bestimmen* kann. Der Grad der persönlichen Abhängigkeit hängt dabei auch von der Eigenart der jeweiligen Tätigkeit ab. Für die Feststellung, ob ein Arbeitsvertrag vorliegt, ist eine Gesamtbetrachtung aller Umstände vorzunehmen.

Berufssportler werden hiernach arbeitsrechtlich dann als Arbeitnehmer eingestuft, wenn sie ihre Leistungen in einem persönlichen Abhängigkeitsverhältnis erbringen, das über das durch die Vereinsmitgliedschaft begründete Abhängigkeitsverhältnis hinausgeht.[2] Dieses kann insbesondere Profisportler betreffen, welche auch über den Trainings- und Spielbetrieb hinaus weitreichende Verpflichtungen für den jeweiligen Verein haben, bei dem sie organisiert sind, wie z. B. die Mitwirkung an PR-Veranstaltungen.[3] Entsprechend werden nach der Rechtsprechung des BAG Lizenzfußballspieler der Bundesliga regelmäßig als Arbeitnehmer eingestuft.[4] Auch Betreiber von Einzelsportarten wie z. B. Tischtennis im Ligabetrieb wurden von der Rechtsprechung als Arbeitnehmer eingestuft.[5] Entscheidungen zu der Arbeitnehmereigenschaft von Sumō-Ringern sind erwartungsgemäß aufgrund der fehlenden Professionalisierung und des Nischendaseins dieses Sportes in Deutschland, soweit ersichtlich, nicht ergangen.

---

1 *Reinecke*, Die Begriffe Arbeitnehmer und Beschäftigter – Entwicklungslinien exemplarisch dargestellt im Sportrecht, NJW (2018), S. 2081 mit Hinweis auf: BAG v. 13. Dezember 1962, AP BGB § 611 BGB Abhängigkeit Nr. 3; BSG v. 23. Juni 1959, BSGE 10, 94; BFH v. 16. März 1951, BFHE 55, 255.

2 BAG v. 10. Mai 1990, NZA (1991), S. 308, BAG v. 17. 1. 1979, AP BGB § 611 Berufssport Nr. 2.

3 *Reinecke* (Anm. 1), S. 2081.

4 BAG v. 24. November 1992, NZA (1993), S. 750; BAG v. 17. Januar 1979, AP BGB § 611 Berufssport Nr. 2; die Arbeitnehmereigenschaft für Vertragsamateure ablehnend: BAG v. 10. Mai 1990, AP § 611 Abhängigkeit Nr. 51.

5 OLG Stuttgart: Urteil v. 17. 11. 1977, BeckRS (1977), 31365739.

2. Japan

Nach japanischem Recht ist ein Arbeitnehmer nach Artikel 9 des japanischen Arbeitsstandard-Gesetzes (労働基準法, *rōdō kijun hō*), wer in einem Unternehmen oder Betrieb beschäftigt ist und hierfür ein Gehalt erhält, unabhängig von der Art der Beschäftigung. Um zu beurteilen, wann eine „Beschäftigung" im Sinne des Artikel 9 Arbeitsstandards-Gesetzes vorliegt, zieht die Rechtsprechung verschiedene Kriterien[6] heran, z. B.:

(i) Ob die Person die Arbeit frei ablehnen oder akzeptieren kann;

(ii) Ob und in welchem Maß die Person entscheiden kann, wann und wo sie arbeitet;

(iii) Ob und in welchem Maß die Arbeit unter Anleitung und Aufsicht ausgeführt wird;

(iv) Ob die Person die Arbeit durch Dritte ausführen kann oder ob sie höchstpersönlich ist;

(v) Ob die Arbeitsregelungen einschließlich Disziplinarmaßnahmen auf die Person angewendet werden;

(vi) Welche Partei die Aufwendungen für Arbeitsmaterialien und Arbeitswerkzeuge für die Durchführung der Arbeit tragen muss;

(vii) Ob die Person für eine Dienstleistung bezahlt wird oder nur für das Ergebnis einer Dienstleistung;

(viii) Ob die Einkommensteuer von dem Gehalt abgezogen wird.

Ein Schwerpunkt wird dabei oftmals auf die Faktoren (ii), d. h. ob die Freiheit, wann und wo die Arbeit durchzuführen, besteht, sowie (iii), die Frage nach dem Ausmaß der Kontrolle und Aufsicht, gelegt.[7] Profisportler, wie Profibaseballer und Profifußballer, werden dabei allgemein nicht als Arbeitnehmer im Sinne des Arbeitsstandard-Gesetzes und des Arbeitsvertrages angesehen.[8] Bei bestimmten semi-professionellen Sportlern kann etwas anderes gelten, wenn der Beschäftigungsvertrag Vorschriften enthält, wonach der Spieler Mitarbeiter des Unternehmens wird, dem der Verein gehört, und nach Beendigung der Sportlerkarriere weiterhin für das Unternehmen tätig werden soll. Wenngleich Profisportler typischerweise arbeitsvertraglich nicht als Arbeitnehmer anerkennt werden, dürfen sie sich kollektivrechtlich organisieren.[9] Nach dem japanischen Gewerkschaftsgesetz ist ein Arbeitnehmer eine „Person, die *unabhängig von der Art der Beschäftigung* von Löhnen, Gehältern oder anderen vergleichbaren Einkünften lebt". Tatsächlich sind die Japan Professional Base-

---

6 *Ouchi*, Labor Law Coverage and the Concept of „Worker", Japan Institute for Labour Policy and Training (JILPT) (2004).

7 *Ouchi* (Anm. 6).

8 Tokyo University Labour Law Study Group, Labour Standards Act Annotated (2003), S. 155.

9 *Sugeno*, Labour Law (2019), S. 832.

ball Players Association und die Japan Pro-Footballers Association als Gewerkschaften gemäß dem Gewerkschaftsgesetz (労働組合法, *rōdō kumiai hō*) anerkannt.[10]

III. Fokus: Sumō-Ringer

1. Allgemeines

Sumō wird in Japan als mehr als nur ein Sport betrachtet. Es wird mit seiner mehr als 1.500 Jahre alten Geschichte als zentraler Bestandteil des kulturellen Erbes Japans angesehen.[11]

Die fundamentale Organisationseinheit für jeden Sumō-Ringer im professionellen Sumō ist das Heya (部屋), oft als Trainingsstall übersetzt. Ein Heya fungiert als gemeinschaftliche Wohn- und Trainingseinrichtung der Sumō-Ringer. In dieser leben und trainieren die Sumō-Ringer unter der direkten Aufsicht und Autorität ihres Stallmeisters, des Oyakata (親方). Alle Heya sind als Mitgliedsorganisationen im Japanischen Sumō-Verband (日本相撲協会, *nihon sumō kyōkai*) organisiert.

Im Heya herrscht eine strenge Hierarchie. Diese orientiert sich am offiziellen Ranking der Ringer, dem Banzuke (番付). Die Rangordnung legt fest, welche Aufgaben jeder Ringer hat. Ringer mit niedrigem Rang erledigen traditionell den Großteil der Hausarbeit und bedienen die höherrangigen Kämpfer. Die strikte Regulierung des Verhaltens erstreckt sich auch auf das öffentliche Auftreten der Ringer. Ein prominentes Beispiel hierfür ist die Kleiderordnung: Ringer sind außerhalb des Heya oder des Trainingsgeländes verpflichtet, traditionelle japanische Kleidung wie Kimono oder Yukata (im Sommer) zu tragen.

Die professionellen Sumō-Ringer nehmen an sechs großen Turnieren pro Jahr teil, den sogenannten Honbasho (本場所, *honbasho*). Diese finden jeweils im ungeraden Monat des Jahres in verschiedenen Orten des Landes statt. Jedes Turnier dauert 15 Tage, beginnend an einem Sonntag und endend am übernächsten Sonntag.

2. Die Rechtsprechung des Tokioter Bezirksgerichts zu der (fehlenden) Arbeitnehmereigenschaft von Sumō-Ringern

a) Überblick

In den Jahren 2012 und 2013 entschied das Tokioter Bezirksgericht in drei Fällen über die Kündigung von Sumō-Ringern durch den Sumō-Verband, in denen die Arbeitnehmereigenschaft von Sumō-Ringern thematisiert wurde.

Hintergrund war ein Wettskandal und die Vorwürfe von illegalem Glücksspiel und Manipulation von Kampfergebnissen. Auslöser war eine polizeiliche Ermittlung bezüglich illegaler Wetten auf Baseballspiele, in die auch Personen aus dem Sumō verwickelt waren. Während der Ermittlungen zu den illegalen Baseballwetten wurden

---

10 Betreffend Baseball: https://jpbpa.net/management; betreffend Fußball: https://www.j-pfa.or.jp/about.

11 Weiterführend: *Ikeda*, Einführung in die Geschichte des Großen Sumo (大相撲史入門, *ōzumōshi nyūmon*) (2020).

Beweise, insbesondere Textnachrichten auf Mobiltelefonen, gefunden, die auch auf Kampfmanipulationen innerhalb von Sumō hindeuteten.

In der Folge wurden diverse Sumō-Ringer vom Japanischen Sumō-Verband beschuldigt, an Kampfmanipulationen beteiligt gewesen zu sein und anschließend zum Rücktritt aufgefordert. Die meisten folgten der „Empfehlung", freiwillig zurückzutreten. Als einzelne Sumō-Ringer sich aber dem verweigerten, wurden sie vom Verband ausgeschlossen. Die Sumō-Ringer Hoshikaze, Sokokurai und Kotomitsuki reichten daraufhin in separaten Fällen Klage gegen den Sumō-Verband ein.

In der ersten Entscheidung vom 24. Mai 2012 (betreffend Hoshikaze)[12] lehnte das Gericht die Feststellungsklage des Sumō-Ringers betreffend die Unwirksamkeit der Kündigung und Zahlungsansprüche gegen den Sumō-Verband ab. Dabei setzte sich das Gericht nicht mit der Natur des Vertragsverhältnisses zwischen dem Sumō-Ringer und dem Verband auseinander, da es die Kündigung – auch unter Anlegung arbeitsrechtlicher Maßstäbe – als wirksam erachtet hat.

In der zweiten Entscheidung vom 25. März 2013 (betreffend Sokokurai)[13] qualifizierte das Gericht die vertragliche Beziehung zwischen den Parteien weder als Arbeitsvertrag, noch als Auftragsvertrag im Sinne des Zivilgesetzbuches. Stattdessen wurde die Vertragsbeziehung zwischen dem Sumō-Ringer und dem Verband als „unbenannter Vertrag" eingestuft. Eine Typisierung anhand der gesetzlich geregelten Vertragstypen sei aufgrund der Besonderheiten der von diversen Traditionen und Ritualen geprägten Beziehung zwischen Sumō-Kämpfer und Verband schwer möglich. Die Wirksamkeit der Kündigung sei stattdessen anhand der Disziplinarvorschriften der Beklagten zu beurteilen, da diese als Bestandteil des Vertrags zwischen den Parteien anzusehen seien. Dabei seien jedoch auch allgemeine Rechtsgrundsätze zu beachten. Im Ergebnis sah das Gericht jedoch ein Fehlverhalten des Klägers (bezüglich des Vorwurfs des „absichtlichen, lustlosen Sumō") als nicht hinreichend erwiesen an, sodass es die Kündigung als unwirksam betrachtete.

In der dritten Entscheidung vom 12. September 2013 (betreffend Kotomitsuki)[14] hat das Gericht die vertragliche Beziehung zwischen den Parteien ebenfalls nicht als Arbeitsvertrag, sondern als „unbenannten Vertrag" qualifiziert, stellte aber auch hier fest, dass die Kündung auch unter arbeitsrechtlichen Maßstäben als wirksam zu betrachten wäre.

b) Zusammenfassung der Entscheidung vom 25. März 2013

Nachfolgend wird die zweite Entscheidung vom 25. März 2013 zusammengefasst, da sich das Gericht in den Entscheidungsgründen dieses Urteils am ausführlichsten mit der rechtlichen Qualifizierung des Vertragsverhältnisses auseinandergesetzt hat.

aa) Die Darlegungen der Parteien

Der Kläger vertrat in seiner Klage die Auffassung, dass der zugrundeliegende Vertrag als Arbeitsvertrag zu qualifizieren sei.

---

12 Heisei 23 (Wa) Nr. 22024.

13 Heisei 23 (Wa) Nr. 20049.

14 Heisei 23 (Wa) Nr. 12298.

Zur Begründung führte der Kläger insbesondere folgende Aspekte an:

- Die Sumō-Ringer seien gegenüber dem Sumō-Verband zur Teilnahme an Sumō-Wettkämpfen verpflichtet gewesen.
- Zudem seien sie jeweils einem Sumō-Stall zugeordnet und unterstünden den dortigen Anweisungen, einschließlich bezüglich der Lebensführung außerhalb von Training und Wettkampf, sowie den Disziplinarvorschriften der Beklagten.
- Sie erhielten ein fixes Monatsgehalt sowie Zulagen entsprechend ihrem Rang, was eine Entschädigung für ihre erbrachte Arbeit darstelle.
- Hinsichtlich der Kranken- und Rentenversicherung behandele die Beklagte die Sumō-Kämpfer sozialversicherungsrechtlich als Arbeitnehmer.

Die Beklagte, der Sumō-Verband, nahm demgegenüber den Standpunkt ein, es handle sich um einen Quasi-Auftragsvertrag und nicht um ein Arbeitsverhältnis. Die Beklagte stützte sich hierbei insbesondere auf folgende Argumente:

- Der grundlegende Vertragsinhalt bestehe darin, dass die Beklagte Wettkämpfe organisiere und die Sumō-Kämpfer an den (Haupt-)Wettkämpfen gegen eine Vergütung teilnähmen, die sich nach ihren individuellen Fähigkeiten richtet, die sie durch ihren freiwilligen Einsatz erworben haben.
- Eine direkte Verpflichtung der Sumō-Kämpfer zur Teilnahme an den Wettkämpfen existiere nicht; ihre Teilnahme erfolge nach eigenem Ermessen.
- Es bestehe kein Weisungsverhältnis zwischen dem Sumō-Verband und den Sumō-Kämpfern bezüglich der jeweiligen Strategie.
- Die Vergütung bemesse sich nach der Leistung und sei unabhängig von der aufgewendeten Arbeitszeit.
- Die Beziehung zwischen den Sumō-Ringern und ihren Sumō-Ställen bzw. Meistern basiere auf der traditionellen Sumō-Tradition, diese sei mit den arbeitsrechtlichen Bestimmungen unvereinbar.

bb) Die Entscheidung des Gerichts

In seinen Entscheidungsgründen setzte sich das Gericht mit den von den Parteien vorgetragenen Argumenten eingehend auseinander.

Das Gericht identifizierte dabei als Kernelement des Vertrages die Pflicht des individuellen Sumō-Ringers, seine Fertigkeiten bei offiziellen Wettkämpfen und anderen Veranstaltungen zu demonstrieren. Als Gegenleistung bestehe die Pflicht der Beklagten zur Zahlung einer Vergütung.

Darüber hinaus umfasse der Vertrag weitere konstituierende Elemente:

- Der Sumō-Verband stelle die personelle und materielle Infrastruktur für die Durchführung der Wettkämpfe bereit.
- Mit Abschluss des Vertrages erlange der einzelne Sumō-Ringer die Mitgliedschaft in der Organisation des Sumō-Verbands und somit eine bestimmte Stellung und Status.

- In diesem Rahmen lebe der Sumō-Ringer in einem Sumō-Stall und unterwerfe sich den dortigen Anleitungen, die auch Aspekte der Lebensführung umfassten.
- Der Sumō-Ringer befolge die von dem Sumō-Verband erlassenen Dienstvorschriften und unterliege den damit verbundenen disziplinarischen Vorgaben, einschließlich Sanktionen bei Verstößen.
- Der Sumō-Ringer sei in die Organisation des Sumō-Verbands eingebunden; dies basiere auf einer kontinuirlichen Beziehung, die auf dem Vertrauensverhältnis zwischen den Sumō-Ringern, ihren Stall-Meistern und dem Sumō-Verband aufbaue.

Ausgehend von diesen Feststellungen gelangte das Gericht zu dem Schluss, dass der Vertrag zwischen den Parteien komplexe Elemente aufweise, die teilweise nur schwer mit den Prinzipien des Vertragsrechts zu vereinbaren und hierunter zu klassifizieren sei. Unter Berücksichtigung der historischen Entwicklung des Sumō seit der Antike, der Weiterentwicklung des modernen Sumō-Systems in der Edo-Zeit sowie der Tatsache, dass die Beziehung zwischen Sumō-Ringern und dem Verband auf einer Tradition beruhe, die älter sei als die Kodifikation des japanischen Zivilgesetzes (民法, *minpō*), erscheine eine Einordnung des Vertrags als typischer Arbeitsvertrag oder Quasi-Auftragsvertrag (準委任契約, *jun'inin keiyaku*) im Sinne des Zivilgesetzes als nicht sachgerecht. Vielmehr sei der Vertrag als ein unbenannter Vertrag des Privatrechts zu interpretieren.

Die Vorschriften des Arbeits- bzw. Auftragsrechts zur Kündigung seien in diesem Fall nicht unmittelbar anwendbar. Stattdessen sei die Rechtmäßigkeit der Kündigung anhand der Disziplinarvorschriften der Beklagten zu beurteilen, da diese als integraler Bestandteil des Vertrags zwischen den Parteien anzusehen seien und die in diesem Fall streitgegenständliche Entlassung als Disziplinarmaßnahme auf dieser Grundlage erfolgt sei.

Bei der Auslegung und Anwendung der Disziplinarvorschriften seien jedoch allgemeine Rechtsgrundsätze zu beachten, wie etwa das Erfordernis der vorherigen Bestimmtheit von Disziplinartatbeständen und -verfahren, das Verbot der Doppelbestrafung sowie der Grundsatz der Verhältnismäßigkeit der jeweiligen Sanktion.

Das Gericht befand schließlich, dass die Beweise nicht ausreichten, um ein Fehlverhalten des Klägers im Sinne eines „absichtlichen, lustlosen Sumō" zu belegen. Da somit die für die Kündigung maßgebliche Pflichtverletzung nicht festgestellt werden konnte, erklärte das Gericht die Kündigung für unwirksam.

IV. Fazit

Zusammenfassend lässt sich festhalten, dass in Japan die rechtliche Einordnung von Profisportlern als Arbeitnehmer tendenziell restriktiv gehandhabt wird. Auch das Verhältnis eines Sumō-Ringers zu seinem Verband, welches durch ein hohes Maß an geschriebenen und ungeschriebenen Regelungen und damit Kontrolle sowie Weisungen betreffend Training, Wettkampf und Lebensführung gekennzeichnet ist, wird nach vorherrschender Rechtsprechung nicht als Arbeitsverhältnis qualifiziert, sondern als Vertrag eigener Art (*sui generis*). Gleichwohl ist bei der Anwendung der relevanten Verbandsvorschriften die Beachtung allgemeiner Rechtsgrundsätze geboten, was dem Gericht implizit eine gewisse Verhältnismäßigkeitsprüfung ermöglicht.

Darüber hinaus zeigt sich, dass Japan in Fällen, in denen Beschäftigungsverhältnisse nicht als Arbeitsverhältnisse qualifiziert werden und damit nicht den arbeitsrechtlichen Schutzvorschriften unterliegen, Vorschriften erlässt, um für diese wachsenden Personengruppe ebenfalls Schutzmechanismen zu etablieren und ihre Position zu stärken. In diesem Zusammenhang ist das „Gesetz zur Gewährleistung fairer Transaktionen mit bestimmten beauftragten Geschäftspartnern“, bekannt als „Freelancer-Gesetz“[15], am 1. November 2024 in Kraft getreten. Dieses Gesetz, dass unter anderem klare Vertragsbedingungen, fristgerechte Zahlungen und eine Verbesserung der Arbeitsbedingungen für unabhängige Dienstleister vorsieht, wurde als Reaktion auf die fortschreitende Diversifizierung der Arbeitsformen und zur Stärkung der Position der wachsenden Gruppe von Freelancern eingeführt. Der Gesetzgeber hatte damit gewiss nicht die exklusive Gruppe von Profisportlern im Sinn, aber die Schaffung eines solchen spezifischen Schutzgesetzes für eine außerhalb des traditionellen Arbeitsverhältnisses stehende Gruppe unterstreicht die generelle Tendenz, auf die fortschreitende Diversifizierung der Arbeitswelt in Japan mit angepassten rechtlichen Rahmenbedingungen zu reagieren.

Literaturverzeichnis

Ikeda, Masao: Einführung in die Geschichte des Großen Sumo (大相撲史入門, *ōzumōshi nyūmon*) (2020).

Ouchi, Shinya: Labor Law Coverage and the Concept of „Worker“, Japan Institute for Labour Policy and Training (JILPT) (2004).

Reinecke, Gerhard: Die Begriffe Arbeitnehmer und Beschäftigter – Entwicklungslinien exemplarisch dargestellt im Sportrecht, NJW (2018), S. 2081.

Sugeno, Kazuo: Labour Law (2019).

Tokyo University Labour Law Study Group: Labour Standards Act Annotated (2003).

15 特定受託事業者に係る取引の適正化等に関する法律 (*tokutei jutaku jigyōsha ni kakaru torihiki no tekiseikatō ni kansuru hōritsu*), Gesetz Nr. 25 von 2023.

Die Europäische Erbrechtsverordnung im Deutsch-Japanischen Rechtsverkehr

Von *Rembert Süß*

Dr. Rembert Süß, Leiter des Referats für Internationales und Ausländisches Privatrecht am Deutschen Notarinstitut in Würzburg. Von 1993 bis 1996 Dozent für Deutsches Recht an der Tohoku Universität in Sendai.

I. Vorbemerkung

1993 hatte ich in Tokyo das Glück, Heinrich Menkhaus kennen zu lernen. Damals leitete er die Rechtsabteilung der Deutschen Industrie- und Handelskammer in Japan, Tokyo. Ich war als frisch gebackener Dozent aus Osnabrück nach Sendai gekommen, um an der Tohoku Universität japanische Studenten im deutschen Recht zu unterrichten. Er hat mich als „Greenhorn" sehr freundlich aufgenommen und unterstützt. Dazu mag ihn vielleicht auch die gemeinsame Herkunft aus dem Osnabrücker Land bewogen haben. Später haben sich die Positionen getauscht: Heinrich Menkhaus hat an deutschen und japanischen Universitäten gelehrt und ich habe in der internationalen Praxis juristisch beraten. Geblieben ist uns beiden die internationale juristische Ausrichtung, das Überbrücken der juristischen nationalen Grenzen. Zu großem Dank bin ich ihm auch verpflichtet, weil er in dem von mir mit Thomas Wachter gemeinsam herausgegebenen Handbuch zum internationalen GmbH-Recht einen Beitrag zum Gesellschaftsrecht in Japan erstellt und regelmäßig aktualisiert hat. Ich freue mich daher nun außerordentlich über die Gelegenheit, ihm zu seinem Geburtstag zu gratulieren, indem ich ihm gerne einen kleinen Beitrag zu praktischen Fragen aus dem täglichen Leben im deutsch-japanischen Rechtsverkehr widme, der wieder *ad fontes* zum Internationalen Privatrecht zurückführt.

II. Ermittlung des Erbstatuts im deutsch-japanischen Rechtsverkehr

Das materielle Erbrecht ist im japanischen Zivilgesetzbuch wie im deutschen BGB im Fünften Buch geregelt. Daran zeigt sich der Einfluss der deutschen Pandektenlehre und der Erlass des BGB als juristisches Jahrhundertwerk im Deutschen Kaiserreich auf das Japan der Meiji-Zeit. Bei genauerem Hinsehen entpuppt sich aber, dass hier unter der deutschen Hülle auch in der Neufassung des japanischen Erbrechts von 1947 viel Gedankengut aus Frankreich zu erkennen ist. Insbesondere bei den Möglichkeiten der testamentarischen Anordnungen (dazu mehr unten). Dass die Ab-

Duncker & Humblot · Berlin | https://doi.org/10.3790/978-3-428-59611-9.2025.418839

kömmlinge in erster Ordnung erben und bei Vorversterben von ihren Abkömmlingen *per stirpes* repräsentiert werden, ist keine Besonderheit des deutschen Rechts. Das gilt weitestgehend überall. Interessanter wird es aber in der zweiten Erbenordnung. Hinterlässt der Erblasser keine Abkömmlinge, so treten in der zweiten Erbenordnung japanischen Rechts gem. Art. 889 Abs. 1 S. 1 ZivilG bei Vorversterben eines Elternteils nicht dessen Abkömmlinge – also die Brüder und Schwestern des Erblassers – an seiner statt in die Erbfolge ein, sondern die weiter entfernten Aszendenten in gerader Linie. Die Geschwister sind dagegen gem. Art. 889 Abs. 1 S. 2 ZivilG erst in dritter Ordnung berufen, also wenn keine Aszendenten – gleich welchen Grades – überlebt haben.

Diese Differenzen im Sachrecht lassen sich durch das Kollisionsrecht lösen: Konkurrieren also Geschwister mit den Großeltern des Erblassers, so entscheidet das IPR, ob mit der Geltung des japanischen Erbrechts die Großeltern erben oder ob mit der Geltung des deutschen Erbrechts die Geschwister die Großeltern aus der Erbfolge verdrängen.

Das Internationale Privatrecht ist in Japan aktuell in dem am 1. Januar 2007 in Kraft getretenen Rechtsanwendungsgesetz vom 21. Juni 2006[1] (jRAG) geregelt. Gem. Art. 36 jRAG unterliegt die Erbfolge dem Heimatrecht des Erblassers. War der Erblasser japanischer Staatsangehöriger, so erben also vorrangig die Großeltern, auch wenn der Erblasser zuletzt in Deutschland lebte.

War er dagegen ein in Japan lebender deutscher Staatsangehöriger, so verweist Art. 36 jRAG auf das deutsche Recht. Diese Verweisung erfasst gem. Art. 41 S. 1 jRAG auch das deutsche Internationale Privatrecht, so dass eine Rückverweisung auf das japanische Recht zu befolgen ist:

Artikel 41 jRAG

Wenn das Heimatrecht der Person anzuwenden ist und nach den Regeln jenes Rechts das japanische Recht anzuwenden ist, so ist das japanische Recht anzuwenden.

Damit wäre auch aus japanischer Sicht zu differenzieren: Ist der Erbfall vor dem 17. August 2015 eingetreten, so beurteilt sich die Erbfolge aus deutscher Sicht nach Art. 25 EGBGB a.F. Diese Vorschrift knüpfte ebenso wie Art. 36 jRAG das Erbstatut an die Staatsangehörigkeit des Erblassers an. Das deutsche Recht nahm die Verweisung also an, so dass entsprechend den Regeln des BGB die Geschwister zur Erbfolge berufen sind.

War dagegen der Erbfall nach dem 16. August 2015 eingetreten, so unterliegt er gem. Art. 83 Abs. 1 EUErbVO den Regeln der Europäischen Erbrechtsverordnung vom 4. Juli 2012. Art. 21 Abs. 1 EUErbVO verweist dann, wenn der Erblasser kein Testament errichtet hat, in dem er die Erbfolge seinem Heimatrecht unterstellt hatte (Art. 22 EUErbVO), für die Erbfolge auf das Recht des Staates, in dem der Erblasser seinen letzten gewöhnlichen Aufenthalt hatte. Lebte der deutsche Erblasser also dauerhaft in Japan, hatte er dort nicht nur eine unbefristete Beschäftigung, sondern auch seine Familie und plante, dort dauerhaft zu bleiben, hatte er dort also seinen

1 Eine Einführung und deutsche Übersetzung zum jRAG findet sich bei *Sakuraga/Nishitani/Schwittek*, Gesetz Nr. 78 über die allgemeinen Regeln über die Anwendung von Gesetzen (Rechtsanwendungsgesetz) vom 21. Juni 2006, in: RabelsZ, Bd. 76, Nr. 1 (2012), S. 170 ff.

Lebensmittelpunkt, so wäre nach der EUErbVO das japanische Recht anzuwenden. Aus japanischer Sicht würde sich hieraus eine Rückverweisung ergeben, die gem. Art. 41 S. 1 jRAG unmittelbar zur Geltung des japanischen Sachrechts führt. Folglich wird der Erblasser aus japanischer Sicht trotz seiner deutschen Staatsangehörigkeit nach den japanischen Regeln von den Großeltern und nicht von den Geschwistern beerbt.

Umgekehrt freilich wäre die Situation aus deutscher Sicht zu beurteilen: Sollte der deutsche Erblasser seinen gewöhnlichen Aufenthalt in Japan haben, so ist vorbehaltlich einer abweichenden Rechtswahl (Art. 22 Abs. 1 EUErbVO) gem. Art. 21 Abs. 1 EUErbVO japanisches Recht anzuwenden. Japanisches Recht würde aber mit Art. 36 jRAG wegen der deutschen Staatsangehörigkeit auf das deutsche Recht zurückverweisen. Gem. Art. 34 Abs. 1 EUErbVO ist – da Japan kein Mitgliedstaat i. S. d. EUErbVO sondern sog. Drittstaat ist – nach Verweisung auf das japanische Recht aus deutscher Sicht ebenfalls das japanische Internationale Privatrecht anzuwenden:

Artikel 34 EUErbVO

Rück- und Weiterverweisung

(1) Unter dem nach dieser Verordnung anzuwendenden Recht eines Drittstaats sind die in diesem Staat geltenden Rechtsvorschriften einschließlich derjenigen seines Internationalen Privatrechts zu verstehen, soweit diese zurück- oder weiterverweisen auf:
   a) das Recht eines Mitgliedstaats oder
   b) das Recht eines anderen Drittstaats, der sein eigenes Recht anwenden würde.

(2) Rück- und Weiterverweisungen durch die in Artikel 21 Absatz 2, Artikel 22, Artikel 27, Artikel 28 Buchstabe b und Artikel 30 genannten Rechtsordnungen sind nicht zu beachten.

Art. 34 Abs. 1 EUErbVO enthält – anders als Art. 41 jRAG und Art. 4 Abs. 1 S. 2 EGBGB – keine ausdrückliche Regelung dazu, wie diese Rückverweisung auf das Recht eines Mitgliedstaats i. S. d. EUErbVO aus europäischer Sicht zu behandeln ist. Denkbar wäre nämlich nicht nur, dass die Verweisungskette in Deutschland oder im entsprechenden anderen Mitgliedstaat abgebrochen würde. Der von der EUErbVO mit dieser Regelung verfolgte Zweck, einen internationalen Entscheidungseinklang zu erreichen[2] würde vielmehr dafürsprechen, im Wege des *double renvoi* die Rückverweisung so zu behandeln wie die Gerichte des Staates, auf den die EUErbVO verwiesen hatte. Entsprechend der japanischen Sichtweise wäre also gem. Art. 41 S. 1 jRAG der Verweisungszirkel im japanischen Recht abzubrechen. Dennoch wird von der zur EUErbVO ergangenen Literatur weithin und ohne große Diskussion angenommen, es gelte die Regel des *single renvoi*, so dass also die Verweisung immer im Inland abzubrechen sei.[3]

---

2 Erwägungsgrund 57, S. 3 letzter Hs. EUErbVO.

3 *Bauer/Fornasier*, in: Dutta/Weber (Hrsg.), Internationales Erbrecht, 2. Aufl. (2021), Art. 34 EUErbVO Rn. 14; *Solomon*, Die Renaissance des Renvoi im Europäischen Internationalen Privatrecht, in: Liber Amicorum, Klaus Schurig: zum 70. Geburtstag (2012), S. 253; *Bonomi/Wautelet* (Hrsg.), Le droit européen des successions internationales, 2. Aufl. (2016), Art. 34 annot. 17.

Folge ist, dass der ursprünglich sich aus der übereinstimmenden Anknüpfung an die Staatsangehörigkeit im deutsch-japanischen Verhältnis ergebende internationale Entscheidungskonsens mit Inkrafttreten der EUErbVO verloren gegangen ist. Stattdessen hat die *lex fori* den Sieg errungen. Jeder Staat wendet sein eigenes Recht an, und zwar unabhängig davon, ob der Erblasser die Staatsangehörigkeit des Gerichtsstaates besaß oder aber zwar Angehöriger des anderen Staates war, sich aber im Forumstaat dauerhaft niedergelassen hatte. Will der Erblasser die damit einhergehenden Differenzen im deutsch-japanischen Verhältnis vermeiden und den miteinander zerstrittenen Hinterbliebenen ein Tor zum *forum shopping* verschließen, so muss er ein Testament errichten und die Erbfolge durch Rechtswahl i. S. v. Art. 22 EUErbVO seinem Heimatrecht unterstellen.

III. Besonderheiten im Ehegattenerbrecht

1. Einführung in die Problematik

Die vorgenannten Probleme mit dem internationalen Entscheidungsdissens setzen sich fort, wenn es um das gesetzliche Erbrecht des Ehegatten geht. Das japanische Recht regelt die gesetzliche Erbquote des überlebenden Ehegatten wie folgt:

Art. 890 ZivilG

Der Ehegatte des Erblassers ist in jedem Fall zur Erbfolge berufen. Er erbt er neben den Erben nach Art. 887 und den Erben nach dem vorangegangenen Artikel im gleichen Rang.

Art. 900 ZivilG

Erben mehrere Personen im selben Rang, so bestimmen sich die Erbquoten nach den Regeln in den folgenden Ziffern:

1. Erben Kinder und der Ehegatte, so beträgt der Erbteil der Kinder und des Ehegatten jeweils ein Halb.
2. Erben der Ehegatte und die Vorfahren in gerader Linie, so beträgt der Erbteil des Ehegatten zwei Drittel und der Erbteil der Vorfahren in gerader Linie ein Drittel.
3. Erben der Ehegatte und die Geschwister, so beträgt der Erbteil des Ehegatten drei Viertel und der Erbteil der Geschwister ein Viertel.
4. …

Regelmäßig hinzu kommt seit der Reform von 2020 gem. Art. 1028 ff. ZivilG ein lebenslanges Nutzungsrecht des überlebenden Ehegatten an der zum Nachlass gehörenden Ehewohnung.[4]

In Deutschland gilt nach § 1931 BGB eine mehrfach differenzierte Regelung. Diese macht die Höhe des Erbrechts des Ehegatten nicht allein vom Grad der Verwandtschaft der mit dem Ehegatten erbenden Angehörigen des Erblassers abhängig. Es kommt auch darauf an, in welchem Güterstand der Erblasser gelebt hatte. Grundsätzlich erbt der überlebende Ehegatte nur ein Viertel, § 1931 Abs. 1 BGB. Lebte er aber

---

[4] Einzelheiten bei *Nagata-Vogelsang*, in: Burandt/Rojahn (Hrsg.), Erbrecht, 4. Aufl. (2022), Länderbericht Japan Rn. 36.

mit dem Erblasser im gesetzlichen Güterstand der Zugewinngemeinschaft, so erhält er über §§ 1931 Abs. 3, 1371 Abs. 1 BGB regelmäßig ein weiteres Viertel (das „güterrechtliche Viertel“) und kommt damit – wie nach japanischem Erbrecht – auf eine gesetzliche Erbquote von ein Halb.

Um dem Ehegatten, der in Zugewinngemeinschaft deutschen Rechts lebte, auch bei Geltung ausländischen Erbrechts – also beispielsweise bei ausländischer Staatsangehörigkeit des vorverstorbenen Ehegatten – die Vergünstigung des güterrechtlichen Viertels zu gewährleisten, wurde in der Vergangenheit nach einer jahrzehntelang in der Literatur und Rechtsprechung geführten Diskussion über die „güterrechtliche“ und die „erbrechtliche“ Qualifikation,[5] die zuletzt vom BGH[6] zugunsten der „güterrechtlichen Qualifikation“ entschieden wurde, das güterrechtliche Viertel „güterrechtlich qualifiziert“. Es wurde demnach bei Geltung der Zugewinngemeinschaft aufgrund Anwendbarkeit deutschen Güterstatuts immer gewährt, unabhängig davon, ob deutsches oder ausländisches Erbrecht galt. Das führte aber vor allem dann zu Problemen, wenn Güterstatut und Erbstatut nicht zusammenpassten. Galt also japanisches Erbrecht und deutsche Zugewinngemeinschaft, so hätte der überlebende Ehegatte aus dem japanischen Erbstatut ein Halb und ein weiteres Viertel aus dem deutschen Güterrecht, insgesamt also drei Viertel des Nachlasses erhalten, während die Kinder lediglich ein Viertel bekommen hätten. Das ist mehr als die Hälfte, die er erhielte, würde ausschließlich japanisches für Erb- und Güterrecht bzw. nur deutsches Recht gelten. Die Rechtsprechung korrigierte daher dieses Ergebnis als Fall der kollisionsrechtlichen „Normenhäufung“ im Wege der Anpassung dadurch, dass sie die Erbquoten auf je ein Halb reduzierte.[7]

Spiegelbildlich stellte sich das Problem, wenn deutsches Recht Erbstatut ist und die güterrechtlichen Beziehungen dem japanischen Recht unterlagen. Qualifiziert man den gesetzlichen Güterstand nach japanischem Recht als „Gütertrennung“ i. S. v. § 1931 Abs. 4 BGB, wonach der überlebende Ehegatte und jedes Kind zu gleichen Teilen erben, ergibt sich zwar eine Erbquote von ein Halb, wenn der Erblasser ein Kind hatte. Hinterlässt er aber zwei oder mehr Kinder, so erhält der Ehegatte nur ein Drittel oder ein Viertel – also weniger als bei Geltung ausschließlich deutschen oder ausschließlich japanischen Rechts (bei gesetzlichem Güterstand jeweils ein Halb). Ob und wie in diesem Fall die Erbquote im Wege der Anpassung angehoben werden kann, war ungeklärt.

Mit Inkrafttreten der EUErbVO am 16. August 2015 wurden die Karten in diesem Spiel neu gemischt. Die EUErbVO genießt als europäisches Verordnungsrecht Vorrang vor dem nationalen Recht der Mitgliedstaaten. Dabei fällt gem. Art. 23 Abs. 2 lit. b EUErbVO die Frage, wie hoch die gesetzliche Erbquote des Ehegatten ist, in den Regelungsbereich der EUErbVO. Eine Modifikation der sich aus der Anwendung des nach den Regeln der EUErbVO bestimmten ergebenden ausländischen Erbstatuts ergebenden gesetzlichen Erbquoten durch das deutsche Güterrecht verbot sich

5 Vgl. z. B. OLG Karlsruhe NJW 1990, 1421und OLG Hamm FamRZ 1995, 1606: Güterrechtliche Qualifikation; OLG Stuttgart ZEV 2005, 443 und OLG Köln ZEV 2012, 205: Erbrechtliche Qualifikation.

6 BGH NJW 2015, 2185.

7 So z. B. OLG Düsseldorf FamRZ (2015), S. 1237 Anm. Dutta.

damit. Die deutsche Literatur kämpfte zunächst für den weiteren Vorrang des Güterrechtlichen Viertels. Konsequent auf der Basis der EUErbVO argumentieren, hat dagegen der EuGH nicht vom nationalen Recht ausgehend, sondern von den Vorschriften und dem Regelungszweck der EUErbVO in der Rechtssache „Mahnkopf" auf Vorlage durch das Kammergericht in Berlin entschieden, dass das „güterrechtliche Viertel" aus § 1371 Abs. 1 BGB erbrechtlich zu qualifizieren sei.[8] Damit ergibt sich nunmehr, dass das güterrechtliche Viertel ausschließlich dann gewährt werden kann, wenn deutsches Recht Erbstatut ist. Wie sich das im deutsch-japanischen Rechtsverkehr auswirkt, sei anhand der folgenden Beispielsfälle illustriert:[9]

2. Beispielsfall 1: Deutsches Erbstatut und japanisches Güterrecht

a) Sachverhalt

Die Erblasserin war japanische Staatsangehörige. Sie lebte seit vielen Jahren in Deutschland. 1970 hat sie in Japan einen japanischen Staatsangehörigen geheiratet. Ein Ehevertrag oder ein Testament liegt nicht vor. Neben ihrem Ehemann hinterlässt sie als nächste Verwandte Geschwister und Kinder vorverstorbener Geschwister.

Gefragt wurde, wie hoch die Erbquote des Ehemannes sei.

b) Bestimmung des Erbstatuts

Da der Erbfall nach dem 16. August 2015 eintrat, ist auf die Erbfolge das nach den Vorschriften der EuErbVO bestimmte Erbrecht anzuwenden. Art. 21 Abs. 1 EuErbVO verweist auf das Recht des Staates, in dem die Erblasserin zum Zeitpunkt des Eintritts des Erbfalles ihren gewöhnlichen Aufenthalt hatte. Ausgehend davon, dass die Erblasserin lange Zeit mit ihrem Mann in Deutschland lebte und hier auch offenbar endgültig verbleiben wollte, liegt ein gewöhnlicher Aufenthalt im Inland nahe. Es gilt dann also deutsches Erbrecht.

c) Ermittlung des auf den Güterstand anwendbaren Rechts

§ 1931 BGB macht die Höhe der Erbquoten im Rahmen der gesetzlichen Erbfolge vom Güterstand der Erblasserin abhängig. Damit ist vorab das auf die güterrechtlichen Wirkungen der Ehe anwendbare Recht zu ermitteln.

Da die Eheleute 1970 geheiratet hatten, ist zur Bestimmung des Güterstatuts Art. 220 Abs. 3 und Art. 229 § 47 Abs. 2 Ziff. 2 EGBGB zu beachten. Hatten beide Eheleute zum Zeitpunkt der Eheschließung die gleiche Staatsangehörigkeit, so ist gem. Art. 220 Abs. 3 S. 1 Ziff. 1 EGBGB für die Zeit bis zum 8. April 1983 und für die Zeit danach gem. Art. 15 Abs. 1, 14 Abs. 1 Ziff. 1 EGBGB in der bis zum 29. Januar 2019 geltenden Fassung auf die gemeinsame Staatsangehörigkeit der Eheleute bei Eheschließung abzustellen. Damit wird auf das japanische Recht verwiesen.

Diese Verweisung erfasst auch das in Japan geltende Internationale Privatrecht. Insb. wäre eine Rückverweisung durch das japanische IPR zu beachten. Gem.

8 EUGH DNotZ 2018, 785 „Mahnkopf".

9 Der Fall ist nicht fiktiv, sondern war Gegenstand der Anfrage eines Notars zum Deutschen Notarinstituts.

Art. 26 Abs. 1 i. V. m. Art. 25 jRAG unterliegen die güterrechtlichen Verhältnisse einer Ehe vorbehaltlich einer abweichenden ehevertraglichen Vereinbarung (Rechtswahl) der Eheleute ihrem gemeinsamen Heimatrecht. Abweichend von Art. 15 EGBGB a. F. sind hierbei die jeweils aktuellen Verhältnisse maßgeblich. Ein Wechsel der Staatsangehörigkeit nach Heirat führt aus japanischer Sicht zu einem Wechsel auch des Güterstatuts. Das japanische IPR knüpft das Güterstatut also wandelbar an. Da die Eheleute im vorliegenden Fall nicht nur zum Zeitpunkt der Eheschließung, sondern auch zum Zeitpunkt des Erbfalls noch beide japanische Staatsangehörige waren, nimmt das japanische Recht die Verweisung an. Die Eheleute haben im gesetzlichen Güterstand des japanischen Rechts gelebt.

d) Gesetzlicher Güterstand des japanischen Rechts

Der gesetzliche Güterstand des japanischen Rechts wird in der westlichen Literatur weithin als „Gütertrennung" bezeichnet. Grundlage dafür ist Art. 762 ZivilG:

Art. 762 ZivilG

(1) Vermögen, das einem Ehegatten schon vor der Heirat gehörte, oder dass er während der Ehe im eigenen Namen erworben hat, ist sein Sondergut.

(2) Vermögen, bei dem nicht klar ist, welchem der Ehegatten es hört, gilt als ihr Miteigentum.

Anders als bei der reinen Gütertrennung wird bei Scheidung der Ehe allerdings das während der Ehe erworbene Vermögen „gerecht geteilt":

Art. 768 ZivilG

(1) Nach einer einverständlichen Scheidung kann jeder der Ehegatten vom anderen die Teilung des Vermögens verlangen.

(2) Wurde keine Einigung über eine Vermögensteilung nach den Vorschriften im vorherigen Absatz erzielt oder können sich die Parteien nicht einigen, so können sie beim Familiengericht eine die Einigung ersetzende Anordnung beantragen. Das gilt aber dann nicht mehr, wenn seit der Scheidung zwei Jahre verstrichen sind.

(3) Im Fall des vorangegangenen Absatzes entscheidet das Gericht unter Berücksichtigung des Wertes des von den Parteien gemeinschaftlich erworbenen Vermögens sowie aller anderen Umstände darüber, ob eine Vermögensteilung erfolgen muss und in welcher Weise diese durchzuführen ist.

Bei dieser Vermögensaufteilung (*Zaisan-Bun'yo*) wird das Vermögen, das die Eheleute während der Dauer Ehe erworben haben, gegeneinander aufgerechnet. Man ging bei Erlass der Vorschrift davon aus, dass auch dann, wenn die Ehefrau zu Hause geblieben ist und das Haus versorgt hat, das Vermögen, das im Namen des Ehemannes während der Ehe erworben wurde, mit ihrer Hilfe geschaffen wurde. Dieses soll deswegen, je nach Umfang der Mitwirkung der Frau, geteilt werden.

Gegenstand der Teilung ist das Vermögen, das während des gemeinsamen Ehelebens erworben wurde. Vermögen, das von Dritten durch Schenkung oder Erbfolge unentgeltlich erworben wurde, wird von der Teilung ausgenommen. Auch Güter, die nach allgemeiner gesellschaftlicher Ansicht als persönliches Sondereigentum gelten, sollen ausgenommen bleiben. Vermögensmehrung durch zufällige Ereignisse wie Lottogewinn, Pferdewetten, Vermehrung der Anzahl von Aktien durch Aktiensplit etc. fällt dagegen in die Teilungsmasse. Die Quote der Mitwirkung einer Vollhausfrau wird mittlerweile grundsätzlich mit 50 % angesetzt.[10]

Eine entsprechende Teilung wird ausschließlich im Rahmen der Ehescheidung, nicht aber im Erbfall durchgeführt.

Insoweit ergibt sich im vorliegenden Fall, dass das System der „Gütertrennung“ des japanischen Rechts weitgehend der Zugewinngemeinschaft des deutschen Rechts vergleichbar ist, bei der die Vermögensmassen der Eheleute ebenfalls zunächst getrennt bleiben und der während der Dauer der Ehe erzielte Vermögenszuwachs der Eheleute – soweit er nicht aus unentgeltlichen Zuwendungen von Dritten herrührt – im Rahmen der Scheidung hälftig ausgeglichen wird, während im Fall der Auflösung der Ehe durch Tod eines der Ehegatten ein entsprechender Ausgleich nicht durchgeführt wird. Vielmehr zeigt sich, dass im deutschen wie im japanischen Recht der überlebende Ehegatte bei Geltung des gesetzlichen Güterstands neben Abkömmlingen eine gesetzliche Erbquote von ein Halb und neben Geschwistern von drei Vierteln erhält, also im internationalen Vergleich relativ großzügig abgefunden wird, so dass quasi der güterrechtliche Ausgleich als abgegolten gilt.

e) Substitution der Zugewinngemeinschaft durch den japanischen Güterstand

Insoweit stellt sich nun die Frage, ob im Rahmen der Anwendung von § 1931 Abs. 3, § 1371 Abs. 1 BGB auch ein ausländischer Güterstand als „Zugewinngemeinschaft“ i. S. d. erbrechtlichen Vorschriften eingestuft werden kann.

Ein Teil der deutschen Literatur möchte die Gleichstellung eines ausländischen Güterstands mit der Zugewinngemeinschaft deutschen Rechts kategorisch ausschließen bzw. davon abhängig machen, dass auch das ausländische Güterrecht ein „pauschales Viertel“ vorsieht.[11] Die andere Ansicht hält eine Substitution grundsätzlich für zulässig und möglich.[12] Einzelheiten sind allerdings umstritten. Weitgehende Einigkeit besteht wohl darüber, dass eine Substitution jedenfalls dann ausscheidet, wenn die Eheleute in einer absoluten Gütertrennung leben, also sowohl im Scheidungs- als auch im Erbfall kein Wertausgleich stattfindet. Für diesen Fall ist § 1931 Abs. 4 BGB zur Bestimmung der Erbquoten heranzuziehen.

---

10 *Nagata-Vogelsang*, Länderbericht Japan, in: Rieck (Begr.)/Lettmaier (Hrsg.), Ausländisches Familienrecht (Std.: 2021), Rn. 20.

11 *Dörner*, Erbrechtliche Qualifikation des § 1371 Abs. 1 BGB durch den EuGH: Konsequenzen und neue Fragen, in: ZEV (2018), S. 307; *Weber*, Ein Klassiker neu aufgelegt: Die Qualifikation des § 1371 BGB unter dem Regime der Europäischen Erbrechtsverordnung, in: NJW (2018), S. 1357 – wobei den Autoren bewusst ist, dass es solche Regelungen außerhalb Deutschlands wohl nicht, jedenfalls aber nur extrem selten geben dürfte.

12 Z. B. *Remien*, Aktuelles zur Europäischen Erbrechtsverordnung, in: Grziwotz/Limmer (Hrsg.), Erbrecht 2019: Perspektiven für die notarielle Gestaltungspraxis, 10. Verleihung des Helmut Schippel Preises (2019), S. 133; *Odersky*, in: Hausmann/Odersky (Hrsg.), Internationales Privatrecht in der Notar- und Gestaltungspraxis, 4. Aufl. (2021), § 15 Rn. 31.3; *Süß*, Die Entscheidung des EuGH in der Rechtssache Mahnkopf: Folgen für das gesetzliche Erbrecht des überlebenden Ehegatten in internationalen Ehen und neue Gestaltungsmöglichkeiten, in: DNotZ (2018), S. 752.

Wesenselement des § 1371 Abs. 1 BGB ist, dass im Erbfall das güterrechtliche Viertel nur zum Zuge kommt, wenn kein güterrechtlicher Ausgleich erfolgt.[13] Auch wenn die Eheleute sowohl im Scheidungsfall als auch im Erbfall auf güterrechtlicher Basis am gemeinsamen Vermögensaufbau partizipieren – wie bei einer Gütergemeinschaft oder Errungenschaftsgemeinschaft ausländischen Rechts – bzw. wenn es auch im Fall der Auflösung der Ehe durch Tod eines der Eheleute zu dem im Scheidungsfall vorgesehenen rechnerischen Geldausgleich kommt – wie z. B. bei der Errungenschaftsbeteiligung nach Schweizer oder türkischem Recht – scheidet eine Substitution aus, damit es zu keinem verdoppelten Ausgleich auf güter- und zugleich erbrechtlichem Wege kommt. In diesem Fall richten sich vielmehr wie bei der Gütergemeinschaft deutschen Rechts die Erbquoten nach § 1931 Abs. 1 BGB.[14]

In der Literatur für möglich gehalten wird eine Substitution allerdings in den Fällen, in denen das ausländische Recht einen güterrechtlichen Ausgleich für den Fall der Scheidung vorsieht, im Erbfall allerdings den überlebenden Ehegatten ausschließlich auf die ihm zugewiesene großzügige erbrechtliche Stellung verweist.[15]

Die Voraussetzungen für eine Substitution sind m. E. auch im japanischen Recht erfüllt. Zwar ergibt sich hier im Vergleich zum deutschen Recht ein erheblicher Unterschied daraus, dass die Berechnung des Zugewinnausgleichsanspruchs nicht so kleinteilig gesetzlich geregelt ist, dass er auf Yen und EURO genau nachprüfbar ausgerechnet werden kann. Vielmehr kommt im japanischen Recht der Bewertung der Umstände des Einzelfalls und dem richterlichen Ermessen eine erhebliche Bedeutung zu.[16] Im Übrigen entspricht das System aber weitestgehend dem deutschen Recht: Es erfolgt ein Ausgleich für den während der Dauer der Ehe erzielten Vermögenszuwachs, soweit dieser auf die Ehe zurückzuführen ist im Rahmen der Scheidung. Bei Beendigung der Ehe durch Tod aber wird der Ausgleich nicht durchgeführt.

---

13 *Odersky* (Anm. 12), § 15 Rn. 313.

14 OLG Frankfurt a. M. FamRZ 2021, 234 (zur Errungenschaftsgemeinschaft chinesischen Rechts); OLG Hamm MittBayNot 2019, 504 (zur Errungenschaftsbeteiligung türkischen Rechts); OLG Brandenburg ZEV 2023, 522 (zur Errungenschaftsgemeinschaft kubanischen Rechts); *Kleinschmidt*, EuGH: § 1371 Abs. 1 BGB ist erbrechtlich zu qualifizieren, Anmerkung zu EuGH, Urt. v. 01. 03. 2018 – C-558/16, in: ErbR (2018), S. 324, 328; *Schmidt*, Abschied von alten Gewissheiten: Die EU-Erbrechtsverordnung in der Rechtsprechung, in: ErbR (2020), S. 95.

15 So z. B. im österreichischen und im englischen Recht: *Sonnentag*, Die erbrechtliche Qualifikation des güterrechtlichen Viertels durch den EuGH und ihre Konsequenzen, in: JZ (2019), S. 664; *Süß*, in: Pfeiffer/Lobach/Rapp (Hrsg.), Europäisches Familien- und Erbrecht (2021), S. 151; *Dutta*, Pauschalierter Zugewinnausgleich nach § 1371 Abs. 1 BGB bei ausländischem Güterstatut? – Vom praktischen Nutzen der funktionalen Rechtsvergleichung, in: ErbR (2020), S. 305; *Schmidt*, in: Dutta/Weber (Hrsg.), Internationales Erbrecht, 2. Aufl. (2021), Art. 1 EuErbVO Rn. 48, verweist darauf, dass bei Ablehnen der Substitution eine „Anpassung" aufgrund Normenmangels durchgeführt werden müsse. In gleicher Weise müsste die Substitution für die separate-property-Systeme der zahlenmäßig meisten Einzelstaaten der USA, das neuseeländische Recht, das australische Recht und das Recht von Korea gelten. Gerichtliche Entscheidungen liegen für diesen Fall aber leider noch nicht vor.

16 Insoweit ergibt sich eine ähnliche Situation z. B. bei der Berechnung des marital property in den US-amerikanischen separate property states oder bei der Ermittlung der „ehelichen Ersparnisse" entsprechend den Regeln des österreichischen Ehegesetzes – wobei in beiden Staaten der gesetzliche Güterstand ebenfalls als „Gütertrennung" etikettiert wird.

Stattdessen wird der überlebende Ehegatte auf das Erbrecht verwiesen. Hier ergibt sich sogar im japanischen Recht eine mit dem deutschen Recht identische gesetzliche Erbquote – jedenfalls dann, wenn der überlebende Ehegatte mit den Abkömmlingen des Erblassers (ein Halb) oder aber mit den Geschwistern des Erblassers (drei Viertel) konkurriert. Zwar wird die hohe gesetzliche Quote nicht davon abhängig gemacht, dass die Eheleute in einem bestimmten Güterstand gelebt haben. Das ist m. E. aber unbeachtlich, denn in der japanischen Praxis kommt ein anderer als der gesetzliche Güterstand kaum vor. Daher sollte der gesetzliche Güterstand des japanischen Rechts der Zugewinngemeinschaft i. S. v. §§ 1931 Abs. 3, 1371 Abs. 1 BGB gleichgestellt und eine Substitution zugelassen werden. Dementsprechend wäre dem überlebenden Ehegatten eine gesetzliche Erbquote von ¾ zuzuerkennen und das verbleibende Viertel des Nachlasses auf die Erben zweiten Grades der Ehefrau zu verteilen.

Würde man die Substitution dagegen ablehnen, weil sich aus dem japanischen Güterrecht kein separates Viertel ergibt,[17] so wäre der Rechtsanwender mit dem Ergebnis konfrontiert, dass sich aus § 1931 Abs. 1 BGB für die Ehefrau eine gesetzliche Erbquote von einem Halb ergibt, sie aber bei Geltung deutschen Rechts sowohl für Erb- und Güterrecht bzw. allein japanischen Rechts sowohl für Erb- und Güterrecht jeweils drei Viertel erhielte. Erst die Kombination von deutschem Erb- und japanischem Güterrecht würde dann dazu führen, dass sich ihre Erbquote um ein Viertel auf ein Halb reduziert. Da dieses Ergebnis sowohl dem japanischen als auch dem deutschen System widerspräche, müsste im Rahmen eine „Angleichung" bzw. „Anpassung"[18] dieser Fall des „Normenmangels" dahingehend behoben werden, dass die überlebende Ehefrau entweder doch eine gesetzliche Erbquote von drei Viertel erhält oder aber – wie nach § 1371 Abs. 2 BGB – neben der nicht-erhöhten Erbquote den rechnerischen Ausgleich nach japanischem Scheidungsrecht geltend machen kann. Da aber hier eine Substitution in Frage kommt, ist m. E. die Lösung über die Anpassung als subsidiären Korrekturmodus auf letzter Ebene versperrt.

3. Beispielsfall 2: Japanisches Erbstatut und deutsches Güterrecht

Problematisch ist auch der umgekehrte Fall: Haben die Eheleute zunächst in Deutschland gelebt, wo der japanische Ehemann bei einer Firma in Düsseldorf gearbeitet und 1994 eine deutsche Staatsangehörige geheiratet hat, und ist er gestorben, nachdem er in den Ruhestand getreten und gemeinsam mit seiner deutschen Ehefrau und den drei Kindern nach Fukuoka zurückgekehrt ist, so ergibt sich aus deutscher Sicht für die Erbfolge aufgrund des letzten gewöhnlichen Aufenthalt eine Verweisung auf das japanische Recht (Art. 21 Abs. 1 EUErbVO. Dieses nimmt die Verweisung an, Art. 37 jRAG, da der Erblasser japanischer Staatsangehöriger war). Für die güterrechtlichen Folgen der Ehe dagegen kommt es aufgrund des Umstandes, dass die Eheleute bei Heirat keine gemeinsame Staatsangehörigkeit besaßen, aber beide ihren gewöhnlichen Aufenthalt in Deutschland hatten, aus deutscher Sicht gem.

---

17 So wohl nach der Ansicht von *Dörner* (Anm. 11), S. 307 und *Weber* (Anm. 11), S. 1357.

18 Dazu z. B. *von Bar/Mankowski*, Internationales Privatrecht Band 1: Allgemeiner Teil, 2. Aufl. (2003), § 7 Rn. 252; *Kegel/Schurig*, Internationales Privatrecht, 9. Aufl. (2004), § 8 III 2 (2), S. 364.

Art. 15 Abs. 1, Art. 14 Abs. 1 Ziff. 2 EGBGB a. F. und Art. 220 § 47 Abs. 2 Ziff. 2 EGBGB zur Geltung des deutschen Rechts.[19] Die Eheleute lebten daher in Zugewinngemeinschaft. Wegen der unwandelbaren Anknüpfung an die Verhältnisse bei Eheschließung ändert aus deutscher Sicht auch der gemeinsame Umzug der Eheleute nach Japan daran nichts.[20]

Aus dem japanischen Recht ergibt sich zugunsten der überlebenden Ehefrau eine gesetzliche Erbquote von ein Halb. Zwar käme wegen Geltung der Zugewinngemeinschaft deutschen Rechts auch ein „güterrechtliches Viertel" aus § 1371 Abs. 1 BGB in Betracht. Aufgrund der Rechtsprechung des EUGH in der Rechtssache Mahnkopf[21] ist diese Regelung aber erbrechtlich zu qualifizieren, so dass sie wegen der Geltung japanischen Rechts für die Erbfolge nicht berufen ist. Damit bleibt es bei der Geltung der sich aus dem japanischen ZGB ergebenden gesetzlichen Quote von ein Halb.

Allenfalls stellt sich nun noch die Frage, ob die Ehefrau, die auf diese Weise vom erbrechtlichen Zugewinnausgleich ausgeschlossen nicht stattdessen von der Erbengemeinschaft Zahlung des Zugewinnausgleichs gem. Art. 1371 Abs. 2 BGB nach den güterrechtlichen Regeln verlangen kann. Das wird von vielen Autoren für möglich gehalten, wenn der Zugewinnausgleich auf der erbrechtlichen Schiene aufgrund Geltung ausländischen Erbstatuts verschlossen bleibt.[22] Freilich wäre in der vorliegenden Konstellation zu beachten, dass das japanische Erbrecht ihr ohnehin schon eine Erbquote von ein Halb gewährt, also so viel, wie sie nach deutschem Recht im Rahmen der Erbfolge mit den Kindern erhalten würde, um neben der erbrechtlichen Beteiligung am Nachlass die Ansprüche aus der Beendigung der Zugewinngemeinschaft pauschal abzufinden. Bei einer Erbquote von ein Halb gehen vielmehr sowohl die japanische als auch die deutsche Rechtsordnung einvernehmlich davon aus, dass für Ansprüche aus Beendigung der Ehe (also sowohl bei Zugewinngemeinschaft als auch des gesetzlichen Güterstands nach japanischem Recht) kein Raum mehr ist. Damit scheidet m. E. im vorliegenden Fall die Geltendmachung des Zugewinnausgleichs auch nach den güterrechtlichen Regeln aus.

---

19 Anders wäre dies wohl aus japanischer Sicht zu beurteilen, da wegen der unterschiedlichen Staatsangehörigkeit der Eheleute und der Verlegung des gewöhnlichen Aufenthalts von Deutschland nach Japan ab dem Zeitpunkt der Aufenthaltsverlegung (wandelbare Anknüpfung) das japanische Recht Güterstatut wäre.

20 Anders wäre dies freilich aus japanischer Sicht zu beurteilen, weil Art. 26 Abs. 1 jRAG auf den jeweils aktuellen gewöhnlichen Aufenthalt der Eheleute abstellen würde, so dass mit Umzug nach Japan die Eheleute aus dem gesetzlichen Güterstand des deutschen in das japanische Recht gewechselt sind. Japanisches Recht wäre daher aus japanischer sich die erbrechtlichen wie auch die güterrechtlichen Beziehungen anzuwenden.

21 Dazu bereits oben Anm. 8.

22 Dazu *Süß* (Anm. 12), S. 751; *Hausmann/Odersky*, § 9 Rn. 206; *Dutta*, ErbR 2020, 304, 305; *Sonnentag*, JZ 2019, 657, 663; *J. P. Schmidt*, ErbR 2020, 91, 95; ablehnend *Weber* (Anm. 11), S. 1358.

IV. Gemeinschaftliche Testamente mit japanischen Beteiligten

Ein weiterer „klassischer Problemfall“ aus dem internationalen Erbrecht vor Inkrafttreten der EUErbVO war die Errichtung von gemeinschaftlichen Testamenten unter Beteiligung von ausländischen Eheleuten.

Man denke hier an einen in Marburg lebenden Deutschen, der sich in seine Japanisch-Lehrerin verliebt hat. Die japanische Dame ist verwitwet. Aus erster Ehe hat sie drei Kinder und erhebliches Vermögen geerbt. Nach der Heirat kommen die Eheleute zum Notar. Sie wollen sich im Rahmen eines Berliner Testaments gegenseitig zu Alleinerben und die Kinder der Ehefrau aus erster Ehe als Schlusserben einsetzen. Der Notar fragt sich, ob sich hier die japanische Staatsangehörigkeit der Ehefrau hier der gemeinschaftlichen Testamentserrichtung entgegensteht.

1. Rechtanwendung vor Inkrafttreten der EUErbVO

a) Ermittlung des Errichtungsstatuts

Gem. Art. 25 Abs. 1 EGBGB a.F. wurde bis zum 16. August 2015 das Erbstatut an die Staatsangehörigkeit des Erblassers angeknüpft. Damit war allein auf Seiten des deutschen Ehemannes das deutsche Erbrecht anwendbar. Für die Erbfolge nach der Ehefrau dagegen hätte das deutsche Recht auf das japanische Recht verwiesen.

Diese Verweisung wurde für die materielle Wirksamkeit einer Verfügung von Todes wegen in Art. 26 Abs. 5 S. 1 EGBGB a.F. modifiziert: Die Gültigkeit der Errichtung einer Verfügung von Todes wegen und die Bindung an sie wurden dem Recht unterstellt, das im Zeitpunkt der Verfügung auf die Rechtsnachfolge von Todes wegen anzuwenden wäre. Das so gebildete „Errichtungsstatut“ fror quasi die Anknüpfung der Wirksamkeit der Verfügung auf den Zeitpunkt der Errichtung der Verfügung ein. Ein Wechsel der Staatsangehörigkeit oder sonstiger für die Anknüpfung des Erbstatuts maßgeblicher Umstände nach Errichtung der Verfügung konnte sich somit nicht mehr auf die Wirksamkeit der Verfügung auswirken.

Auf diese Verweisung auf das japanische Recht war gem. Art. 4 Abs. 1 S. 1 EGBGB eine Rückverweisung durch das japanische Recht zu beachten. Allerdings unterstellt auch das japanische Recht die Erbfolge dem japanischen Heimatrecht der Ehefrau. Dieses nimmt (Art. 36 jRAG), die Verweisung also an. Art. 37 Abs. 1 jRAG bestimmt darüber hinaus:

Art. 37 jRAG[23]

(1) Die Errichtung und die Wirkungen eines Testaments unterliegen dem Heimatrecht des Errichtenden zum Zeitpunkt der Errichtung des Testaments.

(2) Der Widerruf eines Testaments unterliegt dem Heimatrecht des Errichtenden zum Zeitpunkt des Widerrufs.

---

23 Englische Übersetzung von *Anderson/Okuda*, Translation of Japan's Private International Law: Act on the General Rules of Application of Laws, in: ZJapanR, Bd. 12, Nr. 23 (2007), S. 227 ff.

Auch im japanischen Recht wird also das auf die materielle Wirksamkeit des Testaments anwendbare Recht auf das Heimatrecht zum Zeitpunkt der Errichtung eingefroren. In dieser Hinsicht kommt daher – etwa bei Wechsel der Staatsangehörigkeit durch die Ehefrau nach Testamentserrichtung – keine Rückverweisung auf das deutsche Recht in Betracht.

b) Ermittlung des Testamentsformstatuts

Für die Formwirksamkeit von Testamenten gilt sowohl für die Bundesrepublik Deutschland als auch für Japan das Haager Übereinkommen über das auf die Form letztwilliger Verfügungen anwendbare Recht vom 5. Oktober 1961. Das Haager Testamentsformübereinkommen erfasst auch gemeinschaftliche Testamente (Art. 4 des Übereinkommens). Das anwendbare Recht bestimmt sich gem. Art. 1 des Übereinkommens wie folgt:

Art. 1 [Gültigkeit der Verfügung]

(1) Eine letztwillige Verfügung ist hinsichtlich ihrer Form gültig, wenn diese dem innerstaatlichen Recht entspricht:
   a) des Ortes, an dem der Erblasser letztwillig verfügt hat, oder
   b) eines Staates, dessen Staatsangehörigkeit der Erblasser im Zeitpunkt, in dem er letztwillig verfügt hat, oder im Zeitpunkt seines Todes besessen hat, oder
   c) eines Ortes, an dem der Erblasser im Zeitpunkt, in dem er letztwillig verfügt hat, oder im Zeitpunkt seines Todes seinen Wohnsitz gehabt hat, oder
   d) des Ortes, an dem der Erblasser im Zeitpunkt, in dem er letztwillig verfügt hat, oder im Zeitpunkt seines Todes seinen gewöhnlichen Aufenthalt gehabt hat, oder
   e) soweit es sich um unbewegliches Vermögen handelt, des Ortes, an dem sich dieses befindet.

(2) Ist die Rechtsordnung, die auf Grund der Staatsangehörigkeit anzuwenden ist, nicht vereinheitlicht, so wird für den Bereich dieses Übereinkommens das anzuwendende Recht durch die innerhalb dieser Rechtsordnung geltenden Vorschriften, mangels solcher Vorschriften durch die engste Bindung bestimmt, die der Erblasser zu einer der Teilrechtsordnungen gehabt hat, aus denen sich die Rechtsordnung zusammensetzt.

(3) Die Frage, ob der Erblasser an einem bestimmten Ort einen Wohnsitz gehabt hat, wird durch das an diesem Orte geltende Recht geregelt.

Ein in Deutschland den Vorschriften des deutschen Rechts entsprechend notariell beurkundetes gemeinschaftliches Testament wäre mithin aus deutscher wie auch aus japanischer Sicht unabhängig von der unterschiedlichen Staatsangehörigkeit der Testatoren aufgrund Einhaltung der deutschen Ortsform (Art. 1 Abs. 1 lit. a Übereinkommen) formwirksam.

c) Erbeinsetzung nach japanischem Recht

Das japanische Recht kennt keine Einsetzung von Erben. Vielmehr kann die Testatorin ausschließlich in Form von Vermächtnissen Vermögen zuwenden. Insoweit folgt das japanische dem französischen Recht. Ähnlich wie im französischen Recht kann der Erblasser neben dem Einzelvermächtnis bzw. Stückvermächtnis aber auch ein Universalvermächtnis aussetzen (Art. 964 ZivilG), wonach der Vermächtnisnehmer im Wesentlichen eine dem gesetzlichen Erben vergleichbare Stellung erhält.[24] Darüber hinaus wäre im vorliegenden Fall der von der Testatorin zum Alleinerben eingesetzte Ehemann nach japanischem Recht ohnehin zum gesetzlichen Erben berufen, so dass das Testament lediglich seine Erbenstellung ausweiten und Erbenstellung der neben ihm berufenen Kinder der Testatorin ausschließen würden.

d) Zulässigkeit der gemeinschaftlichen Testamentserrichtung

Das japanische Recht kennt Verfügungen von Todes wegen ausschließlich in Form von einseitigen widerruflichen testamentarischen Verfügungen. Das gemeinschaftliche Testament ist dem japanischen Recht nicht bekannt. Art. 975 ZivilG bestimmt vielmehr ausdrücklich, dass ein Testament von mehr als einer Person in derselben Urkunde nicht errichtet werden kann.

Damit stellt sich die Frage, ob die Wirksamkeit der gemeinschaftlichen Testamentserrichtung eine Frage der Form der Verfügung oder aber eine Frage des Inhalts darstellt. Wird die Frage als Frage des Inhalts begriffen, so gilt aufgrund der Staatsangehörigkeit für die Wirksamkeit auf Seiten der Ehefrau das japanische Erbstatut, wonach die gemeinschaftliche Testamentserrichtung nicht zulässig und die Verfügung unwirksam ist. Bei Qualifikation als Formfrage hingegen könnte nach Art. 1 Abs. 1 lit. a Testamentsformübereinkommens auf die deutsche Ortsform zurückgegriffen werden, welche in § 2265 BGB Ehegatten die gemeinschaftliche Testamentserrichtung erlaubt. Diese Frage in der deutschen Literatur und Rechtsprechung bis zur Aufhebung von Art.25 EGBGB a.F. durch die EUErbVO nicht wirklich entschieden gelöst worden.

Prima facie stellt sich die Frage, ob mehrere Personen in einer einzigen Urkunde letztwillig verfügen können und welche besonderen Bedingungen hierbei einzuhalten sind, weniger als eine Frage des Inhalts der Verfügung dar als eine Frage der Art und Weise der Errichtung der Verfügung. Damit wäre sie als eine Frage der Form zu qualifizieren. Folge wäre, dass das gemeinschaftliche Testament trotz Geltung japanischen Errichtungsstatuts gem. § 2265 BGB aufgrund Einhaltung der deutschen Ortsform wirksam wäre. Diese Lösung entsprach z.B. der Auffassung in Frankreich, den Niederlanden, Ungarn und in Polen, wo gemeinschaftliche Testamente ebenfalls verboten waren.

In einigen anderen Ländern ist man dagegen der Ansicht, die strenge Einseitigkeit der letztwilligen Verfügung diene der freien Errichtung und dem freien Widerruf der Verfügung, so dass die Formerleichterungen nicht eingreifen können, sondern das Erbstatut entscheiden müsse (so z.B. die Rechtsprechung und Literatur in Italien und in Griechenland).

Die herrschende Meinung in Deutschland versuchte, diesen divergierenden Ansätzen simultan zu folgen und folgerte, dass die Qualifikation nicht einheitlich erfolgen könne, sondern dem jeweiligen Erbstatut zu entnehmen sei.[25] Das führte im Ergebnis

---

24 *Baum*, Japanische Testamente vor deutschen Nachlassgerichten, in: ZJapanR, Bd.19, Nr. 38 (2014), S. 201, 206.

25 *Dörner*, in: Staudinger (Begr.), Kommentar zum Bürgerlichen Gesetzbuch mit Einführungsgesetzen und Nebengesetzen (2007), Art. 25 EGBGB Rn. 323 m.z.w.N.

nicht nur dazu, dass das deutsche IPR die Qualifikation der Frage aus der Hand gab und das ausländische Recht entscheiden ließ („Qualifikation *lege causae*"). Da die Qualifikation dieser Frage im internationalen Privatrecht vieler Staaten nicht geklärt war bzw. aus deutscher Sicht keine Informationen ermittelt werden konnten (wie z. B. schon in Spanien, in der Schweiz, erst recht aber im Recht „exotischer Staaten" wie in Südamerika), führte dieser Lösungsansatz zu Haarspalterei und Spekulationen, im Ergebnis also zu rechtlichen Unsicherheiten.

Im japanischen Erbrecht würde für die Qualifikation als Frage der Form sprechen, dass Art. 975 ZivilG unter den Titel „Form des Testaments" eingeordnet worden ist. Nach einer Entscheidung des Obersten Gerichtshofs in Tokyo[26] sollen Testamente, die Eheleute jeweils nacheinander auf vier zusammenhängenden Seiten errichtet haben, wirksam sein, wenn jeder Ehegatte die Formalitäten für die Errichtung eingehalten hat. Hier lässt der OGH also die äußere Verbindung und die dadurch vermittelte innere Verknüpfung der beiden Verfügungen nicht schaden, wenn nur jeder Ehegatte die für die Einhaltung der gesetzlichen Formerfordernisse notwendigen Anforderungen eingehalten. Schließlich dürfte der Ursprung der Regel aus dem französischen *code civil* indizieren, dass man auch bei der internationalprivatrechtlichen Qualifikation den gleichen Weg beschreitet wie die französischen Gerichte.

Die neuere Literatur in Japan favorisiert allerdings offenbar eine materielle Qualifikation. Zwischen gemeinschaftlicher Errichtung von Testamenten und Erbvertrag wird nicht differenziert, sondern das Errichtungsstatut gem. Art. 37 jRAG angewandt.[27]

Folge war also, dass aufgrund der herrschenden Meinung in Deutschland trotz Geltung deutschen Testamentsformstatuts auf Seiten der japanischen Ehefrau aus dem Verbot gemeinschaftlicher Testamente im japanischen Errichtungsstatut die Unwirksamkeit der von der japanischen Ehefrau gemeinschaftlich errichteten Verfügungen drohte.

2. Bewertung nach Inkrafttreten der EUErbVO

a) Erbstatut

Gemeinschaftliche Testamente sind in der EuErbVO zwar definiert,[28] ihre Zulässigkeit aber nicht ausdrücklich geregelt. Daher ist es umstritten, ob die Vorschriften über Testamente (Art. 24 EuErbVO) gelten oder die Vorschriften über Erbverträge (Art. 25 EuErbVO).[29] Da sowohl Art. 24 Abs. 1 EuErbVO als auch Art. 25 Abs. 1

26 Saikō Saibansho Kagetsu 46-4-27, zitiert bei *Minamikata*, in: Pintens (Hrsg.), International Encyclopedia of Laws: Family and Succession (2022) Rn. 724.

27 Nachweise bei *Nishioka/Nishitani*, Japanese Private International Law (2021), S. 198.

28 Art. 3 Abs. 1 lit. c EUErbVO.

29 Nach BGH NJW 2021, 1159 soll das gemeinschaftliche Testament als „Erbvertrag" qualifiziert werden, wenn es wechselbezügliche Verfügungen nach deutschem Recht enthält. Ähnlich OLG München ZEV 2021, 33. Hiergegen spricht m. E., dass die Auslegung der Vorschriften europäischen Verordnungsrechts nicht unter Zugrundelegung von Regeln nationalen Rechts erfolgen kann, sondern nach autonomen Regeln erfolgen muss. Dafür hat sich auch bislang schon wiederholt der EUGH ausgesprochen (vgl. hier die Entscheidung des EUGH in der Rechtssache zum güterrechtlichen Viertel). Solange sich der BGH gegen eine

EuErbVO den gewöhnlichen Aufenthalt der Testierenden zum Zeitpunkt der Errichtung der Verfügung von Todes wegen für die Zulässigkeit und die materielle Wirksamkeit des „Erbvertrages" bzw. der „Verfügung von Todes wegen mit Ausnahme des Erbvertrags" für maßgeblich erklären, ergibt sich aber nach beiden Regeln übereinstimmend die Geltung des Errichtungsstatuts, so dass im Regelfall Art. 24 und Art. 25 EUErbVO zur selben Rechtsordnung führen. Dabei wird die Zulässigkeit der gemeinschaftlichen Testamentserrichtung wohl allgemein als Frage der „Zulässigkeit" qualifiziert und damit vom Formstatut ausgeklammert und dem Errichtungsstatut zugewiesen. Die Anknüpfung des Errichtungsstatuts an den gewöhnlichen Aufenthalt der Eheleute hat aber in der Praxis nunmehr zur Folge, dass zum einen auf Seiten beider Eheleute – soweit sie denn nur bei Errichtung im selben Staat ihren Lebensmittelpunkt haben – unabhängig von der Staatsangehörigkeit das gleiche Recht gilt. Zum anderen orientieren sich die Eheleute bei der Wahl der Testamentsform ohnehin zumeist an ihrem aktuellen rechtlichen Umfeld, so dass die gemeinschaftliche Errichtung bei in Deutschland lebenden Eheleuten eher wahrscheinlich sein dürfte als bei in Japan lebenden Eheleuten. Damit dürfte trotz des Ausschlusses des Formstatuts für die Zulässigkeit der gemeinschaftlichen Errichtung die durch die EUErbVO geschaffene rechtliche Situation *de facto* die Wirksamkeit gemeinschaftlicher Testamente von deutsch-japanischen Eheleuten begünstigen.

3. Japanische Perspektive

Hat der Ehemann die japanische Staatsangehörigkeit, so gilt aus japanischer Sicht gem. Art. 37 Abs. 1 jRAG das japanische Recht für die von ihm getroffenen Verfügungen von Todes wegen als Errichtungsstatut. Japan hat das HTestFormÜ ratifiziert und im japanischen Gesetz über das Formstatut der Testamente wortgetreu in das nationale Recht transformiert.[30] Demnach ist auch aus japanischer Sicht die Einhaltung der deutschen Formvorschriften ausreichend. Dementsprechend wäre aus japanischer Sicht die gemeinschaftlich mit ihrem deutschen Ehemann der japanischen Ehefrau getroffene Verfügung nur dann wirksam, wenn aus Sicht der japanischen Gerichte die Zulässigkeiten der gemeinschaftlichen Testamentserrichtung als Frage der Form qualifiziert wird. Bei Qualifikation als materielle Wirksamkeitsvoraussetzung dagegen wäre die Verfügung unwirksam.

V. Schluss

Die EUErbVO bringt für die Behandlung deutsch-japanischer Erbfälle durch die deutschen Gerichte eine erhebliche Vereinfachung. Das Zusammentreffen deutschen Erb- mit japanischem Güterrecht und umgekehrt bei der Bemessung des gesetzlichen Erbquote des überlebenden Ehegatten ist aufgrund der Mahnkopf-Entscheidung des EUGH endlich geklärt und führt zu sachgerechten Ergebnissen. Insbesondere gehören die Unsicherheiten und Probleme aufgrund der güterrechtlichen Qualifikation

---

Vorlage der Frage zum EUGH sperrt, muss allerdings dieses Ergebnis vorläufig im inländischen Rechtsverkehr als Faktum hingenommen werden.

[30] Gesetz Nr. 100 aus dem Jahr 1964.

des BGH, die regelmäßig Anpassungsprobleme bescherte, nun der Vergangenheit an. Gemeinschaftliche Testamente, die in Deutschland lebende Ehegatten errichtet haben, können regelmäßig unabhängig davon als wirksam beurteilt werden, ob der verstorbene Ehegatte die japanische oder die deutsche Staatsangehörigkeit besaß.

Vermehrte Aufmerksamkeit ist bei der Nachlassplanung aber nun angebracht, wenn Vermögen in Japan belegen ist oder gar zu erwarten ist, dass der Erblasser vor seinem Tod nach Japan übersiedelt. Da die EUErbVO den mit Japan bislang bestehenden Gleichklang aufgrund der Anknüpfung an die Staatsangehörigkeit aufgegeben hat, muss sich der Gestalter nunmehr auch mit der japanischen Perspektive und der abweichenden Ermittlung des anwendbaren Rechts auseinandersetzen.

Literaturverzeichnis

Bar, Christian von/*Mankowski*, Peter: Internationales Privatrecht, Bd. 1: Allgemeiner Teil, 2. Aufl. (2003).

Baum, Harald: Japanische Testamente vor deutschen Nachlassgerichten, in: ZJapanR, Bd. 19, Nr. 38 (2014), S. 201–208.

Bonomi, Andrea/*Wautelet*, Patrick (Hrsg.), Le droit européen des successions internationales, 2. Aufl. (2016).

Burandt, Wolfgang/*Rojahn*, Dieter (Hrsg.): Erbrecht, Kommentar, 4. Aufl. (2022).

Dutta, Anatol: Pauschalierter Zugewinnausgleich nach § 1371 Abs. 1 BGB bei ausländischem Güterstatut? – Vom praktischen Nutzen der funktionalen Rechtsvergleichung, in: ErbR (2020), S. 304–305.

Dutta, Anatol/*Weber*, Johannes (Hrsg.): Internationales Erbrecht, Kommentar, 2. Aufl. (2021).

Dörner, Heinrich: Erbrechtliche Qualifikation des § 1371 Abs. 1 BGB durch den EuGH: Konsequenzen und neue Fragen, in: ZEV (2018), S. 305–310.

Hausmann, Rainer/*Odersky*, Felix (Hrsg.): Internationales Privatrecht in der Notar- und Gestaltungspraxis, Handbuch, 4. Aufl. (2021).

Kegel, Gerhard/*Schurig*, Klaus: Internationales Privatrecht, 9. Aufl. (2004).

Kleinschmidt, Jens: EuGH: § 1371 Abs. 1 BGB ist erbrechtlich zu qualifizieren, Anmerkung zu EuGH, Urt. v. 01.03.2018 – C-558/16, in: ErbR (2018), S. 324–330.

Minamikata, Satoshi: Japan, in: Pintens, Walter (Hrsg.), International Encyclopedia of Laws: Family and Succession (2022).

Nagata-Vogelsang, Yohei: Länderbericht Japan, in: Rieck, Jürgen (Begr.)/Lettmaier, Saskia (Hrsg.), Ausländisches Familienrecht (Std.: 2021).

Nishioka, Kazuaki/*Nishitani*, Yuko: Japanese Private International Law (2021).

Süß, Rembert, Probleme der Europäischen Erbrechtsverordnung aus Sicht der notariellen Praxis, in: Pfeiffer, Thomas/Lobach, Quincy C./Rapp, Tobias: Europäisches Familien- und Erbrecht (2020), S. 165–188.

Remien, Oliver: Aktuelles zur Europäischen Erbrechtsverordnung, in: Grziwotz, Herbert/Limmer, Peter (Hrsg.), Erbrecht 2019: Perspektiven für die notarielle Gestaltungspraxis, 10. Verleihung des Helmut Schippel Preises (2019), S. 121–136.

Schmidt, Jan Peter: Abschied von alten Gewissheiten: Die EU-Erbrechtsverordnung in der Rechtsprechung, in: ErbR (2020), S. 91–98.

Solomon, Dennis: Die Renaissance des Renvoi im Europäischen Internationalen Privatrecht, in: Liber Amicorum, Klaus Schurig: zum 70. Geburtstag (2012), S. 253–264.

Sonnentag, Michael: Die erbrechtliche Qualifikation des güterrechtlichen Viertels durch den EuGH und ihre Konsequenzen, in: JZ (2019), S. 657–666.

Staudinger, Julius von (Begr.): Kommentar zum Bürgerlichen Gesetzbuch mit Einführungsgesetzen und Nebengesetzen (online Stand 15.07.2025).

Süß, Rembert: Die Entscheidung des EuGH in der Rechtssache Mahnkopf: Folgen für das gesetzliche Erbrecht des überlebenden Ehegatten in internationalen Ehen und neue Gestaltungsmöglichkeiten, in: DNotZ (2018), S. 742–757.

Weber, Johannes: Ein Klassiker neu aufgelegt: Die Qualifikation des § 1371 BGB unter dem Regime der Europäischen Erbrechtsverordnung, in: NJW (2018), S. 1356–1358.

Ad Calendas Graecas?

Zur Frage einer Reform der Japanischen Verfassung

Von *Dan Tidten*[1]

Dr. Dan Tidten studierte Rechtswissenschaften in München und Kyoto und wurde nach Forschungsaufenthalten an der Universität Tokyo und am Deutschen Institut für Japanstudien, Tokyo, an der Universität Regensburg mit einer Arbeit zu gleichheitsorientierten Politiken in Japan promoviert. Anschließend nahm er seine derzeitige Tätigkeit als Diplomat beim Auswärtigen Amt auf.

Im März 2025 wurde im Bundestag und im Bundesrat die in kurzer Zeit auf den Weg gebrachte 69. Änderung des Grundgesetzes beschlossen, um als Ausnahme zur sogenannten Schuldenbremse Sondervermögen für Verteidigungsausgaben und Infrastrukturmaßnahmen zu ermöglichen. Das Grundgesetz wurde damit seit Inkrafttreten am 23. Mai 1949 durchschnittlich alle 1,1 Jahre geändert, also beinahe jährlich. Verfassungsänderungen in Deutschland sind damit in etwa so selten bzw. häufig wie das jährliche Aufziehen der Winterreifen.

Im Falle Japans hingegen kann man jetzt schon sagen, dass es, falls es überhaupt in mittlerer Zukunft irgendwann einmal zu einer Reform der Verfassung kommen sollte, diese einem Jahrhundertereignis gleichkäme: Die japanische Verfassung (JV)[2] wird im Erscheinungsjahr dieses Beitrags 78 Jahre alt – für eine kein einziges Mal reformierte Verfassung ein bemerkenswertes Alter.

Dieser Beitrag soll weniger die bisherige Entwicklung der nun seit knapp achtzig Jahren im Raume stehenden Frage umfassend darstellen, ob und in welchen Bereichen die japanische Verfassung reformiert werden kann oder soll, sondern vielmehr einen Überblick über die derzeit relevanten zentralen Fragestellungen in diesem Kontext geben – und so hoffentlich auch Anregungen für künftiges wissenschaftliches Arbeiten zum Bereich des japanischen Verfassungsrechts bieten.

---

1 Besonderer Dank gilt Professor Abe Kazufumi von der Universität Sophia, sowie David Malitz vom Deutschen Institut für Japanstudien, ohne deren wertvolle Hilfe und Hinweise dieser Beitrag nicht möglich gewesen wäre. Danken möchte ich auch den Professores Mōri Tōru (Universität Kyoto), Saitō Megumi (Universität Chiba) und Kinoshita Masahiko (Universität Kōbe) für die freundliche Durchsicht des Manuskripts und wertvolle Hinweise. Die Verantwortung für eventuelle Fehler in dieser Arbeit liegt selbstverständlich allein beim Autor. Diese Arbeit ist ein persönlicher wissenschaftlicher Beitrag des Autors, er repräsentiert in keiner Weise die Sichtweise der Institution, der er angehört. Übersetzungen aus dem Japanischen, soweit nicht anders angegeben, stammen vom Autor selbst.

2 Japanische Verfassung (日本国憲法, *nihonkoku kempō*, abgekürzt JV), keine Gesetznummer, 1946 beschlossen, am 3. Mai 1947 in Kraft getreten.

Duncker & Humblot · Berlin | https://doi.org/10.3790/978-3-428-59611-9.2025.418787

Dazu soll zunächst beleuchtet werden, (I.) aus welchen Gründen es bislang zu keiner Verfassungsreform kam, (II.) ob, von wem und zu welchen Regelungsbereichen eine Verfassungsreform in jüngerer Vergangenheit diskutiert und angestrebt wird, und (III.) eine zusammenfassende Einschätzung versucht werden, welche strukturellen Besonderheiten sich aus der über lange Zeit unveränderten Verfassung ergeben und wie wahrscheinlich eine Verfassungsreform in naher Zukunft ist.

I. Warum nicht?

Zu fragen, warum die japanische Verfassung bislang „noch" nie reformiert wurde, ist aus deutscher Perspektive naheliegend. Die Frage, warum „noch" nie, impliziert die Überzeugung, dass eine Verfassung früher oder später zu reformieren ist, dass die Gesetze sich naturgemäß „sacht von Ort zu Ort" bewegen[3] und eben nicht „kein Jota und kein Häkchen vergehen"[4] bis zum Ende der Welt.

Die Überzeugung, dass auch Verfassungen beständig an aktuelle Entwicklungen anzupassen und in unregelmäßigen Abständen zu reformieren sind, scheint weltweit eher die Regel zu sein: Von den großen und etablierten Rechtsstaaten der Gegenwart kann keiner eine ebenso lange unverändert gebliebene Verfassung vorweisen wie Japan.[5]

Die Liberaldemokratische Partei Japans (自由民主党, *jiyū minshu-tō*, kurz: LDP), die in der Nachkriegszeit bis auf wenige Ausnahmen die japanische Regierung stellte, nennt in ihren Materialien zu den Plänen einer Verfassungsreform den Gedanken der Anpassung einer Verfassung an veränderte Zeitumstände, sozialen und kulturellen Wandel als ausschlaggebend: Auch für eine Verfassung seien „Updates"[6] erforderlich.

1. Rechtliche Voraussetzungen

Die japanische Verfassung ist theoretisch reformierbar, die Modalitäten sind in Art. 96 JV geregelt: Eine Änderung müsste in beiden Kammern des Parlaments jeweils mit Zweidrittelmehrheit beschlossen und anschließend in einer landesweiten Volksbefragung bestätigt werden. Inzwischen sind die gesetzlichen Rahmenbedingungen für eine solche Volksabstimmung auch in Kraft, das sog. Volksabstimmungs-

---

3 *Goethe*, Faust. Der Tragödie erste Teil (1808), V 1975.

4 Mt 5, 18.

5 Vergleichende Daten zur sog. Verfassungslebensdauer, i.e. des Zeitraumes, während dessen eine Verfassung unverändert blieb, vgl. *McElwain*, 日本国憲法の普遍と特異：その軌跡と定量的考察 (*nihonkoku kempō no fuhen to tokui – sono kiseki to teiryōteki kōsatsu*, The Universality and Originality of the Japanese Constitution in Quantitative Perspective) (2022), S. 54.

6 *Liberaldemokratische Partei Japans* (自由民主党), 日本国憲法の改正実現にむけて (*nihonkoku kempō no kaisei jitsugen ni mukete*, Hin zu einer Verwirklichung einer Reform der Japanischen Verfassung) (23. Mai 2022), online abrufbar unter https://www.jimin.jp/constitution/document/, zuletzt abgerufen am 25. März 2025, S. 1.

gesetz[7] wurde 2007 beschlossen und zuletzt im Juni 2021 mit Bestimmungen zur vereinfachten Stimmabgabe reformiert.

Wenngleich die japanische Verfassung keine Regelung über unveränderbare Grundsätze der Verfassung – also eine Entsprechung zur Ewigkeitsklausel des Art. 79 III GG – enthält, so besteht doch in Japan Einigkeit, dass eine den grundlegenden Wesenskern der Verfassung antastende Verfassungsänderung wohl unzulässig wäre.[8] Innerhalb dieser Rahmenbedingungen wäre die Verfassung eigentlich relativ rasch reformierbar. Warum passierte das nie?

2. *Il faut qu'une constitution soit courte et obscure*[9]

Erstens scheint der geringere Reformbedarf in der Verfassung damit zusammenzuhängen, dass die japanische Verfassung verhältnismäßig kurz ist. Mit ca. 5.000 Wörtern in 103 Artikeln ist die japanische Verfassung deutlich kürzer als das Grundgesetz (ca. 25.000 Wörter), die französische (ca. 9.000 Wörter) oder die amerikanische Verfassung (ca. 7.500 Wörter, wenn man die 27 Amendments dazuzählt). Angesichts unterschiedlicher sprachlicher Gepflogenheiten und damit einhergehender Schwierigkeiten bei der Zählung der Wörter (ein Verb mit langer Endung in einer agglutinierenden Sprache wie dem Japanischen kann auf Englisch oder Deutsch rasch einen ganzen Nebensatz umfassen) sollte man das Augenmerk freilich nicht zu sehr auf die bloße Zahl der Wörter legen.

Von den 103 Artikeln der japanischen Verfassung entfallen bereits acht auf den Kaiser und seine Rolle, gefolgt von Art. 9, dem sog. Friedensartikel. Der Grundrechtsteil umfasst mit seinen relativ ausführlichen 31 Artikeln beinahe ein Drittel der gesamten Verfassung. Für das Staatsorganisationsrecht und alle übrigen Vorschriften verbleiben somit lediglich 63 Artikel. Zum Vergleich: Das Grundgesetz hat inzwischen mit allen zusätzlich eingefügten Artikeln insgesamt knapp 200 Artikel, wovon auf den für Verfassungsänderungen weniger einschlägigen Grundrechtsteil[10] nur etwa ein Zehntel der Artikel entfallen.

---

7 日本国憲法の改正手続きに関する法律 (*nihonkoku kempō no kaisei tetsuzuki ni kansuru hōritsu*, Gesetz bezüglich des Verfahrens einer Reform der Japanischen Verfassung), Gesetz Nr. 51 aus dem 2007, Inkrafttreten am 18. Mai 2010.

8 Zur Frage, welche Änderungen so weitgehend wären, dass sie unzulässig wären: Unter Bezugnahme auf Art. 79 III GG *Mōri/Koizumi/Asano/Matsumoto*, 憲法I・総論・統治 (*kempō I・sōron・tōji*, Verfassung I. Allgemeiner Teil, Regierung), 3. Auflage (2022), S. 33; ferner *Komamura* in Okudaira/Aikyō/Aoi (Hrsg.), 改憲の何が問題か (*kaiken no nani ga mondai ka*, Was das Problem bei der Verfassungsänderung ist) (2013), S. 31 ff.; *Hasebe*, 憲法 (*kempō*, Verfassung), 8. Auflage (2022), S. 34 ff.

9 Napoleon Bonaparte zugeschrieben.

10 Von den (Stand März 2025) bisher 69 Grundgesetzänderungen betrafen lediglich sieben den Grundrechtsteil: 7. GG-Änderung vom 19. März 1956 (BGBl. I S. 111); 17. GG-Änderung vom 24. Juni 1968 (BGBl. I S. 709); 39. GG-Änderung vom 8. Juni 1993 (BGBl. I S. 1002); 42. GG-Änderung vom 27. Oktober 1994 (BGBl. I S. 3146); 45. GG-Änderung 26. März 1998 (BGBl. I S. 610); 47. GG-Änderung 29. November 2000 (BGBl. I S. 1633); 48. GG-Änderung vom 19. Dezember 2000 (BGBl. I S. 1755).

McElwain legt in umfassenden Vergleichen dar, weswegen die japanische Verfassung strukturell bereits seltener Anlass für Reformdiskussionen bietet: Erstens führe die beschriebene Kürze und das damit einhergehende hohe Abstraktionsniveau der Verfassung dazu, dass selten konkrete Normen als reformbedürftig auffielen.[11] Zweitens seien viele Regularien, die sich in Verfassungen anderer Länder fänden, deswegen in Japan einfachgesetzlich geregelt.[12] Auch Inoue charakterisiert die japanische Verfassung als „kleine Verfassung", die vergleichsweise wenig im Detail regelt und verhältnismäßig viel dem einfachgesetzlichen Gesetzgeber überlässt.[13] Drittens sei v. a. der Grundrechtsteil der japanischen Verfassung in seiner Ausführlichkeit seiner Zeit voraus gewesen und habe bereits Inhalte normiert, die in vielen anderen Ländern erst später durch Verfassungsänderungen hinzugefügt wurden.[14]

Aus deutscher Sicht ließe sich noch ein vierter Punkt ergänzen: Föderale Strukturen führen wohl regelmäßig zu relativ detaillierten Vorschriften über das Verhältnis des Bundes zu den Ländern. Auch hier liegt die Vermutung nahe, dass detaillierte Regeln auch zu erhöhtem Reformbedarf führen, weil die Vorschriften nicht *courte et obscure*, sondern konkret und präzise ausformuliert sein müssen. Umgekehrt bedeutet das für einen Zentralstaat wie Japan entsprechend auch in dieser Hinsicht weniger Reformbedarf.

3. Mit Zweifeln leben

Die japanische Rechtsordnung kennt kein Verfassungsgericht. Die Verfassungsmäßigkeit von Verwaltungshandeln wie auch von Gesetzen kann zwar gerichtlich überprüft werden. Dies geschieht jedoch im Rahmen der ordentlichen Gerichtsbarkeit inzident – also in Verfahren der ordentlichen Gerichtsbarkeit, in denen die Frage der Verfassungsmäßigkeit eines formellen oder materiellen Gesetzes als eine Teilfrage zu klären ist. Eine Entsprechung zur deutschen Verfassungsbeschwerde oder zur abstrakten Normenkontrolle, deren Hauptfragestellung die Verfassungsmäßigkeit eines konkreten Verwaltungshandelns bzw. eines konkreten Gesetzes ist, existiert nicht.

Dies führt dazu, dass die Frage der Verfassungsmäßigkeit eines Gesetzes oder sonst einer rechtlichen oder tatsächlichen Praxis deutlich seltener Gegenstand eines Gerichtsverfahrens wird. Ein aus deutscher Sicht erstaunliches Beispiel dafür sind die Selbstverteidigungsstreitkräfte (engl. Self-Defence Forces, SDF) Japans. Das Gesetz über die Selbstverteidigungsstreitkräfte[15] wurde in seiner Gesamtheit – mangels abstraktem Normenkontrollverfahren in Japan – nie auf Verfassungskonformität überprüft.

---

11 *McElwain* (Anm. 5), S. 55 ff.

12 *McElwain* (Anm. 5), S. 63 ff.

13 *Inoue*, 立憲主義とテクスト—日本国憲法の場合 (*rikkenshugi to tekusuto – nihonkoku kempo no baai*, Konstitutionalismus und Text – Der Fall der japanischen Verfassung), 論究ジュリスト Bd. 20 (2017), S. 114 f.

14 *McElwain* (Anm. 5), S. 79 ff.

15 自衛隊法 (*jieitai-hō*), Gesetz Nr. 165 aus dem Jahre 1954.

Die Frage der Vereinbarkeit von Streitkräften mit Art. 9 JV stellte sich aber bereits in der Vergangenheit. Als Japan – noch vor der eigentlichen Gründung der SDF – auf Anordnung des *Supreme Commander for the Allied Powers* mit dem Aufbau einer Nationalen Polizeireserve begann, gegliedert in Land-, Luft- und Seestreitkräfte, erhob ein Bürger Klage dagegen mit der Begründung, dies sei ein Verstoß gegen Art. 9 Verf. Der Oberste Gerichtshof (OGH) lehnte die Klage ohne materiellrechtliche Prüfung ab mit dem Hinweis, er könne lediglich einen konkreten Streitfall prüfen, keine abstrakte Frage zur Verfassungsmäßigkeit.[16]

Für große Aufmerksamkeit sorgte auch der sog. Sunagawa-Fall aus dem Jahre 1959: Der OGH hob hierin das erstinstanzliche Urteil des Distriktgerichts (DG) Tokyo auf, in dem dieses in der Stationierung US-amerikanischer Truppen in Japan einen Verstoß gegen Art. 9 JV sah – äußerte sich aber darin nur insofern zur Streitfrage der Stationierung von US-Truppen in Japan, dass diese zumindest nicht ganz offensichtlich verfassungswidrig sei, und zu den SDF als solche gar nicht.[17]

Drittens zu nennen ist der sog. „Naganuma-Nike"-Fall, in dem das DG Sapporo im Jahre 1973 zunächst urteilte, die Existenz der SDF in dieser Form verstoße gegen Art. 9 JV.[18] Letztlich bestätigte der OGH zehn Jahre später die Aufhebung des Urteils am 5. August 1976 durch das Obergericht (OG) Sapporo[19] – allerdings ohne sich zur Frage der Verfassungsmäßigkeit zu äußern.[20]

Im Ergebnis ist also eine für den japanischen Staat so zentrale Frage wie die Vereinbarkeit seiner Streitkräfte mit der Verfassung auch nach Jahrzehnten nicht durch höchstrichterliche Entscheidung, sondern lediglich durch nunmehr siebzigjährige Praxis und eine daraus resultierende gefühlte Rechtmäßigkeit geklärt.

Deutschland wäre reich an Gegenbeispielen. Der auch vielen juristischen Laien geläufigen Neuschaffung des Art. 16a GG im Juni 1993 etwa lag der sog. Asylkompromiss vom 6. Dezember 1992 zugrunde: Die Koalition aus CDU/CSU und FDP hatte in einem mit der Oppositionspartei SPD ausgehandelten Kompromiss zur Änderung des Asylverfahrensgesetzes auch eine Änderung des Grundgesetzes beschlossen. Damit wurde die neue Rechtslage bundesverfassungsgerichtsfest gemacht (was dann auch vom Bundesverfassungsgericht in drei Entscheidungen bestätigt wurde)[21].

Die im Vergleich zu Deutschland deutlich eingeschränkteren Möglichkeiten verfassungsrechtlicher Normenkontrollen führen also, wenn man es positiv formulieren möchte, zwangsläufig zu einer gewissen Fähigkeit, mit verfassungsrechtlichen Zweifeln einfach zu leben, ohne sie gerichtlich zu klären. Das verfassungsrechtliche Problem ist aus judikativer Sicht oft *non in actis, non in mundo.* Die in Japan deutlich zurückhaltender gestaltete Regelung gerichtlicher Normenkontrollverfahren verringert also das Erfordernis für Verfassungsreformen weiter, weil der einfachgesetzliche Gesetzgeber im Vergleich zu Deutschland sich deutlich weniger Sorgen um eine

16 OGH Minshū 6, 783.

17 OGH Keishū 13, 3225.

18 DG Sapporo Hanji 713, 24.

19 OG Sapporo Gyōsaireishū 27, 8, 1175.

20 OGH Minshū 36, 1679.

21 BVerfGE 94, 49; 94, 115; 94, 166.

mögliche gerichtliche Verfassungsmäßigkeitsprüfung neugeschaffener Gesetze machen muss.

4. Politisch umstritten

Das in Japan oft zu hörende Argument lautet schließlich: Die Frage, *ob* eine Reform der Verfassung erstrebenswert ist, ist politisch sehr umstritten und parteipolitisch aufgeladen. Dies ist ein weiterer deutlicher zu Unterschied zu Deutschland. Zwar würden in Deutschland politische Akteure je nach politischer Lage sicherlich heiß über die Frage diskutieren, welche Art von Verfassungsänderung erforderlich oder angemessen ist, i. e. *wie* eine Verfassungsänderung sein sollte. Die schlichte abstrakte Aussage hingegen, *dass* die Verfassung reformiert werden sollte, könnte jedoch keinem politischen Lager zugeordnet werden.

In Japan aber ist klar, dass die Reform der Verfassung politisch vom Spektrum Mitte-rechts gewollt ist (zu den Vertretern der These, die jetzige Verfassung sei überhaupt ungültig, da unter dem Einfluss der Besatzungsmacht erstellt, weiter unten). Wer sich in Japan für eine Verfassungsreform ausspricht, wird als politisch konservativ wahrgenommen, und zwar auch ohne dass er sich zur Art der angestrebten Verfassungsänderung überhaupt geäußert hätte. Die eher links orientierten Parteien sehen eine Verfassungsreform hingegen skeptisch; die derzeit (März 2025) größte Oppositionspartei 立憲民主党 (*rikken minshu-tō*, Konstitutionell-Demokratische Partei, im Deutschen oft als KDP abgekürzt) lehnte eine Verfassungsreform, insbesondere eine Neufassung von Art. 9 JV, bei ihrer Gründung im Jahr 2017 ab[22] (zur gegenwärtigen Position weiter unten).

Die KDP trägt den Namen „konstitutionell-demokratisch". Konstitutionalismus beschreibt ein politisches System, in dem die Rechte und Pflichten der Staatsgewalt wie auch der Bürger in einer Verfassung festgelegt werden. Gegenmodelle, die nicht dem Prinzip des Konstitutionalismus entsprechen, wären insbesondere eine absolute Monarchie, aber auch theokratische oder Räterepubliken ohne Verfassung und mit einer unumschränkten Gewalt der jeweiligen Herrscher über Institutionen und Bevölkerung. Aus dem Prinzip des Konstitutionalismus folgt, dass bestimmte allgemeine Prinzipien, die unabhängig von Religion oder individueller Weltanschauung sind, als Minimalkonsens besonders zu schützen sind und als solche besonders zu schützende Prinzipien in der Verfassung verankert und somit regelmäßig deutlich schwerer zu ändern sind als einfachgesetzliche Bestimmungen. In Deutschland ist der Konstitutionalismus inzwischen als Fachbegriff in der aktuellen politischen und verfassungsrechtlichen Diskussion selten geworden, da er seit seinem vollständigen Siegeszug im neunzehnten Jahrhundert schlicht eine Selbstverständlichkeit des deutschen politischen Denkens bedeutet. In Japan ist der Begriff *rikken shugi*[23] in Wissenschaft und Politik wohl (wiewohl in der Sache ebenso unumstritten wie in Deutschland) etwas präsenter.[24]

---

22 *Hoover* (Hrsg.), Historical Dictionary of Postwar Japan (2018), S. 61.

23 立憲主義 (*rikken shugi*, Konstitutionalismus).

24 *Hasebe*, 憲法と平和をといなおす (*kempō to heiwa wo toinaosu*, Überdenken der Verfassung und des Friedens) (2004), S. 11 ff.; *ders.* zusammenfassend dazu auch in der

Der Konstitutionalismus ist so betrachtet sicherlich kein Alleinstellungsmerkmal einer konkreten Partei. Gleichwohl schwingt in dem seit 2017 bestehenden Parteinamen der KDP die Betonung der besonderen Achtung der Verfassung mit (und damit implizit auch die Unterstellung, die anderen – v. a. die konservative LDP – respektiere die Grundsätze der Verfassung wohl nicht ganz so sehr wie die KDP). Der Parteiname kann insofern auch als Statement zur Frage der Verfassungsreform gelesen werden.

Die zwar kleine, aber strukturell stabil aufgestellte Japanische Kommunistische Partei[25] ist ebenfalls eine lautstarke Stimme gegen eine Verfassungsreform:[26] Die Verfassung in ihrer Gesamtheit will sie mit aller Kraft bewahren.[27] Aus deutscher Sicht wirkt dies *prima facie* unfreiwillig komisch: Von einer gestandenen kommunistischen Partei würde man als unbedarfter Beobachter statt der Bewahrung vielmehr den „gewaltsamen Umsturz aller bisherigen Gesellschaftsordnung“[28] erwarten, auf dass „die herrschenden Klassen vor einer Kommunistischen Revolution zittern“[29]. Ins oben beschriebene Bild fügt sich diese Position gleichwohl gut: Die japanischen Konservativen – vor allem die LDP – wollen eine Verfassungsreform und machen dazu konkrete Textvorschläge; die politisch eher links verorteten Kräfte stehen einer Verfassungsreform als solcher skeptisch gegenüber.

Für die Debatte um eine mögliche Verfassungsreform hat dies zur Folge, dass politisch linke Kräfte sich zwar an den Reformvorschlägen der Konservativen abarbeiten und diese mit zahlreichen und teilweise sehr klugen Argumenten kritisieren (dazu weiter unten), aber keine eigenen Vorschläge machen. Für den Bereich des Art. 9 JV beispielsweise könnten politische Kräfte, die entweder gegen das umstrittene Konzept der kollektiven Selbstverteidigung sind (auch dazu weiter unten) oder sogar die SDF als solche explizit ablehnen, ja durchaus auch eigene Reformvorschläge machen, die im Gegensatz zur gegenwärtigen relativ abstrakten Formulierung in Art. 9 JV diese Inhalte verfassungsrechtlich unmissverständlich festschreiben. Ob Vorschläge in der Richtung mehrheitsfähig wären, müsste dann politisch diskutiert werden – aber in jedem Fall wären solche konkreten Textvorschläge ein wertvoller Debattenbeitrag. Bislang bleibt der Reflex der politisch links orientierten Kräfte aber die Ablehnung der Verfassungsreform als solcher.

Anhörung vor dem japanischen Unterhaus am 4. Juni 2015, Protokoll der Sitzung online abrufbar auf der Website des japanischen Unterhauses unter https://www.shugiin.go.jp/internet/itdb_kaigirokua.nsf/html/kaigirokua/025018920150604003.htm, zuletzt abgerufen am 25. März 2025.

25 日本共産党 (*nihon kyōsan-tō*, Japanische Kommunistische Partei).

26 Zusammenfassende Argumentationspunkte in der parteinahen Zeitung „Die Rote Fahne“ 赤旗 *akahata*, online abrufbar unter https://www.jcp.or.jp/akahata/aik21/2022-01-06/2022010605_01_0.html, zuletzt abgerufen am 25. März 2025.

27 „現行憲法の前文をふくむ全条項をまもり、とくに平和的民主的諸条項の完全実施をめざす“, Abschnitt 4 des Parteiprogramms *Manifesto* der Kommunistischen Partei, online abrufbar unter https://www.jcp.or.jp/web_jcp/html/Koryo/, zuletzt abgerufen am 25. März 2025.

28 *Marx/Engels*, Manifest der Kommunistischen Partei (1848), a. E.

29 Ibid.

Der dahinterstehende Gedanke ist also eher, Verfassungsreformen gleichsam als Pandorabüchse zu fürchten. Diejenigen, die Angst haben, in einer Debatte um die konkrete Art einer Verfassungsreform mit ihren Argumenten keine politischen Mehrheiten zu erlangen, bevorzugen scheinbar, lieber gar keine Textvorschläge zu machen. Aus deutscher Sicht mag der Gedanke „lieber keine eigenen konkreten Reformvorschläge machen, damit wir die Pandorabüchse der Verfassungsreformen gar nicht erst öffnen“ (nennen wir diesen Gedanken das „Pandora-Argument“) ängstlich und passiv klingen; in Japan wird diese Linie aber von der KDP, der Kommunistischen Partei und weiteren Verfassungsreform-Skeptikern politisch konsequent vertreten und zumindest von Teilen der Wählerschaft auch als besonnen gutgeheißen.

II. Muss das sein?

Nach dem oben unter I. Gesagten ist also bezüglich der Frage einer Verfassungsreform zur aus deutscher Perzeption naheliegenden Frage „Warum (noch) nicht?“ das wichtige Gegenstück die möglicherweise ebenso naheliegende Frage: „Muss das sein?“ – und falls ja, bei welchen Themengebieten?

1. Reformpläne der LDP bis 2012

Die Liberaldemokratische Partei formulierte bereits bei ihrer Gründung 1955 in ihrer Gründungsproklamation[30]:

> „6. Aufbau eines unabhängigen Regierungssystems
>
> Unter Wahrung der Prinzipien des Pazifismus, der Demokratie und der Achtung der grundlegenden Menschenrechte sollen eine eigenständige Reform der bestehenden Verfassung angestrebt sowie die während der Besatzungszeit erlassenen Gesetze überprüft und entsprechend der nationalen Gegebenheiten geändert oder aufgehoben werden.
>
> Zum Schutz des Weltfriedens, der nationalen Unabhängigkeit und der Freiheit der Bürger soll im Rahmen eines kollektiven Sicherheitssystems eine den nationalen Gegebenheiten und der Wirtschaftskraft entsprechende Selbstverteidigungsstreitkraft aufgebaut und auf den Abzug ausländischer Truppen vorbereitet werden.“[31]

Da die Verfassung (wie auch zahlreiche Gesetze) während der Besatzungszeit ausgearbeitet worden war, wurde hier zunächst einmal im Sinne eines soeben in die demokratische Unabhängigkeit und Freiheit entlassenen Staates das Ziel formuliert, die grundsätzlichen Akte der Gesetzgebung auch durch ggf. für erforderlich befundene Änderungen noch einmal aus eigener demokratischer Überzeugung legislativ nachzuvollziehen. Die Verpflichtung zum Pazifismus, zur Demokratie und zur Achtung grundlegender Menschenrechte als grundlegende Prinzipien der neuen Verfassungsordnung – die sich in diesen drei Grundweichenstellungen fundamental von der Mei-

---

30 立党宣言 (*rittō sengen*), Gründungsproklamation der LDP vom 15. November 1955, online abrufbar unter https://www.jimin.jp/aboutus/declaration/ (zuletzt abgerufen am 25. März 2025).

31 Punkt 6 der Gründungsproklamation der LDP vom 15. November 1955.

ji-Verfassung aus dem Jahre 1890[32] unterschied – machte sich die LDP in ihrer Gründungsproklamation dabei explizit zu eigen. Zu erwähnen ist hier auch, dass insbesondere in der unmittelbaren Nachkriegszeit Teile des nationalkonservativen Spektrums, also insbesondere dann auch in der LDP, die Gültigkeit der jetzigen Verfassung als solche ablehnten: Die japanische Verfassung von 1946 sei unter dem maßgeblichen Einfluss der US-amerikanischen Besatzer auf den Weg gebracht worden, also unter Missachtung der freien und souveränen Willensbildung des japanischen Volkes, und deswegen nicht als wirksame Verfassung anzusehen (sog. 憲法無効論 (*kempō mukō-ron*), wörtl. „Lehre der Unwirksamkeit der Verfassung“).[33] Eine bekannte politische Persönlichkeit in diesem Kontext ist beispielsweise der Politiker und ehemalige Verteidiger Tōjō Hidekis bei den Tokyoter Prozessen Kiyose Ichirō, der als Abgeordneter vor und nach dem Zweiten Weltkrieg verschiedenen Parteien (zuletzt der LDP) angehörte und von 1960 bis 1963 Unterhauspräsident war, und sich im Laufe seines politischen Lebens im Sinne der *kempō mukō-ron* äußerte. Auch aus der nationalistischen Vereinigung Nippon Kaigi sind gelegentlich Äußerungen in der Richtung zu vernehmen, wenngleich die *kempō mukō-ron* in Reinform von keiner größeren politischen Kraft vertreten wird. Dass angesichts prominenter verfassungskritischer Stimmen wie *Kiyose* in den übrigen politischen Lagern auch Zweifel daran aufkamen, inwiefern die LDP die in ihrer Gründungsproklamation für die Verfassungsreform genannten Grundprinzipien der Verpflichtung zum Pazifismus, zur Demokratie und zur Achtung grundlegender Menschenrechte auch wirklich ernst meinte, ist vor diesem Hintergrund vielleicht nicht ganz unverständlich.

Wenngleich die LDP seit 1955, von zwei kurzen Unterbrechungen 1993 – 96 und 2009 – 12 abgesehen, die Geschicke Japans als die eine maßgebliche Regierungspartei prägte, blieb die Diskussion um eine mögliche Verfassungsreform in den darauffolgenden Jahrzehnten vergleichsweise ruhig.

Neue Akzente in der Debatte setzten die 2005 und dann vor allem 2012 veröffentlichten Entwürfe der LDP für einen revidierten Verfassungstext. Vor allem letzterer ist auch für die derzeitige Debatte oft Bezugspunkt, während ersterer in der aktuellen Debatte eher weniger relevant ist.

Der LDP-Entwurf von 2012[34] schlägt umfangreiche Änderungen vor. Die Präambel, die den Tennō betreffenden Vorschriften, Bestimmungen zu Nationalflagge und -hymne, zahlreiche Vorschriften aus dem Abschnitt über die Grundrechte, u. v. m. sollen neugefasst oder neu eingeführt werden. Kimura[35] zählt 53 Regelungsmaterien und weist darauf hin, dass in diesem Umfang auch die zwingend erforderliche und nach Einzelthemen getrennt durchzuführende Volksbefragung enorme praktische

32 大日本帝國憲法 (*dai nippon teikoku kempō*, Verfassung des Kaiserreichs von Groß-Japan), üblicherweise bezeichnet als 明治憲法 (*meiji kempō*, Meiji-Verfassung).

33 Hierzu ausführlich e. g. *Koyama*, 憲法無効論とは何か (*kempō mukō to wa nani ka*, Was die Unwirksamkeit der Verfassung ist) (2006).

34 Online abrufbar unter https://storage2.jimin.jp/pdf/news/policy/130250_1.pdf, zuletzt abgerufen am 25. März 2025.

35 *Kimura*, 増補版　自衛隊と憲法・危機の時代の憲法論議のために (*zōho-ban jieitai to kenpō・kiki no jidai no kenpō rongi no tame ni*, Erweiterte Ausgabe: Die Selbstverteidigungskräfte und die Verfassung: Für eine Verfassungsdebatte in Krisenzeiten) (2022), S. 27 f.

Probleme bedeuten würde. Vor diesem Hintergrund sei der LDP-Entwurf von 2012 eigentlich nicht als im engeren Sinne ernstgemeinter Reformentwurf zu sehen,[36] sondern wohl eher als Diskussionsentwurf, gewissermaßen als in konkrete Normformulierungen gegossene Reformstoßrichtung und Maximalforderung der Regierungspartei. Als solcher Betracht ist er ein sehr hilfreiches Dokument, um den Diskurs ins Konkrete zu lenken.

2. Fokussierte Reformvorschläge der LDP

Deutlich fokussierter ist der Vorstoß der LDP aus dem Jahr 2018. Das für die Pläne zur Verfassungsreform zuständige „Hauptquartier zur Förderung der Verfassungsänderung“[37] in der Parteizentrale der LDP (seit November 2021 nicht nur zur Förderung, sondern zur „Umsetzung der Verfassungsänderung“[38] zuständig) arbeitet stärker fokussierte Vorschläge[39] für vier Themenbereiche aus. Die sog. „Grobentwürfe“ oder „Grundgedanken als Diskussionsgrundlage“[40] umfassen Erläuterungen und konkrete Textvorschläge zu den Themen: a) Die Selbstverteidigungsstreitkräfte, b) Regelungen zum Notstand im Katastrophenfall, c) Wahlkreiseinteilungen und d) Bildung und Erziehung.

Auch wenn dieser erneute Vorstoß der LDP erwartungsgemäß auch von kritischen Stimmen aus der Wissenschaft begleitet wird,[41] so wurde dadurch die Debatte zu einer möglichen Verfassungsreform doch in deutlich konkretere, überschaubarere Bahnen gelenkt.

Zu erwähnen ist, dass in der Folge auch die kleineren Parteien zu den unterschiedlichen Themenbereichen teils eigene[42], teils gemeinsame Vorschläge[43] ausarbeiteten. Selbst die KDP publizierte in der Folge im November 2020 einen ausführlichen Beitrag in Form von „Richtlinien zur Verfassungsdebatte“ eine ausführliche Meinungsäußerung, die sich gleichwohl auf der oben beschriebenen Linie (Pandora-Argument)

---

36 *Kimura* (Anm. 38), S. 28.

37 憲法改正推進本部 (*kempō kaisei suishin honbu*, wörtl. „Hauptquartier zur Förderung der Verfassungsänderung“).

38 憲法改正実現本部 (*kempō kaisei jitsugen honbu*, wörtl. „Hauptquartier zur Umsetzung der Verfassungsänderung“).

39 Online abrufbar unter https://www.jimin.jp/constitution/document/discussion/, zuletzt abgerufen am 25. März 2025.

40 たたき台素案 (*tatakidai soan*), grober bzw. grundlegender Entwurf als Diskussions (wörtl. „für auf den Hackklotz“).

41 *Moto*, 憲法をめぐる情勢と安倍改憲の問題点 (*kempō o meguru jōsei to abe kaiken no mondaiten*, Die Lage der Verfassung und die Probleme von Abes Verfassungsreform), in: 法学セミナー (*hōgaku seminā*) Bd. 761 (2018), S. 18 ff.

42 E. g. die derzeit (März 2025) zweitgrößte Oppositionspartei 日本維新の会 (*nippon ishin no kai*, wörtl. etwa „Gesellschaft zur Erneuerung/Restauration Japans“, kurz: Ishin): https://o-ishin.jp/policy/pdf/kenpoukaisei.pdf, zuletzt abgerufen am 25. März 2025.

43 Gemeinsamer Vorschlag der Oppositionsparteien Ishin und 国民民主党 (*kokumin minshu-tō*, wörtl. Demokratische Volkspartei, kurz: DPFP) zu Notstandsregeln, https://mainichi.jp/articles/20230331/ddm/005/010/104000c, zuletzt abgerufen am 25. März 2025.

im Wesentlichen auf Erläuterung und Begründung der Ablehnung der Pläne der LDP beschränken.[44]

a) Die Selbstverteidigungsstreitkräfte

Größter Streitpunkt in allen Diskussionen zur Frage einer möglichen Verfassungsreform bleibt Art. 9 JV, der in dieser Grundsätzlichkeit tatsächlich ein Unicum der vergleichenden Verfassungsrechtswissenschaft bleibt:

Art. 9

(1) Das japanische Volk strebt aufrichtig nach internationalem Frieden, der auf Gerechtigkeit und Ordnung basiert, und verzichtet für alle Zeiten auf Krieg als Mittel zur Durchsetzung staatlicher Souveränitätsrechte sowie auf die Androhung oder Anwendung von Gewalt zur Beilegung internationaler Streitigkeiten.

(2) Um das in Absatz 1 genannte Ziel zu erreichen, unterhält Japan keine Land-, See- oder Luftstreitkräfte oder sonstige Kriegsmittel. Das Recht des Staates auf Kriegsführung wird nicht anerkannt.

aa) Die SDF und die derzeitige japanische Verfassung

Für den juristischen Diskurs drängend erscheint zunächst die Gretchenfrage, ob denn die Existenz der japanischen SDF mit der Verfassung vereinbar ist. Auf ein japanisches höchstrichterliches *Roma locuta, causa finita* dazu wartet die Juristenwelt bislang vergeblich (s. o.). Da die SDF seit über siebzig Jahren existieren und von einer überwältigenden Mehrheit der japanischen Bevölkerung auch wertgeschätzt werden[45] könnte man in Versuchung geraten, im Jellinek'schen Sinne der seit Generationen geübten Praxis auch normative Wirkung zubilligen und die Frage *ad acta* zu legen. „Das ist alles recht schön und gut; Ungefähr sagt das der Pfarrer auch, Nur mit ein bißchen andern Worten."[46]

Um nicht nur Jellinek, sondern auch Hume und seiner Warnung vor einem naturalistischen Fehlschluss gerecht zu werden, soll hier deswegen kurz die gängige Argumentation zur Vereinbarkeit von Existenz der SDF mit der japanischen Verfassung umrissen werden. Auch wenn im Rahmen dieses Beitrags die Gesamtheit der juristischen und politischen Diskussion zu diesem Thema nicht erschöpfend dargestellt werden kann, so soll doch zumindest im Sinne Gretchens kurz beschrieben werden, mit welchen Worten es denn der Pfarrer (i. e. die japanische Jurisprudenz) nun sagt.

Zu erwähnen ist hier zum ersten die nach dem Juristen und LDP-Politiker Ashida Hitoshi (1887–1959) benannte sog. Ashida-These.[47] Ashida hatte im Rahmen der Beratungen zur japanischen Verfassung die Einfügung der Passage „前項の目的を達するため" (wörtl. „um das in Absatz 1 genannte Ziel zu erreichen") am Anfang von Absatz zwei erwirkt. Die Ashida-These besagt, aus der eingefügten Passage folge, dass Streitkräfte, die nicht i. S. v. Art. 9 I JV (i. e. zur Führung von Kriegen als

44 Online abrufbar unter https://archive2017.cdp-japan.jp/policy/constitution, zuletzt abgerufen am 25. März 2025.

45 *Kimura* (Anm. 38), S. 149 f.

46 *Goethe* (Anm. 3), V. 3459–3461.

47 *Mōri et al.* (Anm. 8), S. 135 ff.

Mittel zur Durchsetzung staatlicher Souveränitätsrechte oder für die Androhung oder Anwendung von Gewalt zur Beilegung internationaler Streitigkeiten) unterhalten werden, sondern zu anderen Zwecken (also der Selbstverteidigung), keinen Verstoß gegen Art. 9 JV darstellen.[48] Die Argumentation ist zweifelsohne hochinteressant, wenn auch grammatisch (im japanischen Originaltext wie auch in der deutschen Übersetzung) etwas gewagt.

Der Kabinettsbeschluss vom 1. Juli 2014[49] fasst demgegenüber die Auffassung der Regierung – die man zumindest in der Frage der grundsätzlichen Verfassungsmäßigkeit der Existenz der SDF (zur davon strikt zu trennenden Frage der Zulässigkeit der kollektiven Selbstverteidigung weiter unten) getrost als herrschende Meinung betrachten kann – zusammen. Demnach ist Art. 9 JV durchaus als ernstgemeinte Ablehnung des Unterhalts von Streitkräften (und zwar nicht nur solcher zur Führung von Angriffskriegen) zu verstehen. Auch andere, gleichrangige verfassungsrechtliche Vorschriften seien aber zu berücksichtigen, insbesondere die aus Art. 13 JV folgende Verpflichtung staatlicher Gewalt zum Schutze von Würde, Leben und Freiheit der Bürger. Damit der japanische Staat auch diesen Verpflichtungen nachkommen könne, seien u. a. Streitkräfte zur Selbstverteidigung erforderlich. Die Argumentation entspricht in ihrem Grundgedanken der auch in Deutschland üblichen Praxis, bei kollidierendem Verfassungsrecht einen Ausgleich im Sinne praktischer Konkordanz zu suchen.

bb) Der aktuelle LDP-Vorschlag (2018)

Konkret schlägt die LDP in ihrem o.g. neuesten Vorstoß von 2018 vor, einen Art. 9a JV einzuführen (bzw. in japanischer Nummerierungslogik einen Art. 9-2 JV), den bisherigen Art. 9 JV hingegen unangetastet zu lassen:

Art. 9-2

(1) Die Bestimmungen des vorhergehenden Artikels hindern Japan nicht daran, Maßnahmen zur Selbstverteidigung zu ergreifen, die notwendig sind, um den Frieden und die Unabhängigkeit unseres Landes zu wahren sowie die Sicherheit des Staates und der Bevölkerung zu gewährleisten. Zu diesem Zweck unterhält Japan eine Streitkraft, die gemäß den gesetzlichen Bestimmungen als Selbstverteidigungskräfte organisiert ist und deren oberster Befehlshaber der Premierminister als Chef des Kabinetts ist.

(2) Die Aktivitäten der Selbstverteidigungskräfte unterliegen der gesetzlichen Regelung und der Kontrolle sowie der Zustimmung des Parlaments.

Der Vorschlag verankert die SDF explizit verfassungsrechtlich, stellt diese unter zivilen Oberbefehl, i. e. den des Premierministers, und legt zudem im zweiten Absatz einen Gesetzes- und (noch zu konkretisierenden) Parlamentsvorbehalt fest.

In den Erläuterungen der LDP wird ausgeführt, dass im Rahmen der Ausarbeitung dieses Vorschlags auch diskutiert wurde, den Art. 9 II JV vollständig zu streichen. Dies würde mangels verfassungsrechtlicher Regelung (und auch mangels verfas-

---

48 *Ashida*, 憲法法解釈 *(kempō hō kaishaku*, Interpretation des Verfassungsrechts) (1946), S. 36; *Kimura* (Anm. 38), S. 47; *Hasebe* (Anm. 8), S. 58 f.

49 Online abrufbar unter https://www.cas.go.jp/jp/gaiyou/jimu/pdf/anpohosei.pdf, zuletzt abgerufen am 25. März 2025.

sungsrechtlichen Verbotes) wohl zu einer einfachgesetzlichen Regelung der notwendigen Punkte wie zivile Kontrolle, Voraussetzungen für den Einsatz etc. führen. Im Vergleich dazu scheint der obige konkrete Textvorschlag – wenngleich Abs. 2 einfachgesetzliche Regelungen für offenbar alle weiteren Kernfragen vorsieht – denjenigen entgegenzukommen, die eine möglichst zuverlässige, i. e. verfassungsrechtliche Beschränkung der Befugnisse des Militärs bzw. der SDF verlangen, in dem zumindest die zivile Kontrolle und der Gesetzes- und Parlamentsvorbehalt verfassungsrechtlich vorgeschrieben wird.

Die LDP hat sich 2018 also gegen den beschriebenen weitergehenden Vorschlag (Streichung von Art. 9 II JV entschieden, und stattdessen eine gemessen an der bisherigen Diskussion verhältnismäßig zurückhaltende Formulierung gewählt.

cc) Vergleich zum LDP-Vorschlag von 2012

Noch deutlicher wird diese etwas zurückhaltendere Position der LDP im Vergleich zum oben erwähnten LDP-Verfassungsentwurf von 2012: Dieser ähnelt dem neueren Vorschlag zwar insofern, als er den Oberbefehl des Premierministers und den Gesetzes- und Parlamentsvorbehalt ebenfalls enthält. Allerdings würde nach dem Vorschlag 2012 Art. 9 II JV (Verzicht auf Unterhalt von Heer, Marine und Luftwaffe) ersetzt durch einen neuen Absatz mit der Bekräftigung des Selbstverteidigungsrecht.

Ein neuer Art. 9-2 JV würde nach dem Vorschlag 2012 zudem die Bezeichnung 国防軍 (*kokubō gun*, wörtl: Armee zur Landesverteidigung) einführen. Semantisch klingt dies *prima facie* unproblematisch; man sollte jedoch bedenken, dass die letzte Institution, die einen vergleichbaren Namen trug, die japanische kaiserliche Armee 日本軍 (*nihon-gun*)[50] u. a. im Zweiten Weltkrieg war. Die Bezeichnung *gun* verursacht auch deswegen bei einem nicht unwesentlichen Teil der japanischen Bevölkerung ein gewisses Unwohlsein. Gerade aus deutscher Sicht ist dieser Punkt nachvollziehbar, haben doch gleich zwei Diktaturen im vergangenen Jahrhundert viele zuvor harmlose oder neutrale Wörter der deutschen Sprache durch ganz spezifische Verwendung gewissermaßen zweckentfremdet und verbrannt – dazu ließe sich eine lange Liste erstellen.

Im Vergleich zu dem LDP-Entwurf von 2012, der für viele eher links orientierte politische Kräfte sicherlich schwer akzeptabel ist und auch in der Wissenschaft auf teils vehementen Widerstand stieß,[51] ist bei den Überlegungen der LDP von 2018 eher der Versuch erkennbar, Vorschläge und Bedenken zu berücksichtigen. Der Vorschlag der zweitgrößten Oppositionspartei Ishin (Anm. 45) etwa ist inhaltlich vom LDP-Vorschlag 2018 nicht allzu weit entfernt.[52]

---

50 Wörtl. „japanische Armee", die Streitkräfte des japanischen Kaiserreiches, bestehend aus Heer und Marine.

51 Zur Kritik insbesondere an den Reformplänen des LDP-Entwurf 2012 zu Art. 9 JV ausführlich *Aoi*, in: Okudaira et al. (Anm. 8), S. 167 ff.

52 https://o-ishin.jp/policy/pdf/kenpoukaisei.pdf, zuletzt abgerufen am 25. März 2025.

dd) das kollektive Selbstverteidigungsrecht

Die Existenz der SDF als Streitkräfte (für die aufgrund von Art. 9 II JV nicht die Bezeichnung „Militär“ oder „Armee“ verwendet wird) als solche scheint nach h. M. unproblematisch zu sein, soweit sie zur Selbstverteidigung dient, i. e. zur Landesverteidigung im Falle des Angriffs Japans durch einen externen Aggressor. Dies entspricht im Prinzip der deutschen Regelung des Art. 87a GG: Wenn Deutschland angegriffen wird, verteidigt es die Bundeswehr.

Heiß diskutiert wurde die Frage nach dem sogenannten „kollektiven Selbstverteidigungsrecht“[53]. Diese entspricht *mutatis mutandis* dem Grundgedanken des Art. 24 II GG: Die Einordnung in ein System gegenseitiger kollektiver Sicherheit (e. g. VN, NATO) kann zum Einsatz der Bundeswehr auch in Fällen führen, in denen Deutschland selbst nicht unmittelbar angegriffen wird,[54] soweit die im Parlamentsbeteiligungsgesetz von 2005 festgelegten Voraussetzungen erfüllt sind. Die japanische Verfassung enthält keine dem Art. 24 II GG entsprechende Vorschrift.

Auch der LDP-Vorschlag von 2018 enthält keine explizite Bestimmung dazu (gleichwohl in Art. 9-2 II JV den besagten allgemeinen Verweis auf die einfachgesetzliche Ausgestaltung zu möglichen Aktivitäten der SDF). Seit 2015 legt die japanische Regierung die geltende Verfassung so aus, dass auch die kollektive Selbstverteidigung zulässig ist. Verschriftlich wurde dies im Kabinettsbeschluss vom 1. Juli 2014[55] und vor allem in der sog. Sicherheitsgesetzgebung von 2015,[56] einem Gesetzespaket, das in diesem Sinne das SDF-Gesetz, das sog. PKO-Gesetz[57] und eine Reihe weiterer Gesetze anpasste und teilweise neu formulierte. Hintergrund ist die zunehmende Verantwortung, die Japan als dritt- bzw. viertgrößte Wirtschaftsmacht der Welt auch in der Sicherheitspolitik übernimmt: Abgesehen von konkreten Auslandseinsätzen der SDF (etwa im Irak, aber auch in einer Reihe weiterer Länder) kann sich in Zukunft zunehmend die Frage stellen, inwieweit Japan auch durch Entsendung der SDF verbündeten Nationen oder engen Partnern zur Seite stehen sollte.

Da die japanische Verfassung keine Vorschrift zur kollektiven Verteidigung enthält, erscheint diese Interpretation vielen gewagt. In einer zum youtube-Hit avancierten Parlamentsanhörung der renommierten Verfassungsrechtswissenschaftler Hasebe Yasuo, Kobayashi Setsu und Sasada Eiji im japanischen Unterhaus vom 4. Juni

---

53 集団的自衛権 (*shūdan-teki jiei-ken*, wörtl. Recht zur Selbstverteidigung im Rahmen einer Gruppe).

54 BVerfGE 90, 286.

55 Online abrufbar unter https://www.cas.go.jp/jp/gaiyou/jimu/pdf/anpohosei.pdf, zuletzt abgerufen am 25. März 2025; Ziff. 3 erläutert die Auffassung zur Vereinbarkeit des kollektiven Selbstverteidigungsrechts mit Art. 9 Verf.

56 Überblick und Gesetzestexte dazu auf der Website des japanischen Kabinettsekretariats https://www.cas.go.jp/jp/gaiyou/jimu/housei_seibi.html, zuletzt abgerufen am 25. März 2025.

57 Gesetz über die Zusammenarbeit bei den Friedenssicherungsaktivitäten der Vereinten Nationen, sog. PKO-Gesetz (国際連合平和維持活動等に対する協力に関する法律, *kokusai rengō heiwa iji katsudō tō ni taisuru kyōryoku ni kansuru hōritsu*), Gesetz Nr. 79 aus dem Jahre 1992.

2015 äußerten diese u. a. *unisono* die Überzeugung, ein Recht zur kollektiven Selbstverteidigung sei *de lege lata* nicht verfassungskonform.[58]

Die Sicherheitsgesetzgebung trat im Herbst desselben Jahres gleichwohl in Kraft, gestützt von einer stabilen parlamentarischen Mehrheit der Regierungsparteien. Aufgrund der beschriebenen strukturellen Unterschiede gerichtlicher Prüfung von Gesetzen auf ihre Verfassungsmäßigkeit (keine abstrakten Normenkontrollverfahren in Japan) befasste sich der OGH trotz einer Klagewelle gegen die Sicherheitsgesetzgebung letztlich nie materiellrechtlich mit der Frage der Verfassungskonformität der Sicherheitsgesetzgebung. Von niedrigeren Instanzen wurde im Laufe der Jahre wiederholt entschieden, mit der Argumentation der Kläger, die Sicherheitsgesetzgebung von 2015 bedrohe ihr Recht auf ein friedliches Leben und persönliche Sicherheit, könne kein staatshaftungsrechtlicher Anspruch auf Schadensersatz begründet werden;[59] auch der OGH blieb in seiner Entscheidung vom 7. September 2023 bei dieser Linie.[60]

Im Rahmen der landesweit parallel betriebenen Klagewelle stellte einzig das OG Sendai materiellrechtlich fest, dass die Sicherheitsgesetzgebung von 2015 verfassungskonform sei.[61] Die Kläger gaben daraufhin gegenüber den Medien bekannt, sie würden von einer Revision beim OGH absehen, da ein rechtskräftiges Urteil des OGH zu der Frage „erhebliche Auswirkungen auf zukünftige Friedensbewegungen haben"[62] würde. Erstaunlicherweise erschien den Klägern also das Fortdauern eines in der Sache höchstrichterlich nicht entschiedenen Zustandes erstrebenswerter als eine mögliche endgültige Entscheidung in der Sache durch den OGH. Unabhängig davon bleibt die Frage, ob der OGH sich im Falle einer Revision überhaupt materiellrechtlich geäußert hätte, natürlich Spekulation.

Die Sicherheitsgesetzgebung von 2015 und die Frage der kollektiven Selbstverteidigung wird weiterhin in Wissenschaft, Politik und Medien kontrovers diskutiert.[63] Nachdem nach wie vor eine stabile Mehrheit (nicht nur der Koalition, sondern auch mehrerer Oppositionsparteien wie der Ishin oder der DPFP (Anm. 46)) im Parlament hinter der Gesetzgebung steht, ist eine einfachgesetzliche Rückabwicklung

58 Protokoll der Sitzung online abrufbar auf der Website des japanischen Unterhauses unter https://www.shugiin.go.jp/internet/itdb_kaigirokua.nsf/html/kaigirokua/025018920150604003.htm, zuletzt abgerufen am 25. März 2025.

59 Exemplarisch OG Takamatsu vom 5. Dezember 2024, Gz. 令和6(ネ)147, online abrufbar unter https://www.courts.go.jp/app/hanrei_jp/detail4?id=93601, zuletzt abgerufen am 25. März 2025.

60 Aus der umfangreichen medialen Berichterstattung zu dem Urteil vgl. Tokyo Shimbun vom 7. September 2023, online abrufbar unter https://www.tokyo-np.co.jp/article/275499, zuletzt abgerufen am 25. März 2025.

61 OG Sendai vom 5. Dezember 2023, Gz. 令和4(ネ)80, online abrufbar unter https://www.courts.go.jp/app/hanrei_jp/detail4?id=92596, zuletzt abgerufen am 25. März 2025.

62 Berichterstattung bei *TBS*, 最高裁判決が確定した場合、今後の平和運動への影響が大きい (*saikōsai hanketsu ga kakutei shita baai, kongo no heiwa undō e no eikyō ga ōkī*, Sollte das Urteil des OGH feststehen, wird es erheblichen Einfluss auf die künftige Friedensbewegung haben), online abrufbar unter https://newsdig.tbs.co.jp/articles/tbc/902576?display=1, zuletzt abgerufen am 25. März 2025.

63 Kritisch dazu *Hasebe* (Anm. 8), S. 60 ff., ebenso kritisch *Mōri et al.* (Anm. 8), S. 150 f.

derzeit nicht in Sicht. Ebenso wenig sind Zeichen für rechtskräftige richterliche Entscheidungen gegen die Vereinbarkeit der Sicherheitsgesetzgebung mit der Verfassung erkennbar. Damit ist das kollektive Selbstverteidigungsrecht vorerst fester Bestandteil der japanischen politischen und juristischen Realität.

b) Regelungen zum Notstand im Katastrophenfall

Die Dreifachkatastrophe vom 11. März 2011 hat in Japan erneut Überlegungen dazu befeuert, wie im Falle einer Großkatastrophe die Regierung handlungsfähig bleiben kann. Japan ist bekanntermaßen stark erdbebengefährdet. Etwa 300 km südöstlich von Tokyo treffen die Pazifische, die Philippinische und die Eurasische Platte aufeinander, weswegen die Region Tokyo auch innerhalb Japans zu den stärker erdbebengefährdeten Regionen gehört.

Tokyo wurde in zuletzt in den Jahren 1703, 1855 und 1923 von schweren Erdbeben über weite Teile zerstört. Das nächste wird früher oder später sicherlich kommen – *certus an, incertus quando* –, und auch wenn Tokyo jetzt sicherlich besser vorbereitet ist als in den vergangenen Jahrhunderten, so ist dennoch mit verheerenden Folgen zu rechnen. Tsunami oder gar kriegerische Angriffe auf Tokyo sind ebenfalls denkbare Katastrophen, die potenziell Regierung und Parlament teilweise oder gänzlich arbeitsunfähig machen könnten.

Der LDP-Vorschlag von 2018 hierzu umfasst die Einfügung zweier neuer Vorschriften (in japanischer Nummerierungslogik 73-2 und 64-2):

Artikel 73-2

(1) Wenn aufgrund eines großen Erdbebens oder einer anderen außergewöhnlichen und großflächigen Katastrophe besondere Umstände vorliegen, die es unmöglich machen, auf die gesetzgeberische Entscheidung des Parlaments zu warten, kann das Kabinett gemäß den gesetzlichen Bestimmungen Regierungsverordnungen erlassen, um das Leben, den Körper und das Eigentum der Bürger zu schützen.

(2) Wenn das Kabinett eine solche Regierungsverordnung erlässt, muss es unverzüglich gemäß den gesetzlichen Bestimmungen die Zustimmung des Parlaments einholen.

Artikel 64-2

Wenn aufgrund eines großen Erdbebens oder einer anderen außergewöhnlichen und großflächigen Katastrophe die ordnungsgemäße Durchführung der allgemeinen Wahl der Abgeordneten des Unterhauses oder der regulären Wahl der Mitglieder des Oberhauses als schwierig erachtet wird, kann das Parlament gemäß den gesetzlichen Bestimmungen mit einer Mehrheit von mindestens zwei Dritteln der anwesenden Mitglieder jeder Kammer eine Sonderregelung für die Amtszeit festlegen.

Die Thematik möglicher Notstandsregeln in der Verfassung wird seit einiger Zeit diskutiert. Parallelen zur Debatte in Deutschland in den späten 1960er Jahren vor dem Hintergrund der am 1. Mai 1968 vom Bundestag beschlossenen Grundgesetzänderungen (sog. Notstandsgesetze) sind eindeutig (wenngleich diese in Deutschland von massiven und teils gewaltsamen Protesten der sog. außerparlamentarischen Opposition begleitet und befeuert wurden). Am LDP-Entwurf von 2018 wird kritisiert, er sei in den Formulierungen zu allgemein, vage und allgemein gehalten: Hier sei

Missbrauch in Form von Perpetuierung eines eigentlich als absolute Ausnahme gedachten Notstandes Tür und Tor geöffnet.[64]

Kritiker des (strukturell anders verorteten, in den Grundgedanken aber ähnlichen, wenngleich bezüglich möglichen Einschränkungen individueller Rechter etwas weitreichender formulierten) LDP-Vorschlags von 2012 zu diesem Themenbereich Bereich kritisieren die Vorschriften auf ähnlicher Linie als zu weit oder zu ungenau gefasst („einer anderen außergewöhnlichen […] Katastrophe“) und bemängeln die fehlende Differenzierung nach Art der jeweiligen „Katastrophe“, die jeweils völlig andersartige Herausforderungen bedeuteten (Erdbeben, Krieg, Pandemie).[65]

c) Wahlkreiseinteilungen

Schwankungen in den Bevölkerungszahlen, insbesondere die zunehmende Landflucht, führen dazu, dass ländliche Wahlkreise oft immer größere, aber bevölkerungsarme Gebiete umfassen. Das Bevölkerungsungleichgewicht ist in Japan teilweise so groß, dass dies erhebliche Ungleichgewichtungen der Stimmen in den Wahlkreisen zur Folge hat. Da in Japan sowohl im Ober- als auch im Unterhaus mehr als die Hälfte der Sitze nach reinem Mehrheitswahlrecht in den jeweiligen Wahlkreisen gewählt wird (und jeweils weniger als die Hälfte der Sitze in reiner Verhältniswahl – sog. echtes Zweistimmensystem oder Grabenwahlrecht), sind die Auswirkungen auf die Sitzverteilung im Parlament insgesamt und die Frage, wie viele Wahlberechtigte ein Abgeordneter vertritt, erheblich. Der OGH muss sich seit Jahrzehnten häufig mit der Frage befassen, inwiefern der Zuschnitt der Wahlkreise einen Verstoß gegen den allgemeinen Gleichheitsgrundsatz des Art. 14 JV darstellt und legt dabei für das Unterhaus einen strengeren Maßstab an als für das Oberhaus.[66]

Die traditionell in ländlichen Gebieten starke LDP verweist auf die Tatsache, dass traditionelle gebietskörperschaftliche Einheiten (Gemeinden oder gar Präfekturen) nicht mehr separat repräsentiert werden können, wenn die Ungleichgewichtung der Stimmen ein gewisses Verhältnis nicht überschreiten darf.[67] Entsprechend schlägt sie in vor, nicht nur die Bevölkerungszahl, sondern auch Verwaltungsgrenzen, regionale Zusammengehörigkeit, topografische Gegebenheiten und weitere Faktoren umfassend zu berücksichtigen. Eine solche Regelung hätte zur Folge, dass eine starke Ungleichgewichtung der Stimmung zulässig sein könnte, wenn sie mit den übrigen Faktoren hinreichend begründet werden kann. Der LDP-Vorschlag von 2018 führt entsprechend aus:

Artikel 47

(1) Bei der Einrichtung von Wahlkreisen für die Wahlen der Mitglieder beider Kammern ist die Bevölkerungszahl als Grundlage zu nehmen. Dabei sind Verwaltungsgrenzen, regionale Zusammengehörigkeit, topografische Gegebenheiten und weitere Faktoren umfassend zu berücksichtigen, um die Wahlkreise sowie die Anzahl der in jedem Wahlkreis

---

64 *Moto* (Anm. 44), S. 22 f.

65 *Okudaira et al.* (Anm. 8), S. 187 f.; auf den S. 188 f. auch mit Vergleichen zu den deutschen Regelungen im GG.

66 *Tidten*, Inter Pares (2012), S. 41 ff.

67 Online abrufbar unter https://www.jimin.jp/constitution/document/discussion/, zuletzt abgerufen am 25. März 2025.

zu wählenden Abgeordneten festzulegen. Falls für die Wahl aller oder eines Teils der Mitglieder des Oberhauses die Gebiete überregionaler Gebietskörperschaften als Wahlkreise bestimmt werden, kann festgelegt werden, dass bei jeder Wahl in jedem Wahlkreis mindestens eine Person gewählt werden muss.

(2) Über die in den vorstehenden Absätzen festgelegten Regelungen hinaus werden Wahlkreise, Wahlverfahren und sonstige Angelegenheiten im Zusammenhang mit den Wahlen der Mitglieder beider Kammern durch Gesetz geregelt.

Artikel 92

Die lokalen Gebietskörperschaften bestehen grundsätzlich aus grundlegenden lokalen Gebietskörperschaften sowie überregionalen Gebietskörperschaften, die diese umfassen. Die Arten dieser Körperschaften sowie Angelegenheiten in Bezug auf ihre Organisation und Verwaltung werden auf Grundlage der Prinzipien der kommunalen Selbstverwaltung durch Gesetz geregelt.

Hierzu könnte man kritisch anmerken, dass die LDP mit einer solchen Regelung vor allem dünn besiedelte, ländliche Regionen im Wahlrecht bevorzugen würde – also genau die Regionen, in denen sie traditionell stark abschneidet. Andererseits ist der Gedanke, dass bestimmte kulturell und historisch gewachsenen Einheiten auch im Wahlkreiszuschnitt nach Möglichkeit berücksichtigt werden sollen, auch nicht von der Hand zu weisen.

So wird auch in Europa beispielsweise bei der Wahl zum Europaparlament die Anzahl der Sitze pro Mitgliedsland nach dem Prinzip der sogenannten degressiven Proportionalität bestimmt, was dazu führt, dass die Stimmen der Wahlberechtigten unterschiedlich starken Einfluss auf die Zusammensetzung des Europaparlaments haben (ein französischer Wahlberechtigter hat rechnerisch etwa das 1,1-fache Gewicht eines deutschen, ein maltesischer sogar das ca. zehnfache)[68], was üblicherweise mit dem Hinweis auf die nationale Zugehörigkeit, also auf traditionell gewachsene soziokulturelle Einheiten, begründet wird: Rein rechnerisch könnte nämlich sonst Malta insgesamt noch nicht einmal einen einzigen Abgeordneten stellen.

Nach dem seit der Bundestagswahl 2025 für die Wahl zum Deutschen Bundestag geltenden Wahlrecht ist es sogar möglich, dass existierende Wahlkreise überhaupt nicht repräsentiert werden, da sog. Überhangmandate nur noch in sehr begrenztem Umfang zugelassen werden.

Angesichts der intensiven höchstrichterlichen Rechtsprechung zur Frage der Ungleichgewichtung der Stimmen in den Wahlkreisen erscheint eine verfassungsrechtliche Präzisierung der Kriterien, nach denen die Wahlkreise *de lege ferenda* dann einfachgesetzlich zu bestimmen sind, ein durchaus nachvollziehbarer Vorstoß zu sein. Welche konkreten Kriterien mehrheitsfähig sind, ist allerdings noch unklar, da auch zu diesem Punkt keine Gegenvorschläge anderer Parteien vorliegen.

Kritische Stimmen auch in der Wissenschaft betonen vor allem die Tatsache, dass die dann zu erwartende Regelung, wonach auch bei Oberhauswahlen jede Präfektur mit mindestens einem Sitz repräsentiert sein muss, zu einer deutlichen Ungleichge-

---

68 Die Ungleichgewichtung ergibt sich aus dem Verhältnis der Zahl der Abgeordneten (Deutschland: 96; Frankreich: 81; Malta: 6) im Verhältnis zur jeweiligen Bevölkerungszahl (Deutschland: ca. 83 Mio.; Frankreich: ca. 68 Mio.; Malta: ca. 0,55 Mio.).

wichtung zugunsten der regelmäßig LDP-nahen ländlichen Regionen führt, ohne deswegen aber eine entsprechende Reform kategorisch abzulehnen.[69]

d) Bildung und Erziehung

Für den Bereich Bildung und Erziehung schlägt die LDP 2018 einen neuen, dritten Absatz zu Art. 26 JV sowie eine Umformulierung von Art. 89 JV vor:

Artikel 26

(3) Der Staat muss sich unter Berücksichtigung der Tatsache, dass Bildung darauf abzielt, die Persönlichkeit jedes einzelnen Bürgers zu entfalten, dass sie für die Verwirklichung individuellen Glücks unverzichtbar ist und dass sie eine äußerst wichtige Rolle für die Zukunft des Landes spielt, um die Verbesserung der Bildungsumgebung bemühen. Dies schließt die Sicherstellung von Bildungschancen unabhängig von den wirtschaftlichen Verhältnissen des Einzelnen mit ein.

Artikel 89

Öffentliche Gelder und sonstiges öffentliches Vermögen dürfen nicht für die Nutzung, den Vorteil oder den Unterhalt religiöser Organisationen oder Gruppen verwendet oder diesen zur Verfügung gestellt werden. Ebenso dürfen sie nicht für wohltätige, erzieherische oder humanitäre Zwecke aufgewendet oder genutzt werden, sofern diese nicht unter öffentlicher Aufsicht stehen.

Die Debatte über diesen Vorschlag hält sich in Grenzen; weder regt sich vehementer Widerstand, noch ist von lautstarker Befürwortung zu hören. Zum Anliegen der verfassungsreformfreundlich gesonnenen Oppositionspartei Ishin, Oberschulen gänzlich ohne Schulgebühren zu finanzieren (bzw. finanzieren zu lassen), fand sich letztlich in der LDP (wohl auch angesichts fiskalischer Zwänge) keine Mehrheit für eine klare Formulierung.[70] Dieser gesamte Themenbereich wäre aber sicherlich ein potentiell verhandelbarer Punkt für den Fall, dass Japans politische Parteien irgendwann in Zukunft einmal an einem konkreten Paket für eine Verfassungsreform arbeiten sollten.

e) Die vorgeschlagene Neufassung des Art. 96 JV

Zu den vier Themenbereichen, zu denen die LDP 2018 Neuformulierungen vorschlug, zählte die sowohl 2005 als auch 2012 vorgeschlagene Neufassung des Art. 96 JV nicht mehr. Dieser Artikel legt die Voraussetzungen für Verfassungsänderungen fest.

Der von der LDP zu Oppositionszeiten 2012 ausgearbeitete umfassende Vorschlag sah vor, den Art. 96 JV in einen neuen (dann Art. 100) umzuwandeln, der statt der Zweidrittelmehrheit in beiden Kammern nur noch die Mehrheit der Mitglieder der jeweiligen Kammer (in Deutschland umgangssprachlich oft als Kanzlermehrheit bezeichnet, um diese Form der Mehrheit i. S. v. Art. 121 GG von der bloßen Mehrheit

69 *Moto* (Anm. 44), S. 21 f.

70 *Moto* (Anm. 44), S. 20 f.

der abgegebenen Stimmen zu unterscheiden) vorsah, die vorgesehene anschließende Volksbefragung aber beibehielt.[71]

Dieser Vorstoß, der die Hürden für eine Verfassungsänderung deutlich senken würde und in Art und Ausführung sehr nah an die einfachgesetzliche Gesetzgebung bringt, ist in der Tat bemerkenswert. Er wurde entsprechend scharf kritisiert.[72]

Verfassungsänderungen künftig mit nur noch der Mehrheit der Abgeordneten auch ohne Zweidrittelmehrheit zu ermöglichen, würde für deutsche Juristen sicherlich auch gewisse Bauchschmerzen bedeuten. In Deutschland sahen die Weimarer Reichsverfassung (Art. 76 WRV) und sieht auch das Grundgesetz (Art. 79 II GG) das Erfordernis einer Zweidrittelmehrheit für Verfassungsänderungen vor. Gleiches gilt für viele weitere Staaten, etwa für Italien (Art. 138 der Verfassung von 1948), Spanien (Art. 167 der Verfassung von 1978) oder die Vereinigten Staaten von Amerika (Art. 5 der Verfassung von 1776). Das Erfordernis einer Zweidrittelmehrheit für besonders weitreichende Entscheidung ist tief verwurzelt in der europäischen Rechtstradition; die Zweidrittelmehrheit ist e. g. seit dem dritten Laterankonzil im Jahre 1179 auch für eine gültige Papstwahl erforderlich.[73]

In Frankreich hingegen reichen gem. Art. 89 der Verfassung 60 % der Abgeordneten (Dreifünftelmehrheit), wobei zu berücksichtigen ist, dass im sogenannten romanischen Mehrheitswahlrecht, nach dem die Französische Nationalversammlung gewählt wird, stabile Mehrheiten und somit auch eine Mehrheit von 60 % im Parlament von der relativ stärksten Partei sehr viel leichter errungen werden können als bei einer reinen Verhältniswahl. Im Falle einer Volksabstimmung ist sogar die einfache Mehrheit ausreichend (Art. 89 der jetzt gültigen französischen Verfassung von 1958). Im Sonderfall Großbritannien – ohne geschriebene Verfassung – können Verfassungsänderungen auch im regulären legislativen Verfahren beschlossen werden, also mit einfacher Mehrheit (bekannte Beispiele für offensichtlich staatsorganisationsrechtliche, also verfassungsrechtliche Gesetzgebung sind etwa die Scotland Act, Northern Ireland Act und Government of Wales Act von 1998 – diese erhielten zwar eine überwältigende Zustimmung, wurden aber im regulären Gesetzgebungsverfahren beschlossen, hätten juristisch betrachtet also auch mit einfacher Mehrheit gültig beschlossen werden können). Somit wären Frankreich und Großbritannien zwei Beispiele für Regelungen, in denen die Hürde für eine Verfassungsänderung genauso niedrig bzw. sogar noch niedriger wäre als im LDP-Entwurf von 2012.

Die Frage nach einer Veränderung von Art. 96 der japanischen Verfassung wird gleichwohl akademisch bleiben: Eine Abschaffung des Erfordernisses der Zweidrittelmehrheit würde wohl niemals Zustimmung bei einer Oppositionspartei finden, da sie damit ja für künftige Verfassungsänderungen jegliche Mitsprachemöglichkeit vergeben würde. Denkbar wäre dies nur in einer Konstellation, in der die Regierungskoalition über eine Zweidrittelmehrheit in beiden Kammern verfügte: Dann könnte sie diese Gelegenheit gewissermaßen beim Schopfe packen und die Hürden für Ver-

---

71 LDP-Entwurf von 2012, online abrufbar unter https://www.jimin.jp/constitution/document/, zuletzt abgerufen am 25. März 2025.

72 *Takami*, in: Keigo, in: Okudaira et al. (Anm. 8), S. 79 ff.

73 Canon 1 des Concilium Lateranense III von März 1179.

fassungsänderungen senken, um dann künftig selbst bei Verlust der Zweidrittelmehrheit auch mit der lediglich absoluten Mehrheit der abgegebenen Stimmen die Verfassung ändern zu können. Die LDP-geführte Koalition hatte im Unterhaus in der Vergangenheit tatsächlich auch schon eine Zweidrittelmehrheit errungen, allerdings nie im Oberhaus (wenngleich sie bei der Oberhauswahl 2016 145 von 244 Oberhaussitzen für sich selbst errang und mit den zu der Zeit eine Verfassungsreform unterstützenden Kräften aus kleineren Oppositionsparteien auch im Oberhaus auf eine Zweidrittelmehrheit gekommen wäre – inzwischen ist das aber bereits wieder nicht mehr der Fall).

Auch wenn eine Zweidrittelmehrheit im japanischen Wahlsystem (s. o.) aufgrund der größeren Bedeutung der nach Mehrheitswahlrecht Wahlkreise zumindest einfacher zu erreichen ist als in einem Wahlsystem wie in Deutschland, in dem die Gesamtzusammensetzung rein nach Verhältniswahl festgelegt wird, so ist es doch insgesamt sehr schwer, als Koalition oder gar als einzelne Partei in naher Zukunft eine Zweidrittelmehrheit in beiden Kammern zu erringen (zum Zeitpunkt des Verfassens dieses Beitrags im Frühling 2025 erscheint in den Umfragen für keine einzelne Partei und auch nicht für die regierende Koalition aus LDP und Kōmeitō (公明党, wörtl. Gerechtigkeitspartei) Aussichten auf eine Zweidrittelmehrheit zu haben).

Gleichwohl: Die LDP machte 2005 und 2012 deutlich, was ihr diesbezüglich vorschwebte. Da die bestehenden Regelungen mit ausschlaggebend dafür waren, dass seit beinahe achtzig Jahren die Verfassung nicht reformiert wurde, ist nicht auszuschließen, dass auch die Frage, nach welchem Verfahren die Verfassung überhaupt zu reformieren ist, irgendwann in Zukunft wieder Diskussionsgegenstand wird. Dann wird sich auch die Frage stellen, ob eine Änderung der Änderungsregeln überhaupt eine zulässige Verfassungsänderung ist, oder ob sie (analog Art. 79 III GG) den Wesenskern der Verfassung antastet und deswegen unzulässig sein könnte.[74] Derzeit wird die Idee einer Reform des Art. 96 JV jedoch nicht weiterverfolgt.

III. Risiken und Nebenwirkungen

Dass eine Verfassung so lange unverändert bleibt, erregt bei deutschen Beobachtern immer wieder Erstaunen. Welche Fragen ergeben sich – abgesehen von den konkreten Vorschriften, zu denen Änderungsvorschläge gemacht oder abgelehnt werden – aus der Tatsache als solche, dass die Verfassung nicht geändert wurde?

1. „Kein Mensch muss müssen“[75]

Von einer Verfassung als grundlegendes Dokument einer Gesellschaft wird oft instinktiv erwartet, dass sie in einer Form von Willensbekundung – durch das Volk

74 Zur Frage, welche Änderungen so weitgehend wären, dass sie unzulässig wären: Unter Bezugnahme auf Art. 79 III GG *Mōri et al.* (Anm. 8), S. 33; *Hasebe* (Anm. 8), S. 34 ff.

75 *Lessing*, Nathan der Weise (1779), Erster Aufzug, Dritter Auftritt, Nathan und der Derwisch.

selbst, durch einen die Staatsgewalt ausübenden Monarchen, durch ein Parlament oder eine Nationalversammlung – angenommen wird.

Die Japanische Verfassung wurde im Oktober 1946 im Parlament – juristisch betrachtet als „Änderung" der Meiji-Verfassung[76] – fast ohne Gegenstimmen, also mit der gem. Art. 73 der Meiji-Verfassung erforderlichen Zweidrittelmehrheit, beschlossen und im November vom Kaiser verkündet.[77] Eine Volksabstimmung war nicht vorgesehen und fand nicht statt – sie wäre nur im Falle einer Verfassungsänderung gem. Art. 96 JV vorgesehen. Solange die Verfassung nicht geändert wird, bliebe also der Zustand bestehen, dass die Bevölkerung sich nie direkt zum wichtigsten Gesetzestext des Staates äußerte. Die LDP verweist in ihren Materialien zur Frage einer Verfassungsreform zudem auf die teilweise sehr hohe Zahl an bereits durchgeführten Verfassungsreformen in anderen Ländern (auch Deutschland ist ein regelmäßig genannter Bezugsmaßstab) und betont, wie erstaunlich es vor diesem Hintergrund doch sei, dass die japanische Verfassung bislang nie reformiert wurde.[78]

Bei nüchterner Betrachtung erscheint dieses Argument per se jedoch relativ schwach: Japan sieht plebiszitäre Verfahren auf nationaler Ebene (abgesehen von Art. 96 JV) nicht vor, ist hier also ähnlich zurückhaltend wie Deutschland. Dies bedeutet keinen demokratietheoretischen Makel, da die gewählte Volksvertretung (im April 1946 erstmalig nach Kriegsende und erstmalig auch von Frauen gewählt) ihre Zustimmung mit überwältigender Mehrheit erteilte. (Zum Vergleich: In Deutschland steht das Grundgesetz, dem das bayerische Landesparlament Ende Mai 1949 als einziges Landesparlament sogar die Zustimmung verweigerte und über das niemals eine Volksbefragung durchgeführt wurde, so gesehen demokratietheoretisch sogar auf wackligeren Füßen. Dennoch wird seine Gültigkeit nicht ernsthaft angezweifelt.)

Keine ernstzunehmende Stimme in Bevölkerung oder Wissenschaft zweifelt die Gültigkeit der Verfassung an, die seit nunmehr achtzig Jahren als rechtliche Wirklichkeit von den japanischen Institutionen gelebt wird.[79] Ein gefühltes Erfordernis für eine Volksbefragung bzw. ein durch eine Verfassungsänderung mit herbeigeführtes Plebiszit, auf dass sich die Bevölkerung durch eine Aktualisierung der Verfassung diese wahrhaft zu eigen mache, lässt sich mit dieser Argumentationslinie wohl kaum begründen oder ableiten. Daraus folgt auch für die Frage des Erfordernisses einer Verfassungsänderung: Kein Mensch muss müssen.

---

76 Zur Frage der denkbaren Formen bei einer Verfassungsreform, insbesondere im Vergleich zum US-amerikanischen System der Verfassungszusätze („appendative model"), lesenswert *Kinoshita*, The Form of Constitutional Amendments in Japan, in: Albert (Hrsg.), The Architecture of Constitutional Amendments: History, Law, Politics (2023), S. 89–104, https://www.bloomsbury.com/us/architecture-of-constitutional-amendments-9781509959082/, online abrufbar unter https://papers.ssrn.com/sol3/papers.cfm?abstract_id=4638706, zuletzt abgerufen am 15. April 2025.

77 *Hasebe* (Anm. 8), S. 49 f.

78 Leserfreundlich als kurzes Manga gestaltet, online abrufbar unter https://storage2.jimin.jp/pdf/constitution/kenpou_force.pdf, zuletzt abgerufen am 25. März 2025.

79 *Yokodaido*, Constitutional stability in japan not due to popular approval, in: German Law Journal, Bd. 20 Sonderausgabe 2 (2019), S. 263–283, doi:10.1017/glj.2019.16.

2. *κείμεθα τοῖς κείνων ῥήμασι πειθόμενοι*

Die Frage, aufgrund welcher Normen Menschen in den Krieg ziehen, aufgrund welcher Normen eine Gesellschaft bestimmte Mitglieder in den Krieg schickt, ist sehr alt.

Berühmt ist der Fall der dreihundert Spartaner aus den Perserkriegen: Als im Spätsommer 480 v. Chr. der Perserkönig Xerxes I. mit einem Invasionsheer enormen Ausmaßes in Griechenland einfiel, stellten dreihundert Spartiaten unter ihrem König Leonídas das persische Heer bei den Thermopylen zum Kampf und fielen dort bis auf den letzten Mann. Sie taten dies, wie später im berühmten, oft Simonides zugeschriebenen Epigramm dazu formuliert wurde, τοῖς κείνων ῥήμασι πειθόμενοι – i. e. „den Worten jener gehorchend", oder in Schillers Übersetzung „wie das Gesetz es befahl".

Herodot beschreibt, dass tatsächlich die Gesetze Spartas während des wichtigen religiösen Festes der Karneia militärische Einsätze im Grundsatz verboten, und dass deswegen lediglich die dreihundert Hippeis, die königliche Leibgarde, aufgrund einer eilig erteilten Sondererlaubnis der Ephoren in den Einsatz geschickt werden durften.[80] Schillers etwas freiere Übersetzung entspricht somit sogar eher den Tatsachen: Nicht *die Worte*, sondern *die Gesetze* Spartas führten dazu, dass nicht Spartas vollumfängliches Heer (mit zumindest einer gewissen Wahrscheinlichkeit, eine Schlacht auch zu gewinnen und zu überleben) ausgeschickt, sondern lediglich 300 Spartiaten in einen (mit an Sicherheit grenzender Wahrscheinlichkeit für diese tödlich endenden) Einsatz ausgesandt wurden, als bewusstes Himmelfahrtskommando, mit dem an der Heimatfront dann wertvolle Zeit gewonnen werden konnte.

Wenn ein Staat von den Staatsbürgern, die der Gemeinschaft als Soldaten dienen, den Einsatz von Leib und Leben verlangt, ist die Frage nicht trivial, auf welcher normativen Grundlage das verlangt wird. Wir können davon ausgehen, dass ein Soldat erwartet, zumindest nach den juristischen Kriterien seines eigenen Landes auch rechtmäßig zu handeln, wenn er sich bereit erklärt, in einen Kampfeinsatz zu ziehen. Die höchste Form der Rechtssicherheit, die ein moderner Staat bieten kann, ist die Verankerung in der Verfassung. Auch einfachgesetzliche Regeln oder materielle Gesetze in Form von Verordnungen, schließlich auch Allgemeinverfügungen oder Verwaltungsakte stehen für sich genommen für Rechtssicherheit – wenn auch in absteigender Rangfolge in der aufgezählten Reihenfolge. Sie können jeweils einfacher geändert werden als die nächste ranghöhere Norm.

Wenn die Hürde für eine Verfassungsänderung zu hoch ist, eine Materie aber gleichwohl geregelt werden muss, wird die politische Führung andere Formen der Regulierung nutzen. Ein anschauliches Beispiel aus dem heutigen Japan ist die oben genannte Interpretationsänderung zu Art. 9 JV. Da zu einer möglichen Änderung der Verfassung absehbar keine Einigkeit zu erzielen war, wurde per einfachem Kabinettsbeschluss festgelegt, dass die sog. kollektive Selbstverteidigung verfassungskonform sei; einfachgesetzliche Regelungen auf dieser Linie folgten in der sog. Sicherheitsgesetzgebung 2015.

---

80 Herodot VII, 206.

Konkret für den Bereich der SDF wurde das Ziel, japanischen Soldaten, die Leib und Leben für Frieden und Freiheit riskieren, eine zuverlässige rechtliche Grundlage für ihre Tätigkeit (was die Möglichkeit von Auslandseinsätzen miteinschließt) zu bieten, in Japan nun also nicht verfassungs-, sondern einfachgesetzlich umgesetzt.

Für einen Angehörigen der japanischen SDF; der in einen Auslandseinsatz geschickt wird, bedeutet das, dass er zunächst davon ausgehen kann, rechtmäßiger Weise in einen solchen Einsatz geschickt zu werden, wenn die gesetzlichen Voraussetzungen erfüllt sind. Sollte der Einsatz allerdings im Rahmen einer kollektiven Selbstverteidigung erfolgen (verschiedene Konstellationen dafür wären vorstellbar), dann bliebe bei dem SDF-Angehörigen das flaue Gefühl, zumindest nach der Auffassung zahlreicher renommierter japanischer Rechtswissenschaftler (s. o.) etwas Unrechtes zu tun. Die innerjapanischen Kritiker einer Anpassung des Friedensartikels der japanischen Verfassung an sicherheitspolitische Realitäten im 21. Jahrhundert nehmen also die beschriebene gefühlte Restunsicherheit für diejenigen, die Leib und Leben für Frieden und Freiheit einsetzen, zumindest in Kauf.

(Eine andere interessante Frage, die man auch hier stellen könnte, wäre, ob in Japan generell eine Tendenz zu niedrigrangigeren Normen besteht: So setzte etwa während der Covid-19-Pandemie die Regierung stark auf Empfehlungen statt auf harte gesetzliche Reglungen wie Lockdowns. Auch im Bereich des Vorgehens gegen Diskriminierung fällt auf, dass kaum harte gesetzliche Vorschriften bestehen, sondern verstärkt auf regelmäßig durch bloße Verwaltungsvorschriften geregelte Schlichtungs- und Beratungsangebote gesetzt wird.[81] McElwain[82] und Inoue[83] beschreiben die japanische Tendenz, *prima facie* durchaus verfassungsrechtlich regelbare Materie stattdessen einfachgesetzlich zu regulieren. Ob daraus tatsächlich auf die Existenz einer allgemeinen japanischen Tendenz zu möglichst niedrigrangigen Normen (bis hin zu jederzeit leicht änderbaren bloß internen Verwaltungsvorschriften oder bloßen freundlichen Ratschlägen der Regierung) gefolgert werden kann, wäre in dieser Grundsätzlichkeit eine tiefergehende Frage, für deren Beantwortung umfangreiche Untersuchungen zum Geist der Gesetze in Japan erforderlich wären und die hier im Rahmen dieses kurzen Beitrages nicht erörtert werden kann.)

3. Jetzt erstmal nicht

Die Debatte zur Frage einer möglichen Reform der japanischen Verfassung ist langsam, wenn auch nicht tot. Die Diskussionslage heute ist eine deutlich andere als vor zwanzig (2005er Entwurf), vierzig (erste Niederlage der LDP) oder siebzig (Gründung der LDP) Jahren. Eine mögliche Verfassungsreform ist inzwischen sehr viel konkreter, diskutierbarer, als sie es in der Vergangenheit war. Mit den vier Themenbereichen der LDP von 2018 und den teilweise konkreten Vorschlägen auch von Oppositionsparteien erscheint die Möglichkeit einer Kompromissfindung in Form einer Paketlösung zumindest perspektivisch denkbar.

---

81 *Tidten* (Anm. 66), S. 108 ff.

82 *McElwain* (Anm. 5), S. 63 ff.

83 *Inoue* (Anm. 13), S. 114 f.

Gleichwohl: Die scheinbar drängenden Probleme, die im Laufe der Nachkriegszeit immer wieder als Argumente genannt wurden, brennen derzeit nicht allzu sehr. Das „sich zu eigen machen“ der Verfassung durch die japanische Bevölkerung wird nicht angezweifelt, die Verfassung wird in Japan nicht als oktroyiert, sondern als wertvoll (wenngleich für den Alltag juristischer Laien meist nicht sonderlich relevant) empfunden. Der rechtliche Status der japanischen Streitkräfte wird von allen seriösen politischen Kräften akzeptiert, und selbst zur umstrittenen Frage der kollektiven Selbstverteidigung wurden wie oben beschrieben juristische Fakten geschaffen. Zum Zeitpunkt der Abfassung dieses Beitrags befindet sich die LDP in einer Minderheitsregierung. Dass die Koalition oder Teile der Opposition das Thema Verfassungsreform in den Vordergrund stellt oder gar mit diesem Thema auf mehr Zustimmung bei Wahlen hofft, ist nicht erkennbar.

Die Debatte wird weitergehen, wenn auch in langsamen Schritten, und auch für die Zukunft auf der Agenda bleiben. Nach einer baldigen Verfassungsreform sieht es im Frühjahr 2025 jedenfalls nicht aus.

Literaturverzeichnis

Ashida, Hitoshi: 憲法法解釈 *(kempō hō kaishaku*, Interpretation des Verfassungsrechts) (1946).

Goethe, Johann Wolfgang: Faust. Der Tragödie erste Teil (1808).

Hasebe, Yasuo: 憲法 (*kempō*, Verfassung), 8. Auflage (2022).

Hasebe, Yasuo: 憲法と平和 をといなおす (*kempō to heiwa wo toinaosu*, Überdenken der Verfassung und des Friedens) (2004).

Hoover, William D. (Hrsg.): Historical Dictionary of Postwar Japan (2018).

Inoue, Takeshi: 立憲主義とテクスト—日本国憲法の場合 (*rikkenshugi to tekusuto – nihonkoku kempo no baai*, Konstitutionalismus und Text – Der Fall der japanischen Verfassung), 論究ジュリスト Bd. 20 (2017).

Kimura, Sōta: 増補版　自衛隊と憲法・危機の時代の憲法論議のために (*zōho-ban jieitai to kenpō・kiki no jidai no kenpō rongi no tame ni*, Erweiterte Ausgabe: Die Selbstverteidigungskräfte und die Verfassung: Für eine Verfassungsdebatte in Krisenzeiten) (2022).

Kinoshita, Masahiko: The Form of Constitutional Amendments in Japan, in: Richard Albert (Hrsg.), The Architecture of Constitutional Amendments: History, Law, Politics (2023), S. 89 – 104, https://www.bloomsbury.com/us/architecture-of-constitutional-amendments-9781509959082/, online abrufbar unter https://papers.ssrn.com/sol3/papers.cfm?abstract_id=4638706, zuletzt abgerufen am 15. April 2025.

Koyama, Tsunemi: 憲法無効論とは何か (*kempō mukō to wa nani ka*, Was die Unwirksamkeit der Verfassung ist) (2006).

Lessing, Gotthold Ephraim: Nathan der Weise (1779).

Liberaldemokratische Partei Japans (自由民主党): 日本国憲法の改正実現にむけて (*nihonkoku kempō no kaisei jitsugen ni mukete*, Hin zu einer Verwirklichung einer Reform der Japanischen Verfassung) (23. Mai 2022), online abrufbar unter https://www.jimin.jp/constitution/document/, zuletzt abgerufen am 25. März 2025.

Marx, Karl/*Engels*, Friedrich: Manifest der Kommunistischen Partei (1848).

McElwain, Kenneth Mori: 日本国憲法の普遍と特異 – 日本国憲法の普遍と特異：その軌跡と定量的考察 (*nihonkoku kempō no fuhen to tokui – sono kiseki to teiryōteki kōsatsu*, The Universality and Originality of the Japanese Constitution in Quantitative Perspective) (2022).

Mōri, Tōru/*Koizumi*, Yoshiyuki/*Asano*, Hironobu/*Matsumoto*, Tetsuji, 憲法I・総論・統治 (*kempō I・sōron・tōji*, Verfassung I. Allgemeiner Teil, Regierung), 3. Auflage (2022).

Moto, Hidenori: 憲法をめぐる情勢と安倍改憲の問題点 (*kempō o meguru jōsei to abe kaiken no mondaiten*, Die Lage der Verfassung und die Probleme von Abes Verfassungsreform), in: 法学セミナー (*hōgaku seminā*) Bd. 761 (2018), S. 18 ff.

Okudaira, Yasuhiro/*Aikyō*, Kōji/*Aoi*, Miho: 改憲の何が問題か (*kaiken no nani ga mondai ka*, Was das Problem bei der Verfassungsänderung ist) (2013).

Tidten, Dan: Inter Pares (2012).

Yokodaido, Satoshi: Constitutional stability in japan not due to popular approval, in: German Law Journal, Bd. 20 Sonderausgabe 2 (2019), S. 263–283, doi:10.1017/glj.2019.16.

Bürgerliches Recht und Arbeitsrecht aus dem Blickwinkel der individuellen Arbeitsbeziehungen

Von *Raimund Waltermann*

Professor Dr. Raimund Waltermann war von 2001 bis 2024 Direktor des Instituts für Arbeitsrecht und Recht der Sozialen Sicherheit der Rheinischen Friedrich-Wilhelms-Universität Bonn und dort Inhaber des Lehrstuhls für Bürgerliches Recht, Arbeitsrecht und Sozialrecht. Nach der Promotion war er 1989 und 1990 Rechtsanwalt in einer OLG-Sozietät in Hamm, nach der Habilitation von 1994 bis 2001 Inhaber des Lehrstuhls für Bürgerliches Recht, Arbeitsrecht und Sozialrecht der Justus-Liebig-Universität Gießen. Seit 2012 regelmäßiger Kontakt mit der japanischen Rechtswissenschaft.

I. Einleitung

Heinrich Menkhaus hat in seiner damaligen Funktion als Vorsitzender der Deutsch-Japanischen Gesellschaft für Arbeitsrecht im Zusammenwirken mit dem damaligen Geschäftsführer der Gesellschaft, Rechtsanwalt und Fachanwalt für Arbeitsrecht Rüdiger Henning, das siebente Gemeinsame Symposion mit der japanischen Schwestergesellschaft, der Japanisch-Deutschen Gesellschaft für Arbeitsrecht, in der Meiji-Universität veranstaltet. Es fand am 3. und 4. September 2012 in Tokyo statt. Durch dieses Symposion entstand ein intensiver und fruchtbarer Gedankenaustausch, der mich auf Einladung von Professor Hajime Wada in den Folgejahren mehrere Male zu Gastvorträgen nach Japan geführt hat. Der entstandene wissenschaftliche und freundschaftliche Austausch mit zahlreichen Wissenschaftlerinnen und Wissenschaftlern des japanischen Arbeitsrechts hält bis heute an. So konnte ich im Januar 2024 an der von Frau Professorin Keiko Ogata geleiteten Übergabe der Festschrift für Hajime Wada als Referent teilnehmen. Die bei dem siebenten Symposion 2012 gehaltenen Vorträge der japanischen und deutschen Referenten und die Begrüßungsansprache von Heinrich Menkhaus sind in dem Band Düwell/Löwisch/Waltermann/Wank (Hrsg.), Das Verhältnis von Arbeitsrecht und Zivilrecht in Japan und Deutschland, 2013, veröffentlicht.

Aufgabe des damals von mir gehaltenen Vortrags war, das Verhältnis von Bürgerlichem Recht und Arbeitsrecht unter dem Blickwinkel des individuellen Arbeitsrechts zu betrachten. Es sollten die Entwicklung des Arbeitsverhältnisrechts, die Entwicklung der rechtstheoretischen Grundlagen des Arbeitsvertragsrechts und die Pluralität der Beschäftigungsformen, namentlich Teilzeitarbeit, Leiharbeit, befristete Beschäftigung und auch Kleine Selbständigkeit rechtsvergleichend betrachtet werden.

Duncker & Humblot · Berlin | https://doi.org/10.3790/978-3-428-59611-9.2025.418929

Das deutsche Arbeitsrecht hat sich, insbesondere was die genannten Beschäftigungsformen angeht, in den Jahren nach dem Symposion von 2012 in einigen Hinsichten weiterentwickelt, in anderen Hinsichten nicht. Das soll, den damaligen Vortrag aus Anlass der Festschrift für Heinrich Menkhaus noch einmal aufgreifend, mit der Rechtslage von 2012 vergleichend dargelegt werden. Heinrich Menkhaus wünsche ich für die Zeit nach dem 70. Geburtstag Gesundheit und Schaffenskraft!

II. Recht der abhängigen Arbeit

1. Begriff des Arbeitsvertrags

In Japan und in Deutschland ist das Arbeitsrecht das „Recht der abhängigen Arbeit". In Deutschland haben sich die Dinge seit 2012 in der Grundsituation nicht verändert. Allerdings wurde 2017 der Rechtsbegriff des Arbeitsvertrags in § 611a Abs. 1 BGB gesetzlich erfasst. Man kann nicht sagen, dass der Begriff des Arbeitsvertrags mit § 611a Abs. 1 BGB „definiert" worden wäre, denn es bleibt dabei, dass sich das Arbeitsverhältnis, welches den Ausgangspunkt für die Anwendung des Arbeitsrechts bildet, nicht im eigentlichen Sinn definieren lässt. § 611a Abs. 1 BGB greift die bis dahin von der Rechtsprechung zugrunde gelegten Maßstäbe auf[1] und verleiht diesen, weiterhin für Entwicklungen offen,[2] Gesetzeskraft.

Mit der Gesetzeskraft der Begriffsbestimmung des Arbeitsvertrags, durch welchen schuldrechtlich das Arbeitsverhältnis als Gefüge entsteht, verbindet sich in meiner Bewertung unter dem Strich eine Stärkung des in § 611a Abs. 1 Satz 6 BGB angeordneten Vorrangs der tatsächlichen Handhabung des Vertragsverhältnisses gegenüber der Bezeichnung im Vertrag, bei der es sich nicht selten um Vertragsdesign handelt.[3] § 611a Abs. 1 Satz 6 BGB bestimmt:

> „Zeigt die tatsächliche Durchführung des Vertragsverhältnisses, dass es sich um ein Arbeitsverhältnis handelt, kommt es auf die Bezeichnung im Vertrag nicht an".

Dieses bis 2017 auf der höchstrichterlichen Rechtsprechung beruhende Auslegungskriterium hat nun Gesetzeskraft und muss bei der Bestimmung, ob es sich um ein Arbeitsverhältnis handelt, berücksichtigt werden.

---

1 BT-Drs. 18/9232, S. 4, 18.

2 Vgl. stellvertretend *Greiner*, Grenzen des Fremdpersonaleinsatzes im Krankenhaus: Die „Honorararzt"-Entscheidungen des BSG – zugleich Besprechung der Leitentscheidung BSG, 4. 6. 2019, B 12 R 11/18 R –, in: NZS 2019, 761 (764); *Preis*, in: Müller-Glöge/Preis/Gallner/Schmidt (Hrsg.): Erfurter Kommentar zum Arbeitsrecht, 25. Aufl. (2025), BGB § 611a Rn. 8; *Roloff*, Scheinselbständig, „scheintypologisch" und „scheinbar" zwingend – Gedanken zum Verständnis des § 611a Abs. 1 BGB, in: Brose/Greiner/Rolfs/Sagan/Schneider/Stoffels/Temming/Ulber (Hrsg.), Grundlagen des Arbeits- und Sozialrechts, Festschrift für Ulrich Preis (2021), S. 1087 (1088); *Waltermann*, Abhängige Beschäftigung in der digitalisierten Arbeitswelt, in: NZA (2021), S. 298.

3 Zum hier vertretenen Standpunkt *Waltermann* (Anm. 2), S. 297 ff.; *ders.*, Beschäftigung und Arbeitsverhältnis – Verschiedenheiten und Gemeinsamkeiten der Rechtsbegriffe, in: Meßling/Voelzke (Hrsg.), Die Zukunft des Rechts- und Sozialstaats, Festschrift für Rainer Schlegel (2024), S. 916 ff.

2. Arbeitsvertrag und Bürgerliches Recht

Das Recht der Arbeitsverhältnisse bleibt in Deutschland auch unter Geltung von § 611a Abs. 1 BGB weiterhin Teil des Besonderen Schuldrechts (§§ 611 ff. BGB). Es findet also nach wie vor im Bürgerlichen Recht und im Bürgerlichen Gesetzbuch (BGB) seinen Ausgangspunkt.

Das Arbeitsverhältnis, das durch den Arbeitsvertrag (§ 611a Abs.1 BGB) begründet wird, ist in Japan und in Deutschland auf fremdbestimmte Arbeit gerichtet. Dabei ist das Arbeitsverhältnisrecht als das Recht der unselbständigen oder abhängigen Arbeit im deutschen Bürgerlichen Recht auch 2025 nur bruchstückhaft erfasst. Das deutsche Bürgerliche Gesetzbuch enthält insoweit seit seinem Inkrafttreten im Jahr 1900 eine beträchtliche Lücke, die man von Beginn an durch ein Arbeitsgesetzbuch hatte schließen wollen – aber bis heute nicht geschlossen hat.

3. Das Arbeitsverhältnis als privatrechtliches Schuldverhältnis

Das Arbeitsverhältnisrecht (auch Arbeitsvertragsrecht) enthält in Deutschland die im Wesentlichen privatrechtlichen Rechtsvorschriften, welche das Arbeitsverhältnis als privatrechtliches Schuldverhältnis ausgestalten – von seiner Begründung durch den Abschluss des Arbeitsvertrags über die inhaltliche Durchführung im Dauerschuldverhältnis mit wechselseitigen Rechten und Pflichten und deren Störung (Leistungsstörung, Haftung) bis hin zu seiner Beendigung (namentlich durch Kündigung). Die Regelungsweise ist im Grundsatz nicht anders als sonst im Privatrecht. Man kann im Arbeitsverhältnisrecht also auf die Erkenntnisse insbesondere der Rechtsgeschäftslehre und des Allgemeinen und Besonderen Schuldrechts zurückgreifen. Das Arbeitsverhältnisrecht kennt jedoch eine Vielzahl von Abweichungen von den allgemeinen bürgerlich-rechtlichen Regeln, die sich überwiegend in speziellen Gesetzen finden.

Nach wie vor hat neben dem Gesetzesrecht die richterliche Rechtsfortbildung im Arbeitsrecht und auch im Arbeitsverhältnisrecht beträchtliche praktische Bedeutung. Denn das deutsche Recht nimmt, weil ein Arbeitsgesetzbuch fehlt und also die allgemeinen Regeln des Bürgerlichen Gesetzbuchs gelten, die über den Leistungsaustausch hinausgehende Dimension des Arbeitsverhältnisses mit seinem Charakter als Dauerschuldverhältnis, mit seiner personenbezogenen Prägung und mit seiner besonderen Risikolage sowie seiner Bedeutung für die Existenzsicherung zu wenig zur Kenntnis. Das habe ich auf dem Symposion 2012 durch ein praxisrelevantes Beispiel zu verdeutlichen versucht: Ein Arbeitnehmer gerät nach jahrzehntelanger unfallfreier Fahrt als Kraftfahrer mit einem neuen und teuren Lastzug infolge leichter Fahrlässigkeit von der Fahrbahn ab. Der Schaden an dem umgestürzten LKW beträgt 150.000 Euro, die der Arbeitgeber ersetzt verlangt. Nach dem Bürgerlichen Recht wäre der Anspruch begründet. Vertragspflichtverletzung (§ 280 Abs. 1 BGB) und unerlaubte Handlung (§§ 823 ff. BGB) führen zur Haftung, wenn der Schuldner wenigstens fahrlässig handelt (§ 276 Abs. 1 BGB). Arbeitnehmer müssten also selbst bei leichtester Fahrlässigkeit dem Arbeitgeber vollen Schadensersatz leisten, auch wenn die Höhe des Schadensersatzes die Leistungsfähigkeit des Arbeitnehmers weit übersteigt. In unserer heutigen Arbeitswelt gibt es eine Vielzahl von Tätigkeiten, bei denen durch eine geringfügige Unaufmerksamkeit sehr hohe Schäden entstehen können. Müsste das Risiko im Arbeitsverhältnis, das Folge der mit Unternehmung verbundenen Arbeitsteilung ist, nicht von dem Grundsatz abweichend verteilt sein, nach dem der Schädiger für jede Fahrlässigkeit einstehen muss? Rechtsprechung und arbeitsrechtliche Lehre haben im Weg richterlicher Rechtsfortbildung seit langer Zeit Grundsätze zur Einschränkung der Arbeitnehmerhaftung entwickelt.[4] Nach diesen richterrechtlichen Grundsätzen, die unter allgemeiner Billigung eine vom BGB abweichende angemessene Risikozuweisung bezwecken, würde der Arbeitnehmer in unserem Fall, weil ihm nur leichte Fahrlässigkeit zur Last fällt, nicht haften.

4. Arbeitsgesetzbuch als „ewiges" Vorhaben

Eine Kodifikation des Arbeitsrechts in einem Arbeitsgesetzbuch wird seit langem angestrebt, aber nicht verwirklicht.[5] Es ist auch heute im Jahr 2025 nicht wahrscheinlich, dass es in Deutschland in absehbarer Zeit zu einem Arbeitsgesetzbuch kommen wird, welches das gesamte Arbeitsrecht einschließlich des Arbeitskampfrechts kodifiziert. Der Einigungsvertrag zwischen der Bundesrepublik Deutschland und der DDR machte es 1990 dem Gesetzgeber immerhin erneut zur Aufgabe, das Arbeitsvertragsrecht sowie das Arbeitszeitrecht möglichst bald einheitlich neu zu kodifizieren und den Arbeitsschutz neu zu regeln. Wenn alle bisher vorgelegten Entwürfe, zuletzt der von den Kölner Professoren Martin Henssler und Ulrich Preis im Jahr 2007 erarbeitete Diskussionsentwurf, nicht verwirklicht wurden, liegt das auch daran, dass die Interessenverbände der Arbeitgeber- und Arbeitnehmerseite (natürlich aus verschiedenen Gründen) stets eine Vielzahl von Kritikpunkten finden werden, wenn man das Vorhaben der Kodifikation des Arbeitsvertragsrechts, wie bisher stets geschehen, mit inhaltlichen Änderungen verbindet. Vielleicht wird ein einheitliches Gesetzeswerk des Arbeitsrechts erst zustande kommen können, wenn man sich allein auf die Kodifikation der bislang verstreuten Gesetzesbestimmungen beschränkt und damit keine Sachreform verbindet. Denn nur so lässt sich erreichen, dass die Interessenvertretungen der Arbeitgeber und der Arbeitnehmer mitziehen. Das klingt bescheidener als es ist, denn auch ein Kodifikationsvorhaben stellt hohe Anforderungen. Und auch hier zeigt sich in meiner Bewertung ein gegenüber dem Erkenntnisstand von 2012 neuer Aspekt: Wie dargelegt, sollten mit § 611a Abs. 1 BGB die von der höchstrichterlichen Rechtsprechung entwickelten Auslegungsmaßstäbe – ohne inhaltliche Reform – kodifiziert werden. Und doch verbindet sich damit insofern eine Veränderung, als diesen Maßstäben nunmehr Gesetzeskraft zukommt. Das hat, wie dargelegt, bei der Auslegung Bedeutung.

---

4 Grundlegend BAGE 5, 1 ff. Aus späterer Zeit BAG, NZA (1994), S. 1083 ff.; BAG, NZA (2011), S. 345 ff.

5 Zusammenfassung bei *Waltermann/Chandna-Hoppe*, Arbeitsrecht, Band 1, 21. Aufl. (2026), Rn. 15 m. Nachw.

III. Arbeitsverhältnis und (Neue) Selbstständigkeit

Das Arbeitsverhältnis beruht auf einem privatrechtlichen Vertrag. Damit dieser privatrechtliche Vertrag ein Arbeitsverhältnis begründet, muss die versprochene Dienstleistung nach überkommenem Verständnis weisungsabhängig zu erbringen sein. Nur dann spricht man traditionell von unselbständiger oder abhängiger Arbeit. § 611a Abs. 1 BGB bringt das seit 2017 in den Sätzen 1 bis 3 zum Ausdruck. Den rechtlichen Gegensatz dazu bilden der (freie) Dienstvertrag, der in der Systematik des deutschen Bürgerlichen Rechts auch Geschäftsbesorgungscharakter (§ 675 BGB) haben kann, und der (freie) Werkvertrag (§§ 631 ff. BGB).

Das Arbeitsverhältnis muss von den angesprochenen Formen der Selbständigkeit, insbesondere vom Dienstvertrag, abgegrenzt werden. Diese Abgrenzung ist in Deutschland von größerer Bedeutung als in anderen Rechtsordnungen, auch von größerer Bedeutung als in Japan. Wer auf der Grundlage eines Arbeitsverhältnisses beschäftigt ist, genießt in Deutschland den Vollschutz des Arbeitsrechts. Das spiegelt sich im Sozialrecht im Hinblick auf die soziale Absicherung in den Zweigen der Sozialversicherung wider. Der mit dem Begriff des Arbeitsverhältnisses im Wesentlichen deckungsgleiche Begriff der Beschäftigung (§ 7 Abs. 1 SGB IV) begründet den Vollschutz der Sozialversicherung. Wer nicht in einem Arbeitsverhältnis tätig und nicht im Sinn von § 7 Abs. 1 SGB IV beschäftigt ist, genießt nur in ausgewählten Hinsichten arbeitsrechtlichen Schutz und ist im Grundsatz nicht in den Schutz der Sozialversicherung einbezogen.[6]

Dass die Abgrenzung in den letzten Jahren wichtiger und schwieriger geworden ist, liegt zum einen daran, dass sich die tatsächlichen Verhältnisse im Arbeitsleben verändert haben und weiter verändern. Die Einbindung in eine Betriebsorganisation geht, zumal in Zeiten neuer Kommunikationsformen, überall zurück; der Fabrikarbeiter der Industrialisierung, dessen Arbeitsplatz sich ganz in der Nähe des Fabrikschornsteins befand, hat seit langem nicht mehr Modellcharakter für die abhängige Arbeit. Die Abgrenzung hat darüber hinaus vor dem Hintergrund von Vertragsgestaltungen, welche die Bindungen des Arbeits- und des Sozialrechts vermeiden wollen, praktische Bedeutung erlangt.

2012 hatte ich dazu angemerkt, dass man nicht nur im deutschen Recht an einem Wegpunkt angekommen sein könnte, der Antworten auf Entwicklungstendenzen erfordert: Das kann man heute, im Jahr 2025, angesichts der mit der Digitalisierung auch im Arbeitsleben verbundenen Veränderungen nur unterstreichen. In der Anfangszeit des Arbeitsrechts und bis weit hinein in das 20. Jahrhundert haben die Kriterien zur Erfassung des Arbeitsverhältnisses die auftretenden Fallgestaltungen gut bewältigt. Die Anknüpfung an das Weisungsrecht als Kennzeichen des Arbeitsverhältnisses war in einer Zeit hierarchischer Strukturen vollkommen geeignet, den arbeitsrechtlichen Schutz zu begründen und den Anknüpfungspunkt für die soziale Absicherung durch die Bismarcksche Sozialversicherung zu bilden. Spätestens seit den 1980er Jahren haben sich jedoch die Fälle rechtlicher Unterordnung (aufgrund Weisungsrechts) und wirtschaftlicher Abhängigkeit, die zuvor im Grunde deckungs-

---

6 Überblick bei *Waltermann*, Digitalisierung der Arbeitswelt und Schutz Kleiner Selbständiger durch das Sozialversicherungsrecht, SGb. (2017), S. 425 ff. mit Nachweisen.

gleich waren, nicht nur in Deutschland, auseinanderentwickelt. Wirtschaftliche Abhängigkeit außerhalb des Arbeitsverhältnisses nimmt zu. Zugleich geht die Bedeutung der Fremdbestimmung im Arbeitsverhältnis aus verschiedenen Gründen, vor allem im Dienstleistungsbereich, angesichts veränderter Kommunikationsmittel, bei Management mit „flachen" Hierarchien oder in „Netzwerkstrukturen" zurück. Heute genügt vielfach die Kontrolle des Arbeitsergebnisses. In der Folge dieser Entwicklung begegnen uns die Schutzgründe des Arbeitsrechts längst auch außerhalb des Arbeitsverhältnisses.[7] Die Unterscheidung zwischen abhängiger Beschäftigung und Selbständigkeit hat an Trennschärfe verloren. Das betrifft vor allem die in den letzten Jahren in Deutschland stark gewachsene sogenannte Neue Selbständigkeit. In vielen Fällen ist in der Praxis aus unterschiedlichen Gründen Kleine Selbständigkeit, insbesondere „Solo-Selbständigkeit", also Selbständigkeit ohne Beschäftigte, an die Stelle von abhängiger Arbeit getreten.

Mit der Neuen (Kleinen) Selbständigkeit verbindet sich nicht mehr die prinzipielle Erwartung wirtschaftlicher Unabhängigkeit. Sie hat häufig nur niedrigen Ertrag und sorgt für das Alter nicht vor. Ein Teil dieser Selbständigen, meist Solo-Selbständigen, ist nicht marktorientiert und lediglich für einen oder für zwei Auftraggeber tätig. Diese neuen Selbständigen sind nur rechtlich gesehen nicht weisungsabhängig und also nicht in einem Arbeitsverhältnis mit den daran anknüpfenden arbeits- und sozialrechtlichen Konsequenzen tätig. Sie halten sich ihrem Auftraggeber jedoch in ähnlichem Maß zur Verfügung wie Arbeitnehmer ihrem Arbeitgeber.

Dieser Befund galt schon 2012. Die Digitalisierung hat dieser Entwicklung nochmals einen Schub gegeben, und sie wird diese Entwicklung weiter vorantreiben. Schon 2012 bestand vor diesem Hintergrund die dringende Notwendigkeit, die Kleinen Selbständigen kurzfristig zu einer Altersversorgung zu verpflichten. Das hatte die damalige Bundesregierung auch geplant, und genauso stand es im Koalitionsvertrag für die 19. Legislaturperiode[8] und für die soeben vergangene 20. Legislaturperiode[9]. Nichts hat sich getan. (Auch) in der soeben vergangenen Legislaturperiode hat das daran gelegen, dass man die Kleine Selbständigkeit nicht in die gesetzliche Rentenversicherung, das Hauptmodell der Altersvorsorge, hat einbeziehen wollen, sondern ausgerechnet diesem Kreis, dessen fragile wirtschaftliche Lage die Corona-Pandemie deutlich unterstrichen hat, eine Wahlmöglichkeit hat geben wollen, mit der die Kleinen Selbständigen „im Rahmen eines einfachen und unbürokratischen Opt Outs ein privates Vorsorgeprodukt" sollten wählen können. Die damit verbundenen beträchtlichen Regelungsbedarfe haben sich erwartungsgemäß nicht bewältigen lassen. Wenn nun der Entwurf des Koalitionsvertrags zwischen CDU, CSU und SPD für die 21. Legislaturperiode die Einbeziehung der Kleinen Selbständigkeit (ausdrücklich) in die gesetzliche Rentenversicherung vorsieht[10], liegt darin die Chance, den seit lan-

---

7 Vgl. bereits (grundlegend) *Wiedemann*, Das Arbeitsverhältnis als Austausch- und Gemeinschaftsverhältnis (1966), S. 11 ff.

8 Koalitionsvertrag zwischen CDU, CSU und SPD für die 19. Legislaturperiode, 7. Februar 2018, S. 93 Nr. 4290 ff.

9 Koalitionsvertrag zwischen SPD, Bündnis 90/Die Grünen und FDP für die 20. Legislaturperiode, 7. Dezember 2021, S. 59.

10 Koalitionsvertrag zwischen CDU, CSU und SPD für die 21. Legislaturperiode, 9. April 2025, S. 20.

gem überfälligen Schritt zu gehen. Würde man die Kleinen Selbständigen zur Altersvorsorge verpflichten, würden sich auch die Preise verändern, zu denen Leistung in Kleiner Selbständigkeit angeboten werden kann, was in vielen Bereichen Rückwirkung auf die Konkurrenzfähigkeit des Arbeitsverhältnisses haben könnte. Dass man, wenn man das Jahr 2012 zum Ausgangspunkt der Überlegung nimmt, nun schon über weitere 13 Jahre diesen Schritt versäumt hat, wälzt in Deutschland weiterhin Lasten in die wirtschaftlichen Spielräume der nächsten Generation weiter. Nur Selbstständigkeit, die sich für die Selbstständigen dauerhaft rechnet, bleibt am Ende ohne nachteilige Folgen auch für die Gesellschaft, die sonst in der Zukunft die (inzwischen aus den geburtenstarken Jahrgängen zahlreicher werdenden) Selbständigen ohne existenzsichernde Vorsorge im Alter aus Steuermitteln wird unterstützen müssen. Es wird erforderlich sein, die Einziehung der Beiträge in einem (digitalen) Quellenabzugsverfahren zu gestalten, wie es auch im Steuerrecht existiert.

Inwieweit arbeitsrechtliche Konsequenzen aus dem angedeuteten Befund gezogen werden sollten, lässt sich nicht pauschal sagen. Ich würde die Trennlinie zwischen abhängiger Beschäftigung und Selbständigkeit in der Grundausrichtung auch 2025 weiterhin nicht einebnen. Das deutsche Arbeitsrecht greift bereits einen Teil der Kleinen Selbständigen heraus und regelt arbeitsrechtlichen Schutz: Als arbeitnehmerähnliche Personen (vgl. zum Begriff § 12a Abs. 1 Nr. 1 TVG) bezeichnet das Arbeitsrecht bestimmte Selbständige, die wirtschaftlich abhängig und vergleichbar einem Arbeitnehmer sozial schutzbedürftig sind. Für diese arbeitnehmerähnlichen Personen gelten neben den allgemeinen Vorschriften des Bürgerlichen Rechts, des Handelsrechts und des Wirtschaftsrechts wegen ihrer Schutzbedürftigkeit einige Regelungen des Arbeitsrechts (z.B. § 2 S. 2 BUrlG, § 6 Abs. 1 S. 1 Nr. 3 AGG). Für Klagen ist unter den Voraussetzungen des § 5 Abs. 1 S. 2 ArbGG der Rechtsweg zu den Arbeitsgerichten eröffnet. Auch die in Heimarbeit Beschäftigten genießen einen begrenzten arbeitsrechtlichen Schutz. Was Zukunftsperspektiven angesichts der Verschiebungen von Arbeit im Arbeitsverhältnis zu Arbeit in Selbständigkeit und angesichts des Hinauswachsens der Schutzgründe des Arbeitsrechts über das Arbeitsverhältnis angeht, gibt es zwei mögliche Wege:[11] Man könnte systematisch die Anknüpfung des Schutzes, wie bei der Heimarbeit geschehen, über das Arbeitsverhältnis hinaus ausweiten, was allerdings beträchtliche konzeptionelle Anforderungen stellen würde. Vorzugswürdig erscheint mir, den Schutz durch arbeitsrechtliche Vorschriften punktuell, wie es zum Teil bereits geschehen ist, auf weitere Beschäftigungssituationen auszudehnen, wie es zum Beispiel in § 6 Abs. 1 AGG, § 2 Abs. 2 ArbSchG, § 26 Abs. 8 BDSG bereits geschehen ist. Auf diesem politisch gut umsetzbaren Weg könnte ein zukunftstauglicher Rechtsrahmen errichtet werden.

---

11 Näher zum hier vertretenen Standpunkt *Waltermann*, Digital statt analog: Zur Zukunftsfähigkeit des Arbeitsrechts, in: RdA (2019), S. 97f.

IV. Arbeitsverhältnisrecht, Arbeitsschutzrecht, kollektives Arbeitsrecht

1. Grundkonzeption

Das deutsche Arbeitsrecht besteht aus drei wesensverschiedenen Teilgebieten. Das Arbeitsverhältnisrecht (oder Arbeitsvertragsrecht) enthält im Wesentlichen privatrechtliche Rechtsvorschriften, die auf dem Bürgerlichen Recht aufbauen. Das Arbeitsschutzrecht folgt einer anderen Regelungsweise, die dem primären Ansatz des japanischen Arbeitsstandardgesetzes ähnlich ist. Es regelt die von ihm erfassten Gegenstände öffentlich-rechtlich. Das Arbeitsschutzrecht ist in seinen wesentlichen Hinsichten Recht der Gefahrenabwehr. Es ist geprägt durch staatliche Aufsicht, Zwang zur Erfüllung der gesetzlichen Vorgaben und durch Bußgeld- und Strafvorschriften, welche die Ausführung der arbeitsschutzrechtlichen Bestimmungen absichern. Während im Arbeitsverhältnisrecht der Einzelne zu entscheiden hat, ob er bestehende Ansprüche, eventuell mit gerichtlicher Hilfe, verfolgen will, wie es dem Bürgerlichen Recht durchgehend entspricht, wacht im Arbeitsschutzrecht der Staat wie sonst im Verwaltungsrecht über die Einhaltung der Gesetzesvorschriften. Die besondere Eigenart des Arbeitsrechts wird in dem dritten Teilgebiet, dem Kollektiven Arbeitsrecht am deutlichsten. Das zur Ausgleichung des Machtungleichgewichts zwischen Arbeitnehmern und Arbeitgebern geschaffene kollektive Arbeitsrecht enthält auf zwei Ebenen, der Tarifebene und der Ebene der Betriebsverfassung, eigenständige Mechanismen für ein Kompromisse findendes Zusammenwirken von Arbeitgeber- und Arbeitnehmerseite im Weg der Selbstverwaltung.

2. Verschiebungen

In der Gewichtung dieser drei Teilgebiete haben sich seit 2012 Verschiebungen ergeben, die in meiner Bewertung belegen, dass die an sich sehr geeigneten Mechanismen des deutschen Arbeitsrechts heutige Gestaltungsaufgaben aus tatsächlichen Gründen nicht mehr bewältigen: Auf der Ebene des Kollektiven Arbeitsrechts erreicht die rechtsvergleichend in besonderem Maß auf Mitgliedschaft aufbauende deutsche Tarifautonomie in der heutigen Lebenswelt wichtige Bereiche nicht mehr, namentlich in der Dienstleistungsarbeit und im Niedriglohnsektor. Der Tarifautonomie fehlt der Rückhalt durch Mitgliedschaft auf Seiten der Arbeitnehmer, auf dem die deutsche Tarifautonomie in ihrem Kern aufbaut.[12] Die Funktionsschwäche der Tarifautonomie hat dazu geführt, dass ein nach der Konzeption des deutschen Arbeitsrechts besonders wichtiges, eigentlich zentrales Gestaltungsmittel – der Tarifvertrag – auf zu großer Fläche für die Regelung in der Praxis ausscheidet. Die Folge ist, dass der Gesetzgeber, nach 2012 verstärkt, Wege zu einer Ausweitung der Wirkungen von Tarifverträgen über die durch Mitgliedschaft an den Tarifvertrag Gebundenen hinaus ausgeweitet hat, zuletzt durch das Tarifautonomiestärkungsgesetz von

---

12 Siehe aktuell die auf Vorträgen eines Symposions der Gesellschaft für Rechtspolitik beruhenden Aufsätze von *Franzen, Höpfner, Jacobs, Schubert* und *Waltermann*, in: RdA Heft 2 (2025).

2014 und durch das Pflegelöhneverbesserungsgesetz von 2018.[13] Es geht dabei um eine Erstreckung von tarifvertraglich vereinbarten Inhalten über die Tarifgebundenen hinaus, namentlich durch Allgemeinverbindlicherklärung unter den Voraussetzungen des § 5 TVG oder durch staatliche Rechtsverordnung nach Maßgabe des Arbeitnehmerentsendegesetzes (AEntG). Ein weiterer Weg liegt in der Erstreckung von Tarifinhalten über Tariftreuegestaltungen bei der Vergabe öffentlicher Aufträge. Dieser Weg ist in der Pflegeversicherung beschritten worden, und bereits bestehende Rechtsgrundlagen für die Vergabe öffentlicher Aufträge allgemein hat in der 20. Legislaturperiode die Bundesregierung für die Auftragsvergabe des Bundes weiterentwickeln wollen.[14] Auch in Nordrhein-Westfalen arbeitet die Landesregierung an der Reform ihres Tariftreuegesetzes.

3. Das deutsche Arbeitsrecht wird staatlicher

In der Gesamtbetrachtung zeigt sich eine Verschiebung der Gestaltungswege innerhalb der drei Teilgebiete Arbeitsverhältnisrecht, Arbeitsschutzrecht und Kollektives Arbeitsrecht, die in besonderer Deutlichkeit an der Gestaltung des 2015 in Kraft getretenen Mindestlohngesetzes abgelesen werden kann. Die arbeitsverhältnisrechtlichen Bestimmungen des MiLoG zum Anspruch auf den Mindestlohn verbindet das MiLoG mit ausführlichen arbeitsschutzrechtlichen Bestimmungen zu Kontrolle und Durchsetzung des gesetzlichen Mindestlohns in den §§ 14 bis 21 MiLoG.

V. Rechtstheoretische Grundlagen des Arbeitsverhältnisrechts

Das Arbeitsverhältnisrecht folgt, wie dargelegt wurde, in der Struktur seiner Rechtssätze im Wesentlichen dem allgemeinen Bürgerlichen Recht. Die speziellen Regelungen des Arbeitsverhältnisrechts bauen auf den Vorschriften des Bürgerlichen Rechts auf und knüpfen an seine Struktur an. Nicht selten kommen Rechtsvorschriften des allgemeinen Bürgerlichen Rechts und des speziellen Arbeitsrechts nebeneinander zur Anwendung. So ist das Recht der Kündigung zu einem Teil dem Kündigungsschutzgesetz zu entnehmen, die Regelung der Kündigungsfristen und die Regelung der außerordentlichen Kündigungsgründe findet sich im BGB (§§ 622, 626 BGB).

Vor allem bei der Rechtsanwendung zeigt sich, dass das Arbeitsverhältnis im Zivilrechtssystem seinen Platz hat. Die Rechtsauslegung und Rechtsanwendung im Arbeitsverhältnisrecht folgt den Regeln und dem begrifflich-dogmatischen Rüstzeug der Zivilrechtsdogmatik. Dabei lässt sich im Arbeitsverhältnisrecht in den letzten

---

13 Dargestellt u. a. bei *Waltermann*, Attraktivität von Tarifbindung – Zur Zukunftsfähigkeit der deutschen Tarifautonomie, in: ZFA (2020), S. 211 ff. m. Nachw.

14 Der Entwurf eines Gesetzes zur Stärkung der Tarifautonomie durch die Sicherung von Tariftreue bei der Vergabe öffentlicher Aufträge des Bundes (Tariftreuegesetz) wurde am 27. November 2024 vom Bundeskabinett beschlossen und in den Bundestag noch eingebracht, siehe BT-Drs. 20/14345. Der Regierungsentwurf der Bundesregierung der 21. Legislaturperiode vom 6. August 2025 ist am 10. Oktober 2025 im Bundestag in Erster Lesung beraten worden.

Jahren durchaus eine kritischer gewordene Haltung gegenüber arbeitsrechtlichen Sonderentwicklungen und eine Rückbesinnung auf eine zivilistische Herangehensweise an Auslegungsfragen des Arbeitsrechts beobachten. Der Blick auf die Entscheidungspraxis des Bundesarbeitsgerichts zeigt das in meiner Bewertung deutlich. Ein anschauliches Beispiel bildet etwa die Rechtsprechung zum Leistungsstörungsrecht.[15] Zahlreiche arbeitsrechtliche Erscheinungen außerhalb des Arbeitsverhältnisrechts (wie Arbeitskampf, Tarifvertrag und Betriebsverfassung) können dagegen mit der Begrifflichkeit des Privatrechts nur zum Teil erfasst werden.

Auch im Arbeitsverhältnisrecht (mehr jedoch im Recht der Verbände und dem Arbeitskampfrecht) fehlt es in einigen Hinsichten an geschriebenen oder für das Arbeitsverhältnis passenden Rechtssätzen. Wo gesetzliche Vorgaben fehlen oder unvollständig sind, müssen die Gerichte das Recht fortbilden. Nur so können sie die den Gerichten vom Grundgesetz (Art. 28 I, Art. 19 IV GG) auferlegte Pflicht erfüllen, jeden vor sie gebrachten Rechtsstreit sachgerecht zu entscheiden. Es wäre aber ein Missverständnis anzunehmen, Lückenhaftigkeit sei sozusagen ein Markenzeichen des Arbeitsrechts. Die allermeisten Fragen des Arbeitsverhältnisrechts sind, wenn auch in einer Vielzahl von Einzelgesetzen, geregelt. Wo Lücken im Gesetz bestehen, unterliegt die Rechtsfortbildung im Arbeitsrecht keinen anderen Kriterien als sonst.

VI. Die überkommene Gestaltung des Arbeitsverhältnisses durch das (Arbeits-)Recht in Deutschland

Das Prinzip der Privatautonomie bildet von jeher die Grundlage des Bürgerlichen Rechts und damit des Arbeitsverhältnisrechts. Seit 1949 ist die für Privatautonomie zentrale Vertragsfreiheit verfassungsrechtlich durch Art. 12 Abs. 1 GG, Art. 2 Abs. 1 GG gewährleistet. Diese Gewährleistung schließt die Arbeitsvertragsfreiheit ein. Neben der Vertragsfreiheit steht die ebenfalls verfassungsrechtlich durch Art. 9 Abs. 3 GG gewährleistete Koalitionsfreiheit. Die Koalitionsfreiheit sichert die Vereinbarung von Arbeitsbedingungen auf einer kollektiven Ebene, gesetzlich unterstützt durch das Tarifvertragsgesetz (TVG) und die darin normierte unmittelbare und zwingende Wirkung der Normen des Tarifvertrags. Privatautonomie und Tarifautonomie wirken im deutschen Recht zusammen. Beide Ebenen sind durch den Gedanken der Autonomie geprägt. Die durch Art. 9 Abs. 3 GG verfassungsrechtlich gewährleistete Tarifautonomie beruht auf dem Gedanken, gesellschaftliche Kräfte zu aktivieren und gesellschaftlichen Gruppen die Regelung von Angelegenheiten, die sie selbst betreffen und die sie besonders sachkundig beurteilen können, zu eigener Verantwortung zu überlassen.[16] Es soll nicht in erster Linie der Staat die Arbeitsbeziehungen gestalten.

---

15 Siehe stellvertretend BAG, NJW (2022), S. 2867 ff. zu § 615 S. 3 BGB.

16 BVerfGE 33, S. 125 (156 f.).

Natürlich kennt die Privatautonomie gerade im Arbeitsrecht Schranken.[17] Das im Geist des Liberalismus entstandene Bürgerliche Gesetzbuch formulierte zunächst nur die für eine freiheitliche Rechtsordnung unverzichtbaren äußeren Grenzen. Dazu gehört, dass gemäß § 138 BGB Rechtsgeschäfte, die gegen die guten Sitten verstoßen, nichtig sind. Das erfasst insbesondere Rechtsgeschäfte, durch welche Zwangslagen ausgebeutet und Unerfahrenheit oder Willensschwäche in dem Bestreben ausgenutzt werden, den anderen Vertragsteil zu übervorteilen. Das Bundesarbeitsgericht hat 2009 für die Grenze zum Lohnwucher höchstrichterlich einen Richtwert gebildet.[18] Danach ist Nichtigkeit der Vergütungsvereinbarung wegen Lohnwuchers gemäß § 138 Abs. 2 BGB gegeben, wenn die Arbeitsvergütung nicht einmal zwei Drittel des in der betreffenden Branche oder Wirtschaftsregion üblicherweise gezahlten Tariflohns erreicht. Auch zwingendes Gesetzesrecht anderer Bereiche als des Bürgerlichen Rechts ist einzuhalten. Gemäß § 134 BGB sind Rechtsgeschäfte, die gegen ein gesetzliches Verbot verstoßen, nichtig. Das sichert die Abstimmung des Bürgerlichen Rechts mit allgemein geltenden öffentlich-rechtlichen Pflichten, im Arbeitsrecht also die Abstimmung des Arbeitsverhältnisrechts und des Arbeitsschutzrechts.

VII. Neue Beschäftigungsformen

1. Kurzer Rückblick

Die auf Deregulierung setzenden Reformen der Jahre nach etwa 1985 haben, nicht nur in Deutschland, neue Beschäftigungsformen in dem Bestreben begünstigt, die Arbeitslosigkeit zu verringern. In vielen Mitgliedstaaten der Europäischen Union hat die Präsenz des Normalarbeitsverhältnisses seit den 1990er Jahren abgenommen, und der Anteil „neuer Beschäftigungsformen" ist (unterschiedlich stark) angestiegen. Diese „neuen Beschäftigungsformen" werden in Deutschland und in Japan allgemein mit dem Begriff der atypischen Beschäftigung belegt. Dazu zählt man vor allem die Teilzeitbeschäftigung, wenn die Beschäftigung einen Zeitumfang von 20 oder weniger Stunden pro Woche hat, die Beschäftigung in einem befristeten Arbeitsverhältnis und die Beschäftigung in Leiharbeit. Bei diesen Formen der atypischen Beschäftigung handelt es sich um Beschäftigung auf der Grundlage eines Arbeitsverhältnisses. Die Zunahme neuer Beschäftigungsformen und deren Konsequenzen war Thema des 68. Deutschen Juristentags 2010 in Berlin. In einem Zusammenhang damit stand das Thema des 74. Deutschen Juristentags „Wen schützt das Arbeits- und Sozialversicherungsrecht? – Empfiehlt sich eine Neuausrichtung seines Anwendungsbereichs?", der 2024 in Stuttgart stattgefunden hat. Die Notwendigkeit von Schutz und Absicherung ist in den Jahren nach 2012 wieder stärker in den Blick gekommen. In diese Richtung geht nun auch die Europäische Union. Die Richtlinie der Europäischen Union über angemessene Mindestlöhne vom 19. Oktober 2022 (RiL (EU) 2022/2041) gibt als Ziel vor, dass 80 % der Beschäftigten unter den Geltungsbereich eines Tarifvertrags fallen sollen.

---

17 Umfassend demnächst *Chandna-Hoppe*, Die Gegenleistung im Vertrag – Gegenstand, Grenzen und Risikoverteilung, Habilitationsschrift Bonn (2024).

18 BAG, NZA (2009), S. 837 ff.

In Deutschland hat nach 2012 der Anteil atypischer Beschäftigung zugunsten des (sozialversicherten) Normalarbeitsverhältnisses abgenommen. Diese Tendenz ist zu begrüßen, und die Tendenz könnte angesichts des Fachkräftemangels stabil bleiben.

2. Teilzeitbeschäftigung und Minijobs

Die nicht nur in Deutschland zu beobachtende Zunahme der Beschäftigungsformen abseits des traditionellen Normalarbeitsverhältnisses beruhte auf verschiedenen Gründen. Von den in meinem Vortrag 2012 angesprochenen „Neuen Beschäftigungsformen" greife ich hier nochmals die Teilzeitbeschäftigung und vor allem die Geringfügige Beschäftigung („Minijobs") heraus.

a) Eine wesentliche Triebfeder der Teilzeitbeschäftigung liegt, weiterhin, in dem Anliegen von Arbeitnehmern und Gesellschaft, Beruf und Familie besser in Einklang zu bringen. Heute, 2025, ist man vor dem Hintergrund des zunehmenden Fachkräftemangels aber bestrebt, Anreiz für den Übergang von einer Teilzeitbeschäftigung in eine Vollzeitstelle oder wenigstens zu einer Erhöhung der Arbeitszeit zu setzen.

b) Anders als bei der „normalen" Teilzeitbeschäftigung liegt es in dem in Deutschland praktisch wichtigen Teilbereich der sog. geringfügigen Beschäftigung. Die geringfügige Beschäftigung ist arbeitsrechtlich Teilzeitbeschäftigung. Sie unterscheidet sich von der üblichen Teilzeitbeschäftigung durch ihre sozialrechtliche und steuerrechtliche Sonderbehandlung bei den Abgaben: Die geringfügige (Teilzeit-)Beschäftigung ist in der Kranken-, Pflege-, Renten- und Arbeitslosenversicherung von der Sozialversicherungspflicht befreit, und sie ist von der normalen Steuerpflicht ausgenommen.[19] Die damit verbundene Abgabenprivilegierung ist, auch im Jahr 2025, beschäftigungspolitisch motiviert. Man wollte bei der Reform dieser sog. „Minijobs" im Jahr 2003 geringfügige Beschäftigungsverhältnisse unter Zurückstellung der ihnen bis dahin entgegengebrachten Bedenken ausweiten und Anreize zur Schaffung bzw. Aufnahme einer solchen Beschäftigung geben, um Arbeit im Niedriglohnsektor zu fördern.

c) Der nicht nur in Deutschland zu beobachtende Anstieg der sozialversicherten Teilzeitbeschäftigung hat auch 2025 weiterhin einige Vorteile. Für Arbeitgeber hat Teilzeitbeschäftigung den Vorteil einer höheren Belastbarkeit der Teilzeitbeschäftigten und flexibler Einsatzmöglichkeiten, was sich mit Motivationsvorteilen bei den Arbeitnehmern verbinden kann. Bei den Arbeitnehmern steht das Anliegen einer besseren Vereinbarkeit von Beruf und Familie im Vordergrund, was in einer Zeit knapper werdender Fachkräfte wiederum günstige Rückwirkung auf Unternehmen hat, weil man Kräfte gewinnt, die für eine Vollzeitstelle nicht zur Verfügung stehen könnten. Zugleich wird heute, 2025, bemerkt, dass Arbeitskräfte, denen man ein größeres Arbeitsvolumen geben möchte, in der Teilzeit verbleiben. Teilzeitarbeit hat in der Praxis vor allem für Frauen Bedeutung. Das deutsche Arbeitsrecht fördert Teilzeitbeschäftigung, in Unternehmen mit mehr als 15 Ar-

---

[19] Überblick zur Rechtslage bei *Waltermannn/Schmidt/Chandna-Hoppe*, Sozialrecht, 16. Aufl. (2025), Rn. 136 ff.

beitnehmern besteht ein Anspruch auf Teilzeitbeschäftigung, soweit betriebliche Gründe nicht entgegenstehen (§§ 6, 8 TzBfG). Das durch Richtlinienrecht der Europäischen Union vorgegebene Verbot der Diskriminierung Teilzeitbeschäftigter ist durch § 4 TzBfG umgesetzt. In der rechtspolitischen Bewertung besteht nach allgemeiner Überzeugung in Bezug auf die sozialversicherungspflichtige Teilzeitbeschäftigung von allen neuen Beschäftigungsformen auch 2025 weiterhin der geringste Anlass, den in Deutschland geltenden Rechtsrahmen zu verändern. Nachteile der Teilzeitbeschäftigung können sich, wenn alle Rechtsvorschriften eingehalten werden, allerdings aus dem geringeren Umfang der Erwerbstätigkeit ergeben. Der geringere Umfang führt zu geringerem Einkommen der Beschäftigten und zu geringerem Beitragsaufkommen in der Sozialversicherung, damit im deutschen Sicherungssystem zu geringerer Altersvorsorge. Das kann zu Problemen führen, wenn die Teilzeitbeschäftigung nicht dauerhaft in einen Haushaltskontext mit weiterem Einkommen eingebettet ist und längerfristig erfolgt. Hier sind mit dem Blick in die Zukunft die veränderten gesellschaftlichen Realitäten in Bezug auf Ehe, Familie und Partnerschaft sowie die zunehmende Instabilität von Ehen und Partnerschaften zu bedenken.

d) Handlungsbedarf erkannte man in Deutschland, ohne dass dies nach 2012 zu Veränderungen geführt hätte[20] im Hinblick auf die abgabenprivilegierte geringfügige Beschäftigung als besonderer Form der Teilzeitbeschäftigung. Bei den „Minijobs“ sind nur pauschale Beiträge zur Kranken- und Rentenversicherung und eine geringe pauschale Steuer zu entrichten. Außer in der Renten- und Unfallversicherung bestehen keine Leistungsansprüche der Beschäftigten. Diese Privilegierung ist jedoch mit beträchtlichen Nachteilen verbunden, denen keine Vorteile gegenüberstehen. Bei ihrer Einführung wurde von einer Brückenfunktion der Minijobs in normale Arbeit ausgegangen. Diese Brückenfunktion ist jedoch bis heute in keiner einzigen Untersuchung bestätigt worden. Das ist nicht verwunderlich, denn Minijobs haben ihre praktische Bedeutung vor allem im Dienstleistungssektor und dort vornehmlich in Branchen, in denen Vollzeitbeschäftigung selten vorkommt (etwa in der Gastronomie oder in der Gebäudebetreuung) und in denen die Vollzeitbeschäftigung gegenüber der Teilzeitbeschäftigung keine Präferenz genießt. Die Zahl der geringfügigen Beschäftigungsverhältnisse in Deutschland liegt heute, wie 2012, bei rund 7,5 Millionen.[21]

Die in anderen europäischen Ländern (außer in Österreich) nicht anzutreffende Sonderbehandlung von geringfügigen Teilzeitbeschäftigungsverhältnissen hat im Spannungsfeld von Bürgerlichem Recht, Arbeitsrecht und Sozialrecht eine weiterhin zu wenig beachtete ungünstige ökonomische Wirkung. Diese ökonomische Wirkung läuft sinnvoller Vertragsfreiheit zuwider. Die ungünstige ökonomische Wirkung hat

---

20 Kritisch insbesondere auch *Schlegel*, Geringfügige Beschäftigung, in: Brose/Greiner/Rolfs/Sagan/Schneider/Stoffels/Temming/Ulber (Hrsg.), Grundlagen des Arbeits- und Sozialrechts, Festschrift für Ulrich Preis (2021), S. 1167 ff. Zum hier vertretenen Standpunkt *Waltermann*, Mini-Jobs – ausweiten oder abschaffen?, in: NJW 2013, S. 118 ff. m. Nachw.

21 Bundesagentur für Arbeit, Beschäftigung – Die aktuelle Entwicklung in Kürze – Juni 2025, abrufbar unter https://statistik.arbeitsagentur.de/DE/Navigation/Statistiken/Fachstatistiken/Beschaeftigung/Aktuelle-Eckwerte-Nav.html.

sich allerdings abgeschwächt. Sie lag 2012 in Folgendem: Die Privilegierung der Minijobs bei Abgaben und Steuern wird ohne jeden Zweifel bei Abschluss des Arbeitsvertrags in Bezug auf die Lohnhöhe einkalkuliert. Unternehmen und Arbeitnehmer haben durch die Abgabenprivilegierung gleichermaßen, kurzfristig betrachtet, Vorteile, worin ein Fehlanreiz liegt. Die Arbeitnehmer bekommen das Geld in die Hand, längerfristige Nachteile für sie selbst und für die Gesellschaft aufgrund der Sozialversicherungsfreiheit liegen außerhalb ihrer Wahrnehmung. Die Unternehmen entrichten zwar pauschalierte Abgaben, sie haben jedoch unter dem Strich betriebswirtschaftlich Kostenvorteile gegenüber einer normalen (Teilzeit-)Beschäftigung. Bei Minijobs liegen die Pauschalbeiträge bei rund 30 %, im nicht abgabenprivilegierten normalen Arbeitsverhältnis müssen die Arbeitgeber betriebswirtschaftlich mit dem vollen Beitragssatz von 40 % kalkulieren, da sie den Arbeitgeber- und den Arbeitnehmerbeitrag abführen müssen (§§ 28d S. 1, 28e Abs. 1, 28g, 28h Abs. 1 SGB IV). Am Ende wurde 2012, als es das MiLoG noch nicht gab, in Kenntnis der ökonomischen Wirkung der Rechtslage eine „Nettoentgeltvereinbarung" geschlossen. Man einigte sich unter Berücksichtigung der Abgabenprivilegierung bei Sozialversicherungsbeiträgen und Steuern auf den Betrag, mit dem in der Tasche der Arbeitnehmer zufrieden war und der dem Unternehmen unter Berücksichtigung der Pauschalabgaben angebracht erschien. Ohne die Abgabenprivilegierung hätte man anders kalkulieren müssen.

Dieser die Privatautonomie und die Vertragsfreiheit betreffende Fehlanreiz führte in seinen Auswirkungen nicht nur zu einer Verzerrung des Arbeitsmarkts mit Auswirkung auf die Lohngestaltung im einzelnen Arbeitsverhältnis. Der Fehlanreiz beeinflusste darüber hinaus in zahlreichen Bereichen die Personalplanung, und er prägte am Ende die Struktur des Arbeitsmarkts in den Bereichen, in denen Minijobs vermehrt anzutreffen sind.

Die skizzierte Abgabenprivilegierung beeinflusst weiterhin das Vertragsgeschehen am Arbeitsmarkt. Es zeigt sich beispielhaft, wie sehr trotz des bürgerlich-rechtlichen Rahmens, in den das Arbeitsverhältnis und das Arbeitsverhältnisrecht eingebettet sind, Einflüsse des Sozialrechts wesentlich werden können und beachtet werden müssen. Allerdings erfolgte 2015 mit der Einführung des MiLoG eine nochmalige Beeinflussung des Privatrechts, dieses Mal durch das Arbeitsrecht und mit der – nicht beabsichtigten – Folge, dass sich der Anreiz, Minijobs zu begründen, für Arbeitgeber (nicht für Arbeitnehmer) verringerte: Denn Arbeitgeber zahlen seither die Pauschalabgaben von rund 30 % mit Bezug auf das Nettoentgelt, während aber durch den nicht abdingbaren gesetzlichen Mindestlohn die bis dahin mögliche „Nettoentgeltvereinbarung" nicht mehr möglich ist. Die Pointe der Minijobs lag bis Ende 2014 darin, dass Arbeitgeber bei Minijobs ein Nettoentgelt anboten und vereinbarten, das mehr oder weniger weit unter dem von 2015 an geltenden Mindestlohn lag.[22] Seit 2015 bildet der gesetzliche Mindestlohn die Untergrenze der möglichen (Nettoentgelt-)Vereinbarung. Für Arbeitnehmer blieb allerdings der Fehlanreiz bestehen, wenn sie aufgrund des Familienkontexts einen höheren Steuersatz als die Pauschalsteuer von 2 % hatten. Seit 2022 ist allerdings dieser Effekt wieder geringer geworden, weil durch eine weitere Detailreform Arbeitgeber im (nun sog.) „Übergangsbe-

22 Näher *Waltermann/Schmidt/Chandna-Hoppe* (Anm. 19), Rn. 143 m. Nachw.

reich" oberhalb der Geringfügigkeitsgrenze (zuvor „Gleitzone" genannt) einen Beitragsanteil von 28 % zu zahlen haben, der dann bei höherem Verdienst des Arbeitnehmers schrittweise sinkt (§ 20 Abs. 2a SGB IV).

3. Arbeitsverhältnisse mit geringen Erträgen

Arbeitsverhältnisse mit geringem Ertrag hatten 2012 eine größere Bedeutung als heute. Hier haben sich Dinge verändert. In Deutschland war 2012 vor dem Hintergrund des Konkurrenzdrucks im globalen Wettbewerb und des Wandels zu Dienstleistungsarbeit die Zahl niedrig entlohnter Arbeitsverhältnisse gestiegen. Daran hatten die Reformen des Arbeits- und Sozialrechts durch die damalige „Agenda 2010" mitgewirkt, die eine Ausweitung des Niedriglohnsektors bezweckt und erreicht haben. In der Folgezeit gelangten die damit verbundenen Probleme in das Blickfeld. 2012 war es bereits zu ersten Reaktionen des Gesetzgebers gekommen. In der Leiharbeit veranlassten die dort verbreitet niedrigen Erträge den Gesetzgeber, einen Mindestlohn für diesen Bereich einzuführen (§ 3a AÜG). 2015 wurde der allgemeine gesetzliche Mindestlohn eingeführt.

Auf einen damals noch wenig wahrgenommenen Gesichtspunkt habe ich in dem Vortrag von 2012 hingewiesen, der das auf Privatautonomie gegründete Aushandeln von Arbeitsleistung und Entgelthöhe ungünstig beeinflusst[23] und den man heute, 2025, im Auge hat: Zum Teil wurden und werden noch heute, allerdings wegen des regelmäßig angepassten gesetzlichen Mindestlohns in geringerem Maß, Arbeitsverhältnisse mit niedriger Vergütung (in geringfügiger Beschäftigung, in der Leiharbeit aber auch in sozialversicherten Normalarbeitsverhältnissen mit geringem Ertrag) durch steuerfinanzierte Aufstockungsleistungen zur Sicherung des Existenzminimums bezuschusst. In Deutschland greift die sozialrechtliche Grundsicherung, die subsidiäre Sicherung des Existenzminimums, auch ein, wenn trotz einer Erwerbstätigkeit Bedürftigkeit verbleibt. Arbeitsentgelt und Sozialleistung können nebeneinanderstehen. Natürlich bildet niedriges Arbeitsentgelt nur eine von mehreren Ursachen, die trotz einer ausgeübten Arbeitstätigkeit sozialrechtlich zu Hilfebedürftigkeit und also zu Leistungen führen können. Andere Ursachen sind ein zu niedriger Arbeitsumfang (auch Teilzeitbeschäftigung Alleinerziehender) und der Haushaltskontext. Zu bedenken ist: Die sozialrechtliche Aufstockung von niedrigen Löhnen beeinflusst die Marktsituation am Arbeitsmarkt im Niedriglohnbereich. Es liegt genauso wie bei der Abgabenprivilegierung der Minijobs. Die Aufstockung ermöglicht es den Vertragsparteien, die aufstockende Transferleistung beim Vertragsschluss mit Einfluss auf die Lohnhöhe im Einzelfall einzukalkulieren, das hat wiederum Auswirkung auf die Personalplanung der Unternehmen, und dies hat am Ende Rückwirkung auf die Stellenstruktur im Bereich des Niedriglohnsektors. Es bedarf keiner langen Darlegung, dass durch dieses Zusammenwirken die Verhandlungsposition der Arbeitnehmer beeinflusst wird. Es bleibt offen, wo der „markträumende Preis" liegen könnte, und es entstehen bedenkliche Mitnahmeeffekte. Das widerspricht dem Kon-

---

23 Ausführlicher *Waltermann*, Abschied vom Normalarbeitsverhältnis? – Welche arbeits- und sozialrechtlichen Regelungen empfehlen sich im Hinblick auf die Zunahme neuer Beschäftigungsformen und die wachsende Diskontinuität von Erwerbsbiographien?, in: Verhandlungen des 68. Deutschen Juristentages, Band I, Gutachten Teil B (2010), S. B 70 ff.

zept der Rechtsordnung. Mit dem in Deutschland 2015, später als in anderen europäischen Ländern, eingeführten gesetzlichen Mindestlohn, der derzeit bei 12,82 Euro liegt, hat sich das Problem verringert. Das Arbeitsverhältnisrecht sorgt hier, flankiert durch eine arbeitsschutzrechtliche Absicherung (§§ 14 ff. MiLoG) für eine Abstützung der Marktsituation am Arbeitsmarkt im Niedriglohnbereich.

VIII. Folgen niedriger Erträge aus Arbeit

Niedrige Entgelte in Arbeitsverhältnissen haben beachtliche ungünstige Auswirkungen auf die sozialrechtliche Altersvorsorge. Mit dem Blick auf die Altersvorsorge, die in Deutschland wie in Japan auf der Versicherung beruht, zeigt sich die Unvereinbarkeit einer Verfestigung niedriger Entgelte und deren Begünstigung durch das Recht in aller Deutlichkeit. Geringe Erträge aus Arbeit laufen dem Konzept einer auf Versicherung beruhenden Altersvorsorge zuwider. Ein auf Versicherung beruhendes Konzept der Altersvorsorge ist auf Erträge aus Arbeit unbedingt angewiesen. Fehlt eine geeignete Entgeltstruktur, müssen in der Zukunft in steigendem und beträchtlichem Maß niedrige Renten zu Lasten der wirtschaftlichen Spielräume der Zukunft aus Steuermitteln zum Existenzminimum aufgestockt werden. Das verschiebt Probleme zu Lasten der nächsten Generation in die Zukunft weiter. Die damit verbundene finanzielle Belastung wird demnächst vor allem die Mittelschicht zu spüren bekommen, welche die (alternde) Gesellschaft wesentlich mitträgt. In allen Demokratien hängt aber die Stabilität der Gesellschaft – und damit auch die Bedingung für geordnetes Wirtschaften der Unternehmen – davon ab, dass sich dieser Personenkreis nicht aus Mangel an Perspektive abwendet. Und es wird zu Recht darauf hingewiesen, dass auch im Bereich des Sozialen in gedanklicher Anwendung der vom Bundesverfassungsgericht zu den Lasten des Klimaschutzes entwickelten Gesichtspunkte[24] eine verhältnismäßige Belastung zwischen den Generationen gewährleistet sein muss;[25] dann darf nicht die zahlenmäßig auch noch kleinere nächste Generation für Einsparungen und Versäumnisse (auch in der Infrastruktur) aus früheren Zeiten geradestehen müssen.

IX. Herausforderungen für das Arbeitsrecht

Das deutsche Bürgerliche Recht hatte nie im Sinn, den Vertragsparteien Vorschriften über die im Austauschverhältnis stehenden Leistungsinhalte zu machen.[26] Deshalb lässt auch das Recht der AGB-Kontrolle (§§ 305 bis 310 BGB), das seit 2002 auch im Arbeitsrecht gilt, Abreden über den unmittelbaren Gegenstand der Hauptleistung (im Arbeitsverhältnis also Arbeitsleistung und Entgeltzahlung) kontrollfrei. Das Privatrecht geht aber selbstverständlich von der Vorstellung aus, dass die Einzelnen eigenverantwortlich die Existenz sichern. Für die eigenverantwortliche Existenzsicherung hat die Rechtsordnung einen geeigneten Rechtsrahmen zu gewährleisten.

---

24 BVerfGE 157, 30 ff. = NJW (2021), S. 1723, Rn. 146, 182 f.

25 *Schlegel*, Zeitenwende auch im Sozialstaat?, in: NJW (2023), S. 2096 f.

26 Ausf. demnächst *Chandna-Hoppe* (Anm. 17).

Was die Arbeitsverhältnisse angeht, ist die Gewährleistung dieses Rechtsrahmens Aufgabe des Arbeitsrechts. Arbeitsleistung und Entgeltzahlung die Struktur zu geben, ist in Deutschland dabei traditionell Aufgabe der Tarifautonomie. Deren Funktionsdefizit im Niedriglohnbereich hat eine gesetzliche Mindestlohnregelung unausweichlich gemacht, um der Privatautonomie zuwiderlaufende Marktverzerrungen durch die sozialrechtliche Absicherung des Existenzminimums zu verhindern. Ohnehin gebietet benötigte und ordnungsgemäß erbrachte Arbeit eine ordnungsgemäße Bezahlung.

Es geht nicht nur um volkswirtschaftliche und politische Fragen, sondern auch um die *Konzeption der Rechtsordnungen* vor dem Hintergrund ihrer Wertmaßstäbe.[27] Der Rechtsvergleich, den Heinrich Menkhaus mit seinem langjährigen beruflichen Engagement im Zivilrecht und Arbeitsrecht Japans und Deutschland sehr unterstützt hat, kann die zukunftsgerichtete und nachhaltige Gestaltung des Arbeitsrechts dabei sehr unterstützen.

Literaturverzeichnis

Chandna-Hoppe, Katja: Die Gegenleistung im Vertrag – Gegenstand, Grenzen und Risikoverteilung, Habilitationsschrift Bonn (2024).

Greiner, Stefan: Grenzen des Fremdpersonaleinsatzes im Krankenhaus: Die „Honorararzt"-Entscheidungen des BSG – zugleich Besprechung der Leitentscheidung BSG, 4.6.2019, B 12 R 11/18 R –, in: NZS (2019), S. 761 ff.

Müller-Glöge, Rudi/*Preis*, Ulrich/*Gallner*, Inken/*Schmidt*, Ingrid (Hrsg.): Erfurter Kommentar zum Arbeitsrecht, 25. Aufl. (2025).

Roloff, Sebastian: Scheinselbständig, „scheintypologisch" und „scheinbar" zwingend – Gedanken zum Verständnis des § 611a Ab. 1 BGB, in: Brose, Wiebke/Greiner, Stefan/Rolfs, Christian/Sagan, Adam/Schneider, Angie/Stoffels, Markus/Temming, Felipe/Ulber, Daniel (Hrsg.), Grundlagen des Arbeits- und Sozialrechts, Festschrift für Ulrich Preis (2021), S. 1087 ff.

Schlegel, Rainer: Geringfügige Beschäftigung, in: Brose, Wiebke/Greiner, Stefan/Rolfs, Christian/Sagan, Adam/Schneider, Angie/Stoffels, Markus/Temming, Felipe/Ulber, Daniel (Hrsg.), Grundlagen des Arbeits- und Sozialrechts, Festschrift für Ulrich Preis (2021), S. 1167 ff.

Schlegel, Rainer: Zeitenwende auch im Sozialstaat?, in: NJW (2023), S. 2093 ff.

Waltermann, Raimund: Abhängige Beschäftigung in der digitalisierten Arbeitswelt, in: NZA (2021), S. 297 ff.

Waltermann, Raimund: Abschied vom Normalarbeitsverhältnis? – Welche arbeits- und sozialrechtlichen Regelungen empfehlen sich im Hinblick auf die Zunahme neuer Beschäftigungsformen und die wachsende Diskontinuität von Erwerbsbiographien?, in: Verhandlungen des 68. Deutschen Juristentages, Band I, Gutachten Teil B (2010).

Waltermann, Raimund: Attraktivität von Tarifbindung – Zur Zukunftsfähigkeit der deutschen Tarifautonomie, in: ZFA (2020), S. 211 ff.

---

27 Näher zum hier vertretenen Standpunkt *Waltermann* (Anm. 23), S. B 112 ff.

Waltermann, Raimund: Beschäftigung und Arbeitsverhältnis – Verschiedenheiten und Gemeinsamkeiten der Rechtsbegriffe, in: Meßling, Miriam/Voelzke, Thomas (Hrsg.), Die Zukunft des Rechts- und Sozialstaats, Festschrift für Rainer Schlegel (2024), S. 907 ff.

Waltermann, Raimund: Digital statt analog: Zur Zukunftsfähigkeit des Arbeitsrechts, in: RdA (2019), S. 94 ff.

Waltermann, Raimund: Digitalisierung der Arbeitswelt und Schutz Kleiner Selbständiger durch das Sozialversicherungsrecht, SGb. (2017), S. 425 ff.

Waltermann, Raimund: Mini-Jobs – ausweiten oder abschaffen?, in: NJW (2013), S. 118 ff.

Waltermann, Raimund/*Chandna-Hoppe*, Katja: Arbeitsrecht, Band 1, Individualarbeitsrecht, 21. Auflage, 2026.

Waltermannn, Raimund/*Schmidt*, Benjamin/*Chandna-Hoppe*, Katja: Sozialrecht, 16. Aufl. (2025).

Wiedemann, Herbert: Das Arbeitsverhältnis als Austausch- und Gemeinschaftsverhältnis (1966).

Arbeitszeitsouveränität und Unternehmensorganisation in Deutschland und Japan

Von *Rolf Wank*

Prof. Dr. Rolf Wank, Emeritus der Ruhr-Universität Bochum, früher Inhaber des Lehrstuhls für Bürgerliches Recht, Handels-, Wirtschafts- und Arbeitsrecht sowie Methodenlehre; seit langem Mitglied der Deutsch-Japanischen Gesellschaft für Arbeitsrecht; häufige Aufenthalte in Japan; Vorträge, Vorlesungen und Seminare in Zusammenarbeit mit Prof. Takashi Araki, Prof. Yoko Hashimoto und Prof. Hajime Wada; umfangreiche Veröffentlichungen in deutsch-japanischen Buchprojekten.

I. Die Interessenlage bei der Zeitsouveränität

Wenn man über eine Reform des Arbeitszeitrechts spricht, ist damit üblicherweise nur die Regelung im Arbeitszeitgesetz gemeint. Tatsächlich ist ein größerer Komplex zu betrachten. Zeitsouveränität auf Arbeitnehmerseite betrifft alle Formen der zeitlichen Bindung im Arbeitsverhältnis. Es geht also u. a. um

- Befristung[1]
- Teilzeit
- Wochenarbeitszeit
- Elternzeit, Angehörigenbetreuung, Kinderbetreuung, Fortbildung (s. u. V.)
- Überstunden (s. u. VII.) und
- ständige Erreichbarkeit (s. u. VI.).

Wichtig ist dabei, dass zwei Interessen miteinander in Einklang gebracht werden müssen: das Interesse des Arbeitnehmers an Zeitsouveränität auf der einen Seite und das Interesse des Arbeitgebers an einer funktionsfähigen Organisation auf der anderen Seite.[2]

1 Zum Befristungsrecht in Deutschland und Japan *Wank*, Rechtskultur im Arbeitsrecht in Japan und Deutschland, in: Takei/Yano/Ogata/Yamakawa (Hrsg.), In Search of Justice in Labor Law, Festschrift für Hajime Wada, Tokio (2023), S. 205 ff.

2 S. Weißbuch „Arbeiten 4.0“ des Bundesministeriums für Arbeit und Soziales (Stand März 2017), S. 119; s. auch § 1 Ziff. 1 ArbZG.

Duncker & Humblot · Berlin | https://doi.org/10.3790/978-3-428-59611-9.2025.418841

1. Zeitsouveränität auf Arbeitnehmerseite

Der Arbeitnehmer würde seine Arbeit am liebsten mit seinem Laptop in Bali am Strand ausüben. Er arbeitet so lange, wie es ihm gefällt. Ist ein Verwandter krank (insbesondere bei Kindern in Kindergarten und Schule regelmäßig der Fall) oder sind Verwandte pflegebedürftig, möchte der Arbeitnehmer sofort und ohne Einschränkungen zur Verfügung stehen. Ist eine Hypothek für ein Haus abzutragen, möchte der Arbeitnehmer fünf Stunden pro Woche länger arbeiten; sind kleine Kinder zu betreuen, möchte er fünf Stunden weniger in der Woche arbeiten. Und wenn der Arbeitnehmer eine Weltreise plant, wünscht er ein Jahr Arbeitsunterbrechung.

Zeitsouveränität auf Arbeitnehmerseite kann auf bestimmten äußeren Anlässen beruhen oder auf freiwilliger Entscheidung. Eine *anlassbezogene Änderung* der Arbeitszeit ergibt sich bei Mutterschutz, Elternzeit, Pflegezeit, Kinderbetreuung, Fortbildung und ähnlichem. Eine anlasslose Änderung der Arbeitszeit besteht z. B. bei einem Sabbatical oder bei einem Teilzeitwunsch. Der Gesetzgeber sollte diese Unterscheidung im Hinblick darauf, was dem Arbeitgeber zumutbar ist – anders als beim verfassungsrechtlich bedenklichen Anspruch auf willkürliche Vertragsänderung hin zu Teilzeit nach § 8 TzBfG – berücksichtigen.

Wichtig ist für Arbeitnehmer auch ein *Wahlrecht.*[3] Als die Deutsche Bahn 2018 ihre Mitarbeiter befragte, ob sie mehr Geld oder mehr Urlaub wollten, entschied sich die Mehrheit für sechs Tage mehr Urlaub im Jahr. Nach einer Studie des Instituts für Arbeitsmarkt- und Berufsforschung würden 40 % der Männer und 30 % der Frauen ihre Arbeitszeit gerne um mindestens 2,5 Wochenstunden reduzieren.[4]

2. Zeitsouveränität auf Arbeitgeberseite

Für Arbeitgeber ist im Hinblick auf den zeitlichen Einsatz von Arbeitnehmern die jederzeitige Einsetzbarkeit und Überprüfbarkeit wichtig. Am liebsten würden sie ihre Arbeitnehmer immer nur dann einsetzen, wenn dafür gerade Bedarf besteht. Dazu sollte es möglichst keine Vorlaufzeit und keine sonstigen Einschränkungen geben; der Aufenthaltsort des Arbeitnehmers sollte möglichst jederzeit unter Kontrolle des Arbeitgebers stehen.

Aus Arbeitgebersicht sind bei der Arbeitszeitgestaltung zu berücksichtigen:

- Kosten: Personelle und organisatorische Mehrkosten z. B. durch Aufteilung einer Vollzeitstelle in zwei Halbtagsstellen. Geringere Kosten bei Teilzeit statt Vollzeit bei bloßem Einsatz zu Stoßzeiten.
- Organisation: Manche Abläufe, insbesondere in der Produktion, laufen nach einem bestimmten zwingenden Konzept ab und lassen keine Zeitvariante zu.

---

3 S. auch *Kümmerling/Postels/Slomka*, Zufriedenheit mit der Arbeitszeit – wie kann sie gelingen? – Eine Analyse der Arbeitszeiten nach Geschlecht und Statusgruppen, Working Paper Nr. 54 Hans-Böckler-Stiftung (2017), S. 74 ff.

4 *Weber/Zimmert*, Arbeitszeit zwischen Wunsch und Wirklichkeit: Wie Diskrepanzen entstehen und wie man sie auflöst, IAB-Kurzbericht 13/2018 (2018), S. 2.

– Planbarkeit: Ein Aspekt, der in Gesetzen, insbesondere im TzBfG, nicht genügend berücksichtigt wird: Jede Änderung der Arbeitszeit setzt eine Umorganisation voraus, die regelmäßig einer längerfristigen Planung bedarf. In den unten vorgestellten Tarifverträgen zur Arbeitszeitsouveränität wird das – besser als im TzBfG – genügend berücksichtigt.

3. Auswirkung auf Dritte, insbesondere Vertreter

In der juristischen Diskussion bleibt eine Person zu Unrecht außer Betracht. Wenn zum Beispiel ein Arbeitnehmer lange Zeit ausfällt, braucht der Arbeitgeber eine Vertretung. Deren Schicksal – im Hinblick auf Befristungsgrund, Dauer der Befristung und Arbeitsaufgaben – hängt davon ab, wie die Regelung für den Vertretenen aussieht. Erlaubt das Gesetz z. B. beim Elternurlaub ein Rückkehrrecht auf den Arbeitsplatz zu jeder Zeit, kann der Vertreter oder die Vertreterin nicht sinnvoll planen. Die Unsicherheit betrifft auch den Arbeitgeber. Welchen Vertrag soll er mit einer Vertretungskraft schließen, wenn unklar ist, wann der Vertretene auf seinen Arbeitsplatz zurückkommt?

II. Das Arbeitszeitrecht der Europäischen Union

1. Die Definition der Arbeitszeit in der Richtlinie

Die Arbeitszeitrichtlinie RL 2003/88/EG (im Folgenden „RL") gibt den Rahmen für das Arbeitszeitrecht der Mitgliedstaaten vor. Geregelt sind unter anderem Arbeitszeit, Ruhezeit, Nachtarbeit und Schichtarbeit (vgl. die Definitionen in Art. 2 RL). Der Zwang, auf die unterschiedlichen Rechtssysteme der Mitgliedstaaten einzugehen und Kompromisse zu schließen, bringt Ungereimtheiten mit sich. Das lässt sich bereits an dem zentralen *Begriff der Arbeitszeit* aufzeigen. Die so genannte Definition in Art. 2 Nr. 1 RL entspricht nicht den Anforderungen[5] an eine Legaldefinition.[6] Darin heißt es: „Arbeitszeit (ist) jede Zeitspanne, während der ein Arbeitnehmer… arbeitet" – offensichtlich eine nichts sagende Zirkeldefinition.[7] Des Weiteren wird die Arbeitszeit dadurch definiert, dass der Arbeitnehmer „dem Arbeitgeber zur Verfügung steht und seine Tätigkeit ausübt oder Aufgaben wahrnimmt". Deutlich wird dadurch zwar, dass es nicht ausreicht, wenn der Arbeitnehmer dem Arbeitgeber zur Verfügung steht. Aber dass er „seine Tätigkeit ausübt oder Aufgaben wahrnimmt" ist nichts anderes als eine Umschreibung dafür, dass er arbeitet. Kennzeich-

5 *Puppe*, Kleine Schule des juristischen Denkens, 5. Aufl. (2008), S. 76 ff.; *Schnapp*, Logik für Juristen, 7. Aufl. (2016), S. 47 ff.; *Wank*, Juristische Methodenlehre (2020), § 8 Rn. 10 ff.

6 Wohlwollende Interpretation bei *Gallner*, in: Franzen/Gallner/Oetker (Hrsg.), Kommentar zum europäischen Arbeitsrecht, 5. Aufl. (2024), RL 2003/88, Art. 2 Rn. 3; Kritik dagegen bei *Sagan*, in: Preis/Sagan (Hrsg.), Europäisches Arbeitsrecht – Grundlagen – Richtlinie – Folgen für das deutsche Recht, 3. Aufl. (2024), S. 812 f.

7 *Puppe* (Anm. 5), S. 77 f.

nend für den Arbeitszeitbegriff des EU-Rechts ist im Übrigen, dass es nur die beiden Begriffe Arbeitszeit und Ruhezeit kennt.[8]

2. Der differenzierte Arbeitszeitbegriff des deutschen Rechts und die Rechtssache Matzak

a) Abstufungen

Gegenüber dieser unergiebigen Definition gab es im deutschen Arbeitszeitrecht folgende Abstufung:[9]

- Ruhezeit
- Rufbereitschaft
- Bereitschaftsdienst
- Arbeitsbereitschaft
- Vollarbeit

Den einen Begriff der Arbeitszeit gibt es nicht. Gemäß der „Relativität der Rechtsbegriffe“[10] gibt es unterschiedliche Begriffe von Arbeitszeit je nach Rechtsgebiet[11] (dazu auch u. II. 2. e)).

Wichtig ist die Trennlinie zwischen Bereitschaftsdienst und Rufbereitschaft,[12] die Unterscheidung zwischen Unionsrecht und deutschem Recht, sowie die Unterscheidung zwischen Gesundheitsschutz[13] und Vergütung (dazu u. II. 2. e)). Auch wenn das – unterkomplexe – Unionsrecht nur Arbeitszeit und Ruhezeit kennt, empfiehlt es sich für ein besseres Verständnis, sich am früheren deutschen Recht zu orientieren.

b) Rufbereitschaft

Rufbereitschaft[14] ist dadurch gekennzeichnet, dass sich der Arbeitnehmer

- nicht an einem vom Arbeitgeber bestimmten Arbeitsplatz aufhalten,
- aber jederzeit erreichbar sein muss.

---

8 S. z. B. EuGH, Urteil v. 10. September 2025 – C–266/14, NZA (2015), S. 1177 – Tyco; *Gallner* (Anm. 6), RL 2003/88, Art. 2 Rn. 4; zur unionsrechtskonformen Auslegung *Roloff*, in: Müller-Glöge/Preis/Gallner/Schmidt (Hrsg.), Erfurter Kommentar zum Arbeitsrecht, 25. Aufl. (2025), § 1 ArbZG Rn. 3.

9 *Roloff* (Anm. 8), § 2 ArbZG Rn. 15–22; *Wank*, Facetten der Arbeitszeit, in: RdA (2014), 285 ff.

10 *Wank* (Anm. 5), § 8 Rn. 46 ff.

11 *Schliemann*, Arbeitszeitgesetz, 4. Aufl. 2020, § 2 Rn. 6; *Wank* (Anm. 9), S. 285 ff.

12 *Gallner* (Anm. 6), RL 2003/88, Art. 2 Rn. 6.

13 *Gallner* (Anm. 6), RL 2003/88, Art. 1 Rn. 6.

14 Dazu *Koberski*, in: Kiel/Lunk/Oetker (Hrsg.), Münchener Handbuch Arbeitsrecht, 5. Aufl. (2021), §§ 181–188 Arbeitszeitschutz, § 182 Rn. 39 ff.; *Buschmann/Ulber*, Arbeitszeitrecht (2019), § 2 ArbZG Rn. 32 f.; *Roloff* (Anm. 8), § 2 ArbZG Rn. 20; *Spengler*, in: Hahn/Pfeiffer/Schubert (Hrsg.), Arbeitszeitrecht, 3. Aufl. (2024), § 2 ArbZG Rn. 10; *Schliemann* (Anm. 11), § 2 Rn. 36 ff.

Nach Unionsrecht[15] und deutschem Recht zählt bei der Rufbereitschaft nur die Zeit der tatsächlich geleisteten Arbeit als Arbeitszeit.[16] Auch nach der EuGH-Rechtsprechung ist ein wichtiges Kriterium für die Abgrenzung, ob der Aufenthaltsort des Arbeitnehmers vom Arbeitgeber bestimmt wird oder vom Arbeitnehmer gewählt wird. Sofern der Arbeitnehmer nicht kurzfristig für eine Arbeit zur Verfügung stehen muss, ist diese Zeit auch nach der Rechtsprechung des EuGH keine Arbeitszeit, sondern Ruhezeit.

c) Bereitschaftsdienst

Bereitschaftsdienst[17] bedeutet, dass der Arbeitnehmer

- nicht durchgängig Arbeitsleistungen erbringen,
- aber sich an einem vom Arbeitgeber bestimmten Ort aufhalten muss.

Beim Bereitschaftsdienst ist im Anschluss an die Rechtsprechung des EuGH eine arbeitsschutzrechtliche Arbeitszeit[18] im deutschen Recht auch dann zu bejahen, wenn der Arbeitnehmer schläft.[19] Entgegen der in Deutschland früher üblichen Differenzierung insbes. beim Bereitschaftsdienst hat der EuGH in seinen Urteilen in den Fällen Simap,[20] Jaeger[21] und Dellas[22] den Bereitschaftsdienst in vollem Umfang arbeitsschutzrechtlich zur Arbeitszeit gezählt.

d) Die Rechtssache Matzak

In seinem Urteil in der Rechtssache Matzak[23] aus Februar 2018 hat der EuGH eine Lösung gefunden, die mit den deutschen Arbeitszeitbegriffen kompatibel und vernünftig ist.[24] Danach verläuft die Trennlinie wie folgt:

Arbeitszeit ist die Zeit, in der der Arbeitnehmer dem Arbeitgeber zur Verfügung steht. Sie ist gekennzeichnet durch

- sofortige Verfügbarkeit[25] und
- Ortsvorgabe durch den Arbeitgeber.

---

15 EuGH, Urteil v. 21. Februar 2018 – C–518/15, Rn. 60, NZA (2018), S. 292 – Matzak.

16 *Schliemann* (Anm. 14), § 2 Rn. 39.

17 *Koberski* (Anm. 14), § 182 Rn. 34 f.; *Roloff* (Anm. 8), § 2 ArbZG Rn. 18; *Schliemann* (Anm. 14), § 2 Rn. 29 ff.

18 Anders für das Vergütungsrecht, *Koberski* (Anm. 14), § 182 Rn. 37; s. u. II. 2. e).

19 EuGH, Urteil v. 9. September 2003 – C–151/02, Rn. 44 ff., NZA (2002), S. 1016 – Jaeger.

20 EuGH, Urteil v. 3. Oktober 2000 – C–303/98, Rn. 46 ff., NZA (2000), S. 1222 – Simap.

21 EuGH (Anm. 19), Rn. 44 ff.

22 EuGH, Urteil v. 1. Dezember 2005 – C–14/04, Rn. 43, NZA (2006), S. 89 – Dellas.

23 EuGH, Urteil v. 21. Februar 2018 – C–518/15, NZA (2018), S. 293.

24 So auch *Bayreuther*, Rufbereitschaft als Arbeitszeit?, in: NZA (2018), S. 348.

25 EuGH (Anm. 23), Rn. 61 ff.: 8 Minuten; dazu *Gallner* (Anm. 6), RL 2003/88 Art. 2 Rn. 5a.

Der Arzt, der im Krankenhaus im Ärztezimmer schläft, bis er zum Einsatz herbeigerufen wird, steht dem Arbeitgeber zur Verfügung; sein Aufenthaltsort ist nicht von ihm gewählt, sondern vom Arbeitgeber bestimmt.

Ruhezeit als Gegenstück zur Arbeitszeit ist demgegenüber dadurch gekennzeichnet, dass der Arbeitnehmer dem Arbeitgeber nicht sofort zur Verfügung steht und dass er seinen Aufenthaltsort selbst gewählt hat. Entscheidend sollte sein, mit welcher Verlässlichkeit sich der Arbeitnehmer während der Abwesenheit von seinem Arbeitsplatz seinen eigenen Interessen widmen kann.[26]

Zwischen Arbeitszeit und Ruhezeit steht eine Fallgestaltung wie in der Rechtssache Matzak: Der Arbeitnehmer kann zwar seinen Aufenthaltsort selbst wählen; er muss aber dem Arbeitgeber innerhalb von 8 Minuten nach einem Anruf zur Verfügung stehen. Da bei dieser Konstellation der Erholungszweck der Ruhezeit nicht gewährleistet ist, wertet der EuGH diese Konstellation zutreffend als Arbeitszeit.

e) Arbeitsschutz und Vergütung

Die Urteile des EuGH beziehen sich allein auf den arbeitsschutzrechtlichen Begriff der Arbeitszeit. Zu Aussagen zur Vergütung der Arbeitszeit fehlt dem EuGH die Kompetenz, Art. 153 Abs. 5 AEUV. Selbst ein dahingehendes obiter dictum des EuGH[27] hat Schliemann kritisiert.[28] Die EuGH-Rechtsprechung ist nur bindend für den Arbeitsschutz, Art. 153 Abs. 2 Buchst. a) i. V. m. Abs. 1 Buchst. a) und b).[29]

Im deutschen Recht richtet sich das Verhältnis von Arbeit und Vergütung[30] nach dem Arbeitsvertrag[31] und nach § 323 BGB: Wenn der Arbeitnehmer nicht arbeitet, erhält er keinen Lohn. Ausnahmen gibt es wegen Verteilung des Unternehmerrisikos nach § 615 BGB sowie aus sozialen Gründen für Fälle von Nichtarbeit nach BUrlG, EFZG, § 616 BGB ua. Eine Vorschrift des Inhalts, dass der Arbeitnehmer auch für seinen Schlaf den vollen Lohn erhalten muss, gibt es nicht. Aus § 611 a BGB sowie aus § 106 GewO folgt für diese Frage nichts. § 611 a Abs. 2 BGB besagt zwar, dass für eine Arbeitsleistung Lohn gezahlt werden muss, aber nicht, dass auch für eine Nichtleistung Lohn anfällt und in welcher Höhe; das bestimmt sich nach dem Tarifvertrag oder nach dem Arbeitsvertrag. Wäre die Gegenansicht[32] richtig, dann wären alle diejenigen Tarifverträge nichtig, die für Bereitschaftsdienst einen geringeren Lohn vorsehen.[33] § 106 GewO besagt nur, dass der Arbeitgeber Ort und Zeit für den Arbeitnehmer bestimmen kann, aber nichts zur Vergütung. Der im Gesetz nicht

---

26 *Bayreuther* (Anm. 24) S. 349.

27 EuGH (Anm. 23), 293.

28 *Schliemann*, Vorlagefragen – Sachantwort des EuGH trotz Nichtkompetenz der EU, in: EuZW (2018), 274; s. aber *Junker*, in: Giesen/Junker/Rieble (Hrsg.), Arbeitszeitmodelle der Zukunft (2019), S. 99, 102 f.

29 *Gallner* (Anm. 6), Art. 1 RL 2003/88/EG Rn. 3, 22.

30 Zu den verschiedenen Arbeitszeitbegriffen je nach Rechtsgebiet s. *Roloff* (Anm. 8), § 2 ArbZG Rn. 8 ff.; *Wank* (Anm. 9), S. 285 ff.

31 *Preis* (Anm. 8) § 611a BGB Rn. 420 ff.

32 *Preis/Schwarz*, Dienstreisen als Rechtsproblem, HSI-Schriftenreihe Band 31 (2020), S. 17, 66 ff.; *Roloff* (Anm. 8), § 2 ArbZG Rn. 21 f.

33 S. demgegenüber BAG, Urteil v. 19. November 2014, Rn. 16, DB (2015), S. 253.

definierte Begriff „Arbeit" wird verstanden als „jede Tätigkeit, die der Befriedigung eines fremden Bedürfnisses dient,"[34] ohne jeden Bezug zum Arbeitsvertrag und zur Entlohnung. Auch aus der EuGH-Rechtsprechung lässt sich kein Gleichlauf von arbeitsschutzrechtlichem und vergütungsrechtlichem Arbeitszeitbegriff herleiten, da der EuGH dafür keine Kompetenz hat. Schließlich lässt sich aus Sondervorschriften über die Arbeitszeit von Kraftfahrern[35] keine allgemeine Aussage herleiten.[36] Wenn daher in Ausführungen zur Lohnhöhe auf den Arbeitszeitbegriff des Arbeitsschutzrechts verwiesen wird, handelt es sich um eine Begriffsvertauschung.[37]

3. Reform des Arbeitszeitrechts der EU?

Wer spekuliert, die Arbeitszeitrichtlinie der EU könnte im Hinblick auf in Deutschland entwickelte Änderungswünsche in absehbarer Zeit geändert werden, sollte diese Hoffnung aufgeben.[38] Kommission, Parlament und Rat konnten sich bis heute nicht auf eine Reform der Arbeitszeitrichtlinie einigen.

4. Arbeitszeit-Richtlinie und Arbeitszeitgesetz: Korsett und Option

Auch wenn die *Richtlinie* eine ganze Reihe bindender Vorgaben macht und der EuGH den Spielraum für Arbeitgeber noch weiter eingegrenzt hat, sollte man nicht außer Acht lassen, dass die Richtlinie auch Optionen enthält, die noch genutzt werden können.

Ein Beispiel bietet die Regelung der Höchstarbeitszeit in der Richtlinie. Der deutsche Gesetzgeber richtet die Höchstarbeitszeit am Arbeitstag aus; er darf höchstens 8–10 Stunden betragen. Demgegenüber lässt die Richtlinie auch eine nationale Regelung zu, bei der sich die Arbeitszeit an einer 48-Stunden-Arbeitswoche orientiert.

Auch das *Arbeitszeitgesetz* gewährt viel Spielraum, zum einen bezogen auf Beruf und Tätigkeiten, wie z. B. die Arbeit im Krankenhaus oder in Verkehrsbetrieben, zum anderen durch Tarifverträge, die den Besonderheiten der jeweiligen Branche angepasst sind; man beachte nur die ausführliche Regelung in § 7 ArbZG.

III. Japan – der rechtliche Rahmen

Ein eigenes Arbeitszeitgesetz gibt es in Japan nicht. Dafür hat uns Japan aber zwei allgemeine Gesetze zum Arbeitsvertrag voraus, nämlich das Arbeitsstandardgesetz

34 *Anzinger/Koberski*, ArbZG – Arbeitszeitgesetz, 5. Aufl. (2020), § 2 ArbZG Rn. 9.

35 *Koberski* (Anm. 14), § 187.

36 A. A. *Roloff* (Anm. 8), § 2 ArbZG Rn. 22.

37 Dazu *Schnapp* (Anm. 5), S. 191 ff.

38 *Krause*, Digitalisierung der Arbeitswelt: Herausforderungen und Regelungsbedarf, in: Verhandlungen des 71. Deutschen Juristentages, Band I, Gutachten Teil B (2016), B 465 f.; *Gallner* (Anm. 6), Art. 1 RL 2003/88 Rn. 11 ff.

(ASG) und das Arbeitsvertragsgesetz (AVG). Das Arbeitszeitrecht ist im ASG geregelt.

Auf Anhieb erscheint manches hier vertraut. Nach Art. 32 ASG darf die tägliche Arbeitszeit nicht über 8 Stunden (in Deutschland über 10 Stunden, Art. 3 Satz 2 ArbZG) und die wöchentliche Arbeitszeit nicht über 40 Stunden hinausgehen (in Deutschland ist die 48-Stunden-Woche zulässig). Nach Art. 35 ASG muss es wöchentlich mindestens einen freien Tag geben, wobei in der Praxis zwei Ruhetage üblich sind (vgl. § 9 ArbZG). Während der Arbeitszeit ist nach Art. 34 Abs. 1 ASG eine Ruhepause von mindestens 45 Minuten zu geben.

Charakteristisch ist, dass vom gesetzlichen Arbeitszeitrecht eine Reihe von Abweichungen durch Vereinbarung möglich sind.

In Betracht kommen:

- eine schriftliche Vereinbarung mit der Mehrheitsgewerkschaft
- eine schriftliche Vereinbarung mit dem Mehrheitsvertreter der Arbeitnehmer
- eine Regelung in der Arbeitsordnung.

Ein Mehrheitsvertreter kann nur dann eine abweichende Vereinbarung treffen, wenn es im Betrieb keine Mehrheitsgewerkschaft gibt.[39]

Eine Bezugnahme auf die genannten Rechtsgrundlagen (teils auf alle drei, teils auf die ersten beiden) findet sich in Art. 32-2 Abs. 1, 32-3 Abs. 1, 32-4 Abs. 1, 36 Abs. 1, 38-2, 38-3 Abs. 1 ASG. Eine Besonderheit ist der Betriebsausschuss nach Art. 38-4 ASG, der sich aus Vertretern des Arbeitgebers und der Arbeitnehmer zusammensetzt. Seine Beschlüsse treten nach Art. 38-4 Abs. 5 ASG an die Stelle der oben genannten Rechtsgrundlagen.

Bei einer *Rechtsvergleichung* muss man außer auf die einzelnen Paragrafen auch auf das Gesamtsystem und auf die Rechtstatsachen achten.[40] Das scheinbar arbeitnehmerfreundliche Bild vom japanischen Arbeitszeitrecht wird stark getrübt, wenn man das Recht der Überstunden und die gelebte Praxis einbezieht (dazu u. VII.). Ein markantes Beispiel ist das *Urlaubsrecht.* Der japanische Urlaubsanspruch nach Art. 39 ASG umfasst nur halb so viel Tage wie der deutsche,[41] und es galt bis vor einiger Zeit als sozial verwerflich, ihn für mehr als die Hälfte der dem Arbeitnehmer zustehenden Tage tatsächlich in Anspruch zu nehmen. Heute hängt die Einstellung von der Generation und vom Unternehmen ab. Bekannt ist auch das Phänomen des

---

39 Zur Organisation der Vertretung der Arbeitnehmer in Japan *Kuwamura*, Die Flexibilisierung des Arbeitsrechts und die Vertretung der Arbeitnehmer in Japan, in: RdA (2012), 155 ff.

40 *Wank*, Rechtsvergleichung und faktische Geltung, in: Arbeit und Recht im gesellschaftlichen Wandel – 25 Jahre Gesellschaften für Arbeitsrecht in Deutschland und Japan – Festschrift zum 25. Geburtstag der Deutsch-Japanischen Gesellschaft für Arbeitsrecht e. V. (2023), S. 103 ff.

41 S. *Kiyono*, Characteristics of and Differences between the Way of Working in Japan and Germany, in: Düwell/Gallner/Haase/Wolmerath (Hrsg.), Auf dem Weg zu einem sozialen und inklusiven Rechtsstaat – Covid 19 als Herausforderung, Liber amicorum Franz Josef Düwell (2021), S. 119 f.

Karōshi: Jemand arbeitet sich zu Tode – das ist wörtlich zu verstehen.[42] Gegenmaßnahmen waren die Reformen der Arbeitsweise durch die Gesetzesnovellen von 2018/19.

In Japan ist der Organisationsgrad der Arbeitnehmer sehr niedrig. Gewerkschaften gibt es in den großen Unternehmen – als Unternehmensgewerkschaften, nicht nach dem Industrieverbandsprinzip.[43] In kleinen und mittleren Unternehmen wird eine betriebliche Vereinbarung mit dem Mehrheitsvertreter geschlossen; dessen demokratische Legitimation ist zweifelhaft. Es fehlt an einer schlagkräftigen Vertretung der Arbeitnehmerinteressen wie nach dem Betriebsverfassungsgesetz.[44]

IV. Modelle flexibler Arbeitszeit

1. Deutschland

Flexible Arbeitszeit[45] ist im Hinblick auf Arbeitnehmer und Arbeitgeber ambivalent zu bewerten. Auf der einen Seite kann sie Arbeitnehmern mehr Zeitsouveränität verschaffen. Andererseits kann sie Arbeitnehmer stärker unter Druck setzen im Hinblick auf Arbeitsleistung, Arbeitsverdichtung und Arbeitskontrolle. Im Einzelfall kann es sein, dass eine flexible Arbeitszeit allein vom Arbeitnehmer gewünscht wird oder allein vom Arbeitgeber. Der rechtliche Rahmen muss dann jeweils die Interessen der anderen Vertragspartei berücksichtigen. Am besten ist natürlich eine Regelung, die den Interessen von Arbeitgebern und Arbeitnehmern in gleicher Weise gerecht wird.

Aus der *japanischen rechtssoziologischen Literatur* zeigt sich, dass eine Reduzierung der Arbeitszeit oder jedenfalls Änderungsmöglichkeiten sich auch *für den Arbeitgeber positiv* auswirken.[46] So führen übermäßig lange Arbeitszeiten zu einer ineffizienten Allokation von Humankapital. Der japanische Arbeitnehmer ist weniger produktiv als der durchschnittliche Arbeitnehmer in der OECD. Zu lange Arbeitszeiten verhindern eine gesunde Balance von Arbeit und Privatleben; sie schreiben das Rollenmodell der Familie fest;[47] sie wirken sich gesundheitsschädlich aus. Auch hat man festgestellt, dass Innovationen und Kreativität am ehesten in einer entspannten Situation entstehen.

---

42 *Josephs*, in: Blanpain/Bisom-Rapp/Corbett/Josephs/Zimmer (Hrsg.), The Global Workplace – International and Comparative Employment Law – Cases and Materials (2007), S. 524 ff.; *Tieste*, Der Tod durch Überarbeitung (2003); s. auch *Wank* (Anm. 1), S. 192, 209 f. zu einem Urteil des Nagasaki District Court.

43 *Wank*, in: Düwell/Löwisch/Waltermann/Wank (Hrsg.), Das Verhältnis von Arbeitsrecht und Zivilrecht in Japan und Deutschland (2013), S. 83 ff.

44 Krit. *Hashimoto*, Arbeitszeitrecht in Japan, in: RIW (2018), S. 564, 565 f.; *Yoshida*, in: Wank/Yoshida, Arbeitsordnung und allgemeine Arbeitsbedingungen – Ein Vergleich der Entwicklung in Deutschland und in Japan (2025), S. 86 ff.

45 Zu Arbeitszeitmodellen *Roloff* (Anm. 8), § 3 ArbZG Rn. 13 ff.

46 Dazu *Ono*, Why Do the Japanese Work Long Hours? – Sociological Perspectives on Long Working Hours in Japan, in: Japan Labor Issues vol. 2, no. 5 (2018), S. 36 f.

47 S. auch *Weber/Zimmert* (Anm. 4), S. 1 f., 6 f.

Im Folgenden werden einige Modelle flexibler Arbeitszeit behandelt.

a) Veränderung der Arbeitszeit

Auch für die Dauer der Arbeitszeit gilt eigentlich der Grundsatz: pacta sunt servanda; anders im Arbeitsrecht. Hier besteht eine Asymmetrie, je nachdem ob der Arbeitnehmer oder der Arbeitgeber eine Veränderung wünscht.

aa) Wünscht ein Arbeitnehmer für eine bestimmte Dauer eine *Erhöhung der Arbeitszeit*, so besteht darauf grundsätzlich kein Anspruch. Aber ein Teilzeitbeschäftigter kann mit einem Vorlauf von drei Monaten verlangen, mit seinem Wunsch berücksichtigt zu werden, § 9 TzBfG.

Geht der Wunsch zur Erhöhung der Arbeitszeit vom Arbeitgeber aus, gilt für die Inhaltskontrolle nicht das TzBfG; nach der Rechtsprechung greift eine Inhaltskontrolle nach § 307 BGB ein.[48] Sie orientiert sich an § 14 TzBfG.

bb) Auf eine *Absenkung der Arbeitszeit* hat der Arbeitnehmer einen Anspruch nach § 8 TzBfG. Ein Rückkehrrecht besteht nach § 9a TzBfG. In der Literatur wird vorgeschlagen, vertraglich eine Erhöhung der Arbeitszeit etwa bei guter Auftragslage vorzusehen, diese aber mit einem *Widerrufsvorbehalt* zu verbinden.[49]

b) Abrufarbeit

Der Gesetzgeber des TzBfG hatte sich vorgestellt, mit dem Instrument der Abrufarbeit nach § 12 TzBfG beiden Interessen gerecht zu werden. Für Arbeitgeber erweist es sich jedoch als störend, dass sie dem Arbeitnehmer die Lage der Arbeitszeit mindestens vier Tage im Voraus mitteilen müssen. Wenn ein Gastronom an einem schönen Sommertag besonders viele Gäste vorfindet, nützt es ihm nichts, wenn er seinen Kellner vier Tage vorher hätte informieren müssen, um ihn heute zusätzlich einsetzen zu können. In der Praxis sind Arbeitgeber daher auf den Gedanken verfallen, bloße Rahmenverträge abzuschließen, die alles offenlassen und dem Arbeitnehmer keine Planung ermöglichen. Diese Verträge halten einer Inhaltskontrolle nicht stand. Aber das BAG weist einen Ausweg.[50] Der Arbeitgeber kann mit dem Arbeitnehmer eine vertragliche Mindestarbeitszeit vereinbaren und zugleich bestimmen, dass eine bestimmte Stundenzahl auf Abruf zu leisten ist. Wie bei der Inhaltskontrolle von Widerrufsvorbehalten darf die Vereinbarung von Abrufarbeit nicht mehr als 25 % der vereinbarten wöchentlichen Mindestarbeitszeit betragen.[51]

c) Beispielhafte Tarifabschlüsse

Im Hinblick auf Zeitsouveränität für Arbeitnehmer einerseits und betriebliche Verträglichkeit andererseits erscheinen zwei neue Tarifabschlüsse[52] bemerkenswert.

---

48 BAG, Urteil v. 8. August 2007, NZA (2008), 223.

49 *Pfrogner*, Flexible Arbeitszeiten in der Industrie 4.0, in: BB (2018), S. 500.

50 Dazu *Pfrogner* (Anm. 49), S. 501 f.

51 BAG, Urteil v. 7. Dezember 2005, in: NZA (2006), S. 423.

52 Zu Möglichkeiten für vom Gesetz abweichende tarifliche Regelungen *Roloff* (Anm. 8), § 7 ArbZG.

aa) Auf der einen Seite ist der Tarifabschluss 2018 der *Metallindustrie* Südwest zu nennen.[53] Er erlaubt es Arbeitnehmern, von der Normalarbeitszeit von 35 Wochenstunden nach unten um ein paar Stunden oder nach oben um ein paar Stunden abzuweichen. Für Arbeitgeber ist das dadurch akzeptabel, dass

- es eine Vorlaufzeit gibt
- nur ein bestimmter Prozentsatz der Beschäftigten von der Arbeitszeitverkürzung Gebrauch machen kann
- das Gesamtkonzept mit dem Betriebsrat abgestimmt wird.

bb) Die Wahlmöglichkeit für Arbeitnehmer wird auch durch das *Potsdamer Modell* im Eisenbahnertarifvertrag gewährt. Arbeitnehmer können danach wählen, ob sie aus der laufenden Tarifrunde mehr Geld oder mehr Freizeit wollen, wobei sich die beiden Lager ungefähr gleichmäßig verteilen.

Die Beispiele zeigen, dass es in erster Linie Aufgabe der Tarifvertragsparteien ist, für sachgerechte Änderungen zu sorgen.

2. Japan

Flexible Arbeitszeitsysteme sind nach dem japanischen ASG in folgender Weise möglich:[54]

- als Arbeitszeit mit Zeitausgleich (Art. 32-2, 32-4 und 32-5 ASG)[55]
- als Gleitarbeitszeit (Art. 38-2, 32-3 ASG)[56] und als
- Ermessensarbeitszeit (Art. 38-2 und 38-4 ASG)[57]
- bei Tätigkeiten in Betrieben, die in einer Rechtsverordnung des Arbeitsministeriums aufgeführt sind, mit Ausschluss von Wochenarbeitszeit und Pausenregelungen (Art. 40 ASG).[58]

Bei der *Arbeitszeit mit Zeitausgleich* kann der Arbeitgeber im Einvernehmen mit der Mehrheitsgewerkschaft (oder aufgrund der anderen oben genannten Rechtsgrundlagen) innerhalb eines bestimmten Zeitraums die über 40 Stunden pro Woche nicht hinausgehende Arbeitszeit frei vereinbaren. Insoweit kann der Arbeitgeber einen Arbeitnehmer mehr als 8 Stunden täglich beschäftigen.

Bei der *Gleitzeitarbeit* kann der Arbeitnehmer Beginn und Ende seiner Arbeitszeit frei wählen. Arbeitgeber und Mehrheitsgewerkschaft legen im Vorfeld ein Modell fest, das den Ausgleichszeitraum, die maßgebliche tägliche Arbeitszeit sowie Beginn

53 Info *Wank*, Flexibilisierung der Arbeitszeit in der Metallindustrie, in: RdA (2018), S. 189.

54 *Hashimoto* (Anm. 44), S. 566 f.

55 *Hashimoto* (Anm. 44), S. 564.

56 *Hashimoto* (Anm. 44), S. 566, 567.

57 *Hashimoto* (Anm. 44), S. 567 ff.

58 *Hashimoto* (Anm. 44), S. 568.

und Ende der Kernarbeitszeit festlegt. Der Ausgleichzeitraum beträgt bei § 32-3 ASG bis zu drei Monaten, bei § 32-4 ASG bis zu einem Jahr.

Beim Modell der *Ermessensarbeitszeit* gilt die tatsächlich geleistete Arbeitszeit als vertraglich geschuldete Arbeitszeit, und zwar unabhängig davon, wie viele Stunden der Arbeitnehmer tatsächlich arbeitet. Das Modell gibt es in zwei Varianten, als Ermessensarbeitszeit für Spezialisten, 38-3 ASG,[59] und als Ermessensarbeitszeit für Arbeitnehmer in Planungsabteilungen, § 38-4 ASG.[60]

V. Vereinbarkeit von Beruf und Familie

1. Deutschland

Die Richtlinie 2019/1158 zur Vereinbarkeit von Beruf und Privatleben für Eltern und pflegende Angehörige v. 20. 6. 2019 (Vereinbarkeitsrichtlinie)[61] wurde durch Gesetz vom 19. 12. 2022[62] in Deutschland umgesetzt.[63] Elternzeit, Elterngeld und ElterngeldPlus erleichtern das Zusammenspiel von Familie und Beruf. Die Gesetzesänderung brachte u. a. eine Begründungspflicht für Arbeitgeber bei Ablehnung eines Antrags auf Verringerung der Arbeitszeit, erweiterten Kündigungsschutz und eine erweiterte Zuständigkeit für die Antidiskriminierungsstelle des Bundes. Ein Thema ist insbesondere die Verteilung der sog. Sorgearbeit.[64]

Bemerkenswert ist, dass jedenfalls in Deutschland und hier insbesondere bei der jüngeren Generation ein Gesinnungswandel stattfindet.[65] Statt wie bisher vor allem Status und Lohnhöhe, fassen heutige Jugendliche auch die Lebensqualität ins Auge, und dabei insbesondere auch Zeiten für die Familie und in der Familie. Das bedeutet allerdings nicht, dass die jungen Leute nicht fleißig wären. Die Erwerbsquote der 20- bis 24-Jährigen ist seit 2015 um über 6 Prozentpunkte gestiegen.[66]

Folgende typische arbeitszeitrechtliche Konfliktfälle zum Bereich Beruf und Familie werden genannt:

Kinder müssen zu einer Zeit zum Kindergarten gebracht werden, die mit dem Beginn der Büroarbeitszeit kollidiert. Zu dem Zeitpunkt, zu dem das Kind abgeholt wer-

---

59 *Hashimoto* (Anm. 44), S. 567 f.

60 *Hashimoto* (Anm. 44), S. 568.

61 Dazu *Dohrmann*, New Work nach der Corona-Pandemie, in: DB (2022), S. 664 ff.; *Thoma*, in: Nebe/Gröhl/Thoma (Hrsg.), Der Diskriminierungsschutz von Sorgeleistenden (Teil II), in: ZESAR (2021), S. 210 ff.

62 BGBl. 2022 Nr. 54 v. 23. Dezember 2022, S. 2510.

63 S. zum Thema allgemein *Meier-Gräwe/Motozawa/Schad-Seifert*, Family Life in Japan and Germany (2019); *Wank*, Untersuchung arbeitsrechtlicher Normen zu Familienfreundlichkeit und Gleichstellung, in: Klammer/Motz (Hrsg.), Neue Wege – Gleiche Chancen, Expertisen zum Ersten Gleichstellungsbericht (2011), S. 125 ff.

64 Dazu *Thoma* (Anm. 61), S. 441 ff.

65 S. z. B. Der Spiegel 26/2017, S. 76, 78.

66 *Hellwagner/Weber*, Generation Z – noch ein Klischee weniger (Stand 17. Februar 2025), verfügbar unter www.iab-forum.de/generation-z-noch-ein-klischee-weniger.

den muss, sind die Arbeitszeiten des Tages noch nicht abgeleistet. Der Vater oder die Mutter müssten die Arbeit kurz für das Abholen der Kinder unterbrechen und dann entweder im Büro oder zuhause weiterarbeiten können.[67] Da kleine Kinder häufiger krank sind, als das SGB V sich das vorstellt, müssten Eltern kleiner Kinder mehr Arbeitsbefreiung erhalten können.

In allen diesen Fällen sollte es möglich sein, die Arbeitszeit entsprechend anzupassen. Die im Beispiel genannte Unterbrechung der Arbeitszeit wäre möglich, wenn das Arbeitszeitgesetz statt der Tageshöchstarbeitszeit eine Wochenhöchstarbeitszeit vorsehen würde, was unionsrechtlich zulässig wäre.

2. Japan

Nach dem Gesetz zur Eltern- und Pflegezeit ist der Arbeitgeber verpflichtet, Maßnahmen zur Verkürzung der Arbeitszeit bei solchen Arbeitnehmern zu treffen, die keine Elternzeit in Anspruch genommen haben, § 23 Abs. 1. Insofern bestehen auch Begrenzungen bei der Zulässigkeit von Überstunden, § 16-8 des Gesetzes.

Für die Pflege des pflegebedürftigen Ehepartners, der pflegebedürftigen Eltern, Kinder oder Schwiegereltern[68] hat der Arbeitnehmer das Recht auf Pflegezeiten von dreimal bis zu 93 Tagen, § 11 Abs. 2 des Gesetzes zur Eltern- und Pflegezeit.[69] Auf Antrag eines Arbeitnehmers, der ein Kind im Alter von unter drei Jahren betreut, darf der Arbeitgeber keine Überstunden anordnen, § 16-8 des Gesetzes zur Eltern- und Pflegezeit.

VI. Ständige Erreichbarkeit

1. Deutschland

Schon in der analogen Welt war es möglich, dass der Chef einen Mitarbeiter nach Feierabend anrief. Die „ständige Erreichbarkeit“[70] ist also kein neues Problem des digitalen Zeitalters. Aber wenn statt gelegentlicher Telefonate den ganzen Tag über E-Mails und SMS ausgetauscht werden und auch in der Freizeit die Internetnutzung allgemein verbreitet ist,[71] liegt die Verführung nahe, sich ihrer auch nach Feierabend zu bedienen.

Die Rechtslage ist – wenn man nur den Wortlaut der einschlägigen Vorschriften zugrunde legt – eindeutig. Wer nach Feierabend 5 Minuten lang eine dienstliche

67 S. zu „coworking spaces“ ULA-Nachrichten 2/2018 S. 8, 9.

68 Zu Arbeit und Pflege *Ogata*, Familiäre Pflege und das Arbeitsrecht unter dem Genderaspekt – Abschied vom Modell des Mannes als Ernährer, in: Wada/Waltermann (Hrsg.), Nachhaltiges Arbeits- und Sozialrecht in der alternden Gesellschaft in Japan und Deutschland (2018), S. 113 ff.

69 Gesetz Nr. 76 v. 15. Mai 1991; dazu *Hashimoto* (Anm. 44), S. 564, 571.

70 *Krause* (Anm. 38), B 28; *Schwemmle/Wedde*, Alles unter Kontrolle? Arbeitspolitik und Arbeitsrecht in digitalen Zeiten, WISO-Diskurs 2/2018 (2018), S. 11.

71 *Däubler*, Digitalisierung und Arbeitsrecht, 8. Aufl. (2022), S. 33 ff.; *Freyler*, Arbeitszeit- und Urlaubsrecht im Mobile Office (2018), S. 9 f.; *Krause* (Anm. 38), B 14 f.

E-Mail liest, arbeitet. Nach dem Ende der Arbeitszeit stehen ihm nach § 5 ArbZG 11 Stunden Ruhezeit zu. D. h. wer die E-Mail um 23:00 Uhr liest, darf am nächsten Tag erst um 10:00 Uhr morgens zum Dienst erscheinen.[72]

Zu der Frage, ob das so zutrifft, gibt es zwei Meinungen. Auch wenn sämtliche Methodenlehren behaupten, der mögliche Wortlaut stelle die Grenze der Auslegung dar, sagt die eine Meinung, durch Auslegung ergebe sich, dass solche Bagatellarbeit nicht zähle[73] oder dass jedenfalls eine freiwillige Kommunikation nicht anzurechnen sei.[74] Nach anderer Meinung ist die Regelung in der Arbeitszeitrichtlinie und im Arbeitszeitgesetz bindend, Ausnahmen sind nicht vorgesehen.[75] Eine Mittelstellung findet sich in einer BAG-Entscheidung, nach der die Kenntnisnahme einer Weisung in der Freizeit keine Arbeitszeit bedeutet.[76]

Solange die Richtlinie und das Gesetz nicht geändert werden und sich auch der EuGH noch nicht geäußert hat – zum Beispiel in der Weise, dass kurzfristige Arbeitszeiten bis zu 10 Minuten die Ruhezeit nicht erneut in Gang setzen – bedeutet die derzeitige ungewisse Rechtslage ein erhebliches Risiko für Arbeitgeber.

Es besteht eine rechtliche Verpflichtung, Vorgesetzten und Mitarbeitern dienstliche Kontakte nach Feierabend zu untersagen, und dies beispielsweise durch eine Betriebsvereinbarung festzulegen. Offen sind vor allem zwei Punkte. Wie steht es, wenn der Arbeitnehmer selbst *freiwillig* nach Feierabend kommuniziert? Ebenso wie der Arbeitgeber Arbeitnehmer daran hindern muss, außerhalb der gesetzlichen Höchstarbeitszeit zu arbeiten, muss er sie auch daran hindern, in der Freizeit über den zulässigen Rahmen hinaus zu arbeiten.

Ein anderes Problem betrifft den Fall, dass eine Nachricht aus dem *Ausland* und damit aus einer anderen Zeitzone das Unternehmen erreicht.[77] Arbeitgeber meinen, es müsse möglich sein, im Unternehmen zu jeder Tageszeit einen Ansprechpartner zu haben.[78] Das überzeugt nicht. Auch Ausländer wissen, dass es auf der Welt verschiedene Zeitzonen gibt und müssen das in ihre Geschäftstätigkeit einplanen.

---

72 *Anzinger/Koberski* (Anm. 34), § 5 Rn. 3a f.; *Baeck/Deutsch/Winzer*, ArbZG Arbeitszeitgesetz, 4. Aufl. (2020), § 5 Rn. 13; *Wank* (Anm. 9), S. 285; a. A. *Freyler* (Anm. 71), S. 165 f.

73 *Anzinger/Koberski* (Anm. 34), § 5 ArbZG Rn. 13 f.; *Baeck/Deutsch/Winzer* (Anm. 72), § 5 ArbZG Rn. 14; *Bissels/Wisskirchen*, BlackBerry & Co.: Was ist heute Arbeitszeit?, in: DB (2010), S. 2054; Literaturnachw. bei *Freyler* (Anm. 71), S. 106 f.; *Krause* (Anm. 38), B 35 f., Fn. 183.

74 *Schlegel*, Grenzenlose Arbeit, in: NZA Beil. 1/2014 (2014), S. 16, 19.

75 *Däubler* (Anm.71), § 5 Rn. 15; *Falder*, Immer erreichbar – Arbeitszeit- und Urlaubsrecht in Zeiten des technologischen Wandels, NZA (2010), S. 1150, 1152 f.; *Freyler* (Anm. 71), S. 118; *Gaul*, Leistungsdruck, psychische Belastung und Stress, in: DB (2013), S. 61 f.; *Krause* (Anm. 38), B 36; *Schuchart*, Ständige Erreichbarkeit im Arbeitsverhältnis – Ist das Arbeitszeitgesetz noch zeitgemäß?, in: *Latzel/Picker*, Neue Arbeitswelt (2014), S. 207 f.; *Wank* (Anm. 9), S. 285, 289; *Zöll/Kielkowski*, Arbeitsrechtliche Umsetzung von „Bring Your Own Device“, BB (2012), S. 2625, 2628.

76 BAG, Urteil v. 23. August 2023, NZA (2023), S. 1607; zust. *Salamon/Iser*, Erreichbarkeit des Arbeitnehmers außerhalb der Arbeitszeit – leistungssichernde Nebenpflichten, in: NZA (2024), S. 242.

77 *Däubler* (Anm. 71), § 5 Rn. 29.

78 S. den Hinweis bei *Krause* (Anm. 38), B 40.

Von der aktiven Kommunikation nach Feierabend ist die ständige Erreichbarkeit i. e. S. zu unterscheiden, also die bloße Online-Verfügbarkeit. Teilweise wird die entsprechende Zeit als Bereitschaftsdienst qualifiziert.[79] Richtigerweise ist hier Rufbereitschaft anzunehmen.[80]

2. Japan

Ständige Erreichbarkeit wurde in Japan weitgehend als selbstverständlich angesehen. Nach einer Untersuchung des japanischen Gewerkschafts-Dachverbands RENGO (*Nippon Sōrōdō Kumiai Sōrengō Kai*) im Jahre 2023 hat nur ein Viertel der Unternehmen eine betriebliche Regelung über die Erreichbarkeit am Wochenende.

VII. Überstunden

1. Deutschland

a) Arbeitszeit und Überstunden im Systemzusammenhang

Wenn von Arbeitszeit die Rede ist, wird meist nur auf die gesetzliche und die vertragliche Arbeitszeit Bezug genommen. Überstunden bleiben außen vor. Das gilt z. B. für Statistiken zur Arbeitszeit, wenn etwa die Arbeitszeiten deutscher und japanischer Arbeitnehmer miteinander verglichen werden. Ein ganz wesentlicher Aspekt betrifft aber die Überstunden, so dass sich ein sinnvoller Vergleich auf die tatsächliche Arbeitszeit aus regulärer Arbeitszeit und Überstunden beziehen müsste.

Rechtstatsächlich ergibt ein Arbeitszeitreport des DGB für Nordrhein-Westfalen:[81] Fast die Hälfte der Beschäftigten leistet nach eigenen Angaben regelmäßig Überstunden, ein Fünftel ohne Entlohnung. Unbezahlte Überstunden finden sich häufig in Lehr- und in Ausbildungsberufen, aber auch in den Bereichen Einkauf, Verkehr, Handel, Hotel und Gaststätten.

b) Überstunden aus Arbeitgebersicht

Bei realitätsnaher juristischer Betrachtungsweise sollte immer von einem Systemkomplex ausgegangen werden. So müssen z. B. Kündigungsrecht, Befristungsrecht und Leiharbeitsrecht als Teile eines Systems betrachtet werden. Ist das Kündigungsschutzrecht zu rigide, weichen Arbeitgeber auf Befristungen und Leiharbeit aus. Ist das reguläre Arbeitszeitrecht zu starr, nehmen Arbeitgeber Zuflucht zu Überstunden.

Für Arbeitgeber gehören Überstunden zum Gesamtkomplex flexible Arbeitszeit. Überstunden sind unter einem Organisationsaspekt und unter einem Kostenaspekt zu sehen. Arbeitsanfall und reguläre Arbeitszeit gehen nicht immer konform. Am besten wäre es, wenn Arbeitnehmer immer nur dann eingesetzt werden könnten,

---

79 *Buschmann/Ulber*, ArbZG, 8. Aufl. 2025, § 2 Rn. 26.

80 *Falder* (Anm. 75), S. 1150, 1151; *Freyler* (Anm. 71), S. 95 ff.; *Gaul* (Anm. 75), S. 60, 61; *Kohte*, Arbeitsschutz in der digitalen Arbeitswelt, in: NZA (2015), S. 1423; *Krause* (Anm. 38), B 38; *Wank* (Anm. 9), S. 288 f.; s. auch *Däubler* (Anm.71), § 5 Rn. 8 ff.

81 DGB NRW Arbeitszeitreport, nach Kölner Stadt-Anzeiger v. 31. Januar 2018, S. 8.

wenn Bedarf besteht. Organisatorisch lässt sich ein erhöhter Arbeitsanfall und ein Arbeitsanfall außerhalb der regulären Arbeitszeit entweder durch zusätzliche Arbeitskräfte (Teilzeitbeschäftigte, Leiharbeitnehmer, befristet Beschäftigte) auffangen oder durch Überstunden der Stammbelegschaft.

c) Überstunden aus Arbeitnehmersicht

Aus Arbeitnehmersicht ist die Anordnung von Überstunden ambivalent. Auf der einen Seite gibt es Arbeitnehmer, die gerne Überstunden leisten, um entsprechend mehr zu verdienen und die auch klagen, wenn zwar anderen Arbeitnehmern Überstunden angeboten werden, ihnen aber nicht. Dem stehen andere Arbeitnehmer gegenüber, die schon die Normalarbeitszeit als erhebliche Belastung betrachten und jede Überstunde vermeiden möchten.

d) Die Rechtslage

Das BAG betrachtet Überstunden unter drei Aspekten: Rechtsgrund, Transparenz der Regelung und Vergütung.

Es besteht allgemeine Einigkeit darüber, dass es für Überstunden, wenn sie nicht ad hoc zwischen Arbeitgeber und Arbeitnehmer vereinbart werden, einer Rechtsgrundlage bedarf, die sich aus einem Tarifvertrag oder einem Arbeitsvertrag ergeben kann. Besteht sie nicht, braucht ein Arbeitnehmer keine Überstunde zu leisten.

Ist eine Rechtsgrundlage zur Ableistung von Überstunden vorhanden, so verlangt das BAG, dass die Regelung transparent ist. Der Arbeitnehmer muss vorhersehen können, welche Belastungen in welchem Umfang und zu welchen Zeiten auf ihn zukommen. Wie so oft, werden teilweise Transparenzüberlegungen auch hier als Vehikel für eine inhaltliche Kontrolle herangezogen.

Vor allem geht es um die Frage der Vergütung. Die Regelung im Arbeitsvertrag mag noch so transparent sein – wenn der Arbeitnehmer für seine Überstunden keinen zusätzlichen Lohn erhält, nützt ihm die Transparenz auch nichts. Hier muss erstaunen, dass nach Rechtsprechung und Literatur überhaupt unbezahlte Überstunden zulässig sind. Argumentiert wird, dass der Arbeitsvertrag eine bestimmte Zahl von Überstunden im Monatslohn mit abdecke. Das verstößt zum einen gegen das Transparenzgebot: Bei unbezahlten Überstunden ist der reale Stundenlohn oder Monatslohn entsprechend geringer, ohne dass dies gemäß dem Nachweisgesetz oder in sonstiger Weise zum Ausdruck käme. Vor allem aber dürfte es unbezahlte Überstunden eigentlich gar nicht geben. Der Arbeitgeber ist nach § 611a Abs. 2 BGB verpflichtet, dem Arbeitnehmer für seine Arbeit Lohn zu zahlen. Dem kann er sich nicht durch eine willkürliche Umbenennung (pauschale Abgeltung, unbezahlte Überstunden) entziehen. Daher muss der Überstundenlohn im Arbeitsvertrag oder im Tarifvertrag gesondert ausgewiesen werden.[82]

---

[82] Zum Ganzen *Maties*, Überstunden im Arbeitsverhältnis, Vortrag vom 19. September 2022, Universität des Saarlands, abrufbar unter https://irp.cdn-website.com/42d07635/files/uploaded/Druckfassung.

Es gibt allerdings Berufe, wie beim leitenden Angestellten[83] oder beim Freiberufler, bei denen es üblich ist, dass sie auch jenseits des vertraglichen zeitlichen Rahmens arbeiten, und zwar ohne Entgelt. Das BAG grenzt insofern ab, ob unentgeltliche Überstunden erwartet werden oder nicht. Auf *Erwartungen* abzustellen, gehört zwar zum Instrumentarium von Soziologen, die mit der Konstruktion von zwingendem Gesetzesrecht nichts anzufangen wissen. Aber ein Gericht darf das Entstehen eines Lohnanspruchs nicht davon abhängig machen, ob alle gegen das Gesetz verstoßen und deshalb niemand die Einhaltung des Gesetzes erwartet.

2. Japan

Nach § 33 ASG kann die *Aufsichtsbehörde* eine Erlaubnis für Überstunden erteilen, wenn anderenfalls eine Katastrophe droht oder andere zwingende Gründe vorliegen. Von dieser Regelung macht so gut wie niemand Gebrauch, da es einen einfacheren Weg gibt, die Möglichkeit einer Vereinbarung mit der Mehrheitsgewerkschaft oder mit dem Mehrheitsvertreter oder mit dem Betriebsausschuss, Art. 38-4 Abs. 5 ASG.

Es gab lange Zeit keine Obergrenze für die Mehrarbeit. Inzwischen beträgt sie bei Überstunden während eines Monats 45 Stunden und 360 Stunden pro Jahr.

In Japan wurden Überstunden bis vor kurzem als sozial begrüßenswert angesehen, da sie vom Fleiß und vom Verantwortungsbewusstsein des Arbeitnehmers zeugen. In Japan gab es zudem das *tsukiai zangyō*, das gemeinsame in Überstunden arbeiten, allerdings eher als Zeichen von Kollegialität.[84] Früher war es zudem üblich, dass Arbeitgeber und Belegschaft nach der Arbeitszeit noch gemeinsam ein Lokal aufsuchten. Da ein Großteil der Bevölkerung im Großraum Tokyo arbeitet, in dem Wohnraum unbezahlbar ist, kommt für viele Arbeitnehmer eine tägliche Zeit des Pendelns von mehr als 2 Stunden zur Arbeitszeit hinzu.

Wenn man das Arbeitszeitrecht in Deutschland und in Japan miteinander vergleicht, muss man neben der gesetzlichen Arbeitszeit auch die gelebte Arbeitswelt in den Blick nehmen.

Literaturverzeichnis

Anzinger, Rudolf/*Koberski*, Wolfgang: ArbZG – Arbeitszeitgesetz, 5. Aufl. (2020).

Baeck, Ulrich/*Deutsch*, Markus/*Winzer*, Thomas: ArbZG Arbeitszeitgesetz, 4. Aufl. (2020).

Bayreuther, Frank: Rufbereitschaft als Arbeitszeit?, in: NZA (2018), S. 348 ff.

Bissels, Alexander/*Wisskirchen*, Gerlind: BlackBerry & Co.: Was ist heute Arbeitszeit?, in: DB (2010), S. 2052 ff.

---

83 Zu Führungskräften s. *Bundesministerium für Arbeit und Soziales* (BMAS), Forschungsbericht 505 Arbeitsqualität und wirtschaftlicher Erfolg: – Längsschnittstudie in deutschen Betrieben, Stand: 30. November 2017 (2017), S. 82.

84 S. auch die Beiträge in *Kurishima/Wolff/Kaspar* (Hrsg.), Individualität und Kollektivität (2025).

Blanpain, Roger/*Bisom-Rapp*, Susan/*Corbett*, William R./*Josephs*, Hilary K./*Zimmer*, Michael J. (Hrsg.), The Global Workplace – International and Comparative Employment Law – Cases and Materials (2007).

Bundesministeriums für Arbeit und Soziales: Weißbuch „Arbeiten 4.0“, Stand: März 2017 (2017).

Bundesministerium für Arbeit und Soziales (BMAS): Forschungsbericht 505 Arbeitsqualität und wirtschaftlicher Erfolg:– Längsschnittstudie in deutschen Betrieben, Stand: 30. November 2017 (2017).

Buschmann, Rudolf/*Ulber*, Jürgen: Arbeitszeitrecht (2019).

Däubler, Wolfgang: Digitalisierung und Arbeitsrecht, 8. Aufl. (2022).

Dohrmann, Vanessa Dorothea: New Work nach der Corona-Pandemie, in: DB (2022), S. 664 ff.

Düwell, Franz-Josef/*Löwisch*, Manfred/*Waltermann*, Raimund/*Wank*, Rolf (Hrsg.): Das Verhältnis von Arbeitsrecht und Zivilrecht in Japan und Deutschland (2013).

Falder, Roland: Immer erreichbar – Arbeitszeit- und Urlaubsrecht in Zeiten des technologischen Wandels, in: NZA (2010), S. 1150 ff.

Franzen, Martin/*Gallner*, Inken/*Oetker*, Hartmut (Hrsg.): Kommentar zum europäischen Arbeitsrecht, 5. Aufl. (2024).

Freyler, Carmen : Arbeitszeit- und Urlaubsrecht im Mobile Office (2018).

Gaul, Björn: Leistungsdruck, psychische Belastung und Stress, in: DB (2013), S. 60 ff.

Giesen, Richard/*Junker*, Abbo/*Rieble*, Volker (Hrsg.): Arbeitszeitmodelle der Zukunft (2019).

Hahn, Frank/*Pfeiffer*, Gerhard/*Schubert*, Jens M.: Arbeitszeitrecht, 3. Aufl. (2024).

Hashimoto, Yoko: Arbeitszeitrecht in Japan, in: RIW (2018), S. 564 ff.

Hellwagner, Timon/*Weber*, Enzo: Generation Z – noch ein Klischee weniger (Stand: 17. Februar 2025), abrufbar unter: www.iab-forum.de/generation-z-noch-ein-klischee-weniger.

Kiyono, Kohei: Characteristics of and Differences between the Way of Working in Japan and Germany, in: Düwell, Nora/Gallner, Inken/Haase, Karsten/Wolmerath, Martin (Hrsg.), Auf dem Weg zu einem sozialen und inklusiven Rechtsstaat – Covid 19 als Herausforderung, Liber amicorum Franz Josef Düwell (2021), S. 113 ff.

Koberski, Wolfgang: in Kiel, Heinrich/Lunk, Stefan/Oetker, Hartmut (Hrsg.), Münchener Handbuch Arbeitsrecht, 5. Aufl. (2021), §§ 181 – 188 Arbeitszeitschutz.

Kohte, Wolfhard: Arbeitsschutz in der digitalen Arbeitswelt, in: NZA (2015), S. 1417 ff.

Krause, Rüdiger: Digitalisierung der Arbeitswelt: Herausforderungen und Regelungsbedarf, in: Verhandlungen des 71. Deutschen Juristentages, Band I, Gutachten Teil B (2016).

Kümmerling, Angelika/*Postels*, Dominik/*Slomka*, Christine: Zufriedenheit mit der Arbeitszeit – wie kann sie gelingen? – Eine Analyse der Arbeitszeiten nach Geschlecht und Statusgruppen, Working Paper Nr. 54 Hans-Böckler-Stiftung (2017).

Kurishima, Tomoaki/*Wolff*, Daniel/*Kaspar*, Johannes (Hrsg.): Individualität und Kollektivität (2025).

Kuwamura, Yumiko: Die Flexibilisierung des Arbeitsrechts und die Vertretung der Arbeitnehmer in Japan, in: RdA (2012), S. 155 ff.

Maties, Martin: Überstunden im Arbeitsverhältnis, Vortrag vom 19. September 2022, Universität des Saarlands, abrufbar unter https://irp.cdn-website.com/42d07635/files/uploaded/Druckfassung.

Meier-Gräwe, Uta/*Motozawa*, Miyoko/*Schad-Seifert*, Annette: Family Life in Japan and Germany (2019).

Müller-Glöge, Rudi/*Preis*, Ulrich/*Gallner*, Inken/*Schmidt*, Ingrid (Hrsg.): Erfurter Kommentar zum Arbeitsrecht, 25. Aufl. (2025).

Nebe, Katja/*Gröhl*, Stefanie/*Thoma*, Nicole: Der Diskriminierungsschutz von Sorgeleistenden (Teil II), in: ZESAR (2021), S. 210 ff.

Pfrogner, Julia: Flexible Arbeitszeiten in der Industrie 4.0, in: BB (2018), S. 500 ff.

Preis, Ulrich/*Sagan*, Adam: Europäisches Arbeitsrecht- Grundlagen – Richtlinie – Folgen für das deutsche Recht, 3. Aufl. (2024).

Preis, Ulrich/*Schwarz*, Katharina: Dienstreisen als Rechtsproblem (2020), HSI-Schriftenreihe Band 31.

Puppe, Ingeborg: Kleine Schule des juristischen Denkens, 5. Aufl. (2008).

Ogata, Keiko: Familiäre Pflege und das Arbeitsrecht unter dem Genderaspekt – Abschied vom Modell des Mannes als Ernährer, in: Wada, Hajime/Waltermann, Raimund (Hrsg.), Nachhaltiges Arbeits- und Sozialrecht in der alternden Gesellschaft in Japan und Deutschland (2018), S. 113 ff.

Ono, Hiroshi: Why Do the Japanese Work Long Hours? – Sociological Perspectives on Long Working Hours in Japan, in: Japan Labor Issues vol. 2, no. 5 (2018), S. 35 ff.

Salamon, Erwin/*Iser*, Laura: Erreichbarkeit des Arbeitnehmers außerhalb der Arbeitszeit – leistungssichernde Nebenpflichten, in: NZA (2024), S. 242 ff.

Schlegel, Rainer: Grenzenlose Arbeit, in: NZA Beil. 1/2014 (2014), S. 16 ff.

Schliemann, Harald: Arbeitszeitgesetz, 4. Aufl. (2020).

Schliemann, Harald: Vorlagefragen – Sachantwort des EuGH trotz Nichtkompetenz der EU, in: EuZW (2018), S. 274 ff.

Schnapp, Friedrich E.: Logik für Juristen, 7. Aufl. (2016).

Schuchart, Uta: Ständige Erreichbarkeit im Arbeitsverhältnis – Ist das Arbeitszeitgesetz noch zeitgemäß?, in: Latzel, Clemens/Picker, Christian (Hrsg.), Neue Arbeitswelt (2014), S. 207 ff.

Schwemmle, Michael/*Wedde*, Peter: Alles unter Kontrolle? Arbeitspolitik und Arbeitsrecht in digitalen Zeiten, WISO-Diskurs 2/2018 (2018).

Tieste, Oliver: Der Tod durch Überarbeitung (2003).

Wank, Rolf: Facetten der Arbeitszeit, in: RdA (2014), S. 285 ff.

Wank, Rolf: Flexibilisierung der Arbeitszeit in der Metallindustrie, in: RdA (2018), S. 189.

Wank, Rolf: Juristische Methodenlehre (2020).

Wank, Rolf: Rechtskultur im Arbeitsrecht in Japan und Deutschland, in: Takei, Hiroshi/Yano, Masahiro/Ogata, Keiko/Yamakawa, Kazuyoshi (Hrsg.), In Search of Justice in Labor Law, Festschrift für Hajime Wada, Tokio (2023), S. 192–215.

Wank, Rolf: Rechtsvergleichung und faktische Geltung, in: Arbeit und Recht im gesellschaftlichen Wandel – 25 Jahre Gesellschaften für Arbeitsrecht in Deutschland und Japan – Festschrift zum 25. Geburtstag der Deutsch-Japanischen Gesellschaft für Arbeitsrecht e.V. (2023), S. 103 ff.

Wank, Rolf: Untersuchung arbeitsrechtlicher Normen zu Familienfreundlichkeit und Gleichstellung, in: Klammer, Ute/Motz, Markus (Hrsg.), Neue Wege – Gleiche Chancen, Expertisen zum Ersten Gleichstellungsbericht (2011), S. 125 ff.

Wank, Rolf/*Yoshida*, Mariko: Arbeitsordnung und allgemeine Arbeitsbedingungen – Vergleich der Entwicklung in Deutschland und in Japan (2025).

Weber, Enno/*Zimmert*, Franziska: Arbeitszeit zwischen Wunsch und Wirklichkeit: Wie Diskrepanzen entstehen und wie man sie auflöst, IAB-Kurzbericht 13/2018 (2018)

Zöll, Oliver/*Kielkowski*, Jacek: Arbeitsrechtliche Umsetzung von „Bring Your Own Device", in: BB (2012), S. 2625 ff.

„Künstliche Intelligenz“

Chance und Herausforderung für die Arbeitswelt

Von *Peter Wedde*

Prof. Dr. Peter Wedde ist Professor für Arbeitsrecht und Recht der Informationstechnik im Fachbereich Informatik und Ingenieurwissenschaften der Frankfurt University a. D., Wissenschaftlicher Leiter des Instituts für Datenschutz, Arbeitsrecht und Technologieberatung – d+a consulting in Wiesbaden, Wissenschaftlicher Berater des Anwaltsbüros Mittländer in Frankfurt sowie Autor zahlreicher Fachaufsätze und Fachbücher zu arbeits-, datenschutz- und technikrechtlichen Themen.

Dieser Beitrag gibt einen Überblick über Chancen und Herausforderungen, die sich im Zusammenhang mit der Ausbreitung der „Künstlichen Intelligenz“ (kurz „KI“) in der Arbeitswelt verbinden. Zugleich skizziert er kollektivrechtliche Lösungsmöglichkeiten und erste praktische Erfahrungen mit deren Umsetzung auf.

I. KI überall

Der Weg zur Digitalisierung fast aller Lebens- und Arbeitsbereiche wird durch die Diskussion um verschiedenste Systeme und Lösungen aus dem Bereich der „KI“ dominiert. Die Möglichkeiten für den Einsatz von KI-Anwendungen scheinen im Moment fast grenzenlos zu sein. In der Arbeitswelt steuert KI-Software beispielsweise bereits komplexe Logistiksysteme, Fahrzeuge, Maschinen oder Personalinformationssysteme. Für Beschäftigte stehen verschiedenste KI-Werkzeuge zur Verfügung, mit denen sich beispielsweise Texte und Ausarbeitungen anhand von wenigen Stichworten erzeugen lassen. Alternativ lassen sich eigene Entwürfe mit Hilfe von KI-Tools verbessern oder in einen bestimmten Sprachstil umsetzen.

Die aktuell verfügbaren KI-Anwendungen sind das Ergebnis jahrzehntelanger Forschung in diesem Bereich, die ihre Ursprünge in den fünfziger Jahren des letzten Jahrhunderts haben.[1] Ursprünglich zielte diese Forschung darauf, „Starke KI“ zu entwickeln, deren intellektuelle Fertigkeiten und Fähigkeiten denen der Menschen gleichen oder diese sogar übertreffen sollte. Bei den aktuell zur Verfügung stehenden Anwendungen handelt es sich hingegen durchgängig um „Schwache KI“. Dieser Begriff steht für Systeme, die auf der Basis von Methoden aus der Mathematik und Informatik zur Lösung konkreter Anwendungsprobleme in der Lage sind und die sich dabei selbst optimieren können. Diese KI-Systeme können Aspekte menschlicher Intelli-

---

1 Vgl. etwa *Kurzweil*, The Age of Intelligent Machines (1990).

Duncker & Humblot · Berlin | https://doi.org/10.3790/978-3-428-59611-9.2025.419797

genz nachbilden und formal beschreiben bzw. menschliches Denken simulieren und unterstützen.[2]

In der Arbeitswelt sind KI-Anwendungen in einzelnen Bereichen längst etabliert, etwa im Bereich Personalmanagement.[3] In der breiten Öffentlichkeit sind Entwicklungen wie diese allerdings nicht nachhaltig wahrgenommen worden. Und dass KI-Anwendungen Teil unserer alltäglichen Lebenswelt werden, das war für viele Menschen lange nicht vorstellbar. Das hat sich mit der Freigabe der kostenlosen Nutzung der KI-Software „ChatGPT" Ende 2022 durch die Firma OpenAI schlagartig geändert. Dieses Ereignis hat einen bis heute andauernden Hype zum Thema „KI-Anwendungen" ausgelöst. Alle großen „Tech"-Konzerne befassen sich intensiv mit dem Thema und versuchen entweder, ChatGPT über Lizenzen in die eigene Softwarewelt zu übernehmen oder Parallelentwicklungen an den Markt zu bringen. Als mögliche Alternative zu ChatGPT wurde Anfang 2025 die chinesische KI-Software DeepSeek vorgestellt, für deren Entwicklung deutlich weniger Kosten angefallen sein sollen als bei OpenAI. Im Moment scheint es keine Grenzen mehr für die Anwendung und Nutzung derartiger KI-Technik zu geben. Die Zahl der KI-Komponenten und -Systeme, die für die private oder berufliche Nutzung angeboten werden, wächst rasant. Im Internet stehen verschiedenste KI-Anwendungen für Text- oder Bildbearbeitung der breiten Öffentlichkeit als Basisversion kostenlos oder gegen eine geringe Gebühr zur Verfügung. Wer das volle Leistungsspektrum nutzen will, muss teilweise tief ins Portemonnaie greifen. Und die Nutzer kostenloser Angebote „bezahlen" regelmäßig mit der Zurverfügungstellung ihrer persönlichen Daten.

II. KI in der Arbeitswelt

In der Arbeitswelt sind Grenzen für den Einsatz von KI-Anwendungen derzeit nicht erkennbar. Die dort stattfindende Entwicklung verändert viele Arbeits- und Tätigkeitsfelder grundlegend. Sachbearbeiter- und Verwaltungstätigkeiten werden von dieser Entwicklung ebenso erfasst wie Serviceangebote in Call-Centern oder Arbeit in Produktionsbereichen. Steuern KI-Anwendungen beispielsweise Prozesse oder Arbeitsaufgaben, ist ein menschliches Eingreifen vielfach nur noch für Stichproben oder beim Auftreten von Problemen oder Fehlern vorgesehen.

Beschäftigte können KI-Anwendungen insbesondere für die Erledigung von Routinetätigkeiten oder zur Verbesserung ihrer persönlichen Arbeitsleistungen einsetzen. Deutlich wird dies etwa im Informatikbereich, wo KI-Systeme für Programmierarbeiten für den Test von Programmen ebenso zum Einsatz kommen wie bei der Fehlersuche in komplexen IT-Anwendungen. Im Dienstleistungsbereich werden Kun-

---

2 Zur Definition vgl. Die Bundesregierung, Strategie der Künstlichen Intelligenz der Bundesregierung, Stand November 2018 (2018), S. 4, elektronisch abrufbar unter https://www.ki-strategie-deutschland.de/?file=files/downloads/Nationale_KI-Strategie.pdf&cid=728 (Abrufdatum 1.12.2025).

3 Vgl. *Wedde*, Automatisierung im Personalmanagement – arbeitsrechtliche Aspekte und Beschäftigtendatenschutz (2020), elektronisch abrufbar unter https://algorithmwatch.org/de/wp-content/uploads/2020/03/AlgorithmWatch_AutoHR_Gutachten_Arbeitsrecht_Datenschutz_Wedde_2020.pdf (Abrufdatum 1.12.2025).

denkontakte zunehmend durch „KI-Bots“ abgewickelt, die mit Anfragenden „sprechen“ können. Menschliche Kontakte gibt es dort teilweise nur noch bei schwierigeren Problemen im „Second-Level-Support“ oder gegen Zahlung einer Extragebühr.

KI-Anwendungen betreffen praktisch alle Berufsfelder und Beschäftigtengruppen. Sie werden in der Arbeitswelt ebenso Standard sein wie es PC, Notebooks oder Smartphones bereits sind. Teilweise werden KI-Systeme dazu beitragen, menschliche Fähigkeiten zu stärken und auszubauen. Vielfach werden sie menschliche Arbeit vollständig ersetzen.

Für die Steuerung von Arbeitsprozessen eingesetzte KI-Anwendungen sind aber auch in der Lage, die menschlichen Arbeitsanteile von Gesamtprozessen „nebenbei“ umfassend zu analysieren und zu bewerten. Es ist ihnen möglich, sowohl den Verschleiß der verwendeten Maschinen oder die Qualität und Richtigkeit verfasster Texte zu erkennen, als auch die individuelle physische und psychische Leistungsfähigkeit der in Prozesse eingebundenen Beschäftigten festzuhalten. Die Grenzen für die möglichen personenbezogenen Erkenntnisse werden allein durch rechtliche Vorgaben bestimmt, nicht aber durch die bereits vorhandenen technischen Möglichkeiten der KI.

III. Chancen und Risiken

1. Gewinner und Verlierer

Wer die Gewinner und wer die Verlierer der aktuellen Entwicklung im KI-Bereich sein werden, dass können auch die derzeit zur Verfügung stehenden KI-Anwendungen nicht verbindlich voraussagen, sondern nur vermuten. Die Ursache dieser Prognoseschwäche ist struktureller Natur: Das „Wissen“ vieler KI-Anwendungen basiert darauf, dass sie die aus der Vergangenheit vorhandenen Informationen auswerten und aufbereiten. Das gilt insbesondere für die sog. „*Large Language Models*“, kurz „*LLM*“. Der Begriff steht für Software, die auf der Basis spezieller Algorithmen die Wahrscheinlichkeit berechnet, mit welchen Wort-, Satz- oder Textfolgen sich Anfragen vermutlich richtig beantworten lassen. Damit das funktioniert, muss die Software in einer Trainingsphase mit einer möglichst großen Menge an Beispieltexten „gefüttert“ werden. Anschließend wird in einem Testverfahren geprüft, ob die errechneten Antworten plausibel sind. Funktioniert das, lassen sich auf der vorhandenen Grundlage zwar solche Entwicklungen vorhersagen, die Erfahrungen aus der Vergangenheit fortschreiben, beispielsweise, dass immer mehr Menschen Smartphones nutzen oder Elektroautos fahren. Zu tiefergehenden Prognosen zu Zukunftstrends, für die es in der Vergangenheit keine unmittelbaren Vorbilder gibt, sind KI-Anwendungen aber ebenso wenig in der Lage wie zu sicheren Abschätzungen aktuell gerade beginnender Entwicklungen. Deshalb bleiben auf die Zukunft bezogene Aussagen der KI vielfach allgemein. Das macht ein kleiner Versuch mit ChatGPT deutlich: Diese KI-Anwendung beantwortet beispielsweise die Anfrage „*Beantworte bitte in vier Sätzen und im wissenschaftlichen Stil die Frage ‚Wer werden im Jahr 2030 in der Arbeitswelt die Gewinner und wer die Verlierer der aktuellen Entwicklung im KI-Bereich sein?*‘“ mit der folgenden Feststellung:

„Die Entwicklung der KI wird bis 2030 sowohl Gewinner als auch Verlierer in der Arbeitswelt hervorbringen. Technologische Berufe, kreative Tätigkeiten und Unternehmen mit starker KI-Integration profitieren von Effizienzsteigerungen und neuen Möglichkeiten. Gleichzeitig sind Routineberufe, geringqualifizierte Arbeitskräfte und Unternehmen ohne digitale Anpassung stark gefährdet. Um langfristig erfolgreich zu bleiben, sind gezielte Investitionen in Bildung und Weiterbildung entscheidend."

Diese Antwort ist zwar grundsätzlich richtig, erfolgt aber auf einem hohen Abstraktionsniveau. Vergleichbares hätten auch mit dem Thema „Zukunft der Arbeitswelt" halbwegs vertrauten Fachleute ohne großes Nachdenken so oder so ähnlich formulieren können. An der Allgemeinheit der von ChatGPT errechneten Aussage ändern auch weitere Abfragen (neudeutsch „Prompts" mit der Bitte um Konkretisierung nichts. Vor diesem Hintergrund spricht nichts dagegen, sich bei der Abschätzung von Chancen und Risiken der KI und der hieraus abgeleiteten Prognose, wer die künftigen Gewinner und Verlierer dieser Entwicklung sein werden, auf menschliche Intelligenz zu verlassen.

Allgemein lässt sich als uneingeschränkt positive Möglichkeit der KI beispielsweise die Möglichkeit der einfachen und schnellen Informationsgewinnung oder die Aufhebung von Sprachbarrieren durch KI-Übersetzungstools benennen. Dem steht als kritischer Punkt insbesondere die mangelnde Transparenz der in KI-Systemen ablaufenden Entscheidungsprozesse gegenüber. Zudem zeichnet sich ab, dass eine Reihe von Menschen mit der rasanten Entwicklung der KI-Technik persönlich nur noch begrenzt oder gar nicht mehr Schritt halten kann. Ob Chancen oder Risiken sich die Waage halten werden oder ob sich ein Ungleichgewicht ergeben wird, ist derzeit ungewiss, aber nicht unwahrscheinlich. Zu den möglichen Verlierern werden insbesondere die Menschen gehören, denen der Zugang zur KI-Technik nicht oder nur teilweise möglich ist.

2. Arbeitswelt

Ambivalent fällt die Bewertung der Verteilung von Chancen und Risiken auch bezogen auf die Arbeitswelt aus: In Abhängigkeit von individuellen Faktoren wie der Einstellung zur KI-Technik, dem Kenntnisstand zur stattfindenden Entwicklung, der Ausstattung mit IT-Ressourcen, der fachlichen Qualifikation oder der beruflichen Position gibt es bei Beschäftigten bezogen auf die Entwicklung der KI einerseits hohe Erwartungen und große Hoffnungen und andererseits vielfältige Sorgen und Ängste.

Insbesondere technikbegeisterte Beschäftigte versprechen sich von KI-Anwendungen Hilfe und Unterstützung bei der Erledigung ihrer Arbeitsaufgaben, Entlastung von Routinetätigkeiten oder die Erweiterung der individuellen Gestaltungsmöglichkeiten. Sie erwarten, dass KI-Anwendungen ihnen bei der Lösung beruflicher Probleme sowie der Erledigung von Aufgaben helfen und sie bei Recherchen oder Analysen unterstützen. Dieser Gruppe von Beschäftigten stehen eher „KI-kritische" oder „KI-ängstliche" Arbeitnehmerinnen und Arbeitnehmer gegenüber, die sich angesichts der undurchschaubaren Arbeitsabläufe in KI-Anwendungen um den Wert ihrer fachlichen Qualifikation sorgen und die fürchten, mit der schnellen technischen Entwicklung nicht mehr Schritt halten können. Nicht selten ist auch das Gefühl der

Unterlegenheit gegenüber der KI-Technik oder der permanenten Überforderung vorhanden, weil KI-Programme Aufgaben schneller und umfassender lösen als Beschäftigte selbst dies können. Folge kann die pauschale Ablehnung der neuen technischen Möglichkeiten sein, ohne dass eine offene Befassung mit den gebotenen Chancen erfolgt. Soll dieser Effekt vermieden werden, sind individuell angepasste Aus- und Weiterbildungsangebote erforderlich, die in Qualität und Intensität über heute in der Arbeitswelt vielfach übliche „One size fits all“ Online- oder Self-Learning-Angebote hinausgehen.

3. Rechtsfragen

Welche juristischen Auswirkungen das Vordringen von KI-Anwendungen in der Arbeitswelt hat, dazu gibt es bezüglich vieler Einzelthemen derzeit keine klare Antwort. Hieran ändert auch die seit dem 2. August 2024 geltende Europäische Verordnung über künstliche Intelligenz (KI-Verordnung)[4] nichts, die sich auf grundlegende Vorgaben und Regelungen des Einsatzes und der Anwendung von KI-Systemen beschränkt. Zu den offenen Fragen gehört beispielsweise das individuelle Haftungsrisiko, das bestehen kann, wenn Beschäftigte von KI-Anwendungen fehlerhaft erzeugte Ergebnisse oder Lösungen für die Erledigung ihrer Aufgaben verwenden. Derzeit stellt sich die Haftungssituation wie folgt dar: Entscheiden Beschäftigte allein über die Nutzung eines KI-Systems bzw. nutzen sie eine ihnen privat zur Verfügung KI-Anwendung für die Lösung dienstlicher Aufgaben, haften sie für den Fall einer aus dieser Nutzung folgenden Schädigung des Arbeitgebers oder Dritter nach den allgemeinen Grundsätzen der Arbeitnehmerhaftung. Gleiches könnte bei der Verwendung eines vom Arbeitgeber für die Arbeitserledigung vorgegebenen dienstlichen KI-Systems gelten, wenn Beschäftigte einen durch dieses System erzeugten Fehler hätten erkennen können oder müssen. Anders stellt sich die Situation dar, wenn es sich um KI-Anwendungen handelt, deren Funktionsweise weder die Beschäftigten noch die Arbeitgeber kennen oder begreifen und bei denen es keinen Nachweis für die Richtigkeit der gefundenen Ergebnisse gibt. Resultieren Fehler aus der Verwendung eines solchen KI-Systemen, die im weiteren Prozess der betrieblichen Aufgabenerledigung einzelnen Beschäftigten zugeschrieben werden, könnte diesen der Nachweis schwerfallen, dass die auf Anweisung des Arbeitgebers verwendete KI-Software ursächlich für den entstandenen Schaden war.

Juristisch problematisch ist auch, dass das Vorliegen eines für jede Verarbeitung personenbezogener Daten notwendigen datenschutzrechtlichen Erlaubnistatbestands bei der Verwendung von KI-Systemen vielfach nicht mehr eindeutig und abschließend festgestellt werden kann. Beispielsweise ist nicht erkennbar, welcher der in Art. 6 Abs. 1 Datenschutzgrundverordnung (DSGVO) abschließend benannten Erlaubnistatbestände die Verarbeitung von Beschäftigtendaten für ein betriebsinternes Training von KI-Anwendungen legitimieren würde. Zudem stellt eine solche Verwendung von Beschäftigtendaten eine Zweckänderung dar, die ebenfalls einer datenschutzrechtlichen Legitimation bedarf. Ob diese im Einzelfall gegeben ist, bleibt

---

4 Verordnung (EU) 2024/1689 des Europäischen Parlaments und des Rates vom 13. Juni 2024 (Verordnung über künstliche Intelligenz), Amtsblatt der Europäischen Union Reihe L vom 13. Juni 2024.

vielfach offen. Schließlich steht die Verarbeitung von Beschäftigtendaten in betrieblichen KI-Anwendungen oft im Widerspruch zu den in Art. 5 Abs. 1 DSGVO verankerten Grundsätzen zur Transparenz, zur Zweckbindung sowie zur Datensparsamkeit. Diese Grundsätze lassen insbesondere eine zweckfreie Verarbeitung personenbezogener Daten für Trainingszwecke von KI-Systemen nicht zu. Entsprechendes gilt für die datenschutzrechtlichen Vorgaben zur Datenlöschung oder zum „Recht auf Vergessenwerden", deren Anwendung in der betrieblichen Praxis den Informationsgehalt und die Konsistenz des „Wissens" von KI-Systemen negativ beeinflussen könnte.

IV. KI-Gestaltung in der Arbeitswelt

Der Erfolg von KI-Anwendungen in der Arbeitswelt hängt entscheidend davon ab, ob es gelingt, Beschäftigte von den Vorteilen dieser neuen Technik zu überzeugen. Dafür müssen nicht nur die Chancen der KI für Betriebe und Unternehmer betont, sondern auch die Sorgen und Ängste von Beschäftigten ernst genommen werden. Diesbezüglich wird in der aktuellen Diskussion teilweise verkannt, dass Belegschaften nicht nur aus „KI-Enthusiasten", aus „Nerds" oder aus „IT-Freaks" bestehen, die ohne ihre „Handhelds" und „Smartphones" nicht mehr arbeiten können, sondern auch aus Beschäftigten, die konventionelle Arbeitsformen oder Kommunikationswege wie selbst verfasste Dokumente oder Telefongespräche weiterhin bevorzugen – und damit ähnlich effektiv arbeiten wie technikaffinere Kolleginnen und Kollegen. Insbesondere für diese „konventionell orientierten" Beschäftigten kann eine nicht durch angemessene Schulungs- und Weiterbildungsmaßnahmen flankierte Einführung von KI-Anwendungen Frustration erzeugen oder die Befürchtung begründen, dass es zu einer Entwertung beruflicher und persönlicher Qualifikation kommt. Und tatsächlich kann es ernüchternd sein, wenn ein von einer KI-Software generierter Text fachlich und sprachlich viel besser klingt als eine mühsam selbst erstellte Ausarbeitung. Verfestigt sich in dieser Situation das Gefühl der Frustration, kann eine ablehnende Haltung gegenüber KI-Software das Ergebnis sein.

Um eine prinzipielle Ablehnung zu vermeiden und um skeptische oder unsichere Beschäftigte auf dem Weg in die KI-Arbeitswelt mitzunehmen, sind ganzheitliche und gezielte Einführungsstrategien und individuelle Unterstützungsmaßnahmen notwendig. Statt „Learning by doing" oder „Self Learning" anhand vorgefertigter Videoclips sollten gerade den KI-kritischen Beschäftigten auf der Basis gezielter und individuell angepasster Aus- und Fortbildungsmaßnahmen eine Unterstützung in der Einarbeitungsphase angeboten werden, bei denen beispielsweise arbeitsplatznah eine persönliche Unterstützung durch „Key-User" zur Verfügung steht, die bei auftretenden Problemen schnell weiterhelfen.

Erste Praxiserfahrungen zeigen, dass es eine weitere bedeutende Voraussetzung für die erfolgreiche betriebliche Etablierung von KI-Anwendungen ist, dass von Anfang an klare arbeitsrechtliche Rahmenbedingungen für Einführung und Anwendung geschaffen werden. Hierzu gehören beispielsweise „KI-Richtlinien", die bei Einführungen und Änderungen von allen KI-Anwendungen eingehalten werden müssen. Derartige Richtlinien finden in der Praxis große Akzeptanz, wenn sie im Zusammenspiel von Arbeitgebern und betrieblichen Interessenvertretungen und unter Berücksichtigung der Bedürfnisse der Beschäftigten entwickelt werden.

Gibt es Betriebsräte, ist für die betriebliche Umsetzung von „KI-Richtlinien“ in der Regel der Abschluss einer „KI-Betriebsvereinbarung“ oder einer „KI-Rahmenvereinbarung“ unumgänglich, die einerseits bestehende Regelungsmechanismen aus vorhandenen „IT-Vereinbarungen“ in die KI-Welt überführen und die andererseits die Besonderheiten von KI-Anwendungen in standardisierten Mitbestimmungsprozessen berücksichtigen. Für von beiden Betriebsparteien für unproblematisch gehaltene KI-Systeme können in dem kollektivrechtlich vorgegebenen Rahmen vereinfachte Einführungs- und Änderungsprozesse vorgesehen werden. Umfassendere Einzelregelungen müssen nur noch für KI-Anwendungen getroffen werden, die umfassende Verhaltens- oder Leistungskontrollen ermöglichen oder durchführen sollen.

Weiterer Regelungsbestandteil von KI-Rahmenbetriebsvereinbarungen ist die Konkretisierung datenschutzrechtlicher Gestaltungsvorgaben. Hierzu kann – unter Beachtung des in Art. 88 Abs. 2 DSGVO benannten Rahmens – auch die Legitimation bestimmter Verarbeitungsprozesse gehören, beispielsweise die Verwendung bestimmter Leistungs- oder Verhaltensdaten für die inhaltliche Präzisierung von KI-Anwendungen. In bereits abgeschlossenen KI-Rahmenbetriebsvereinbarungen finden sich regelmäßig umfassende Vorgaben zur Aus- und Weiterbildung. Hierzu gehört teilweise auch die Verpflichtung von Arbeitgebern, einen Teil der betriebswirtschaftlichen Einsparungen, die aus der Einführung von KI-Anwendungen resultieren, für Weiterbildungsangebote zur Verfügung zu stellen.

Zu den Inhalten von KI-Rahmenbetriebsvereinbarungen gehören in Abhängigkeit von der betrieblichen Situation weiterhin spezifische Einzelthemen wie etwa die Reduzierung des Haftungsrisikos von Beschäftigten bei der Nutzung von „selbstlernenden“ KI-Anwendungen. Teilweise verbinden sich diese Regelungen mit Vorgaben zur betriebsinternen Qualitätskontrolle oder durch Verpflichtungen des Arbeitgebers zum Abschluss entsprechender Versicherungen.

Durch gute KI-Richtlinien und KI-Rahmenbetriebsvereinbarungen lässt sich Beschäftigten verdeutlichen, dass ein Teil der Sorgen, die sie mit dem Thema „KI im Betrieb“ verbinden, nicht unberechtigt sind bzw. dass sich erkennbare Probleme durch gezielte Absicherungen und Aus- und Weiterbildungskonzepte begrenzen lassen. Im Ergebnis kann so die Akzeptanz der Beschäftigten für neue KI-gesteuerte oder -unterstützte Arbeitsmittel erhöht werden.

Hilfreich bei der Bewertung können „KI-Beratungsgremien“ sein, deren Gründung Betriebsparteien in einer Reihe von bereits abgeschlossenen KI-Vereinbarungen vorgesehen haben. Die Hauptaufgabe dieser Gremien besteht darin, den Betriebsparteien Hinweise und Empfehlungen zum Umgang mit aktuellen Entwicklungen im KI-Bereich zu geben. Diese haben zwar regelmäßig nur Empfehlungscharakter, werden aber zumindest dann bei der operativen Umsetzung berücksichtigt, wenn die unterschiedlichen Positionen der Betriebsparteien angemessen berücksichtigt werden.

V. Fazit

KI beinhaltet für praktisch alle Lebensbereiche neue Chancen und eröffnet neue Möglichkeiten. Diese Feststellung gilt auch für die Arbeitswelt. Hier kann das volle Potential der neuen Technik optimal ausgeschöpft werden, wenn die Betriebsparteien sich den bestehenden Gestaltungsherausforderungen gemeinsam stellen. Ihnen fällt jenseits kollektivrechtlicher Regelungsmechanismen und Normen die Aufgabe zu, eine Situation zu schaffen, in der die KI-spezifischen Chancen allen Beteiligten und Betroffenen gleichermaßen zugutekommen. Die hierfür notwendigen Modelle gibt es (noch) nicht, weshalb menschliche Intelligenz bei ihrer Entwicklung besonders gefordert ist. KI kann eben doch nicht alles.

Literaturverzeichnis

Bundesregierung: Strategie der Künstlichen Intelligenz der Bundesregierung, Stand November 2018 (2018).

Kurzweil, Ray: The Age of Intelligent Machines (1990).

Wedde, Peter: Automatisierung im Personalmanagement – arbeitsrechtliche Aspekte und Beschäftigtendatenschutz (2020).

Ansatzpunkte für einen wertschätzenden Umgang am Arbeitsplatz

Von *Martin Wolmerath*

Dr. Martin Wolmerath, Vertretungsprofessor für Bürgerliches Recht, Handels- und Gesellschaftsrecht, Arbeitsrecht an der FH Dortmund, Rechtsanwalt, ist Gründungsmitglied der Deutsch-Japanischen Gesellschaft für Arbeitsrecht e. V. und war der erste Geschäftsführer dieses Vereins (1997–2002). Mit der Mobbingproblematik in der deutschen Arbeitswelt beschäftigt er sich seit den Anfängen ihrer Diskussion und Aufarbeitung.

Vor allem die Diskussion der Mobbingproblematik und der weiteren Erscheinungsformen der psychosozialen Belastungen in der deutschen Arbeitswelt hat verdeutlicht, dass es Verhaltensweisen und Umgangsformen am Arbeitsplatz gibt, die sich für die davon betroffenen Personen als äußerst fatal erweisen können. Aber auch das Arbeitsklima leidet darunter. Zudem zeigen sich immer wieder negative Auswirkungen hinsichtlich der wirtschaftlichen Lage sowie Entwicklungsmöglichkeiten von Unternehmen. Als ein gutes Beispiel lässt sich insoweit der am 13. März 2025 vorgestellte Gallup Engagement Index Deutschland 2024[1] anführen. Hiernach sei die emotionale Bindung der Beschäftigten in Deutschland auf ein Rekordtief gefallen. Noch nie zuvor hätten so viele Personen Dienst nach Vorschrift verrichtet. Der deutschen Wirtschaft seien infolge von innerer Kündigung und daraus resultierenden Produktivitätsverlusten 113,1 Milliarden Euro entgangen. Diese wenigen Ausführungen verdeutlichen bereits, dass es in der deutschen Arbeitswelt einen dringenden Handlungsbedarf gibt, diesen Entwicklungen Einhalt zu gebieten. Ein Ansatzpunkt hierbei ist die Verwirklichung eines wertschätzenden Umgangs am Arbeitsplatz.

I. Mit den Erkenntnissen von Heinz Leymann fing es an

Mit seinem Buch „Mobbing"[2] eröffnete Heinz Leymann im Jahr 1993 eine Diskussion zu einem Thema, das es zwar schon vor dem Zeitpunkt des Erscheinens seines viel beachteten Werkes gab – zumindest seit etlichen Jahren oder vielleicht sogar schon seit mehreren Jahrzehnten –, zu dem es bis dahin allerdings keinen schlagwortartigen und leicht einprägsamen Begriff gab, mit dem das Phänomen auf den sprichwörtlichen Punkt gebracht werden konnte. Von „Mobbing" war die Rede. Gemäß

1 Vgl. https://www.gallup.com/de/472028/bericht-zum-engagement-index-deutschland.aspx.

2 *Leymann*, Mobbing. Psychoterror am Arbeitsplatz und wie man sich dagegen wehren kann (1993).

Duncker & Humblot · Berlin | https://doi.org/10.3790/978-3-428-59611-9.2025.418885

Leymann wird darunter „eine konfliktbelastete Kommunikation am Arbeitsplatz unter Kollegen oder zwischen Vorgesetzten und Untergebenen verstanden, bei der die angegriffene Person unterlegen ist und von einer oder einigen Personen systematisch, oft und während längerer Zeit mit dem Ziel und/oder dem Effekt des Ausstoßes aus dem Arbeitsverhältnis direkt oder indirekt angegriffen wird und dies als Diskriminierung empfindet.“[3]

Aufbauend auf seine wissenschaftlichen Erkenntnisse, die er hauptsächlich in Schweden gewann, beschrieb Leymann bis dahin in der Arbeitswelt nicht wahrgenommene Verhaltensweisen von Vorgesetzten, Gleichgestellten sowie Untergebenen, die nahezu gesetzmäßig dazu führten, dass die von Mobbing betroffenen Personen mit fortschreitender Dauer ihres Martyriums in einem zunehmenden Maß erkrankten, am Arbeitsplatz immer mehr isoliert wurden und letzten Endes nahezu regelmäßig ihre bislang inne gehabte Position räumen mussten. Im schlimmsten Fall konnte das Mobbing in einem Suizid(-versuch) enden, da die Betroffenen keinen anderen Ausweg sahen, ihrer scheinbar aussichtslosen Lage entfliehen zu können.

Die von Leymann ausgelöste Diskussion und von vielen Akteuren in der Arbeitswelt erkannte Notwendigkeit, gegen dieses nicht hinnehmbare Phänomen aktiv zu werden, führte unter anderem dazu, dass in zahlreichen Betrieben der Privatwirtschaft, der Dienststellen des öffentlichen Dienstes sowie der in kirchlicher Trägerschaft befindlichen Einrichtungen Betriebs- bzw. Dienstvereinbarungen geschlossen wurden, um mit deren Hilfe dem Mobbing am Arbeitsplatz zu begegnen.[4] Solche Vereinbarungen, die zeitlich nachfolgend nicht selten weiterentwickelt wurden, verfolgten regelmäßig sowohl einen intervenierenden als auch einen präventiven Ansatz. Erfolge in der Bewältigung von konkreten Mobbingsituationen sowie in der Prävention von Mobbing gaben den betrieblichen Akteuren recht. Daneben konnte immer wieder eine Verbesserung des Arbeitsklimas, eine Senkung des Krankenstandes sowie eine Reduzierung der Fluktuationsquote festgestellt werden.

Seit dem Erscheinen des (ersten) Buches von Leymann im Jahre 1993 und den Anfängen der Auseinandersetzung mit dem Mobbingphänomen sind inzwischen mehr als 30 Jahre vergangen. In dieser Zeit hat sich einiges in Bezug auf die Mobbingproblematik getan, letzten Endes aber noch viel zu wenig. Der deutsche Gesetzgeber hat sich mit dem Problem in all der Zeit nicht befasst, so wie es etwa in Schweden und Frankreich der Fall gewesen ist.[5] Zwar gab es in der Vergangenheit immer wieder einzelne parlamentarische Anfragen[6] und Anträge.[7] Auch wurden von der Bundesanstalt

---

3 *Leymann* (Hrsg.), Der neue Mobbing-Bericht. Erfahrungen und Initiativen, Auswege und Hilfsangebote (1995), S. 18.

4 Siehe dazu *Wolmerath*, Mobbing im Betrieb. Rechtsansprüche und deren Durchsetzbarkeit (2001), mit einer Dokumentation von elf Betriebs- und Dienstvereinbarungen im Anhang (S. 323–368).

5 Siehe dazu *Däubler-Gmelin*, Warum hat Deutschland (bisher) kein eigenständiges und umfassendes „Anti-Mobbing-Gesetz“?, in: Wolmerath/Esser (Hrsg.), Werkbuch Mobbing. Offensive Methoden gegen psychische Gewalt am Arbeitsplatz (2012), S. 39.

6 Vgl. Antwort der Bundesregierung auf die Kleine Anfrage der Abgeordneten Werner Dreibus, Dr. Lothar Bisky, Dr. Barbara Höll, weiterer Abgeordneter und der Fraktion DIE LINKE vom 25. Juli 2007, BT-Drucksache 16/6139; Antwort der Bundesregierung auf die Kleine Anfrage der Abgeordneten Beater Müller-Gemmeke, Markus Kurth, Brigitte Pothmer,

für Arbeitsschutz und Arbeitsmedizin zwei Forschungsaufträge[8] und von dem Bundesministerium für Arbeit und Soziales eine Studie in Auftrag gegeben.[9] Doch ein Gesetzgebungsverfahren wurde bis heute nicht auf den Weg gebracht, mit dem der Gesetzgeber ein Zeichen hätte setzen können, dass Mobbing in der deutschen Arbeitswelt weder akzeptiert noch hingenommen wird. Aber genau dieses bisherige Versäumnis kann in gewisser Weise als Vorteil gewertet werden, falls das Bundesministerium für Arbeit und Soziales in der neuen Legislaturperiode 2025 bis 2029 – entgegen allen bislang gemachten Erfahrungen – in Sachen Mobbing aktiv werden und einen Gesetzentwurf auf den Weg bringen sollte. Insoweit kann der im Februar 2025 von dem Bundesministerium für Arbeit und Soziales vorgelegte „Mobbing-Report 2024“[10] als ein erster Hoffnungsschimmer gewertet werden. Dabei sollten Ministerium, Bundesregierung und Parlament die nachfolgenden Ausführungen beachten, die auch für interessierte Leserinnen und Leser in Japan von Nutzen sein können. Denn auch in Japan ist das Mobbingphänomen bereits seit vielen Jahren Anlass zur Diskussion.[11]

II. Zur aktuellen Situation der betrieblichen Interessenvertretung

Die betriebliche Interessenvertretung kann in Deutschland auf eine lange Tradition zurückblicken, die bis in die Weimarer Republik zurückreicht.[12] Für den Bereich des öffentlichen Dienstes gibt es mit der Personalvertretung eine Interessenvertretung, die dem föderalen Aufbau der Bundesrepublik Deutschland folgt. Für den Bund existiert ein Bundespersonalvertretungsgesetz, für die einzelnen Bundesländer eigenständige Landespersonalvertretungsgesetze. Dies hat zur Folge, dass die Einflussnahme- und Handlungsmöglichkeiten der Personalvertretungen – nicht nur in Sachen

weiterer Abgeordneter und der Fraktion BÜNDNIS 90/DIE GRÜNEN vom 12. März 2014, BT-Drucksache 18/779.

7 Antrag der Abgeordneten Beate Müller-Gemmeke, weiterer Abgeordneter und der Fraktion BÜNDNIS 90/DIE GRÜNEN vom 28. November 2018, BT-Drucksache 19/6128; Antrag der Abgeordneten Jutta Krellmann, weiterer Abgeordneter und der Fraktion DIE LINKE vom 14. Januar 2020, BT-Drucksache 19/16480.

8 Vgl. *Meschkutat/Stackelbeck/Langenhoff*, Der Mobbing-Report. Repräsentativstudie für die Bundesrepublik Deutschland (2002); *Eisermann/de Costanzo*, Die Erfassung von Mobbing – Eine Konstruktvalidierung aktueller Datenerhebungsverfahren (2011).

9 Vgl. *Bundesministerium für Arbeit und Soziales*, Mobbing in der Arbeitswelt. Bedeutung, Verbreitung und Prävention (Mobbing-Report 2024) (2025). Der Mobbing-Report 2024 findet sich als pdf unter https://bmas.de/DE/Service/Publikationen/Broschueren/report-mobbing-in-der-arbeitswelt. Der Forschungsbericht der Universität Leipzig „Repräsentative Studie zum Thema Mobbing in der Arbeitswelt in der Bundesrepublik Deutschland“ (2024), ist unter https://bmas.de/DE/Service/Publikationen/Forschungsberichte/fb-655-repraesentative-studie-mobbing-in-deutschland.html dokumentiert.

10 Vgl. *Bundesministerium für Arbeit und Soziales* (Anm. 9).

11 Vgl. *Sumida*, Mobbing in Japan, in: Wolmerath/Esser (Hrsg.), Werkbuch Mobbing. Offensive Methoden gegen psychische Gewalt am Arbeitsplatz (2012), S. 261.

12 Vgl. *Däubler/Kittner*, Geschichte und Zukunft der Betriebsverfassung, 2. Aufl. (2022), S. 151 ff.

Mobbing – von Gesetz zu Gesetz unterschiedlich ausfallen. Ähnlich verhält es sich im Bereich der kirchlichen Einrichtungen.

Einfacher ist es auf der Ebene der Privatwirtschaft. Dort findet bundesweit das Betriebsverfassungsgesetz Anwendung, das traditionell vor allem von Seiten der Gewerkschaften eine breite Befürwortung sowie Unterstützung erfährt. Diese sind immer wieder Treiber für punktuelle Aktualisierungen sowie Nachbesserungen des Gesetzes. Ihr berechtigter Wunsch nach einer umfassenden sowie tiefgreifenden Überarbeitung des Betriebsverfassungsgesetzes wurde vom Gesetzgeber in der letzten Legislaturperiode nicht erfüllt, zumal die Sozialpartner zu gegensätzliche Vorstellungen hinsichtlich eines neuen Betriebsverfassungsgesetzes haben.[13]

Warum sollte sich der Gesetzgeber einer umfassenden Reform des Betriebsverfassungsgesetzes annehmen? Neben den zahlreichen inhaltlichen Gründen ist zu bedenken, dass es nur noch in sieben Prozent aller betriebsratsfähigen Betriebe einen Betriebsrat gibt.[14] Dabei zeigt sich, dass die Wahrscheinlichkeit, dass in einem Betrieb ein Betriebsrat eingerichtet ist, in dem Maße wächst, wie die Zahl der dort beschäftigten Arbeitnehmer steigt. Dies bedeutet, dass es in vielen Unternehmen, die als KMU[15] bezeichnet werden, aufgrund ihrer Größe keine betriebliche Interessenvertretung gibt.[16] Will der Gesetzgeber (etwa auch in Sachen Mobbing) tätig werden, so muss er eine Lösung für das Problem finden, dass Betriebsräte nur noch in den wenigsten Fällen in der betrieblichen Lebenswirklichkeit anzutreffen sind. Für die betriebsratslosen Betriebe muss es daher etwas anderes als den traditionellen Betriebsrat geben.

Weiter ist zu bedenken, dass der in § 2 Abs. 1 BetrVG verankerte Grundsatz der vertrauensvollen Zusammenarbeit der Betriebsparteien von einer Unterstützung des Betriebsrats seitens der Gewerkschaft und einer Begleitung des Arbeitgebers durch seinen Arbeitgeberverband ausgeht. Dieser Wunsch des Gesetzgebers entspricht nicht mehr der realen Lebenswirklichkeit. Sofern von einem gegenwärtigen Organisationsgrad der Beschäftigten in Höhe von rund 15 Prozent ausgegangen wird,[17] ergibt sich für die deutsche Arbeitswelt ein erschreckendes Bild mit gravie-

---

13 Vgl. *Däubler/Kittner* (Anm. 12), S. 641 ff., die den Gesetzentwurf des DGB zunächst vorstellen und sodann auf die Chancen seiner Realisierung eingehen.

14 *Stettes*, Verbreitung von Betriebsräten und der Wunsch nach Interessenvertretung. Eine Analyse auf Basis der IW-Beschäftigtenbefragung 2024 (IW-Report 1/2025), Institut der Deutschen Wirtschaft (2025), S. 4.

15 KMU bezeichnet und umfasst Kleinstunternehmen, kleine Unternehmen sowie mittlere Unternehmen. Das Statistische Bundesamt definiert diese in Anlehnung an die Empfehlung (2003/361/EG) der Europäischen Kommission nach Umsatz- und Beschäftigtengrößenklassen. Kleinstunternehmen umfassen bis neun tätige Personen und einen Jahresumsatz bis zwei Millionen Euro. Kleine Unternehmen haben zehn bis 49 tätige Personen und einen Jahresumsatz bis 10 Millionen Euro. Mittlere Unternehmen weisen 50 bis 249 tätige Personen und einen Jahresumsatz bis 50 Millionen Euro auf. Siehe auch https://www.destatis.de/DE/Themen/Branchen-Unternehmen/Unternehmen/Kleine-Unternehmen-Mittlere-Unternehmen/Glossar/kmu.html.

16 *Stettes* (Anm. 14), S. 7.

17 Siehe auch *Fulda*, Gewerkschaften: Weniger Repräsentativität durch Strukturdefizite?, IW-Kurzbericht 83/22, Institut der Deutschen Wirtschaft (2022), die für das Jahr 2021 einen Netto-Organisationsgrad in Höhe von 17,4 Prozent angibt.

renden Folgen: Etwa 85 Prozent der Arbeitnehmer gehören keiner Gewerkschaft an. Ist in dem betreffenden Betrieb nicht zumindest ein Gewerkschaftsmitglied anzutreffen, ist es der für den Betrieb zuständigen Gewerkschaft nicht möglich, die erstmalige Wahl eines Betriebsrats anzustoßen.[18]

Sind Betriebsräte und Gewerkschaften in vielen Betrieben nicht mehr anzutreffen bzw. präsent, so muss es für die betroffenen Arbeitnehmer eine andersartige, besondere Anlaufstelle geben, deren Aufgabe es ist, die Interessen der Arbeitnehmer in betriebsratslosen Betrieben zu vertreten. Insoweit bietet es sich an, über das Modell der Arbeitnehmerkammern nachzudenken, wie es sie in der Bundesrepublik Deutschland im Saarland und in Bremen gibt. Die Gesetzgebung könnte solche Arbeitnehmerkammern flächendeckend in allen Bundesländern einrichten und sie mit den nötigen Aufgaben sowie Werkzeugen ausstatten, so dass sie unter anderem auch in Sachen Mobbing zum Schutz der Arbeitnehmer aktiv werden können.[19]

III. Der Fortgang der Diskussion zum Mobbing am Arbeitsplatz

In den ersten Jahren der Auseinandersetzung mit der Mobbingproblematik wurde der Fokus eng auf das Mobbing gelegt und dieses Phänomen einer Beantwortung der zahlreichen damit verbundenen Fragen zugeführt. Alsbald zeigte sich jedoch, dass es Verhaltensweisen am Arbeitsplatz gibt, bei denen es sich zwar nicht um Mobbing handelt, die aber durchaus geeignet sind, sich zu einer konkreten Mobbingsituation weiterzuentwickeln. In einer vergleichbaren Weise können sie im Einzelfall geeignet sein, die davon betroffenen Personen krank zu machen. So kann eine Benachteiligung wegen eines in § 1 AGG genannten Grundes[20] Bestandteil eines konkreten Mobbinggeschehens sein. Aber nicht jede Benachteiligung im Sinne des § 1 AGG ist automatisch Mobbing, etwa weil es sich um eine nur einmal vorgekommene Verhaltensweise gehandelt hat, wie es beispielsweise bei einer schikanösen Weisung eines Vorgesetzten[21] gegenüber einer ihm untergebenen Mitarbeiterin der Fall sein kann.

Die von Leymann arbeitswissenschaftlich geprägte Definition des Begriffs Mobbing[22] unter gleichzeitiger Abgrenzung von anderen nicht hinnehmbaren Verhaltensweisen am Arbeitsplatz führte dazu, Mobbing als eine Erscheinungsform psychosozialer Belastungen am Arbeitsplatz zu begreifen.[23] Unter Letzteren werden Beein-

18 Vgl. §§ 17 Abs. 3, 17a Nr. 3 BetrVG.

19 Siehe auch *Wolmerath*, Es ist an der Zeit – Ansatzpunkte für eine Reform des Betriebsverfassungsgesetzes, in: Düwell/Gallner/Haase/Wolmerath (Hrsg.), Auf dem Weg zu einem sozialen und inklusiven Rechtsstaat – Covid 19 als Herausforderung, Liber amicorum Franz Josef Düwell (2021), S. 848.

20 § 1 AGG zählt insoweit abschließend auf: Rasse, ethnische Herkunft, Geschlecht, Religion, Weltanschauung, Behinderung, Alter, sexuelle Identität.

21 Siehe dazu *Ruberg*, Schikanöse Weisungen. Psychosoziale Gefährdung am Arbeitsplatz im Blickfeld der Gerichte für Arbeitssachen – nicht nur! – bei „Mobbing" (2004).

22 Siehe auch *Wolmerath*, Mobbing. Rechtshandbuch für die Praxis, 5. Aufl. (2019), S. 24, mit einer Begriffsbestimmung, die arbeitsrechtliche Aspekte berücksichtigt.

23 Alternativ dazu kann auch der Begriff der psychischen Belästigung am Arbeitsplatz verwendet werden. Vgl. *Wolmerath* (Anm. 22), S. 31.

trächtigungen seelischer Art verstanden, die ihre Ursachen im Kontakt mit anderen Menschen am Arbeitsplatz haben.[24] Mit dieser (damals neuen) Sichtweise war die weitere Erkenntnis verbunden, dass die psychosozialen Belastungen den psychischen Belastungen zuzuordnen sind, so dass das Mobbing sowie die weiteren Erscheinungsformen psychosozialer Belastungen – wozu insbesondere auch die in § 1 AGG aufgezählten Benachteiligungsformen zählen – den psychischen Belastungen unterfallen. Dies wiederum war der Anknüpfungspunkt für eine Anwendbarkeit des Arbeitsschutzgesetzes auf alle Formen der psychosozialen Belastungen. Denn nach § 5 Abs. 3 Nr. 6 ArbSchG kann sich eine für die Beschäftigten mit ihrer Arbeit verbundenen Gefährdung durch psychische Belastungen bei der Arbeit ergeben, was der Arbeitgeber gemäß § 5 Abs. 1 ArbSchG bei einer von ihm vorzunehmenden Gefährdungsbeurteilung und dem nachfolgend bei der Ergreifung von gegebenenfalls erforderlichen Arbeitsschutzmaßnahmen und deren Evaluierung laut § 3 Abs. 1 ArbSchG zu berücksichtigen hat.

In der betrieblichen Praxis führten diese Erkenntnisse vielerorts zu einer neuen, erweiterten Sichtweise des Mobbingphänomens. Mit Blick zunächst auf das seit dem 21. August 1996 geltende Arbeitsschutzgesetz und das nachfolgend am 18. August 2006 in Kraft getretene Allgemeine Gleichbehandlungsgesetz (AGG) wurde als Begrifflichkeit bzw. sprachlicher Ansatzpunkt das partnerschaftliche oder respektvolle Verhalten am Arbeitsplatz – bzw. der dortige Umgang miteinander – gewählt und auch in den Überschriften zahlreicher Betriebs- und Dienstvereinbarungen zum Ausdruck gebracht.[25]

Wer sich die Worte „partnerschaftlich“ sowie „respektvoll“ von ihrer Bedeutung her vergegenwärtigt, der kann beide Begriffe als nicht wirklich zutreffend empfinden. Mit einem Partner befinde ich mich auf derselben Ebene, quasi auf Augenhöhe, was aber in einem Arbeitsverhältnis nicht der Fall ist. Der Arbeitgeber und seine Arbeitnehmer stehen nicht auf derselben hierarchischen Stufe, vielmehr befinden sie sich in einem Unter-/Überordnungsverhältnis. Dies verdeutlicht vor allem das arbeitgeberseitige Weisungsrecht gemäß § 106 GewO. Gemäß dessen Satz 1 kann der Arbeitgeber Inhalt, Ort und Zeit der Arbeitsleistung nach billigem Ermessen näher bestimmen, soweit diese Arbeitsbedingungen nicht gegen höherrangiges Recht verstoßen. Nach § 106 Satz 2 GewO gilt dies auch hinsichtlich der Ordnung und des Verhaltens der Arbeitnehmer im Betrieb. Lediglich Personen, die auf derselben hierarchischen Ebene stehen, können sich auf gleicher Augenhöhe begegnen. Insoweit kann ein partnerschaftlicher Umgang lediglich unter Vorgesetzten, unter gleichgestellten Arbeitskollegen sowie unter Auszubildenden in Betracht kommen.

Das Wort „Respekt“ kann mit „Achtung“ sowie „Ehrerbietung“ beschrieben werden.[26] Laut Wikipedia äußert es sich durch verschiedene Verhaltensweisen: Achtung,

---

24 *Wolmerath* (Anm. 22), S. 31.

25 Insoweit war die Betriebsvereinbarung „Partnerschaftliches Verhalten am Arbeitsplatz“ bei der Volkswagen AG vom 27. Juni 1996 ihrer Zeit weit voraus, zumal das Arbeitsschutzgesetz vom 7. August 1996 datiert.

26 Vgl. *Duden*, Band 1, Die deutsche Rechtschreibung, 28. Aufl., Berlin (2020), S. 952. Im *Duden*, Band 5, Das Fremdwörterbuch, 12. Aufl., Berlin (2020), S. 977, wird „Respekt“ als auf Anerkennung oder Bewunderung beruhende Achtung verstanden.

Höflichkeit und Anerkennung können Ausdrucksformen des Respekts sein. Die Autorität anderer Personen oder auch die Angst vor der Macht anderer können jemandem Respekt abverlangen. Toleranz gegenüber den Ansichten anderer kann ebenfalls Ausdruck von Respekt sein.[27] Wer die hierarchische Lebenswirklichkeit in der Arbeitswelt bedenkt, dem zeigt sich, dass allenfalls Vorgesetzte von ihren Untergebenen Respekt einfordern können. Untergebene wiederum verhalten sich ihren Vorgesetzten gegenüber regelmäßig respektvoll, da sie sich ihrer untergeordneten Rolle und der Macht der ihnen übergeordneten Person bewusst sind. Zum Ausdruck kommt beides in dem bereits angesprochenen arbeitgeberseitigen Weisungsrecht gemäß § 106 GewO.

Als passendere Wortwahl erachte ich die „Wertschätzung“. Mit diesem Begriff geht eine positive Bewertung einer anderen Person einher. Die Wertschätzung fußt auf einer inneren allgemeinen Haltung anderen Personen gegenüber. Sie umfasst den Menschen als Ganzes und betrachtet diesen eher losgelöst von einzelnen Handlungen sowie Leistungen, auch wenn solche die subjektive Einschätzung einer Person und damit ihre Wertschätzung beeinflussen.[28] Als wertschätzenden Umgang am Arbeitsplatz kann in einem weiten Sinn jedes Verhalten verstanden werden, das den jeweils anderen als eine Person begreift, die von mir in einer Art und Weise behandelt wird, wie ich selbst von der betreffenden Person behandelt werden möchte. Der wertschätzende Umgang mit einem anderen verbietet mithin jedes Verhalten, das eine Herabsetzung seines menschlichen Wertes zum Ausdruck bringt. Mobbing verbietet sich damit in der gleichen Weise wie jede andere Form psychosozialer Belastung. Zu einem wertschätzenden Miteinander am Arbeitsplatz gehört es mithin auch, auftretende Meinungsverschiedenheiten, Streitigkeiten und Konflikte in einer fairen und zielführenden Art und Weise zu bewältigen. Die zu beantwortende Frage lautet stets: Welche Behandlung und welches Verhalten würde ich mir in der gegenwärtigen Situation wünschen, wenn ich selbst bzw. meine Person betroffen wäre.

IV. Gesetzlicher Handlungsauftrag

Betriebs- bzw. unternehmenspolitische Gründe, in Sachen wertschätzender Umgang am Arbeitsplatz tätig zu werden, gibt es viele. Die Steigerung des Betriebs- und Arbeitsklimas sollte in der gleichen Weise Anlass für Aktivitäten sein wie die Senkung des Krankenstandes sowie der Fluktuation. Hinzu kommt, dass gesunde und motivierte Belegschaften bessere Arbeitsergebnisse liefern, was sich sowohl in deren Quantität als auch in deren Qualität widerspiegeln dürfte.

Als zentraler gesetzlicher Handlungsauftrag ist § 75 BetrVG anzuführen, wobei zu berücksichtigen ist, dass diese Norm auch der Arbeitgeber zu beachten hat, in dessen

27 Vgl. Wikipedia-Eintrag zum Stichwort Respekt, abrufbar unter https://de.wikipedia.org/wiki/Respekt#:~:text=Respekt%20(von%20lateinisch%20respectio%20,Rückschau,%2C%20Ressentiment%2C%20Frechheit%20und%20Verachtung.

28 Vgl. Wikipedia-Eintrag zum Stichwort Wertschätzung, abrufbar unter https://de.wikipedia.org/wiki/Wertschätzung.

Betrieb kein Betriebsrat eingerichtet ist.[29] § 75 Abs. 1 BetrVG verpflichtet den Arbeitgeber – gleiches gilt für einen gegebenenfalls existierenden Betriebsrat –, darüber zu wachen, dass alle im Betrieb tätigen Personen nach den Grundsätzen von Recht und Billigkeit behandelt werden. In einem beispielhaften und nicht abschließenden Sinn zählt das Gesetz hierzu das Unterbleiben von jeder Benachteiligung von Personen aus Gründen ihrer Rasse oder wegen ihrer ethnischen Herkunft, ihrer Abstammung oder sonstigen Herkunft, ihrer Nationalität, ihrer Religion oder Weltanschauung, ihrer Behinderung, ihres Alters, ihrer politischen oder gewerkschaftlichen Betätigung oder Einstellung oder wegen ihres Geschlechts oder ihrer sexuellen Identität auf. Ergänzt wird diese Pflicht in Abs. 2 durch die Aspekte des Schutzes und der Förderung der freien Entfaltung der Persönlichkeit der im Betrieb beschäftigten Arbeitnehmer sowie der Förderung der Selbständigkeit und Eigeninitiative der Arbeitnehmer und Arbeitsgruppen.

V. Handlungsmöglichkeiten der Betriebsparteien

In Betrieben, in denen kein Betriebsrat eingerichtet ist, kann der Arbeitgeber von seinem Weisungsrecht gemäß § 106 GewO Gebrauch machen und seine Beschäftigten zu einem gegenseitigen wertschätzenden Umgang anhalten. Das schließt die Vorgesetzten mit ein. Der Arbeitgeber kann den wertschätzenden Umgang am Arbeitsplatz mit Blick auf die in § 105 Satz 1 GewO zum Ausdruck kommende Vertragsfreiheit zum Inhalt eines jeden Arbeitsvertrags machen. Bei mündlich geschlossenen Arbeitsverträgen sollte der zwingend anzufertigende Nachweis nach § 2 Abs. 1 NachwG dazu genutzt werden, die arbeitgeberseitig gewünschten Verhaltensregeln bzw. -anforderungen in diesen Nachweis zu integrieren und somit schriftlich zu dokumentieren. In der weiteren Folge können Verstöße gegen die Verhaltensanforderungen zum Gegenstand arbeitsvertragsrechtlicher Sanktionen (z.B. Abmahnung, Versetzung) gemacht werden.

Ist in dem Betrieb ein Betriebsrat eingerichtet, so können die Betriebsparteien von der Regelung des § 88 BetrVG Gebrauch machen und eine sogenannte freiwillige Betriebsvereinbarung zum wertschätzenden Umgang am Arbeitsplatz schließen. Da eine solche Vereinbarung den beiderseitigen Willen von Arbeitgeber und Betriebsrat voraussetzt, kann der Rückgriff auf § 88 BetrVG nur dort von Erfolg gekrönt sein, wo beide Betriebsparteien an dem sprichwörtlichen gleichen Strang ziehen.

In allen Fällen, in denen dies nicht möglich ist, ist § 87 BetrVG heranzuziehen. § 87 Abs. 1 Nr. 1 und Nr. 7 BetrVG – Letzteres in Verbindung mit § 3 Abs. 1 und § 5 Abs. 1 ArbSchG – sind die einschlägigen Vorschriften, mit denen der Arbeitgeber den Betriebsrat bzw. der Betriebsrat den Arbeitgeber zur Aufnahme von Verhandlungen zum Abschluss einer Betriebsvereinbarung zum wertschätzenden Umgang am Arbeitsplatz auffordern kann.[30] Bei einer etwaigen Weigerung des angesprochenen Betriebspartners kann gemäß § 87 Abs. 2 BetrVG die Einigungsstelle ange-

29 Vgl. *Berg*, in: Däubler/Klebe/Wedde (Hrsg.), BetrVG, 19. Aufl. (2024), § 75 Rn. 13; *Lorenz*, in: Düwell (Hrsg.), Betriebsverfassungsgesetz, 6. Aufl., Baden-Baden 2022, § 75 Rn. 2.

30 Vgl. *Klebe* (Anm. 29), § 87 Rn. 67, 258 für Mobbing.

rufen werden. Dieser Weg eröffnet der die Einigungsstelle anrufenden Betriebspartei die Möglichkeit, das Thema unter Hinzuziehung einer bzw. eines unparteiischen, neutralen Einigungsstellenvorsitzenden zu diskutieren und einer Betriebsvereinbarung zuzuführen. Der denkbare Erfolg eines solchen Vorgehens ist allerdings von der fachlichen Kompetenz der bzw. des Einigungsstellenvorsitzenden abhängig, zumindest aber von einer adäquaten fachlichen Begleitung des Einigungsstellenverfahrens durchexterne Experten bzw. Personen mit einem besonderen Fachwissen.

VI. Zentrale Eckpunkte einer Betriebsvereinbarung zum wertschätzenden Umgang am Arbeitsplatz

Sofern sich die Betriebsparteien dazu entschließen, in Sachen wertschätzender Umgang am Arbeitsplatz tätig zu werden, wird sich ihnen die Frage stellen, wie eine entsprechende Betriebsvereinbarung inhaltlich ausgestaltet werden kann. Zu ihrer Beantwortung werden im Folgenden zentrale Eckpunkte einer solchen Betriebsvereinbarung vorgestellt, die bisweilen um Formulierungsbeispiele ergänzt werden. Letztere sind mit einer Einrückung versehen.

Als zentrale Eckpunkte einer Betriebsvereinbarung zum wertschätzenden Umgang am Arbeitsplatz lassen sich anführen:

- Überschrift bzw. Titel
- Anlass und Ziele
- Geltungsbereich
- Grundsätze für einen wertschätzenden Umgang
- Beschwerderecht
- Betriebliche Beschwerdestelle
- Verschwiegenheitspflicht
- Maßregelungsverbot
- Schlussbestimmungen

1. Überschrift bzw. Titel

Wird bedacht, dass eine Betriebsvereinbarung von allen im Betrieb tätigen Akteuren verstanden werden soll, dann liegt es auf der Hand, dass die Überschrift bzw. der Titel leicht verständlich auf den sprichwörtlichen Punkt gebracht werden sollte. Allein schon aus diesem Grund verbieten sich komplizierte Formulierungen sowie die Verwendung von Fremdwörtern. Zudem sollte die Vereinbarung nicht gegen, sondern vielmehr für etwas stehen und insoweit eine positive Formulierung aufweisen. Dies vor Augen bietet sich beispielhaft als Überschrift bzw. Titel der Vereinbarung an:

> „Betriebsvereinbarung für einen wertschätzenden Umgang am Arbeitsplatz".

Alternativ dazu könnte es unter Hinzufügung der Firma des Unternehmens heißen:

„Betriebsvereinbarung für einen wertschätzenden Umgang bei der ...[31]".

2. Anlass und Ziele

Damit vor allem später in den Betrieb eintretende Personen erfahren können, aus welchen Gründen und mit welchen Zielen die Betriebsvereinbarung seinerzeit geschlossen wurde, sollte viel Wert auf eine möglichst treffende Formulierung gelegt werden. Auf diese Weise lässt sich bei den jeweiligen Lesern ein hohes Maß an Sensibilisierung erzielen. Beispielhaft könnte es heißen:

„Ein wertschätzender Umgang am Arbeitsplatz ist eine wichtige Voraussetzung für den Erfolg der ...[32] Dazu gehört, dass im Zusammenhang mit der Arbeit aufkommende Probleme, Differenzen und Konflikte offen, ehrlich und fair bewältigt werden. Hierzu soll diese Betriebsvereinbarung einen wertvollen Beitrag liefern."

Der bereits unter IV. angesprochene § 75 Abs. 1 BetrVG wurde im Jahr 2006 aus Anlass des Inkrafttretens des Allgemeinen Gleichbehandlungsgesetzes neu gefasst. Integriert wurden die in § 1 AGG aufgeführten Benachteiligungsmerkmale. Diese inhaltliche Nähe der beiden Vorschriften kann dazu genutzt werden, die nach § 13 Abs. 1 AGG einzurichtende betriebliche Beschwerdestelle mit weiteren Aufgaben zu versehen und in die Thematik des wertschätzenden Umgangs am Arbeitsplatz einzubinden. Eine weitere Folge ist, dass es keiner speziellen, weiteren Betriebsvereinbarung zu der in § 13 Abs. 1 AGG angesprochenen betrieblichen Beschwerdestelle bedarf, die zumindest hinsichtlich der Verfahrensregelungen der Mitbestimmung des Betriebsrats gemäß § 87 Abs. 1 Nr. 1 BetrVG unterliegt.[33] Wer diese aufgezeigte Möglichkeit nutzen möchte, der kann insoweit anfügen:

„Zugleich wird mit ihr der gesetzlichen Vorgabe, betriebliche Beschwerdestellen im Sinne des § 13 Abs. 1 AGG bei der ...[34] einzurichten, Rechnung getragen."

Zum Zweck der Klarstellung und Transparenz kann zudem die Überschrift bzw. der Titel der Betriebsvereinbarung um den in Klammer gesetzten Hinweis

„(Betriebliche Beschwerdestelle gemäß § 13 Abs. 1 AGG)"

ergänzt werden.

3. Geltungsbereich

In der Betriebsvereinbarung muss niedergelegt werden, für welchen Personenkreis sie gelten oder nicht gelten soll. Dabei ist dem § 5 Abs. 3 BetrVG Beachtung zu

---

31 Anmerkung: Hinzuzufügen ist die Firma bzw. der Name des betreffenden Betriebs.

32 Anmerkung: Hinzuzufügen ist die Firma bzw. der Name des betreffenden Betriebs.

33 Vgl. BAG, Beschluss v. 21. Juli 2009 – 1 ABR 42/08, wobei der Erste Senat übersieht, dass die personelle Besetzung der betrieblichen Beschwerdestelle nicht losgelöst von der inhaltlichen Ausgestaltung des Beschwerdeverfahrens geregelt werden kann, sofern die betriebliche Beschwerdestelle ihren gesetzlich auferlegten Zweck soll erfüllen können.

34 Anmerkung: Hinzuzufügen ist die Firma bzw. der Name des betreffenden Betriebs.

schenken, wonach das Betriebsverfassungsgesetz, und demzufolge auch die Betriebsvereinbarung, auf leitende Angestellte keine Anwendung findet. Vergleichbares gilt für Dienstleister und Kooperationspartner, auf die die Betriebsvereinbarung ebenfalls keine Wirkung entfalten kann. Ferner kann die zeitliche Geltungsdauer festgeschrieben werden, sofern die Betriebsparteien eine zeitlich befristete Geltung der Betriebsvereinbarung etwa aus Gründen ihrer Erprobung wollen. Mithin kann sich folgende Formulierung anbieten:

„(1) Diese Betriebsvereinbarung gilt für alle Beschäftigten der …[35]

(2) Die …[36] verpflichtet sich, auf von dem Geltungsbereich dieser Betriebsvereinbarung nicht erfassten Personen (z. B. leitende Angestellte, Dienstleister, Kooperationspartner) dahingehend einzuwirken, dass sich diese und deren Mitarbeiter gemäß den Vorgaben dieser Betriebsvereinbarung verhalten. Sofern dies nicht erfolgt, verpflichtet sich die …[37], geeignete Maßnahmen zum Schutz der Beschäftigten zu ergreifen (z. B. Versetzung eines leitenden Angestellten, Kündigung eines Dienstleistungsvertrags, Forderung nach Austausch eines Fremdfirmenbeschäftigten).

(3) Aus Gründen ihrer Erprobung soll die Betriebsvereinbarung am …[38] in Kraft und am …[39] außer Kraft treten, wobei eine Nachwirkung der Betriebsvereinbarung ausgeschlossen ist."

4. Grundsätze für einen wertschätzenden Umgang

Je größer die Belegschaft ist, desto mehr werden die Ansichten und Meinungen auseinandergehen, was unter einem wertschätzenden Umgang am Arbeitsplatz zu verstehen ist. Daher ist es unabdingbar, in der Betriebsvereinbarung darzulegen, was darunter zu begreifen ist. In der gleichen Weise ist auszuführen, welche in der konkreten betrieblichen Lebenswirklichkeit anzutreffenden Verhaltensweisen als nicht wünschenswert betrachtet werden und daher zu unterlassen sind. Diese können konkret benannt und aufgeführt werden. Probleme, Differenzen und Konflikte werden oftmals in einer Art und Weise angegangen bzw. ausgetragen, die in einem krassen Gegensatz zu einem wertschätzenden Umgang stehen. Insoweit ist zu empfehlen, den Umgang mit Problemen, Differenzen und Konflikten anzusprechen und die Verfahrensweise damit zu thematisieren. Eine Formulierung kann wie folgt aussehen:

(1) Jeder wertschätzende Umgang am Arbeitsplatz folgt dem allgemeinen Grundsatz angewandter Ethik: Behandle andere so, wie Du selbst behandelt werden möchtest. Diesem Grundsatz folgend sind Verhaltensweisen zu unterlassen, die einen anderen verletzen bzw. von einem anderen als verletzend empfunden werden können. Dazu zählen vor allem: …[40]

---

35 Anmerkung: Hinzuzufügen ist die Firma bzw. der Name des betreffenden Betriebs.

36 Anmerkung: Hinzuzufügen ist die Firma bzw. der Name des betreffenden Betriebs.

37 Anmerkung: Hinzuzufügen ist die Firma bzw. der Name des betreffenden Betriebs.

38 Anmerkung: Hinzuzufügen ist das Datum des Inkrafttretens.

39 Anmerkung: Hinzuzufügen ist das Datum des Außerkrafttretens.

40 Anmerkung: Einzuarbeiten sind typische Beispiele, wie sie in dem Betrieb anzutreffen sind.

(2) Ein wertschätzender Umgang am Arbeitsplatz zeichnet sich weiter dadurch aus, dass Probleme, Differenzen und Konflikte offen angesprochen und sodann in einer fairen sowie ehrlichen Art und Weise bewältigt werden."

5. Beschwerderecht

Das Recht, sich wegen einer bestimmten Situation am Arbeitsplatz zu beschweren, ist in §§ 84 bis 86 BetrVG normiert. Auch wenn es in dem betreffenden Betrieb keinen Betriebsrat gibt, kann sich jeder Arbeitnehmer an die dafür arbeitgeberseitig festgelegte Stelle wenden und sich dort beschweren.[41] Insoweit trägt § 84 Abs. 1 Satz 2 BetrVG nur dem besonderen Umstand Rechnung, dass ein Mitglied des Betriebsrats zur Unterstützung oder Vermittlung herangezogen werden kann, wenn es in dem Betrieb einen Betriebsrat gibt. § 85 Abs. 1 BetrVG eröffnet dem einzelnen Arbeitnehmer die Möglichkeit, seine Beschwerde an den Betriebsrat zu richten, sofern ein solcher in dem jeweiligen Betrieb eingerichtet ist. § 86 BetrVG ermächtigt die Betriebsparteien, die Einzelheiten des Beschwerdeverfahrens mittels Betriebsvereinbarung zu regeln und eine betriebliche Beschwerdestelle an Stelle der in § 84 Abs. 2 BetrVG vorgesehenen Einigungsstelle zu installieren. Soweit es den Anwendungsbereich des Allgemeinen Gleichbehandlungsgesetzes betrifft, räumt § 13 Abs. 1 BetrVG den Arbeitnehmern das Recht ein, sich wegen eines in § 1 AGG genannten Grundes bei der betrieblichen Beschwerdestelle zu beschweren. Da jede Benachteiligung wegen eines in § 1 AGG genannten Grundes den Grundsätzen eines wertschätzenden Umgangs widerspricht, bietet es sich – wie bereits ausgeführt – an, das Beschwerderecht nach § 13 Abs. 1 AGG mit in die Betriebsvereinbarung aufzunehmen. Eine entsprechende Formulierung kann beispielsweise lauten:

„(1) Jede und jeder Beschäftigte der …[42] hat das Recht, sich bei der betrieblichen Beschwerdestelle zu beschweren, wenn sie bzw. er sich im Zusammenhang mit dem Beschäftigungsverhältnis vom Arbeitgeber, von Vorgesetzten, von Arbeitskollegen oder von Dritten (z. B. Kunde, Dienstleister) wegen der Rasse oder der ethnischen Herkunft, des Geschlechts, der Religion oder Weltanschauung, einer Behinderung, des Alters oder der sexuellen Identität benachteiligt fühlt.

(2) Darüber hinaus kann sich bei der betrieblichen Beschwerdestelle beschweren, wer sich aus sonstigen Gründen im Zusammenhang mit seinem Beschäftigungsverhältnis diskriminiert, gemobbt oder in anderer Weise benachteiligt oder nicht wertgeschätzt behandelt fühlt oder einer (sexuellen) Belästigung oder einer Nachstellung ausgesetzt sieht."

6. Betriebliche Beschwerdestelle

Es wurde bereits darauf hingewiesen, dass es sich anbietet, die in § 13 Abs. 1 AGG angeführte betriebliche Beschwerdestelle in die Betriebsvereinbarung zu integrieren. Hierzu bietet sich beispielsweise der folgende Passus an:

---

41 Vgl. *Buschmann* (Anm. 29), § 84 Rn. 1.

42 Anmerkung: Hinzuzufügen ist die Firma bzw. der Name des betreffenden Betriebs.

„Bei der …[43] wird mit Wirkung zum …[44] eine betriebliche Beschwerdestelle im Sinne des § 13 Abs. 1 AGG eingerichtet. Ihre Aufgabe ist es, den an sie auf der Grundlage dieser Betriebsvereinbarung gerichteten Beschwerden nachzugehen sowie Beschäftigte bei der Bewältigung von Problemen, Differenzen und Konflikten, die im Zusammenhang mit ihrem Beschäftigungsverhältnis stehen, zu unterstützen. Weiter kann sie der Geschäftsführung sowie dem Betriebsrat Maßnahmen vorschlagen, die den Zielen dieser Betriebsvereinbarung dienen."

Als weitere Aspekte, die einer inhaltlichen Ausgestaltung in der Betriebsvereinbarung bedürfen, sind vornehmlich zu nennen:

- Personelle Zusammensetzung der Beschwerdestelle;
- Sachausstattung der Beschwerdestelle sowie der arbeitgeberseitigen Kostentragung;
- Fortbildung der Mitglieder der Beschwerdestelle sowie der arbeitgeberseitigen Kostentragung;
- Verfahrensgrundsätze für die Arbeit der Mitglieder der Beschwerdestelle;
- Coaching und Supervision der Mitglieder der Beschwerdestelle sowie der arbeitgeberseitigen Kostentragung;
- Angebote der Beschwerdestelle für die Beschäftigten des Betriebs sowie der arbeitgeberseitigen Kostentragung;
- Unterbreitung von Vorschlägen der Beschwerdestelle an die Betriebsparteien (z.B. Schulung der Beschäftigten, Ergreifung von Maßnahmen, Evaluierung und Fortschreibung der Betriebsvereinbarung).

7. Verschwiegenheitspflicht

Jede Person, die sich an die betriebliche Beschwerdestelle wendet, muss darauf vertrauen können, dass ihre Anliegen vertraulich behandelt werden. Die Akzeptanz der betrieblichen Beschwerdestelle, ihrer Mitglieder und deren Arbeit ist insoweit abhängig von der Verschwiegenheit der Mitglieder der betrieblichen Beschwerdestelle. Sie erfordert daher ein besonderes Augenmerk. Beispielhaft kann die Verschwiegenheitspflicht wie folgt geregelt werden, wobei die Pflicht zur Verschwiegenheit nicht mit der Beendigung der Mitgliedschaft in der betrieblichen Beschwerdestelle enden sollte:

„Die Mitglieder der betrieblichen Beschwerdestelle sind zur Verschwiegenheit verpflichtet, soweit sie nicht im konkreten Einzelfall von der betreffenden Person von ihrer Verschwiegenheitspflicht entbunden worden sind. Die Verschwiegenheitspflicht gilt über das Ende der Ausübung des Amtes als Mitglied der betrieblichen Beschwerdestelle und bei einem Ausscheiden aus dem Unternehmen über das Ende des Beschäftigungsverhältnisses hinaus."

---

43 Anmerkung: Hinzuzufügen ist die Firma bzw. der Name des betreffenden Betriebs.

44 Anmerkung: Hinzuzufügen ist ein konkretes Datum.

8. Maßregelungsverbot

In einer vergleichbaren Weise, wie es bei der Verschwiegenheitspflicht der Fall ist, müssen die Beschäftigten darauf vertrauen können, dass sie vor einer Maßregelung geschützt sind. Aufbauend auf § 612a BGB sowie § 16 AGG kann es daher beispielhaft lauten:

„Die …[45] darf Beschäftigte wegen der Inanspruchnahme von Rechten nach dieser Betriebsvereinbarung oder wegen der Weigerung, eine gegen diese Betriebsvereinbarung verstoßende Anweisung auszuführen, nicht benachteiligen. Gleiches gilt für Personen, welche Beschäftigte bei der Inanspruchnahme von Rechten nach dieser Betriebsvereinbarung oder bei der Weigerung, eine gegen diese Betriebsvereinbarung verstoßende Anweisung auszuführen, unterstützen.“

9. Schlussbestimmungen

Als Schlussbestimmungen einer Betriebsvereinbarung werden regelmäßig Aspekte genannt, welche die nachfolgend aufgeführten Themen zum Gegenstand haben, wobei auf Formulierungsvorschläge verzichtet wird:

- Inkrafttreten der Betriebsvereinbarung, sofern ihre Laufzeit nicht bereits unter „3. Geltungsbereich“ geregelt ist oder ein Inkrafttreten nicht mit der Unterzeichnung der Betriebsvereinbarung erfolgen soll;
- Kündigung und Nachwirkung der Betriebsvereinbarung;
- Evaluation und Fortschreibung der Betriebsvereinbarung;
- Salvatorische Klausel.

VII. Resümee und Ausblick

Wer sich dem Thema des wertschätzenden Umgangs am Arbeitsplatz annimmt, der hat die Möglichkeit, im Betrieb unerwünschte Verhaltensweisen wie Mobbing und den sonstigen Erscheinungsformen der psychosozialen Belastungen am Arbeitsplatz wirksam zu begegnen. Sowohl intervenierende als auch vorbeugende Maßnahmen werden zudem bewirken, dass sich das Klima am Arbeitsplatz verbessert und negative Folgen eines schlechten Betriebsklimas, wozu vor allen der Krankenstand sowie die Fluktuation zählen, verringern. Daneben kann es dem Arbeitgeber bei der Rekrutierung von neuen Mitarbeitern helfen, die aufgrund des demografischen Wandels sowie des vielerorts anzutreffenden Fachkräftemangels immer weniger werden. Eine Betriebsvereinbarung zum wertschätzenden Umgang am Arbeitsplatz dürfte das Image des Arbeitgebers im Allgemeinen und seine Attraktivität bei solchen Personen steigern, die sich in beruflicher Hinsicht verändern möchten. Schlussendlich kann der in dem Gallup Engagement Index Deutschland 2024 aufgezeigten Entwicklung begegnet werden.

---

[45] Anmerkung: Hinzuzufügen ist die Firma bzw. der Name des betreffenden Betriebs.

Literaturverzeichnis

Bundesministerium für Arbeit und Soziales: Mobbing in der Arbeitswelt. Bedeutung, Verbreitung und Prävention (Mobbing-Report 2024) (2025).

Däubler, Wolfgang/*Klebe*, Thomas/*Wedde*, Peter (Hrsg.): BetrVG – Betriebsverfassungsgesetz, 19. Aufl. (2024).

Däubler, Wolfgang/*Kittner*, Michael: Geschichte und Zukunft der Betriebsverfassung, 2. Aufl. (2022).

Däubler-Gmelin, Herta: Warum hat Deutschland (bisher) kein eigenständiges und umfassendes „Anti-Mobbing-Gesetz"?, in: Wolmerath, Martin/Esser, Axel (Hrsg.), Werkbuch Mobbing. Offensive Methoden gegen psychische Gewalt am Arbeitsplatz (2012), S. 38 ff.

Düwell, Franz Josef (Hrsg.): Betriebsverfassungsgesetz, 6. Aufl. (2022).

Eisermann, Jens/*Costanzo*, Elisabetta de: Die Erfassung von Mobbing – Eine Konstruktvalidierung aktueller Datenerhebungsverfahren (2011).

Fulda, Carolin Denise: Gewerkschaften: Weniger Repräsentativität durch Strukturdefizite?, IW-Kurzbericht 83/22, Institut der Deutschen Wirtschaft (2022).

Leymann, Heinz (Hrsg.): Der neue Mobbing-Bericht. Erfahrungen und Initiativen, Auswege und Hilfsangebote (1995).

Leymann, Heinz: Mobbing. Psychoterror am Arbeitsplatz und wie man sich dagegen wehren kann (1993).

Meschkutat, Bärbel/*Stackelbeck*, Martina/*Langenhoff*, Georg: Der Mobbing-Report. Repräsentativstudie für die Bundesrepublik Deutschland (2002).

Ruberg, Bernd: Schikanöse Weisungen. Psychosoziale Gefährdung am Arbeitsplatz im Blickfeld der Gerichte für Arbeitssachen – nicht nur! – bei „Mobbing" (2004).

Stettes, Oliver: Verbreitung von Betriebsräten und der Wunsch nach Interessenvertretung. Eine Analyse auf Basis der IW-Beschäftigtenbefragung 2024 (IW-Report 1/2025), Institut der Deutschen Wirtschaft (2025).

Sumida, Kunishige: Mobbing in Japan, in: Wolmerath, Martin/Esser, Axel (Hrsg.), Werkbuch Mobbing. Offensive Methoden gegen psychische Gewalt am Arbeitsplatz, Frankfurt am Main 2012, S. 261 ff.

Wolmerath, Martin: Es ist an der Zeit – Ansatzpunkte für eine Reform des Betriebsverfassungsgesetzes, in: Düwell, Nora/Gallner, Inken/Haase, Karsten/Wolmerath, Martin (Hrsg.), Auf dem Weg zu einem sozialen und inklusiven Rechtsstaat – Covid 19 als Herausforderung. Liber amicorum Franz Josef Düwell (2021), S. 845 ff.

Wolmerath, Martin: Mobbing. Rechtshandbuch für die Praxis, 5. Aufl. (2019).

Wolmerath, Martin: Mobbing im Betrieb. Rechtsansprüche und deren Durchsetzbarkeit (2001).

Verzeichnis der Schriften von Prof. Dr. Heinrich Menkhaus

I. Selbstständige Werke

1. Kreditsicherung beim Dokumenteninkasso. Bankrechtliche Sonderveröffentlichungen des Instituts für Bankwirtschaft und Bankrecht an der Universität zu Köln, Band 34, Köln (1984).

Besprechung: Nielsen, Jens, in: ZIP (1985), S. 777 ff.

2. *Hōmushō Keiji Kyoku* (Abteilung für Strafsachen im Justizministerium) (Hrsg.): *Hōritsu yōgo taiyaku shū – doitsugo hen* (Zweisprachiges Lexikon juristischer Fachtermini – Japanisch/Deutsch), Tokyo (1992) (zusammen mit Toda Nobuhisa).

3. Der japanische Kapitalmarkt, Reihe Japanwirtschaft des Deutsch-Japanischen Wirtschaftsförderungsbüros, Heft 25, Düsseldorf (1992).

4. Egalität und Individualität im gegenwärtigen Japan – Untersuchungen zu Wertemustern in Bezug auf Familie und Arbeitswelt, Monographienreihe des Deutschen Instituts für Japanstudien, Band 7, Iudicium, München (1994) (zusammen mit Helmut Demes, Ulrich Möhwald, Hans Dieter Ölschleger, Annelie Ortmanns-Suzuki und Bettina Post-Kobayashi).

Besprechungen: Meier, Bernd, in: Informationsdienst des Instituts der deutschen Wirtschaft 24 (1995), S. 6; Manzenreiter, Wolfram, in: Minikomi – Informationen des Akademischen Arbeitskreises Japan 2 (1995), S. 9–14; Mehl, Margaret, in: Japan Forum 8 (1996), S. 134.

5. Die Verfassungskultur in Japan aus deutscher Sicht, Konrad Adenauer Stiftung, Japan Office, Tokyo (2016).

6. Verein der Förderer der deutschsprachigen katholischen Kirchengemeinde St. Michael Tokyo (1969–2019) – 50. Gründungsjubiläum und Auflösung, OAG (Deutsche Gesellschaft für Natur- und Völkerkunde Ostasiens), Tokyo (2020) (OAG Aktuell Nr. 150).

II. Herausgabe

1. Das Japanische im japanischen Recht. Monographienreihe des Deutschen Instituts für Japanstudien, Band 5, Iudicium, München (1994).

Besprechungen: Heuser, Robert, in: ZaöRV (1995), S. 1267; Kliesow, Olaf, in: Mitteilungen der Deutsch-Japanischen Juristenvereinigung 15 (1995), S. 132; Süß, Rembert, in: RIW 8 (1995) II; Heath, Christopher, in: GRUR Int 5 (1995), S. 439; Lehner, Monika, in: ZfRV (1996), S. 172; Kaffsack, Annette, in: VRÜ 1 (1996), S. 113; Marfording, Annette, in: Japanese Studies Bulletin (Australia) 16 (1996), S. 95; Hohmann, Harald, in: The American Journal of Comparative Law 44 (1996), S. 151; Steenstrup, Carl, in: Monumenta Japonica 51 (1996), S. 252; Großfeld, Bernhard, in: RabelsZ (1997), S. 177; Heath, Christopher, in: IIC (1997), S. 431; Pape, Fabian, in: DZWir (1997), S. 264.

Duncker & Humblot · Berlin | https://doi.org/10.3790/978-3-428-59611-9.2025.423784

2. 20th Anniversary – Past, Present and Future of the European Association for Japanese Studies, 1973–1994, EAJS, Leiden (1994) (zusammen mit Adriana Boscaro, Jan van Bremen und Tom Harper).

3. Japanischer Brückenbauer zum deutschen Rechtskreis, Festschrift für Koresuke Yamauchi zum 60. Geburtstag, Duncker & Humblot, Berlin 2006 (zusammen mit Fumihiko Satō).

4. Vom Ungleichen in Japan. Untersuchungen zu wachsenden Disparitäten in Gesellschaft, Wirtschaft und Recht. Referate gehalten auf dem 14. Deutschsprachigen Japanologentag in Halle, 29.9.–2.10.2009, Band I: Wirtschaft und Recht, Bier'sche Verlagsanstalt, Bonn (2012) (zusammen mit Günther Distelrath und Hans Dieter Ölschleger).

5. Japanischer Vorkämpfer für die Rechtsordnung des 21. Jahrhunderts, Festschrift für Koresuke Yamauchi zum 70. Geburtstag, Duncker & Humblot, Berlin (2017) (zusammen mit Midori Narazaki).

6. The Law of Public Procurement in Japan, Germany and the EU. Duncker & Humblot, Berlin (2025), erscheint demnächst (zusammen mit Shigeki Kusunoki).

III. Wissenschaftliche Aufsätze

1. Der Oberste Gerichtshof der Vereinigten Staaten nimmt Stellung zum Verhältnis von Handels- und Steuerbilanz, in: JZ (Juristenzeitung) (1979), S. 359.

2. Das Drama ‚Gemeinnützigkeit', in: ZfgG (Zeitschrift für das gesamte Genossenschaftswesen) 32 (1982), S. 163–182 (zusammen mit Bernhard Großfeld).

3. Der Vertriebsvertrag, in: Deutsche Industrie- und Handelskammer in Japan (Hrsg.): Investitionsfibel – Juristische Ratschläge für das Japangeschäft. Deutsche Industrie- und Handelskammer in Japan, Tokyo (1985), Teil A, S. 24–29.

4. Sicherungsrechte der kreditgebenden Einreicherbank am Inkassoerlös im Konkurs des Dokumenteneinreichers beim Dokumenteninkasso – Anmerkung zum Urteil des BGH vom 1. 7. 1985 II ZR 155/84, in: ZIP (Zeitschrift für Wirtschaftsrecht) (1985), S. 1309–1314.

5. Dokumentäre Zahlungsabwicklung im Außenhandel, in: Yamauchi, Koresuke (Hrsg.): Beiträge zum japanischen und ausländischen Bank- und Finanzrecht, Veröffentlichungen des Japanischen Instituts für Rechtsvergleichung, Universität Chūō, Band 10, Tokyo (1987), S. 151–172.

6. Der Vertriebsvertrag, in: Deutsche Industrie- und Handelskammer in Japan (Hrsg.): Investitionsfibel – Juristische Ratschläge für das Japangeschäft, 2. Aufl., Deutsche Industrie- und Handelskammer in Japan, Tokyo (1987), S. 41–45.

7. Anerkennung und Vollstreckbarkeitserklärung deutscher zivilgerichtlicher Entscheidungen in Japan, in: RIW (Recht der Internationalen Wirtschaft) (1988), S. 189–193.

8. *Tōkyō ofu shoa māketto* (Der off shore-Markt in Tokyo), in: Yamauchi, Koresuke (Hrsg.): 1987 *nendo kokusai kin'yūhō zemināru ronbunshū, Chūō daigaku hōgakubu* (Sammlung der Beiträge zum Seminar Internationales Finanzrecht an der Rechtswissenschaftlichen Fakultät der Universtät *Chūō* im Jahr 1987), Tokyo (1988), S. 217–225.

9. Internationalisierung und Liberalisierung der japanischen Finanzmärkte?, in: Lokowandt, Ernst (Hrsg.): Referate des 1. Japanologentages der OAG in Tokyo,– 7.–8. 4. 1988, Iudicium, München (1990), S. 173–189.

10. Die Bedeutung der devisenrechtlichen Regelungsmechanismen für die internationale Verbreitung des Yen, in: Japanstudien (Jahrbuch des Deutschen Instituts für Japanstudien) 1 (1989), S. 211–236.

11. Zeit ist Geld – Zum Stand des bargeldlosen Zahlungsverkehrs in Japan, in: Japanstudien: (Jahrbuch des Deutschen Instituts für Japanstudien) 2 (1990), S. 53–87.

12. Strukturwandel auf den japanischen Finanzmärkten, in: Bachmayer, Eva u. a. (Hrsg.): Japan von Aids bis Zen – Referate des 8. deutschsprachigen Japanologentages vom 26.–27. 9. 1990 in Wien, Beiträge zur Japanologie, Band 29, 2. Teil, Institut für Japanologie der Universität Wien, Wien (1991), S. 403–425.

13. *Takokuseki kigyō to kin'yūhō* (Multinationale Unternehmen und Finanzrecht), in: *Takokuseki kigyō no hōkisei, Kubo Kin'ya sensei taikan kinen ronbunshū* (Juristische Schranken für multinationale Unternehmen, Jubiläumsfestgabe anlässlich der Emeritierung von Prof. Kin'ya Kubo), *Chūō Keizaisha*, Tokyo (1993), S. 173–182.

14. *Doitsu renpō kyōwa koku hōsōzai seirei* (Die Verpackungsverordnung der Bundesrepublik Deutschland), in: *Hikakuhō Zasshi* (Zeitschrift für Rechtsvergleichung der Universität *Chūō*) 27/1 (1993), S. 51–64.

15. *A sō* – Einblicke ins japanische Namensrecht, in: Erlinghagen, Susanne u. a. (Hrsg.): Die Freuden des jungen Bäckermeisters Lehmann – Prof. Dr. Bernhard Großfeld zum 60. Geburtstag, Eigenverlag, Münster (1993), S. 147–158.

16. Zulassung fremder Juristen als Rechtsanwälte für ausländisches Recht in Japan, in: Mitteilungen der Deutsch-Japanischen Juristenvereinigung 9 (1993), S. 7–9.

17. Vertrieb, Transport und Lagerhaltung, in: Baum, Harald/Drobnig, Ulrich (Hrsg.): Japanisches Handels- und Wirtschaftsrecht, Walter de Gruyter, Berlin u. a. (1994), S. 145–184 (zusammen mit Shūhei Maruyama).

18. Einführung, Diskussionen, Das Japanische im japanischen Finanzrecht und Zusammenfassung, in: Menkhaus, Heinrich (Hrsg.): Das Japanische im japanischen Recht, Monographienreihe des Deutschen Instituts für Japanstudien, Band 5, Iudicium, München (1994), S. 1–11, 281–310 und 537–556.

19. Gründung einer Tochtergesellschaft in Japan, in: Lutter, Marcus (Hrsg.): Die Gründung einer Tochtergesellschaft im Ausland, 3. Aufl., ZGR-Sonderband 3, Walter de Gruyter, Berlin u. a. (1994), S. 338–373 (zusammen mit Koresuke Yamauchi).

20. Zulassung fremder Juristen als Rechtsanwälte für ausländisches Recht in Japan, Teil II, in: Mitteilungen der Deutsch-Japanischen Juristenvereinigung 11 (1994), S. 12–15.

21. Die Struktur der japanischen Finanzmärkte nach dem 1. April 1993 – das Ende des Trennungsprinzips?, in: Klopfenstein, Eduard u. a. (Hrsg.): Referate des 9. deutschsprachigen Japanologentages in Zürich, Asiatische Studien XLVIII – 1–1994, Peter Lang: Bern u. a. (1994), S. 595–602.

22. *Kokusai kaishahō o meguru shomondai* (Probleme des Internationalen Gesellschaftsrechts), in: *Meijō Hōgaku* (Juristische Zeitschrift der Universität *Meijō*, Nagoya) 44/2 (1994), S. 1–10 (Vortragsmitschrift von Fumihiko Satō).

23. Working Regulations for Foreign Workers in Foreign Affiliated Companies in Japan, in: Labour Issues Quarterly 32 (1996), S. 1.

24. *Kaisha no keitai no hyōki de kangaeru koto* (Nachdenkliches über die Angabe der Rechtsform der Handelsgesellschaften), in: *JETRO Sensâ* (Zeitschrift der japanischen Außenhandelsförderungsorganisation JETRO) 6 (1996), S. 94–95.

25. *Seizōbutsu sekininhō wa shin no shōhisha hogo ka?* (Dient das Produkthaftpflichtrecht wirklich dem Verbraucherschutz?), in: *JETRO Sensâ* (Zeitschrift der japanischen Außenhandelsförderungsorganisation JETRO) 9 (1996), S. 94–95.

26. Marktzugangsbedingungen Japan, in: Ostasiatischer Verein und Deutsche Industrie- und Handelskammer in Japan für den Asien-Pazifik-Ausschuß der Deutschen Wirtschaft, (November 1996), S. 8 (zusammen mit Carsten Güntner).

27. Japanisches und deutsches Produkthaftpflichtrecht – Ein Vergleich, in: *Kakehashi*/Die Brücke (Zeitschrift der Japanisch-Deutschen Gesellschaft e. V.), Tokyo 1 (1997), S. 1.

28. *Doitsu no junkan keizai – haikibutsuhō to jisshi seirei* (Die deutsche Kreislaufwirtschaft – Abfallbeseitigungsgesetz und Ausführungsverordnungen), in: *JETRO Sensâ* (Zeitschrift der japanischen Außenhandelsförderungsorganisation JETRO) 4 (1997), S. 94–96.

29. Die ‚japanische' Verpackungsverordnung, in: Japan-Markt (Zeitschrift der Deutschen Industrie- und Handelskammer in Japan) 7 (1997), S. 19–20.

30. Japan, in: Detzer, Klaus/Zwernemann, Dieter (Hrsg.): Ausländisches Recht der Handelsvertreter und Vertragshändler, Schriftenreihe Recht der Internationalen Wirtschaft, Band 54: Recht und Wirtschaft, Heidelberg (1997), S. 207–212 (zusammen mit Klaus Detzer und Dieter Zwernemann).

31. Investitionsbedingungen in Japan, in: DSWR (Datenverarbeitung, Steuer, Wirtschaft, Recht) 1/2 (1998), S. 29–33.

32. Liberalisierung des Devisenverkehrs zum 1. April – aber!, in: Japan-Markt (Zeitschrift der Deutschen Industrie- und Handelskammer in Japan) 3 (1998), S. 18.

33. Liberalisierung des Devisenverkehrs zum 1. April – aber! (2. Teil), in: Japan-Markt (Zeitschrift der Deutschen Industrie- und Handelskammer in Japan) 4 (1998), S. 24.

34. Die rechtliche Bewältigung von Marktzugangsproblemen, in: Riesenhuber, Heinz/Kreiner, Josef (Hrsg.): Japan ist offen, Springer, Berlin (1998), S. 123–137.

35. Japan – Besonderheiten der bilateralen Beziehungen aus der Sicht der Deutschen Industrie- und Handelskammer in Japan, in: Ostasiatischer Verein e. V. (Hrsg.): Wirtschaftshandbuch Asien-Pazifik (1998/1999), S. 243–247 (zusammen mit Manfred Dransfeld).

36. Recruitment of Foreigners by Foreign Affiliated Enterprises in Japan, Labour Issues Quarterly 39 (1998), S. 1.

37. Deutsch-Japanisches Sozialversicherungsabkommen, in: Japan-Markt (Zeitschrift der Deutschen Industrie- und Handelskammer in Japan) 6 (1998), S. 3–5.

38. *Kigyō hō ni okeru Nihon to Doitsu – omo ni kenrishutai ni tsuite* (Unternehmensrecht in Japan und Deutschland – insbesondere zu den Rechtsträgern von Unternehmen), in: *Hikakuhō* (Rechtsvergleichende Zeitschrift der Universität *Tōyō*, Tokyo) 36 (1999), S. 59–68.

39. Wortbeitrag von Dr. Heinrich Menkhaus, in: *Nichidoku Rōdōhō Kaihō* (Zeitschrift der Japanisch-Deutschen Gesellschaft für Arbeitsrecht) 2 (1999), S. 84–85.

40. Deregulierung aus juristischer Sicht, in: Schaumann, Werner (Hrsg.): Japans Kultur der Reformen, Referate des 6. Japanologentages der OAG in Tokyo, Iudicium, München (1999), S. 49–57.

41. Japan, in: Henrich, Dieter (Hrsg.): Internationales Ehe- und Kindschaftsrecht mit Staatsangehörigkeitsrecht, 6. Aufl. 1983 ff., Verlag für Standesamtswesen, Frankfurt/Main u. a. (Loseblatt), 139. Lieferung (2000), S. 1–57 (zusammen mit Koresuke Yamauchi und Fumihiko Satō).

42. Marktzugangsbedingungen aus der Sicht der Deutschen Industrie- und Handelskammer in Japan, in: Ostasiatischer Verein e. V. (Hrsg.): Wirtschaftshandbuch Asien-Pazifik (1999/2000), S. 249–255 (zusammen mit Manfred Dransfeld).

43. Der deutsch-japanische Austausch der Gegenwart und die Juristen, in: Manthey, Barbara u. a. (Hrsg.): JapanWelten – Aspekte der deutschsprachigen Japanforschung, Festschrift für Josef Kreiner zu seinem 60. Geburtstag von seinen Schülern und Mitarbeitern, Bier'sche Verlagsanstalt, Bonn (2000), S. 261–277.

44. Marktzugangsbedingungen aus der Sicht der Deutschen Industrie- und Handelskammer in Japan, in: Ostasiatischer Verein e. V. (Hrsg.): Wirtschaftshandbuch Asien-Pazifik (2000/2001), S. 244–247 (zusammen mit Manfred Dransfeld).

45. M & A in Japan – Fremdinvestitionen, Unternehmenskäufe, Zielbranchen, in: Pohl, Manfred (Hrsg.): Japan 1999/2000 – Politik und Wirtschaft, Institut für Asienkunde, Hamburg (2000), S. 172–186 (zusammen mit Holger Schmitt).

46. *Nihon ni okeru doitsu kigyō to nichidoku ibunka komyunikēshon* (Deutschkapitalisierte Unternehmen in Japan und das Verständnis japanisch-deutscher Kulturunterschiede), in: *Rikkyō daigaku doitsu bungakuka kenkyūshitsu* (Germanistisches Seminar der *Rikkyō*-Universität Tokyo) (Hrsg.): Aspekt – *Rikkyō daigaku doitsu bungakuka ronshū* (Aufsatzsammlung Germanistisches Seminar der Universität *Rikkyō*) 34 (2000), S. 355–361 (Vortragsmitschrift von Mayumi Takahashi).

47. Deutsch-Japanisches Sozialversicherungsabkommen, in: Gössmann, Hilaria u. a. (Hrsg.): 11. Deutschsprachiger Japanologentag in Trier 1999, Band I: Geschichte, Geistesgeschichte, Politik, Recht, Wirtschaft, LIT-Verlag, Münster u. a. (2001), S. 401–410.

48. *Nichidoku shakai hoshō kyōtei – saisho no keikenteki jirei* (Das japanisch-deutsche Sozialversicherungsabkommen – Erste Erfahrungen), in: Seki, Hideaki u. a. (Hrsg.): *gendai kigyōhō no shin tenkai – Kojima Yasuhiro kyōju taikan kinen* (Neue Entwicklungen des Unternehmensrechts der Gegenwart, Festschrift zur Emeritierung von Yasuhiro Kojima), *Shinzansha*, Tokyo (2001), S. 535–547.

49. Marktzugangsbedingungen aus der Sicht der Deutschen Industrie- und Handelskammer in Japan (DIHKJ), in: Ostasiatischer Verein e. V. (Hrsg.): Wirtschaftshandbuch Asien-Pazifik (2001/2002), S. 255–259 (zusammen mit Manfred Dransfeld).

50. German Global Player – Deutsch in deutschkapitalisierten Unternehmen in Japan, in: *Doitsugo kyōiku* (Deutschunterricht in Japan) 6 (2001), S. 123–139.

51. Japanisches Recht und Japanwissenschaften, in: Japanforschung – Mitteilungen der Gesellschaft für Japanforschung e. V. 1 (2002), S. 6–11.

52. Rechtsverfolgung in Zivil- und Handelssachen in Japan, ab 2003 auf der Homepage der Deutschen Botschaft in Japan.

53. Literatur zum japanischen Arbeitsrecht in westlichen Sprachen seit 1990 – eine teilannotierte Auswahl, ab 2003 auf der Homepage der Deutsch-Japanischen Gesellschaft für Arbeitsrecht (zusammen mit Falk Meinhardt).

54. *Doitsu ni okeru 2002 nen no hōsō yōsei kaisei ni tsuite* (Die Änderungen der deutschen Juristenausbildung aus dem Jahre 2002), in: *Hōritsu Jihō* (Juristische Fachzeitschrift in Japan) 76 (2004), S. 65–71.

55. „Neues“ Kündigungsschutzrecht in Japan!?, in: ZIAS (Zeitschrift für ausländisches und internationales Arbeits- und Sozialrecht) 3 (2004), S. 201–215 (zusammen mit Falk Meinhardt).

56. History of German-Japanese Scientific Relations in the Area of Legal Science, in: Deutsche Gesellschaft der JSPS-Stipendiaten e. V. (Hrsg.): 10th Anniversary of the Deutsche Gesellschaft der JSPS-Stipendiaten e. V. – German-Japanese Scientific Exchange, Deutsche Gesellschaft der JSPS-Stipendiaten e. V., Bonn (2005), S. 107–122.

57. Die japanische Beschäftigung mit dem deutschen Rechtswesen, in: Japanstudien (Jahrbuch des Deutschen Instituts für Japanstudien) 17 (2005), S. 133–163 (zusammen mit Yamauchi Koresuke).

58. *Kōeki hōjinsei kenkyū – doitsu to nihon no hikaku* (Studien zu gemeinnützigen juristischen Personen- Vergleich zwischen Japan und Deutschland) in: *Hitotsubashi daigakuin hōgaku kenkyūka, sōgō hōseisaku jitsumu teikei sentā,* (Rechtsgraduiertenschule der Universität *Hitotsubashi*, Allgemeines Zentrum für die Kooperation zwischen Rechtspolitik und -praxis (Hrsg.): *Heisei 17 nendo projekuto I, hōkokusho: hikakuhō no shomondai* (Bericht des Projektes 1 aus dem Jahre 2005: Verschiedene Probleme der Rechtsvergleichung), *Hitotsubashi daigakuin hōgaku kenkyūka* (Rechtsgraduiertenschule der Universität *Hitotsubashi*), Tokyo (2006), S. 35–38.

59. *Māburgu daigaku ni okeru nihon no jinbunkagaku kenkyū no rekishi* (Die Geschichte der geisteswissenschaftlichen Auseinandersetzung mit Japan an der Universität Marburg), in: Suma, Kozo u. a. (Hrsg.): Tawara's Opera, Revisited (II), Proceedings of the 4th Tawara-Aschoff Symposium, 17.–18. 11. 2005 in Tokyo, Japan. Organizing Committee of the 4th Tawara-Aschoff Symposium: Tokyo (2006), S. 15–21.

60. Japan, in: Süß, Rembert/Wachter, Thomas (Hrsg.): Handbuch des internationalen GmbH-Rechts. Zerb: Angelbachtal (2006), S. 923–934.

61. Alternative Streitbeilegung in Japan – Entwicklungen bis zum ADR-Gesetz 2004, in: Hengstl, Joachim/Sick, Ulrich (Hrsg.): Recht heute und gestern, Festschrift zum 85. Geburtstag von Richard Haase, Harrassowitz, Wiesbaden (2006), S. 281–291 (Philippika – Marburger Altertumskundliche Abhandlungen, Band 13).

62. *Doitsugoken ni okeru nihonhō he no gakumonteki torikumi* (Das deutschsprachige Studium des japanischen Rechts), in: *Hōsei Daigaku Kokusai Nihongaku Kenkyūsho* (Forschungsinstitut zu den internationalen Japanwissenschaften der Universität *Hōsei*) und Forschungsstelle Modernes Japan der Universität Bonn (Hrsg.): *Doitsugoken ni okeru nihon kenkyū no genjō* (Die Situation der Japanstudien im deutschsprachigen Raum), *Hōsei Daigaku Nihongaku Kenkyū Sentā* (Forschungszentrum Japanwissenschaften der Universität *Hōsei*), Tokyo (2006), S. 49–70.

63. Allgemeines Gesellschaftsrecht in Japan, in: Menkhaus, Heinrich/Sato, Fumihiko (Hrsg.): Japanischer Brückenbauer zum deutschen Rechtskreis, Festschrift für Koresuke Yamauchi zum 60. Geburtstag, Duncker & Humblot, Berlin (2006), S. 229–252.

64. *Doitsu ni okeru nihon hō kyōiku* (Die Vermittlung des japanischen Rechts in Deutschland), in: *Hitotsubashi daigaku* (Universität *Hitotsubashi*) (Hrsg.): *nichiō kōshingata no kōtō hōgaku kyōiku ni mukete* (Auf dem Weg zu einer qualitativ hochwertigen Juristenausbildung für den Austausch zwischen Japan und Europa), *nichiō kōshingata hōgaku kenkyūsha yōsei puroguramu* (Programm zur Ausbildung von Rechtswissenschaftlern für den Austausch zwischen Japan und Europa), *hassoku kinen shinpojium* (Symposium aus Anlass der Einführung des Programmes), abrufbar unter http://www.law.hit-u.ac.jp/home/research/project/post-9.html.

65. *Doitsu renpō kyōwa koku no hōsō yōsei ni okeru shokugyō rinri kyōiku* (Vermittlung der Berufsethik der juristischen Berufe in der Ausbildung der Bundesrepublik Deutschland),

in: Muraoka, Keiichi (Hrsg.): *kamoku ōdanteki hōsō rinri kyōiku no kaihatsu purojekuto* (Projekt zur Ausbildung in juristischer Berufsethik quer durch alle Fachgebiete).

66. Das Studium des Japanischen Rechts in Marburg, in: Ölschleger, Hans Dieter (Hrsg.): Referate des 12. deutschsprachigen Japanologentages, Band II: Wirtschaft, Gesellschaft, Recht, Bier'sche Verlagsanstalt, Bonn (2008), S. 67–76.

67. Deregulierung in Japan – Eine Einführung, in: Distelrath, Günther (Hrsg.): Referate des 13. deutschsprachigen Japanologentages, Band II: Sozial-, Geschichts- und Rechtswissenschaft, EB-Verlag, Berlin (2009), S. 217–230.

68. Vom *Jagatarubumi* zum *Japayukisan* – Japanische Staatsangehörigkeit von Kindern aus Beziehungen zwischen Japanern und Ausländern, in: *Meiji* Law Journal 16 (2009), S. 1–17.

69. *Doitsu no daigaku in okeru nihon kenkyū no kōzoteki shomondai* (Strukturprobleme der universitären wissenschaftlichen Auseinandersetzung mit Japan in Deutschland), in: *Kokusai nihonbunka kenkyū sentā* (International Research Center for Japanese Studies) (Hrsg.): *Nihon bunka kenkyū no kako, genzai, mirai – atarata na chihei wo hiraku tame ni* (Japanstudien: Vergangenheit, Gegenwart und Zukunft – Erschließung neuer Territorien für die Erforschung der japanischen Kultur), *sōritsu niju shunen kokusai shipojium* (20. Internationales Symposium), *Kokusai nihonbunka kenkyū sentā* (International Research Center for Japanese Studies), Kyoto (2009), S. 23–32.

70. Halbwertige Kinder?! – Zum Erbteil des nichtehelichen Kindes in Japan, in: *Meiji* Law Journal 17 (2010), S. 21–39.

71. C. Illies & Co. – Das älteste deutsche Unternehmen in Japan?!, zugleich eine Besprechung der Bücher: Bähr, Johannes/Lesczenski, Jörg/Schmidtpott, Katja: Handel ist Wandel. 150 Jahre C. Illies & Co. Piper: München 2009; Bähr, Johannes/Lesczenski, Jörg/Schmidtpott, Katja: *Winds of change: On the 150th anniversary of C. Illies & Co.* Piper: München 2009; Kikkawa, Takeo: C. Illies & Co. – Die Anfänge in Japan/*Irisu 150nen – Reimeiki no kioku* (zweisprachig deutsch/japanisch), Selbstverlag Irisu, Tokyo 2009, in: OAG Notizen 1 (2011), S. 27–35.

72. Zwingende Vorgaben für grenzüberschreitende Arbeitsverträge im transnational operierenden Unternehmen nach dem Recht der Rechtsträger im deutsch-japanischen Rechtsverkehr, in: Yamada, Shozo/Ishii, Yasuo (Hrsg.): *Rōdōsha jinkaku no kenkyū. Sumida Kunishige sensei koki kinen. Jōkan* (Studien zum Persönlichkeitsrecht des Arbeitnehmers), Festschrift für Kunishige Sumida zum 70. Geburtstag, Band 1, Shinzansha, Tokyo (2011), S. 177–190.

73. „Götter ohne Mietvertrag" oder unentgeltliche Gebrauchsüberlassung von Grundstücken im Eigentum einer öffentlichrechtlichen Gebietskörperschaft an eine Gemeinde von Gläubigen zur Verehrung von Göttern – Jüngste Entwicklungen zum verfassungsrechtlichen Grundsatz der Trennung von Staat und Religion in Japan –, in: *Meiji* Law Journal 18 (2011), S. 11–37.

74. Japan, in: Süß, Rembert/Wachter, Thomas (Hrsg.): Handbuch des internationalen GmbH-Rechts, 2. Aufl., Zerb, Bonn (2011), S. 995–1020 (zusammen mit Sebastian Pawlowski).

75. Insassenwechsel im Schuldturm – Erfolge der japanischen Zivilrechtsprechung bei der Bekämpfung wucherischer Zinsen in Kreditverträgen, in: *Meiji* Law Journal 19 (2012), S. 25–38.

76. *Dokkyō* Universität und Vermittlung deutschen Rechts in Japan, abrufbar seit Januar 2012 auf der Homepage der *Dokkyō* Universität unter http://www.dokkyo.ac.jp/kokuse/pdf/2011/menkhaus_all.pdf.

77. Verbraucherkreditrecht in Japan nach der Reform aus dem Jahre 2006, in: Distelrath, Günter/Menkhaus, Heinrich/Ölschleger, Hans Dieter (Hrsg.): Vom Ungleichen in Japan. Unter-

suchungen zu wachsenden Disparitäten in Gesellschaft, Wirtschaft und Recht. Referate gehalten auf dem 14. Deutschsprachigen Japanologentag in Halle, 29.9.–2.10.2009, Band I: Wirtschaft und Recht, Bier'sche Verlagsanstalt, Bonn (2012), S. 171–182.

78. Zwischen Scylla und Charybdis – Der rechtliche Rahmen für das Fahrradfahren in Japan, in: Distelrath, Günther/Lützeler, Ralph/Manthey, Barbara (Hrsg.): Auf der Suche nach der Entwicklung menschlicher Gesellschaften, Festschrift für Hans Dieter Ölschleger zu seinem 60. Geburtstag von seinen Freunden und Kollegen, EB-Verlag, Bonn (2012), S. 305–317.

79. *Doitsujin nihonryūgaku keikensha dōsōkai* (Alumnivereinigung der Deutschen mit Auslandsstudienerfahrung in Japan), in: *DAAD tomo no kai* (Japanischer Freundeskreis des DAAD) (Hrsg.), Echo 28 (2012), S. 49–51.

80. Deutsche Juristen in Japan während der *Meiji*-Zeit – Probleme bei der wissenschaftlichen Aufarbeitung ihrer Arbeit, in: Shin, Yu-Cheol (Hrsg.): Rezeption europäischer Rechte in Ostasien, *Bobmunsa*, Seoul (2013), S. 71–85.

81. Die Stellung des deutschen und europäischen Rechts in der japanischen Juristenausbildung, in: Shin, Yu-Cheol (Hrsg.): Rezeption europäischer Rechte in Ostasien, *Bobmunsa*, Seoul (2013), S. 151–156 (zusammen mit Holger Finken).

82. Die deutsche wissenschaftliche Beschäftigung mit dem japanischen Recht, in: Yamauchi, Koresuke/Ebke, Werner (Hrsg.): *Chūō daigaku myunstā daigaku kōryū 25 shunen kinen* (25 Jahre Universitätspartnerschaft *Chūō* Münster), *kokusai kankei shihō no chosen* (Herausforderungen für das Zivilrecht im internationalen Bereich), Meilensteine im Internationalen Privat- und Wirtschaftsrecht, Festgabe für Bernhard Großfeld und Otto Sandrock, *Chūō daigaku shuppanbu* (Verlag der Universität *Chūō*), Tokyo (2014), S. 77–128.

83. Rechtsstaat Japan? Konstitutive Elemente und Gefährdungen, in: Yamaguchi, Karin/Wördemann, Raimund (Hrsg.): Länderbericht Japan, Bundeszentrale für politische Bildung, Bonn (2014), S. 221–236.

84. Blick zurück im Zorn – Japanisches Recht in Marburg, in: Gornig, Gilbert (Hrsg.): Rechtspolitische Entwicklungen im nationalen und internationalen Kontext, Festschrift für Friedrich Bohl zum 70. Geburtstag, Duncker & Humblot, Berlin (2015), S. 239–255.

85. *Oyatoi gaikokujin no naka no doitsujin hōritsuka* (Die deutschen Juristen unter den Kontraktausländern, in: *Kokuritsu rekishi minzoku hakubutsukan* (Nationalmuseum für japanische Geschichte) (Hrsg.): *Doitsu to Nihon wo musubu mono – nichidoku shūkō 150nen no rekishi:* Was Deutschland und Japan verbindet – 150 Jahre Freundschaft zwischen Deutschland und Japan, *Kokuritsu rekishi minzoku hakubutsukan* (Nationalmuseum für japanische Geschichte), *Sakura* (2015), S. 92–93.

86. Japan, in: Süß, Rembert/Wachter, Thomas (Hrsg.): Handbuch des internationalen GmbH-Rechts, 3. Aufl., Zerb, Bonn (2016), S. 999–1024.

87. Der Wert eines Japaners im heimatlichen Großstadtdschungel. Das aktive Wahlrecht im Einpersonenwahlbezirk bei den japanischen Unterhauswahlen im Spannungsfeld der Grundrechte Gleichheit und Freizügigkeit sowie der Verfassungsgrundsätze Demokratie und Rechtsstaat, in: *Meiji* Law Journal 23 (2016), S. 1–23.

88. *Doitsu mibun shōmeisho* (Der deutsche Personalausweis), in: *Kakehashi*/Die Brücke (Zeitschrift der Japanisch-Deutschen Gesellschaft Tokyo) 10 (2016), S. 8–9 (zusammen mit Rosalia Mulara).

89. *Saiban?* – Nein, *Shinpan!* Ein weiteres Instrument der japanischen Judikative? Hier: Verwaltungsrechtliche Streitigkeiten, in: Menkhaus, Heinrich/Narazaki, Midori (Hrsg.): Japani-

scher Vorkämpfer für die Rechtsordnung des 21. Jahrhunderts, Festschrift für Koresuke Yamauchi zum 70. Geburtstag, Duncker & Humblot, Berlin (2017), S. 341–366.

90. Images of Japan Held by German Legal Experts in the *Meiji* Period, in: Saaler, Sven/Kudō, Akira/Tajima, Nobuo (Hrsg.): Mutual Perceptions and Images in Japanese-German Relations 1860–2010, Brill, Leiden/Boston (2017), S. 180–191.

Besprechung: Dobson, Sebastian, in: OAG Notizen 1 (2019), S. 48–54.

91. 20 Jahre Deutsch-Japanische Gesellschaft für Arbeitsrecht – Rückblick und Ausblick, in: Düwell, Franz-Josef/Haase, Karsten/Wolmerath, Martin (Hrsg.): Digitalisierung der Arbeitswelt in Deutschland und Japan. Herausforderungen für das Arbeitsrecht, Festschrift zum 20. Geburtstag der Deutsch-Japanischen Gesellschaft für Arbeitsrecht e. V., Delgany Publishing, Hamm (2018), S. 17–25.

92. Die deutsch-japanischen Beziehungen im Ersten Weltkrieg aus juristischer Perspektive, in: *Meiji* Law Journal 27 (2020), S. 9–29.

93. Das Verhältnis zwischen dem Deutschen Reich und dem Großjapanischen Reich im Ersten Weltkrieg, in: Gornig, Gilbert/Michel, Adrianna (Hrsg.): Der Erste Weltkrieg und seine Folgen für das Zusammenleben der Völker in Mittel- und Ostmitteleuropa, Teil 3. Duncker & Humblot, Berlin (2020), S. 201–220.

94. Das richterliche Dienstrecht im Licht der Staatsformmerkmale Rechtsstaat und Demokratie/*kokkakeitai toshite no hōchikokkasei to minshusei ga terasu han'i nai no saibankan shokumu kengen ni kan suru kitei*, in: *Hōgaku ronsō* (Juristische Fachzeitschrift der Juristischen Fakultät der Universität *Meiji*) 93/1 (2020), S. 231–237.

95. *Doitsugoken oyatoi gaikokujin* (Kontraktausländer aus dem deutschen Sprachraum), in: Ishida, Yuji u. a. (Hrsg.): *doitsu bunka jiten* (Lexikon der Deutschen Kultur in Japan), Maruzen, Tokyo (2020), S. 298–299.

96. Das japanische Rechtsstaatsverständnis, in: Rosenau, Henning/Kunig, Philip/Yildiz, Ali Kemal (Hrsg.): Rechtsstaat und Strafrecht. Deutsch-Japanisch-Türkisches Symposium zum Rechtsstaat, Mohr Siebeck, Tübingen (2020), S. 23–50.

97. Der Japanisch-Preußische Freundschafts-, Schifffahrts- und Handelsvertrag von 1861 – Eine juristische Analyse anlässlich der offiziellen Feier des 160. Jubiläums des Beginns der japanisch-deutschen Beziehungen, Teil 1, in: *Meiji* Law Journal 38 (2021), S. 35–45.

98. Recht der Beschäftigung versus Pandemiebekämpfung oder Der Corona-Virus kennt keinen Feierabend – Gleichzeitig ein Beitrag zum Rechtsstaatsprinzip in Japan –, in: Düwell, Nora/Gallner, Inken/Haase, Karsten/Wolmerath, Martin (Hrsg.): Auf dem Weg zu einem sozialen und inklusiven Rechtsstaat – Covid-19 als Herausforderung, Liber amicorum Franz Josef Düwell, Nomos, Baden Baden (2021), S. 23–44.

99. Japan, in: Süß, Rembert/Wachter, Thomas (Hrsg.): Handbuch des internationalen GmbH-Rechts, 4. Aufl., Zerb, Bonn (2021), S. 1113–1139.

100. Der Japanisch-Preußische Freundschafts-, Schifffahrts- und Handelsvertrag von 1861 – Eine juristische Analyse anlässlich der offiziellen Feier des 160. Jubiläums des Beginns der japanisch-deutschen Beziehungen, Teil 2, in: *Meiji* Law Journal 30 (2023), S. 47–60.

101. Demokratische Legitimation der Staatsgewalt in Japan. Verfassungsrechtliche Vorgaben, gesetzliche Regelungen und tatsächliche Handhabung, in: Hilpold, Peter/Perathoner, Christoph (Hrsg.): Völkerrecht, Europarecht, Deutsches Recht, Festschrift für Gilbert Gornig, Band II, Nomos/Facultas, Wien (2023), S. 197–228.

102. Introduction, in: Menkhaus, Heinrich/Kusunoki, Shigeki (Hrsg.): The Law of Public Procurement in Japan, Germany and the EU, Duncker & Humblot, Berlin 2025, erscheint demnächst.

103. Der Japanisch-Preußische Freundschafts-, Schifffahrts- und Handelsvertrag von 1861 – Eine juristische Analyse anlässlich der offiziellen Feier des 160. Jubiläums des Beginns der japanisch-deutschen Beziehungen, Teil 3, in: *Meiji* Law Journal, erscheint demnächst.

IV. Buchbesprechungen

1. Ebenroth, Carsten-Thomas: Die verdeckten Vermögenszuwendungen im transnationalen Unternehmen, Gieseking, Bielefeld 1979, in: NJW (Neue Juristische Wochenschrift) (1981), S. 1138–1139.

2. Oda, Hiroshi/ Grice, Geoffrey (Hrsg.): Japanese Banking, Securities and Anti-Monopoly Law, Butterworth, London 1988, in: Japanstudien, Jahrbuch des Deutschen Instituts für Japanstudien 1 (1989), S. 432–437.

3. Nihon Tosho Sentâ (Hrsg.): History of the Nonmilitary Activities of the Occupation of Japan 1945–1951, *Nihon Senryō GHQ Seishi*, *Tokyo* 1990, 55 Bände, in: Japanstudien, Jahrbuch des Deutschen Instituts für Japanstudien 2 (1990), S. 397–403.

4. Foundation for Advanced Information and Research (FAIR) (Hrsg.): Japan's Financial Markets, FAIR Fact Series II, Look Japan, Tokyo 1991, in: ZKW (Zeitschrift für das gesamte Kreditwesen) (1992), S. 348.

5. Zweisprachige Wörterbücher zur juristischen Fachsprache – Deutsch/Japanisch und Japanisch/Deutsch, in: Japanstudien, Jahrbuch des Deutschen Instituts für Japanstudien 4 (1992), S. 279–291.

6. Deutsch-Japanische Wörterbücher zur juristischen Fachsprache – Neuerscheinungen 1993, in: Japanstudien, Jahrbuch des Deutschen Instituts für Japanstudien 5 (1993), S. 524–534.

7. Marburger Hefte zur japanischen Umwelt, in: Japan-Markt (Zeitschrift der Deutschen Industrie- und Handelskammer in Japan) 11 (1997), S. 31.

8. Kaffsack, Annette: Die Stellung des Rechtsanwalts und der Rechtsanwaltsschaft in Japan, Münsteraner Studien zur Rechtsvergleichung, Band 15, Münster 1996, in: Japan-Markt (Zeitschrift der Deutschen Industrie- und Handelskammer in Japan) 7 (1998), S. 32.

9. Schütze, Rolf A.: Rechtsverfolgung im Ausland, 2. Aufl., Verlag Recht und Wirtschaft, Heidelberg 1998, in: Japan-Markt (Zeitschrift der Deutschen Industrie- und Handelskammer in Japan) 10 (1998), S. 30.

10. Kudō, Akira: Japanese German Business Relations – Cooperation and Rivalry in the Inter-War Period, Routledge, London 1998, in: Japan-Markt (Zeitschrift der Deutschen Industrie- und Handelskammer in Japan) 12 (1998), S. 32.

11. Koch, Iris: Außergerichtliche Streitbeilegung im japanischen Wirtschaftsverkehr unter besonderer Berücksichtigung der Schiedsgerichtsbarkeit, Schriftenreihe der August Maria Berges Stiftung für Arbitrales Recht, Band 2, Peter Lang, Frankfurt/Main 2000, in: Japan-Markt (Zeitschrift der Deutschen Industrie- und Handelskammer in Japan) 10 (2000), S. 17–18.

12. Araki, Takashi: Labor and Employment Law in Japan, Japan Institute of Labor, Tokyo 2002, auf japanisch, in: *Nihon Rōdō Kenkyū Zasshi* (The Japanese Journal of Labour Studies), Nr. 512 Heft 2/3 (2003), S. 76–79.

13. Kliesow, Olaf/Eisele, Ursula/Bälz, Moritz: Das japanische Handelsgesetz, Carl Heymanns, Köln u. a. 2002, in: RabelsZ (Rabels Zeitschrift für ausländisches und internationales Privatrecht) 69 (2005), S. 593–598.

14. Spang, Christian/Wippich, Rolf-Harald (Hrsg.): Japanese-German Relations, 1895–1945, Routledge, London/New York 2006, in: Japanstudien. Jahrbuch des Deutschen Instituts für Japanstudien 19 (2007), S. 245–250.

15. Brauneder, Wilhelm/ Takii, Kazuhiro (Hrsg.): Die österreichischen Einflüsse auf die Modernisierung des japanischen Rechts, Peter Lang, Frankfurt/Main 2007, und Takii, Kazuhiro, The *Meiji* Constitution. The Japanese Experience of the West and the Shaping of the Modern State, International House of Japan, Tokyo 2007, in: ZNR (Zeitschrift für neuere Rechtsgeschichte) 30 (2008), S. 320–324.

16. Pantzer, Peter/Saaler, Sven: Japanische Impressionen eines Kaiserlichen Gesandten. Karl von Eisendecher im Japan der *Meiji*-Zeit, Iudicium, München 2007, in: ZJapanR (Zeitschrift für japanisches Recht) 25 (2008), S. 275–278.

17. Osiander, Anja: Der Fall Minamata. Bürgerrechte und Obrigkeit in Japan nach 1945, Iudicium, München 2007 (Monographien aus dem Deutschen Institut für Japanstudien, Band 41), in: ZJapanR (Zeitschrift für japanisches Recht) 26 (2008), S. 223–229, und im Bulletin des Deutschen Instituts für Japanstudien 31/32 (2012), S. 105–112.

18. Wörterbücher zur juristischen Fachsprache Deutsch-Japanisch und Japanisch-Deutsch, 3. Teil, in: Japanstudien, Jahrbuch des Deutschen Instituts für Japanstudien 20 (2008), S. 359–363.

19. Kaiser, Andreas: Das japanische Zivilgesetzbuch in deutscher Sprache, Carl Heymanns, Köln/München 2008, in: Japanstudien, Jahrbuch des Deutschen Instituts für Japanstudien 21 (2009), S. 342–348.

20. Dettmer, Hans Adalbert: Der *Yōrō*-Kodex. Die Gebote. Einleitung und Übersetzung des *Ryō no gige*. Buch 1, Harrassowitz, Wiesbaden 2009 (Veröffentlichungen des Ostasien-Instituts der Ruhr-Universität Bochum, Band 55), in: OAG Notizen 2 (2010), S. 37–43.

21. Krebs, Gerhard: Das moderne Japan 1868–1952, Oldenbourg Wissenschaftsverlag, München 2009, in: Bochumer Jahrbuch zur Ostasienforschung 33 (2009), S. 282–285.

22. C. Illies & Co. – Das älteste deutsche Unternehmen in Japan?!, zugleich eine Besprechung der Bücher: Johannes Bähr/Jörg Lesczenski/Katja Schmidtpott: Handel ist Wandel. 150 Jahre C. Illies & Co., Piper, München 2009; Johannes Bähr/Jörg Lesczenski/Katja Schmidtpott: Winds of change: On the 150th anniversary of C. Illies & Co., Piper, München 2009; Kikkawa, Takeo: C. Illies & Co. – Die Anfänge in Japan/Irisu 150nen – *Reimeiki no kioku* (zweisprachig deutsch/japanisch), Selbstverlag *Irisu*, Tokyo 2009, in: OAG Notizen 1/2011, S. 27–35. (Siehe auch wissenschaftliche Aufsätze Nr. 71).

23. Koltermann, Till Philip: Der Untergang des Dritten Reiches im Spiegel der deutsch-japanischen Kulturbegegnung 1933–1945. Unter Mitarbeit von Abe Yasuko, Harrassowitz, Wiesbaden, 2009 (Freiburger Fernöstliche Forschungen, Band 9), in: Bochumer Jahrbuch zur Ostasienforschung 34 (2010), S. 308–310.

24. Sokolowski, Christoph: Der sogenannte Kodifikationenstreit in Japan, Iudicium, München 2010, in: OAG Notizen 3 (2012), S. 43–46.

25. Kazuhiro, Takii: *Itō Hirobumi* – Japan's First Prime Minister and Father of the *Meiji* Constitution, Routledge, London/New York 2014, in: OAG Notizen 5 (2014), S. 35–37.

26. Jochem, Clemens: Der Fall Foerster: Die deutsch-japanische Maschinenfabrik in Tokio und das Jüdische Hilfskommitee, Hentrich & Hentrich, Berlin 2017, in: OAG Notizen 1 (2018), S. 56–58.

27. Trollmann, Christian: Nationalsozialismus auf Japanisch? Deutsch-Japanische Beziehungen 1933–1945 aus translationssoziologischer Sicht, Frank & Timme, Berlin 2016, in: OAG Notizen 2 (2019), S. 33–38.

28. Meyer, Harald/Zöllner, Reinhard (Hrsg.): Die Sammlung Trautz. Visuelle Schätze aus dem Nachlass des Japangelehrten Friedrich M. Trautz (1877–1952), Iudicium, München 2019, in: OAG Notizen 10 (2019), S. 39–42.

29. Meißner, Kirstin: Strategische Experten. Die imperialpolitische Rolle von ausländischen Beratern in *Meiji*-Japan (1868–1912), Campus, Frankfurt/New York 2018, in: OAG Notizen 9 (2020), S. 52–55.

30. Schwentker, Wolfgang: Geschichte Japans, C. H. Beck, München 2022, in: OAG Notizen 6 (2024), S. 34–45.

31. Krämer, Hans Martin: Geschichte Japans, C. H. Beck, München 2024, in: OAG Notizen (2025), erscheint demnächst.

V. Berichte, Nachrufe, Laudationes, Kommentare, Gruß-, Vor- und Nachworte

1. Wahlstation bei der Deutschen Industrie- und Handelskammer in Japan, Tokio, in: JuS (Juristische Schulung) (1987), S. 590–591.

2. Japan, in: Großfeld, Bernhard/Vieweg, Klaus (Hrsg.): Jurastudium und Wahlstation im Ausland, Regensberg & Biermann, Münster (1987), S. 80–91.

3. Das Ende der Einbahnstraße – nun auch im Recht, in: *Shiosai* – das Magazin über Japan 5 (1987), S. 3–4.

4. *Sekai no kyanpasu, dai rokkai, nishi doitsu, vesutofērisshe viruherumsu daigaku* (Universitäten der Welt, 6. Folge, Bundesrepublik Deutschland, Westfälische Wilhelms-Universität), in: *Chūō Daigaku Toshokan Dayori* (Zeitschrift der Bibliothek der Universität *Chūō*) 12 (1988), S. 1.

5. Philipp-Franz-von-Siebold-Stiftung/Deutsches Institut für Japanstudien, Tokyo, in: Mitteilungen der Deutsch-Japanischen Juristenvereinigung 3 (1989), S. 42–46.

6. Deutsche Juristen zu Gast in Japan (I), in: Mitteilungen der Deutsch-Japanischen Juristenvereinigung 3 (1989), S. 48–49.

7. Erstes Symposium des Global Economic Action Institute in Japan, Tokyo, 17. 1. 1990, in: Bulletin des Deutschen Instituts für Japanstudien 3 (1990), S. 46–48.

8. Juristenausbildung in Japan, Teil 1: Bewerbung um einen Studienplatz, in: Mitteilungen der Deutsch-Japanischen Juristenvereinigung 4 (1990), S. 28–32.

9. Philipp-Franz-von-Siebold-Stiftung/Deutsches Institut für Japanstudien, in: Mitteilungen der Deutsch-Japanischen Juristenvereinigung 5 (1991), S. 64–69.

10. Deutsche Juristen zu Gast in Japan (II), in: Mitteilungen der Deutsch-Japanischen Juristenvereinigung 5 (1991), S. 69–71.

11. Gründungsversammlung der Inter-Pacific Bar Association (21.–24. 4. 1991), in: Mitteilungen der Deutsch-Japanischen Juristenvereinigung 6 (1991), S. 8–9.

12. Japan, in: Großfeld, Bernhard/Vieweg, Klaus (Hrsg.): JuS-Auslandsstudienführer, 2. Aufl., C. H. Beck; München (1991), S. 73–91.

13. *Doitsu ni okeru hōsō yōsei no jitsujo* (Die Juristenausbildung in der Bundesrepublik Deutschland), in: *Jurisuto* (Juristische Fachzeitschrift in Japan) 1020 (1993), S. 89–91.

14. *Doitsu no bengoshi seido* (Die Rechtsanwaltschaft in der Bundesrepublik Deutschland), in: *Jurisuto* (Juristische Fachzeitschrift in Japan) 1021 (1993), S. 86–89.

15. Nachruf auf Prof. Kawashima Takeyoshi, in: Mitteilungen der Deutsch-Japanischen Juristenvereinigung 9 (1993), S. 3–4.

16. Prof. Dr. Mikazuki Akira japanischer Justizminister, in: Mitteilungen der Deutsch-Japanischen Juristenvereinigung 11 (1994), S. 16.

17. Permanent Office, in: Boscaro, Adriana u. a. (Hrsg.): 20th Anniversary – Past, Present and Future of the European Association for Japanese Studies (EAJS), 1973–1994, EAJS, Leiden 1994, S. 66–71.

18. Permanent Office in Leiden – 20th Anniversary of the European Association for Japanese Studies, in: International Institute for Asian Studies Newsletter 3 (1994), S. 55.

19. Bericht über das Symposium ‚Kontinuität und Fremdbestimmung': Zum Einfluß der Besatzungsmächte auf die deutsche und japanische Rechtsordnung 1945–1950 im Deutschen Institut für Japanstudien, Tokyo, 6.–9. 4. 1994, in: Mitteilungen der Deutsch-Japanischen Juristenvereinigung 15 (1995), S. 16–21.

20. Recht und Steuern in: Deutsche Industrie- und Handelskammer in Japan (Hrsg.): Jahresbericht (1995), S. 19–21.

21. Praktikantenbedarf in Japan – Umfrage bringt neue Erkenntnisse, in: Japan-Markt (Zeitschrift der Deutschen Industrie- und Handelskammer in Japan) 7 (1996), S. 4–8 (zusammen mit Tanja Fuß, Tim Goydke, Udo Link, Felix Treibmann und Thorsten Wolf).

22. *Doitsu sangyōkai no Japan inishiachibu* (Die Japan-Initiative der Deutschen Wirtschaft), in: JETRO *Sensâ* (Zeitschrift der japanischen Außenhandelsförderungsorganisation JETRO) 12 (1996), S. 94–95.

23. EU-Japan Legal Dialogue (Bericht über die 1. Tagung europäischer und japanischer Juristen zum Thema Vertragsrecht), in: Japan-Markt (Zeitschrift der Deutschen Industrie- und Handelskammer in Japan) 1 (1997), S. 29.

24. *Nyūâsu '96 ni sanka shite* (Die Beteiligung an der Umweltmesse New Earth 1996), in: Rite Now (Zeitschrift des japanischen Research Institute of Innovative Technology for the Earth) 22 (1997), S. 14.

25. Recht und Steuern, in: Deutsche Industrie- und Handelskammer in Japan (Hrsg.): Jahresbericht (1996), S. 22–25.

26. Interview mit Rechtsanwalt Reinhard Einsel, in: Japan-Markt (Zeitschrift der Deutschen Industrie- und Handelskammer in Japan) 4 (1997), S. 33–37 (zusammen mit Manfred Dransfeld).

27. Interview mit dem Perlenhändler Rudolf Voll, in: Japan-Markt (Zeitschrift der Deutschen Industrie- und Handelskammer in Japan) 11 (1997), S. 32–35.

28. Recht und Steuern, in: Deutsche Industrie- und Handelskammer in Japan (Hrsg.): Jahresbericht (1997), S. 24–27.

29. Interview mit Alfred Stüber, in: Japan-Markt (Zeitschrift der Deutschen Industrie- und Handelskammer in Japan) 11 (1998), S. 36–37.

30. Recht und Steuern, in: Deutsche Industrie- und Handelskammer in Japan (Hrsg.): Jahresbericht (1998), S. 25–29.

31. 30. Jahrestag der Gründung des Vereins der Förderer der deutschsprachigen katholischen Kirchengemeinde in Tokyo am 21. April 1969, in: Gemeinde St. Michael (Hrsg.): Gemeindebrief 5 (1999), S. 25–29.

32. Recht und Steuern, in: Deutsche Industrie- und Handelskammer in Japan (Hrsg.): Jahresbericht (1999), S. 30–33.

33. *Hakodate de no Aruberuto Mosse – tsuma ni ateta tegami kara* (Albert Mosse in Hakodate – aus Briefen an die Ehefrau), in: *Chiikishi Kenkyū Hakodate* (Studien zur Regionalgeschichte – Hakodate) 31 (2000), S. 67–83.

34. *Chiikiteki na hogoken wa jiyū na shōhin ryūtsū o samatageru* (Störung des freien Güterverkehrs durch regional unterschiedliche Schutzrechte), in: Shimizu, Keisuke u. a. (Hrsg.): *Chiteki sōzō jidai no chiteki zaisan* (Geistiges Eigentum im Zeitalter geistiger Kreativität), *Keio Gijuku Daigaku Shuppankai* (Verlag der Universität *Keio*), Tokyo (2000), S. 197–198.

35. Bericht aus dem Ressort Recht, Personal, Grundstücke und Gebäude, Jahresbericht der Deutschen Gesellschaft für Natur- und Völkerkunde Ostasiens 1999/2000, in: OAG Notizen 5 (2000), S. 48–51.

36. *Zainichi doitsu shōkō kaigisho yori saishin nyūsu*/Neues von der Deutschen Industrie- und Handelskammer in Japan, in: *Kakehashi*/Die Brücke (Zeitschrift der Japanisch-Deutschen Gesellschaft e. V.), Tokyo 3 (2000), S. 10.

37. Die japanische Verwaltungs- und Kabinettsreform 2001, in: OAG Notizen 4 (2001), S. 25–31 (zusammen mit Andreas Bach).

38. Recht und Steuern bzw. *hōmubu* (zweisprachig), in: Deutsche Industrie- und Handelskammer in Japan (Hrsg.): Jahresbericht (2000), S. 29–37.

39. Bericht aus dem Ressort Recht, Personal, Grundstücke und Gebäude, Jahresbericht der Deutschen Gesellschaft für Natur- und Völkerkunde Ostasiens 1999/2000, in: OAG Notizen 5 (2001), S. 48–50.

40. Berufung auf die Professur für Japanisches Recht in Marburg, in: JSPS Rundschreiben aus Wissenschaft und Forschung 1 (2002), S. 15.

41. Japanisches Recht in Marburg, in: Marburger Uni Journal 12 (2002), S. 34.

42. Bericht des Geschäftsführenden Direktors, in: Japan-Zentrum der Philipps-Universität Marburg (Hrsg.): Jahresbericht 2001/2002, S. 3–6.

43. ‚Mitglieder laden Mitglieder ein' – eine neue Clubaktivität, in: JSPS Rundschreiben aus Wissenschaft und Forschung 2 (2003), S. 7–8.

44. Bericht des Geschäftsführenden Direktors, in: Japan-Zentrum der Philipps-Universität Marburg (Hrsg.): Jahresbericht 2002/2003, S. 3–6.

45. Bericht des Geschäftsführenden Direktors, in: Japan-Zentrum der Philipps-Universität Marburg (Hrsg.): Jahresbericht 2003/2004, S. 3–6.

46. Die Geschichte der Deutsch-Japanischen Gesellschaft für Arbeitsrecht, ehemals auf der Homepage der Deutsch-Japanischen Gesellschaft für Arbeitsrecht.

47. Wissenschaftsressourcen in Fernost – Marburgs Verbindungen nach Japan sind vielfältig und umfassen Partnerschaften mit mittlerweile fünf japanischen Hochschulen, in: Marburger UniJournal 22 (2005), S. 48.

48. The History of the JSPS-Club, in: Deutsche Gesellschaft der JSPS-Stipendiaten e.V. (Hrsg.): 10th Anniversary of the Deutsche Gesellschaft der JSPS-Stipendiaten e.V. – German-Japanese Scientific Exchange, Deutsche Gesellschaft der JSPS-Stipendiaten e.V., Bonn (2005), S. 15–22 (zusammen mit Uwe Czarnetzki), auch abgedruckt in: Deutsche Gesellschaft der JSPS- Stipendiaten e.V. und JSPS Bonn Office (Hrsg.): 10th Japanese-German Symposium: Prospects of Japanese-German Scientific Cooperation, Deutsche Gesellschaft der JSPS- Stipendiaten e.V. und JSPS Bonn Office, Bonn (2005), S. 7–12.

49. Bericht des Geschäftsführenden Direktors, in: Japan-Zentrum der Philipps-Universität Marburg (Hrsg.): Jahresbericht 2004/2005, S. 3–6.

50. Message from Former JSPS Fellow (2): JSPS fellowship begins a long-lasting encounter with Japan, in: JSPS Quarterly 14 (2005), S. 12.

51. Bericht des Geschäftsführenden Direktors, in: Japan-Zentrum der Philipps-Universität Marburg (Hrsg.): Jahresbericht 2005/2006, S. 3–8.

52. Bericht aus der Arbeitsgruppe Juristenausbildung, in: Murakami, Jun'ichi u. a. (Hrsg.): Globalisierung und Recht – Beiträge Japans und Deutschlands zu einer internationalen Rechtsordnung im 21. Jahrhundert, De Gruyter, Berlin (2007), S. 271–273.

53. Bericht der Geschäftsführung, in: Japan-Zentrum der Philipps-Universität Marburg (Hrsg.): Jahresbericht 2006/2007, S. 3–8 (zusammen mit Katja Schmidtpott).

54. German JSPS-Club, in: *Gakujutsu Geppō* (Japanese Scientific Monthly) 61/3 (2008), S. 125–126.

55. Veränderungen im Vorstand, Wechsel des Club-Vorsitzenden, Prof. Dr. Heinrich Menkhaus, nach Japan und ERA-Link mit Japan gestartet, in: Neues vom JSPS-Club 2 (2008) S. 1–4.

56. Marburg im Manga, in: Marburger Uni-Journal 31 (2008), S. 28–30 (zusammen mit Jürgen Seitz).

57. JSPS-Club wird Mitveranstalter des Wissenschaftlichen Gesprächskreises (WGK) in Tokyo, in: Neues vom Club 2 (2009), S. 1.

58. German Innovation Award, in: Neues vom Club 2 (2009), S. 4.

59. Die Parteigenossem ins rote Zimmer, die Volksgenossen an die Bar! – In memoriam Rudolf Voll, in: OAG-Notizen 5 (2009), S. 61–64.

60. Japanischsprachige Festschrift für Mitglied Prof. Dr. Gerhard Ries, in: Neues vom JSPS Club 3 (2009), S. 2–3.

61. Welcome Address, in: Széll, György/Széll, Ute (Hrsg.): Quality of Life and Working Life in Comparison, Lang, Frankfurt/Main u. a. (2009), S. 7–8.

62. In memoriam Reinhard Einsel, in: OAG-Notizen 9 (2009), S. 63–69.

63. 14. Deutschsprachiger Japanologentag in Halle (Saale), in: Neues vom JSPS Club 4 (2009), S. 6.

64. Besuch des Vorsitzenden der deutschen und schwedischen JSPS Alumni Vereinigung im JSPS Headquarter in Tokyo, in: Neues vom JSPS Club 5 (2009), S. 4.

65. WGK in Tokyo – Ein Jahr erfolgreicher Mitveranstaltung durch den JSPS-Club, in: Neues vom JSPS Club 5 (2009), S. 4–5.

66. *Meiji* University Law in Japan Program, in: Neues vom JSPS Club 5 (2009), S. 5–6.
67. Bridge – Das neue Wiedereinladungsstipendium für die Mitglieder der JSPS Alumni Vereinigungen, in: Neues vom JSPS Club 5 (2009), S. 6.
68. Mitglied Yasuo Tanaka erhält Verdienstorden des Landes Nordrhein-Westfalen, in: Neues vom JSPS Club 1 (2010), S. 1.
69. Mitglieder Harald Baum und Urs Matthias Zachmann erhalten JaDe-Preis, in: Neues vom JSPS Club 1 (2010), S. 1.
70. Hohe japanische Auszeichnung für Mitglied Yasuo Tanaka, in: Neues vom JSPS Club 3 (2010), S. 2.
71. German Innovation Award, in: Neues vom JSPS Club 3 (2010), S. 2.
72. *Shagai kansayaku toshite* (Als unternehmensfremder Aufsichtsrat), in: *Bairīn Nyūsu* (Nachrichten des Unternehmens Nihon Vilene) 452 (2010), S. 2.
73. Ehrung für Mitglied Gernot Frenking, in: Neues vom JSPS Club 4 (2010), S. 1.
74. Katja Schmidtpott neues Vorstandsmitglied, in: Neues vom JSPS Club 4 (2010), S. 1.
75. Der Wissenschaftliche Gesprächskreis im Jahre 2010, in: Neues vom JSPS Club 4 (2010), S. 2.
76. Grußwort, in: Erstausgabe der Zeitschrift Wissenschaft und Forschung – Japan 1 (2011), S. 5.
77. Global 30 Aktivitäten an der *Meiji*, in: Neues vom JSPS Club 1 (2011), S. 5.
78. Bericht aus dem Referat Personal, in: OAG Notizen 5 (2011), S. 57–58.
79. *Doitsu hōsōkai no naka no bengoshi no shikaku* (Die Stellung des Rechtsanwalts unter den deutschen Juristen), in: *Meiji Daigaku Hōsōkai* (Vereinigung der Volljuristen der *Meiji*-Universität (Hrsg.): *Meiji Daigaku Hōsōkai setsuritsu 50 shunen kinenshi* (50. Gründungsjubiläum der Vereinigung der Volljuristen der *Meiji*-Universität), *Meiji Daigaku Hōsōkai*, Tokyo (2011), S. 73–75.
80. Die Deutsche Gesellschaft der JSPS-Stipendiaten e. V., in: Curt-Engelhorn-Stiftung für die Reiss-Engelhorn-Museen und Verband der Deutsch-Japanischen Gesellschaften (Hrsg.): Ferne Gefährten – 150 Jahre deutsch-japanische Beziehungen, Schnell und Steiner, Regensburg (2011), S. 191.
81. *Mata, kondo!* (Wir sehen uns!), in: Kōso, Toshiaki (Hrsg.): *Rūmeru famirī kaisō. kurausu rumeru shinpu tsuito bunsho* (Erinnerungen an Pater Klaus Luhmer S. J.), *Gakuensha*, Tokyo (2012), S. 213–214.
82. Erstes Treffen der in Japan arbeitenden Clubmitglieder im Oktober 2011, in: Neues vom JSPS Club 1 (2012), S. 1–2.
83. Der Wissenschaftliche Gesprächskreis (WGK) im Jahre 2011, in: Neues vom JSPS Club 1 (2012), S. 2.
84. JSPS Orientations, in: Neues vom JSPS Club 1 (2012), S. 2–3.
85. JSPS-Club-Infostand in Tokyo anlässlich der 150-Jahrfeier der deutsch-japanischen diplomatischen Beziehungen am 23. 10. 2011, in: Neues vom JSPS Club 1 (2012), S. 3.
86. Verabschiedung von JSPS-Präsident Ono Motoyuki, in: Neues vom JSPS Club 1 (2012), S. 3.

87. Ehrendoktorwürde für Bundesministerin Prof. Dr. Annette Schavan von der *Meiji*-Universität, in: Neues vom JSPS Club 1 (2012), S. 4.

88. Bericht aus dem Referat Personal, in: OAG Notizen 5 (2012), S. 53–54.

89. German Innovation Award – Gottfried Wagener Prize 2012, in: Wissenschaft & Forschung Japan 5 (2012), S. 18.

90. Änderungen im Ausländerrecht, in: Japan-Markt 7/8 (2012), S. 30–31 (zusammen mit Kumiko Yamaguchi).

91. German Innovation Award – Gottfried Wagener Prize 2012, in: Neues vom JSPS Club 2 (2012), S. 2.

92. St. Michael und ich, in: Markert, Vera/Yamauchi, Ann-Christin (Hrsg.): Festschrift zum 50. Jubiläum der Gemeinde St. Michael in Tokyo, Selbstverlag, Tokyo (2012), S. 29–32.

93. JSPS-Empfang auf dem 15. Deutschsprachigen Japanologentag in Zürich, in: Neues vom JSPS Club 3 (2012), S. 1.

94. Wie die Erdbebenspenden des JSPS-Clubs verwendet wurden: Ein Rechenschaftsbericht vom Club-Vorsitzenden Prof. Dr. Heinrich Menkhaus, Tokyo, in: Neues vom JSPS Club 3 (2012), S. 1–4.

95. Das Verhältnis von Arbeitsrecht und Zivilrecht in Japan und Deutschland: Bericht vom 7. Arbeitsrechtliches Symposium der Deutsch-Japanischen Gesellschaft für Arbeitsrecht und ihrer japanischen Schwestergesellschaft, der *Nichidoku Rōdōhō Kyōkai*, in: Zeitschrift Wissenschaft und Forschung – Japan 8 (2012), S. 6.

96. Der WGK im Jahre 2012, in: Neues vom JSPS Club 1 (2013), S. 2.

97. Deutsches Festival in Tokyo, in: Neues vom JSPS Club 1 (2013), S. 3.

98. Bericht aus dem Referat Personal, in: OAG Notizen 5 (2013), S. 50.

99. Grußwort zum 7. Gemeinsamen Symposium der Deutsch-Japanischen Gesellschaft für Arbeitsrecht und der Japanisch-Deutschen Gesellschaft für Arbeitsrecht, in: Düwell, Franz Josef/Löwisch, Manfred/Waltermann, Raimund/Wank, Rolf (Hrsg.): Das Verhältnis von Arbeitsrecht und Zivilrecht in Japan und Deutschland, Lang, Frankfurt/Main u.a. 2013, S. 6.

100. Deutsche Professoren als Gastgeber in Japan, in: Neues vom JSPS Club 2 (2013), S. 3–5.

101. 7. Deutsch-Japanischer Youth Summit, in: Neues vom JSPS Club 3 (2013), S. 1.

102. Der Wissenschaftliche Gesprächskreis im Jahre 2013, in: Neues vom JSPS Club 4 (2013), S. 3.

103. Der japanische Rechtswissenschaftler Zentarō Kitagawa und Marburg – ein Nachruf, in: Marburg Law Review (2013), S. 114–115.

104. *Zenkoku nichidoku kyōkai rengōkai sōritsu 25 shunen: doitsujin sankaisha aisatsu* (Grußwort anlässlich des 25. Jubiläums der Gründung des Verbandes der Japanisch-Deutschen Gesellschaften), in: *Hokkaidō nichidoku kyōkai kaihō* (Berichte der Japanisch-Deutschen Gesellschaft *Hokkaidō*) 30 (2013), S. 32.

105. Nachruf auf Professor Saburō Kuwata, in: ZjapR (Zeitschrift für japanisches Recht) 37 (2014), S. 327–329 (zusammen mit Koresuke Yamauchi).

106. Interview mit dem Botschafter der Bundesrepublik Deutschland in Japan, Herrn Dr. Hans Carl von Werthern, in: Neues vom JSPS Club 2/3 (2014), S. 1–2.

107. Club-Ehrenmitgliedschaft für Kato Hisashi, in: Neues vom JSPS Club 2/3 (2014), S. 4–5.

108. 26. Jahrestagung des Verbandes der japanisch-deutschen Gesellschaften, in: Neues vom JSPS Club 2/3 (2014), S. 6–7.

109. Eröffnung der DLR-Ausstellung „A New Perspective on Mars“ in Tokyo, in: Neues vom JSPS Club 2/3 (2014), S. 8.

110. Horizon 2020. Das neue Forschungsprogramm der EU, in: Neues vom JSPS Club 2/3 (2014), S. 8–9.

111. European Higher Education Fair in Japan, in: Neues vom JSPS Club 2/3 (2014), S. 9.

112. 8. Deutsch-Japanischer Youth Summit in Tokyo, in: Neues vom JSPS Club 2/3 (2014), S. 11–12.

113. 6. Verleihung des German Innovation Award, in: Neues vom JSPS Club 2/3 (2014), S. 12–13.

114. Interview mit Matthieu Py, neuer Leiter des EURAXESS Links Japan Büros, in: Neues vom JSPS Club 4 (2014), S. 1–2.

115. Grußwort zum 12. Symposium der Deutsch-Japanischen Gesellschaft für Sozialwissenschaften in der Werner Reimers Stiftung, Bad Homburg, in: Trommsdorff, Gisela (Hrsg.): Proceedings of the 12th Meeting of the Deutsch-Japanische Gesellschaft für Sozialwissenschaften e. V.: Interdisciplinary Aspects of Well-Being in Changing Societies, German Japanese Society for Social Science, Konstanz (2014), S. 8–9.

116. Nachruf auf Hans Adalbert Dettmer, in: ZjapR (Zeitschrift für japanisches Recht) 38 (2014), S. 301–303.

117. Editorial: Erstes Editorial im NvC – Der JSPS Club, in: Neues vom JSPS Club 1 (2015), S. 1–2.

118. Änderungen im Vorstand – Kooptation Chantal Weber, in: Neues vom JSPS Club 1 (2015), S. 2.

119. Introductory Remarks to the Commemorative Volume Celebrating the 20th Anniversary of the German JSPS Alumni Association, in: German JSPS Alumni Association (Hrsg.): Deutsche Gesellschaft der JSPS Stipendiaten e. V., 20th Anniversary – German Japanese Scientific Exchange, Deutsche Gesellschaft der JSPS Stipendiaten e. V., Bonn (2015), S. 14–16.

120. History of the JSPS Club – Continued, in: German JSPS Alumni Association (Hrsg.): Deutsche Gesellschaft der JSPS Stipendiaten e. V., 20th Anniversary – German Japanese Scientific Exchange, Deutsche Gesellschaft der JSPS Stipendiaten e. V., Bonn (2015), S. 17–22 (zusammen mit Sabine Ganter-Richter).

121. Country Representative Japan, in: German JSPS Alumni Association (Hrsg.): Deutsche Gesellschaft der JSPS Stipendiaten e. V., 20th Anniversary – German Japanese Scientific Exchange, Deutsche Gesellschaft der JSPS Stipendiaten e. V., Bonn (2015), S. 23–26.

122. Future Perspectives for the Activities of the JSPS Club, in: German JSPS Alumni Association (Hrsg.): Deutsche Gesellschaft der JSPS Stipendiaten e. V., 20th Anniversary – German Japanese Scientific Exchange, Deutsche Gesellschaft der JSPS Stipendiaten e.V., Bonn (2015), S. 51–58.

123. Editorial: Ausstellung „Was Deutschland und Japan verbindet“ in Japan, in: Neues vom JSPS Club 3 (2015), S. 1.

124. 9. Deutsch-Japanischer Youth Summit, 23.-30. 08. 2015, Berlin, in: Neues vom JSPS Club 3 (2015), S. 5.

125. Eröffnung der Ausstellung „Was Deutschland mit Japan verbindet – 150 Jahre Freundschaft zwischen Deutschland und Japan“, in: Neues vom JSPS Club 3 (2015), S. 7.

126. German Innovation Award 2015, in: Neues vom JSPS Club 3 (2015), S. 8.

127. Editorial: Unternehmerische Forschungsförderung in Japan, in: Neues vom JSPS Club 4 (2015), S. 1.

128. Club-Mitglieder als Wissenschaftsvermittler: Erfolgreiche Zusammenführung von deutscher und japanischer Rechtswissenschaft, in: Neues vom JSPS Club 4 (2015), S. 11–12.

129. Editorial: 5. Japanischer Basisplan für Wissenschaft und Technologie, in: Neues vom JSPS Club 1 (2016), S. 1.

130. Editorial: Deutsch-Japanischer Energierat, in: Neues vom JSPS Club 2 (2016), S. 1.

131. Gesprächskreis: Wissenschaftsaustausch soll grenzenlos sein – Aber lernen Deutsche und Japaner genug voneinander?, in: Neues vom JSPS Club 2 (2016), S. 3–5 (zusammen mit Sabine Ganter-Richter).

132. Editorial: Deutsche Richtlinie zur Förderung von innovativen Konzepten zur deutschlandweiten Fach-Alumniarbeit mit China, in: Neues vom JSPS Club 3 (2016), S. 1.

133. Falling Walls Lab am 29.08.2016, in: Neues vom JSPS Club 3 (2016), S. 3.

134. Wissenschaftlicher Gesprächskreis am 16.09.2016, in: Neues vom JSPS Club 3 (2016), S. 4.

135. Verabschiedung von Frau Dr. Ursula Toyka-Fuong als Leiterin der Außenstelle des DAAD in Japan am 16.09.2016, in: Neues vom JSPS Club 3 (2016), S. 4–5.

136. Editorial: Neo-Protektionismus – auch bei der Stipendienvergabe, in: Neues vom JSPS Club 4 (2016), S. 1.

137. Second European Research Day in Japan, in: Neues vom JSPS Club 4 (2016), S. 6–7.

138. Japanologen-Arbeitskreise in Japan, in: Neues vom JSPS Club 4 (2016), S. 8–9.

139. Editorial: Atomkraftwerke Fukushima: Abbau auch mit deutscher Hilfe, in: Neues vom JSPS Club 1 (2017), S. 1.

140. *Doitsujin hōritsuka no mita nihonkoku kenpō* (Die japanische Verfassung aus der Sicht eines deutschen Juristen), in: *kaze* (Der Wind), *Shonan Nichidoku Kyōkai Kaihō* (Zeitschrift der Japanisch-Deutschen Gesellschaft *Shonan*) Vortragszusammenfassung von Nakajima Bin, 19/3 (14.5.2017), S. 3–4.

141. Editorial: Ainu-Gebeine zurück nach Japan, in: Neues vom JSPS Club 2 (2017), S. 1.

142. 10 Jahre European Research Council, in: Neues vom JSPS Club 2 (2017), S. 3.

143. Editorial: Förderung der wissenschaftlichen Befassung mit Japan, in: Neues vom JSPS Club 3 (2017), S. 1.

144. Laudatio für Prof. Dr. Koresuke Yamauchi zum 70. Geburtstag anlässlich der Verleihung der Festschrift „Japanischer Vorkämpfer für die Rechtsordnung des 21. Jahrhunderts“ an ihn, in: *Hikakuhō Zasshi* (Comparative Law Review: Zeitschrift des Institute of Comparative Law in Japan) 51/3 (2017), S. 23–32.

145. Editorial: Deutsche Richtlinie zur Förderung von innovativen Konzepten zur deutschlandweiten Fach-Alumniarbeit mit Chinabezug – Teil II, in: Neues vom JSPS Club 4 (2017), S. 1.

146. Blue Planet Prize an deutschen Wissenschaftler, in: Neues vom JSPS Club 4 (2017), S. 2.

147. Horizon 2012 – Work Program for Research & Innovation 2018–2020. Cooperation Opportunities for Japanese Researchers, in: Neues vom JSPS Club 4 (2017), S. 2–3.

148. Orden des Heiligen Schatzes für Prof. Dr. Keiichi Kodaira, in: Neues vom JSPS Club 4 (2017), S. 3–4.

149. European Research Day 2017, in: Neues vom JSPS Club 4 (2017), S. 6–7.

150. Deutsche Gesellschaft der JSPS-Stipendiaten e. V., in: OAG Notizen 1 (2018), S. 10–11.

151. Wendepunkt Kanazawa Resolution 2018?; in: Neues vom JSPS Club 2 (2018), S. 1–2.

152. Gedenkfeier für Yasuo Tanaka, in: Neues vom JSPS Club 2 (2018), S. 3–4.

153. Deutsch-Japanische Hochschulpartnerschaften und der JSPS Club, in: Neues vom JSPS Club 2 (2018), S. 7–8.

154. *Murayama Masayuki sensei no koto* (zu Professor Masayuki Maruyama), in: *Hōritsu Ronsō* (japanischsprachige Fachzeitschrift der juristischen Fakultät der Universität *Meiji*), 91/1 (2018), S. 13–15.

155. Editorial: Engere diplomatische Deutsch-Französische Zusammenarbeit in Drittländern, in: Neues vom Club 3 (2018), S. 1.

156. 12. Deutsch-Japanischer Youth-Summit, in: Neues vom Club 3 (2018), S. 5.

157. European Research Day (2. 10. 2018), in: Neues vom Club 3 (2018), S. 6.

158. Editorial: Klare Worte von japanischen Nobelpreisträgern, in: Neues vom Club 4 (2018), S. 1.

159. Nachruf auf Yoshiko Watanabe-Rögner, in: Neues vom Club 4 (2018), S. 6.

160. Editorial: Protektionismus in der Wissenschaft, in: Neues vom Club 1 (2019), S. 1.

161. Nobel Prize Dialogue, in: Neues vom Club 1 (2019), S. 4.

162. 30th Anniversary Postdoctoral Fellowships for Research in Japan, in: Neues vom Club 1 (2019), S. 4–5.

163. Message from a JSPS Alumnus, Revisiting the Program Three Decades Ago, in: Overseas Fellowship Division, Japan Society for the Promotion of Science (Hrsg.), 30th Anniversary Postdoctoral Fellowships for Research in Japan, JSPS, Tokyo (2019), S. 4.

164. Editorial: Wissenschaft in den Angeboten der Deutsch-Japanischen Gesellschaften, in: Neues vom Club 2 (2019), S. 1–3.

165. Editorial: Bedeutung der Mitglieder für einen Verein, in: Neues vom Club 3 (2019), S. 1–2.

166. 13. Deutsch-Japanischer Youth Summit: 22.8.–1.9.2019, Frankfurt, Weimar, Berlin, in: Neues vom Club 3 (2019), S. 2–3.

167. Gottesdienst mit Papst Franziskus im Tokyo Dome am 25. 11. 2019, in: Gemeinsamer Gemeindebrief der Kreuzkirche und der katholischen deutschsprachigen Kirchengemeinde St. Michael Tokyo, (Februar/März 2020), S. 20–23.

168. Editorial: Unentgeltliche höhere Bildung in Japan, in: Neues vom Club 4 (2019) und 1 (2020), S. 1–2.

169. JANET-Treffen 2019, in: Neues vom Club 4 (2019) und 1 (2020), S. 3–4.

170. *Hikakuhō kenkyūjo goaisatsu* (Begrüßung seitens des Direktors des Instituts für Rechtsvergleichung), in: *Meiji Daigaku Hōgakubu Ethics Law Medicine Kenkyūjo (ELM)/Meiji*

Daigaku Hōugakubu Hikakuhō kenkyūjo (MICL) (Institut für Ethik, Recht und Medizin der juristischen Fakultät der Universität *Meiji*/Institut für Rechtsvergleichung der juristischen Fakultät der Universität *Meiji* (Hrsg.): *Atarata na yakuji seido wo motomete: Nichidoku seido no hikaku kara* (Forderung nach einem neuen System zur Regulierung von Arzneimitteln und medizinischen Geräten: Rechtsvergleichend aus der Sicht des japanischen und deutschen Rechtssystems), *Meiji Daigaku Hōgakubu* (Juristische Fakultät der Universität *Meiji*), Tokyo (2020), S. 2–3.

171. *Shikai* (Conferencier): *Meiji daigaku shakai kagaku kenkyūsho kōkai kōenkai* (Öffentliche Vortragsveranstaltung des Instituts für Sozialwissenschaften der *Meiji* Universität): *jidō unten wo meguru hōseibi no genzai* (Der gegenwärtige Stand der Regulierung des autonomen Fahrens), in: *Meiji Daigaku Shakai Kagaku Kenkyūsho Kiyō* (Zeitschrift des Instituts für Sozialwissenschaften der *Meiji* Universität) 92 (2020), S. 232–233.

172. Editorial: Corona und die Folgen, in: Neues vom JSPS Club 2 (2020), S. 1.

173. COVID 19 in Japan oder Die Bekämpfung einer Pandemie durch eine Fremdsprache, in: OAG Notizen 9 (2020), S. 42–46.

174. Editorial: Corona und die Folgen II, in: Neues vom JSPS Club 3 (2020), S. 1–2.

175. Franziskanerinnen vom Heiligen Märtyrer Georg – 100 Jahre Mission in Japan (1920–2020), in: Gemeinsamer Gemeindebrief der Evangelischen Gemeinde Deutscher Sprache und der Deutschsprachigen Katholischen Gemeinde St. Michael in Tokyo 11/12 (2020), S. 22–24.

176. Editorial: Freiheit der Wissenschaft, in: Neues vom JSPS Club 4 (2020), S. 1–2.

177. Editorial: 160 Years of Japanese-German Diplomatic Relations, in: Neues vom JSPS Club 1 (2021), S. 1.

178. Changes on the Board, in: Neues vom JSPS Club 1 (2021), S. 1–2.

179. Greeting address on behalf of the German JSPS Alumni Association, in: Hitzer, Eckard/ Kimura, Christoph Goro/Shukuya, Masanori/Takeuchi, Ayano (Hrsg.): For A Sustainable World: Energy Efficiency, Renewable Energy and the Engagements of Univerities in Japan, Bookmondo – Osiander (2022), S. 19.

180. Editorial: Academic Awards, in: Neues vom JSPS Club 3 (2021), S. 1.

181. Editorial: Travel Restrictions for Scientists, in: Neues vom JSPS Club 4 (2021), S. 1–2.

182. The 10th Club Meeting in Japan, in: Neues vom JSPS Club 4 (2021), S. 2.

183. Editorial: A Look into the Future of the JSPS Club, in: Neues vom JSPS Club 1 (2022), S. 1.

184. Worldwide Japan Alumni Conference, in: Neues vom JSPS Club 1 (2022), S. 4–5.

185. Bar Camp during the Yearly National Assembly of the Member Associations of the Federation of German Japanese Societies in Frankfurt/Main, 28. 5. 2022, in: Neues vom JSPS Club 1 (2022), S. 5–6.

186. *Doitsu renpō kyōwa koku kenpō to nihon koku kenpō* (Vergleich der deutschen mit der japanischen Verfassung), in: *kaze* (Der Wind), *Shōnan Nichidoku Kyōkai Kaihō* (Zeitschrift der Japanisch-Deutschen Gesellschaft Shonan) 24/3 (11. 9. 2022), S. 3 (Zusammenfassung eines Vortrages durch Susumu Miyazaki).

187. Editorial: Agreement of Scientific and Technological Cooperation between the Governments of Japan and Germany, in: Neues vom JSPS Club 2/3 (2022), S. 1.

188. European Research Days 2022, in: Neues vom JSPS Club 2/3 (2022), S. 4–5.

189. Editorial: The 45th Anniversary of the DAAD Tokyo Office, in: Neues vom JSPS Club 1 (2023), S. 1–2.

190. 3rd Japan Alumni Conference, in: Neues vom JSPS Club 1 (2023), S. 2–3.

191. Meeting with the EU Ambassador in Tokyo, in: Neues vom JSPS Club 1 (2023), S. 3–4.

192. Editorial: European Scientists in Japan, in: Neues vom JSPS Club 2 (2023), S. 1–2.

193. Editorial: European Scientists in Japan II, in: Neues vom JSPS Club 3 (2023), S. 1–2.

194. Editorial: The Office, in: Neues vom JSPS Club 1 (2024), S. 1.

195. Visit to Okinawa Institute for Science and Technology (OIST), in: Neues vom JSPS Club 1 (2024), S. 5–6.

196. Editorial: Academic Freedom Index, in: Neues vom JSPS Club 2 (2024), S. 1.

197. EURAXESS Japan, in: Neues vom JSPS Club 2 (2024), S. 6–7.

198. Report on the 2nd Symposium of the four European Researchers Associations in Japan, Neues vom JSPS Club 2 (2024), S. 8–9.

199. First Home Made Science Circle, in: Neues vom JSPS Club 2 (2024), S. 12–13.

200. *Tobitate* Japan (Study Abroad Initiative of Japan), in: Neues vom JSPS Club 2 (2024), S. 16–18.

201. Nachruf auf Pater Franz-Josef Mohr SJ, in: OAG Notizen 3 (2025), S. 70–71.

202. Editorial: Orientations, in: Neues vom Club 1/2 (2025), S. 1–2.

203. *Tobitate* Japan (Study Abroad Initiative of Japan) 2025, in: Neues vom JSPS Club 3 (2025), erscheint demnächst.

204. European Contest for Young Scientists (EUCYS), in: Neues vom JSPS Club 3 (2025), erscheint demnächst.

205. Changes in the Board in 2025, in: Neues vom JSPS Club 3 (2025), erscheint demnächst.

206. Editorial: 30 years JSPS Club, in: Neues vom JSPS Club 3 (2025), erscheint demnächst.

VI. Interviews, Gespräche, Grussworte und Diskussionsrunden in Druckmedien

1. *Gaikokujin kara mita senkyo – sōzōshii gaitō enzetsu* (Wahlen aus der Sicht eines Ausländers – Laute Wahlreden auf der Straße), Interview für die Zeitung *Shizuoka Shinbun*, in: *Shizuoka Shinbun* (1. 1. 1991).

2. *Jurisuto zadankai: shakai ga kitai suru hōsōzō* (Diskussionsrunde der Zeitschrift Der Jurist: Welche Rolle erwartet die Gesellschaft von Juristen), in: *Jurisuto* (Jurist) 984 (1991), S. 14–28 (zusammen mit Shindō, Kōji/Matsuo, Kōya/Rokumoto, Kahei und Hori, Ryūji).

3. *Doitsu ni okeru hōsōzai haikibutsu no taisho* (Deutsche Maßnahmen gegen Verpackungsabfälle), Interview für die Tageszeitung *Asahi*, in: *Asahi Shinbun* (11. 12. 1992).

4. *Hōsōzai shori no tame no dyuaru shistemu* (Das duale System für die Beseitigung von Verpackungsabfällen), Interview für die Zeitschrift *Trigger*, in: *Trigger* 13/5 (1994), S. 30–32.

5. Interview with Dr. Menkhaus on the European Association for Japanese Studies (EAJS), in: UEN (Unilever Expatriate Network) 7/8 (1995), S. 2–3.

6. *Jāmani: sumūzu ni gokaku shite mo 20dai kōhan – erīto e no michi wa nintai hitosuji* (Deutschland: Auch wenn die Examen reibungslos laufen wird man Ende 20 – Der Weg zur Elite erfordert Geduld auf dem einzig möglichen Weg), Interview für die Zeitschrift *type* über die Ausbildung zum Juristen, Wirtschaftsprüfer und Steuerberater, in: *type* 2 (1996), S. 21.

7. *Chihō tainichi tōshi kaigi in Kitakyūshū '96* (Podiumsdiskussion: 1. Konferenz über ausländische Investitionen in den ländlichen Regionen Japans, veranstaltet in der Stadt *Kitakyūshū* 1996), in: *Chihō tainichi tōshi kaigi in Kitakyūshū '96 hōkokusho* (Bericht über die 1. Konferenz über ausländische Investitionen in den ländlichen Regionen Japans, veranstaltet in der Stadt Kitakyūshū 1996) (1996), S. 111–112.

8. *Gaishikei kigyō no chihō tenkai ni tsuite* (Die Entwicklung ausländisch kapitalisierter Unternehmen in den ländlichen Regionen Japans), Interview für die japanische Tageszeitung *Nikkei Sangyō Shinbun*, in: *Nikkei Sangyō Shinbun* (27. 3. 1996).

9. *Anata no machi no rōsei* (Podiumsdiskussion: Die Arbeitsplatzbeschaffungspolitik ihrer Stadt), in: *Tōkyō no Rōdō* (Zeitung Arbeit in Tokyo) (25. 7. 1997).

10. Personnel and Labour Management for Foreign Affiliated Enterprises in Japan, Podiumsdiskussion am 17. und 20. 3. 1998 im Japan Institute of Labour in Osaka und Tokyo, in: Labour Issues Quarterly 40 (1998), S. 2–8.

11. *Doku kigyō no jōken mitasu* (Die Bedingungen für deutsche Unternehmen sind erfüllt), Interview für die japanische Wirtschaftstageszeitung *Nihon Keizai Shinbun*, in: *Nihon Keizai Shinbun* (10. 6. 1998).

12. Japan – Firmen im Ausverkauf, Interview für die Tageszeitung Rheinischer Merkur, in: Rheinischer Merkur (7. 5. 1999).

13. *Zadankai: Nichidoku shihō no genjō to kadai – 21seiki no shihō wo mezashite* (Diskussionsrunde der japanischen Zeitschrift für Rechtssprechung: Gegenwärtiger Zustand und Aufgaben der Rechtspflege in Japan und Deutschland), in: *Hanrei Jihō* (Japanische juristische Fachzeitschrift) 1708 (2000), S. 3–26 (zusammen mit Ebihara, Akio/Mimura, Ryōichi/Miyazaki, Kimio/Fukuda, Takahisa und Hieda, Masahiro).

14. Neue Professoren in Marburg: Heinrich Menkhaus – Japanisches Recht, Interview für die Zeitschrift der Philipps-Universität Marburg, in: Marburger Uni Journal 11 (2002), S. 54.

15. *Ōbei no hōshisutemu* (Fernsehdiskussionsrunde: Die Rechtsysteme Europas und der Vereinigten Staaten von Amerika), in: *Rokumoto, Kahei: Hikakuhō shisutemu ron* (Theorie der Rechtsvergleichung), *Hōsō daigaku kyōiku shinkōkai* (Vereinigung zur Förderung der Erziehung an der Fernuniversität), Tokyo 2002, S. 145–159 (zusammen mit Rokumoto, Kahei/Daniel H. Foote/Kitamaru, Ichirō und Yamaguchi, Kōichirō).

16. Professor hilft Experten, in Nippon klarzukommen, Interview für die Tageszeitung Frankfurter Rundschau, in: Frankfurter Rundschau (8. 8. 2002).

17. Neuer Studiengang soll Fachkräfte für Einsatz in Japan qualifizieren, Interview für die Tageszeitung Oberhessische Presse, in: Oberhessische Presse (16. 8. 2002) (zusammen mit Erich Pauer).

18. Japaner haben deutsches Recht ergänzt und ihrer Kultur angepaßt, Interview für die Tageszeitung Marburger Neue Zeitung, in: Marburger Neue Zeitung (27. 8. 2002).

19. Menschen – Heinrich Menkhaus: Unser Problem!, Interview für das Marburger Magazin Express, in: Express 35 (2002), S. 5.

20. Jubiläum – Japanforscher mit guten Aussichten, Interview für die Tageszeitung Frankfurter Rundschau, in: Frankfurter Rundschau (10. 5. 2003).

21. Vor 125 Jahren legte Geograph Rein Grundstein für heutige Japanforschung, Interview für die Tageszeitung Oberhessische Presse, in: Tageszeitung Oberhessische Presse (15. 5. 2003) (zusammen mit Erich Pauer).

22. Kein Raum für Exotik, Interview für die Tageszeitung Marburger Neue Zeitung, in: Marburger Neue Zeitung (27. 5. 2003) (zusammen mit Erich Pauer).

23. Uni für einen Tag im Zeichen der aufgehenden Sonne, Interview für die Tageszeitung Oberhessische Presse, in: Oberhessische Presse (31. 5. 2003).

24. Marburger Japanforscher haben sehr gute Aussichten, Interview für die Tageszeitung Gießener Anzeiger, in: Gießener Anzeiger (31. 5. 2003).

25. Japan-Zentrum setzt auf erklärten Wunsch der Uni zur Profilbildung, Interview für die Tageszeitung Marburger Neue Zeitung, in: Marburger Neue Zeitung (21. 10. 2003).

26. Deutschland in Japan – Der Direktor des Japan-Zentrums, Professor Dr. Heinrich Menkhaus, nimmt teil am „Deutschlandjahr in Japan" des Auswärtigen Amtes in: Marburger Uni-Journal 22 (2005), S. 48–49.

27. Japankompetenz auf allen wissenschaftlichen Gebieten, in: Japan-Magazin 6 (2006), S. 21 (zusammen mit Ingrid Fritsch).

28. *Manesuman saiban chūshi – kigyōtōchi kaikaku, mada tesaguri* (Abbruch des Mannesmann-Prozesses – Immer noch Vortasten bei der Reform der Unternehmenskontrolle), in: *Nikkei Kin'yū Shinbun* (japanischsprachige Fachtageszeitung Finanzen des japanischen Medienunternehmens Nikkei) (1. 12. 2006).

29. Auf Dienstreise mit der Bundesbildungsministerin – Nach einem Japanbesuch mit Annette Schavan gehört Heinrich Menkhaus jetzt auch ihrem Japan-Arbeitskreis an, in: Marburger UniJournal 28 (2007), S. 12.

30. Marburger Modell für Japan-Zentrum bedroht bzw. Das Japan-Zentrum wird abgewickelt, in: Tageszeitung Oberhessische Presse (24. 5. 2007).

31. Studieren ohne Bücher. Weiter Ärger über Zentrenbildung in Hessen, in: Tageszeitung Frankfurter Allgemeine Zeitung (FAZ): Beilage Rhein-Main Zeitung (23. 10. 2007).

32. *Nihon kenkyū: tenkan ka suitai ka. nichibunken kokusai shinpo de jitsujō hōkoku* (Japanstudien: Veränderung oder Abnahme. Berichte eines internationalen Symposiums am Nationalen Japanischen Institut für Japanstudien), in: *Yomiuri Shinbun* (japanischsprachige Tageszeitung) (7. 11. 2007).

33. Japanese studies facing the chop on Europe, in: *Daily Yomiuri* (englischsprachige Tageszeitung in Japan) (8. 12. 2007).

34. Japan entdeckt das deutsche Recht neu – Vertragsabschlüsse nach englischem Recht verlieren in Nippon an Beliebtheit, in: Tageszeitung Handelsblatt (24. 6. 2009).

35. Soldaten prägen Deutschlandbild – Ausstellung in Marburg erinnert an deutsche Kriegsgefangene in Japan, in: Tageszeitung Marburger Neue Zeitung (2./3. 10. 2009).

36. Kriegsgefangenen-Ausstellung in Marburg, in: OAG-Notizen 11 (2009), S. 59–60.

37. *Hōgakubu Meiji University Law in Japan Program 2009 wo oete* (*Meiji* University Law in Japan Programm 2009 der juristischen Fakultät), in: *Meiji Daigaku Kōhō* 614 (2009), S. 6.

38. Sciences un colloque bien nourri, in: Magazin L'Alsace (22. 5. 2010).

39. Im Land der Perfektionisten. Mit einer Mischung aus Bewunderung und Verwunderung erleben Deutsche ihre Wahlheimat Tokio, in: Tageszeitung Frankfurter Allgemeine Zeitung (FAZ) (24./25. 7. 2010).

40. *Waga tenpyo. Dai 11 kai. Do no yo na koto de mo, tatoe jozu kuika nakute mo isshokenmei yareba yoi. Kansakuyaku Hainrihhi Menkuhausu san* (Unser Punkt Nr. 11: Wer immer strebend sich bemüht, den können wir erlösen), in: *Bairin Famiri* (Zeitschrift des Unternehmens Nippon Vilene) 112 (2011) 2.

41. „Wie ein Vaterlandsverräter". Gebürtiger Hollager Heinrich Menkhaus erlebte das Erdbeben in Japan, in: Tageszeitung Neue Osnabrücker Zeitung (28. 3. 2011).

42. Der Ex als Botschafter, in: Deutsche Universitätszeitung (DUZ) 11 (2011), S. 30–31.

43. *Dai 23 kai Dokkyō intānashonaru Fuōramu: Nichidoku kōryū no rekishi kara mirai wo misueru: shakai, gakumon, bunka* (23. Internationales Forum der *Dokkyō* Universität: Die Zukunft des Japanisch-Deutschen Austausches aus historischem Blickwinkel: Gesellschaft, Wissenschaft, Kultur), in: *Dokkyō Daigaku Gakuhō* (Zeitschrift der Universität *Dokkyō*) 28 (2011), S. 115–133.

44. *De ra sāru daigaku (hi) no hōgakubusei ni tanki ukeire puroguramu „Law in Japan" kaikō* (Einrichtung des Kurzzeitlehrprogramms „Law in Japan" für Studierende der juristischen Fakultät der De La Salle Universität der Philippinen), in: *daigaku kōhō* (Zeitung der Universität *Meiji*) (1. 8. 2015).

45. *Sekai no mikata: tsuyoi kengen motsu doku kenpōsai* (Die Sicht der Welt: Das mit starken Rechten ausgestattete deutsche Verfassungsgericht), in: *Mainichi Shinbun* (Japanische Tageszeitung) Morgenausgabe (16. 8. 2015).

46. *Sengo 70 nen – kengen kōshi takamaru koe* (Stimmen, die eine stärkere Ausübung von Rechten fordern), in: *Mainichi Shinbun* (Japanische Tageszeitung) Morgenausgabe (23. 10. 2015).

47. *Doitsugoken nihon gakujutsu shinkōkai kenkyūsha dōsōkai: enerugī wo tēma ni, meidai de 20shunen shinpo* (Deutsche Gesellschaft der JSPS Stipendiaten: Das Symposium anlässlich des 20. Gründungsjubiläums hat Energie zum Thema), in: *Meiji daigaku kōhō* (Zeitung der *Meiji* Universität) (1. 11. 2015).

48. German JSPS Alumni Talk about Past and Future Successes of their Association, in: JSPS (Japan Society for the Promotion of Science) Quarterly 54 (2015), S. 10.

49. *Nihon no hōritsu to gaikokuhō* (Japanisches und ausländisches Recht), in: *Fukushima kenritsu iwaki sakurgaoka kōtō gakkō* (*Iwaki Sakuragaoka* Oberschule der Präfektur Fukushima) (Hrsg.): *shinro jānaru* (Zeitschrift Route), *gōgai* (Sondernummer) (14. 9. 2016).

50. Blick zurück nicht nur im Zorn, in: Frankfurter Allgemeine Zeitung (FAZ) (27. 12. 2016).

51. *Meiji* University Ethics, Law, Medicine (ELM) Institute/*Meiji* University Institute of Comparative Law (MICL) *kyōsai shinpojiumu: iryōhin – iryōkiki wo meguro nichidoku shoseido no hikaku* (Internationales gemeinsames Symposium der Institute ELM und MICL – Vergleich der Systeme zur Regulierung von Arzneimitteln und Medizinprodukten in Japan und Deutschland), in: *Meiji daigaku kōhō* (Zeitung der *Meiji* Universität) (1. 4. 2019).

52. Kaspar, Johannes: Festveranstaltung aus Anlass der neugegründeten Kooperation mit der Universität *Meiji*, Japan, in: Jahresbericht 2017/2018 der juristischen Fakultät der Universität Augsburg (2019).

53. *Kansō: doitsu kihon hō to nihon koku kenpō no hikaku – nihon koku kenpō wo kaisei subeki ka?* (Meinung: Auf der Basis eines Vergleichs des Deutschen Grundgesetzes und der Verfas-

sung des Staates Japan – Bedarf die Verfassung des Staates Japan einer Änderung?)/Discourse: Based on Comparison of the Japanese and German Constitution – Does the Japanese Constitution need change?, in: International Medical News (Zeitschrift der Internationalen Medizinischen Gesellschaft Japans) 509 (2021), S. 11/12 bzw. 24/25.

54. Ex-Hollager lehrt und lebt in Japan, in: Tageszeitung Neue Osnabrücker Zeitung (15. 9. 2023).

55. Law in Japan Program for *sanpauro daigaku* Online 2024 *wo jisshi* (Programm „Law in Japan" für die Universität Sao Paulo im Jahre 2024 online verwirklicht), in: *Meiji Daigaku kōhō* (Zeitung der University *Meiji*) 789 (2024), S. 4.

VII. Interviews, Gespräche, Grußworte und Diskussionsrunden in anderen Medien

1. *Doitsu shikei kigyō no tainichi tōshi* (Investitionen deutschkapitalisierter Unternehmen in Japan), ausgestrahlt am 22. 7. 1997 im NHK (*Nippon Hōsō Kyōkai*) Fernsehen News-Shuttle *Kitakyūshū.*

2. *Nihon o nerauōshū chūshō kigyō* (Auf Japan zielende kleine und mittlere europäische Unternehmen), ausgestrahlt am 8. 6. 1998 im NHK (*Nippon Hōsō Kyōkai*) Satellitenfernsehen Kanal 1 BS 22.

3. Deregulation in Japan, Japan VIP Series, Channel J, ausgestrahlt am 23. und 24. 2. 2001 in den Vereinigten Staaten von Amerika von den Fernsehsendern Direct TV 440 ch und NHK (*Nippon Hōsō Kyōkai*) World Premier.

4. *Hōsō daigaku jugyō bangumi* (Unterrichtsprogramm der Japanischen Fernuniversität), *hōshisutemu I* (Serie Rechtssyteme I), *dai 5 kai: doitsu no hōshisutemu* (Nr. 5: Das Rechtssystem der Bundesrepublik Deutschland), *dai 8 kai: ōbei shokoku no hōshisutemu* (Nr. 8: Die Rechtssysteme Europas und der Vereinigten Staaten von Amerika), ausgestrahlt für vier Jahre ab 1. 4. 2002 von NHK (*Nippon Hōsō Kyōkai*) World Premier.

5. Marburg: Philipps-Universität bietet neuen Studiengang Japanwissenschaften, Radiointerview für hr 4 Mittelhessen-Journal, ausgestrahlt am 5. 9. 2002 (zusammen mit Erich Pauer, Anne Holzapfel und Akiko Sawatari).

6. Marburg: An der Philipps-Universität begann vor 125 Jahren die deutsche Japan-Forschung, für hr 4 Mittelhessen-Journal, ausgestrahlt am 30. 5. 2003 (zusammen mit Erich Pauer, Anne Holzapfel und Akiko Sawatari).

7. Lernen von Japan – Die Japan Society for the Promotion of Science hat zum Erfahrungsaustausch nach Bonn eingeladen, für Deutschlandfunk, ausgestrahlt am 22. 4. 2005 (zusammen mit Ingrid Fritsch, Arnulf Jaeger-Waldau und Andreas Marx).

8. Gewinner und Verlierer des Hochschulpaktes in Hessen, für Deutschlandfunk, ausgestrahlt am 3. 6. 2005 (zusammen mit Erich Pauer u. a.).

9. Sag mir, wo die Blumen sind. Über die Zukunft der Orchideenfächer, für Deutschlandfunk, ausgestrahlt am 25. 1. 2007 (zusammen mit Eva Nonnast).

10. Introductory Remarks, 15. Gemeinsames Symposium der Japan Society for the Promotion of Science und der Deutschen Gesellschaft der JSPS-Stipendiaten e. V. zusammen mit der Association Française D'anciens Boursiers de la JSPS zum Thema: Food Science and Society, Université de Strasbourg, abrufbar unter http://www.canalc2.tv/video.asp?idVideo=9312&voir=oui.

11. Interview mit Prof. Dr. jur. Heinrich Menkhaus. In dem Interview mit NaJ erläutert Vorsitzender Prof. Dr. Heinrich Menkhaus die Arbeit und Zielsetzungen der Deutschen Gesellschaft der JSPS-Stipendiaten e. V., in: Neues aus Japan 104 (2013), abrufbar unter http://www.de.emb-japan.go.jp/NaJ/NaJ1307/jsps.html und http://www.jsps-club.de/fileadmin/aktuelles/Neues_aus_Japan_07.2013.pdf.

12. *Goaisatsu menkuhausu hainrihhi kyōju meiji daigaku hikakuhō kenkyūjo shochō* (Grußwort als Vorsitzender der Deutschen Gesellschaft der JSPS-Stipendiaten e. V. anlässlich des Symposiums: SUDem2020 Sustainable University Development – Education and Management), International Christian University, Tokyo (22. 2. 2020), abrufbar unter https://www.youtube.com/watch?v=c_p9vcpwwWQ&feature=youtu.be.

13. Closing Remarks as Director of *Meiji* Institute of Comparative Law of the symposium: Climate Change Law and Policy in the Asia Pacific 2020, jointly organized by *Meiji* University School of Law and *Meiji* Institute of Comparative Law (MICL) (11. 9. 2020), abrufbar unter https://www.youtube.com/watch?v=Jy1Zh8G5lJo&feature=youtu.be.

14. Auf den Spuren der Eulenburg-Mission, Vortrag vor der Deutschen Gesellschaft für Natur- und Völkerkunde Ostasiens (OAG) (20. 1. 2021), abrufbar unter Prof. Dr. Heinrich Menkhaus: „Auf den Spuren der Eulenburg-Mission“ | Veranstaltungen | OAG – Deutsche Gesellschaft für Natur- und Völkerkunde Ostasiens (Tokyo).

15. Wie das deutsche Recht nach Japan kam, Vortrag vor der Deutsch-Japanischen Gesellschaft (DJG) Bonn und der DJG der Studierenden der Universität Bonn (30. 1. 2021), abrufbar unter Prof. Dr. jur. Heinrich Menkhaus: Wie das deutsche Recht nach Japan kam – YouTube Deutsch-Japanische Gesellschaft Bonn e. V. – YouTube.

16. Auf den Spuren der Eulenburg-Mission: Führung der Botschafterin der Bundesrepublik Deutschland Ina Lepel am 23. 2. 2021 an die Stellen in Tokyo, die Mitglieder der Eulenburg Mission aufgesucht haben, abrufbar unter 先日レーペル大使は明治大学のメンクハウス教授と共にオイレンブルグ使節団の足跡を辿… – ドイツ連邦共和国大使館・総領事館 (facebook.com) und ドイツ大使館DEさんはTwitterを使っています 「先日レーペル大使は明治大学のメンクハウス教授と共にオイレンブルグ使節団の足跡を辿ったので、その様子をご紹介します。 #散歩の日 https://t.co/BUyzXwSYVM」 / Twitter.

17. Interview zu den juristischen Aspekten des Preußisch-Japanischen Freundschafts-, Schifffahrts- und Handelsvertrages vom 24. 1. 1861 anlässlich der virtuellen Ausstellung der Deutschen Botschaft Tokyo „160 Jahre Deutsch-Japanische Freundschaft“, abrufbar seit dem 26. 7. 2021, abrufbar unter www.germanyinjapan160.com.

18. COVID 19 Pandemic from a School of Law Point of View – Challenges for the Legal Systems with Special Consideration of the Constitutions: Vortrag vor den Mitgliedern der Deutschen Gesellschaft der JSPS-Stipendiaten e. V. anlässlich des 10. Club-Treffens in Japan am 18. 12. 2021, abrufbar unter 10th JSPS Club „Meeting in Japan“ 2021 | Prof. Dr. Menkhaus – YouTube.

19. 50 Schriften zu Wallenhorst. Prof. Dr. Heinrich Menkhaus überreicht Bücher an Archivgruppe, HP der Gemeinde Wallenhorst (3. 9. 2023), abrufbar unter 50 Schriften zu Wallenhorst – Gemeinde Wallenhorst.

20. Diskussion des Vortrages von Prof. Dr. Alexander Graser über „The Legal Structures of the German Welfare State“ am 24. 9. 2024 am Institut für Rechtsvergleichung der Universität *Meiji*, abrufbar unter 2024年9月24日（火）「社会保障法II」における特別講演：Prof. Dr. Alexander Graser (Universität Regensburg).

21. Rechtsberater und OAG-Sportkegler. Erinnerung an den Kontraktausländer Albert Isaac Mosse: Vortrag vor der Deutschen Gesellschaft für Natur- und Völkerkunde Ostasiens (OAG) am 4. 6. 2025, abrufbar unter https://oag.jp/events/prof-dr-heinrich-menkhaus-rechts berater-und-oag-sportkegler-erinnerung-an-den-kontraktauslaender-albert-isaac-mosse/.

VIII. Redaktion

1. Deutsches Institut für Japanstudien, Bulletin 1 (1989) – 3 (1990).
2. Deutsch-Japanische Juristenvereinigung, Mitteilungen 3 (1989) – 11/12 (1994).
3. Deutsches Institut für Japanstudien, Jahrbuch 2 (1990).
4. European Association for Japanese Studies, Bulletin 40 (1994) – 41 (1995)
5. Occasional Papers des Japan-Zentrums der Philipps-Universität Marburg, Takahashi, Shigeru: Rechtliche und politische Aspekte der Kernenergienutzung in Japan, Occasional Paper 31 (2005).
6. Occasional Papers des Japan-Zentrums der Philipps-Universität Marburg, Shibata, Masashi: Struktur, Aufgaben und Arbeit der japanischen Familiengerichte, Occasional Paper 32 (2005).
7. Festschrift der Deutschen Gesellschaft der JSPS-Stipendiaten e. V. zum 10. Gründungsjubiläum (2005) (zusammen mit Sabine Ganter-Richter).
8. Occasional Papers des Japan-Zentrums der Philipps-Universität Marburg, Akademische Feier aus Anlaß der Überreichung der Festschrift „Japanischer Brückenbauer zum deutschen Rechtskreis an Prof. Dr. Yamauchi Koresuke“ am 2. 5. 2007, Alte Aula der Philipps-Universität Marburg. Occasional Paper Nr. 33 (2008).
9. Festschrift der Deutschen Gesellschaft der JSPS-Stipendiaten e. V. zum 20. Gründungsjubiläum (2015) (zusammen mit Wolfgang Staguhn).
10. Festschrift der Deutschen Gesellschaft der JSPS-Stipendiaten e. V. zum 30. Gründungsjubiläum (2025) (zusammen mit Daniela Winkler).

IX. Beiträge zu Ausstellungen

1. *Oyatoi gaikokujin no naka no doitsujin hōritsuka* (Die deutschen Juristen unter den Kontraktausländern), Panel Nr. 7 der Ausstellung: *Doitsu to Nihon wo musubu mono – nichidoku shūkō 150nen no rekishi*: Was Deutschland und Japan verbindet – 150 Jahre Freundschaft zwischen Deutschland und Japan. Vom 7. 7. – 6. 9. 2015 im *Kokuritsu Rekishi Minzoku Hakubutsukan* (Nationalmuseum für japanische Geschichte), *Sakura, Chiba,* vom 19. 9. – 29. 11. 2015 im *Nagasaki Rekishi Bunka Hakubutsukan* (Museum für Geschichte und Kultur der Präfektur Nagasaki), *Nagasaki*, vom 9. 12. 2015 – 24. 1. 2016 im *Narutoshi Doitsukan* (Deutsches Haus der Stadt Naruto), *Naruto*, Präfektur *Tokushima* und vom 3. 2. – 10. 4. 2016 im *Yokohama Kaikō Shiryōkan* (Archiv zur Hafenöffnung in der Stadt Yokohama).